Political Ideas and Ideologies

POLITICAL IDEAS AND IDEOLOGIES

A History of Political Thought

Mulford Q. Sibley

Professor of Political Science / University of Minnesota

Harper & Row, Publishers

NEW YORK · EVANSTON · LONDON

Political Ideas and Ideologies:
A History of Political Thought
 For information address Harper & Row, Publishers, Inc., 49 East 33rd Street, New York, N.Y. 10016

Library of Congress catalog card number: 73-113492

Contents

Preface

This book is designed to give some impression of the scope and nature of political discussion in the so-called Western tradition during the past 3000 years or more. It is not intended to be a specialized study of any one problem nor does it purport to be even a cursory examination of all issues. Instead, it is an admittedly selective treatment, as all such ventures must be, of what the author regards as a few of the major streams of political ideas and ideologies, "major" being defined both as those which have been historically influential and as those whose importance lies in their analytical strength. Some tendencies have been important both historically and analytically; others are chiefly significant in one way only. Even with respect to the questions explored, the author is acutely conscious of omissions, ambiguities, and other shortcomings, some of them due to the relatively brief space available (the original manuscript had to be cut about one third). Then, too, anyone who is foolhardy enough to attempt a book of this scope becomes all too aware of the limitations of language in the communication of ideas: every sentence, as it were, is a venture in faith which at times one wishes one could recall.

The volume sees ideas as both responding to and shaping historical crises and developments. Systems of thought, moreover, while often heavily conditioned and narrowly bound by cultural biases and class interests—a fact stressed by the so-called sociology of knowledge—may also transcend these limitations and get at something of "reality." But the nature of political reality is itself a problem and one which is in certain respects probably no nearer solution today than in the time of Aristotle. Political ideas, too, it is assumed throughout the volume, ought to be considered from the viewpoints of biography, history, philosophy, and science; and there is no one magic formula for understanding their background, implications, influence, and criticism.

Certain general patterns emerge when one examines major tendencies in political thought as a whole. Some of these patterns persist almost from the beginning down to our own day, indicating a basic continuity for frameworks of thought: the threefold nature of collective experience—prepolitical, political, and postpolitical—may be cited as one example. Other patterns are more characteristic of particular time spans. Although these periods have something of the arbitrary about them (as, indeed, all historical divisions do), they are not wholly arbitrary. From the viewpoint of political thought, the study suggests four periods, to each of which a Part is devoted. Some of the significant identifying patterns of the period under consideration are indicated in each Part Introduction, and the chapters following discuss details.

It need hardly be said that a book of this kind can only be suggestive. The serious student of political ideas and ideologies may use it as a point of departure for study, criticism, and discussion. But he must go beyond it if his inquiries are to be most fruitful. It is no substitute, in other words, for reading original treatises or other and more detailed analyses and criticisms.

It is impossible to thank adequately all those who have contributed to this book. There are the many, many typists who copied and recopied its several versions, among whom was my son Martin. Others helped with valuable criticisms, among them Professor Benjamin Lippincott, who read and commented on the Introduction, and Professor Arthur Kalleberg, who went through the entire manuscript, asking helpful questions in the process. Many assisted in research, in proofreading, and in other ways—especially Laurence Golden; also Barbara Golden, Dr. Ernest Katin, Dr. Daniel Kieselhorst, Rafiqul Choudhury, Michael McGrath, Donald Moon, Henry Rempel, Russell Dondero, and Muriel Welch.

But the book would never have been finished had it not been for the hard work and, above all, the inspiration of my wife, Marjorie H. Sibley. Not only did she do much of the original criticism but she kept insisting, in the face of my frequent doubts and discouragement, that it was worth while to write the book.

MULFORD Q. SIBLEY

introduction

Politics and the History of Political Ideas

What is politics?

It is impossible to provide an answer that will satisfy everyone, for the very scope and meaning of the term will depend in large measure on one's general outlook. A Marxist will define it in one way; a Platonist in yet another. Many identify it with "power" phenomena; but when we inquire into the definition of power, the ambiguities confront us once more. For some, politics is virtually equivalent to action in accordance with expediency rather than principle. To others, it constitutes the means whereby we attain the ends set up by our ethics. Although it is used as an epithet of opprobrium by many, for some it has highly favorable connotations.

Here we shall provisionally use the term to indicate man's deliberate efforts to order, direct, and control his collective affairs and activities; to set up ends for society; and to implement and evaluate those ends. Politics is to collective affairs what the striving for autonomy is in personal matters. In both instances man is seeking, often without success, to cast off unconscious and externally imposed patterns of conduct. Just as in the development of his personality an adolescent will try to emancipate himself from uncriticized governance by his family, so in collective matters a time arises when men begin to reject nondeliberative ways of direction and control and to embrace deliberative ones.

In this sense the term "political" arises when ordering by mere custom and mores breaks down. Men are then compelled to work out standards of action to take the place of habit patterns that no longer govern. In prepolitical or nonpolitical governance, human beings act unreflectively, observing the guidelines provided by deposits of folkways, which are themselves developed through slow and subdeliberative evolution. Political governance, by contrast, implies deliberation, aspiration for rationality, and subjecting governance by folkways to questioning and criticism. It also entails a dissatisfaction with rule by accident or fortuitous concatenation of social forces, which tends to follow the breakdown of nonpolitical governance.

Obviously, no given group of men is wholly prepolitical or completely political. In any historical society, one will find methods of governance tending in one direction or the other. Primitive societies presumably reduce the political to a minimum, even though it is always present to some degree. On the other hand, complex and urban cultures witness a vast extension of the political—or at least an expansion of a consciousness of the possibilities for political ordering.

Political ordering may exist at different levels and in a variety of contexts. Thus wherever men seek deliberately to plan ecclesiastical affairs, the political is present, as it is when they strive to do the same in labor, commercial, industrial, or other collective matters. Even the family has a political aspect; for insofar as its arrangements are not the result merely of biological or habitual determination, the possibility of politics is opened up. To be sure, we often think of the "State" as peculiarly political; but is this not primarily because the aspirations for deliberate ordering are often exhibited more dramatically and on a larger scale in this context? As primitive division of labor declines, the public area expands, with increasing interdependence, and the potentially political is correspondingly magnified.

In any historical community, political elements will be in tension with the nonpolitical. Decisions made politically will often become part of the folkways or mores and sink below the level of what we may call the political consciousness, only to be made part of it again in times of crisis. Thus the Constitution of the United States is a product of the political process; but it has tended during a large part of its history to take on a sacred character which—except in times of acute division and testing—pushed it below the line of the political. In periods of rapid social change, everything tends to be summoned before the political bar and may become subject to renewed policy-making; for if governance by deliberately formulated policy does not take place, rule by accident or happenstance is its substitute. Periods of religious skepticism, rapid urbanization, commercialism, and industrialism tend to be associated with expanded politics. By contrast, the political declines in ages of faith, slow social change, and a preponderantly rural existence.

Politics and Political Ideas

As man reflects, often with perturbation, on the breakdown of prepolitical and nonpolitical ordering (juvenile delinquency appears, for example, or commerce is constantly breaking up the cake of custom), seeking to establish foundations for political governance and to explain the phenomena connected with it, he is confronted by challenges at several levels. These problems of thought include the metaphysical, epistemological, and logical; the empirical and scientific; the normative; and the practical. In other words, every more or less developed system of political ideas will, if often only implicitly, include these elements.

Metaphysical, Epistemological, and Logical. The metaphysical, epistemological, and logical are closely interrelated. Generally speaking, *metaphysics* concerns itself with first or starting principles of thought and tries to envision the nature of reality; *epistemology* attempts to inquire into the nature of knowledge and principles for obtaining it; and *logic* has to do with such questions as how propositions are connected with one another, the distinction between fallacious and valid reasoning, and how to evaluate a mode of reasoning. We must bring to the study of politics, in other words, principles which are regarded as the foundation of all thinking; some kind of a conception as to how, if at all, we can know; and a framework of thought which prescribes, for example, how we can validly deduce one statement from another, proceed from the particular to the general, and evaluate thought in terms of such criteria as internal consistency.

At the metaphysical, epistemological, and logical levels, the political thinker must think about the process of his thinking and clarify in his own mind the notions upon which the whole structure of his thought is to be based.

Empirical and Scientific. Given his metaphysical, epistemological, and logical framework, the political thinker then proceeds to the task of describing, explaining, and, in some sense, predicting events in the political world. In one way or another, he makes judgments about political history and, in varying degrees, endeavors to discover some measure of regularity behind the apparently irregular movements of politics. Many political thinkers endeavor to develop *if–then* statements: If, in other words, we have conditions *xyz*, then, under circumstances *bbb*, we tend to get results *aaa*. Here the apparent purpose is to explain and account for political conduct and to predict it within the limits laid down. Why do men act as they do under given conditions and how can they be expected to behave under postulated circumstances?

How to *know* politics empirically is, of course, a problem in itself. Certainly we cannot know it directly through the five senses. Some suggest that if modern scientific method is developed fully, we can indeed come to understand the political world. Others, however, deny that the means characteristic of science can in themselves ever enable us to know. "At the center of his existence," remarks Eric Voegelin, "man is unknown to himself and must remain so, for the part of his being that calls itself man could be known fully only if the community of being and its drama in time were known as a whole."[1] Voegelin's view would not deny, presumably, that aspects of political reality can be clarified in part through scientific analysis. It would, however, argue that the whole, being more than the sum total of all its parts, escapes full analysis and can be grasped in one of its dimensions only through direct experience expressed in symbolization and analogy.[2]

Questions of this kind are, of course, central. Here we simply note their existence and point out the lack of agreement among thinkers.

Normative. Politics involves value systems of every type. It particularly implies moral valuation; for once the ordering of human affairs is in some measure deliberate, we confront immediately the question of what *kind* of order ought to be constructed. This issue in turn depends on what we deem to be right and good in general. When we ask this question, we are then forced to ask how we can account for our moral experience as a whole and whether moral valuations are intuitive, rational, merely "emotive," or a combination of these and other elements. How do we validate a proposition about morals? We are also confronted by the problem of whether the good to be attained by the individual is the same as that for the community. Should individual ethics be pursued as a separate inquiry or, by contrast, are they inextricably tied to social and political ethics? One scholar suggests that the history of Western political thought can be read in terms of the varied answers given to this last question, with men in the earlier period thinking of morals and politics as inseparably bound together and with students in later epochs seeking to separate them.[3]

The domain of religion, too, is relevant here, as elsewhere (in, for example, all inquiries into the basis of community). Insofar as religious commitments also involve moral valuations—as they often do—then religion and political theory will and should be intertwined.

Practical. The purpose of inquiry into the philosophical, scientific, and normative realms is a practical or, as some say, a "legislative" one. Although it may be valuable in itself to understand the foundations of knowledge, to be able to make valid historical and hypothetical statements, and to set up normative principles, these inquiries remain at a somewhat abstract level. If the political domain is that wherein we seek consciously and deliberately to direct and control collective affairs, then abstract statements or investigations are not enough, indispensable though they may be. A further step is needed: We must be able to relate these propositions to the day to day problems of human collectives. A scientific statement, for example, will be couched in terms of possible situations which may not in fact occur in that particular combination in actual life. But if we are to order human affairs, we must correct this statement in light of the particular conditions present in a given culture and at a certain time. This is somewhat like the problem the natural scientist confronts when he attempts to correct his statements about actions of particles in a vacuum in face of the fact that no completely airless situation exists.

We must, moreover, attempt to relate normative principles to the possibilities revealed by scientific inquiry. If, that is to say, we argue that men should conduct themselves quite

1. *Israel and Revelation*, vol. 1, *Order and History*, Baton Rouge: Louisiana State University Press, 1956, p. 2.
2. *Ibid.*
3. C. E. M. Joad, *Guide to the Philosophy of Morals and Politics*, New York: Random House, 1937.

differently from the ways in which they have acted in the past, then we must show how, given our abstract knowledge corrected by ingredients from the nonabstract world of the here and now, they can actually attain this goal. Thus in the struggle for racial equality, we are guided by the normative principle of equality, sociological generalizations as to how men are likely to act under given conditions, and practical judgments as to what conditions in fact are likely to exist.

In doing this, we shall have to take into account not merely the hypothetical (if–then) statements of the scientists but also our over-all assessment of the human condition, both in general and in particular. And this over-all assessment can be the product only of experience and the study of history. We cannot, in other words, get an account of the actual political universe simply by adding scientific hypothetical statements together. Judgments about practical affairs which concern the policymaker are propositions about things that are or probably will be: They are not, unlike scientific statements, assertions about abstracted and controlled parts. In dealing with the nonabstracted universe of the here and now, we shall have to resort to the very uneasy method of historical analogies. And inevitably, the further we descend from hypothetical statements, the greater our uncertainty will be. Political decisions, like personal choices, are determined by general evaluations of what we deem to be good and over-all judgments about the interrelatedness of the facts to potentialities; and beyond a certain point, scientific judgments are helpless to assist us. This is why great thinkers like Aristotle have told us that we cannot expect the degree of certainty about politics or, indeed, any practical study—e.g., medicine—that we expect from purely theoretical or hypothetical alleged knowledge.

Systematic Theory and Political Ideas in General

A system of political ideas in its most complete sense might be called a political theory or philosophy. It would embrace discussions of all the elements we have noted and would endeavor to make all its propositions as explicit and as documented as possible. It would include philosophical, scientific, normative, and public policy considerations; and it would strive for consistency as well as verifiability in its account.

Very little political thought, however, has achieved this goal, even the great systems emphasizing some aspects to the virtual exclusion of certain others. This does not mean, though, that because most political thought is not systematic, there are no political ideas worth studying outside the few great systems. The contrary is true; some of the most suggestive and influential ideas are outside the important systems. Political ideas may be said to exist on a continuum between a few great systems, on the one hand, and sporadic, isolated reflection, on the other. Even the person of lowest political consciousness will have some ideas—for example, "politicians are corrupt," "old ways are best," and so on—but either he will not or he cannot relate them to one another and to life experience as a whole. From another point of view, of course, even the simplest observation is an idea which implicitly entails other ideas. Thus "World War II began in 1939" appears on the surface to be a simple statement of "brute fact"; but implicit in any understanding of it are such ideas as those of time, meaning of "war," and "number."

The more thorough the attempt to develop the interrelatedness of things and of ideas, the more systematic and the higher—if we think of higher as somehow involving unity behind diversity—will be the body of political thought. The less the conscious effort to relate ideas to one another, the less systematic and the lower the scheme. Seeing the world as a phenomenon of utterly unrelated facts is perhaps the lowest form of thinking; but most notions about politics will stand somewhere on the continuum between this position, on the one hand, and such systematic efforts as those of Plato and Hobbes, on the other hand.

The student of political ideas should, of course, be interested in every level of thinking from the lowest to the most systematic and complete. The former will usually embrace what might be called popular thought and it will often be an excellent clue to the kinds of considerations which move men in politics. It will, in fact, be an indispensable aspect of the study of culture in general and of politics in particular. At the higher levels, of course, one might expect to find the schemes most useful for a sophisticated understanding; but the nonpopular thought of one generation often becomes the popular thought of a later period.

In the history of political ideas, the subject of the pages which follow, we are concerned with the development of thought at every level in the context of Western culture. We shall be interested in seeing ideas not only in their abstract form, but also as they are related to the economics, politics, religion, and institutions in a given age. Every body of political ideas includes within it notions which are "culture-bound"—that is, which are peculiar expressions of the way of life of a given region and time and which deal with particular issues that may disappear in another age—as well as propositions which might conceivably have more universal applicability. And the history of political ideas will endeavor to distinguish between the two.

With respect to the more systematic thinkers, we shall be very much concerned with biography, since part of history is the relation of ideas to the development of personality; and the experiences of a man's life will help account for many of the peculiarities of his thought, just as his thought will assist in explaining his actions. Seen in the context of his life, his thought will often be clearer than if viewed simply in the abstract: Thus Plato's attitude toward the several factions of the Athenian *polis* is to be understood not only through a reading of his *Dialogues* but also by a study of the *Seventh Letter*. Moreover, as one interprets systems of thought "ideologically"—sees them as in part an expression of some particular or class interest—biography as well as general history will become indispensable.

But we should beware of confusing biographical, historical, sociological, and psychological explanations of a body of ideas with issues involving the validity of the ideas themselves. We may trace Hobbes' great concern with security back to his experiences of early childhood; but this is a different question from the issue of whether his account of human nature is correct or whether his prescription for attaining security is supportable. The historian of ideas is concerned with both questions, but he should keep them distinct.

We shall not hesitate in this volume to criticize particular viewpoints, not only through the medium of analyzing the alternative positions—in the ongoing dialectic so central to the history of ideas—but also in terms of the present writer's own judgments. Some ideas are to be preferred to others on philosophical, empirical, normative, or practical grounds. Political theorists, Benjamin Lippincott has observed, are obviously interested in knowing what a writer has said; but they are "still more interested in determining its truth."[4] The present writer believes that he has an obligation, then, to scrutinize thought for its truth value not merely through the lenses of others but through his own as well.[5] A merely descriptive history of political ideas is not enough.

What value may we attribute to the history of political ideas as conceived here?

One school of thought, at least in American political science circles, would see little. It tends to argue that "understanding politics" is a matter of developing scientific models and then testing them empirically. As we gradually accumulate a body of if-then or hypothetical statements, we shall (so one infers) eventually have some understanding of the complex world of political institutions, views, dynamics, and struggle.

Now obviously much of the controversy results from what we mean by an understanding of politics. We have already suggested that from the viewpoint of the present volume, understanding is much more than science. Political ideas are as much in the realm of the humanities as they are in the social sciences; and imaginative literature may be as significant a source of ideas as formal treatises. Intuitions must be compared with intuitions; direct experience with direct experience; and mythological representation with mythological representation—all this goes beyond science, as that term is usually understood.

More specifically, however, let us assess the

4. "Political Theory in the United States," in *Contemporary Political Science, A Survey of Methods, Research and Teaching*, UNESCO, 1950, p. 216.
5. One of the criticisms frequently directed at past essays in the history of political ideas is that they rarely provided a critical judgment on the schemes examined. They seemed to offer no standards for evaluation and even to deny that such standards existed. See Lippincott, *op. cit.*, pp. 213–216. This is also a complaint made familiar to students by David Easton, *The Political System*, New York: Knopf, 1953.

possible value of the history of political ideas in the context of this humanities-social-science conception of understanding.

We may suggest first of all that politics is an important aspect of human culture and that culture obviously has a past. Men reflect on their cultures and an understanding of how they have reflected is patently a part of our comprehension of both culture and politics. If the study of history in general has value for a grasping of the human condition, then that segment which examines the history of political ideas must be held to have a similar importance for its particular sphere. "Like literature," John Morley once observed, "the use of history in politics is to refresh, to open, to make the mind generous and hospitable; to enrich, to impart flexibility, to quicken and nourish political imagination and invention, to instruct in the common difficulties and the various experiences of government. . . ."[6]

For those accustomed to using physics as a model and who therefore argue that the history of political ideas is as irrelevant for understanding politics as the history of physical ideas allegedly is for understanding physics, a significant observation is offered by John Plamenatz. Our social and political theory, he argues, will affect our conduct, whereas what we believe about the physical universe will not change the nature of that universe. Political beliefs, whether erroneous or not, need study if only to help explain why and how political behavior of a particular type took place. This can be understood, we may suggest, only in the context of a variety of cultural and historical conditions.

Our social theory, Plamenatz goes on, can affect conduct in two ways: "by causing us to believe that society is so and so constituted and thus to act on that belief, and by changing our ideas about what is right or desirable. This it may do though rooted in ignorance and arrogance."[7] The history of political ideas, by attempting to relate even erroneous notions to human deeds in particular and diverse cultures, can help us understand the politics based on those ideas. This assumes, of course, that men's images of the world about them affect the way they behave, a proposition which, while some may question its proof, is surely a plausible one.

The history of political ideas, moreover, like the history of thought in general, will illustrate in concrete terms how one system arises in response to, and acts as a corrective for, others. This is an important empirical datum and yet another of the many elements which enter into an understanding of politics in its broadest sense.

Besides, the portrayal of ideas historically can make for a critical spirit and open-mindedness, which should be important values in any study. Seen historically, many bodies of ideas can plausibly be interpreted, at least in part, as rationalizations of a given *status quo;* and this should put one on guard about one's own thinking and the degree to which it can transcend the pressures of class, cultural, and national interest. The history of political ideas dramatizes the fragility of every system of thought as it is tested against logic and experience. One learns to raise questions about every scheme, however plausible it may have seemed. As one sees Thomist undermined by Ockhamite views, for example, and Lockean ideas challenged by Burke, one becomes more dubious about the incontrovertibility of any single body of thought but, at the same time, aware of a degree of validity in every analysis. In addition, one sees how the speculations of great minds are often distorted by their followers to mean something radically different—in part, at least, because the original systems contained so many ambiguities. But one comes also to appreciate that any attempt to think profoundly will always exhaust the resources of language, thus making inconsistencies and ambiguities virtually inevitable.

Some students of politics seem to imply that their efforts should be confined to an examination of the contemporary world. But what is contemporary? No sooner does an event take place than it is past and a part of the historical record. The materials of all political science come from the past, even those gathered by so-called behavioral methods. The present, to be sure, may be a necessary way of speaking; but it is quite ephemeral. While the past no doubt exists, it is also true that any given generation will in considerable degree, through its own selective consciousness, make its own past; just as ideas developed in the past—those of Locke, for instance, or of Marx—become ineluctable constituents of the future, often being implemented long after they were first formulated. The history of political ideas assumes a seamlessness in human experience, the so-called present and the future shaping the past, just as the past is organically embodied in the future.

The history of political ideas can also give us perspective with respect to the vexing problem of novelty. It is easy enough to claim that a modern hypothesis or a moral conception is new. But truly novel ideas in the domains of morals and politics are extremely rare and the history of political thought can demonstrate just how uncommon they are. Much of what we take to be new may simply be rebaptized concepts as old as the history of thought. Knowing this we gain humility, without which there can be little understanding.

Finally, the history of political ideas can be defended as a liberal art whose study is intrinsically interesting. Aside from all other values which one might allege, it is enough to say that men's reactions to the political universe have a fascination analogous to that which the student of some ancient dialect may find in his subject or a student of art before a great painting. One will find the development of meaning in political language; the struggle of men to understand the social context of their lives; the foolishness and the wisdom which are often combined in the same system; the interaction of ideas with institutions; mixtures of magic, religion, and science in speculation about politics; and the frustrations of even great minds when they discover their inability to communicate without ambiguity.

One should not, of course, expect too much. In morals and politics, there is no clear-cut development which supposedly betokens progress. Nor are there definitive solutions to most of the questions which men have asked themselves: One ends, perhaps, in greater doubt than when one began. But these very limitations are enlightening.

Themes and Perspectives

In Part I, we sketch the beginning of political speculation in ancient times and its main lines of development to the rise of Christianity: The notion of organic, intimate community is a central theme. In Part II, which treats political thought in the so-called Christian centuries, a tension is set up between the claims of temporal authority and those of spiritual rule: a conflict unlike preponderant streams of thought in ancient times. With Part III, we enter the heyday of "individualism," when the point of departure for analysis tends to be the discrete individual; community is seen increasingly as an artifact until the end of this epoch just before the French Revolution. In Part IV, all important streams of thought since the Revolution must respond to the traumatic effect of the Revolution itself, to the phenomena connected with the National State, and to the fever-heat development of industrialization which makes political—deliberate—answers more imperative than ever, but which at the same time often tends to make them improbable in the light of technological and other imperatives. Finally, beyond Part IV, we seek to recapitulate certain major issues which have arisen throughout the volume.

6. "A Few Words on French Revolutionary Models," *Nineteenth Century* 23 (1888), 480.
7. "The Place and Influence of Political and Social Philosophy" (mimeographed), address delivered to the Rome Congress of the International Political Science Association, 1959, p. 13.

part I

THE EMERGENCE OF POLITICS AND THE IDEA OF THE ORGANIC COMMUNITY

The early history of ancient politics and political thought is the story of the issues arising when primitive tribal life gradually dissolved, to be succeeded by the problems characterizing the thrust to deliberate—or political—ordering. Among most beasts, affairs are governed by instinct or native tendencies. In human tribal existence, communities are ruled largely by immemorial custom, and the extent of deliberate or conscious ordering of affairs is strictly limited. With the break-up of tribal life, however, men are squarely confronted (as they are in their personal lives during late adolescence) with the question of how they can order their affairs rationally; for they do not have the instinctual equipment of the beasts, nor can they simply restore the ancient customs. At first, they seek to avoid the issue of deliberate ordering, hoping that the gods or medicine men will supply easy answers. But as human experience grows, at least some men eventually decide that only through thought can they develop substitutes for ordering by wont and immemorial custom.

In the Hebrew experience, this pattern of emergence from tribal to political (or historical) ways was a slow and painful one. From Abraham to the Judges, their tradition was largely a tribal one, with communication mainly oral. Men were attached to their clans and, later on, would look back to them as reflections of an almost idyllic existence. However, political consciousness began to develop at least by the time of Moses, and by the age of Saul had been greatly accentuated. With the expansion of commerce under Solomon, tribal governance broke down still more; and after the downfall of the Kingdom of Judah in the sixth century B.C., Hebrew thinkers had an opportunity to reflect on a long history of sociopolitical experience.

Meanwhile, in Greece, the small and rather isolated communities of the peninsula were going through stages of change reminiscent, in many respects, of Hebrew development. Tribal-clan systems of human relations were the order of the day for centuries. Even when the tribal way of life broke down and the phenomena associated with "individuality" arose, men did not wish to recognize what was taking place. They called on the gods to save them, but in vain. By the seventh and sixth centuries B.C., they were beginning to understand the imperatives for a deliberate construction of social order, and by the fourth century, were producing the classical Greek systems of political thought.

After the fourth century, large-scale empires increasingly began to supersede the intimate life of the city-state. With the development of these complex structures came the phenomena of what moderns call alienation, with the individual feeling more and more politically helpless and divorced from society.

How did men respond to these experiences from the time of Moses to the age of the Antonines?

In general, the early period was characterized by views which saw individual and community as organically interconnected: The tribe might be dead but man could, nevertheless, consciously resurrect something of its warmth in political form. In ancient Hebrew thought this organicism is reflected in the development of the idea of the Covenant, or *berith*. Associated with it was a conception of law, a theory of history, and a vision of how men can eventually reconcile the intimacy of the clan with the imperatives of civilization. But Hebrew thought did not develop great systematic speculations; instead, it expressed itself mythologically or through prophetic utterances.

In Greece, by contrast, preclassical, classical, and postclassical thought were all characterized by efforts to build intellectual systems. To be sure, the preclassical schemes were sketchy and incomplete. The effort, however, was there. In classical thought, Plato and Aristotle sought to give philosophical form to the idea of a small, closely knit community, which, while allowing considerable development in division of labor, still controls the economic aspect of life and subordinates it to political, aesthetic, and ethical considerations. Problems of ethics and politics, which the modern world has often tended to separate from each other, were regarded as different sides of the same coin.

But with the break-up of the city-state and the domination of empire, man's alienation was expressed in philosophies like those of Cynicism and Stoicism, which, to some degree, appear to think of individual fulfillment as achievable apart from the community. Ethics and politics were, to be sure, not completely divorced from each other, but an uneasy tension was set up between them, which would be continued and developed after the rise of Christianity.

Man's efforts to think politically in the Alexandrian and Roman empires were characterized by this tension, which existed in the context of such significant factors as the polarization of classes, the growth of slavery, the rise of large cities, and the quest for universal norms of law. By the time of Marcus Aurelius, more than a few thinkers had sought to synthesize elements of Greek speculation with aspects of Hebrew social and political thought. To the Hebrew conviction that "history" and particulars are significant was annexed—somewhat uneasily—the classical Greek notion that it is the "form" or the idea or the permanent which is the goal of the political and social adventure.

In summary, Part I begins with the emergence of political from tribal life, continues through the working out of organic conceptions of political community, and ends with a kind of eclecticism which is reflected in the first phases of Christian thought.

chapter 1

Politics and Ethics Among the Ancient Hebrews

Reflection on social and political experience is very old in one sense yet relatively recent in another. It is old in that long before the great systems of thought produced by the ancient Greeks, political consciousness was developing among the Egyptians (fourth millennium B.C.) and such peoples as the first Chaldeans (about the third millennium B.C.).[1] It is relatively recent in that even the earliest recorded attitudes to politics, law, and social organization do not appear until the human species has lived on the earth more than three-fourths of its total span.[2]

Over a fairly wide area of the earth, human beings first appeared living in small bands and protecting themselves from nature by rather crude devices. There would seem to be no evidence whatsoever that men ever lived isolated from one another—they always existed in bands or herds of some kind. In the earliest epochs, they managed to support life by hunting and fishing, although it was always a precarious existence. Later, they became pastoral, moving from pasture to pasture with their flocks and organizing themselves in tribes and clans. At this stage of social evolution, kinship played the decisive role in the structuring of human societies; and wont and custom provided virtually the only guidance for both individual and collective life. Even when pastoral peoples begin to lead more stationary lives and take up agricultural occupations, their manners, morals, and law are almost always customary and unquestioned; and any distinction between and among morals, law, religion, and magic was largely absent. As the primitive agricultural civilizations begin to construct cities, however, governance by wont tends to break down; and societies, instead of being held together only by immemorial custom, must in part find other bases for their guidance. Wont, it is true, still predominates in an overwhelming fashion; but it is no longer as unquestioned as in earlier stages of development. The social use of physical force to counteract rebellious activities on the part of self-conscious individuals becomes more and more an ingredient in compelling cohesion, and great military empires are the external manifestations of the central role which force comes to play. Meanwhile, primitive political thinkers seek to provide an intellectual and mythological foundation for the new kinds of cohesion which in late agricultural and early city civilizations begin to contest the supremacy of the kinship principle.

In many respects, the ancient Hebrews constitute an excellent example of this general pattern of growth, and because their modes of thought are to be so decisive in the later development of Western culture, their emergence as a "political" society is an event of unusual significance. They pass through the economic and social stages common to Egyptians, Assyrians, and Babylonians; for a brief time they even constitute an empire, having characteristics very much like the others. In their intellectual life, too, the Hebrews have much in common with their powerful neighbors.

But while in some respects the Hebrews are typical, in certain others they seem to be unique. Their independent political life, for example, was more precarious than that of their great rivals. They were an empire for only the brief period of Solomon's reign. But what is of even greater significance, they seem to have had an unusually acute religious and ethical sensitivity; and they thought of their own history as having, in some peculiar sense, a universal significance.

Politics from Moses to the Maccabees

From the viewpoint of politics and political theory, it would seem helpful to divide the ancient Hebrew experience into four phases. The first extends, roughly, from the middle of the thirteenth century B.C. to the close of the eleventh; the second, that of the united monarchy, from the eleventh to the last third of the tenth; the third, which embraces the divided monarchy, from the latter part of the tenth to the beginning of the sixth; while the fourth, initiated by the fall of the monarchy, ends in the second century B.C. with its revival in modified form.

The Pastoral-Judges Stage. The outlines of Hebrew social evolution can hardly be discerned much before the time of Moses (thirteenth century) and even then the picture is not entirely clear. Apparently, the loose aggregation of tribes known as the Hebrews had been welcomed into Egypt under a dynasty which was closely akin to them ethnically. No doubt other wandering desert tribes were from time to time also provided with living space in Egypt during the same period. With the coming of the Nineteenth Dynasty (about 1328 B.C.), however, the attitude of the Egyptian government changed. Rameses II (c. 1300–1234 B.C.) was particularly insistent that outsiders like the Hebrews not be recognized as the equals of Egyptians. The period of slavery is said, therefore, to have begun in his reign.

Under his successor the Exodus took place. Thereafter, for nearly half a century, the tribes were wandering in the desert. Having just emerged from conditions of servitude, they were ill prepared for an independent social existence. At times, they seemed to reject any discipline whatsoever; while at other points they appeared receptive to a restoration of servitude.[3] Their organization was in terms of clans and tribes; and each family was ruled by the father, the combined fathers of tribes and clans constituting councils of elders. For many years, no doubt, such laws as they possessed were customary. With no fixed place of habitation, nothing resembling a "State" in the Egyptian sense was possible.

Under these conditions, the figure of Moses emerged as the symbol of a more closely knit social organization and body of laws. According to tradition, he actually initiated the flight from Egypt, although the evidence for his historicity is slight indeed. If he did exist, however, he must have been a commanding figure. Men followed him because there was something about him which gave him an air of authority.

Economically, the wandering tribes were sustained by their sheep and cattle. Division of labor was extremely primitive, of course; and trade, if it existed at all, must have been very limited in extent. Every family was virtually self-sustaining.

After a generation of sometimes aimless roving, the tribes reached Palestine and then began their long and slow conquest of the "Promised Land." Some of the Old Testament accounts imply that the triumph of the Hebrews over the ancient cultures of Palestine was a rapid matter, but nothing could be further from the truth. The territory had to be gained foot by foot over a period of perhaps more than a hundred years; and even then, the original inhabitants were constantly revolting. It was not, indeed, until the time of David (about 1010 B.C.) that the last stronghold, Jerusalem, was taken.

Each of the twelve tribes occupied a different part of the country. Two tribes clustered together in the southern portion; several others constituted a kind of central strip; while the remainder gradually settled down in the northern area. There were jealousies and conflicts between and among individual tribes and a very basic tension between the southern tribes, on the one hand, and the central and northern clusters, on the other. Tribes and individual clans would carry on raiding expeditions against the still remaining Canaanite towns and in the process a kind of informal leadership was developed. The "Judges" were originally leaders of plundering clans and tribes and often came to be highly regarded, primarily because of their military prowess. But they were much more than military leaders. They were also arbitrators of clan and tribal disputes and were looked up to as intellectual leaders as well. Not chosen to fill an established office, they rather asserted their own superior qualities and in a sense created their own offices.[4]

It is clear that during the period of the Judges—roughly, from 1150 to 1025 B.C.—there was no centralized organization whatsoever. While a given Judge might be widely respected among all the twelve tribes, his relation to the tribes and to individuals within the tribes was not a superordinate-subordinate one. Although Joshua had to some extent been a leader of all the tribes, there were relatively few who fol-

1. A recent work which treats of ancient Egyptian and Near Eastern political thought is Eric Voegelin, *Order and History: Israel and Revelation*, vol. 1, Baton Rouge: Louisiana State University Press, 1956. See also R. T. Rundle Clark, *Myth and Symbol in Ancient Egypt*, London: Thames and Hudson, 1959.
2. When human beings became "human," as we know them today, is, of course, a point much disputed. Oral speculation, of course, preceded expression of written attitudes.
3. Such, it would seem, is illustrated by the worship of the "golden calf." Even servitude appeared appealing compared with the harshness and uncertainty of desert life.
4. Perhaps they had "charisma," as that term is used today—they appeared to possess extraordinary physical, psychic, and spiritual qualities or "divine gifts."

lowed in his footsteps. Any common action by the tribes as a whole would have to be initiated by ad hoc consultations among the elders; and decisions might or might not be accepted by the often unruly and highly independent tribesmen.

In the latter half of the eleventh century, however, pressure from relatively powerful surrounding peoples began to be felt. The Philistines particularly became a matter of concern to all of the tribes; and the story of the judge Samson is largely built around his successful exploits against them. But the Judges, however able, had no permanent machinery to assist them. Each developing situation had to be treated on an ad hoc basis, which to increasing numbers of critics among the tribes was not a satisfactory arrangement. Moreover, the desire to imitate surrounding peoples, most of whom possessed more permanent organizations, was a factor in the growing unrest within most of the tribes. This combination of an alleged need for regular leadership and the ever-present tendency of the Hebrews to imitate older cultures in matters of religion and politics led to the pressure for a monarchy.

But there was apparently vigorous opposition to the demand for a king. Certain shrewd observers noted that Philistines and others were subjected to many more onerous regulations than the Hebrews. Their kings conscripted them for war, and taxes, which were almost nonexistent in the twelve tribes, were levied ruthlessly in surrounding monarchies. It is small wonder that antagonism to kingly rule was so great.

Only the pressure of events, with which the opponents of monarchy could not deal, can account for the fact that the tribes eventually succumbed to the cry for a king, and thus Saul was chosen about 1025 B.C. The theory of the monarchy we shall deal with below.[5] Now, however, we should note some of the problems which the newly established kingdom confronted.

The United Kingdom. The first question, undoubtedly, with which King Saul had to deal was the continuing lack of harmony among the tribes themselves. This remained throughout the period of the united kingdom a political factor of great importance. On the whole, Saul attempted to unite the tribes primarily through successful leadership in war.

A second and related question of some importance had to do with the relationship between tribal and the newly emerging political government. This is an issue which always confronts a society in the transition stages between kinship-organization and a scheme which endeavors to transcend clan and tribal loyalties. How much authority will be retained by the traditional family and tribal elders in the face of pressures making for centralized controls? It is unclear from the record how issues of this kind were resolved in detail. In the time of Saul, however, it seems evident that tribal ties remained very strong indeed; and even under his successor David, the centrifugal tendencies continued powerful. Only under Solomon did they give way to some extent.

In the time of David, the ancient capital of the Jebusites, Jerusalem, was finally taken and this served to strengthen the centralizing tendencies of the monarchy. In the reign of David, too, trade and commerce tended to provide an economic basis for greater interdependence. By this time, the Canaanite inhabitants were being absorbed by the Hebrews culturally; or perhaps it would be more accurate to say that the synthesis between Hebrew and Canaanite culture was being completed. David may be thought of as the consolidator of the united kingdom, provided that we keep in mind the continuance of strong tribal attachments. At the same time, the boundaries of the kingdom were enlarged.

Solomon's reign was characterized by a great expansion of commerce, the establishment of diplomatic alliances, and a centering of power in Jerusalem. The development of commerce had as one of its results a growing gulf between rich and poor, with conservatives pointing back to the premonarchical days as a time when men were equal. Class unrest apparently made its appearance.

Diplomatic and economic alliances strengthened the position of the united monarchy externally and provided the period of peace so essential for such gigantic public works as the royal palace and the Temple. The ancient chronicler tells us that David was not allowed to build the Temple because he had "shed much blood."[6] Under Solomon, the external bloodshed, for the most part, ceased and it is now possible to speak of a Hebrew Empire.

In his last years, Solomon seemed to insist more and more on acting in an arbitrary fashion, disregarding ancient customs and no doubt antagonizing tribal elders. His critics pointed out that his royal palace was much more elaborate than the Temple which he had constructed for religious purposes. The old feeling for tribal and personal freedom clashed with the demands of royal taxation and conscript labor. Thus, an accumulation of resentments made the last days of Solomon unhappy ones. Toward the end, a general of the army, Jeroboam, sought to revolt. Unsuccessful, he managed to take refuge in Egypt, from which he no doubt carried on a correspondence looking to an eventual overthrow of the Davidic house.

The Two Kingdoms. When Solomon died, Jeroboam saw his opportunity. Returning from Egypt, he placed himself at the head of the opposition and challenged Solomon's son and successor, Rehoboam. The latter was apparently a man of little political sagacity. He might have been able to have saved the united kingdom with a little more wisdom. But instead of wisdom, he accentuated the coercion of Solomon, telling a protesting delegation that whereas his father had "chastised" the Israelites with "whips," he would "chastise" them with "scorpions."

This was too much for the northern and central clusters of tribes. As we have noted, they had always been restive, even in the days of the Judges. Now, in 933 B.C., under the leadership of Jeroboam, they revolted against Rehoboam and established the independent kingdom known as Israel. The rump of what had been the Davidic kingdom came to be called Judah, the name of its largest constituent tribe. During more than two hundred years, the two Hebrew monarchies existed in uneasy relations with each other. Both were beset by pressures from the outside—from Assyria, Syria, Egypt, and Babylonia. Both sought to maintain their integrity and independence by a series of hazardous alliances and by playing off the great empires against one another. Both were under a constant temptation to succumb to foreign cultures and religions.

The northern kingdom's career was the briefer of the two. Unlike Judah, its royal house did not remain in any single family. Often ambitious generals like Jehu (about 842 B.C.) seized the kingdom and proclaimed themselves its rulers. The period of its greatest prosperity and temporal power occurred during the reign of Jeroboam II (about 783–743 B.C.). But after his death, Israel began to decline in power very rapidly. It tried desperately to avoid absorption by Assyria. But in 722 its capital, Samaria, fell to the armies of the Assyrian king, and many of its inhabitants were taken captive and scattered throughout the Assyrian domain.

Meanwhile, the politics of Judah were equally complex. While the royal family remained Davidic until the dissolution of the kingdom, Judah was beset by numerous domestic and external conflicts. Internally, there was a tendency for its kings to absorb the religious customs of surrounding peoples, possibly because they were less demanding than those of the stern Jewish moralists. It is in Judah that most of the great prophets originate, beginning in the ninth and extending through the seventh and sixth centuries. It is in Judah, too, that "prophecy" is most closely associated with the course of domestic and international politics.[7]

In 607 B.C., the Assyrian Empire fell and men hoped—particularly in such fragile states as Judah—that this meant relief from a long period of uncertainty and warfare. But already the new Babylonian Empire (founded in 625 B.C.) had begun to rise, becoming the chief opponent of Egypt after the destruction of Assyria. After King Josiah had denied the Egyptian king permission to pass through his country in order to attack his giant rival, the Egyptian monarch defeated the army of Judah at Megiddo (608 B.C.) and, after the fall of Assyria, also attacked the Babylonians. During the period between 608 and 605 B.C., Judah became a tributary to Egypt. In the latter year, however, the Babylonian general Nebuchadrezzar triumphed over the Egyptians and forced the king of Judah to become a puppet of the Babylonian monarch. Thereafter, until the second "fall of Jerusalem" in 587, both the internal and the external politics of Judah were dominated by the question of what to do about the problem of political subservience to Babylon.

From the Fall of Judah to the Reestablishment of Monarchy. Many Jews were taken to Babylon both after the first fall of Jerusalem in 597 and following its final capture in 587. Those who remained in Judah were put under

5. See pp. 19–22.
6. 1 Chronicles 28:3. Another reason given is that David had been a "man of war."
7. It may, indeed, be asserted that the *occasion* for prophecy in Judah is almost always political.

the control of a governor appointed by the Babylonian Empire.

In terms of politics, the next generation was characterized by attempts on the part of many in Babylon to return. As a matter of fact, the center of religious and political interest shifted almost completely to Babylon, whither most of the Jewish intellectuals had been transported. Some exiles did return in 538, with permission of the Persian king who by now had conquered Babylon; and in 516, the Second Temple was dedicated. But politically, Judah remained a part of the Persian Empire.

By the middle of the next century another group of exiles returned, first under Ezra and then under Nehemiah. While the status of the Jews still remained one of subordination to the Persian Empire, they were apparently granted considerable autonomy. Under the influence of strict priestly minded men like Ezra, they built an ecclesiastical organization and in most matters were governed by their own religiously inspired laws. As a matter of fact, we may think of them in some sense as a kind of "church-state" within the confines of the Persian Empire.[8]

When Jerusalem surrendered to Alexander the Great in 332 B.C., the Macedonian master maintained and apparently even extended their privileges. It was only under his successors that tension developed. In 167 B.C., Antiochus Epiphanes of Syria, whose father had taken Palestine from the Egyptian Ptolemaic successors of Alexander, attempted to suppress Jewish religion, apparently in the interests of Greek cultural supremacy. This led to the great Maccabean revolt, first under Mattathias and then under the leadership of his sons Judas, Jonathan, and Simon. By 165, with the recapture of Jerusalem, the Maccabees could restore Temple worship. Thereafter, the politics of the Jews became more complicated than ever. There were tensions within the Maccabean family itself; and often these conflicts led to alliances and counter-alliances with combatting elements in the Syrian court. Generally speaking, the Maccabeans became high priests, and by virtue of this office had political as well as ecclesiastical influence, if, indeed, it is legitimate to differentiate the two in Jewish thought. Although Jerusalem and its surrounding territory gained a kind of independence from Syria in 142, it was a precarious autonomy and was always profoundly affected by the politics of Syria and of Egypt.

Finally, in 105 B.C., Aristobulus, a grandson of Simon Maccabaeus, proclaimed himself king and thus, in form at least, reestablished the monarchy. We do not need to go into the vicissitudes of the Maccabean monarchy. Allied at times with the rising Roman power and at other times opposed to it, it maintained a kind of spurious independence until weakened by Pompey's conquest of Jerusalem and the rise of the rival claims of the Herods in the next century.

Reconstructing the Ancient Hebrew Outlook

It is no easy task to reconstruct what ancient Hebrew thinkers thought about society and politics. This is true for a number of reasons.

In the first place, and most basically, the literary sources from which the reconstruction must be developed—chiefly the Old Testament and the Hebrew Apocrypha—are in a confused state. The Old Testament is neither a logically nor a chronologically arranged series of books. Indeed, within each of its divisions one will find deposits from widely diverse ages. Biblical scholars have, to be sure, sought to identify these sources and to establish, as nearly as possible, the time to which they may be attributed.[9] They have endeavored, too, to identify the authors of the several books, going behind the often fictive names under which they have been traditionally known. Thus, one of the earliest efforts at "Higher Criticism" of the Bible was to demonstrate that the so-called "books of Moses" could not have been written by Moses—that they were, indeed, a compilation of many documents and traditions stretching out over a period of a millennium.

But even with their best efforts, students of Hebrew literature find themselves unable to reach agreement about many problems involved in Biblical interpretation.

A second general difficulty in reconstructing the political positions of ancient Hebrew thinkers turns on what we shall understand politics to mean in the context of Hebrew life. The religious consciousness, it has long been recognized, is central in any interpretation of Hebrew development and that consciousness refused to make the distinctions which are customary in modern times or even among the ancient Greeks. "Law," for example, was intimately bound up with religious ceremonial as well as with the concerns which we should today classify as "secular." In their whole development, as a matter of fact, the Hebrews remained *theocratically* oriented—that is, they conceived themselves to be governed, either directly or indirectly, by Yahweh. Hence, they were constantly seeing in the events of political history the finger of the deity. The religious, political, and historical dimensions of consciousness, then, are so inextricably interwoven in Hebrew thought as to be virtually inseparable.

Finally, both in literary development and in terms of political thought, many scholars think of the date 621 B.C. as extraordinarily significant. It was in that year that the militant social and religious reformer, King Josiah of Judah, instructed the high priest to supervise repair of the Temple. As its precincts were being searched, an allegedly ancient "book of the law" was discovered and brought to the king. Josiah read the book and ordered its proposals carried out immediately. It is widely thought today that the scroll was a large part of Deuteronomy and that much of it had been written either shortly before Josiah or in the early part of his reign, although it was ascribed to the ancient lawgiver Moses.

The significance of this event is many-fold. Historically, it reflected the work of eighth- and seventh-century prophets, who had as their objective little less than a revolution in Judah's way of life. For Deuteronomy advocated a complete centralization of worship in Jerusalem and a simultaneous destruction of local shrines and "high places." We have already seen that since the days of Solomon, the Temple at Jerusalem had assumed greater and greater importance. But in the three hundred years between Solomon and Josiah there had never been a time when both Temple and local shrines had not been regarded as legitimate for purposes of worship. Now, however, after the "discovery" of Deuteronomy, a pious Jew could theoretically offer sacrifice only in the capital. This meant not merely a religious centralization but also an enhancement of the political centralization which had begun in the days of King Solomon; for the king, as the agent of Yahweh, could use the monopolistic position of the Temple for political purposes as well as religious rites. Deuteronomy theoretically sanctioned centralization in order to keep pure the religion of Yahweh, which, according to the prophets, had been so frequently corrupted during the eighth and seventh centuries. But it also meant that if a bad king should ever reign, his power to effect a religious revolution in the reverse direction would likewise be enhanced. It made easier the establishment of institutionalized religion—the reduction of the ancient faith to a series of external ceremonies.

But Deuteronomy also had a second significance. It provided an up-to-date version of the ancient law which stressed ethical and political justice rather than merely religious ritual. One will also find portrayed in Deuteronomy a whole cluster of social, legal, and political ideals which were probably unknown in the days of Solomon, let alone in those of Moses.[10] Thus such principles as those involving land tenure, economic organization, and social structure may represent the goals of the reformers of the seventh century rather than primitive Hebrew notions.[11] And these Deuteronomic ideals inform other parts of the Old Testament which on the surface purport to represent deposits of an older day. Some parts of I and II Samuel, to cite one instance, were probably written, or at least edited, by reformers who helped shape the ideals of Deuteronomy. It is possible, too, that the famous statement of Samuel which purported to predict the evils of monarchy[12] was actually written during the seventh century, some four hundred years after Samuel, and therefore with four centuries of monarchical rule as a background. All this, of course, enhances the difficulty of interpreting Hebrew thought.

We may also observe in conclusion that the Deuteronomic documents—both those in Deuteronomy itself and those purportedly

8. Indeed, scholars like Julius Wellhausen tend to think of Jewish ecclesiastical organization in the empire as the beginning of the "church" idea which would be so important in the later history of thought. See Julius Wellhausen, *Prolegomena to the History of Ancient Israel*, New York: Meridian Books, 1957.
9. See, for example, *The Interpreter's Bible*, 4 vols., New York and Nashville: Abingdon Press, 1962. See also S. R. Driver, *An Introduction to the Literature of the Old Testament*, New York: Meridian Library, 1956 (originally published in 1897).
10. Thus parts of Deuteronomy reflect the rise of commercialism and its problems.
11. In the reign of Manasseh, which preceded that of Josiah, the reformers would have been out of favor at court and would thus have had much time to speculate.
12. 1 Samuel 8: 11–18.

scattered throughout other parts of the Old Testament—represent the beginnings of both literary and political self-consciousness. True, there were oral traditions which go far back into Hebrew history; and there were also other important documents—for example, the Book of Amos, dating from about 760 B.C.—which antedated the Deuteronomic reforms. But it was the impetus of Deuteronomic speculations which was to set in motion not only immediate social and political reforms but also an almost continuous literary history from the beginning of the seventh century through the long period of postexilic creativity to the reestablishment of the monarchy in 105 B.C.

Keeping in mind, then, the difficulties of imposing order on the mass of documents known as the Old Testament, the inseparability of law, religion and politics in the Hebrew view of things, and the significance of the Deuteronomic reforms and documents, let us examine three historically important Hebrew sociopolitical notions: the conception of the Covenant, the doctrine of monarchy, and the prophetic theory of political history.

The Conception of the Covenant

As we have noted earlier,[13] the ancient Hebrew mind, apparently from a very early period, saw the key to an understanding of God in all his ramifications in a study of human history and particularly in Hebrew history. History revealed the "will of God" and exhibited Yahweh's intentions for the Hebrew people. In the prophetic theory of history, which we shall examine presently,[14] this notion underwent considerable development and its formulation was closely connected with politics of the seventh and sixth centuries B.C.

But the root of political-historical interpretation lay in the conception of the Covenant (*berith*). "Covenant" is used with considerable frequency in designating agreements between the deity and individual men. Thus God makes a Covenant with Noah promising protection from the coming Flood.[15] But it is the Covenant between the tribes of Israel and Yahweh which is of greatest political and historical importance. Thus in Genesis we probably have reflected a very ancient tradition of Yahweh promising Abraham: "I will bless you, and make your name so great that it will be used for blessings. I will bless those who bless you, and anyone who curses you I will curse; through you shall all the families of the earth invoke blessings on one another."[16]

And long centuries later, after the death of Rameses II, the Israelites are represented as "groaning under their bondage" and crying for help: "And their cry because of their bondage came up to God. God heard their moaning, and God remembered his covenant with Abraham, Isaac, and Jacob; God saw the plight of Israel, and took cognizance of it."[17] Moses, as a matter of fact, becomes God's agent in carrying out the Covenant.

During the period of the Judges, an angel of God restates the two-way Covenant, with its rights and obligations on each side: "I will never break my covenant with you, but you on your part must make no covenant with the inhabitants of this land; you must tear down their altars."[18] When Deuteronomy itself is discovered during the reign of Josiah, the reforming scribe reports how the king read the ancient agreement to the assembly.[19] And in the Psalms, God is represented as never forgetting his Covenant with Israel.[20]

In Amos, the Covenant seems to be much broader than that merely between the Israelites and God. Rather, it appears to be an agreement with all nations. For the Lord, in condemning Tyre, states that his condemnation is because the Tyrians "handed over a whole people as captives to Edom, and did not remember the covenant of brotherhood."[21] Malachi apparently conceives that there is a special subordinate Covenant between God and the priests, for he condemns those priests who do not perform their functions well; they have violated the Covenant which God has made with Levi.[22]

Finally, the greatest of the prophets, Jeremiah, is reputed to have spoken of a new Covenant between Israel and God. For in the thirty-first chapter of the Book of Jeremiah, the prophet (or some later editor using his name to support the idea) reports the "oracle" of the Lord:

> Days are coming . . . when I will make a new covenant with the house of Israel and with the house of Judah, not like the covenant which I made with their fathers on the day that I took them by the hand to lead them out of the land of Egypt . . .; but this is the covenant which I will make with the house of Israel after those days. . . . I will put my law within them.[23]

But having cited relevant passages dealing with the Covenant idea, it is not easy to reconstruct what must have been its development. In the beginning, we may suggest, the Covenant was closely associated with ritualistic religion as well as with the endeavor to promote social solidarity by magical incantations. If only the Israelites would offer the proper sacrifices, God would keep his Covenant with them; and they would not fall apart as a people. We see here an endeavor, primitive though it may be, to develop consciously a conception of organic unity, when that unity is threatened with disruption due to the breakdown of social solidarity of wont and custom. At the same time, one seems to discern the notion that the basis of such unity as the tribes did achieve was not due either to a contract among themselves or to nature, but rather to a special kind of agreement with deity. The basis for law lay neither in rational calculations, nor merely in custom, but rather in divine guidance to ad hoc leaders like Moses. Or at least so such leaders seem to teach.

When direct theocratic conceptions decline and the monarchy is established, the Covenant is thought to be a kind of contract between the king, as bearing in his person the corporeity of Israel, and Yahweh. When Josiah discovers the "book of the Covenant," he thinks it his obligation to carry it out with great thoroughness. His massacre of antagonistic elements among the priesthood and his almost fanatical centralization of worship in Jerusalem are examples of his effort to execute the Deuteronomic version of the berith.

In the prophetic writing, while the Covenant tends to remain one primarily between the people of Israel and Yahweh, its implications are often quite different from those of earlier days. Although variations in the prophets should be noted, their tendency is to think of the Covenant not as an agreement between a jealous God and an Israel who must propitiate him through semimagical rites and seemingly irrational massacres but rather as a description of the conditions under which political and social stability and development in human life can be achieved. The great prophets such as Amos, the first Isaiah, and Jeremiah, were not only deeply religious figures but also shrewd observers of politics. They were searching for regularities in social and political life, very much as the Greeks of the fifth century B.C. were beginning to do. But the Hebrew prophets sought to fit their observations on international and domestic politics into the religious frame of reference which they inherited—that of a peculiar Covenant between Israel and Yahweh. In doing so, they reinterpret the corporate mission of Israel,[24] connecting it very distinctly with such problems as the relation between "right" and "might" and the distribution of income and power. Some of them, as, for example, Amos and the figure known as the postexilic "second" Isaiah, even seem to think of the Covenant as one between not merely Israel and God but also as a contract, in some sense, between God and humanity. Indeed, insofar as the prophets grope for universal ethical and political explanations and norms, they all seem to move in this direction.

Monarchy in Hebrew Thought

It is only in light of Covenant ideas that Hebrew conceptions of monarchy in general and of the Hebrew monarchy in particular can be understood. For both those who supported the monarchy and those who opposed it believed that they were fulfilling the Covenant.

Those who sustained the monarchy thought of it, apparently, as the most effective way by which Israel's obligations under the Covenant could be fulfilled. Thus, the king is consecrated to God and is anointed by a priest as both an instrument of God and as the figure symbolic of the people.[25]

That the king is both the instrument of God and in some sense the agent of the people must often create uncertainty as to his role. Suppose the will of God, for example, conflicts with that of the multitude? That it could do so is illustrated in the case of Saul. He is instructed by God to attack the Amalekites and utterly destroy them—to "slaughter both man and

13. See pp. 16–17.
14. Pp. 21–27.
15. Genesis 6:18.
16. AT Genesis 12:2. AT refers to *The Complete Bible: An American Translation. Old Testament* trans. by J. M. Powis Smith and a group of scholars. Copyright 1939 by The University of Chicago. All rights reserved. Composed and printed by The University of Chicago Press, Chicago, Ill.
17. AT Exodus 2:23, 24, 25.
18. AT Judges 2:1, 2.
19. 2 Chronicles 34:30, 319.
20. Psalms 105:8, 9.
21. AT Amos 1:9.
22. Malachi 2:4, 5.
23. AT Jeremiah 31:31, 32, 33.
24. See pp. 22–28.
25. Samuel initiates the practice when he anoints Saul. 1 Samuel 10:1.

woman, child and infant, ox and sheep, camel and ass."[26] Saul does indeed carry out these orders, except that he spares Agag, King of the Amalekites, and also "the best of the sheep, the oxen, the fatlings, the lambs, and all that was good. . . ."[27] For this seemingly minor (in the eyes of the people) disobedience, the monarchy is taken away from Saul's house and given to that of David.

On the other hand, the sanction merely of God is not sufficient for rulership. Thus the monarchy itself, while eventually blessed by God, is originally established at the behest of the people; for God apparently prefers direct rule, as do his spokesmen. Nevertheless, he sees the people clamor for a king and succumbs to the inevitable. While God sanctions the house of David in the person of Rehoboam, it is obvious that a large part of the people do not assent to his rule and God is represented as permitting Jeroboam and the ten tribes to withdraw. Rehoboam's house remains on the throne of Judah, it is true, but the popular will ordains that most Israelites no longer obey him.

Those, then, who support the monarchy (either enthusiastically or reluctantly), see it as the agency of God and the people for the implementation of the Covenant which has promised prosperity and temporal success to Israel. In his dual role, the king, as the anointed of God, reminds the people of God's promises and stipulations; while as the person who reflects the people, the monarch must be aware of their purposes and objectives.

The ideal king, in Hebrew theory, must be a native and not a foreigner. He must not enter into relations with Egypt—a reflection, no doubt, of the distrust with which the Deuteronomic reformers viewed the tendency of Judah's kings to rely on Egyptian power.[28] He ought not to marry many wives, "so that his heart may not be estranged." Nor should he have "great quantities of silver and gold." When he assumes the throne, he must write down a copy of the Deuteronomic code and get the approval of the "levitical priests." He must be guided by this code throughout his life. He should not consider himself more exempt than his countrymen from observance of the law. A king should not be above law but rather under it, and if he acts in this manner "he and his descendents may continue long on the throne."[29]

Since ancient Hebrew thought is so centrally concerned with problems of religion, the relation of the king to the priesthood becomes unusually interesting. The monarch is always conceived to be subordinate to the Torah, or law, of course, and his office is closely connected with religious rites. But throughout most of their political experience and speculation, Hebrew thinkers repudiate the notion that the priestly and royal functions should be exercised by one man. The high priest is to be descended from Aaron; the king comes from an entirely different line. No doubt this separation of functions is in part to be attributed to the very ambivalence with which Hebrews tended to look at kingship. It is also possibly rooted in a feeling that the priesthood must be independent of direct royal control if it is to be a critic of kingly government.

This formal separation of the ecclesiastical establishment from the monarch makes it easier, when the Davidic monarchy is abolished in 587 B.C., for the Jewish community to rebuild itself, even in exile, under the leadership of the priesthood. While the king is gone, and with him a rallying point for patriotic effort, the assembly of those who follow Yahweh still remains. Indeed, it has been argued that the idea of the "church" is first developed during the Babylonian captivity and that it is upon this early Jewish experience and theory of the independence of the religious community that the later Christian conception of the church is built.[30]

Later, during the Maccabean period, the theory that the "secular" ruler should not also be a priest is abandoned. This first occurs under Jonathan, brother of Judas Maccabeus, but is celebrated chiefly under Simon, another brother. And, as we have seen, the civil governorship held by Simon is transformed into a kingship by his son Aristobulus. Neither Simon nor Aristobulus was a descendant of Aaron, of course; nor was either of the house of David. Apparently the reestablishment of monarchy is not an act which can be accounted for by doctrine. Rather is it a kind of reward to the Maccabees, particularly to Simon, for their vigorous resistance to Antiochus and his successors. And the union of kingship and priesthood in the same person is to be explained similarly.

Despite the idealizations of the Maccabean period, however,[31] and its apparent willingness to merge priesthood with kingship, classical Hebrew thought is undoubtedly hostile to monarchy, at least as that institution is understood from the eighth to the sixth century B.C.

to allow their personal ambitions and their enjoyment of wealth and power to obscure the duties of their office. The critics of monarchy see them associated with social complexity and connect their activities with such phenomena as class differentiation, economic inequality, and the triumph of "might" over "right." To check these tendencies, the authority of prophets is set up as a method for reminding kings of their ethical and legal obligations.

The Prophetic View of Society and History

But the prophets did not warn and chastise kings and princes in an arbitrary fashion. Either explicitly or implicitly, they worked out an over-all framework within which they sought to fit the events of political history.

They were apparently never conscious about problems of method in the analysis of political events; yet it would not be correct to think of them as mere fortune-tellers claiming to predict developments of the future. As a matter of fact, they were concerned primarily with events of their own day and of the past and only incidentally and rather generally with the future course of history.

It would be a mistake to think of the prophets as being substantially like one another, either in background or in teaching. In background they vary widely in terms of class status, political influence, and personality. Thus, Amos (whose prophecy dates from about 760 B.C.) was a shepherd and looks at the state, society, and politics from the viewpoint of one who does not share in the luxury and pomp of Jeroboam II's court. The first Isaiah,[38] who flourished a little later than Amos, was apparently a man of high social status, with close connections at court and yet possessing a keenly critical attitude to politics. Hosea, another eighth-century prophet, came from the northern kingdom rather than from Judah and again reflects "lower-class" attitudes. As for Micah, the fourth of the great eighth-century prophets, one senses in his prophecy an accent on agrarian reform and a criticism of existing rulers for their neglect of the farmer.

Jeremiah came from the priestly class and flourished from about the middle of the seventh century to a period sometime after the final capture of Jerusalem.

As for the second Isaiah, we know almost nothing about his background except that he taught after the Exile, possibly in the period from about 545 to 530 B.C. He seems to have come from the "intellectual" or "upper" classes, however, and thus is to be distinguished from such early prophetic figures as Hosea and Amos.

The prophets differed widely not only in background, but also in the specifics of their moral and political teachings. Thus for a man like Samuel, the pressing political issue was whether to sanction the establishment of monarchy despite his inclinations to discountenance it. He was concerned only to a slight degree with the broad issues of world politics.

The burden of eighth-century prophecy, by contrast, tended to be concerned with two major questions: the nature of social justice and the political role which small nations like Israel and Judah should play in a world politics dominated by such giant states as Assyria. Amos, Hosea, and Micah were preeminently concerned with the first question; the first Isaiah centered his attention on the latter.

The background for the problem of social justice in the eighth century can be discovered in the growing prosperity of the northern kingdom and the rise of sharper class distinctions in both Israel and Judah. In Israel, the economy reached its height during the reign of Jeroboam II, while Syrian and Assyrian kings were preoccupied with other matters. At the same time, class differences became sharper and the lot of the agricultural worker more difficult. In Judah, some of the same tendencies were discernible. The growth of city life made the traditional gulf between the country dweller and his city cousin even wider than in the past and the resentment of the peasant at the prosperity of the urban citizen correspondingly greater.

As for international politics in the eighth century, we have already referred to the general pattern. Both Hebrew kingdoms were regarded by the kings of Assyria as obstacles to their expansion: Not that Israel and Judah had enough power to triumph over Assyria, of course, but simply that they were a nuisance, particularly when Assyria wished to attack Egypt. All the eighth-century prophets were aware of this fact of political life, and Isaiah makes it the center of his prophecy. In the period immediately before 721 B.C., when most of Israel was taken captive by Assyria, Isaiah was calling attention to what he regarded as the inevitable doom of the ten tribes, and after

One ground of its opposition is its belief that Yahweh should rule directly as it pictured him governing in the time of the Judges. Then, too, the actual experience with monarchy must have shattered many. While we can never be certain about the conditions that actually prevailed in premonarchical times, the critics of monarchy picture an epoch somewhat like the myth of the "primitive age" which runs through so much of Western political literature. This ideal kingless state supposedly allowed great latitude and freedom to each man and tribe. Commercialism had not developed, moreover, and in its absence, each man was roughly the social and economic equal of his neighbor. While there were conflicts within Israel, they were about relatively simple and uncomplex issues and could be settled without an elaborate judicial structure and the machinery of centralized coercion characteristic of monarchy.

But according to the republican thinkers of the eighth to sixth century, this idyllic situation was destroyed after the monarchy was established. With the king come commerce, a money economy, the seductions of strange gods and equally strange women, and ungodly class differentiations. With monarchy also appear strong standing armies and a royal court which suck the very life out of humble people. Some unknown writer of possibly the seventh century puts all this into the prophet Samuel's stirring speech supposedly made on the eve of the monarchy's establishment:

> This will be the procedure of the king who shall reign over you: he will take your sons and appoint them for himself for his chariots and for his horsemen; and they shall run before his chariots; and he will appoint for himself commanders of thousands and commanders of hundreds, and some to do his plowing and to reap his harvests and make his implements of war and the equipment for his chariots. He will take your daughters for his perfumers, for cooks, and for bakers. He will take the best of your fields and your vineyards and your olive orchards, and give them to his servants.[32]

As a matter of fact, scattered throughout the "historical" books of the Old Testament are constant criticisms of royal conduct. In such accounts as those of 1 and 2 Chronicles—products of a late stage in Hebrew intellectual development—one discovers an almost continuous animosity to kings and ruling classes. Relatively few kings do that "which is right in the sight of the Lord God"; even when, on the whole, their acts are sanctioned, the approval, as in the case of Amaziah,[33] is sometimes qualified.

One reason the prophet comes to be so highly valued by those who reflect on Israel's politics is that he is thought of as a spokesman for God who is entitled to chastise and speak freely to the king. In the absence of adequate machinery for control of the monarch's activities, the prophets assert the right and, indeed, the duty of attempting to keep the king within limits of legitimacy. Thus, when King David sends Uriah the Hittite to the front lines to be killed in order that the monarch might marry his wife, the prophet Nathan appears before the king and forces him to repent.[34] It is a prophet who forbids Rehoboam to make war on Jeroboam, when the latter has established the northern kingdom.[35]

Even when kings "do right in the sight of the Lord," the prophets are active. Indeed, it is possible that the kings "do right" precisely because the prophets do not hesitate to give blunt advice about moral and political matters. Thus, the prophet Isaiah is a vigorous counsellor in the reign of King Hezekiah,[36] and Jeremiah, besides his well-known political work under such a bad king as Zedekiah, also plays an important role in shaping the public policies of Josiah.[37]

In general, it seems clear, the prophet conceives his role to be a political one. His task is to relate his religious insights to the politics of his time. While the priests guard and perpetuate the ritual, prophets assert their prerogative of stating the "will of God" for king and people.

Monarchy, then, while accepted by the ancient Hebrews, is almost never received enthusiastically. An ideal king is hardly ever to be found; and kings as they actually reign tend

26. AT 1 Samuel 15:3.
27. AT 1 Samuel 15:9.
28. AT Deuteronomy 17:15, 16.
29. AT Deuteronomy 17:17–20.
30. See Wellhausen, *op. cit.*
31. See 1 Maccabees 14.
32. AT 1 Samuel 8:11–19.
33. 2 Chronicles 25:2.
34. 2 Samuel 12:1–15.
35. 1 Kings 12:21–24.
36. Isaiah 36 and 37.
37. He begins his prophecy, as a matter of fact, in the reign of Josiah.

the fall of Samaria—some years following 721—the prophet was concerned with the impact of Assyrian politics on Judah.

In the seventh century, of course, world politics became even more complicated and the position of Judah, as the sole remaining Hebrew kingdom, correspondingly more difficult. During the early part of the century, Assyria dominated the stage, but because of constant revolts, maintained its supremacy uncertainly. Its greatest political opponent was Egypt, which in the early part of the century sought to regain Syria and to supplant Assyria as the dominant power in Palestine. Egyptian manipulations account for many of the complexities of international politics down to 661 B.C. In that year, the king of Assyria managed to subdue Egypt, which now became an Assyrian province. But this status did not last long. By 650, Egypt was revolting and from this date, we may trace the gradual decline of Assyrian power.

The gigantic clashes between Egypt and Assyria and, later, between Babylonia and Egypt, coincide almost exactly with the life of Jeremiah. The revival of Egyptian power began about the year of his birth and by the time he began his prophetic career, the Assyrians were declining rapidly. It took no astounding prescience to foretell their doom, as Jeremiah did; nor did it require remarkable insight to suggest that Judah might be likely to find its political existence in jeopardy. After 630 B.C., the Assyrian Empire was invaded by Scythian tribes and by 609 or 608, the rising Babylonian power, allied with the Median Empire, felt strong enough to attack the Assyrian capital, Nineveh. Meanwhile, a much strengthened Egypt asked permission of Judah to use its territory in order to gain a share of the Assyrian spoils for itself. The King of Judah, Josiah, opposed the Egyptian request, contrary to the advice of Jeremiah. The result was the battle of Megiddo, in which Josiah was killed and Judah made a vassal of the Egyptian power. Meanwhile, the Assyrian capital had fallen and the Babylonians attacked the Egyptians at Carchemish in 605 B.C. The Egyptians were defeated and Judah was now forced to accept Babylonia as its suzerain. Judah revolted in 598 but was defeated in 597. The king and many leaders were then deported to Babylon. Jeremiah was the leader of what was alleged by the patriots to be the "pro-Babylonian" party because he resisted those who advocated a second revolt. However, the latter were successful, the result being the destruction of Jerusalem in 587 B.C. and the subsequent exile of thousands in Babylon.

Prophetic effort after the exile down to the middle of the fifth century B.C. centered on the significance of the whole political history of the Hebrews for religious faith. In terms of practical politics, of course, many of the prophets were undoubtedly active in seeking a return to Judah. With the rise of the Persian Empire, this became a reality. But despite the gradual return of many Hebrews (many others remained in Babylon, possibly for commercial reasons), the postexilic prophets came to see the Return not as an end but as a means to some more nearly ultimate goal. This is in part the significance of the second Isaiah.

Despite the different emphases and backgrounds of the prophets from the eighth century to the fifth, there arose a more or less common framework for their political speculations. We may consider it as threefold: the significance and goals of political history; the role of human effort in achieving the goals; and the ultimate achievement of the ends of history despite many human efforts to frustrate them.

Significance and Goals of Human History. As has been noted earlier,[39] ancient Hebrew thought in general tends to see the social and political changes and conflicts of history within a religious framework. That is to say, it assumes that Yahweh expresses his will for human beings in events which superficially might seem to be meaningless. Every event, if understood within the context of what has gone before, is like a word in the larger sentences and paragraphs which he writes in the vicissitudes and triumphs of man. God is thus primarily revealed in the concrete episodes of the human story, rather than through the speculations of "reason."

The central problem of political history

38. Scholars usually distinguish between at least two Isaiahs. The first is reflected in the Book of Isaiah, Chapters 1 through 35, while the second inspires Chapters 40 through 66. The first Isaiah lived in the eighth century; the second possibly in the postexilic sixth. And there are other materials in the Book of Isaiah which belong to neither of the two identifiable Isaiahs.

39. See p. 18.

throughout seems to be how to interpret it in light of the Covenant idea. If Yahweh does indeed have a peculiar relation to the Hebrew people and has made them definite promises that he will preserve and protect them, how, then, the prophets ask, can we account for the political disasters which have befallen them? And in a broader context, many of the prophets seem to be asking how one can explain the existence of social "evils" such as war and class stratifications and at the same time believe, with every good Hebrew, that Yahweh is the Lord of History.

In answer to questions of this kind, the prophets worked out what is sometimes called a *theodicy*—that is, a justification and vindication of God despite his apparent callousness about the fate of Judah and, in later prophetic thought, of all men. In developing this theodicy, the prophets suggest that God had certain goals which he sets up for human history but that at the same time he allows man—who is endowed with freedom—to reject those goals or intentions. When and if he rejects them, however, he must pay the penalty in terms of political disintegration, the destruction of community, and war. Moreover, the structure of collective humanity is such that the errors and rejections of one historical epoch affect the lives of future generations as well. There is an organic interconnection between and among generations and, within each generation, between and among individuals as well. This seems to be what is meant by the expression "The fathers have eaten sour grapes and the children's teeth are set on edge."[40]

But what are the goals which Yahweh sets up for human achievement and the rejection of which brings about individual and political disintegration? Here one can discern a very slow development in Hebrew thought, including the doctrine of the prophets. In the beginning, as reflected in the more ancient layers of the Old Testament, the goal is seen to consist largely in the right performance of ritual and magic;[41] and, indeed, this remains a factor throughout. In earlier thought, too, the utter massacre of political opponents seems to be insisted on by Yahweh as the price for his fulfillment of the Covenant.[42] But at the peak of the prophetic movement, and particularly at the time of the Deuteronomic reforms, other goals ascribed to Yahweh came into view. In the "law" of Deuteronomy, for example, certain principles begin to be stated for the government of Hebrews in war.[43] An invested city is to be offered conditions of peace and if the terms are accepted, the lives of its inhabitants are to be spared (although they will become forced laborers). Fruit trees are to be spared in construction of siegeworks.

How far these regulations reflect the views of the eighth- and seventh-century prophets we do not know. They are cited here because modern scholarship tends to suggest that some at least of the principles embodied in the Deuteronomic code represent positions which might have been and probably were accepted by the prophetic movement.

There is a similar problem with respect to the economic and social ideals embodied in the Code. Here, however, it would seem relatively clear that most of the preexilic prophets agree in principle, since very similar notions are put forward by Amos and Micah in the eighth century. Generally speaking, the social ideal of the prophets is an egalitarian one. Great disparities in income are to be wiped out or held within strict limits by legislation and religious sanctions; and there is a strong antagonism to commercialism. The political acts of such rulers as Jeroboam II of Israel are in part traced to the spirit of wealthy upper-class domination of social and political life. The poor are exploited and those who already have great economic and political power are never satisfied.[44]

It seems, according to Micah (writing, it will be remembered, in the eighth century) that the possession of power, instead of satiating a ruler, only goads him to gain more for himself. The rich begin every morning to work out methods whereby they can gain more land, thus depriving the poor peasant of his livelihood.[45]

Hosea is even more eloquent as he puts into the mouth of Yahweh denunciations which couple monarchy with idolatry:[46]

They made kings; but it was not of my doing;
They made princes; but without my knowledge.
Of their silver and their gold they made
Idols for themselves, that they might be cut off.

Writing at the height of eighth-century prosperity, when trade and commerce had further enriched the owning classes, Isaiah denounces rulers for sanctioning and abetting exploitation:[47]

The Lord will bring an indictment
Against the elders and princes of his people.
"It is you that have ravaged the vineyard;
The plunder of the poor is in your houses."

It would seem, then, to be the prophetic analysis of class conflict and exploiting ruling classes which leads to the provisions of the Deuteronomic code; and at the same time, those provisions possibly reflect the kinds of rules which the prophets would approve as (possibly with some exceptions) in accordance with the spirit of their teaching. Justice is to be administered in the several tribes impartially and judges are to be forbidden to take bribes.[48] There is to be a remission of debts every seventh year: "Every creditor who has a claim against his fellow-countryman is to remit it."[49] No Hebrew is to be enslaved for more than six years; in the seventh year he must be manumitted.[50] Interest on loans to fellow-countrymen is forbidden, although it is permitted on money extended to non-Israelites.[51] (Evidently the Deuteronomic legislator feels that he must make some concessions to the spirit of commercialism, for in the earlier version of this prohibition of usury [Exodus 22:25] the distinction between Hebrew and non-Hebrew is not mentioned.)

Throughout all the provisions dealing with the "property" problem, it seems evident that the author of Deuteronomy—and the prophets would not contradict him—has in mind as an ultimate ideal the elimination of private ownership and a complete mutual sharing of resources.

In its criminal law provisions, the Deuteronomic code is a combination of severity and carefully contrived restrictions on vengeance. Although it includes the classic "life for life, eye for eye, tooth for tooth, hand for hand, foot for foot,"[52] this is apparently to be interpreted not merely as an exhortation to severity but also as a limitation on vengeance; instead of taking two lives for a life, for instance, one is to take only one. This would seem to be borne out when we remember that it is also in the Deuteronomic code that we have enunciated the principle of individual responsibility: "Fathers are not to be put to death with their children, nor are children to be put to death with their fathers. Everyone is to be put to death for his own sin."[53] The idea of individual responsibility is thus vindicated, whereas in ancient Hebrew thought, the whole of the criminal's family is wiped out along with the violator of the law himself.[54]

This concern for the individual and the effort to separate individual from corporate responsibility runs through the criminal code. An effort is made, too, to distinguish between accidental killing and intentional murder; and "cities of refuge" are set aside to which the unintentional killer can flee and be protected from the revenge of his unfortunate victim's family.[55]

But we should always keep in mind that the rules stated in Deuteronomy remain largely ideals. To some extent, it is true, they are no doubt carried out, particularly during the reign of Josiah. The implementation, however, is always sporadic at best.

In postexilic prophecy, the conceptions of God's will in history depart even more widely from political reality than during the two centuries before 587 B.C. The views of the prophets in exile are indeed anticipated by Jeremiah (or by an author of the sixth century who uses Jeremiah's name) when he suggests that it is Yahweh's intent to create a society based on a "new Covenant."[56] The provisions of this novel arrangement center on the elimination of those conditions which make children suffer for the mistaken political and moral decisions of their parents. This interdependence of generations—the fact, for example, that King Manasseh's wrongful choices should be a factor in forcing men of Josiah's day into war—is always a problem for the prophets. They recognize it as a reality but cannot fully accept it. Why should an infant be impaled on

40. AT Jeremiah 31:29.
41. An imperative, it would seem, of all primitive peoples.
42. Thus the Lord is represented as instructing the Israelites to take Ai and utterly destroy it, with all its inhabitants, just as they destroyed Jericho. Joshua 8:1–2.
43. See Deuteronomy 20; 21:1–14.
44. Amos 8:4–6.
45. Micah 2:1, 2.
46. AT Hosea 8:4.
47. AT Isaiah 3:14, 15.
48. Deuteronomy 16:18–20.
49. AT Deuteronomy 25:1, 2. This provision could, of course, be interpreted as a complete cancellation of debts; but scholars on the whole seem to agree that a moratorium is intended.
50. Deuteronomy 25:12, 13.
51. Deuteronomy 23:19, 20.
52. AT Deuteronomy 19:21.
53. AT Deuteronomy 24:16.
54. Joshua 7:22–26, which relates the story of Achan.
55. Deuteronomy 19:1–13.
56. Jeremiah 31:29, 30.

the sword of a Babylonian soldier because certain political decisions of three generations before had set in motion forces which made it difficult to halt the enmity between Judah and Babylon? Surely there must be something unjust about a social world constructed on such lines. Yet despite the fact that Yahweh is responsible for this suffering of the innocent, his intent is somehow to overcome those conditions which make it inevitable. Thus the ideal is one where men will no longer say "The fathers have eaten sour grapes, and the children's teeth are set on edge"; but everyone shall die for his own guilt—"everyone who eats the sour grapes shall have his own teeth set on edge."

While the priests of the postexilic period continue to stress the necessity of minute regulations for the government of human conduct (although at the same time accepting many prophetic ideals), Jeremiah's conception of spontaneously achieved social harmony is reflected in such postexilic figures as the second Isaiah and possibly others who use the name Isaiah. After the appearance of a righteous judge who uses coercion to eliminate the unrighteous, a kind of free harmony and cooperation will unite men and beasts:[57]

Then the wolf will lodge with the lamb,
And the leopard will lie down with the kid;
The calf and the young lion will graze together,
And a little child will lead them.

The substance of prophetic sociopolitical ideals, then, changes considerably from the days of Samuel to those of postexilic figures. In the early days, the stress is on chaining the tendency to tyranny and limitless lust for power on the part of kings. In the intermediate stage of prophecy—during the eighth and seventh centuries—the prophets, assisted by the prophetically inspired legislator of Deuteronomy, endeavor to broaden and make more specific the goals which they discern in the will of Yahweh. They indicate their lack of confidence in a commercial society; suggest as a goal a classless social order; hint at communism as an economic ideal; see the rise of royal tyranny and idolatry as in part a product of class differentiation and its concomitant luxury for the ruling classes; and, in the theory of criminal law, stress the responsibility of the individual as over against attribution of guilt to the whole family or clan. Toward the end of the seventh century a tendency is initiated to think of the political ideal as one not only of classlessness but also of the absence of external regulation. During the postexilic epoch, this "utopian" goal is enlarged so that the historic order of things becomes almost completely revolutionized.

Human Effort and Divine Judgment. But however they define the ends which Yahweh intends, the prophets agree that societies are constantly rebelling against the divine will. And rebellion inevitably, again according to the will of Yahweh, results in wholesale destruction. Man is free to follow the intentions of Yahweh or to spurn them. If he accepts them his political life will be harmonious and he will not find his children's lives subject to the conqueror. If, however, he rejects Yahweh's goals by setting up ends contrary to God's will, his triumphs will turn to dust. Judgment inevitably follows disobedience.

These observations are amply documented by a sampling of prophetic utterances. Amos foresees destruction for Damascus, Gaza, Edon, Ashrod, and the Ammonites.[58] At the same time, he sees the history of the northern kingdom as a series of repeated chastisements through which it is reprimanded for its departure from the norms of social justice.[59] Speaking about a generation before the dissolution of Israel, and at the time of its greatest prosperity under Jeroboam II, he sees its catastrophe as complete:[60]

I saw the Lord, standing upon the altar,
And he said, "Smite the capitals, . . .
And smash them on the heads of them all."

When "false prophets" berate him for not differentiating Israel from other states, he makes the Lord answer:[61]

Are you not like the Ethiopians to me,
O Israelites?

It is pride in power which leads states astray, thinks Hosea. After the Lord fed the Israelites in the wilderness, they "became arrogant, and so they forgot me. So I will be unto them like a lion, or like a leopard by the road I will lurk. I will rend them like a bear robbed of its cubs. . . ."[62]

Running through many of the prophets is the theme that destruction will come because of reliance on "might" and war. And connected with this notion is a profound skepticism about military alliances as methods of protection. "You have eaten the fruit of lies," remarks Hosea, "In that you trusted in your chariots, and in your great might."[63] And the postexilic prophet Zechariah announces that it is "Not by arms, nor by force, but by my spirit" that social objectives are to be attained.[64]

But it is in an apocalyptically inspired passage from Isaiah, undoubtedly of postexilic origin, that condemnation of war and bloodshed is clearest. Men will be punished by God, asserts the prophet, "because they have transgressed laws, violated statutes, broken the everlasting covenant."[65] By the everlasting Covenant, the prophet apparently means not the contract between Yahweh and Israel, but that which was made between Noah and God after the flood. After Noah and his family had been saved from the flood, according to Genesis,[66] God insists that he will "hold men accountable for one another's lives; whoever sheds the blood of man, by man shall his blood be shed; for God made man in his own image." This Covenant is apparently a universal one, for Noah is not reputed to have been a Hebrew, and the judgment, according to the prophet, will be correspondingly universal.

God, according to the view of the prophets, can use political structures which he condemns to judge other societies which he equally condemns. Thus Assyria, which has no moral compunctions whatsoever in its quest for empire, can yet be regarded by the prophets as an instrument of God. For while men may not legitimately use certain methods to gain their objectives, God may turn means which he regards as evil to ultimately good ends.[67]

The apparent chaos of international politics is thus seen by the prophets to have in it an implicit pattern. Each state, itself a violator of the canons of social and international justice, is regarded as an organization for vindicating the will of God. Preexilic and postexilic prophecy clearly anticipate the over-all views of the Book of Daniel in this respect. Daniel is written during the political turmoil of Maccabean days and in its symbolic "beasts" it portrays vividly the general notions of judgment which the prophets sketch out long before.[68]

History as Educator. Yet judgments and political calamities imposed because of man's failures to discern or execute the will of Yahweh have two aspects, according to many of the prophets. On the one hand, they demonstrate that man cannot run counter to the divine intention with impunity. On the other hand, the very punishments inflicted during the course of political history have the capacity of making human leaders aware of "reality." Rulers have been caught up in their own arrogance and the more they have sought to frustrate the divine will, the greater is the difficulty of persuading them to mend their ways by gentle means. Radical and harsh judgment comes in the form of wars and social disintegration because ruling classes have completely lost touch with, to use an expression of modern Freudians, the "reality principle." But men do learn from judgments and historical experience, however slowly; eventually, so several of the prophets hold, they will no longer seek to attack the intentions of Yahweh. At that time, the political and social goals exalted in prophetic teaching will become secure and judgments presumably will cease. History, as the record of broken covenants and punitive politics, will end.

This is the general picture of how God through the historical process educates states and civilizations. Because Yahweh is the Lord of history, his will is to be accomplished, even against the many obstacles set up by men and particularly by the ruling classes of states.

But the expression of the exact way in which this is to be accomplished differs from prophet to prophet. Some prophets, indeed, seem to see only judgment unconnected with education.

Hosea thinks of Israel as a prostitute who has wandered away from her husband. Yahweh tries to redeem her by appeals to reason but, this failing, sends harsh judgments in the form of deprivation of wealth and ornaments. When the harlot is stripped of those things

57. AT Isaiah 11:6.
58. Amos 1.
59. Amos 5.
60. AT Amos 9:1.
61. AT Amos 9:7, 8.
62. AT Hosea 13:6–8.
63. AT Hosea 10:13.
64. AT Zechariah 4:6. Compare Isaiah 31:1, 2: "Woe to those who go down to Egypt for help, and rely on horses; those who trust in chariots because they are many, and in horsemen, because they are very numerous; but look not to the Holy One of Israel, nor consult the Lord! Yet he is the wise one, and brings calamity. . . ."
65. AT Isaiah 24:5.
66. AT Genesis 9:5, 6, 7.
67. See Isaiah 10:5–11, for the full judgment.
68. See particularly Daniel 7.

and taken to the "wilderness" she eventually sees her errors and responds "as in the days of her youth."[69] It is the very harshness of the chastisement which strips her of illusion and induces her once more to observe the law.

Amos, however, seems to doubt the educative effects of political and social ruin. He paints a graphic picture of the many "chastisements" to which Israel has been subject in history. But the nation continues to rebel against justice. Finally, Yahweh becomes disgusted and predicts utter destruction, unalleviated, apparently, by hope:[70]

> Fallen, never to rise again, is the virgin Israel;
> Prostrate on her own soil, with none to raise her up.

Only some postexilic writer using the name of Amos sees the disaster as possibly an educative factor.[71]

In Jeremiah, of course, the note of judgment predominates as he observes the manipulations of international politics. But unlike the preexilic Amos, the effect of judgment is not only destruction but also moral and political education. Thus the neighbors of Judah are warned that they face judgment because they, along with Judah, have violated Yahweh's intentions. But Jeremiah represents God as telling them that after he has "plucked them up," he will give them another chance, the implication being that the preliminary "plucking" will lead them to change their social and political orders radically.[72]

But the classical prophetic passages which appear to suggest that corporate political disaster, with its accompanying human suffering, may serve as a moral and political educator are the "Suffering Servant" chapters of the postexilic Isaiah.[73] Although there has been a vigorous scholarly dispute as to whether Isaiah means to describe an individual or a collectivity, considerable agreement exists now that he has in mind the corporate Israel. Political and physical disasters to the people of Israel are seen as stripping away illusion, pride, and confidence in violence and military might.

It is in the Suffering Servant passages that the notion of class and state conflicts as educational reaches its height. Divine imperatives for the social and political order will be achieved by men themselves as they become increasingly aware that historical conflicts are not meaningless. And as their historical and political consciousness is enlarged, men will themselves attain the kind of order which the prophets proclaim as the will of Yahweh.

This prophetic view should be contrasted with another tendency in Hebrew thought which is sometimes called the eschatological. By contrast with the classical prophetic conception, the eschatological position tends to maintain that the goals of Yahweh are to be attained by direct divine intervention. Human history is "saved" from its perversions, not by human insight and effort which have been enlightened through corporate suffering, but rather by Yahweh's putting an end to his fruitless educational endeavors. There are final political and military conflicts, followed by the appearance of a divinely sent Messiah who cuts through clumsy and rebellious human politics and institutes divine government. The prophet, then, sees man as eventually discovering and implementing the divine will for corporate life; the eschatologist, by contrast, thinks of God as impatient with man. In modern language, the prophet conceives the deity as a Lord of political history exercising indirect leadership; the eschatologist appears to hold that Yahweh begins to despair and takes direct control of affairs.[74]

But we should beware of making the distinction between prophecy and eschatological conceptions too sharp. In practice, many prophets seem often to be ambivalent as to their position; and the same would seem to be true of some who are primarily eschatological. We should perhaps think of the prophetic and the eschatological as ideal types to which no one speculator conforms completely.

As the classical age of prophecy passes—sometime after the middle of the fifth century B.C.—there is a tendency for conservative priestly thought to dominate Hebrew intellectual life.[75] The vigorous critical attitude of the prophets gives way to the spirit of conservation. The political Messiah who will restore the kingdom is often conceived as a military figure who will ensure Israel's domination of the world by methods similar to those through which Israel has been dominated. In the second century, of course, the politics of the Maccabean period constitute the background for several eschatological treatises. For the most part, however, these do not revive in major degree the spirit of prophetic teaching.

The Significance and Impact of Hebrew Conceptions

It should by now be abundantly clear that there was no body of ideas among the ancient

Hebrews which could be called a systematically formulated theory of politics. Interest in knowledge (whether natural or social) as an end never even approximated the level it was to attain in classical Greece. One might have expected the study of political history to have developed markedly from 600 B.C. onward, since Hebrew thinkers were so profoundly convinced of the significance of their collective past. But such was not the case, for treatment of political history was almost always primarily a *midrash*—that is, examination of the past in poetic and moralistic terms. Under such conditions, respect for what moderns might regard as "historical truth" was often subordinate to ideological purposes.

In part, the intense Hebrew conviction that divinity was present in all aspects of social and political life served to inhibit the development of particular sciences. Emphasis on the unity of things made the Hebrew mind suspicious of the analysis of particular phenomena so indispensable to science. The disinterested pursuit of "facts" was discouraged by the tendency to think of "knowledge" in oracular terms. There was often a premature attempt to fit things poorly understood in themselves into the larger "religious" whole which was the primary object of consciousness.

On the other hand, the notion that "religion" and divinity were not things apart from everyday individual life and social conflict saved the Hebrews from that "other-worldly" view of politics which was much later to characterize some interpretations of Plato and certainly many versions of "Christianity." Hebrew organicism, too, was so strong that the conception of one morality for the individual and another for the state—an idea which became prominent after the classical age of Greece—hardly ever took root.

Whatever the shortcomings and ambiguities of Hebrew speculation analytically, there can be little doubt as to its importance in the history of political ideas. The conception of the Covenant provided a tradition which was to be adapted by Christian thinkers when they sought to identify the Church with the "new" Israel operating as a leaven in the midst of political conflict. Hebrew notions of monarchy were to play a vital role in both the theory and practice of kingship during the Middle Ages. And the conviction that political history somehow revealed larger purposes and intentions was to become so much a part of the warp and woof of thought that it helped shape such diverse systems as those of St. Augustine and Karl Marx. The prophetic theory of history, under many different guises, has been with us from the time of the great eighth-century prophets to the twentieth century.

Meanwhile, as the Hebrews were wrestling with the notion of meaning in history and formulating, however unsystematically, conceptions of social justice, systematic political thought was being born in Greece.

69. Hosea 2:2–23.
70. AT Amos 5:1, 2.
71. Amos 9:9–15.
72. Jeremiah 12:14–27.
73. Isaiah 42:1–4; 49:1–6; 50:4–9; 52:13; 53:12.
74. The eschatological note in politics is struck in such Hebrew writings as Daniel. The idea of the coming of the Messiah is often associated with eschatology. On the notion of the Messiah, see Joseph Klausner, *The Messianic Idea in Israel from Its Beginning to the Completion of the Mishnah*, New York: Macmillan, 1955.
75. Illustrated, perhaps, in Ezra and Nehemiah. But it should always be remembered that prophetic teaching affected the priests and vice versa.

chapter 2

Growth and General Conception of the Polis

While the Hebrew prophets were elaborating their characteristic views of political history, the institutional and intellectual history of the Greek city-states was giving birth to the great systematic political theories of ancient times. We have already observed that, for the most part, Hebrew political doctrine was primarily implicit, that it was intimately connected with the evolution of Hebrew religious ideas, and that no Hebrew thinkers could be called primarily "political." By contrast, while the development of political thought in Greece down to the fourth century B.C. was implicit and unsystematic, the fourth century produced two of the most influential systems in the entire history of speculation—those of Plato and Aristotle.

The Greek Way of Life

It is no easy task to transpose ourselves from the life of the twentieth century A.D. into a material and nonmaterial culture of the period from the second millennium to 400 B.C. The story of the migration of the various Greek tribes into the Hellenic peninsula is well-known.[1] We know relatively little about the Hellenic tribes, however, before the eighth century B.C., and our information even about that is rather unsatisfactory. Geographically, of course, Greece is a mountainous country, the various fertile patches of which are separated from one another by natural barriers which, in ancient days, made communication difficult and at times almost impossible. Perhaps this is one of the basic factors which led later on to the sharp political separation of the many city-states into which the Greek peninsula and the adjoining islands were to be divided. And yet geographical separateness was combined with a generally uniform language and, on the whole, with common religious traditions. Those religious beliefs, as is well-known, included a multiplicity of gods, with Zeus as a kind of chairman and Apollo as the god perhaps closest to the Greek heart.[2]

Most of the isolated Greek communities, while primarily tribal in character, had some kind of leader known as the king (*basileus*), but we know very little about the kings of early days. By the eighth century, most of the kings, with the exception of the Spartan, had vanished, although the title remained in some of the Greek cities as a kind of religious dignity.

During the very early period, Greeks were first hunters and then shepherds. While sheep-herding remained an important occupation, it was combined later on with agriculture. There is no way of knowing just when the vine and olive trees were introduced, but it must have been at a very early stage of development. Grape and olive culture became staples of Greek economic life, for even after the rise of commerce, the farmer continued to be in considerable degree the backbone of city life. For centuries, then, pastoral and agricultural life, together with governance by what sociologists would call the folkways and mores, were characteristic of the ancient Hellenes, whatever their tribe. The few social decisions which were consciously made were matters for the traditional Council of Elders, *gerusia*, which we find mentioned in Homer.

During these early days, communication of tradition was mainly a matter of passing on patterns of action through word of mouth, as in most tribal societies.

If Homer was an historical personage at all, he probably lived about 950 B.C. and it is in his pages that we catch glimpses of early Greek life and foretastes of the life to come. The tradition of the Trojan wars, moreover, became the basis for a common Greek poetry and primitive philosophy, even though tribal patterns remained predominant.

Another factor which eventually led Greeks to compare their respective ways of life was undoubtedly the common Olympic festivals. The games were supposedly established in 776 B.C.—about the time of the prophet Amos and shortly before the traditional foundation of Rome—and constituted the occasion for a gathering of Greeks from many varying backgrounds. No doubt there was some discussion of divergent customs, although again this comparison was not sufficient in itself to cause radical changes in the mores of such diverse Hellenic peoples as the Thebans, Corinthians, Athenians, and Spartans.

There were, however, two factors which, in combination with interchanges in religion and athletics, were to create literal revolutions in many Greek peoples. These were the population problem and the beginning of extensive trade and commerce.

Before we can note the effect of population growth and of trade, however, we must look a little more closely into the life of a typical polis before the revolution began. It is difficult for us in the twentieth century to envision the small scale of social life in the eighth century B.C. In Attica, the total area occupied by the Athenian tribes was perhaps not more than that of a moderate-sized American county. Tribal life was carried on in very small villages, tended to be self-sufficient economically, and was, as we have said, governed largely by custom. If it is legitimate to use political terminology on the verge of the revolution, we could term the life of Attica conservative in extreme degree.

But such self-sufficient communities were growing rapidly in population and finding it difficult to support the increment. Since most Greek communities were not far from the sea, it was quite natural that their inhabitants should begin moving beyond their traditional borders in the quest for additional food supplies. They had, of course, learned the art of navigation long before (perhaps from Egyptians and Phoenicians) and now it stood them in good stead. Some bold men turned to piracy and began to rob communities normally outside their ken. Others drifted to uninhabited places and began to live as separate communities. In some instances, the tribes dwelling within a given area—Athens, for example, or Corinth—would deliberately decide to plant colonies elsewhere in order to ease the economic strain.

Thus was set in motion the great era of colonization, which for centuries was to people southern Italy, northern Africa, Asia Minor, and the isles of the sea with new cities of Hellenic extraction.

Meanwhile, the bold mariners setting out to found new colonies could not help but touch other and non-Hellenic countries. From early days, there had been communication with Egypt. New Hellenic ships began to traverse the seas in greater and greater numbers. Some of them were ships bearing colonists. Others were pirate boats preying on both Hellenic and non-Hellenic communities. Yet others began to be interested in foreign trade. Indeed, the line between piracy and trade was a thin one in those days, for some ships would combine piracy with commerce, and others might carry on piracy under the guise of trade.

Throughout the period of the eighth to the sixth centuries, then, colonization, piracy, and trade were beginning to revolutionize the ways of life of dozens of Hellenic communities. What was the nature of the revolution and what was its effect on the communal and intellectual patterns of the conservative tribes which it affected?

We may note the following major effects: (1) the rise and development of individuality; (2) the tendency to disruption of the ancient tribes; (3) the development of the "citadel" as the center of polis life; (4) the penetration of foreign customs and beliefs, particularly in religion; (5) the rise of science and philosophy. Actually, of course, these effects interacted on one another.

(1) When we say that individuality developed, we mean that many men now began to conceive themselves as somehow divorced from the traditional ways of life. Taking up careers of piracy or trade, they tended to lose that strong consciousness of attachment to a given community which characterizes tribal living. They began to imagine other possible ways of existence. Some of them, moreover, acted on the basis of their imaginations and violated many of the tribal *tabus* which hitherto had been deemed sacred. Slowly, but certainly, many Greek cities witnessed a decline of what modern sociologists call the "sacred" society and the rise of "secularism" in areas which had hitherto been deemed beyond criticism.

1. See Morton Smith, *The Ancient Greeks,* Ithaca, N.Y.: Cornell University Press, 1960, pp. 5–8; and Emily Vermeule, *Greece in the Bronze Age,* Chicago: University of Chicago Press, 1964, pp. 58–77, 106–110, 233–279.
2. See H. J. Rose, *A Handbook of Greek Mythology,* New York: 1959; Samuel Kramer, *Mythologies of the Ancient World,* Chicago: Quadrangle Books, 1961, pp. 220–276; and Edith Hamilton, *Mythology: Timeless Tales of Gods and Heroes,* New York: Mentor, 1962.

In the eighth century itself, the poet Hesiod[3] both reflects this tendency and is a critic of it. He reflects it, in that he consciously reacts as an individual to the tendencies he sees about him. He is a critic, insofar as he wonders what will become of the Hellenes now that the ancient ways are being disrupted. The gradual weakening of family and tribal ties he cannot explain, but somehow he thinks of it as a degeneration from the good old days when men's paths were prescribed for them by immemorial tradition. A modern commentator calls the mind of Hesiod a "peasant mentality."[4] Now, as Hesiod complains, force tends to rule, and he sees life as having degenerated through five stages—a foreshadowing of the later doctrine of the fall of man, which will be so momentous for Christian political thought.

(2) What is meant, though, when we say that the tribal way of life was being disrupted? In the first place, the rise of the individual posed in dramatic form the problem of social order. Up to now, the reconciliation of the claims of individuality with the demands of order had been relatively simple, for individuality itself had been only incipient. Now, however, with traditional modes of governance declining, men had to *think* about the issue of the individual in relation to social order.

In the second place, the decline of the tribal way of life meant for the individual a loss of that relative certainty which he must have possessed in more primitive days. Not only did he have to think about the social order (he could no longer take it for granted) but he had to speculate about his own place in the universe.

Thirdly, the gradual disappearance of the tribal ways implied the whole property question and the problem of class struggle. We need not go so far as Winspear and modern Marxists in accepting the notion of a tribe as largely lacking in property consciousness to recognize, nevertheless, that in primitive tribal Hellenic society the tradition tended to be one of common ownership of land, little private accumulation, and a largely moneyless economy. Now, however, as tribal systems disintegrated and private property in land became a part of the economic system, both the institutions and the intellectual consciousness of the Hellenes underwent rapid transformation.

(3) As the tribal way of life disintegrated, the deliberate planning for social order which took its place tended to center around the citadel, or fortified spot from which the small Hellenic community could be defended. Most of the villagers were outside the city (*asty*, or inner city) walls, but when the danger of outside attack became great, they would take up their residence within the walls and the citadel became the center of active defense. From it came the orders which organized the polis for military activity; and it, too, was transformed into the basis for the gradually developing political life. As tribal ways declined, the political life tended to be its partial substitute.

(4) When we speak of the penetration of foreign customs and beliefs, we note a phenomenon which also affected the Hebrews. As trade grew and the maritime life of Greece became a larger and larger factor in affairs, it would have been surprising had cultural and religious imports not accompanied trade in material goods. Men became acutely aware that there were other ways of life than their own and that foreign customs quite often stressed values repudiated by Greek cultures. What was good in one culture could be deemed bad in another; and the easy identification of a given polis' way of life with the absolute good could no longer be made.

This growing familiarity with foreign cultures was particularly significant in the realm of religion[5] and, through religion, philosophy. The Greeks from time immemorial had given reverence to several oracles of the gods which purportedly could give advice on all things temporal and spiritual. The most famous of these oracles was that at Delphi, where Apollo was revered as the god who could aid statesmen in their dilemmas and generals in their strategy. From all parts of Greece, whatever the polis, commoners and leaders alike would journey to Delphi to consult the oracle. Plutarch tells us, for example, that Lycurgus, the traditional founder of the Spartan constitution, consulted the Delphic voice with respect to his political reforms.[6] And later on even Socrates cited the oracle in connection with his teaching.

Now in the sixth century a new kind of religious syncretism began to develop around the oracle at Delphi. Apollo was not ousted from his domain but he began to share it with another god—Dionysus. The cult of Dionysus was to be one of the importations most influential in the spiritual and intellectual development of preclassical Greece. Brought, so it is said, from Thrace or Lydia, a whole theology was built around it with the aid of the mythical Orpheus, the founder of the Orphic cult associated with Dionysus.

According to this theology, Dionysus, an ox, was torn to pieces by the Titans, who swallowed his limbs. Only his heart was saved. Athena seized the heart and brought it to Zeus, who thereupon proceeded to make a new Dionysus from the heart of the old. Zeus also blasted the Titans with lightning and from their ashes men were produced. Thus human beings are composed of a Titanic element, the body, and a Dionysiac element, the soul. The eternal soul is imprisoned in an earthly body as punishment for a transgression committed during the divine existence. The Orphic cult went on to aver that the soul is constantly born and reborn into new bodies, the several transmigrations presumably giving it an opportunity to purge itself of the offenses of long ago. After the sixth century, it came to be held that during the winter months Apollo was absent from the temple at Delphi and Dionysus took his place.

The implications of Orphism for popular religion and the birth of philosophy were enormous. The cult was a missionary one and thousands of Greeks now became familiar with one version of the "soul-body" problem. Before the rise of Orphism the ordinary Greek view had held that the body was real—indeed, the very distinction between soul and body had not been made. Now, however, under the impact of foreign notions, the notion of the immortality of the soul began to receive wide credence. From Orphism it is but a relatively short step to some aspects of Pythagoreanism in the sixth and fifth centuries, and from Pythagoreanism the transition to Platonic teaching in the fourth century is not a great one.

(5) The rise of science and philosophy in the sixth century and their progress during the fifth and fourth centuries can be thought of, then, as the product of the development of individual consciousness, the tendency to disrupt the ancient tribes, the growth of urban as against village life, and the stimulation of foreign cultures, particularly of Orphism.[7]

The basic question which disturbed the Greek mind of the sixth century was the issue of flux versus permanence. Now that the tribal way of life had been breaking down for two centuries and the sacred society was more and more a thing of the past, men were led to inquire whether everything was not change and nothing was permanent. If even the most sacred things of the past could now be shown to be relative to time and place, what, if anything, was *not* relative? The Greek imagination of the sixth and fifth centuries could not let questions of this kind die.

In the sixth century and the first half of the fifth, many kinds of answers were given in the realm of "natural science." In the fifth and fourth centuries, the scene shifted largely to what we should today call the "social sciences."

During the sixth century, Thales suggested that the basic and permanent substance from which all others came was water; Anaximander thought of the "permanent" as motion itself; while Anaximenes held the beyond-change "stuff" to be air.

A little later, the basic query asked about "nature" came to be, "Assuming there is a Basic One of some kind, how does this One become the Many?" In other words, "How do the particulars in flux, whether in biology or physics, arise out of some kind of Fundamental Stuff (whether air, or water, or fire, or motion)?"

Questions of this kind were particularly pointed after Xenophanes, studying in Malta and Sicily, had called attention to the fossils of sea animals found far inland (about 500 B.C.). About the same time Heraclitus[8] was suggesting that all things come into being and pass away through conflict. In strife, opposites

3. See John Symonds, *Studies of the Greek Poets,* New York: Barnes & Noble, 1920, and *Hesiodus: The Works and Days,* Richmond Lattimore, trans., Ann Arbor, Mich.: University of Michigan Press, 1959.
4. A. D. Winspear, *The Genesis of Plato's Thought,* New York: J. A. Russell, 1956, p. 42.
5. See, for example, Gilbert Murray, *Five Stages of Greek Religion,* New York: Doubleday, 1955; and Martin Nilsson, *History of Greek Religion,* New York: W. W. Norton, 1964.
6. Plutarch, "Lycurgus," in *Lives,* John Dryden, trans., New York: Modern Library, 1932.
7. See W. K. C. Guthrie, *Orpheus and Greek Religion,* London: Methuen, 1952; and Leon Robin, *Greek Thought and the Origins of the Scientific Spirit,* New York: Knopf, 1928.
8. Note particularly Abel Jeanniere, *La Penssée d'Heraclite d'Ephése et la Vision Presocratique du Monde,* Aubier: Editions Montaigne, 1959; and Philip Wheelwright, *Heraclitus,* Princeton, N.J.: Princeton University Press, 1959.

combine to produce harmony. Only Becoming—not Being—is real. Yet Heraclitus at the same time seemed to hold that there was a "central fire" which never died.

When Parmenides came to discuss the question, he maintained that sense experience is an illusion and that the problem was to get beyond the senses to the "One" which lay beyond them. He seemed to be asserting, in other words, that the world of flux was unreal; but he had no answer to the question as to how the illusion arose that things were in flux.

Later on in the fifth century (about 450 B.C.), we find Empedocles[9] offering the hypothesis that evolution through fortuitous combinations is the key to nature.

Meanwhile, Pythagoras[10] had begun to ask questions not only about the realm of nature but also about human relations. Just as the earlier physical philosophers of the sixth century had puzzled about the One and the Many, so Pythagoras (who died about 500 B.C.) began to inquire about justice and injustice in human affairs. If justice or righteousness could no longer be equated with the traditional tribal pattern—for that way of life had been shown to be relative to time and place—did any permanent good remain? If there was a permanent good, how did one identify it amidst the conflict and flux of a rapidly changing society? Or was it an impossible assignment? Pythagoras thought that the task was not impossible. Number, he concluded, is the nature of all things; and righteousness is a square number. He thought, in other words, that he had found the root of all things, natural and human, in pure mathematical forms, which were unchangeable; and the Pythagoreans in the fifth century developed this notion in the realm of politics and law.

From the middle of the fifth century and onwards, Greek scientific inquiry turned increasingly to the social sciences. True, speculation in the physical studies did not die, but it was overshadowed by social thought. Why, we may ask, did this come about? Why, in the period between 450 and 300, did moral and political issues assume a central place? The answer to questions of this kind can be found in the fact that political turbulence was increasing and intellectuals were eager to find explanations and remedies for it.

In order to comprehend the kinds of crises which led men to ask themselves social science questions in the latter part of the fifth century and throughout the fourth, some understanding of the specific development of Greek political life is necessary.

The Constitution of Sparta

As the political scientists and philosophers of the fifth and fourth centuries looked about them, the example of Sparta appeared unusually instructive. Many of the early social scientists admired its institutions. Others conceived of it as the design of what a polis ought not to be. Yet others, as for example Plato, both approved it in part and in some measure repudiated it. But there was no doubt about their thinking of it as some kind of model or point of departure for speculation.

Why did Sparta possess this character?[11]

There were several reasons. First of all, legend had it that Sparta was the earliest deliberately constructed polis. Its institutions were thought to have been inaugurated by the half-mythical figure Lycurgus in the ninth century B.C. He was supposed to have laid down the main lines of Spartan development and to have demonstrated what self-conscious law-making could do. If Sparta could deliberately erect a scheme of institutions which appeared to resolve the apparently contradictory claims of individuality and social solidarity, why could not other cities do the same?

But secondly, Sparta was admired—if not always thought worthy of emulation—because of the discipline which it had apparently so successfully established. Critics of the Athenian constitution particularly could point to Sparta with pride, for Athens in the classical period was notoriously a community of violent party wrangles.

Finally, Sparta became a "model" in many respects because its internal discipline was deemed to be such that it conduced to success in war. Since the Greece of the sixth and fifth centuries was constantly at war, the Lacedemonians appeared to provide the key to military victory everywhere.

Beyond merely utilitarian considerations, however, the Greek mind found something aesthetically pleasing about the constitution of Sparta. It represented, in some measure, a kind of perfection and harmony of parts in the whole, as even its critics recognized.

The Sparta known to classical political thinkers was a union of five Dorian villages. As was true of most Hellenic polis structures, the area inclosed within the city walls was relatively limited and the number of full citizens rather few. The villages surrounding the town proper were composed of the *perioeci*, or the "dwellers round about," who were autonomous in their own villages but had no political rights in the Spartan polis. They were obliged to render military service, however, and many of them were engaged in farming the royal domains.

Rulership of Sparta had been traditionally vested in two kings, whose powers by the fifth and fourth centuries had been considerably circumscribed. Whereas the office of king, or *basileus*, had long ago been abolished completely in Athens, the kings of Sparta in classical times were still commanders of the army and apparently acted also as high priests of Apollo.

Lycurgus by tradition had introduced the Gerusia, or council of elders (Senate) to act as a kind of buffer between the kings and the people. Its functions seem to have been to present issues to the Apella and to act as a court of justice for criminal cases.

In Sparta, the assembly of the people was known as the Apella. Composed of every full Spartan citizen who had passed his thirtieth year, it met once every month and "acclaimed" proposals submitted to it by the kings and ephors. In addition to its validating or acclaiming prerogatives, the Apella chose the Gerusia, the magistrates, and the ephors.

Plutarch tells us that one hundred thirty years after Lycurgus the institution of the ephorate was established, although later students of Spartan constitutional history have suggested that it dated back to the eighth century. Some maintain that in its origin, the ephorate was an effort to relieve the kings of burdensome duties—or perhaps to clip the wings of monarchy as popular and oligarchical tendencies began to emerge. At any rate, the five ephors, chosen by lot, were initially without much independent political power and began to emerge with substantial prerogatives only in the seventh century. We may think of them after that period as a "popular" element in the administrative machinery of the Spartan polis.

In addition to being inspectors general for the citizenry, the ephors constituted the supreme civil court and were also criminal judges in cases involving the *perioeci*. Undoubtedly their most important role, however, was that which made them the disciplinarians of Sparta. If ancient historians are to be believed, it was they who kept the Helots in order, maintained the spirit of the Lycurgan scheme of things, and instilled into all citizens proper ideals of conduct.

Before the sixth century, the Spartan polis had seemingly been relatively liberal; the nobility had possessed some of the luxuries which aristocrats in all centuries have valued; and there were even Spartan poets of a sort. By the end of the sixth century, however, the liberal features of the Spartan constitution had largely vanished.

What catastrophe—for catastrophe it must have been—could have produced this change? Plutarch and other ancient historians were puzzled, too, and there were many hypotheses. Plutarch himself suggests that a great earthquake had occurred and that (although he does not become explicit about this) the Helots (or Spartan serfs) took advantage of the social disorganization which accompanied the earthquake to revolt against their masters. They were joined in this rebellion by the Messenians. The whole country was laid waste and, for a time, it seemed that the continuance of the city was in danger. However, the Spartan citizenry eventually regained the upper hand and, presumably with the aid of the *perioeci*, began to administer the Lycurgan institutions with a harshness not known previously.

The most marked change, perhaps, occurred in the lot of the Helot. While before the sixth century revolution, he had existed in a mild form of serfdom—punctuated, perhaps, by a cruelty not unknown in such relationships—

9. See Kathleen Freeman, *Pre-Socratic Philosophers*, Cambridge, Mass.: Harvard University Press, 1947; and Werner Jaeger, *The Theology of the Early Greek Philosophers*, New York: Oxford University Press, 1947.
10. Consult Freeman, *op. cit.;* William Guthrie, *History of Greek Philosophy*, vol. 1, New York: Cambridge University Press, 1962; and Robert Scoon, *Greek Philosophy Before Plato*, Princeton, N.J.: Princeton University Press, 1928.
11. Note K. Atkinson, *Ancient Sparta*, Manchester: Manchester University Press, 1949; George Huxley, *Early Sparta*, Cambridge, Mass.: Harvard University Press, 1962; H. Michell, *Sparta*, Cambridge: Cambridge University Press, 1952; and E. N. Tigerstedt, *The Legend of Sparta in Classical Antiquity*, Stockholm: Almquist & Wiksell, 1965.

the serfdom now became extraordinarily severe.

The economic relationship of the Helot to his master was that of a poor sharecropper whose first order priority was to provide for the needs of the master's family. Each Spartan had a lot which passed from father to son and could not be divided or sold. Every year the owner of the lot was entitled to 70 medimni of corn for himself and to 12 medimni for his wife; and there were comparable allotments of wine and fruit. The hard manual work required to produce this food was assigned to the Helots. After the master's portion had been provided, the Helot could have what remained. The theory, apparently, was that he would work more intensively if he knew that he would obtain only residual amounts.

There was a kind of secret police known as the *Krypteia,* one of whose major functions seems to have been the disciplining of Helots. The Helot was not protected by a code of law, and after the sixth century Spartan opinion seemed to hold that the occasional commission of acts of violence against Helots was desirable; it was believed they had to be instilled with fear if they were to remain submissive.

The educational system, unlike schooling in most other city-states, was a public one. Its purpose was to prepare the youth for war; and everything which did not minister to this objective was regarded as superfluous. At the age of seven the boy was given to a polis official and up to twenty he was trained in a huge barracks-like school. Hierarchies of officials stood over him to make sure that the school discipline was rigorously enforced. The captains and prefects were more than twenty years of age and under thirty; the theory was that they would not only train their charges but make love to them. It was assumed that homosexual affection would develop between each boy and his mentor and that these relations would assist in inculcating the spirit of the constitution.[12]

The Spartan attitude to sex and marriage was a good reflection of the polis culture. Just as young men were prepared by harsh discipline for the rigors of military life, so were young women compelled to strengthen their bodies systematically in order to bear healthy future soldiers. Girls had to learn to wrestle, throw quoits, and cast darts. They often exercised naked beside the young men. In certain solemn festivals, moreover, young men and women alike marched entirely unclothed so that Spartans would become used to the idea of nakedness, and the exercise in the nude, it was held, would toughen against the elements. We are told by the ancients, moreover, that while these Spartan practices alarmed the uninformed in Athens, no young women were more modest than those of Sparta.[13]

Several measures were designed to make certain that an increasing supply of soldiers would be forthcoming for the future. Those who remained bachelors incurred civic disabilities, including a prohibition against attending the festivals. When, at twenty, the young Spartan was permitted to marry, he was not to think of his wife as an exclusive possession, for by Spartan custom, it was deemed fitting for a husband to lend his wife to any man whom he might deem eugenically fit. Older men, particularly, who were married to young wives, were encouraged to recommend some appropriate young man by whom the wife could bear a future soldier.

As for the economic basis of the Spartan constitution, it, too, was designed primarily to minister to the needs of the military. Throughout the classical period, no polis was more hostile to trade than was Sparta, for its statesmen, as they looked upon what they regarded as the foreign economic entanglements of cities like Corinth and Athens, vowed that the inevitable consequences of foreign trade would not be experienced in their city.

To discourage foreign commerce, and indeed, domestic trade as well, the Spartan scheme during classical times provided for an iron currency. Being far less valuable than gold and silver, iron would have to be possessed in enormous and awkward quantities to carry on even minor exchange. Hence, while neither foreign nor domestic trade was prohibited entirely, the inconvenience of the currency, along with the more general hostility of the polity, effectively discouraged it.

Unfortunately, from the viewpoint of those who supported the Lycurgan system, the very military virtues which were the raison d'être of the Spartan scheme were to prove its undoing. Successful in war after war as it was, Sparta found itself, despite the constitution, confronted by the customs and manners of the enemies over whom it had triumphed. It had succeeded in banishing trade only to find that war itself provided possibilities for corruption hardly less dangerous than those of commerce, and while for centuries it was able to circumvent those temptations, the long Peloponnesian War, which ended in 404 B.C. with the triumph of Sparta over Athens, proved the beginning of the end for the Lycurgan constitution.

The process of decline was a slow one, however. Throughout the first half of the fourth century, the growth of economic inequality, while real, was hardly perceptible. This was the period when Plato and his students in the Academy were to look favorably on many aspects of the Spartan constitution, apparently only dimly aware that the old scheme of things was dissolving. Later on in the century came the Macedonian conquest and with it a still greater disruption of the Lycurgan order. Class differentiations began to appear in sharp form; the distinction between rich and poor among citizens, which the Lycurgan constitution had endeavored to prevent, developed rapidly.

Not until the middle of the third century—from about 250 to 240 B.C.—did a leader appear who could rally defenders of the old order. The energetic King Agis endeavored to restore the main features of the ancient regime by proposing a redivision of lands and the elimination of class distinctions. But by then it was too late and Agis, together with several members of his family, was murdered by the now completely triumphant oligarchic faction.

But in the classical period of Greek political philosophy—roughly from 450 to 322 B.C.—the ultimate fate of Sparta was seen but vaguely, if at all.

The Constitution of Athens

The second great historical example available for fifth- and fourth-century political thinkers was Athens. In many respects, no constitution was more unlike that of Sparta than the constitution or *politeia* of Athens.

In terms of over-all constitutional development, Athenian life reflected, in a form which was to become classical, conflict between landed and commercial classes; the struggle between rich and poor; the tension rising between those who were aristocrats by birth and those who claimed aristocracy by intellect; and the rise of ancient democracy. Some modern students of Athenian development have sought to give it a Marxist or "class-struggle" interpretation.[14] Yet others, as for example, Grote in the nineteenth century, have seen in Athenian politics a foreshadowing of the conflict between Whigs and Tories in British political history.[15] So rich, in fact, is Athenian development in apparent analogies or parallels to modern affairs that there is always a danger of forgetting that we are dealing with ancient and not twentieth-century politics.

We may speculate—for our information is not accurate and even the knowledge which we do have is colored by the partisan struggles of the fifth and fourth centuries—that the beginning of the era of colonization already found Athens with some elements of the constitution that it possessed in the seventh century. The monarchy had long ago been destroyed; and the relatively rapid social changes connected with colonization were already disrupting the tribal way of doing things. By the seventh century, the issues which were to plague Athenian politicians for the next three hundred years were already coming to the forefront, albeit vaguely.

For convenience, we may divide the constitutional development of Athens into four epochs: (1) from about 700 to the reforms of Draco in 621, (2) from Draco to the constitution of Cleisthenes, (3) from the constitution of Cleisthenes (about 500 B.C.) to the overthrow of the Thirty Tyrants (in 403 B.C.), and (4) from the deposition of the Thirty to the death of Aristotle in 322 B.C. In 700 B.C., democracy was noteworthy largely by its absence; by the time of Aristotle, however, it had become triumphant.[16]

To the Reforms of Draco. As political development emerges in the seventh century, the traditional status system of the polis included four classes. The *Eupatridae* were composed of the large landowners and in effect constituted the nobility. Below the *Eupatridae* in

12. Plutarch, "Lycurgus," in *Lives, op. cit.*
13. *Ibid.*
14. For example, Alban Winspear, *op. cit.*
15. George Grote, *History of Greece*, 12 vols., London: J. Murray, 1846–1856. (One-volume edition condensed and edited by J. M. Mitchell and M. O. B. Caspari, London: Geo. Routledge, 1907.)
16. See Walter Agard, *What Democracy Meant to the Greeks*, Madison, Wis.: University of Wisconsin Press, 1960; T. R. Glover, *Democracy in the Ancient World*, New York: Cooper Square Publishers, 1966; and A. H. Jones, *Athenian Democracy*, Oxford: Basil Blackwell, 1957.

terms of social status were the *Georgi*, or the peasants who cultivated their own farms. The *Demiurgi* were those who lived by trade and commerce. While citizens, their political rights were very limited. Finally, there were freemen who were not citizens at all. These included agricultural laborers, restive under their inferior status, and craftsmen. Much of the subsequent history of politics was to turn on the status of the craftsmen and farm workers.

Meanwhile, throughout the seventh century, this classification of the free population in terms of traditional status was giving way to an aristocracy of wealth. Athenians began to view their fellow freemen not through eyes which centered attention on birth but rather from the perspective of money. This was a sure sign that a money economy was coming to the fore and that the amount of material goods which one possessed, not the status into which one was born, was to become crucial in determination of political prerogatives. By the end of the century, this aristocracy of wealth was fourfold.

First came the *Pentacosiomedemni*, or those whose income was at least 500 medemni of corn, or of corn and oil or wine.

The *Knights* were those who had an income of at least 300 medemni, roughly the amount necessary to maintain a horse and take part in war.

The *Zeugitae*, or "Teamsters," possessed minimum incomes of 200 medimni. We may think of them as the well-to-do farmers, who, together with less well-off peasants, still constituted the economic backbone of Attic life.

Finally, the *Thêtes*, while citizens, had no rights of political participation. These were ordinary peasants who, however, were becoming restive because of their lack of status.

In the next century, then, the political struggles are to center on the conflicts between the aristocracy of birth and the aristocracy of wealth. But cutting across this conflict was to come the ever-increasing pressure by the vast group of poverty-stricken citizens for an improvement of their economic status and political prerogatives.

Toward the end of the century, in 621 B.C., the "lawgiver" Draco introduced changes in its constitutional structure. That scheme had consisted of an *Ecclesia* or Assembly—roughly corresponding to the Apella of Sparta, a Council (*Boule*), a Council of the Areopagus, and a number of archons who apparently had for many years been exercising functions formerly carried out by the ancient king. There was in addition a Polemarch, who had both judicial and military functions.

Whatever had been the powers and functions of these bodies and magistrates before Draco, Aristotle tells us[17] that Draco defined their spheres more explicitly. It is obvious, too, that Draco was operating in a context which revealed an increasing influence by the aristocracy of wealth, although the aristocracy of birth was by no means ignored.

Apparently, full political rights—that is, permission to sit in the Ecclesia—were granted to those who could provide themselves with military equipment.

The Draconian laws provided for a Council (corresponding to the Gerusia of Sparta) to consist of 401 members chosen by lot from those possessing full rights of citizenship. Those who failed to attend sessions of the Council or Assembly were to be fined, the fine to be graded according to the census (or category of wealth) of the individual.

The Council of the Areopagus, under the Draconian scheme, apparently retained prerogatives of criminal justice and guardianship of the laws. It consisted of former archons and hence was a very aristocratic body. As such, it was to be subjected in subsequent centuries to the attack of the poor and the "democrats."

Draco's redefinition of constitutional relationships represented an attempt at greater certainty in the proliferating political structure. The emphasis it gave to the aristocracy of wealth, moreover, indicated clearly that political power by the end of the seventh century had become, even formally, largely a function of one's economic status.

The great power of new men of wealth was also revealed in the criminal law reforms associated with the name of Draco. Our term "draconian" has connotations of harsh or severe. And indeed the legal code of Draco was hardly mild. Stealing a cabbage, for example, was punishable by death. But viewed in the perspective of legal evolution we may also think of the code as an endeavor to make more exact differentiations between and among types of crime and to establish greater certainty in the law. It was Draco's code, for example, which first made a careful distinction between murder and manslaughter. Greater exactitude in law was a need felt by the growing class of traders, who found traditional law often inappropriate and all too frequently lacking in the clarity so essential for men of commerce.

To the Constitution of Cleisthenes. Meanwhile, the condition of the small landholders had become steadily worse. This was a product of many factors. In the first place, the relative economic position of all except a few landholders had probably been declining for about half a century or more. Some time in the past, in all probability, most if not all land had been held in common; but gradually a few powerful men had been able to enclose much of the commons, leaving only the poorer land to the masses of peasants. The growth of population, even though somewhat alleviated by colonization, had pressed hard upon the scant resources of Attica.

Moreover, a series of wars toward the end of the seventh century was accompanied, as usual, by inflation in the currency and by profiteering. Those who possessed much of this world's goods gained yet more as a result of the profiteering; while the lot of those who had little wealth became a hard one indeed. The law of Athens permitted men to pledge their bodies for payment of debts. With inflation, war, and the increase of poverty, thousands of small peasants and free laborers were compelled to borrow money, giving as security only themselves. When they found they were unable to pay, they were reduced to a condition of what Aristotle calls "serfdom"[18] and what some modern commentators term "slavery." The debt structure had increased beyond anything hitherto known. Interest rates, always high, had become ruinous.

Although we do not know the exact circumstances of Athenian politics at this time, later tradition suggested (and the view is reflected in Aristotle's *Constitution of Athens*) that the party of the rich and the party of the poor decided to appoint a "mediator" whose task it would be to prevent even more severe civil discord. The mediator chosen was Solon. In 594 B.C., he was elected archon—and the choice, under the constitution of Draco, was a matter for the wealthy classes—and was given extraordinary powers. In the light both of political history and of the political theory of classical Greece, the choice of Solon was significant, for he came from the middle class, those of moderate wealth, and according to Greek tradition was able to understand both the viewpoint of the wealthy and that of the poor.

Solon was a figure who reflected the ideal of Greek popular culture in that he is represented as taking literally the advice of the Delphic oracle "Nothing in excess." Besides being an able representative of the middle class, he was something of a poet and he reflected his conception of moderation when he criticized the profiteers and *pentacosiomedemni* for their lack of restraint.

Holding these views, it is not surprising that he proceeded very rapidly to redress the wrongs which he discerned in the social situation. A merchant himself, he saw that unless the economic imbalances were corrected, the class of merchants itself would be wiped out.

He therefore utilized his extraordinary powers to cancel all debts for which persons had been pledged. All, moreover, who had become serfs because of failure to discharge debts, were freed—apparently without compensation. What was more important, he decreed that for the future it would be illegal to mortgage one's person.

But he went even further; he wiped out all debts, public and private, even when the person was not pledged for payment. He also limited the size of landholding and, because of the desperate domestic need for food, prohibited exportation of all Attic products except olive oil.

In the factional struggles of later Athenian politics, the Solonic reforms were to be the subject of much acrimonious debate. On the whole, the "popular" party was to be pro-Solonic while its opponents were antagonistic.

The Solonic changes in their other dimensions also represented a gain for those economically less well-off. The Thêtes were now admitted to the Ecclesia, whereas it will be remembered that the Draconian measures had excluded them.

Certain other aspects of the Solonic revolution also deserve note. He established, for example, the first form of what was to be so typical an Athenian institution—the "popular courts." All those eligible for the Ecclesia could now be chosen, by lot, to serve on large

17. Kurt von Fritz and Ernst Lapp, trans., *Aristotle's Constitution of Athens and Related Texts,* New York: Hafner, 1950, pp. 71–72.
18. *Ibid.*, ch. 5.

judicial panels. Each jury might consist of several hundred jurors, and the popular courts were to have power to hear appeals from the judicial decisions of the archons.

The aristocratic Council of the Areopagus lost ground, as one might expect. It was deprived of certain deliberative functions. But it still retained its power to see that the laws were observed by all officials and it continued to act as a kind of moral censor.

Finally, the moderation of Solon is again illustrated in his provisions for the establishment of a new Council to take the place of that which had been decreed by Draco. This body was to consist of 400 members—100 from each of the four tribes—and was to be chosen by lot. The method of choice was, of course, ultra-democratic, according to Athenian notions. At the same time, however, Solon limited its democratic features severely by excluding the Thêtes from membership.

Solon did for Athens what Lycurgus is reputed to have accomplished for Sparta—he laid down the main lines along which constitutional evolution was to develop, with some setbacks, for the next two centuries.

But while the general tendency of his lawgiving was democratic, he was unable to please all the leaders of the democratic faction. They apparently resented the restraint with which he extended political powers to the disenfranchised and above all his failure to effect a radical realignment of property relations. Opponents of the popular faction, the great *eupatridae* families and the *pentacosiomedemni* and knights, were likewise dissatisfied: they correctly saw that their preeminent position was on the wane.

Apparently Solon became disgusted with the attitude of both factions. His poems reflect this disillusionment and at the same time reiterate his adherance to the Delphic creed of moderation:

Take the mid-seat and be the vessel's guide;
Many in Athens are upon your side.

He claimed that in fact his legislation had united force with justice: "with force and justice working both in one."

Because of his increasing disillusionment with both factions, he decided to abdicate power and leave Attica for Egypt, announcing that he would not return for ten years and would rely for the interpretation of his laws on others.

Solon's departure was the signal for eruption of factional strife, as there seemed to be no one leader who could mediate. Now arose those parties which were to become classical in the political discussions of the fifth and fourth centuries. Aristotle tells us[19] that there were three factions. One, known as the Party of the Plain, was bent on reestablishment of oligarchy. It apparently was composed of the remnants of the ancient *eupatridae* together with some of the nouveau riche. The second faction was called the Highlanders. It was the radical democratic group, pressing for greater redistribution of property. Finally, the supporters of Solon grouped themselves in the Party of the Shore or the Coast. As is true of most middle-of-the-road parties in time of acute crisis and in the absence of outstanding leadership, the Party of the Coast tended to be squeezed out by the more extreme groups. Moreover, the democratic faction developed a rather remarkable leader in Pisitratus, who, chosen Polemarch in 570 B.C., managed to be successful in a war with Salamis and thus enhanced his reputation greatly.

In 561 B.C., Pisistratus was able to seize the "tyranny"—that is, to gain power by extra-legal means. He remained tyrant for a period of about nineteen years. The remaining part of his life he spent in exile, for despite his commanding presence, he was never able to abate completely the conflict of factions.

After the death of Pisistratus, the tyranny fell into the hands of his sons, Hippias and Hipparchus. The latter was soon murdered and Hippias, plagued by uncertainty and insecurity, tended to increase the harshness of his regime. His political opponents, in turn, eventually allied themselves with Sparta and, seventeen years after the death of Hipparchus, overthrew the tyranny.

The struggle in Athens then centered on the conflict between the partisans of Isagoras and those of Cleisthenes. However, the active contest was at first not carried out in the open but rather in the political "clubs"—debating associations whose members came mainly from the aristocratic and oligarchic factions in Athenian politics. They often wielded a power quite disproportionate to their membership. We may think of them as an ancient version of the Union League Club in the United States or the Carlton Club in Great Britain.

In the clubs, then, the partisans of Isagoras and Cleisthenes proclaimed the merits of their respective leaders. Meanwhile, in the marketplace and among ordinary citizens, suspicion of the clubs was growing, since they had been known for a long time as hotbeds of *eupatrid* and *pentacosiomedemni* manipulations. It was feared that the victory so hardly won against the tyrants would be largely lost in a new triumph of aristocrats and oligarchs.

But the bitter struggle in the clubs weakened the cause of both the eupatrids and the oligarchs. When eventually Cleisthenes found himself defeated in the clubrooms, he sought a political alliance with leaders of the "popular" faction. At this, Isagoras took alarm and summoned the kings of Sparta to his aid. Cleisthenes fled the country and the Spartan rulers appeared and expelled seven hundred families who constituted the leading supporters of Cleisthenes. The Spartans thereupon attempted to dissolve the Council and to impose the rule of Isagoras. But the Council resisted, and, supported by the citizenry, besieged the Isagoran forces in the Acropolis. After several days of siege, the Spartans were allowed to withdraw, the popular forces emerged triumphant, and Cleisthenes was recalled from exile, together with his leading supporters. Cleisthenes thereupon assumed the unofficial position of leader of the people and, adopting a Solon-like stance, proceeded to remold the Athenian life.

His reforms were radical and moved still further in the direction of dominance by the democracy. In order to lesson the traditional power of the leading families which had been exercised through the ancient four tribes, he abolished the tribes altogether.

Finally, Cleisthenes was responsible for the law establishing ostracism. According to this, the Ecclesia, under certain limitations, could exile political leaders. Whoever had the most ostraka (an ostrakon was a piece of potsherd on which the name of the leader was written) against him was compelled to leave Attica within ten days. According to the notions of the time, this was an ultrademocratic device which would prevent any revival of *eupatrid* or oligarchic claims.

To sum up, we may say that by about 500 B.C., when the Persian Wars began, the "democracy" of ancient Athens had become triumphant. Citizenship had been extended about as far as it was to be granted; social order by contrivance rather than by traditional and unconsciously created folkways had made great strides; the Ecclesia's powers had been greatly enlarged; while they could still be chosen only from the two highest classes, selection of magistrates by lot rather than by election had been extended; the old tribal ways had been largely disrupted; the powers of the ancient Council of the Areopagus had been severely limited; and, to all appearances at least, the possibility of a revival of *eupatrid* and *pentacosiomedemni* political power had been wiped out.

From Cleisthenes to the Overthrow of the Thirty. Yet the triumph of the democracy was in part more apparent than real. During the Persian Wars (500–479 B.C.), for example, the aristocratic Council of the Areopagus, which had hitherto declined both in prestige and in formal powers, won renewed respect because of its leadership in planning such engagements as the battle of Salamis. After the wars, it continued to maintain this prestige for a time, despite the overwhelming tide of democratic sentiment.

Then, too, while more citizens were now eligible for the position of archon and while all could sit in the popular courts, it was a real burden to serve the public when one's private business had to be neglected in the process, for down to the middle of the fifth century most positions were not paid. Traditionally, of course, the offices had been open only to those having considerable financial means and for them the question of public compensation had not even arisen.

Finally, the character of the Athenian Empire which flourished during the generation following the Persian Wars led eventually to a revival of aristocratic and oligarchic sentiment.

The period from the end of the Persian Wars to the beginning of the Peloponnesian War (479–431 B.C.) is the time to which later Greeks were to point as the epoch of glory. It was an age in which Athens emerged triumphant as a sea power and as the leader of a confederacy of city-states banded together to prevent the recurrence of foreign invasion. Within these few years, all the arts flowered under the patronage of the Athenian polis.

Meanwhile, the figure of Pericles dominated the political scene during the latter part of the imperial period down to his death in 429 B.C. Originally from the middle class like Solon, he became the champion of the popular cause and sought to remove the last obstacles in the

19. *Ibid.*, ch. 13.

way of a triumphant democracy.[20] It was under his leadership, for example, that the Council of the Areopagus finally lost its remaining powers. Its brief revival during and immediately after the Persian Wars now came to an end under the onslaughts of the "popular" party.

Of even greater importance was the effort of Pericles to ease the strain of public service. He provided for a salaried archonship and also for payment of the popular judges, whose powers by now included not only appellate but also original jurisdiction.

The nature of the Athenian Empire was both an expression of democracy and a cause of its disintegration toward the end of the century. According to the agreement which Athens reached with its allies, the latter were to contribute regular sums to the Confederate treasury, in return for which Athens would guarantee their defense against foreign invasion. This seemed reasonable enough at the time but was later to be the cause of much acrimony and the basis for renewed factional struggle.

By the middle of the century, it was clear that Athens, instead of being merely "first among equals" in the confederacy, was actually becoming the dominant party. The supporters of Pericles took pride in its dominance, claiming that it would always control the confederacy for the benefit of all members. The democrats increasingly became the imperialists, glorying in the subordination of other cities to Athens and rationalizing that subordination in ways familiar to ruling groups throughout the centuries.

It was in this atmosphere that Pericles decided to take the funds deposited in the Confederacy's treasury and use them to complete the public buildings of Athens. Supported strongly by his faction in the Ecclesia, he accordingly had the gold removed and proceeded to construct the Parthenon and the other noble piles which we still admire on the Acropolis. Athens, hitherto a rather poor city in economic terms, began to assume the appearance of a very wealthy metropolis.

But the removal of the common funds and their use for Athenian improvements was the signal for bitter conflict. It was to be expected that the confederate cities would protest. They argued with force that Pericles' use of the imperial gold represented a misappropriation of money, that the funds of the confederacy were to be utilized solely for its defense.

The cry was taken up in Athens by the opponents of Pericles—mainly the remnants of the aristocratic party. Led by Thucydides (not the historian), they sought to impeach Pericles for misconduct and to depose him from leadership. But Pericles defended his employment of confederate funds, arguing that by the agreement with its fellow-confederates, Athens had been given a carte blanche to use the gold in any way it saw fit, provided that it performed its part of the contract, which was to defend the confederacy.

Eventually the whole issue came to an ostracism. Feeling ran high. The imperialist democrats stood pitted against the anti-imperialist aristocrats. Led by the political acumen of Pericles, the former emerged triumphant and Thucydides was ostracized. But the conflict left ugly sores on the body politic, which would be reopened during the war with Sparta.

When the war began in 431 it seemed that Athens would find fortune favoring its cause. It had grown in wealth and power during a generation of peace; it had amassed a reserve of gold which seemed to be adequate for any contingency; and the opponents of the war, whatever their numbers, were largely inarticulate at the outset of the struggle.

We need not go into the details of the Peloponnesian War. But it is important to note its effects on the political and constitutional life of the Athenian polis, for much of what classical theory had to say about democracy was based on its judgments of the wartime *demos.*

The death of Pericles in 429 B.C. removed the one leader who could have given a measure of restraint to the seething passions released by the war. Moreover, the great plague, to which Pericles succumbed, so disorganized the crowded city of Athens that a way was opened for a different kind of democratic leadership. Power passed from the middle class to such leaders as Eucrates, a rope seller; Hyperbolus, a lamp maker; and Cleon, a leather merchant.

The term democracy was to connote, for many of the Greek political thinkers of the late fifth and the fourth centuries, the kind of regime characteristic of Athenian life during the Peloponnesian War. While this rule was in part the product of the two-century development which we have traced, it was also informed by the peculiar spirit characteristic of post-Periclean leadership. In addition to the particular kind of democratic leadership evidenced between 429 and 403, there were certain general marks of the democracy which intelligent men could not help but note.

One was, of course, the selection of almost all higher administrators by lot rather than by vote.

Another characteristic which came to be associated with democracy was the moral right of the Ecclesia to change rules of procedure hastily and to overturn even the decisions of law courts. The Ecclesia often tended to think that rule by the *demos* meant that the people were subject to no moral limitations—that sovereignty not only meant absence of legal restrictions but also the elimination of moral bounds. Thus what English law has called bills of attainder came to be looked upon by the triumphant democracy as entirely permissible.

Finally, a democratic *politeia* was associated in Athens with wide latitude on the part of the popular courts. Just as the Ecclesia when sitting as a policy making body regarded itself as subject to no moral limitations so the popular courts tended quite often to interpret the law in accordance with their emotions of the moment. Sometimes they seemed to disregard the plain intent of the law. In criminal cases they were wont to place great weight on the tears of supplicants, even in the face of evident guilt. All this was democracy, according to its critics.

By 421, when a temporary truce obtained, the citizen population of Athens had been reduced through plague and war from about 100,000 to fewer than 75,000, and to the opponents of democracy this was at least partially due to the cardinal characteristics of democratic politics domestically and to the aggressive tendencies of that same politics in foreign affairs. During the decade between 421 and 411, anti-democratic forces grew in influence and power. Once the war had been resumed—the peace of 421 was short-lived—the opponents of democracy were increasingly identified as the peace party.

This coupling of peace and oligarchy became particularly close after the disastrous Sicilian expedition of 414 to 413.

When news of the expedition's fate reached Athens in the autumn of 413, those who advocated overthrow of the democracy were greatly strengthened. By 412 B.C. they were able to push through the Ecclesia measures which fundamentally changed the constitution. The Committee of Ten, which had been given conduct of the war, was to be enlarged to thirty. The new Committee of Thirty was then to draft proposals for "the salvation of the country." When it finally acted, the Thirty shook up the political order quite radically: public revenue was to be used only for the conduct of the war; most public officials would serve without pay until the end of the war (a clearly aristocratic provision); and the administration of the country was to be entrusted to the 5000 most propertied Athenians.

The Five Thousand now delegated constitution-making prerogatives to a Committee of One Hundred, and this Committee proceeded to draw up an elaborate scheme which, in general, tended to be strongly aristocratic. All this, however, remained unimplemented. Meanwhile, the day-to-day business was entrusted to a new Council of Four Hundred, which elected the magistrates and supervised the public accounts.

What disaster had initiated disaster was to undo. Aristotle tells us that the rule of the Four Hundred lasted only four months (in 411). Just as the Sicilian failure had established its power, so a naval battle off Eretria and the revolt of the Euboeans destroyed it. The Ecclesia, disgusted and disillusioned, abolished the temporary oligarchy and turned over authority to the Five Thousand. Although this was not exactly a return of the democracy, as that had been known before, it did mean that confidence in the oligarchy had abated. The Ecclesia once more assumed an active role.

About the same time, the Spartans offered to conclude a peace on very favorable terms, only to be spurned by the leadership of the Ecclesia. Again, the peace party felt that the decision had been stupid and, indeed, immoral.

A year after this refusal of peace by the Athenians, they lost the great battle of Aegospotami, which opened the way for the Spartans, under Lysander, to enter Athens and support the claims of the oligarchical faction. The presence of the Spartans accordingly intimidated the Ecclesia to establish the rule of

20. See Aagard, *op. cit.;* A. R. Burn, *Pericles and Athens*, London: Hodder & Stoughton, 1948; Glover, *op. cit.;* Jones, *op. cit.;* C. Mackenzie, *Pericles*, London: Hodder & Stoughton, 1937; Plutarch, "Pericles," in *Lives, op. cit.;* and Charles Robinson, Jr., *Athens in the Age of Pericles*, Norman, Okla.: University of Oklahoma Press, 1959.

a Committee of Thirty, who came to be called the "Thirty Tyrants." This was in 404 B.C.

The rule of the Thirty was apparently moderate at first. They tried to limit the sweeping powers of the popular judges in interpreting the laws and to make the texts of the laws more exact. And they attacked the powers which demagogues had come to possess.

But this moderation was a pretence. Once their rule was firmly established, they proceeded to attack their political enemies and all those who, by reputation, might challenge their authority. Within a relatively short time, they had ordered executed some 1500 persons, a large number when one remembers that the total citizen body at this time was no more than 100,000.

But the democratic exiles, with their forces, shortly afterwards defeated a force sent by the Thirty to combat them. Meanwhile, 3000 leading citizens, taking heart, deposed the Tyrants and gave full authority to a Committee of Ten to bring the civil conflict to an end. But the Ten, according to their critics, betrayed the purpose for which they had been chosen, actually asking Sparta for assistance. Eventually the Committee of Ten was deposed in favor of a body which did effect reconciliation.

Gradually, during the course of several months in 403, the democratic constitution was restored. Aristotle, not noted for his democratic sympathies, praises the reestablished popular party for its moderation; there was a wide extension of amnesty and an endeavor to heal the wounds which had been created by more than a year of active civil conflict.

The Ecclesia was established on its old footing and by 401 to 400 it had set up a new and ultrademocratic constitution.

It was this constitution which was in effect when Socrates was executed, Plato was writing his dialogues, and Aristotle was conducting his scientific, moral, and political investigations. It was under this scheme, too, that Athens began to lose its political independence after the middle of the century, as the power of Macedonia waxed and that of the Greek cities gradually declined.

Constitutional Development and Intellectual Evolution

At the outset of this chapter, we noted the slow disintegration of the tribal way of life, the rise of class distinctions, the age of colonization, and the growth of trade and commerce as important factors in the evolution of Greek life as a whole. We also observed the beginning of self-conscious intellectual life in the eighth century and its flowering in the seventh and sixth. We pointed out that the first intellectual curiosity was exhibited about the world of external nature, as over against the world of men; and that this probing took the form of the classic attempt to reconcile our experience of diversity in the physical world with our quest for some kind of unity which we somehow think must lie behind and beyond that diversity. This question of the Many and the One was developed into the issue of how the One, whatever it was, became the Many. Some thinkers seemed to conceive of the Many, or flux, as the only Reality, while others thought that they saw, behind the Many, a One of some kind (whether fire, water, or another) out of which the Many grew.

Meanwhile, we continued, the minds of leading Greeks were by the latter part of the sixth century turning not only to physical but also social speculation. Thus, Pythagoras, who died about 500 B.C., was taken as a symbol of a tendency in Greek thought to unite the emotionalism of the Orphic cult with rationality and to add to the current doctrines about physical life equally sharp speculations regarding the moral, social, and political realm.

But it is impossible, we suggested, to comprehend the full dimensions of the social speculations that began in the late sixth century and flowered in the fifth, without a fairly good understanding of the increasing instability of Greek political life. Hence we turned to the Constitution of Sparta and saw how it had attempted to contrive a political order strongly infused with military ideology, an order, moreover, which sought stability and success in war as the objectives of collective life. Meanwhile, in Athens, the slow and tortuous evolution from the seventh century to the end of the fourth century had begun. It was characterized by a bewildering variety of social phenomena which even able thinkers found hard to comprehend: the conflict between an aristocracy of birth and a newly rising aristocracy of wealth; the struggle between poor peasants, caught in the vise of a money and war economy, and the class of newly rich, largely the product of trade, commerce, and war speculation; the break-up of traditional tribal divisions; and the slow and painful process of attempting to contrive an order which would once more provide a framework within which the life of Athenians could have meaning and a measure of stability. The constitutional evolution of Athens, we suggested, was an effort to provide answers to the political problems posed by social disintegration and economic development; and from the constitution of Draco (about 621 B.C.) to that of the year 400, Athenian politicians had wrestled with diverse forms of the distribution of power—schemes which were to be the point of departure for the speculations of the fifth and fourth centuries.

Meanwhile, interest in moral and social questions was evidenced as early as the time of Pythagoras and had grown with the complexity of division of labor, constitutional and economic struggles, and the apparent inability of men to contrive systems of government possessing any measure of stability. Moreover, the long Peloponnesian War was simply illustrative of the fact that war, as Zimmern puts it,[21] was never exceptional. To the instability of internal polis life was added the ever-present possibility of armed conflict between two or more cities.

These were the circumstances, then, in which thinkers gradually turned from central interest in natural science to primary concern for social studies.

How did men conceive the sociopolitical transformations through which the fifth and fourth centuries passed so rapidly? How did they explain those changes? How did they fit the phenomena of social change into the ancient conviction that there must be an unchanging something from which all change proceeded? Yet how account for diversity of moral and political values if justice or righteousness were one?

These are only a few of the questions which puzzled the moral and political thinkers of the fifth century to whose reactions we turn in the next chapter.

chapter 3

Political Thought and Opinion from Hesiod to Socrates

The institutional developments which have been traced out in Chapter 2 were paralleled by intellectual tendencies that partly reflected and partly shaped them.

As far as we can discern, men's original reflections on the social and primitive political worlds were conditioned strongly by the tribal way of things. Custom—or as the Greeks called it, *nomos*—ruled almost completely. To follow custom was *diké,* which may be interpreted as righteousness or justice. To disregard custom was *hubris* which signified outrage or unrighteousness or violence. The customary way of life of a people or individual or primitive ruler, then, was both nomos and diké and it was inconceivable, probably, to the mind of the ninth century, that there could ever be any conflict between what we should today call the folkways and what we would term ethical and political justice.

This general position would seem to be the one taken by the writings of Homer. In the *Iliad* and the *Odyssey* we get elaborate pictures of tribal, semipolitical societies, in which *hubris* is thought of as running contrary to custom and hence to diké as well. The will of the gods was equivalent to the custom of a people as well as to righteousness.

As social and economic differentiations began to grow, however, and the rigid tribal patterns of conduct proceeded to crack, a great measure of disorder succeeded the primitive stability.

In the eighth century, the poet Hesiod began to reflect man's puzzlement about social development. Hesiod witnessed the growth of

Chapter 2

21. Alfred Zimmern, *The Greek Commonwealth,* Oxford: Clarendon Press, 1911, p. 340.

piracy and the beginnings of sharp class differentiation and in many respects may be compared to his great Hebrew contemporary, Amos, who was also puzzled by the social evolution of his people.

Thus he portrays in his poetry five ages of degeneracy through which mankind have come from the postulated age when diké and custom were identical. The age in which he lived he termed the epoch of iron, for "justice" seemed to be simply a matter of superiority in strength. Those who had no strength, Hesiod complains, have no diké; while those—the now increasingly differentiated nobility—who possess force arrogantly equate that force with diké. Diké in the old sense of "equality" as between and among men, has retreated to Olympus.

In his poem *Works and Days*, Hesiod expresses this attitude in dramatic form: "Diké shall be in the strength of a man's hands, and reverence shall be no more." Or again, in comparing the relation of a landlord to a small peasant with that of a hawk to a nightingale, he makes the hawk say: "A far stronger than you holds you in his grasp; and you must go wherever I take you, well though you sing. I will make a meal of you, if I please, or let you go. He is a fool who strives to withstand the stronger."[1]

In the century and a quarter between Hesiod and Solon, the discussion of ethical and political questions, while still rather incidental and sketchy, was undoubtedly a factor of some importance in Greek intellectual life. The Hesiodic influence was present, and, in the sixth century, the popular Dionysiac cult was accustoming ordinary Greeks to the notion of a separation of body from soul—a division very much like that which Hesiod was beginning to discern between diké, which now seemed to be a possession of the gods alone, and sheer power which appeared in the "practical" world to be the sole appeal. Meanwhile, the Draconic reforms at the end of the seventh century may be interpreted as primitive efforts to contrive a kind of diké in an order of things which had become more and more political and which was retreating significantly from family and clan conceptions.

Solon appeared on the political scene as archon early in the sixth century;[2] he came to symbolize for later Greeks not only legal and economic reform but also a kind of political theory seeking to reconcile the claims of the aristocrats with those of the popular party. The doctrine of Solon now also claimed to reintroduce in the contrived, or political, order the diké which Hesiod had thought of as having retreated to the gods. Solon himself thought of his work in this way, as he reflected in later years on his significance.

But Solon declined to accept any arbitrary power and even before he became archon, he had the reputation among the many of being a thinker who understood the true meaning of the Delphic admonition "nothing in excess":

> Solon surely was a dreamer, and a man of simple mind;
> When the gods would give him fortune, he of his own will declined;
> When the net was full of fishes, over-heaving thinking it,
> He declined to haul it up, through want of heart and want of wit.[3]

When finally he did accept leadership, it was with the understanding that he was to be a kind of arbitrator between the claims of the *eupatrids* and the wealthy and those of the dispossessed peasants and workers. Thus there appeared for the first time in Greek political thought the notion that the polis might be impartial and somehow might discover a diké transcending the claims of all the contending factions in city life.

Solon maintained that his greatest claim to fame lay in his tying justice to force. Whereas, according to Hesiod, diké had fled to the gods and force now falsely paraded in its robes, Solon suggested that he had done everything possible to unite diké with force. It is interesting to note that he conceived diké to be something above and beyond mere force and that he regarded the great political problem as being one of marrying the righteousness about which Hesiod had talked to the mere force which landlords and the nobility had equated with righteousness.

Finally, Solon went down in the Greek political tradition as one who felt that men themselves could discover what diké demanded. One could not expect the gods to intervene in the construction of the political order. The old order of custom had gone and righteousness had fled, it is true, but it was possible for men to recapture the righteousness which had formerly been embodied in the customary order of things.

While Solon, then, had stated the political problem as one of uniting power of every kind to diké and had clearly seen that the political order had to be contrived and would not be imposed, as it were, fullblown from *outside* the human community, he had accepted a rather conventional notion as to the meaning of diké. He had simply received the Delphic statement on moderation and given it his own interpretation. For him, justice in his time was to restore material goods to those who had been dispossessed of them while at the same time recognizing legitimacy, up to a degree, in the claims of the *eupatrids* and the oligarchs.

But *was* justice really a balance between groups which had either economic or physical power? Or was Solon acting in the way he did simply because he *had* to do so, and not because the diké which had fled to the gods was involved? Was he really looking *beyond* the Delphic oracle and attempting to discover the nature of justice; or was he accepting the oracle uncritically, despite his claim that a just political order depended on human contrivance alone? Finally, if his actions represented simply a realistic recognition of power relations baptized under the name of diké, in what sense did his conception of justice differ from that which Hesiod had associated with those who possessed power in the world? In other words, was not Solon's notion of "balance" of powers in the polis simply a variant of the view that there is no distinction between diké and force—that diké has in fact not retreated to the gods but is in reality possessed by those who have the most power?

It was questions of this kind which the generations after the death of Solon in 558 B.C. were to ask themselves. While their answers were to vary widely and many peripheral (though important) issues were to be raised, we may think of the basic problem as turning after the middle of the sixth century on the relation between nomos, or convention, and *physis*, or nature. And this issue, in turn, was the "social science" expression of the old "physical science" question of the relation between the One and the Many.

Insofar as answers to the nomos-physis controversy were given at all (and some simply tried to clarify the issue and did not profess to provide a solution), they may be grouped into two schools of thought. According to the one school, nomos—or convention—defined the only justice there could be. It was futile to seek for a universal One behind the many expressions of nomos to be found in the varied cultures of the time. At the risk of oversimplification, we might designate this school in the sixth and fifth centuries as the *relativist*.

The second school, by contrast, sought for and believed it could find a "one" universal lying behind the many customs and conventions reflected in ancient cultures. For the sake of convenience, we may call those who held this view the *absolutists*.

Some modern critics—notably, Winspear and Popper—claim that political thought in the fifth century (and in the fourth as well) was in large degree closely correlated with the ongoing political power struggle, particularly in Athens. The popular party, this contention avers, was represented intellectually by the relativist political thinkers; while the aristocrats, on the other hand, found their philosophy in the absolutist school. Certain critics even seem to suggest that absolutist and relativist positions were simply *ideologies*—that is, rationalizations of the power interests of popular and antipopular factions respectively.

To rephrase this argument, one might say that it was to the interest of popular leaders to stress the desirability of change, for until the end of the fifth century, change, in terms of practical politics, would probably be in a democratic direction. Therefore, the allegation goes on, the democrats attached themselves to the relativists whose social and political philosophy seemed to think of diké as simply a matter of convention.

On the other hand, the aristocrats—if one accepts the ideological interpretation of the history of political thought—had an interest in absolutist views because they were losing out in the political struggle, and if they could somehow spread abroad and get accepted the notion that there was an absolute justice differing from the predominant tendencies in the direction of popular rule, they might conceivably preserve a part of their traditional privileges.

If the ideological interpretation of intellectual history is to be taken in its extreme form,

1. "The Works and Days," in *Hesiod*, Richmond Lattimore, trans., Ann Arbor: University of Michigan Press, 1959, pp. 205–215.
2. See John E. Rexine, *Solon and His Political Theory*, New York: William-Frederick Press, 1958.
3. "Solon," in Plutarch, *The Lives of the Noble Grecians and Romans*, John Dryden, trans., New York: Modern Library, 1932.

those who engaged in the great debates of the fifth century were under the illusion that they were searching for the truth about moral-political relations. In reality, this extreme version would seem to suggest, they were, whether they knew it or not, simply spokesmen for factional groups within the polis, and their attitudes to the increasingly acute issues of ancient political theory were shaped wholly by ideological factors.

There is, of course, a measure of validity in the ideological interpretation of Greek political thought, whether in the fifth or the fourth centuries.

At the same time, it would seem questionable to regard any thinker or scheme of thought simply as an expression of partisan social and political conflict. While systems of thought in the fifth and fourth centuries were no doubt used as weapons, the burden of proof must be on those critics who allege that they were no more than weapons. Certainly the ancient formulators conceived their scientific and philosophical schemes to be efforts to explain political reality, discover political norms, and escape from mere rationalizations.

Although strictly speaking there was no system of Greek political thought before Plato, many serious efforts were made in the latter part of the sixth century and throughout the fifth to explain political phenomena and to find moral norms. Here let us note six of those efforts as undertaken by (1) Pythagoras and the Pythagoreans, (2) Herodotus, (3) the great tragedians, (4) Aristophanes, (5) the "sophists," and (6) Socrates.

Pythagoras and the Pythagoreans

We know very little about the life of Pythagoras and it is often difficult to separate his teaching from that of his disciples, the Pythagoreans.

In political terms, moreover, there has been, as with Plato, a great controversy as to the precise relation between Pythagorean teaching and the political events of his time. Hegel was one, for example, to minimize both the practical political activities of Pythagoras and his alleged political teaching. On the other hand, recent scholars like Winspear[4] profess to find the genesis of Pythagoras' mathematics in his political predilections.

Pythagoras was born apparently about 582 B.C. (during the archonship of Solon) on the island of Samos and spent the early part of his life there. About 535, the tyrant Polycrates seized power in Samos and Pythagoras, disliking his activities, left Samos in 532 to take up his residence in the Greek Italian polis of Croton. He spent the rest of his days in Croton, apparently being both an activist and an academic. He died about 507, roughly about the time of the Cleisthenian democratic revolution in Athens.

It is fairly certain that Pythagoras was active in religious affairs. He was particularly interested in the Orphic cult and did much to spread its influence in Italy. Apparently he actually organized Orphic brotherhoods, and it was the influence of Orphism which helped shape all aspects of his teaching.

Politically, too, Pythagoras was not idle. While it is doubtful that he ever held public office, it is almost certain that he helped organize some of the political "clubs" which played an important role in the politics of many Greek city-states, and these organizations no doubt served to spread the influence of Pythagorean teaching throughout all the Greek world.

The tendency in Orphism to separate sharply the soul from the body was taken up by Pythagoras and made the basis of much of his science and political teaching. His cosmological views as well as his social theory seemingly turned on this rather sharp dichotomy.

Now in cosmological terms, Pythagoras apparently thought that the "whole" was "number." Hence he spent a great part of his life looking into the nature of number and endeavoring to express things in numerical and geometrical formulae. Number was the beginning or *arché* of things and was therefore that which was true reality. It was the "ordering principle" behind the flux; the One behind the Many.

In the relationship between soul and body, the soul was the *arché*. Men found themselves imprisoned in the body and unduly separated from the soul; for it was the soul which was the essence of man, as number was the essence of the universe. The Pythagoreans, and apparently Pythagoras also, held to a doctrine of the transmigration of souls, according to which the soul would be gradually purified of the body which sought to dominate it. It was the task of man, in the moral and political realm, to free the soul as much as possible from bodily restrictions so that it might assume its rightful place as the "governor" of human action.

The Pythagorean view of politics was closely associated with its conception of the cosmos and of human personality. The turbulence which the Pythagoreans witnessed in the party struggles of the polis was like the chaos which was the appearance of the universe.

Pythagoras thought of righteousness as mathematical proportion and expressed it as a "square number." It was literally a right triangle, in which the square of the hypotenuse was always equal to the sum of the squares of the other two sides. This was true no matter how long the other two sides happened to be.

Having identified justice or righteousness with a square, the Pythagoreans apparently proceeded to show what this implied for politics. For one thing, it seemed to involve a theory of proportionate rather than absolute equality in the polis. Some modern critics have taken this as proof that Pythagoras and his followers were always anti-democrats in the struggles of the sixth and fifth centuries, and, indeed, such seems to have been the case in many instances. It also appears to have been true that many of the Pythagoreans were hostile to social change in general, apparently because they regarded it as a still further departure from the arché of things. On the other hand, it should likewise be pointed out that they were frequently persecuted for their religious innovations, which would seem to cast doubt on the proposition that they were against all change in society.

The basic contentions of the Pythagoreans were of enormous importance for later views of society and politics. Both the cosmological and the social doctrines of Pythagoras appear to have influenced the system of Parmenides (b. 514 B.C.), for example, and the whole school of the Eleatic philosophers. And they are central for the great Platonic structure, as we shall see presently.

Herodotus

Herodotus was of some significance in the development of ancient Greek thought, not because he was primarily a political speculator, but because his great *History* established a kind of frame of reference for the questions put by both popular and professional thinkers in the fifth and fourth centuries. Born in the early part of the fifth century (c. 484 B.C.), Herodotus lived until well after the beginning of the Peloponnesian War, dying (425 B.C.) about four years after the death of Pericles.

His great *History,* as is well known, was designed to be a kind of epic which would detail the rise and fall of the Persian Empire when confronted by the indomitable opposition of the Greeks and particularly of the Athenians. In the process of developing his major theme, however, Herodotus felt that he had to introduce much material giving the geographical, anthropological, and economic backgrounds of the various peoples with whom he dealt—the Medes, for example, and the Lydians, Libyans, Persians, and even the Indians. The result is that one obtains in his *History* not only a narrative tracing out the attempt of the Persians to conquer Greece but also a rather amazing study of comparative customs.

As the ideological spokesman for democratic Athens, Herodotus conceived himself to be the vindicator of the Athenian *politeia* against the claims of autocracies like those of Persia.

But secondly, Herodotus was one of the many observers of the fifth century who dramatized so vividly that cultures and political systems differ widely. His own extensive travels had led him to this position, and his recitations before the Athenians no doubt heightened their awareness of this fact. Thus he portrays the Persian King Darius as asking some Greeks what they would take to eat their dead fathers. This naturally horrified the Greeks, who were by now cremating the dead. To ask them whether they would be willing to eat the dead, and particularly their fathers, was little short of sacrilege to them. It was not according to nature to eat one's dead father.

But Darius then proceeded to call in representatives of a tribe of Indians who allegedly ate dead parents. The king asked the Indians how much they would take to burn their parents. The Indians were outraged by this proposal, replying that nothing could induce them to violate nature by burning the dead.

Herodotus then points out the moral—and a most effective one it is. The diverse burial customs of Indians and Greeks simply illustrate the observation of the poet Pindar, for he said that "custom is king." And he seems to imply that there is nothing beyond nomos or

4. Alban Winspear, *The Genesis of Plato's Thought,* New York: S. A. Russell, 1956.

custom, that there is no one best burial custom, that all such practices are relative to the culture of a given time, place, and tradition.

His study of comparative anthropology tended, therefore, to make Herodotus a relativist in terms of the exciting nomos-physis controversy of the fifth and fourth centuries.[5] This relativism, moreover, is strongly supported by his frequently expressed religious skepticism. While on the one hand he accepts the stories of gods and portents when and if they are sufficiently removed from contemporary events, he tends to be doubtful about any alleged intervention of the gods in the recent historical happenings which he studies. Moreover, he thinks that if the gods had ever communed directly with men, it must have been long before the time alleged by the common Greek tradition.

The Tragedians and the Political Problem

While Herodotus was casting the light of comparative anthropology on questions of fifth-century political opinion and thought, the great tragic dramatists were dealing with similar issues within the limits of the dramatic conventions which had developed in the previous century. Aeschylus (525–456), Sophocles (496–406), and Euripides (480–406), together with others whose scripts for production have been lost, could not avoid at least an implicit treatment of political subjects.

Although the themes of the great tragedies were by convention usually taken from Homeric stories—an exception is Aeschylus' *The Persians*—the dramatist was given great freedom in their development. He undoubtedly had in mind, as he dealt with Homeric legends, many of the sixth- and fifth-century problems confronting Greek society. Thus the role of force in politics was an important thread running through many of the tragedies; and it is not difficult to see in this theme more than a casual reference to the tyrant—the man who, with a show of force, would take control of a polis illegally. While many tyrants, once in power, ruled mildly and beneficially (as, for example, Pisistratus), there was never any assurance that they would do so. So also one finds mirrored in the tragedies the almost constant warfare which went on among the city-states and against the "barbarians."

The productions of Aeschylus, Sophocles, and Euripides represent a characteristic general attitude to collective as well as to individual life and treat moral and political obligations in their multifarious aspects.

(1) The tragic attitude to political life could hardly be separated from its position on personal vicissitudes and human nature in general. Recognizing that with the rise of individuality, human choices become more and more significant, tragedy thinks of them, however, as frequently involving decisions between courses of action almost equally undesirable. The life of the individual is so enmeshed with that of his ancestors and his contemporaries, the tragic viewpoint holds, that alternatives set before political leaders might all be unacceptable. Yet leaders have to make choices.

At the heart of the tragic sense of political life is the Greek notion of hubris, to which we have already referred in connection with the Delphic oracle. The tragedians see man emerging from the closely-knit, tradition-governed life of the tribe with no sure guides for action. As differentiations of wealth and power develop, individuals or groups make wealth and power the end. The man or polis acquiring riches or power tends to embody hubris, which sometimes is thought of as insolent pride. Hubris implies arrogance and a willingness to utilize means which violate the emphasis on moderation—or *sóphrosyné*—which is so central an emphasis in Greek popular culture.

But once hubris is present in man or polis, the tragedians see human events as in considerable degree shaped by it. Retribution inevitably will follow hubris, but those who carry out the retribution will in turn take on hubris characteristics. And later generations will find their choices limited by what took place in their fathers' and grandfathers' time. Thus the tragedian can look beyond any simple assessment of responsibility and moral guilt. Instead of holding tyrants or kings responsible for the chaos which so many see in Greek politics, the tragedians suggest that both tyrants and kings are caught up in forces and "curses" that restrict their choices and often make them do evil in order to expel evil.

In the *Agamemnon*, for example, Aeschylus has the Chorus say:

> It has been made long since and grown old among men,
> this saying: human wealth
> grown to fulness of stature
> breeds again nor dies without issue.
> From high good fortune in the blood
> blossoms the quenchless agony.[6]

And the Chorus in the same tragedy thinks of the Trojan War in the following terms:

The god of war, money changer of dead bodies,
held the balance of his spear in the fighting,
and from the corpse-fires at Illium
sent to their dearest the dust
heavy and bitter with tears shed
packing smooth the urns with
ashes that once were men.[7]

The tragic view sees both political and individual life as often governed by sheer arbitrary force or might, which the tragedians sometimes identify with Zeus. Thus the myth of Prometheus is treated by Aeschylus as an example of the vengeance of Zeus for Prometheus' benefitting mankind by giving them fire. In retaliation for the arrogance of this act—for fire was originally solely under the control of the gods—Zeus orders Prometheus to be chained tightly to a rock, there to suffer for his misdeeds. The dramatist significantly symbolizes the agents of Zeus as Might and Violence.[8]

The tragedians, however, while they emphasize the dilemmas that the hubris of previous generations might create for men, also see human beings, whether in their political or in their private roles, responding with a certain inner dignity to the narrow choices which are thrust before them. Thus Electra in Euripides' play of that name, while she has doubts about whether she should slay her mother in retaliation for her mother's killing her father, in the end, once having made her choice, supports her brother in the act.

In the legend of Prometheus, as treated by Aeschylus, Prometheus may be said to symbolize, among other things, the revolt of rational and political man against dominance by force and violence. Even when chained to his rock, he stands in defiance of might and violence, agents of Zeus. Prometheus is protesting undoubtedly against the tyranny, which, in the struggle of Athenians for a political order, so often runs counter both to traditional nomos and to men's conceptions of a diké beyond any given nomos.

(2) The dilemmas of choice which the tragic interpretation sees in collective life are well illustrated in Sophocles' play *Antigone*. Here the whole issue of nomos, physis, and diké is raised in the context of a conflict between obligation to the polis as over against loyalty to traditional convention. Like the later discussion of political obligation by Socrates in prison, the *Antigone* examination of the issue is extraordinarily pointed.

The story of *Antigone* is well known. Polynices and Eteocles, sons of King Oedipus, have fallen out. Eteocles supports the successor of Oedipus, Creon, as king of Thebes, while Polynices raises an army to attack the forces of Eteocles and Creon. Eventually Polynices is defeated before the walls of Thebes and his corpse lies unburied. The body of Eteocles, on the other hand, is given a traditional burial by King Creon. Creon not only refuses to bury Polynices but issues a proclamation saying that anyone who dares to bury him should suffer death. Antigone, sister of Polynices, defies this order and is eventually condemned to death by Creon. A son of Creon, Haemon, commits suicide rather than allow his fiancée, Antigone, to depart to the Shades without him.

The problem of obligation central throughout the drama is whether one should obey the commands of the political rulers when they run counter to the tradition of the pre-political society. Involved, too, is the perennial question of how one can discover "objective" standards for righteousness.

Very early in the play, the issue is joined on one level when Antigone asks her sister Ismene to help her defy the king by burying Polynices. Ismene turns down this request, saying in effect that *force majeure*, as reflected in the power of the king, must be triumphant despite one's objection.[9] It is interesting to note that Ismene does not allege that obedience to the king is right in this instance, but rather that she fears death if she doesn't obey. Also there is an undercurrent of the feminist issue

5. "Herodotus," in J. B. Bury, *Ancient Greek Historians*, New York: Macmillan, 1909, Dover Publications, 1958.
6. *Oresteia, Agamemnon, The Libation Bearers, The Eumenides*, Richmond Lattimore, trans., Chicago: University of Chicago Press, 1954, p. 58, lines 750 ff.
7. *Ibid.*, p. 48, lines 437 ff.
8. Aeschylus, "Prometheus Bound," David Grene, trans., in *The Suppliant Maidens, The Persians, Seven Against Thebes, Prometheus Bound*, Chicago: University of Chicago Press, 1956, p. 139, lines 1 ff.
9. "Antigone," in Sophocles, *The Theban Plays*, E. F. Watling, trans., New York: Penguin Books, 1951, p. 128.

which was beginning to appear in some Athenian literature—how can women stand up against men?

In reply, Antigone states her intentions:

Go your own way; I will bury my brother;
And if I die for it, what happiness . . .
Live, if you will;
Live, and defy the holiest laws of heaven.[10]

And Ismene reiterates:

I do not defy them; but I cannot act
Against the State [polis]. I am not strong enough.[11]

Throughout the play the Chorus, composed of the Elders of Thebes, feels that it must support the king in all his decisions. Like Ismene, it cannot see beyond the decrees of him who has command of the superior force.[12] The Chorus actually symbolizes the tendency for the mass of men to allow themselves to be directed by the wills of others—a point which Aristotle later developed in his theory of slavery.

Yet the king, in attempting to assess blame for the defiance of his order (Antigone has not yet been discovered), sees defiers on every hand. He is the archtype of the ruler troubled always by the problem of gaining obedience, always fearful of plots which might be directed against him.[13]

Antigone, once discovered, states her position strongly to the king:

I did not think your edicts strong enough
To overrule the unwritten unalterable laws
Of God and heaven, you being only a man.[14]

This is an extremely interesting passage, for it maintains that there are laws beyond the decrees of the king or even, apparently, beyond traditional nomos (although this is not clear). But Antigone does not profess to account for these unwritten laws: All she knows is that they exist and that somehow she has an insight into them.

But even the king, despite his apparent certitude, is not sure of his obligation, for he defends his action in terms of the rule of law. Once he has decided, he cannot change his will (which probably means that he has serious doubts about that will).[15]

Sophocles seems to conclude that there is very little an individual can do about the conflicts in loyalties posed by his drama. He thinks that the choices put before men in political life are not determined by themselves but rather by social forces working out a kind of destiny which at least appears to be chance. Thus the messenger toward the end of the drama meditates:

What is the life of man? A thing not fixed
For good or evil, fashioned for praise or blame.
Chance raises a man to the heights, chance casts him down,
And none can foretell what will be from what is.[16]

Sophocles, like the other tragedians, cannot see a certain way in which the life of the community, now pulling away from government by sheer custom and tradition, can be established on a basis in which diké, clearly comprehended, will emerge triumphant.

Thus the tragedians add yet another note to the widespread discussion of the ethical-political problem which characterizes fifth-century Athens. While the Pythagoreans saw the clue to a righteous political order in a square number and men like Herodotus wondered whether there is indeed anything universal beyond nomos, the tragic view seems to see men in community striving to comprehend a hidden universal justice but being entrapped in the meshes of their own necessarily limited decisions.

The Comedy and Politics: Aristophanes

Meanwhile, on quite a different level, the comic view of political life was arising. A younger contemporary of the tragedian Euripides, Aristophanes (448–380 B.C.), was affording the Greek mind yet another perspective.[17] On the whole, Aristophanes may be interpreted as a conservative in his political philosophy in that he saw the chaos of the period between 431 and his death as the result of departure from ancient nomos. But one should be wary of making Aristophanes perfectly consistent; for, although there is a serious undertone in his plays, he wrote his comedies not primarily as essays in political opinion but rather as efforts to provoke mirth at the expense of politicians and policies he happened to dislike.

There can be little doubt about the position of Aristophanes with respect to the practical politics of his time. He is (1) a bitter antagonist of the democracy and all that it was assumed to stand for, and (2) a vigorous opponent of the war with Sparta. Although the ultimate philosophical basis for his attitude to democracy and the war is not evident to us, and perhaps was not even clear to him, his

I intend that women shall belong to all men in common, and each shall beget children by any man that wishes to have her.[18]

In one sense it is curious that Aristophanes, in his own day and in ours, is classified as a defender of the old against existing and proposed innovations. True, he looks with suspicion on the democracy and ridicules proposals for community of goods. In taking these positions, however, he is defending the recent old as against what many innovators might have called the ancient old. There is little doubt, for example, that many of those who proposed community of goods thought that they might be restoring at least the spirit of the prepolitical Athenian institutions. Much of the appeal of the radical democrats was to the still-lingering tribal traditions which were suspicious of private property and particularly of sharp class distinctions. The radical democrats, in other words, appealed from both the Athens of democracy and the Athens of the pentacosiomedemni oligarchs to a half-mythical, half-historical tribal society in which property, trade, and class distinctions had been relatively unknown. Aristophanes, from their point of view, did not go back far enough for his model of what Athenian polis life should be.

Yet in one respect, at least, the political ideology of Aristophanes does seem to take its cue from the tribal model. He associates wars and imperialism with the Cleonic democracy and appeals to those forces in Attica which see in the whole conception of the Athenian Empire a degeneration from the days when Athens was self-sufficient and its wars presumably few. This may be said to be part, at least, of the meaning of the great drama *Lysistrata,* in which the reactionary Aristophanes attacks the Peloponnesian War and turns to radical solutions to end it. Aristophanes throughout seeks to connect the democracy with the very idea of war.

He imagines a situation in which the women of Athens, led by Lysistrata, and cooperating with the women of other cities (including Sparta), strive to put pressure on the ruling men to bring an end to the war. Their technique is essentially the withdrawal of sexual favors from all men who refuse to work for immediate peace. The activities of the women in effect constitute a strike against men and much of the play turns on the anguish of male warmakers when they discover that their women are serious. We cannot doubt that Aristophanes sympathizes with the objectives of the women in his play. In the end, their techniques win out, a peace is concluded, and great rejoicings—including the restoration of sexual favors—constitute the climax of the drama.

We are not told what the reaction to *Lysistrata* was, nor can we guess how it influenced Athenian thinking on war and peace. The war dragged on another seven years after its production and the attitude of the fourth-century democracy to war as an institution did not differ substantially from that of the Cleonic *demos.* But the brilliant attack of Aristophanes certainly pointed up dramatically the whole issue of the relationship between the form and spirit of the polis, on the one hand, and the existence of external disorder, on the other. For Aristophanes, there was nothing natural about war. That it destroyed so large a part of Athenian life was due to the fact that men had departed from the paths of justice, which had somehow been formerly enshrined in the traditional order. If only we could restore the old order, Aristophanes seemed to say, we would eliminate both the diseases of the polis internally and the disintegration caused by war in the external scene.

In taking this position, Aristophanes undoubtedly spoke for a substantial portion of Athenian and Greek opinion. Unsystematic and inconsistent though the position may have been, it was one which appealed to all those who felt alarmed by the tendencies of politics and who were yet unable or unwilling to seek for answers in a more radical and philosophically less naive analysis. Such an analysis was already being offered in the time of Aristophanes by the Sophists and by the enigmatic philosopher Socrates.

The Sophists and Ethical-Political Thinking

Just what the Sophists taught has been a matter of controversy for generations. Portrayed by some fourth-century thinkers almost as intellectual prostitutes, they have been praised by others—including modern critics like Popper and Winspear—as profound thinkers who established a firm basis for social change and democracy. Part of the difficulty in interpreting the Sophists lies in the fact that there were many of them and that their teaching was by no means uniform.

comments on the practical politics of the Athens of 431 to 380 add another dimension to our understanding of the political speculations of the fourth century.

His bitter opposition to the radical democracy which succeeded the moderate regime of Pericles is well known and is perhaps best illustrated as a whole in his play *The Knights*. Produced fairly early in the war, in 424, it ridicules the democracy without mercy. Aristophanes symbolizes the Athenian people in the character Demos, a weak-willed individual without principles and always seeking to gratify his own immediate desires. He has had several servants—political leaders—to do his bidding, the current one being Cleon, the tanner. Throughout the play, the comic poet castigates Demos for his lack of principles and character and equally criticizes Cleon as the demagogue who caters to the whims of his master. During the course of the action, Nicias and Demosthenes, admirals in the fleet, challenge a sausage-seller to depose Cleon; and much of the plot turns on the methods by which the sausage-seller is successful. Meanwhile, of course, the sausage-seller has been portrayed in colors as black as those of Cleon. Aristophanes concludes that Demos has simply exchanged one demagogue for another and implies that it must be ever thus so long as Demos is in control.

Long after the *Knights* was performed—in fact, after the 400 B.C. constitution had been firmly established—Aristophanes continued his attack on the democracy, levelling his shafts at its supposed tendencies to abolish private property and the institution of marriage. By this time, of course, proposals for a communistic way of life were undoubtedly well known. Hippodamus, the great city planner of the fifth century, had suggested the abolition of private property and Plato had already delivered his lectures on the *Republic* (although the book itself was not yet published). When, therefore, Aristophanes satirized communism of goods and women in the *Ecclesiazusae,* he must have had an appreciative audience.

He imagines a situation in which Athenian women, disguised as men, go early to the Ecclesia meetingplace. When the Ecclesia opens, they are able to command a majority of votes for their revolutionary proposals and thereafter the play concerns itself with problems and dilemmas arising out of community of goods and women. The exponents of communism, through Praxagora their clever feminine leader, allege that it will abolish poverty, eliminate the ubiquitous Athenian lawsuits, introduce genuine equality, and destroy crime. Praxagora explains all this to her irate husband Blepyrus whose cloak she has stolen to provide herself with a disguise for the Ecclesia session:

Praxagora: There will be no more thieves, nor envious people, no more rags nor misery, no more abuse and no more prosecutions and lawsuits.

Blepyrus: By Posidon! 'tis grand, if true.

. . . .

Praxagora: . . . I want all to have a share of everything and all property to be in common; there will no longer be either rich or poor; no longer shall we see one man harvesting vast tracts of land, while another has not ground enough to be buried in, nor one man surround himself with a whole army of slaves, while another has not a single attendant; I intend that there shall only be one and the same condition of life for all. . . . I shall begin by making land, money, everything that is private property, common to all. Then we shall live on this common wealth, which we shall take care to administer with wise thrift.

Blepyrus: And how about the man who has no land, but only gold and silver coins, that cannot be seen?

Praxagora: He must bring them to the common stock, and if he fails he will be a perjured man. . . .

The poor will no longer be obliged to work; each will have all that he needs, bread, salt, fish, cakes, tunics, wine, chaplets and chick-pease; of what advantage will it be to him not to contribute his share to the common wealth? . . .

Blepyrus: If someone saw a pretty wench and wished to satisfy his fancy for her, he would take some of his reserve store to make her a present and stay the night with her; this would not prevent him claiming his share of the common property.

Praxagora: But he can sleep with her for nothing;

10. *Ibid.*, p. 128.
11. *Ibid.*, p. 128.
12. *Ibid.*, p. 132.
13. *Ibid.*, p. 134.
14. *Ibid.*, p. 138.
15. *Ibid.*, p. 144.
16. *Ibid.*, p. 157.
17. See Maurice Croiset, *Aristophanes and the Political Parties at Athens*, London: Macmillan, 1909; and Leo Strauss, *Socrates and Aristophanes,* New York: Basic Books, 1966.

They began to appear on the Athenian scene during the Periclean age and were usually foreigners attracted to Athens by the brilliance of its culture and by the welcome it gave to discussion. Because they were foreigners, however, they often came under the suspicion of patriotic Athenians. If the United States in the twentieth century were to admit large numbers of Soviet Union or Chinese dialectical materialists who would teach on the street-corners in a provocative way, perhaps we might get some impression of the role which the Sophists played in fifth- and fourth-century Athens.

Through the eyes of Plato and of Plato's Socrates, the Sophists appear as teachers who charged for their services and were therefore suspected of making their teaching conform to the interests of their pupils. And many of the Sophists were, indeed, paid substantial fees by young Athenians seeking both practical and theoretical or scientific wisdom.

In terms of practical wisdom, the Sophists fulfilled an important role in democratic Athens because they helped train citizens in their functions as members of the Ecclesia and participants in the popular courts. In a very real sense then, the Sophists were political and legal men. They gave advice as to how one might more effectively appeal to one's fellow-members of the Ecclesia. They were keen students of political human nature and attempted to understand the manner in which one might persuade one's fellow citizen to pursue a given course of action.

Similarly, they became unofficial advisers to litigants appearing before the popular courts and counselors of the courts themselves. While there was no legal profession in the fifth and fourth centuries, the Sophists in effect performed some of the functions which later became associated with the bar.

It is not farfetched to suggest that the Sophists' economic interests became so entwined with those of democracy that it would have been unusual for many of them to have become antidemocrats. By and large, they may be thought of as the philosophical supporters of the democratic order as it developed during the latter half of the fifth century; and while some of them ran into conflict with defenders of the demos, most found that their chief opposition came from men who espoused an antidemocratic ideology.

Unfortunately, much of what we know about Sophistical teaching has come down to us through their opponents. It is therefore not easy to reconstruct a picture of what they actually believed. Although several of the dialogues of Plato, for example, are ostensibly devoted to them,[19] we cannot be at all sure that the Sophists appearing in them have any necessary relationship to the historical figures bearing their names.

Protagoras is often looked upon as the earliest of the Sophists. Born in 481 B.C. in Abdera, he apparently came from a family of little means. Very early he was attracted to the life of an itinerant teacher, later taking up his residence in Athens. He served by appointment of Pericles as commissioner to draw up laws for the colony of Thurii. When the Oligarchy came to temporary power in 411, he was accused of atheism and banished. He died shortly thereafter, probably in 410.

The teaching of Protagoras was apparently sharply opposed to that of such men as Pythagoras and, indeed, to all the devotees of the cult of Orpheus. Protagoras was a *materialist:* that is, he held that the explanation of all things lay in matter. Men perceive matter, however, in accordance with widely varying perspectives; their social position, birth, and training all contributing to widely diverse views of its nature. Thus, Protagoras is a relativist in the sense that he believes that our perceptions of the stuff of things are always relative to time and circumstance. It is, therefore, impossible to see phenomena as they really are. They are always strained through our widely differing perceptions. Hence man is "the measure of all things."

Beyond this general relativist proposition, however, the details of his teaching are not clear. He does hold, of course, that human institutions are relative to historical circumstance. They do not embody *physis* or nature, but are rather simply conventions which have grown up in particular historical circumstances. Presumably, according to Protagoras, man can never get at the basic matter but must always be conditioned by time, space, tradition, and culture. More clearly than Herodotus, Protagoras seems to hold that righteous-

18. Aristophanes, *The Eleven Comedies,* New York: Liveright, 1943, vol. 2, pp. 370–372.
19. The *Protagoras,* the *Gorgias,* and the *Hippias.*

ness or justice is simply what a given society says it is. And in this view, he was apparently joined by most of the later Sophists, although there were wide variations in the way the teaching was stated.

Because so many of the Sophists were skeptical about the possibility of knowing a diké beyond that defined by what we should today call the folkways and mores, they laid the groundwork for the moral and political philosophy of the fourth century. And the link between the theory of the Sophists and the systematic structures of the fourth century was the teaching of the still largely enigmatic Socrates.

The Politics of Socrates

Three significant versions of Socrates have come down to us. One is the burlesque offered by Aristophanes in his drama the *Clouds*, where the comic poet pokes fun at Socrates for his investigations into geology, geography, and other subjects; he obviously dislikes the perpetual questioning of conventional morality that he associates with Socrates. A second account of Socrates is given to us by Xenophon in the *Memorabilia*. Here the ancient historian seeks to make Socrates simply a purveyor of acceptable or conventional morality. Xenophon does this, apparently, in order to defend the memory of Socrates against the charge that he had corrupted the youth of Athens. Finally, we have the picture drawn for us by Plato in so many of his dialogues. This is the Socrates who is always asking questions but rarely giving definite answers; the man who asserts his own ignorance as well as the ignorance of every other man; the philosopher who, while he attacks the Sophists, also has in his own views an element of their skepticism.

Which of these versions of the historical Socrates shall we accept?

As A. E. Taylor points out in his study, the three versions are not necessarily contradictory.[20] Xenophon had little direct knowledge of this hero and his treatment of the subject is frankly apologetic. If we assume that Socrates was only the conventional figure given to us by Xenophon, it is difficult to account for the criticism levelled at Socrates historically. Perhaps Xenophon was reading into his subject his own rather conformist notions of morals and politics; he was interpreting the enigmatic Socrates through his own relatively narrow perspective.

On the other hand, Aristophanes cannot have been wholly unhistorical in his burlesque because the *Clouds* was presented to an audience which knew the central character. And the very nature of burlesque is that it takes certain central characteristics of its subject and exaggerates them. Although the picture of Socrates given in the *Clouds* is undoubtedly a caricature, it must have borne some resemblance to the historical character if it was to have any point at all.

As for the Platonic version, it was worked out by a man who actually knew Socrates intimately; one who, moreover, while he was not present at his death, had talked extensively with those who did witness the execution. The difficulty with the Platonic account, of course, is that we do not know exactly to what degree the figure presented is simply a peg on which to hang Plato's ideas and to what extent it is historical. Many nineteenth-century scholars tended to deny that we could rely on Plato for a picture of the historical Socrates. On the other hand, critical scholarship on Plato is now coming to an increasingly widespread acceptance of the notion that in the earlier Platonic dialogues at least—among them, the *Apology* and the *Phaedo*—we do have a fairly accurate picture of the historical Socrates.

We know relatively little of Socrates before the age of fifty-five, although in some of the Platonic dialogues there are autobiographical references to his earlier career.

Apparently he was born about 470 B.C. He came from a family of comfortable economic status and on the death of his father inherited a modest competence. This enabled him to qualify for service in the army as a *hoplite*—a heavily armed infantry soldier the equipment for whom had to be purchased by the soldier himself. We know that Socrates served in several campaigns, possibly in 432 to 431, and that he stood the rigors of campaigning extraordinarily well.

Meanwhile, he had already evidenced that keen interest in intellectual matters which was to characterize his later life. His early concerns lay in physical science and only in middle life did he turn increasingly to what we today call social and moral study. Plato portrays him as having conversed and argued with Protagoras and it would seem that this was undoubtedly an important episode in his life. Indeed, we may well imagine that it was the Sophists who gave him much of his stimulus.

Like Aristophanes, Socrates was not in sympathy with the Cleonic democracy, although he tells us that his "inner voice" forbade him to mix in politics lest his mission be imperiled.

This does not mean, however, that he refused to serve in offices to which he might be called by his fellow citizens. Hence he was chosen a member of the Council of Five Hundred toward the end of the Peloponnesian War. When his tribe held the Presidency of the Council (the *pyrtanes*) he of course took his part as a member of the presiding committee and one account says that he was actually chairman of the committee. It was when he was a member of the *pyrtanes*, in 406, that we first hear of him as a public man. That was the year in which the generals were haled before the Ecclesia for failing to rescue men cast adrift after the Athenian naval victory at Arginusae. We saw earlier that the Ecclesia condemned the generals, over the protest of many who believed that constitutional procedure had been violated. Apparently the protest was not against condemnation by the process known as *eisangelia*, a bill of attainder, which was recognized by the democratic constitution as legitimate. Rather the constitutional objection turned on the fact that the accusers demanded the condemnation of the eight generals en bloc. This was a violation of due procedure.

It was at this point that Socrates made his appearance. The *pyrtanes*, of which he was a member, refused to put the question of en bloc condemnation to a vote, thus defeating the efforts of the prosecutors. But the latter would not be frustrated and threatened to include the members of the *pyrtanes* among the accused. This led to the surrender of the *pyrtanes*, all of whom, with the exception of the lone figure of Socrates, now submitted the question of en bloc conviction to a vote. The result was that six of the generals were executed. Socrates remained adamant to the end, however, and the action of his fellow committee members strengthened his convictions that the Cleonic democracy could not be trusted.

A little later he again appeared as the champion of "due process," this time against the Thirty Tyrants, two of whose members were former students of his. As we have seen, some 1500 Athenians died as a result of the Tyrants' outrageous activities. During the course of the proscriptions, Socrates was asked to arrest Leon of Salamis. He absolutely refused to do so and was fully prepared to be executed by the wrathful Thirty. At this point, however—in 403—the Thirty were overthrown and the death of Socrates was postponed.

From the viewpoint of Socrates' politics, it is significant that in the case of the generals he was opposing an act of the democracy; while in his refusal to arrest Leon, he was challenging an order of the antidemocratic faction. In both instances, he appealed from the decisions of the governing powers to standards which he thought ought to limit democrats and antidemocrats alike. Politically, he came to be highly distrustful both of the democracy and of the political opponents of the demos.

After the democracy was restored, Socrates appeared to be a menace to many of the triumphant party. True, he had sought to protect the legal rights of one of their number (Leon), but he continued to ask embarrassing questions and, in the process, to attack pillars of the restored regime.

Meanwhile, however, the democratic leaders moved slowly. They were busy revising the laws and restoring Athens to some semblance of prosperity after the generation of warfare. It was not until 400 that proceedings against Socrates were instituted. Anytus, who began them, was a moderate democrat—perhaps we might say a democrat of the school of Pericles—and did not intend that Socrates should be killed. He apparently hoped that the philosopher, getting wind of the indictment, would flee Athens in the interests of his own safety.[21] Perhaps Anytus thought that a criminal indictment was the only sure way of preserving the life of Socrates while yet satisfying the demands of the more extreme members of the democratic faction.

Perhaps it was the very vagueness of the charges—of not worshipping the state gods and of corrupting the youth—which led so many of Socrates' judges to vote for acquittal. The vote for conviction was 280 to 220 against. After the Court rendered its verdict, Socrates had the right to suggest an alternative to the death penalty. He proposed that he pay a *mina* fine, although many thought—and some hoped—that he would suggest banish-

20. A. E. Taylor, *Socrates*, Garden City: Doubleday, Anchor Books, 1953.
21. *Ibid.*, p. 102.

ment. He did not offer the alternative of banishment for he believed that his mission to Athens had been such a benefit that the polis ought to have offered him a lifetime seat at the public tables (as it did eminent generals and Olympic victors). To have suggested a punishment, given these beliefs, would have meant that he was untrue to his convictions. But a fine, he thought, was no real evil and hence he offered to pay it.

Because he took this adamant position and refused to offer it the easy way out by proposing banishment, the Court seems to have stiffened its attitude. More members voted for the death penalty than had approved conviction. The ballot indicated that 360 thought Socrates should suffer death, while only 140 opposed it.

We may think of Socrates' teaching as consisting of a method or approach and certain doctrines about true rulership.

Broadly speaking, we may divide his general method and approach into three parts: (1) the doctrine of dialectic; (2) the teleological notion; (3) the theory of Forms.

(1) In Plato's dialogue the *Phaedo*, there is a famous autobiographical passage in which Socrates recounts his intellectual development. He says that when he was young he was deeply interested in the department of philosophy known as the "investigation of nature." He was concerned with such questions as the growth and decay of animals, the problem of the seat of thought, and the effect of heat and cold on phenomena. He asked himself, furthermore, what was the meaning of greater and less in the investigation of nature. He could not understand, moreover, how adding one to one gave two, while dividing one equally also gave two. The problem of number puzzled him, as it had Pythagoras.

Then he read Anaxagoras (d. 428 B.C.), he says, and thought that he had discovered the basic causes of phenomena. For Anaxagoras, instead of suggesting that air, or water, or fire, was the fundamental cause of all, proposed mind as the "disposer." From this, Socrates deduced that Anaxagoras must necessarily conclude that mind disposes all things for the best, and that the science of the good is the basic science. But he found Anaxagoras disappointing in his application of the principle of mind as cause. Instead of using the mind, Anaxagoras in fact had resorted to such eccentricities as ether and water to explain natural phenomena. His actual explanations departed from the principle he laid down.

Socrates thereupon began to search for a new method which would use mind as the basis of explanation. Instead of looking at things in themselves, he would try to get at reality by examining the statements or doctrines (*logoi*) we develop about things. Truth, he held, can be reached only as a result of debate, or conversation, or dialectic, and not by examining the things in themselves. The hypothesis is to be taken as the beginning of an argument; it will then be called in question, in which case it will have to be examined in the perspective of some broader hypothesis. Whether the hypothesis is true or not must be kept separated from the issue of what consequences follow if we accept it. Socrates thus states for the first time certain rules for the formulation of scientific theory. While he does not deal with the problem of verifying the theoretical consequences of an hypothesis in terms of observed fact, this aspect of the problem of scientific inquiry would be taken up by Plato in the Academy; and of course Aristotle would develop it still further.

(2) The teleological explanation of things is also characteristic of Socrates. One of his reasons for disappointment in the actual application of Anaxagoras' doctrine of mind was that Anaxagoras, after having suggested mind as the cause of all, did not proceed to show in detail how this worked out. Instead, he continued to explain things in terms of antecedent *conditions*. Socrates' own statement of his disappointment is a classic passage in the *Phaedo:*

> I might compare him to a person who began by maintaining generally that mind is the cause of the actions of Socrates, but who, when he endeavoured to explain the causes of my several actions in detail, went on to show that I sit here because my body is made up of bones and muscles; and the bones, as he would say, are hard and have joints which divide them, and the muscles are elastic, and they cover the bones, which have also a covering or environment of flesh and skin which contains them; and as the bones are lifted at their joints by the contraction or relaxation of the muscles, I am able to bend my limbs, and this is why I am sitting here in a curved posture—that is what he would say; and he would have a similar explanation of my talking to you, which he would attribute to sound, and air, and hearing, and he would assign ten thousand other causes of the same sort, forgetting to mention the true cause, which is, that the Athenians have thought fit to condemn me, and accordingly

I have thought it better and more right to remain here and undergo my sentence. . . .[22]

If mind is indeed the cause as Anaxagoras had contended, Socrates thinks that teleological explanations—which center on purpose or goal (*telos*)—are the only ones compatible with the Anaxagoran contention.

(3) Socrates' conviction—shared with the Pythagoreans and all those in the fifth century who had some absolutist viewpoint—that the universe is somehow ordered for the best could we but know it leads him to formulate in a sketchy and inadequate way the doctrine of Forms. Concerned as he always is to explain how qualities of things come and go, he suggests the notion that things participate in eternal Forms in varying degrees. The things themselves perish, but the Forms in which they participate endure. No representation of a triangle, for example, is a pure triangle, for the representation of lines requires thickness and breadth, whereas the Form of the triangle does not depend on its representation. Thus, too, a thing is beautiful because it participates in the Form of beauty. A polis is just to the degree that it participates in the Form of diké, which is eternal.

The objects which we seek to know in science, then, are the Forms; and sense experience in itself can give us only a distorted image of these Forms. Like Pythagoras, Socrates is fond of using geometry to illustrate his propositions. Just as there are Forms of the square and triangle and line imperfectly reflected in our sense representations, so also are there Forms of the polis, harmony, and diké imperfectly reflected in the political societies of history.

Socrates applies his doctrine of knowledge primarily to the area of human relations. Giving up his early primary interest in the physical sciences because of the pressing moral and political problems which he saw besetting the Athenian polis, he provides the foundations upon which the moral and political theory systematizers of the fourth century are to build. While denying that anyone, including himself, has any real knowledge of the Form of diké or righteousness, he sees promise of discovering more about it through the utilization of dialectic and the teleological approach. Sharing Protagoras' doubt about what he really knows, he still thinks it possible to know something about the eternal Forms which lie beyond the flux of political experience.

Socrates holds that "goodness" in the moral and political sense is knowledge, "evil" is essentially ignorance, and the ordering of a polis can come about only as a result of control by men of knowledge.

The view that moral goodness is knowledge is based on the assumption that all men are searching implicitly for the good, which, once they see it, they will embrace. Men cannot truly see the good and then do evil.

Contrariwise, failure to act righteously is due to ignorance of what is right.

How, then, is the good to be taught? Socrates here makes a distinction between the imparting of technical knowledge and the teaching of goodness. The former can be taught directly, for it is simply passing on skills—"how to do it" knowledge. The Sophists could teach how to win an argument in the Ecclesia, for example. But goodness can be taught only indirectly. The teacher must be able by questions to elicit a recollection of the Form of goodness in the pupil. Knowledge of right moral conduct, then, can come only as a result of the teacher stimulating the student to *remember* things which his soul has forgotten. This is obviously akin to some aspects of Orphism and Pythagoreanism, which held that the soul had forgotten its divine origin.

But learning in this indirect way involves the right use of dialectic in which a person must receive rigorous training. True ordering of the polis can arise only through those who know. The good of the polis, like the good of the soul, is a matter of understanding the conditions under which "righteousness" develops in society and above all a comprehension of the teleological *causes* of a right social order.

The application of these views can be illustrated by turning to Socrates' implicit criticisms of Cleonic democracy.

In Plato's dialogue the *Gorgias*, Socrates asks Callicles whether he (Socrates) should be the "physician" of the polis who strives to make the Athenians as good as possible or the "servant and flatterer" of the polis. Callicles replies that he ought to be the "servant," for if he is anything more he will run the risk of popular enmity. But this is no reason for denying one's

22. "Phaedo," in *Dialogues of Plato*, Benjamin Jowett, trans., Philadelphia: Random House, 1937, vol. 1, pp. 98–99.

mission, Socrates avers. He knows what the Athenians are capable of and how their leaders have flattered members of the Ecclesia in order to retain power. Those leaders are not, in fact, true politicians at all, for they are not searching primarily for the political good but rather for ways by which they can retain their ascendancy in the Ecclesia. And he concludes rather bitterly: "I think that I am the only or almost the only Athenian living who practises the true art of politics; I am the only politician of my time."[23]

Socrates even attacks such traditional political giants as Themistocles and Pericles. After maintaining that rhetoric is of two kinds—that which is "mere flattery and disgraceful declamation" and that which "strives to say what is best, whether welcome or unwelcome, to the audience"—he asks Callicles whether any contemporary orator uses rhetoric in its "best" sense. Callicles can think of none. Well, then, Socrates suggests, perhaps some Athenian of a former generation used rhetoric for "noble" ends. Callicles says that Themistocles, Cimon, Miltiades, and Pericles had such reputations and that Socrates himself had heard Pericles "who is just lately dead." But Socrates will not agree that even these heroes were good in the noble sense. "If . . . the satisfaction of some desires makes us better, and of others, worse, and we ought to gratify the one and not the other, and there is an art in distinguishing them,—can you tell me of any of these statesmen who did distinguish them?"[24]

At other points Socrates becomes more specific in his indictment of most past statesmen. Pericles corrupted the Athenians by giving them pay for public service and "encouraged them in the love of talk and of money"; all the older statesmen, while no doubt better than Socrates' contemporaries in terms of satisfying popular desires, were no better than they in relation to the end of righteousness. Pericles and Themistocles were clever "at providing ships and walls and docks, and all that," it is true,[25] but none of them had any notion of the good apart from what the populace thought to be the good.

While some scholars have wondered whether these harsh strictures on democracy were those of the historic Socrates or of the Platonic Socrates, authorities like A. E. Taylor argue that "the severity of these verdicts comes from Socrates rather than from Plato."[26] And there would seem to be evidence to support this view.

At the same time, we should remember that Socrates had no word of praise for any nondemocratic leader. Apparently no politician even approximated his standards of training in dialectic and ability to discern the Form of the political good.

We should be careful, in assessing Socrates' political attitude, not to ignore his important doctrine of political obligation, which is the first Greek philosophical treatment of the subject. While he could not accept the conception of a democratic polis, as that was interpreted in Athens, he did not believe that he was justified in evading the penalties of its laws, even though he were unjustly convicted. When it is proposed to him, in prison, that he escape (which was perfectly feasible), he refuses to do so. When he is told that public opinion would not condemn him for such an act, he replies that he does not take his notions of political obligation from public opinion but rather from his own understanding of the good. When it is pointed out that by allowing the polis to execute him he would be deserting his family and evading the responsibility for educating his children, he replies that his obligation not to evade the laws is greater than any obligations he might have to his family.

If a particular application of the law is unjust, he maintains, that does not absolve me of my obligation to respect the *principle* of law, for by continuing to live in the polis after I have attained my majority, I have implicitly accepted voluntarily the yoke of the laws. For me to evade them now would be to violate an "implied contract" promising obedience.[27]

Socrates seems to hold that escaping would be returning evil for evil and we are never justified in committing evil simply because evil is done to us. To use evil means is to tend to destroy that which is best in a man—to deny the Form of manhood. Even though the law, therefore, is administered by evil men and I suffer as a result, it is better to suffer evil than to commit it.

This theory is not without its difficulties, of course. Is Socrates, for example, contending that the system of laws was not responsible at all for the miscarriage of justice in his case? After all, it was the system which had established a defective procedure that contributed to the result. While one might accept the notion that it is never just to return evil for evil, Socrates hardly furnishes us with a clear standard for identifying evil. What is one to do, moreover, if and when the whole *system*—

as contrasted with a few laws or policies—becomes thoroughly corrupt and suffused with the spirit of lawlessness? Is one still obliged to accept its penalties for violating particular laws? Was it wrong for men to violate Nazi laws in secret, evading the punishment?

But unsatisfactory as Socrates' doctrine of obligation may be, it represented historically a clear victory for the political man as over against the man having primary attachments to tribe and family. In Sophocles' *Antigone,* for example, the claims of polis and family seemed to clash on about equal terms. But Socrates appears to give clear priority to the claims of the polis.

By the beginning of the fourth century, moral and political speculation had clearly become of central importance in the intellectual life of Greece. Most of the basic questions which Plato and Aristotle were to ask in the century had already been put in the fifth century, Socrates laying the foundations for a truly philosophical treatment of politics.

Plato and Aristotle will rephrase the basic questions, inquire more deeply into their meaning, and treat more systematically the possible answers. In doing this, they will draw heavily on the background of discussion built up between the time of Pythagoras and that of Socrates.

chapter 4

Plato and the Rational Polis

While Socrates laid the foundations for fourth-century theories of morals and politics, and the fifth-century historians, tragedians, Sophists, and comedians incidentally formulated many of the important questions, it was Plato who worked out the first of the great systems of political thought. He endeavored to establish a coherent metaphysical basis and to suggest several different levels of political analysis.

Plato's Political Biography

Modern critical study has not infrequently sought to find clues to the genesis of Plato's political thought in the circumstances which surrounded his childhood and youth. Thus his well-known dislike of the Athenian democracy has often been said to root in his upbringing by an antidemocratic family. But this thesis can hardly stand, for his family had associations with all political factions.

Born in May, 427 B.C., Aristocles (for Plato was his nickname) came into the Athenian world shortly after the beginning of the Peloponnesian War. Pericles had just died, and while the plague was still taking its toll, there was at this time a measure of optimism about the possibility of Athenian victory. Later legend had it that Plato was descended through his father from the ancient kings of Athens and through them from the god Poseidon. On his mother's side, one of his ancestors was Dropides, a close kinsman of Solon. Perictione, his mother, however, was a sister of

Chapter 3

23. "Gorgias," in *Dialogues of Plato,* vol. 1, p. 521.
24. *Ibid.,* p. 503.
25. *Ibid.,* p. 517.
26. A. E. Taylor, *op. cit.,* p. 150.
27. "Crito," in *Dialogues of Plato,* vol. 1. p. 51.

Charmides, who was to be one of the Thirty Tyrants.

When Plato was very young, his father, Ariston, died, and his mother later married Pyrilampes. It was in the home of his stepfather, then, that the future philosopher grew up, and while we know hardly anything about his childhood, he must from a very early age have listened to vigorous political discussion in the intimacy of his home. Pyrilampes had been a close personal friend of Pericles and continued to be a supporter of the Periclean faction after the death of the moderate democratic leader. No doubt Plato heard his stepfather propound arguments in support of the democratic viewpoint, while at the same time he must have become acquainted very early with Charmides and have had ample opportunity to reflect on firsthand statements in criticism of both Periclean and Cleonic democracy. This mixed political background of his family would appear to undermine the argument that he was propagandized from an early age exclusively in favor of eupatrid and oligarchical viewpoints.

Just when Plato first met Socrates we do not know but perhaps it was in beginning adolescence. This is the period when so many religious conversions occur and one's political consciousness is often first aroused. At any rate, Plato's higher education was certainly gained in conversations with Socrates, after a good formal schooling provided by his stepfather. Because of illness, he was not present at the final prison scene in which Socrates discussed so many important questions with his friends. After the execution, Plato withdrew to the city of Megara.

In 398, he began his first series of travels, visiting Cyrene, Italy, and perhaps Egypt. About 388, he was in Sicily where he had an opportunity to observe the tyranny of Dionysius I in Syracuse. He also met Dion, the brother-in-law of the tyrant, thus beginning a close association which was to persist until Dion's assassination in 353. Plato was repelled by the luxury of Sicily—a life, as he put it in his *Seventh Epistle*, "full of Italian and Sicilian dishes, with eating a big meal twice a day and never sleeping alone by night, and all the entertainments that go with this kind of life."[1] Already, apparently, there was an ascetic streak in his character.

When he spoke openly against the tyranny of Dionysius I, he was sold as a slave by that monarch. His friends ransomed him and he returned to Athens in 387. Shortly after this, he founded the Academy, the first great center of higher learning in the western world.

Originally, Plato had intended to pursue a career in politics but precisely at the time when he would normally have begun it, the Thirty Tyrants had come into power. Their actions had repelled him and he felt he could not honestly collaborate with them. He tells us that the Thirty had "made the previous regime [that of the radical democrats] appear like gold by comparison."[2] After the restoration of the democracy, he had once more contemplated entering the political arena; he remarks that initially "those who returned to the city conducted themselves with much decency."[3] But the execution of Socrates had again led him to withdraw from his projected lifework. Moreover, he had seen no opportunity to acquire reliable political associates for a reformation of the city. Hence he "finally had to realize that all the states of our time without exception are badly administered." He hoped that the discoveries of the Academy would provide the knowledge without which, he was convinced, no righteous state could be established.[4] This series of episodes appears to emphasize that he was as critical of nondemocratic polities as he was of the so-called democracies.

He continued, however, to be a keen observer and student of practical politics. Hence his interest in Syracusan politics never died and he made at least two trips to that city after the initial visit of 388 to 387. Thus, in 367, at the age of 60, he returned at the behest of Dion, who thought Plato might be of assistance in training Dionysius II. A few years later, in 361 or 360, he returned again, this time to prepare a provisional draft of a constitution for a proposed federation of Greek city-states in Sicily. But Dionysius, not unlike rulers in all ages, was suspicious of all academics and forced Plato to withdraw. Even after this last frustrating venture in practical politics, however, he maintained a strong interest in Sicilian affairs, particularly when Dion succeeded in expelling Dionysius II and himself assumed the rulership of Syracuse. In fact, Plato was far more directly involved in practical politics than Aristotle was to be, despite the latter's subsequent reputation as the more "practical" of the two.

Meanwhile, in the long years between 387 and his death in 347, his major attention was devoted to teaching and research. Like Socrates before him, his intellectual inquiries were stimulated by the moral or political questions put by ordinary men; and after Plato pursued these questions back to the ultimate problems of epistemology and metaphysics, he always returned to them. Moral and political issues remained central to him, all other branches of philosophy occupying an instrumental status.

Plato's last days were spent in the twilight of the Athenian polis. Within a decade after his death, the independence of Athens would be destroyed by the rising Macedonian power, and his last lectures in the Academy might well have been filled with references to current political events. Unfortunately, his lectures have not survived, although he himself thought that oral discourse was probably a more appropriate method of moral and political teaching than formal written dialogues or treatises. But the dialogues reflect at least some of his informal treatment, even though they probably cannot convey all of its spirit.

Plato's Politics: Perspective and Method

Modern scholars, in attempting to reconstruct the development of Plato's political thought, have often differed about the time of composition of the several dialogues.[5] Much work in the nineteenth and early twentieth centuries dealt with this problem. While differences still exist among the several interpreters, there seems to be fairly general agreement that the *Apology*, *Crito*, and *Phaedo*—which report the trial, prison scenes, and death of Socrates—are the products of Plato's late twenties or early thirties. It would also appear that these three dialogues come closest to reflecting the teaching of the historical Socrates and that when Plato introduces Socrates into the later dialogues he may be using the figure of his great teacher, in greater or lesser degree, as a mouthpiece for his own particular teaching.

The three greatest political dialogues represent quite different periods in Plato's life and thought. The *Republic*, for example, was probably finished about 386, just after the foundation of the Academy. Still later he wrote the *Politicus* or *Statesman*, probably when he was in his fifties or early sixties. Finally, the *Laws*, by far the longest of the dialogues, was completed in his late seventies and not published until after his death. While these are the dialogues of central interest to the student of the history of political thought, almost all of the others are also of considerable relevance—the *Gorgias*, for instance, the *Protagoras*, and the *Symposium*.

Now if Plato's political speculations developed over the long period between, say, 386 and about 348, it would be surprising if in some respects his position did not change. His particular emphases in his forties and fifties were often quite different from those in his sixties and seventies. His explanations of certain phenomena in the *Laws* sometimes differed from those in the *Republic*. In his last dialogue, too, he appeared to be much more interested than in earlier writings in historical questions. During the years between the *Republic* and the *Laws*, his students in the Academy were engaging in both empirical and nonempirical investigations and it would have been astonishing had their conclusions not affected the outlook of the man who was so open to new insights.

But while any treatment of Plato's political theory must clearly recognize development and change, it must also, on the basis of the evidence we have, be careful not to exaggerate them. It is doubtful, for example, whether there is a basic epistemological and methodological difference between the *Republic* and the *Laws*, however great Plato's change in political emphases. Actually, the chief distinction between the former and the latter is one of *level* of analysis: In the *Republic*, he seeks to suggest the outlines of an ideally righteous polity; in the *Laws*, he retains the essential features of the ideal typical picture but seeks to show the degree to which it might be implemented in light of the limitations and recalcitrancies of collective experience.

Let us explore this more fully. Plato sees any given historical polis as a mixture of psychological, social, physical, and ethical factors in which no *pure* democracy or *pure* tyranny or *pure* oligarchy has ever arisen or can ever

1. *Seventh Epistle*, 326c, in *The Collected Dialogues of Plato*, Edith Hamilton and Huntington Cairns, eds., New York: Pantheon Books, 1961.
2. *Ibid.*, p. 324d.
3. *Ibid.*
4. *Ibid.*
5. On the problem of chronology, see A. E. Taylor, *Plato: the Man and His Work*, Cleveland: World Publishing, 1966.

develop. In creating an ideal-type concept of a righteous or just polis, the philosopher or scientist will seek to understand through simplification. Thus he will ask himself "What is the logic and psychology of democracy when divorced from the nondemocratic elements with which it is mixed in any given historical polis?" Or, "What, if he ever existed, would a pure tyrant be—a tyrant unchecked by the nontyrannical elements present in any existential polis?" In the *Republic*, this ideal-type level of abstraction is very high. Plato does not pretend that he is dealing in the *Republic* primarily with *historical* cities. Rather does he find mirrored in historical cities in impure guise the *pure* aristocracy, let us say, embodied in the Form of aristocracy.

Now the doctrine of the Forms, as we have seen, was apparently formulated by Socrates. As developed by Plato, it may be said to suggest both a scientific method of studying complex and involved phenomena and a doctrine involving assertions about degrees of reality. In the former sense, the theory resembles the *ideal typology* of such modern social scientists as Max Weber, who seek to enlarge our understanding of historical and political reality by imagining institutions and situations relieved of their actual mixture with opposing or contrary tendencies. As a doctrine of reality, the theory of Forms has both metaphysical and ethical implications. It maintains that the Forms are permanent, objective *facts* and not merely convenient human constructs. In ethical terms, the Forms are the implicit goals of their imperfect historical representations and therefore establish a standard by which to judge the world of flux.

From the viewpoint of Plato's method, the *Republic* may be looked upon as an attempt to deal with ideal types or forms in a relatively pure state. In the *Laws*, however, Plato takes us down several notches in the scale both of abstraction and—according to his metaphysics—of reality. Most of the so-called differences between the *Republic* and the *Laws* do not, therefore, represent a fundamental change in Plato's account of politics, whether scientifically or normatively. The *Laws* simply look at the Forms in a somewhat less pure state—partway between the corrupt and recalcitrant historical polis, on the one hand, and the pure Forms of the *Republic*, on the other. Using the mathematical figures of which both the Pythagoreans and Plato were so fond, the *Republic* is analogous to a pure line or triangle, uncorrupted by breadth, thickness, or irregularity, while the *Laws* is like a line or triangle placed on the blackboard, with distortions of thickness and irregularity which representation makes inevitable. But the triangle of the *Laws* is still purer than the situation which men confront in historical politics, which by analogy is an imperfect triangle with bulges and with distorted squares and circles cutting across it.

In the *Timaeus*, Plato's great cosmological treatise, the philosopher imagines the gods seeking to impose the Forms on the unformed stuff—or matter—which needs shaping. But "matter" is always resisting. The legislator is like the gods—he must first discover the Forms (the *Republic*) and then seek a way to mold the rather conglomerate chaotic stuff of historical politics into at least a semi-formed or semi-righteous order (*Laws*) in face of the constant recalcitrance and resistance of the unformed or chaotic.

To change the figure, the modern physicist has never known a pure vacuum. Yet he imagines its existence, describes how bodies would act in it without air resistance (*Republic*), and then corrects his description for the impurity of air (*Laws*).

Here we first examine the Form of the polis and then turn to the way in which Plato seeks to correct it at a lower level of analysis.

Justice or Righteousness: The Problem

Earlier we showed how the problem of diké—righteousness or justice—had puzzled Athenian intellectuals of the fifth century and then suggested the several answers they had given in a rather uncertain way. In fact, the debate upon which Plato built was almost a commonplace in the life of his own day as well as of four or five generations preceding him.

In initiating his inquiry, a modern scholar has suggested,[6] Plato deliberately places the dialogue in the Piraeus, seaport of Athens, whither Socrates had gone to participate in the rites of the goddess Bendis. Both Bendis and the Piraeus symbolized the corruptions of Athenian life, the former because she was an imported divinity beloved of sailors and merchants, the latter because it lacked social and political integration except in terms of making money. Going "down" to the Piraeus, then, meant descending from the goals which true righteousness demanded; and the whole inquiry into righteousness was an endeavor to discover the steps up which Athens could ascend to the Form of Justice from which it (and all other cities) had been separated.

Plato uses a number of figures to symbolize several current conceptions of justice, all of which Socrates rejects. Thus the old rich man Cephalus represents the viewpoint of the Piraeus chamber of commerce: justice is simply speaking the truth and paying your debts,[7] which obviously begs the question as to the definition of truth and the ultimate meaning of a debt (aside from the issue of whether debts should always be repaid). Polemarchus argues that righteousness is doing good to one's friends and harm to enemies,[8] but Socrates maintains that doing harm to any human being causes him to deteriorate in his distinctively human trait—rationality—and that therefore injuring even one's enemies must be excluded, since righteousness must surely imply a characteristically human quality, which destruction of manhood can only undermine. In the figure and doctrine of Thrasymachus, Plato symbolizes all those in fourth-century Athens who, looking upon the political development of the previous century and a half, saw in it primarily the domination in succession of special-interest groups. Is it not reasonable, Thrasymachus asks, to think of righteousness as simply the interest of the stronger? How can one get beyond the notion that right is basically the possession of might? But Socrates points out that the stronger may easily err about where their "interests" actually lie and thus, in effect, be working *against* their interests. How can justice be both working for one's interests and using force against them?

Thrasymachus' is obviously a naïve force theory exhibited in every generation of political thought. Glaucon now takes over and attempts to make the Thrasymachean view more sophisticated by stating a position in which he does not necessarily believe: justice is a kind of compromise between the desire to be "unjust" and the fear of consequences to oneself if one is unjust.[9] If, asks Glaucon, each of us could make himself invisible as did Gyges in the legend, would any man hesitate to seize the prettiest women, steal, or murder for gain? We are restrained from doing these things only by the fear of being found out. Righteousness is simply a convention or contract representing those practices and customs which experience has told us enable each to maximize his own ego while avoiding death or embarrassment at the hands of others. There is thus nothing natural about righteousness: one cannot get beyond a given custom, and the custom itself is ultimately grounded on an uneasy balance between lust for pleasure and power and fear of the consequences if we push our desires too far.

It is not doing violence to the spirit of the Glauconian argument (a position also supported in the dialogue by Adeimantus) if we rephrase it in Freudian terminology.[10] We may say that each man wishes above all to express his *id* (desires, passions) and that the id is naturally limitless. However, each man's id must soon confront the fact of other ids having similar objectives and through the ego (or calculating reason), each sees that unless he restrains his id to some degree it is likely to be wiped out altogether. Out of this awareness there arise habits and patterns of conduct to which men give the name justice. They represent the super-ego. The habits, customs, and laws become so numerous and complex that their original reason for existence is often forgotten, but when we strip them away we see that they are simply efforts to keep open an opportunity for each man to get as much for himself as possible without running the very serious risk of annihilation. The fact that conventions differ so widely—as both Herodotus and Thucydides observed—indicates that there is no "justice" by "nature."

It is obvious that Plato is very much impressed by the Glauconian position. Putting it in the strongest way possible, he tends to identify it with the Sophists and, in considerable measure, with the exponents of Athenian democracy. His Socrates sees in it a good argument—so good, in fact, that he announces he can refute it only indirectly. He must, he says, examine the nature of the polis before he can return to the question of personal righ-

6. Eric Voegelin, *Order and History: Plato and Aristotle*, Baton Rouge: Louisiana State University Press, 1956.
7. *Republic*, in *The Dialogues of Plato*, Benjamin Jowett, trans., New York: Random House, 1937, vol. 1. Bk. I, 331.
8. *Ibid.*, I, 332.
9. *Ibid.*, II, 359.
10. Freud himself was steeped in the ancient classics and the affinities between his analysis and that of Plato are at certain points quite remarkable. The differences are obviously of equally great significance.

teousness. He must do this because justice in the individual—whatever it is—must be assumed to be the same as justice in the polis. With this proposition even his opponents agree, thus indicating the extent to which the Greek mind unites ethics with politics.[11]

Origin and Nature of the Polis

Yet the proposition that justice must be the same in individual and organized society is an astonishing one in light of the later history of political thought. Aristotle, of course, will continue to accept it without much question. But post-classical Greek thought will in some respects question it and Christianity will tend to create a tension between the individual and political society.

From the viewpoint of modern terminology, Plato begins his enquiry by asking an ethical question—what is justice or righteousness? But in attempting to discover an answer, he characteristically turns to politics, seeing in it the ethical dilemmas of the individual "writ large." To certain modern critics—for example, Warner Fite[12] and Karl Popper[13]—this has seemed to put Plato in the position of subordinating the good life of the individual to the political ends of the state. But this is to misconstrue both the purpose and method of Plato. He never loses sight of the original ethical question. *Both* polis and individual soul are subject to a common Form of righteousness; and the individual is no more subordinate to the polis than the polis is to the individual. To be sure, individual means rational person—one who is truly human—just as polis means the essence of political society, not its historical accidents.

In order to discover the essence of political society and, through it, justice writ large, Plato seeks to show how the polis arises psychologically and how teleologically it fits into the implicit ends of human nature. Again, some modern critics appear unjustifiably to have interpreted Plato as giving an historical account of the origin of the polis.[14] Hence they sometimes criticize his statement for historical inaccuracies. While Plato was not unacquainted with history—and in the *Laws* speculates on its major epochs—to interpret him in the *Republic* as being primarily interested in any literal history of political institutions is almost totally wrong. If we maintain that he is giving an historical account, for example, we must impute to him the view that men once lived isolated lives, that they were at one time nonsocial creatures. But this interpretation, in light of what we know of Plato's general theory of man,[15] cannot be sustained. Insofar as he thinks historically at all, there is no evidence that he ever believed in a presocial state. He *assumes*, when he talks of man, that we are always referring to "man-in-society."

This does not mean, of course, that there is not a wide latitude within which social relations can develop. Man's social nature can express itself, for example, in relatively simple social structures or in highly complex ones. His life may be one either of elementary or of advanced division of labor. The polis arises out of the wants of men, he points out. Some men specialize as farmers, others as builders and weavers. Manual laborers are also necessary. But human nature (both in terms of implicit origins and in those of implicit ends) is never satisfied with relatively simple division of labor. No sooner does it acquire the bare necessities than it seeks luxuries. We then get sofas, perfumes, gold, ivory, embroidery. Ironically, Plato observes—perhaps remembering his experiences in Sicily—the luxurious state will now call for the occupation of physician to cure the ills created by overeating, excessive drinking, and lack of exercise.

In the thrust to the luxurious state, Plato sees the psychological roots of war. The desire for gain and luxury will tend to lead man to seek additional territory. Hence he will seize a slice of his neighbor's land and physical conflict will result. The lust for unlimited accumulations of wealth tends to produce war and conflict of all kinds; and the same cause is at the root of almost all evils within the polis, whether those evils be public or private.[16]

Thus Plato sees in human nature, in one of its aspects, a tendency to insatiability of wants; and he emphasizes the large role which economic factors must play in any political society. He is saying, in effect, that if this were all there is to human nature, then we would be seeing only part of it. As it is, however, the very economic quest which is accompanied by division and conflict (competition for scarce goods) exists alongside man's social nature which is as basic as the economic. Man's telos includes the need for companionship of other men and women as well as the desire to acquire material goods. Both are aspects of distinctively human purposes and therefore both are equally natural. They coexist and the soul of man is often torn between them; for economic competition, in itself, tends to undermine the quest for fellowship and the latter makes us forget our need for scarce or economic goods.

But just as friendship and desire for economic gain are often at war with each other, so the quest for harmonization of the two is equally basic. Economic strife and the search for congenial companions do not give rise to a desire for a mere compromise; rather does the quest for harmony and justice suggest an ordering going beyond any simple balancing of interests. Justice or righteousness is that aspect of man's telos which, by relating friendship and the need for material goods to each other, seeks to subordinate both to the Form of the Good. Justice is an over-all quality whereby each person and group performs the task which each is best equipped by nature to carry out. Given justice in a polis, man's natural quest for friendship and sociality is no longer in conflict with his equally natural desire for material goods and the pleasures of sense. Knowing justice in all its ramifications, each man will find his own ostensibly warring elements at peace with one another and as a whole he will find himself in harmony with his fellows. Psychological peace is a function of communal peace and vice versa, and neither is possible without justice.

But the specific contents of justice can be discovered only by looking more exactly at the functions which the several kinds of souls in a polis naturally perform. In examining the types of souls and their diverse kinds of possible interrelationships we are also looking at alternative kinds of political relationships. For alternative polis types will mirror diverse kinds of souls, and the souls will tend to reflect particular polis types. In a special way of relating souls to one another we shall discover justice or righteousness.

Soul and Polis: Their Types and Relations

A. E. Taylor[17] has maintained that Socrates was the first to formulate the conception of the soul (psyche) that was to be so influential in the later development of thought. In Greek speculation before Socrates, the notion of the *psyche* had been identified with a diversity of views. Homer, for example, thought of it as a kind of wraith, the real person being the body; the psyche which departs from the body retained no consciousness but was rather a breath which man exhaled for the last time when he died. Some of the early Greek physicists thought of the psyche simply as divine air which had become individualized in a human being but which, when the being died, returned to be reabsorbed into the common stock of air.

By contrast, Orphism, as we have seen, thought of the psyche as the real man who has been condemned to life in a body but who by proper training can emancipate himself from the body. Both Orphics and Pythagoreans tended to conceive the psyche as unconnected with the ordinary thinking, acting self—rather was it that something which manifested itself in dreams and visions. Thus while it was real and permanently individual, as compared with the Homeric psyche, it still had but little to do with the active and contemplating everyday individual. Indeed, it was in considerable measure in conflict with that individual.

Now Socrates, by contrast with both Orphism-Pythagoreanism and the Homeric tradition, initiated the notion of the psyche as the residence of the whole character and intelligence of a man in all his emotional and thought life. He agreed with the Pythagoreans that the soul is individual and he further argued that it is immortal. But, as over against both Orphism and Pythagoreanism, the characteristic human task is not to purify the soul through various rituals and dietary restrictions (the Pythagoreans prescribed a vegetarian diet, for example) but rather to cultivate it through rationality. The central function of the psyche is to know and understand; and particularly to know and understand the distinction between good and evil and to direct

11. *Republic*, II, 369.
12. Warner Fite, *The Platonic Legend*, New York: Scribner's, 1934.
13. Karl Popper, *The Open Society and Its Enemies*, vol. 1: *The Spell of Plato*, New York: Harper & Row, 1963.
14. See Popper, *op. cit.*, and Alban D. Winspear, *The Genesis of Plato's Thought*, New York: Russell, 1956.
15. See John Wild, *Plato's Theory of Man*, Cambridge, Mass.: Harvard University Press, 1946.
16. *Republic*, II, 373.
17. *Socrates*, New York: Doubleday, Anchor, 1953, 133–140. See also Jane Harrison, *Themis, A Study of the Social Origins of Greek Religion*, Cleveland: World, 1962.

its actions in such a way that good is enhanced.

Plato, generally speaking, adopts the Socratic notion of the soul and conceives it to be his task to show its relation to the polis, while spelling out in greater detail how the principles of governance in the city are reflected also in the psyche.

He does this by asking himself what are the basic tasks which any polis must perform. Is it possible, in other words, to get beyond the wide variety of constitutions as Herodotus had observed them, and to discover underlying functions which make polis resemble polis and Greek political society resemble barbarian? He thought that one can indeed discern such common functions and ends.[18]

Every polis must have a material base, in the first place. Plato places great stress on the necessity for material goods and, indeed, as we have seen, sees the luxurious state taking shape as a result of men's demands for refinements in the economic realm. Yet implicit in the striving for material goods is an end beyond the economic—the goal or telos of knowledge. Economic goods, in other words, are not ends in themselves but means of sustaining life while man pursues the Form of the Good.

But secondly, every polis requires some type of protection and ordering. Economic activities in themselves are blind and tend to chaos and disruption of the social, as we have seen. Unchecked and uncontrolled by noneconomic principles and ends, in other words, the polis would soon disintegrate inwardly and be in perpetual war externally. It therefore needs guards who can look beyond the economic in order to save economic activities—however desirable in their proper place—from self-destruction. There must be a *will* for order and this will must be embodied in a group of functionaries. Plato calls them "soldiers" but it seems clear that he intends more by the term than the military as narrowly conceived: He also implies what we would call legislative leadership, the police, and, indeed, public administration in general.

Finally, every city needs *principles* of ordering. How are soldiers and administrators and technicians, for example, to discriminate between right and wrong, the prudent and the imprudent? What guides shall be provided for policy? How and by whom shall the system of training for future generations be established? These are questions which the *ruling* element in the polis must consider.

Now these three aspects of every polis Plato finds also present in the souls of men. Every soul has some tendency to desire material goods, to establish some kind of order and protection for its own life, and to search for a ruling principle or guide. To be sure, these tendencies are present in different proportions: for some, the quest for material goods and sense pleasure is central; for others, the search for honor, the exemplification of will, and the active life; for yet others, the telos of knowledge. But while appetitive men are characterized by acquisitive capacity, they also reflect some capacity for will and a certain level of knowledge; although spirited men exhibit will at the center of their being, they also have limited degrees of ability for knowledge and acquisition; and while noetic men show chiefly a passion for understanding the Forms, they are not without some potentiality for producing material goods and for willing the good.

Although Plato remains rather vague about precisely what occupations are natural to these three types of souls, it is doing no injustice to his view to suggest that appetitive men will be most in harmony with their true selves as farmers, merchants, mechanics, barbers, tanners, realtors, bankers, and seamen. Spirited men, if they find their natural places, will tend to become physicians, technicians, soldiers, administrators, policemen, teachers, and professional speech writers. Men of knowledge will not be at home except as scientists, philosophers, scholars, prophets, artists, and seers.

In relating basic functions of the polis to types of souls, it should always be remembered that Plato is speaking in terms of ideal typology as well as of the morally good. In the politics of existence, the relationships are always scrambled and confused, as Plato thought he saw particularly in Sicily and in Athenian constitutional history. Hence, when he deals with those relationships in essence (as contrasted with the impure existence), he is attempting to understand first, what the Form of the Good would require a pure polis to be; and, secondly, what varying types of nonpoleis —those which have fallen away from the good —would look like. In neither case is he talking of cities which have existed in history.

Thus when he speaks of the *idea* or *form* of the polis, he has in mind the interrelations between soul and soul and souls and community which are natural, in the sense that they conform to the Form of the Good which one can discover through reason, observation, and dialectic. All existing poleis are in varying degrees not poleis from the perspective of those who know the Form of the polis; for Athens and Sparta and Thebes are to the Form of the polis as pencilled representations of the triangle are to the Form of the triangle.

Similarly, when Plato examines the types of nonpoleis—those which depart completely from the natural polis—he also has in mind ideal types and not historic poleis; for the latter always have elements of the natural in them. Thus when he examines democracy and proceeds to criticize it from the perspective of the natural or true polis, he is not thinking of the so-called democracy of Athens. The democracy of Athens suggests to him, it is true, certain tendencies which, if separated from nondemocratic elements, would produce ideal type democracy. But the ideal type should not be equated with historic schemes designated by that name, for they are always admixtures of the Form of the Good and of patterns which have fallen away from the Good.

At this point a serious problem is created by Plato's analysis. Are the patterns which have been completely separated from the Form of the Good themselves a part of reality, or are they simply negative fallings-away from the good? Impliedly, this raises the ancient question of evil. If Plato says that the nonforms exist independently of the Forms, then he has destroyed the notion of a universe and created a duoverse, or, in theological terms, he has embraced a type of Zoroastrianism, which saw the world as divided between an uncreated good and an uncreated evil. If, on the other hand, Plato says that the negative patterns are simply a negative departure from good, he must seemingly account for the fallings away. Why could evil exist in a universe ruled by good? On the whole, Plato does not answer this question with any clarity, either in his political dialogues or in such treatises as the *Timaeus*.[19]

At one point he notes that the Form of the State or polis is "laid up in heaven."[20] By this he meant that in existential reality as contrasted with essential reality (the world of the Forms), the Form of Justice is always impressed upon the stuff of flux or matter in only a distorted way. But it is equally true that ideal-type nonpoleis are not reflected perfectly in existential reality. Thus neither Athens nor Sparta has ever been a polis, but by the same token neither has been wholly a nonpolis. Whatever their actual political structures and tendencies—whether under Pericles or the Thirty, under Lycurgus or Lysander—they have never been just. It is equally true to say that they have always embodied justice in some degree.

It is important to stress this aspect of Plato's political thought because certain modern critics (notably Karl Popper) seem to think that he was eager to restore some order which had hypothetically existed historically.[21] But this is to misread Plato's doctrine. True, he held that existing orders were degenerate, but only because they all fell short of the Form of Justice and not because some historical order embodied that Form in any pure sense. Plato is not "idealizing" the past—as did Aristophanes, for example—but rather is seeking to discern some immutable principles by which all historic orders can be judged. He is thus doing in the moral and political realm what Greek physicists attempted to do in the physical world—to grasp something of the allegedly permanent behind the change observed in the universe. The Form of the Good in the moral-political universe is both a norm and what we might call a statement of fact—a metaphysically real fact which lies behind the immediate experience of moral and political life.

The Form of the Polis

The Form of Justice, which the existential polis is seeking to embody, is, according to Plato, a coordinating one. When it is present, noetic men concentrate on the predominant

18. In this objective, Plato is engaging in a task somewhat like that which modern economists like Frank Knight essay for the economy. Thus Knight in *The Economic Organization*, Chicago: Augustus M. Kelley, 1951, identifies five functions which *any* economic system must perform—fixing standards; organizing production; distribution; maintenance and economic progress; and adjustment of consumption to production within very short periods. These five functions must be performed in some way, whether the economy is primitive or highly developed.
19. In the *Timaeus*, he seems to suggest the eternal nature of the "formless" or "matter." The gods try to impress the forms on this matter.
20. *Republic*, IX, 592.
21. See Popper, *op. cit.*, and Winspear, *op. cit.*

tendency of their souls, that of knowledge or wisdom; spirited men center their primary activities on doing, acting, and ordering; appetitive men devote their main energies to getting and spending and sensual enjoyment. For noetic men to devote their primary energies to getting and spending and sensual enjoyment would not only make them unhappy (for they would be frustrated in their true vocation), but would also clearly mark them as unrighteous; they would not be doing what nature best equipped them to do. Similarly, if appetitive and spirited men should endeavor to understand the Forms, they would not only find that they "messed things up" but that they were frustrated and unhappy, for their satisfaction and achievement of true selfhood lie in getting and guarding, respectively.

When each type of soul is carrying on the activity for which it is best fitted, then, justice pervades the polis and righteousness and happiness the individual soul. Justice in relation to the polis and soul is like health to the physical body: When achieved, it is recognized as that for which men have been implicitly striving. The uneasiness and perturbations of historical so-called poleis as well as the frustrations and unhappiness of souls are simply indications that justice has not been achieved. Hence justice is not primarily instrumental. Rather it is an ultimate, metaphysically real goal (a Form) working within every person and every polis and seeking to impress itself more clearly on them.

Although some modern commentators have asserted the contrary, it would appear that Plato does not think of appetitive men as "inferior" in all respects to spirited and noetic souls; nor does he conceive the latter to be superior in every way. Throughout he is concerned to point out the organic interdependence of the three kinds of souls.[22] Thus, the noetic in a just society are completely dependent on the appetitive for their scant material goods, while appetitive men rely on the noetic for principles of coordination and of morals.

Keenly aware as he is of the economic problem, Plato gives considerable attention to the issue of wealth and poverty. The righteous polis, he holds, will be neither poor nor rich because just as poverty tends to produce viciousness and meanness, so excessive wealth breeds luxury and indolence. This is, of course, a restatement of the Delphic oracle's "nothing in excess." Harmony and justice are impossible if a polis is really two cities, one of the rich and the other of the poor, for then the interests of citizens become diverse and the common or civic consciousness declines. Again and again the Platonic writings emphasize this theme.

Economic or appetitive men, one gathers, would constitute by far the most numerous group of Plato's three categories. While he does not say so explicitly, it seems reasonable to assume (despite the argument of modern writers like Max Beer to the contrary[23]) that Plato would preserve the institutions of private property, contract, marriage and the family for those fulfilling the economic function. By definition, the appetitive is predominant in their souls; and since the desire for gain is, within limits, indispensable for society, Plato combines the psychic desire for material goods with the social need for material subsistence. Without private property and families it is difficult to see how appetitive men could achieve their central telos. But they will be limited by two factors. First, the whole spirit of righteousness, applied by the rulers, will circumscribe the extent of gain for any given person as well as for appetitive men as a group, lest the city once more be divided into the rich and the poor. Secondly, since the appetitive will have no share in ruling but instead will be the ruled, their activities will be limited by principles which they themselves do not formulate. But presumably the limitations, being based on an understanding of the Form of the Good, will take into account the necessity for a considerable measure of freedom to attain the appetitive telos.

While economic men can get and spend but have no share in governance, spirited and noetic souls share in governance but do not get and spend. The price appetitive man pays for freedom to buy, sell, and accumulate is surrender of any share in governance. The price nonappetitive man pays for a share in government is deprivation of any freedom to buy, sell, and accumulate. Governing men, moreover, must live, in terms of material goods, on what is virtually an ascetic level. In no sense can they risk the possibility that private economic interest may interfere with public duty; their asceticism will preserve them against sloth, love of ease, and any tendency to make food and drink other than unfortunate instrumental necessities. They are utterly dependent on appetitive men for what they eat, drink, and wear, and the material goods they do possess are held in common and distributed in accordance with individual need. Plato's economic communism, however, is not a communism of abundance, such as is advanced by modern communists and socialists, but rather a communism of common poverty designed to encourage a group of disciplined, dedicated, and selfless men.

Just as they must renounce wealth and private property, so much spirited and noetic men spurn family life and monogamous marriage. Here the purpose is not to liberate them for "free love" but rather to eliminate the burdens of private obligations. How can a man (or woman) devote full time to the public interest, asks Plato, when he is constantly distracted by children's illnesses, debts, or family conflicts? Women must be regarded as the equals of men and must share in the obligations of rulership. Sex relations for purposes of procreation will be arranged by a Planning Committee which will seek the best combinations; and all those conceived at a given public hymeneal rite will be regarded as the children of the adults participating in the rite.

It will be noted immediately how radically the life of Plato's guardians differs from that of the rulers of his day. The former are ascetics; the latter in considerable measure are acquisitive. The former include women as equals; the latter exclude the feminine sex (in Athens) altogether. The former have no private property; the latter are deeply involved in the property system. The former must renounce ease and comfort in order to rule; the latter often use office to enhance their ease and comfort. And these observations apply to the Athenian *demos* as well as to the *aristoi*.

It will be obvious, too, how little Plato's communism resembles the communism so ridiculed by Aristophanes.[24] The great dramatist painted a communism designed primarily to "share the wealth and share the women." To the degree that Aristophanes' communism reflects accurately the proposals of radical social reformers in his day, it points up the vast gulf between Plato's system and those of Athenian democratic radicals.

What are the specific tasks of noetic and spirited men?

The former are by nature and training equipped to (1) contemplate the Forms and (2) apply their knowledge of the Forms to the function of coordination and governance.

Contemplation of the Forms is, of course, "beyond politics." It is the pursuit of the permanent ideas which are the reality of the physical and moral universe.[25] Yet the conditions for contemplation of the Forms are political in that without ordering, organization, and education, those trained to contemplate could never do so.

The very fact that their ability to contemplate depends so largely on the organization of the polis creates an obligation in noetic men to guide the polis in accordance with their understanding of the Form of the Good. While they may not like this task—indeed, the more they contemplate the more they would like to flee from it—justice clearly requires that they perform it.

In his conception of this political task, Plato suggests that the Form of the State is that of a wisdom-polis rather than a law-polis. The noetic, in other words, do not govern through what Plato regards as the clumsy devices of positive law, but rather have the insight and knowledge to treat every instance as a matter of what we would call equity. Rigid rules always violate justice by compelling the ruler to assimilate unique individuals and unique cases to a pattern which in pure justice does not fit them at all.

This makes the noetic political task an enormously difficult and delicate one. There is no refuge in such formulae as "the law says" or "it has been ruled in the past." Instead, the ruler has no precedent to guide him but must act in accordance with the wisdom applicable to each situation.

While noetic men contemplate and guide, the spirited execute. Their souls are such that they can understand the relevance of the decisions of the noetic even though they do not have the capacity to contemplate the Forms in themselves. Moreover, their potentiality for "righ-

22. *Republic*, IV., 442–443. See also, Wincenty Lutoslawski, *The World of Souls*, London: Allyn and Unwin, 1924.
23. See *General History of Socialism and Social Struggles*, vol. 1: *Social Struggles in Antiquity*, New York: Russell and Russell, 1957.
24. See Aristophanes, *The Ecclesiazusae*.
25. See particularly the *Timaeus* (Jowett trans.), 28–31.

teous indignation" and action is developed to a high degree. The noetic understand what to do and thus specialize in decision-making rather than action; the spirited act but must depend on the noetic for standards of action.

But how are these extraordinary noetic and spirited souls discovered and educated?

Educating the Political Man

It is clear that Plato's discussion of education applies primarily to noetic and spirited souls and not to economic man. But does this mean that those who produce the material goods are to remain uneducated? The answer is unclear, but it would seem from the context that appetitive men, too, would be educated up to their capacities.[26] At least some testing machinery appears to be implied; Plato suggests that children of the appetitive might be expected on occasion to qualify for the guardian category, while the souls of some guardians' children might be found to fit them best for primarily economic tasks. In essence, the scheme is a public one—itself a revolutionary proposal for the Athens of the time, which knew only privately financed education—in which every child is carefully nurtured to the extent of his capacity, dropping out only when his proper level has been attained.

But right education for either economic or political man cannot be understood without taking into account the nature of the soul with which the educator must deal. Already we have taken note of Plato's doctrine of the soul, which he developed on foundations laid by Socrates. Here let us point out how education is dependent on our judgment of the soul.

The soul, as we have already seen, is a living entity constantly striving for the good (no soul voluntarily does evil) but tending often to be frustrated in its quest. It is a dynamic spiritual organism, an immortal one, which, while it cannot be killed, can be distorted, warped, and poorly nourished. It is shaped in considerable degree by its environment and particularly, in the absence of a public education system, by a fickle public opinion. While the "eye of the soul" is always looking for the Form, there is an overwhelming probability that it will not attain its goal in any society whose cultural emphasis is primarily on sense experience rather than on the Forms which lie beyond sense. Only a powerful and well supported educational scheme which looks beyond immediate sensual satisfaction can be expected to counteract those tendencies which keep the soul away from the good. The soul, Plato suggests, is like a stringed instrument which a right education will tune correctly. But an untuned instrument, however sound by nature, cannot be expected to produce harmony in either soul or polis.

Broadly speaking, the task of education for the political man is to liberate him from subservience to the "shadows" of mere appearance and sense. In the famous Parable of the Cave in Book VII of the *Republic*, Plato compares our usual understanding of the world about us to that of prisoners chained for life in a "den." Their necks are so tied that they cannot turn around. Behind them is a bright fire and between them and the fire a stage and puppet screen before which objects are dangled. The prisoners view the images of the objects on the wall of the cave but cannot see the objects themselves. Moreover, they cannot discern the central fire. They take the shadows for the substance of things. They must be released by education to see the things in themselves.

There are several stages in the soul's development. It proceeds from "perception of images" to "belief" or "conviction" to "knowledge" and "understanding." Each stage represents a different level of apprehension, the final being sight of the Form of the Good (the *Agathon*). This highest level can be attained only by a few and after long years of toil, study, and experience.

Given this general conception of educational development, Plato proceeds to suggest the kinds of discipline it entails. Here he is undoubtedly influenced in some measure by the example of Spartan institutions, although the differences between his proposals and the practices of Sparta are also important. While Spartan education hoped to produce disciplined warriors, Platonic has as its goal the development of contemplator-rulers who will have been cultivated in the arts and sciences as well as in the "master science" of "dialectic." Plato looks with horror on the Spartan objective, much as he admires many aspects of Sparta's educational system.[27]

Down to the age of twenty, the young citizen is to be educated primarily in what Plato calls *mousikê* and gymnastic. The former, which includes both music proper and literature, will be taught not only to acquaint the child with his cultural heritage but also to discipline his emotions. Only that literature which both disciplines and stimulates is to be emphasized. Plays which simply titillate the emotions, which lead men to laugh or cry at random and without relation to a central noble theme, are to be suspect; and poets who stress the alleged horrors" of the afterlife are to be "expelled" from the classroom. It is precisely because the passions are so vital in human life that they need regulation from an early age.[28]

Gymnastic, likewise, has several roles to play. It includes not only systematic physical exercise but also the development of proper habits of diet. Although it is, of course, designed to strengthen the muscles, it will also, if successful, help to discipline the spirit. Together with music and literature, it will make the body a pliable instrument of the soul for good ends.[29]

One infers—although unfortunately Plato is not clear—that appetitive souls leave the formal educational process at the age of twenty and take their places in economic society. Their souls are attuned to it and their education has prepared them to accept their particular stations in life.

Those who remain students will from twenty to thirty have their souls nourished on the sciences, mainly arithmetic, geometry, astronomy, and harmonics. The first period, to the age of twenty, has taken the child and youth beyond the world of mere shadows or images to certain convictions or beliefs which he has developed through literature and the contemplation of heroes on whom he has modeled himself. The purpose of education in the sciences is to show him that, while beliefs and convictions about the existence of things beyond shadows are important, true understanding is still more significant.[30]

The sciences take one from descriptive sense perception to the *relations* which underly things. The youth begins to see that behind the particular triangles with which he deals, there is a *form* of the triangle; that beyond the wide variety of sounds in music proper there is a *form* or essence of harmony to be discovered. Given his metaphysical views, so much like those of the Pythagoreans, Plato would understand the real factors of the universe as ideas or forms behind the appearances. He sees the "whole phenomenal world," in the words of Nettleship, "as the symbol of an intelligible order."[31]

By the age of thirty, the auxiliaries, or men of spirit, will presumably drop out of the educational system. They have now had the rigorous training of the body which equips them for the life of action and the discipline of soul through the separate sciences which provides them with "understanding." But they do not have the capacity to move from understanding to ultimate knowledge.

This last stage is reserved for the very few. From thirty to thirty-five, they are put through a rigorous course of dialectic, the basic notion of which we have seen Socrates suggesting. Plato, carrying on the Socratic tradition, believes that by a concentrated effort and searching questions noetic man can get at the "inter-connectedness" of the Forms studied during his scientific education. He can move, in other words, from "conditioned" to "unconditioned" hypotheses; from if-then statements, as we would say today, to propositions in which the "if" has been eliminated through a final act of intuitive—some would say mystic—knowledge. On the way toward a grasping of the Form of the Good which underlies all other Forms, the student would, of course, imbibe deeply of logic, metaphysics, and reli-

26. It is more plausible to assume this than the reverse. While appetitive men do not govern, they obviously constitute most of the governed; and throughout his political works Plato makes formal education and training the central factors in rule. Education of the body and emotions, the first rung of the *Republic's* educational ladder, would clearly appear to be particularly appropriate and necessary for appetitive men.
27. This is true both in the *Republic* and in the *Laws*. Note the following passage in the *Laws* (*Dialogues of Plato*, Jowett trans.), I, 644: "For we are not speaking of education in this narrower sense, but of that other education in virtue from youth upwards, which makes a man eagerly pursue the ideal perfection of citizenship, and teaches him how rightly to rule and how to obey. This is the only education which, upon our view, deserves the name; that other sort of training, which aims at the acquisition of wealth or bodily strength, or mere cleverness apart from intelligence and justice, is mean and illiberal, and is not worthy to be called education at all."
28. *Republic*, VIII, 559.
29. *Ibid.*, III, 403-404, 410.
30. *Ibid.*, VII, 525-532, 537.
31. R. L. Nettleship, *The Theory of Education in Plato's Republic*, London: Oxford, 1951, p. 129.

gion. The ultimate grasping of the Agathon, however, is more than all these and more than all the individual sciences—it is like the recognition of a long-lost friend; we remember a previous experience of the ultimate basis for knowledge. Knowledge of any of the Forms, as a matter of fact, is an act of recalling what we once knew (perhaps in a previous incarnation), and a grasping of the Agathon is simply a supreme example of this.

Having successfully mastered the dialectic, the guardian at the age of thirty-five is prepared for a period of public service. From thirty-five to fifty he devotes most of his time to ruling, although he occasionally retreats to his academy. His very reluctance to rule—for by now he is so enamored of the Forms that other tasks seem humdrum by comparison—is a high qualification for ruling: It means that he is immune to the temptations of demagoguery, special pleading, and making political power an end rather than a means, which have corrupted rulers historically.

His final stage of life begins at fifty, when contemplation becomes central and he is summoned back to the polis only occasionally for purposes of consultation. His character is formed, he has tested his intellectual capacities under rigorous conditions, and his reluctant immersion in politics has dramatized for him the difficulties of applying the Forms to human affairs. He has earned not rest, but rather the opportunity to concentrate on contemplation.

Thus the educational system serves both to undergird and sustain the idea of political order and to provide a ladder, so to speak, up which those who have the capacity can climb to escape the contingencies and limitations of political life. These two purposes, according to Plato, are not contradictory. Rather do they support and sustain each other. Without political order, the life of contemplation would be impossible, for conflicts and near chaos would be forever interfering with the calm required for study and mystic experience. Without study and mystic experience, the wisdom necessary to sustain the political order would be lacking.

But the ideal-type polis and soul are no sooner imagined than we begin to comprehend what their degenerate expressions can be. Understanding the political expression of the good immediately suggests what ideal-type falling away from the Good would imply. Indeed, the nature of the political good itself cannot be fully comprehended, Plato avers, unless we picture graphically what the non-good, or evil, would be.

Degenerate Soul and Polis

For centuries many students of Plato's political theory seem to have misinterpreted his discussion of degenerate souls and states. They have assumed, in some instances, that he is interested in historical rather than in psychological and logical descriptions. Hence they have sought to identify his degenerate societies with particular Greek political forms. They have seen *timocratic* man as Spartan and democratic man as Athenian. But this interpretation is as erroneous as to identify his idea or Form of the polis with an actual historical order that has vanished. In treating degenerate states, as we have seen, Plato is dealing in ideal types, without implying that those types are metaphysically real.

At the very outset of his discussion of degenerate societies, he is puzzled as to the way in which the Form of the polis may be held to be challenged by degeneracy. If it is pure and eternal, what is the source of the types which fall away from the Form of the Good? Already we have touched on this issue and have suggested that Plato's answer is not clear. Mistakes are somehow made, he hints rather lamely, in the planned mating of men and women; why and how the errors arise in a pure polis he does not say. Once they occur, however, the ruling class is split and groups other than noetic men take control. This is somewhat analogous, of course, to the "war in heaven" of Hebrew thought.

The first stage in degeneracy is represented by a conflict within the souls of the noetic which is mirrored in a political fission. Their grasp on the world of Forms is lost and spirited men step into the breach, claiming rulership from the noetic. Since the hallmark of the spirited is honor and reliance on might, these goals are now the telos of the semipolis. Reason becomes instrumental for the achievement not of the Form of the Good, but rather of status. Organization and maintenance of discipline become ends in themselves to which reason (now denuded of dialectic and mystical experience) becomes prostituted. And thus we have a timocracy which permeates both polis and soul.[32] In an ideal-type timocracy no offices would be filled by lot. Technique would be exalted at the expense of science and military service would be regarded as the noblest calling. The timocratic soul would find its incentives in ribbons and medals and other awards.

But since timocratic men's wills are no longer governed by the natural ruling principle, they will find it progressively more difficult to subordinate the lust for sensual pleasure and material gain. Even "honor" will decline as the integrating factor, in the degree that men more and more think of accumulation as the end of life. When this spirit becomes predominant, an oligarchy arises, where size of fortune and income becomes the standard for emulation and the basis for rule. Both will and reason then serve the needs of acquisition.[33]

But just as the seeds of destruction were planted in a timocracy, so similar bases for fission are implicit in an oligarchy. Wealth is even less than honor an adequate basis for integration or wholeness in soul and polis. An oligarchy, in denigrating reason and will, weakens its own ability to pursue even its own goal. Eventually a democracy takes its place—an order in which the appetites become "free and equal," so to speak. In an oligarchy, the ruling appetite is material gain and other passions are subordinate to it. But as the oligarchy deteriorates, the governing passion itself is overthrown and the democratic principle of no order—absolute equality of men and equality of passions within men—takes its place. The goal of integration is itself overthrown, polis and soul swaying and changing with shifts in the several passions. Quantity rather than quality tends to be the keynote of the society, with pleasures measured in such terms as intensity and duration rather than intrinsic and differentiated merit.[34]

Within a democratical disorder, however, the basis for a new kind of ordering is inevitably bred. The very absence of hierarchy and order tends to make men subject to those souls who can satisfy their momentary passions and desires, but they pay a terrible price for this satisfaction because in effect they become tools for the satisfaction of their overlords' erratic passions. Thus a tyranny arises. The tyrant is a dominating soul exploiting the needs of others for his inconstant and increasingly demanding desires. For him to flourish, of course, the bulk of the population must be willing to make themselves virtual slaves, in return for the tyrant's provision of a specious security.

In all the pages of political and psychological literature, it is difficult to think of a more graphic portrayal of tyranny than that presented by Plato in Book IX of the *Republic*. As in all of his picturizations of ideal types, it shows both the factors at work in the soul of the tyrant and those which operate in the structure of society. Everyone is possessed of "certain unnecessary pleasures and appetites" which are "unlawful." In a soul where reason is in command, these desires are controlled in the interests of the whole or even banished entirely. All men have them, however, and they emerge to the surface from time to time to plague the natural ordering of the soul. When reason is weakened, they become graphically evident, particularly in sleep:

> Then the wild beast within us, gorged with meat and drink, starts up and having shaken off sleep, goes forth to satisfy his desires; and there is no conceivable folly or crime . . . which at such a time, when he has parted company with all shame and sense, a man may not be ready to commit.[35]

But when the beast emerges, the tyrant appears; and with the tyrant, the tyrannical polis. Beginning by enslaving himself to lust, drink, or acquisition, the tyrant ends by becoming a far greater danger to the body politic than ordinary thieves and murderers. As he gains followers and political power, he becomes more and more enamored of his desires. As his power grows, his fears also multiply; for he is ever disturbed by the possibility that he may be overthrown. But fear and suspicion produce isolation, isolation leads to separation from reality, and mounting ignorance of the world makes the tyrant stupid, even in terms of his own interests. Meanwhile his own fear of conspiracy and his growing irrationality have stimulated the conspiracy which will lead to his overthrow.

And so ideal-type constitutions and souls have completed the circle. Between the just and the tyrannical polis and soul there is an enormous gulf. It is a distance, Plato maintains, which has never been traversed by any earthly polis, although we may catch glimpses of each type in the always mixed political-ethical contexts of history.

32. *Republic*, VII, 548–550.
33. *Ibid.*, 550–554.
34. *Ibid.*, 561–564; and the *Gorgias* (Jowett trans.), 483d.
35. *Republic*, IX, 571.

On the whole, Plato holds, the Forms of the polis and the human soul are laid up in heaven and cannot be attained existentially, however well they may serve as models for emulation and stimuli for action. But would it not be possible to achieve an ordering somewhat closer to the model than the cities of history? It is to this task that Plato turns in his discussion of what we might call his conception of the less distorted commonwealth.

The Less-Distorted Commonwealth

The commonwealth less distorted than those of history lies part way between the Form of the polis (or soul) and historical societies. Plato suggests that it differs basically from the pure Form in two respects: First, it is a law-state and not a wisdom-state; and second, its citizens have private property and individual family life.

As we noted earlier, Plato is always suspicious of positive law, thinking of it as an encumbrance in the quest for exact justice. Thus in his dialogue *The Statesman*, speaking through "the Stranger," he observes:[36]

> The best thing of all is not that the law should rule, but that a man should rule, supposing him to have wisdom and royal power. . . . The law does not perfectly comprehend what is noblest and most just for all and therefore cannot enforce what is best. The differences of men and actions, and the endless irregular movements of human things, do not admit of any universal and simple rule. And no art whatsoever can lay down a rule which will last for all time.
>
> . . . The law is always striving to make one;—like an obstinate and ignorant tyrant, who will not allow anything to be done contrary to his appointment, or any question to be asked—not even in sudden changes of circumstances, when something happens to be better than what he commanded for some one. . . .
>
> A perfectly simple principle can never be applied to a state of things which is the reverse of simple.

And he analogizes the statesman to a ship's pilot who guides the boat by wisdom and not in accordance with fixed rules. Both pilot and ideal-type statesman watch continually over their charges, "not by laying down rules" but by making their respective arts a "law."[37]

Unfortunately, however, such statesmen cannot be found in the mixed situations which constitute human history. Even if a man can be discovered who knows what is best for human society, he may not always be able or willing to do what is best.[38] Men also find it difficult to understand that the "true art of politics" is concerned not with the private but rather with the public good: They tend to confuse the two.

It is because we either cannot discover men of knowledge or, if we do find them, they tend to be corrupted by political power, that we must accept a system of laws. This does not alter the fact that the Form of the polis is governance by reason and wisdom. "But then there is no such mind anywhere, or at least not much; and therefore we must choose law and order, which are second best."

Any law-state, Plato implies, will inevitably do injustice to individuals and groups. It will cause pain where pain violates the Form of Justice, and it will often create situations which, because law is such a clumsy instrument, cannot be reconciled with righteousness. Yet the alternative is giving political power to men who never have the requisite wisdom and who, if they do have a modicum of knowledge, find it swiftly pass away when united with political power—an alternative surely worse than a polity of laws.

And just as we must choose a commonwealth of laws, so must we abandon the community of material goods, women, and children. For communism, Plato seems to be saying, while still the norm for noetic and spirited men, demands so much of the imperfectly noetic and spirited that the latter are likely to rebel and create disorder far worse than a less-than-communist arrangement.

The device which Plato uses in sketching his law-state is one which must have been quite familiar to him and to his students in the Academy. He was called upon frequently, it will be remembered, to help work out constitutions for new cities. Now he imagines an Athenian giving advice to a constitutional commission which has been appointed by the city of Cnossus (Crete) to establish a scheme for a Cnossus-sponsored colony.

In process of developing this advice, it is significant that Plato is much more historically oriented than in the *Republic*. There he set up ideal types, as we have seen, in the interest of understanding and also because he held the good types to be metaphysically real. Now, while not forgetting the types, he seeks first to reconstruct the evolution of society historically rather than psychologically or logically.

For aeons of time, he guesses, men were without civilization or the arts—he suggests that this period must have extended over at least 100 million years![39] He adopts the view current in Greek mythology that there was at one time a deluge which destroyed an incipient civilization that had developed. Hence mankind had to start anew.

Beginning as peaceable roaming small bands, men later adopted a pastoral life and had little occasion for quarrels, since pastures were abundant and both milk and flesh were plentiful. There were no wars and no poverty. Lawgivers were unneeded, since life was governed by the "customs of their ancestors." There may have been a sketchy kind of lordship (the Greek *kyrios*), but it was devolved upon the parents. When smaller communities merged into larger ones, it was because men enjoyed one another's company and also had to fend off attacks of wild beasts. Husbandry developed but the old rule continued. Later, the need for legislators arose as rule by tradition was no longer adequate, in view of the development of thickly settled communities and cities. Eventually, cities themselves established associations with one another, particularly for protection.[40]

After this review of the history of political society, Plato sketches out the basis for his law-commonwealth. Generally speaking, it will be a polity combining the wisdom of ideal monarchy, as reflected imperfectly in Persia, with the liberty sketchily suggested by the democracy of Athens. Basically, Plato argues, all states in history are variants of either monarchy or democracy. The task of the lawgiver is to blend the two in such a way that men can combine their actual tendency to wish to be free of onerous restrictions with some recognition of the limitations which ideal wisdom—were it to be known—would place on activities. The constitution of the polis will never forget this proposed combination.

Because the city is a "law" and "property" commonwealth, Plato goes into great detail about regulations essential to preserve a measure of harmony and justice in a situation which is always fraught potentially with conflict and injustice. Laws must be prolific, he suggests, where conflicts between public and private interests are likely to arise. The price we pay for a regime of private property and the private family is minute regulation and complexity in legislation.

The city is to consist of exactly 5040 households and each family is to have an approximately equal plot of land which will be inalienable.[41] The land will descend to that child whom the father deems most worthy, and excess children in any given household will be turned over to those families which have few offspring of their own. If the city should develop an over-all superfluity of population, it will have to launch schemes of colonization. Meanwhile, it will encourage methods of birth control when population seems to be increasing unduly. But when famine or war have reduced the numbers of human beings perilously, policy will establish a system of rewards for large families. In general, every man will be expected to marry by the age of thirty-five. If he remains unmarried, he will be required to pay an annual fine or tax.

As in the *Republic*, Plato sees the economic as a vital factor in the problem of political order. He wishes it were possible that those who colonize the city were equal in economic goods, for this would obviate many difficulties. But since this is unlikely, given human beings and cultures as they are, he settles for some inequality, hoping that it can be carefully regulated by the laws. It will even be the basis, in some measure, for distribution of political power.[42]

On the other hand, wealth is always to remain a third-rate good, ranking below the second-rate body and the first-rate soul. This inferior position of mere wealth even in the "second-best" state is reflected in a number of regulations. In the first place, the disparity between highest and lowest possessions is to be in the ratio of four to one. The limit of poverty will be the value of the ancestral lot; no man can be allowed wealth of more than four times this value. If by trade or other means an individual should acquire additional possessions, the excess will revert to the public treasury. All citizens are to be required to

36. *Statesman* (Jowett trans.), 294a, b.
37. *Ibid.*, 297.
38. *Laws*, IX, 875.
39. *Ibid.*, III, 677.
40. *Ibid.*, 683–688.
41. *Ibid.*, V, 737–738.
42. *Ibid.*, 742–745.

register their possessions with a public agency and the records are to be open, apparently, to public inspection.[43]

Moreover, there are to be strict regulations about gold and silver as well as kinds of acquisition permitted. No man will be allowed to possess the precious metals except in the form of money, which Plato reluctantly admits to be some kind of a necessity. There are to be no dowries and interest on money is strictly prohibited. Plato does not examine the bases for the forbidding of usury but presumably they are similar to those which Aristotle will later advance—indeed, it is not far-fetched to suggest that in this, as in so much else, Aristotle is indebted to his teacher.[44]

Over-all, the economy of the polis is to be strictly subordinate to the ends of both soul and body. The legislator will not consider seriously what the "many" in their erratic moods deem to be desirable. He will not—and here Plato obviously directs his shafts at the imperialism of both Periclean and Cleonic democracy—think that the state "should be as great and as rich as possible, and should possess gold and silver, and have the greatest empire by sea and land."[45]

Just as the economy reflects the principles of the blended or mixed constitution, so does the governing structure. All who are eligible and fit for military service shall vote for the guardians of the law. First, 300 "candidates" shall be selected in the election. Then this number shall be reduced to 100 through a second ballot. Finally, the thirty-seven guardians shall be chosen from the 100 in a third election.

The Council will consist of 360 persons selected by an equally elaborate process. Candidates—360 in number—shall be chosen by the entire citizen body from each of the four classes into which the city has been divided on the basis of wealth. In a second election all the citizens reduce the candidates from each class to 180. Finally, ninety shall be selected by lot from each of the four categories. It will be noted how cleverly Plato tries to blend oligarchical, aristocratic, and democratic (choice by lot) elements in the elections.

He is not entirely happy about this scheme. But once he admits economic disparities into the citizen body, he feels he must reflect these disparities openly in the governing structure. And he can argue that poorer citizens would be better off politically than they would be in a system which did not require candidates to be chosen by categories. In that event, one would probably find the wealthier elements able to "rig" the elections, thus producing councillors most of whom would come from the upper income and status groups. And if one looks at politics in modern times, Plato would seem to be vindicated. The American Congress, for example, is not elected according to a class system, yet in the end hardly any congressmen come from those groups most numerous in the community—manual workers and white-collar salaried employees.

Throughout his proposals for public administration, which we need not detail here, Plato tries to blend aristocratic nomination procedures with popular election. He obviously does not subscribe to what modern theorists of public administration would term an hierarchical doctrine. Literally scores of officers—wardens of the city, wardens of the agora, interpreters, priests—are to be selected by mixed devices, with candidates often limited to members of the upper two categories but election to be by the whole citizen body.

The leading officer of the state will be the Minister of Education who must be fifty years of age and the father of children. He will be chosen by the whole body of magistrates from among the thirty-seven guardians of the law and hold office five years.

As always, Plato sees education as the key to the maintenance of the polis and to such improvement of the laws as is possible. We may think of his educational system as beginning even before the birth of the child. The guardians of the law are to appoint a Committee of Women who, by suggestion and gentle pressure, will see that the marriage laws are observed and that couples at least reproduce themselves. If there are no children after ten years of marriage, divorce is to be urged. At the same time, certain of the Committee of Women will act as matrons supervising the very young children and their nurses. The child begins formal education at the age of three and until six amuses himself under very loose supervision. During this period Plato warns against rigidity in training. Children are to be allowed to follow their "natural" bent as much as possible.

After six, the sexes will be separated. But both boys and girls will receive a long public education under teachers paid by the polis. In general, Plato's educational philosophy has not changed from that which he associated with the Form of the polis. There is a curious contradiction which runs through his scheme and theory, however. On the one hand, he appears to be utterly suspicious of change, contending that innovations in children's games, for example, when made by the children themselves, might portend revolutionary leadership later. On the other hand, he ridicules those who would restrict free enquiry into the nature of the universe and of religion.[46] This uncertainty about change is characteristic of Platonic political doctrine as a whole. He seems to be searching for principles which will provide social and political stability yet at the same time admits that the scientific investigations and contemplation which he advocates will inevitably shake up men's world outlooks and possibly their political systems. He never completely resolves this problem.

Although throughout his analysis he stresses the possibilities of legislation and the relatively favorable situation of a law-state, he always retains some doubt about the possibilities of deliberately ordering human affairs. On the one hand, he holds that "there is nothing which tends more to the improvement of mankind than legislation and colonization."[47] On the other hand, he wonders whether, in the end, it is not true to say "that man never legislates, but accidents of all sorts . . . legislate for us in all sorts of ways. The violence of war and the hard necessity of poverty are constantly overturning governments and changing laws."[48] A powerful argument can he made that in human affairs "change is almost everything."

Between these two positions—that human legislation can be vital and decisive and that only "chance" can legislate—Plato thinks that there is a kind of middle point, which he seems to defend. It is here that the art of politics and legislation resembles that of the skilled pilot when confronting a storm. The pilot prays for favorable external conditions; but whether the gods grant him propitious or unpropitious circumstances, his art can always help to control the situation to some extent. So, too, human reason reflected in laws *can* be decisive; but we ought always to remember that it must be exercised within conditions and limitations *not* established by deliberate human contrivance.

Laws, within these basic limitations, have both an educational and a coercive function. They are educational in that they instruct good men "how they may live on friendly terms with one another."[49] They are coercive because they compel "those who refuse to be instructed, whose spirit cannot be subdued, or softened, or hindered from plunging into evil."[50]

The theory of law as both educative and coercive is illustrated further in Plato's distinction between the "preamble" and the "law pure and simple." In the former, the lawgiver should endeavor to be persuasive by explaining the purpose of the legislation, its relation to reason, and its social justification. For most men, this will take the arbitrary note out of the "law pure and simple." At the same time, the law pure and simple viewed as command will inevitably appear to the irrational as a restraining factor.[51] Plato obviously hopes that if greater and greater skill is used in drafting the preamble, the law will increasingly be accepted through the coercion of reason alone.

He suggests that perhaps the longest preamble to a law will be that which introduces the legislation on impiety. This preface will have to persuade men that the gods exist, that they are concerned with the affairs of men, and that men can in no sense appease them. The law on impiety indicates that Plato believes in the necessity for a public profession of religion, with sanctions for disobedience. He apparently thinks not only that the simple threefold theology can be proved, but also that civic harmony would be disrupted if all do not at least say they believe it. Although quite aware of deistic and atheistic claims—positions which were openly avowed in the Athens of the fourth century—he thinks that, in addition to their invalidity, they do not comport with the maintenance of that solidarity which must underlie any system of legislation. Those who by act or word violate the official theology are to be either imprisoned or put to death.

Somewhat inconsistently, Plato introduces the wisdom-state into his law-state, when, almost as an afterthought, he establishes the Nocturnal Council. This body is to have wide powers to reconsider the laws and to "tell

43. *Ibid.*
44. See Chapter 5, pp. 95–96.
45. *Laws*, V, 742.
46. *Ibid.*, VII, 821.
47. *Ibid.*, IV, 708.
48. *Ibid.*, 709.
49. *Ibid.*, IX, 880.
50. *Ibid.*
51. *Ibid.*, IV, 722–723.

what is the aim of the state, and . . . how we are to attain this, and what law or what man will advise us to that end."[52] While Plato is not too clear as to what the council will do, he does specifically mention that it will send out investigators to study the laws of other lands to provide information on which it can base its own legal revisions.

Although he is ambivalent in his attitude to social change, as we have seen, the institution of the Nocturnal Council seems to indicate that every polity must consider change, at times, to be a relative good. To the degree that the council is interpreted as a body which can suspend laws (and there are hints of this function) in the name of "wisdom," it would appear to be in contradiction to the notion of the law-state. It could easily become—assuming that its members are not fully noetic, as is the premise of the law-state—a body of semi-tyrants.

Plato's Critics: Ancient and Modern

Plato in his own day was a controversial political thinker and has remained one throughout the subsequent centuries. During the past generation alone, the critical literature dealing with his politics has been enormous, which would seem to be a tribute to the lasting impression he has made on mankind.

Space limitations prevent our thoroughly examining all the issues which have aroused the interest of ancient and modern scholars. Let us attempt, however, to suggest a few of the general lines of critical analysis, commenting in the process on their merits.

Plato's Method and Assumptions. From the time of Aristotle onward, Plato has been attacked by those who question his theory of knowledge and the means he uses to understand politics. This issue is, of course, broader than his political theory as such; but his approach in political theory nicely illustrates the epistemological and methodological questions involved.

The critics have tended to maintain that Plato's ontology, which allegedly led him to identify "reality" with the Forms or Ideas and to deny reality to the world of sense experience, is an unjustified dichotomy and one which is incompatible with a true science of politics. Without careful observation of the empirical world, it is asserted, and at least the assumption that that world shares in reality, we cannot develop those explanatory hypotheses without which any science is impossible. Plato, by tending to be suspicious of sense and to place his primary confidence in reason and dialectic, puts himself in the position of claiming that he can explain politics by mere armchair speculation.

Even if the sharp dichotomy between the reality of the Forms and the unreality of sense experience is a misinterpretation of Plato, the critics continue, he certainly gives sense experience only a kind of relative reality status and does not show how the world of change can be connected with the presumably eternal Forms. Aristotle particularly was dissatisfied with his teacher at this point.[53]

There would seem to be merit in these criticisms provided they are not pushed too far. Plato was so impressed by the order which he saw lying behind apparent disorder and so unsatisfied by those views which doubted that any knowledge of politics (whether explanatory or "normative") was possible, that he too easily dismissed the problem of the exact relation between the Forms and the appearances.[54]

But it should not be imagined that Plato ignored the empirical dimension. As we have pointed out, the Academy was for years engaged in a comparative study of constitutions and when it came to give advice on the foundation of new colonies it considered such mundane issues as water supply, geography, proximity to the sea, the cultural heritage of potential inhabitants, climate, and economic possibilities. Plato in the *Laws* illustrates the fact that he could be very cognizant of history and of the diversity of human conditions. And we must always remember, too, that in attempting to determine the natural end of an institution or a human being, he had first to examine the institution or the person before concluding which of its or his activities were natural and which distorted. Some study of the world of flux was indispensable, if only to give hints of the universe of Forms.

Although Plato provided too little guidance for the empirical investigator, he did see that a true science of politics must attempt to provide explanations of political conduct and not merely record isolated facts. The doctrine of the Forms is the first extended statement of the notion of science as the discovery of the way in which things are related to one another. Political phenomena can be explained, in other words, only if we think of them, not as discrete and isolated, but rather as expressions of a whole or wholes which somehow join them together.

The Problem of Cultural and Class Bias. Every thinker is to some extent blinded by cultural and class presuppositions. But the reverse observation is also true—that every thinker *believes,* at least, that he is attempting to transcend cultural limitations and prejudices. Unless one is to assume, with certain Marxists, that every system of political thought is simply an ideology (or defense of an economic or class interest) and cannot be fruitfully investigated from the viewpoint of validity or invalidity, it is incumbent on the student to discover both the ways in which the thinker is culturebound and the respects in which he manages, often with great difficulty, to depart from his culture.

Now Plato appears to have been blind in certain respects, meaning by this that he did not probe vigorously enough into widely accepted but questionable beliefs. Thus he seems to have accepted with little question the popular distinction between Greek and barbarian, even though his search for a universal human nature would appear to run counter to it. He followed, moreover, without adequate questioning (except, perhaps, in the *Republic*), the predominant cultural judgment that slavery must be inevitable or a given;[55] in the *Laws,* he seems to anticipate Aristotle's argument that slavery is natural. Just as he accepts the inevitability of slavery, so he apparently finds it impossible even to conceive of a social condition in which war is abolished—hence the great emphasis in both the *Republic* and the *Laws* on military training and on discussion of military matters. In the *Republic* at least, the critic can validly argue, where he purports to treat the Form of the polis, he ought surely to have envisioned a state in which war has vanished. Yet despite his emphatic attack on timocratic integration and his splendid critique of Sparta, warfare is assumed to continue even in the "idea laid up in heaven." How he could accept war and reject demagoguery in his Form of polis, when both were rife in Greek polities of the time, is a mystery that still remains—apart from seeing it as a case of acute intellectual and moral blindness.

On the other hand, in many respects he challenged predominant cultural valuations in no uncertain terms—in his judgment of women, for example, and in his insistence on systems of public education. To be sure, he had a kind of model for these things in the institutions of Sparta; but his intellectual defense went far beyond anything Sparta had produced and, when all is said, he was still challenging some of the most deeply rooted prejudices of Athens.

Was Plato a Totalitarian? Certain modern critics, Karl Popper,[56] R. H. S. Crossman,[57] and Bertrand Russell[58] among them, have contended that Plato was a totalitarian. How shall we evaluate this charge?

The difficulty turns, of course, on what we mean by the term. If it is understood to designate an advocate of a sociopolitical order that appeals for its sanctions primarily to physical force or to such emotional slogans as "blood and soil," then Plato's thought is clearly not totalitarian. The order outlined in the *Republic* is based upon reason and understanding; and the emotions are integrated around these qualities. In the *Laws,* Plato specifically attacks those who, like the Spartans, make the military the center of polis life.

If "totalitarianism" implies a view which places great emphasis on the need for unity as a foundation of political order, then Plato was in a certain sense a totalitarian (although the word is hardly appropriate). In some respects, his society was, to use an expression of Popper, a "closed" one: Commerce was restricted and drastic innovation eschewed as incompatible with harmony, mental health, and the pursuit of the good. But it should be reemphasized

52. *Ibid.*, XIX, 962.
53. See pp. 87–88.
54. The literature critical of Plato's theory of the Forms is enormous. But note particularly W. D. Ross, *Plato's Theory of Ideas,* New York: Oxford University Press, 1951; John A. Stewart, *Plato's Doctrine of Ideas,* New York: Russell, 1964; and Karl Popper, *op. cit.*
55. On Plato's attitude to slavery see Glenn R. Morrow, *Plato's Law of Slavery in its Relation to Greek Law,* Urbana: University of Illinois Press, 1939.
56. Karl Popper, *op. cit.*
57. R. H. S. Crossman, *Plato Today,* New York: Oxford University Press, 1959.
58. See Russell's discussion in his *History of Western Philosophy,* New York: Simon & Schuster, 1945.

that Plato's unity and justice were grounded on discovering the role for which each citizen was most suited and then giving the citizen appropriate responsibilities. Although each citizen is to be subordinate to the "good of the whole," he will at the same time be attaining his own highest possible level of righteousness and happiness. Thus, the personalities even of appetitive men are considered: Their potentialities are allowed scope for development within the larger framework of the social order. Far from being coerced into nonappetitive roles, Plato in effect tells them to be themselves. We should also remember that Plato's suspicion of law is grounded on its inability to take account of individual circumstances and unique personalities—hardly a view which could be identified with the kind of unity that runs roughshod over human eccentricity.

Was Plato Antagonistic to Freedom? Akin to the charge of totalitarianism is a common criticism that Plato was opposed to freedom for the person. The answer to this will, of course, depend on how one defines freedom. If it is conceived to be the right to do what one desires at any given moment, without external restraints and without reference to what one ought to do, then indeed Plato can be said to have rejected freedom, for to him expression of desires unrelated to justice and to one's natural functions was the antithesis of freedom—it was, in fact, a kind of slavery to the appetites like that exemplified in tyranny. If, however, freedom consists in emancipation from domination by the appetites and in the opportunity to carry out one's true function and to attain one's highest self, then one of the major purposes of Plato's polis was to make freedom possible. In fact, in his conception of freedom as action in accordance with reason and justice, he provided the basic text for one of the most influential conceptions of freedom in history—a view of which in modern times was to deeply affect the thought of men like Rousseau and Hegel.

Was Plato Hostile to Change? Fite, Popper, Winspear, and others have asserted that Plato looked forward to the creation of an order in which social change would be completely eliminated.

To some extent, as we have seen, Plato does indeed frown on change. But in the *Laws*, ambivalent as he often is, he definitely makes provision for it, hoping only that it can be carried out with the least possible hardship.[59] Where he does hope to regulate the rapidity of change, it is because he thinks that in this way men are more likely to control their own social destinies. If change is too rapid and too drastic, men become its victims rather than its masters. Certainly this has happened in modern times where we have allowed technological change to develop an autonomy of its own and have then insisted that men must adjust to the demands of the machine. Plato, unlike many moderns, doubted that change in itself is necessarily good.

Was Plato Restoring a Past Order? Some critics aver (and here again Popper and men like Winspear come to mind) that one of Plato's primary purposes was to create a propaganda and an ideology which would unite the aristocrats of the fourth century behind a plan for restoration of some past presumably ideal order. This order would be either one which supposedly existed in the remote past or one which was more recent—perhaps the arrangement of things which flourished in Athens before the Solonic reforms began. Plato, so the argument goes, was such a bitter opponent of the democracy that he regarded it as his mission to reestablish a united front of antidemocrats. In Winspear's version, "He wanted land-owning aristocrats and wealthy merchants to combine; by combining they could check the democratic movement and make life again secure for those who possessed great wealth—whether wealth in land or wealth in moveable property."[60]

In support of such contentions, critics note both the circumstances of Plato's life and his statements in the dialogues. We have already called attention to his partially antidemocratic family background. In his opposition to the tyrants of Syracuse, too, he was attacking men who had considerable popular support—as did many of the ancient tyrants, including Pisistratus, who gained power illegally but often introduced much-needed reforms. Many of Plato's friends, moreover, came from families having eupatrid antecedents. We know, too, that he deeply resented the execution of Socrates by the restored democracy.

But the contention that Plato did *not* intend to restore any given historic order would seem to have much greater support than the position ascribed to him by the critics. It will be recalled, for example, that he was as hostile to the conduct of the Thirty as he was to certain actions of the restored democracy. It is difficult to read his dialogues, moreover, without emerging with the impression that he rejected not only all political factions of his own day but also those of previous generations. While there is no question that he attacked both ideal-type and existential democratic man,[61] he was equally vehement in excoriating men of wealth. When Winspear alleges that one of Plato's objectives was to "check the democratic movement and make life again secure for those who possessed great wealth," he passes over far too lightly the evidence of the dialogues. In the *Republic,* as we have seen, rulers are to own nothing and to be ascetics; in the *Laws,* all citizens are to be landowners and no person is to have more than four times the wealth of another—a disparity far less than that in most modern nations, including the United States. And in the *Laws,* Plato apologizes for allowing any disparity at all.

Although some critics admit that Plato had little love for rule by the wealthy, they may still aver that he did have an historic model in Sparta. In certain respects this is indeed true, as we have suggested—in his attitude to women, for example, and in his respect for a system of public education. Sparta, moreover, was integrated around a definite goal, thus enabling it to order its affairs in a way which was impossible for Athens. But Plato was far from admiring the focus for Spartan integration—war and the subordination of intellectual and spiritual ends to the supreme goal of military triumph. "No one," he says through the Athenian Stranger, "can be a true statesman, whether he aims at the happiness of the individual or state, who looks only, or first of all, to external warfare. . . ."[62] Although we have elsewhere criticized Plato for not envisioning the elimination of war in his idea of the state, at no point does he sanction the notion that war is or ought to be the supreme end of polis life. As a matter of fact, it is when ideal-type timocratic man—the merely military or technological mind—usurps the authority of noetic man that the polis begins its psychological degeneration.

Was Plato Peculiarly "Antidemocratic"? Because so many moderns tend to look at the past in terms of what the twentieth century calls democracy, let us examine briefly the charge—offered by men like Fite, Popper, Winspear, and Crossman—that Plato was peculiarly antidemocratic.

We have already touched on the issue in the previous section. Here let us continue by noting the ways in which he was indeed antidemocratic according to definitions of his own day. For the ancients democracy included the appointment of officials by lottery, rule by mere numbers rather than by principles or law, bills of attainder, and decisions arrived at by caprice and emotion rather than by reason. Plato's ideal democratic man represents his picture of these characteristics pushed to their logical and psychological extremes. Now there can be no question that Plato, if these hallmarks be taken as the criteria, was vigorously antidemocratic.

On the other hand, it should also be pointed out that he accepted—indeed, urged—many proposals whose principles are intimately associated, rightly or wrongly, with modern democratic thought. For example, he generally favored choice of officials by ballot rather than exclusively by lot, thus providing for some conscious discrimination among candidates. Other instances would be his emphasis on equality of women; his insistence that all decisions be made rationally; and his recognition of vertical social mobility in the *Republic.*

What Was the Purpose of Plato's Political Teaching? The import of what we have been saying is that Plato did not write his political dialogues to sustain the claims of any Athenian political factions; nor can he be identified with any modern ideologies or movements.

How, then, did he intend his dialogues to be used? The answer would seem to be that he hoped to instruct men in the underlying issues of politics and to suggest, in tentative ways only, the bases for possible answers. His political dialogues, like his dialogues in general, should be read as the works of a scientist and philosopher who was also a poet. In the *Timaeus,* for example, he is constantly suggesting that the foundations of the physical universe "may be like this but we don't really know." So, too, in ethical-political dialogues like the *Gorgias, Protagoras, Republic, Statesman,* and *Laws,* while at points he appears to be dogmatic, basically he seems simply to be

59. *Laws,* XII, 951-952.
60. A. D. Winspear, *op. cit.,* 306.
61. Although some modern scholars, notably John Wild, *Plato's Theory of Man,* New York: Octagon Books, 1964, seem to argue that he was implicitly a democrat in the twentieth century sense of the term.
62. *Laws,* I, 638.

suggesting and dramatizing possible alternatives as foundations for further discussion. His constant resort to myths, as in Book X of the *Republic*, is an indication that the most profound questions of politics and ethics cannot be stated in prosaic, literal terms, but to some extent must be couched in poetic form.

Looked at in this way, Plato's politics, then, must be seen as a framework within which political issues can be examined and not as a series of final answers to the questions posed. Even where he is most emphatic and controversial—as in his defense of censorship and the "noble lie"—he seems to be telling us that the truth must in any system be diluted or seemingly distorted for those still in the cave and that the problem is how to dilute it in such a way that souls can ultimately transcend the dilutions, and while he appears to give us an answer, he is really illustrating a possible answer to a basic question.

Throughout the dialogues, too, recurs the constant theme that answers to political issues are not easy; that, in fact, the questions posed are ones which are divine in nature—the imposition of the Forms on recalcitrant matter—but must be answered by mere human beings. Plato thinks that with the framework he has provided we are more likely to grasp the awful dimensions of political ordering and righteousness and to reject the kinds of superficial solutions—whether by eupatrids, oligarchs, or democrats—so common in his day. Once the plausible but spurious answers have been spurned, we are ready to pursue true knowledge, without which there can be no political justice.[63]

The Historical Impact of Plato

It is difficult to exaggerate the impact which Plato had on subsequent generations. Although in later ancient times the Academy would be taken over by non-Platonic schools of thought,[64] in the epoch immediately following the death of Plato his students continued his work in giving advice to cities and in refining his conceptions. Aristotle was one of those students; and while he founded his own school, the basic ingredients of his thought were in the end to be very Plato-like.

The period following the death of Aristotle was, of course, one in which Platonic teaching came to be criticized by a wide variety of viewpoints to be treated later.[65] Despite this criticism, however, men continued to read the *Republic* and to imitate its style if not its contents. Zeno, the Stoic, for example, would entitle his great utopian work—now unfortunately lost—the *Republic*. Much later on, when Cicero came to develop his political philosophy in the declining days of republican Rome, he would be inspired in his political thought by the teaching of Plato. And there were many other imitators in the ancient world.

The political Plato continued to be read in ancient times down to the disintegration of the western Roman Empire in the fifth century A.D. As late as the middle of that century, Proclus was still commenting on the works of the ancient Athenian. The Academy itself was not abolished until A.D. 529, when the Emperor Justinian, fearing that its spirit of criticism was dangerous to Christianity, issued a decree dissolving it.

But the Platonic dialogues themselves came to be read, after the first century A.D., in the context of intellectual and social conditions radically different from those obtaining in the fourth century B.C. Now they had to compete with the expanding mystery religions, an influential Stoicism, and various attempts to combine classical Greek with postclassical Greek and Hebrew thought. In this syncretic and eclectic period, which we shall touch upon later, it would have been surprising had pure Platonism flourished. Its influence tended, by the third century A.D. to be transmitted through the movement of thought known as neo-Platonism, which was inseparably connected with the writings of Plotinus (A.D. 205–270).[66] Although Plotinus himself at one point in his career attempted to found a republic-like experimental community in Italy (he was dissuaded by the then emperor on the ground that the land was infested by malaria), the tendency of later neo-Platonism was to retreat from the world of politics and to afford a philosophical basis for later ancient thinkers to eschew social questions.

It was through neo-Platonism, however, that a form of the Platonic outlook was made familiar to St. Augustine, who did so much to lay the foundations for the political outlook of the early medieval world.[67] After Augustine, however, the direct impact of Platonism (as contrasted with its indirect influence through later ancient thinkers) began to fade. As the Western World became more and more isolated from the East, the former was left largely to its own devices and eventually ceased to possess even the texts of the political Plato. While he continued to be read (although hardly followed) in the Byzantine Empire, the western world had to be satisfied primarily with mere fragments of his writings. And it was precisely in this long period—roughly from A.D. 500 to 1450—that the utopian impulse in Western Civilization was at its nadir. Many factors contributed to this phenomenon, of course, and we shall deal with some of them later, but surely one important element in the decline of political imagination was the loss of the ancient world's greatest political thinker.

When in the fifteenth century Plato came again to be read by scholars in western Christendom, his impact on men's imaginations was almost immediate. A whole rash of utopian speculations followed his rediscovery—most of them stimulated by the *Republic*. Since 1500, his influence has continued to be an extremely important factor in the political imaginations of social thinkers. Such twentieth-century utopists as H. G. Wells, for example, were profoundly influenced in their political speculations by the ancient philosopher. Even where writers violently reacted against Platonic political teaching, they often confessed to having been deeply impressed. Thus Warner Fite, a pioneer twentieth-century critic of the political Plato, remarked that despite his revulsion, he could not teach his course in politics at Princeton without using Plato's *Republic*. And the very vehemence with which the politics of Plato has been debated during the past generation is itself an indication of his wide-ranging impact.

Despite the difficulty of giving an exact or certain answer, we might well ask what features of the political Plato have caused him to be so influential.

The first is perhaps the boldness with which he cuts through nonessentials to get at primary issues. Politics in any generation are always so complicated that this is a feat which has always been admired. The third- or fourth-level political issues may be peculiar to a given age, but underlying them are essentials that transcend the particularities of any given generation. It is Plato's ability to identify these essentials which influenced men.

We might suggest, too, that the radical quality of Platonic theory has been significant. Not only does he cut through to the essential questions but the responses he suggests—even if he intended them to be merely stimuli for further

thought, as we have argued—are radical in the sense that they seem to deal with the roots of possible answers.

Finally, Plato's confidence in the possibility of knowledge as the key to the dilemmas of politics has in every age constituted a challenge of first order. In defining man himself as rational, Plato challenges all those views which would see the human being as simply an expression of primitive nature. Plato's implication that we cannot understand man except in terms of his often unachieved purposes or goals lays the groundwork for all those views of morals and politics which doubt that humanity can ever be explained in wholly scientific terms, as these are usually understood. Knowledge is breaking down into parts, as the scientist correctly asserts, but it is also accounting for a phenomenon in terms of a purposeful whole which itself shapes the parts and cannot be reduced to them.

While Plato was putting his writings in order before his death in 347, his thirty-seven-year-old pupil, Aristotle, was no doubt meditating on those criticisms which he was to direct at his master. Already, too, Aristotle had manifested that love of biological study which was to provide him with quite a different emphasis and model from that of Plato. And Aristotle would develop yet further the doctrine of Forms which Socrates had suggested and Plato elaborated.

In Aristotle, as we shall see in the next chapter, ancient classical political thought is rounded out and Platonic insights are completed.

63. Cf. Leo Strauss, "On a New Interpretation of Plato's Political Philosophy," *Social Research*, September 1946.
64. On the development of the Academy, see Pan Aristophrōn, *Plato's Academy*, London: Oxford University Press, 1938. See also Harold Cherniss, *Aristotle's Criticism of Plato and the Academy*, New York: Russell and Russell, 1962 and *Riddle of the Early Academy*, New York: Russell and Russell, 1945.
65. See Chapter 6.
66. See W. R. Inge, *The Philosophy of Plotinus*, London, and New York: Longmans, Green, 1918.
67. See Chapter 10.

chapter 5

Aristotle and Political Society

If Plato may be said to have worked out what he regarded as a schematic analysis of the rational polis, we may think of Aristotle as the one who attempted in a greater detail to supply the missing links between the Forms and the world of ordinary political experience. Basically, Aristotle, despite a difference in emphasis, accepted most of Plato's ontology and epistemology. But he sought to make them less ambiguous than they were in the hands of his predecessor. In his political theory, too, despite important criticisms of his master, he built upon Plato's work.

Aristotle and the Politics of the Fourth Century

Born in 384 B.C. in Stagira to the court physician of Macedonia's king, Aristotle grew up in medical circles and early became acquainted with the biological knowledge of the time. Intellectually, this had a profound effect on him, for in his ethical and political discourses we shall note the influence of biological and medical analogies. He probably received at least the initial training of a physician and possibly completed his formal medical studies.

It is important in examining the formative influences on Aristotle's early life to keep in mind the rapidly shifting political situation. He was born halfway between the beginning of Sparta's decline and the final elimination of Spartan hegemony by Thebes. The decline of Sparta must have left a deep impression on the Greek mind, which, as we have noted, tended to admire so many aspects of the Laconian way of life. At the same time, all who knew Thebes probably realized that its hegemony would be short lived, as indeed it was. Meanwhile, Macedonian power was growing and the only hope, militarily speaking, for fending off its possible triumph was for the Greek city-states to unite in an effective fashion. This they seemed unable to do, despite temporary leagues and alliances.

The acute mind of the boy Aristotle could not have been unaware of these political facts of life when he was sent at the age of seventeen to study at the Academy in Athens. The year was 367 B.C., and it is probable that when Aristotle arrived Plato was on leave from the Academy for his political maneuvers in Sicily.

For twenty years he remained in and about the Academy, first as a student (primarily of biology and politics) and then, possibly, as a member of the staff. His association with Plato was a close one, although toward the end of the period, as we have seen, he began to be critical of certain aspects of Plato's philosophy.

On the death of the head of the Academy, Aristotle began to reside in the city of Atarneus in Asia Minor. There a former student of the Academy, Hippias, had become the political leader. He welcomed his friend Aristotle and the latter married the niece of Hippias. Hippias was engaged as an active politician in fending off possible pressures by the king of Persia, although he had apparently not given up his scholarly interests entirely. Meanwhile, Aristotle studied marine biology for a period of more than three years.

In 343, Hippias was killed by an assassin hired by the king of Persia. This naturally made a deep impression on Aristotle, both from the political point of view and in terms of his long personal friendship. Aristotle is said to have written a hymn extolling the memory of Hippias. Some time after this, however, he decided that he had best accept an invitation to join the Macedonian royal court, in which he was called upon to be tutor to the crown prince.

The prince was, of course, Alexander, then a boy of about thirteen. In both ancient and modern times, there has been much speculation about what the exact relations were between the future king and the eminent scientist and philosopher. The fact is that we know very little about the matter. Modern authorities like A. E. Taylor think that "it is . . . improbable that Aristotle's influence counted for much in forming the character of Alexander."[1] On the other hand, such ancient writers as Plutarch apparently believed that Aristotle was in part responsible for the shaping of Alexander's political mind.

When Alexander's father, Philip of Macedon, was assassinated, in 336, the accession of Alexander to the throne meant that he would no longer have time for study. Hence Aristotle now returned to Athens.

The Athens in which he took up residence was already within the shadow of the Macedonian power. The battle of Chaeronea had been fought in 338 and it was evident that all Greece would soon be a part of the rapidly developing empire. These events, curiously enough, seem to have made little impression on the by now maturing political views of Aristotle. In 335, Speusippus, president of the Academy, died and some think that Aristotle may have been a candidate for the position. Instead, Xenocrates was chosen. This was the signal for Aristotle to found his own school, the Lyceum. From 335, therefore, until a year before his death he was preoccupied with research and administrative duties.

It is significant, although not surprising, that the central studies carried on in the Lyceum were biology and history. Aristotle had collected a large variety of biological specimens (some of them sent by Alexander with his compliments) and his students travelled all over Greece to add to the collection. His historical investigations emphasized what we should today call "constitutional history." In this field, he and his students managed to compile and probably publish accounts of the development of some 158 Greek city-states. So far as we are aware, however, no one at the Lyceum wrote an account of the changes which the conquests of Alexander were bringing about.

Alexander himself had by 326 grown increasingly cool to his old mentor. The climax of his increasing hostility came in the affair of Callisthenes, who had been close to Aristotle and was at Alexander's court in the capacity of an adviser on historical matters. He was an independent soul and while always respectful of Alexander was extraordinarily frank in his statements. He let everyone know, for example, that he disapproved of Alexander's assuming the trappings of Oriental monarchy. Refusing to adore Alexander after the manner of the Persians, he aroused the admiration of many young men at court. Plutarch relates that one of them asked Callisthenes "what he should do to be the most illustrious person on earth." Callisthenes is said to have replied that the readiest way "was to kill him who was already" the most illustrious man on earth.[2] Although Callisthenes did not participate in the subsequent conspiracy, his remark came to be discovered. The philosopher was thereupon imprisoned and was either executed or died in prison. Alexander immediately blamed Aristotle for the attitude of Callisthenes; and had it not been for the time-consuming nature of his preparations to invade India, he might have arrested his former tutor.

At the same time, Aristotle's position in Athens was a precarious one. While he had little sympathy with Alexander's political ambitions and although Alexander had become hostile to him, public opinion in Athens associated him, for understandable reasons, with the pro-Macedonian faction. After Alexander's death in 323, therefore, Aristotle was indicted for "impiety." The technical charge was based on the poem he had written after the death of his friend Hippias. Although the poem had been composed before his association with Alexander, it virtually made a god of his friend and hence afforded a pretext for the anti-Alexandrian faction to bring the indictment against him.

But Aristotle was no Socrates. Once he had been informed of the indictment, he decided to flee, "lest," he is reported to have said, "the Athenians sin twice against philosophy."

The last year of his life was spent in Chalcis in Euboea. Here he resumed his researches but was troubled by digestive complaints. When he died in 322, his physician reported that death was due to "chronic indigestion rendered acute by overwork."

Neither his political nor his ethical doctrine (which are so interwoven that it will be impossible to separate them) can be understood without some attention to his general philosophy. Let us first, therefore, examine his theory of causation.

Causation and Transformation of Platonic Forms

Aristotle is one of those who criticized Plato's doctrine of Forms rather severely. Yet while he begins in a critical vein, he ends by being basically at one with his teacher.

1. A. E. Taylor, *Aristotle*, New York: Dover Publications, 1955, p. 9.
2. "Alexander," in Plutarch, *The Lives of the Noble Grecians and Romans*, John Dryden, trans., New York: Modern Library, 1932, p. 841.

His criticism of Plato's theory of the Forms is threefold. First, he asks how the "general" can be "substantial" and, of course, suggests that it cannot be. Second, he attacks Plato for his seeming to make the "properties" of things *outside* the things of which they are properties. How do the properties, he asks, get themselves *into* the things if they are outside them? Finally, he queries Plato as to how the Forms or Ideas, lacking a moving force, can be "causes" of phenomena.[3]

In setting about to remedy the Platonic ambiguities, Aristotle develops the classical distinction between matter and form. Matter he thinks of as the raw stuff out of which specific things emerge or are made. It is shapeless and undefined in itself. However, *within* all matter, there are latent forms of some kind which are seeking to differentiate a particular thing from other things. Aristotle emphasizes that the form is in the matter and not outside it, thus seeking at the beginning to differentiate his view from that of Plato.

The relationship between matter and form is expressed dynamically by suggesting that matter is "potentiality" and form is "actuality." Matter as potential is shaped by the form within it in such a way that matter becomes less and less shapeless and undifferentiated and more and more definite and differentiated. Aristotle's researches as a biologist undoubtedly suggested to him this conception of the relation between matter and form as potentiality and actuality. It is possible that he compared the early embryos of pigs with those of cattle and found that, in terms of seeming composition, physical structure, and appearance, they seemed to be the same. By examining them simply as they were, one could easily conclude that they were not distinguishable from each other. Yet one embryo would, in normal circumstances, become a hog and the other a cow.

How account for the fact that two apparently similar pieces of matter should become different things? The explanation, says Aristotle, is the "Form" within each, which is impressing itself on the apparently undifferentiated matter.

We should be careful in interpreting Aristotle at this point not to confuse matter with body. When he speaks of the "material," he does not mean to identify it only with those things which have extension in space. Matter can also embrace such phenomena as raw psychological "potentialities," or the "spiritual" stuff out of which "character" develops. Matter, as Aristotle uses the term, is simply all that which is relatively undifferentiated or shapeless.

Form, then, is an "immaterial" principle which has the capacity to shape matter to a given end or goal. Matter is just as real as form. In fact, there is no matter within which there is not implanted some form that is changing the matter from what it now appears to be into something which it is potentially capable of becoming.

But neither can anything achieve its actuality without being attached to what Aristotle terms an "efficient" cause. The embryo of the pig, for example, cannot provide the matter upon which the form can work unless a male and a female hog "cause" it through the act of procreation. The embryo of the calf is not possible unless procreated in a similar manner. These are "efficient" causes.

But to what end does form act? And why does the form of hogness shape things in a way different from the form of bullness or cowness? Why is the form of oakness present in the acorn so radically different from either the form of hogness or the form of cattleness? It is because each form is itself but the reflection of a final cause. In a sense, as it were, the final cause provides the form which works within the matter that is launched by the efficient cause. Thus the final cause of the particular acorn is an oak tree which does not yet exist, but the materials and the shaping principles for which are present.

This theory of causation, it will be noted, develops the Socratic notion that a complete account of a thing can be given only if we examine it not merely in terms of its parts but also by reference to its implicit purpose or end. Thus the analytical work of the scientist, in the usual sense of that term, can give a very complete account of a hog embryo in terms of its physics, chemistry, and biology. The scientist can look at the structure of the tissues, note the coloration, measure the size. But this method can never give us a complete account of the embryo. For these things are caused by the whole form in the embryo and the form is a reflection of the hog which does not yet exist.

Thus far we have been dealing with the Aristotelian doctrine as if it were a theory which sought to account for phenomena only in the biological and physical worlds. We have not specifically related it to the world of human life and relations. But Aristotle, of course, thinks that the theory is universally applicable.

How shall one account for a bowl, for example, if we accept the fourfold theory of causation? The material cause is the raw and unformed silver which has been made available to the bowlmaker. The silver in its natural state is, of course, changing in accordance with inner forms which are shaping it through rain, geological upheaval, and other efficient causes into some final end that is implicit in the inner form. But here all causation is in natural forces. Man has not yet entered the picture.

When the bowlmaker takes the raw silver, he initiates a process which will supplant the forms operating within the silver in its natural state. For the nature of silver is such that it is capable of being shaped into a bowl, given the proper efficient cause. It has now found that cause in the work of the silversmith or bowlmaker. As he hammers it, the form of the bowl gradually separates the silver used by the silversmith from its sister-silver which remains under the control of other forms in nature. The silversmith sees what the silver can become under his blows and the particular shape which it assumes eventually is the result of a combination of his hammering and the Form which he sees as possible or potential in the silver.

Aristotle thinks of man as imitating nature through art. He becomes an efficient cause as an artist and can discern many alternative potential forms in matter, depending upon the end for which the artistic production is to be used. Man intervenes in the process of causation, in other words. But the same fourfold process is involved.

We should be careful, however, not to impute to Aristotle the notion that man can be completely arbitrary in dealing with matter. Although human purposes can through formal and efficient causes shape matter, there are limits to the potential forms present in matter. The inherent qualities of the material will condition the kinds of forms into which it is capable of being shaped. Thus if one wishes to erect a durable statue, one could hardly discern the form in a piece of ice or a block of pine wood. On the other hand, the form of a durable statue is clearly present in a block of marble and Phidias could see this. Just as in nature, outside man, one would not expect the form of a fig tree to be present in a thistle tree seed, so man is limited in fashioning his world.

All this implies that to understand a thing in the ethical, social, and political domain means to know it not merely in its origins and in its history, not only in its parts, as it were, but to know it also in its implicit purpose and its goal. In the biological world, including man, every species has characteristic functions to perform—functions, that is, which set it apart from other species; and within any given organism, each part exists to carry out a specific function or functions. To perform its function well, whether in biology or in social life, makes a thing virtuous, whether it be the seeing of an eye, the winning of a race by an athlete, the cleaning up of filth by a fly, or the winning of victory by an army. Knowledge, therefore, implies an understanding of how every object of knowledge relates to the ordering of the whole; for its function connects its own activities with the purpose or *telos* of the whole.

Theoretical and Practical Science

Now while all knowledge, according to Aristotle, involves investigation in terms of the fourfold "causative" principle, there is a basic distinction between what he calls "theoretical" knowledge and wisdom, on the one hand, and "practical" knowledge and wisdom on the other.[4]

Theoretical Science. The truths which theoretical or speculative science studies are those which could not be "otherwise than they are." They are truths which can be deduced by the necessities of logic from principles which are self-evidently true:

> The object of scientific knowledge is of necessity. Therefore it is eternal; for things that are of necessity in the unqualified sense are all eternal; and things that are eternal are ungenerated and imperishable.[5]

Aristotle, unlike Plato (who thought of theoretical science as one), divided speculative

3. Aristotle, *Metaphysics,* Alpha, 9, Richard Hope, trans., Ann Arbor: University of Michigan Press, 1960.
4. *Metaphysics,* Alpha, 1, and Aristotle, *Nicomachean Ethics,* W. D. Ross, trans., London: Oxford University Press, 1954.
5. Aristotle, *Nicomachean Ethics,* Bk. VI, ch. 3.

science into First Philosophy, Mathematics, and Physics. What Aristotle terms "first philosophy" later came to be called, in the Middle Ages, metaphysics. First philosophy treats of "being qua being," as Aristotle puts it. It thus includes what might be termed today, or in the Middle Ages, theology; for insofar as first philosophy examines the nature of the first cause it is dealing with the "science of God."

Mathematics deals with being as reflected in the forms of number and geometry. It is more narrow than "being qua being" since it is qualified by the characteristics of number and figure. The objects which first philosophy studies are entirely separate from matter and have no motion; whereas the things studied by mathematics, though in themselves not capable of "motion," are "inherent" in matter.

Physics, according to Aristotle, is concerned with the examination of material objects which can move. As we move "down" from first philosophy to physics, the range of studies grows more narrow. First philosophy for Aristotle is roughly what mathematics is for Plato; for unlike Plato, Aristotle does not conceive mathematical forms as separable from matter. Aristotelian mathematical forms are *in* matter but, as we have seen, are not capable of motion themselves. Physics, then, the most narrow in range of theoretical sciences, is qualified as to its subject matter by the requirement that its object of study be matter which has the capacity for movement.

Practical Science. Now while the object of theoretical or speculative science is to know as an end in itself, the object of practical science or wisdom is both to know and to use the knowledge gained in order to control events. In ethics and politics, for example, which constitute for Aristotle the center of practical science, we wish to know about human relations both teleologically and nonteleologically; but we do not stop there, for our knowledge is also designed to help man be an efficient cause in changing what, without man, would be the ordinary course of development.

Aristotle tells us that we should not expect the certainty in the area of deliberative or practical knowledge that we have a right to expect in the speculative area. As A. E. Taylor puts it, the truths of practical science for Aristotle

> because they relate to what "can be otherwise," are never rigidly universal; they are general rules which hold good "in the majority of cases," but are liable to occasional exceptions owing to the contingent character of the facts with which they deal. . . . Thus for Aristotle the distinction between the necessary and the contingent is real and not merely apparent, and "probability is the guide" in studies which have to do with the direction of life.[6]

Politics: The Science of the Good

Within this framework of causation and knowledge, then, Aristotle proceeds to examine politics.

At the very outset, he tells us that it is "the master art." What does he mean by this expression?

He maintains that every art, action, and inquiry aims at some good or has some purpose. There is a multiplicity of arts and actions and hence a multiplicity of ends at which they may be conceived to aim. But among ends themselves a distinction must be kept in mind, for some ends lie in the activities themselves while other ends are products "apart from the activities that produce them." Where the end of an action is "outside" itself, the end is "better" than the action which produces it: the action, in this event, gains whatever goodness it has from the product for the sake of which it has taken place. Of course, Aristotle would maintain, some activities are "goods" in themselves and also are "goods" because they contribute to ends outside themselves. In this case, while we will acknowledge the activity as having a certain value for its own sake, we will never lose sight of the fact that it also exists for a more inclusive and all-embracing good. Thus Aristotle would say that a certain amount of physical exercise can be an enjoyable activity in itself; but it must also be viewed as a means—and one means only—which is simply instrumental to the more inclusive or higher end of health.

Many pursuits, however, would seem to exist *only* for more inclusive goods. Thus they derive whatever good they may have entirely —or at least almost entirely—from ends outside themselves. Hence Aristotle suggests that bridle-making could hardly be an activity that one would pursue for itself. Instead, it is good only insofar as it contributes to the art of riding. Although riding might conceivably be regarded as having some value apart from the act itself, its main good lies in the fact that it helps perfect military action. But military action is of many kinds, only one of which is riding. Now military action of all kinds exists primarily to serve the art of strategy. As one rises in the hierarchy of ends, one moves to arts which, relatively speaking, are "master" arts. Thus strategy is a master art relative to military action; military action relative to riding; and riding relative to harness-making.

So all human actions and pursuits and all human arts can be looked upon from the perspective of hierarchies of ends. Even if the actions are regarded from one point of view as ends in themselves, they are also to be thought of as subserving higher ends—higher meaning more inclusive and more fundamental. Thus while the art of household management (*oeconomica*) may give its practitioner a certain satisfaction, it can never be regarded *solely* as an end in itself; for its product, wealth, is primarily instrumental to ends outside household management.

Is there an "end," Aristotle asks, which we are pursuing *only* for itself and which cannot by any means be regarded as instrumental to other and more inclusive ends? If we can find such an end, it will be regarded as the end of ends, so to speak, and its art as the master of all the subordinate arts.

Now the art which Aristotle identifies as the master of master arts, as it were, is that of politics.[7] It has this status, Aristotle thinks, because it is the art

> that ordains which of the sciences would be studied in a state, and which each class of citizens should learn and up to what point they should learn them; and we see even the most highly esteemed of capacities to fall under this, e.g., strategy, economics, rhetoric.[8]

This is one of the key passages of Aristotle's political writing. In it he gives political science, for the realm of practical science, roughly the same status as first philosophy in the domain of speculative science.

He is also maintaining that such studies as military science, economics, and medicine, become most "meaningful" if we place them within the framework of the study—politics—which treats of man's primary or general good. For even if military science should achieve "victory," military triumph is not a goal in itself; even if economics tells us the conditions under which wealth can best be produced, wealth is not an end in itself; and while "health," the product of medicine, is certainly from one point of view more nearly an end, yet physical and mental health points primarily to a still more basic end—namely, the "good life."

The Nature of Eudaimonia

But what, we might ask Aristotle, is the "good"; and, a matter of even greater importance, how do we assure that men will become "good"? In answer to the first question, Aristotle calls the good which we commonly strive to attain "happiness," or *eudaimonia.* As for the second question, we make certain that men become good by education, a branch of politics, and we take into consideration the nature of the soul with which we have to deal. Let us now note how Aristotle deals with these two questions.

Eudaimonia. It does not get us very far, Aristotle suggests, simply to equate the good of the community and of the individual with happiness. For we must ask what kind of life deserves to be called happy. And in order to get at this question, we must ask, in turn, what is the characteristic function of man in the universe. What can man do which other species cannot do?

Aristotle makes it clear that the happiness we seek in pursuit of characteristically human functions is an expression of the soul's activity and not a "bodily" virtue. Here he uses soul very much as Socrates and Plato employed the term:

> By human virtue we mean not that of the body but that of the soul. . . . The student of politics, then, must study the soul, and must study it with these objects in view. . . .[9]

Now the soul of man clearly exhibits two aspects—an irrational and a rational. Aristotle proceeds to examine the irrational expression in order to show to what extent its natural functions connect it with the souls of other animals.

He divides the irrational into two parts: a

6. Taylor, *op. cit.*, p. 17.
7. It is instructive to compare Aristotle's discussion at this point with that of Plato in the *Statesman* (*Politicus*), Benjamin Jowett, trans., New York: Random House, 1937, pp. 304–305.
8. *Nicomachean Ethics*, Bk. I, ch. 2.
9. *Ibid.*, ch. 13.

vegetative and an appetitive. The vegetative is that part of the irrational which men share with both plants and animals and which shapes the growth of a man unconsciously and without his having anything to do with it. Nutrition, excretion, and the other bodily functions Aristotle conceives to be controlled by the vegetative. He suggests that it functions best "in sleep" when the conscious aspect of the soul is not in control; but he also points out that the movements of the good and bad, associated normally with the conscious aspect of the soul, may affect the unconscious. Thus the dreams of good men are better than those of ordinary or bad people; for in dreams we reflect to some extent the motions of our waking and conscious life. Like Plato, Aristotle is very aware of the importance of the unconscious elements of human personality.

The appetitively irrational in the soul of man may be thought of as the emotional.

The rational aspect of the soul, by contrast with the irrational, is conscious and deliberate. It is developed to its full potentialities only under purposeful direction and discipline (by contrast with the vegetatively irrational which we may think of as simply "growing," like Topsy). Although the appetitively irrational may be searching naturally for the good, it can be sure only with the assistance of the rational element of the soul; and, as we have seen, the mere inclination of the appetitively irrational to the good can be easily sidetracked unless firmly grounded in rational activity.

If the human soul be thus constituted, Aristotle asks, what is peculiarly "human" about it? What, in other words, does it have potentially which other souls do not possess? His answer is the rational aspect. Man, therefore, in addition to being vegetative and appetitive—characteristics which he shares in some measure with all vegetables and animals—is also rational.

Now if man in this sense is a rational animal, his peculiar telos must be to exercise his rationality to its fullest. Just as it is the function of the eye to see and the ear to hear and the nose to smell and life, in general, to live, so it is the particular natural function of man to contemplate and to act rationally. If happiness is an "activity of the soul," as Aristotle has suggested, then the human soul, as such, will be happy only when it is carrying out its peculiar function—contemplation and rational action—in the highest degree.

It will be noted that throughout his discussion of eudaimonia, Aristotle thinks that it can be achieved only *indirectly* and not directly. It is, as it were, a by-product of the activity of the soul directed to its highest potentialities. Just as the eye is happiest when it is seeing well, so the human soul is happiest when it is exercising its peculiar capabilities—embraced under the term rationality—to the maximum extent.

In this by-product theory of happiness, Aristotle gives classical formulation to a doctrine which will be highly important for the later development of moral and political thought. Happiness, as we may put the doctrine in other terms, is to be sought, not by concentrating consciously on its achievement but rather by pursuing almost at "fever heat" that activity for which we are by nature best qualified. The New Testament saying "Seek ye first the Kingdom of God and all these things will be added to you" comes to mind. The late George Bernard Shaw once put the same principle facetiously: "The only way to avoid being miserable is not to have leisure enough to wonder whether you are happy or not."

If, then, the highest telos for man is rational activity and contemplation, how is it to be attained? What conditions are entailed for the community to be integrated around this peculiar human function, as a by-product of which we may expect happiness?

Many prerequisites are required, most of which, insofar as they involve external organization and arrangements, we shall deal with later.[10] Here, however, it is important to note Aristotle's distinction between intellectual and moral virtue. The former, involving knowing of final causes and first philosophy, is, of course, the objective of human life, insofar as it is characteristically human. Through intellectual virtue we can know things as they are, including the ultimate basis for those matters of conduct which are so essential for the activity of contemplation. We may equate intellectual virtue in Aristotle's thinking with the knowledge of dialectic in Plato's guardians. Intellectual virtue can be taught and, indeed, owes both its "birth" and its "growth," according to Aristotle, to teaching.[11]

Moral virtue (*ethike*), by contrast, cannot be taught directly but is rather the product of right actions developing an habitual mode of conduct (*ethos*). We can never develop moral virtue, in other words, simply by admonition or instruction but only by practicing the kinds of conduct which build into us the patterns that will make right actions easier in the future. *Doing* the right is to be sharply distinguished from merely *knowing* it.

In casting about for a rough guide to the kind of conduct which should be embodied in habit (*ethos*), Aristotle elaborates the doctrine of the "mean." In his formulation, he is, of course, only putting somewhat more exactly the Greek cultural ideal which we have already seen stemming from the Delphic oracle —"nothing in excess." It is the nature of things to be impaired "by defect and excess," he thinks. Both too much exercise and too little, for example, will destroy bodily health; and similarly too much or too little food or drink. In like manner, as a rough principle, we can say that courage is a mean between recklessness and timidity; and meanness and extravagance are the extremes of generosity. The *via media*, he holds, is as close as we can get to any *general* formulation of rules of right conduct or moral virtue.

Obviously, this does not get us too far, as Aristotle himself recognizes. For how can we identify the extremes in any given situation? Every action would seem to be related to every other action and our judgments of right in any given particular might vary enormously. Moreover, judgments of the mean would seem to turn, in some degree at least, on what the likely consequences of given acts might be. How are we to gain some uniformity in all this? Who determines the mean and how the various means shall be related to one another in patterns of conduct?

These are central questions. Aristotle's answer, in general, is that the constitution-maker and ruler must determine the mean. The ruler, too, must use all the devices at his command to see that the principle of the mean is actually embodied in the habits of men and women, so that, for the most part, they themselves will not have to decide—perhaps because they are in part incapable of deciding—what the mean is in any given instance. And the ruler—guided, presumably, by the "political scientist," as Aristotle uses that term—will act through the educator.

Making Men Good. The role of education is thus crucial in Aristotle's scheme of moral and political thought. Here we shall not deal with the specifics of his educational system but rather examine the function of education as related to the establishment of the habits that provide the conditions necessary to attain human eudaimonia.

The moral, social, and civic role of the educator is to train the emotions and impulses of men—the appetitive side of the irrational—in the direction of the good as defined by the legislator and ruler. For the emotions, as we have seen, are in themselves neither good nor bad but are the material cause of what might be *either* good or bad actions. Embedded in the emotions, in other words, are the forms of either good or bad activities. The efficient cause of good actions is the training offered by the educator who seeks to implement or bring into effect the final cause as defined by the legislator. The function of the educator, as Joad points out,[12] is to develop habits which will make good citizens, and, in a good polis, good men. While the soul, if conditions are appropriate, will incline to good action, it has its uncertain moments in which, without strong habit patterns, it will tend to fall away from the good.

It will be noted that throughout, the general formula of the mean is used but that its application differs with each individual. No two circumstances are exactly alike, so that the ruler must not only discover the mean in general but must establish an educational system and environment which so mold each soul that it desires to do what is right and can immediately see how the right applies to each instance. The pattern of the mean is impressed on the soul; but in addition to this, institutions and education are so to conspire that no man will or can go far wrong in applying it to his own particular circumstances. For Aristotle, as A. E. Taylor puts it, "The final aim of education in goodness is to make our immediate judgment as to what is right coincide with the spirit of a wise legislation."[13]

But what is the basis of the rule which identifies the good and which establishes the educational and cultural systems that implement the judgments of the legislator? To answer this question, we must turn to Aristotle's conception of the function and role of the polis in human life.

10. See below, particularly pp. 100–103.
11. *Nicomachean Ethics*, Bk. II, ch. 1.
12. C. E. M. Joad, *Guide to the Philosophy of Morals and Politics*, New York: Random House, 1937, p. 91.
13. A. E. Taylor, *op. cit.*, p. 96.

The Polis and Human Association

Aristotle begins by repeating that every community is established for some good; and therefore the political community, being the highest (that is, most comprehensive) of all, must aim at the highest good. This, of course, he has already said in other connections.

But a problem arises for him when he notes that there are those who assert that the rule in every type of community is the same. They maintain that the relationship between ruler and ruled in the household, for example, is identical with that between the ruler and ruled in the political community. Or they say that the tie between husband and wife is like that between political ruler and political subject.

Aristotle denies the legitimacy of these comparisons and in order to differentiate the political from other relations proceeds to inquire into the origin of political institutions. He discovers the natural origin of society in the union of male and female, for without this combination there could be no society at all. However, the union is not a deliberate one but rather one shared with other animals. Soon after the union of male and female comes that of master and slave; for the former naturally controls the latter to the degree that the slave cannot effectively manage himself. The family is thus born through this combination of two kinds of rule—male over female and master controlling slave. But Aristotle anticipates his later argument by admonishing us not to confuse the two relationships.

Once the family is in existence, it is obvious that it flourishes to provide everyday wants. It is born of a "biological" urge which is undeliberative but implicitly looks forward to an end (supply of everyday wants) of which men become more and more conscious. The family is the basic reflection of man's dependence on man.

But no sooner are elementary wants gained by this combination of the undeliberate and deliberate (or instinctual and conscious) than the family begins to look—first implicitly, then semideliberately—beyond itself to a more inclusive community, the village. Men, by nature (teleologically), strive for self-sufficiency in community and only that community in which they are "self-sufficient" will produce harmony of body, spirit, and human relationships which men are seeking without at first being aware of their search. The final cause is working, then, when villages are established.

But villages obviously do not provide a self-sufficiency, at least at all levels. Here we should note that when Aristotle uses the term self-sufficiency (*autarky*), he refers not merely to what we should call economic goods but also to what he discerns as the implicit tendency in men to wish to specialize in their labors. Hence there is a kind of "pull" present in human beings to establish that community in which each man can find his true or natural level, those who are least characteristically human making it possible for those who are most human to develop the intellectual virtues.

Thus is born the political community out of a union of villages. It is in the political community that man finds it possible both to specialize and at the same time maintain the ties of friendship which bound him together at more primitive levels. Of course, Aristotle would say, not every political community which proclaims itself to be such has in fact attained the true political status. Only when one inquires into what is implicit in the notion of the political—investigates, that is, the nature of the ideal community—can one discover how far any given actual polis is from the true polis. The historical polis—Athens, or Sparta, or Thebes—is in this view always *becoming* but never *is* a polis. Yet all the activities of commerce, family life, male-female relationships, and social intercourse in general are "caused" by the polis.

Or, as Aristotle puts it in a classical expression, "the polis is by nature prior to the family and to the individual, since the whole is of necessity prior to the part."[14] By this he obviously does not mean *chronologically* prior to the part but rather teleologically. Man is so constituted, in other words, that his individual parts (men and women) cannot become characteristically human except in a polis. Without the political community, individuals are, as Aristotle observes, either beasts or gods,[15]—they cannot be men.

Only man lives in a state of indeterminacy, in the sense that although his true nature calls for a given kind of order in the polis, he is capable of falling away from that order. While he shares the vegetative part of the irrational aspect of his soul with the beasts, the appetitive part is capable either of following nature and thus establishing justice in the polis or of going wild and doing things which the beasts are incapable of accomplishing. Man is furnished at birth with "arms," which are meant by nature to be used by intelligence and virtue. Unfortunately, these same arms—the human body and emotions—may also be used for ends which are against nature. In such circumstances—"when separated from law and justice"—man is the "worst of all" animals.[16]

The relation between master and slave is to be differentiated from that between political ruler and subject in that while the slave is simply an instrument of the master, the political subject is not to be regarded as a mere tool of the ruler. To show this, Aristotle examines the contention of those (some of the Sophists, for example, were already suggesting this viewpoint) who allege that slavery is unnatural. On the contrary, argues Aristotle, slavery is natural. Some individuals, while born with the physical bodies of human beings, have souls which are incapable, even potentially, of directing their own actions. Natural slaves share with all human beings, of course, the vegetatively irrational and also the appetitively irrational; but the rational aspect of their souls is capable of developing only to the point where they can recognize a command and obey it. They lack the capacity of giving directions to themselves but instead must be directed by others.

Aristotle makes a careful distinction, of course, between slaves by nature and those who are enslaved by convention. It is not necessarily true, he observes, that because the fortunes of war enslave a man, he is a slave by nature. Aristotle does not suggest what should be done with those who are conventional but not natural slaves, although it is of some interest to note that in his will he directed that his own slaves be freed.

As for the relation between husband and wife, it, too, is to be distinguished from the political tie. Although the man is by nature superior to the woman and therefore rules her, his rulership, unlike that of the political governor, is a permanent one. In the political community, in other words, subjects and rulers may change places, depending upon circumstances and the particular dictates of justice; but in male-female relations the man is more gifted for command and the woman for obedience. This does not mean, however, that the woman is the slave of the man; for she is not by nature the mere instrument of the man but rather his complement. He directs her "constitutionally," Aristotle observes, and not "despotically."

But what of father and children? Here once more Aristotle seeks to give precision to the differentiation from political rule, as well as to show how paternal differs from masterly and husbandly rulership. Children are subject to the rule of a father because the latter, through greater experience by virtue of age, is presumed to be by nature fitted to train them. But it is a temporary relationship, Aristotle emphasizes, and is meant to prepare the children for lives as free men. By contrast with political relations, the subjects never exchange places with the rulers; unlike the situation in husband-wife relations, the connection is temporary.

Like Plato, Aristotle thinks of economic activity as highly significant in any analysis of political relations. Certain ways of obtaining wealth and distributing economic goods will tend to corrupt an otherwise good constitution. By nature, economic activity should be strictly subordinate to the political, for the polis is concerned with the good life as a whole—or, as we should say today, with a multiplicity of values—whereas the economic realm has to do with a single good.

Discussing the acquisition of wealth, he distinguishes between natural and unnatural modes. The natural will include the pastoral occupations, hunting, and agriculture. Hunting Aristotle subdivides into brigandage, fishing, and the pursuit of birds and beasts. He apparently thinks of these occupations as natural because they are direct applications of human labor to the things which the earth spontaneously produces. They supply man's needs and only his needs. They can hardly become ends in themselves.

However, as society increases in complexity, products come to be exchanged through barter. Shoes, for example, begin to have both an "exchange" and a "use" value.[17] At this stage, shoes continue to be made primarily to be used and the exchange of them is still secondary: trade does not become an end. Hence, Aristotle argues, barter, while not strictly speaking natural, is not against nature.

14. Aristotle, *Politics,* Benjamin Jowett, trans., New York Modern Library, 1943, Bk. I, ch. 2.
15. *Ibid.*
16. *Ibid.*
17. *Ibid.*, ch. 9.

The use value of the shoe or the food is kept central. Human need is not forgotten.

But more complex exchange through money is in part unnatural. In a celebrated passage, Aristotle contends that this is true because "there is no bound to the riches which spring from this art of wealth-getting."[18] He appears to think that although there are natural limits on desire when one produces directly or exchanges through barter, the limits tend to be cast away when money and retail trade enter the picture. Man's desires run wild; the accumulation of money becomes an end; and the natural purpose of production—human need—is often forgotten.

Aristotle reserves his most pointed criticism for that form of acquisition which involves the taking of interest. It is unnatural enough for one to make money-getting and exchange ends in themselves, thus pushing aside human need. But when it is assumed that money can have offspring (*tokos*), like cattle, the height of an unnatural situation has been attained. Here the gulf between acquisition as an end and the natural purpose of wealth-getting, which is the supply of human necessities, has become enormous. Aristotle is both bitter and sarcastic in attacking "usury."[19]

Thus the subordination of slave to master, female to male, and child to father are shown to have within them natural elements; although one should also remember, Aristotle reminds us, that there are "conventional" arrangements for subordination—in the institution of slavery, for example—which may have little to do with nature. The acquisition of wealth, too, if confined to grazing, hunting, husbandry, and barter exchange, is not an unnatural aspect of household management; but if it takes the primary form of retail exchange through money or of interest-taking on money, it is clearly against nature.

Households united with other households in villages find themselves completed in the polis, the negative condition for which is the observance of the distinctions between natural and unnatural acts. But while this is the condition without which political community cannot exist, what, more positively, is the constitution (*politeia*) or way of life of the polis itself?

Political Community and Justice

Aristotle attacks many aspects of Plato's conception. Thus, he wonders whether the proposal in the *Republic* for a community of women, children, and property does not provide too much unity. The nature of the state, he contends, is to be a "plurality"—a kind of harmony of diversities. But Plato would, in effect, make it something like a family, or even an individual. The nature of the state is not to be as integrated as either the family or the individual. In attacking Plato at this point, Aristotle seems to be forgetting, as W. D. Ross argues,[20] that the author of the *Republic* was quite aware of the problem of diversity versus unity. Indeed, Plato had made elaborate provision for "plurality" in his threefold division of the society.

But even if unity be natural, Aristotle goes on, it is doubtful whether Plato is providing it. It takes more than a formal decree abolishing family life and private property to provide a sense of oneness. Love will be "watery" in a state having women and children in common;[21] for one cannot extend common possession to large numbers and expect the same intensity of feeling which one has in the private family. Moreover, what is everybody's business is nobody's business—"that which is common to the greatest number has the least care bestowed upon it."[22]

With respect to private property, Aristotle develops what we should expect of him, considering his discussion of economic society and his criticism of Plato. Property is natural in the sense that love of self is natural; and a certain amount of material goods is essential to provide for the legitimate ends of the self. The human personality obtains a modicum of innocent pleasure in possessing goods. True, selfishness is rightly censured; but selfishness should be distinguished from the natural love of self—it is rather an excess love of the self. Moreover, all men have a natural tendency to wish to be kind and of service to their fellows. How can this end of generosity and kindness be served without the private possession of material goods?

Nature thus requires private property, he concludes, but its use should be common. That is to say, material goods should, for the most part, be distributed privately; but each person ought through the right system of education to be encouraged to use the goods for community ends.

But the examination of property relations immediately leads us to ask, What is Aristotle's notion of ideal justice? Negatively he has already told us much—that property, slavery, and certain kinds of wealth-acquisition are not unnatural. More positively, indeed, he has rather vehemently defended the natural character of private property against those, like Plato, who would destroy it.

Justice, of course, has to do with human relations in general. It is complete virtue—"not absolutely, but in relation to our neighbor."[23] The social character of virtue, therefore, is what Aristotle calls "universal" justice—or lawfulness. But this universal justice is reflected in what he terms "particular" justice, which he attempts to analyze in its ideal sense. Particular justice is divided into two kinds—that which is concerned with the distribution of "honor or money or safety" and that which is "rectificatory" or remedial.

Distributive justice is one of Aristotle's classical notions. By it he means that offices and wealth ought to be distributed, not in accorddance with "arithmetic" but rather with "geometric" proportion. In other words it is just to distribute offices or wealth in accordance with the merits of the persons involved.

But what do we mean by merit? Here Aristotle points out that our definitions vary in accordance with the spirit of the constitution. Thus in an oligarchy, merit is graded in accordance with wealth. In an aristocracy, by definition, it is measured in relationship to virtue.

Now Aristotle maintains that in a true polis, distributive justice would have virtue as its standard of merit. Those of greatest virtue would control the key offices, while those possessing lesser degrees would be awarded the lower ones. And apparently the same principle would apply in distribution of other honors and of wealth. For the virtuous soul can be expected to keep both economic goods and the goods of honor in a subordinate position; while he who is of lesser virtue may be expected to waver in the ability to administer goods and honors in accordance with the chief end of man.

By contrast, rectificatory or remedial justice —that which is meted out by the judge—is according to the standard of arithmetical proportion. That is to say, in matters of contracts or torts, or even criminal law, we ought not to ask what the merits of a person may be but rather treat all persons as if they were of equal merit.

Almost as an afterthought, Aristotle suggests yet another sense in which justice can be used. For he speaks of the exchange of goods and the pressure of supply and demand (as expressed in money values) as working out a kind of rough justice in the commercial realm. But in this sense justice is not a virtue but a type of stabilizer. We can almost see here a foreshadowing of Adam Smith's "invisible hand" doctrine.

While Aristotle is confused and ambiguous at many points, there is little doubt that the Form (to use Plato's expression) of his polis is a monarchy or at least an aristocracy. If we can find, he suggests, "some one person, or more than one, although not enough to make up the full complement of a state, whose virtue is so pre-eminent that the virtues or the political capacity of all the rest admit of no comparison with his or theirs,"[24] we should "joyfully obey" such a ruler or rulers. In a situation of this type the aristocratic ideal of distributive justice according to virtue would rule supreme. We should have a state not unlike Plato's in the *Republic*, one "laid up in heaven."

Aristotle never draws out the implications of his ideal polis to any great extent. He does suggest that it must not be too large—a herald should be able to be heard by all the citizens at once. On the other hand, it should not be too small to lack self-sufficiency—since this, as we have seen, is a characteristic of the polis-end to which all other communities point. There should be some communication with the sea. The citizens will be men combining a high degree of intelligence with spirit.

The citizen body will alternate as rulers and subjects, by which he apparently means that when out of office they will engage, as leisured gentlemen, in contemplation and the pursuit of knowledge as an end. When called to office, they will reluctantly, like Plato's guardians, assume the burdens of administration and adjudication. They will differ from the guardians chiefly in the fact that they will possess sub-

18. *Ibid.*
19. The reader will recall the similar attack of Hebrew thinkers. See particularly Deuteronomy 8:17–19. See also Chapter 1 of this volume.
20. W. D. Ross, *Aristotle*, London: Methuen, 1949, p. 244.
21. *Politics*, Bk. II, ch. 4.
22. *Ibid.*, ch. 3.
23. *Nicomachean Ethics*, Bk. V., ch. 1.
24. *Politics*, Bk. III, ch. 13.

stantial private estates and have their own families. Of course, women will occupy a subsidiary position from the time they marry, at eighteen, until their death.

Although Aristotle places a central emphasis on education, deeming it crucial for both soul and polis, his discussion of it in the ideal state is a sketchy and incomplete one.[25] As in Athens and Sparta historically, deformed children will be exposed to die; while couples who have too many children already will be encouraged to have abortions.

In Aristotle's conception of citizen education we have an excellent reflection, not only of his own view, but also of the doctrine characteristic of educated Greeks as a whole. The objective of education is primarily to prepare the citizen for leisure (*scholē*); and leisure is the purpose for which an occupation (*ascholia* —"absence of leisure") is performed. Actually, the citizens of Aristotle's ideal polis, confiding most of their land-holding responsibilities to deputies, will have little else but leisure. But with this leisure will go the obligation of ruling and the equally great responsibility for pursuing the arts and sciences as ends.

Constitutions and Political Diseases

Even less than Plato with respect to the achievement of his Form of the State and Justice does Aristotle believe that the attainment of his own ideal is probable. Present in any given historical politics are not only the final causes tending to shape things for the good but also factors (ignorance, passion, and the inertia of institutions) which cloud the working out of those causes. The attainment of any good tends to be partial; and there are always but few if any men of outstanding virtue. Means—money, acquisition of wealth, entertainment—are forever becoming ends.

In view of these complex probabilities, then, Aristotle's chief attention is directed not to the sketching out of ideal justice and community but rather to the discovery of that political pattern which will maximize justice while at the same time it provides a certain stability. What are the factors which tend to pull men and institutions away from the ideally just and would it be possible, by recognizing them, to limit and control their effect? These are the questions which Aristotle asks himself.

To answer them, he makes his celebrated inquiries into the actual constitutions of states and the causes for change in constitutions. A constitution (*politeia*) is for him—as for the Greek political mind—the way of life of the polis. It embraces such matters as the manner in which honors and wealth are distributed, the spirit of the community, and the definition of merit embodied in a culture. One gets at such matters, he holds, by examining in some detail the history of a given polis. Really to know the constitution of Corinth, for example, one must be familiar with its evolution, its economy, its legal system, its religion, and its attitude to life as reflected in its literary productions.

The significance of the 158 constitutions which Aristotle and his students examined and described lies in the fact that they furnished the raw material for the generalizations of his political theory. His statements dealing with the "pathology" of states, for example, are based on this minute inquiry. In doing all this, of course, he is simply carrying on the tradition established by Plato in the *Laws*, for the *Laws* is based upon as much careful empirical study as Aristotle's *Politics*.

Aristotle builds on Plato's classification of constitutions in the *Statesman*. The key to any constitutional system, he thinks, is to be found in asking where the ultimate seat of authority lies: This will both shape and be a general reflection of the culture as a whole. "True" governments are those, he maintains, which, generally speaking, have primary concern for the general or public interest; distorted or deviant governments are those whose principles are designed chiefly to advance the interest of their respective ruling classes. In each of the true and deviant forms, merit, in the system of distributive justice, will be defined in a characteristic way.

The first of the true forms is kingly, or rule by the one. As we have seen, Aristotle thinks that it is conceivable that one man will so excel all others in virtue that he will obviously be the one whom all should obey. Moreover, by reason of his very virtue, he can stand outside the law and be a kind of single guardian. Here the public interest would be safeguarded without law. But in historical monarchies, he points out, the public interest is best secured through a system of rules which lies outside the king—law presumably laid down by the legislator, who set the city in motion, as it were. Although law is a clumsy expedient from the viewpoint of exact equity (*epieikeia*), since it seeks classifications which cannot possibly fit every case, it is on the whole better to rule through law—given the probable absence of a man of supreme virtue—than to risk giving political power to a single man without the law.

Actually, according to Aristotle, monarchies tend to fade into aristocracies, which represent the second true form of rule. In practice, it is never possible for a king to dispense with the services of other well-equipped persons; and "what difference does it make whether these subordinates always existed or were appointed by him because he needed them?"[26] When the few well-equipped rule for the public interest, through law—and the public interest historically can be attained only through law, which is "reason unaffected by desire"—one has an aristocracy.

The third form of true rule Aristotle calls "polity." Since he uses the same word for the third type of unperverted rule as he employs for "constitution" in general (*politeia*), there is necessarily a certain amount of confusion in his discussion. For at times polity means the generic constitution, while at other times it refers to the specific polity. In its specific sense, polity means a kind of mixed rule, in which the claims of the many and the propertied are blended under law. Because Aristotle thinks of this kind of constitution as the best possible under probable historical circumstances, we shall reserve a more detailed discussion of it for the following section.

Meanwhile, let us now turn to his examination of perverted constitutions. The first is *tyranny*, which in its most typical form is the "counterpart of the perfect monarchy." He defines tyranny as "just that arbitrary power of an individual which is responsible to no one, and governs all alike, whether equals or better, with a view to its own advantage, not to that of its subjects, and therefore against their will."[27]

When aristocracy is perverted it becomes an *oligarchy*—that is to say, rule in their own interests by the few who are rich. In an oligarchy, as we have noted, the standard of merit comes to be wealth alone; and distributive justice, therefore, is informed by this criterion.[28]

The third perverted type is *democracy*. Aristotle rejects any definition which would identify democracy simply with that constitution in which the "greater number" are sovereign. He suggests that in oligarchies, as indeed in all governments, "the majority rules." This is a rather enigmatic statement, but apparently he means that the majority must at least acquiesce if any kind of rule is to be effective; and a given rule consists of the standards and the spirit which are determined by the particular form of government, whether of the best or of the wealthy.

We should not, he goes on, call a city in which a thousand rich men rule three hundred poor men a democracy. Nor would we say that a few poor ruling the wealthy many could be termed an "oligarchy." At this point, he suggests that a democracy is the form of constitution in which all the free are rulers and an oligarchy one in which the rich control; "for it is only an accident that the free are the many and the rich are the few."[29]

Yet Aristotle is not satisfied by the criteria of wealth and freedom. Suppose, he asks, that one finds a society in which the freemen are few in number and yet rule over the many who are not free, as at Apollonia or in Thera. Would this be a democracy? Or is it a democracy where the rich, simply because they constitute the larger number, possess the government?

He finally settles for a definition that combines quantitative with qualitative criteria, but even then, as other parts of his analysis show, he is dissatisfied with it. "The form of government," he suggests, "is a democracy when the free, who are also poor and the majority, govern, and an oligarchy when the rich and the noble govern, they being at the same time few in number."

On the whole, Aristotle thinks that democracy is the "least bad" of the perverted forms, just as tyranny is the worst of the three. In defending this position, he develops an argument which is one of the most famous in the history of political thought. The "many," he thinks "when they meet together may very

25. Aristotle's disquisition on ideal education will be found in Books VII and VIII of *Politics*. See also Harold Cherniss, *Aristotle's Criticism of Plato and the Academy*, New York: Russell and Russell, 1962; Thomas Davidson, *Aristotle and Ancient Educational Ideals*, New York: Scribners, 1892; and William Frankena, *Three Historical Philosophies of Education*, Chicago: Scott, Foresman, 1965.
26. *Politics*, Bk. III, ch. 17.
27. *Ibid.*, Bk. IV, ch. 10.
28. *Ibid.*, ch. 5.
29. *Ibid.*, ch. 4.

likely be better than the few good, if regarded not individually but collectively, just as a feast to which many contribute is better than a dinner provided out of a single purse."[30] This may be so because each individual, however poor or dishonest, brings to the meeting some little virtue, prudence, and experience. When the total virtues and experience of the many are brought together in the assembly, the compound produced is likely to be greater than the goodness of a single individual or of a small group. The many can thus be better judges, not only of policy, but even of "music and poetry." "Some understand one part, and some another, and among them they understand the whole."

This is, of course, an astonishing doctrine coming from one who, by and large, distrusted the demos. But we should remember that the theory itself was foreshadowed in Plato's *Laws*, albeit implicitly. We should also note the qualifications which Aristotle introduces. He is not sure, in the first place, that "this principle can apply to every democracy, and to all bodies of men." He makes it clear, secondly, that he distinguishes between judgment of policy and the holding of executive office. In the latter capacity the individual's lack of virtue and incompetence could easily show up and militate against good conduct. Moreover, he asks whether it does not take a good physician to judge another physician, a good geometrician to pass on the merits of another, and so on. Is not the function of judging magistrates, which democracy assigns to the assembly, analogous to the problem of evaluating the work of a scientist?

Aristotle attempts to answer these latter questions by suggesting that there are some arts whose products are not best judged by the artists themselves. He instances the building of a house, for example. Although the builder has some capacity to judge of its merits, the user of the house is an even better judge. The pilot who actually utilizes the rudder of a ship, too, will be better able to pass on its usefulness than the carpenter who constructed it; and "the guest will judge better of a feast than the cook."

The democrat argues, with some plausibility, that the relation between policy validation—*to kyrion*, as the Greeks put it—and policy proposal, is like that between guest and cook.

Presently we shall return to these arguments. Now, however, let us turn more explicitly to an examination of the constitution which he believes is the closest approximation to the ideal attainable within historical reality.

The Polity as Relatively Ideal

It is highly characteristic of Aristotle that his third of the three true forms of government should be a combination of two perversions. For he makes the polity, in his specific usage of the term, a blending of oligarchic and democratic elements. Although Aristotle's exact position is often, here as elsewhere, a confusing one, his general reasoning would seem to run roughly as follows. All historical forms of government, whether in the true category or in the perverted, "fall short of the most perfect form."[31] Hence the true are themselves perversions of the ideal and the perversions are perversions of perversions. When we say, therefore, that a polity or constitutional government is a union of perversions, it is not too startling.

Since Aristotle has argued for the natural character of property, he could not very well contend that it would be possible or desirable to attain the elimination of rich men. A wealthy class is inevitable, he thinks. So also is a group of relatively poor citizens. The hope for political stability lies in the enlargement of that group in the population which is neither wealthy nor extremely poor. With this group large, it would sit in the assembly along with poorer and richer elements and the blending of viewpoints would result in the best achieveable constitution. The wealthy elements could not control the act of final validation, nor could the very poor create disorder by attempting the in the long-run impossible task of destroying the wealthy. At the same time, the large middle group would, in terms of political decisions, reflect the mean of Aristotle's ethical goal.

He points out, too, that the problem of political community in the realm of historical possibility is not merely one of discovering good laws but also one of getting the laws obeyed. Given an ideal polis, of course, the right could and would be determined by those of supreme intellectual virtue, those of lesser virtue fitting into the organic whole without difficulty. The problem of obedience would conceivably not exist. But granted the probable absence of a distinctly superior group and the fact that those who possess wealth are not necessarily the ones who have intellectual virtue (they have the leisure but may not possess the souls which equip them for the task), the problem both of discovering relatively good laws and of getting relatively widespread obedience is ever-present. It would seem, then, that, in relation to the possibilities, some participation of all in political life is desirable and that choice of the Council and magistrates should combine the principle of selection through lot (democratic) with election (aristocratic-oligarchic).

There are various ways of combining the oligarchic with the democratic. He points out that in those constitutions which tend to be oligarchic, the rich are fined if they do not serve as judges and the poor are given no pay, whereas in democratic constitutions the poor are paid and the rich are not fined. Perhaps some combination can be found in which the poor are given moderate pay while at the same time the rich are fined. Or a mean may be discovered between the enactments of oligarchy and democracy—thus democracies require no property qualification or only a small one for membership in the assembly; oligarchies require a high one. Would it not be possible to have a property qualification higher than that of democracies but lower than that of most oligarchies? This would allow the middle group to dominate the Ecclesia.

The point of this whole discussion is, of course, that there are many ways of blending the two elements. Aristotle is simply suggesting some of the possibilities. Throughout, however, he hopes to combine lot, election, property qualifications, and relative merit in such a mosaic that the best possible policies will be formulated (keeping the ethical ideal of the mean in mind) and probably obeyed. The argument in favor of the democratic theory of validation is balanced by recognition of an inevitable differentiation in wealth.

Professor W. D. Ross[32] thinks that if Aristotle had any historical model in mind for the polity, it was the form of government drafted in 411 B.C. at the time of the temporary eclipse of the democracy. One of the authors of the 411 arrangements was Theramenes, whom the philosopher admired very much; and the combination of democratic and oligarchic elements (members of the Ecclesia were not to be paid, for example) reminds one of Aristotle's theoretical discussion.

However, it is not necessary that we seek a particular model for the arrangements proposed by Aristotle. The polity reflects a kind of condensation of his practical political wis-

dom. Much of its basis is to be found in Plato's *Statesman* and *Laws;* and no doubt many of the constitutions so assiduously examined by Aristotle and his students approached, if they did not exactly attain, the ideal of the polity. In its balance, caution, and absence of any adventurous spirit, the polity is almost a perfect epitome of Aristotle's ethical-political position.

The Dynamics of Politics

One of the most celebrated aspects of Aristotle's political theory is his explanation of revolution and change.

Broadly speaking, he inquires first of all into the theory of change and revolution in general. Then he examines the matter with respect to particular constitutions. Finally, he asks himself how violent changes, or revolutions, can be averted. Throughout his discussion, one of his leading values is stability; for while he is under no illusion that things can remain what they have always been, he seems to assume that the pace of change can be controlled and kept within definite limits.

As for revolutions and change in general, he thinks that democracy arises out of the "notion that those who are equal in any respect are equal in all respects; because men are equally free, they claim to be absolutely equal." Oligarchy, by contrast, is established on the belief that those who are unequal in one respect "are in all respects unequal; being unequal, that is, in property, they suppose themselves to be unequal absolutely."[33] Of course, both democracy and oligarchy, although they possess a "kind of justice," fall far short of any absolute standard. Because of this, the demos in an oligarchy and the oligarchs in a democracy will tend always, other things being equal, to be moving in a revolutionary direction. For in each case, there will be some merit in the contention that the constitution, not reflecting absolute justice, needs correction.

Aristotle believes that the basic cause of revo-

30. *Ibid.*, Bk. III, ch. 11.
31. *Ibid.*, Bk. IV, ch. 8.
32. W. D. Ross, *op. cit.*, p. 259. See also Aristotle's *Constitution of Athens*, ch. 29 and 30.
33. *Politics*, Bk. V, ch. 1.

lutionary feeling is the desire for equality. Men think that they are the equals of those who have more than themselves and seek revolution to implement their desires. Or, feeling themselves superior, they seek to overturn a situation in which that superiority is not recognized. "Inferiors revolt in order that they may be equal, and equals that they may be superior."[34]

But there are many other causes of the revolutionary spirit. Insolence and avarice may be involved, for magistrates who develop an insolent outlook conspire against their colleagues and against the constitution.

Fear, too, may play a vital role. Men who have committed wrong fear punishment and seek revolution in order to avoid the retribution. Or they fear that they may suffer injustice in the future and lead a faction which will prevent what they fear. Oligarchs fear the disorder and anarchy which tend to become uppermost in democracies.

A disproportionate increase in any part of the state, too, may lead to fundamental change. In Tarentum, Aristotle points out, a large number of the oligarchs were slain in battle just after the Persian wars; and this so reduced the "notables" element in the state that what had hitherto approached a polity became a democracy. In Athens, too, the city became more democratic after many citizens of leading families had died in the Peloponnesian wars.

Even apparent trifles may be highly significant when they affect rulers; for they may produce divisions and it is fissions in the ruling class which frequently initiate revolution. He cites the example of Syracuse, whose constitution was once changed because of a homosexual love dispute.

Another very vital cause of revolution is the polarization of the state into rich and poor classes. When the middle class is squeezed out and rich and poor seem to be about equal in strength (the poor in terms of numbers, the rich in economic power), civil war and revolution are usually close at hand. If either the rich or the poor were obviously superior, of course, the other faction would not dare to attack. It is when they are substantially equal that the student of politics can almost always predict disturbances and some vital change.

The methods of revolution, according to the philosopher, are either force or fraud. Force may be applied at the time of the revolution itself or later after it has been successful. Fraud, he thinks, is of two kinds: The citizenry may be deceived into acquiescing in a change, afterwards being dominated against their will (as in the manipulations of the Four Hundred in 411); or, on the other hand, the people may be swayed by a constant repetition of slogans. It might be observed in passing that Aristotle's categories would seem to fit nicely such modern coups d'états and revolutions as those of Napoleon III, Adolf Hitler, and Benito Mussolini. Clearly, he is anticipating or even stating the role of what modern political thinkers call propaganda.

As for the analysis of revolution under particular constitutions, Aristotle discerns the root cause of change under democracy to be the activities of demagogues. Typically, the demagogue attacks the rich, thus compelling the latter to combine and hence destroy the democratic constitution. In early history, the demagogue was also a military man and out of this combination rose the military tyrant who came to dominate what was hitherto a democratic society.

Revolutions in oligarchies, Aristotle contends, arise if and when the oligarchs impose almost unlimited exactions on the people, of which there are many historical examples. Then, too, there may be personal rivalries between and among the oligarchs themselves. This opens a breach in the ruling class, the rival oligarchs often becoming demagogues and seeking alliances with the people. But the support of the demos, of course, comes high; for it will often lead to a complete overthrow of the oligarchy itself.

In politics and aristocracies, radical changes are often brought about because there is a deviation from justice. There may be, for example, a bad mingling of democratic and oligarchic elements in the polity; and in the aristocracy, the blending of democracy, oligarchy, and virtue may be at fault.

As for the means of preserving constitutions, Aristotle thinks that the most important is the development of respect for law even in seemingly trivial matters. Small breaches of the law lead insidiously to larger ones, just as large fortunes are dissipated by seemingly slight expenditures. The ruler should discover ways of dramatizing the dangers of revolution, which are ever near even when they seem to be remote.

Of equally great importance is the principle that officials of the polis should not be allowed to make money out of their offices. Thus there should always be a careful accounting and auditing of expenditures. In oligarchies, for example, the people often do not resent not participating in the affairs of the state; but they do object violently if they think the rulers are stealing money which ought to belong to the public. Hence, if oligarchic rulers wish to remain in power, they should do everything possible to show that they are not stealing.

In a democracy, the assembly must take particular care not to despoil the rich. For nothing can unite a class more completely, politically speaking, than a concerted attack on its possessions. On the other hand, democratic polities ought to prevent the rich from giving "choruses, torch-races, and the like"; for Aristotle thinks, not without reason on the basis of historical experience, that such expenditures could easily corrupt the demos and open the way to an oligarchy.

It is in his characterization of the ways by which tyrants can preserve themselves that Aristotle perhaps exhibits most acutely his vast historical and political knowledge. The tyrant should "lop off" all those who are "too high" and he must not hesitate to execute all men of spirit. He must be suspicious of any activities which bring men together in clubs or which cause them to develop common meals or educational curricula. He has to keep an eye out for anything which might lead his people to become courageous or to develop self-confidence. It is very important, too, that he prohibit discussion groups, literary activities, or any close association among his subjects which might promote mutual confidence; for so soon as men are no longer divided from one another by mutual suspicion, the basis of tyrannical rule is challenged. Furthermore, the tyrant must develop a good system of spies, perhaps like the "female detectives" who existed at Syracuse.

It is vital, too, thinks Aristotle, that the tyrannical ruler engender discord among his subjects. Every method must be used to break up incipient friendships, for example. Rich men living under a tyranny ought to be kept in perpetual feuds with one another, lest they unite to oppose the tyrant. The poor should be kept hard at work so that they will find no time for conspiracy; and Aristotle thinks that the construction of the pyramids of Egypt illustrates very well how a tyrant can keep men busy.

Throughout, Aristotle holds, the tyrant should *appear* to be as much like a king as possible, while eschewing the reality of kingly rule where necessary. He should be careful, for instance, not to expend revenues publicly on such items as high-class courtesans or artists; for this might arouse a public spirit among the citizenry. Of course, it is perfectly appropriate for him to use the monies privately, provided the fact is not noised abroad.

To carry on his appearance of being a truly royal ruler, he must erect great public works which will be admired by the populace. No one, moreover, should excel the tyrant in his public homage to the gods and in his observance of all religious rites. These public religious ceremonies tend to lead the public to believe that the tyrant cannot be unjust (even though many of his acts seem to be so).

Throughout Aristotle's discussion of political change and revolution, there is nothing to lead one to believe that he has anything resembling a doctrine of what the modern world calls progress. While his analysis is based on a vast knowledge of Greek political history, he apparently sees no "pattern" in that history which is moving either in the direction of a long-lasting polity or of an ideal "rule of the best."

Aristotle's Significance

Both in terms of his general philosophy and in terms of his political theory, Aristotle has been the center of controversy. Each generation has seen him in a somewhat different light depending upon the state of its science and the problems with which it has been confronted. In the twentieth century, after a long period of revolt against his influence, Aristotelian ways of thinking have had a revival which still persists.

In assessing his over-all place in the history of political thought, as well as his role as a thinker whose political doctrine still lives, it is not possible to divorce his political theory entirely from other aspects of his philosophy. Nor can we within a relatively brief compass deal with all the issues which any assessment involves.

Aristotle versus Plato? In both ancient and modern times, many scholars have tended to

34. *Ibid.*, ch. 2.

draw sharp contrasts between either the method or the substance of Aristotle as compared with Plato. Aristotle himself, as we have noted, often seems to think of his doctrine as sharply distinguished from that of his teacher. In our own day, such historians of science as George Sarton[35] and such teachers of political philosophy as Warner Fite[36] have sought to draw out the points of difference. On the other hand, scholars like A. E. Taylor[37] have tended to minimize the alleged contrasts, at least of method.

As is so often true of controversies of this kind, there would seem to be a measure of validity in each contention. Those who make the gulf between the two thinkers a wide one are, of course, right in suggesting that Aristotle throughout his whole career paid much more attention to detailed and careful observation of particulars than did Plato. In what we should today call biology, for example, he was so meticulous that he won high praise from such modern scientists as Charles Darwin. So, too, in morals and politics, he tends to provide much more explicit documentation for his statements of "fact" than does Plato.

But it is very easy to exaggerate the differences in approach between Plato and Aristotle and here those scholars who tend to narrow the gulf between the two thinkers have much to support their contentions. As Taylor has pointed out,[38] while Aristotle begins by denouncing Plato's theory that ideas transcend sense experience, "his final conclusions on all points of importance are hardly distinguishable from those of Plato, except by the fact that, as they are so much at variance with the naturalistic side of his philosophy, they have the appearance of being sudden lapses into an alogical mysticism." And Taylor goes on: "He is everywhere a Platonist *malgre lui*, and it is just the Platonic element in his thought to which it owes its hold over men's minds."[39]

But it is not only in method and approach that the two men are in close alliance. Their substantive analysis of moral-political issues is very similar, despite a certain difference in emphasis. Both see ethics and politics as inseparable. Hence they are to be pursued as one study. When Aristotle suggests that political science is the master study among the subjects of practical philosophy, he echoes Plato in somewhat different terms. Both think that it is impossible to give a complete account of morals and politics without resort to teleological explanations; although Aristotle elaborates the meaning of the conception more fully than either Plato or Socrates. Both have approximately the same notion of what the ideal polis would be, although Aristotle, because of the difference in his emphasis, gives us a less complete picture. Then, too, Aristotle's account of the soul vis à vis the polis parallels the Platonic version.

The similarity between Plato and Aristotle is evident, too, in what we might call their common prejudices, although here Plato managed to be less culture-bound than his student. Both seemingly accepted as significant the distinction between "Hellene" and "barbarian."[40] Both, living in the twilight of the city-state as an institution, clung to the polis as the teleologically natural expression of man's social characteristics.

In some respects, Aristotle was less able than Plato to transcend certain culturally circumscribed views. Thus he assumed, without any real endeavor to defend, the so-called inferiority of women, whereas Plato boldly and vigorously attacked the commonly accepted judgments of Athenian society. With respect to sex relations in general, as a matter of fact, Plato was far less circumscribed in his views than Aristotle, tolerating many forms of sexual deviation which the later philosopher rigidly excluded.

As for the vital question of property, the distinction between Plato and Aristotle is equally marked. While neither accepted contemporary property relations without serious reflection and criticism, the "natural" for Plato differed from that of Aristotle in that the former saw a distinction depending on the nature of the particular soul, while the latter discerned a common human nature. Souls capable of truly rational governance, according to Plato, had the capacity to emancipate themselves from particular property entanglements, whatever might be true of souls incapable of fully human achievements. For Aristotle, on the other hand, all souls were alike in requiring private possession of material goods for the expression of their souls—all souls, that is, except (presumably) natural slaves.

What Is Living and What Is Dead in Aristotle? From the viewpoint of any analytical and critical student, it is always important to ask whether a given approach to politics is of interest simply to the antiquarian or historian of ideas or whether, in addition, the system of thought has something to offer to students of any generation. This question is eminently appropriate in the case of Aristotle, for no man in any generation has aspired to do so much; nor has any thinker ever conceived his own scheme in terms of such finality.

There are several respects in which the theory of Aristotle gives us hypotheses or offers perspectives which, while they have been questioned in subsequent generations, are still alive in the sense that they offer useful points of departure for investigation and frameworks within which significant questions can be asked:

(1) While teleology tended to become passé with the repudiation of Aristotle's scientific conceptions in early modern times and down to our own age, many are once more asking whether Aristotle's teleological mode of explanation is not particularly appropriate in accounting for human actions. Can one really explain human society without resort to the notion of an implicit purpose or purposes which it is seeking to fulfill?

The same question may be asked about personality. Is it not the type of whole which is more than the sum total of its parts? Can one really dispense with final causation, relying merely on material and efficient causation?

(2) Connected with teleology is, of course, the notion that norms for both public and private conduct can be discovered rationally. Aristotle, together with Plato, becomes a founder of what later is called "natural law." After a long history, this notion came under highly critical scrutiny in early modern times, and, under the attacks of men like Hobbes, Hume, and Kant, tended to fade in the nineteenth century. In our day, however, we are asking again whether there is not, in one sense, such a body of norms as natural law implied which can be discovered by rational inquiry into human nature.[41]

(3) For political scientists, Aristotle's conception of a constitution as the pattern of life of a people, as well as its formal system for distribution of offices and honors, is of inestimable value in getting at the spirit of institutions. A better clue to the actual functioning of governance, he tells us, can be gained by studying the class structure of a people than by elaborate examinations of its legal system in the abstract. No one has emphasized more than Aristotle what would seem to be cardinal in any empirical account of politics—that the

investigator should know the psychology, sociology, family structure, and economy of a people before venturing to pronounce on the tendencies of its politics.

(4) Aristotle, like Plato, placed much emphasis, as we have seen, on the notion that a healthy city is a just one. The parallel between sociopolitical health and personal health, both physical and mental, is a central theme in Aristotle's political analysis. Here again, eighteenth and nineteenth centuries tended to discard any such proposition, at least as Aristotle formulated it. But in the twentieth century we are not so sure. Will the constitution of a people (in Aristotle's sense) in part determine whether they are mentally healthy or not? Aristotle's "organic" account of the interdependence of individual and corporate health tends to take on new meaning in an age when one out of every two beds in American hospitals is occupied by a mental patient. Can one, in other words, isolate the individual's well-being and integration from the well-being, justice, and integration of the society?

(5) His brief treatment of the argument for democracy in Book III of the *Politics* is still one of the classic statements. And the analogy he draws between aesthetic and political judgments remains a living challenge: certainly, it is difficult to refute it.

(6) His drawing out of the meaning and implications of citizenship helped delineate more sharply a conception which Plato left rather vague. Aristotle endeavored to show how citizenship was to be differentiated from

35. George Sarton, *History of Science: Ancient Science Through the Golden Age of Greece*, New York: Wiley, 1964.
36 Warner Fite, *The Platonic Legend*, New York: Scribner's, 1934.
37. A. E. Taylor, *op. cit.*
38. *Ibid.*, p. 30.
39. *Ibid.*, pp. 30–31.
40. Although here one should be careful. Plato is critical of the distinction in the *Statesman*, insofar as there is any implication that "barbarians" are a single unit with no divisions.
41. Here the works of Erich Fromm might be cited, particularly *The Sane Society*, New York: Holt, Rinehart and Winston, 1955. See also Lawrence K. Frank, *Society as the Patient*, New Brunswick: Rutgers University Press, 1948, for another modern example.

mere subjection to political rule—the citizen helped shape that rule—and from other social relations.

Of equal importance was his distinction between the "good citizen" and the "good man." Only in the ideal polis was there no conflict between the two, since the demands of citizenship in it would not run counter to the requirements of individual righteousness. Below this level, however, the requirements of good citizenship might well be in tension with those for good men. For if one of the demands of the former was cheerful obedience of the laws and values of the polis and if the polis happened to be an oligarchy, there would obviously be a conflict between true righteousness (as defined by Aristotle) and the imperatives of a constitution emphasizing the (false) values associated with acquisition of wealth as an end.

For Aristotle, of course, the conflict could exist only for the relatively small number of men who might possess intellectual virtue—the many had to be content with good citizenship and could only hope that the political order itself was good. But the problem itself was and is an important and perennial one, even though Aristotle was not very helpful in telling the good man living in a bad polis what his obligations might be.

(7) Modern "liberal" critics have often attacked Aristotle for his economic and social views. He was a "reactionary," it has been said, and his suspicion of commerce, money, and economic forces generally represented simply a defensive ideology of the land-owning classes.

But Aristotle, like Plato (in Book II of the *Republic*), saw that economic forces, if left to themselves, tend to be blind. Beyond a certain stage of complexity in division of labor, money values tend to obscure human values and mere technique often becomes an end in itself. Thus in highly industrialized societies, complex technology frequently sets the pace: men must adjust to it rather than requiring it to adjust to them. When economic considerations are allowed to reign supreme, human beings—who by nature are more than merely economic animals—are prevented from attaining their true *telos*. Aristotle understood all this and his subordination of economic life to the political realm was an effort to ensure that noneconomic values remained uppermost.

Even Aristotle's theory of natural slavery may have a certain viability. Modern liberals and socialists explain the general passivity and slavishness of many men in terms of lack of education, leisure, and adequate material income. But after a hundred years of increasing leisure, magnified incomes, widespread education, and extended suffrage in the industrialized nations, can it be said that active participation in public affairs has really increased greatly? If the answer is negative, then Aristotle's doctrine of natural slavery can hardly be dismissed out of hand.

(8) Finally, for modern political scientists, Aristotle's word of caution about the limitations of practical science and philosophy would seem to be badly needed. Too often do modern political scientists forget that theirs is not a theoretical or speculative study, in Aristotle's sense of the term. To be sure, they may expect to become more and more exact by using the controlled experimental method—a method which neither Plato nor Aristotle suggested—but they pay the price, in the process, of getting exactitude in minute segments of life without telling us how we can add up—at least "scientifically"—the segments for purposes of policy-making.

Aristotle's Impact on Ancient Political Thought. Returning to the evolution of political theory, it is now appropriate to ask what impact Aristotle had on ancient moral-political speculation and events.

In terms of affecting the actual course of political events it is doubtful if his grand system had much influence. Although he undoubtedly intended that his *Politics* should be primarily a handbook for statesmen, telling them what to avoid as well as what to encourage, few statesmen seem to have followed its advice. Alexander the Great, while not familiar with the *Politics* itself, was surely acquainted with the general moral and political outlook of his former teacher. Yet, as we have seen, the gulf between him and Aristotle grew steadily until, in the end, Alexander was on the verge of arresting Aristotle for countenancing sedition.

Nor were most other statesmen very much affected by either the *Politics* or the *Ethics.* The counsels of moderation offered in the latter, as well as the legal and policy judgments of the former, fell on deaf ears.

But while his teaching was not an efficient cause for making politicians into men of wisdom, it was profoundly influential in the world of thought itself. His school, the Lyceum, continued to carry on his political studies. His classification of constitutions was taken up and developed by later ancient thinkers, some of whom undoubtedly sought to apply it to the empire-form which succeeded the city-state. When Polybius, in the second century B.C., came to study the evolution of the Roman constitution, he was profoundly influenced by the Aristotelian analysis of politics.

Aristotle's Impact on Later Political Thought. Neither Plato nor Aristotle was to survive antiquity in pure form. During the long period of the early Middle Ages, for example, both ancient thinkers were largely forgotten, except insofar as they were embodied, imperfectly, in Roman and early Christian thinkers. And of the two, Aristotle suffered the most.

On the other hand, when in the eleventh, twelfth, and thirteenth centuries A.D. ancient science and philosophy began to be revived, it was Aristotle who first reappeared. In general philosophy, his revival created little less than a revolution. In terms of ethical and political theory, his resurrection was to be only less important; for in men like St. Thomas Aquinas, he lived again.

Meanwhile, remaining in the stream of ancient political and intellectual history, what developments followed on the death of Aristotle?

chapter 6

Political Thought and Attitudes from Alexander to the Triumph of Rome

While Aristotle was penning his classical moral-political analysis and idealizing the notion of the polis, little less than a revolution was taking place about him. That revolution characterized both practical politics and political attitudes and thought. Radical changes in political power relations provided the stimulus for intellectual positions sharply different from those of the two great classical political thinkers. At the same time, the new intellectual climate paved the way for the politics and political thought of the Roman principate and empire as well as for many of the social attitudes of first-century Christianity.

The epoch under examination in this chapter may be said to extend from 338 B.C., when Philip of Macedon triumphed over the Greek cities at the battle of Chaeronea, to 146 B.C., when Roman predominance in the Hellenistic world was assured by the destruction of Corinth.

The Culture and Politics of the Age

The Hellenistic Age, as it is sometimes called to distinguish it from the history of "classical" Greece, was one in which Greek culture tended to become triumphant in the whole eastern part of the ancient world.[1] The strands of the story are many, complex, and closely interwoven.

The very mingling of Macedonians and Greeks was in itself significant, for it meant that for the first time in history, those who were products of the polis way of life rubbed

1. The bibliography on the Hellenistic Age is, of course, very extensive. On its general impact, see, for example, William W. Tarn, *Hellenistic Civilization*, 2nd ed., London: E. Arnold, 1936; and Arnold J. Toynbee, *Hellenism: The History of a Civilization*, New York: Oxford University Press, 1959.

shoulders on a large scale with men whom they had often been taught (as in the orations of Demosthenes, for example) to think of as exemplars of an inferior way of life. The common objectives of battle, however, tended to submerge any differences between Greek and Macedonian. At the same time, each learned to appreciate the strengths and weaknesses of the other.

The Alexandrian conquest was so rapid that neither Greek nor Macedonian was prepared for the problems which would confront them when they had to deal socially with the Persians. Both had been taught to think of the Persians as somehow inferior. Yet when they actually began to mingle with Persians, they found that their image was in many respects mistaken. Could it be, Greek soldiers must have asked themselves, that the distinction between Greek and barbarian, which they had been taught from babyhood, was an invalid one?

The question became even more pointed as they observed the ways in which their commanders were acting. Many of them took Persian mistresses and began to ape the Persian style of dress. And it was even rumored that Alexander himself was about to take a Persian wife. When this rumor proved to be well founded and when further Alexander advised his subordinate officers to do likewise, old traditions began to crumble.

The effect of this social mingling was, of course, to extend Greek cultural and political ideals into areas where they had formerly been known only in the abstract, if at all. Some Greek soldiers settled down in Persia with their foreign wives and must have been objects of great curiosity to the surrounding barbarians. Permanent settlers are to be distinguished from mere traders. While for centuries Greek merchants had traveled to parts of the Persian empire, relatively few had become permanent residents (although the Greek cities in Asia Minor often paid tribute to the Persian king, of course). On occasion the new Greek residents of the ancient Empire would no doubt return to the "old country" to relate the wonders they had seen, the beauty of the barbarian women, and the marvels of marrying a foreigner. In a previous generation, the teaching of the foreign Sophists had shocked opinion. Now it was shaken up by even more severe *traumata*.[2]

Economically, too, the Alexandrian triumph shook the foundations of polis life. Greek economies had, on the whole, been ones of extreme scarcity. Athens, for example, was throughout most of its independent history a poor country which had become even poorer as a result of the Peloponnesian wars. Now, however, the Alexandrian conquest opened up vistas of wealth undreamed of either by the old landowning classes, represented by men like Aristotle, or by the well-to-do Athenian commercial groups.

The immediate impact of the conquest was, of course, to accentuate the gulf between rich and poor. The injection of so much hitherto hoarded gold into the streams of commerce and trade led to a vast increase in prices, but one which was not matched by corresponding increments in compensation for artisans and other free workers. The "terms of trade" favored the newly rich. Relatively speaking, the poor became poorer.

The conquest, moreover, undoubtedly led to an important shift in ownership of the land. Those who had benefited from the Persian plunder could offer good prices for land still possessed by many of the old Greek families. As the land changed hands, so was the traditional landowning power weakened. The new owners, while they undoubtedly hoped to gain the social prestige that went with possession of land, could hardly hope to acquire overnight that political preeminence so often associated with it. Meanwhile, those who sold their land either sought quick fortunes through investment of the proceeds or went adventuring themselves in the vast territories now opened to them both psychologically and politically.

It was probably the greatly accentuated fission between rich and poor which partly accounts for the political disturbances so characteristic of the Alexandrian and post-Alexandrian empires.[3] Inheriting as they did the long tradition of democratic dominance, the masses in such cities as Athens now found themselves not only deprived of polis independence but also saw those newly enriched through the fortunes of war lording it over them in a way which rivalled the actions of the old oligarchies. The newly affluent were associated with the politics of empire, and many of the demos, no doubt, found their only escape from poverty to lie in an attack on that empire and on the economic forces which supported the new order.

Alexander and his successors (on his death, the empire began to be divided into several major parts) sought in the beginning to conciliate polis patriotic sentiment. Thus each city was to be granted a wide degree of autonomy, its domestic institutions remaining what they had been before the rise of Macedonian supremacy.[4] The Alexandrian rulers hoped by these measures, no doubt, to build up a body of supporters which would be immune to the calls of those who advocated forcible measures against foreign rule. And for many cities these measures appeared to be successful.

Particularly after the death of Alexander, however, the factors making for an undermining of Macedonian rule began to assume greater importance. Quarrels within the royal court itself tended to encourage political alliances against the Alexandrians, thus illustrating the classical Greek contention that revolution usually springs from a division of the ruling class. In the third century, too, the patriotic factions of many cities seemed to regain a measure of self-confidence which was aided and abetted, as we have noted, by the hostility of the poor against the ostentation of those enriched by the spoils of empire. The popular assemblies once more rang out with the cries of Demosthenes-like orators shouting imprecations against the Macedonian power.

Opposition to the empire was particularly reflected in such alliances of cities as the Achaean and the Aetolian leagues.[5] The former went back, in its original form, to the sixth century, when certain city-states around the Gulf of Corinth combined in a loose alliance to rid the neighborhood of pirates. The Achaean League had been active in opposing Philip of Macedon at the battle of Chaeronea. After that disastrous defeat, however, it had dissolved. A little later, about the end of the century, it was revived and carried on activities for mutual defense against possible domestic tyrannies. Around the middle of the third century, the league was joined by several other cities of Greece, the result being that the Macedonian soldiers were driven from Corinth. So powerful did the opposition to the empire now seem that many believed it was possible to liberate all of Greece. But internecine conflicts among the Greek cities prevented this wholesale expulsion, particularly after Sparta began to attack the league.

Meanwhile, the Aetolian League of cities north of the Gulf of Corinth had been founded in the fourth century. By the time the Achaean League became embroiled with the Spartans, the Aetolians had achieved considerable power and influence in Greek politics. They allied themselves with Sparta against the Achaeans, who had meanwhile asked the Macedonians for assistance. The Spartans and the Aetolians were relatively successful against the Achaeans and Macedonians, the Achaean League tending to fade from the political picture for a number of years.

In the intervening years, Roman power was beginning to make its influence felt in Greece. Allying itself with the Aetolian League against Macedonia, it soundly defeated Philip V at the battle of Cynocephalae in 200 B.C. But soon afterwards, the Aetolians, growing suspicious of Rome, made an alliance with Antiochus III of Syria. When that monarch was defeated in 189, the political power of the Aetolian League was destroyed.

The Achaean League, early in the second century, had turned to a Roman alliance. The Romans, however, were suspicious of the league, deported its leaders in 168, and, after resistance by the Achaeans, wiped out the league and the city of Corinth in 146.

One cannot fail to be impressed, in surveying the whole of Greek political history between the beginning of the Peloponnesian wars in 431 and the final extinction of independent polis life in 146, by the large role which almost perpetual war played in bringing about the destruction of civic autonomy. The long war between Athens and Sparta, ostensibly waged

2. For a general discussion of East-West commingling, see William W. Tarn, *Alexander the Great and the Unity of Mankind*, London: H. Milford, 1933; note also Pierre Jonguet, *Macedonian Imperialism and the Hellenization of the East*, translated from the French by M. R. Dobie, New York: Knopf, 1928.
3. See, for example, Max Beer, *Social Struggles in Antiquity*, Boston: Small, Maynard and Co., 1922; and Mikhail I. Rostovtzeff, *Social and Economic History of the Hellenistic World*, New York: Oxford University Press, 1941. See also Tarn, *Hellenistic Civilization*, *op. cit.*
4. On Alexander's policies with reference to the cities, see, for example, William W. Tarn, *Alexander the Great*, 2 vols., Cambridge: Cambridge University Press, 1950–51.
5. On the constitutional theory and practice of the Achaean and Aetolian Leagues, see Edward A. Freeman, *History of Federal Government in Greece and Italy*, 2nd ed., J. B. Bury, ed., London: Macmillan, 1893. Consult also, André Aymard, *Les Assemblées de la Confédération Achaienne*, Bordeaux: Féret et Fils, 1938.

to preserve freedom, actually laid the foundations for an undermining of both civic and personal liberty. Those Greek conservatives, like Aristophanes, who argued for "peace at any price," were, in the light of subsequent events, almost certainly right. In the end, it was not Macedonia and Rome which destroyed Greek liberty—it was the Greeks themselves.

Political Attitudes in the Hellenistic Empires

Much of the theory of the Hellenistic empires was implicit rather than explicit, unsystematic rather than highly organized.

The Theory of Kingship. As we pointed out earlier, monarchy proper had died out as an institution in the Greek polis long before relatively certain political history begins. True, it survived in Sparta in the form of the dual kingship; but Greeks looked upon the Spartan monarchy as simply a dignified military commandership limited and controlled by the Ephorate and by the other institutions established by Lycurgus. In general, Greek attitudes, whether at Athens or elsewhere, were extremely hostile to monarchy; in the period just before the Alexandrian conquests, it was regarded as little less than a tyranny.[6] To be sure, the kings of Macedonia, like those of Sparta, were said to have sprung directly from Zeus himself through Heracles and Aeacus, his sons. But the common view still was that the Macedonian monarchy was "un-Greek," for did not the king of Macedon have the power to order the killing of even free citizens without trial and without forms of law and did not Macedonia lack a true Assembly of Citizens and any doctrine of limited rule?

What, therefore, must have been the shock to Greek attitudes, when Alexander, who professed to be a Greek and yet inherited the Macedonian monarchy, came to demand the obedience of all his Hellenistic subjects? When, in addition, Alexander added to the Macedonian idea of kingship certain notions absorbed from the Persians and the Egyptians, the traditional Greek political mind was horrified.

We do not know, of course, exactly how Alexander would have formulated his notion of kingship. But we can infer what it probably was both from his practices and from the comments of his critics. There is no doubt, for example, that he connected his rule and his empire with a destiny which had been fixed for him by the gods. Plutarch tells us that while in Egypt he visited the shrine of the god Ammon and that when Alexander asked the high priest whether the god had reserved the empire of the world for him, the pontiff replied emphatically in the affirmative.[7] While his ancestors had ruled, by descent from Zeus, the little kingdom of Macedonia, he, by decree of all the gods, was designated to rule the world.

Although he may have had private doubts, he certainly permitted himself for a time to be adored after the manner of Oriental monarchs; and while he later gave up this practice under the unwelcome prodding of men like Callisthenes,[8] the exalted ideas of monarchy which he took over from the Persians and Egyptians persisted under his successors. Whether in Macedonia and Greece, in Syria, or in Egypt—the successor kingdoms to the Alexandrian Empire—the theory of kingship owed not a little to Alexander's borrowed conceptions.

By and large, what emerged from the Alexandrian experience was a doctrine of monarchy which owed something to both Macedonian and Oriental theories of kingship. The monarch came to be conceived as in a peculiar sense the son of a god and as such entitled to the obedience of the lesser sons who were his subjects. He was exalted far above the mass of men, the distance between his throne and them being greater than that between god and the king. Although the king had an enormous responsibility for the welfare of his subjects, there was no machinery whereby he could be held accountable. To a much greater degree than had been true of the old Macedonian monarchy, the king was thought of as distinct from his subjects.

Historically, the implementation of doctrines of this kind in Greece was not without elements of irony and even of tragedy. In some respects, it was as if the Persian wars of the early fifth century had never been fought. Those wars had been portrayed by Herodotus as conflicts in which the Greek "way of life" was at stake; and the ultimate victory of the confederated cities was conceived to be the triumph of free citizenship over Oriental despotism. And yet, only a century and three quarters after the end of the Persian wars, the Greeks became subject to kings whose conceptions of monarchy were very much like those presumably held by Xerxes. What then, the ancient pacifist must have asked himself, had been the value of the military defeat of Xerxes?

Political Attitudes in the Polis. While the old-new conception of kingship was being evolved and implemented, what happened to the polis tradition itself? And what were the public reactions to the triumph of Orientalism?

It was not easy, of course, to kill the idea of the polis, even though as a living force, the institutions of the city-state had been declining for years. Many of the characteristic features of the old way of life persisted, in form, long after Oriental-Macedonian conceptions and practices of kingship had taken root. But the spirit tended more and more to be drained from civic life.

In these circumstances, it was not surprising that citizens, who were now increasingly becoming merely subjects, should begin to question whether they had any role at all in political life. As decisions came increasingly from the royal center and debates in the assembly settled only secondary issues, active civic participation became a thing of the past for most men. Some, indeed, welcomed the new state of affairs, for the rise of empire and the new theory of rule gave them a wider scope for their economic enterprise and travel. Political and administrative decisions could be left to the efficient bureaucracy which tended to grow up around the monarch.

As for the intellectual, who for so long had been tied to political life, his *scholē*, or prized leisure, could now be wholly devoted to contemplation rather than being divided between study and civic activity.[9] The monarch, for the most part, did not call on him for advice, being even less likely than rulers in Plato's day to be a philosopher; and while he might counsel the city on its own now-petty problems, this, too, seemed relatively fruitless.

Generally speaking, we may say that the ties of man with man tended now to have a wider outreach but at the same time a much lower level of intensity and intimacy. Men's horizons were enlarged but at the same time the bonds which held them to others were more tenuous. As they became more and more conscious that they had but a small role to play in public affairs, they began to ask increasingly what, indeed, their role should be.

What disturbed many men even more was the apparent fact that there was very little they could do to control political events. Although they recognized, of course, the role of Nemesis and tragedy in previous political history, men in the earlier days could at least shape substantial segments of their collective destiny through deliberation in the Ecclesia and through common counsel together. Now, however, even this modicum of collective control seemed to be evaporating altogether. Plato and Aristotle had warned that a complicated money economy would tend to militate against man's ability to direct his own collective destiny and that it would create a situation in which material gain could become an end. Events seemed to be demonstrating in dramatic form the soundness of these classical views.

Even more fundamental than the decreasing possibility of deliberate collective control was the growing intellectual doubt that there were any knowable principles in accordance with which one could say that affairs *should* be controlled. The old debates between Socrates and the Sophists, which Plato and Aristotle had thought they had settled in favor of Socrates, were revived; and now the moral and political doctrines of men like Protagoras began to eclipse Platonic and Aristotelian teaching. Even the Academy came under the influence of men hostile to much of Plato's doctrine.

Cynics, Skeptics, Epicureans, and Stoics emerged as the intellectual leaders of the new age; and to their political outlook, as related to their moral doctrine, we must now turn.

From Cynics to Stoics in Politics

The general tendency of the new moral-political ideas was to put into more or less philo-

6. Note Tarn, *Alexander the Great*, and Toynbee, *op. cit.*, for examples.
7. Plutarch, "Alexander," in *The Lives of the Noble Grecians and Romans*, New York: Modern Library, 1932.
8. See p. 87.
9. Even in classic days, of course, scholars felt a tension between the call of civic obligation—the life of activity—and the vocation of pure inquiry, as the writings of Plato indicate. And, indeed, the tension between the two kinds of existence is a common theme in ancient thought.

sophical form the widespread but vague sense of alienation from the political world of the third and second centuries.[10]

The Cynical Position. The Cynical attitude stemmed from the teaching of Antisthenes (444–365 B.C.) and was carried on in a later generation by Diogenes, who died in the same year as Alexander (323). Throughout the second and first centuries Cynical teaching continued to be influential, although often in altered form and in combination with other emphases.

In general, Cynicism begins by attempting to give content to "the good," which Socrates, it will be remembered, thought could be discovered by insight after rigorous training. But Socrates was vague as to what the good might be in specific terms. What, asked Antisthenes and the Cynics, is the nature of a virtuous or good life? Their general answer, not dissimilar from that of Socrates, is to make virtue a necessary condition for happiness. This does not get us very far. But the Cynic proceeds now to ask under what circumstances a man can be most assured of virtue for himself and answers, "When he gives the fewest hostages to external circumstance." Now how does a man go about cutting himself off from control by external forces that might interfere with his virtue and hence with his happiness?

The answer of the Cynic is "When he reduces his wants to the very bare minimum." He will, as it were, in his own life, strip off the accretions of culture—the things which he has gained as a result of the division of labor which Plato describes in Book II of the *Republic.* He will live on the coarsest fare and particularly on the food which he can gain by his own labors. He will inure himself to hardship.

In effect, Cynicism is a repudiation of civilization and its institutions. The Greek mind in the classical age, of course, was keenly aware of the close connection between the polis or city and the good life which entailed a substantial material basis. Even though Plato and Aristotle sought to control economic expansion, both conceded that the development of the arts and of that rational deliberation which they associated with politics were dependent on some economic development.

When the Cynic, therefore, held up as the ideal of the virtuous man a destruction of all desire and entanglement, he was attacking the very citadel of the classical theory of culture and politics. That doctrine, as we have noted, saw the fulfillment of personality in community. The Cynic, by contrast, sees it in a repudiation of most communal ties. The classical doctrine saw some men, at least, as requiring civic activity for the attainment of their potentialities. The Cynic, on the contrary, maintains that he who is wise and covets a life of happiness will not involve himself in politics any more than he will become entangled in commercial endeavor.

The picture of the Cynic which has come down to us from antiquity is, in sum, one of a man clad in coarse clothing who lives on a little rough food. He sees conventions and laws as devices to entrap him into domination by his desires. He views the intimate life of the polis as unnatural in that it wipes out his quest for self-sufficiency. He is indifferent or hostile to the claims of all political factions and to all schemes for ideal republics.

Historically, the Cynic attitude to politics and civilization is significant because it formulates for the first time, although in sketchy fashion, that ideal of individual self-sufficiency which is to be so important for later antiquity. It also gives expression to a widespread view that nature should be conceived in primitive terms. The wise man is self-sufficient and is therefore natural. The life of civilized and hence of political man is unnatural in that it is a departure from the simplicity of the primitive.[11]

Cynicism could, and undoubtedly did, exist at many different levels of consciousness. In a Diogenes, for example, the degree of awareness was high. But there was probably also much popular, unreflecting Cynicism. Whether in Diogenic or in popular form, however, it represented the largely negative belief-system of men who felt themselves utterly alienated from the kind of life which developed in the ancient world after the beginning of the Alexandrian triumphs.

More positive statements of Cynicism's sociopolitical attitudes were to await the formulations of Epicureanism and Stoicism.

Skepticism. Basically, Skepticism doubted that knowledge of anything is possible. It had a long history. It was implied to some degree in the teachings of Protagoras and many of the Sophists. Socrates himself gave hostages to the view in that he was constantly emphasizing how little he knew or, apparently, could know. But Socrates' skepticism was merely a preliminary stage in his quest for knowledge; we must, he seemed to say, doubt everything before we can know anything.

Classical Skepticism went much further than this. It was elaborated by Pyrrho of Elis (360–270 B.C.), who is usually regarded as its founder, and by Timon, one of his students (320–230 B.C.). Pyrrho accompanied Alexander to the Orient and is said by some to have engaged in a profound study of both Persian and Indian philosophy. It was Timon's role to preserve the teachings of his master and to pass them on to posterity. After Timon's death, significantly enough, Skepticism became an important factor in the Platonic Academy.

Skepticism was bottomed on the proposition that every assertion about the world can with plausibility be contradicted. Neither empirical investigation nor rational activity can tell us about the true nature of things, whether in the physical and biological worlds or in that of social relations. All we can really know, the Skeptic said, is the state of our feelings induced by the things of the universe outside us. In a sense, then, all the so-called sciences are simply representations of our feelings, and understanding of phenomena as they really exist is impossible.

But if we cannot know, we obviously cannot act on an unattainable knowledge. The Skeptic will, then, in matters of morals and politics, always seek to avoid judgment about actions; for unless he keeps his judgments suspended (and the Skeptics were often nicknamed "suspenders"), he will be acting on the basis of pure feeling and desire.

But how can one avoid action? The Skeptic admits that this is difficult; yet he thinks that in a measure it is possible. One can, by not allowing external events to trouble one, build up an inner imperturbability—a kind of folded arms attitude to moral and political decisions. By concentrating solely on one's own inner feelings (the only possible object of knowledge, it will be remembered), it is possible to approach the kind of self-sufficiency held up by the Cynic as the goal of the wise man.

In the end, of course, the Skeptic is forced to admit that some action may be unavoidable. The ideal of imperturbability is never completely achievable; we are thrust by the circumstances of life into positions where we must stand for or against something—where apparent choices confront us. In these events our only guides can be our feelings at the time or the tradition of the community. The latter acts as a guide, not in the sense that we deem it to reflect the "right"—for there is no right which we can know—but rather because of its convenience.

Politically, the outcome of the Skeptical view tends to be an attitude of conservatism. No more than the Cynic does he regard the state, law, and convention as natural. But unlike the Cynic, he cannot see political institutions as unnatural either; for the distinction between the natural and the unnatural is meaningless in a cognitive sense. The Skeptic allows himself to be directed in his few and reluctant actions by law, convention, and tradition because, aside from feeling, they are the only possible guides. They possess no positive value.

Skepticism historically reflects dramatically that despair about the ordering of life which we have noted in varying degrees from the time of Hesiod onward. All ancient political thinkers, indeed, began with an attitude of doubt about the possibility of either explaining political phenomena or of "knowing" anything normatively. But classical thinkers like Plato and Aristotle thought they had in part resolved these doubts. Now, in the Hellenistic period, the Skeptics begin with the same doubts; but, unlike the classical political thinkers, they end with them also.

The Epicurean Position on Politics. The Epicurean attitude toward politics contains in it strains both of Cynicism and of Skepticism. Unlike the former, it does not seek to wipe out completely the life of desire. But against the latter, it seems to hold that the wise man can at least know what is useful.

Epicurus himself (341–270 B.C.) was born in

10. Eduard Zeller remains one of the best scholars dealing with the thought of this epoch. See particularly the new edition of his *Stoics, Epicureans, and Sceptics*, Oswald J. Reichel, trans., New York: Russell and Russell, 1962.
11. Every age, we might say, produces the equivalent of the Cynic, although in some epochs the general attitude of Cynicism is more common than in others. In the modern era, the Nihilists of Czarist Russia resembled the Cynics in many respects; and in twentieth-century United States, the Beatniks and Hippies have some of their coloration.

Samos, the son of an Athenian colonist in that island. We know almost nothing about him. Whether he participated in politics or not is left very vague in the fragmentary accounts we have of him; but a good guess would be that, on the basis of his general attitude, he remained aloof.

Epicurean teaching begins with the Cynical position, accepting in principle that the wise man ought to be free from the encumbrance of desire if he would be master of himself. But the Epicurean analysis is more subtle and explicit than that of the Cynic. Desires are of three kinds—the natural, which we cannot escape; the unnatural, which completely destroy self-sufficiency; and those which, while not being unnatural, may be given expression or not depending upon the insight of the wise man. Natural desires, of course, are unavoidable. Purely conventional desires—those wild and excessive demands so often encouraged by a culture or by kings—are to be avoided. But most desires may be used by the wise man or not used by him, depending upon circumstances, to enhance his pleasure. The test, as with the Cynic, is still whether one becomes the slave of desire; but Epicurus seems to hold that under certain circumstances, one becomes less of a slave if one surrenders to the desire than if one excludes it altogether.

Given this hedonistic morality (a hedonism which values such pleasures as conversation and wit more highly than purely "physical" enjoyment) combined with the idea of personal self-sufficiency, Epicurus' attitude to society and politics might be expected. Social relations, he thinks, have their roots in utility; we associate with others because it will enhance our pleasure. At the same time, we have the capacity to renounce that intercourse when and if it begins to destroy our pleasure or to wipe out our self-sufficiency. Even friendship, which Aristotle had seen as natural and not a matter of mere utility, Epicurus tends to regard in a utilitarian light.

It is not surprising, then, to learn that the Epicureans think of the state as based on a contract. It is constructed to enhance the possibility of enjoyment for the individual. Its laws are mere conventions which, when they no longer serve the purposes of individual pleasure (as defined by Epicurus), can be disregarded by the "wise man." Unlike the Cynic, the Epicurean maintains that public life may under certain circumstances be necessary from a utilitarian point of view. On the whole, however, he assumes an attitude of aloofness. The life of politics is, at best, a kind of tool; and when at all possible, the discriminating man will avoid it.

Consistent with this position is the Epicurean attitude toward religion and its place in the life of the community. The gods are simply instruments, like the laws and the state, which men may use to secure the civic order essential for the highest pleasures of wit and conversation. Because of its tendency to Skepticism, Epicureanism does not admit that we can know the gods, if indeed they exist at all. Religion is a kind of artifact which may or may not prove useful; and it is to be evaluated solely in these terms.

The Impact of Stoicism on Political Thought. Both Cynicism and Skepticism were largely negative in their attitude to politics, although they arrived at their negations by means of different routes. Even Epicureanism, with its conception of political institutions as based on agreement or contract, remained largely indifferent to society and state; for the social and political obligation of the emancipated or wise man under its system was a marginal or exceptional one. Stoicism, by contrast, attempted to make a place for political man, while yet beginning largely with a Cynical framework.

Its traditional founder was Zeno, a Cyprus Phoenician who was born in 336 and committed suicide, when told he had an incurable disease, in 264. For many years Zeno taught in Athens, where he attracted a large following among the politically disillusioned young men of a city whose "glory" had now passed. Perhaps the most creative of the later Stoics of the Hellenistic age was Chrysippus (280–207 B.C.), who reformulated and expanded the Zenoic teaching. In the second century, Panaetius of Rhodes was responsible for introducing the doctrine to Rome, which by now was well on its way to its days of imperial supremacy. Posidonius, a disciple of Panaetius, was one of Cicero's teachers and Cicero was, of course, a contemporary of Julius Caesar in the first century B.C. Thus for a period of two hundred years, the ethical-political doctrine of Stoicism was shaped by a series of Greek teachers through whom it was transmitted to Roman politicians and judges.

Zeno himself was profoundly influenced by Cynical teaching on the state and the world and in his early career adopted their bluntness of speech and outrageous statements in polite society which so shocked old-fashioned Athenians. Like the Cynics, he sought emancipation from convention and law and felt himself alienated from the kind of society represented by the Hellenistic empires. But unlike the Cynics, he—and those who developed his doctrine in later generations—sought to construct a coherent system of thought upon which to base ethical and political views.[12]

Stoicism, like so many of the post-Aristotelian systems of thought, saw knowledge as divided into three major categories: ethics, logic, and physics. Politics is regarded as a subdivision of ethics, and this is a significant reversal of the Aristotelian scheme, where, it will be remembered, ethics was conceived to be a branch of politics. Ethics itself tends to be the predominant interest of the Stoics, and their logical and physical inquiries are largely attempts to provide what they think is a needed basis for their ethical and political views.

A full understanding of their political position must place it in the context of their general theory of knowledge and of the universe. With respect to the former, they deny the Skeptical contention that no knowledge except that of one's feelings is possible. Sense perception does give us some certain knowledge; and while our impressions differ in clearness and distinctness, the wise man can distinguish between those which cannot afford certainty and those, on the other hand, which can provide sure knowledge (the "grasping impressions," in Stoic terminology—*katalēptikā phantasia*).

These sense impressions tell us that the universe is one material substance. The Stoics conceive it to be a single body, which they identify with a subtle fiery ether, equivalent to reason and also, some held, to God. But somehow the ether partly "depotentiated," the result being the world as we see it and human history as we know it. However, the ether still envelops the world as its soul and the differentiated or depotentiated parts of the universe are, in varying degrees, still trying to return to their undifferentiated potentiated state. Among human beings, the wise men or sages so prominent in Cynical, Skeptical, and Epicurean thought, are conceived by Stoicism to have present in them a large measure of the ethereal fire of reason and therefore to be closer to the undifferentiated soul.

The operations of nature in its many parts—including human nature—are the reflections of the logos, or word, or law, which proceeds from the fiery soul that still surrounds the world. Stoicism originally borrowed its logos doctrine from Democritus (460–370 B.C.), but it was subjected to many permutations and modifications during the course of the centuries. One form was to be developed by Philo of Alexandria, for example, and applied to political history.[13]

But if the universe is governed by reason through the logos, then what is the significance of ethical-political choices? If all is shaped by the universal soul, why be concerned about morals and politics? These were questions which the ancients continued to put to the Stoics and to which the latter gave varying answers. In general, they contended that, while from the perspective of God or the fiery soul all acts, including human acts, are determined by sovereign reason, from the perspective of humanity, our choices are real. There are levels or degrees of adherence to the natural ruling principle; and our peace of mind depends upon the degree to which we direct our wills in conformity with the goals of the divine will. To be "in harmony with God" means to be "in agreement with nature"; and to be in agreement with nature implies that we are determined to be governed by the highest ruling principle.

This is the Stoic version of "natural law," whose germs we have already seen in the doctrines of Plato and Aristotle. What are the contents of natural law according to the Stoic interpretation? Like classical doctrine, and unlike that of Epicurus, Stoic theory sees society as natural. Man is born for society and can develop only in community. But what society and what community? The Stoic answer is that the end or goal of human beings is a *cosmopolis*—or a city of the world. This, however, is no historic community. Rather

12. Unfortunately only a small fragment of Zeno's *Republic* has come down to us. It was, however, presumably somewhat modeled on Plato's great treatise in form. See A. C. Pearson, *The Fragments of Zeno and Cleanthes*, London: C.J. Clay, 1891.
13. See Chapter 7, pp. 134–137.

it is a community of all men held together by the common possession of reason and transcending all historic divisions. For at least some Stoics, particularly in later phases of the school's development, this may even embrace the souls of men who are no longer "alive" in given cities but who, presumably, are somewhat closer to the undifferentiated reason at the heart of things. The community in which man becomes himself, then, is a universal one, in which the ancient distinction between Greek and barbarian is broken down and men are united solely by the common flame of reason.

But it is universal in another sense, too. Not only does it transcend the barrier between Greek and barbarian but it also overcomes any natural differentiation between the freeman and the slave. Earlier we have noted Aristotle's emphasis on the naturalness of slavery.[14] Plato, too, while not in explicit terms, seemed to imply a similar view. But the Stoic sees reason—however depotentiated—in all men. Slavery becomes unnatural in the cosmopolis.

There is thus but one "life and order" (*kosmos*) and a single flock "feeding together on a common pasture" (*nomos*). Here, of course, nomos is used in its dual meaning of "pasture" and "law." The pasture is the universal community of souls, while the law is the ordering of that community in accordance with reason.

The Stoic theory of the cosmopolis and of natural law would seem on the surface to have had revolutionary implications politically. If natural distinctions between Greek and barbarian no longer exist and if Aristotle's differentiation between freeman and slave is shown to be invalid, one might expect the Stoic to have been a leader in political movements having for their objective the overthrow of all constitutions based on social inequality. And, indeed, some modern scholars have seen in Stoicism the inspiration for an ancient politics of reform and radical change. Thus Max Beer suggests that Zeno's theory meant that there were to be "no political government, no courts of justice, no man-made laws, but goods in common, equality of the sexes, brotherhood of all mankind."[15] Stoicism, he avers, taught the doctrines of "anarchist communism." And he goes on to cite as an example of what Stoicism implied, the writings of Euhomeros, a contemporary of Zeno.

But such interpretations of Stoic politics are almost certainly mistaken. It is true, of course, that the strong emphasis on equality found in the doctrine of natural law and cosmopolis appears to point to egalitarian social and political arrangements. Yet it is pure guesswork to say that Zeno specifically advocated the destruction of traditional political institutions or even the abolition of slavery.

With respect to the general doctrine of Stoicism, moreover, there would appear to be many elements within it not compatible with the politics of social reform or revolution. And historically, we have few if any records of Stoics who actually interpreted their doctrines as if they implied radical change in the existing situation.

In what ways, then, does Stoic doctrine itself check or even completely frustrate what appear to be its revolutionary political implications? Two aspects of the doctrine stand out at this point. In the first place, the cosmopolis which plays so large a part in Stoic teaching is thought of primarily as a community held together by a common inner principle present in all men. Here inner implies spiritual. The notion of self-sufficiency which the Stoics took over from the Cynics makes outer conditions a matter of relative indifference. So long as men are aware that they are members of the cosmopolis, the particular political institutions under which they happen to live become relatively unimportant.

But there would seem to be a second basis for the Stoic aversion to fundamental change. As we have noted, Stoic doctrine stresses necessity and the control of the world by reason. It is but a short step from this position to the view that, however much existing institutions may fall short of nature, they are somehow ordained by nature. Many later Stoics, or Stoic-influenced thinkers, will elaborate this thesis and develop a theory of political history to give expression to it.[16]

When the over-all political attitude of Stoicism from 275 B.C. to about A.D. 100 is evaluated, it is evident that while it began by repudiating the Epicurean notion of society as a mere convention and by attacking Cynical negativism, it ended by affirming some of the positions espoused by both the Epicureans and the Cynics. While society is natural, one should not become too involved in it; while one should make abstention from social and political activity the exception rather than the rule, one must never allow oneself to become so entangled that withdrawal is not a possibility; while the cosmopolis transcends all lines of class and city, there is nothing very much we can do in the here and now to change the essentials of political society.

Ethics and Politics in Post-Classical Theory

By the time of Corinth's destruction in 146 B.C., Cynical, Skeptical, Epicurean, and Stoic attitudes to society and politics probably predominated in intellectual circles. Even the Academy, as we have noted, was not unaffected by the major trends. Although some of the explanatory structure in classical theory was retained, its normative aspects were in considerable measure discarded.

One of the most striking tendencies in the four schools of thought was the effort to separate the study of ethics from that of politics.[17] Whereas in the classical thinkers, the good for the individual and the good for the community had to be pursued together, post-classical thought often implied their fission. The individual's salvation—to use religious terminology already employed in the second century—was attainable apart from political justice. His ends lay beyond the goals sought by princes and senates.

It was attitudes of this kind that were to be so profoundly influential in intellectual circles of the Roman principate and empire. But the social, political, and intellectual evolution of Rome contributed its own elements to political theory and attitudes in the imperial period. Although much was Greek, much, too, was the product of Roman experience. How that experience affected typical post-classical Greek attitudes and conceptions and how Greek doctrine in turn helped shape the thinking of Roman intellectuals will be the subject of the chapter which follows.

chapter 7

Roman Experience and Political Thought

A student of political theory and attitudes living near the beginning of the third century A.D. (perhaps in the reign of Caracalla) would undoubtedly, if he were treating his subject historically, reflect systematically on both the political experience of the Romans and on the interrelationship between that experience and the Greek philosophical and political doctrine which had been influential in the Roman world for the previous three centuries or more.

The Economics and Politics of Roman Evolution

The destruction of Corinth was the military event, as we have seen, which in effect spelled the doom of all Greek efforts to restore political independence. Thereafter, the Roman *imperium* was to remain predominant in the eastern world.

Meanwhile, the city of Rome itself had gone through a political evolution astonishingly similar, in many respects, to that which we have noted of the Greek polis. Like the polis, the city began as a struggling fortified village under a kingship. The king was advised by a council of elders known as the Senate. But by the latter part of the sixth century B.C. (roughly 509), the last king of Rome was

Chapter 6

14. See pp. 94–96.
15. *The General History of Socialism and Social Struggles*, vol. 1, New York: Russell and Russell, 1957, p. 120.
16. See pp. 130–132.
17. To be sure, the split was never complete, as it tended to become by the time of the Renaissance. But the tension set up in post-classical thought between individual good and social welfare provided a climate unlike that of the classical age.

deposed and the republican period was initiated. Thereafter, two Consuls took the place of the king; the Senate, while theoretically remaining advisory only, gradually began to initiate and direct action; and the political power of the plebeians, who corresponded roughly to the demos of the polis, was slowly extended.[1]

The Populus in the Roman Constitution. Broadly speaking, the evolution was one in which control by landowners and inheritors of social status gave way in part to direction by the plebeians. But despite the growth in plebeian power, Rome never became a democracy, even in the Greek sense of that term. There were undoubtedly thrusts in the democratic direction; but before they could be completed, foreign conquest, the growth of a slave economy, and the rise of the power of a professional army contributed, along with other factors, to the complete frustration of democratic efforts.

It is a complicated story and much of its early part is very cloudy indeed. Traditionally, in addition to the council of elders, or Senate, there had been an assembly of the people known as the *comitia curiata.* Organized on the basis of inherited family and religious groupings and including members of all social classes, it may have had at one time some political significance. But by the classical period of the Roman Republic, the comitia curiata had ceased to have any influence.

Meanwhile, the power of a second assembly known as the *comitia centuriata* had grown. This was the "people in arms" and consisted of all men of military age. Down to 287 B.C., the comitia centuriata had two major functions—it elected the chief magistrates and it approved proposed laws (or validated them, in Greek terminology) laid before it. After 287, it lost its law-approving function to the *comitia tributa*, which had in the meantime grown up out of the struggles between patricians and plebeians.

Throughout its history, the comitia centuriata was an assembly in which the wealthy classes had overwhelming influence; for while all arms-bearing men could vote, they did so only through their "centuries," and the centuries were based on distinctions of wealth. Thus long after the plebeian element in Roman society began to have greater influence, the comitia centuriata could be effectively dominated by a few men of property. After 241, for example, when the comitia centuriata underwent reform, the wealthy businessmen, or *equites,* were divided into eighteen centuries; and the proletariat (far more numerous) had only five. Since voting was by centuries rather than individuals, this meant that a few thousand equites had more than three times the weight of the many thousand proletariat.

While the comitia centuriata was assuming this form, the plebeians had been effective in securing the formation of yet another assembly called the comitia tributa. The social conflicts between patricians and plebeians are well known to every student of early Roman history. Shortly after the destruction of the monarchy, the plebeians had conducted their famous "general strike" (494 B.C.) against the patricians and this had won them the right to elect two tribunes who were to have the veto power against decrees of the magistrates. The tribunes (later increased in number) were chosen by the *concilium plebis,* which was the assembly of plebeians. In this assembly, voting was by tribes (or districts of the city of Rome) rather than by clans, as in the curiata, or by centuries arranged according to wealth. This tribal voting system was apparently established about 471.

In the concilium plebis, it became customary for the plebeians not only to elect the tribunes but also to talk about public affairs in general. While this debate was, of course, purely unofficial, it came to have greater and greater informal effect throughout the fifth century. The tribunes had the power to ask for the advice of the concilium plebis through a vote, which came to be called a *plebiscitum.* By the middle of the century, resolutions of the *concilium* could be given the force of law, but only when the proposals were submitted by the Senate.

For the next century and a half (after 449), the concilium plebis struggled to remove this senatorial control. Only after many wars had led to social disorganization and the plebeians had engaged in another mass exodus from the city, in 287, did their agitation succeed. In that year the Hortensian Law changed the name of the concilium plebis to comitia tributa and gave to the new comitia the comitia centuriata's prerogative of approving laws.

On the surface, it would seem that the passage of the law of 287 had established democracy in Rome. Was this indeed the fact? Was Rome after 287 a democracy either in the Athenian or in the modern sense?

The answer must be in the negative. In the first place the comitia centuriata still elected the magistrates, with the exception of the tribunes and their assistants the Aediles.

Secondly, the Senate continued to be a highly aristocratic body composed of the old families and of the ex-magistrates who had been chosen by the centuriata.

But thirdly, the comitia tributa, although not based formally on distinctions of wealth, could usually be easily manipulated by the landowners and other rich men who dominated the Senate and the magistracies.

By 146, then, both comitias could be effectively controlled—barring very exceptional circumstances—by wealthy men. Rome, on the verge of the great disturbances of the next century, was what Aristotle would have called an oligarchy. But the oligarchy itself hid behind a semi-democratic institutional mask.

The Senate. While popular institutions had assumed this form by the middle of the second century B.C., the ancient Senate had not remained stationary. Originally advisory to the king, after the Republic it became the council with which the two consuls conferred before they took important actions. As it emerges into the historical period, we seem to see in it a body in many respects similar to the Spartan Gerusia. In the beginning, it was appointed by the king and later, by the two consuls. Its membership came from the patrician classes—those who, like the eupatridae in ancient Athens, had an inherited social status. By 312 B.C., the censors (who had been created in 444) took over the functions of striking senators from the rolls if they were "unworthy" (a task formerly performed by the consuls) and of filling vacancies. During the third and second centuries the custom of filling vacancies from the ranks of ex-magistrates became hardened, so that it was assumed without question that after a year in each of certain offices one would then enter the ranks of the Senate.

Although the Senate throughout this period nominally remained merely an advisory body, its social status and the experience of its members were such that its advice was rarely disregarded, particularly after the beginning of the third century. From that time until the troubles of the first century, it was the Senate which played the crucial role in diplomatic negotiations, allotment of the budget, approval of proposals for laws (which had, of course, to be validated by the comitia), and conduct of the innumerable wars of conquest.

After 146, to be sure, senatorial domination came increasingly to be challenged by those whom the senators customarily thought of as demagogues—popular leaders who attacked the increasing division between rich and poor and who demanded redress of grievances.

Evolution of the Magistracies. The consuls remained the leading magistrates throughout the Roman Republic. Two in number, it was common Roman sentiment that they acted to check one another (even in the conduct of military campaigns) and thus to prevent a revival of the hated ancient monarchy. Every Roman politician aspired to be a consul; but that dignity was usually reserved for those who had first passed through certain inferior magistracies.

In the third and second centuries, as the influence and power of the Senate waxed, the independent decision-making of the magistrates tended to wane.

Social Revolution and Politics. Between 264 B.C., the beginning of the First Punic War, and 44 B.C., when Caesar was assassinated, not only were formal institutions profoundly affected but the very spirit of Roman life was radically changed.

By the time of Caesar—indeed, long before then—the city-state was no longer an intimate community of villagers and outlying countrymen. It had become the political center for a vast empire. Just as Athens emerged from the Persian wars the pivot of a commercial and naval empire, so the city of Rome came out of the Punic, Eastern, and Italian wars an administrative and political hub for a society which included all of Italy, much of northern Africa, and most of the Hellenistic world. But although the extent and nature of the Roman state had thus changed drastically, the way in

1. Ancient Roman political institutions have been treated in a number of works. See, for example, Frank F. Abbott, *A History and Description of Roman Political Institutions*, New York: Biblo and Tannen, 1963; *Ibid., Roman Politics*, New York: Cooper Square Publishers, 1963; *Ibid., Society and Politics in Ancient Rome*, New York: Charles Scribner's Sons, 1909; Frank E. Adcock, *Roman Political Ideas and Practice*, Ann Arbor: University of Michigan Press, 1959; and Leon P. Homo, *Roman Political Institutions: From City to State*, M. R. Dobie, trans., New York: Barnes & Noble, 1962.

which the Roman citizen viewed his political society had not been altered comparably: he still continued to think that it was a city *dominating* the world and not one which had to subordinate its life to the necessities of a wider society. This rigidity of thought became an endless source of difficulty.

The inadequacy of thought about practical matters is illustrated very well in the struggles centering on the agrarian problems of the second century B.C. With the wars of conquest, farmers, who traditionally had been the economic backbone of the Republic, now found themselves either bought or pressured (often by soldiers with abundant booty) off their lands, many of which were consolidated and worked by slave labor.[2] When the resources of the ex-farmer gave out, he often found himself an urban dependent of some wealthy senator or knight. While still a citizen, his vote was at the command of his patron. Meanwhile, his farm came under the control of an absentee landlord who ran it as a big business, the bailiff being his manager and the slaves his factory workers.

The importation of new supplies of gold and other precious metals enlarged the power of the ruling classes—patricians, *equites*, senators—and caused inflation of prices. Since wages of laborers did not rise correspondingly and alternative occupations were lacking, economic dependence on patrons was enhanced.

Then, too, the two centuries preceding the death of Caesar had witnessed much soil erosion. Although the early Roman farmer was usually very careful and certainly hard working, the exhaustion of the soil in the absence of enough fertilizer often tended to drive him from his traditional homestead. Small farms would then be consolidated into large cattle ranches; and the soil which had formerly grown wheat would become pasture land. This process had several effects: it accentuated even more the power of wealthy men; it accelerated the flight to the city, which was stimulated by conquest and slavery; and by reducing the supply of Italian grown grains, it forced the Roman polity to seek its wheat elsewhere—in Sicily or in Egypt. But to have to depend on foreign sources for the staff of life created a precarious situation both economically and politically. Economically, it clearly implied the loss of that independence which was so praised in lore and legend; politically, it meant that that demagogue who could make the most plausible promises about continuation of the grain supply would be well on his way to political power.

With respect to traditional public land policy, the practice had been to lease out newly acquired lands to private cultivators. While there was theoretically a limit (since the Licinian-Sextian Law of 367 B.C.) of 500 *iugera* (about 312 acres) on the size of a lease-hold, in practice this was often disregarded; for administration of the law was in the hands of the very classes who were tending to enlarge the size of farms everywhere.

In the second century, agitation for a real limitation on the extent of lease-holds achieved more and more support among the populus; and this was accentuated by the demands of soldiers returning to civilian life. The so-called veteran problem was intimately interwoven with the demands of the agrarians. Traditionally, land had been given, or at least rented, to war veterans as a kind of pension or retirement allowance. Now, however (after 146 B.C., the end of the third Punic War and also the date when Rome triumphed over Greek resistance), at the very time when veterans were becoming more numerous than ever before, the land available was more limited than in previous centuries. Hence, the land reformers, supported strongly by the veteran bloc, insisted that workable limits be imposed on lease-holds of public lands and that substantial quantities be rented to veterans as small farmsteads.

It was, of course, at this point that the appeals of the Gracchi proved most attractive. Tiberius Gracchus (163–133 B.C.) and Caius Gracchus (153–121 B.C.) regarded it as their mission in life to solve the agrarian problem through a deliberate and well-planned public policy.[3] The gist of it was a rigorous limitation on size of farms and provision for distribution of land to veterans. Although the policy met with some success (some 80,000 new homesteads were created), the process of consolidation had already gone too far and the power of the Gracchi's opponents was too great. Both men were murdered and concentration of economic power seemed only to be enhanced.

Another factor in the revolutionary ferment characteristic of the last days of the Republic was the rise of the military as an important political force. In an immediate sense, this was the product of events of the second and first centuries B.C. But seen in perspective, its genesis is to be traced back into the third century, with the first and second Punic wars. Had Rome not been in a state of almost perpetual war, a caste of near-professional warriors might not have arisen; for certainly the ideal held up by most Roman political thinkers was that of a citizen army recruited in accordance with immediate need and of an officer corps drawn from the patrician classes.

But most Romans were not perspicacious enough to understand that virtually constant warfare, either Italian or foreign, was destroying whatever remained of the ideal. Romans could not see that they could not have, at one and the same time, a Republic on the old model and an expansive and aggressive foreign policy. Had they given up the latter, they might have preserved subordination of the military to civil power. Instead, the tendency to what Plato had called timocratic rule was accelerated.

The politics of the period following the death of Caius Gracchus (121 B.C.) became, therefore, increasingly a politics of contesting military powers. While struggling politician-generals often appealed to various class interests (Sulla was an aristocrat; Marius a democrat), their methods were similar. Impatient, as were their followers, with the slow processes enshrined in the republican constitution, they sought quick military solutions. The result in the first century B.C. was a long series of civil wars, often fought not in Italy but in the lands so recently conquered under the aegis of senatorial control. As the power of the military waxed, that of the Senate waned; for even when military "champions" of the Senate arose they soon made it apparent that they, and not the senators, were the masters of the situation.

When Octavian was finally victorious, no particular political ideology triumphed with him. Instead, he and his successors were to work out rationalizations of their acts—or have their intellectuals do so—throughout the following century and a half.

Principate and Empire to the Third Century. The political history of the Roman world from 27 B.C. to the early part of the third century is one of slow and steady eclipse of republican institutions. Ostensibly a "savior" of the Republic, Octavian (who was soon given the title "Augustus" by the Senate) was too keen-witted to believe that the republican spirit could really be preserved in the kind of society which had developed in the previous century and a half.

However, the Republic still had about it an aura of sanctity and he dared not show contempt for it openly. His general policy, as is well known, was to attempt a revitalization of the forms of republic life while at the same time he made sure that his own power as commander of the army (Imperator) was not disturbed. In some respects, indeed, he seems to have had a genuine reverence for the traditions of the Republic, so that not all his acts need be interpreted as hypocritical. The old republican offices were continued, consuls still serving their prescribed year of office; praetors supervising administration of the law; and quaestors directing the *fiscus.* Augustus himself agreed to accept certain offices in addition to his imperatorship or commandership of the Army. Thus he eventually became *princeps senatus* (chief of the Senate) for life; and it was this office which gave the empire its early designation—the "principate." Roman hostility to the kingship forbade the new ruler to use the hated *rex;* but princeps (which we often translate as prince) seemed not to labor under these handicaps.

As one notes the politics of Augustus, it is amazing how well they exemplify those which Aristotle admonished his tyrant to pursue. Like the Aristotelian tyrant, the Prince showed publicly, in every way possible, his reverence for tradition; yet he was never loath to put new wine into the carefully preserved bottles of old customs. Again, although probably an agnostic, he praised religion, provided new temples for the gods, and sought to set an example for the public by his public piety.

In general, of course, the political apathy, which was in part the result of the long period of blood-letting, continued to exist and was itself the foundation for much of Augustus'

2. These problems have been treated extensively by many writers. See particularly Arnold H. M. Jones, *The Later Roman Empire*, Norman: University of Oklahoma Press, 1964; Frank Tenny, *An Economic Survey of Ancient Rome*, Paterson, N.J.: Pageant Books, 1959; and Mikhail I. Rostovtsev, *The Social and Economic History of the Roman Empire*, Oxford: Clarendon Press, 1957.
3. On the lives and doctrines of the Gracchi, consult Gregory Odin, *Caius Gracchus, A Tragedy*, New York: Boni and Liveright, 1920; and Howard H. Scullard, *From the Gracchi to Nero*, New York: Barnes & Noble, 1963.

success. But in addition, the Imperator made sure that the landless and largely unoccupied proletariat received an abundance of oil and wheat, the staples of their physical existence. Nothing was left to chance in this respect: there must always be a steady stream of ships bearing grain from Egypt to Rome.

As for the spiritual needs of the proletariat, the Imperator tried to assure them through ample provision for amusements. Augustus understood that man does not live by bread alone; but he also felt that the spiritual wants of most men would be satisfied by ample supplies of gladiatorial combats, races, and gaudy spectacles. Greek political culture, too, had understood the need for public amusements and entertainment but for the most part this had been satisfied by genuine contests of athletic skill and the intellectually stimulating comedy and tragedy. Roman popular culture, by contrast, was by the time of Augustus well on the road to those gigantic displays of cruelty which seemed so characteristic of it.[4]

The Augustan policies laid the foundations for the activities of his successors. For them, he was a model of the successful politician; and while most of them failed to approximate his successes in the political realm, many of them certainly tried to do so. Under his immediate successors—Tiberius, Caligula, Claudius, and Nero—the relative political status of the Imperator continued to grow, despite the weak and often despicable characters of those who held the imperial office.

It was under Emperor Hadrian (117–138 B.C.) that what we today call bureaucracy really began to take root. The demands of complex administration, the variegated nature of the empire, and the philosophical nature of the emperor himself all conspired to assist in the growth of an hierarchical administration divided into departments or ministries. The expertise of second-century administration contrasted strongly with the amateur quality of administration in the second century B.C. And as the effective influence of Senate, populus, and magistrates continued to decline, the power of the civil service waxed.[5]

Meanwhile, as the principate and empire gradually cast shadows over the ancient Republic, what was happening to the cultural life of the Roman world? What of its morals and manners and its general intellectual climate—all of which factors Aristotle thought of as such vital parts of the constitution or way of life of a people?

Stoicism as a philosophy, we observed earlier, entered Rome in the second century B.C. Already, of course, the cultures of Greek cities in southern Italy had not been without their effect in shaping the Roman mind, although often against the opposition of leading senators who looked upon Greek culture as effete and grossly un-Roman. These tendencies were aided and abetted, as one might expect, by the conquests of the East. Just as the world of the Greek polis had not been unaffected by the triumphs of Alexander, so the Roman *civitas* was shaped culturally through the activities of a Flamininus.[6]

Here, of course, we are primarily interested in the ways through which general speculation was reflected in political theory and attitudes. As men looked at the evolution of Roman institutions from the Punic wars to the third century, how did they seek to explain and account for the events and struggles which we have sketched? Into what larger patterns did they fit them? What kind of continuity can be discerned between the political attitudes of the late Hellenistic world—before the destruction of Corinth—and the opinions and views of men living in the first and second centuries A.D.?

In seeking to interpret the political thought of the period, we shall find that, while the method and categories of that thought tended to be Greek, it was the stuff of Roman political history upon which men reflected. The evolution of Rome from city-state to empire was as impressive to the political thinkers of these three hundred years as it is to us; and while many of the questions which they asked about it may seem to be characteristic only of the ancient world, others surely are more universal in nature.

A Greek Examines Roman Politics: The Speculations of Polybius

It is fortunate for the historian of political theory that at the very juncture when Rome was becoming a world state an extraordinarily acute mind pondered the meaning and significance of Roman politics and of the Roman constitution as he had come to know it. Polybius was an historian, a world traveller, a politician, and a military strategist. A Greek coming from an area bitterly hostile to Rome, he yet lived to be an adviser to Roman generals and a confidant of Roman statesmen.

He was born in 203 B.C. in Megalopolis, a city

which participated actively in the Achaean League during the period when it was endeavoring to preserve some remnants of independence for Greek cities. His father was a leader in the affairs of the league and Polybius seems from a very early age to have been brought up as a diplomat destined for the league's service. At the age of thirty-four, during the very period when the Roman power was beginning to be suspicious of his family, he was elected Hipparch (commander of cavalry) by the league's assembly.

Eventually (in 167), along with other prominent leaders of the league, he was taken to Italy by the Romans, who had with some justification become suspicious of the league, even though some of its leaders appeared to be pro-Roman.

Once in Italy, Polybius obtained special privileges, in part because of his friendship with Aemilius Paulus, whom he had met in Greece, and in part by reason of his personal charm. He was allowed to remain in Rome, while most of his fellow-exiles had been forced to reside outside the metropolis. He became tutor to the sons of Aemilius Paulus and initiated that long study of the Roman constitution which was to affect so profoundly his political theory and attitudes.

In 149, he was asked by the Romans to become their adviser in the campaigns of the third and last Punic War. He may have known the Carthaginian language and he was certainly a close student of military strategy. He was present when Scipio burned the city in the spring of 146 and noted the melancholy reflections of the Roman commander as he forecast a possible like fate for the city of Rome.[7]

The remaining part of his life was spent in travel and in composition of his *Histories*, which are the main source of his political theory. On occasion he appears to have continued to advise Roman leaders, who seem to have had great respect for his sagacity, despite the still-prevalent Roman hostility to Greek culture. He died in the year of Caius Gracchus' assassination (121 B.C.).

Polybius' was not a political doctrine woven in the secluded shade of a Stoic porch but rather one hammered out on the anvil of a long career in politics and diplomacy. Unlike the Stoics of his time, who were just beginning to affect Roman thought, he has very little to say of the remoter implications of political activity: he does not endeavor to connect his ethical and political views, for example, with any particular cosmology. But he does share, in some measure, the fatalistic position so often espoused by Stoic teachers.

He carries over from classical Greek political thought an admiration for the Lycurgan constitution and a classification of constitutions very much like that of Aristotle. The *permissible* forms are kingship, aristocracy, and democracy. The *degenerate* constitutions include tyranny, oligarchy, and what Polybius calls "mob-rule."

As a close student of Roman politics, Polybius was interested in determining the reasons for the "success"—as he calls it—of the Republic. By success, he apparently means the ability to conquer most of the world within a relatively short period of time[8] and, of equal importance, the "stability" supposedly achieved in Roman institutions.[9] He finds the key to that success in the "balance" of the constitution; the Roman polity, he argues, does not rest on "one species of power." It is a "mixed" constitution.

It is significant that Polybius examines Roman politics at the end of the third century and not toward the close of the second. Although he is writing in the second, he tells us explicitly that

4. Cf. Otto Kiefer, *Sexual Life in Ancient Rome*, London: Routledge, 1941. Kiefer argues that desire to inflict pain was characteristic of Roman culture under both the Republic and the Empire.
5. By the end of the second century, many of the hallmarks of "ideal-type" bureaucracy as described by modern scholars like Max Weber are nicely illustrated. See Frank F. Abbott, *Municipal Administration in the Roman Empire*, Princeton: Princeton University Press, 1926; and Harold Mattingly, *The Imperial Civil Service of Rome*, Cambridge: Cambridge University Press, 1910.
6. Flamininus (229–174 B.C.) was the "liberator" of Greek cities from the tyranny of Alexander the Great's successors and helped introduce Greek culture into Italy.
7. Polybius, *Histories*, 2 vols., Evelyn S. Shuckburgh, trans., London: Macmillan, 1889, Bk. XXXIX, Ch. 5. "At the sight of the city utterly perishing amidst the flames Scipio burst into tears, and stood long reflecting on the inevitable change which awaits cities, nations, and dynasties, one and all, as it does every one of us men."
8. *Ibid.*, ch. 1.
9. *Ibid.*, ch. 10.

he is looking at the Roman constitution as it existed at the time of the battle of Cannae (216 B.C., in the Second Punic War). At the same time, it is evident that he thinks of the constitution as a living developing thing which, despite its relative excellence, is subject to decay.

The Roman polity as he conceives it, has a "despotic" aspect in the consuls, an "aristocratic" element in the Senate, and a popular one in the comitias. When not leading the legions, the consuls remain in Rome supervising the administration and the other magistrates. They are responsible for calling the Senate together, for introducing ambassadors to that body, and for summoning the comitia. Their powers of discipline over the army are almost absolute.

At the same time, Polybius points out, the Senate has important prerogatives which limit and condition the consuls, as well as other magistrates. The quaestors, for example, cannot release money from the treasury without a decree of the Senate; and that body is also responsible for the granting of money for construction and repair of public buildings. Crimes committed in Italy—including treason, conspiracy, poisoning, or murder—are "in the hands of" the Senate.

However, Polybius would not have us believe that the popular element is inconsequential. The people, as a matter of fact, are the "sole fountain of honour and of punishment." Appeals on matters of life and death go to the people. It is they who elect the magistrates and who pass or repeal laws in the ultimate sense. And when terms are proposed for alliances or treaties, the people must ultimately accept them if they are to have validity.

But what interests Polybius is not merely the diversity of functions found in the three parts of the state. He is equally if not more concerned to show that the parts "can, when they choose, oppose or support each other."[10] Thus the consul, while ostensibly supreme in his command of the army, is dependent on the Senate for the voting of supplies. Then, too, the Senate can, by its actions, emphasize or deemphasize the merits and demerits of respective generals and thus make or break them in their careers.

Likewise are Senate and people mutually interdependent. The former, for example, must get the consent of the latter for decrees which punish offences with death. In general, as a matter of fact, the people are final in passage or rejection of new laws. Of even greater importance is the fact that the tribunes have a veto on acts of the Senate; and the tribunes are in a peculiar sense the agents of the people.

Polybius shrewdly suggests, too, that the people are in some respects very much dependent on the consuls. For "men do not rashly resist the wishes of the Consuls, because one and all may become subject to their absolute authority on a campaign."[11]

So far does Polybius go in praise of the Roman constitution that he thinks no other historical polity can match it. The tests of a good constitution are whether its customs and laws conduce to "holy and pure" private lives and whether the public life of the state is "civilized and just." By these standards, the Roman is clearly the superior of the Cretan constitution and even of the Spartan system. The Cretan scheme allowed unlimited possession of land and placed great emphasis on the value of money: the result was treachery and avarice in private affairs and inequity as the half-mark of public life. The Spartan constitution avoided these pitfalls, it is true; but Polybius, like Plato and Aristotle before him, points out that the very scheme which made Spartans "disinterested and sober-minded" in relation to their own way of life tended to produce aggressiveness and desire to dominate externally. Yet the constitution which they possessed did not permit them to be "successful" as aggressors, in part because their economic system, by failing to establish a money economy, did not provide flexibility for trading purposes.

In his comparison of Roman and Spartan constitutions, it is difficult to discover whether Polybius favors the expanding state or not. He can be interpreted as an apologist for Roman imperialism. On the other hand, he also hedges his statements in such a way that he can be thought of simply as a scientist seeking to show the conditions under which a state can succeed in a career of conquest. He makes it clear that if the objective be the preservation of "freedom" alone, and not external expansion, there has never existed a constitution "preferable to that of Sparta." On the other hand, "if one is seeking aggrandisement . . . the Spartan constitution is deficient and that of Rome superior and better constituted for obtaining power."[12]

One of the central superiorities of the Roman constitution is the way in which it uses religion. The "fear of the gods" means something to Romans, whereas it had become a mere superstition to sophisticated Greeks. If one could ever construct a nation of "philosophers," he speculates, religion might not be necessary. But so long as most men are not philosophers, their fickleness, "lawless desires, unreasoning anger, and violent passion" must be restrained by the "mysterious terrors and scenic effects" of religious rites. Religion is for him, then, primarily a civic device—an instrument for government.

It is highly significant, however, that Polybius recognizes the possible seeds of "decay" in the Roman constitution. Even the most balanced polity, he thinks, cannot long resist a "high pitch of prosperity and undisputed power." The way of life of the majority will tend to be filled with envy, jealousy, ostentation, and rivalry for office. The people will be suspicious and will be flattered by ambitious politicians. At the same time, they will covet the wealth of the few. Under such circumstances, Polybius argues, "mob-rule" will be imminent.

He did not live to see the disorder of the first century, of course; but in his assertion that even the most "balanced" of constitutions might be subject to decay, he gives us a clue as to how he might have reacted to the events of the two generations from his own death to the time of Julius Caesar.

In some measure, it might be observed, his picture of balance in Roman politics is overdrawn, even for the time of which he purports to speak. Thus he gave the people a somewhat greater independence than they ever possessed; and despite his great emphasis on economic factors, he seems not to have understood how the wholesale extension of chattel slavery would help alter the social basis of Roman political life.

Issues of this kind were bequeathed to the generation of Cicero, who in many respects failed, as did Polybius, to understand them.

Cicero and the Idea of the Commonwealth

Cicero was neither an original nor a particularly profound social and political thinker.

Born in 106 B.C., only fifteen years after the deaths of Caius Gracchus and Polybius, he came from a rising family of Arpinum, a town lying about twelve miles northwest of Rome. Politically, this middling, suburban birth was later to make him suspect both to the aristocratic faction of Roman politics and to the increasingly influential proletariat. The first period of his life might be said to extend to 77 B.C. These were the years of his basic education, under skilled tutors, and of some travel. In 89, too, he underwent a brief spell of military service in the army of Sulla. His legal studies were directed by Q. Mucius Scaevola, one of the early great jurisconsults who were to play so large a role in the evolution of Roman law. In 79 he travelled and studied in the East, partly for reasons of health; and it was during this tour of Asia and Greece that he became profoundly impressed by the Stoic attitude to society in the teaching of Posidonius of Rhodes (the student of that Panaetius who, as we observed earlier, had first introduced the teaching of Zeno to the Roman world).

Returning to Rome in 77, Cicero very soon embarked upon his political career. But he entered politics by way of the law, just as is so true of many American politicians.

By 66, he had been chosen praetor and thus gained additional legal experience as supervisor of the law-courts. After this step up the ladder, he was prepared to run for the consulate, to which he was elected for the year 63.

As Consul, he appeared to be confronted by almost every kind of crisis, but undoubtedly the most significant was the so-called "conspiracy of Catiline." Catiline, an aristocrat fallen upon evil days, apparently placed himself at the head of a group of dissatisfied commoners and demanded debt-cancellation laws and a revival of Gracchus-like land reforms. Unsuccessful in gaining office, he was alleged by Cicero to have planned a military rebellion, which Cicero's private investigators uncovered in time. Four of the so-called conspirators were strangled by Cicero's orders (after he had consulted the Senate) and Catiline himself was killed in the battle which ensued when Roman legions were sent to pursue the troops that had rallied to his banner. In later years Cicero was to point to the crushing of the Catilinian conspiracy as one of his greatest accomplishments as consul.

10. *Ibid.*, ch. 15
11. *Ibid.*, ch. 17.
12. *Ibid.*, ch. 50.

After his year's consulship had expired, Cicero's political fortunes began to wane. Although he was immensely popular in certain middle-income circles, the aristocrats never really trusted him; and the populus, many of whom had sympathized with the Catilinian proposals, resented his savage attacks on proposals for radical agrarian reform. This hostility was undoubtedly used by certain politicians for their own advantage. Thus Julius Caesar, who had carefully cut himself off from Catilinian connections in the nick of time, appealed as a good demagogue to the anti-Ciceronian sentiments of the comitia.

After a period of exile from Rome, Cicero was recalled and asked to be governor of Cilicia. No sooner did he return from that assignment in 49, however, than he was confronted by the incipient civil war between the forces of Caesar and those of Pompey. He could hardly remain neutral between the two and eventually decided—reluctantly, as we must suppose—to cast in his lot with Pompey, who had secured his return from exile. When Pompey was defeated in 48, he might have expected to be on a list of the proscribed. But Caesar, shrewd politician that he was, decided that Cicero's still considerable following might be useful to him. He made great professions of friendship for the aging republican orator. Cicero, however, felt that his position was now too precarious for him to participate actively in politics. Hence he retired once more to his study, now more convinced than ever that the Republic was being subverted.

And indeed, the demise of republican institutions was not far away. Already their strength had been sapped over the course of the preceding century. The balanced constitution which Polybius had seen was, assuming it had ever existed at all, a thing of the past. Military power now overshadowed the traditional institutions. The Senate was packed by Caesar; and the tribunes, ostensibly reflecting an independent position in Roman politics, were also his creatures by virtue of his control of the comitia which elected them.

It was this scene which confronted Cicero as he meditated and wrote during the last years of his life. Then suddenly there came the news of Caesar's assaisination (in 44) by a small band of men who were undoubtedly devoted to republican institutions. Was the Republic saved? Cicero apparently thought that there might still be hope, strange as that may appear to us who have the wisdom of hindsight. He returned to his seat in the Senate. But he was quickly made aware that the manipulations of Marcus Antonius, far from strengthening the republican cause, were leading only to more civil war.

He was soon informed that his safety was in jeopardy and made preparations to flee. But before he could board his ship, he was overtaken by a squad of Antony's soldiers, who butchered him without mercy in December of 43.

Some appreciation of Cicero's political biography is indispensable for an understanding both of his political attitude and of his theory. For the practical politics in which he was involved set for him the problems, or at least posed the alternatives, which led to the questions that he had to answer as a political thinker. We first inquire into his position on the constitutional issues of his day and then turn to his more general political theory.

The clue to his stand on the Roman constitution will be found, at least in part, in his social background and education. As we have noted, he came from a family relatively well-off financially but who were not members of the ancient aristocracy. At the same time, his family connections were such that they permitted very little identification with the cause of those who were attacking what they regarded as the property inequities of the time. Throughout his career, Cicero aspired to be accepted by the aristocracy and yet in the end never really made the grade, despite his many services to the families of social status.

On the other hand, his very ambition to "arrive," as we should say today, led him to be cautious about associating with the causes dear to the heart of the populus.

His education, too, served to strengthen his frequent ambivalence. He had thorough training in the traditions of the Republic, of course, but in addition was shaped by the teaching of the New Academy—then under control of the Skeptics—and of the Stoics through Posidonius. Through the Skeptic side of his education, Cicero came to doubt the possibility of any certain knowledge, even of what Aristotle called speculative science, let alone of practical philosophy. It became difficult for him, then, to develop an independent view which he might hold to be based on any definite truth. This tended, in politics, to make him fall back on the "traditions of the Republic" as the only rock upon which one might stand politically.

On the other hand, his Stoic training had in

some measure counteracted the impact of Skepticism, since Stoicism held (as we have seen) that sensation afforded some certain cognition and that in ethics and politics men, by understanding nature, could live according to reason. Cicero was never able to work out a view either of the world as a whole or of politics in particular which could integrate these diverse strands of his education.

Keeping these factors in mind, then, let us endeavor to understand Cicero's attitudes toward the constitutional crises of his time. Basically, he seems to have accepted Polybius' view of the Roman constitution as a balance of social, economic, and political power. The "image" in his mind was of a society held together by an ancient tradition which assigned to each part of the polity its due bounds. Cicero does not tell us how this constitution came to be, whether by reason or by trial and error. He simply accepts it as the norm by which all good Romans should live. All drastic proposals for change, whether coming from the aristocracy or from the populus, he tends to reject as likely to disturb the balance.

Let us note, for example, his attitude to the Catilinian conspiracy. Here was a scheme which purported to change rather fundamentally the economic relations of the classes as Cicero had seen them through early manhood. It is, of course, difficult to know whether the conspirators had any articulate social and political philosophy and, if so, just what it was. Scholarship is not certain. On the one hand, there are those who, like F. R. Cowell,[13] think that Catiline was a "seedy aristocrat" striving by debt cancellation laws to wipe out his own enormous personal debts which had been incurred through riotous living.

A drastically different view of Catiline and his followers is taken by Max Beer, who thinks of them as exemplars and exponents of the class struggle in ancient Rome. The sentiments of the Roman masses, argues Beer, were "revolutionary"; and Catiline, in addition to being an aristocrat by birth, was a noble-minded leader seeking to give political effect to this revolutionary fervor. Catiline was "leader of the dispossessed and . . . a reformer, whose proposals aimed at securing a share in the land to all the dispossessed."[14]

To students like Cowell, Cicero's attitude toward the Catilinian conspiracy was an effort to defend the *principle* of the Republic. He was battling a decadent aristocracy many of whose members—including Catiline—did not know how to manage material resources in a money economy and hoped to use the machinery of the state to eliminate their private difficulties. The fact that many of the populus followed Catiline is no indication that either the leadership or its followers were attached to any universal principles of "justice." They were out simply to "feather their own nests."[15]

By contrast, the Beerian position is that Cicero was a "representative of the property interests" and had no conception of the merits of those views which argued for a redistribution of land and a cancellation of debts. To support his interpretation of Cicero's position, he cites[16] a passage from the Senator's essay *Duties*[17] in which protection of material possessions seems to be exalted as the chief concern of any good state:

> But they who wish to be popular, and upon that account either attempt the agrarian affair that the owners may be driven out of their possessions, or they that borrowed money shall be released to the debtors, sap the foundations of the constitution; for this is the peculiar concern of a State and city, that every person's custody of his own property be free and undisturbed.

It would seem that both Beer and Cowell manage to get at something of Cicero's attitude. There can be no question about his position on the "property question" which had been agitating Rome for some three generations. The *first* duty, he avers, of the governor of a state is to make sure that each individual is preserved in the "quiet enjoyment" of "his own." "For to what end were cities and commonwealths established," he asks, "but only that every one might be safer and securer in the enjoyment of his own?"[18]

Significantly enough, Cicero makes the second

13. F. R. Cowell, *Cicero and the Roman Republic*, 1948; Penguin edition, 1956, pp. 231–233.
14. *General History of Socialism and Social Struggles—Social Struggles in Antiquity*, Vol. 1, New York: Russell & Russell, 1957, p. 145.
15. F. R. Cowell, *op. cit.*, 234–235.
16. Max Beer, *op. cit.*, 145–146.
17. Book II, ch. 22–24. The *Duties* is usually translated *The Offices*. See also the translation of *De Officiis* (Offices) by Thomas Cockman in *Cicero's Offices*, Int. by Joseph Warrington; London: J. M. Dent, 1909, 1955, pp. 108–111.
18. Cicero, *De Officiis*, II, 21.

important duty of the governor that he not impose taxes, unless absolutely necessary. Our forefathers, it is true, he observes, did have to levy taxes to carry on their wars and when the treasury was low. But this should always be looked upon as a last extremity. And it is true, of course, that by Cicero's time Italy was beginning to be immune from taxation—a situation which was not to change until the declining days of the empire.

The third function of the governor, he holds, is to furnish the commonwealth "with all the conveniences and necessaries of life."[19] He seems to assume that his readers know what these are and how they can be provided; and he is much more concerned that public officials do not develop "sticky fingers" in ensuring the necessities than he is in identifying the conveniences. Moreover, he does not even deal with the problem of reconciling his admonition against taxation with the presumed duty to provide necessities.

With Beer, however, we can agree that he is a staunch defender of property rights in the abstract and has but little understanding of the surging masses of the cities who were rootless and traditionless and who were struggling desperately to discover a "place in the sun."

On the other hand, Cicero is not *merely* the spokesman of "property" interests, if by this it is meant that he had no wider concerns in discoursing on the commonwealth; and to the degree that interpreters like Cowell call attention to this fact, they are providing a much-needed balance for the extreme "class-warfare" expositors.

Cicero's dilemma about the property question in relation to preservation of the Republic was not, of course, an untypical one. It is the problem of anyone living in an era of rapid change who seeks "order." Historically, one contrasts current disorder with past stability. Among the characteristics of the disorder are attacks on established property relationships. What is more "reasonable" in one sense than to conclude that the attacks are causes rather than expressions of the disorder?

In taking this position, Cicero did not or could not see that in vindicating property he was supporting that very disorder which, as he correctly saw, was destroying the Republic. In defending property as it had come to exist in the Rome of 50 B.C., he was in effect sustaining those very forces of plunder, proletarianization, and "alienation" that were rapidly turning Rome first into a regime which Polybius would have called mob-rule and then into a despotism. He legitimately railed at Caesar for the latter's demagogic promises of land distribution which were largely unfulfilled. But he did not see that the republican order for which he searched required, above all, that men be given once more a stake in society if they were to act responsibly.

Had he been the profound political thinker he professed to be, instead of a rather hapless moralist caught in a web out of which he could not escape, he would have understood that only a radical social and economic solution might have conserved the Republic. Instead, he reduced his cry to one which constantly repeated "save the Republic" but did so in a social and economic context utterly incompatible with republican politics.

As for Cicero's systematic and academic reflections on politics,[20] his philosophical position is an eclectic one; for he drew something from Platonists, Skeptics, and Stoics without committing himself to any one position. At the same time, we may be sure that when he deals with such notions as "justice" he is never too far removed from his study of Roman political experience.

He traces the beginning of political society to the need of the "poorer sort" of people for protection against the oppression of the rich.[21] Kings originally were obeyed, then, because they provided through their virtue and "justice" a necessary safeguard for the mass of men; for the mass saw in royal rulers the principle of equity against that of sheer force. So long as men could obtain equity by personal rule, they were quite content, and, indeed, Cicero implies, this royal rule ideally is the best.

It is curious that he should make the origin of politics and law lie in the oppression of the poor by the rich, when in his own day he seemed so blind to the economic realities which underlay the struggles of the dying Republic. But the fact that he did hold this view (ascribing it to Herodotus) is clear.

Once the notion of justice arose and had found eventual embodiment in law, the idea of the "commonwealth" or Republic was born, according to Cicero. A true populus, in the political sense, he defines as an assemblage associated by a common acknowledgment of right and by a community of interests. When men violate the justice which theoretically is reflected in law, they begin to dissolve the *respublica;* and what was formerly a populus becomes simply a mob or an aggregate.

Cicero attempts to illustrate his meaning through examples from Greek and Roman history. It is human nature, he contends, to desire the society of other men; and when governors appeal to this nature by acting with justice and equity, the bonds of society are strengthened. The endeavor of every ruler who seeks to perpetuate the ideal of the *respublica* should be to obtain men's love rather than their hate. "Obedience, proceeding from fear, cannot possibly be lasting; whereas that which is the effect of love will be faithful for ever."[22]

Illustrating this thesis, he argues that so long as the republic "supported itself, not by the methods of injustice and violence, but rather by actions of kindness and gentleness, wars were undertaken to protect its allies, or defend its honour. . . ."[23] But after the victory of Sulla (82 B.C.), Cicero argues, "people began to think nothing could be unjust to their confederates and allies, when once they had seen so great cruelties exercised even on their very fellow-citizens." While Sulla's cause was "just," his victory was "cruel and unjust." He established the precedent whereby the Republic fell away from the "justice" of its early days; until by the time of Caesar, "whose cause was impious, and his victory yet more scandalous and inhuman [than that of Sulla]" the commonwealth "is absolutely sunk into ruins and nothing."

Cicero conceives law as a reflection of justice, which, as with Plato, is "eternal." Certain norms are universal and no people can "repeal" them; and it is these norms which the Roman people have violated. In *De Republica*, for example, he gives a Stoic-like definition of law as transcending all human enactments yet at the same time judging those enactments:

> True law is indeed right reason, conformable to nature, pervading all things, constant, eternal.[24]

And in *De Republica*, too, Scipio, through whom Cicero speaks, praises "reason" with which law in this universal sense is identified:

> As, among the different sounds which proceed from lyres, flutes, and the human voice, there must be maintained a certain harmony which a cultivated ear cannot endure to hear disturbed or jarring, but which may be elicited in full and absolute concord by the modulation even of voices very unlike one another; so, where reason is allowed to modulate the diverse elements of the state, there is obtained a perfect concord from the upper, lower, and middle classes as from various sounds.[25]

As the Roman Republic ceased gradually to be that populus which Cicero's doctrine of law and justice exalted, his conviction that there was a universal standard for law seemed to grow. Through all his ethical and political essays there runs the same refrain. It was perhaps the conflict between Cicero the aspiring politician and Cicero the philosopher which accounts for his serious ambiguities and ambivalences—his assertion, on the one hand, that the state arose to protect the poor from the rich, while, on the other, he seems to see no injustice in the Republic of his day; his contention that wars of conquest are against nature, accompanied, though, by his seeming blindness to the fact that many of Rome's military expeditions long before the days of Sulla were wars of conquest; his conception of a populus held together by common interest under justice-informed law as over against any basic economic and social reform which could alone have given reality, in his day, to the conception; his emphasis on legal and political tradition combined with his fundamental acceptance of a social and economic structure antagonistic to that tradition.[26]

Toward the close of his life, Cicero became more and more of a Stoic in his attitude to political life. As he despaired of any restoration of the republican scheme of things, he began to look upon the world of actual law and politics with resignation. Those influenced by later Stoicism were to develop more fully Cicero's confidence in the notion of universal law and at the same time were to give voice to

19. *op. cit.*, II, 21, 106.
20. See George Holland Sabine and Stanley Barney Smith's Introduction to Cicero's *On the Commonwealth*, Columbus: Ohio State University Press, 1929.
21. *De Officiis*, II, 12.
22. *Ibid.*, II, 7.
23. *Ibid.*, II, 8.
24. *Ibid.*, III, XXII, 33.
25. Compare with Cicero's quote in Sabine and Smith, *op. cit.*, p. 193.
26. See particularly Books I and III in Sabine and Smith, *op. cit.*

his despair about affecting the course of political evolution under the Empire.

Stoicism, the Primitive, and Politics

It has sometimes been asserted that the Stoicism of the first two centuries of the Empire was the philosophy which shaped and molded the whole intellectual life of Rome and its provinces. If one understood developments in later Stoicism one might well comprehend the ethical and political "mind" of the Empire down to the end of the second century. In considerable degree, of course, this contention is not without foundation. But we should be wary in our interpretation of it. If by the statement we mean that all those who reflected on moral and political issues *consciously* and *deliberately* adopted Stoic explanations and attitudes, we should almost certainly be mistaken.

Actually, almost all the positions to be adopted by the Stoicism of the first two centuries A.D. were foreshadowed by Cicero. But the emphases were often different; and the political context in which they were developed was a radically changed one. Whereas Cicero speculated in the decaying Republic, such men as Seneca, Epictetus, and Marcus Aurelius looked out upon a world in which the principle of monarchy had been firmly established.

It was a world, too, in which the social and economic relations taking shape in Cicero's day were now taken for granted. True, large slave raids were largely of the past (although there were important exceptions, as with the capture of Jerusalem in 70 A.D.). But the widespread use of slaves for agricultural purposes, as well as for many of the skilled trades, continued. The *latifundia* or large estates, which so many called in question during the time of Polybius and Cicero, had almost completely supplanted small-peasant farming. The proletariat of the cities, now swollen even more in numbers, were kept docile by regular corn and oil supplies and by even more elaborate public entertainments.

A typical Stoic thinker of the epoch is Seneca (4 B.C. to A.D. 65), the Spanish-born son of the rhetorician Seneca. Part politician, part man of letters, and part philosopher and political thinker, he was educated in Rome, became tutor to the young Nero, and was influential during the earlier part of the latter's reign.[27] He managed to "feather his own nest" financially in the process and at the same time to write essays on morals which exalted the virtues of honesty and public responsibility. The contrast, indeed, between the Stoic moral views of Seneca, on the one hand, and his public activities, on the other, is a remarkable one.

Characteristically enough, later Stoic doctrine, as with Seneca and Marcus Aurelius, stressed the gulf between the "material" and the "spiritual." While earlier Stoicism had tended to think of man in "anthropologically monistic" terms—that is, as wholly matter, even though somewhat "depotentiated"—the Stoicism of the Empire moved in the direction of "anthropological dualism." That is, the gulf between matter or flesh and spirit grew; and the former came to be associated with evil while the latter was good. In many respects, the Stoicism of the first two centuries A.D. comes to conceive of a kind of war between the flesh and the spirit.

This general framework is, of course, not without significance for its political position. Inheriting as it does from earlier Stoicism the notion of the world as a cosmopolis of equal men and women, it seeks to account for the fact that men in the Empire as it knows it are not equal. It observes the miserable condition of slaves, for example; and it notes the increasing separation of ruler from ruled—a fission which was to extend much further, of course, in the third century but which was already significant in the second. It is aware, too, of course, that the economic independence of most Romans has been lost. Just as political man finds himself without a field of action in which he can preserve his dignity, so the economic man discovers himself dependent on the arbitrary actions of others.

The fatalist tendency which we noted in earlier Stoicism does not allow the Stoic-thinking men of the first two centuries to become radical social reformers. They can hardly seek, therefore, to lessen the gulf between the notion of cosmopolis and the political reality of their day. Yet somehow they must account for that reality. Why, if men by reason can discover a "law of nature" which transcends the inequalities of society, cannot that society eliminate those inequalities? Why, if slavery is unnatural—as all Stoics teach—does the political society tolerate it?

Gradually, the thought of the empire, in order to answer these questions, evolves the notion that there must have entered a kind of corruption into human nature. The cosmopolis which is so natural was somehow destroyed and the *civitas* of history is the result. And once the original nature has been lost, the particular manifestations of corruption, such as slavery and tyranny, must be accepted by the wise man as inevitable fruits of the corruption. He will seek to mitigate, it is true, the lot of the slave and to do what he can to limit the effects of tyranny; but he is important, by reason of the general corruption, to make fundamental changes.

This general climate of opinion, in great part Stoic but to some degree transcending Stoicism, can be illustrated in many ways. Thus the historian Sallust, writing in the first century B.C., yearns in his treatise on Catiline, for the time when men were free and living in harmony—an age which he apparently associates with an historical epoch. And the poet Virgil paints in his *Georgics*[28] the picture of a society still under the rule of Saturn and before the days of Jove, who reduced men to conditions of subordination:

> Before the rule of Jove no tillers used to subdue the fields. It was impious then e'en to mark the field or distinguish it by bounds. Men's gains were for the common stock; of her own free-will more readily the earth did all things bear when none solicited her gifts.

The satirist Horace does not disagree. He, too, exalts the primitive and finds it yet present among the Scythians.[29]

And Seneca himself actually seems to believe that there was an idyllic age in which freedom was combined with plenty and mutual sharing with harmony.[30]

While there were many ways of expressing the notion of corruption in human nature and society, the entry of "avarice" into the life of man seems to symbolize for literary men and Stoics alike the end of primitive nature.

The poet Ovid, a contemporary of Augustus, gives most vivid expression to the notion of the degeneracy of man from the primitive. As do so many from the time of Augustus to the end of the second century, Ovid thinks of human history in terms of "ages." The first age is "golden." It gives place to "silver," which leads to "bronze" and then to "iron":

> Then sprang up first the golden age, which of itself maintained
> The truth and right of everything, unforced and unconstrained.
> There was no fear of punishment, there was no threatening law

> In brazen tables nailed up, to keep the folk in awe.
> . . . .
> Men knew none other countries yet than where themselves did keep:
> There was no town enclosed yet with walls and ditches deep.
> No horn nor trumpet was in use, no sword nor helmet worn.
> The world was such that soldier's help might easily be forborne.
> The fertile earth as yet was free, untouched of spade or plough,
> And yet it yielded of itself of every thing enow.
> . . . .
> Of iron is the last
> In no part good and tractable as former ages past;
> For when that of this wicked age once opened was the vein
> Therein all mischief rushed forth, the faith and truth were fain
> And honest shame to hide their heads; for whom stepped stoutly in.
> Craft, treason, violence, envy, pride, and wicked lust to win.[31]

Although Ovid in explicit terms makes the age of iron the prelude to a gigantic destruction of the world through flood, the gods having become angry with humankind, many social thinkers during the first two centuries apparently think of the cycle repeating itself. Ovid himself suggests that a new race of men emerges after the flood, although he does not tell us explicitly whether the antedeluvian "ages" are duplicated. We do know that it was the Stoic tendency to think of political and social history as an almost monotonous repetition of the "fall" from a golden age.

In the whole idealization of primitive simplicity, one notes again, as in the days of the Hellenistic monarchies, a tendency to question the values of "civilization." While the classical Greeks maintained that human life could be fulfilled only in the polis or *civitas*—hence in

27. Francis C. Holland, *Seneca the Philosopher and His Modern Message*, London: Longmans, Green, 1920.
28. *Georgics*, Bk. I.
29. Horace, *Complete Works*, Casper J. Kraemer, Jr., ed., New York: Book League of America, 1938, III, 24, pp. 259–260.
30. *Letters*, 90.
31. "Metamorphoses," in *Ovid: Selected Works*, J. C. and M. J. Thornton, eds., translated by Arthur Golding, London: J. M. Dent, 1939, pp. 134–136.

politics and civilization—the later Stoics see an enormous tension between the goals of individual morality and the apparently inevitable practical necessities of political society. Even more than the earlier Stoic schools, they endeavor to carve out an individual world of private morality which will be immune to the shocks and violence of the kind of politics which they know. In so doing, they lay the groundwork for that attitude to the state and the world which will characterize early Christianity.[32]

Meanwhile, as the philosophers and literary men increasingly set up a dualism between the good "primitive" and the fallen "political," the Roman courts are wrestling with the problems of moral and legal thought at an entirely different level.

"Natural Law" and the Growth of Roman Legal Thought

The occasions which gave rise to the speculations of the Roman jurists cannot be fully understood without some reference to the development of Roman legal and judicial machinery from the foundation of the city to the end of the second century A.D. The growth of Roman law and the proliferation of the machinery for its administration both reflected and in part shaped the political expansion of the Empire.[33] In the process, the legal system had to make adjustments to relatively rapid social change and develop conceptions that might hold together the multiplicity of nationalities which constituted the Empire. At the same time, it could not help being affected by the transition from republican to imperial institutions; and the tension which so commonly exists between political rulers, on the one hand, and judges, on the other, was to be a factor of some importance. The creative work of the great Roman jurists—men like Papinian, Paul, Ulpian, Gaius, and Modestinus—ended, however, in the first quarter of the third century and thereafter the conceptions worked out in the earlier epochs remained a fixed and relatively unchanging tradition in ancient times.

The earliest Roman law—that which arose under the monarchy—was largely customary, as one might expect. About the middle of the fifth century B.C.—approximately two generations after the founding of the Republic—the main provisions of the traditional law were codified in the famous Twelve Tables. Meanwhile, the consuls had superseded the king as general supervisors of the legal machinery. The duties of the consuls apparently included formulation of procedural rules for the courts as well as administration of the judicial department.

By the early part of the fourth century B.C., it was becoming evident to many that the consuls, occupied as they were with political, military, and general administrative duties, could no longer adequately attend to their judicial functions. In 367, therefore, the office of praetor was created to relieve them. Subsequently the number of praetors was increased as the territory of Rome expanded and the administration of the law became more complex. In 247, the office of *praetor peregrinus*, or praetor for foreigners, was created. As the title of his office indicates, his was the task of overseeing the administration of the law which sought to reconcile and adjudicate claims of persons living under diverse legal systems (for Rome, as it expanded, generally continued to recognize the legal systems of the people it conquered). The older *praetor urbanus*, or the praetor of the city, continued, of course, to supervise the legal machinery which administered the law that applied to Roman citizens.

No sooner had the Twelve Tables been established than they required interpretation, particularly because subsequent generations were living through a period of relatively rapid social change. At the beginning of each year, the praetor announced publicly the principles which would guide him in administering the law. This announcement, called the *edictum*, afforded him an opportunity to meet probable new situations as they might arise and allowed him, through such devices as the legal fiction, to put new meaning into a law which ostensibly remained the same.

Meanwhile, however, praetors, whether urban or those for foreigners, began to recognize the inadequacy of their technical knowledge. Laymen as they were—for they were usually aspiring politicians intent on the consulship—they began to seek the advice of men who presumably knew more than they did about the law. These were the *iuris consults*, Roman gentlemen of leisure who originally took up the study of law as a kind of hobby; for the law was to a Roman gentleman what philosophy was to his Greek analogue. In reply to the questions of the praetors, the jurists would return advisory answers known as *responsa prudentium*, or "answers of the learned."

As the Republic became the Empire, the annual edict of the praetor, enriched by the advice of the jurists and grappling with practical problems of commerce and family relations, became longer and more complex. The power of the praetor to affect the nature of the law became correspondingly greater.

But the rather wide prerogatives vested in the praetor soon created jealousy on the part of the Emperor who, as republican institutions faded, tended to think of himself as the sole source of law. The annual *edictum* was in effect a device through which law was not only interpreted but also made. Yet the emperor, as delegate of the populus, conceived of his office as the center for making of *leges*. The conflict between emperor and praetor was somewhat like that which developed between the king and the lord chief justice in early seventeenth-century Britain or between Franklin Roosevelt and the Supreme Court in the twentieth century. In the end (A.D. 125), the Emperor (Hadrian) ordered his jurists to draw up and promulgate what was called an *edictum perpetuum*, which was theoretically to supersede all previous edicts and also to eliminate the necessity for revisions in the future. It was, in effect, a kind of codification.

As is true of all codifications, of course, the *edictum perpetuum* was subject to interpretation and it was soon apparent that interpretation was very necessary. Again, the process of developing the law soon put new meaning into the allegedly perpetual edict.

The law itself was theoretically divided (after 247 B.C.) into the *ius civile* and the *ius gentium*, the former consisting of the rules which governed Roman citizens, and the latter of principles whereby the praetor peregrinus settled differences among those living under two or more different legal systems. Precedent was important in the development of both systems, of course, but because of its relatively late beginning and the fact that the praetor peregrinus could more frequently start *de novo*, the *ius gentium* tended to be more flexible and adaptable to changing situations. Very early, as a matter of fact, the rulings of the praetor urbanus began to be affected by those of the praetor peregrinus, until eventually the *ius gentium* for all practical purposes merged with the *ius civile*. In the process, of course, it meant that the law of Rome now found many of its ancient principles modified by the legal systems of Babylon, Phoenicia, and Greece. Just as foreign gods were imported into the Pantheon, so did foreign legal notions help to change the traditional Roman legal system.

As the jurists worked out their doctrines from the first century B.C. to the third century A.D., a central problem associated with their general political and legal doctrine was that of the relationship between and among natural law (by now a common notion, of course), the *ius civile*, and the *ius gentium*. Sometimes we are led to believe by certain modern scholars that the jurists were in agreement about this major concern. But it is obvious that there were wide disagreements if we compare the doctrines of three of the leading jurists—Ulpian, Paul, and Gaius. Ulpian is quoted in the Justinian *Digest* as follows:

> Private law is threefold; it can be gathered from the precepts of nature, or from those of the nations, or from those of the city. Natural law is that which nature has taught all animals; this law indeed is not peculiar to the human race, but belongs to all animals. . . . From this law springs the union of male and female, which we call matrimony, the procreation of children and their education. . . . The law of nations is that law which mankind observes. It is easy to understand that this law should differ from the natural, inasmuch as the latter belongs to all animals, while the former is peculiar to men.[34]

Paul, however, treats the matter in this way:

> We can speak of law in different senses; in one sense, when we call law what is always equitable and good, as in natural law. In another sense, what in each city is profitable to all or to many, as is civil law [*ius civile*].[35]

Gaius, a jurist of the second century—about the time of Marcus Aurelius—has yet a different formulation:

> All peoples who are governed by law and by custom observe laws which in part are their own and in part are common to all mankind. For those laws which each people has given itself are peculiar to each city and are called the civil law

32. See Chapter 8.
33. See Arnold H. M. Jones, *Studies in Roman Government and Law*, New York: Praeger, 1960.
34. I, i, 1.
35. I, i, 11.

[*ius civile*]. . . . But what natural reason dictates to all men and is most equally observed among them is called the law of nations, as that law which is practised by all mankind.[36]

An important conflict would appear to invólve the respective conceptions of *ius naturale*. In Ulpian, "nature" is instinctual and the natural law is therefore that order which man shares with all non-human animals. In Paul and Gaius, by contrast, *ius naturale* is a dictate of "natural reason" which is presumably not vouchsafed to animals other than men. Moreover, while Ulpian distinctly says that *ius naturale* is different from *ius gentium*, Gaius virtually indentifies the two when he asserts that "natural reason" is "called the law of nations."

Assuming for the moment that these statements attributed to the three jurists are genuine (and some scholars have asserted that later interpolations have corrupted the texts),[37] it seems clear that some jurists at least differed with the Stoic conception of natural law and that there must have been serious debates in the second and third centuries as to what the juristic position would be. We should always remember, of course, the *purpose* which natural law served in juristic activity. While philosophical Stoics might use the notion to discover what positive law (if uncontaminated by corruption) ought to be, the jurists think of it as a device to remove ambiguities in the *leges* of the emperor or in the edicts of the praetor. There is no suggestion in the classical jurists that positive laws which violate *ius naturale* are null and void; for this notion does not enter political thought until much later, partly under the influence of Christian thinking. Instead, the jurists seem to be asking themselves, "What shall we understand this word or phrase in the edict or *lex* to mean?" Or, if the edict or *lex* is silent on a given matter of importance, "What would the populus or emperor be likely to say if asked to rule on this issue?"

In endeavoring to fill up interstices of this kind, jurists like Gaius, Paul, Ulpian, and Modestinus do not wish to act in an arbitrary fashion but seek rather some basic substance from which they can, so to speak, mix the legal mortar. They find this substance in the notion of normal human conduct; and although they differ on whether "normality" is to be determined by reference to "instinct" or to "reason," they are united in the view that there *is* a normality that can be discovered. If at some points they seem to identify *ius naturale* with *ius gentium*, it is because they think that a good evidence of normality is to be found in practices which all mankind have in common; and *ius gentium* is built on the assumption that, however varied the *ius civile* may be, there still are *common* elements in the diverse customs of human beings. In interpreting the meaning to be given to words or the absence of words, we must assume that the lawgiver does not intend to prohibit normal conduct nor encourage the abnormal. The standard of normality as against abnormality we find in the *ius naturale*.

Any examination of the classical juristic view must emphasize the nonrevolutionary quality of this outlook. There is no hint in it of natural rights which men can claim against political society; there is no platform from which one can attack such institutions as slavery and war.

The very ambiguities we have noted in the classical juristic conceptions of natural law and of its relations to *ius civile* and *ius gentium* were to constitute texts from which refinements of natural law doctrines could grow when creative legal and political thinking reemerged during the Middle Ages. Nine hundred years after the end of the classical juristic period, the doctrines of Ulpian, Gaius, Paul, Modestinus, and Papinian, transmitted through the Justinian *Digest*, would lead to the great creative epoch of canonical and civilian legal and political thinking. By that time, too, the unrevolutionary doctrines of the jurists would sometimes be given a revolutionary interpretation.

Meanwhile, in the classical age itself, the existence of diversity of cultures and laws—so important for both the Stoics and the jurists—was helping to shape the political philosophies of other thinkers. The common working conceptions of nature, logos, reason—the stuff out of which so much political theory and so many attitudes were made—affected not only Roman politicians, Greek philosphers, and Latin judges, but were also taken up by Jewish thinkers of the first and second centuries. An excellent example of the latter is Philo Judaeus.

Philo Judaeus and the Logos in Political History

Philo Judaeus came from a prominent Jewish family in Alexandria, one of the leading centers of the *diaspora*, and flourished from about

20 B.C. to A.D. 50. He was evidently a spokesman for the Alexandrian Jews in their political relations with the Romans; and we read in Josephus[38] that he was the "principal of the Jewish embassage" in a mission to the Emperor Caligula. That ruler (who occupied the principate from 37 to 41) had initiated the custom of having divine honors paid to the emperor while the latter was yet alive. Many of the Greeks living in Alexandria had charged the Jews with refusing to give proper honor to the emperor and Philo's mission in Rome was to persuade Caligula that the charges were false. In carrying out that mission, he became involved in the intrigues of the imperial court and learned that the emperor had instructed the governor of Syria to erect a statue of Caligula in the Temple at Jerusalem. Eventually this plan failed, in part because Caligula died before he could impose his will by force. This incident, occurring as it did in the midst of Jewish difficulties in Alexandria, made a profound impression on every self-conscious Jew, including Philo. The death of Caligula was to him a providential event and in his political writings he makes much of it. He treats the Alexandrian Jewish problems and his mission to Caligula in two works, *In Flaccum* and *Legatio ad Caium*, and in the process offers reflections on the nature of politics in his day.

But his more profound speculations are to be found in other works. For centuries these treatises were regarded as virtually without political significance, but modern scholars have shown that their political content is considerable and that Philo deliberately veiled much of his meaning in order to avoid prosecution by Roman authority.[39] He is thoroughly familiar with classical Greek political theory and with Cynic and Stoic treatments of nature and natural law. In his attitude to the Roman power and to political history, he anticipates much that was to be characteristic of early Christianity.

Philo can be best understood if we first examine his general conception of the state and of the individual's relation to it. Let us then analyze his understanding of nature and natural law, since no political philosophy of the first two centuries can possibly avoid the terms. Finally, his doctrine of the logos in political history will illustrate his blending of Jewish and Greek conceptions and at the same time emphasize his general attitude to imperial politics.

Like so many of the Stoics, Philo is exceedingly ambivalent with respect to the State and the role of the individual in it. He is torn between his frequently emphasized position that the "highest" life consists in the mystic contemplation by the individual of the good and his equally strong view that the individual cannot be abstracted from the network of relations which constitutes society. His political consciousness is both Greek and Hebrew: Greek, in that he continues much of the Platonic-Aristotelian stress on the organic character of society; Hebrew, because he cannot rid himself of the conviction that God reveals himself in political history.

In one of his most complex allegories—and much of his political teaching assumed allegorical form—he interprets Hebrew Scripture to mean that men are children of two parents, who represent radically different tendencies in human experience. The father or male is "right reason" or "natural law." He pulls men in the direction of pure or naked rationality uncorrupted by custom or merely positive law. Philo seems to think of the "male" principle, in other words, as directing men away from the concrete experiences of history and political controversy and into the world of abstractions or, in Platonic language, of pure Forms. By contrast, the mother, in the words of one of Philo's leading modern interpreters, "is the encyclical course of studies, those based upon human observation and inference."[40] The female commands us to obey the laws of cities, observe customs, and make compromises.

Philo thinks that all human beings fall into

36. I, i, 9.
37. See the brief discussion in A. P. D'Entreves, *Natural Law*, London: Hutchinson's University Library, 1952, ch. 1.
38. Flavius Josephus, *Antiquities of the Jews*, William Whiston, trans., in *The Life and Works of Flavius Josephus*, Philadelphia: John C. Winston Co., 1957, Book XVIII, ch. 8.
39. See particularly Erwin R. Goodenough, *An Introduction to Philo Judaeus*, 2nd ed., Oxford: B. Blackwell, 1962; *Ibid.*, *The Politics of Philo Judaeus: Practice and Theory*, New Haven: Yale University Press, 1938; and Sterling Tracy, *Philo Judaeus and the Roman Principate*, Williamsport, Pa.: The Bayard Press, 1933.
40. Erwin R. Goodenough, *The Politics of Philo Judaeus*, *op. cit.*, 74.

four categories. The first consists of those who obey both "parents" and is the highest of all; the second is composed of those who pay no attention to either and is the lowest; in the third are beings who are obedient only to the father; while the fourth contains men who obey the mother but not the father. If one has to choose between obedience to the male principle as over against conformity to the female, Philo thinks that the male is the better choice. But the wise man or "sage"—and here again the familiar Stoic figure appears—will know how to be obedient to both.

Through this allegory, Philo hopes that he has resolved the dilemma which had puzzled Stoic thinkers almost from the beginning and was of particular concern to those of the first century. How could their sense of an independent individuality be reconciled with their equally profound experience—not shared by the Epicureans—that society was natural? Philo calls men "alien residents" in mortal affairs (a phrase which strikingly anticipates St. Paul) who will flee inwardly from the contentions and passions of political life. Yet outwardly they will participate actively in politics and legislation, seeing these as necessary but not sufficient goods.

In Philo's view of natural law, we find again that blending of Greek and Hebrew elements which is so characteristic of his thought as a whole.[41] The absolute itself is the "archetypal pattern of laws, just as the conceptual sun is of the sensible sun, for from the invisible source the conceptual sun furnishes visible brilliance to the sun that is seen." Although God himself cannot be law, he constitutes the origin of all law and legal institutions. The logos or word proceeds from God and is the highest expression of law. This law of nature is the source, ideally, of all civil law; although in actuality, Philo admits, the laws of existing cities do not conform to natural law. However, Philo goes beyond the Roman jurists in suggesting that all positive law must be tested by the standard to be found in the logos of nature. He certainly implies that positive law not in conformity with the law of nature is not binding on men.

Actually, Philo contends, positive laws may be looked upon, so to speak, as "additions" to the law of nature:

> The Megalopolis, or Great City, . . . uses a single constitution and a single law, and this is the Logos of Nature which enjoins what is to be done, and prohibits what is not to be done. But the variously situated states are unlimited in number and use different constitutions and dissimilar laws; for the different states various customs and laws have been invented and enacted in addition [to the law of Nature].[42]

Here Philo apparently means that civil laws, being diverse and conditioned by such contingencies as wars, tyranny, and luxury, are an expression of the mother. Any man, he suggests, who accepts them (or their parallel customs) without criticism is virtually a slave.

Because he is "divine" and "spiritual," man is a member of the cosmopolis and is subject to the law of nature. In his "material" nature, however, he lives in cities and hence is subject to the inevitably corrupt civil laws which usually reflect the arrogance of the *politicus* and the chance factors of human history. There is thus the *civitas* (or city) of the universe, and the *civitas* of ordinary polities, including the Roman Empire. Man is always torn between the two "cities" and Philo himself suggests that he is constantly tempted to flee the latter *civitas* because of its many corruptions.

Yet he thinks that there are possibilities within the corrupt *civitas*. The law can be an educator, as Plato had seen; and the wise man can, by participating in the "virtue" of the heavenly city, help transform the corrupt city of history. While there is always a warfare between the two cities, it is still possible for civil law to be somewhat modified in favor of the law of the logos. Hence Philo's idealization of the man who can be the son of both father and mother.

But it is in his theory of political change that Philo is perhaps most original. The idea of the logos, or the word or law proceeding from and connecting God with man, was common currency among the intellectuals of the first century. But by no means all of them sought to relate it to the dynamics of political history.

The logos, Philo contends, is in "constant flux." It will on occasion concentrate in one political power, and sometimes in another, depending upon factors which man cannot wholly understand, since the monarch of the universe, God, remains basically a mystery. As political predominance passes from Egypt to Assyria to Babylon to Persia to Macedonia, we witness the movement of the logos from one concentration to another. The injustices of one system are counter-balanced by those of another. In historical time, political power is transferred from one empire to its successor. All given systems pass away as new ones emerge on the horizon. History is thus what Philo calls a gigantic "democracy" held in balance by the logos.

At no point in his examination of the rise and fall of empires does Philo mention Rome. The omission is no doubt deliberate; for anything more than a veiled allusion might have led to prosecution and to more difficulties for the Alexandrian Jews. But we cannot doubt that he would have conceived Rome to be subject to the same Logos flux which controlled all other political concentrations.

If we ask ourselves whether he conceives the flux as having an ending point, the only answer can be that he shares the belief of all pious Jews in the coming of a direct Kingdom of God which will supplant the indirect rule of the logos. The Jews are to be to the human race what the Stoic wise man is to the mass of mankind—a group destined to connect the cosmopolis with the cities of history. In the new era, not only will the lion lie down with the lamb, as in Isaiah, but bears, lions, leopards, and tigers will wag their tails when man comes near them.[43]

Philo apparently conceives this epoch as arising through a quick transformation rather than a slow development.

It seems clear that in his conception of the *way* in which the Messianic Age will arise, Philo has much in common with the Jewish eschatologists. The Jews are quickly transformed, their leaders almost overnight become philosophers, and the slavery of Hebrews everywhere is quite unexpectedly ended. Here Philo is obviously going far beyond the usual modes of Greek and Roman thought and importing into the first century of the Roman principate notions like those of Daniel.

The Theory of Empire

It would be a mistake, of course, to think that most men conceived of the Empire in eschatological terms or even within the somewhat negative framework of the Stoics. As we have seen, the creative jurists continued their work until the early part of the third century; and practical statesmen and permanent administrators, insofar as they thought in large scale fashion at all, were doubtless more concerned about such problems as what some have called the "engineering of consent" than they were with golden ages, degenerate states, or the relation between history and deity. Their speculations would concern themselves with the Empire as a going concern and with its positive role in human life.

No one thinker in the period between Julius Caesar and the age of the Antonines deals with all questions of this kind, although biographers like Suetonius (private secretary to the Emperor Hadrian) and administrators and historians like Dio Cassius (d. 235) seek answers to many of them. Even though the materials are scattered, however, it would seem possible to piece together an implicit theory of empire.

Caesarism and the Theory of Rulership. As was noted earlier, the Empire emerges, according to official ideology, as a device for saving the Republic. Yet from the very beginning characteristically republican tendencies fade into the background. Augustus conceives himself simply as one who holds several republican magistracies; and the Senate, ostensibly at least, subscribes to the same doctrine. Important decrees continue to be issued in the name of the Senate, Augustus still campaigns for his candidates in the comitia,[44] and governors for "senatorial" provinces are chosen by lot from among those ex-magistrates who are eligible. If we are to believe the ancient accounts, Augustus is himself concerned to develop a theory of rulership which will guide him.

In pursuit of such a doctrine, he asks Agrippa and Maecenas, two of his intimates, to state for him alternative conceptions. Agrippa pleads eloquently for a complete restoration of republican institutions and ideologies; while Maecenas states the argument for a kind of disguised monarchy.

Agrippa maintains:

> Equality before the law has a pleasant name and its results are a triumph of justice. If you take men who have received the same nature, are of kindred race to one another, have been brought up under the same institutions, have been trained in laws

41. See Erwin Goodenough, *By Light, Light,* vol. 2, New Haven: Yale University Press, 1935.
42. *De Josepho*, 28.
43. *De Praemiis et Poenis*, 89.
44. Note Suetonius, "Augustus," in *Lives of the Twelve Caesars.* An unexpurgated English version. With notes and an introduction by Joseph Gavorse, ed., New York: Modern Library, 1931.

that are alike, and yield in common the service of their bodies and of their minds to the same State, is it not just that they should have all other things, too, in common? Is it not best that they should secure no superior honors except as a result of excellence? . . .[45]

Agrippa cannot understand why Augustus should even consider being sole ruler. For one thing, he maintains, such a system would not accord with the spirit of Roman institutions. And besides, it would be "unpleasant" for Augustus himself. Romans very early tried a monarchy and found it wanting. On the other hand, they discovered that republican institutions enabled them to achieve greatness and preserve liberty. "The Senate debated, the people ratified, the force under arms showed zeal, and the commanders were fired with ambition."[46] The Romans know from experience, then, the results of both monarchy and republic and they obviously preferred the latter.

Agrippa then proceeds to show how the ruler in a monarchy will be harassed in his personal life. He will be so engrossed in public business that all private enjoyments will have to be eliminated. He will never be free from "biting grief." He will be "subject to many fears, enjoy very little pleasure, but hear and see, perform and suffer, always and everywhere, what is most disagreeable."[47]

Because of these considerations, Agrippa concludes, Augustus should restore to the people "the arms, the provinces, the offices, and the funds." If he does so voluntarily, he will be famous and worthy indeed. But if he has to be forced, he will go down in political history as a person of ill repute.

Maecenas puts the case for monarchy much more verbosely, perhaps because he realizes that tradition is against him and that the benefit of any doubt must be given to the republican argument. He begs Augustus not to be deceived by "fine-sounding names" but rather to examine realistically the results likely to spring from the alternative proposals of Agrippa and himself. Those alone who are "most prudent" should deliberate and only the "most qualified" should become generals. The people should be confined to their everyday occupations and not be allowed to disturb the public business.[48]

The plain fact, Maecenas shrewdly observes, is that while we Romans were "few" in numbers and confined in territory, we could get along very well with our republican government. When we were few, we did not quarrel with our neighbors and were not plagued by factionalism at home. However, once we began to spread beyond the peninsula, "nothing good has been our lot." Our population has become heterogeneous—there are many races and "the most diversified tempers and desires."[49] Such a polity cannot be expected to "rule" itself. Indeed, it will be difficult enough for you to rule it.

Maecenas concludes that if Caesar wishes to avoid the charge of establishing a "kingdom," he can do so by spurning the title "king" but in effect introducing monarchical institutions. Keep only the designation "Caesar," he argues, and perhaps ask the Senate to add to it "Imperator." In so doing "you may obtain all the advantages of a kingdom without the disfavor that attaches to the term itself."[50]

It is, of course, doubtful whether the speeches of Agrippa and Maecenas were ever actually delivered as they are reported to us. But they do at least give us a clue as to what an historian and political thinker two hundred years after Augustus thought were the basic issues which confronted Octavian when he established the principate.

That Augustus tended to follow the advice of Maecenas rather than that of Agrippa is, of course, evident. But it would be a mistake to think of the implicit theory of the Empire as a carbon copy of Maecenean propositions. In the first place, Augustus repudiates certain arguments altogether—those, for example, which contend that elections should be abolished and all non-Roman local institutions eliminated. Secondly, the working out of the doctrine is a matter of time.

In the beginning, the office of emperor is conceived to be a combination of republican offices conferred on a given person for limited periods—a year, ten years, or life. These grants of power are dependent on the Senate and people. The titles of Imperator and Princeps Senatus are bestowed by the Roman people and Senate; and what is given can be taken away. But by the age of the Antonines, the *lex regia* (the law conferring authority on the emperor) represents a grant of power which is virtually irreversible.

So, too, is there an evolution of doctrine with respect to succession in the imperial office. Initially, the imperator is the choice of Senate and people, with the assent of the army. By the beginning of the third century, it becomes a central doctrine, violated rarely in practice, that the army nominates the imperator and the Senate gives consent.

The theory and practice of the role which the emperor shall play also change. At the outset, he is *primus inter pares*—a member of the Senate who respects his colleagues as equals but who has greater responsibilities than they. But this status is not maintained for long. By the latter part of the reign of Tiberius, certainly, the emperor is elevated, both in his own eyes and in those of the populus and Senate, above the ancient magistrates. Although Augustus would exchange informal social calls with his fellow senators,[51] this is no longer true by the time of Domitian. The secular tendency undoubtedly is for the emperor's office to embody a social, legislative, executive, and military authority which by the age of the Antonines completely overshadows what remains of Senate and people.

But of even greater importance for political theory is the religious significance increasingly attached to the office of emperor and to the persons who hold the office. Roman public office, of course, even under the Republic, was always deeply involved in religious or quasi-religious ceremonies. The auspices had to be discovered before a battle; and politicians were always looking for signs and portents of success or failure in their ventures. The Roman gods were civic deities. With the Empire, however, this deep involvement in religious language and practice takes on a new dimension, first very slowly but later on with gathering momentum. When Julius Caesar dies, he is proclaimed *divus Iulius* by a formal decree of the Senate and is thus admitted into the ranks of the gods.[52]

The triumph of Octavian at Actium is the real beginning of the cult of what will later constitute the deification of the emperors. For the ancient world Actium represents the triumph of peace over a generation of civil war and tumult. Several years after the victory, Horace can write of the emperor as the incarnation of the fertility goddess' son:

> O thou, fair Maia's winged son appear,
> And human shape in prime of manhood wear;
> Declared the guardian of the imperial state,
> Divine avenger of great Caesar's fate.[53]

At his death, of course, the former Octavian is made Divus Augustus by decree of the Senate.

It is only in the reign of Caligula, however, that a ruler dares assert his own divinity during his lifetime; and at first the doctrine apparently shocks all good Romans, possibly in part because of the character of Caligula but also because the deification of a living ruler is to them still rather novel. At any rate, Caligula avows that he has had intimate converse with the Moon Goddess and establishes a Caligulan religious order with priests and priestesses.[54]

Despite initial opposition by Romans to the doctrine of the living deified Caesar, the conception rather swiftly makes its way into the generally accepted theory of the Empire. It is associated with the fading of the republican tradition and is accompanied by the eventual designation of Caesar as *dominus* (lord). This word under the Republic was employed to describe the owner of a slave and originally carried with it connotations not dissimilar to those of Aristotle's master-slave relationship: The slave was the complete tool of his owner. Given this meaning, *dominus* is spurned as a title by the early Caesars, including Tiberius. Caligula, however, begins to accept it and Domitian insists on it. By the time of Trajan, early in the second century, it is regularly employed as the form for addressing the emperor.

The growth of the ascription of divinity to the living Caesar and the use of the formerly-hated *dominus* as a title owe much, of course, to the influence of Oriental doctrines. Just as Alexander the Great was shaped in his thinking about his office by Persian and Egyptian theories of kingship, so the Roman conquest of the East is also a partial triumph of the East over Rome; for there can be little doubt that attributing "godhood" in some peculiar sense to the ruler is a central eastern belief which clashes with traditional Roman notions.

But while the transformation of the Roman

45. Dio Cassius, *Roman History*, Herbert B. Foster, trans., Troy, N.Y.: Pafraets Book Company, 1905, Bk. LII, ch. 4.
46. *Ibid.*, ch. 9.
47. *Ibid.*, ch. 10.
48. *Ibid.*, ch. 14.
49. *Ibid.*, ch. 15.
50. *Ibid.*, ch. 40.
51. Suetonius, *op. cit.*, "Augustus."
52. Suetonius, *op. cit.*, "Julius Caesar," pp. 49–50.
53. Horace, "Odes," in *Complete Works of Horace*, Casper J. Kraemer, Jr., ed., New York: Book League of America, 1938, I, 2, p. 130.
54. Dio Cassius, *op. cit.*, Bk. 59, ch. 28.

theory of rulership is a fact, it is almost certainly true that the language of deification is interpreted in diverse ways. A basic division, of course, is between those who think that the *office* is divine and those, on the other hand, who attribute divinity to the *person* of the ruler. It is difficult to believe that Roman intellectuals, for example, could really accept the latter interpretation. Indeed, if we are to believe Suetonius, some of the emperors could joke about their divinity. Thus Vespasian is quoted as jesting, only minutes before his death, "Woe's me. Methinks I'm turning into a God."[55]

But whatever the intellectual viewpoint might be, it is almost equally certain that millions of subjects would associate divinity with the person of the emperor as well as with the office. During the first two centuries of our era there is a hungering of men for "salvation"—of this there can be no doubt, as the flourishing "mystery" religions attest. While salvation might mean many things, one of its contexts is political. The monarch "saves" mankind because he overcomes the chaos always threatening society. He is the "author"—initiator, originator—of order; and, whatever his personal failings might be, he is, as the creator of order, a divine being.

At this point, it might be well to point out some of the psychological ramifications involved in the theory of deification. Along with his status as divine, the emperor is usually conceived to be the *pater patriae*, or "father of the country." The divinity which thus comes to hedge him about is combined with the imagery of fatherhood. The god is a father and the father is a god. Modern doctrines which suggest that for many men, the "father image" lives on in the figure of the ruler would seem to cast an interesting light on the whole theory of imperial rulership.

The Idea of Citizenship. Accompanying the evolution of Caesarism and the theory of rulership is the changing face of the theory of citizenship. Oriental monarchies, of course, never really developed a doctrine of citizenship, if by that term is signified the notion of active participation in civic and political affairs. It was in the polis that the conception of citizenship was first nourished.

In republican Rome and, indeed, in early imperial Rome as well, the idea of Roman citizenship is one of privilege. Roman citizens are immune from the more humiliating forms of punishment such as crucifixion. They share in the political power of the comitia and are eligible for the magistracies. They govern provinces. Their rights of judicial appeal to the emperor are extensive, as is illustrated by the case of St. Paul.[56] The extension of Roman citizenship is, therefore, regarded with jealousy down to the first century A.D.

But the theory of citizenship undergoes a slow evolution as the nature of the Empire changes. The thrust is in the direction of assimilating the private rights of citizens to those of non-citizens and vice versa. The influence of the *ius gentium* on the *ius civile* in the first two centuries shapes doctrines of private law which narrow the gulf between the citizen and non-citizen. And the number of citizens tends to be increased as soldiers of diverse nationalities, for example, are granted the boon. The process will culminate with the famous decree of Caracalla which in 212 extends citizenship to virtually all subjects of the Empire.

As the proportion of citizens grows, however, the significance of citizenship, particularly in the sphere of politics, declines. The idea of citizenship becomes diluted as the theory of universal citizenship takes root. Thus participation in politics becomes virtually meaningless and the magistracies, now largely manipulated by the emperor, cease to have any independent influence and power. It is this decline of the idea of active citizenship which is, of course, the occasion for the formulation of so many doctrines of political despair, including those of later Stoicism. When, therefore, Caracalla extends citizenship to most subjects, he is primarily enlarging the responsibilities and burdens of men (particularly with respect to certain taxes) and not basically expanding their political privileges and rights.

The City and the World. Of the Empire during the first two centuries it can truly be said that it is a structure growing out of a civitas without planning and often with curious inconsistencies. The city is transformed into the world but with no clear constitutional doctrine appropriate for the world. In the beginning, it seems to be assumed that the city is simply the *dominus* of the world. Despite Stoic doctrine, Romans are in fact to be dominant over non-Romans. At the same time, there is always implicit in the doctrine of empire the idea that the city is dependent on the world. Very early, for example, the army ceases to be purely "Roman" and we have noted the impact on Roman legal conceptions of the laws of Egyptians, Phoenicians, and Greeks. Is the emperor beholden to the Roman people only for his *auctoritas* or is he in some sense the mouthpiece of the world? How can the Senate, in conception only a kind of municipal council, claim authority to issue decrees for the whole world?

Roman constitutional and political thought never gives clear answers to such questions. One might expect that it would develop a theory of imperial representation, for example, but there is no indication that either administrators or scholars give this central issue of politics any thought. In the republican constitution, the bare notion of representation is perhaps reflected in the tribunate; but it is avowedly a kind of class representation and then only very imperfectly related to the general theory of the constitution. The comitia itself is not representative and under the Empire it soon fades away in any event.

Generally speaking, the implicit theory of the empire allows for wide diversity in relationships between the city and that world of which it is the *dominus*. The principle seems to be that once military supremacy has been achieved, political and administrative connections between Rome and the kingdoms, provinces, and municipalities which constitute the Empire depend upon such varied factors as local historical tradition, the mood of the Senate or emperor, or even the requests of local magnates. A given territory might be ruled by its own king, his relations with Rome depending on particular stipulations unique for him. The rule of the Herods in Palestine seems to be of this nature. The connection between the city and a given kingdom might be loose or close so long as the supremacy of Rome continues to be recognized. On the other hand, indirect rule through local kings can be supplanted by tranformation of the kingdom into a Roman province, under the direct control of a governor, "president," or proconsul.

Even where a given land is directly ruled, many traditional local institutions persist and given cultural groups might be granted autonomy for certain purposes. Legal traditions are usually respected, for example. Religious and racial communities like the Jews might be awarded special guarantees of their own peculiar practices. In Alexandria during the first century, for example, they exist as a kind of enclave in the midst of the predominantly Greek population; and except in unusual crises, they manage their religious and cultural affairs and even have their own courts and officials.[57]

One of the more interesting aspects of the relation between the city and the world is the nature of municipal life under the early Empire. Despite the fact that the Senate of Rome gradually declines, living as it does under the shadow of the imperator, municipal autonomy and institutions outside Rome retain some of their earlier spirit. Just as Rome's relations with the several nationalities and territories vary widely, so, too, is there a diversity of ties to municipalities. There are "free," "federate," and "stipendiary" cities. There are ancient Greek municipalities which still retain their archons and demarchs. Many municipalities possess Curiae or Senates, some of which have traditions antedating those of Rome. While magistracies and senates are open only to the wealthy, very often elections to magistracies are by the populus. Inscriptions uncovered at Pompeii indicate that the election campaigns must often have been quite lively. Thus while the city of Rome itself finds its republican institutions fading, provincial municipalities, ironically enough, often retain a large degree of civic spirit.[58]

The conception of empire, too, is conducive to a wide degree of toleration with respect to religion. In part this is to be associated with the acceptance of cultural diversity and a variety of municipal institutions. Insofar as the idea is shaped by philosophically minded men, it may be thought of as the product of indifference to all the gods. But the notion of toleration must also be seen as part of that tendency to eclecticism in both philosophy and religion which characterizes so much thought between the time of Augustus and the end of the second century. It is hardly necessary to add, of course, that acceptance into the Roman Pantheon of a myriad of foreign

55. Suetonius, *op. cit.*, "Vespasian," p. 335.
56. See Acts, Apostles 25:11–27; 28:17–20.
57. See E. R. Goodenough, *The Jurisprudence of the Jewish Courts of Egypt*, New Haven: Yale University Press, 1929.
58. On doctrines and practices of municipal life, see Samuel Dill, *Roman Society from Nero to Marcus Aurelius*, London: Macmillan and Co., 1905, Bk. II, ch. 2.

divinities owes something to sheer utilitarian considerations: adopt and respect their gods, the ruling class seems to be saying, and men are more likely to obey us.

The conception of toleration must be qualified in some respects, however. It is conditional on acceptance of the basic premises of the Empire and of the imperial cult. Both the premises and the cult reject the notion of exclusiveness in religion: if the Empire tolerates your cult, you must in turn respect all other cults, including that of the emperor.

Meanwhile, of course, a peculiar religious sect has arisen which challenges the dominant religious-political notions of the Empire. The Christians are by the second century already disturbing the politics of urbs and orbs alike; and their peculiar doctrines about society and state both amaze and puzzle the civilization presided over by the Caesars. We turn to the evolution of those doctrines in the following chapter.

chapter 8

The New Testament and Early Christianity

In general, it may be said that the political attitudes and doctrine found in the New Testament and early Christianity are significant, not because they are systematically stated, clear, and analytically important, but rather because of the great historical impact of Christianity. Even if we take the position of some scholars and assert that early Christianity, or at least Jesus himself, had no positive political ideas,[1] the basis for its alleged negations would be of no inconsiderable import in light of its later place in the history of both institutions and thought.

Among the issues which confront us as we seek to reconstruct the political attitudes of first and second century Christians are the eschatological problem, Jewish versus Greek antecedents, conflicts within the New Testament and early Christianity themselves, and the relation of both explicit and implicit political notions to the politics of the time. Questions of this kind are, of course, closely interrelated.

The eschatological problem has to do with the relative weight which we are to give to the undoubted fact that early Christians anticipated an early end of history. Should we interpret their attitudes to the state, for example, as being completely shaped by this anticipation; or should we, on the contrary, minimize it as a factor?[2]

Then, too, while we may agree that first and second century Christianity represents a union of Jewish and Greek notions, the exact weight to be given to each is not easy to determine. St. Paul, for example, was obviously profoundly influenced by both the Platonism and the Stoicism of the first century; yet he did not leave behind the Pharasaic Judaism which constituted the context of his youth and early manhood.

Within the New Testament and among early

Christians themselves there was obviously a conflict as to how they should view social and political institutions. Some Christians, for example, were probably anarchists and took their stand on certain passages of the Gospels. On the other hand, men like St. Paul were concerned to combat anarchistic tendencies within the primitive Christian communities.

Finally, the meaning of early Christian doctrine can hardly be fully understood without some knowledge of both Jewish and Roman politics in the period between Herod the Great and the age of the Antonines. In certain respects, for example, the teaching of Jesus as it bears on politics referred not only to the relations of Jews to Romans but also to the conflicts between and among the several sects of Jews.

The Setting of Jewish Politics and Political Thought

The political attitudes of Jesus must be seen against the background of Jewish politics from the time of the Maccabees to that of Herod the Great. After Judas Maccabeus had restored the Temple in 165 B.C.,[3] it appeared for a time that Syrian control had been eliminated and that the peculiar religious institutions of the Jews were once again to be free from foreign domination. In the course of the subsequent Syrian civil war, however, an army was once more sent against the Jews led by Judas and he was killed in 161. Succeeded by his brother Jonathan, there was again a period of success. When Jonathan, in turn, was killed, Simon, the third of the original Maccabean brothers, came into control of affairs and managed to maintain an often precarious rule. He was succeeded by his son, John Hyrcanus, as high priest and civil leader. At the death of John (about 105 B.C.), one of his sons, Aristobulus, became high priest and a little later proclaimed himself king. Ecclesiastical and royal powers were thus formally united in the person of a Maccabean (or Asamonean) ruler.

Jewish domestic politics from 105 onward become incredibly complicated, including as they do the struggles between the politico-religious factions known as the Sadducees and the Pharisees. The latter seem to have originated about the time that Aristobulus assumed the royal title and they objected to his union of priestly and royal powers in a dynasty which, in their view, was becoming increasingly worldly. The Sadducees, on the other hand, were the faction associated with the priestly families supporting the Asamonean priesthood and rulership.

In the first century B.C., about the time (63 B.C.) when Pompey carried on his activities in Palestine, the Roman power was allied with the Pharisees against the Sadducean-dominated priesthood. At the same time, a rising politician of Idumea by the name of Antipater was giving refuge to John Hyrcanus II, the current Asamonean priest-king. Antipater gained increasing influence over John, until he virtually became his "mayor of the palace" or prime minister. It was Antipater's son, Herod, who, with the assistance of the Romans, deposed the Asamoneans and reigned under the Roman power as Herod the Great.

When Herod died in 4 B.C., his was a considerable monarchy. He had rebuilt the Temple, partly to conciliate Jewish leaders who had regarded him as a foreigner. He had also reestablished the Sanhedrin or Sanhedrins,[4] thus attempting to show his goodwill to those priestly families who had been predominant during the long period of Asamonean predominance.

In his will, Herod made provision for a division of his kingdom among his sons. Herod Antipas, for example, was to become ruler of Galilee and Peraea; Archelaus controlled all Palestine south of the Vale of Jezeel; Philip became tetrarch of the area east of Galilee and proceeded to a rapid romanization of his kingdom. In A.D. 6, the Jews of Judaea protested against the rule of Archelaus, and the Emperor Augustus, in response to their petition, removed this son of Herod, establishing instead

1. For example, Charles Guignebert, in his great critical work *Jesus*, maintains: "It seems a waste of time to demonstrate at length that Jesus was not interested in what we call political morality." S. H. Cooke, trans., New York: University Books, 1956, p. 385.
2. On the eschatological problem from the viewpoint of modern scholarship, see Amos N. Wilder, *Eschatology and Ethics in the Teaching of Jesus*, New York: Harper & Bros., 1939, the bibliographies in which are particularly helpful. See also Charles Guignebert, *op. cit.*
3. See Chapter 1, p. 16.
4. Many authorities think that there were two Sanhedrins, one for civil and political matters and the other for religious affairs (the so-called Great Sanhedrin of 71 members).

direct Roman government under a procurator. During the brief period of Jesus' teaching, of course, this procurator was Pontius Pilate.

It is difficult to determine the exact status of religio-political affairs from the death of Herod the Great (in 4 B.C.) to the supposed date of Jesus' execution (in A.D. 29). The political rulers familiar to New Testament readers are, of course, Herod Antipas, the tetrarch of Galilee, and Pilate, the Roman procurator of Judaea. But exactly what was the role of the Sanhedrin or Sanhedrins in Jewish affairs? And to what degree did the high priest exercise not merely functions which we should regard as ecclesiastical but also civil and political powers?[5]

But however uncertain we may be as to the exact prerogatives of Herod in Galilee, the Sanhedrin in Jerusalem, and Pilate in Judaea, it is safe to say that their interrelations were not defined precisely. The over-all tendency was for direct Roman rule to be expanded; but Jewish autonomy was still very real both in civic and in religious affairs.

The political positions developed by Jews from the time of Herod the Great to the death of Jesus must be understood, of course, in the context of the social struggles from 105 B.C. onward. The events of the previous century and a quarter were interpreted differently by the Jewish factions; and the politics of those parties cannot be divorced sharply from their religious differences.

In one sense, the most radical position is represented by followers of Judas the Galilean. Shortly after the introduction of direct Roman rule in A.D. 6, they revolt against payment of taxes to the alien power. God, they argue, is to be their only ruler and Jews ought not to pay taxes to mere men. The Jewish law is sufficient both for personal holiness and for political rule; and those Jews who compromise either with the Romans or with Jewish kings such as Herod Antipas are betraying the Hebrew heritage.[6]

In many respects, the Pharisees seem to resemble the followers of Judas. They, too, insist on strict observance of the law. As we noted earlier, they are antagonistic to Jewish monarchy, particularly of the kind represented by the Asamonean and Herodian dynasties. But unlike the followers of Judas, they tend to look for a solution of the political problem not in active revolt but rather through the coming of a Messiah. Meanwhile, the task of Jews is to live as a people apart, attracting Gentiles to their way of life by the manner of their living but never acquiescing in permanent non-Jewish rule. The governance of the heathen, suggests the Pharisee, is here but for a time. If the Jew will observe the law in all its strictness, God will not desert the Chosen People.[7] Through divine intervention, the political enemies of Hebrews will be overthrown.

The Pharisee cannot accept the position of the Sadducee, who is traditionally associated with the old Asamonean priestly families. Jewish government—by contrast with Herodian and Roman rule—is largely in the hands of the Sadducean group. Now the peculiarity about this faction is that, while ostensibly connected with the official religious establishment, it is primarily concerned with maintaining its own power position. Outwardly conforming to Hellenic-Roman culture and skeptical in religious matters, it is determined to manipulate politics in such a way that no challenge to its authority will come either from the Roman overlords or from the serious religious-political Pharisees. The Sadducees may be regarded as "minimalists" with respect to the law, whereas the Pharisees are maximalists and are far more popular with the masses.

As for the Essenes, they are one of the most atypical of Hebrew groups. With a strong tendency to asceticism (most of them repudiate marriage), they are communist in their economy. Josephus points out that they dwell in no one city, but make provision in every city for reception of their wandering brothers. An outsider joining the Essenes must first go through a probationary period before he is admitted to final vows. They renounce the oath as being unnecessary to men whose word is their bond, and they also apparently repudiate use of the sword; Josephus tells us that an Essene must promise to "do no harm to any one, either of his own accord, or by the command of others." By contrast with Zealots and Pharisees, they adopt attitudes of passive obedience to government; the Essene is called upon to "show fidelity to all men, and especially to those in authority, because no one obtains the government without God's assistance."[8]

Finally, the supporters of the Herods are frankly philo-Roman. To them, Roman rule is indeed ordained of God, as is evidenced by His permitting the city on the Tiber to control so much of the world.

The difficulties involved in reconstructing what Jesus actually thought are great indeed. In the first place, the Gospels themselves were compiled many years after his death and often by editors who had had no firsthand acquaintance with him.[9] Secondly, any one Gospel was probably based on several distinct sources which might date from different periods of time. It is thought, for example, that some of Jesus' sayings apparently predicting the Fall of Jerusalem in A.D. 70 were inserted into the record by one who experienced the siege.[10] And the interpolations of later monks—some of them living possibly far beyond the Apostolic Age—should also be mentioned. Thirdly, the Gospels themselves differ in the ways they report the teachings of Jesus and in the ordering of events related to those teachings.

But if the reconstruction of his life and thought in general is fraught with problems, the difficulty of interpreting his political position is even greater.[11] For in addition to the questions noted above, one must attack a prevalent tradition that Jesus did not even have an attitude to political issues. Textbooks on political theory often tend to hold this; and the religious tradition of Christianity has so emphasized the spirituality of its founder that some commentators appear to think of any attempt to link politics with Jesus as little short of blasphemy. To them, to be spiritual and political at the same time is a contradiction.

Against the traditional view, it can be pointed out that Jesus grew up with a Jewish heritage and that that heritage, as we have suggested elsewhere, conceived "religion" to be involved in all aspects of daily life. Religion was ethics, it was politics, it was economy—even though it may have been more than these also.[12] For the pious Jew, moreover, his own particular version of religious faith was inextricably bound up with national aspirations.

Very early, too, Jesus probably came to think of himself as the Messiah. Now the notion of the Messiah in Jewish thought, while interpreted in widely different ways, almost always involved politics. As was noted in the previous section, the Pharisees made the Messiah a figure whose coming would herald the triumph of the Jews and the reduction of non-Jews to politically inferior positions. And the Zealots, likewise, thought of the Messiah as a political leader. Much of the literature of the Jewish Apocrypha portrayed him as primarily a temporal savior who, of course, was also "religious."[13]

In the absence of adequate proof to the contrary, it would seem fairer to assume that Jesus accepted, as a good Jew, the interweaving of ethics, politics, and religion, than that he advocated their separation. When he dealt with ethical issues, in other words, he took for granted that his teaching was applicable to social organization and to politics, just as he assumed that he came not to "destroy" the law but rather to "fulfill" it.[14] And when he spoke of inner attitudes as being significant for "moral" conduct, he *assumed* that the same principle applied to political activities.

5. See Stephen Liberty, *The Political Relations of Christ's Ministry*, London: Oxford University Press, 1916, Appendix to Ch. 6, pp. 141–157.
6. Note the account in Josephus, *op. cit.*, Bk. XVIII, ch. 1, and *Wars of the Jews, op. cit.*, Bk. II, ch. 8.
7. In the past, the Pharisee has often been portrayed, at least in Christian literature, as a mere pretender to piety. Actually, he was more often than not a religious idealist, one who took religious commitments seriously. For recent analysis of the Pharisees, see Hugo Odeberg, *Pharisaism and Christianity*, J. M. Moe, trans., St. Louis: Concordia Publishing House, 1964, and Samuel Umen, *Pharisaism and Jesus*, New York: Philosophical Library, 1963.
8. *Wars of the Jews, op. cit.*, Bk. II, ch. 8.
9. The literature on general New Testament criticism is, of course, enormous. On this point, the student might wish to consult such works as Charles Guignebert, *op. cit.;* E. J. Goodspeed, *The Formation of the New Testament*, Chicago: University of Chicago Press, 1926, and *Introduction to the New Testament*, Chicago: University of Chicago Press, 1937; Frederick C. Grant, *The Growth of the Gospels*, New York: Abingdon Press, 1933; Adolf Harnack, *New Testament Studies*, 4 vols., J. R. Wilkinson, trans., New York: G. P. Putnam's Sons, 1907, 1908, 1909, 1911; and James Moffatt, *An Introduction to the Literature of the New Testament*, 3rd ed., revised, Edinburgh: T. and T. Clark, 1949.
10. Not all students agree with this interpretation, of course. See Amos N. Wilder, *op. cit.*
11. One of the best recent studies is Oscar Cullmann, *The State in the New Testament*, New York: Scribner's, 1956. See also, for example, W. Bieder, *Ekklesin und Polis im Neuen Testament und in der Alten Kirche*, 1941.
12. See Chapter 1, pp. 16–17.
13. See particularly the Apocalypse of Baruch and the Second Esdras.
14. Matthew 5:17.

In interpreting Jesus' attitude to politics, then, it is argued here that he basically accepted the notion that collective life and individual conduct are subject to the same principles; that God is revealed in political history, as He was for the Prophets of Israel; and that, while obviously there is an other-worldly aspect to Jesus' teaching, yet the this-worldly side is equally important. All these are propositions which could, of course, be made about any pious Jew teaching in the first century of our era. Jesus was no exception.

Messiah and Kingdom. Just when Jesus came to conceive that he was the Messiah is difficult to determine. But one account has it that immediately after his baptism by John the Baptist, the latter called the attention of others to the fact that the "Holy Spirit" in the form of a dove had alighted on Jesus. The next day John was standing with two of his disciples and, seeing Jesus pass, called him "God's lamb." The two disciples followed Jesus. One of them was Andrew, who immediately sought out his brother Simon and said to him, "We have found the Messiah!—that is to say, the Christ."[15] And some time later, when Jesus was talking to the Samaritan woman, she said "I know that the Messiah is coming—he who is called the Christ. When he comes, he will tell us everything!" This time Jesus acknowledged that he was indeed the Messiah: "I who am talking to you am he!"[16]

Now the idea of the Messiah was a Jewish national conception; and it was, as we have seen, closely associated with the religious and political beliefs of both the Zealots and the Pharisees. Jewish views of what the Messiah would be differed considerably from one another. Some pictured him as a military leader appearing on horseback and putting himself at the head of Israel's revived military forces. Others thought of him as descending from heaven and bringing about vast changes in the fortunes of the Chosen People. But there can be no doubt that he was envisioned by most versions as a political figure as well as a religious leader—he was a "savior-figure" in the literature of the Hebrews which developed after the Babylonian exile.

No doubt Jesus begins by conceiving himself in the traditional terms. Certainly there is ample evidence to show that he thinks of himself in the beginning as primarily a Jewish leader. Most of his teaching is before Jews and he seems reluctant to get outside Jewish conceptions—as appears evident in the story of his conversation with the woman at the well.[17] Later on, it is true, the Messiah for him becomes a somewhat trans-national figure. But this seems to take place only after he is convinced that the Jews are to reject him as a national leader. Then his role as Messiah becomes a universal one, although he describes it in terms of the Suffering Servant poetry in the second Isaiah.[18]

Meanwhile, Jesus has talked much of the Kingdom of God or the Kingdom of Heaven. The Gospels make evident that this term means several different things to him. It is primarily theocratic rule of human beings—the old Hebrew notion of a society governed directly by God without the intermediation of earthly kings. In this meaning, the Kingdom of Heaven is in the future but it is at the same time an earthly ordering of affairs and not some scheme of rule beyond the concrete relations of history. It is thus Jewish in a very literal sense.

At the same time, Jesus thinks of the Kingdom in the present tense. It is here "now" and not merely in the future. Is this a contradiction in his thinking? When he prays "Thy Kingdom come . . . on earth" is he in flat opposition to his reiteration that the "Kingdom is within you" and among you? If it is in the future, how can it also be in the here and now? The answer seems to lie in Jesus' notion of growth. When he says that the Kingdom is here, he would appear to mean that it is here potentially; that God has revealed its nature through the Christ or Messiah. But how it grows will depend on men. He likens it to a mustard seed, for example, which can grow into a giant mustard tree.[19] Now if we think of Jesus as above all a Jewish thinker, this parable of the kingdom is to be read not merely in terms of individual development toward perfection but also of social and political growth. In the latter sense, the Kingdom will come when direct theocratic rule is established and the kingdoms of the Herods and the Romans will have passed away.

It is this sociopolitical goal, associated with his conviction that he is the Messiah, which at first attracts multitudes to him. They join him in the belief that he is the Anointed One who has been designated by God to emancipate them from the Herodians, the Temple rulers, and the Roman Empire. Some of them undoubtedly think of him as another Judas of Galilee—and at times he himself possibly wonders whether he should not try to emulate

Judas. When in the end he decides that his Christhood or Messiahhood will not permit him to be a Zealot, the masses tend to fall away. Deprived of popular support, the Sadducean Jewish rulers join with jealous Herodians and Romans to eliminate him as a dangerous revolutionary. They see him in this light—although Pilate claims to have doubts[20] —both in religious and in political terms. And it is significant that in the judgment scene he does not deny that he is "King of the Jews."[21]

Ethical and Political Standards. But it is only with difficulty that Jesus comes to his particular attitude. The Gospels of Matthew and Luke record for us in the temptation story the conflicts to which he is subject.[22] According to Matthew, he spends forty days in the desert and is there subjected to at least three "temptations."

In the first, the "tempter," after noting that he has fasted for the forty days, suggests that he turn the stones about him into bread. He is "God's son." Why not, therefore, use God's power and alleviate his hunger? To this temptation Jesus replies, "The Scripture says, 'Not on bread alone is man to live, but on every word that comes from the mouth of God!' "[23]

It is possible, of course, to interpret this discourse literally and to conclude simply that Jesus refuses to use his alleged power to help himself. But the whole ring of the story leads us to believe that its symbolic meaning may be far more important. Jesus may be thought of as tempted by the securely established position of the "worldly" Sadducean ruling class, which values above all the maintenance of its prestige and status in the Sanhedrin. In rejecting the invitation to turn the stones into bread, he is also renouncing the notion of politics and property divorced from central considerations of Hebrew religion—for such is indeed the attitude of the Sadduceans. The bread symbolizes material possessions and the economic and political power which guarantee them. The Sadduceans never seem to get beyond the bread. They are like Plato's appetitive men severed from any organic connection with ultimate purpose. Jesus repudiates any temptation that the Messiah should be simply a Sadducean.

But the tempter now subjects him to a second trial. He takes him to the top of the Temple—the great edifice constructed by Herod the Great—and mockingly asks him to "throw himself down" if he is God's son. He will not be injured, for angels will rescue him and prevent his head from striking the stones below. To this Jesus replies, in the words of the Old Testament, "You shall not try the Lord your God."[24]

Now again we can interpret all this either in literal terms or as symbolism. Conceivably, Jesus may have in mind the position of some (although not all) Pharisees when he rejects the temptation. In their particular version of the "coming age" (a term familiar to all pious Jews), the role of the human being to many is that of one who pulls divine strings. He observes the law, but then awaits the day when the Messiah will be sent by God to transform all the kingdoms of the world and restore the political supremacy of the Jews. He throws himself into the arms of angels, as it were, and claims that he is confident of God's protection. He tries to hasten the day of the "final conflict" by rash action and thus "tries" or "tempts" God. He is in effect manipulating the divine power; for his great insistence on rigid observance of the law is a kind of arrogance or pride.

But it is the third temptation which is most directly political. After failing to persuade Jesus to adopt either a Sadducean attitude or a version of the Pharisaic notion of Messianism, the devil wafts him to a "high mountain" and shows him "all the kingdoms of the world and their splendor." And he tells Jesus, "I will give all this to you, if you will fall on your knees and do homage to me." But Jesus replies, "Begone, Satan! For the Scripture says, 'You must do homage to the Lord your God, and worship him alone!' "[25]

15. AT John 1:41. AT refers to *The Complete Bible: An American Translation. New Testament* and *Apocalypse* trans. by E. J. Goodspeed. Chicago: University of Chicago Press, 1939.
16. AT John 4:25, 26.
17. John 4:6–26.
18. Matthew 12:15–21.
19. Matthew 13:31–32.
20. John 18:39; 19:6–12.
21. John 27:11–12.
22. This "political" interpretation of the temptation story draws heavily on Liberty's suggestive analysis. See Stephen Liberty, *op. cit.*, ch. 4; C. J. Cadoux, *The Life of Jesus*, Harmondsworth, Middlesex: Penguin Books, 1948, has also been extremely helpful throughout.
23. AT Matthew 4:4.
24. AT Matthew 4:7.
25. AT Matthew 4:8, 9, 10.

Of the three temptations, this is the one which most obviously has to be interpreted symbolically. In the first temptation, the stones could undoubtedly be seen and Jesus is represented as being desperately hungry. In the second story, a leap from the Temple could be regarded as a literal "tempting of God." But in the third trial, "all" the kingdoms of the world surely cannot be seen nor can their splendor. From a mountain, one could perhaps see Galilee and Judaea and the trans-Jordan country These stand for or represent independent political power, for all are part of the giant Roman Empire. In the context of Jesus' ethical teaching, it would seem that "worshipping Satan" to gain the "splendor" of the "kingdoms" means to use characteristic methods of Satan. And there is little doubt that Jesus associates these methods with the physical violence so often reflected in political struggle. There is no evidence that he regards obedience to political rulers—even foreign political rulers—as illegitimate. Indeed, the story of the tribute money[26] would seem to indicate that he thinks payment of taxes is a moral as well as a legal obligation. But to gain a kingdom by war and fighting he appears to characterize as "satanic." It smacks of the Herodians and those whom they support, the Romans.

But none of the three temptations can be fully understood except in the context of Jesus' general ethical teaching. His repudiation of the Sadducean position, for example, cannot be completely comprehended outside his attitude to property; his spurning of many Pharisees must be seen as part of his conception of Hebrew law; and his rejection of the violence of politics and the political compromises of the Herods is conditioned and interpreted by his ethic of love and righteousness as well as by his apparent doctrine of passive obedience.

Jesus idealizes both the "poor" in spirit (identified somewhat with the *am-haares* or common people) and the "poor" in this world's goods.[27] There runs through all his teaching almost an idealization of the poverty-stricken masses. Possession of many material goods is frequently seen as a bar to the growth of the Kingdom of Heaven and of theocratic government. He implies that rich men possibly can understand God's purposes, but he doubts that many of them actually *will* do so; for their very riches are an impediment to their understanding.[28] When a "rich ruler"—probably a Pharisee—asks him what he must do to perfect himself (for he had strictly observed all the law), Jesus tells him immediately to sell all his material goods.[29]

Yet we should beware of thinking that he denies the necessity of some material things. Thus in the first temptation story, where he is represented as saying, "Man shall not live by bread alone," the key word is not "bread" but "alone." It is *assumed* that bread is the first indispensable—and this is quite in accordance with the Hebrew prophetic spirit. No less than Amos is Jesus concerned that all men have bread and thus the material basis of life; for without it, the major ends of existence cannot be fulfilled.

At no point in the Gospels, however, do we find any formula by which bread can be assured to all. Later on, after the death of Jesus, some in the early church are to interpret his words as implying a kind of "communism," and in subsequent centuries, "Christian communism" is a position accepted by many as an outcome of Jesus' ethical teaching. But Jesus himself is silent on the whole issue.

His attitude to the law may be described as one which accepts its principles but believes that its purposes can best be attained by not necessarily insisting on literal observance. The Torah is always central to Jewish life; and for Jesus, as no doubt for most Jews of his day, it means not only religious law but also what we should today call criminal and civil law. Much of the administration of the law is, of course, left to Jewish authorities under the over-all supervision of the Romans. Jesus sees law in general as a utilitarian device to achieve certain ends—peace, harmony, and justice. He comes to "fulfill" the law and not to destroy it, in the sense that it is his mission as Messiah to keep before man's attention the ends which the law supposedly serves rather than to ask for obedience without understanding. Moreover, the external act of obedience, without inner motivation and understanding, will eventually defeat the goals of the law itself. Jesus has a keen comprehension of the idea that law, to fulfill its major purposes, must be renewed again and again in the consciousness of men. Law, he thinks, is not primarily "will" but is rather an attempt to state the conditions under which life can be lived most "abundantly." When a particular observance of the law violates its original purpose, then the purpose should take precedence over the ostensible observance. "The Sabbath was made for man and not man for the Sabbath."[30]

Finally, his general ethical teaching casts light

on the third temptation in that it helps us to understand what he means when he repudiates the "worship" of Satan in order to gain political power. His attitude is sufficiently ambiguous to permit a considerable variety of interpretations; and it is not surprising that his followers in subsequent centuries might find justification for several alternative positions.

His doctrine seems to run counter to almost everything which we associate with historical politics. Thus it is the "humble-minded" or the "meek" who will eventually "possess the land."[31] The aspiring Jewish nationalist of his day would probably spurn such statements as "Blessed are the peacemakers, for they will be called God's sons."[32] And what would an advocate of "retributive" justice do with "But I tell you not to resist injury, but if anyone strikes you on your right cheek, turn the other to him too"?[33] Moreover, he tells men that they should reject statements like "You must love your neighbor and hate your enemy." Instead, he commands his followers to "Love your enemies and pray for your persecutors."[34] And the term "enemies" used here refers both to personal and to political and national enemies.

He later admonishes his listeners that they should "Pass no more judgments upon other people, so that you may not have judgment passed upon you. For you will be judged by the standard you judge by, and men will pay you back with the same measure you have used with them."[35] How can one administer even a small society on such principles, let alone an empire? Yet it seems that Jesus intended this "no judgment" command to apply both to private and to public condemnations. His disciples are not to "judge" either in the role of magistrate or in that of an ordinary citizen.[36]

Nor are they to use violent coercion as a method of bringing in the Kingdom. If there is any central teaching of the third temptation, it would seem to be this. And the Gospels as a whole are filled with statements of like import. Thus, on the road from Gethsemane, one of those with him takes his sword and cuts off the ear of the high priest's slave. Jesus immediately reprimands him: "Put your sword back where it belongs! For all who draw the sword will die by the sword."[37] The commands to "resist not evil" and "love your enemies" seem to be followed literally by Jesus himself. Thus for the most part he stands mute in court, avowing, when asked, that he is indeed "King of the Jews" but saying little else.[38] And just as he does not succumb to the temptation of worshipping Satan in order to gain "the kingdoms of this world," when he is arrested he refuses to summon "legions" who might help him.[39] At the crucifixion, he asks God to forgive his enemies, for they "know not what they do."[40]

While the ethic of no judgments and nonresistance is not explicitly applied to the institution of war, it would seem that Jesus' attitude could not be reconciled with the act of war. It is true that he commands a legionary for his faith,[41] saying nothing about his profession; but this is not untypical of him. He always sees the man behind the "office" or "role," dining, for example, with Herodian taxgatherers even though he probably has little sympathy with their activities. His rigorous insistence on the prohibition of killing, even to the extent of forbidding inner "anger," would also seem to indicate his exclusion of warmaking to his disciples.[42]

In general, he seems to differ with all the existing Jewish positions in his attitude to the state, although in some respects he is close to the doctrine of the Essenes. His disciples are

26. Matthew 22:16–22; Luke, 20:20–25.
27. Matthew 6:19–34.
28. Matthew 6:19–25; Mark 10:23–25.
29. Mark 10:17–22.
30. Mark 2:27.
31. AT Matthew 5:5.
32. AT Matthew 4:9.
33. AT Matthew 5:39.
34. AT Matthew 5:44, 45.
35. AT Matthew 7:1, 2, 3.
36. Matthew, 7:1, Romans 14:10, and 1 Corinthian 2:15. From this point of view, the well-known "judge not" passages make no distinction between public officials and private citizens.
37. AT Matthew 26:52.
38. Matthew 27:14.
39. Matthew 26:51–56.
40. Luke 23:34.
41. Matthew 8:5–10.
42. There has been much modern discussion of Jesus' view of war. See, for example, Jean Lasserre, *War and the Gospel*, Oliver Coburn, trans., Scottsdale, Pa.: Herald Press, 1962, particularly pp. 1–71; C. H. C. Macgregor, *The New Testament Basis of Pacifism*, Nyack, N.Y.: Fellowship Publications, 1950; Roland H. Bainton, *Christian Attitudes Toward War and Peace*, New York: Abingdon Press, 1960; and H. A. Fast, *Jesus and Human Conflict*, Scottsdale, Pa.: Herald Press, 1962.

not to cooperate in any attempt to bring about his Kingdom by violent coercion, including war. They are, in general, to obey the existing political authorities without a murmur. Their obedience is not to be a matter merely of expediency but is to be founded also on principle. Although, as we have seen, his disciples are not permitted to be magistrates, they are not to resist ordinary conscript labor. Indeed, they are to do more than is required of them by the official; to go "two miles" when asked to go only one.[43]

Carrying out this general attitude, they are to recognize a sphere which legitimately belongs to the earthly ruler, as over against a jurisdiction which belongs to "God." Thus, unlike the Pharisees, who submit tentatively and expediently to Herodian and Roman authority but expect later to take up arms against it, Jesus advocates genuine submission. And unlike the followers of Judas, he forbids all military attempts to overthrow the regime.

The confrontation between Jesus and the Pharisees on the tax problem is well known and will become a center for dispute in later ages. The New Testament tells us that the Pharisees deliberately lay a trap for him, seeking to force him into either a statement countenancing Roman rule, which would antagonize the Jews, or, on the other hand, a ringing pronouncement proclaiming his antagonism to imperial control. Instead, he sidesteps the trap, in the process seeming to demarcate a jurisdictional sphere both for the emperor and for God:

> "Master, we know that you tell the truth, and teach the way of God with sincerity, regardless of the consequences, for you are impartial. So give us your opinion: Is it right to pay the poll-tax to the emperor, or not?"
>
> But he saw their malice, and said,
>
> "Why do you put me to such a test, you hypocrites? Show me the poll-tax coin!"
>
> And they brought him a denarius. And he said to them,
>
> "Whose head and title is this?"
>
> They answered,
>
> "The emperor's."
>
> Then he said to them,
>
> "Then pay the emperor what belongs to the emperor, and pay God what belongs to God!"
>
> And when they heard it they were amazed, and they went away and left him.[44]

What amazes his questioners is apparently that Jesus should advocate the payment of imperial and Herodian taxes cheerfully. While he carefully avoids any precise definition of the two spheres, he does seem somewhat grudgingly to accept even the hated Roman government. Jews are to pay their "secular" taxes just as, on another occasion, he advises his disciples to pay the "Temple-tax."[45]

Jesus advocates this attitude despite his awareness that government activity includes much in which his disciples ought not to participate personally. He is no doubt aware, for example, that most of the taxes are used to support a military establishment whose violent coercion he cannot approve for himself or his followers. As much as any Greek political critic, he is suspicious of all rulers. Thus the flowers of nature are more splendid than Solomon in all his finery.[46]

While Jesus does not explicitly say as much, he seems to give a kind of limited justification to government, pending the day when most men will become his disciples and the institutions of violently coercive government themselves will no longer exist. This consummation will, in effect, be the "Kingdom of God."[47]

Political History and Eschatology. The political thought of Jesus is also suffused with the Jewish notion of history as the "revelation" of God. The will of God is to bring about the non-coercive, non-hierarchical Kingdom and the Jews are called upon to carry out this mission. But eventually Jesus seems to give up hope that the Jewish nation either will or can understand his doctrine. It is too intent on restoring the alleged glories of Jewish overlordship or on military revolt against Rome. It does not comprehend the true role of Messiah as he who will establish the direct theocracy; nor does it see that, pending the rise of that theocracy, one should cheerfully obey those who are in political authority. Because the Jews will not accept his ethical and political doctrine, Jesus thinks that they will inevitably suffer the judgment of God. That judgment will include elimination of the last vestige of autonomy and also the destruction of Jerusalem. Jesus also apparently believes that after his own death, he will return rather quickly and that his disciples should prepare for this day. In any event, political history as known in the empire will come to an end—possibly within a generation.

Much modern scholarship has seen in Jesus' eschatology—or his doctrine of the end of things—perhaps the most significant aspect of his outlook.[48] His ethical-political teaching is to be understood, according to some, almost wholly in this light. Thus when he teaches love of enemies, non-resistance, passive obedience, and idealization of poverty, he is to be thought of as suggesting an "interim ethic" suitable for the very brief period which will exist before the end of human history as we have known it. According to this point of view, then, Jesus does not see himself as providing standards for an indefinite epoch of historical time.

Other students who recognize the importance of eschatology in the teaching of Jesus would yet suggest that we should not subordinate all of his doctrine to his theory of the possibly imminent cataclysmic conclusion of political history. After all, they would point out, while he undoubtedly thinks of the end as coming soon, yet he also specifically says that we "know not the hour." The kingdoms of this world will be judged by God but only God knows the moment. Meanwhile, and regardless of time span until the *eschaton*, the disciples are to live in accordance with the ethic of the new order, rendering obedience to those to whom it is due while spurning the devil's methods of violent coercion. To those who might suggest[49] that Jesus intended his standards to apply only to a perfect world, this school reasonably replies that in a perfect world there would be no enemies to love, no judgments to be spurned, and no political authorities to which one would be expected to submit. Moreover, Jesus admonishes his disciples to be perfect even as God is perfect; and such a command would make sense only in a world which is far from perfect.

It is difficult to determine just what role Jesus did intend his eschatology to play in his ethical and political thinking. That he expected an imminent end of history is fairly clear. At the same time, the fact that he did not profess himself to know the time exactly would seem to suggest that his ethical and political teaching would be regarded by him as binding whether the period turned out to be long or short. He seems to believe, however, that neither the Jews nor the Gentiles will observe his teachings sufficiently to prevent devastating judgments by God. And these terrors will fall first on the Jews because they have not accepted his conception of nonresistance but instead have fallen a prey to political attitudes like those of the Zealots or followers of Judas of Galilee.

The Gospels are filled with his portrayals of judgments on the Jews; and although some of the passages may have been added after his death (just before the fall of Jerusalem in A.D. 70), others are as genuine as any sayings attributed to him. In Mark, he is represented as leaving the Temple and replying to someone who comments on the splendor of the Temple stones: "Do you see these great buildings? Not one stone shall be left here upon another that shall not be torn down."[50] And he is also reported as advising his disciples to flee when the Temple is about to be desecrated.[51] Toward the close of his life he weeps over the political and military catastrophe which he sees coming to Jerusalem:

> If you yourself only knew today the conditions of peace! . . . A time is coming upon you when your enemies will throw up earthworks about you and surround you and shut you in on all sides, and

43. Matthew 5:41.
44. AT Matthew 22:16–22. We are not to infer that when Jesus says "Pay the emperor what belongs to the emperor, and pay God what belongs to God," he necessarily looks upon the two realms as equal in the claims they have on men. Indeed, Cullmann, *op. cit.*, pp. 35–36, maintains that "if Jesus had really attributed to Caesar's sphere the same value as God's, then he would have placed himself on the side of the Herodians. For this is exactly what the collaborationists maintained: Caesar is God's counterpart. Actually Jesus . . . merely recognizes that within its sphere the state can demand what belongs to it: money, taxes. But it is not placed on the same level as God. Give God what is his! That means: your life, your entire person."
45. Matthew 17:24–27.
46. Matthew 6:28–30.
47. This interpretation of Jesus' teaching on the state owes much to C. J. Cadoux, *The Early Church and the World*, Edinburgh: T. and T. Clark, 1925. The argument of this book seems to me persuasive in most respects. Cullmann, *op. cit.*, p. 18, suggests a very similar interpretation when he observes: "In Jesus . . . we see that he certainly does not regard the State as in any sense a *final*, divine institution: on the other hand, we see that he accepts the State and radically renounces every attempt to overthrow it."
48. To cite all the works dealing with the eschatology of Jesus is impossible within the space of one short footnote. See footnote 2.
49. For bibliography pro and con, see Wilder, *op. cit.*
50. AT Mark 13:2. Also Matthew 24:2.
51. Matthew 24:15–16, 19.

they will throw you and your children within you to the ground! . . .[52]

It seems at times that Jesus thinks of the fall of Jerusalem as the end of all history. At other points, he appears to hold that the *eschaton* and his own return will not necessarily coincide with the destruction of the city. But whatever the relation of this present age to that of the future and to the fate of the Jews, he warns that all manner of violent politics will precede the terminus of history.

In foreseeing a catastrophic end, Jesus follows in the steps of the Jewish eschatologists.[53] But he also lays the groundwork for that peculiar social and political outlook which will characterize those who follow him for more than a century. It will be a view that will color their attitude both to the Roman state and to such institutions as slavery and property.

The Politics of Paul and the New Testament Epistles

The great bulk of the New Testament outside the four Gospels and Apocalypse of John is devoted to the Epistles of St. Paul. Besides the letters of Paul, there are included such documents as Acts, Hebrews, 1 and 2 Peter, 1 and 2 John, and James.

Within the early Christian community itself, a number of factors conditioned the outlook of men like Paul, Peter, and their immediate successors. One was undoubtedly the struggle between those who saw the new movement as primarily Jewish and those who, on the other hand, conceived it as escaping the bounds of the Judaic tradition. After the Council of Jerusalem (about A.D. 45) decided that there was room for both the Jewish particularists and the Pauline universalists, the way was cleared for the ultimate triumph of the latter. But much of the social and political imagery of Judaism remained, being united, sometimes incongruously, with the frequently Hellenistic views of men like Paul and "John."

A second factor of major importance was undoubtedly the fall of Jerusalem in 70. We have already seen how Jesus presumably predicted this event, connecting it somehow with his belief in the probable early end of history. The final desecration of the Temple by the Roman armies was of enormous symbolic significance to both Jews and Christians. For the former, it meant that they would now have to think of themselves as wholly of the Diaspora. No longer would the Hebrew congregations scattered throughout the Empire send their Temple-tax to Jerusalem and look to the Temple authorities for both religious and political guidance. The Temple-tax was replaced by a 38-cent poll levy imposed by the Romans, the proceeds of which would support the Temple of Jupiter on Capitoline Hill. But most of all, the destruction of Jerusalem increased the traditional bitterness of the Jews against the empire. As for the Christians, the wiping out of the sacred city accentuated the triumph of the "universalistic" wing; for the Christians (largely Judaizers), following the advice of the Master, "fled to the hills" and were largely dispersed.

Finally, the beginning of Roman persecution of the Christians as such made its appearance. Early conflicts between the primitive Christian community and external authority were largely with Jewish politico-ecclesiastical rulers. It was they, for example, who ordered the stoning of Stephen.[54] And Paul apparently thought of them, rather than the Romans, as his primary antagonists. But several years before the Council of Jerusalem, the Emperor Caligula had inaugurated the cult of reverence for the emperor's image; and this created serious conflict with the Jews both in Jerusalem and in such cities of the Diaspora as Alexandria. While Christians as such were not directly affected by the Caligulan decree, it made its impress on St. Paul, despite his generally favorable attitude to the Roman authorities. In 64, of course, came the Neronian persecution of the Roman Christians. This was a temporary and local phenomenon but it must have affected powerfully the ideology of the early church and its attitude to the Empire.

Eschatology and Politics in the Epistles. Although early Christians differ as to the exact meaning of the "end of history"—some believe it completely beyond human understanding while others conceive it as a kind of "new age" in which true theocratic controls will be in effect—it seems to be the notion which conditions all sociopolitical conceptions in Paul, Peter, and the other writers of the New Testament. The goal of history, as a modern scholar has expressed it, is seen as that in which "the full purpose of God would disclose itself in an event which should conclusively express both His justice and His mercy."[55]

The outlook would inevitably affect the attitude of Christians to all historical institutions. If the end of all is at hand, why bother about work, contractual and political obligations, or the proper education of children? Why, indeed, worry about the distinction between right and wrong either in personal or in public relations? Paul himself seems to make much of his general teaching turn on the expectation of history's end. Thus he writes with an intensity of conviction which cannot be doubted:

> But this I do say, brothers. The appointed time has grown very short. From this time on those who have wives should live as though they had none. . . . For the present shape of the world is passing away.[56]

This attitude might logically seem to be fatal to the development of any social ethics. Indeed, such seems to have been the case in many of the early churches. There is a strong "antinomian" tendency based in part on Paul's own teaching about the "liberty" of men in Christ.[57] Many early Christians appear to think that Christ has released them from all social obligations: some become "free lovers"; others rebel against even the loose ecclesiastical authority of the first century; yet others adopt attitudes which might roughly be termed "anarchistic" with reference to the state.

In order to clarify the notion of the "end" itself, Paul writes one of his letters which is most fraught with political meaning. Apparently the *ecclesia* at Thessalonica is disturbed by those who think of the *eschaton* as likely to occur within a few weeks or months. They have received letters purporting to come from Paul himself which seem to bear out this belief. Many Thessalonians, therefore, are indifferent to their work and to family responsibilities. They look with eagerness to the expected "day of the Lord." Paul in his letter sympathizes with them and praises them for their "steadfastness" in belief. It is true, he remarks, that the "Lord Jesus" will soon appear from heaven "with his mighty angels in a blaze of fire," and take "vengeance" on the godless who will not listen to the "good news of our Lord Jesus."[58]

But the main burden of his letter is that the Thessalonians do not understand that this will occur only after the "lawless one" or the "adversary of every being that is called a god or an object of worship" makes his appearance. The "lawless one" will enter "God's sanctuary" and proclaim "himself to be God."[59]

There has been much dispute as to the identity of the "lawless one" although it seems

clear that Paul thinks of him as a specific political personage.[60] Some believe that Paul has in mind a Jewish ecclesiastical ruler, while others see the passage as referring to a temporal ruler resembling Caligula.

At any rate, the Parousia will not occur until this political ruler is unleashed and is made free to persecute. The Thessalonians, therefore, are to be diligent in their tasks and fulfill their ordinary obligations until they recognize the "lawless one"—as they will undoubtedly do. He will not be released to do his damage, thinks Paul, until that which is checking him disintegrates.[61] What, then, is holding the lawless one in check? Here, curiously enough, Paul seems to be referring to the Roman Empire, as a kind of embodiment of order and relative righteousness. We may think of him as suggesting that, until imperial institutions undergo a fundamental breakdown, the tendencies within civilization which will precede the Parousia cannot come to fruition.

The State and the Christian's Obligation. The role of the state is, of course, connected in the apostles' minds with their general attitude to the "world." They think of Christians as temporary pilgrims in the dimension of historical events—"aliens and exiles here," as Peter puts it.[62] The "world" outside the little band of Christians is destined to be lost so long as it rejects Christ; and, indeed, the New Testament position (outside the Gospels) appears to be that most non-Christians will reject Christ just as the Jews have spurned him. Wickedness afflicts all society; sin is ubiquitous. And the

52. AT Luke 19:42–44.
53. See, for example, Mark 13, which in turn carries on the tradition of such Jewish Books as Daniel, Tobit, and 3 Maccabees.
54. See Acts 7:59.
55. C. H. Dodd, *Gospel and Law: The Relation of Faith and Ethics in Early Christianity*, New York: Columbia University Press, 1951, p. 27.
56. AT 1 Corinthians 7:29–32.
57. See Galatians 4:9; 5:1.
58. AT 2 Thessalonians 2:6–9.
59. AT 2 Thessalonians 2:3, 4.
60. See the discussion in A. S. Peake, ed., *A Commentary on the Bible*, London: Thomas Nelson and Sons, 1919, pp. 879–880; and see Cadoux, *The Early Church and the World*, *op. cit.*, pp. 88-89.
61. 2 Thessalonians 2:7.
62. AT 1 Peter 2:11.

state and all political institutions reflect this sin.

At the same time, the Apostles are aware that the Empire has in many respects assisted them to preach the gospel. It has provided an admirable system of roads, which facilitates apostolic missions and the intercommunication of congregations. It establishes tribunals which, on the whole, are reasonably fair. This is certainly reflected in the often good experiences of Paul with Roman courts of justice.

Thus the apostolic attitude to the state is torn between, on the one hand, its general evaluation of the non-Christian world as "wicked" and about to produce antichrist and, on the other hand, an appreciation of the concrete benefits present in the political system. On one side, the whole pagan civilization is doomed to destruction at the forthcoming end of history; on the other, that very civilization has produced an ordering of things which is somehow providential insofar as it allows the Gospel to be spread and pagan wickedness to be restricted.

This ambivalence is best reflected, of course, in the letters of St. Paul. In writing to the Romans, he is evidently concerned to counteract certain antinomian tendencies which exist in the capital. Many members of the Roman church, no doubt, are Jews who have been unable to shed the typical Jewish hostility to the Empire. Others think that the "freedom" in Christ about which Paul has so often spoken[63] means emancipation from all external controls, whether of morals or of law. Paul is addressing himself to these groups and tendencies and in the process he tries to define what the Christian's conception of the state and "worldly" society ought to be.

Members of the Roman church must, he suggests, not succumb to the customs of the "world" but instead, as independent spirits, find out the will of God for themselves. We must all see ourselves in relation to the group, he points out, and not think of the "individual" as separate from the community. He is clearly stating one form of the "organic" notion of society in these words:

> For just as there are many parts united in our human bodies, and the parts do not all have the same function, so, many as we are, we form one body through union with Christ, and we are individually parts of one another.[64]

While he is no doubt thinking primarily of a Christian's relations with fellow Christians, he does not exclude "non-Christians" from the admonitions. It would be entirely foreign to his spirit to suggest that although Christians should not act with vengefulness in their relations with fellow-Christians, they might wreak "vengeance" on their non-Christian neighbors.

It is in the light of these statements that one must read the classic language of the thirteenth chapter. One sees in Paul's words a reflection of his own relatively pleasant experiences with the Roman authorities.

> Everyone must obey the authorities that are over him, for no authority can exist without the permission of God; the existing authorities have been established by him, so that anyone who resists the authorities sets himself in opposition to what God has ordained, and those who oppose him will bring down judgment upon themselves.[65]

And Peter, it should be noted, deals in very much the same way with the issue:

> Submit to all human authority, for the Master's sake; to the emperor, as supreme, and to governors, as sent by him to punish evil-doers, and to encourage those who do right.[66]

If we look more closely at passages like these, we note that the duty to obey rests upon the notion that political authority could not be established without God's "permission." The emperor and governor, as a matter of fact, exist in order that "evil" and "evil-doers" may be restrained. In defying commands of political authority one is, therefore, resisting the orders of God Himself. So long as one does "right" one need not fear the magistrate. It is only when one becomes a wrong-doer that one should become uneasy; for the magistrate bears a sword to restrain wickedness and the sword can cause pain. The magistrate in inflicting this suffering is really acting as the agent of a vengeful God.

It is significant that neither Paul nor Peter sees any obligation on the part of the Christian to become a magistrate himself. The obligation is confined to that of passive obedience in the interest of order and peace.

While we can go this far in an analysis of Paul's and Peter's conception of the state's role and the Christian's obligation, many questions are obviously left unanswered. Suppose, for example, that the authorities, instead of being "agents to do you good" or governors sent "to punish evil-doers," begin to be agents for the encouragement of evil or rulers for the suppression of good. Where, then, is the Christian's obligation? Neither Paul nor Peter tells us—and, indeed, comment on this point is to fill later Christian political treatises.

While we cannot be certain, it appears that the primitive Christian community is as hostile to Christians bearing the sword for purposes of war as for ends of civil coercion. It is true that we do not have in the New Testament epistles any unambiguous statement ruling out the military profession. But in addition to the twelfth chapter of Romans, we have certain slim if negative evidence which would support indirectly the idea that the early Christian cannot be a soldier. There is no record, for example, either in the New Testament letters or elsewhere, of converted Christians ever entering the army down to the end of the Apostolic Age.[67]

The Apostolic View of Property and Slavery. The early Christian's position on property and slavery, like his attitude to the state, is profoundly affected by eschatology. If the "end" is near, the general view seems to be, "external" matters such as possession of material goods or birth into the slave status, are matters of relative indifference. At the same time, however, Jesus' hostility to wealth and his tendency to idealize poverty are reinforced.

But the position is somewhat more complicated than these general statements would indicate. The Acts and the Epistles appear to portray a condition in which there is some division of opinion. Although all deprecate riches, some seem to think of the ideal Christian life in "communist" terms as over against others who have a "trusteeship" theory of wealth. The first emphasis is to be found in the church of Jerusalem, composed primarily of Jewish Christians. There we are told that "The believers all shared everything they had with one another, and sold their property and belongings, and divided the money with all the rest, according to their special needs."[68]

Supporting this Jewish Christian view is the Epistle of James, which, whatever its date (some see it written about the middle of the first century, while others think it dates from the early part of the second), clearly reflects the spirit of the Jerusalem church on material goods and property. The rich, James tells us, ought to "rejoice" when they are reduced in circumstances, "for the rich will disappear like the wild flowers."[69] The poor and the men of low social status are really in positions of eminence from the viewpoint of true understanding.

Already when James is writing, it seems clear that the "communism" of the early church has begun to break down. Apparently the surrender of private possessions is never a firm principle, although many, no doubt, think of it as virtually such. But almost from the very beginning, the second attitude to property makes its appearance. Modern critics like Max Beer associate its rise with "the increase in the number of Christians, the diffusion of the communities, the ascendance of the Pauline propaganda and conception of Christianity."[70] To some extent, it seems, this is true. But it would be a mistake to think of the contrast as too sharp, particularly with respect to Paul's position. True, Paul assumes and does not question the legitimacy of private property, just as he assumes at least the relative legitimacy of the state. But he, too, depreciates the value of wealth and insists on the importance of almsgiving for the believer. He stresses also the obligation to share material possessions.

One might expect apostolic Christians to take a hostile attitude to the institution of slavery. After all, most slaves owe their status in the end to the violent coercion of war that is implicitly repudiated during the apostolic age. Moreover, Pauline Christianity breaks down all barriers between Jew and Greek, bond and free, male and female. There is much discussion of the "freedom" which Christ brings to men. And there are, no doubt, some early Christians who believe that slaveholding is incompatible with the teaching of the Gospels.

But it is equally true that most apostolic teaching acquiesces in the institution of slavery. This is partly due to its eschatological

63. For examples, note particularly Galatians 4:9; 5:1.
64. AT Romans 12:4–5.
65. AT Romans 13:1–2.
66. AT 1 Peter 2:13–15.
67. It is true that Peter converts the soldier Cornelius (Acts 10) and Paul baptizes the jailer of Phillipi (Acts 16:30–34). But in neither case are we told whether the soldier involved either remains in the army or leaves.
68. AT Acts 2:44, 45.
69. AT James 1:10.
70. *Social Struggles in Antiquity*, pp. 195–196.

view of history. But there are other considerations as well. Paul's strong emphasis on "faith" and the "inner" as against the "outer" condition leads him to think that the vital fact about a human being is his attitude to Christ rather than his positive legal status. While slavery is undoubtedly a secondary evil, and Paul hints that perhaps Philemon should emancipate his runaway slave Onesimus,[71] he will not countenance any repudiation by the slave of his position. Indeed, writing to the Corinthian church where apparently some slaves were insisting that conversion entitled them to freedom, he maintains: "Everyone ought to remain in the station in which he was called. If you were a slave when you were called, never mind. Even if you can gain your freedom, make the most of your present condition instead."[72]

The position of Paul strongly resembles that of his contemporaries, the Stoics, who, it will be remembered, think of slavery as contrary to nature and yet see no reason to destroy the institution. The strong emphasis on the inner state as over against the outer condition is, of course, common to Paul and such Stoics as Seneca.

Paul and the apostles seem to be saying, in other words, "Why bother to legislate against the existing order of things, since Christ will soon legislate in a far more radical manner than we could ever hope to do?" It is this hope which apparently explains the wide attraction of primitive Christianity for slaves and those of low income and status.

A New People. Already in the epistles and in first-century Christian teaching generally, the conception begins to develop that the Christians are a separate people. We have noted Peter referring to them as "pilgrims" who are here for a time only. They are citizens, argues Paul, of a separate "commonwealth": "But the commonwealth to which we belong is in heaven."[73] And the writer of the epistle to the Hebrews agrees: "We have no permanent city here on earth, but we are in search of the city that is to come."[74] In a positive sense, too, Christians think of themselves as sharing a morality higher than that of the pagans among whom they are temporarily residing.

This notion that they constitute a separate people or nation is, as Harnack argues,[75] a definite political consciousness. Its presuppositions, he goes on, are Jewish apocalyptic, which views the external world as devilish; the "rapid transference of the gospel from the Jews to the Greeks"; and "the fall and ruin of Jerusalem and the Jewish state."[76]

Broadly speaking, by the end of the first century the scattered Christian communities have come to think of themselves as the successors of the Jewish nation. Although their polity is as yet sketchy and their traditions go back for only two generations, their consciousness of solidarity as over against the "world" forces them to develop "policy" almost despite themselves. As the "new" Jews, they are, of course emancipated from the particularities of Hebrew history; but they also inherit the Jewish sense of mission.

It is at the end of the first century, during the persecution of Emperor Domitian, that this Christian "political consciousness" is to undergo its first severe test, the problems of which are reflected in the rather bitter Apocalypse of John.

Politics in the Apocalypse of John

The clash of the infant Christian movement with the state during the reign of Nero had been, as we have seen, short-lived and local. In 64, the issue of image-worship had not yet come to the fore. True, Augustus had been deified after his death. But it was not until the reign of Caligula that the claim to living divinity was made; and most sensible Romans rejected it in view of Caligula's character. But with relative rapidity the notion developed that a cult should be built up around the *office* of emperor, as over against his person. The dead Caesar seems to have been deified as a person and at first rather discriminatingly—Augustus was a "Savior" and "God" because of his deeds and not by reason of his office. By Claudius' death, the deification of the emperor who had died seemed to be associated with the office he had held. By the age of Domitian (A.D. 81–96), of course, the emperor is once more claiming divine honors while yet alive, and we may date from his reign the real "Caesar cultus" centering around the living person who happened to be holding the office of imperator.

As the cultus first of the dead and then of the living Caesar developed, Christians increasingly came into conflict with its demands. Unlike the Jews, they were not exempted from it (and even the Jews, as we have seen, clashed with Caligula over the issue). But from the beginning, their position seems to have been clear. As Harnack has put it:

From the practical point of view, what was of still greater moment than the campaign against the world and worship of the gods, was *the campaign against the apotheosis of men. Christianity tore up political religion by the roots.*[77]

By the end of the first century, we may say, Christian attitudes to the state, relatively benevolent in the time of Paul, have become much more hostile. True, the emperor is still "reverenced" in the churches and prayers are offered for his safety and prosperity. But in many respects these tokens of civic allegiance become purely formal.

It is in this light that the Apocalypse of John must be read. John is presumably a Hebrew Christian who has been exiled by Domitian to the island of Patmos for failure to observe the rules of the imperial cultus. In the context, too, is apparently Domitian's fears that descendants of David, as claimants to the throne of Israel, might challenge his imperial supremacy. He gives orders, therefore, that all those belonging to David's house should be put to death.[78] While this may seem an extraordinarily tyrannical act in a ruler allegedly governed by principles of the Roman law, we should remember that where "political" matters are involved, Roman rulers and magistrates have sweeping prerogatives. Moreover, Domitian remembers the difficulties his father Vespasian and his brother Titus experienced in suppressing the relatively recent Jewish revolt.

The Apocalypse itself is conceived after the manner of the great Hebrew eschatological treatises and many of its modern students think of it as a document written in code which will encourage the "nation" of Christians in its repudiation of the imperial cult. The imagery and symbolism are such that they might have meaning for Christians, familiar as they are with Hebrew history and doctrine, whereas Roman officials would probably find the book incomprehensible. While the Revelation of St. John will be used in later generations for a diversity of purposes, many of them having to do with prediction of remote political events, it would appear that John has in mind only circumstances of his own generation.[79]

Down to the fourth chapter, the Apocalypse consists of a general prologue and of "letters" to the "seven churches" of Asia Minor commending them for their respective virtues and condemning them for their several sins. Thus the writer praises the church of Ephesus because it has been antagonistic to the Nicolaitan sect—a group very much like the "libertarian" or "antinomian" Christians whom Paul castigates in several passages.

He then proceeds to a specific discussion of recent and future politics under the imagery and symbolism of the "seven seals," the "seven trumpets," the "two witnesses," the "dragon," the "two beasts," the "bowls," the destruction of the "beast," and the overthrow of Satan. While the exact meaning of the pictures he paints is not always clear, it would seem to be possible, with the aid of "higher" Biblical criticism, to outline the major propositions.

The "seven seals" keep hidden in a book a series of natural and political events which, when revealed, show the course of the world.[80] When the first seal is opened, a white horse rushes forth—the symbol of conquest and domination by the military. Then appears, under the second seal, a red horse which represents the mass killing involved in war and

71. AT Philemon 21. After advising Philemon to be kind to his converted slave whom Paul has sent back, the apostle says: "I write you in full reliance upon your obedience; I know that you will do even more than I ask." This might be interpreted as a plea for manumission.
72. AT 1 Corinthians 7:21.
73. AT Philippians 3:20.
74. AT Hebrews 13:14.
75. Adolf Harnack, *op. cit.*, vol. 1, p. 256.
76. *Ibid.*, pp. 256–57.
77. *Ibid.*, p. 295.
78. Eusebius, *Ecclesiastical History*, Hugh J. Lawlor and John E. L. Oulton, trans., London: Society for Promoting Christian Knowledge, 1927, Bk. III, ch. 19.
79. The literature bearing, directly or indirectly, on the politics of the Apocalypse is extensive. See Robert H. Charles, *Lectures on the Apocalypse*, London: Oxford University Press, 1922, and *Studies in the Apocalypse*, Edinburgh: T. & T. Clark, 1913. By no means all authorities will agree, however, that the Apocalypse refers to temporal events. Thus E. Lohmeyer, *Die Offenbarung des Johannes*, 2nd ed., C. BornKamm, 1953, contends that the Revelation of John is completely mythological. Cullmann, however, does not disagree with the statement in the text. "Underlying the whole of the Johannine Apocalypse," he avers, "is the outlook which sees powerful engagements between invisible warlike powers taking place behind earthly happenings." *Op. cit.*, pp. 72–73.
80. Apocalypse 4–6.

conquest. When the black horse shows up in the third seal, we are prepared for the famine which always accompanies war; and the pale horse in the fourth seal suggests the pestilence that in ancient times almost always follows the famine and social disorganization associated with war. At this point the scene shifts from political and social catastrophes symbolized by horses to the fate of those who have refused to observe the requirements of the imperial cult; for on the opening of the fifth seal, we get a picture of the souls of those who have perished by reason of their failure to give religious honors to the emperor. When the sixth seal is removed, a great earthquake is seen and persons of all social classes begin to flee from the impending destruction. The Apocalypse is very vivid in describing the wiping out of class differentiations near the close of political history: "The kings of the earth, the nobles, the officers, the rich, the strong—everybody, slave and free—hid themselves in the caves and among the rocks of the mountains."[81] All are aware that the Lord is about to appear and are blinded by his light.

While the classes wait for the end—which will be revealed later in the seventh seal—the 144,000 "saints," or 12,000 from each of the twelve tribes of Israel, are "sealed" to protect them from serious spiritual injury. And later the "seven trumpets" portray largely natural calamities which accompany political disintegration—the turning of the sea to blood, the mountain cast into the sea, the falling of a great meteor which cuts off fresh water. The "two witnesses" appear—perhaps reincarnations of Moses and Elijah or of Peter and Paul—to prophesy during the "forty-two months" or "1260 days" of the persecution. John claims that the length of the state persecution will total the exact duration (three and a half years) of the persecution under Antiochus Epiphanes (168–165 B.C.). This parallelism seems to corroborate the notion that the Christians consider themselves as the "successor nation" of the Jews (who after the destruction of the Temple are barred from political significance).[82]

The "two beasts" appear in the thirteenth chapter of the Apocalypse and obviously refer to the politics of the Empire. The first beast is described as coming out of the sea. It is equipped with

> ten horns and seven heads, and with ten diadems on its horns, and blasphemous titles on its heads. One of its heads seemed to have received a mortal wound, but its mortal wound had been healed. And the whole earth followed the animal in wonder. . . .[83]

As for the second beast, the description is equally vivid:

> It had two horns like a lamb, but it spoke like a dragon. It exercises the full authority of the first animal on its behalf. It makes the earth and its inhabitants worship the first animal, whose mortal wound had been healed. . . . And it makes everyone, high and low, rich and poor, freemen and slaves, have a mark stamped on their right hands or on their foreheads, and permits no one to buy or sell anything unless he bears the mark, that is, the animal's name or the number corresponding to its name. . . . Let everyone of intelligence calculate the animal's number for it indicates a certain man; its number is 666.[84]

While the interpretation of the first animal is open to some question, it would appear that either the horns or the heads or both stand for Roman emperors. Thus, if one reckons the Empire as beginning with Augustus, there are ten emperors through Titus, the immediate predecessor of Domitian.[85] This would mean that the beast symbolizes the Empire before "the end" which is identified with the reign of Domitian. The "seven heads" conceivably could stand for the emperors since Caligula first made the claim to divinity.[86]

But whatever interpretation one adopts, the head which seemed to receive a "mortal wound" that nevertheless healed almost certainly represents Nero, who stands in the latter part of the first century for all that is diabolical and tyrannical in politics. Very soon after his death, it was claimed that Nero had not really died,[87] and at the time John is writing there are undoubtedly many who still accept the legend of Nero *redivivus*. As we shall see, John himself apparently believes the myth in some sense. Nero only *seemed* to die; but his "wound" really healed.

The second beast clearly represents the whole power and influence of the state cult, for while it appears to be gentle like a lamb, it speaks like a dragon or Satan. It is the enforcing power for the first beast, the authority which compels every man to bow low to the monster. Those who do not have the "mark" of the beast—are not certificated as having sacrificed to the image of the emperor, in other words—are subjected to boycott in the marketplace (very much, one might note, as Jehovah's Witnesses in the twentieth century find themselves subject to official and unofficial pressures for their refusal to salute the flag). The "number" of the second beast, 666, is a symbol for Nero, whose spirit animates the second animal.[88]

The remaining chapters of the Apocalypse are devoted to a portrayal of the fates of the two beasts, the "return" of Nero, and the destruction of the Empire. The imagery throughout remains extraordinarily vivid and reveals what an impression the politics of the late-first-century Empire made on the growing numbers of Christians.

"The great city," Rome, breaks into three pieces. God remembers "to give mighty Babylon the cup of the wine of his fierce anger."[89] And one of the seven angels conducts John to witness the details of Rome's destruction. Apparently the still-living Nero has returned from his exile in Parthia and seeks to recapture the Empire from Domitian.

John hears a voice from heaven comment on the destruction of the city of "seven hills" and the statement is one of the most bitter ever to be delivered against an historical political power-structure:

> For her sins are piled up to the sky, and God has remembered her crimes. Pay her back in her own coin, and give her double for what she has done. . . . The kings of the earth who have joined in her idolatry and luxury will weep and lament over her when they see the smoke from her burning.[90]

There follows the binding of the "dragon" or Satan for a thousand years. This would seem to represent, among other things, the wiping out of political power structures. Christ and the Christians who have refused to accept the mark of the "beast" (the Empire) sit on thrones and establish a theocracy for the earth. It is apparently to be a regime very much like that idealized in the time of the Judges or, perhaps, like that which first-century Stoics portrayed as the primitive "golden age."

When Satan is released at the end of the "millennium," he once more roams the earth. But then comes the final judgment. Satan musters the "heathen"–living and resurrected –for the "final conflict." "God's people" oppose them, assisted by fire which rains down from heaven. Finally, Satan is cast into "the fiery, sulphurous lake, where the animal and the false prophet were, there to be tortured day and night forever and ever."[91]

The Apocalypse is an excellent example of how a Christian, using a framework largely reminding one of such Hebrew apocalyptic works as Daniel, can discuss his attitude toward political power in general and to the Roman state and culture in particular. Running throughout the document there is a positive hatred of "civilization" and its agent the *civitas* or "state." Bitterness against the military power of the Empire is particularly evident; and an egalitarian ideology, in which the humble (largely identified with Christians) will be exalted, is developed.

The Apocalypse, as a matter of fact, becomes a good introduction to Christian political thought in the second century. For once more those who read John are disappointed: the "beast" remains strong and, indeed, tends more and more to regard the embryonic Christian "nation" as his political rival.

The Second Century

Among the early "apologists" of the church examining the Christian attitude toward political institutions in the second century are Justin Martyr (100–165), who in his *Apology* replies to those who allege that Christians are "seditious"; Tatian, a pupil of Justin, who about the middle of the century attacks Greek civilization and institutions in his *Oratio ad Graecos*, in the process defending the Christian position on civil and political affairs; and Athenagoras,

81. AT Apocalypse 6:15.
82. See Chapters 8 through 10.
83. AT Apocalypse 13:2–3.
84. AT Apocalypse 13:11–12; 16–17; 18.
85. Augustus, Tiberius, Caligula, Claudius, Nero, Calba, Otho, Vitellius, Vespasian, and Titus.
86. Claudius, Nero, Calba, Otho, Vitellius, Vespasian, and Titus.
87. Tacitus, *History*, Book II, ch. 8.
88. Not all interpretations would agree with this version of the famous number, although it seems to the writer the most plausible one. A. Deissmann, *Licht vom Osten*, 4th ed., Tübingen: T. C. Mohr, 1923, p. 238, n. 3, maintains that 666 signifies Kaisar Theos, or Caesar is God. The argument that 666 symbolizes Nero is based on assigning numerical values to letters of the Greek alphabet and adding the result. See Cullmann, *op. cit.*, pp. 79–83.
89. AT Apocalypse 16:19. "Babylon" is, of course, Rome.
90. AT Apocalypse 18:5–6; 9.
91. AT Apocalypse 20:10.

an Athenian philosopher who in works like *Legatio Pro Christianis* and *De Resurrectione* deals with such divers issues as non-resistance, tyranny, and the theory of law.

In general, the second century witnesses an increase in the intensity of persecution, development of ecclesiastical organization as a protective device, and growing concern on the part of the emperors for the church as a rival political organization. It is the age of the so-called "good" emperors—able and devoted men like Trajan, Hadrian, and Marcus Aurelius—who because of their very devotion and conscientiousness take seriously the challenge of the church. On the whole, the attitude of Christian apologists remains hostile to the "world," and to the state as the chief reflector of that world; but at no point does the extreme bitterness of the Apocalypse reappear. It is as if the church, having become accustomed to persecution, assumes that the state can act in no other way. At the same time, the new cult, which in the first century was largely confined to slaves and those of lower social status (although obviously there were many exceptions), now begins to penetrate the higher orders to a greater degree. Greek philosophers become Christians, as in the case of Athenagoras, and use their philosophical learning as a weapon in defense of the Christian "nation."

It is plain in the second century that the state tends to regard profession of Christianity as an act of hostility to itself. At the same time, the government attempts to safeguard individuals against purely mob action. An act of sacrifice to the emperor is usually sufficient to absolve one of all legal charges. It has been rumored since the middle of the first century that Christians commit such crimes as cannibalism and incest and the emperors are careful to point out that crimes of this kind, if proven, must be punished.

Many of these issues are brought out and discussed in the well-known correspondence between Pliny the Younger, governor of Bithynia, and the Emperor Trajan. They are also adverted to in the Rescript of the Emperor Hadrian to Gaius Fundanus, Proconsul of Asia (A.D. 125).

Pliny reports that he is puzzled as to what attitude he should take to the growing number of Christians in his province. He wonders, among other things, whether "the name itself, even if innocent of crime, should be punished, or only the crimes attaching to the name." Pending advice from the emperor, he notes, he asks the accused three times if they are Christians, threatening them with death. If they continue to insist that they are indeed Christians, the governor sentences them to execution, for "I do not doubt that, whatever kind of crime it may be to which they have confessed, their pertinacity and inflexible obstinacy should certainly be punished."[92] He points out that an anonymous pamphlet has been issued in the province and that it contains the names of many alleged Christians.

In his reply, the Emperor Trajan commends his governor for the care he has exhibited in his dealings with the Christians. No "hard and fast" rule can be laid down, he believes. If a person denies that he is a Christian and "proves" it by "worshipping our gods," he should be pardoned. Anonymous pamphlets should "carry no weight in any charge whatsoever. They constitute a very bad precedent, and are also out of keeping with this age."[93]

Hadrian's general attitude seems to resemble that of Trajan. He attacks "slanderous informers" who practice their "vile trade" and is particularly vehement in his criticism of mob action. Clear crimes are, of course, to be punished. "On the other hand, I emphatically insist on this, that if anyone demand a writ of summons against any of these Christians, merely as a slanderous accusation, you proceed against that man with heavier penalties, in proportion to the gravity of his offense."[94]

In the first century, the state's hostility was sporadic and sometimes without respect for the forms of law. In the second, it is more systematically hostile, but there is a tendency to observe legal procedures more rigorously.

Christian thought, for its part, carries on most of the basic attitudes exemplified in the latter half of the first century. There is still a strong eschatological note, for example, although some interpret the future Kingdom as a state of blessedness beyond the "resurrection," and in "heaven," while others continue to think of it as an earthly society which has been transformed. Among the latter is the writer of the second-century II Peter, who expects "new heavens and a new earth, where uprightness will prevail."[95] Justin Martyr anticipates a literal resurrection of the flesh, the reconstruction of Jerusalem, and the rule of Christ on earth; and Montanus thinks that the earthly "kingdom" is very near.

With respect to attitudes to external society, the Christian "nation" continues to regard itself as set apart. It is more moral than the pagans. The ways of "heathen" society are not for it. Thus Justin Martyr says: "We pray for our enemies, and try to persuade those that hate us unjustly. . . ."[96] This attitude, Christian thinkers argue, sharply differentiates the followers of the Gospel from those who view the pagan culture and state with complacency.

Since they accept the inevitability of persecution, as we have seen, it would be surprising if second-century Christians should exhibit much affection for state institutions. They criticize human laws because they are inconsistent, the implication apparently being that some among them must be wrong.[97] The laws are also weak and ineffective in preventing wrongdoing. "What the laws of man have not been able to effect, that the Logos, being Divine, would have wrought," asserts Justin Martyr, "if the wicked demons had not scattered many lies and godless charges, . . . not one of which applies to us."[98]

With respect to the state as such, however, the general attitude of the second century seems to be one of passive obedience. Despite the fact that many Christians still think of it as "antichrist" and expect its early demise, the command to obey is an apostolic one and the state, moreover, has a kind of relative justification in the restraint of wrong.

As for any usual and positive assistance to the state, however, it is clear that the second-century Christian retains his opposition to service in any public civil office and, probably, to military service as well. With respect to public office, a careful modern student of Christian political views during this age summarizes the situation in these words:

> . . . the Christians of that time stood almost entirely aloof from political life.[99]

Passive submission to the state's orders, in other words, continues to be sharply differentiated from any active participation in its administration.

As for the Christian attitude to war, the writings of the early apologists are filled with encomiums to "peace" and to the conditions which make for it. It seems probable, too, that very few if any Christians enter the army before the middle of the century; and even after that period, when we hear of the first legion which contains Christians (the Legio Fulminata, which serves under Marcus Aurelius in 173), the position of the apologists makes it doubtful that most Christian thinkers condone military service. Harnack thinks that down to the reign of Marcus Aurelius or that of his son Commodus, "Christian soldiers were still few and far between."[100]

The writings of Justin Martyr lend support to the theory that Christianity is regarded as incompatible with military service. Tatian remarks "I decline military command."[101] Athenagoras maintains that Christians cannot justify any man's being put to death, even justly.[102] And Celsus, a pagan antagonist of Christianity in the second century, seems to underline the Christians' theoretical position on war and military service when he virtually calls upon them to give up their obdurate refusal to serve. If they do not do so, he argues, the Empire will be conquered by savages and barbarians.[103]

The First Two Centuries: A Summary

By way of recapitulation, let us characterize the development of Christian political ideas during the first two centuries of our era.

Jesus himself, we have suggested, grew up in the Jewish political atmosphere, with its strife among Sadducees, Pharisees, Zealots, Herodians, and Essenes. He conceived his mission as being associated first of all with the Jews. He continued to think of himself as "king" of the Jews, although later in his life he began to believe that this kingship also had a universalistic quality. He expected, in line with Jewish apocalyptic, an early end of political history. Meanwhile, he looked with relative benevolence on the claims of the state, even those of foreign officials. Thus he thought that it was

92. Pliny, *Letters*, Baltimore: Penguin Books, 1963, X, xcvi.
93. *Ibid.*, X, xcvii.
94. Rescript of Hadrian to Caius Minucius Fundanus.
95. AT 2 Peter 3:13.
96. *Apology*, XIV, 3.
97. Such is the position, for example, of Tatian, *Oratio ad Graecos*, 23, 112.
98. *Apology*, X, 6.
99. C. J. Cadoux, *The Early Church and the World, op. cit.*, pp. 255–256.
100. A. Harnack, *op. cit.*, II, p. 52.
101. *Oratio ad Graecos*, 11, 48.
102. *Legatio Pro Christianis*, 35, 178.
103. Origen, *Contra Celsum*, VIII, 68, 73.

an obligation to pay taxes to the emperor, though there were at the same time obligations which one owed to God. Hence Jesus laid down a principle distinguishing political from sacred obligations. Insofar as his "kingdom" was thought of as "earthly," it was to be a transformation similar to that sketched by many Jewish thinkers, with existing political institutions receding and the direct theocracy of God taking their place. But there were no shortcuts to the Kingdom.

After the death of Jesus, Christian attitudes to politics as expressed by Paul, Peter, and other first-century Apostles expanded on the supposed teachings of Jesus. On the whole, they represented an ideology of the dispossessed and powerless: Meekness and patience were exalted and the poor were thought to be superior in virtue to those who possessed high social and economic status. Men were "free" in Christ; but this was an inward freedom and had little to do with any possible repudiation of social and political obligations. Although the *eschaton* was momentarily expected, this was no reason for an attitude of antinomianism and anarchism: Indeed, the imminence of the end was seen as calling Christians to lead a life of passive obedience to the state. At the same time, one should not use the pagan lawcourts for civil suits (although it was legitimate to take advantage of them for appeals in criminal cases). Nor should one, apparently, serve the state in public office, whether civil or military. Christians were pilgrims on earth and their real citizenship was in heaven.

In the Apocalypse, hatred of political power reached its height. While Paul had thought of the major menace to the Christian movement as coming from the Jewish leadership, the writer of the Apocalypse, confronted by the persecution of Domitian, saw in it the Roman state.

After the Apocalypse, Christian views of the state were never quite as violent. When persecution became much more systematized in the second century, the church increasingly regarded it as inevitable. Expectation of the "end" still continued and the early apologists reiterated the necessity for passive obedience, while repudiating positive collaboration. Active participation in civil life was refused because of the association of public office with violent coercion and worldly ambitions; and military service seems to have been largely spurned because it led to bloodshed in war, the capital punishment of criminals, and the worship of the gods, including the "genius" of the emperor.

By the end of the second century the Roman authority confronted in the ecclesia and its theory an embryonic challenge to the theory and practice of pagan antiquity that all realms of life were in principle subject to the polis, civitas, or state. Thereafter much of the discussion of politics would turn on the problem of how the realms of Caesar and ecclesia were to be differentiated.

Part I Selected References

(in addition to those mentioned in footnotes)

1. *Politics and Ethics Among the Ancient Hebrews*

ALBRIGHT, WILLIAM F. *From Stone Age to Christianity: Monotheism and the Historical Process*, 2nd ed. Garden City: Anchor Books, 1957.

ANDERSON, BERNHARD W. *Understanding the Old Testament*. Englewood Cliffs: Prentice-Hall, 1957.

BRIGHT, JOHN. *A History of Israel*. Philadelphia: Westminster Press, 1959.

Cambridge Ancient History, vol. IV. Cambridge: Cambridge University Press, 1960.

DANIEL-ROPS, HENRY. *Israel and the Ancient World*. London: Eyre & Spottiswoode, 1949.

DENTEN, ROBERT CLAUDE, ED. *The Idea of History in the Ancient Near East*. American Oriental Series, vol. 38, edited by Henry M. Hoenigswald. New Haven: Yale University Press, 1955.

FRANKFORT, H., AND H. A. FRANKFORT. "The Emancipation of Thought from Myth." In H. and H. A. Frankfort *et al.*, *The Intellectual Adventure of Ancient Man*. Chicago: University of Chicago Press, 1956.

GOLDBERG, ISRAEL. *A History of the Jewish People*. New York: World Publishing, 1949.

GUTHRIE, HARVEY H. *God and History in the Old Testament*. Greenwich: Seabury Press, 1960.

HASTINGS, JAMES, ED., WITH JOHN A. SELBIE. *A Dictionary of the Bible*, 5 vols. Edinburgh: T. and T. Clark, 1909.

HENSHAW, THOMAS. *The Later Prophets*. London: Allen & Unwin, 1958.

HESCHEL, ABRAHAM J. *The Prophets*. New York: Harper & Row, 1962.

IRWIN, WILLIAM A. "The Hebrews" In H. and H. A. Frankfort *et al.*, *The Intellectual Adventure of Ancient Man*. Chicago: University of Chicago Press, 1946.

JOSEPHUS, FLAVIUS. *The Life and Works of Flavius Josephus*. William Whiston, trans. Philadelphia: John C. Winston, 1936.

KLAUSNER, JOSEPH. *The Messianic Idea in Israel from Its Beginning to the Completion of the Mishnah*. New York: Macmillan, 1955.

KUHL, CURT. *The Prophets of Israel*. Rudolf J. Ehrlieb and J. P. Smith, trans. Edinburgh: Oliver, 1960.

MACMURRAY, JOHN. *The Clue to History*. New York: Harper, 1938.

METZGER, BRUCE M. *An Introduction to the Apocrypha*. New York: Oxford, 1957.

MORGENSTERN, JULIAN. *The Message of Deutero-Isaiah in its Sequential Unfolding*. Cincinnati: Hebrew Union College Press, 1961.

NORTH, CHRISTOPHER R. *The Old Testament Interpretation of History*. London: Epworth Press, 1946.

PATTERSON, CHARLES H. *The Philosophy of the Old Testament*. New York: Ronald, 1953.

PEAKE, A. S. *The People and the Book*. New York: Oxford, 1925.

RAY, GERHARD VON. *Old Testament Theology*. D. M. G. Stalker, trans. New York: Harper, 1962.

ROBINSON, THEODORE H. *The Decline and Fall of the Hebrew Kingdoms*. New York: Oxford, 1939.

SANDMEL, SAMUEL. *The Hebrew Scriptures: An Introduction to their Literature and Religious Ideas*. New York: Knopf, 1963.

STRACHEY, SIR EDWARD. *Jewish History and Politics in the Times of Sargon and Sennacherib*. London: W. Ibister, 1874.

WALLIS, LOUIS. *God and the Social Process*. Chicago: University of Chicago Press, 1935.

WALLIS, LOUIS. *A Sociological Study of the Bible*. Chicago: University of Chicago Press, 1912.

WEBER, MAX. *Ancient Judaism*. Hans H. Gerth and Don Martindale, trans. and ed. Glencoe, Ill.: Free Press, 1952.

WELCH, A. C. *Deuteronomy, The Framework to the Code*. New York: Oxford, 1932.

2. *Growth and General Conception of the Polis*

BONNER, ROBERT J. *Aspects of Athenian Democracy*. Berkeley: University of California Press, 1933. *Ibid. Lawyers and Litigants in Ancient Athens*. Chicago: University of Chicago Press, 1927.

BOTSFORD, G. W. *The Development of the Athenian Constitution*. Boston: Ginn & Co., 1893.

BURY, J. B. *A History of Greece*. New York: Modern Library, 1937.

CALHOUN, G. M. *The Growth of Criminal Law in Ancient Athens*. Berkeley: University of California Press, 1927.

DICKINSON, G. LOWES. *The Greek View of Life*. New York: Doubleday, Page, 1925.

DURANT, WILL. *The Life of Greece*. New York: Simon & Schuster, 1939.

FERGUSON, W. S. *Greek Imperialism*. Boston: Houghton Mifflin, 1913.

GLOTZ, GUSTAVE. *The Greek City and Its Institutions*. New York: Knopf, 1929.

GREENIDGE, A. H. J. *A Handbook of Greek Constitutional History*. New York: Macmillan, 1896.

3. *Political Thought and Opinion from Hesiod to Socrates*

ARISTOPHANES. *The Acharnians; The Birds; The Clouds; The Ecclesiazusae; The Knights; Lysistrata; Peace; The Wasps*.

BARKER, ERNEST. *Greek Political Theory: Plato and His Predecessors.* New York: Barnes and Noble, 1960.
BURNET, JOHN. *Greek Philosophy.* London: Macmillan, 1960. Particularly Ch. 2, "Pythagoras," and Ch. 3, "Heraclitus."
CLEVE, FELIX M. *The Giants of Pre-Sophistic Greek Philosophy.* The Hague: Martinus Nijhoff, 1965.
CORNFORD, FRANCIS. *Before and After Socrates.* Cambridge: University Press, 1932.
CORNFORD, FRANCIS. *From Religion to Philosophy.* New York: Harper & Row, 1957.
DUPREEL, EUGENE. *La Legende Socratique et les Sources de Platon.* Bruxelles: R. Sand, 1922.
GOMPERZ, THEODOR. *Greek Thinkers.* 4 vols. L. Magnus, trans. London: J. Murray, 1949. Vols. 1 and 2.
JAEGER, WERNER W. *Paideia: The Ideals of Greek Culture,* 2nd ed. Gilbert Highet, trans. New York: Oxford University Press, 1948.
RALPH, LESLIE. *Pythagoras: A Short Account of his Life and Philosophy.* London: Krikos, 1961.
SOPHOCLES. *Oedipus the King; Oedipus at Colonus.*
WEIL, SIMONE. "The Illiad: The Poem of Force." *Politics,* November 1945.
ZELLER, EDUARD. *Outlines of the History of Greek Philosophy.* New York: Harcourt, Brace, 1931.
ZELLER, EDUARD. *Socrates and the Socratic Schools.* London: Longmans, Green, 1885.
ZELLER, EDUARD. *Stoics, Epicureans, and Sceptics.* London: Longmans, Green, 1870.

4. *Plato and the Rational Polis*

ADAMSON, JOHN E. *The Theory of Education in Plato's Republic.* London: S. Sonnenschein, 1903.
BARKER, ERNEST. *The Political Thought of Plato and Aristotle.* New York: G. P. Putnam's Sons, 1906.
BARKER, ERNEST. *Greek Political Theory: Plato and His Predecessors.* New York: Barnes & Noble, 1960.
BURNET, JOHN. *Platonism.* Berkeley: University of California Press, 1928.
DEMOS, RAPHAEL. *The Philosophy of Plato.* Chicago: Scribner's, 1939.
FOSTER, MICHAEL B. *The Political Philosophies of Plato and Hegel.* New York: Oxford, 1935.
GOMPERZ, THEODOR. *Greek Thinkers.* 4 vols. L. Magnus, trans. London: J. Murray, 1949. Vols. 3 and 4.
GROTE, GEORGE. *Plato, and the Other Companions of Socrates.* London: J. Murray, 1888.
JAEGER, WERNER W. *Paideia: The Ideals of Greek Culture,* 2nd ed. Gilbert Highet, trans. New York: Oxford University Press, 1948.
JOSEPH, HORACE W. B. *Knowledge and the Good in Plato's Republic.* New York: Oxford, 1948.
LEON, PHILIP. *Plato.* London: T. Nelson, 1939.
LEVINSON, ROLAND. *In Defense of Plato.* Cambridge: Harvard University Press, 1953.
LUTOSLAWSKI, WINCENTY. *The Origin and Growth of Plato's Logic.* London: Longmans, Green, 1897.
MARCUSE, LUDWIG. *Plato and Dionysus.* New York: Knopf, 1947.
MORE, PAUL E. *Platonism.* Princeton: Princeton University Press, 1921.
MORE, PAUL E. *The Religion of Plato.* Princeton: University Press, 1921.
NETTLESHIP, RICHARD L. *Philosophical Lectures and Remains.* Vol. 2. *The Republic of Plato.* London: Macmillan, 1897.
PLATO. *Apology; Phaedo; Symposium; Timaeus; Critias; Euthydemus.*
RITTER, CONSTANTIN. *The Essence of Plato's Philosophy.* London: Allen & Unwin, 1933.
SHOREY, PAUL. *Platonism, Ancient and Modern.* Berkeley: University of California Press, 1938.
SHOREY, PAUL. *What Plato Said.* Chicago: University of Chicago Press, 1933.
SOLMSEN, FRIEDRICH. *Plato's Theology.* Ithaca: Cornell University Press, 1942.
TAYLOR, A. E. *Platonism and Its Influence.* Boston: Marshall Jones Co., 1924.
WILD, JOHN. *Plato's Modern Enemies and the Theory of Natural Law.* Chicago: University of Chicago Press, 1952.
ZELLER, EDUARD. *Plato and the Older Academy.* London: Longmans, Green, 1888.

5. *Aristotle and Political Society*

BADAREU, DAN. *L'individuel chez Aristotle.* Paris: Boivin, 1936.
BLACKIE, J. S. *Four Phases of Morals: Socrates, Aristotle, Christianity, Utilitarianism.* New York: Scribner, Armstrong, 1872.
CHERNISS, HAROLD F. *Aristotle's Criticism of Presocratic Philosophy.* Baltimore: Johns Hopkins University Press, 1944.
EHRENBURG, VICTOR. *Alexander and the Greeks.* London: Oxford University Press, 1938.
GOMPERZ, THEODOR. *Greek Thinkers.* 4 vols. L. Magnus, trans. London: J. Murray, 1949. Vol. 4.
GRIFFIN, ARTHUR K. *Aristotle's Psychology of Conduct.* London: Williams & Norgate, 1931.
HAMBURGER, M. *Morals and Law: the Growth of Aristotle's Legal Theory.* New Haven: Yale University Press, 1951.
JAEGER, WERNER. *Paideia: The Ideals of Greek Culture.* 2nd ed. Gilbert Highet, trans. New York: Oxford University Press, 1948.
JAEGER, WERNER. *Aristotle.* Oxford: Clarendon, 1934.
LOOS, ISAAC. *The Political Philosophy of Aristotle. Annals of the American Academy,* vol. 10. Philadelphia: American Academy of Political and Social Science, 1897.
LOOS, ISAAC. *Studies in the Politics of Aristotle and the Republic of Plato.* Iowa City: University of Iowa Bulletin, 1899, vol. 1.
MURE, GEOFFREY. Aristotle. London: E. Benn, 1932.
ROBIN, LEON. *Aristotle.* Paris: Presses Universitaires de France, 1944.
SHUTE, CLARENCE W. *The Psychology of Aristotle.* New York: Columbia University Press, 1941.
SPICER, EAULLIE E. *Aristotle's Conception of the Soul.* London: University of London, 1934.
STOCKS, JOHN L. *Aristotelianism.* Boston: Marshall Jones, 1925.
ZELLER, EDUARD. *Aristotle and the Earlier Peripatetics.* London: Longmans, Green, 1897.

6. *Political Thought and Attitudes from Alexander to the Triumph of Rome*

BRÉHIER, ÉMILE. *Chrysippe et l'ancient stoicisme.* Nouv. ed. rev. Paris: Presses Universitaires de France, 1951.

CARY, MAX. *The Legacy of Alexander: a History of the Greek World from 323 to 146 B.C.* New York: Dial Press, 1932.

CLOCHÉ, PAUL. *Alexandre le Grand et les essais de fusion entre l'Occident gréco-macédonien et l'Orient.* Neuchâtel: H. Messeiler, 1953.

DAVIDSON, WILLIAM L. *The Stoic Creed.* Edinburgh: T. and T. Clark, 1907.

FLACELIÈRE, ROBERT. *Les Aitoliens à Delphes; contribution à l'histoire de la Grèce au IIe siècle.* Paris: E. de Boccard, 1937.

LIVINGSTONE, SIR RICHARD. *Greek Ideals and Modern Life.* Cambridge: Harvard University Press, 1935.

POLYBIUS. *The History of the Achaean League as Contained in the Remains of Polybius.* Edited by W. W. Capes. New York: Macmillan, 1888.

REESON, MARGARET B. *The Political Theory of the Old and Middle Stoa.* New York: J. J. Augustin, 1951.

TCHERIKOVER, VICTOR. *Hellenistic Civilization and the Jews.* Philadelphia: Jewish Publication Society of America, 1959.

WENLEY, ROBERT M. *Stoicism and Its Influence.* Boston: Marshall Jones, 1924.

7. *Roman Experience and Political Thought*

ADCOCK, SIR FRANK EZRA. *Roman Political Ideas and Practice.* Ann Arbor: University of Michigan Press, 1959.

ARNOLD, EDWARD VERNON. *Roman Stoicism.* Cambridge: Cambridge University Press, 1911.

BEVAN, EDWYN ROBERT. *Stoics and Sceptics.* Oxford: Clarendon, 1913.

DAVIS, C. H. S. *Greek and Roman Stoicism and Some of Its Disciples: Epictetus, Seneca, and Marcus Aurelius.* Boston: H. B. Turner and Co., 1930.

FOWLER, WILLIAM WARDE. *The City-State of the Greeks and Romans.* New York: St. Martin's Press, 1963.

FRITZ, KURT VON. *The Theory of the Mixed Constitution in Antiquity.* New York: Columbia University Press, 1954.

GIBBON, EDWARD. *The Decline and Fall of the Roman Empire.* 4 vols. Edited by H. N. Milman. London: Ward, Lock and Co., n.d. Vol. 1.

GLOVER, T. R. *The Conflict of Religions in the Early Roman Empire.* London: Methuen, 1909.

GUMMERE, RICHARD MOTT. *Seneca, the Philosopher and His Modern Message.* New York: Cooper Square Publishers, 1963.

HASKELL, HENRY JOSEPH. *The New Deal in Old Rome.* New York: Knopf, 1947.

LARSEN, JACOB A. O. *Representative Government in Greek and Roman History.* Berkeley: University of California Press, 1955.

MARCUS AURELIUS. *Meditations.*

PLINY THE YOUNGER. *Letters.* 2 vols. William Melmoth, trans. London: Loeb Classical Library, 1915.

SCULLARD, HOWARD H. *From the Gracchi to Nero.* New York: Barnes & Noble, 1963.

WALBANK, FRANK WILLIAM. *A Historical Commentary on Polybius.* Oxford: Clarendon, 1957.

ZELLER, EDUARD. *The Stoics, Epicureans, and Sceptics.* New and rev. ed. Oswald J. Reichel, trans. New York: Russell and Russell, 1962.

8. *The New Testament and Early Christianity*

ALBRIGHT, WILLIAM F. *From the Stone Age to Christianity.* 2nd ed. New York: Anchor Books, 1957.

BRANDON, SAMUEL. *Jesus and the Zealots.* New York: Scribner, 1968.

BULTMANN, RUDOLF. *The Theology of the New Testament.* K. Grobel, trans. New York: Scribner's, 1951.

CANFIELD, LEON H. *The Early Persecutions of the Christians.* New York: Columbia University Press, 1913.

COCHRANE, CHARLES N. *Christianity and Classical Culture: A Study of Thought and Action from Augustus to Augustine.* Oxford: Clarendon, 1940.

COHEN, A. A. "*The Past and Future of Eschatological Thinking.*" In Harold Stahmer, ed., *Religion and Contemporary Society.* New York: Collier Books, 1963.

CULLMANN, OSCAR. *Christ and Time: The Primitive Christian Concept of Time and History.* Floyd V. Filson, trans. Philadelphia: Westminster Press, 1950.

DEISSMANN, GUSTAV A. *The New Testament in the Light of Modern Research.* Garden City: Doubleday, Doran, 1929.

DUCHESNE, L. *The Early History of the Christian Church.* 3 vols. London: J. Murray, 1909–1922.

FAST, H. A. *Jesus and Human Conflict.* Scottsdale, Pa.: Herald Press, 1962.

GILBERT, GEORGE H. *Greek Thought in the New Testament.* New York: Macmillan, 1928.

GRANT, F. C. *Roman Hellenism and the New Testament.* New York: Scribner's, 1962.

KAUTSKY, KARL. *Foundations of Christianity.* Henry F. Mins, trans. New York: S. A. Russell, 1953. [Jesus as a "class warfare" advocate.]

KIDDLE, MARTIN. *The Revelation of St. John.* New York: Harper, 1941.

KLAUSNER, JOSEPH. *From Jesus to Paul.* William Stinespring, trans. New York: Macmillan, 1943.

KLAUSNER, JOSEPH. *The Messianic Idea in Israel from Its Beginning to the Completion of the Mishnah.* W. F. Stinespring, trans. New York: Macmillan, 1955.

MCGIFFERT, ARTHUR C. *A History of Christianity in the Apostolic Age.* Rev. ed. New York: Scribner's, 1914.

MORE, GEORGE FOOT. *Judaism in the First Centuries of the Christian Era and the Age of the Tannaim.* 2 vols. Cambridge, Mass.: Harvard University Press, 1927.

MOWRY, L. *The Dead Sea Scrolls and the Early Church.* Chicago: University of Chicago Press, 1962.

ODEBERG, HUGO. *Pharisaism and Christianity*. J. M. Moe, trans. St. Louis: Concordia Publishing House, 1964.

SCHWEITZER, ALBERT. *The Quest of the Historical Jesus*. New York: Macmillan, 1948.

UMEN, SAMUEL. *Pharisaism and Jesus*. New York: Philosophical Library, 1963.

WALLIS, LOUIS. *God and the Social Process*. Chicago: University of Chicago Press, 1935.

WALLIS, LOUIS. *A Sociological Study of the Bible*. Chicago: University of Chicago Press, 1912.

WILLIS, H. E. *The Good Society, the Goal of Law, and the Religion of Jesus*. New York: Vantage, 1958.

WORKMAN, HERBERT H. *Persecution in the Early Church*. 4th ed. London: Epworth Press, 1923.

part II

THIS WORLD AND THE NEXT: POLITICAL THOUGHT IN THE CHRISTIAN CENTURIES

The late classical world feverishly searched for "salvation," whether religious or political. Man's sense of alienation led him to seek assurance in the mystery religions, in civic religious cults, or in political redeemers who promised to preserve "civilization."

This quest for salvation was grounded in the very nature of institutional development. After the second century A.D., it became obvious to the perspicacious that the classical Republic was not to be restored and that the kind of organic community envisioned by Plato and Aristotle was indeed laid up in heaven. Political tyranny became increasingly central and wars against the so-called barbarians—and every age has its barbarians or tends to invent them—both strengthened this tyranny and made men fearful of challenging it.

It was into this environment that the Christian sect was born. Originating about the time of Tiberius, it had gained great social and political strength by the age of Aurelian in the third century. As the Roman Empire disintegrated, organized Christianity increasingly began to preside in its place. It guided the Eastern Empire and for several centuries provided the central element of unity in the West. Developing from its status as a small sect to a position of political power, it encountered countless problems of adjusting its early ideology to the presumed necessities of the world while at the same time attempting not to surrender its basic principles.

Christian thinkers faced a world which, after the fifth century, became more and more disintegrated socially and politically. We may think of the period from the fifth to the end of the eleventh century as the epoch during which an ecclesiastical organization, originally strong but later demoralized, strives to achieve a universal status against the pull of feudal and decentralist forces dominated by Germanic kingdoms and fiefdoms.

Around 1100, the Church managed to achieve a central position which persisted until about 1300; and this two-hundred-year period some have called the High Middle Ages. It was characterized by the revival of universities, the renewed influence of Aristotle, the expansion of urban life, and the development of philosophy. Two universal institutions struggled for mastery—the Church and the Holy Roman Empire (whose birth we usually date as 962). But both were constantly challenged by the centrifugal forces of the feudal-manorial system.

The epoch of the declining Middle Ages may be said to extend from 1300 to the early part of the sixteenth century. Town life continued to expand and feudal modes of existence began to contract. The foundations of commercial capitalism were laid. The structure of the Church Universal, so painfully built up in the years before 1100, showed signs of weakness: for two generations, the popes were subject to the influence of French kings at Avignon and immediately thereafter the Great Schism rent the Church asunder, with two popes and then three contesting for the allegiance of Christendom. To ecclesiastical division was added a corruption of the clergy greater than in the High Middle Ages. Even when the Church was reunited (in 1417), the corruption persisted. By 1500, the way had been prepared for the politics of the sixteenth century, with its wholesale onslaught on things medieval.

Meanwhile, how were political thinkers reacting?

The political thought of the New Testament stressed submission to political authority but refusal to participate actively in the things of this world. Thus in the beginning no Christian could be a magistrate or wage war. There was a widespread belief, too, in the imminent end of history. Life, as with certain of the pagan schools of thought, was a pilgrimage, in which Christians partook with great reluctance and out of a sense of obligation.

Attitudes of this kind continued, in greater or lesser degree, until the middle of the third century. Gradually, however, as the Church gained converts from the official and higher economic classes, tentative concessions to the "world" were made. As belief in the imminent end of history declined, accommodation to the world had to be made. This was all the more essential after the Church had triumphed politically in the early part of the fourth century. It was the task of St. Augustine to attempt a synthesis of early Christian attitudes with later views that sustained some Christian participation in politics.

St. Augustine's political doctrine was an overshadowing one during the first period of the Middle Ages. He was quoted widely by those who helped shape canon law and it was through him that late Stoic and Neoplatonic notions became part of the warp and woof of political thought down to the early part of the twelfth century. In the great eleventh-century struggle for a unified Church, he was cited to support papal apologists; and Pope Gregory VII could use him effectively in denigrating merely temporal authority.

Meanwhile, the Gelasian doctrine of spirituals and temporals had been laid down, the foundations of a monastic view of the social world had been established, and implicitly the feudal-manorial system suggested its own social and political theory. In the great Investiture struggle of the eleventh century, a gigantic ideological battle was carried on between territorial church conceptions, on the one hand, and the argument for ecclesiastical universalism, on the other.

After about 1100, with the beginning of the High Middle Ages, political thought became more sophisticated. The impact of Arabic and Jewish learning was important, as were the Crusades. But heresy, too, conditioned the growth of doctrine. By 1200, indeed, the issue of heresy was a central one, at the very time—under Innocent III—when the papacy reached its apogee. In the first part of the High Middle Ages, speculation was dominated by the civil and canon lawyers, who debated vigorously the respective roles of spiritual and temporal authority in the single society known as Christendom. After 1200, however, while the debate of the lawyers continued, scholastic philosophy—particularly as reflected in St. Thomas Aquinas—came to the fore.

During the period of the disintegrating Middle Ages, from 1300 to 1500, discussion centered on the ideologies of the sects, on the political implications of nominalistic philosophy, and on the theories of the conciliar movement. Strong cases for the Holy Roman Empire and the Papacy continued to be made (by Dante and Boniface VIII, for example) but the predominant outlook increasingly became one which subverted typically medieval notions in favor of the sovereign national-state conception and a church subordinated to temporal authority. By 1500, the world was prepared for Machiavelli, who epitomized in political thought many of the intellectual tendencies of late medieval and early modern conceptions.

Seen in the perspective of history, among the most important contributions of medieval thought and institutions to politics were the stress on man's duality, as both temporal and spiritual; the subordination of economic to noneconomic ends; the notion of corporate life as integrated by religion; the development of ideas of representation (in religious orders, in the rise of parliaments, and during the conciliar movement); the expansion of the idea of natural law; the conception of liberty, born in part out of the clash between temporals and spirituals and nourished by certain sects; and the growth of pluralistic views of law and social life. Although the shadow of the Inquisition hovered over later medieval life, it is also true that medieval men began to struggle against it and that many inquisitorial practices were adopted reluctantly. The Middle Ages have often been characterized as superstitious, but we should remember that, at least by the thirteenth century, there was a great stress on reason in natural law. Modern political thought is not without its debts to the medieval mind.

chapter 9

Christian Attitudes and Politics: Tertullian to Augustine

After the time of the Antonines the disintegrating factors of imperial politics began to make themselves felt, and the centuries from 200 to 400 were to witness a near revolution in the structure and spirit of the Empire.

While the Empire was struggling for its very existence, the ecclesiastical structure within it was waxing, until by the end of the fourth century, an observer returning from the year 100 would scarcely have recognized it.

With this transformation of the Church came not only a shift in the politics of secular-ecclesiastical relations but also an important transformation in the political attitudes of members and leaders of the rapidly expanding Christian body.

This chapter sketches out the main lines of these developments.

The Politics of the Imperium

Four interrelated characteristics appear to stand out in the transformation of imperial politics.

Growth of Violence in Politics. Nothing is more characteristic of the two centuries under consideration than the development of violence as a political weapon. Emperors strove for power and many were assassinated. Marcus Aurelius' son Commodus was assassinated, as were his successors, Pertinax and Didius Julianus.

This tendency to violence was, of course, inseparably connected with the enormous role which the army came to play in politics. From the very beginning of the principate, military force had been of great importance. Now, however, it became central. Eventually emperors were made and unmade either by the elite corps, the Praetorian Guard, or by armies in the field. The Senate, if it was consulted at all, gave an automatic approval to the nominees of the military forces.

Elimination of Republican Restraints. Under these circumstances, naturally, such republican institutions as the Senate and magistracies, already greatly weakened, suffered even more drastically.

Development of Oriental Conceptions. The task of controlling an increasingly unruly Empire menaced by military threats from the outside was the occasion for two developments of enormous importance: first, by the closing years of the third century "East" and "West" were beginning to be administered by different emperors or "Caesars," this contributing, it was hoped, to more vigorous and effective control. Second, about the same time it was evident that ancient republican simplicity in the office of imperator, already seriously undermined, had received its coup de grace.

The Empire and the Christian. Closely related to these phenomena was the long struggle between a disintegrating Empire and an ecclesiastical organization moving in the direction of integration. At first, the Empire saw in the growing complexity of church organization a competitor which must be crushed—hence such persecutions as those under Septimius Severus toward the end of the second century and under Aurelian and Decius in the third. Even as late as the early part of the fourth century, Diocletian was attempting to wipe out the "nation" of Christians.

After this last ferocious effort had failed, however, Constantine began to tolerate the Church (313) and even asserted a claim to preside over Church councils, as at the Ecumenical Council of Nicaea (324). Gradually during the fourth century (except for the brief reaction under Emperor Julian in 360–362) the state conferred privileges on the Church, hoping, no doubt, to utilize its organization to strengthen its own position and prestige. By the end of the fourth century, the circle was complete: the state, no longer merely tolerating the Christian organization, began to suppress all its rivals, the pagan cults.

The Politics of the Ecclesia: Theory and Practice

References to the "church" in the New Testament are comparatively few and even then their implications and meaning are often difficult to understand.[1] In the first century and a half, organization was relatively loose; and while Christians very early, as we have seen, began to think of themselves as a separate "nation," this was apparently a conception confined to the spiritual realm. Between the middle of the second and the end of the fourth century, however, theory and practice of the *ecclesia* were radically altered. What factors were present in this transformation?

Social Transformation. Broadly speaking, much higher proportions of upper-class men and women began to enter the Church, thus creating problems for Christian ideology as well as for the Empire, which led Emperors like Aurelian (258) to decree harsh punishments for high-status persons who became Christians.[2]

In a sense, the ultimate decree of toleration became indispensable, for long before it, aristocratic Christians were serving in high administrative positions and the emperors apparently decided that if they could not force them to renounce their faith (and they tried unsuccessfully to do so), toleration was the only avenue open.

The Growth of Hierarchy. To the student of politics and social structure, the transformation of the church in organizational terms is a fascinating study which must consider religious beliefs, the necessity for communication, the effect of persecution, and the rise of schism and heresy.

Religious belief contributed to more closely-knit and hierarchical organization in that the bishop (*episcopus*), after the deaths of the original Apostles, claimed the prerogative of distinguishing between true and false deliverances of the Holy Spirit. All Christians in the beginning felt that the Spirit might speak through any and all men. Suppose, however, that it spoke in diverse ways? In Apostolic days, presumably, the Twelve Apostles could distinguish between true and false by virtue of their closeness to the historical Christ. Once the Apostles were gone, this prerogative passed to the ecclesiastical hierarchy and helped contribute to its growth and prestige.

The political organization of the ecclesia developed, too, because it helped widely scattered and diverse churches communicate with one another more effectively, especially after Christians became more numerous. Greater concentrations of Christians seemingly called for more elaborate organization.

Persecution stimulated more closely-knit structure, since the beleaguered ecclesia could more effectively preserve the faith, combat hostile officials, and encourage often fainthearted pilgrims under conditions of tight rather than loose organizational ties. In all times and cultures, it would seem, severe external pressure always has a tendency to promote centralization of control and heightened solidarity among persons and associations subject to the attack.

Finally, a word should be said about the schisms and heresies which, like external pressures, tended to demand firmer ecclesiastical organization. In the first century, the belief that all Christians should observe Jewish ritual eventually became a kind of heresy. Later on, the Gnostic movement asserted that Jesus was not actually a "material" embodiment; and certainly no teaching could challenge orthodoxy more fundamentally than this. In the second century, the Montanists attempted to check what they saw as the growing worldliness of the Church; and they persisted in their attack well into the third century, counting among their leading men the great Tertullian. In the fourth century, the struggle between the heretical Arians and the orthodox Athanasians disturbed both ecclesiastical and secular politics. The fourth century, too, saw the birth of the schismatic Donatist movement, which persisted about one hundred years and which would be interwoven with the life and teaching of St. Augustine. Donatism arose out of dissensions in Carthage and originally held that the authority of a priest or bishop depended on his personal purity and probity rather than merely on his office in the church. This theory, of course, was a heart-thrust at the orthodox hierarchical notion which made authority to administer the sacraments turn simply on whether the ecclesiastic had been properly appointed: his personal virtues were irrelevant.

1. For examples of the different uses of the term, see Acts 1:15, 1:25, 19:39 and 1 Thessalonians 1:1.
2. The decree is quoted by Adolf Harnack, *Mission and Expansion of Christianity*, Vol. 2, New York: G. P. Putnam, 1908, p. 38.

Confronted as it was by these many schisms and heresies, the Church responded to the internal crises thus created by strengthening its own organization and eventually, if reluctantly, calling on the state for assistance. Particularly after the Council of Nicaea (A.D. 325), when Arianism was condemned and Athanasianism emerged officially triumphant, was the close association of Empire and Church increasingly central.

While imperial and ecclesiastical politics were thus reshaping the Empire from the second century to the end of the fourth, what was happening to Christian outlooks on politics? How were they affected by transformations in imperium and ecclesia?

The End of History

Broadly speaking, Christian thought after 200 still expects the end of political history momentarily and some thinkers even venture to predict the time. But during the third and fourth centuries, most thinkers become more and more uncertain about the exact date of the end. Some (Tertullian, for example), continue to think that it is imminent, to be sure, but many (Origen, for instance) by now, instead of believing that the end implies a new "earthly" kingdom, interpret eschatology in a purely "spiritual" sense.[3] The "earthly" interpretation is often called a "chiliastic" view.

The eschatological hope in a transformed earthly kingdom does not disappear entirely after the third century, but its impact on general Christian thought tends to be much less important than in an earlier day.

The Patristic Attitude to Property

While the belief in the end tends to be attenuated, the early Christian view of property and wealth continues to be manifested in the writings of the pre-Augustinian Fathers. In theory, at least, the Fathers do not attempt to justify in any elaborate way private property institutions, and many of them refer with approval to the first-century experiment in "communism" at Jerusalem.

Clement of Alexandria (late second and early third century) maintains: "Let it then be granted that good things are the property only of good men, and Christians are good. Accordingly good things are possessed by Christians alone. But what is possession? It is not he who has and keeps it, but he who gives away, he is rich."[4]

Tertullian, stating undoubtedly the ideal and not necessarily the practice, observes:

> Only those are good brothers who are good men. But on this very account perhaps we are regarded as having less claim to be held true brothers that no tragedy makes a noise about our brotherhood, or that the family possessions which generally divide brotherhood among you [the pagans] create fraternal bonds among us. One in mind and soul, we do not hesitate to share our earthly goods with one another. All things are common among us but our wives.[5]

Basil the Great, in the fourth century,[6] compares the property institutions of man unfavorably with the practices of the beasts:

> We who are gifted with reason show ourselves to be more cruel than the animals. The latter make use of the natural products of the earth as common things.

And he goes on to commend Lycurgus for the communist institutions of ancient Sparta.

A similar attitude is taken by St. Ambrose (late fourth century).[7]

The Fathers and the State

Throughout the third and fourth centuries, Christian thinkers remain somewhat divided on their attitude to the state and its institutions. Down to the very end of the third century—particularly in the case of those, like Tertullian, who have been influenced by Montanism—they remain bitterly hostile. This animosity is grounded on the association of public authority with violent coercion and the tendency, as they see it, for the possession of political authority to "corrupt" the holder. But the antagonism is reinforced by virtue of the fact that the state is the persecutor, and is perhaps not uninfluenced by the vigorous disapproval with which men like Tertullian view the steady influx of Christians into public administration. Often governments and kings are regarded as instruments of the devil. Yet the Christian is bound, for the most part, to obey them, while abstaining from active participation.

Just on the verge of the third century, Tertullian reflects a fundamental antagonism to the state and its rulers: "But as those in whom all ardour in the pursuit of glory and honour is dead, we have no pressing inducement to take part in your public meetings, nor is there aught more entirely foreign to us than politics. We acknowledge one all-embracing commonwealth—the world."[8]

While Origen as a broadly read scholar devoted to the nonliteral interpretation of Scripture is not as harsh as Tertullian, his judgment of the state would appear to be no less firm.[9]

A recurrent theme in political literature before the decree of toleration is the Christian expectation and hope of vengeance. But it is always God who is to be responsible for the vengeance. Christians, although permitted to associate together to oppose the state nonviolently, are not allowed by the law of Christ to offer violent opposition. The figure of the Antichrist is often associated with the expected fall of Rome as a punishment of persecution; and St. Cyprian, curiously enough, brackets heretics and men like the persecuting Emperor Decius as either the offspring or "pioneers" of Antichrist.[10]

Despite the vigor with which Christian writers attack state institutions during the third and even the fourth century, there is a division of opinion as to whether members of the church ought to hold public office. In the third century, apparently a majority of Christian thinkers hold that for a Christian to become a magistrate or in any other way use instruments of violent coercion is to violate basic principles of the Gospel. Some ecclesiastical disciplines, indeed, specifically exclude magistrates from church membership.[11] And Lactantius, as late as the early fourth century, seems to frown on acceptance of any public honor or administrative post.[12]

Yet in the third century, and certainly in the fourth, there is another school of thought which justifies acceptance of at least some public offices. Confronted by the growing participation of Christians in public life, particularly after 313, this school seeks to vindicate, sometimes reluctantly, active participation in public authority. Some point out that Daniel and Joseph accepted high office; and since the Old Testament is authoritative for Christians this is regarded as a favorable precedent. Already in the middle of the third century Cyprian complains that bishops think it is legitimate to act as agents of secular rulers. Eusebius claims, too, that some of the emperors have relaxed the rules commanding sacrifice to idols in order to permit appointment of Christians as governors of provinces.[13]

Probably the gulf between general patristic teaching on the state and actual practice of Christians is to be largely explained in terms of the tendency of men in all ages to act in ways other than those which they might profess. Although it can be argued, of course, that the great Fathers do not accurately reflect general Christian thinking of the third century, it would be difficult to prove this contention. In the fourth century, of course, the official Church begins to give its blessing to active participation in the state;[14] but even here we must not assume that there are not many dissenters. Lactantius, for example, whose life extends to A.D. 340—long after the preference given to Christianity by Constantine—argues that "The just and wise man . . . does not long for any power or honour, lest he inflict injury on any one; for he knows that all men, having been made by the same God and in the same condition, have been joined together by the law of brotherhood."[15]

There are various ways in which, after the Constantinian revolution, the earlier tradition of hostility to participation in the state seeks to maintain itself. One is, of course, the effort on

3. Note, on this whole matter, Cadoux, *The Early Church and the World,* Edinburgh: T. and T. Clark, 1925, pp. 308–310.
4. As quoted by Max Beer, *Social Struggles in Antiquity*, Boston: Small, Maynard and Co., 1922, p. 201, from Clement's *Paedagogicus,* III, 6.
5. *Apology*, ch. 38.
6. Quoted by Beer, *op. cit.*, pp. 204–205.
7. See *De Nabuthe*, 1, 2, as quoted by Beer, *op. cit.*, pp. 206–207; and *Exposition in Lucam,* XII, 15, 22, 23.
8. *Apology*, ch. 38. See also his *Idolatry*, ch. 19.
9. Origen, *Contra Celsum*, I, 1.
10. Note Cadoux's discussion of this point, *op. cit.*, pp. 518–520.
11. The "Egyptian Church-Order," for example, as pointed out by Cadoux, *op. cit.*, p. 536.
12. Lactantius, *Institutes*, V. XXII, 14.
13. *Ecclesiastical History*, VIII, 1.
14. Thus the Synod of Arles, in 314 (one year after Constantine's edict), seems to assume that it is legitimate for a Christian to hold the office of governor and participate in active political life. But it urges those who do hold public office to observe Christian "discipline"—a rather vague limitation, though indicating dubiety.
15. *Institutes*, V. XXII, 7.

the part of a few writers to refuse compromise at all. Another, on the plane of action, is reflected in the movements which advocate retreat from civil society altogether (monachism), lest the new political arrangements force one to violate Christian morality. A third is to essay to preserve the old position but to apply it rigidly only to those who elect the "highest" religious life. Thus Eusebius, writing in the fourth century, suggests that there are two standards of Christian morality. For those who wish to attain the highest piety, he argues, celibacy, abstention from commerce, and avoidance of public office and military activity are called for. Men of this stamp would preserve intact the early Christian attitude to the state and the world. On the other hand, he maintains, it is possible to be a kind of second-class Christian and yet participate in marriage, politics, military service, and trade.[16] As Cadoux rightly remarks, we have in the position of Eusebius "the definite beginning of the age-long Catholic distinction between religious and lay morality."[17]

The Problem of War

At no point, perhaps, are Christian attitudes to political institutions transformed more thoroughly than with reference to the problem of war. As we have seen, the first century and a half, so far as we can determine, is characterized by an adamant rejection of its legitimacy. After Marcus Aurelius, however, while the great apologists maintain the earlier position, the practice of individual Christians increasingly departs from it; and by the first part of the fourth century, the Church makes it clear that there is no longer any doctrinal bar to military service. The details of this transformation cast considerable illumination on the general social thought of the Church.

War in Human History: The Position of the Patristic Writers. While the patristic writers will deny the legitimacy of military service for Christians, they by no means confine their discussion of the subject to this problem. They ask themselves, how, given what they regard as the Christian position, the Christian is to reconcile his attitude of condemnation with the apparent approval of war in the Old Testament (which is, of course, accepted as part of God's revelation). Moreover, they attempt to relate war as an institution to the prophetic view of history and to see it, despite their moral condemnation, as an agency which prepares the way for the Christian revelation. They tend to conclude that God can utilize morally reprehensible means even though those methods are specifically forbidden to men. Here the patristic thinkers obviously carry on the Hebrew prophetic view of history: War as an institution is to them what Assyria and Babylonia were to the ancient prophets.

In general, there is no question that the Fathers attack war as an institution, although their reasons are sometimes curious. Cadoux points out, for example, that Clement of Alexandria makes one of his chief bases for opposition the fact that war relies on the artificial stimulus of music.[18] Other thinkers, of course, are far less eccentric. Thus Tertullian raises the problem of means and ends and suggests that "deceit" and "harshness," which he regards as the inevitable accompaniments of war, cannot be compatible with "gentleness" and "justice," which are Christian objectives.[19]

Yet the Fathers are confronted with the fact that God apparently approved the wars of the Hebrews. How could God (through Christ) condemn the bloodshed of war and at the same time approve it through another part of Scripture? Could one reconcile the Sermon on the Mount with God's command to Saul to destroy the enemy utterly? The Fathers wrestle with issues of this kind and come out with varying answers. Origen argues that the command to make war in the Old Testament is to be interpreted spiritually. Old Testament struggles symbolize mental and spiritual struggles for the good and the constant tendency of men, both individually and collectively, to fall away from the good. While Origen is not entirely consistent in this interpretation, it seems, on the whole, to represent his best attempt.[20]

Broader than the issue of Hebrew wars is, of course, the role of war in general. Many of the Fathers recognize, for example, that wars have played a crucial role in building the Roman Empire and that without the Empire the teaching of Christianity would have been much more difficult. Does this imply a kind of "relative" justification for war? Then, too, there can be no question that even the Empire of a Commodus or a Caracalla provides a kind of peace which benefits men—yet it seems to be sustained by constant foreign wars or the threat of war. How can the Christian fit these observations into his general view which would make the institution illegitimate?

In dealing with questions of this order, the Fathers cut a wide swath. They reexamine Hebrew history in the light of prophetic teaching and try to relate it to the politics of their own and immediate past generations. The outcome is that they tend to look on war as a method which God uses to discipline the human race. Like ancient Assyria for the prophets, it is his "branding-iron." Both Hebrew and Roman wars can be interpreted in this way.

Thus Origen sees Hebrew, Assyrian, and Babylonian military conflicts as "scourges" sent by God to punish human sin.[21] Theophilus, Tertullian, and Origen alike look upon the Roman destruction of Jerusalem as a punishment for Jewish national sins, particularly the murder of Jesus, although Origen warns against interpreting God's punishment in materialistic terms. While corporate sins may be punished by God through the scourge of war, those who carry on the war are still to be condemned.[22] God allows rulers to use war as chastisement because, in the Divine Providence, corporate man has employed his freedom contrary to the intentions of God for human history.

As is usual, it is Origen who discusses the subject in the broadest and most scholarly way and who shows most appreciation for an ethic which he himself cannot accept as a Christian. In his reply to Celsus, for example, he admits frankly that the growth of the Christian Church would have been impeded had not a single unified Empire existed; and he recognizes that that Empire was built up by war.[23] Existing as they do with no insight into Christ's law, pagans are relatively justified in taking up arms and their acts of heroism are seen by Origen as praiseworthy in relation to the inferior ethic under which they live.

The Fathers Reject Military Service for the Christian. That the Fathers do in fact believe military service to be incompatible with Christian beliefs would seem to be supported by their works, however they might have viewed the relative justification of war for the Hebrews or for non-Christian Romans. At the very time when Christians are increasingly entering the Roman army, the pre-Augustinian Fathers are in effect denouncing them for doing so.

Thus, Tertullian says flatly that it is the duty of Christians to be killed sooner than to slay.[24] And at another point, when he is still an orthodox Catholic, he would seem clearly to be stating the incompatibility between Christian belief and military service: "How shall he wage war, nay, how shall he even be a soldier in peace-time, without the sword which the Lord has taken away?"[25]

In another of his works, written after he had become a Montanist, Tertullian is about as explicit as any of the Fathers become:

> Is it right to occupy oneself with the sword, when the Lord proclaims that he who uses the sword shall perish by the sword?[26]

The careful modern scholar Harnack, who has little personal sympathy with Tertullian's position on the issue, concludes that the great Montanist undoubtedly regards the military vocation as "irreconcilable" with Christianity.[27] And he summarizes Tertullian's reasons as his condemnation of judicial duties inherent in the work of the officer; incompatibility of the loyalty oath, or *sacramentum*, with allegiance to Christ; and Jesus' denial of the use of the sword to any Christian.

It is obvious, too, as Harnack argues,[28] that Origen takes a similar position. In answering Celsus' charge that Christians are averse to military service, Origen in effect admits the charge but argues that Christians contribute as much or more to the ostensible goals of political rule and of war through their prayers and their godly lives:

> And we, in putting down by our prayers all demons—those who stir up warlike feelings and

16. Eusebius, *Demonstratio Evangelica*, I. VIII, 29b–30b.
17. Cadoux, *op. cit.*, p. 469.
18. *Ibid.*, pp. 403–404.
19. *De Corona Militis*, 12 (i. 448).
20. *Contra Celsum*, VII, 18.
21. *Ibid.*, IV, 9.
22. *Ibid.*, 70.
23. *Ibid.*, II, 30.
24. *Apology*, 37 (i. 251). "Cui bello non idonei, non prompti fuissemus, etiam impares copiis, qui tam libenter trucidamur, si non apud istam disciplinam magis occidi liceret, quam occidere?"
25. *De Idololatria*, 19 (i. 101 ff.).
26. *De Corona*, II (i. 442–446). This work was written in 211.
27. *Ibid.*, 55, *n.* 2.
28. *Ibid.*, 56.

prompt the violation of oaths and disturb the peace—help the Emperors more than those who to all appearance serve as soldiers.[29]

In general, while Origen admits the relative justification of war, as we have noted before, he sees the Christians appealing to a higher ethic which has the potentiality of overcoming that which governs most Romans. As Romans and barbarians become Christians and repudiate military service, Origen thinks that social order will be constructed on firmer and more durable bases than under the ethic of violence which prevails. For Christianity will, by removing the roots of war and all violent conflict, make even the relative justification of war obsolete.

Although the late third and early fourth centuries are rightly regarded as the age in which Christian approval of military service increases, we should not fail to note that even in this period there is strong patristic condemnation. The most notable voice is that of Lactantius who would appear to be even more explicit than Tertullian and Origen:

> When God prohibits killing, He not only forbids us to commit brigandage, which is not allowed even by the public laws, but He warns us not to do even those things which are regarded as legal among men. And so it will not be lawful for a just man to serve as a soldier. . . .[30]

The objection to military service is evidenced not only by passages like those from Lactantius but also in several of the martyrdoms, the judicial records of which have been preserved. When Maximilianus is conscripted for military service in 295, for example, he refuses to don the military garb and is brought before the Proconsul Dion. The following colloquy ensues:

> *The Proconsul Dion said:* "What are you called?"
> *Maximilianus answered:* "But why do you want to know my name? I dare not fight, since I am a Christian."
> *The Proconsul Dion said:* "Measure him."
> *But on being measured Maximilianus answered:* "I cannot fight, I cannot do evil; I am a Christian."
> *The Proconsul Dion said:* "Measure him."
> *And after he had been measured, the attendant read out:* "He is five feet ten."
>
> . . . .
>
> *Dion to Maximilianus:* "Serve and accept the badge [the leaden badge with the Emperor's effigy on it and worn by all soldiers]."
> *Maximilianus answered:* "I do not accept the badge; for I have the badge of Christ my God."
>
> . . . .
>
> *The Proconsul Dion said:* "In the sacred retinue of our lords Diocletian and Maximian, Constantius and Maximus there are Christian soldiers and they do war service."
> *Maximilianus answered:* "They know what is fitting for them, but I am a Christian and I cannot do evil."
> *Dion said:* "What evil do they do who do military service?"
> *Maximilianus answered:* "You know quite well what they do."
> *The Proconsul Dion said:* "You had better serve; else if you continue to go on refusing, you will certainly come to a bad end!"
> *Maximilianus answered:* "I shall not perish; and when I shall have left this world, my soul shall live with Christ my lord.[31]

Maximilianus is executed shortly afterward and buried near the tomb of St. Cyprian, who had probably taken a position on war service very much like that of the young man.

Nor is his the only record of men refusing military service, in part, at least, for reasons of conscientious objection to the peculiar tasks of soldiers. Harnack mentions the names of several who apparently share Maximilianus' convictions, although usually the reasons are not as clearcut as those in his case.[32]

The Gradual Change and the Constantinian Revolution. But from the middle of the second century onward, it is evident that Christian practice has begun to diverge from the predominant doctrines of the early thinkers. Before the time of Marcus Aurelius, as Harnack admits, "Christian soldiers were still few and far between."[33] Only toward the end of the second century does the issue of military service become a pressing moral problem. After that time, despite the major Fathers, Christians become more numerous in military life, although, as the instance of Maximilianus demonstrates, there are still young men more than a century after Commodus who adhere to earlier principles. And Lactantius is a figure of the late third century and early fourth.

After the Constantinian revolution, however, Christians became soldiers with the full sanction of the Church, despite the stubborn adherence to earlier doctrines of men like Lactantius. The turning point with respect to official doctrine seems to be the Synod of Arles in 314 (one year after Constantine's edict of toleration), which enacts a canon saying "Those who discard their weapons during peace shall be excluded from communion."[34] Almost exactly a century later—in 416—the process is completed when the Theodosian Code forbids *non-Christians* to serve in the army.[35]

Needed: A Synthesis

As the fourth century draws to a close, Christian social and political doctrines and practice embody many diverse, and sometimes contradictory, tendencies. While hope in the imminence of the *eschaton* has now almost completely faded, the notion that political history, as hitherto known, will end remains a part of Christian belief. The conception of the ecclesia as somehow withdrawn from the world has not died, yet the fact remains that ecclesiastical and worldy affairs are now inextricably combined. As the Church has gained numbers and political power, the rigor of its ethical standards has declined: Profession of a detailed creed has become the hallmark of the Christian; and the notion of Christian life as radically different from worldly society is in retreat. Men are working out formulae for adjustment of the Christian outlook to the post-Constantinian situation, but only against the strenuous opposition of heretics like the Donatists and severe critics like the leaders of the monachist movement.

Intellectually, Christian thinkers have borrowed heavily from the Hebrew prophetic theory of history as well as classical Greek thinking. And they have sought to weave together, not too successfully, the apparently incompatible strands of Christian political ideas which at times stress passive obedience and at others violent antagonism to the state. The traditions of early Christian "communism" mingle with those which, following some of the Greeks, would stress the need for property institutions.

However reluctantly, Christians by the end of the fourth century, feel an almost desperate need to reconcile the politics of "Christian" empire with the politics of apocalyptic: a seemingly impossible task. Equally difficult would appear to be the problem of making a place both for the view that war is incompatible with Christian teaching and for the position that military conflict is permissible to the devotee of the Gospel.

As the century comes to an end, Christians also find themselves in need of a more positive theory of the state. Can the state, for example, be looked upon as an agency for the advancement of good as well as a force for the restraint of evil? Before Constantine, this issue is not pressing, for while Christians have long served in the civil service their role as policymakers has been a limited one up to the fourth century. After Constantine, however, they begin to dominate leading policy making positions, command armies, and preside over courts. How shall they view their roles in the light of Christian teaching and particularly how shall they reconcile their past antagonism to Roman institutions with their present control of imperial politics?

For nearly a century, Christian princes refrain from using the power of the state to suppress their religious rivals. Then they begin to do to the cults of paganism what Diocletian had done to the followers of Christ. Will they develop a theory to justify such an action and, if so, upon what foundations will it be established?

Finally, for the first time since the ancient Jewish monarchy, the problem of "heresy" arises.

It is with questions of this kind that St. Augustine will deal in the early years of the fifth century. Inheriting the many schemes of non-Christian ancient thought and impressed

29. *Contra Celsum,* VIII, 73.
30. *Divinae Institutiones,* VI, XX, 15–17.
31. Harnack reprints the record of the hearing, in Latin, in *Militia Christi: Die Christliche Religion and der Soldatenstand in den ersten drei Jahrhunderten,* Tubingen: J. C. B. Mohr (Paul Siebeck), 1905, pp. 114–117.
32. *The Mission and Expansion of Christianity,* vol. 2, pp. 61–62. Harnack rightly points out that we should beware of forgeries in this field, but he regards the case of Maximilianus as genuine and he seems to hold the same about the record of Marcellus' martyrdom, which resembles that of Maximilianus in many respects.
33. *Ibid.,* p. 52.
34. Note, for a discussion of the controversies surrounding the meaning of this canon, Cadoux, *op. cit.,* p. 588; Harnack, *Mission and Expansion of Christianity,* vol. 2, p. 64; and Harnack, *Militia Christi,* pp. 86–88.
35. Codex Theodosianus, XVI, X, 21, as quoted by Andreas Bigelmair, *Die Beteiligung der Christen am offentlichen Leben in vorkonstantinischer Zeit,* Munich: Lentner, 1902, p. 201.

by much of what he finds, he will attempt to develop a system of Christian historical-political doctrine which can make room both for the diverse strands of the Christian social outlook and for those aspects of ancient non-Christian thought which are most compatible with the Hebraic-Christian heritage.

chapter 10

Augustine and the Politics of the Two Cities

Saint Augustine was the greatest systematic political thinker since Aristotle. He evolved his scheme of politics and history under stress of considerable personal emotion and in a political world which was rapidly disintegrating. While we often think of him as setting the keynote for the social speculation of the early Middle Ages, it is equally true to assert that he looks back and weaves together many of the major strands which we have seen in ancient attitudes and ideology.

His major role historically was to provide a system within which Christians could pay their respects to the outlook of early Christianity while accepting the many political compromises which developed after the Constantinian revolution.

Augustine and the Politics of His Day

Augustine spent his early days in a time which was crucial for both ecclesiastical and secular politics. Born in 354, in Tagaste, Numidia, he was seven years old when the Emperor Julian ascended the throne and began to develop his anti-Christian policies. The Church, which by now occupied a very privileged position in the imperial system, was aghast. True, Julian proposed only to put Christians on a parity with all other religious faiths. But for the Church this would have meant a retrogression to mere toleration; and by now it had tasted the fruits of political power and liked them. What would have happened had Julian's reign extended longer than two years, we cannot tell. Perhaps he would have succeeded.

No doubt Augustine's mother, who was a Christian, viewed imperial politics with some interest and, like most Christians, rejoiced when Julian was killed in battle and the privileges of the Church were restored. But she evidently had relatively little immediate influence on her son, who became the father of an illegitimate child at the age of seventeen and was an ardent student of pagan thought and culture.

It was Augustine's father who shaped his early life by making great sacrifices in order to send the young man to school and to provide him a higher education in Carthage. In the Punic city, he became a Manichaean, the sharp conflict between good and evil principles in Manichaean theology no doubt appealing to his sensitive mind. He returned to his native village to teach grammar and, according to his autobiography, to be prayed over by his mother who was eager to make him an orthodox Christian.

He was at home only a year, however, for the attractions of Carthage were too much for him. In the life of the big city, those doubts about his Manichaean beliefs which were later to beset him were probably born; although it was not until he moved to Rome in 383 that his whole world-view began to change. The crucial factor at this point in his intellectual evolution was his study of natural science, which apparently led him to be critical of Manichaean dualism. The Manichaean notion that matter is evil also came under his critical scrutiny.

But his dualist friends persisted in attempting to keep him in their fold. He was so plagued by their zeal, as a matter of fact, that he eventually decided to leave Rome for Milan. There he taught rhetoric and began to doubt the possibility of any knowledge. For a time he became a thoroughgoing Skeptic—a not unnatural reaction to the certainty which many of his Manichaean friends professed to see.

Yet his inquiring mind could not stop with Skepticism. It was too negative. Surely, he thought, as he went about his daily teaching rounds, there must be the possibility of some knowledge. It was at this point that he began to study, and eventually to be convinced by the Neoplatonists, who, of course, asserted the unity of the world and the possibility of knowing it through a kind of mystic insight. Neoplatonism was at the opposite end of the continuum from Manichaeanism.

To those who would interpret intellectual evolution in terms of a dialectic, Augustine's biography might be a good case study. Manichaeanism led him eventually to embrace its opposite, Neoplatonism. But he must have brought to his new beliefs a doubt as to whether his earlier position was wholly wrong. Neoplatonism disposed of the problem of evil, he began to think, all too easily; yet Manichaeanism destroyed the unity which Augustine so eagerly sought. Was it possible to preserve both the acute sense of evil represented by the Manichaeans and at the same time keep intact the basic unity exalted by Neoplatonism? This seems to have been the question with which he wrestled for some time.

His ultimate resolution of the difficulty is a classic page in the history of thought. He heard Bishop Ambrose preach in the Milan Cathedral and was strangely moved by the combination of learning and emotion represented in the bishop's sermon. Taking up the serious study of the Pauline epistles, he began to find in them hints as to a solution for his Manichaean-Neoplatonic conflict. At the same time, he seemed to see in Paul an assurance of genuine knowledge which had not been satisfied even by Neoplatonism.

Meanwhile, he had become acquainted through a friend with the monachist movement, which exalted withdrawal from the world and which sought, as we pointed out earlier,[1] to counteract what it regarded as the Church's fatal compromises with the Empire. Even the civil service was being affected by the flight to the desert; and Augustine was profoundly moved when he learned that two young officials had decided to renounce the world, give up their secure positions, and isolate themselves from the political society. Augustine was on the verge of doing likewise when he was converted to Catholic Christianity.[2] He was baptized and in 388 returned to his native town of Tagaste, where he became the head of a small religious community composed mostly of his friends.

In 391 the Christian community of Hippo needed a presbyter and the people chose him for the position (the local ecclesia still had considerable powers in the choice of bishops and presbyters). In 395 he was chosen Coadjutor Bishop of Hippo and a few years later became Bishop, continuing in this position until his death.

1. See p. 174.
2. After reading Romans 18:13, 14.

Augustine was a vigorous and devoted administrator. But he was also a controversialist of note. Many of the intellectual conflicts in which he engaged helped shape his political views, both with respect to ecclesiastical politics and in reference to the politics of the Empire. For example, when he took up the cudgels of battle against his old friends the Manichaeans, he did so as an ardent Catholic eager to defend both the intellectual and the political position of the Church. Similarly, when he attacked the Donatists, whose position we have already noted in connection with the theory of the Church,[3] he stood on ground which justified the significance of the office of bishop and which denied that personal virtue should play a vital role. It was in connection with the Donatist struggle, too, that he called upon the state to assist the Church in forcible suppression if necessary.[4] Finally, his debates with the Pelagians were central to what we might call his theology of politics; for Coelestius, a student of Pelagius, had formulated the doctrines of "Pelagianism" in terms of three propositions which are theological antitheses of all that later came to be called Augustinianism—that Adam's sin was purely personal, that each man is born uncorrupt, and that children who die in infancy are untainted by sin and can be saved without baptism. Augustine wrote fifteen treatises against the Pelagian propositions and these were to lay the foundations for much that passed as orthodoxy from the time of Augustine to that of St. Thomas Aquinas.

While Augustine was engaging in these doctrinal battles and administering his diocese, the political state of the Empire was going from bad to worse. Although the adoption of Christianity as the preferred religion had temporarily strengthened the hands of the government, its benefits had not been unmixed. For the emperors were not the complete masters of the Church and had, indeed, given many hostages to the latter in return for its support. The Church increasingly insisted, for example, that Christianity not only be the preferred religion but that all others be prohibited. This demand, of course, ran counter to the whole Roman tradition and had within it implications of political strife.

Then, too, imperial settlement of internal ecclesiastical conflicts was not without its deleterious effects on the authority of the emperor. The long and bitter struggle against the Arians, for example, had definite secular political implications. Not only did the government antagonize the many supporters of the defeated Arius within the empire but the prosecutions drove scores of Arians into the lands of the barbarians, many of whom were converted to Arian Christianity. When the barbarians penetrated the Empire, therefore, they were opposing not merely the imperial political structure but also the victorious Athanasian faction. The monopolistic Christian religion had become a monopolistic Christian faction which excluded not merely the pagans but also all other Christians; and the barbarians took advantage of this situation in many ways.

In 410, Alaric and his hosts occupied Rome and a great cry went up that the conquest of the imperial city had been due to the displeasure of the gods who had been displaced by Christianity. How seriously pagan intellectuals believed this we do not know. But undoubtedly many found this charge very useful politically in an empire which still included millions of pagans and many who looked back with admiration at the policies of Julian. And thousands of devoted pagan rural dwellers must have taken the charge at its face value. Even many converts to Christianity were probably beset by doubts; for their knowledge of Roman history would remind them that the mighty city had not been under alien control for many centuries.

At any rate, Augustine was impressed by the apparently widespread attribution of political decline to Christianity. While he could not immediately proceed to deal with the problem, he undoubtedly reflected seriously on it between the fall of the city and 413, when he began to write the *City of God*. The composition of his great work occupied his spare time for thirteen years and when he had completed it he had provided the Western tradition not only an important theological work, but also an historical-political treatise of great significance. Augustine died in 430.

The Problem of Augustine as a Political Thinker

Anyone who examines Augustine's conceptions carefully must be impressed by the fact that he was not primarily a political thinker nor, indeed, a philosopher, as that term is ordinarily employed. His political thought was quite incidental, even though profoundly influential.

We should also remember that Augustine was by nature a very emotional man who felt deeply about the issues he confronted during his stormy career and who sometimes allowed his feelings to dominate his analysis. His convictions were often passionately held but sometimes not adequately buttressed by reason and empirical knowledge. Although, for example, a large part of the *City of God* is devoted to what might be called the philosophy of history—an essentially political theme—Augustine's knowledge of actual history was relatively scanty.

Then, too, while we earlier referred to him as "systematic," this was only relatively so. By comparison with most early Christian thinkers, he did, of course, build a system of thought. But it was a highly shaky structure at many points, since his main objective was to be an apologist for the Church, rather than to construct a scheme which would be immune to logical attack. Augustine's inconsistencies and ambiguities have plagued his commentators from medieval times to the present day; and the conflict about what he really meant is still very much alive. Thus, some would see him as an "individualist" and mystic having but little sense of corporeity; while others think of him as the great champion of the institutional church.[5] Some view him as identifying the Church Militant with the Kingdom of God; to which others reply that the Kingdom is only the invisible community of the saved.[6] One approach holds that he condemns all earthly states as without genuine authority; while another maintains that he supports and justifies them.[7]

Here we may note in a preliminary way that in process of working out his political and social views, Augustine develops a philosophy of history which roots in Hebraic conceptions; a theory of natural law which owes much to the Stoics and earlier Church Fathers; and a doctrine which makes but little room for the chiliasm so characteristic of early Christian thought, the belief in the imminent return of Christ having faded by Augustine's day.

The Mythology and Politics of Paganism: A Christian View

While the stage for Augustine's drama is a much broader one than that upon which pagan claims are denounced, the refutation of the charges that Rome's fall was due to the adoption of Christianity is a central aspect of his philosophy of history. Essentially, he seeks, first, to answer the contention that material and political disasters are due to the abandonment of paganism; and second, to demonstrate that, whatever may be true of the temporal scene, belief in the gods is not essential if we are to enjoy the life to come. In developing his argument, Augustine ranges far into the realm of comparative mythology and makes ample use of pagan writers.

With respect to temporal calamities, he contends that the history of Rome abounds in them, despite all the gods and the religious-civic ceremonies of Republic and Empire. Pagan apologists delude themselves if they really believe that the sack of 410 is unique. Virtually all the kings of ancient Rome, for example, died violent deaths. And Augustine ironically points out that when the Capitol was saved from the Gauls (390 B.C.), it was the geese, and not the gods, who preserved it. Moreover, from the time of the Gracchi to the establishment of the principate, there was almost perpetual civil war which all the divinities of Rome seemed powerless to limit, let alone avert. He also appears to think that the notorious divisions between rich and poor are to be regarded as a disaster.[8]

While it is true, he goes on, that on the whole the Romans have been remarkably successful

3. See p. 171.
4. See Hugh Pope, *Saint Augustine of Hippo*, New York: Doubleday, 1958, for a discussion.
5. This problem is touched upon in J. N. Figgis, *The Political Aspects of St. Augustine's "City of God,"* London: Longmans, Green, 1921, pp. 68–72 and elsewhere. Herbert Dean, in his recent study *The Social and Political Theory of St. Augustine*, New York: Columbia University Press, 1963, would seem to side with the "individualist" interpretation.
6. To the former school of interpretation belongs W. Cunningham, *St. Augustine and His Place in the History of Christian Thought* (1885), while H. Reuter, *Augustinische Studien*, exemplifies the latter.
7. Thus Dorner, *Augustinus*, Berlin, 1873, and T. Rischl, "Uber die Methode der älteren Dogmengeschichte," *Jahrbücher für Deutsche Theologie*, Bk. XVI, Gotha, 1871, pp. 191–214, take the first position. Figgis, *op. cit.*, on the other hand, adopts the second.
8. See *The City of God*, Marcus Dods, trans., New York: Hafner, 1948, II, 20.

in war, it should be pointed out that they have suffered many military disasters which have caused untold suffering. What is more, Augustine goes on, we should ask ourselves whether great empire is to be regarded as a sign of felicity. The Romans have possessed the world by wars, but does this constitute "success" in a moral sense? Augustine thinks not and he asks who has greater "peace of mind," the rich man always worrying about his possessions, or the man of moderate wealth living at peace with similar neighbors who do not envy one another. It is so with states. Small ones living side by side in harmony, with no lust for dominion, are to be preferred to a large empire. For if the empire is built up without "justice," it is essentially nothing but "robbery" on a large scale[9]—*remota justitia quid regna nisi magna latrocinia.* This becomes one of the great but often puzzling phrases in Augustine's political conception which will be examined more closely below.

He points out that the Assyrian Empire existed for many hundreds of years without the assistance of the Roman gods; but after this long span it fell to the Medes. And its destruction came, he reminds his pagan readers, at a time when Christianity had not even been born.[10] If Roman wars were, indeed, for the most part, just—and Augustine seems to think that they were—good men will not particularly rejoice, although they may be grateful that those more righteous have triumphed. But what relation do the Roman gods have to the process?[11]

In light of considerations like these, he thinks, there is no ground for believing that the acts of Constantine and Theodosius in tolerating and establishing Christianity had anything to do with the capture of the city in 410. The Roman gods are certainly not essential for empire, as the history of other political structures shows; and it cannot be demonstrated that the gods of other nations (of the barbarians, for example) are responsible for their victories.

Nor can it be proved, he goes on, that the gods are essential for the achievement of eternal felicity. His point of departure for this discussion is the treatise on the gods written by Marcus Terentius Varro (116–27 B.C.). Varro had pointed out that there were three kinds of "theology"—varieties, that is, of explanations for and justifications of the gods. The gods may first be looked upon from the viewpoint of the poets, who use them in their stageplays to fill out and help with the plots. This is called the mythical or fabulous interpretation. Secondly, one may see them from the viewpoint of the philosophers who seek in the postulation of gods explanations for the creation and maintenance of the universe. This Varro calls physical or "natural" theology. The ancient Greek thinkers, for example, were constantly trying to find the "one" basis of the world—whether in fire or in water or air.[12] Finally, civil or political theology concerns itself with the forms of worship and sacrifice prescribed by law and custom. Here one will infer the nature of the gods from the ways in which, whether by formal decree or immemorial custom, they are worshipped.

Augustine goes on to point out that the representations of the gods in mythical and civil theology closely resemble each other. Fabulous theology makes alleged divinities simply men writ large. They have all the passions associated with human beings: they lust, make war, conclude alliances, and struggle for power among themselves. If these pictures presented by the poets are indeed portraits of the gods, how can such alleged beings confer eternal felicity or peace?

As for the nature of the gods as presented by law and custom, it, too, is not prepossessing. If we assume that the conventional modes of worship indicate what the gods are, then we can have little more confidence in the political divinities than in those of the poets and dramatists. Here again we see lusting, conflicting beings who give no evidence that they understand either peace of soul or peace of society. Frequently their worship is associated with lewd rites, as, for example, with Liber.[13]

Augustine ponders the problem as to how belief in the gods of the poets and politicians could have arisen and suggests that possibly it developed out of respect or fear of certain men. Gradually the characteristics of these men were expanded and extended, their humanity was forgotten, and they came to be called gods though having the passions and weaknesses of men.[14]

In addition to these considerations, Augustine points out that pagans themselves admit a conflict of jurisdictions among the gods. How can such a conflict arise among beings who are necessary to eternal felicity? If pagans point out in reply that there is a kind of chief god—Jove or Jupiter—why cannot he keep order within the society of divinities? The whole situation is absurd.

Augustine admits, to be sure, with Varro (himself highly dubious about the gods), that physical theology has a certain point. It seeks to discover a unity behind the apparent diversities of the world—a unity without which the universe and human life could have no significance. Yet the philosophers themselves differ as to the kinds of gods responsible for the world and the human race. Plato's view—and here Augustine is obviously thinking of Neoplatonism which played so important a role in his own intellectual development—is the closest to that of Christianity in this respect.[15]

It is at this point, of course, that Augustine sees the superiority of Christianity even to the Platonism which he so respects. For Christian teaching, by asserting that God voluntarily limited himself and became man, recognizes both the inscrutability and transcendence of divinity and also gives a kind of divine significance, through the Incarnation, to the struggles of human history. In effect, Augustine is suggesting, the Christian position, with its doctrine of the Incarnation, combines Platonic and Greek notions of the ultimate with Hebrew consciousness of the significance of history.

Once this is done, Augustine thinks, we see history in a new perspective. We will no longer try to associate temporal "fortune" with worship of any god or historical disaster with desertion of a particular divinity. The one God is never completely understandable in his historical judgments and we can never interpret his actions with any certainty. We know, indeed, that since he is sovereign, his Providence overrules all; and the Christian understands through the Incarnation that, however remote divinity may be from fallen man, the history of the human race is important in the eyes of God. To the Christian, broadly speaking, social and political disaster cannot affect eternal felicity, although it may, like fire, make gold (that is, righteous men) shine. Because of men's interdependence, calamity may visit good and bad alike; for we are bound together in this life both to our contemporaries and to all those who have gone before.

Meanwhile, the choices which men make, whether individual or collective, can be "free"—in the sense that they are not specifically dictated by God. Despite the fact that nothing happens historically outside the will of God, "necessity" is not in conflict with man's freedom. Here Augustine makes his famous distinction between God's foreknowledge and any allegation that he tells men or nations what to do. He knows what choices men will make before they make them and he foresees what answers he will give to their prayers which he also predicts. But this foreknowledge does not mean that he determines their individual choices. Those choices are undetermined and free, even though God, being omniscient as well as omnipotent, foresees, through his knowledge of human beings and of himself, how that freedom will be used.[16] Whatever one may think of this alleged reconcilement of "necessity" with "freedom," there can be no doubt that it plays an important part in Augustine's view of the relation between God and human history.[17]

Thus, after God had suffered the "kingdoms of the East" to be "illustrious" for a "long time," it "pleased" him that there should also arise a "Western empire, which, though later in time, should be more illustrious in extent and greatness."[18] Augustine suggests that God has good and sufficient reasons for his political dispositions, some of which he has revealed to men. But even though there has been a partial revelation to men—so that, for example, longstanding pride or lust will undoubtedly be chastised—the purposes of God can never be understood completely. This is true not only because God, being God, is always far beyond men, but also because men cannot see one another's motives, which are known only to God.[19]

In sum, Augustine sees political history as a gigantic struggle of forces the whole of which can be understood only by God. But in some

9. *Ibid.*, IV, 4.
10. *Ibid.*, IV, 6, 7.
11. *Ibid.*, IV, 15.
12. See Chapter 2, pp. 32–33.
13. *City of God*, VII, 21.
14. *Ibid.*, VII, 18.
15. *Ibid.*, VIII, 5.
16. *Ibid.*, V, 10.
17. On the many and complex ramifications of the Augustinian conception of freedom, see Mary T. Clark, *Augustine, Philosopher of Freedom: A Survey in Contemporary Philosophy*, New York: Desclee Co., 1958.
18. *City of God*, V, 13.
19. *Ibid.*, V, 21.

measure He has given us clues as to the significance of this struggle. Those clues are to be found in Scripture and in the Christ of the Incarnation. It is upon the foundation of these indications, together with pagan insights not incompatible with them, that Augustine spells out in greater detail his political conceptions.

Civitas Dei versus Civitas Terrena

As he constructs his conception of the "two cities," Augustine does not build *de novo*. As a matter of fact, at no point do we find better illustrated the fact that he is a kind of agent for synthesis in the history of historical and political thought.

Later Stoic notions of the cosmopolis or *mundus* constitute one of the foundation stones.[20] Briefly recapitulated, Roman Stoicism tended to think of society very broadly as a series of concentric circles, the innermost of which is the *domus*, or household. Every *civitas*, or city in the ordinary sense of the term, is composed of a number of households and is in turn connected with all other earthly communities in the *orbis terrae*. But there is also a yet more all-embracing society—the cosmopolis or *mundus*—which unites all the communities of the *orbis terrae* with all the souls of the departed and the angels. It is to this "city of the world" that the late Stoic believed his primary allegiance belonged.

The second source for Augustine's great conception is, of course, the New Testament and early Christian thought. We have already suggested that Christians very early thought of themselves as pilgrims and exiles on earth[21] and that some of them actually called the Christian community a separate nation. In Philippians, St. Paul, it will be remembered, states that "the commonwealth to which we belong is in heaven."[22]

Thirdly, we should note once more the impact of Neoplatonism. Plotinus (A.D. 205–270) and the whole Neoplatonic school, while stressing the basic unity of the world, had made much of the distinction between those who were ever conscious of the "lower" value of matter and sense and those, on the other hand, who made sensation and enjoyment of the material sphere their end.

A fourth antecedent for Augustine's portrayal of the two cities is the Hebraic-Christian story of Adam and Eve. This was capable of a variety of interpretations and many ancient thinkers, whatever they may have thought about it as a literal account of history, were acutely aware of its symbolical and mythological significance.[23] St. Augustine makes it a central foundation stone for his whole view of history and of the struggle between the two cities.

From the very creation, Augustine argues, the cosmopolis which Stoics had seen to be one, was potentially two. True, at the beginning God created all the angels with a "good" nature—good being adherence to God. But he also brought them into being with wills capable of "falling away" from God. When many of the angels did indeed fall away, they became evil. Evil is thus not a positive independent force in the universe, as the Manichaeans argue, but rather a negative one. There is no "efficient" cause of evil, Augustine maintains (using the terminology of Aristotle), but rather a "deficient" one.[24]

Augustine is troubled by the problem of where the inordinate pride or evil will of the originally good angels came from. Although his answer is not very convincing, he seems to hold that while all angels were created good and that all had an equal measure of "grace," when the pride of some led them to fall, "the others were more abundantly assisted, and attained to that pitch of blessedness at which they became certain they should never fall from it."[25] Thus in the very act of falling through pride, Lucifer and his associates brought into effect a divine ordinance punishing them eternally through a decree saying that never again should they see God; while by the same token, those angels who resisted the temptation to fall were strengthened by additional grace so that they now had assurance that they were permanently with God. This seems to be an early example of the Scriptural statement "To him that hath shall be given and from him that hath not shall be taken away even what he hath."

The scene is thus set for the Fall of Man, which could not have taken place, presumably, had not the higher creation already been divided. But there are a number of points which Augustine makes about the Fall itself which are very significant for his social and political thought.

First, he stresses the role of woman in the episode. It is Eve who is first "tempted" to eat of the fruit by the fallen angel. To Augustine, as to many of his contemporaries, woman seems to symbolize the temptations of the world as over against adherence to God.[26] At the same time, however, it should be remembered that woman is also, by virtue of the very temptation, the leader or initiator. Man follows because he cannot get along without woman; and he knows full well what the results of his following the woman will be. This appears to place woman in the paradoxical position of being responsible for the separation from God and at the same time the indispensable factor in human history.

But secondly, Augustine makes the central factor in the Fall (which operates initially through woman) that of lust. By this term he means many things—pride of intellect, the urge to dominate, the overweening desire for knowledge, the envy of God for his overarching knowledge of the universe and of man. But above all, as Augustine explicitly states,[27] lust is represented in sexual desire—which again is associated primarily with woman and only secondarily with man. Before the forbidden fruit was eaten, as Augustine interprets the Adam and Eve story, everything that Adam and Eve desired could be good—or close to God. Their wills were good and their desires were always subordinated to their wills. Thus Adam could have sexual intercourse with Eve and not allow the desire for her to triumph over his rationality and his closeness to God. The first man and woman could use the fruits of the earth to sustain themselves; but the gathering of fruit did not become an obsession and neither had any desire to enclose the fields in order to prevent the other from acquiring the material possessions enclosed. Adam did not rule Eve nor did Eve rule Adam; but both controlled and administered animal and plant life for the good of human beings as a whole. The "nature" of Adam and Eve before the Fall—and hence pure "human nature"—was cooperative. Neither political *dominion* nor private property existed—a fact which Augustine will make much of when he comes to develop his theory of state and property.

A third aspect of the Fall in the Augustinian version is that the problems of human choice are made infinitely more complicated. Before Eve succumbed, the only real issue was whether or not to eat the fruit of one particular tree out of the many which existed in the Garden. So long as they stayed away from that tree, man and woman were confronted by no decisions in which their choices could

violate the will of God. This meant that the purposes of God for human society were directly fulfilled through every choice of man. At the same time, it implied that man did not really "know" either good or evil since he had not as yet experienced the falling away through which Lucifer had already gone.

Once the fruit was eaten, however, human choices became infinitely more involved. The possibility of great knowledge was opened up but also the probability of a perpetually renewed falling away from good. Every step in the former direction was to be matched by another in the latter. For the first time, men would become acquainted with misery, grief, death, and the domination of lust in all its aspects—even while they were asserting their own independence of God through scientific knowledge and philosophy. Their loss of innocence was like the passage of childhood into manhood: while the man becomes autonomous he must bear the responsibility for this autonomy and the penalties which go with wrong choices. His choices are now always mixed ones, in which good and evil are intermingled. He cannot, in fact, really make choices which do not entail some evil—so Augustine seems to be saying.

But thus far the two cities are not clearly defined on earth, although the angelic communities are already in existence. On earth, however, after the Fall, all mankind are involved in the departure from God. Presumably, for example, Cain and Abel share in both the potentialities and the penalties in-

20. See pp. 130–132.
21. See p. 156; note 1 Peter 2.
22. Philippians 3:20.
23. Note William R. Inge, *The Philosophy of Plotinus*, New York: Barnes & Noble, 1948, particularly ch. 4 and 5. Among these thinkers was Origen, who tends throughout to adopt figurative interpretations of the Old Testament.
24. *City of God*, XII, 7.
25. *Ibid.*, 9.
26. Cf. W. E. H. Lecky, *History of European Morals from Augustus to Charlemagne*, vol. 1, New York: D. Appleton, 1929, for a portrayal of temptations of the world through a woman's charms.
27. *City of God*, XIV, 16–18.

volved in the sin of Adam and Eve. Yet there is a difference, for Scripture tells us that while Abel was always something of a "pilgrim" on earth,[28] Cain was from the beginning at home. It was Cain who constructed the first *civitas*, for example; and Augustine seems to imply that in so doing he sought to cut himself off even from God's grace, and from natural or uncomplex society. Then Cain killed Abel.

At this point Augustine discovers the beginnings of the two cities on earth which are connected with their respective counterparts among the angels. Seth—whom Eve bore after Abel was murdered—becomes the founder of the heavenly and Cain of the earthly community;[29] and thereafter, while the *civitas dei* is at certain points to be distinguished from the *civitas terrena*—thus Augustine traces the descent of the *civitas dei* through Noah to Abraham and in the subsequent history of Israel—the exact limits of the two communities are not to be discerned in human history. Throughout, however, the coming of the embodied Christ is prophesied, not only by insightful spirits in Israel but also by gentiles.[30]

What are the hallmarks of the two cities as they work their way through human history? At no one point does Augustine describe them. Rather will the characteristics be found scattered throughout his writing. The city of the world is sustained by pride in man's own achievements, for the devil told this city that its citizens should "be as gods." Their very striving to be more than men, however, makes them less than the men they ought to be.[31] The pride in sin is worse than the sin itself. The descendants of Cain, moreover, include the names of women, which is a sign that the citizens of the *civitas terrena* engage in acts of copulation, and hence sin, but do not have any regeneration.[32] They create false gods whom they serve by sacrifice, even going to the extent of making gods out of men (an obvious reference to emperor-worship and to the theory, already mentioned, that all the gods were originally mere men). The chief pleasures of the earthly city are sexual relations, acquisition of riches, and enjoyment of social intercourse; and along with these might be included the itch for dominion over men. Citizens avert their faces from God.

By contrast, citizens of the *civitas dei* are characterized by humility, for they realize that they are but men and cannot be as gods. This very humility enables them to achieve in greater degree the full good potentialities of human nature. While they, too, must copulate in order to bear children, they are saved from this sin by regeneration:

> The sexual intercourse of man and woman, then, is in the case of mortals a kind of seed-bed of the city; but while the earthly city needs for its population only generation, the heavenly needs also regeneration to rid it of the taint of generation.[33]

Although the earthly city is "at home" in the warring, conflicting society characteristic of history, the heavenly always feels out of place. The *civitas dei* holds that "life eternal" is the *summum bonum* and that "death eternal" is undoubtedly the *summum malum*. Yet to live for the true supreme good requires faith, and faith is given by God. Would-be citizens of God can never be certain that they will indeed be heard by God, for even members of the *civitas dei* are ultimately descendants of Adam and need divine grace to be "naturalized" in that city. And, as Augustine has observed earlier, God knows from the beginning those whom he will "save" and those, on the other hand, whom he cannot "elect."

Throughout his enquiry into the two cities, Augustine emphasizes that they are commingled on earth and that the struggles and conflicts of history are due to this commingling. For the members of the *civitas terrena* will be constantly warring with one another, either physically or psychologically, seeking to gain preeminence both over their fellow citizens of the earth and over those who are citizens of God. Citizens of God, in turn, must resist the too great encroachments of the earthly city both for the sake of their own integrity and for that of a precarious peace in the society of the commingled. It is at this point, of course, that politics and the problem of the social order as such enter the system of St. Augustine. But his treatment of them will remain without depth if it is too much abstracted from the general drama of the two cities.

The Church and the Two Cities

While the general picture of the two cities is relatively clear, St. Augustine is by no means entirely lucid when he comes to give an account of the Church in society. Yet historically there can be no question that this problem is one of the most important in his social and political outlook.

In earlier chapters we have endeavored to

show how the general notion of the ecclesia as an independent factor in society took root. By the time of Augustine, of course, the hierarchical principle has been fully established and the Church is closely associated with the state in the task of governing.

The general problem with which Augustine is confronted may be stated as one of reconciling his doctrine of predestination—the notion that the citizens of God are elected by God—with his defense of the idea that the Church Militant is essential for salvation and entitled to the support of the state in its struggle with schismatics and heretics. If election is individual and a matter of grace, it would seem that the Church as a visible body is irrelevant, as is any support of it by the state.[34] On the other hand, in his controversy with the Donatists, Augustine clearly forges a doctrine which emphasizes the authority and significance of the *office* of bishop, as over against the Donatists' claim that it is the character of the individual ecclesiastical official which is crucial. This would seem to place him in the position of underlining the great importance of the "visible" Church, as would his stress on the universal character of the Church by contrast with the sectional nature of the Donatist schism.[35] Moreover, his attack on the Donatists includes one on their political allies, the Circumcellionists. The latter were composed, at least in part, of exploited peasants who revolted against the oppressions of their landlords and claimed more extended property rights in land. In criticizing both the Donatists and the Circumcellionists, Augustine contends that only those who submit to authority are entitled to property rights. Since both the Donatists and the Circumcellionists have attacked authority, they are not entitled to protection of their property. This comment of Augustine has significance for his theory of property but here its importance is due to the fact that he links the authority of Church and state. He seems to reinforce his argument that the authority of the visible Church is a vital factor in his social and political outlook.

This ambiguity regarding his theory of the visible Church is never entirely cleared up. Nevertheless, he seems in general to regard the "city of God" as coterminous with the "invisible Church," which includes Christians as well as those who have never known Christianity. The visible, hierarchical Church, however, embraces members of both cities.[36] This distinction between visible ecclesia, consisting

of citizens of God *and* citizens of the world, and invisible ecclesia, which is identical with the City of God, is pointedly made: "Where both classes exist, it is the Church as it now is, but where only the one exists it is the Church as it is destined to be when no wicked person shall be in her."[37]

But while the visible Church includes both cities, as a whole it is apparently ruled by "saints." The "tares grow in the Church along with the wheat," yet they do not reign with it. The "kingdom militant"—the visible Church—is set up by God to carry on conflict with the enemies of God, even though within it there are undoubtedly earthly citizens; and right to pronounce judgment is given to rulers of the visible Church, as is evidenced in the famous text assigning them the prerogative of forbidding or permitting acts according to their own insights.[38]

If we interpret Augustine correctly, there is a divine authority in the visible Church which will enable it to distinguish between the "tares" and the "wheat" at the time of the "first resurrecton" and this will inaugurate the millennium. Meanwhile, the Church presumably has full authority over its members and those who would be true Christians and eligible for grace must be members of it. Indeed, Figgis asserts that while "the actual expression *extra ecclesiam nulla salus*" is not Augustine's, "the principle he definitely states."[39] The visible Church is in truth the Second Coming of

28. See Genesis 4:2.
29. *City of God*, XV, 15.
30. Thus he claims that the Erythraean sibyl, speaking about the time of Romulus, clearly predicted the advent of Jesus Christ. XVIII, 23.
31. *City of God*, XIV, 13.
32. *Ibid.*, XV, 17.
33. *Ibid.*, XV, 16.
34. Thus Ernst Troeltsch argues that while Augustine accepts the visible Church, he does not place a high value on it. *Social Teaching of the Christian Churches*, New York: Macmillan, 1949, I, 1, pp. 156-159.
35. The Donatists, it will be remembered, dominated large sections of Africa, but possessed few if any adherents elsewhere.
36. Note *City of God*, XX, 9.
37. *Ibid.*
38. Matthew 18:18; see *City of God*, XVIII, 18.
39. Figgis, *op. cit.*, p. 72.

Christ, its rulers being the deputies of Christ; and the saint attacks those chiliastic views which expect a literal return of Christ in physical form.

We are now prepared to examine Augustine's attitude to the role of the secular power in relation to the visible Church, particularly with respect to persecution. At least a fifth of all his letters deal with the problem of the Donatist dissidents and the Circumcellions. At first, apparently, he believes that they should be persuaded to return to the fold of Holy Mother Church without threats from imperial authority. Moral suasion alone should be used. Gradually, however, his views begin to change and by 408, he has reached the conclusion that it is legitimate for secular rulers to assist the visible Church in dealing with heretics and schismatics.[40] His watchword now becomes the text "Compel them to come in."[41]

The imperial edicts commanding Donatists to return to the Church and to surrender their own church edifices had originally been issued without St. Augustine's approval. In fact, he and his faction had petitioned the emperors only for decrees which would protect against Donatist and Circumcellion violence, allowing the heresy as such to be legally tolerated.[42] However, the emperors went beyond this and ordered suppression of the heresy. Augustine tells us that once he saw the effects of the decrees, he began to reflect on the role of coercion in religious matters and eventually came to the conclusion that a "preliminary dose of fear and force" may be essential.[43] Thus he sees the suppression of religious schism and heresy by secular authority as an expression of God's love: coercion may be essential to shock the heretic into a full realization of his terrible offense.

But while the saint thus comes to justify support of the visible Church by the secular power, he remains uneasy about the kinds of penalties to be imposed on heretics and schismatics, even those who have been convicted of acts of violence. Although he has now come to accept, rather reluctantly, the principle of coercion, he thinks that it should not be administered vindictively. Thus he writes to his personal friend Marcellinus, who is also a Roman judge, admonishing him not to administer the law in accordance with the principle of "an eye for an eye and a tooth for a tooth." Anger is to be tempered with the "claims of humanity." Although it is legitimate to restrain heretics, they should not suffer "loss of life or limb."[44]

Thus Augustine's theory of the role and purpose of the visible Church is filled with difficulties. He attempts to combine in a rather uneasy alliance the proposition that (1) the visible Church is a commingling of the two cities, which will not be separated until the end of political history with the view that (2) the visible Church is also the Kingdom of Heaven or of Christ whose rulers have authority given by God and whose judgments will establish the millennial kingdom.

Perhaps it is not unfair to say that Augustine is torn between his role as a philosopher and theologian endeavoring to understand God and history and, on the other hand, his position as a political-ecclesiastical controversialist seeking to defend the immediate interests of the visible Church. In the former capacity, he sees the visible Church as a voluntary society of the commingled cities—important, indeed, but not playing the crucial role, which is occupied by the relation between the individual soul and God. In the latter role, by contrast, the emphasis is on corporeity and authority, compulsion and judgment; the visible ecclesiastical rulers combine with the governors of the Empire to "compel them to come in" and to carry on the battle with earthly citizens (even though many of those are in the Church itself).

It is obvious that the very ambiguities of St. Augustine provide a fertile source for later controversy. Individualists can argue, on the basis of Augustinian texts, that it is the soul's relation to God which is of vital significance, not the organization of an hierarchical Church with its supporting civil authority. But advocates of clerical predominance can also make a good case for the contrary position. They can point to the visible Church as the Kingdom of God, to the necessity for unity, and to the implied notion that the state is to be an agent for ecclesiastical purposes. Augustine's theory of the Church is in part important precisely because it reflects the very imperfect and sometimes muddle-headed synthesis of these two positions.

Slavery, War, and Rule

By nature, Augustine holds, man is made for society and harmony. To be fully itself, an individual soul will subject the irrational to the rational, the fleshly appetites to the beatific vision. At the same time, its perfect union with God will mean its equally perfect and harmonious concord with other souls. The division of the cities lies in the fact that the heavenly city aspires to vertical union with God and horizontal union with men, whereas the earthly city makes temporal joys its end.

But in the general society of history, the two cities are commingled, just as they are in the Church. It is the historical destiny of the citizens of God, in other words, to be conditioned in their acts and institutions by the fact that the overwhelming mass of mankind are citizens of the earth. Although heavenly citizens are destined for ultimate unity or integration, they, too, are descendants of Adam and therefore cannot expect to escape the miseries of historical society to which they have been doomed by Adam's fall.

All this means that, while Augustine stresses the social nature of man, he finds that nature so corrupted by the entry of sin that the kind of peace achieved in the commingling of the two cities is always precarious. The peace of society before the Fall is spontaneous, unforced, and sure: in it, there is no conflict between man's freedom and his social character, between his desires and God's will. After the Fall, by contrast, while he cannot escape the longing for peace, both of soul and of society, he is compelled as a punishment to accept a kind of secondary and precarious peace. This is the peace gained by conquest, characterized by slavery, and ordered by the state. It is the peace of separation from God, forced and unspontaneous and ever menaced by shifts in fortune and in power.

Augustine descants at length on the uneasy harmony characteristic of historical society after the Fall. It is reflected, first of all, in the *domus*, or household, which should be "the natural refuge from the ills of life,"[45] but is frequently instead an exemplification of its miseries. Marriage itself is often sheer misery and children constitute a burden which often weighs us down. But as we move into the next circle of society—the *civitas*—how much more is the precarious and mixed nature of historical peace exemplified! There are the lawsuits which divide man from man. There is always the risk of civil war and insurrection. And Augustine portrays vividly the dilemmas of the judge who, compelled to ascertain the truth in the criminal cases coming before him, is often ignorant and utterly incapable of discovering the facts. He may put men to the torture and in the process injure the innocent despite his objective of protecting society! There is a kind of tragedy in civil society; for in the name of preserving peace—the peace of the sinful state—we are always committing injustice.[46] The third circle of the Stoics, it will be remembered, is the *orbis terrae;* and just as the miseries and dilemmas of the *civitas* greatly exceed those of the *domus*, so those of the larger society of nations magnify those of the *civitas*. Fissions due to language, war, and injustice characterize it. Finally, even the *mundus* or cosmopolis exemplifies the pain and frustrations of human existence, in that men are led by demons into believing that they themselves are good, thus cutting off human beings from the society of good angels.[47]

But although the peace and harmony of the four circles thus rest on such uneasy foundations and are connected with so much misery, Augustine would have us also look at the other side of the coin. For the very fruits of that sin which all men share with Adam constitute, by God's providence, a series of partial correctives for the sin. Thus, while the Fall gives birth to war among men, war itself is ordained as a check on the war-like and as a means to preserve a kind of peace. Augustine no longer holds in any sense to the early Christian view that military service must be barred to the Christian, for he sees in war an instrument which may be essential to achieve the only kind of civil concord possible in the fallen state.[48] He lays the foundations, in fact,

40. See J. B. Bernardin, "St. Augustine as Pastor," in R. W. Battenhouse, ed., *A Companion to the Study of St. Augustine*, New York: Oxford University Press, 1955.
41. Luke 14:23.
42. St. Augustine, Letter 95.
43. *Ibid.*
44. St. Augustine, Letter 133.
45. *City of God*, XIX, 5.
46. *Ibid.*, XIX, 6.
47. *Ibid.*, XIX, 9.
48. *Ibid.*, XIX, 12. In Letter 189, he remarks that while peace is the object of our desires, we may have to wage war to attain peace. By subduing those whom one attacks in war, one may bring them back to "peace."

for that theory of the "just war" which is to be developed in medieval Christendom. Like Athanasius and Ambrose, he would call his fellow religionists to arms both to protect the Empire and to wipe out heretics. Unlike Origen, he does not view Christian life as a vehicle through which, by means of refusing military service, wars will be made to cease. The Sermon on the Mount does not demand nonresistance but rather simply an inner attitude exalting good will toward the aggressor.

It is providential, he thinks, that while the enslavement of man by man is a fruit of the Fall, it is also a corrective. Before Eve succumbed, men had dominion over beasts and the other lower creation, but not over man. Once, however, desire was no longer subjected to the good, it apparently had free reign to make human beings the tools of their fellow humans. Thus servitude entered the world. But no sooner did it appear than it enslaved not only the chattel but also the master. This dual enslavement is in effect the erection of a limitation on slavery itself; for the master, in becoming enslaved to his own lusts, is in a worse position than the technical slave, who, because he is an integral part of a sinning society, has been reduced to his status through war.[49]

Augustine, in other words, like most of the early Fathers, puts himself squarely against Aristotle's view that there is a natural slavery. He is more aligned with the Stoic position, which, while deeming the institution unnatural, still justifies its existence in the actual state of human society. But Augustine fits the Stoic notion into the mythology of the Fall and thus gives slavery, like other institutions, a religious significance which it did not have for philosophers like Seneca.

With respect to property institutions, the view of Augustine would seem to be similar to that of his attitude to slavery. Before the Fall, of course, there was no engrossment of material goods by individuals and no lust for material possessions. After the Fall, however, men began to make a distinction between "mine" and "thine." While this was the fruit of sin, it also constitutes a limitation. Although many men lust after complete ownership of the earth, the similar lusts of other men serve to check them in their desires. Thus in property relations there is a kind of power balance similar to that between master and slave, the acquisitive urge of one helping to limit, at least in a measure, that of others.

Finally, the *civitas*, as the *ordo* or order which encircles and guards property, defends the institutions of slavery, and makes war for the sake of peace, is itself both the fruit of sin and a limitation on evil. The state exemplifies how, even though men in their freedom rebel against God, the divine being can use the instruments of evil for his own ends.[50] In the society of the commingled cities, the primary role of the state, in Augustine's view, is suppressive and negative. Arising, like slavery, out of men's pride and lust, it turns upon those who have created it and controls the degree to which they can destroy themselves in their egoistic pretensions.

In the whole of Augustine's discussion of war, slavery, property, and the state, one will note emerging a kind of *ordo* which, while not natural, is yet justified. This has led some writers, notably Troeltsch,[51] to speak of an Augustinian doctrine of "relative natural law." That is, natural law is the divine order of things present before the Fall. Relative natural law is that *ordo* which is appropriate for man after sin has infected his every act.

The implication is clear that, under such a relative *ordo*, for human beings to rebel against service in war would be "relatively" immoral; and for them to seek a wholesale abolition of slavery would be to commit another rebellion. Similarly, if they should try to institute a communist order of society, it would simply mean that they would inevitably fail and in the process create enormous destruction. Finally, if they should question the principle of political authority, they would be flying in the face of the system of relations which God himself had ordained for the post-Fall society.

Justice and the Republic

One of the most celebrated apparent ambiguities in the Augustinian treatment of politics is the saint's analysis of the relation between justice and the state or the republic. He introduces the subject very early in the *City of God*[52] and develops the theme at much greater length in Book XIX. Moreover, considerable light is cast on his attitude in his treatises against the Donatists and elsewhere.[53]

The central issue is whether there can be a populus, and therefore a *respublica*, without justice. In Cicero's dialogue *De Republica* (modeled on that of Plato, to some extent), the ancient Roman orator had put into the mouth of Scipio Africanus the words "*Populum autem non omnem coetum multitudinis sed coetum juris consensu et utilitatis communione sociatum esse determinat*"—that is, a people is a multitude of men or an assembly associated together by a common acknowledgement of right (*juris*) and by a community of interests. Augustine then proceeds to interpret this Ciceronian statement. *Juris*, derived from *jus*, he interprets as meaning *justitia*—"righteousness" or "justice." And he is at pains to show that he believes Cicero meant *vera justitia*—true righteousness or justice. If legal right must be based on *justitia* and *justitia* is, in fact, *vera justitia*, then one vital aspect of *vera justitia* is surely the recognition which man must accord to the one true God. "Is he who keeps back a piece of ground from the purchaser, and gives it to a man who has no right to it, unjust," asks Augustine rhetorically, "while he who keeps back himself from the God who made him, and serves wicked spirits, is just?"[54]

In sum, if we are to accept the Ciceronian-Augustinian conception of a republic, only those "multitudes" which are united by law based on "true justice" can be regarded as commonwealths; and an integral part of *vera justitia* is public worship of the true God and a thoroughgoing repudiation of pagan deities. In negative terms, a so-called republic without true justice is simply robbery writ large. Or, as Augustine puts it, "Justice being taken away, then, what are kingdoms but great robberies?"[55] *Remota justitia quid regna nisi magna lactrocinia.* And he cites with great glee the story of Alexander the Great and the pirate who had been captured by that monarch. When the ruler asked the robber how he could have so much presumption as to dominate the sea and prey upon men, the pirate replied: "What do you yourself mean by seizing the whole earth, not merely the sea? But because I do it with a petty ship, I am called a robber, whilst you who do it with a great fleet are styled emperor." Generally speaking, if one commits robbery on such a large scale that all opposition is overcome, one is called a ruler and statesman; while if one merely succeeds in carrying on small-scale larceny, one is eventually captured and called a criminal. Augustine at this point seems to be utterly convinced that almost all historical political systems are simply results of the successful use of force and deception and can in no wise be called commonwealths.[56]

By this standard, it is obvious, there could hardly be an obligation on the part of citizens to obey rulers. Most political history would be simply the story of the *civitas terrena* and the Fall would have led to such depravity that all remembrance of nature before the Fall would have been wiped out. Moreover, had Augustine confined himself to his interpretation of Cicero, he would appear to have denied God's overriding providence after the Fall; for human nature would have departed so far from deity that even a secondary *ordo*, such as is assumed in the so-called doctrine of relative natural law, would have been excluded.

It is undoubtedly considerations of this kind which lead Augustine to search for another "definition" of *respublica*. He must somehow recognize the large element of force, chicanery, and sheer sin in all human institutions and at the same time preserve (in order to be consistent with his view of the Fall) a relatively natural character for the major institutions as they have actually evolved in history. He must recognize the exploitative nature of all sociopolitical organization but also see in it a providential ordinance which preserves a little of that which has been, in its pure form, irretrievably lost.

The clue to his second definition of the *respublica* will be found in his statement that, while kingdoms without justice are but gigantic robberies, robber bands are themselves but little kingdoms. That is to say, even within a pirate band there must be some kind of *ordo* if the objectives of the robbers are to be attained. A piratical expedition, for example, is ruled by a prince and there has to be some kind of agreement or contract to hold the alliance together; for example, Augustine argues, if there is no clear understanding about the division of booty one of the major purposes of the group will be frustrated. There is a separation

49. *Ibid.*, XIX, 15.
50. Note particularly XIX, 15.
51. Troeltsch, *Social Teaching of the Christian Churches*, I, 1, pp. 158–161.
52. *Ibid.*, II, 21.
53. See his commentaries on the Psalms, and refer to Father Hugh Pope, *op. cit.*
54. *City of God*, XIX, 21.
55. *Ibid.*, IV, 4.
56. *Ibid.*, XIX, 23.

of rulers from ruled but also a consensual basis for the very existence of rulership.[57]

Thus there are two sides to the piracy-republic comparison. On the one hand, it is clear that almost all earthly societies have fallen far short of the requirement of *vera justitia* and, from the viewpoint of the prime Cicero-Augustine standard, are little better than piratical bands. On the other hand, all human aggregates, including those whose objective is sheer plunder, must have internal peace of a kind if they are to attain their goals. And this peace cannot be gained without at least an incipient legal system, a differentiation between rulers and ruled, and some provision for the division of economic goods.[58]

It is this second aspect of the piracy-republic analogy which Augustine makes the basis for his alternative definition of republic. We can, he believes, formulate a minimal standard which has been attained by most historical kingdoms and republics. He uses this language: *Populus est coetus multitudinis rationalis, rerum quae diligit concordi communione sociatus.* That is to say, "a people is an assemblage of reasonable beings bound together by a common agreement as to the objects of their love."[59] Here *justitia* is not even mentioned and thus Babylonia, Egypt, Assyria, Athens, Sparta, and Rome have been commonwealths if we accept this definition.

Obviously, the two Augustinian definitions are separated from each other by a very wide gulf. The former would exclude virtually all historical political societies from the designation republic; the latter would embrace all of them and would in addition include many not usually so termed. If we interpret Augustine from the viewpoint of individual moral and political obligation, the former would apparently sever the righteous individual from any obligation to obey the historical republic; while the latter, by the same token, would seem to afford no basis for opposition to any ruling class. The successful application of force on a large scale, if we accept the second definition, would *ipso facto* entitle its user to the title of legitimate governor.

But while wide separation between the two definitions is, broadly speaking, true, we should also note a common bond. It lies in the fact that both definitions assume an association of *human* beings (not of subhuman creatures) and that both see an element of consent. As a matter of fact, Augustine seems to suggest, the successful use of physical force is itself dependent on a minimum of agreement; for soldiers and policemen or pirates and robbers must consent to obey their commanders if the enterprise, even under the second definition, is to achieve its goals. And that a substantial segment of the population will positively agree to obey must mean that many others will also at least passively acquiesce.

But to complicate the picture still further, it can be argued that Augustine suggests yet a third notion of a true republic—one which lies beyond even his first. For he contends that "true justice has no existence save in that republic whose founder and ruler is Christ, if at least any choose to call this a republic; and indeed we cannot deny that it is the people's weal."[60] Whether he means by this a society like that of humanity before the Fall or one which may presumably arise after citizens of the world have been separated from the citizens of God we cannot tell.

For all practical purposes, we may disregard this third notion of republic in Augustine and confine the remaining part of our analysis to the first two statements. In attempting to relate the two to each other and to the conception of the two cities, we might ask ourselves whether Augustine intends to identify the state with the *civitas terrena.* There can be no doubt that at times he speaks as if the two were indeed identical. All historical political societies have fallen so far from God and *vera justitia*, he repeatedly says, that their only inner bond of unity has been the pursuit of those common interests which have represented, for the most part, the goals of iniquity.

But just as there is an ambiguity about his identification of the visible Church with the *civitas dei*, so it would be a mistake to interpret Augustine as equating the state with the *civitas terrena.* If general political society were indeed coterminous with the earthly city then there would be nothing whatsoever in it to remind us of God and the good. But both Scripture (chiefly St. Paul and St. Peter) and our own observation tell us that the authority of the political society is in some sense "of God." It provides a peace which, while it must not be confused with that of the *civitas dei,* is still, St. Augustine seems to say, an eighth or tenth carbon copy of that godly harmony. And while political institutions are produced by sin, their very nature is such that they serve to limit some of the worst effects of the Fall.

Throughout his analysis, Augustine tends to emphasize political institutions as primarily negative in function. They restrict some of the worst effects of sin but can hardly in themselves contribute to a positive good. Here the Augustinian position is obviously widely separated from that of Plato and Aristotle, for whom political society is a positive expression of and necessity for the growth of the soul. Augustine, like so much of Christianity, tends in some measure to separate the quest for the individual good from politics and to think of the positive search for salvation as a personal matter for which organized society has only an indirect and secondary relevance.

Augustine and Medieval Thought

John N. Figgis has rightly said: "Clearly we cannot understand the Middle Ages on its political and social side without Augustine."[61]

While scholars are divided as to the exact degree to which Augustine was characteristically "ancient" or "medieval" in his thought and outlook,[62] there would seem to be widespread agreement that he had considerable influence in shaping the medieval mind. It is always difficult to document such assertions, but here it may be suggested that that impact was twofold—general and specific. It was general in that the Augustinian thought-pattern as a whole tends to run through the world-outlook of early medieval times down to at least the thirteenth century. It was specific in that leading medieval thinkers cited St. Augustine either as authority for their views or as corroborating positions which they had arrived at independently.

With respect to his general influence, it is not easy to say whether the Middle Ages tended to think like Augustine because of him or whether the general religious and political atmosphere conditioned both Augustine and the medieval mind. Perhaps it is safest to suggest that the affinities between the Augustinian system and views of the early Middle Ages are striking, however we account for them in explicit terms.

In the first place, Augustine's whole notion of the commingling of the two cities here on earth was a common belief. With it went a general conviction that in Adam's Fall was to be sought the explanation for many social and political phenomena. This alone was enough to distinguish both Augustine and early medieval thought from a major current of intellectual history after the thirteenth century.

Secondly, while Augustine, as we have seen,

sought to reconcile the antiworldly attitude of early Christian thought with the presumed necessity for accommodating Christian viewpoints to the post-Constantinian political situation, the tension between this world and the other world remained, both in his own writings and in the outlook of the first medieval centuries.

Thirdly, the argument of Augustine that secular institutions originated in sin provided an ideal weapon for exponents of the notion that the Church was somehow higher than nonecclesiastical institutions. Although Augustine did not, at least on the whole, identify the *civitas terrena* with the state, his severe attacks on actual historical states provided a veritable armory of weapons for advocates of medieval clericalism.

But finally, Augustine also afforded arguments for the anticlericalists. We have noted his ambiguity about visible versus invisible Church and his frequent tendency to emphasize the "commingling" of the two cities in the visible ecclesia. Attention has also been called to his contention that it is individual souls who are elected and that their election took place before there was any visible hierarchical church order. Obviously, considerations of this kind could, and did, furnish numerous

57. *Ibid.*, IV, 4.
58. Compare with a modern analysis like that of Charles Merriam, *Political Power*, New York: McGraw-Hill, 1934, ch. 3, "Law Among the Outlaws."
59. *City of God*, XIX, 24.
60. *Ibid.*, II, 21.
61. Figgis, *op. cit.*, p. 100. In the generation immediately following the death of St. Augustine, Paulus Orosius, a Spanish theologian who had resided for a time with the Bishop of Hippo, sought to emphasize the Augustinian contention that Christians were not responsible for the disintegration of the Roman Empire. At the suggestion of Augustine himself, he completed a general history of the world, *Adversus Paganos Historiarum Libri VII*, in which he portrayed the heathen epoch in even bleaker terms than those of St. Augustine. During the Dark Ages this study—now regarded by scholars as of little value—enjoyed a considerable popularity and may be said to have helped reinforce the world view of the author of the *City of God*.
62. Troeltsch, for example, tends to stress his affinities with ancient thought.

ideological swords for all those—whether pro-imperialists in the eleventh century, Joachimites in the thirteenth, or Wycliffites in the fifteenth—who attacked the temporal claims of the Church.

In fact, it is often the very ambivalence and division within the mind of Augustine itself that foreshadow the political and ideological battles of the Middle Ages. His initial reluctance to call upon civil authority to suppress the Donatists, for example, is matched by the frequent uncertainty, in the early Middle Ages, as to what role kings should play in eliminating heresy. But his ultimate conviction that Catholic Christianity is entitled to the support of the *regnum* seems to anticipate the firm establishment of the Inquisition and its close links with temporal authority.

More explicitly, scholars have been ingenious in tracing out the degree to which Augustine was cited by medieval thinkers and rulers.

If the reading matter of kings influences their conduct, then Charlemagne was profoundly indebted to the *City of God,* which was one of his favorite works. He was particularly fond of Book V, Chapter 24, which outlines the "ideal" of a Christian emperor. The many pamphlets produced during the course of the struggle between Gregory VII and Henry IV are filled with references to St. Augustine and apparently both sides could use him to support their respective positions.[63]

In the development of canonical views of society and politics,[64] Augustine was, of course, to carry great weight indeed. The unofficial but profoundly influential *Concordia Discordantium Canorum* of Gratian, in the twelfth century, includes at least 530 references to his works. His authority is particularly cited to support the idea of compulsion in dealing with heretics. Augustine had argued that the only reason coercion was not used by the early Christians had been the fact that they were so weak in numbers. Statements of this kind, no doubt, assisted the frequently uneasy consciences of thinkers who were constructing an intellectual edifice within which persecution could be housed. For the same reason, Augustine's defense of war[65] was undoubtedly a godsend.

It would take us too far afield to inquire with greater detail into this absorbing subject, but for the student of the history of political thought the lesson would seem to be that the historical importance of Augustine can scarcely be exaggerated.

The Universal and Analytic Significance of Augustine

Later medieval thought was to depart in considerable measure from Augustinian viewpoints. But with the rise of Lutheranism and early Calvinism both his general position and his political notions were to be given a new lease on life. After the early eighteenth century, however, Augustine's political doctrine began to be looked upon as a relic of superstition and the general temper of modern times has tended to support this judgment.

However, by the middle of the twentieth century, men were again asking themselves whether his hypotheses were indeed as useless as the liberal mind had argued. The hopes of the nineteenth century for social and moral progress seemed to be at least dimmed by such phenomena as the two World Wars. And the general anti-Augustinian argument that it was culture and ignorance which were responsible for war, slavery, and seemingly irrational conflict did not seem as plausible as it had appeared in the time of Queen Victoria.

More explicitly, Augustine's challenge to modern political thought may be said to lie in his assertions that there is something stubborn in man's present nature which resists enlightenment; that irrational rebellion remains a characteristic of political man whatever the structure of the society or however enlightened its rulers; that there is no method and no device which can ensure that powerholders will not make their own self-perpetuation their end; that while economic factors do indeed play a large role in explaining political phenomena, including the division of society into classes, economic problems themselves must be seen in the light of an even more fundamental fact—that historical man is basically egoistic and that it is impossible for him to return through social reorganization of some kind to a spontaneous, free society; that while communism of goods is indeed the ideal, human effort is powerless to attain it; that with every ostensible step in the direction of moral progress, there is always the probability of another Fall; that the very knowledge made possible by the Fall is a two-edged sword which can be used either to enhance human life or to destroy it; and that greatly magnified technological power is as likely to be employed to pollute and kill human beings as it is to benefit them.

It is at least not self-evident that propositions

of this kind are false to social and political experience; and insofar as the twentieth century begins once more to appreciate them, the conceptions of St. Augustine are hardly dead in our day.

chapter 11

Main Currents from Augustine to the High Middle Ages

There was no great system of what could be dignified as political theory from the death of Augustine to the twelfth century. Nevertheless, ample ground existed for political controversy and the development of rival attitudes. For seven hundred years, competing political views are to be discovered in the compilations of ecclesiastical editors, the comments of often obscure monks, the encyclicals and other writings of the Popes, the proclamations of kings and emperors, and, toward the end of the period, in the polemics of rival pamphleteers. Implicit political doctrine must also be read into the practices of such institutions as feudalism and the manorial system.

Ecclesia and Imperium from Augustine to Gregory I

As was noted in Chapter 10, the authority of Augustine can be cited in support of the notion that the visible Church is highly significant as well as to sustain the proposition that it is only the invisible Church which matters. His frequent ambivalence with respect to temporal institutions arises because, while they have their origin in sin, they are also God's ordinance for the correction and chastisement of sin. When he stresses the invisible Church, Augustine tends to emphasize the individual pole of social thought; while his utterances which buttress the visible ecclesia pave the way for all those doctrines which will exalt the authority of an hierarchically organized body of believers.

Chapter 10

63. See C. Mirbt, *Die Stellung Augustine in der Publicstic des Gregorianischen Kirchenstreits*, Leipzig, 1888.
64. See Chapter 12.
65. Discussed in Gratian's *Concordia*, ch. 23, i, 2.

Above all, he leaves dangling the vexing issue of what precisely belongs to the visible church and what to the *regnum* or temporal rule. In the fifth and sixth centuries this question becomes particularly acute in view of the tangled relationships between a Church continuing to wax in influence and a state which is often drawn into the vortex of theological controversy.

Indeed, the context of fifth- and sixth-centuries struggle cannot be fully understood unless we go back to the fourth century. After the time of Julian the Apostate, it will be remembered, there was no longer any organized challenge to the preferred position of the Church which had been established under Constantine and continued under his immediate successors. And by the end of the century, not only was the church preferred but all other public professions of religion were prohibited by the Emperor Theodosius.

The same emperor, however, clashed with the divine institution he did so much to exalt. The most famous episode involved his conflict with St. Ambrose over the suppression of a riot at Thessalonica. Certain residents of that city had engaged in violent acts against the authorities and in retaliation, the emperor had ordered the random massacre of its citizens (A.D. 390). This shocked the Bishop of Milan, who excommunicated the ruler and excluded him from the Church until he should repent of a deed which, according to Ambrose, violated Christian morality. In reply, Theodosius asserted the proposition that he was the ruler over the Church and that no bishop could presume to chastise him for his alleged sins. He could, of course, use the authority of Constantine to sustain his attitude, for that emperor had flatly asserted "Whatever I will, that is to be considered a canon."

In response to this argument, St. Ambrose endeavored to refute the Constantinian theory and thereby to lay the groundwork for the idea that the Church is, in some respects at least, the superior of the ruler, and not merely his subordinate. The emperor is in the Church, argues Ambrose, and not over it—at least for purposes which are the primary concern of the ecclesia. And he goes on to censure Theodosius for daring to deny liberty of expression to a holy bishop.[1]

While Ambrose triumphed in that he secured an act of repentance from the emperor, his doctrine of the exact jurisdictions of spirituals and temporals is not very explicit or pointed.

Meanwhile, the history of theological doctrine has certain political implications. In the first place, the long series of formal definitions of the natures of God and of Christ raises the issue of whether the state will use its authority to impose the orthodox view. Secondly, the question is put as to whether it is the bishops or the emperor (as sustainer of the organized Church) who in the last analysis may be said to have the right to formulate authoritative doctrine.

With respect to the first issue, both implicit and explicit doctrine answer the question in the affirmative.

As for the second question, the ambiguity arises because of the very fact that the emperors have had a large share in the summoning and conduct of the Councils which deal with questions of creed. Constantine presides over the Council of Nicaea in 325; and insofar as the Constantinian "Whatever I will, that is to be considered a canon" is accepted, it would seem logical to hold that the emperor may, if he wills, not only support doctrine proclaimed by the councils but also define the doctrines themselves.

After the conclusion of the long Athanasian-Arian controversy, with the triumph of the notion that God is triune and that Christ is both man and God, theological speculation turns to the question of exactly how man and God are united in Christ. Eventually, there come to be three rather well-defined positions: the Monophysite, the Nestorian, and the Orthodox. Briefly, the Monophysite definition maintains that Christ is one person with a partly divine and a partly human nature. Nestorianism can be rephrased as asserting that he is "two persons in one"—divine and human. The Orthodox position, formulated by the Council of Chalcedon in A.D. 451, defines Christ as one person who is perfectly divine and perfectly human.[2]

The Chalcedonian decree is a condemnation of both Monophysitism and Nestorianism. It was intended, however, to provide a ground of reconciliation through a formula which might appeal to many in both parties.

But historically it did not completely succeed in this objective and out of its failure emerges the great controversy that culminates in the Gelasian doctrine. After Chalcedon, the Monophysite interpretation remained particularly strong in Egypt and undoubtedly constituted not only an ecclesiastical thorn in the side of the Eastern emperor but a political one as well. Secular rulers endeavor, where possible, to conciliate divergent theological positions in the interests of political unity and strength. The Emperor Zeno had actually suffered exile for two years, while his rival was supported by the Monophysites, so that he had an unusually strong motivation to conciliate the opposing faction when at length he was restored to the throne. The result was that, under the advice of Acacius, Patriarch of Constantinople, he issued (A.D. 482) the *Henoticon*, in which he sought to reconcile the Monophysite position with that which had been promulgated at Chalcedon, while at the same time suggesting that that Council was not beyond error.

There can be no question that in the *Henoticon* Zeno proclaims his right to define theological doctrine. The document asserts that the emperor is convinced that "the source and stay" of his sovereignty, "its strength and impregnable safeguard," is that "only genuine and true faith which, by the inspiration of God, was published by the 318 holy Fathers assembled at Nicaea, and confirmed by the 150 holy Fathers who, in like manner, met in council at Constantinople." He is, he avows, very much concerned with correct theological doctrine, because the right understanding and worship of "our great God and Saviour Jesus Christ, who was incarnate and born of Mary, the holy Virgin and God-bearer" will ensure that "the power of our enemies will be overwhelmed and dispersed, and the blessings of peace, of favorable weather and abundant crops, and all that is to man's benefit, will be freely bestowed upon us."

Because, then, true faith "is the safeguard of ourselves and of the Roman commonwealth" and the basis for unity with peace, Zeno proceeds to develop a formula which he thinks will not be incompatible with unity and orthodoxy. God took on manhood in Jesus Christ, "who in respect of his Godhead is consubstantial with the Father, and consubstantial with us in respect of his manhood." He is "one, not two." And the emperor then proceeds to anathematize "anyone who has held or holds any other opinion, either now or at any other time, whether at Chalcedon or at any synod whatsoever. . . ."[3]

The whole document is, of course, a challenge to those within the Church who see the ecclesia as not subject to kings in its doctrinal life and who resent the attempt of any emperor to settle theological disputes, even in the interests of political peace.

The reaction of Western ecclesiastical leaders to the *Henoticon* was almost instantaneous and continued for several years. They objected, of course, to its theological formulations; but even more did they oppose the idea that the emperor might legitimately overturn the decrees of a council. In the opposition of the Bishops of Rome, one sees reflected an attitude to imperial authority which was to sharply differentiate Western developments from those in the East. In the Eastern Empire, the imperial claim to define doctrine was seemingly unchallenged; and the Church increasingly became virtually a department of state in the later Byzantine Empire. In the West, by contrast, Popes Felix II and Gelasius I took such vigorous exception to the act of Zeno that they inaugurated the long tradition which would stake out claims to a spiritual jurisdiction separate from that of royal and imperial authority.

Felix II anathematized Acacius for the advice he had given to Zeno, and when Gelasius I succeeded Felix, he continued the controversy.

Gelasius in a series of letters endeavored to formulate a whole theory of the relations between spiritual and temporal authority as a framework for opposing the assertion of imperial authority represented in the *Henoticon*. Broadly speaking, he avers, there is a sphere of authority appertaining to the emperor by virtue of his grant from the Roman people and another allotted to the Church through Christ. In temporal matters, the pope is subject to the emperor; but in spirituals, the emperor must submit to bishops and the pope.

In supporting this general theory, Gelasius cites as authority the Scriptures and the precedents established by previous bishops in their relations with emperors. The Gelasian doc-

1. Epistle 40 to Theodosius.
2. Council of Chalcedon, Actio V.
3. Zeno's *Henotikon*, reprinted in *Documents of the Christian Church*, Henry Bettenson, ed., London: Oxford University Press, 1963, pp. 123–126.

trine is chiefly notable for its employment of the story of Melchizedek in Genesis; for this establishes a precedent of considerable importance in later medieval thought. Melchizedek was both king and priest, Gelasius argues, which was one of the reasons that Abraham paid him obeisance. And this union of the priesthood with royal authority, he goes on, established a precedent for the merging of the two offices before the coming of Christ. Satan himself imitated the Melchizedekan union when he ordained that the pagan emperors should also hold the office of Pontifex Maximus.[4]

When Christ came, he was of the order of Melchizedek and combined perfectly the offices of priest and king. However, Christ was aware of the many weaknesses of human nature and ordained that after his departure, the two offices should never again be united in a single man. They were, instead, to be associated with two separate institutions, at least until the return of Christ.

Because of this ordinance of Christ, then, the Christian emperor is absolutely dependent on the ecclesiastic for eternal life. At the same time, the priest relies on the government of the emperor for temporal felicity.

Gelasius points out that there are notable precedents in ecclesiastical and imperial history for such an interpretation. Thus St. Ambrose excommunicated Theodosius,[5] St. Leo rebuked Theodosius the Younger, Pope Hilary condemned the Emperor Anthemius, and Pope Simplicius anathematized the usurper Basiliscus. Gelasius mentions, too, the action of his predecessor against the Emperor Zeno.

Thus the relation between Church and Empire is one of separate authorities and distinct jurisdictions but at the same time of mutual interdependence and subordination. For the emperor to assert the prerogative of defining the exact nature of Christ is as outrageous, Gelasius implies, as it would be for the pope to regulate the imperial exchequer.

Like almost all medieval doctrines of spiritual-temporal affairs, the Gelasian theory is unclear at many points. No more than many later writers, for example, does Gelasius state who is to determine the respective spheres in the event of a dispute. But, significantly enough, he does maintain that the burden of responsibility for the priest is heavier than that of the king, for in the divine judgment the ecclesiastic must give an account not only of his own life, but also of the actions of kings.

If priests will have to give an account of kings at the divine judgment, the corollary would seem to be that kings are not directly responsible to God. While Gelasius does not deal explicitly with the problem of the source of imperial authority, he appears to think that its credentials, in case of dispute, are less worthy than those of ecclesiastical rulers.

Yet we should not conclude that those who succeed Gelasius in the sixth century necessarily follow his apparently qualified judgment of temporal rule. Indeed, Pope Gregory I (590–604) would appear to think of temporal authority in very high terms indeed. Although he follows St. Augustine in holding that the state arises out of the sin of Adam while at the same time being a correction of that sin, he also argues that the ruler obtains his authority directly from God and not through the mediation of the community.

Gregory thus exalts almost beyond measure the authority of the secular ruler. Even the evil ruler must be respected, for did not David refuse to touch the wicked ruler Saul who was the anointed of the Lord?

Implicitly, Gregory's theory would seem to be radically at odds with the Gelasian doctrine. Whereas Gelasius refuses to recognize or proclaim an order of the emperor which violates ecclesiastical authority, Gregory promulgates decrees against which he has protested but in which he believes he must acquiesce. Unfortunately, Gregory does not spell out an exact theory of ecclesiastical-temporal relations, so that we cannot compare his position in precise terms with that of Gelasius.

Certain it is that Gelasius does not stand in awe of kings in the same degree as Gregory. While the former interprets the history of Israel in such a way as to emphasize the authoritative role of prophet against king, the latter stresses the king as the anointed of God who must not be questioned even by good men. Although the former makes the priest accountable for the actions of kings, the latter explicitly sees the secular ruler as directly accountable to God.

While later in the Middle Ages the Gregorian statement will be used by some apologists for the imperial cause, it is the Gelasian theory which is the more influential of the two. By and large, Gregory's doctrine of royal authority and his implicit theory of spirituals and temporals will not appear again until, in the time of Luther, a wholesale onslaught against medieval notions is carried out.

While Gregory I was asserting the power and prerogatives of the Roman See and at the same time developing a theory of passive obedience to the secular ruler, conditions of life in the West were changing rapidly. Broadly speaking, the Roman bishop in practical terms began to exercise much of the leadership which had formerly been associated with the imperial office; for while the Eastern emperor continued to claim jurisdiction in the West without challenge from a rival Caesar until 800 (with the crowning of Charlemagne), the politics of Western civilization were in fact ceasing to be imperial. Germanic monarchies took the place of imperial authority, even though nominally they might continue to recognize a vague universal jurisdiction on the part of the Eastern emperor. Meanwhile, men were actually governed increasingly at the local level, and general ties, whether economic, social, or political, became more and more tenuous.

The new order which developed in the seventh and eighth centuries and spread rapidly in the ninth cannot be characterized adequately in a few words; and since it never really had a philosophical expositor, any theory about it must be discovered by generalizing on the basis of its practices. No one term is adequate to describe it and any analysis must necessarily do injustice to its complexities. From the viewpoint of the student of the history of political theory, however, we may characterize its "notes" as localism, feudal and manorial institutions, and a conflict between barbarian and Roman legal conceptions.[6]

By localism, we mean that the center of life and existence tends to be in the individual agricultural village rather than in the city, which now rapidly declines in significance. Whereas the relatively large *civitas* is the essence of classical Roman civilization, this is no longer true by the ninth century. And the small communities which do exist are isolated from one another and even from the shadowy authority of the king who claims to rule them.

As a substitute for the civic sense and imperial citizenship of the past, there arises a series of complex personal relationships which both expresses and shapes a kind of socioeconomic and military organization. Scholars have debated almost endlessly the origins and nature of the feudal and manorial systems and we are still by no means clear as to all of their implications. But they are interwoven with the localism we have noted and with the conception of a society organized and graded in terms of classes—the nobility, the clergy, the workers on the land (or peasants) and, later on, the town dwellers or burgesses. And accompanying these class divisions are the practice and ideology of almost constant warfare between and among rival feudal lords.

The feudal relation itself is essentially one whereby one man vows fealty to another and is in turn given a "fief." The vow of fealty usually involves personal service of some kind —assistance in military activity, for example, and in the administration of justice. The fief granted by the feudal superior may be land, but it also may be simply an honor or an office. Or it may consist of the right to fish or hunt or to escort pilgrims or merchants on their way. While the manorial system—peculiar arrangements for living on the land built around the manor and including payment of feudal dues and performance of service on the part of the serf in return for protection by the lord—seems to be inseparably connected with the Western feudal system as historically developed, it should not be equated with feudalism itself.

Historically, it would seem that the roots of feudalism and the manorial system are to be found in both German and Roman custom and law, although students are not yet agreed as to the exact weight to be given to each. The institutions of feudalism seem to owe something to the Roman conception of *precarium*, whereby the impoverished landholder would turn his land over to a wealthy patron and receive it back as a conditional lease or *precarium*. The use of slave labor begins to decline in the third century and by the third and fourth the Empire is enacting laws "freezing" allegedly free workers to their occupations as they become restive under the unsettled conditions of the times. Thus many of the *coloni* (or free tenants) begin to leave the land and

4. Tractate IV, Letter 12, of Gelasius.
5. See p. 196.
6. Otto F. von Gierke's *Natural Law and the Theory of Society, 1500 to 1800*, Cambridge: Cambridge University Press, 1958, treats some of these problems.

Constantine in the fourth century promulgates laws which make them "compulsory tenants." They are attached to the soil, as are their children after them. If they try to flee they are treated as fugitive slaves. The law, in fact, describes the flight of a *colon* as theft, for the fugitive, in the words of the statute, "steals his own person." The State also finds it convenient to make the proprietor of the land worked by the *coloni* a tax collector, the administrator of conscription, a chief of the local police, and even the fount of justice in minor matters, certainly anticipations of the theory and practice of feudalism.

In the ancient Roman conception of *patrocinium,* too, we have foreshadowed the sociopolitical system of the ninth century. The wealthy senator or landowner would extend "protection" (economic and social) to a client in return for various services which the latter might render. And the German notion of *comitatus,* which included provision for protection, on the one hand, and for rendering of military service, on the other, has similar implications.[7]

But whatever the legal and customary roots of feudal and manorial systems—and we can at least say that they long antedate the systems themselves—it would seem clear that the conception of government involved implies lack of integration over any wide geographical area and absence, too, of what might be called the bureaucratic principle. The ideas of a uniform citizenship and of a justice administered by ostensibly impartial public bodies under rules which have been carefully developed and reconciled are obscured. In their place arises a scheme where public and private rights are confused and the law to be administered is itself a mass of inconsistencies.

This leads us directly to an examination of the nature and theory of law. Broadly speaking, it may be said that with the collapse of the Roman order, legal complexity is greatly enhanced. Roman law, to be sure, continues to remain as an important governing factor, particularly in some portions of the former Empire; but even there it is imperfectly understood and, in the several codes through which it is transmitted (for example, the Theodosian), is often affected by local practices which are difficult to reconcile with its principles. Although, contrary to some earlier scholarly belief, its formal study never wholly dies out (there is even some evidence, for example, that the ancient law school of Rome maintains at least a shadowy kind of continuous existence), men learned in its niceties become very few in number and lose their critical spirit.

But the most profound impact on the new legal order is made by the laws of the barbarians (*leges barbarorum*). The legal systems of the several Germanic tribes are often said to be *volk* law. That is to say, the rules govern the activities of tribes as such, regardless of the territory in which they may dwell. Since it is a period of great migrations, each tribe takes its law with it.

Another characteristic of volk law is that it is based almost wholly on custom. In fact, the line between custom and law is hardly drawn at all. A Lombard will carry his governing customs, law, and moral standards with him, just as he will transport his body and his physical characteristics. The customary basis of volk law is, of course, enormously significant in that it implies a new beginning of legal history itself. Roman law has passed through the early customary stages to codification and then to juristic development. Volk law returns to the beginning.

But there is yet a third kind of law, less important, it is true, than the vestiges of the Roman system and the primitive volk law, but nevertheless necessary to note. This is the legislation of the Germanic kings, who claim to inherit the prerogatives of the Roman emperor in the "making" of law. Overwhelmingly, of course, the Germanic theory is that law is discovered in custom and not imposed by an act of will. Hence we are to see Germanic royal legislative activity as peripheral and marginal, even though it should be observed in passing.

The historian of political thought will note certain important distinctions between the conceptions and assumptions behind Germanic law as contrasted with those which govern the Roman. Besides the vital contrast between the volk basis of the former as against the territorial foundation of the latter, we should mention the Germanic theory that the king is "under" the law as opposed to the Roman doctrine that the emperor is "above" it. Implicit in the customary basis of Germanic legal systems, in other words, is the view that the monarch is simply the servant of immemorial tradition which binds him as it controls his subjects. Roman legal theory, on the other hand, holds that because the Roman populus have delegated legislative power to the emperor (through the *lex regia*), he must stand above the *leges* which he creates; thus, for example, not only can he issue new *leges* but he can also remold the legal rules which have been developed as a result of juristic activity.

While the Germanic king can, as we have seen, promulgate what would correspond to the Roman *leges*, he can do so only under carefully circumscribed conditions. Almost all Germanic tribal traditions require that he consult his wise men and in some sense make sure that the members of the tribe approve; or, as the *Edictum Pistense* of 864 puts it, "*Quoniam lex consensu populi et constitutione regis fit.*"

The general effect of Germanic legal conceptions, combined with the rapid growth of feudal and manorial institutions during the ninth century, is to challenge the universalism both of the Roman legal tradition and of the conceptions of canon law as held by such Popes as Gelasius I and Gregory I.

Landeskirche Idea and the Investiture Struggle

The tendency of volk law to break up canon law is in large degree the basis for the gigantic struggle between papacy and Empire in the eleventh century. The contest is accompanied by the revival of Roman legal study, the almost contemporary revival of canonical law, the first faint reestablishment of the city as a factor in culture, and the growth of a church-reform movement which has significant political implications. The interrelation of these developments prepares the way for the civilization of the High Middle Ages and for the typical political theory discussions which accompany it. The institutional church emerges as the strongest factor in governance, but in the process its very success engenders new forms of opposition and novel ways of expressing the old.

From the viewpoint of those who see the Catholic Church as the vital factor in civilization as well as the necessary vehicle for individual salvation, the most serious attack on catholicity comes from the rise of what is known as the territorial church. Its development is intimately connected with Germanic conceptions of law and the establishment of feudal relations. As we have already noted, Germanic volk law tends to obscure the distinction between public and private right which was so carefully nurtured by the Roman system.

Now the Germanic views, in merging public and private authority and law, root both public and private rights of the person in landed property. With the possession of land goes not only its use for purposes of a livelihood but also authority in criminal, civil, and religious jurisdiction. We have observed already that the feudal lord under the system is able to establish courts, try offenses, and impose the feudal version of conscription. He does all this, not by virtue of an office to which he is appointed by an emperor or king but because he holds real property. Thus we speak of land ownership as the fount of governmental right as well as of private power.

Under this conception of things, if a nobleman or lord builds a church or establishes a monastery, he thinks of himself as their owner. He also maintains that by virtue of his ownership he can control their income, appoint and depose their priests, and, if the church is a cathedral church, choose the bishop. The Germanic king—and that Germanic ruler who, after the establishment of the Holy Roman Empire in 962, happens to be emperor—tends to regard all episcopal churches as part of his estate and hence subject to his regulation. Thus he holds that ecclesiastical prerogatives, as well as civil and criminal authority, flow from his possession of land and he challenges the canonical conception that the church as such is outside the Germanic-feudal scheme of things. Obviously, if the claims of secular rulers (including the emperor) to control ecclesiastical establishments and "invest" persons with clerical status are pressed to their logical conclusion the Church becomes but an aspect of land ownership and its ministers simply servants of the temporal power. Neither the views of Gregory I nor those of Gelasius could be reconciled with these claims, however much the former exalts the status of the king.

That Germanic rulers are prepared to press these claims to the utmost is shown particularly in the acts of emperors from the foundation of the Holy Roman Empire to the time of the Emperor Henry IV, in the eleventh century. Thus the Emperor Otto begins to prefer

7. Some see *comitatus* as the essence of feudalism.

bishops as holders of the imperial fiefs because, having no legitimate descendants, the titles of the fiefs would turn to him at the death of their holders. Hence, operating within the limits of the feudal scheme of things, he can maximize the extent of his own personal control by making certain that the hereditary principle does not limit his effective rights. He even begins to assert the power to invest laymen with clerical status in order to secure the same objective. And this policy is continued by most of his successors.

Moreover, the emperors become greatly concerned about ecclesiastical reform. By the tenth century, the Church is filled with clergymen who have violated their vows of celibacy and who may pretend, under certain conditions, to be legitimately married. To the extent that their claims to marriage are recognized, they can presumably have legitimate children. Thus, to make doubly sure that those clergy who hold fiefs can never have legitimate heirs, the emperors begin to carry on a vast campaign to make the clergy celibate in fact. And the reform party in the Church can hardly be less zealous in this respect than the emperors.

As part of the same process, the emperors also attack simony—the practice of buying clerical office—for it, too, would tend to attenuate their own political status by introducing a factor of corruption which would make clerics less amenable to imperial control. And here again, the reform party within the Church can hardly be less committed to the attack on purchase of the "gift of the Holy Spirit" than its imperial rival.

The whole imperial claim to investiture—the alleged right of the temporal ruler to install a cleric in his office—with its accompanying zeal for reformation of the clergy, is thus, from the viewpoint of the eleventh-century popes, a gigantic attempt to merge ecclesia with *imperium.* If it were to succeed completely (and by the end of the tenth century it has been successful in considerable degree), the efforts of Gelasius to establish a theoretically clear line of division between ecclesia and *imperium* would go for naught, as would the great practical efforts of popes like Gregory I to extend the prerogatives of the Roman See.

The whole future of Western Christendom thus turns on the great struggle. And the conflict itself is intensified after 1050, when the tenuous bonds which have united Western to Eastern churches are snapped. The Western Church is now free to concentrate on the serious imperial and secular challenge to its claims.

In preparing for the battle, it is not without valuable temporal and ideological assets. It has the support of many town potentates who are restive under both imperial and feudal claims. Internally, moreover, it has tightened its own organization partly under the inspiration of the Cluniac reformers (a reorganized Benedictine group) whose zeal for ecclesiastical autonomy is equalled by their intelligence.

In terms of ecclesiastical-political ideology, too, the Church is well-served. For one thing, it has what later are to be called the "forged decretals" written in the eighth century, which purport to be a genuine part of canon law and upon which the Church can base its claims not only for spiritual supremacy (which few question, in any event) but also for temporal power.

As the ideological groundwork for the struggle is laid, the internal politics of the Church undergo a transformation. Ironically enough, the changes begin when the Emperor Henry III uses his influence to elect a pope who assumes a posture of independence with reference to local Italian secular politics. Whereas the papacy had become almost a puppet of contending Roman families, it now moves to reform the method of electing the pope so that this will no longer be possible. Thus in 1059, a decree of Pope Nicholas II establishes choice of the pope by the cardinals and attempts to safeguard the procedures in such a way that temporal lords will no longer control the machinery.

By the middle of the eleventh century, then, the stage is set for the acute contest between Gregory VII and Henry IV. While up to now the Empire has often assisted the Church in its reform (although, as we have said, for its own ends), the contest toward the end of the century becomes one between a strengthened and reformed Church, on the one hand, and an Empire seeking to check the encroachments of that Church, on the other.

With the details of the actual conflict we are not concerned. How Pope Gregory VII humiliates the emperor and then deposes him in 1076 is a familiar story. It indicates that during the previous century both papacy and Church had done much to overcome those tendencies which in the first half of the tenth century had reduced the Church universal to a position of near extinction. But while we are not concerned to detail the politics of the struggle, we are directly interested in the social and political theory which emerges from it. What are the principles which seem to govern the Church? And what does it profess as the doctrine which will control it in the eventuality of ultimate political "victory"? We can see the answers to these questions best reflected in the theories of Gregory himself.

Gregory VII's Conception of Spirituals and Temporals

During the course of his controversy with Henry IV, it becomes clear that the whole investiture issue is but a convenient foundation upon which Gregory builds a doctrine of Church supremacy, even in temporals. It is equally clear that when Gregory says Church, he tends to mean pope. His opponents, who include bishops associated with the "territorial church" conception, tend to think of the church as a free association of regional churches, with the Bishop of Rome as a kind of *primus inter pares;* by contrast, Gregory sees the initiating and sustaining factor of the Church to be the papacy itself.

Gregory's views are best expressed in a letter which he writes to Bishop Hermann of Metz in 1081, just after he has himself been deposed by councils subservient to the emperor. Nothing in the letter indicates that he is depressed by his situation; indeed, his statement of ecclesiastical and papal claims seems to be made against a background of belief in his ultimate triumph.

He begins by denouncing those who assert that the Roman See has no power to excommunicate Henry or to depose him and absolve his subjects of their oaths of fealty. Men of this kind, he avers, must totally ignore all the warrants for the power of Holy Church and of its ruler, the pope. And he proceeds to list the grounds on which he asserts both the spiritual and temporal supremacy of the Church and as a consequence opposes Henry's view of investiture and of imperial prerogatives.

We may classify Gregory's considerations as Scriptural, the writings of the Fathers and the decrees of Councils, the example of the Emperor Constantine, historical precedents, and empirical observations on the nature of kings. He develops each of these in what might be called a typically medieval fashion. Certainly we are now far removed from the spirit of classical antiquity.

With reference to supporting Scriptural authority, Gregory cites the well-known passage in Matthew,[8] where Jesus is represented as telling Peter that upon this "rock" he will build his church; and Gregory interprets the "rock" as meaning Peter. Jesus furthermore goes on to assert that Peter shall have the power to "bind and loose" in earth and heaven.[9]

Scripture also shows, thinks Gregory, that kings are essentially allies of the Devil. God's Son despised a "secular kingdom, which makes the sons of this world swell with pride, and came of His own will to the priesthood of the cross." He rejected the "kingdoms of this world" when tempted by the Devil; and this surely signifies that those kings who seek to reject the authority of priests are but sons and associates of the Devil.

The writings of the Fathers and the decrees of Councils are cited by Gregory to attest to the fact that the Holy Roman Church is a divine institution before which all other churches must bow down. They have called the Roman Church "the universal mother" and have agreed "with one spirit and one voice" that "judgments over all churches ought to be referred to it as to a mother and a head; and from it there was no appeal. . . ." Here, obviously, Gregory is turning from the supremacy of Church over Empire to the clear assertion of the hegemony of the Roman Church over all other churches.

Constantine the Great is venerated throughout the Middle Ages as the great political savior of the early Church and it is not surprising, therefore, to find Gregory pointing out that that monarch, "lord of all the kings and princes of nearly the whole world," deferred to the bishops at the Council of Nicaea in 325. He addressed the bishops "as gods and decreed that they should not be subject to his judgment but that he should be dependent upon their will. . . ."

The historical references to depositions and excommunications of kings and emperors are imposing. He calls attention to the excommunication of the Emperor Arcadius by Pope

8. Matthew 16:18, 19.
9. Gregory's Letter to Bishop *Hermann* is reprinted in Doeberl, *Monumenta,* III.

Innocent I because the monarch had assented to the expulsion of St. John Chrysostom; to the deposition of a king of the Franks by Pope Zachary because the Pope thought that the king was incompetent; and to the excommunication of Theodosius by St. Ambrose.

Finally, there is a long discussion of observations which presumably all men can and do make on the actual conduct of kings. Secular rulers do not emerge with enhanced reputation from this survey, although the critic may well wonder how the pope can avoid at least mentioning similar tendencies in priests, bishops, and popes. In a passage which demonstrates his acute understanding of power, Gregory calls attention to what he holds to be the fact "that earthly glory and the cares of this world usually tempt men to pride, especially those in authority." In such situations humility is lost and the "glory" of the powerholder becomes the major end; he seeks "to lord it over" his brethren.

The antagonist of Henry IV then proceeds to judge kings and emperors by the standards of medieval piety—criteria such as those which might be exalted, for example, by Bernard of Clairvaux.[10] Powerholders can with difficulty enter into the kingdom of heaven; and those who are eventually saved attain that state only through the mercy of God.

In his diatribe against kings and emperors, it is instructive to note that Gregory includes the charge of war-making. "If the judgment of the Holy Church severely punishes a sinner for the slaying of one man, what will become of those who, for the sake of worldly glory, hand over many thousands to death?" he asks. Yet for the most part such persons seem never to regret what they have done; and in fact they rejoice "at the extension of their so-called fame." In Gregory's condemnation of war one finds almost the exact language of the fourth-century Lactantius[11] but the attitude of bitterness to secular rulers reminds one strongly of those passages in St. Augustine which clearly emphasize the sinful origin of all dominion.

It is noteworthy that at no point in the construction of his argument does the Pope refer to the Gelasian doctrine. In the heat of the eleventh-century controversy he has forgotten the rather carefully worked out formulae of the fifth-century pontiff.

In Gregory VII we see vanish that vast respect for royal authority which was the keynote of Gregory I's political attitude. It is as if the great ecclesiastical reforms of the century, the growth of religious piety, and the extension of the power of the visible church have convinced him that he should eliminate Augustine's occasional ambiguities and definitely identify purely temporal rulers with the *civitas terrena.*

The Concordat and After

The Concordat of Worms between Pope Calixtus II and the Emperor Henry V (1122), which is usually said to end the struggle about investitures, is in one sense a mere incident in the politics and political thought of empire and papacy. While under its terms the Pope emerges with the greater share of what is essentially a compromise—he now invests by "ring and staff," has all Church property restored, and leaves the conferring of the lesser "regalia" to the temporal power—this simply formalizes what has been an increasingly accomplished fact during the previous twenty years. Moreover, the triumph of the Church only sets the stage for a new series of debates whose purpose it is to clarify the exact spheres of ecclesia and temporal authority. While it is true that Gregory VII made claims which, if fully accepted, might have obviated the necessity for this battle of wits, the Gregorian assertions were put forth in the heat of battle and were not systematically related to any body of general thought.

The task of political controversialists after 1100, therefore, is to attempt more thoroughly to explore the implications of the high medieval view that Christendom is a single society governed by two autonomous universal authorities. All politically conscious men are concerned about this issue, not least of all ecclesiastical and secular rulers themselves. But much of the discussion now shifts to the universities which have just made their appearance and out of which comes some of the most vigorous thought characteristic of the twelfth and thirteenth centuries.

And within the universities, it is the systematic study of law which above all constitutes a framework for the revived interest in political theory. To the political doctrines of the lawyers, therefore, we turn in the following chapter.

chapter 12

Medieval Law and the Political Theory of the Lawyers

The High Middle Ages, once inaugurated, became an age of law and lawyers; and neither political institutions nor political theory can be understood except by reference to them. In this chapter, we examine the complexity of legal systems, the evolution of Roman and canon law in medieval institutional and intellectual development, and the political doctrine of civil (Roman) and canon lawyers. In the variety of law, we see what many have suggested is an implicit pluralistic theory of society; in the evolution of Roman and canonical systems, the major ideal would seem to be the overcoming of fissaparous tendencies in medieval life; and in the political theories of the lawyers themselves—who are in effect the Middle Ages' social scientists—we find mirrored the most important issues of social doctrine as a whole.

Pluralism and the Network of Legal Relations

The institutional life of the High Middle Ages is governed by an amazingly complex body of law, only part of which is the Roman law which began to be studied again in the eleventh century. For the most part, as a matter of fact, the network of legal relations at many points has little to do with the development of Roman and canon law, let alone the speculations of civilian and canonical thinkers.

First of all, it is extremely important to remember that feudalism and feudal law retain their strong hold on the greater segment of medieval life, despite the rise of competing systems. With them are associated many elements of ancient Germanic volk law and particularly the law of the local marketplace. The "law of the fief," as we have suggested, governs the relation between lord and vassal, whether or not land and the manorial system are involved. In some measure, this law may be said to be based on contract, since in the beginning the protection of the lord was given in return for specified services on the part of the vassal. But while a contractual basis is present historically, deliberate agreement is engulfed by custom having the force of law; and thus a man is born into a definite status, lives his life in that status, and cannot "contract" out of it.

A key aspect of the feudal and manorial systems and of their corresponding law is the position of the king during the High Middle Ages. Often medieval political thinkers will discuss kingship as if the ruler were in direct relations with his ostensible subjects; and it is a temptation of the modern mind to take these statements literally, thus assimilating the kingship to that of a modern government. But typically, the king does not deal with most of his subjects directly. Instead, he has immediate relations with only those few who are his feudal vassals. If he wishes to participate in a Crusade or attack another feudatory, he does not conscript his subjects as would a modern ruler, but calls upon his vassals—who, in turn, request the help of sub-vassals—to assist him.

Both in theory and in practice, then—within the limits of the feudal system—the king is simply a "lord of lords" rather than a direct ruler of all those who are in the kingdom; and since many of his immediate vassals compete with him in numbers of vassals and extent of land (the key to social, political, and economic relations under feudalism), they can by virtue of their power often avoid their customary and legal obligations and thus effectively limit the activities of the king. And the emperor himself is simply a great feudal lord.

Feudal relations are essentially personal. While there is a law and a custom which endeavor to transcend the emotional ties characteristic of feudal life, feeling and sentiments

Chapter 11

10. On Bernard, see Henry Daniel-Rops, *Saint Bernard et ses fils*, Paris: Mame; and the modern edition of Saint Bernard's works, *Bernard de Clairvaux*, edited by the Cistercian Abbey of Clairvaux, France, preface by Thomas Merton, Paris: Editions Alsatia, 1953.
11. See p. 176.

of personal loyalty play much more important roles than they do under the impersonal bureaucracy of the late classical Empire or of modern states. This is not to say that law and the relations of sub- and superordination are ever divorced entirely from emotion and personality but rather that they are much more directly involved in feudal than in nonfeudal situations. One has duties to a warm, sometimes cruel, sometimes erratic living person rather than to an abstraction like the state; and in turn one can expect that, for good or ill, one's lord will see one as a creature of flesh and blood rather than as a statistic or a legal category.

But very early in the Middle Ages, tendencies are present which begin to undermine the theory and practice of feudalism. We have noted how the Church struggles to secure its emancipation in order to be governed by the canon law whose principles it then seeks to extend even beyond ecclesiastical organization. This is, of course, a factor of overwhelming political significance; for it implies that theocratic conceptions of governance, seen through the eyes of jurisprudence, strive to subordinate all other legal relations and organizational schemes.

Aside from the canon law, however, other kinds of law assume considerable importance as larger and larger numbers of persons cease to be subject to feudal law. With the growth of trade and commerce, for example, the merchants, like the clergy, gradually develop their own "law merchant." For the most part, it is not enacted by any king, any more than the law of the fief. It is not even administered by any state in the usual sense of that term, but rather by associations or corporations of merchants or leagues of trading cities. From the viewpoint of political theory, this would seem to cast an interesting light on the ever-present question of the relationship between state and law. As Jenks has well put it:

> Occasionally, some special rule of the Law Merchant receives official sanction from king or *seigneur*. But, for the most part, the Law Merchant is obeyed, no one knows why. It is simply one of several authorities of different origin. . . .[1]

The "several authorities of different origin" include corporate groups of many types, each of which is regarded as generating its own law. Because there is no uniform law which theoretically applies equally to all groups, each vocational and social category tends to develop its own spirit of solidarity and standards which are both moral and legal in nature.[2]

While modern exponents of pluralism and the conception of group-generated law[3] have perhaps exaggerated the significance and extent of corporate autonomy during the Middle Ages and have sometimes romanticized the general notion, any legitimate qualification of their stress still leaves us with an institutional fact and a doctrine of enormous importance. In the absence of any state-structure as understood either by the men of A.D. 200 or those of today, human beings in quest of social solidarity and order discover law in the day-to-day economic and social relations which arise parallel to the feudal scheme of things. And this law is obeyed not primarily because it is sanctioned by threat of physical force (for this sanction is almost nonexistent in the law of corporations) but because men see the order which it embodies as an expression and condition of their social solidarity and economic relations.

At the same time, it must be admitted that a multiplicity of authorities such as is implied in corporation-generated law will lead to the probability of conflict. And that this conflict is a fact during the High Middle Ages few will deny. Hence medieval man seeks, both consciously and unconsciously, to overcome the clash of rival laws in a thrust toward greater integration. But the quest for higher and broader levels of integration in turn involves alternative political doctrines. On the plane of institutional development, kings either consciously or unconsciously seek to burst the limitations of their feudal status and, in feudal language, to make all persons in their realms their direct feudal vassals. Severely restricted in their financial resources to the customary feudal dues which they can collect and to whatever reluctantly awarded grants they can obtain from the estates of the clergy, nobility, and burgesses, they seize every opportunity to extend king-declared law as more individuals are freed from fief law.

The actual political theory connected with the idea of royal supremacy and national (as against feudal) bonds must wait for the declining Middle Ages and will be dealt with later.[4] Meanwhile, as the royal-state notion of integration remains latent in formal expression and its institutional progress relatively slow, the general discussion of what society ought to be is largely a matter for examination by those broadly educated men of the High Middle Ages, the civil and canon lawyers. They seek to give voice to that great quest for unity which, despite existential centrifugal forces, is still so central for an understanding of the medieval political outlook. Until the development of scholastic theology and philosophy, they are the most articulate political thinkers.

Roman Law, Society, and Politics

Paul Vinogradoff, the great student of medieval law, has justly remarked that "Altogether, the history of Roman Law during the Middle Ages testifies to the latent vigour and organising power of *ideas* in the midst of shifting surroundings."[5] In this section, we indicate how Roman legal scholarship developed and what general impact it had on both the practice of law and on political institutions.

The basis for the whole development was, of course, the great *corpus* of the Emperor Justinian, who reigned from 527 to 565. His legal advisers had represented to him the sad state into which the study and practice of law had fallen during the previous century. Despite the *edictum perpetuum* of the Emperor Hadrian, to which we have referred in a previous chapter,[6] juristic activity and the *leges* of emperors had by the end of the fifth century created a veritable maze of rules the understanding of which was beyond the skill of even the best lawyers. There were contradictions and ambiguities which compounded the difficulties; and courts, no less than the practitioners of law, were frequently confused as to which rule was applicable.

The Emperor appointed a commission headed by the jurist Tribonian to study the whole situation and out of the labors of this body, actively encouraged by the ruler, emerged what in medieval society and modern times alike is often referred to as the "Code." But the results constituted much more than a code. In fact, the whole *corpus* consisted of four separate and distinct parts. There was, first of all, the *Codex* proper, which organized and arranged all the imperial *leges* down to 535, when it was issued.

In addition to the *Codex*, however, Tribonian's commission edited the *Digest*, which contained well-arranged extracts from the classical jurists (men like Paul, Ulpian, Gaius, and Modestinus, to whom we have referred earlier) bearing on all the complex issues of both public and private law. Since juristic activity had been so vital in shaping Roman conceptions of law and state, it is obvious that the *Digest* was an extremely crucial aspect of the entire endeavor.[7]

The third portion of the *corpus* was called the *Institutes*.[8] This was the Tribonian Commission's contribution to legal education. In it, the law student found textbook-like discussions of problems raised by *Codex* and *Digest*, as well as elementary expositions of *leges* and juristic commentaries.

The *Codex* had included *leges* down to 535. After its publication, the Emperor continued his lawmaking activity, of course, so that before the death of Justinian the *Codex* was already out of date. Hence the *Novella*, the new laws issued since 535, constituted the last part of Justinian's creative work.

The fourfold *corpus* thus became in a sense a vast summary of the legal civilization of antiquity. Without it, much that the medieval mind eventually came to learn about the classical Empire might have been lacking. But possessing it, the reviving legal and social studies of the eleventh century found themselves with a ready foundation upon which to build.

It is significant that when the well-known law schools of the Middle Ages did make their appearance, they were often associated initially with political causes. Thus the school at Ravenna was apparently founded by partisans of Henry IV and used its Roman legal learning as a kind of propaganda weapon in behalf of the imperial interests. When the partisans of the papacy saw that the principles of the Justinian *corpus* could be used to sustain the

1. Edward Jenks, *Law and Politics in the Middle Ages*, London: John Murray, 1913, p. 30.
2. Compare Ernst Troeltsch, *The Social Teaching of the Christian Churches*, vol. 1, New York: Macmillan, 1949, pp. 248–249.
3. Writers, for example, like Otto Gierke, J. N. Figgis, and, to some extent, R. H. Tawney.
4. See Chapter 15.
5. Paul Vinogradoff, *Roman Law in Medieval Europe*, London and New York: Harper, 1909, p. 131.
6. See Chapter 7, p. 133.
7. For a modern translation of the Digest, see Charles H. Monro, *Corpus Juris Civilis: Digesta*, Cambridge: Cambridge University Press, 1904.
8. J. B. Moyle, trans., *Corpus Juris Civilis: Institutiones*, 5th ed., Oxford: Clarendon Press, 1913.

emperor, they began to wonder whether the good Christian emperor's compilation could not be used equally well against the imperial claims. Hence, under the original patronage of the Marchioness Matilda, a leading noblewoman of the time and ardent in her support of Gregory VII, the law school at Bologna was founded to counteract the influence of the Ravenna school.

This does not mean, of course, that the whole revival of legal study was politically motivated nor that it was always the pure Roman law which was studied. In some law schools, for example, both Germanic and Roman law were analyzed and efforts made to reconcile their frequent divergencies. This was notably true, for example, of the revival in Lombardy.

The economic and social context, too, should not be overlooked. The study and practice of Roman law revived at a time when the new stirrings of town life began to make their appearance, aided and abetted by the Crusades and by the slow but steady growth of trade. The ancient law had developed in a civilization of towns, cities, and commercial intercourse and was hardly suited to one of isolated villages and the absence of a money economy. While we must beware of seeing any simple cause and effect relationship between the enthusiastic study of Roman law, on the one hand, and the faint emergence of a town and commercial civilization, on the other, it is hardly to be doubted that the new law both encouraged these developments and was in some degree embraced because of them.

But we should not make the mistake of asserting that the reception of Roman law occurred everywhere at the same time nor that it did not meet vigorous opposition. As a matter of fact, it began to penetrate Germanic dominated culture in any authoritative way only in the fifteenth century. At first, it had its greatest impact on those parts of Western Christendom where the Roman tradition had had a somewhat uninterrupted although not uncorrupted existence.

And often, as in England, there was vigorous objection. Although at first the Roman law was enthusiastically studied at Oxford (in the twelfth century), there were soon many pressures against it. The Church sometimes dissented, for it was interested in pushing the integrating potentialities of canon law. Thus popes Honorius III and Innocent IV, both of them eminent canon lawyers, denounced the teaching of Roman law in Paris and "neighbouring countries."[9] But opposition from incipient nationalism was even stronger: Like German feudal lords, English kings tended to view with suspicion Roman legal and political notions.

Despite all this opposition Roman rules and conceptions made steady progress, aided as they were by social and economic developments and by the struggles of monarchs against the centrifugal forces of feudalism. In England, Bracton and Glanvil, although deeply devoted to the common law, were not uninfluenced by both the legal and the political conceptions implicit in Roman law; and even in the German territories of the Empire, the local courts were by the late fifteenth and early sixteenth century applying Roman rules—after the central Imperial Court had been instructed to use them.

Although revivalists of the eleventh century rejoiced that they were now in possession of a text which for them was near-Scripture, they could not for long ignore the fact that a *corpus* drawn up in the sixth century and embodying notions much older would need interpretation. The very words used by Justinian's compilers had often changed their common meaning; or the medieval scholars were sometimes unacquainted with their ancient signification.

Out of this situation and need rose the "gloss" and the school of medieval Roman lawyers known as the "Glossators." St. Isidore of Seville (560–636), in the period of disintegrating Roman legal study, had written a vast *Etymologies* or kind of encyclopaedia of ancient learning, including law. In the endeavor to explain legal institutions and principles, St. Isidore had laid great stress on the supposed etymology of words; but already the decline of learning had made some of his statements fantastic. Now, in the eleventh century, with several versions of the Justinian *corpus* before them, the early Glossators sought to correct the errors of men like St. Isidore and to restore the law as it was supposed to have been in ancient times. Their first task was to compare the several versions of the Justinian text and to reach agreement on a common version to be used in the schools. They endeavored to clear up inconsistencies and to restore the completeness of the legal scripture.

Then they proceeded to exercise their dialectical skill on it. Just as the theologians and canonists made deductions from Holy Scripture, so the lawyers used the Justinian *corpus* as the basis for legal deductions. First they sought through interlinear glosses to explain words and phrases, very much as students of the Bible throughout the centuries have done. But soon they found that their brief statements between the lines of the text were insufficient. Hence they turned to the margins for extended glosses or long notes. The notes might be simply explanations of words or paragraphs in the *Codex* or *Digest* but they might also endeavor to deduce how the principle should be applied in the social life of the time. From marginal glosses as isolated comments came a consecutive or running commentary on the text. The earlier or simple glosses were characteristic of great jurists like Irnerius and Bulgarus; while the later running commentaries came to be associated with the names of Azo and Accursius toward the end of the Glossatorial period in the first half of the thirteenth century. By this time, it could be said that "the law is what is contained in the gloss."

But the very strength of the Bologna school of law, to which medieval study owed so much, was also, in one sense, a weakness. While it restored the Roman law, it was in many respects far removed from the sources of living law in medieval custom. Although its logical analysis was admirable, the foundation for its reasoning was, after all, an ancient compilation which could not take account of the intricate network of customary relations that had been built up for six centuries. It was so impressed by the ancient framework as a rational construct, that it tended to minimize the notion that law is more than logic, that it must also be connected with day-to-day experience. While in the abstract, the Glossators might recognize that concrete customs could reflect a kind of reason, their basic mission was to stress deductions derived from the Justinian *corpus* alone.

But we have seen that in their declining age —toward the middle of the thirteenth century— their glosses became long commentaries on the text.

We usually say that Roman law enters another period of development after about 1250. The school of the Glossators is succeeded by the Postglossators or Commentators, the greatest of whom was perhaps Bartolus of Sassoferrato (1314–1357).[10] It was the task of the Commentators down to the end of the active juristic period (about 1400) to take account more explicitly of feudal, Germanic, and Church law and to forge connecting links between Roman law proper and these characteristic products of medieval civilization. This does not mean that Roman law was abandoned but rather that it was fitted into a yet wider framework erected through the use of the scholastic method.

Using a familiar analogy, we may compare the method of Roman legal development—and, indeed, the way in which all law grows—with that of language. It is a well-known fact, for example, that the written language of any culture tends to be different (and sometimes radically different) from that which is spoken; and that the former is much more influenced by formal grammatical, spelling, and rhetorical rules than the latter. It is in the area of spoken language that "slang" arises and that new idioms are invented. At first these developments are resisted by the grammarians and the rhetoricians; but if they persist, eventually those whose task it is to formulate the principles of the language will take account of the customary mode of speech, trying to fit its innovations into the general framework which they have developed for the preservation of language purity. The grammarians and rhetoricians are analogous to the Glossators, Commentators, and teachers of law; while the unplanned development of common or vulgar speech may be compared with the growth of that binding custom which is recognized as having the force of law.

In this whole analogy, of course, we have left out of account another factor in language and law alike: namely, the role of the conscious innovator. While both language and law in the Middle Ages (and in other periods as well) are largely shaped by the systematizers and rationalists, on the one hand, and the unplanned forces of ordinary life, on the other, the systematizers and others may deliberately introduce changes; and ordinary community life is always searching for a formal summary of its tendencies. The role of the legislator (king, emperor, creative author, jurist), in greater or lesser degree (greater in modern

9. Note Vinogradoff, *op. cit.*, p. 85.
10. See C. S. N. Woolf, *Bartolus of Sassoferato*, Cambridge: Cambridge University Press, 1913.

times than in the Middle Ages), must always be recognized. From this point of view, law and language are in some measure acts of will, rather than merely those of systematic formal summaries or of custom. Hence medieval legal scholars (and students of language), no less than their modern counterparts, are constantly debating the respective roles of reason and logic, custom, and will.

Indeed, this debate about the nature of law itself will constitute one of the most important aspects of the Roman lawyers' political theory. Although in the course of their discussions, they go far beyond this problem, in one way or another they always return to it both as a foundation and as a capstone.

Meanwhile, as the institutions and scholarship of Roman law were running through their course from 1100 to 1400, the great and often competing system of the canon law was establishing itself. And it, too, became a large factor both in the organization of medieval life and in the way men viewed the issues of political philosophy.

Canon Law, Society, and Politics

Adolf Harnack, the great historian of dogmatics, has emphasized that before the middle of the thirteenth century, the papal theory of the Church, which had come to the fore with Gregory VII, was advanced hardly at all by theology but rather by jurisprudence. "For the Curia," he observes, "only the student of law was of any account . . . the great majority of the Cardinals were well-equipped jurists, not theologians, and the greatest popes of the Middle Ages, Alexander III, Innocents III and IV, Boniface VIII, etc., came to the papal chair as highly-esteemed legal scholars."[11]

Unless we remember this, we are likely to miss an important clue to medieval social and political theory, at least down to the opening of the fourteenth century.[12] The authoritative theory of the Church in the twelfth and thirteenth centuries was shaped largely by experts in the canon law; and since the Church was claiming increasingly to direct not only spirituals but temporals this meant that the rising governing elite were largely ecclesiastical lawyers.

What later came to be known as canon law developed in its earlier stages almost imperceptibly. In earlier chapters we have seen that from the first century onward, many in the infant Christian movement had thought of the churches as a separate nation. By the second century certain writing had begun to be accepted universally by the churches (for there was yet no "Church" in the medieval sense) as authoritative; and just as the Jewish nation had developed a sacred "canon" (relatively late in its history), so the Christians, who, as we have seen, thought of themselves as the successors of the Jews, gradually recognized a "Scripture" peculiar to themselves—one which included but also went beyond the Jewish canon.

After the official recognition of Christianity, of course, ecclesiastical *leges* were freely issued by the emperors. Earlier, we quoted Constantine to the effect that what he willed was "canon"; and while many of the Fathers disputed this claim, there is little doubt that in practice the external discipline of the churches after Constantine owed much to Roman legal conceptions as well as to the specific constitutions of the emperors. And Roman imperial notions of organization and administration profoundly affected ecclesiastical organizational and administrative theory, just as Roman dress of the fifth century became fixed as the costume of the clergy. In addition to Scripture, then, canon law had as a source ancient secular law and legislation, some of it embodied in the Justinian *corpus*.

But as the idea of the Church universal grew, ecclesiastical councils came to be seen as additional sources of law. This was particularly true of the great ecumenical or universal councils like that at Nicaea in 325; but local synods or councils were not entirely excluded. By the time of Gregory I, certainly, several conciliar or synodal pronouncements had been accepted not only as bases for faith but also for discipline. Thus conciliar decrees might be regarded as a third basis for canon law.

This was particularly true of the regular clergy, or those associated with monasteries. Meanwhile, the collapse of imperial authority in the West led to the popes' exercising increasingly large powers; and their decretals came to be accepted by many if not most of the clergy as authoritative sources for Church discipline.

Then, too, as secular sources for ecclesiastical legislation disappear, the writings of the Fathers who lived from the second century to the end of the sixth (the time of Pope Gregory I) come to be looked upon by much of the Church as genuine guides for its visible organization as well as for its eternal goals. Along with decretals of the popes and decrees of councils they gain increasing respect in the confusion of the seventh, eighth, and ninth centuries.[13]

But while—as Jenks points out—the initial reaction of the barbarians to ecclesiastical organization was one of awe and general refusal to tamper with it, by the time of Charlemagne or earlier, the Frankish rulers begin to issue "Capitularies" regulating ecclesiastical matters. At first, apparently, the Church does not object, for the decrees are generally favorable to the claims of the bishops; but even at this time, there are undoubtedly many ecclesiastics who look with suspicion upon the pretensions of the new Caesar. After the collapse of the Carolingian Empire, of course, the development of feudal institutions and the growth of the territorial church conception increasingly subject churches to the conditions of feudal control and begin to precipitate the demand for radical reform, as we noted in the last chapter.

Up to this point (roughly the middle of the ninth century), the various elements which went to make up canon law had not been codified or arranged in any systematic way. True, there was the Dionysian collection of conciliar decrees, but this was four centuries old and embraced, moreover, only a part of what the ecclesiastical reformers regarded as canon law. The reformers' version of that law awaited a Justinian who could reconcile inconsistencies and establish a platform upon which the church-political reformers could stand. Although the ninth century did not produce such a legislator, it did give birth to what were later to be called the "Pseudo-Isidorean" Decretals and these in turn were to constitute significant elements in the development of canonical ideology.

The False or Pseudo-Isidorean Decretals play an important role in the controversies of the eleventh century and provide a rallying point for all those who sustain the papal ecclesiastical point of view. Part of a larger collection that embraced many genuine papal decrees, the False Decretals include among other forgeries—and the forgeries are accepted as genuine during the early Middle Ages—the so-called Donation of Constantine which was itself originally a product of the eighth century. In the Donation, the Emperor Constantine I purportedly gave temporal authority over much of the West to Pope Sylvester I, who then passed it on to his successors in the papacy. Obviously, documents of this type tend to support papalist and many canonical arguments, furnishing ingredients both for codification and for ideology. They represent one of the most famous examples of that tendency in both religious and political literature to ascribe authorship of documents which the apologist hopes to be authoritative to well-known literary or historical figures (in this instance, to men like Constantine and St. Isidore of Seville). We have already noted such possible false attribution in the case of Deuteronomy[14] and in other instances.

By the end of the Investiture controversy early in the twelfth century, the age is ripe for an initial grand summary of the elements which by now go to make up the canon law. This is undertaken by Gratianus who about 1145 publishes his systematization of canon law (including scriptural, conciliar, imperial, decretal, patristic, and "false" decretal sources). Soon given a short title as the *Decretum Gratiani,* this becomes the fundamental basis of all canonical speculation in subsequent centuries, although it is supplemented from time to time by other collections—that of Gregory IX, for example, in 1234. As canon law becomes defined with increasing exactitude, its scholars and practitioners make greater and greater claims for it. Originally designed to be a body of rules governing the Church and ecclesiastical persons, its more extreme exponents eventually argue that it sums up all knowledge. Thus Cardinal Hostiensis of Ostia argues in the thirteenth century that "If canon law is well known and understood, the mastery of all spiritual and temporal matters is assured." And he goes on to contend that it includes everything that might bear on the governance of man, whether ecclesiastical or not.

Obviously such conceptions make of law, and particularly of canon law, something much

11. Adolf Harnack, *History of Dogma,* New York: Russell and Russell, 1958, VI, 128.
12. For a useful and relatively brief discussion of the relation of Roman to Canon Law, see H. D. Hazeltine, "Roman and Canon Law in the Middle Ages," *The Cambridge Medieval History,* 8 vols., Cambridge, 1915–1938, vol. 5, pp. 697–762.
13. Jenks, *op. cit.,* pp. 26–27.
14. See Chapter 1, p. 17.

broader than that which we associate with the term today. It becomes more nearly analogous to a combination of social science and law (in the way that word is understood in the twentieth century). Many of the canonists, for example, seem to equate law with knowledge or learning (*sapientia*) and science (*scientia*) in general. Thus they classify all learning into three branches. There is *civilis sapientia*, or civil learning, which embraces Roman and natural law and the *ius gentium*, together with economics (*iconomica*) and political science (*politica scientia*). The second division, *theologica scientia*, embraces the laws which underlie all civil learning (presumably basic assumptions), prophecy, Jewish law, and the gospel and apostolic writings. *Canonica scientia* is a kind of synthesis of civil and theological learning and science. It sees both of them in the light of a higher wisdom, which, while comprehending all they can teach, unifies them in a whole which is more than the sum total of its parts.[15]

Claims of this kind did not endear the canon lawyers to either civil lawyers or the theologians (who by the last half of the thirteenth century were beginning to come to the fore). Yet there can be no question that canon law assumptions and reasoning control the machinery of the Church as a whole during the twelfth and thirteenth centuries. To such an extent is this true that the popes of the time (many of them eminent canon lawyers themselves) begin to restrict the extent to which the clergy may even study the inferior civil learning. Thus Alexander III prohibits monks from leaving their cloisters to attend scientific and Roman law lectures; and in 1219, Pope Honorius extends the decree to embrace all "beneficed clerks."[16]

But whatever the jealousies and animosities between the two systems of law and the two sets of lawyers, they share a common world outlook, to which, before examining more closely their political doctrines, we now turn. It is a general view, we might add, that tends to be accepted by all medieval men, whether lawyers or not.

The General View

There are various ways of expressing the world outlook of medieval thinkers but here let us note its Christianity, universalism, dualistic ethic, and high view of law.

Christianity. By Christianity, we mean that the medieval mind, both general and legal, conceived of society as animated by Christian beliefs and ethical principles. Orthodox religion as contained in Scripture and interpreted by the Fathers, general councils, and the Church, is held to be mandatory on all those living in Christendom (except, of course, the Jews). Christianity as thus conceived is the common platform, so to speak, upon which stand lawyers, legislators, judges, priests, and emperors; or to change the figure, the point of departure for all discussions of law, politics, economics, and morals.

But Christianity also means something even more explicit. It implies that all non-Jews are automatically members of a visible Church and that the Sacraments administered by that Church are somehow essential for salvation. As we noted earlier,[17] there was a conflict within the mind of Augustine between the notion of the Church as an invisible society of the predestined elect and the conception of a visible *ecclesia* as somehow essential for salvation. During the High Middle Ages, this doubt—at least for most men, including the lawyers—is resolved in favor of the visible hierarchical organization. This does not mean that the invisible Church is ignored but simply that the center of attention is directed to the activities of the by now greatly strengthened visible organization.

It is this organization through which the seven sacraments are administered: baptism, confirmation, the eucharist, penance, extreme unction, priestly ordination, and marriage. If, either through deliberation or by accident, these sacraments are not available, the medieval Catholic is disturbed, to say the least. And while the exact import of each sacrament is debated by scholastic theologians, good Christians are agreed as to the significance of the seven and as to the notion that their administration should be regulated by the Church. It is this general acceptance of the sacraments as vital, combined with the equally universal agreement that they are to be administered under Church auspices, which provides the Church with a weapon of enormous political importance. For by making the sacraments unavailable—through excommunication or the "interdict"—it can cow even powerful princes into submission.

Universalism. By the universalism of the High Middle Ages, we mean the generally accepted view that society and civilization are fundamentally one, despite feudal class gradations, conflicts between town and country, and latent national ideas. This, of course, is a basically Stoic and Christian position.

But although the society is fundamentally united, it is shaped toward its ends by two authorities, one having charge of "temporal" or earthly interests, the other presiding over the eternal fate of the soul. In principle, the apex of temporal authority is in the Holy Roman Empire, all other jurisdictions ranking below it. The medieval empire, which is conceived to be the successor of the classical Roman Empire by way of Charlemagne (crowned emporer by the pope in 800) and Otto (installed by the pope in 962), waxes and wanes in power and influence. But whatever its acceptance in everyday affairs—it is weakened by feudal fissiparousness, widespread warfare, and rejection of it in practice by many holders of temporal power—it remains for both canonists and civilians the embodiment of the idea of temporal universality. Ideologically, Christendom remains one on its temporal side.

The eternal fate of the soul is, of course, under the care of the universal Church. During the twelfth and thirteenth centuries it is much better grounded in the everyday experience of men—and much better organized—than the Empire. Its universalism is far less attenuated than that of the ostensible ecumenical temporal authority; and while many of its branches are interwoven with and affected by feudal institutions, it is always vigorously seeking to transcend this involvement. In one sense, it represents the bureaucratic idea of organization against the decentralist, feudalistic principle.

The fundamental problem of the dualism in this conception of authority arises when one attempts to define the respective spheres of temporal versus spiritual rule. This is not an issue peculiar to medieval lawyers and political philosophers, of course, but is inherent in any conception that thinks of man as having goals which in some measure escape confinement to ends in time and space. What is or should be the relation between the time-bound and the timeless in human society?

The notion, then, of a single society governed by two cooperating authorities, while accepted by both canon and civil law and, indeed, by the medieval mind generally, bristles with difficulties when we have to define more exactly the spheres of those authorities. For the spiritual authority can with some plausibility claim that all temporal aspects of the soul-body affect, however indirectly, its possibility of eternal salvation; while the temporal governor can often with equal justification contend that the spiritual state of a man will profoundly affect his ability and willingness to fulfill civic, legal, and political obligations.

But there is yet another difficulty in the single-society–two-authorities formula. It is all very well to construct one's speculations as if society and civilization were fundamentally one, both horizontally and vertically. But what is one to do about the fact of sharp divisions, which literally make the world of the serf quite different in many if not most respects from that of the pope? How is one to treat slavery or serfdom in light of the fundamental Christian premise of equality?

Dualistic Ethic. Always in the background, too, in any medieval discussion touching on law and politics, is the assumption, rarely questioned, that life in the world of politics, war, and the general economy is morally inferior to the withdrawn existence of the cloister. The history of the dualistic ethic is a long one and at several points we have touched on its genesis and development. There is the contrast, in the New Testament, between life according to the commands of the law and life which would be perfect; thus the rich young ruler, praised by Jesus because he has faithfully observed the law, is yet dissatisfied and is told that if he would be perfect he must sell all his goods and give the proceeds to the poor.[18] There is the frequent tendency in Augustine to equate political life with the *civitas terrena*, even though his view as a whole would not do so. There is the obvious conflict between a Gospel ethic which appears to forbid war and bloodshed and a feudal world in which war and bloodshed are almost endemic and yet to some extent justified by the prevalent view. The medieval conscience wrestles with such questions and comes to the conclusion that there are two standards. The first is a kind of minimum morality appropriate for the competitive and power relations of social, eco-

15. For a discussion of the extreme claims of canonists like Hostiensis, see Walter Ullmann, *Medieval Papalism*. London: Methuen, 1949.
16. Jenks, *op. cit.*, 29.
17. See Chapter 10.
18. See Matthew 19:16–22.

nomic, and political life; the second is the "more perfect" or higher morality of a life lived in the monastery according to the alleged Gospel precepts of poverty, nonaggression and nonresistance, renunciation of marriage (for did not Jesus suggest that some would be "eunuchs" for his sake?).[19]

The first or minimum ethic represents medieval Christian civilization's concession to the world which it had originally scorned but which it now feels it must accept, for original sin has so discolored man's original nature that most men are not capable of conforming to a first-order morality. Hence their wars must be limited by the "Peace of God"; but it is impossible to abolish military conflict. Their economic operations must be governed through prohibition of usury,[20] restriction of advertising, establishment of social control of wages and of avarice; but because of sin, pure communism can never be attained in the general society.

In other terms, man's interdependence both vertically (back to Adam) and horizontally (with all other men living at a given time) means that however innocent an individual may be in the beginning, he is born into a context weighted down by all mankind's sins of the past and by the fact of his contemporaries' offenses. He must act within this context and the choices placed before him are those made inevitable by his organic interdependence with others. The choices are limited; in selecting between alternatives, morally perfect courses are never available. In his very choosings, then, the individual is tainted by corporate sin. While temporal rulers can, to be sure, restrain some of the more egregious egoistic actions of others, they are themselves strictly limited by man's original sin in what they can do. Indeed, their very efforts to restrain unrighteousness will themselves take on some of the characteristics of injustice, as when lords, endeavoring to restrict the violence of others, hope to gain booty for their own coffers. Or again, although rulers have an obligation to regulate economic life for the good of all—particularly in an economy of unusually limited resources—the measures which they take to achieve this objective often have a tendency, however incidentally, to benefit the special interests of the governors. The problems placed before us as political beings have been produced by countless generations of sinful men; our efforts to respond to those problems, while essential, will create yet new dilemmas for mankind. By God's design, political institutions help correct the sin out of which the institutions arise; but since the chief of the seven deadly sins, pride, is always present in the very act of carrying out the restraint, institutions and rulers contribute to future occasions for sinning.

By contrast, the higher-level ethic seeks to approximate conditions which Augustine ascribes to the human situation before the Fall. The life of the monastery is satisfied with no minimum morality but aspires to the perfection reflected in common ownership and use of goods, celibacy, complete obedience to the will of God, and abstention from outward fighting and bloodshed. Only a comparatively small number might expect to live according to counsels of perfection, by withdrawing from such entanglements of the general society as marriage. While life in the world, according to the Augustine-like aspect of medieval thought, is relatively justified, the withdrawn existence is still better.

In one sense it is the spirit of monasticism which triumphs in the Church after the time of Pope Gregory VII. It is the impetus given by asceticism that helps initiate and sustain the ecclesiastical reforms of the eleventh century; and the renunciation of the world which it implies comes to mean rejection of all relations not strictly governed by the Church. As Harnack has put it so well, "Abandonment of the world in the service of the world-ruling Church, dominion over the world in the service of renunciation of the world,—this was the problem and the ideal of the Middle Ages!"[21]

We should always remind ourselves, of course, that while this is a central tendency in medieval thought as a whole, the degree and implications of its impact vary widely. Civilians will differ from canonists in many respects, and the revival of Aristotle will seriously modify details and even serve to cast doubt on certain basic aspects of the view.

The Ubiquity of Law. The High Middle Ages are an epoch in which the notion of a lawful universe dominates not only canon and civil lawyers but the entire civilization. The word "law" itself is used in many different contexts and sometimes writers are not too clear as to exactly how it is being employed. Broadly speaking, it is a term which may be either descriptive or prescriptive. Thus, it may describe a principle which is in fact working in the universe as we immediately experience it, as when we speak of the law of sin operating within human beings; or it may suggest a standard of attainment which is presumably binding in pure nature but which is not yet or perhaps cannot be achieved existentially. Law is used to describe the regularities of physiological and physical processes and it is also employed to prescribe ethical standards.

But when we make this distinction between description and prescription, it is a rather artificial one from the viewpoint of the medieval thinker. For to him, all law tends to be discovered and the distinction between description and prescription fades: one discovers both the *is* and the *ought* by examining an objective universe of "fact" and "value." Even when the king makes a law, he is essentially declaring it and not imposing it as a sheer act of arbitrary will. It is obvious that this is true of the Germanic view, in which courts and kings look to custom and tradition as the source of positive law; and it is significant, for example, that the English parliamentary estates are called "the High Court of Parliament."[22] In Roman and canon law too—despite deceptive appearances to the contrary—it would seem that most thinkers conceive of law as at least primarily discovery. The Roman lawyers theoretically discover their law in the Code and in the jurists and the canon lawyers theirs in such sources as decretals and conciliar decrees.

This widespread consciousness of law and the parallel notion that law is discovered rather than made are, of course, closely connected with the acute religious consciousness of twelfth and thirteenth centuries. Religion shapes the legal awareness just as jurisprudence tends often to provide the categories within which religion is discussed. While in his ultimate reaches God is no doubt inscrutable, to the human mind he can be sufficiently understood through his many manifestations in law to give him a kind of reality not vouchsafed to modern man.

The Nature and Types of Law

There are several terms, which, while differently defined by given civil and canon lawyers, play an important role in the discussion of the nature of law. One is *aequitas*, another *justitia*, and the third *jus*. If we are to generalize about the three, we can say that on the whole, medieval students of law think of the first as ultimate good. Some suggest that it is identical with God. Some tend to equate *aequitas* with *justitia*, while others associate *justitia* with will. The relation between *aequitas* and *justitia*, would seem to be analogous to that which Plato discerns between the "rational" and the "spirited" aspects of the soul.

As for *jus*, or law, it represents an attempt to translate *justitia* into the concrete conditions of human existence. Both civilians and canonists agree with this fundamental proposition, although they will differ as to the specific contents of *jus* and the exact way in which *jus* may be analyzed.

From the Justinian Code and the Roman law tradition generally, the medievalists tend to inherit and accept a tripartite division of *jus* into *jus naturale*, *jus gentium*, and *jus civile*. To them the Middle Ages add *jus canonicum*.

Jus Naturale—Natural Law. The Middle Ages are above all the centuries of natural law theory; it is particularly important, therefore, that we note the ways in which the civilians and canonists try to define it.

1. The Civilian View. Earlier we have noted that the ancient Roman jurist Ulpian associated *natura* with instinct.[23] The dictates of natural law are, then, according to this view, those which come to us through the primitive urges.

On the whole, the civilian thinkers never accept association of *natura* wholly with the primitive. Nature is not, in other words, simply that which drives man in certain directions. Rather is it an *ordo* in which rationally derived principles govern; and its law is, therefore, that body of generalizations derived from a study of all the attributes—both instinctive and ideal—characteristic of man. This would appear to mean that natural law embraces both the principles which seem to be implicit in instinct and those which can be derived by assuming that man must and can control and order his instincts in accordance with principles which transcend the instinctual. This

19. See Matthew 19:16–22.
20. See Benjamin Nelson, *The Idea of Usury from Tribal Brotherhood to Universal Otherhood*, Princeton: Princeton University Press, 1949.
21. Harnack, *op. cit.*, VI, 6.
22. See C. H. McIlwain, *The High Court of Parliament*, New Haven: Yale University Press, 1910.
23. See p. 133.

certainly seems to be in part the meaning of Azo, one of the greatest civilian thinkers of the time.[24]

The extent of the civilians' consensus on the meaning of natural law may be indicated when we suggest that they all accept the notion of natural law as a body of moral norms which is everywhere held by human reason to be binding. They also contend that it is unchangeable and cannot be supplanted by any other *jus*. Generally speaking, too, the civilians hold that any positive law (presumably including canon law) clearly in violation of natural law is void. And some of the civilians specifically contend that prescripts of the emperor issued in violation of civil law are void on the ground that one of the principles of natural law is that the ruler must observe the general human law which has been promulgated.

2. The Canonical Position. In general, the canonical discussion of natural law is more complex and subtle than that of the civilians. There is somewhat greater specificity and agreement among canonical writers and also a greater awareness of the difficulties of natural law thinking.

Gratian, of course, is the great point of departure for canonical thinking. He seems to equate divine law—that which is found in the Jewish law and the Gospels—with natural law, as do most of the canonists who follow him. Both natural law and divine law tell us, for example, that we should do to others what we would have them do to us. This is, indeed, the central statement of the Gospels as it is of natural law. What is left ambiguous in Gratian's discussion, however, is the exact relation between the authority of reason and that of divine law. Do we accept the Gospels, for example, because they embody a rational principle or simply because God ordained that we accept them?

Meanwhile, such canonists as Rufinus and Stephen of Tournai, building upon Gratian, think of natural law as containing three kinds of statements. First of all, it has injunctions, such as that we should love one another; secondly, it embraces prohibitions, such as the universal command not to kill; and thirdly, it includes what are usually termed *demonstrationes,* or admonitions, which are usually thought of as axioms of expediency—that, for example, we ought to enhance human liberty and to hold material things in common.[25] The exact relationship between and among the injunctions, prohibitions, and expediential counsels is, of course, a matter for much debate by those concerned with drawing out the implications of natural law doctrine.

One great difficulty arises out of the great canonical treatment of natural law. It has to do with the widespread acceptance of the position that the *jus naturale* is to be found both in the Old Testament law and in the Gospels.

The question might be put in this way. There are many ordinances of the Old Testament which are not followed by good Christians and all Christendom is told that these ordinances need not be obeyed. Animal sacrifices, for example, are clearly commands of the Old Testament but not of positive law in the twelfth century. Does this mean, therefore, asks Gratian, that good Christians are violating natural law in their positive law (which includes canon law)? Obviously not, he answers. The reason is that while *jus naturale* is to be found in the Hebrew law and the Gospels, Scripture includes *more* than natural law. All natural law, in other words, is in Scripture, but not all Scripture is natural law. Here Gratian (and canonists in general) draw a careful distinction between the external observances required by Scripture and the inner or moral law of which it gives a complete account. The former Gratian identifies as *mistica,* which may be appropriate to a certain stage of human development but inappropriate at another. Here some of the canonists seem to approach a doctrine of legal and social evolution: at a particular stage in the evolution of the *mores,* in other words, the external command to prepare food only through "kosher" methods may best symbolize and dramatize an inner moral truth. But the moral truth is not to be equated with its externalization: the former is immutable while the latter is changeable, depending upon such factors as the level of understanding present within a given people and their particular material achievements.

Another canonical question asks whether any parts of natural law, which in principle is held to be immutable, can ever be suspended.

In the discussion of this problem, canon lawyers, including the great lawyer-popes, show great ingenuity in their casuistry. With respect to the Gospels, for example, Pope Innocent IV (whose pontificate extends from 1243 to 1254) asserts that the successor of Peter has the authority to suspend the letter, although not the spirit. All the teachings of Christ contained in the parables are included within this dispensing power; but the injunctions and prohibitions—for example, the command to love one's neighbor and the principle which forbids divorce—are exempt.

The extreme canonists, too, like Alexander III (pontificate 1159–1181), Innocent III (pontificate 1198–1216), and Innocent IV tend to assert that the pope has the right to suspend the natural law contained in the Pauline Epistles, except those "apostolic ordinances" defined as articles of faith. And if one asks who defines articles of faith the answer is the pope himself. Canon lawyers who defend this particular dispensing power in connection with the epistles tend to uphold it by contending that the pope is above St. Paul, since he is the successor of St. Peter who is the Christ-ordained Prince of the Apostles.

It is often difficult, of course, to distinguish between an interpretation by the pope of natural law and a suspension of the law itself. Thus many medieval heretics refuse to take oaths, on the ground that the Gospel and natural law forbid them.[26] But Pope Innocent III, in arguing against such heretics as the Waldensians, maintains that the Gospel passage is not a prohibition of oaths themselves; for it only bars those oaths which forbid one to swear by heaven, earth, Jerusalem, or the human head. Nowhere does it say that one shall not swear by "God." Hence oaths taken in the name of God are not a violation of natural law.

The whole problem of applying natural law principles to given situations will always involve casuistry, of course; for no principle is ever so clear and unambiguous as to make its implementation an exact matter. Even such Gospel (and Mosaic) principles as the prohibition of killing, which would seem on the surface to be so transparently definite, can, and do, give rise to vast debates when the issue of applicability arises. Why, for example, do human institutions permit killing in war? The answer of the great Fathers of the third and fourth centuries is, as we have seen, that there is no Christian distinction between killing in war and slaying a private person. But the medievalists attempt to make such a differentiation through the doctrine of the "just war" and thus to make the exact meaning of the natural law principle much more complicated.

Jus Gentium—The Law of Nations or Peoples. Originally, the distinction between *jus civile* and *jus gentium* developed, it will be remembered,[27] in order to differentiate the body of traditional Roman law from the law,

administered by the *praetor peregrinus*, which governed relations between and among the diverse peoples within the Empire. During the Middle Ages, this remains the basic dividing line between the two, except that *jus civile* is not thought of as Roman law but the particular positive law of any entity as contrasted with the positive law common to all mankind (*jus gentium*). Both *jus civile*, in other words, and *jus gentium* are positive law or, as many jurists put it, customary law.

But a few peculiar twists are given to the notion of *jus gentium*—interpretations due largely to Christian mythology. Several of the canon lawyers,[28] for example, seeking to distinguish between *jus naturale* and *jus gentium* (which often tend naturally to be equated in some thinkers), think of the former as having existed from the beginning of rational beings. *Jus gentium*, by contrast, arose at the time when men began to live with one another in more or less formally organized societies.

In the effort to recreate what medieval lawyers, both civil and canon, thought about the relations between and among *jus naturale*, *jus gentium*, and *jus civile*, we may suggest that they see a continuum of increasing specificity from general principles which express eternal norms to specific regulations appropriate for a given time, place, and culture. Thus it is a principle of human nature that men and women are attracted to one another—it is natural for them to live together in close physical, intellectual, and spiritual communion (*jus naturale*). This universal principle, then, is reflected in the similarly universal institution of marriage (*jus gentium*). This does not mean that this institution is exhibited in identical ways at all times and in all places but simply that all peoples have marriage institutions of some kind which may be held to mirror the search for an ideal as well as be considered an expression of primitive nature.

24. In his *Commentaries* on the *Institutes* of Justinian.
25. In addition to Rufinus and Stephen of Tournai, this tripartite division is accepted by such canonists as Huguccio and Johannes Faventinus.
26. Matthew 5:34–36.
27. See Chapter 8.
28. Gratian, for example, and Rufinus.

Finally, the diversity of external rites, customs, and beliefs about the marriage institution is almost legion (*jus civile*). Here again the medieval civilians and canonists tend to make the same distinction between externals and inner or moral principles which we have seen earlier in another connection.[29]

From one point of view, the *jus-naturale–jus-gentium–jus-civile* link may be thought of as disembodied universal principles giving birth to embodied universal customs, which in turn constitute a common basis for a wide diversity of practices and specific regulations.

The Conception of Jus Civile. Both civilians and canonists think of *jus civile* as that which binds a particular society, as contrasted with the *jus* which is common to all mankind. And the key terms used by all lawyers in analyzing *jus civile* are *mos* (or *consuetudo*) and *lex*. The former is unwritten custom while the latter is, on the whole, law which is written.

It is the relation between *consuetudo* and *lex* which chiefly exercises the ingenuity of men like the civilians Azo and Irnerius and the canonists Gratian and Rufinus. On the whole, there is widespread agreement that *consuetudo* is the original law and that *lex*, in its various forms, comes much later in the history of legal evolution. *Lex* itself, however, is employed in a variety of ways. Some lawyers identify it with the "decree" of the Roman populus (its narrow meaning). But others (both civilians and canonists) give all written statements of law the status of *lex*, thus embracing the *edictum*, the *constitutio* (constitution) of the Roman Emperor, and the *statutum* of the populus.

What is astonishing to the modern mind, accustomed as it is to thinking of law as manufactured or made, is the medieval conviction that by and large it is custom which is the key factor. Thus Azo, the civilian, goes so far as to say that *consuetudo* "creates, abrogates, and interprets" law. (*Et quidem videtur quod consuetudo sit conditrix legis, abrogatrix et interpretatrix.*)[30] And Gratian, the canonist, while not without his ambiguities, maintains that even where a formal "law declaring" authority exists (a prince, for example, or an emperor), his *leges* must be confirmed by *consuetudo* or may be rendered void by it.

Of course, we must remember that in saying this all canonists and civilians assume that custom contrary to *jus naturale* is void. And we must also be ever mindful of the fact that, in the thirteenth century, the assertion of papal "dispensing" power (with respect to natural law) grows. As medieval papalism waxes, both in theory and in practice, we can expect some of the popes to limit the large role assigned to custom. Thus Pope Gregory IX, just before the middle of the thirteenth century, maintains that custom cannot override *leges* unless it is "reasonable" and has existed over a considerable period of time.[31]

The Conception of Canon Law. The problem of canon law is peculiar to the Middle Ages; for although the emperors after Constantine had clearly given much of the ecclesiastical law the force of *jus civile* and this had been recognized in the Justinian *corpus*, the issue in medieval political thinking is whether or to what degree the canon law has an independent binding effect. No one denies that in purely ecclesiastical affairs the Church possesses law which binds all Christians. But what are "purely ecclesiastical affairs" and what is the exact relation of canon law to *jus civile?*

1. Views of the Civilians. On questions of this kind the civilian lawyers seem to be fairly united. With respect to the superiority of that aspect of canon law embodied in Scripture, for example, all the civilians maintain that it takes precedence over civil law. The ambiguity is, of course, whether the Scriptures are to be regarded as *jus naturale* and divine law or whether, in a certain sense (as the canonists argue) they also take on the character of that positive branch of law known as canon law.

But what of other sources of canon law? There would seem to be unanimity that the decrees of the first four ecumenical councils of the Church are *jus* both in its civil and in its canonical sense. But it should be remembered that these decrees were given the force of law by Justinian and hence are accepted by the civilians by virtue of the declaration of the emperor. They do not possess the status of *jus* in the civil sphere, presumably, independently of the emperor's authority.

2. The Canonists View Canon Law. The canonists' treatment of the subject is, of course, much more prolix than that of the civilians and, on the whole, they are concerned to show that the law of the Church is a body of rules having an authority equal to that of civil law. It is, in fact, at the level of civil law; for just as the latter is subordinate to natural and divine law, so is canon law. And earlier we have seen that the tendency of the canonists, and particularly of Gratian, is to identify divine with natural law.

But canon law itself is arranged in a hierarchy ranging from those parts which are generally held to be immutable to those subject to change. Insofar, for example, as the canons are to be found in the teaching of the Gospels, they are unchangeable; and anything in later canonical rules contradicting the "evangelical" precepts will be void. So, too, the canonists hold that "apostolic" canons—those found in St. Paul, for example—are generally immutable; although we should remember our earlier statement that the Pope is held to have the power under certain restricted circumstances to dispense from observance of apostolic statements on the ground that the authority of the successor of St. Peter is higher than that of St. Paul.

One cannot help being impressed by the efforts of the canonists to distinguish between what they regard as fundamental canon law and what, by contrast, they think of as secondary or derivative. In the former category, as a rule, will be the Gospels, apostolic teaching, and the decrees of the Four Councils; in the latter the decretals, decrees of other general councils which are not definitions of faith, and, presumably, the writings of the Fathers.

In the whole discussion, of course, the role of *mos* or *consuetudo* cannot be ignored, for like both canon and civil lawyers with respect to the *jus civile*, so the canon lawyers in viewing canon law give a large role to tradition. They even maintain that tradition and custom may overrule what we have called secondary canon law, although as has been observed elsewhere,[32] Gregory IX in the thirteenth century contends that custom can abrogate decretals or other secondary canon law only when it is reasonable and when it has persisted over a long period of time.

Another question which exercises the canonists is the problem of priority with respect to papal constitutions themselves. Here the answer of Damasus, and apparently that of most of the other canonists as well, is that in the event of conflict the older constitution takes precedence, apparently because it is closer to apostolic times and often has the virtue of simplicity.

By and large, the canonists tend to make the authority of the pope equal to that of a council. The decrees of councils must be approved by the pope and independently of the council he can issue decretals having the force of law. Indeed, some of the canonists begin to assert quite flatly that even the older councils derived their authority from the Roman Church

and hence conclude that the pope, as Bishop of Rome, stands above the council. But this position is not widespread in the twelfth and thirteenth centuries.

Because canon law regulation of what later generations were to think of as secular is so unique a feature of the Middle Ages, there has been a tendency to hold that medieval speculators and particularly canon lawyers must be perfectly clear in their own minds as to the theory of the law itself. But any close study of the subject leaves one with the impression that there are considerable divergencies among thinkers and that within any one exposition the ambiguities are usually of considerable significance. "Nothing, indeed, has been, from the strictly historical point of view," the Carlyles write, "more mischievous than the notion that the Middle Ages had a clear-cut and precise notion of the nature and authority of canon law."[33] This will become even clearer when we turn later on to the theory of spirituals and temporals.

Political Authority and Political Institutions

When medieval jurists, whether civilian or canonical, come to examine the nature and function of political authority and institutions, they build, as elsewhere, on two sometimes divergent traditions—the legal and the patristic. In ancient times, of course, the legal tradition was shaped in part by Stoicism, even though we should never assume that the Stoic element was predominant. As for the patristic attitude, we have, in dealing with St. Augustine, suggested some of its main positions, particularly those which place great emphasis on the Fall of Man.

Political Authority. With respect to the nature and justification of political authority, the main line of divergence between civilians and canonists would appear to be that whereas the former tend to build their doctrine within

29. See p. 216.
30. *Summa Codicis*, VIII, 53, 6.
31. See the discussion in R. W. Carlyle and A. J. Carlyle, *Medieval Political Theory in the West*, vol. 2, Edinburgh and London: Blackwood, 1936, p. 150.
32. See p. 218.
33. Carlyle and Carlyle, *op. cit.*, p. 160.

the framework of the Justinian *corpus*, the latter follow the Fathers, or at least some of them.

1. The Civilian Debate. The civilians make their point of departure the relation between the emperor and the populus. According to Roman theory the ruler is the delegate or "vicar" of the people who originally possessed the sole political authority in the community. With the foundation of the principate, however, the populus is held to have transferred its authority to the imperator. All civilians are in agreement up to this point.

Beyond this, however, there is disagreement. One group of civilians maintains that the populus transferred its power completely while the other argues that it only partially gave up its authority.[34] To the former, the people have engaged in an irreversible process and cannot retrieve the authority which they have delegated; and they cannot even act unconsciously and implicitly through custom to restrict it. The second interpretation, by contrast, holds that the populus cannot be held to have passed authority to the emperor without reservation, for, it maintains, there is no way of transferring authority to make mores. Therefore the authority of the emperor—and presumably of kings and political authority generally—is a contingent one which must necessarily always be exercised within the severe limitations of *consuetudo*.

It is important to remember that no civilian exempts the emperor (and presumably other rulers as well) from the control of *jus naturale* or *jus divinum*. Thus while for many civilians the people can no longer exercise their authority, even through custom, their ruler as well as they are fully subject to natural and divine law; and for many civilians, the ruler stands limited both by the divine and natural law above him and by long-standing custom below.

2. Canonical Doctrine. In the previous chapter, we cited the famous letter from Pope Gregory VII to Bishop Hermann of Metz, in which the Pope denigrates in very extreme form all secular authority. If the canonists are to follow Gregory, they can hardly have a very exalted estimate of secular authority. Yet at the very height of the High Middle Ages, Pope Innocent III, himself one of the greatest of the canonists, indites a letter[35] in which he claims that God himself has established two great "luminaries" or dignities—the "pontifical" authority and the "regal" power. On the one hand, in other words, Gregory VII makes political authority as black as it has ever been painted—some passages of his letter, as a matter of fact, might well have been written by a modern anarchist. On the other hand, Innocent III, about a century later, makes the royal and imperial authority God-ordained. We might well ask ourselves the question, Do the two Popes contradict each other or is there some way of reconciling their positions?

The answer to this question will give us the general canonical view of political authority. It is a position built generally on that of Augustine and continuing in the tradition of Pope Gelasius I. The canonists, unlike the civilians, are not primarily interested in the Roman theory of political authority but seek to discover both its roots and its fruits in the general experience of man. To them, there is little question that man's dominion over man is one expression of that sin which came into the world with Adam's Fall. Subjection of men to the rule of others was not characteristic of Eden. As Gratian puts it, at the Creation but before the Fall, man was under the direct control of *jus naturale*. With the Fall, however, men came together in formal organization and with formal organization arises the *jus gentium* and the diverse expressions of civil law. Coercion of all kinds is the fruit of the Fall.

But the reverse of the coin is that God can make even sin to praise him. For out of the Fall comes correction for its worst excesses: Both Gregory VII and Innocent III are right. Political authority and institutions to the canonists are awesome phenomena precisely because, although they have their origins in sin and are exercised by sinful men, they also restrict and drastically curb the effects of sin. It is for this reason that Innocent III and other canonical writers are constantly emphasizing the divine nature of political authority.

This, then, is the preponderant refrain running through canonical theory. But we should not forget either that while the canonists endow political authority with divine attributes and condemn those who would dare rebel against it, they also tend to argue that there is one authority which can judge it—the pope. Although private persons may not rebel (for even though the secular ruler is under divine and natural *jus*, the canonists place no stress on nonofficial interpretation of *jus naturale*), the Pope, as supreme interpreter of *jus divinum* and *jus naturale*, may in some respects and in some measure limit even the divinely ordained secular ruler. Canonical writers differ as to the degree, method and justification of his control, it is true, but most of them do not doubt that both naturally and divinely he possesses the prerogative. With these theories we shall deal in the next section.

Political Institutions. Let us now examine the civilian and canonical conception of such political institutions as slavery, property, and war.

1. Civilian Doctrine. The conflict between certain Roman law and the patristic viewpoints is illustrated in civilian attitudes. With respect to slavery, there is general agreement among the legists that it violates *jus naturale* and yet is justified under *jus gentium* and *jus civile*, as an institution which, relative to the actual human condition, can be maintained. However, the civilians are eager to support all provisions in the Justinian *corpus* which mitigate the lot of the slave or of the serf. Thus slaves who flee from their masters to churches can be returned to the master only when the latter has sworn not to punish his servant; and some civilians hold that if the master is cruel, the slave must be sold forthwith.

As for property, the civilian view is divided between the position that it is an institution of *jus naturale* and the contention that it is not. The former is associated with many of the ancient jurists, while the latter is sustained by a few of the ancient thinkers and, of course, by the central stream of patristic speculation.

The civilian view of war is not very explicit, although again there is no disposition to question its legitimacy under certain circumstances. Since the ancient Empire was built up largely through wars, it would be surprising if medieval civilians were to question an institution which, moreover, is so ubiquitous throughout the High Middle Ages. It is assumed that under certain circumstances war may be necessary, although the lawyers fail to provide us with sure guidance for identifying the circumstances.

2. Canonical Doctrine. The canonical teaching regarding slavery is clearly patristic, thus making both slavery and serfdom institutions of relative natural law. By nature, men are free and equal; and slavery has arisen because, since the whole of human life was disordered by original sin, liberty shared in this fate. At the same time, however, the formal acceptance of and acquiescence in slavery assists men to restrain the passions unleashed by sin: the master becomes, as it were, an instrument of God for the correction of evil, just as the political ruler serves in that capacity. What is puzzling, however, the critic may maintain, is the question of who restrains the master.

Nor is this acceptance of slavery merely theoretical. The Church in the early Middle Ages owns slaves and, of course, under the feudal system its bishops are often the feudal lords of serfs. True, canonical teaching, like civilian, endeavors to limit the effects of slavery in some measure by the Law of Sanctuary and by implementing ancient rules restricting separation of families. But in the end, there is no evidence whatsoever of a radical reformist spirit in canon law.

In general, the same observation may be made about the canonical view of property. Unlike the civilians, the canonists never hold that it is in accordance with *jus naturale.* It is always for them both the consequence and the corrective for the Fall—a device which will presumably maintain some measure of order in a situation which otherwise would result in a few men engrossing the entire earth.

Yet the tension between the view that property is unnatural and the position that it is, nevertheless, relatively justified, remains, and is reflected in the practices of monasticism. In the monastery, canonical views suggest, there is some approximation of the situation in Eden, even though the secular clergy must exist in a general society that necessarily supports private property. The Middle Ages never accommodate themselves ideologically to the view, which sometimes seems to dominate modern life, that private property institutions are a kind of absolute around which all other concerns must turn.

With respect to the institution of war, the attitude of the canonists does not radically differ from their teaching on slavery and property. We have noted Gregory VII

34. Among the civilians belonging to the first group are Irnerius, Placentinus, and Roger; taking the second position are such lawyers as Bulgarus, Joannes Bassianus, Azo, and Hugolinus.

35. To the Eastern Emperor, Alexius. "Ad firmamentum igitur coeli, hoc est universalis ecclesiae, fecit Deus duo magna luminaria, id est, duas magnas instituit dignitates, quae sunt pontificalis suctoritas, et regalis potestas."

bitterly castigating secular rulers for their killing in war and in an earlier chapter have emphasized the opposition of pre-Constantinian Fathers to war and to Christians serving in the army.[36] By the era of the High Middle Ages, the early Christian view has been transmuted to one which sees war as the fruit of sin but at the same time its remedy. But canon law insists that the clergy shall not shed blood, and the Church endeavors to restrict private war through such devices as Truces of God on holy days. St. Augustine's view that war may be an instrument of justice in a sinful world is supported, in varying degrees, by canonical writers. The tension between the early Christian view, however, and the acceptance of war implied in the feudal system and in the preaching of Crusades never entirely dies out.

As a whole, the discussion of political institutions among civilians and canonists turns, then, on how the several thinkers combine Stoical, patristic, and Roman law views. If they emphasize Stoical and patristic positions, they will tend to make the Fall of Man and its effects a central aspect of their discussion; for it is the Fall which legitimates institutions which would otherwise be unnatural. In terms of that canonical view which divides *jus naturale* into commands, prohibitions, and *demonstrationes*, the natural law condemnation of slavery, property, and war would fall within the latter category: political institutions constitute an expedient and necessary means for gaining the ends of nature which have been made opaque by the Fall. By contrast, some traditional Roman legal views would see no tension between nature and relative nature. For these the Fall (or Stoical versions of it) plays no role.

Sacerdotium and Imperium

The most characteristic problem for medieval political thinkers, as we have seen, is that which involves the theory of temporal-spiritual relations. What exactly are to be the relations between the two autonomous authorities which coexist in the single society?

Gelasius I at the close of the fifth century had answered the question, as we have seen,[37] by proclaiming separation but mutual interdependence, with the secular ruler to be subordinate to the spiritual in "spirituals" and the spiritual ruler to submit to the emperor in "temporals." The Gelasian doctrine became a kind of text upon which Western political theory would build in subsequent centuries.

But it was at best a general formula, the exact interpretation of which posed many difficulties. It is with these problems of application that the major legal and political thinkers in twelfth and thirteenth centuries are concerned.

The Attitude of Civilians. The civilians never doubt that the emperor, and secular rulers generally, must move within the limits prescribed by God and Holy Writ nor that, when acting in this way, the holder of secular authority is a divine agent. While his divine authority is always mediated through the community, as we have seen, it is not thereby weakened. But the very fact that he recognizes his inferiority to God puts the emperor, according to civilians like Azo, in the position of a kind of vassal. God is his feudal superior and what vassal would dare question his obligations to his Lord?

But civilian thought goes beyond this and recognizes a wide scope for canon law. In part, the jurisdiction of ecclesiastical tribunals has been defined in the Code, of course, and where possible the civilians attempt to follow its guidance, as they do in all matters. Irnerius may be taken to typify the civilian view. According to him, ecclesiastical courts have complete jurisdiction over the clergy as clergy; but they have no jurisdiction over the laity in purely secular matters. The difficulty of this formulation is to distinguish between the clergy as clergy and their character as simply human beings; and at the same time, to differentiate between laity with respect to secular matters and the laity in relation to ecclesiastical affairs.

The line of thinking on distinctions of this kind may be indicated if we examine more closely specific civilian assertions regarding use of ecclesiastical and secular courts. When an ecclesiastic is to be prosecuted for a canonical or spiritual offense, the court of the bishop will clearly have jurisdiction. So, too, when one clergyman brings civil proceedings against another, will the episcopal tribunal hear the complaint. By and large, the civilians argue that when a layman brings suit against an ecclesiastic, it must be heard in the church court; and as authority they cite the *Novels* of Justinian.

But beyond this, there is some disagreement among the civilians. Suppose that criminal charges are brought against the clergy. Where will they be heard? Some of the Roman lawyers hold that they may be taken to either an ecclesiastical or a secular court. If the bishop finds the clergyman guilty of a crime, the punishment is to be carried out by the secular arm; if, on the other hand, the case has gone to the civil court in the first instance and the clergyman is found guilty, he cannot be punished by the secular arm until he has been degraded by his bishop.

Certain of the civilians, though, apparently hold that criminal cases against the clergy must always be heard before a civil court. This is the position of men like Irnerius and Azo; but the latter adds that the clergyman cannot be condemned until he is first deprived of his clerical status by the bishop.

If a layman violates canon law, the case is, of course, one for the ecclesiastical court; but many of the civilians argue that the civil authority must be consulted before the episcopal judge actually renders a decision.

From the law of the classical empire, the civilians derive another important principle. In order to provide some check on the activities of their widely ramified administrative and judicial bureaucracy, the post-Constantinian emperors had made increasing use of ecclesiastical officials as imperial agents in secular matters; and these provisions had been enshrined in the Justinian *corpus.* One of the most important was the decree which provided that if a lay suitor should doubt the justice and equity of a secular court, he might ask that a bishop be added to the imperial court to ensure fairness. The medieval civilians carry on this principle in their interpretation of canonical and secular jurisdictions. Theoretically, if the bishop cannot get justice from the secular judge, he is supposed to give the offended suitor a letter to the emperor, who will then hear the case, apparently *ab initio.* To what degree this principle is actually applied during the Middle Ages we do not know exactly. But from our point of view, it illustrates one way in which, despite the Gelasian doctrine, even the civilians maintain that the Church may intervene in secular affairs. In some sense, it seems to imply that the Church is a better guardian of justice than secular authority; and the canonists can build upon this civilian concession to give the Church even greater prestige in secular jurisdiction.

In the post-Glossatorial period, the commentaries of Lucas de Penna (1320–1390) afford an interesting example of the way in which later civilians reasoned about jurisdictional problems. [38] They show, too, how eager civilians are to extend Roman law into areas which many canonists would deem subject to canonical legislation.

Lucas' "solution" of the jurisdictional problem in marriage cases illustrates the difficulties which troubled both civilians and canonists with respect to the dual nature of the marriage relationship. On the one hand (as both Glossatorial and post-Glossatorial civilians would agree), marriage is "secular" for it profoundly affects the secular peace and only through it can the immortality of the human race be guaranteed. Lucas, in fact, terms it a "*publica utilitas.*" On the other hand, there can be no doubt that matrimony is a divine institution, since it was established by God even before the Fall. It is a sacrament, and yet a sacrament which has important secular implications. Because marriage is a sacrament and primarily spiritual, Lucas holds, the ecclesiastical judge quite rightfully has jurisdiction in all cases involving the institution; but because of its vast secular ramifications, the bishop's court should always apply the Roman law unless it is quite clearly opposed to canonical principles.

One of the great problems involved in the notion of a single society with two co-equal authorities is that of determining who makes the final decision as to which authority governs. So long as agreement exists on definition of the respective spheres and on practical application of the principles accepted, there is no difficulty. But suppose disagreements arise. Who, then, can give an authoritative pronouncement? Will the emperor or king decide, or the pope? The civilians never seem to answer this question clearly, thus leaving an almost unobstructed field for the ardent papalists to occupy. The one recognized as the person who can finally delimit jurisdictions and authoritatively establish spheres of action

36. See Chapters 10 and 9.
37. See pp. 197–198.
38. See Walter Ullmann, *The Medieval Idea of Law, as Represented by Lucas de Penna: A Study in Fourteenth Century Legal Scholarship,* London: Methuen, 1946. This is an invaluable study and has been extremely useful in the preparation of this chapter. In fact, all of Ullmann's works contribute to our understanding of the medieval conception of law as well as to other political themes of the High Middle Ages.

is what early modern political theory would call a "sovereign." During the High Middle Ages, however, the only sovereign in this sense may be said to be God; and short of divine interposition in some form, there is no earthly authority who is generally accepted as fulfilling this role.

Many of the papalists, of course, believe that they have an answer to the question; and it is, indeed, they who set the pace for the whole discussion between 1100 and 1300. They are the dynamic thinkers, tending to be less bound by classical precedents than the civilians. It is to the conceptions of men like Huguccio, Johannes Faventinus, Vincentius Hispanus, Gratian, Alexander III, Innocent IV, and Gregory IX that we now turn.

Canonist Conceptions. It is with canonical positions that we usually associate typical high medieval notions of spirituals and temporals. Those views, however, are much more complex and qualified than critics of the theocratic idea sometimes recognize. While they have a common background not only in canonical thought but also in the general intellectual atmosphere of the High Middle Ages, each canonist may differ widely from his brother in the way he applies a given principle.

All analyses of the issue should keep in mind two separate but interrelated questions. The first is that which ponders the degree to which the Church may be said to possess authority in temporals and the second recurs to the problem of the extent to which the pope controls or is identified with the Church. Or, in other terms, what is the relation of *sacerdotium* (priesthood) to *imperium* (secular or imperial authority) and what is the authority of the supreme pontiff over the priesthood?

General Intellectual Atmosphere. The "climate of opinion" which leads medievalists to espouse so many canon law political principles should be noted before we turn to the general position of the canonists themselves. Here let us emphasize (1) the "spirit-matter" dichotomy as a way of viewing human life; and (2) the impact of Aristotle's revival early in the thirteenth century.

1. Spirit and Matter. While orthodox theology theoretically repudiates anything that smacks of Manichaean "dualism," which teaches the wicked character of matter and thinks of evil as an uncreated factor in the universe, in practice the medieval outlook often draws a sharp line between matter and spirit. With Augustine, it expatiates on St. Paul's conflict between "fleshly lusts" and spiritual yearnings;[39] and Augustine's stress on sex as particularly lustful seems to identify the material with evil. Although Augustine is careful to make "pride"—a spiritual attitude—responsible for the Fall, it is often easy to ignore this ultimate and to think of the spirit as good and the body as evil.

This general tendency to depreciate the material and temporal is responsible for many attitudes and institutions which we have come to regard as typically medieval. In some measure, perhaps, monasticism is its fruit; and the not infrequent occurrence of popular self-inflicted punishments is justified and explained by reference to monastic-like standards, however much the modern mind may see in these events evidences of mass masochism.[40]

2. The Rediscovery of Aristotle. In the next chapter we shall deal more fully with the effect of Aristotle's revival on medieval political theory. Here, however, we should note that the Greek philosopher's treatise on the soul, *De Anima*, was once more made available in 1210, at the very height of the "canonical" centuries. We cannot say, of course, exactly what impact it had on the thinkers of the time. But certainly Aristotle's teaching that the spiritual is something divine and the most distinctive of all man's attributes,[41] when interpreted in light of the medieval gulf between "material-temporal" and "spiritual-eternal," does nothing to discourage the tendency to deprecate fleshly and time-bound things. True, Aristotle would have been horrified had he known the use to which his treatise on psychology could be put. But advocates of ecclesiastical and papal supremacy are often not wellrounded philosophers and are seemingly immune to the subtleties of ancient thought.

The Foundation of Canonical Thought. Building upon and refining this widespread intellectual attitude, canonical writers in general tend to exalt Church over temporal authority, although in varying degrees, and pope over the priesthood as a whole.

In the twelfth century, for example, a great English ecclesiastic and jurist, John of Salisbury (1115–1180), argues in his *Policraticus* (1159) that society is like a biological organism. In this organic whole, the spiritual appears to be the vital and ultimate authority. Temporal rulers govern with a certain autonomy, to be sure, but only so long as they remain within the law and under the judgment and aegis of

Holy Church. Spiritual authority can remove tyrants.

Certain specific doctrines of ecclesiastical prerogatives come to be associated with the political notions of the canonists and, indeed, affect high medieval thought as a whole. Here let us note a few of them:

1. Excommunication of Rulers and the Theory of the Interdict. As the Church becomes more and more hierarchical and membership in its visible communion correspondingly more important, the life of the Christian is governed increasingly by reference to participation in the sacraments; and the administration of the sacraments is controlled by Holy Church. The ancient period had handed down only two definite sacraments–the eucharist and baptism.[42] Although a number of other rituals were regarded as in some sense "sacred," they had not been accepted as possessing the holy and mysterious character attributed to the Lord's Supper and the initiating rite of baptism. From the eleventh to the thirteenth centuries, however, partly under the influence of the ancient notion that seven is a sacred number, the sacraments gradually came to include not merely the ancient twain but also penance, marriage, ordination, confirmation, and extreme unction. Here we are not primarily concerned with the intricate theories of the sacraments worked out particularly in the thirteenth century,[43] but rather with the relation of those doctrines and of corresponding popular beliefs to the claims of the Church in political affairs.

That relation is one in which, because the priest is held to be the administrator of the sacraments (although the layman may administer baptism), the *sacerdotium* has enormous potential prerogatives by virtue of its ever-present threat to withhold what is essential for salvation. If participation in the sacraments is a condition for the reception of Grace (as the hierarchical conception holds), then he who possesses the right to give or to withdraw them has an enormous power. In an age when the spiritual is accented, it implies a sanction as effective as the power to control material goods in our own day. Like a Rockefeller who owns and wields the power of a quasi-monopolistic petroleum corporation in a world organized to depend on oil, the priest during the High Middle Ages possesses the threat of the spiritual sword in a universe which values the spiritual goods which only he can dispense.

To be sure, excommunication simply ex-

cludes one from the sacraments and does not directly affect temporalities. But among its spiritual consequences is the command that all good Christians should shun the company of the excommunicated, thus opening the way for economic deprivation. Excommunication may also affect his legal status, depriving the excluded of certain rights. Thus for the Christian, its effect is to cut him off from the society of his fellows and, what is of even greater importance, to deny him the means of that grace which may save him from eternal damnation. All this is the fruit of the medieval notion of the sacraments and of the effects of their deprivation.

But if the effect of excommunication on the ordinary layman may be disastrous, its impact on a ruler is even greater. In theory, none of his officials can now associate with him, the business of government must necessarily come to a standstill, and literally thousands of the ruler's subjects may be deprived of the benefits which supposedly flow from his rule.

If this is not sufficient to restrain the ruler from his canonically wrongful acts, the spiritual weapon of the interdict may be used: originally a restraining order issued by the praetor in his administration of the *jus civile*, for Holy Church it now becomes a papal restriction on access to the sacraments in which whole segments of the population may be denied the means of grace. As a spiritual weapon for the restraint of rulers, its importance can hardly be exaggerated; for by depriving dying Christians of extreme unction, young people of marriage, and all Christians of the eucharist, baptism, confirmation, and penance, it can arouse an almost united action against the offending king or emperor.

2. Deposition of Rulers. Throughout the twelfth and thirteenth centuries, the canonists sustain the principle that the pope may depose secular princes and even, under carefully cir-

39. *Epistle to the Romans*, ch. 7.

40. For a popular and sometimes witty discussion of this question see Frederick D. Kershner, *Those Gay Middle Ages*, Chicago: Willett, Clark & Co., 1938.

41. *De Amina*, II, 2, and III, 3.

42. Note Harnack, *op. cit.*, VII, pp. 201–202.

43. *Ibid.*, pp. 200–275.

cumscribed circumstances, appoint them. On the whole, the assertion of the right to depose and appoint grows stronger as we approach the end of the thirteenth century.

The principle itself is supported on two grounds—historical and philosophical. Historically, the canonists maintain, there is a long tradition of removals and appointments which justifies similar action on the part of medieval popes. Thus it was the popes who translated the Frankish Kingdom from the Merovingians to Pippin; and Pope John VIII, with his episcopal colleagues and the Senate, is said to have chosen Charles the Bald as Emperor in 877.[44] Innocent III repeats the assertion of papal authority in his decretals when he maintains that it was by the authority of the Chair of Peter that the Empire was taken from the Greeks—the Eastern Empire—and given to the Germans, the Holy Roman Empire.

But the assertion of these claims is not only grounded on tradition; it is also based on the philosophical principle that the spiritual authority is higher than that which governs temporals. The Gelasian doctrine that the priest's responsibility is greater than that of the prince is the text for innumerable commentaries which justify deposition when the king sins or violates natural law or defies a legitimate canonical command of his spiritual superior, the pope.

In Innocent III, however, and generally in the canonists of his time, claims which involve the right to depose or appoint are left vague and inexplicit at many points. It is later popes like Innocent IV who are responsible for initiating the vast and less qualified claims of late thirteenth century canonists. Whereas the canonical writers of 1100 to about 1240 make papal authority over secular rulers rather indirect, negative, and residuary, many (although not all) later canonists become bold and flatly assert that the pope has positive temporal authority by virtue of Christ's delegation.

Underlying all the contentions of extremists like Innocent IV and Cardinal Hostiensis is the notion that, while secular authority is still "divine," it possesses only a kind of second-level divinity. By this they mean that the pope obtains his authority directly from God (Christ), while the authority of the emperor is admittedly mediated through the community. Or, as Innocent IV puts it, "*Imperium habet auctoritatem a populo Romano*," but the pontiff's authority is the direct result of a divine "ordinance." One of the great commentators on the canon law[45] well reflects this view when he remarks that while the Roman people can "deprive the emperor of his power . . . all the churches taken together could not do the same to the pope, since he does not receive his power from them, but they from him."

3. Release from Oaths of Allegiance. The oath, to the medieval mind, is an indispensable ingredient in the organization of society, despite the New Testament admonition against swearing.[46] Oaths of fealty presumably become matters of conscience; and to keep an oath is regarded as one of man's highest social and political obligations. Yet through the sacramental system and by virtue of the notion that it is the Church which is the "keeper" of a man's conscience,[47] the Church claims the authority to absolve from the duty of fulfilling evil oaths or at least the right to declare that certain kinds of oaths are null and void *ab initio*. But if the Church can absolve in general, it can obviously relieve subjects of a ruler from keeping their oaths of allegiance. In one form or another, this is clearly stated by most canonists.

In the struggle against heresy which becomes an increasingly great part of the medieval scene after 1150, the right to release from oaths is a weapon of great importance in the papal armory. Thus the Fourth Lateran Council (1215) decrees that if a secular ruler should refuse to do his duty and purge his territory of heretics, the pope should be immediately informed of the fact. It would then be the pontiff's obligation forthwith to release all subjects of the recalcitrant ruler from their oaths of allegiance.

When later political thinkers come to look back on the Middle Ages, one of its shocking doctrines to them is the notion that a priest, however high, can cut off subjects from their ruler, whether by excommunication or by absolution from oaths. Yet we should not be surprised or astonished by the theory, for it is wholly consistent with the general claims which canonists make for Church and papacy. And we should always remember that its effectiveness depends basically upon an intricate system of beliefs and not upon the direction of physical force. If the Middle Ages had not sanctified the oath and believed generally that the Church was the keeper of conscience, the absolution of subjects from their oaths would have had no practical effect.[48]

4. Military Crusades. Although the clergy, according to canon law, cannot shed blood,

this does not mean that the pontiff may not demand from secular rulers the shedding of blood under certain specified circumstances. This claim becomes particularly prominent, in a formal sense, after Innocent IV and extreme canonical apologists like Hostiensis come to draw out the implications of assertions made by popes like Innocent III.

But from the eleventh century onward, the popes and their canonical supporters act as if it is one of the prerogatives of the papacy to demand military service for particular causes, not merely in lands directly under the control of the pope (the states of the Church) but throughout Christendom. If given rulers refuse to render the military service demanded, they may be excommunicated and their lands placed under interdict.

Thus it is the popes who initiate the military Crusades against infidel Moslems, thereby turning the military spirit of feudalism against enemies of the Church. It is Innocent III who excommunicates Count Raymond of Toulouse for his failure to proceed against the Albigensians and who then proclaims a Crusade against the heretics. Or again, the Emperor Frederick II promises to proceed on a Crusade against the Moslems in the thirteenth century.

In addition to formal Crusades against infidels and heretics, the popes maintain that they have the authority to demand military action of one kind or another when disputes arise between and among Catholic princes. Thus Innocent III becomes concerned about the actions of King Sverre of Norway against the Church. When the King refuses to obey his behests to cease and desist, he excommunicates the King's followers and also orders the King of Denmark to take military action against him. And one might cite other cases of the same nature.

5. The Administration of Justice. Earlier we noted that the ancient Roman law had made provision for association of bishops with secular judges when, on the complaint of a suitor, the latter were not rendering justice. We pointed out, moreover, that the medieval civilians generally acquiesced in this ecclesiastical prerogative. Let us now examine very briefly the canonical view of such matters.

It would be surprising to find it restricting ecclesiastical claims. The canonical writers agree with those civilians who support the Justinian view that if a suitor thinks the judge or governor is biased he has the right to ask that the bishop sit with the secular official.[49] But many canonists—notably Gratian and Innocent III—go far beyond this and claim that if one party to a suit thinks that the secular judge will not do justice he has the right to demand that the cause be transferred entirely to the episcopal court. Most of the canonists do not allow a general right of appeal, however, but suggest that the canon law courts can take controversies from the secular tribunals only on a plea of denial of justice.

But denial or defect of justice is a rather vague expression and we find that the canonists are not too explicit in defining it. We can assert, however, that they go beyond the civilian doctrine in that they maintain a right to transfer secular cases entirely from the civilian tribunal to the ecclesiastical court on the ground that justice is a spiritual good.

6. Significance of the Papal Extremists. It is not surprising that extreme claims for papal authority should arise, as we have seen, after the middle of the thirteenth century. The modern mind frequently inclines to the view that the arguments of men like Innocent IV and Hostiensis are those of thinkers simply rationalizing a limitless quest for power by their particular political faction. No doubt there is an element of truth in this: Papal claims were partly "ideological," or rationalizations of "special interests." But from another point of view, the contentions of the

44. For the Latin text, see Carlyle and Carlyle, *op. cit.*, p. 201.
45. Laurentius.
46. Matthew 5:33–36.
47. Cf. Troeltsch, *op. cit.*, vol. 1, p. 233: "Out of it (the sacrament of Penance) there develops the whole Christian ethic of the Church as self-examination and direction of conscience, as absolution, and as the key to the whole system of satisfactions and merits, as the unification of all ethical problems and inconsistencies by the authority of the Church, which removes the responsibility for the unification of the duties of life from the individual, and takes it on its own shoulders."
48. We should not assume, of course, that papal absolution from oaths is always effective. Indeed, by the thirteenth century, subjects in many parts of Christendom have begun in rather widespread fashion to ignore papal pronouncements in this and other matters. See, in general, Walter Ullmann, *The Growth of Papal Government in the Middle Ages*, New York: Barnes & Noble, 1962.
49. Ivo represents this interpretation.

extreme papalists represent one plausible answer to the perennial difficulty of implementing the Gelasian doctrine. It is all very well to lay down the proposition that each of the two authorities is supreme in its own sphere, but who is to define exactly the sphere of each? The Middle Ages learned early that the answer to this question is not an easy one; yet down to the time of Innocent IV, thinkers insist, on the whole, that the Gelasian theory must guide political thought and even most canonists hesitate to give more than a rather indirect and strictly limited authority to the Church in temporals. True, Innocent III often acts in accordance with implicit theories which go beyond his explicit formulations; but the extreme formulations await specific statement at a later date. Down to about 1243, in other words, most canonists are moderates in their claims for papal jurisdiction.

Why, then, do the extremists come to the fore after that date? Certain developments in practical politics, no doubt, help provide the conditions under which there will be greater receptivity to the advanced position. For one thing, the constant problem of the Moslem seems to call for united effort of some kind and for a leadership which will unite temporals with spirituals. But the dramatic rise of heretical movements is of equal importance. Medieval Christendom at the turn of the thirteenth century is divided in its consciousness of heresy and what to do about it: On the one hand almost all agree in the abstract that it should not be tolerated, for it is a menace to that doctrinal unity deemed so important to most good Christians; on the other hand, secular and local ecclesiastical jurisdictions can find many good reasons for not proceeding against particular heretics. When the Inquisition is founded during the pontificate of Gregory IX, this schizophrenia is to some degree alleviated (at least in the beginning) but at the time the stage is set for vast expansion of papal power which the theorists then proceed to explain and justify.

But while the politics involved in the Moslem and heresy problems no doubt plays an important role as a conditioning factor in extremist theory, the unsatisfactory nature of the Gelasian formula itself is surely of equal importance. For a civilization which exalts unity (even though centrifugal forces are always destroying that unity in practice), Gelasius provides division and no method for defining precisely the spheres of the two authorities. In life and society, spirit and body are mingled and mutually interdependent; and if we divide them for certain purposes (as when we distinguish between such spirituals as religion, free expression, and education, on the one hand, and material goods and power, on the other), the severed parts cry out for a new coordination.

It is at this point that papal extremists come to the fore. It is the Chair of Peter, they argue, which is endowed with authority to provide this defining and coordinating power. The other alternative would be to assign the authority to the emperor. But in view of the general medieval consciousness that spirituals are higher than temporals, this answer is not suggested, even by most of the civilians, who for the most part remain vague about the issue. Hence extreme papalism grows as the crises in the Gelasian theory and in political life develop.

From this perspective, it is not at all surprising, then, to find some advocates of papalism supporting doctrines which would have astonished early medieval thinkers as much as they provoke modern critics. Thus Innocent IV contends that the pope can punish even non-Christians when they violate the *jus naturale;* and the same canonist argues that the Jews come under papal jurisdiction whenever they defy the moral code of the New Testament. The Fourth Lateran Council calls upon secular princes to order Jews and Saracens to wear badges which will distinguish them from Christians—and this as early as 1215.

The general import of papal extremism, then, is to contend that the pope is the source of all authority within the Church and that because Christ possessed both temporal and spiritual authority the pope must, through Peter, be entitled to it also. True, for purposes of convenience, the occupant of Peter's chair may delegate his temporal authority to princes, kings, and emperors; but he may also reclaim it at any time. It is he who delimits temporal and spiritual spheres and he does this because he himself is lord of both, by virtue of the power of the keys.[50]

Thus the extreme papalists grant the coordinating and delimiting authority to the *sacerdotium,* the *imperium* to exist on its sufferance. After the sixteenth century, of course, cries of outrage against this doctrine fill the world; and those alarms continue to reverberate today in Protestant, radical Catholic, and secularist circles. Yet when we compare views like those of Hostiensis with the basic theory of the modern state, it would seem that the former makes no greater claims for the ecclesia than its exponents (like Hobbes, for example, or even modern liberals) make for the national state which succeeds the medieval theocracy. Just as the medieval doctrine holds that spirituals and temporals are separate and grants the delimiting authority to the pope, so modern theory contends that religion is a private matter and delegates the defining authority to the state. In the end, modern theory seems to hold, the state must authoritatively decide what is "Caesar's" and what is "God's"; and if it should restrict God's realm beyond what some might approve, the latter can suffer as did the medievalists who opposed extreme papal claims.[51]

This is not to say at all that Innocent IV and his canonists were right in assigning the coordinating and defining authority to the Church. But it is to maintain that the conflict between temporals and spirituals, which we regard as the distinctive mark of medieval political theory, is a perennial issue. The medieval papalists assign the defining power to the spiritual authority and we give it to the temporal; but it would appear that the temporal power is intrinsically no better equipped to demarcate the two spheres than is the spiritual. The medieval Church is no more and no less arrogant in claiming to have "both swords" than the secular national state.

The Decline of Legist Approaches

After the thirteenth century, while civil and canon lawyers continue to play important roles in the formulation of political conceptions, their place as central figures is no longer undisputed. The rise of scholastic philosophy, the revival of Aristotelean studies, and the quest for some resolution of the problem posed by the relation between reason and faith come to occupy a greater place in the discussion of both general and political questions.

And among the thinkers whom we call the scholastics, St. Thomas Aquinas is undoubtedly the most important from the viewpoint of social and political theory. While he, too, is a canon lawyer of note, his role as a philosopher and theologian overshadows his status as a lawyer. To his conceptions we now turn.

chapter 13

Scholasticism and the Political Mind of Thomas Aquinas

In the last chapter we suggested that it was the lawyers who first began to debate political issues seriously during the High Middle Ages. Aligning themselves either with the tradition of the Roman law or with the new and more flexible canonical system (itself partly based on Roman legal notions), they thought of political issues within the context of their glosses or of their comments on Gratian.

Scholastic philosophy emerged in the late stages of the Glossatorial period and soon began to affect the way in which the civilians analyzed the law, helped shape the period of post-Glossatorial legal scholarship, and gradually came to assume the leadership in political thought; and the man who best reflects scholastic philosophy at its height, and with it high scholastic political theory, is St. Thomas Aquinas. Building upon the Fathers, St. Augustine, and Aristotle, Thomas works out the most systematic of all high medieval theories of politics.

The Background of Thomas's Thought

While the Church was waxing in both spiritual and temporal power during the twelfth

Chapter 12

50. Matthew 16:18–19.
51. Thus no modern state will admit that there is a basic moral right to refuse military service (although some states will grant concessions as a matter of grace) even though individuals may maintain that such service is contrary to their religion; even supposedly liberal states like the United States maintain that the state is justified in overruling citizens who claim their religion demands that they have more than one wife.

century and its apologists were working out a *rationale* upon which the extreme claims of the thirteenth century were to be built, heretical and foreign intellectual currents were emerging with which the later Middle Ages had somehow to come to grips. Reserving treatment of the heretical currents for the next chapter, let us note here the foreign influences.

During the first part of the seventh century, Mohammed (d. 632) had laid the foundations of Islam. Built upon Jewish and Christian traditions and inculcating a fierce monotheism, the new faith rapidly penetrated northern Africa in the years immediately following the death of the prophet. Those ancient parts of the Roman Empire which were so important for early Christianity, including Carthage and Augustine's Hippo, were thus severed from their early Christian allegiance and Islamic institutions replaced the network of churches.

The victorious Moslems did not rest content until they had pushed into Spain and perhaps would have penetrated France had they not been militarily defeated at Tours a hundred years after the death of Mohammed. After the first quarter of the eighth century, Islam consolidated its position in Spain; and from then on through the ninth and tenth centuries, Afro-Spanish Moslem life and culture became in effect one civilization.

In terms of intellectual development, this civilization was far in advance of anything known in Europe during the same epoch. While Europe was plunged into the territorial-church period and building the institutions of feudalism, Islamic culture was constructing universities, engaging in scientific experimentation, and attempting to relate ancient Greek philosophy to the Revelation embodied in the Koran. There was a considerable advance in medical science, at a time when European medical knowledge was far below the level it had attained during the days of Galen.

When one reflects on Islamic developments between 750 and 1000, as a matter of fact, one wonders whether the defeat at Tours in 732 was the "blessing" most Christian apologists have termed it. Had the Moslems not been resisted, it is entirely conceivable that the intellectual history of Europe might have taken a different turn. The revival of learning might have appeared two centuries or more before it actually occurred; the papacy might never have come to occupy its commanding position; the Inquisition might never have been founded (there was no such institution under Islam); and many of the features in medieval life criticized by subsequent generations might never have been established.[1]

The two civilizations could not remain completely separated, however. There were travellers moving from one area to the other, even before the days of the Crusades; and lines of communication developed between the flourishing Jewish communities of Islamic civilization and medieval European Jewry. As early as the eleventh century, Europeans were beginning to hear of the great Arab physician and philosopher Avicenna (980–1037) and during the twelfth century some students were reading Averroes (1126–1198), another Moslem thinker who also happened to be a physician. During the eleventh and twelfth centuries, too, some Christians and Jews were aware that Avicebron (Solomon ben Judah ibn Gabirol, 1021–1058) and Maimonides (Moses ben Maimon, 1135–1204) were discussing philosophical issues in the context of Jewish and Greek thought and with the encouragement and help of Islamic scholars. While European thinkers were preoccupied with the issues of the early spirituals-temporals controversy, Arabic and Jewish scholars, in the congenial climate of Islamic culture, were debating the meaning and application of Aristotle.[2]

Islamic students and their Jewish colleagues were concerned with a number of issues. In the first place, they noted a considerable divergence between classical Greek thought and the ways in which both the Jewish and Islamic traditions looked at philosophical and political questions. The Greeks (and this was true even of Aristotle) had tended to stress the abstract and the rational and to look upon the material as somehow less real than what Plato called the Form of a thing. For both Jews and Moslems, on the other hand—as we have seen earlier in the case of the ancient Hebrews—the concrete events of history were significant as revealing the "will" of Yahweh or Allah. History was not meaningless and not simply repetition. And sense experience was not an inferior kind of reality. A modern Moslem scholar, exaggerating a little perhaps, has put the matter well:

> The first important point to note about the spirit of Muslim culture then is that for purposes of knowledge, it fixes its gaze on the concrete, the finite. It is further clear that the birth of the method of observation and experiment in Islam was due not to a compromise with Greek thought but to a prolonged intellectual warfare with it.[3]

At any rate, there was a tension between rationalism and empiricism, and between history as insignificant and history as revelation; and both Islamic and Jewish thought had to grapple with the controversies which grew out of this tension.

But secondly, Islamic and Jewish scholars were concerned about the relation between theology and philosophy. That is to say, if theology works out systematically the implications of religious revelation and revelation be assumed to give us the truth about the world, what room is left for philosophy which presumably is the life of reason? If theology leads us to make one statement and philosophy another and seemingly contradictory one, which is to take precedence? Is theology to be absorbed by philosophy or philosophy by theology? If either solution is accepted, one would seemingly have to reject revelation in the name of reason or reason in favor of revelation; and neither of these answers satisfied the Islamic thinkers. Averroes, as a matter of fact worked out a system—the celebrated "double truth" theory—whereby he seemingly claimed that what might be entirely true for philosophy could be false for theology and vice versa. If one were to accept this view—and some modern scholars have maintained that it was a distortion of what Averroes had actually said—the human mind would apparently be in a perpetual state of bifurcation.

As these controversies of the Arabic world began to penetrate the Christian civilization of late twelfth and early thirteenth centuries they confronted a culture only beginning to be interested in systematic reflection of any kind. At the same time, however, the importation of Arabic and Jewish learning coincided with the beginning of the university movement, which meant that regular seats of learning would now be able to give due attention both to Arabic and Jewish thought and to the Aristotle who had so stimulated men like Averroes. We have already pointed out that Aristotle's treatise on the soul (*De Anima*) was made available at the height of the High Middle Ages (1210) and that it was seized upon by those who sought to prove the superior authority of the Church. More than a generation later (about 1250) the *Nicomachean Ethics* and the *Politics* began to be read once more.

The impact of Arabic-Jewish learning, combined with the close study of Aristotle, was enormous. The philosophical controversies which had exercised Arabic thinkers for more than two centuries now shook up the intellectual life of the High Middle Ages. The Augustinian synthesis, based so largely on an uneasy combination of Neoplatonism, Stoicism, and Hebrew thought, was now confronted by the system of Aristotle and his Arabic and Jewish commentators. The wisdom of the early Middle Ages had been informed by a monastic and spiritual learning. Now, however, the experimental science of Islamic life and the rationalism of Aristotle challenged the complacency of the monks and somewhat destroyed their self-confidence.

Underlying the whole scholastic movement was, of course, a critical spirit. It was unsatisfied with the wisdom of the early Middle Ages and it was uneasy about the philosophical naivete which it saw dominating intellectual life down to the thirteenth century. Although fully committed to the Christian revelation, it could not be satisfied until it had come to grips with the philosophical issues raised by Aristotle and the Arabs.

The social context for medieval political philosophy was, of course, the revived town. While scholasticism seemingly accepted the feudal system, it did so uneasily and with a clear preference for those forms of organization which were nonfeudal in nature. As it became more and more absorbed by Aristotle's *Ethics* and *Politics* its preferences for town life tended to increase and the medieval rural village became for it an inferior form.

Thomas and Thirteenth-Century Society

By the time of Thomas's birth in 1225, Arabian learning had been seeping into Christen-

1. Judgments of this kind, of course, involve might-have-beens which can be neither confirmed nor denied. But rationalizations for the terrible cruelty of so-called victorious wars, whether in medieval or in modern times, have been so ubiquitous that it would seem valuable to imagine what either nonviolent resistance or nonresistance might have accomplished.
2. On the political aspects of Islamic thought, see E. I. J. Rosenthal, *Political Thought in Medieval Islam*, Cambridge: Cambridge University Press, 1958.
3. Sir Mohammad Iqbal, *The Reconstruction of Religious Thought in Islam*, Lahore: Shaikh Muhammad Ashruf, 1954, p. 131.

dom for about a century. Thomas was born into a noble family of the Kingdom of Naples, the Counts of Aquino being related to the Emperors Henry VI and Frederick II.[4] The latter connection is particularly ironical, for if any medieval ruler ran counter to what Thomas was to teach about religion and politics it was Frederick, the semi-pagan opponent of the papacy.

At the age of five, the future saint was sent to receive his first education from the Benedictine monks at Monte Cassino and very soon gave evidence of his precocity in things of the mind. By the age of eleven, he was attending the recently established University of Naples, where he took the regular medieval course of study—the trivium (grammar, logic, rhetoric) and the quadrivium (music, mathematics, geometry, and astronomy). It was while he was at the University of Naples that he apparently decided to embrace the religious life—against the violent opposition of his family who hoped for a legal or political career of some kind. By 1240, he had received the habit of the recently founded order of St. Dominic, the garb of a poor friar, which indicated his intentions of becoming eventually a full-fledged Dominican.

In 1245 he went to study under Albertus Magnus at Cologne. Albertus was, of course, one of the great figures of the thirteenth century involved in the critical examination of Arabian and ancient Greek philosophy; and, like many others, he was at this time exercised by the problem of how faith and reason were to be related. Although Thomas would eventually reject a part of the Albertan solution, he was much impressed by the great doctor and for three years remained his student.

In 1251, Thomas was made sub-regent in the Paris Dominican *studium* and began his teaching career. By 1257 he was a Doctor of Theology and thereafter his life consisted almost wholly of teaching, preaching, and writing. While he was offered the Archbishopric of Naples by Pope Clement IV in 1265, he declined the honor, no doubt believing correctly that his best contributions were not to be made in the field of administration.

His own personality was a striking combination of the mystical and the earth-centered. While we usually (and rightly) think of him as one of the great devotees of reason, he had frequent mystic and ecstatic experiences of the kind made familiar to the modern mind by writers like William James and Evelyn Underhill. Although in his philosophy he rejected what he regarded as Platonism and embraced an earth-centered version of Aristotle, his life experiences included long periods of trance which would have delighted a Neoplatonist.

In 1273, Pope Gregory X summoned a General Council of the Church, to which Thomas was invited as one of the leading teachers of his time. On his way to attend the Council, in the early part of 1274, he became seriously ill and was nursed by Cistercian monks, to whose monastery he had been invited. But their efforts were unavailing and he died in March, 1274.

While St. Thomas was to have an enormous influence on later generations, including our own, we should not forget that his cultural roots are in the century of Frederick II and Pope Gregory IX. Like Gregory, we shall find him defending the eradication of heretics and like Frederick we shall discover that he has a sceptical side which ill comports with the modern picture sometimes drawn of him as a man of naive faith. In a sense, indeed, the thirteenth is one of the most intellectually critical of all the centuries; for in it medieval man tries to look frankly and honestly at his faith in the light of those masters of reason, the ancient Greeks—and Thomas is preeminently a medieval man in this respect.

The Context of Thomas's Politics

Every great system of political thought tends to be developed because tensions and inconsistencies have become evident in previous views or because conflicts within the body politic have grown to such a point as to become intolerable. Both these observations are appropriate in the case of St. Thomas Aquinas.

We have already had occasion to point out the many conflicts within the body of Christian thought itself. There was its ambivalence with respect to the world, which had been resolved during the first century in one direction, in the early Constantinian period in quite another, and with Augustine (and, generally, during the early Middle Ages), in yet a third. Nor had the perennial tension between the Old Testament and the New—so prominent in the early Christian epoch—ever been eliminated. Then again, with Augustine (and the early Middle Ages), the contrast between natural law in its pure sense and natural law after the Fall was a statement, which, while generally accepted (some of the civilians, of course, seemed to dissent in certain respects), was not without its difficulties. And now, with Arabic learning and the overshadowing figure of Aristotle, came the dramatic tension between the role of revelation and that of reason. To complicate the situation still further, Aristotle himself could be interpreted in two rather different directions: on the one hand, he might be looked upon primarily as a Platonist who emphasized rationality as over against sense experience; by contrast, the criticisms of Plato in Aristotle might become central, the Aristotelian thesis thus becoming one stressing the empirical and sensory world rather than that of the Forms.

In constructing his systematic political theory, too, Thomas had to take account not only of the metaphysical and ethical tensions present in the Christian tradition, but also to see these in the light of contemporary political conflicts, such as the struggle between Empire and papacy. In one sense, his problem was to join Aristotelian learning to Christian revelation, so that the parts of the whole would not clash. But from another point of view, his task was what today might be called ideological in that, as a convinced moderate papalist, he must make the cause of papalism plausible. He must go beyond the typical arguments of traditional canonical learning, based as it sometimes was on bad historical lore and on philosophically uncriticized pronouncements of popes and councils, and ground his statements on propositions which would appeal to the philosophically sophisticated.

In accomplishing these objectives, we should always remember, Thomas deliberately accepts what he conceives to be Aristotle's philosophy—even though he knows that several of the popes attack the "philosopher" and that some of his philosophical colleagues opt for a supposedly Platonic rather than an Aristotelian position. In fact, the acceptance of Aristotle is a matter of so much doubt that in some cities his works are publicly burned and it is only after Thomas's death, and partly in response to his system, that the Aristotelian system is finally received as the typical late medieval framework.[5]

While others could not see how the life of reason exalted by the ancient thinker could possibly be reconciled with the notion of knowledge based on the inspiration of Scripture as interpreted by the Church, Thomas finds the key in the Aristotelian distinction between the potential and the actual; at the same time, and in deference to the revelation of man's sin, he holds that the life of reason, which enables us to understand the natural tendencies of things, needs completion by the grace that lies beyond reason and whose administration is in the hands of the Church.

The basic foundations of this formulation are to be found in the organization of the *Summa Theologica* itself. There Thomas tells us that he proposes in the first part of his work to treat of God and of how all substances proceed from God. Revelation is seen in the light of Aristotle's philosophy. While reason cannot, of course, tell us about the ultimate mystery, it can, once the Revelation is given, seek to relate God's message to the human understanding. It can, granted the basic faith in Revelation, seek to justify the ways of God to man.

In Part II, of course, Thomas's basic theme is man. While in Part I he shows us how man, along with other creatures, proceeds from God according to revealed truth, in the second part he is concerned to explain how man through reason can and does seek to return to God. Part II is essentially a treatise on moral and political philosophy, broadly conceived. In it one will discover how very far indeed Thomas goes in sustaining the claims of reason.[6]

Despite his emphasis on reason, Thomas at least thinks that he has made ample room for

4. On the biography of Thomas in general see Walter J. Burghardt, *Saints and Sanctity*, New York: Prentice-Hall, 1965; William Barclay, *Master's Men*, Nashville: Abingdon, 1959; Gilbert K. Chesterton, *St. Thomas Aquinas*, New York: Doubleday, 1956; Martin Cyril D'Arcy, *St. Thomas Aquinas*, Westminster, Md.: Newman Press, 1953; Kenelm Foster, ed., *Life of St. Thomas Aquinas*, New York: Taplinger Publishing Co., 1959; and Jacques Maritain, *St. Thomas Aquinas*, Cleveland: World Publishing Co., 1962.

5. It should always be remembered, of course, that most of Plato was not available to Western philosophers during the High Middle Ages. The *Timaeus* was in circulation, but such dialogues as the *Republic* and the *Laws* were known only indirectly and imperfectly through the Fathers, and particularly through Augustine.

6. John Wild, a modern critic, in *Christian Ethics and the Social Order*, Durham: Duke University Press, 1959, takes Thomas severely to task for allegedly completely insubordinating Faith to Reason..

grace, for the third part of the *Summa* dedicates itself to the task of explaining how Christ, as a living reality in the sacraments, completes the process of reason.

This is the general picture. Now let us note a little more explicitly how Thomas treats the nature of the universe as a prelude to his examination of politics and society. This is, he avers, only one world and those are wrong who suggest that it is plural.[7] He supports this by citations from Scripture as well as from Aristotle. Evil is not caused by God, for God cannot be the cause of things tending to nonbeing. Evil which consists of defect is caused by the defect of the agent.[8] Between God and man there is a whole hierarchy of three orders of angels, all of whom are incorporeal. The angelic superiors illumine and guide their inferiors and angels have the capacity for illumination of man.[9]

An important key to the understanding of St. Thomas is his view of the Fall. With Augustine, it will be remembered, Eve had been the primary agent in promoting the separation of man from God, thus leading to the destruction of the equality and spontaneous freedom of Eden. Thomas's analysis is more involved and shows how much Aristotle has influenced him.

His discussion of woman is an excellent example of the way in which he considers both the Aristotelian position and that of the Christian tradition. He begins by suggesting that God had perhaps made a mistake by creating women, for Aristotle avers that the female is a "misbegotten male."[10] And he cites Genesis, 3:16, to show that after sin entered the world, woman was put under man's power, which seems to demonstrate that it might have been better had woman never been created.

Thomas refutes these considerations by pointing out that in Genesis, 2:18, it is said that God made woman because it was not good for man to be alone. Woman, he goes on, is a helper for man, not in general but primarily in the "work of generation."[11] Among animals and plants, generation is the "noblest" function; but in man, the fact that coition lasts only a brief time indicates God's intention that man should have a yet nobler purpose. Woman was designed to help man in the work of generation, so that man could specialize, as it were, in intellectual matters; for rationality, as Aristotle always said, is the characteristic which sets the human species off from all other orders of animals and plants.

Thomas also observes that if God had deprived the world of all creatures which had in any way been connected with sin, the universe would have been imperfect. Moreover, the common good should not be destroyed in order to avoid "individual evil." This is particularly true in view of the fact that God can use even evil for good ends.

Thomas also asks whether the "image of God" is present in every man and woman. Characteristically enough, he answers that it is, but he immediately qualifies his statement by distinguishing a threefold image. God is present in all men and women in the sense that all possess a natural aptitude for loving God and for thought. It is only when this aptitude is actually implemented and made a part of our habit pattern, however, that it is really effective; and this cannot take place without the assistance of grace—at least since the Fall. When, therefore, our wills learn, through a combination of natural reason and supernatural grace, to love God and to carry out his will habitually, however imperfectly, we are recreated as human personalities; and the image of God, instead of being merely potential, is made actual.

The division between the sexes is, of course, the beginning of human society and Thomas demonstrates that by nature woman, imperfect as she is individually, has the image of God but is at the same time the natural civil subordinate of man. Her subordination is not a consequence of the Fall. Thus, relatively speaking (by comparison with certain other medievalists, particularly some of the ascetics), Thomas has vindicated the "rights of women."

But what is the exact relationship between man and God in Eden? Earlier medieval thought, as we have repeatedly stressed, tended, following Augustine, to emphasize the results of the Fall in accounting for man's present psychological and social state. In Paradise, the earlier position appeared to say, man knew God perfectly.

By contrast, Thomas stresses that even before the Fall, man did not "see" God through his "essence." He bases this statement on Paul's words: "That was not first which is spiritual, but that which is natural."[12] Thomas's comment is that "to see God through His essence is most spiritual. Therefore the first man, in the first state of his natural life, did not see God through his essence." Adam knew God more perfectly than we do today, but if he had really known him in his essence he would have possessed "beatitude" and could not have sinned. The fact that he had the potentiality of sinning meant that he did not have this beatitude. Although man was happy in Eden, it was "not with that perfect happiness to which he was destined, which consists in the vision of the divine essence."

Very succinctly Thomas draws out the distinction between the pre-Fall and the post-Fall states, when he observes that "after sin man requires grace for more things." Even before the Fall "man required grace to obtain eternal life, which is the chief reason for the need of grace. But after sin man required grace also for the remission of sin, and for the support of his weakness."[13]

This tendency to narrow the gulf between pre-Fall and post-Fall man—and hence to enhance the dignity and potentialities of autonomous reason in post-Fall man—is to be noted, above all, in Thomas's analysis of the problem of human equality before and after the Fall. Basically, social order is an integral aspect of pure nature. But order demands inequality of various kinds, for the social whole cannot be directed if each entity is not subordinate, in some respects, to the whole. In Paradise, moreover, some would have had greater justice or knowledge than others. There were differences in bodily strength, too. In other words, inequality is a part of nature, and not merely of nature after the Fall.[14]

But not all types of inequality are natural. Thomas explicitly excludes slavery from the type of inequality which would be present in pure nature; for the slave is an instrument of private gain and not of social weal. Hence slavery must be assumed to be a fruit of the Fall. On the other hand, the types of inequality present among the angels are present among men. Surely the state of man before the Fall was not more exalted than that of the angels, Thomas contends; and he has already observed that these pure Forms are arranged in hierarchies, with those closest to God illuminating the inferior orders as the latter may be held to illuminate man. In Paradise, too, souls differed in "glory," the naturally higher spontaneously ruling the lower for their own or the social good, their rule being in turn spontaneously accepted by those inferior in glory.[15]

It will be noted that here we have again an illustration of the way in which Thomas tends to minimize the results of the Fall. For most early canonists, there was nothing which could be called government before the Fall and although animals were ruled by men, man himself

was not subject to man. For Thomas, on the contrary, both men and animals were subject to the rule of certain men before the Fall. Although the Fall undoubtedly affected the nature of rule to some extent, just as it gave grace more things to do, the principle that some men are, by nature, subordinate to others, remains the same both before the Fall and after the commission of original sin. Thomas makes the ground for thinking of government as natural the assertion that man is naturally a social being. At another point he states, Aristotle-like: "To be a social and political animal living in a crowd is even more natural to man than to the other animals."[16]

In Aristotelian-Thomist terms the potentiality which is either the pure natural or fallen natural man can become the actuality of a being who is not merely created in the image of God or re-created as a just man, but who can take on the very likeness of God himself.[17] Where, then, in this whole process from potentiality to actuality, are we to put politics? The best clue to Thomas's answer will be found in his conception of law, to which we now turn.

Thomas's Conception of Law

Thomas shares the general medieval view that the universe is literally flooded by law. But we should carefully note that he thinks of law in general as both normative and descriptive. At its highest reaches, of course, the normative and descriptive merge: thus at the level of the law which is identical with the divine nature, to describe the divine nature is at the same time to provide a standard or norm. In general,

7. St. Thomas Aquinas, *Summa Theologica* I, Q. 47, Art. 3.
8. *Summa*, I, Q. 49, Art. 2.
9. *Summa*, I, Q. 111, Art. 1.
10. The reference is to Aristotle's *De Generatione Animalium*, II, 3 (737a, 27). See also the *Summa*.
11. *Summa*, I, Q. 92, Art. 1.
12. 1 Corinthians 15:46.
13. *Summa*, I, Q. 95, Art. 4.
14. *Summa*, I, Q. 96, Art. 3.
15. *Summa*, I, Q. 96, Art. 4.
16. Opusc. XI, I *De Requimine Principum and Regem Cypri*, I.
17. *Summa*, I, Q. 93, Art. 4.

Thomas defines law as "An ordinance of reason for the common good, made by him who has the care of the community, and promulgated."[18] Since God "has the care" of that organic community which is the universe, of which human communities constitute but a small part, it is from God that all law is ultimately derived.

More specifically, he discerns four levels of law—eternal, natural, divine, and human. A correct understanding of each will help us grasp not only his theory of law but also his conception of the place of political society in the whole scheme of things.

Eternal Law. Everything in the universe is subject to eternal law, which Thomas seems to equate with the divine nature or essence itself. Thomas would contend that the eternal law is the type of order for the world which exists in the divine mind. No one but God himself can understand its full nature, but men in various ways can "participate" in it.[19]

Natural Law. When men look at the eternal law through reason, they can obtain certain self-evident propositions or moral axioms which provide norms for human conduct. Thomas thinks of natural law, then, as somewhat analogous in the realm of Aristotle's "practical" reason to "first principles" in the area of speculative science or philosophy. The moral axioms of the natural law provide a framework within which to think legally and a standard against which to check the enactments of the human lawmaker. In the realm of speculative or theoretical science, for example, such propositions as "things equal to the same thing are equal to each other" and "every whole is greater than any of its parts" are first principles in thinking for such sciences as mathematics and physics. In the sphere of law and morals, parallel propositions would be "the good is to be followed once discovered," "evil is to be avoided," and "self-preservation is a good."

Man's reason tells him that some goods he shares with all substances—such a good is that of self-preservation. Other goods he shares only with certain kinds of animals—sexual intercourse, for example. But some goods are peculiar to man himself—the good, for example, of knowing God and of pursuing truth. By right reason, Thomas thinks, it is possible for human beings to arrange these goods in a hierarchy and thus to discover what human beings should prefer in the event of a clash of goods.

Practical intelligence, of course, deals with contingent matters—those which could be otherwise than they are. The principles of both speculative and practical science are universal; but since the latter has as its end conduct of particular individuals, Thomas points out that "although there is necessity in the common principles, the more we descend towards the particular, the more frequently we encounter defects."[20]

Thomas illustrates this observation by pointing out that in the realm of speculative science it is always true that three angles of a triangle taken together equal two right angles (even though many may not know this), but that there is no contingency in the principle itself. It is as true of every case as it is true in general. If one turns to practical reason, the general notion that we should always act according to reason leads to the conclusion that goods which have been entrusted to another person should be restored to their owner. Thus far, the parallelism between speculative and practical reason holds. But if we ask whether in all circumstances goods entrusted to another man should be returned to their rightful owner, the answer becomes more doubtful. In a particular case, injury might result if the goods were returned. And he instances the return of goods when the temporary possessor knew that they might be used to fight against one's country.[21]

But the contingent nature of human affairs leads him to ask himself whether the natural law can be changed. If its practical implementation may lead to radically different applications, in other words, may it not be necessary and naturally legitimate to change the principles themselves? Supporting an affirmative answer to this question, he quotes a gloss on Ecclesiasticus[22] to the effect that a ruler changed the positive law in order to "correct" the law of nature. He also quotes St. Isidore of Seville as saying that common possessions and freedom are ordained by natural law; yet, as Thomas points out, the human law has obviously permitted private property and serious restrictions of freedom.

In raising the whole question as to whether natural law can be changed, Thomas is, of course, attempting to anticipate objections of those who are dubious about the existence of a discoverable universal law which reasserts its authority despite human violations. While the Middle Ages produced few if any legal positivists, it did have many who, following the

Augustinian conception of pure nature, found it difficult to reconcile the positive institutions which they supported with the presumed commands of natural law. We have already seen how they sought to support both the institutions and the law by the conception of a sin-created relative nature.

Thomas replies to the contentions of those who say that the natural law can be changed by first distinguishing between violations of natural law and additions to it. Many things, he contends, which are beneficial to human existence have been added "over and above" the natural law. These additions have come through human law itself and as a result of divine law. This does not mean that natural law has been changed but only that it has been supplemented. A little later we shall see how Thomas applies this principle to the theory of property.[23]

In the second place, Thomas observes, change may conceivably mean "subtraction" from the requirements of natural law. Obviously, he asserts here, any subtraction from the standards of the law's "first principles" is not permitted, these being the universals without which the whole idea of natural law would be but a mockery. But it is different with the "derived" principles which arise, as we have seen, as one descends from the general to the particular. Here subtraction is allowed in order to take account of individual circumstances.[24]

Answering the contention that human law has apparently changed natural law through its restrictions on freedom and its establishment of private property, Thomas lays it down that things are commanded by natural law in two ways. In the first, there is a positive inclination to do what is natural—for example, to do no harm to another human being. In the second, natural law is in a sense negative in that it may ordain one thing but not specifically forbid its contrary. Thus man is naturally naked, as Thomas points out, but there is nothing in nature which "inclines" man to object to clothes. Hence clothes can be "added" to nature without violating natural law.

Whatever one might think of these distinctions, it must be admitted that they are ingenious and that they represent an awareness of ambiguity in the term nature and of serious questions as to the congruity of actual human institutions with natural law. Thomas might, of course, have resolved these difficulties by taking a revolutionary position and denouncing certain human institutions as "unnatural" (as many medieval heretics were to do increasingly after his day). But this would have been contrary to his whole general outlook, as we shall see more explicitly later on.

In the course of his inquiry into natural law, he is concerned with another problem that exercises medieval moral and political thinkers —namely, the exact extent to which an awareness of natural law's precepts might be abolished in the human soul. Extreme advocates of the notion that original sin radically changed nature would tend, of course, to suggest that man's consciousness of law has grown exceedingly dim. But Thomas is obviously not one of these. Here again, he distinguishes between the basic, general principles of the law, and the secondary and particular propositions. The former cannot and have not been erased, he maintains, as abstract statements of the law; but they may be obscured or blotted out in varying degrees "in the case of a particular action, in so far as reason is hindered from applying the common principle to the particular action because of concupiscence or some other passion." As for the secondary propositions, they can be covered over "either by evil persuasions, just as in speculative matters errors occur in respect of necessary conclusions; or by vicious customs and corrupt habits. . . ."[25]

One can hardly help noting how much more careful Thomas is in his examination of natural law than most of the civilian and canon lawyers. His qualifications are more clearly put, his awareness of difficulties is much keener, and his perspective is broader and deeper. In his discussion, we see, of course, the fruits of the great philosophical revival.

Divine Law. While the doctrine of natural law always tends to be the center of high medieval political speculation, many of the lawyers, as has been suggested, tend sometimes to identify it with another term widely used—

18. *Summa*, II-I, 2, 90, Art. 2.
19. See *Contra Gentiles*, III, 111-116.
20. *Summa*, II-I, Q. 94, Art. 4.
21. *Summa*, II-I, Q. 94, Art. 4.
22. *Summa*, XVII, 9.
23. See Chapter 000.
24. *Summa*, II-I, Q. 94, Art. 5.
25. *Summa*, II-I, Q. 94, Art. 6.

that of divine law. Thomas clearly separates the divine from the natural law and in so doing develops some of the most characteristic of his understandings.

By contrast with natural law, which is discovered by human reason, Thomas identifies divine law with Revelation and particularly with revelation found in the Old and New Testaments. If any person should argue that divine law is unnecessary in view of the admitted fact that man by reason can discover natural law, which is, of course, man's participation in the eternal law, Thomas, characteristically enough, has four reasons to justify the need for divine law.

In the first place, he argues that the "last end" of man cannot be discovered by reason and hence is not in natural law. Secondly, while we may be directed by natural law to our earthly ends, it is evident that human judgment is often very uncertain as to the application of principles to specific instances, or, as he expresses it, to "contingent and particular matters."[26] In the important questions, then, divine law presumably overlaps natural law to some extent, especially where issues of application are concerned. A third consideration has to do with the inability of mere human law to direct "interior movements," or, as we should say today, to "judge motives and intentions." Yet any rectitude must depend not merely on exterior acts performed or not performed—with which human law can deal—but also with the internal dispositions of the human soul which ultimately can be judged only by God. Finally, human law cannot really punish everything that is evil. This proposition in effect makes a distinction between law and morality. Human law presumably punishes all acts in violation of positive ordinances (assuming those ordinances are not contrary to natural law, of course) but the positive ordinances themselves do not and, indeed, ought not punish all acts which are evil. If human law should attempt to do so, it might actually, in view of the contingencies which Thomas constantly stresses, "hinder the advance of the common good."[27] But God never intends that evil should go unpunished. Hence the sanctions of divine law implement the prohibitions and commands for which human law cannot punish.

In Thomas's answer to his questions, we have a clue not only to his conception of divine law in the scheme as a whole but also one to his general conception of social and political development. We also obtain his response to those unorthodox Christian thinkers who have seen clear conflict between the law of the Old Testament and the love proclaimed in the New.

Broadly speaking, Thomas sees the old law, so-called, as a preparation for the new. It ordains an order of things which disciplines man through fear of punishment, so that he will be prepared to transcend that order and to live according to the law of love. The Old Testament tends to emphasize a temporal good, while the New establishes the principles of the heaven which lies beyond earthly welfare. The old law concentrates on external actions which make for justice; while the new directs its attention primarily to internal acts. Thomas sums up the roles of the two laws by quoting from that favorite of medieval thinkers, the *Sentences* of Peter Lombard: "The old law restrains the hand, but the new law controls the soul."

The attempt to fit divine law into a conception of development is at no point better illustrated than in Thomas's threefold classification of the old law. It contains, he asserts, moral, liturgical or ceremonial, and judicial precepts. Each kind will show the help which God gives to man in his effort to become a person and attain the ideal of community which will be exalted by the new law.

The moral precepts, such as those contained in the Ten Commandments, embrace all the commands of natural law but include others as well. The divine law presupposes the natural law in the same way that grace presupposes nature.[28] While man's reason can discover the common principles of natural law and hence is not subject to error universally, it often, because of sin, becomes confused as to what should be done in particular instances. Moreover, men go astray with respect to the secondary principles derived from the general rules. Divine law steps into the breach to assist reason.

The theory of liturgical or ceremonial law in the Old Testament is one which sustains the need for implementation of the natural and divine law principle that God should be worshipped. How he should be worshipped is the function of positive law to prescribe. The ceremonial precepts involving sacrifice are examples, in the context of Jewish law, of the universal need felt by man for a system of regular ceremonial which will dramatize the distinction between piety and impiety.[29]

Father Gilby, in his study of the political philosophy of St. Thomas,[30] has rightly pointed out that the scholastic philosopher is simply recognizing something universal in all civil polities, whether religious in an orthodox sense or not. Every society establishes ceremonies to dramatize the distinction between that which is sacred and that which is not. Thus the Jews have an untouchable Ark, the ancient Romans the Vestal Virgins and the ceremonies connected with them, the Soviet Russians the elaborate ceremonial surrounding Communist Party meetings, and the Americans flag salutes and Tombs of Unknown Soldiers.

Finally, Thomas distinguishes judicial precepts as the third element in old law. By these he signifies what Aristotle would probably call the "constitution" or polity of the Jewish people.[31] He seeks to show that the constitution of the ancient Jews satisfied Aristotle's requirements for a polity in his specific sense—that is, there was a balance among monarchy, aristocracy, and democracy.

A vital problem for all Christian thinkers who consider the relation between old and new laws has always been the extent to which Old Testament regulations bind men after the coming of Christ. This also involves the issue of how particular Jewish institutions can be related to other polities. Thomas deals with these questions subtly and with care. With the coming of Christ, he contends, the ceremonial precepts of the old law are not only dead but deadly.[32] That is to say, they not only no longer bind but if any ruler seeks to make them bind he is impeding human development. The ceremonial precepts have served their purpose in foreshadowing the mysteries of Christ.

On the other hand, the judicial precepts are dead but not deadly. They were not designed to be figures but rather to "shape the state of the people." They were, in other words, founded that men might perform certain deeds. They no longer bind as such. But if a ruler wishes to institute them for the good government of his people, thus making their binding effect the result of a new positive human law, their observance "is not prejudicial to the truth of faith."[33]

But, we might well ask, if so large a part of the old-law aspect of divine law is either dead or both dead and deadly, why does Thomas devote so substantial a part of his analysis to it? He seems to relish the details of ancient ceremonial and judicial precepts and one finds it difficult at first to discover why he does so. The answer will be found, it would seem, in his use of ancient Jewish liturgical and constitutional regulations not only as prefigurements and disciplines for the coming of the historical Jesus but also as illustrations of the general proposition that ceremony and external rule represent a kind of middle stage between governance simply by instinct or by uncriticized tradition (as with the animals and with early man) and the ultimate social perfection of heaven. As Gilby has pointed out, St. Thomas thinks of political society—and for this purpose organized ecclesiastical rule is associated with and indispensable from the political stage—as including elements of both the prepolitical phase of governance (by instinct, immemorial folkways and mores, and emotion) and of the postpolitical ultimate end when, with the assistance of grace, souls associate freely and at different levels but without any element of disorder or coercive domination.[34]

Just as the human being of political history is an imperfectly shaped person who aspires to the freedom beyond political history, so is the community one of semi-persons. Every political community, Thomas holds, is a combination of coerced with free association. Government is never wholly a matter of coercion, for in Eden it existed as a coercionless hierarchy of natural subordination and direction. On the other hand, even in Eden the ultimate spiritual end of man was beyond the state.

When St. Thomas says that the peculiarly Jewish ceremonial laws are abolished, he clearly does not mean that all public ceremonial of a religious nature is to be wiped out. Rather does he contend that, since the "priest-

26. *Summa*, II–I, Q. 91, Art. 4.
27. *Ibid.*
28. *Summa*, II–I, Q. 99, Art. 2.
29. *Summa*, II–I, Q. 99, Art. 3.
30. Thomas Gilby, *Between Community and Society: A Philosophy and Theology of the State*, London: Longmans, Green, 1953. See also Gilby's *Political Thought of St. Thomas Aquinas*, Chicago: University of Chicago Press, 1958.
31. *Summa*, II–I, Q. 104, Art. 1.
32. *Summa*, II–I, Q. 104, Art. 3.
33. *Ibid.*
34. Note, for Gilby's interpretation, *Between Community and Society*, *op. cit.*, particularly pp. 49–74. See also Jacques Maritain, *Scholasticism and Politics*, New York: Macmillan, 1941.

hood" has been "translated," the ceremonial is now to be established by the successor of the Jewish nation, the Church. Christian liturgy helps to dramatize the demands of the imperfectly realized new law just as Old Testament ceremonial law prefigured the coming of the new dispensation. But the ceremonies of the Church still exist at the political-ecclesiastical stage of development and are not to be thought of as final in any sense.

Similarly, while the particular judicial precepts of the Jews no longer bind as such (although they may be reenacted, as we have seen), they illustrate through the medium of divine law some of the characteristics of any political society which stands between the prepolitical stage of human community and the postpolitical. Thus the polity of the Jews helps us to understand the political implications of natural law precepts by giving us particulars; and while we are to distinguish carefully between those details of the Jewish polity which were appropriate by reason of peculiarly Jewish cultural conditions and those general aspects that illustrate universal principles, both are important as reflecting the general problems of legal regulation in any political community.

But we should always keep in mind that any given political or ecclesiastical organization is historical; and that while it mirrors universal reason in a measure, it also looks beyond reason to the final end. It is in the new law that one will find stated the principles toward which all political society points—the final end which is even now reflected in the seemingly meaningless conflicts of history.

In treating his view of the New Testament as it relates to social and political development, Thomas is careful not to identify it with natural law and he is equally certain that its full "consummation" will not take place until the end of the world. Natural law is that which is "instilled" into man's nature. But the "law of love" is "added to" nature by grace. The new law not only tells man what he should do but it also helps him "to accomplish it."[35] Although some men have lived implicitly by the New Testament long before the historic appearance of Jesus, in its explicit fullness the new law did not appear until men, through the discipline of the old law, were in a measure prepared for it. Here again we find in Thomas the notion of development: Nature precedes the spiritual historically just as in personal development we become aware of right and wrong first through the external commands imposed by the family.[36]

But Thomas is no advocate of progress in the modern sense; and this brings us to his doctrine of the relation which the New Testament bears to the question of consummation. At the very moment Thomas is writing, heretics are already beginning to teach that the evolution from old law to new will be followed by the appearance of the Holy Ghost who will destroy all organized subordination in Church and state. With their specific doctrines we shall be concerned in the next chapter. Here, however, we must note Thomas's vigorous denial of their contentions. His voice is that of Orthodoxy denouncing those who would subvert social order.

He does, however, state fairly the argument of those in the thirteenth century who are beginning to construct what Eric Voegelin has called the "new science of politics."[37] It runs about as follows: the Trinity is reflected in stages of human history. The old law, with its external penalties and its emphasis on prohibitions, represents the age of the Father; the coming of Christ, with the new law, reflects the Son, who institutes a hierarchical priesthood for the governance of mankind; but soon the age of the Holy Ghost will arrive in which all hierarchies will be swept away, including the priesthood of the Church.

To Thomas, such an interpretation is "senseless." He admits that the state of mankind with respect to the new law may change: At certain times, in other words, societies may seem closer to the spirit of the Gospels than at others; "nevertheless, we are not to look forward to a state wherein man is to possess the grace of the Holy Ghost more perfectly than he has possessed it hitherto. . . ."[38]

The vigor with which Thomas denounces incipiently progressive views of history is a measure of his basic attachment to the conservative political position. Even though political society is a preparation for the state of heaven in which some characteristics of politics—organization, dominion, coercion—will be transcended, the revelation embodied in the new law does not support the position that this state can be attained on earth. While one might, to be sure, reject what Voegelin calls heretical "gnosticism" and still have some hope for earthly improvement—and Thomas has more than many medievalists—the basic thrust of Thomistic scholasticism is at least moderately conservative.

How, then, does the new law affect human governance? Here Thomas is clear that it seeks primarily to rule "interior movements." The old law restrained the hand, as he suggests, but the new law seeks to control the will; and in this observation he follows Peter Lombard.[39] The new law both fulfills and is contained in the old. It is the law of liberty not only "because it does not bind us to do or avoid certain things, except such as are of themselves necessary or opposed to salvation," but also because "it . . . makes us comply freely with these precepts and prohibitions, inasmuch as we do so through the promptings of grace."[40] Its major purpose is to provide an opening for grace and it commands only those acts which open the way for grace.

One of the great issues of medieval social and political debate is whether the new law is to be observed by all men in the same degree. We have already pointed out that, in general, medieval thinkers conclude that it prescribes a dualistic ethic. Thomas agrees with this position and tries to justify it philosophically. Again, he resorts to the notion of development, distinguishing between the imperfect and the perfect. Thomas sees man hanging between material and spiritual goods, often uncertain as to which he is to prefer, yet knowing basically that if he clings to the former he will lose beatitude. The commandments clarify his position and seek to prevent his making material things ends in themselves. Hence Thomas will accept Aristotle's attitude to private property yet emphasize that those who wish to attain eternal happiness more speedily will give up their material goods, thus following the advice of Christ to the rich young ruler.[41] Human institutions will accept the one principle; but those who seek a rapid advance to perfection will adopt the other.

The new law teaches, he observes, that there are three basic desires—modern man would probably say drives—"concupiscence of the eyes," or desire for external wealth; "concupiscence of the flesh," or desire for "carnal" pleasures; and "pride of life," or overwhelming desire for honor or status. Perfection, which may be thought of as the negation of these lusts, thus consists in poverty, chastity, and obedience—all of which go beyond nature and yet for which nature is a preparation. Positive institutions, which must be built on nature, cannot, of course, require supernatural acts—to do so would itself be unnatural. But individual souls or communities can go further than nature requires and thus seek to observe the transnatural counsels of the new law.

Thomas's Conception of Human Law. Thomas thinks of human law as a kind of lower level expression of natural law. Just as in speculative science we begin with certain indemonstrable principles and from these proceed to the conclusions of the specific sciences, so in practical reason we start with the indemonstrable but common principles of the natural law and descend to particularistic statements of the human law, explicit rules for everyday life.

Then, too, Thomas thinks that while all men naturally desire virtue, the principle needs fixing through habit. Moreover, since men can find their vision of virtue obscured through sin, they must be restrained at times through force and fear operating under control of the specific rules of human law. This is true of young and old alike. Human law disciplines through fear of punishment. Animals do not possess laws in this sense because they are not rational; but man, while he inclines to virtue naturally and can use his reason to support and implement that virtue, can also employ his great rational capacities to satisfy "his lusts and evil passions, which other animals are unable to do."[42] It is this ambivalence as to how he should employ reason which is in large part at the root of man's construction of positive legal systems.

That the positive law, to be law, must be derived from natural law is to Thomas beyond question. To the objection that natural law is universal while positive laws differ widely, he replies that a given principle of natural law may require diverse positive laws in order to give expression to its objectives under widely varying social and economic conditions. Again and again he stresses the contingent factor in

35. *Summa*, II–I, Q. 106, Art. 1.
36. *Summa*, II–I, Q. 106, Art. 3.
37. Cf. Eric Vogelin, *The New Science of Politics*, Chicago: University of Chicago Press, 1952.
38. For Thomas's entire discussion of this problem see *Summa*, II–I, Q. 106, Art. 4.
39. *Sentences*, III, xi, I (II, 734).
40. *Summa*, II–I, Q. 108, Art. 1, Reply, Objection 2.
41. Matthew 19:21.
42. *Summa*, II–I, Q. 95, Art. 1.

human experience. Thus natural law may prescribe that every offense against a human enactment should be punished. But the particular punishment will have to be a matter shaped in considerable degree by the stage of cultural evolution which a society has attained; here, then, there is room for an enormous growth and change in the idea of what the specific punishment ought to be.

Then, too, the fact that positive law is derived from natural law and that the discovery of the latter is a matter of reason does not mean that literally every element of human law can be demonstrated to be right. Sometimes we must rely on the undemonstrated judgment of the prudent and those experienced in life. Their comments on what the positive law ought to contain should be regarded with great respect, for, on the basis of their wide knowledge of men and affairs, they may "see at once what is the best thing to decide."[43]

The role of the prudential in his system is particularly noteworthy when he comes to discuss the degree to which human law should seek a repression of all vices. He points out that vices of all kinds are contrary to natural law. Since, therefore, human law is derived from natural law, it might appear that statutes should seek to prohibit all things which are vicious under the law of nature. In a sense, of course, this is exactly what the Puritans of the seventeenth century tended to conclude, except that for natural law they substituted what Thomas calls the old law branch of divine law. Thomas, however, is quite clear that it is not within the province of positive law to prohibit everything which is contrary to the law of nature. The many nonvirtuous might react violently to any law which sought to compel standards radically beyond those appropriate for their stage of perfection. Here Thomas quotes Scripture: "He that violently bloweth his nose, bringeth out blood."[44] He also uses the analogy of new wine in old bottles: If new wine, in the form of completely unrealistic positive law commands, is put into the old bottles of human imperfection, the bottles break. In other terms, if human law demands too much of human beings, the attempt to enforce it may lead to the very violence, disorder, and rebellion which law is ostensibly supposed to prevent.

In a sense, then, human law must necessarily wink at most vices—and hence allow the devil considerable freedom—in order that a few very serious offenses (like those of murder and theft) might be effectively restrained. In the process of learning to obey positive enactments dealing with a few matters, men are educated by the law to achieve yet higher standards.

However, this is not to say that all purported human laws are really laws; for if they are unjust, they do not have a binding effect. And they may be unjust in two ways: They may be contrary to the common good or they may be promulgated by a ruler in excess of his power or in a form which is against natural law (as when they impose unequal—irrationally unequal—burdens on the community). In such cases the alleged laws are really acts of violence and can in no sense be binding on the conscience.[45]

While it is clear that obedience to such alleged laws is not required under natural law, Thomas is not at all certain as to who makes the decision on the justice or injustice of a particular law. Some light will, indeed, be cast on this problem in his discussion of political authority and of spiritual-temporal relations, but even there one remains in doubt. He does, however, make it clear that even an unjust law should perhaps (and the very use of this word seems to indicate doubt) be obeyed if disobedience would provoke scandal or disturbance, citing, curiously enough, that New Testament passage which tells one to give a cloak as well as the coat and to go two miles when forced to go one.[46]

As for the relation of law to the ruler, Thomas is confronted by two alternative positions with which, as we have seen, medieval thinkers are constantly grappling. The tradition stemming from the Justinian *Digest*[47] held flatly that the sovereign was not subject to the laws. How could he be, asked those who took this position, since it was he who made the laws? On the other hand, the Germanic outlook, thinking of law as primarily custom, could not see why ruler and subject alike were not bound by the law. Thomas, as is his wont, makes careful distinctions in arriving at his own position. He draws a line between the law in its "coercive power" and, on the other hand, the law as a "directive force." With respect to the former, the ruler is not subject to the law; but he is fully bound by the law in its directive capacity. His exemption is due to the sheer fact that no person can coerce himself; his subjection to the natural and divine law principles that rules made by a man for other men should also be observed by the maker. Basically, it would seem, Thomas thinks of the supreme ruler as bound by law morally and hence subject to divine sanctions if he should disregard it. What the community can do politically if he should violate the law will be examined elsewhere.[48]

At no point is Thomas's balanced view of the political world better reflected than in his analysis of the problem of change in law. Here he seeks to give due recognition both to the eternal characteristics of natural law and to the obviously shifting situations of human history. On the whole, it is clear, he is dubious about the value of change—like most medieval thinkers he is emphatically no social reformer—and yet, because he is keenly aware of impermanence in historical life and possesses a strong pragmatic and utilitarian consciousness, he knows that he must make the problem of change a central question.

Change in law comes about, he maintains, for two reasons. In the first place, human reason and contrivance are ever seeking to develop greater and greater degrees of perfection. But secondly, social and psychological conditions are constantly changing, thus necessitating a different application of natural law norms. Human laws may, therefore, have to be changed from time to time.

But, like Aristotle, Thomas utters a strong word of caution. The mere fact that a new social contrivance might in the abstract seem better than what a community possesses at the moment does not justify change in positive law.[49] This does not mean that Thomas holds all old laws and practices to be *ipso facto* sacred and beyond the reach of the lawmaker. It does imply, however, that he always gives the benefit of the doubt to the old, since it is ever difficult to establish habits of conformity to new law. Thus, as he puts it, "the mere change of law is of itself prejudicial to the common welfare, because custom avails much for the observance of laws."[50]

This analysis of the relation between custom and innovation leads Thomas to ask whether custom itself may change law. His answer is in the affirmative. Custom, he avers, is a kind of will and reason in deeds instead of speech; and since all human law is an expression of the reasonable will of man, custom can be regarded, along with the decrees of the sovereign, as an expression of that reasonable will. Of course, custom which is contrary to either divine or natural law cannot have the force of positive law any more than the decrees of the ruler.

Throughout his discussion of human law, Thomas seems always to be aware that he is attempting to unite in one coherent whole Roman, patristic, Hebrew, and Aristotelian views. Insofar as he accents the need for a definite law-declaring authority he is Roman, as he is also when he stresses the reasonable will. In his consciousness of positive law as subordinate to the law of nature, he combines Aristotelian and patristic positions. Insofar as he looks upon positive law as an externally imposed discipline for the training of mankind, Augustinian and Hebraic elements are present, as they are to the degree that he thinks of legal and political development as an expression of the will of God in history.

In his outlook on law, as in so much else, Thomas reflects a catholic and eclectic viewpoint which spurns *either-or* positions.

Thomas's General Theory of Political Authority

But Thomas's conception of law must be closely related to his analysis of political authority.

As we have seen, political society is for him an arena of paradoxes and tensions, in which a potentially rational man is torn between subpolitical and unreflective subordination of the individual to the group and superpolitical association in which personality is completed in freedom and "community" is achieved in an uncoerced harmony.

The medieval context of his theory is evident in his tracing the authority of the ruler to either the community as a whole or to a "superior." When he maintains that rulers gain their authority through the community and

43. *Summa*, II–I, Q. 95, Art. 2.
44. Proverbs 30:33.
45. *Summa*, II–I, Q. 96, Art. 4.
46. Matthew 5:40, 41.
47. *Digest*, I, iii. 31 (I, 34b).
48. See pp. 244–245.
49. Here he cites Gratian, *Decretum*, I. xii. 5 (I, 28).
50. *Summa*, II–I, Q. 97, Art. 2.

ultimately from God he is, of course, reflecting both the Roman legal tradition and canonical thinking. With respect to political authority conferred by a superior, he would seem to be referring to feudal conditions, whether the feudatory be subordinate to the papacy or to a feudal lord.

As to his exact political ideal, we have already referred to his citing Aristotle as an authority for the notion of mixed government; and it is clear that St. Thomas thinks that that form of political rule is best which takes account both of the superior wisdom of the few and of the necessity for obedience by the many. Moreover, he has great confidence, as we have also seen, in the legislative capacity of the many through custom. He is above all looking for stability, which can best be attained through a monarch who rules with the assent of the whole community and after seeking the advice of an aristocratic body of some kind.

Thomas is torn between Christian reverence for the "powers that be," on the one hand, and a great Aristotelian and Augustinian awareness of the possibilities of tyranny, on the other. Thus he emphasizes that rulers are to be held in great honor, even though they be evil men in a personal sense; for, as he puts it, "*gerunt vicem Dei et communitatis*"[51]—they bear the person of God and the community.

At the same time, his view of natural law and of the nature of justice will not permit him to view all the acts of an alleged ruler as legitimate. We have already noted his differentiation between a just and an unjust law.[52] He makes a similar distinction between a legitimate and an illegitimate ruler. Thus the decrees of a ruler may be unjust on two grounds; he may, in the first place, have obtained his office contrary to law and hence to be a usurper. But secondly, even though his title to office is clear, he may command unjust things.[53]

Hence Thomas feels obliged to discuss the problem of how to treat an obvious tyrant—a favorite theme of medieval thinkers. While he is clear that sedition is a grave sin, he is not so certain that tyrannicide is to be ruled out. The idea that it is legitimate to kill the tyrant is, of course, an old one in the history of political thought. The ancients accepted it without much difficulty. In the twelfth century, John of Salisbury explicitly supported it, thus helping to revive the idea for high medieval thought.[54]

In his *Commentary on the Sentences of Peter Lombard*,[55] Thomas, too, appears to endorse the idea that killing a tyrant is legitimate. There he quotes without disapproval Cicero's favorable comments.

By the time he pens *De Regimine Principum* (or at least part of it), however, he devotes no attention to tyrannicide and is perhaps very dubious as to whether it is to be given moral approbation. In this work, he stresses methods which can be adopted to prevent tyranny from arising in the first place. Thus he discusses the selection of a virtuous ruler and suggests that constitutional arrangements should be established which would prevent his becoming a tyrant. The implication is that the ruler should always be chosen by the community—or at least be approved by it—and that standards for appointment of subordinates should be established by positive law.

In arguing that the ruler ought to be selected by the community, Thomas is not necessarily suggesting that the hereditary principle be discarded entirely. As medieval political thought develops, and the hereditary notion is established in such areas as England and France, inheritance of royal status is usually accompanied by the idea that the community must approve, in some way, the succession of the son to the throne of his father. Heredity, in other words, is not enough—it must be coupled with participation by the whole populus to determine whether the son is worthy to rule. Even a new pope, although selected according to the decree of 1059 by the Cardinals, is acclaimed by the people of Rome.

When Thomas, therefore, suggests selection of the ruler by the community, he is probably not discarding heredity altogether but rather stressing the vital part which community participation should play. He deems it to be essential if the ruler is to be kept constantly reminded of his responsibility to those whom he rules.

If there are legally established methods for removing the tyrant, of course, Thomas sees no objection to their being used fully. The ancient Roman Senate he regards in this light. Even in the absence of formal organs and positive law he seems to think that corporate action by the populus may, under certain circumstances, be essential. But he carefully distinguishes between corporate, and individual or fractional removal of the ruler. Just what he means by community or corporate action in the absence of formal legal provision is, of course, unclear; but Thomas can be interpreted as advocating, in some sense, a right of revolution. Indeed, some modern scholars do see his doctrine in this light; and it is probably this aspect of his teaching which leads Lord Acton to characterize him as "the first Whig in politics."[56]

Given his view that political authority is natural and is not merely the fruit of man's sin, Thomas tends always to see it in a more positive light than St. Augustine. For the latter it is primarily repressive and negative. For the author of the *Summa* it is the positive guardian of the social order; and its negative functions, while no doubt still important, fade into the background. It is one level of the hierarchy of authority which stretches from the demons, whose superordinate and subordinate relations exist for the purpose of drawing souls from God, to the highest reaches of the angels, who illumine those below them through the light they receive from the greatest authority.

Thomas and the Socioeconomic Order

At no point is Thomas's effort to marry Aristotle to early medieval Christian attitudes better illustrated than in his examination of such institutions as slavery and property. He distinguishes the rule of master over slave from that of prince over subject by arguing that while the latter has for its objective the public weal, the former is for private gain. The latter is natural, sin merely introducing distortions. The former, however, is unnatural and is only relatively justified by the coming of sin into the world: here it is clear that Thomas follows Augustine very closely and is also in the tradition of both the civilians and the canonists.

With respect to the institutions of property, however, he develops a theory which is neither that of the Fathers and most of the canonists nor exactly that espoused by Aristotle.

He admits that in nature there are no institutions of private property.[57] However, it is also true that natural law does not positively forbid the development of private property arrangements; and as a matter of fact these devices have been added to nature for the convenience of men. Thus Thomas accepts Augustine's position that community of goods exists naturally and rejects Aristotle's view that private property is positively natural. But he reaches Aristotle's conclusion in substance by holding that man's reason has added to Augustine's nature the institutions of property. Indirectly, we may say, property for Thomas is natural in the sense that reason is the distinctive characteristic of the human species and that where nature does not forbid such action it is permissible for man to add to its ordinances through positive law. Man has added property in material goods to nature because he has concluded that "every man is more careful to procure what is for himself alone than that which is common to many or to all. . . ."[58] Moreover, it seems that human affairs can be more orderly if every man has a definite responsibility for care of material things. Finally, peace is more likely where there is a distribution of goods through property institutions than where things are held in common.

But while property is justified as more than relatively natural, Thomas is careful to point out, following Aristotle, that its use must be common. He interprets St. Ambrose's saying "Let no man call his own that which is common" as an admonition about "ownership as regards use."[59]

His theory of property can be understood more fully if we look not merely at his statement of the general principle but also at its implications for specific conduct. What he does essentially is to work out a philosophical justification for those legal rules, so characteristic of the late Middle Ages, which regulate the use of private property. As many scholars

51. A. P. D'Entreves, ed., *Aquinas: Selected Political Writings*, J. G. Danson, trans., Oxford: Basil Blackwell, 1948, pp. 50–51.
52. See p. 242.
53. See "Commentary on the Sentences of Peter Lombard," in A. P. D'Entreves, *op. cit.*, pp. 182–183.
54. See John of Salisbury, *Policraticus*. Books 4, 5, and 6, with selections from 7 and 8 have been translated by John Dickinson (as *The Statesman's Book of John of Salisbury*), New York: Knopf, 1927; Books 1, 2, and 3, with selections from 7 and 8 have been translated by Joseph B. Pike, Minneapolis: University of Minnesota Press, 1938.
55. A. P. D'Entreves, *op. cit.*, pp. 184–185.
56. *History of Freedom and Other Essays*, London: Macmillan, 1907.
57. *Summa*, II–II, Q. 66, Art. 2.
58. *Summa*, II–II, Q. 66, Art. 2.
59. *Ibid.*

have pointed out,[60] the "medieval synthesis" includes as one of its vital aspects the notion that the economic order and social organization connected with it are subject to the principles of natural law and to the positive law which adds to the provisions of nature but which is not contrary to them. Many canon lawyers contend that economic activities are in a peculiar sense subject to the ecclesiastical courts, for material things are of right subject to spirituals. And in practice it is true that canon law tribunals do supervise such diverse regulations as those which prohibit the taking of interest, establish minimum wages, fix maximum prices, and even prohibit anything resembling advertising. With these general tendencies Thomas is in undoubted sympathy.

He illustrates the general subjection of economic affairs to moral principles by asking whether it is ever lawful to steal through stress of need. He has previously distinguished between robbery and theft by identifying the former with an open taking of things which belong to another while the latter is an unlawful taking carried out secretly.[61] Both are sins, although robbery is the more grievous for it always involves an act of violence, whereas theft is a matter of cunning. While public authority, within the limits of natural law and justice, can forcibly take spoils of war in a just war and seize the goods of a citizen if authorized to do so by natural and positive law, the seizure of another's goods by private persons cannot be permitted.

But no sooner has St. Thomas barred the taking of another's material goods than he begins to hedge his statement about with qualifications. It is neither theft nor robbery, he asserts, if one person should steal from another under "stress of need."[62] He reasons that all things "are common property" insofar as need arises. If those who possess the right to administer material goods do not use them for the common benefit, then he who has an urgent and manifest need can "succor his own need by means of another's property, by taking it either openly or secretly; nor is this, properly speaking, theft or robbery."

The relation between human and divine law is nicely illustrated in his discussion of buying and selling. He lays it down, following the scriptural injunction: "Whatsoever you would that men should do to you, do you also to them,"[63] that it is never right to "sell a thing for more than its worth."[64] No one wishes to buy for more than the worth of a thing and if we apply the Golden Rule it follows that no one ought to sell a material good for more than its worth. How one measures worth Thomas does not tell us, although it is obvious that he is here dealing with what is later to involve moral and economic science in the whole "theory of value" as applied to material goods. But however worth is to be measured specifically, Thomas, like Marx, appears to think of it as something objective.

With respect to usury, Thomas bases his argument against it primarily on Aristotle, although he also takes account of the classical passage in Deuteronomy.[65] He makes a careful distinction between those things "the use of which consists in their consumption," like food and drink, and those other things "the use of which does not consist in their consumption," like the utilization of a house. If a person were to sell wine "separately from the use of the wine," he would, according to St. Thomas, "be selling the same thing twice." On the other hand, the use of a house does not destroy it and hence a man can legitimately make a charge for its use by another person. Rental of a house, in other words, is to be distinguished from double payment for wine or food.

Now money, according to Thomas, is like food or wine rather than like houses. Its consumption is its use in exchange; its use cannot be distinguished from its consumption. For this reason "it is by its very nature unlawful to take payment for the use of money lent, which payment is known as usury."[66] If, therefore, a man has taken usury in this sense, he is bound by both natural and divine law to restore his illegitimate gains to the man from whom he has taken them.

It is significant that in his distinction between a house and food, Thomas has opened the way for usury on invested money. There are certain things, like houses or landed property, "whose use is not their consumption." Such items "admit of usufruct" and hence can have legitimate "fruits" for which payment should be made.[67] It would seem but a relatively slight leap from such propositions to the notion that money used directly for capital goods is entitled to usury, for is not a ship, for example, like a house or land? Does it not have its own usufruct? Although Thomas does not spell this out, it will later become a basis for the admission of usury on money.

In general, Thomas's view of social life is one which deprecates agrarian existence and exalts the urban. He thinks that village and farm life are confining and not conducive to those temporal conditions which are a necessary though not a sufficient condition for the growth of the soul. He is not contemptuous of the business man and, indeed, unlike "the Philosopher," thinks that the insights gained in commercial life can make a real contribution to governance. Although Thomas's whole conception of the hierarchy of souls seems to follow feudal imagery, there can be no doubt that in his general outlook he does not exalt the feudal way of life.

The Politics of the Ecclesia

For a medieval thinker like Thomas the capstone of any sociopolitical discussion must be an examination of the relation between temporal and spiritual power.

It is not easy to classify St. Thomas with respect to this overwhelmingly important political question of the thirteenth century; and it has been suggested, indeed, that his earlier position conflicts with that which he takes in later life.[68] Involved ultimately are the political implications of his theoretical statement on nature and super-nature and the relation between natural and divine law. Then, too, this is an issue on which Thomas has no direct guidance from "the Philosopher," although Aristotle's treatise on the soul undoubtedly affects his attitude as it does that of other thirteenth-century thinkers.

Law and Ecclesiastical Authority. Earlier in this chapter we stressed the fact that natural and divine law are not in conflict with each other but rather that the latter completes and fulfills the former by taking the soul and society into an area beyond reason although not contrary to it.

But general principles must always be administered and applied to particulars, as Thomas is always reminding us. Law by its nature deals with broad categories, yet its subjects are individualized. Hence there must be machinery which will implement the law of nature and artifacts not contrary to it, on the one hand, and the divine law with its institutions, on the other. The former will be the realm of temporal power, the latter that of spiritual government. And because divine law treats of ultimate goals while the natural and human law can only rule in secondary matters, the administration of the latter is inevitably below the direction of the former.[69]

This might superficially be interpreted as subordinating temporal to spiritual authority without limitations. Yet further inquiry into treatment by Thomas of particular issues will suggest that there is a certain and important autonomy in temporals.

Thomas and the Infidels. For example, he is very clear about a matter which exercised the canonists of the thirteenth century—the relation of Christians to infidels. Are Christians bound in conscience to obey Muslim rulers? Or is the duty to obey colored by the religion of the ruler, so that good followers of Christ need not feel any political obligations with respect to princes who profess the faith of the Prophet? If all kings are literally vassals of the Church, as Thomas seems to argue in one passage,[70] does it not follow that the legitimacy of secular rule turns in part on whether the prince is a professed Christian?

In reply,[71] the Angelic Doctor calls attention to his consistently held view that temporal rule springs from nature and that the dictates of nature are universal, transcending any distinctions between Christian and Muslim. Muslim rulers, then, provided they do not violate natural law, are entitled to the cheerful obedience of their Christian subjects and sedition on the part of the latter would be a grievous sin.

At this point it might be asked how Thomas reconciles his attitude on Christians' subjection to Muslim rulers with his equally emphatic assertion that Christian rulers who apostasize have no claim on the obedience of their sub-

60. For example, R. H. Tawney, *Religion and the Rise of Capitalism*, New York: Mentor, 1963; Max Weber, *The Protestant Ethic and the Spirit of Capitalism*, New York: Charles Scribner's Sons, 1948; and Henry O. Taylor, *Medieval Mind*, 2 vols., Cambridge: Harvard University Press, 1959.
61. *Summa*, II–II, Q. 66, Art. 4.
62. *Summa*, II–II, Q. 66, Art. 7.
63. Matthew 7:12.
64. *Summa*, II–II, Q. 77, Art. 1.
65. Deuteronomy 23:19–20.
66. *Summa*, II–II, Q. 78, Art. 1.
67. Note *Summa*, II–II, Q. 78, Art. 3.
68. Such seems to be the view of the Carlyles, *Medieval Political Theory in the West*, Edinburgh and London: Blackwood, 1936, vol. 5, p. 353.
69. *Regimine Principum*, II, 110.
70. *Quaestiones Quodlibetales*, XII, 19.
71. *Summa*, II–II, Q. 10, Art. 10.

jects.[72] A notable example was the case of the Emperor Frederick II (a relative, as we have seen, of St. Thomas) who, while the future saint was yet a boy, was excommunicated by Pope Gregory IX.

Thomas would, of course, have supported the Pope in the general proposition that Gregory could absolve Frederick's subjects of their oaths to him on the ground that the emperor had ceased to be a Christian. Yet he would denounce disobedience of Muslim rulers if the reason alleged were to be their non-Christian faith. To put it another way, had Frederick become a Muslim, his subjects would not have been bound by their oaths; but the Christian subjects of Muslim rulers were to respect them. This would appear to be a clear inconsistency on Thomas's part.

Actually, of course, he holds that it is no inconsistency. He makes a sharp distinction between those who have been among the faithful and fall away from Catholicism and those, on the other hand, who have never been Christians. Once a man has embraced Christianity he comes under the jurisdiction of spiritual government, whether he is a temporal ruler or simply a private person; and if he becomes a heretic (denies the Articles of Faith, or some of them) or a schismatic (accepts the Articles of Faith but denies the authority of the Church of Rome) he is subject to the sanctions of that government.

The Church in General and the Pope in Particular. In dealing with ecclesiastical authority in temporals, Thomas appears to make a clear distinction between the Church as a whole and the pope, as supreme ruler of the ecclesia, in particular. Spiritual power, in general, can intervene in temporal affairs only in those matters where the secular ruler is clearly subject to control by the Church. That is to say, it is normally the principle that temporal rulers can govern, under natural law, of course, without interference by the Church. But insofar as the secular ruler is subject to the government of the Church in spirituals—and any Catholic is in the same position—he may be threatened with sanctions of Holy Church; and if he does not submit, he can be excluded from communion and denied the obedience of his subjects. Thomas explicitly uses the soul-body analogy to justify this attitude.[73]

If this were all, Thomas would simply be restating the Gelasian doctrine. But he proceeds to differentiate the general authority of spiritual government from the particular authority of the pope. In this, of course, Gelasius himself set the precedent and the Thomist statement is from one point of view a comment on the Gelasian distinction. It will be remembered that while Gelasius enunciated the doctrine of separation of the two spheres accompanied by mutual subordination, he also suggested that the pope was in some sense exempt from the general principle. Because this is one of the most controversial aspects of Thomas's political doctrine, it is important to quote his exact words:

> In matters pertaining to salvation of the soul we should obey spiritual rather than temporal authority, but in those which pertain to the political good we should obey the temporal rather than the spiritual, for, as Matthew says, "Give unto Caesar, etc.," unless when it happens that the spiritual and the civil power are joined in one person as in the case of the Pope, who holds the summit of power both spiritual and secular, because of the will of Him who is both King and Priest, Priest unto Eternity according to the order of Melchisedech.[74]

The *Commentary on the Sentences of Peter Lombard,* in which this quotation is found, was an early work; and because the claim that pontifical authority includes both spiritual and temporals is not repeated in later works, many commentators on St. Thomas take the position that he really does not mean what he appears to say.[75] He is essentially restating the Gelasian position, on the whole, these commentators continue, and the passage in the *Commentary* is not in accord with his later views; or he may be referring only to the temporal authority of the pope in the states of the Church rather than to a plenary authority over all mankind.

On the other hand, it is difficult to see why a man of Thomas's high intelligence and frankness does not explicitly state that he has changed his position, if he intends to do so, especially on a matter of such importance. In expounding his "Melchisedechian" view of the papacy in the *Commentary* Thomas becomes very explicit, as the following passage will show:

> Two powers may be such that both arise from a third and supreme authority, and their relative rank then depends upon the will of this uppermost power. When this is the case, either one of the two subordinate authorities controls the other only in those matters in which its superiority has been recognized by the uppermost power. *Of such nature is the authority exercised by rulers, by bishops, archbishops, etc., over their subjects, for*

all of them have received it from the Pope and with it the conditions and limitations of its use.[76] [Italics added]

Here he seems to be saying clearly that ultimately "rulers" (and he must mean temporal rulers) as well as inferior ecclesiastics are assigned their respective jurisdictions by the pope. The papacy, it would appear, is a kind of arbiter in defining both temporals and spirituals; and this certainly confirms a broad interpretation of the Melchisedechian powers.

Although it is true that this passage is from his earlier treatise, in the later political work *DeRegimine Principum* he at no point explicitly contradicts what he has said in the *Commentary*. In a statement from *De Regimine* he maintains that all kings must be subject to the "Roman Pontiff" just as they are subject to Our Lord Jesus.

In the *Summa* itself, moreover, Thomas maintains that "Mankind is considered like one body, which is called the mystic body, whose head is Christ, *both as to soul and as to body*."[77] This particular statement lends some considerable support to the view that Thomas did not in fact change his basic view on the temporal authority of the papacy between the *Commentary* and the *Summa*.

If we reach this conclusion, however, it does not imply that his theory and that, for example, of Hostiensis, are the same. The latter maintains that the *imperium* is inferior to the *sacerdotium* intrinsically and that temporal authority is derived from the *ecclesia* as a whole. Thomas, by contrast, sees temporal authority as divine because it is an ordinance of natural law which is an expression of God understood without the assistance of the Church. The latter, seen as the corporate "body of Christ," does not control temporals. However, the pope, who is head of the Church as the Vicar of Christ, also possesses Christ's supreme authority to define what are "Christ's" and what "Caesar's." In this sense, then, kings are subject to him in temporals as they are admittedly in spirituals.

It must be admitted that this interpretation of Thomas's views is not beyond criticism, but it would seem to be the most reasonable, considering all the factors involved. Nor is it incompatible with the Gelasian position, if the full analysis of Pope Gelasius be kept in mind.

Thomas on Heresy. It is because Thomas's attitude to heresy represents a relatively sophisticated statement of the view almost universally held in his time that it is important to examine it. St. Augustine, as we have seen,[78] accepted secular suppression of religious heresy only after great travail of mind. By the time of Pope Leo I, however, in the middle of the fifth century—scarcely a generation after the death of St. Augustine—the highest authorities of the Church had come to adopt the notion that the Church has an obligation to call upon temporal power for suppression.[79]

Unlike Augustine, Thomas never seems to entertain doubts about the matter—and this is, perhaps, a measure of the way in which moral and political thought has been transformed from the fifth to the thirteenth century. The Angelic Doctor's statement becomes, indeed, an important basis for the philosophic defense of suppression. No one would argue, he contends, that it is not within the prerogatives of the secular ruler to issue edicts against debasing the coinage. How much more necessary, then, is it to punish those who would debase the soul! Nor is the Church wanting in charity in so doing. It has given the heretic warning, in the first place; and secondly, even after he has been abandoned it is always ready, if the heretic repents, to grant penance, so that as he dies he will know that he may win the life eternal. Indeed, if he abandons his heresy, he will, even in the face of condemnation, find that Holy Church is willing to spare his life. If, despite this generosity, he later retracts his recantation, he must then die, though the Church is still willing to allow absolution should he repent at the last moment.

Throughout his analysis,[80] Thomas emphasizes the service which the Church is render-

72. *Summa*, II–II, Q. 12, Art. 2.
73. *Summa*, II–II, Q. 60, Art. 6.
74. *Commentary on the Sentences of Peter Lombard*, II. D. 44, Q. 2, Art. 3.
75. Cf. Thomas Gilby, *Between Community and Society*, pp. 56–57; Carlyle and Carlyle, *op. cit.*, pp. 352–354; and Cardinal Bellarmine, *De Romano Pontifice*, vol. 5, p. 5.
76. *Commentary on the Sentences of Peter Lombard*, II, D. 44.
77. *Summa*, III, Q. 8, Art. 1.
78. See p. 188.
79. H. C. Lea, *A History of the Inquisition of the Middle Ages*, New York: Russell & Russell, 1958, I, p. 215.
80. *Summa*, II–II, Q. 11, Art. 3 and 4.

ing in taking a stand. It is being charitable to those who deny the faith by warning them several times; by saving their lives after condemnation, if they abandon their contumacy; and by granting absolution and the possibility of eternal life to the relapsed who see their errors. At the same time, the Holy Church must and does keep in mind the great danger to souls if false beliefs should be expressed in wholesale fashion.

The fate of the heretic as solemnly expounded by Thomas is a good illustration of what might be termed medieval utilitarianism. That is to say, in the calculations which all governance involves, the weighing of probable goods against evils which may result from a given line of action, the medieval thinker takes into account much more than the modern utilitarian would consider. The latter would try to determine the likely results of a political decision in terms of its effect on living human beings and their descendants; by contrast, the medievalist is concerned not only with the living but also with the fate of the so-called dead.

Peace and War

Thomas shares the view of the canonists that a right relation between Holy Church and temporal authority can assure the kind of peace appropriate for the world here below. Unfortunately, those right relations rarely obtain. One must, therefore, examine more closely the meaning of peace and the issue of whether war is legitimate.

Thomas's conception of peace and war sums up centuries of intellectual evolution in that it gives scholastic form to a position which by the thirteenth century had become widely accepted. In it we see remnants of the early Christian discussion[81] as well as deposits of medieval experience and debate.

All strive for peace, he argues, in that all hope to attain what they desire without hindrance.[82] In general, peace consists of the union of rational appetitive and natural appetitive tendencies; and those who make war really desire peace, their war-making indicating that they can no longer bear the specious peace in which their ends and those of others are not truly meshed. War, then, becomes a means of breaking false concord and presumably establishing true peace. Inevitably, all wars are waged to discover a more nearly perfect peace than that which existed before.[83] But true peace cannot be attained save where the appetite moves in the direction of what is really or objectively good. There is indeed a kind of seeming peace among the wicked, but actually it is always a precarious one.

Thomas distinguishes between perfect and imperfect peace. The former, he argues, consists in the "perfect enjoyment" of final good and "unites all one's desires" by enabling them to find rest in one object or goal.[84] Obviously peace of this kind can be attained only in heaven. Imperfect peace, which may be had in this world, is the harmony based on the fundamental movement of the soul to rest in God, which harmony is, however, periodically disturbed by certain factors within and without the psyche of a human being. Only justice can remove these disturbances to peace,[85] but more positively and directly an indispensable condition is love or charity; for love is a "unitive force."

We might reword this paraphrase of Thomas by saying that in his view of human nature, all tend to be searching for the "perfect peace," which, as with Augustine, can be found only in God. But men are forever discovering that their search is frustrated—by the deposit of original sin, which, despite Thomas's confidence in rationality, still affects human life; by conflicts and uncertainties about ends, which characterize the inner psyche of man; and by what we might call institutional and group imbalances and differences arising out of both ignorance and perverseness.

Thomas is aware, of course, of the moral problem created by the existence of war and he attempts to restate all the traditional arguments which would see it as un-Christian. Thus some say that all wars are unlawful, for the New Testament warns that they that take the sword shall perish with the sword; others maintain that since Scripture admonishes us to resist not evil and not to take vengeance, wars must necessarily be ruled out; while yet others contend that, since nothing but sin is against virtue and war is contrary to peace, therefore war is always sinful.[86]

Relying partly on the authority of St. Augustine, Thomas seeks to refute the absolutist case. Thus when Scripture admonishes against taking the sword, it is really referring to private persons and not to public authority; it is necessary, moreover, to resist evil for the common good, if not for our own; and just wars, moreover, since they aim to establish a more nearly perfect or just peace, can be defended as not sinful.[87]

What, then, is a just war? St. Thomas, again building on earlier Christian moralists, lays down three conditions. It must be declared by a sovereign. Thus it cannot be a private war, as presumably many medieval wars were in fact. Since a private individual can gain redress of wrongs through the courts of his political superior, war is excluded to him.[88]

A second condition for the justice of a war is that it must have a just cause. Those who are warred against must deserve it on account of some fault.

Finally, the intentions of the belligerents must be rightful—that is, they must be seeking to advance good and avoid evil. Even if a war is declared by a lawful authority, then, and for a just cause, it may lack the third ingredient and hence be unjust. If the motivation be mere vengeance, or a restless spirit, or the lust for power, the intention is obviously wrong.[89]

It is clear that Thomas's discussion is shot through with ambiguities and puzzles. Who, for example, is to decide when an authority is public and when private? The answer is not obvious, particularly in the context of the feudal system. How, moreover, can we determine the true motivations of the warmaker? He cites no concrete examples of unjust wars in history, and rulers, no doubt, could with perfect honesty claim that all their wars met the requirements of the Angelic Doctor.

Yet we should not be too harsh in our criticisms of St. Thomas. Those in the twentieth century who defend the legitimacy of war hardly excel him in their statements; and rationalizations for the monstrous wars of our day show how easy it is for the human mind in any generation to defend what initially may appear to be indefensible. In one sense, Thomas epitomizes the way in which intellect at all times has been used to discover reasons for collective outrages.

The Significance of Thomas

Historically, the significance of St. Thomas for political theory is many-faceted. In the first place, he restored philosophy to political speculation in the sense that he reintroduced the reflective and critical spirit. Before the formulation of his great system, such social speculation as had existed in the Middle Ages flourished within the often narrow frameworks of the lawyers and the monks. Thomas shook the intellectual world out of those frameworks; and while we might well question whether he succeeded in fitting Christian social attitudes into the highly developed Aristotelian scheme without leaving serious tensions, the result was a magnificent—and, from the viewpoint which had been predominant in the early Middle Ages, a somewhat subversive —attempt to vindicate reason in human affairs.

Thomas made the medieval Christian more at home in the world of economics and politics in the sense that he restored the political order to a place it had not had since the decline of ancient thought. Although the Augustinian scheme had grudgingly assigned to the economy and the polity a relatively significant role, their position was viewed as essentially negative: Augustine's was a monastic view of the social and political orders. Thomas, by erasing the sharp distinction between pure and relative natural law which had been developed by the Augustinians, gave a positive value to such institutions as law, political rule, and property.

While the Thomist attitude to society and politics was not immediately accepted, it later became the basis upon which official Roman Catholic political thinkers were to build. Although men like Cardinal Bellarmine, Suarez, Vitoria, and, in modern times, Popes Leo XIII and Pius XI, do not follow St. Thomas slavishly, his propositions usually constitute their point of departure and, in considerable degree, their point of return as well.[90]

While it is difficult, then, to exaggerate the importance of St. Thomas in the history of political theory, it should also be remembered that his system became a point of attack—

81. See Chapter 9.
82. *Summa*, II–II, Q. 29, Art. 2.
83. *Ibid.*, Reply, Objection 2.
84. *Ibid.*, Reply, Objection 4.
85. *Summa*, II–II, Q. 29, Art. 3, Reply, Objection 3.
86. *Summa*, II–II, Q. 40, Art. 1.
87. *Ibid.*, Replies, Objections 1, 2, and 3.
88. *Summa*, II–II, Q. 40, Art. 1.
89. *Ibid.*
90. Leo XIII, "Encyclical on the Condition of Labor" and "On Liberty," in Ann Frendautte, *The Papal Encyclicals,* New York: Mentor-Omega, 1963.

whether implicitly or explicitly—in the two centuries which followed his death. During the immediately ensuing chapters we shall, as a matter of fact, be concerned to trace the development of political ideas in the disintegrating Middle Ages, when heretics and the more orthodox alike conspired to alter drastically the predominant late medieval and partly Thomist outlook.

chapter 14

The Ideologies of the Medieval Sects and the Papal Inquisition

While Thomas was developing his grand synthesis and the canon and civil lawyers continued to debate within their respective traditions, forces were at work in the medieval world which were to make that synthesis and those colloquies, as they related to practical politics, increasingly hollow. From the sectarian movements of twelfth and thirteenth centuries were to spring views of the social and political world at odds with the carefully contrived Thomist scheme and equally antagonistic to many aspects of the civil and canonical outlooks.

In response to the rise of sectarian doctrine and practice, the papal Inquisition was founded and its administrators and apologists worked out a rationalization, practice, and ideology which sought to counter the subversive views of the sects. The struggle between the sects on the one hand and the Inquisition on the other served gradually to undermine any semblance of actual medieval unity and to open the way for yet other doctrines that would impair the achievements and shatter the theories of civilians, canonists, and philosophers alike.

In this chapter we examine the major tendencies of sectarian ideology and the vigorous response of the Inquisition, reserving the following chapter for yet other currents which helped to destroy the high medieval synthesis.

The Medieval Manichees

Undoubtedly one of the most significant manifestations of heterodoxy was that of the Cathari, whose beliefs were generally Manichaean in nature.

Before we examine their religious and sociopolitical outlook, however, it might be well to call attention to the interweaving of religious and political questions following the triumph of the Church at the beginning of the High Middle Ages. The significant fact which emerges is that no sooner does the Church gain its formal supremacy and forge the doctrines upon which the extreme papalists are to base their claims to both temporal and spiritual supremacy than the attacks on ecclesiastical controls begin.

During the second quarter of the twelfth century, for example, Arnald of Brescia attacks the corruption of the clergy and their tendency to seek power over temporals. He calls for a purification of the Church and a restoration of true ecclesiastical poverty. At first allied with the temporal power in opposition to the papacy, he is eventually abandoned by the former and is burned to death in 1154.[1]

But while he failed in his attack on the clergy and in his effort to reestablish a Roman republic, a rich merchant of Lyons, Peter Waldo, establishes a movement during the latter half of the century which will grow rapidly and become a real challenge to medieval theocratic ideas. Waldo abandons his lucrative life in the world, makes provision for his family, and wanders about with his followers teaching doctrines which soon make the Waldensians objects of severe censure. Although they are originally perfectly orthodox in their beliefs, their attacks on abuses in the Church eventually lead to their classification as heretics. They come to criticize the authority of the pope; deny that priests have a higher status than laymen; assert that women as well as men can preach; appeal from the authority of men to that of God; and maintain that prayers are as efficacious when uttered outside of a church building as within. To undergird their attacks on the priesthood, they claim that confession to a layman is as valid as it is when rendered to a priest.

One notes, too, in the Waldensians, an effort to return to what they deem to be the purity of first and second century Christianity. Their claim that the Church should be poor is founded upon their conviction that it was in this state immediately after the Apostles. Their rejection of oaths, even in a court of justice, reposes on the New Testament prohibition of swearing. Finally, they follow the preponderant view of first and second century Christian writers in forbidding war and capital punishment, basing their contentions upon Scripture as well as on the attitude of the early Church.[2]

Theologically and perhaps in terms of political outlook the Waldensians are much less sophisticated than the Albigensians or Cathari who inherit from ancient times the creed of the Manichaeans. This body of beliefs, so vigorously attacked by St. Augustine, while suppressed through an alliance of state with Church, never really died out. Banished to the periphery of the ancient Eastern Empire, it absorbed certain elements of early Gnosticism and was sometimes called Paulicianism after Paul of Samosata, one of its early expositors. As it revives in Thrace during the tenth century, it takes on many of the characteristics of ideological militancy, appealing on its social side to the lower economic and social strata. When the Crusaders invade Macedonia during the first Crusade, they learn that whole cities are controlled by Paulician heretics and in one instance the defenders of orthodoxy capture an heretical city and put all its inhabitants to the sword. Yet some of the Crusaders were themselves possibly affected by heretical doctrines.

By the time that medieval Manicheeism becomes politically important in the twelfth century, its religious and political outlook, while not completely homogeneous, is fairly well settled. The Cathari (from the Greek *Katharoi*, or "the pure") are unsatisfied by the medieval synthesis which tends to remove the tension between the Old and New Testaments and between the world and the believer; and their religious tenets lead them to social and political attitudes equally repugnant to those of good orthodox Christians. According to the Cathari, God and Satan are two uncreated beings struggling for mastery of mankind, the former being of the spiritual domain while the

1. See George W. Greenway, *Arnold of Brescia*, New York: Cambridge University Press, 1931; and Arsenia Frugoni, *Arnaldo da Brescia Nelle Fonti Del Secolo XII*, Roma: Nella Sede dell'Instituto, 1954.
2. On the Waldensians see, for example, J. A. Wylie, *The History of the Waldenses*, London and New York: Cassel & Co., 1880. The beginning of the Waldensians is usually dated at 1170 when the merchant Peter Waldo gave away all his goods and began to preach apostolic poverty and service. His followers went further than he and eventually repudiated many of the essentials of medieval Catholicism. The Waldensians were excommunicated as heretics by the Council of Verona in 1184.

latter controls the material. The God of the Old Testament is not that of the New, for he is Lord of such robbers as the ancient patriarchs and is thus to be identified with Satan. The Old Testament emphasis on force and coercion is a direct contradiction of the New Testament exaltation of the spirit and of love. Far from being a kind of prelude or preparation for the New Testament (as medieval thinkers, including, as we have seen, St. Thomas, tend to argue), the Old Testament is actually in irreconcilable conflict with it. The New Testament, by contrast, reveals a God of spirit and love who is at war with the Satan who has created matter. Christ, in this view, could not have been a material being of flesh and blood, for that would have contracted his status as pure spirit at war with matter. Hence the Cathari, following the Paulicians, probably hold that Christ is a ghost or phantasm—he is God as revealed to the spiritual side of man but can have nothing to do with the evil matter in which the spirit is typically embodied.

We have here, quite obviously, all the necessary ingredients for a sharp antithesis between temporals and spirituals and can almost predict, without knowing them explicitly, the social and political attitudes of the Cathari. They are extreme ascetics, in the first place, holding that anything which mortifies the flesh or matter is an exemplification of God's battle with the Devil. All human institutions, therefore, which tend in any way to allow the flesh considerable scope, are prohibited to the good Cathar. Hence the Cathari attack the institution of marriage and look with disfavor on women as vessels which reflect the operations of Satan. While their opponents often accuse the Albigensians of being exponents of free love, their doctrine as such gives no countenance to such views. When they criticize marriage it is because they think of it as sinful and not because they believe that its sex relations should burst the bounds of monogamy.

Like certain other medieval heresies, Catharism appeals from the nature which it identifies with the material and hence with wickedness, to the admonitions of the Gospels that human beings should be perfect. And it interprets this perfection as an effort to combat an evil nature controlled by Satan. A Church which believes that nature or the material can somehow be made compatible with the God of the New Testament Albigensianism looks upon as lost, particularly when the ecclesiastical hierarchy itself employs material force. But the very notion of ecclesiastical hierarchy is anathema to the mind of the Albigensian, for it means that the inequalities of nature—and hence of evil—are institutionalized. While the Cathari themselves differentiate between and among their members in accordance with the degree of perfection achieved, they would distinguish their ranks in terms of proximity to spirit rather than in those of the external distinctions characteristic of the earthly ecclesia.

Just as the Albigensians repudiate medieval sacerdotalism so, too, do they regard many political institutions as impermissible. Unlike St. Augustine and St. Thomas, who in their sometimes divergent ways attempt to reconcile Christian social and political outlooks with property and war, the Cathari see both institutions as evil. While we do not know whether actual community of goods was practiced in widespread fashion among the Albigensians, there is no question about their advocating it in principle. Although all material things are to them afflicted with wickedness, they seem to believe that common ownership can best suppress those tendencies present in all humanity which would tend to deify the material.

As for war, with which the medieval Church wrestles through the just war theory, the Cathari will in principle have none of it. To them, it is a manifestation of nature and therefore of the Devil; and it is prohibited by the Gospel teachings on love of enemies and forgiveness.

In sum, when we look at Catharism as a whole, we find in it a thoroughly ascetic morality which repudiates family, property, war, and the coercive state and which attacks conceptions of the hierarchical Church at a fundamental level. And just as it is radical in its attitude to social and political questions so is it heretical in the more narrow sense of religious doctrine. In effect, it denies the Incarnation, for how could God take on the evil flesh?[3]

That Cathari teaching was revolutionary in a social and political sense is confirmed by scholars like the nineteenth-century historian Dollinger. In one of his well-known works, he has this to say of all medieval sectarian tendencies:

> Every heretical doctrine which arose in the Middle Ages had explicitly or implicitly a revolutionary character, that is, in the measure that it attained to a commanding position, it threatened to dissolve the existing political order and to effect a political and social transformation. Those Gnostic sects, the Cathari and the Albigenses, which specifically pro-

voked the harsh and ruthless legislation of the Middle Ages . . . were the Socialists and Communists of that time.[4]

Joachimites and Amalrichites

The revolutionary nature of Cathari teaching, both religiously and politically, shakes the complacency of Christendom; and it is not surprising that Innocent III (pontificate from 1198 to 1216) makes their elimination one of his major objectives. Nor is the pope without apparent success: The temporal protectors of the Albigensians in southern France are routed and the ferocity of Inquisitors makes certain that the heresy does not again appear, at least as an organized movement.

Meanwhile, however, the ideological cauldron has been brewing other potential dangers to the predominant outlook. At the very time that the Crusade is being preached against Albigensians and their allies, a new ideological movement is emerging from within the Holy Church that will have far-reaching consequences in thirteenth and fourteenth century politics.

Joachim of Flora was born during the second quarter of the twelfth century (about 1130) and was given a thorough education in the classics of that day. He grew up during the enthusiasm of the great Crusades, made the pilgrimage to Palestine (a kind of "grand tour" which became the thing to do for potential leaders of the twelfth century), and later settled down to the life of a monastery in southern Italy where he died in 1202.

During his lifetime, his teaching was not deemed to be particularly heretical, although there were undoubtedly many who questioned the implications of his theory of history. But after his death his doctrines become of importance in a practical sense, for they are taken up by one wing of the Franciscans and through the Franciscans penetrate the lowest social strata. In 1254 appears a work called an *Introduction to the Everlasting Gospel,* whose authorship is ascribed to John of Parma, a Franciscan.[5] The ideals of the *Everlasting Gospel* are admittedly based upon those of Joachim of Flora, but we must be careful not to attribute to Joachim all the conceptions which it advocates. Just how far they may be identified with the preaching of Joachim and to what degree they are original with John (or those associated with him) is still not entirely settled. But it is fairly clear that Joachimite conceptions of history and politics do not become widespread until after 1254.

Here it is best to blend Joachim's doctrines with those of the Joachimites; for from the viewpoint of late thirteenth and early fourteenth century political ideologies, the disciples are as significant as the master. The serfs and town laborers and, indeed, all those at the bottom of the medieval hierarchy who tend to embrace Joachimite teaching, are not particularly concerned as to whether Joachim of Flora or some later interpreter is responsible for the slogans which they follow.

Broadly speaking, the Joachimite ideology represents a strong revival of the chiliastic outlook on politics and history. At the same time, it is combined with a mystical approach to religious experience which always makes the medieval Church suspicious; for mysticism implies that man may relate directly to God and that priests, ritual, and sacraments are unessential.

Joachim himself apparently had much sympathy with those in his day who were criticizing the wealth of the Church; and while he regarded the Albigensians as heretics, at many points his own social teaching seems to parallel theirs. His theology, however—unlike that of the Cathari—is orthodox Christian.

But although his theology may be conformist in name, the social and political implications which his disciples draw from it go far to deny typically medieval views of the social and po-

3. See Sir Steven Runciman, *The Medieval Manichee*, New York: Viking Press, 1961. R. G. Collingwood, in *The New Leviathan,* Oxford: Clarendon Press, 1944, maintains that the Albigensians were not, strictly speaking, heretics but rather were megalomaniacs. See ch. 43.
4. Johann Dollinger, *Kirche and Kirchen. Papsttum und Kirchenstaat,* 1861, p. 61.
5. Actually, John was the leader of what came to be left-wing Franciscanism, and the *Everlasting Gospel* became a kind of textbook of great importance in the politics of the Franciscan order. Joachim of Flora had stated many of his political and historical notions in his *Expositic in Apocalipsim*, but it was the *Everlasting Gospel* which publicized them and helped to agitate the politics of the next two generations. The interweaving of Joachimite, Franciscan, and other eccentric social and political ideas is one of the characteristic hallmarks of the latter part of the thirteenth century and the first half of the fourteenth century.

litical world. Indeed, modern critics like Eric Voegelin see in the teaching of the Joachimites anticipations of characteristically modern political thought, particularly with respect to the idea that a just social order can and will be established on earth.[6]

Like Thomas Aquinas, the Joachimites use the theological nation of the Trinity as a framework for interpreting political experience. In their particular conception, there are three epochs in the history of mankind, the first identified with the Father, the second with the Son, and the third with the Holy Ghost. During the age of the Father, men are governed largely through fear: Threats of vengeance keep them in some kind of order; and externally imposed laws are sanctioned by physical coercion which, while it may injure the lawbreaker, is at the same time relatively justified considering the harsh characteristics of the epoch as a whole. Mankind, the Joachimite seems to say, are like obstreperous children who need chastisement if they are to grow up. The emphasis is on the "thou shalt nots" of the Old Testament. Wars are in some sense to be justified during the age of the Father, as is illustrated in the divinely sanctioned battles of the Jews.

The Joachimites see the age of the Son as arising with organized Christianity. It, too, is integral to the development of mankind and is not to be looked upon as in any sense an aberration. We may interpret this phase of human history as one in which God, taking on the attributes of humanity, comes to know human beings at first hand; and as he sees them from their perspective he understands the harshness and absence of freedom characteristic of the Father's age. God as Son, then, ordains that instead of allowing fear and physical coercion to remain the predominant sanctions, he will establish an hierarchical Church, whose discipline will gradually replace the harsher penalties inevitable in the age of the Father. The Church at its best is seen by the Joachimites as a kind of social and political educator.

At the same time, they recognize that the rule of the Church is felt by many to be an unjust discipline. This is particularly true when, as in their own day, it gathers to itself material goods the possession of which tends to corrupt the very discipline so essential for government in the age of the Son. Indeed, the good Joachimite sees in the degeneration of the Church during the latter part of the thirteenth and the first half of the fourteenth centuries a sign that the age of the Son is about to come to an end. With priests becoming more and more grasping and the distorted discipline of the Church corrupting rather than curing souls, it cannot be long before the age of the Holy Ghost will dawn. The Joachimites originally fix the date as 1260.

It is at this point, of course, that Joachimite ideology becomes "chiliastic" or millennial. While it is much more explicitly political in its interpretation of previous history than the similar chiliastic outlook of the early Christians, it shares with the Apocalypse of John the notion that great disparities of wealth and power and political disasters of various kinds betoken a new age and a novel condition for mankind. The new era, however, is apparently not to be the result of conscious human striving, of collective planning as it were, but rather a kind of intervention from outside history itself. Thus while it is legitimate to describe Joachimite theory as belonging to that kind of outlook which foresees a revolutionary transformation of social and political relations, it would be a mistake to discern in it a clear doctrine of evolutionary progress as that term is understood in modern political thought.

When the age of the Holy Ghost does dawn, however, no good Joachimite can fail to recognize it. All hierarchical distinctions will be abolished, including those of the Church and feudal system. No man will be subordinate to another—apparently even for functional purposes. The material goods of mankind will be held as they were in the Augustinian natural state—that is, there will be a complete absence of the property concept.

Joachim himself apparently thinks that the third phase can be hastened by world teaching orders whose members will devote themselves to a reformation of the Church. The teachers are to embrace voluntary poverty and to call upon the Church to do likewise. When their mission has been accomplished, the Holy Ghost will assume control; and the spirit of man will be released from all external fetters. Freedom will be real.

The ideology of the Joachimites is particularly appealing to many Franciscans who have also begun their missions with mystical religious experiences. At the same time, Joachimites themselves find they are attracted by the doctrines of another medieval ideologist, with whose theories the Joachimite outlook often becomes rather confusedly blended. It is

Amalrich of Bena (died c. 1204) who propounds both religious and political doctrines that challenge medieval orthodoxy at even more fundamental levels.

For Amalrich and what might be called the Amalrichites are pantheists in theology and hence heretical in the strict sense of that term. Theologically, they claim to base their views on those of John Scotus Erigena (died about A.D. 877), one of the few able early medieval philosophers. While many scholars deny that Erigena is pantheistic in his teaching, it must be admitted that the followers of Amalrich have ample grounds for thus interpreting him. Note, for example, the following passage:

> Just as the air appears to be all light, and the molten iron to be all fiery, nay, fire itself, their substances nevertheless remaining, so it is understood by the intellect that after the end of this world every nature, whether corporeal or incorporeal, will seem to be only God, the integrity of nature remaining, so that God, who is in himself incomprehensible, will be somehow comprehended in the creature.[7]

Amalrichites, seizing upon passages of this kind, conclude that all distinctions between and among men—whether religious or political—are purely conventional. If God is in everything—in Jesus as well as in Ovid—then all hierarchies based upon alleged differentiations between those possessing the truth and those devoted to falsehood are without importance. Hence the Amalrichites, like the Joachimites envisioning the third age, tend to minimize the sacraments, law, and political subordination.

It is not surprising that those who claim to follow Amalrich and those who are essentially Joachimites find much in common. The former think of themselves, indeed, as harbingers of the third age of Joachim, since they understand that godhood is to be found in all men and that ecclesiastical doctrine and discipline deny this basic oneness.

Both Joachimite and Amalrichite tendencies make deep inroads into the ranks of orthodox Christendom and often the Inquisition has a difficult time keeping track of their ideologies' progress and permutations. Appealing particularly to restless serfs, ambitious townsmen, and, indeed, to all hopeless men caught in a rigid status system, their millennial emphasis puts their visions in the category of what modern writers like Mannheim call "chiliastic utopias."[8]

But we should always remember that Joachimite and Amalrichite ideologies are not embodied in organized social movements like modern Marxism. A loose kind of informal solidarity exists among their followers, but little in the way of formal organization. They represent tendencies in popular and semipopular thought but are not enshrined in anything like nineteenth and twentieth century political parties. They are still partly medieval in spirit, even though their teachings imply a revolution in medieval society and politics.

Spiritual Franciscans and Evangelical Poverty

Joachim of Flora, it will be remembered, had called for dedicated preachers who would travel throughout the length and breadth of Christendom preaching the imminence of the third age and demanding a return to the evangelical poverty which he identified with primitive Christianity. Only four years after his death, the future of St. Francis of Assisi (1182–1226), troubled by the social situation and by the gap between it and primitive Christian ideals, gathered about him a few persons who had given up all their possessions and agreed to follow him. This may be regarded as the beginning of the Franciscan movement. Originally Francis had in mind a rebellion against the economic and political power of the Church and the corruptions which he discerned in the monasticism of the thirteenth century.

With these objectives in mind, he established standards which required that no friar could accept money for labor, but only perishable goods. At the end of each day, the friar would have to give any surplus food to the poor and for the next day's provisions would have to rely on more labor. Formal organization was to be kept to a minimum and even the clothes of the friars were to be patched until they literally fell apart. In these principles we see a

6. Cf. Eric Voegelin, *The New Science of Politics*, Chicago: The University of Chicago Press, 1952, pp. 110–113.
7. John Scotus Erigena, "The Division of Nature," as partly translated by George Bosworth Burch in *Early Medieval Philosophy*, New York: King's Crown Press, 1951.
8. Cf. Karl Mannheim, *Ideology and Utopia: An Introduction to the Sociology of Knowledge*, New York: Harcourt, Brace, 1959.

clear rebellion against the increasing power of money in the revived town life and at the same time evidence of a desire to avoid both the pitfalls of a hierachical Church and the dangers of the collective egoism which Francis saw enshrined in the old monastic orders.

Unfortunately for his objectives, however, others of his earlier followers—committed though they were to his purposes—thought that some formal organization was essential. When Francis was absent from Italy in 1219, one of his disciples drew up a plan which became the basis for the Order of Franciscans and confronted Francis with a *fait d'accompli* when he eventually returned. While he revolted against the foundation of any order, he accepted the pope's decree of establishment in the hope that the disadvantages of organization—and no one in history has been more conscious of what moderns call the "iron law of oligarchy"—could be overcome by the spirit which he hoped would be maintained.

When the Friars Minor began to multiply and to extend their labors over a wide area, it is not surprising to learn that they were at first mistaken for Albigensians in many communities. Their conceptions of ecclesiastical power resembled those of the Cathari and their attitude to property, while not yet fully articulated, was not unlike that of many formal heretics. From its very birth, then, the Franciscan Order was tainted by a revolutionary ideology and despite the formal papal approval was obviously a focus for many of those within the Church who questioned the claims of men like Innocent IV and later thirteenth-century popes.

After the death of Francis, in 1226, the politics of the order turn on the interpretation of his intentions. The numbers of Franciscans have increased amazingly within a relatively few years and with numbers, as might be expected, come diversity of outlook and what the German sociologist Troeltsch would call a church-type orientation. Members of the order divide into three major factions, the essential differences among which turn on interpretations of what the organization should be; and from 1226 until far into the fourtenth century, the internal politics of the Franciscans are interwoven with both papal and secular political struggles.

Generally speaking, what might be called the right wing of the order envisions a structure and outlook approximating an ideal monastic order of the old type. That is to say, the order itself might be able to own property even though its individual members would be committed to strict evangelical poverty after the instructions of Francis. Many Franciscans, however, constitute a kind of center faction on the spectrum of internal politics: they are wary of too many compromises with the traditional monastic outlook and yet are willing to make some concessions to the strong pressures moving in that direction. Finally, the left wing, as it might be called, is adamant in attempting to maintain in full vigor both the notion of evangelical poverty and the conception of the Church as a purely spiritual power. Left-wing Franciscans—or, as many of them will later be called, "spiritual Franciscans"—tend to argue that those dedicated to a full implementation of the Christian life must surrender ownership of material goods, both individually and in a collective sense. Left-wing Franciscan teaching, in other words, would leave all the administration of temporals in the hands of non-ecclesiastical authorities.

After the death of Francis, management of the order passes for several years into hands of the middle faction, which aspires to combine collective ownership with individual poverty while at the same time avoiding extremes in corporate possessions. Even this position, of course, clearly violates the intentions of Francis and of many early Franciscans. Control by the moderates meets stiff opposition of the right wing and of the larger numbers of left wing members. The latter continue to make appeals for a return to the ideals of the founder. Eventually they are successful in a political sense, for in 1247, John of Parma, the spearhead of radical policy, is elected General of the Franciscans.

John is an ardent admirer of Joachim of Flora and it is under his sponsorship that the *Introduction to the Eternal Gospel* is published.[9] In 1254, the Archbishop of Paris, suspecting that the *Introduction* might be heretical (as well as revolutionary in a social and political sense), submits it to Pope Innocent IV for judgment. A papal commission agrees with the archbishop and later John of Parma is deposed from his generalship.

But the deposition of their leader does not discourage the Spirituals. Wedded to the eternal Gospel and to its chiliastic teaching about the imminence of the third age, they continue to announce the doom of all existing polities and particularly of the hierarchical Church. With "evangelical poverty" as their watchword, they call upon the Church to renounce its temporals and to return to primitive Christianity before the dawn of the age of the spirit.

When, therefore, they take up their intellectual weapons against Pope John XXII (pontificate 1316–1334), who endeavors to defend the secularist position of the Church, it becomes evident that it is a struggle which is of vital concern not only to the participants themselves but also to politicians and political thinkers as a whole. In terms of traditional discussions within the Christian stream of thought, the Spirituals in effect are appealing from the Thomist attitude to property to the patristic. For them, the Thomist-Aristotelian view that property is not unnatural tends to be superseded by the Augustinian view that it is against nature and only relatively justified because of sin. And indeed, a very learned Franciscan of moderate persuasions, John Duns Scotus (d. 1308), is arguing for this position even before the great flareup under John XXII.

Pope John is, of course, victorious in the short-run. With the vigorous support of his efficient inquisitors, he subjects the Spiritual Franciscans to coercion of all types, not excluding burning at the stake.[10]

But the immediate victory of the papacy is purchased at an enormous price. The Spirituals have evoked considerable support not only from those who are severe critics of the thirteenth and fourteenth century Church but also from those who are espousing the cause of national and imperial politics. The latter are attracted by the theory of evangelical poverty because they see in it an opening for a greatly enhanced temporal sword. If the spiritual power, whose claims over temporals have advanced so far during the thirteenth century, is to be deprived of its hard-won status, the apologists for kings and emperors see in the cause of "evangelical poverty" an outlook which will prepare the way for magnified royal and imperial jurisdiction. True, most of the secular defenders of the Spirituals do not support them openly, for that would be too dangerous; but they are better prepared, as a result of the Spirituals' agitations, to carry on their own ideological struggle when the time shall prove ripe.

Meanwhile, as the fissions created by the outlooks of Cathari, Joachimites, Amalrichites, and Spiritual Franciscans grow wider, the Inquisition has been founded and proceeds to strike back in the name of that theological and ideological unity which is so important a desideratum for the High Middle Ages. In carrying out its suppression, however, the Inquisition creates an ideology of its own and, what is more, in some measure exacerbates the divisions it is designed to eliminate.

The Inquisition: Institution and Doctrines

Given its religious and political premises, it is not surprising that the High Middle Ages reacted to its heretics with vigor and severity, and the character of the Inquisition reflects the seriousness with which the medieval mind viewed attacks on its religious and social solidarity. If ecclesiastical and temporal society were to be regarded as an organism, with hierarchies extending from demons through earth to heaven, then any denial of this organic nature and any questioning of the hierarchies must be looked upon as a kind of disease. All this was made concrete in the functioning of the inquisitorial system.

The Inquisition illustrates not only the deep repugnance with which predominant medieval currents viewed heresy but also the theory of spiritual and temporal power. In its actual operations we find dramatically exhibited almost all the difficulties confronted by the medieval statesman when he came to apply the notion of the two swords. At the level of legal administration and in the political struggles turning on the administration of the Inquisition, civil and canonical authority were confused, and the line between spiritual and temporal coercion became a thin one indeed.

Let us examine the formal basis of the Inquisition in the legal and administrative theory of the Middle Ages; the political and jurisdic-

9. Earlier we have identified the *Introduction* with John. Whether he actually wrote it or not is still a matter of some doubt. Beer, in "Social Struggles in the Middle Ages," *The General History of Socialism and Social Struggles*, *op. cit.*, p. 108, contends that John's close friend Gerard of San Donnino was the author. The exact authorship is not of great importance so long as we remember that it was certainly sponsored by left-wing Franciscanism.
10. On rulership among the early Franciscans, see Rosalind Brooke, *Early Franciscan Government*, New York: Cambridge University Press, 1959.

tional conflicts between episcopal and inquisitorial authority; the jurisdictional tensions within the Mendicant Orders themselves; and finally, issues of spiritual and temporal power posed by the existence of the inquisitorial system.

The universal Inquisition grew up because successive popes were dissatisfied with the efforts of bishops and secular rulers to suppress heresy. For more than a generation before the establishment of the papal Inquisition in the second quarter of the thirteenth century, the successors of Peter had made repeated efforts to stimulate bishops, princes, and feudal lords to greater vigilance. The theory that heretics should be subject to coercion and even death had long ago been established, as had the notion that it was the task of every ruler, whether ecclesiastical or secular, to rid his domain of dissidents. Yet all this papal zeal proved ineffective. Secular rulers were themselves frequently in league with the heretics, and episcopal leaders were often either phlegmatic or dependent on the goodwill of temporal princes. The revival of towns, moreover, provided social conditions which enabled heretics to conspire more effectively and to exchange ideas. Thus even when a bishop or prince happened to be zealous he might find the obstacles increasing. For all these reasons, a universal mechanism of some kind seemed essential if the subversive thinkers were to be silenced.

Yet when the papal Inquisition was finally established, it was not as the result of a well-planned policy, but rather the fruit of a series of isolated measures. In 1227, Pope Gregory IX had called to his attention the situation in Florence, Italy, where a repentant heretical bishop had relapsed, to the great scandal of the faithful. And Gregory was asked, in effect, what he proposed to do about it. Having only recently ascended the papal throne and hoping to make a good impression from the very outset of his pontificate, he issued a commission to the prior of the Dominican house of Santa Maria Novella and two other clerics to proceed with full vigor against the relapsed ecclesiastic. The commissioners were to have full powers to call upon lay and clerical authorities to assist them. In 1230, on the prior's death, the Pope appointed a successor. Gradually thereafter, the provincials in the great Mendicant Orders—the Dominicans and Franciscans, but particularly the former—were endowed with larger and larger spheres of authority which tended to make them independent of the bishops.

Meanwhile, the papacy was meeting resistance from the Emperor Frederick II. While that ruler at one point issued very severe statutes for the suppression of heresy, he was himself suspected of heretical tendencies, as we have seen. Until his death, in 1250, the popes had to take into account his possible attitudes and hence the slowly proliferating inquisitorial organization was often hampered in its effectiveness. After Frederick's death, however, the way was paved for a more substantial organization, which was provided in Innocent IV's momentous bull, *Ad Extirpanda.*

Issued in 1252, this famous document systematized the law of the Inquisition and elaborated many details for its administration. While it was never applied formally in all parts of Christendom, (it was addressed to the bishops and secular princes of Italy only), its provisions may be said to represent the papal ideal. All spiritual and temporal governors were instructed to ban heretics and, by a legal fiction, to treat them as if they were sorcerers. Every temporal ruler, not later than three days after taking over his office, was to appoint a kind of inquisitorial commission—today we should probably call it an administrative tribunal with quasi-judicial powers—whose duty it would be to round up heretics, take charge of their material goods, and turn them over to the episcopal jurisdiction. The personnel of the board was to consist of twelve pious men, together with two secretaries and several assistants, and was to be nominated to the temporal ruler by a panel composed of the bishop and four Mendicants (two Dominicans and two Franciscans). There was apparently no provision for the magistrate's refusing to accept the nominees of the ecclesiastical group: His was essentially the rubber-stamp function of endowing the ecclesiastically appointed board with temporal authority. Moreover, the board, once appointed, was to hold office for six months only and might be replaced at any time by new nominees. All these provisions clearly made the temporal authority primarily an instrument of the Church.

The bull went on to require the ruler to draw up a list of heretics in quadruplicate (the techniques of bureaucracy were best reflected in ecclesiastical rather than temporal organization). A copy was to be kept by the ruler himself, and one each was to be furnished to the Dominicans, the Franciscans, and the bishop. Within ten days of sentence, the houses of heretics were to be destroyed and within three months all fines were to be paid, on pain of indefinite imprisonment. Fines and confiscations were to be divided into three parts: one would go to the city where the heretics had lived, another to those who had informed against them, and the third to the bishop and inquisitors in order to finance future prosecutions.

If for any reason temporal rulers should refuse to obey the requirements of *Ad Extirpanda*, together with any other decrees against heresy issued by the popes, they were to be excommunicated and their cities to be placed under interdict.[11]

While the historian of political theory is not concerned primarily with the details of legislation and with its executive and judicial administration, those details often furnish prime illustrations of a general theory. The whole political and administrative pattern of the Inquisition, as illustrated by Innocent IV's famous bull, is an excellent example. Although it was never formally accepted beyond Italy, the attachment of medieval Christendom to the cause of orthodoxy was sufficient to secure establishment of not unsimilar relationships elsewhere.

When one moves from the formal structure of the Inquisition to the tensions which developed within its confines, one finds ample illustrations of the thesis that, while extreme canonists demanded a kind of monolithic theocracy, such a structure never developed fully in practice. It was not possible to implement radical papalism even within the ecclesiastical structure itself. Thus, while the popes tended to exalt the Inquisition at the expense of episcopal jurisdiction, throughout large parts of Christendom the bishops continued to resent the competition. The theory of the Inquisition was, indeed, one which formally associated the bishop with the inquisitor—as we have noted in connection with *Ad Extirpanda* —but since the inquisitor was not in any sense subordinate to the local bishop but ultimately accountable to the pope alone and since, moreover, the legal weapons of the inquisitor were so much greater, it is not surprising that recurring tensions should arise. The bishop felt that he was being reduced to a subordinate position; while the inquisitor, as the special agent assigned to the inspiring task of uprooting heretics, thought of himself as having a more exalted role than that of the bishop.

There was, then, a kind of implicit and sometimes explicit administrative warfare within Holy Church itself which, while it did not prevent the growth of the Inquisition into one of the most thorough instruments of coercion in administrative history, certainly illustrated the conflicts which inevitably arise within any bureaucracy. To emulate the zeal of the inquisitors and at the same time to preserve some measure of their own autonomy, bishops sometimes reinvigorated their own tribunals for the prosecution of heretics; and in such instances, the episcopal and inquisitorial courts afforded the spectacle of two agencies of Holy Church contending for the bodies and souls of those on the way to perdition.

There were tensions not only between bishops and inquisitors but also between the rulers of Mendicant Orders and their inquisitors. The papal practice was, as we have seen, to grant to the generals and provincials of Dominican and Franciscan orders commissions to appoint inquisitors with wide and far-reaching powers. Once designated, there was a strong tendency for the inquisitors to become independent not merely of episcopal jurisdiction but also from the control of their ostensible superiors. The problem of whether or not an inquisitor could be removed by his general or provincial exercised later thirteenth-century popes and for many years they were undecided or issued contradictory instructions. While eventually the rule came to be (in the pontificate of Boniface VIII) that the inquisitor could be removed by the appointing authority, it was also accepted quite widely that he could not lose his status except for cause and after a trial.

There was, then, a tendency for inquisitors to become completely a law unto themselves: No one could excommunicate them while they were in line of duty and as early as 1261 they were given the power to remove excommunication from one another in the event that some ecclesiastical ruler should see fit to deny them the sacraments. If their spies and police (their "familiars") violated canon law through bru-

11. For a fuller discussion of *Ad Extirpanda* and its relation to the Inquisitional structure elsewhere, see H. C. Lea, *A History of the Inquisition of the Middle Ages*, New York: Russell and Russell, vol. 1, 1958, pp. 336–344.

tality or excessive zeal, the Inquisitors themselves were authorized to wipe out their guilt.

The formal structure of the Inquisition and conflicts between bishops and inquisitors and between Mendicant Orders and their inquisitors challenged both the extreme canonists and the devotees of more moderate Gelasian doctrines. For the former, the theocratic ideal remained only a remote possibility so long as the papal Inquisition, as a direct expression of pontifical prerogatives, was not fully accepted by both ecclesiastical and temporal governors. For the Gelasians, among whom we can perhaps number Thomas Aquinas, the theory and practice of the universal Inquisition raised in a very practical form the issue of how Caesar's and God's realms could be kept separate and distinct while yet maintaining intact the unity of Christendom and the cause of orthodoxy. For the student of modern politics, accustomed as he is to what he thinks are clear distinctions between Church and state and voluntary and involuntary associations, the task of differentiating between temporal and ecclesiastical administration under the Inquisition is frequently almost impossible.

If one notes the whole inquisitorial process from start to finish one discovers an intermingling of authorities, and an uncertainty in the moral and legal theory which underlies them, which must have led the moderate Gelasian to wring his hands in frustration. While the institution was, of course, established formally by the pope, its effectiveness depended upon a whole complex of belief systems and unquestioned conventions without which the physical force employed by the inquisitors would have proved unavailing or perhaps unavailable. The ecclesiastical and secular authorities who wielded the inquisitorial weapon were not imposing a system by force on an entirely unwilling population. Although those caught within its toils naturally resented its operations and, as we have seen, the administrative tensions became acute, the *principle* of prosecution and punishment for unorthodox beliefs was an integral part of the predominant climate of opinion.[12]

Once the principle was widely accepted, it became the task of the moral and political philosopher and the jurist to construct devices which would attain the objective with the least possible violation of other doctrines that were equally a part of the medieval world outlook. How, in other words, could the Gelasian theory (at least in some of its versions) be reconciled with an administrative system in which the pope prescribed the manner in which secular officials were to act? And how could the traditional repugnance of the Church for the shedding of human blood and the administration of torture be squared with the supervision of torture by a cleric and specific commands to the secular authority to kill human beings?

We have already cited the bull *Ad Extirpanda* as an illustration of the detail with which popes asserted the authority to define the obligations of the secular power. Here was the exercise of no mere indirect or negative authority which might allow temporal rulers to develop their own devices. The inquisitorial commissions established by that bull were set up by canonical authority and the temporal ruler was in effect acting as a narrowly circumscribed administrative agent of the pope. Were he to default in his obligations, he would be automatically excommunicated and could be subject to the temporal penalties for heresy. All local statutes, whether issued by ecclesiastical or lay authority, which contradicted the provisions of rules promulgated by the central Inquisition were *ipso facto* null and void. Parish priests were, by an ordinance of the Council of Beziers in 1246, set up as policemen who could forcibly enter houses in the search for heretics—despite the fact that in theory priests had only spiritual functions. Here, obviously, the term spiritual embraced activities far beyond those usually understood to be included. The methods sanctioned and used—under supervision of Holy Church—included bringing wives and children into the cells of the accused in order that they might by their tears secure confessions. And, as Lea has pointed out, "Alternate threats and blandishments were tried; he would be removed from his foul and dismal dungeon to commodious quarters, with liberal diet and a show of kindness, to see if his resolution would be weakened by alternations of hope and despair."[13]

There never seems to have been any question about the legitimacy of torture which did not actually shed blood. But when it came to the issue of using the rack and other forms of torment to elicit confessions, the Church at first hesitated. As we have repeatedly noted, the tension between the early Christian ideal of nonviolence and the later attitude which made not inconsiderable concessions to the world was never entirely removed down to the High Middle Ages. While temporal authority might be forced to use physical coercion, the Church hesitated for a long time before it permitted clergymen to sanction and preside over torture. Thus Gratian asserts that no confession is to be forced from a person through the use of deliberate torture.

But the revival of Roman law brought with it, ironically enough, the utilization of methods employed by the ancient jurisprudence and the Church was confronted by a new crisis in its morality. It should always be remembered that, while we think of the Roman law as a highly developed system showing real concern for exact justice, it did support use of the rack and of other similar techniques. Moreover, with its revived study, typically Germanic devices, such as the ordeal, began to decline. In fact, the Fourth Lateran Council, presided over by the great canonist Innocent III, forbade ordeals and thereby implicitly raised the question as to whether the tortures of the Roman legal system ought not to be adopted.

Torture began to be used during the second quarter of the thirteenth century and *Ad Extirpanda* legitimated its employment for the uncovering of heretics.

At first the Church took refuge in the view that it was the temporal power alone which administered torture and that therefore Holy Church could not be held responsible. Inquisitors were not to administer it nor were they to be present at its administration. Any inquisitor who violated these rules was held to be engaging in serious irregularities and he could not act thereafter in his role as a priest without being dispensed and purified. But these limitations were irksome to the administrators of the Inquisition, who felt that the effectiveness of the institution was greatly impaired by undue emphasis on fine points of moral doctrine. Since in the politics of the medieval papacy, the Inquisition began to be an extremely influential power rather early, it is not surprising to learn that Pope Alexander IV addressed himself to the issue in 1256. In a bull of that year, he authorized the inquisitors to absolve one another of all irregularities, thus opening the way for direct administration of the torture which his illustrious predecessor Innocent IV had authorized for temporal administrators in 1252.

While the ultimate penalty of burning at the stake could be administered only by the temporal power to which the heretic had been "relaxed," wielders of the secular sword were so closely supervised by ecclesiastical authority at all stages—including the final one—that implicitly the doctrines of the extreme papalists would seem to have been upheld in practice. Only the most tenuous casuistry could possibly claim that the spiritual power was merely admonishing or advising the temporal authority to act in a certain way. Instead, the Church was in effect using temporal coercion directly—for spiritual ends, no doubt, but also, insofar as common belief systems were deemed basic to worldly peace, for temporal goals as well. Spirituals and temporals were inextricably mingled both as to means and ends.

We thus emerge with a theory and practice whereby ecclesiastical administration is indistinguishable, in effect, from temporal government. This, together with the intricate involvement of the Church in the feudal system, will more and more lead to a confusion of authorities until it is almost impossible to distinguish the things of God from those of Caesar. At the level of high theory, Gelasianism still holds sway, despite men like Cardinal Hostiensis; but in the day-to-day operations of organizations like the Inquisition, it is difficult to distinguish between the two realms.

The theory and practice of the Inquisition thus lead to fissions within the Church itself; to a denial of traditional moral and political theory; and to intellectual doubt, even on the part of some of the orthodox. In a sense, the devices employed by the Inquisition defeat its ends; and the divisions created by ideologies like those of the Cathari, Amalrichites, and

12. Indeed, the principle has been defended by certain twentieth-century writers as appropriate. See, for example, Elpheqe Vacandard, *The Inquisition: A Critical and Historical Study of the Coercive Power of the Church*, Bertrand L. Conway, trans., New York: Longmans Green, 1908, particularly p. vii. And A. Hyatt Verrill contends: "It is nothing short of appalling to speculate on what might have been the results had the Catholic Church not carried on its campaign, had the Inquisition not been inaugurated and maintained during those long centuries when, on every hand, innumerable fantastic, weird, and often most repulsive and horrible forms of religion were springing up and winning converts by the tens of thousands." *The Inquisition*, New York: D. Appleton, 1931, p. 11.
13. *Op. cit.*, p. 418.

Spiritual Franciscans are matched by the rifts produced in the wake of the institution designed to suppress them.

Meanwhile, other currents of thought are helping to undermine the orthodox theory and ideology of the High Middle Ages, as we shall see in the next chapter.

chapter 15

The Decline of Medieval Thought and Attitudes

While thirteenth-century sects were sapping the foundations of orthodox medieval outlooks in religion and politics and the Inquisition was justifying its counterattacks, powerful secular rulers and their apologists were preparing to do battle with extreme papalist claims. At the same time, the world-enlarging impact of the Crusades, the expansion of trade, and the continued growth of town life were slowly but certainly eating away at feudal institutions and making feasible a great enlargement of the king's "estate."

Both at the level of speculation and in the power struggles which characterize all politics, men were embracing the new and turning their backs on old formulas and social structures. Although popes and emperors often spoke as if the earlier schemes of thought and practice were still viable, the end of the century saw growing recognition that a new social universe was striving to be born. The mounting restlessness of serfs, the rise of town burgesses to influence, the unhappy state of the papacy, and the persistence of heresy despite the Inquisition—all these factors both reflected the disintegration of the old order and themselves constituted causative agents.

As the disintegration proceeded, men were struggling with the problem of what the new order would or should be. Those (like Boniface VIII and Augustinus Triumphus) who looked backward hoped that a vigorous papalism could be restored; but as they surveyed the world about them, they saw with dismay that men no longer seemed to be attached to the universal policy which had been the ideal of canonists like Hostiensis.

While the papalists and imperialists were bemoaning the fate of their ideals and calling attention to the disorders which accompanied the disintegration of medieval life, other thinkers were attempting to understand the newer factors which appeared on the scene. Men like Marsilio of Padua, William of Ockham, and John Wycliffe sought in their several ways both to express and to shape those factors.

Throughout the latter part of the fourteenth century and down to the middle of the fifteenth, some of the most important political discussions turned not on the nature of secular politics but rather on the problems of ecclesiastical government. But to men of that age, it should be remembered, analysis of political problems within the Church could be applied, without much modification, to secular issues; and similarly debates turning on temporals might often have direct relevance for ecclesiastical politicians. Hence the "Conciliar Movement," which superficially seems to us a purely ecclesiastical affair, becomes, on closer inspection, of great importance for the history of the theory of constitutional government in general.

If we keep in mind this general picture of life and thought from 1300 to the time of Machiavelli, we can see in a larger perspective the issues which emerge in the conflict between Philip IV of France and Pope Boniface VIII; the arguments of Dante for a world state; the secularist conceptions of Marsilio of Padua; the nominalism of men like William of Ockham as it relates to political and social thought; the nationalism and property theories of Wycliffe; and the ideological struggles which accompany and shape the Conciliar Movement.

National State versus Universal Papacy

Earlier we have pointed out that feudal theory implies that private right, and particularly the right to land, confers what we (and the Romans) should call public authority.[1] In a technical sense, of course, as Professor Figgis has pointed out, "under feudalism there is no public law; all rights are private, including those of the king."[2] What we call public rights—the authority to hold court, administer the police, and regulate conduct—are simply regarded as aspects of, let us say, the private tenure of land. To the extent that a feudal lord expands the number of vassals immediately holding from him and perhaps having no vassals of their own, to that degree is his estate enlarged. During the High Middle Ages, the king, so far as the feudal system is concerned, is simply another lord.

But he is a lord ever aspiring to enlarge his estate as against the estates of others. In England, his estate is great, for there the feudal system has always been relatively weak. In France, by contrast, the king must struggle throughout the latter part of the thirteenth century to enlarge the royal estate and is beginning to succeed by the time of Pope Boniface VIII (whose pontificate extends from 1295 to 1303).

In his efforts to expand the royal estate, the king of France at that time, Philip IV, finds himself in serious conflicts both within and without. Within, of course, he must deal with other feudal lords who resist his incursions and who fear that he will tend to overshadow them. Moreover, his wars, particularly with England, make great demands on his treasury —requirements which he cannot satisfy merely by means of the feudal dues upon which he customarily relies. Looking with great longing at the estates of bishops and other ecclesiastical magnates, he begins to assert the right to tax them. This leads to his greatest external conflict—that with Pope Boniface VIII.

But we should not imagine that Boniface surrenders in any sense. Indeed, more than any pope since Gregory VII does he assert claims for plenary papal power; and he causes other papal partisans to reformulate theocratic doctrine in such a way that even Innocent III might well have retreated from its implications.

The occasion which initiates the political and ideological struggle is a series of wars which offend the papal yearning for political harmony. Thus in 1295, Lombardy, Venice, and Genoa are at war and are commanded by Boniface to make peace on threat of excommunicating their rulers. In the same year he writes to the kings of England and France announcing that he is sending representatives who will be instructed to make peace between them. At the same time, he peremptorily calls upon the Empire to cease its battles. England, France, and the Empire are to cease their fighting for at least a year and if they refuse to do so, their rulers will be excluded from communion.

1. See Chapter 11.
2. J. N. Figgis, *From Gerson to Grotius*, Cambridge: Cambridge University Press, 1956, pp. 9–10.

Such a command would have been treated with great respect a half century before but now there is hesitancy, particularly on the part of King Philip. To reinforce his position, Boniface issues a bull, *Ineffabilis Amoris,* in which he contends that the issues between and among France, England, and the Empire involve questions of sin and are therefore within the jurisdiction of the Holy See. But this assertion, in its particular context, is denied by Philip IV who maintains, in 1297, that the problems are purely temporal in nature and that he as king has no temporal superior—not even the emperor, let alone the pope.

Meanwhile, Philip has asserted the right to tax the clergy of France in order to carry on the wars which are opposed by the pope. It is at this point that Boniface formulates his first great statement bearing on the general issues involved. "The history of olden times teaches," he asserts in *Clericis Laicos* "and daily experience proves, that the laity have always felt hostile to the clergy and have constantly striven to overstep their bounds by wickedness and disobedience." Stupid as they are, he goes on, lay rulers seem not to be aware that all power over the clergy and over the "persons and property of the Church" is "denied them" by canon law and the precedent of ages.

The reception of the bull by secular rulers is anything but cordial. There is widespread and vigorous opposition to it in England and France, and the king of England goes so far as to put all the clergy of his realm beyond his protection. Latent nationalism in both England and France is clearly a factor which undergirds the attitudes of kings.

Faced by this unmistakable opposition, Boniface now begins to hedge. The bull was not intended, he asserts, to forbid necessary taxation for defense; nor did it seek to interpose barriers to the reception of feudal dues by the king. And in 1297, to show his goodwill, Boniface grants the "first-fruits" of many French ecclesiastical revenues to Philip for conduct of his wars. Meanwhile, French political writers have taken up the cause of royal against papal authority and have sought to show that many of Boniface's acts are without precedent in custom or law.

As is characteristic of his whole development in his conflict with Philip, the pope now begins to reconsider his previous hedges and to reinterpret his revised interpretations of the bull. Apparently he believes that opinion is rallying to his support and that he can probably win the battle only if he retracts some of his concessions. In 1301, therefore, we find him suspending the "first-fruits" decree. In another bull, *Asculta Fili,* he attempts to summarize his criticisms of Philip and to define more explicitly his authority as pope.

Philip's reply to *Asculta Fili* is not unlike that of other medieval kings who either need money or find themselves in conflict with the Holy See. He summons the first "States General"—a body representing the several estates of the realm—hoping that it will support him against the pope. In this hope he is not disappointed for he does indeed find widespread sentiment, even among the clergy, in favor of his attitude to Boniface.

The pope's reply to the States-General and to Philip's defiance is almost instantaneous. In one of the most sweeping and aggressive pronouncements of papal history, he claims spiritual and temporal powers alike for the chair of Peter. He is far more explicit than Innocent III; and since *Unam Sanctam* (1302) is a bull, it has a much higher status than the famous but unofficial letter of Gregory VII to Bishop Hermann.[3] It is, in fact, perhaps the greatest defence of theocracy in the history of political theory.

Boniface VIII begins with a statement of faith—that there is only one "holy Catholic and apostolic Church, outside of which is neither salvation nor remission of sins." While he is not clear as to whether he is referring to the spiritual society of St. Augustine or to the hierarchical Church as organized in medieval society, the whole context of the bull leads one to believe that it is the latter.

Addressing himself to the problem of spirituals and temporals, the pope avers that there are indeed two swords. To support this contention, he cites the words of Jesus at the Last Supper. It will be remembered that Jesus discoursed at some length to his disciples at that time, telling them that they would be sent to teach his message and that those would be greatest who served others best. At one point in the discourse, he uttered these words: "When I sent you out without any purse or bag or shoes, was there anything you needed?" The disciples replied: "See, Master, here are two swords!" His answer was "Enough of this."[4] Some translations make his answer read "It is enough."

Boniface interprets this incident as showing

that two swords are enough and he furthermore thinks of the swords shown by the disciples to Jesus as symbolical of temporal and spiritual power. The fact that Jesus said "It is enough" or "Enough of this" meant that he thought there were not more than two powers established for the government of the world.

The pope goes on to make much of another scriptural passage. It will be remembered that after Jesus was betrayed by Judas, one of those accompanying him drew a sword and cut off the high priest's servant's ear. Jesus immediately commanded him to put up his sword, for, he said, "All who draw the sword will die by the sword."[5] Boniface attacks those—and many medievalists do so—who think that Jesus' command and statement bar the Church from exercising temporal power, although he gives no cogent reason for his opinion.

Boniface goes on to draw out the full implications of this idea. The temporal sword is under the spiritual because the apostle says that the powers that be are of God. By this he means that while both temporal and spiritual authority come from God, the former can be exercised only under the supervision of the latter. Boniface apparently intends to suggest that two swords of co-equal rank would be bound to clash. Hence there must be a coordinator, as it were.

In concluding *Unam Sanctam*, the pope tries to show that denial of the plenary authority of the papacy may smack of Manichaeanism. When Jesus gave the "binding and loosing" power to Peter,[6] he indicated that there was a single ordination or ordinance for the government of the world. Now Boniface has shown to his own satisfaction that this single governance is in the hands of the pope as successor of Peter. Only if one is a Manichaean, he avers, can one think that there may be a dual government; for the Manichaean, in obvious denial of that Genesis which asserts that "in the beginning God created the earth," in effect says, "in the beginnings" and thus through his dualism splits the universe.

All this leads the pope to state quite frankly: "We declare, announce and define, that it is altogether necessary to salvation for every human creature to be subject to the Roman pontiff." And that this subjection is to be both temporal and spiritual *Unam Sanctam* has been at great pains to demonstrate.

The publication of the bull creates great consternation throughout all Christendom. Naturally, it alarms Philip's partisans most of all, for if the doctrines of *Unam Sanctam* are to be accepted, the pretensions of kings must wither on the vine. The king therefore sends a force of soldiers into Italy for the purpose of arresting the pope. The soldiers attack the palace, the pope remains firm, and a rising of the Romans on behalf of the successor of Peter compels the invaders to withdraw. But the trauma is too great even for Boniface and toward the end of 1303 he dies.

The passing of Boniface, of course, does not end the controversy, however much it may indicate a political victory for the king. Throughout the exchanges between pope and monarch, apologists for both sides have been active and remain so after the death of Boniface. One of the best-known partisans of the royal cause is John of Paris, who seeks in such pamphlets as *Tractatus de Potestate Regia et Papali*, *Quaestio in Utramque*, and *Quaestio de Potestate Papae* to show that the temporal claims of the papacy are ill-founded and that the king of France is beholden to neither pope nor emperor for his authority.

One of John's most basic attacks on the whole papalist position turns on his denial of the thesis that legitimate royal authority is confined to rule of bodies only. It will be remembered that a favorite papalist contention, after the first quarter of the thirteenth century, is the view that, since Aristotle makes the soul superior to the body, the pope must necessarily be superior to the king or emperor. If the king may be held to rule over bodies only, John says, this analogy might be correct. But Aristotle also views the state and legislator as means whereby man is made good: The community is for the development of virtue in all men. If this is true, then the king must necessarily concern himself with souls as well as bodies; for goodness or virtue is a matter of the soul and not primarily of the body.

Meanwhile, a whole series of papalist apologists flourishes, both in the years just preceding the death of Boniface and immediately thereafter. Many of them simply repeat the

3. See pp. 203–204.
4. Luke 22:35–38.
5. Matthew 26:52.
6. Matthew 5:19.

formulas of the thirteenth-century radical canonists. But some of them—notably Egidius Colonna, Henry of Cremona, James of Viterbo, and Augustinus Triumphus—attempt to expand and enrich the argument. In so doing, several of them are "led by excess of zeal," according to a modern Catholic writer,[7] "to formulate absurd and preposterous propositions." Thus James of Viterbo, in his *De Regimine Christiano,* maintains that the office of priest is itself "royal," so that the distinction between king and priest has only a limited validity. In Christendom, James continues, all statutes ordained by temporal power must be sanctioned by the spiritual.

No one of the papalist writers goes further than Augustinus Triumphus in exalting the position of the papacy. Although some of his writings take us several years beyond the immediate context of the struggle between Boniface and Philip, his *Tractatus Bravis de Duplici Potestate Prelatorum et Laicorum* may have been written about the time of Boniface's death or a little earlier.[8] In addition to many of the usual apologetics, he makes the astonishing assertion that the authority which appertains to the pope is always, by nature, right. By contrast, temporal authority may be wrong (although it is apparently not necessarily in error). Because of this inerrancy of papal authority and the uncertainty of temporal power, the latter is and ought to be controlled and educated by the former.

Curiously enough, the greatest claims for the papacy are made at a time when the actual temporal potency of the pope reaches its low point. After the death of Boniface, the holder of the chair of Peter comes under the direct sway of the French king—that monarch whose theoretical position so alarms men like Henry of Cremona and James of Viterbo. With Pope Clement V (1305–1314), the headquarters of the papacy are translated to Avignon and until 1377 the head of Christendom resides on French soil.

As the popes accommodate themselves to their new surroundings, claims for a kind of unity radically different from that of the papalists begin to be made. The Empire has been in decline since the middle of the thirteenth century. But as the papacy sinks more and more into a state of dependence on secular power, some men look with longing to a revived imperial concept; and as they reflect on the extreme claims of papalists and royalists, their adherence to the imperial idea becomes even firmer. Among those who, in the twilight of imperial influence, exalt a secular universalism the Italian poet Dante stands out as preeminent.

The Universalism of Dante

Dante's political experience must have been similar to that of many others in the declining years of the thirteenth century. Born in Florence in 1265, he comes from a family which has been attached to the papal cause and which therefore, in the Italian politics of the time, has been supporting the faction known as the Guelfs. The Guelfs emerge victorious.

In 1293, the constitution of Florence is changed so that the nobility are deprived of formal political power and the plebeians of the city are admitted to the seats of political authority. Dante himself is active in the General Council of the city-state, where he becomes a spokesman of those who have been enthusiastic in the popular cause. In 1300, he is elected one of the six Priors or Magistrates and to all appearances has a long political career before him.

At this point, however, external and internal politics conspire to prepare the way for his downfall and political exile. Legates of the pope (Boniface VIII) are active in support of the antipopular faction, which in the current struggle is upholding the papal cause. This alliance between his family faction of the Guelfs and the ambitious aristocracy leads Dante to repudiate the pope along with the hated aristocrats. He identifies himself completely with the fortunes of the Bianchi, the party which adheres to the constitution of 1293; while those who sustain the papacy and the nobility organize themselves as the Neri.

It is clear that Dante is one of the leaders of the Bianchi; for when the Neri seize power in 1302, with the support of the troops of Charles of Valois and the pope, the poet is fined and sentenced to indefinite exclusion from office. The sentence includes exile and a threat of burning at the stake should he ever set foot again on the soil of Florence.

From 1302 until his death in 1321, Dante is completely excluded from participation in Florentine affairs. After his withdrawal to Verona he seems, indeed, to have decided to abstain from political affairs altogether. But, as in the case of another great Florentine, Machiavelli, two centuries later, the politics of his time are so vital and momentous that he finds it impossible to keep his vow. This is particularly true after 1308, when Henry of Luxembourg is chosen emperor as Henry VII. Dante becomes an ardent partisan of Henry and writes his greatest purely political treatise, *De Monarchia*, to provide a theoretical foundation for what he hopes will be a revived imperial concept—hopes, of course, which are not to be realized.

His political doctrine is a curious combination of medievalism with anticipations of characteristically modern outlooks and it is for this reason that many have thought of him as one of the great intellectual links between the age of St. Thomas and that, for example, of such exponents of modernity as Hobbes. He is medieval in the way he uses authorities to sustain his case but modern in his foreshadowing of secularism.

Like most medievalists, he maintains that the end of man is twofold—happiness in this life and felicity in the life eternal. Like St. Thomas, too, he sees eternal happiness as possible only with the aid of divine light; for natural reason, while it may take us far, cannot lead us to see God as he is in himself—only the assistance of Revelation can provide this boon.

In developing his major theme, Dante strongly emphasizes the organic character of human society, employing biological analogies to stress the great significance of division of labor and the mutural interdependence of all mankind. Nature produces the thumb for one purpose and the whole hand for another. Similarly each part of the body has a particular function to perform. The human race as a whole is like the biological organism and man has the special capacity to apprehend the relation of parts to the whole.

But Dante, as befits one who has been exiled for the popular cause, emphasizes that the characteristically human attribute of rationality must be operative in many men if the work of the human race is to be accomplished. Conversely, the rationality of one man can be fully developed only if the potentialities of others are likewise drawn out: My development as a human being, to put it another way, depends as much on the efforts of others as it does upon my own endeavors.

The perfection of knowledge and the training of the will, he argues, require peace for the individual and peace also for that human race to which the individual is so intimately tied. If the individual is interrupted in his quest for wisdom by conflicts within his personality, the achievement of the goal will be impaired. Likewise, if humanity finds itself divided by wars and tumults it cannot pursue what Dante thinks of as its divine work.

It is small wonder, therefore, that the Florentine poet makes ecumenical peace the highest political value. Nor is it for him merely political. For if eternal felicity is in some measure dependent on the growth of personality, and if the development of individual potentialities is impossible in the absence of external peace, then peace becomes not merely the central temporal or political value but also a high-order desideratum for eternal felicity.

But how is the harmony of individual and human race to be attained? To answer this question, Dante turns to "the Philosopher." He points out that Aristotle has laid it down that where discrete things are ordered for a single end, one of them must somehow direct the others. Thus the harmony of the home is established through the governance of the father and that of the village through its archon or governor. Human organization, as it radiates outward, always discovers a necessity for coordination. Order, indeed, implies an arrangement whereby some men obey others for the sake of the whole. But the ultimate whole cannot be anything less than the human race, since the quest for knowledge and the development of will are dependent on the participation of all mankind.

Because this is true, he maintains, the conclusion must be that the human race should have a single ruler. Universal monarchy is essential for the well-being of humanity and each man.

But before he discusses the specifics of his universal monarchy, he turns to suggest other arguments for its establishment. Many of these reasons we should probably say are characteristically medieval. For example, he argues that God intends every human being to be in his own likeness and has the same intention with respect to the human race. But the essence of deity is unity. Therefore, the human race is

7. Ludwig Pastor, *The History of the Popes*, vol. 1, London: Kegan Paul, Trench, Trubner and Co., 1891, p. 80.
8. According to the Carlyles, in *Medieval Political Theory in the West*, Edinburgh: Blackwood, 1936, vol. 5, p. 417.

most like God—and hence is most nearly in accordance with the divine will for man—when it is closest to unity.

Once Dante has established both the human and the divine foundations for universal peace and shown that it cannot be attained except under world monarchy, his next task is to demonstrate that unitary rule is and ought to be in the hands of the Romans. From this point on, much of the analysis depends on his interpretation and uses of history and the modern student of political thought may find his arguments exceedingly tenuous.

The Roman people, he suggests, lawfully gained their Empire over mankind, as is proven by the miracles connected with its development. That it was the Romans who were especially fitted to command the world is shown, according to Dante, by the fact that they were indeed successful. He does not tell us what the disintegration of the Empire indicated. Throughout this part of his analysis, in fact, there seems to be a naive identification of military success with evidence of divine pleasure and an unwillingness even to ask whether later failure does not reveal anger on the part of God. In these respects, Dante is far less penetrating in his view of political history than, for example, St. Augustine.

There are numerous indications, however, that he never wavered in this belief that the Roman people and their emperors are of right the rulers of the universe. The fact, for example, that his guide through hell and purgatory is Virgil is evidence not only of affinity between poets but also of the Florentine's almost mystical attachment to the notion of Roman supremacy. We find also that he places Caesar in limbo rather than in hell, thus showing that he believes the founder of the Roman Empire to be a pre-Christian righteous man. Hence "armed Caesar with the falcon eye" is saved from hell proper along with men like Plato and Socrates.[9]

On the other hand, opponents of the Empire's founder, men like Brutus and Cassius—who in their own day were widely regarded as the would-be preservers of their people against the tyranny of Caesar—are consigned to the lowest parts of hell along with Judas Iscariot:

"That soul up there to the worst penance brought
Is Judas the Iscariot," spoke my Lord.
"His head within, he plies his legs without.
Of the other two, hanging with head downward,
Brutus it is whom the black mouth doth maul.
See how he writhes and utters not a word!
Cassius the other who seems so large to sprawl."[10]

Nor are his judgments confined to those political personages who may be in limbo or hell. It is equally revealing to note the rulers whom he places in purgatory. While Boniface VIII (who has not yet died when Dante takes his tour of hell) is to be consigned to the third chasm of the eighth circle of the Inferno,[11] that reserved for simonists, his great opponent, Philip IV of France, although condemned for his treatment of the Vicar of Christ, ends in that part of Purgatory planned for the avaricious.[12]

In the sixth heaven of the Paradise—the sphere of Jupiter—Dante again develops a very elaborate political symbolism. He imagines many spirits forming themselves into the shape of an eagle's head and neck. The eagle, symbol of Roman power, passes judgment on Pope John XXII for his devotion to temporals, particularly money.[13] Here it seems clear that temporal authority—particularly the universal power of the emperor—is set above that of the pope; and that the latter is to be held accountable to the former for his betrayal of the spiritual trust.

Throughout the development of his political attitude, Dante takes great pains to show that the emperor receives his authority directly from God and that the Church is not permitted to exercise any temporal power.

In the higher reaches of Paradise, the poet significantly finds Justinian, and the Roman lawgiver offers the medieval Christian a lesson in the interpretation of both sacred and profane history. He reiterates the glorious achievements of the Roman eagle from the destruction of Troy to the fall of Jerusalem under Titus. Again, the history of Roman conquest is seen as divinely ordained.

The Dantean view of politics, then, is one which views the Roman Empire as the divinely inspired coordinator of mankind; and ultimately, the poet implies, the imperial conception and papal claims will be reconciled in a unity of the world. National pretensions, one gathers, are temporary aberrations if God intends unity. But the unity, when it comes, will be radically different from that postulated by canonical writers and by Pope Boniface VIII. Spiritual power will be responsible and accountable to him who represents the Roman eagle, the emperor being the final adjudicator of differences between spiritual and secular realms.

Modern critics of Dante, like James Burnham,[14] maintain that the Italian poet's version of politics is naive and that he totally fails to take account of political realities in his construction of the argument for imperial unity. In short, his politics ignores the actual forces which are molding the political world and his ideal has no congruence with things as they are.

Such critics are right, of course, in certain respects. There is little in Dante of that minute analysis of political manipulation which is to characterize his great fellow-citizen two centuries later. Like most medievalists, too, he is not interested in looking at politics as if it could be divorced from considerations of morality. He has little sense of the modern view that economic life and political activity must be studied as abstractions before one can know enough about them to implement ethical goals.

Yet from another point of view and in a different way Dante is highly realistic. His picture of the basic unity of mankind and of the ultimate mutual dependence of all men and women on one another cannot be excelled in all political literature. He has a keen appreciation of the social facets involved in the development of rationality.

But although he attacks the claims of embryonic state monarchs to unqualified allegiance, he apparently does not see the creation of a universal empire and the corresponding destruction of effective ecclesiastical opposition as likely to create a situation in which the emperor will take on all the undesirable characteristics which Dante associates with the pope. Given the attenuation of ecclesiastical power, who will resist the tendencies to tyranny and corruption?

It is with questions of this kind, although in the context of emerging national rather than imperial politics, that thinkers like Marsilio of Padua become increasingly concerned.

Secularism and Representation in Marsilio

In 1324, Lewis of Bavaria, around whom opponents of Pope John XXII tended to rally, published a document in which he charged the Pope with heresy. The indictment was based on the contention that the Avignon Pontiff, by repudiating the doctrine of evangelical poverty—which, as we have seen,[15] was ardently espoused by the Spiritual Franciscans—had in effect surrendered his orthodoxy by disagreeing with the manner of life sustained in practice by Christ and his Apostles. In a vigorously-worded section of the document, Lewis (or rather a Spiritual Franciscan who probably wrote it) appealed from the man "who calls himself Pope" to the higher authority of a General Council and to some future pope who will have ceased to be heretical.

Politically, it is obvious, Lewis hopes to gain influence with all those elements in Christendom who by now are thoroughly alarmed about the continued residency of the papacy in France. But religious elements cannot be divorced from the political: The violent controversy over evangelical poverty has split Holy Church itself and the Franciscans see in Lewis an ally who might move the Church to change its attitudes with respect to its position on the property question. Then, too, the demand for general reform of the clergy has mounted to proportions which cannot well be ignored; and Lewis is seen by many as the political leader who, by intervening in ecclesiastical affairs, can bring about that purification which the critics of the later High Middle Ages see as increasingly necessary.[16]

It is against this background that one must see the political ideas of Marsilio of Padua, one of the most revolutionary figures of the age. Born about 1270, Marsilio studied philosophy, medicine, and theology at the University of Paris, where he met the future philosopher William of Ockham. He apparently became imbued with French ideas during his residence in the capital of the rapidly expanding royal estate, so that it is not surprising to find him taking an extreme secularist position in his *Defensor Pacis*, published in 1326. Following as it does the Manifesto of Lewis, it is designed to strengthen the argument of all those who discern fundamental wrongs in the papacy.

9. *Inferno*, Canto IV, *The Divine Comedy*. Laurence Binyon, trans., New York: Viking Press, 1947.
10. *Inferno*, Canto XXXIV.
11. *Inferno*, Canto XIX.
12. *Purgatorio*, Canto XX.
13. *Paradiso*, Canto XVIII.
14. See James Burnham, *The Machiavellians*, Chicago: Henry Regnery Co., 1963, ch. 1.
15. See pp. 258–259.
16. Cf. particularly Henry C. Lea, *The History of Sacerdotal Celibacy in the Christian Church*, New York: Russell and Russell, 1957, ch. 21.

Marsilio is very much concerned about the problem of where ultimate authority lies and how it is to be exercised. His answer is that the supreme power must be held to reside in the people, or at least in the *valencier pars* of the populus. Going on, he explains what he means in words which have become near-classic: "*Valenciorem inquam partem, considerata quantitate personarum et qualitate in communitate illa super quam lex fertur.*" We may roughly interpret these words as meaning that ultimate authority reposes in the preponderant part of the people, taking into account both quantitative and qualitative considerations. Apparently he has in mind a weighting of the populus in accordance with status and possibly educational qualifications, so that the voice of the community is not only representative of numbers but also of what he calls qualitative factors. Modern theories of representation tend to make sheer numerical preponderance the only element; Marsilio, by contrast, tries to combine both a straight nose-count (as we would say today) and a medieval-like recognition of status differences. But he does not spell out the details and has thus puzzled scholars for six centuries as to his precise meaning.

Much of his doctrine is, of course, rooted in medieval notions. Where he does depart from general medieval theory is in his explicit statement that the people (however defined), in order to wield their authority effectively, must delegate it to some kind of representative assembly which will then choose the ruler and hold him accountable. The notion of representation is present in medieval thought and practice; but the idea of subordinating what Marsilio calls the *principans* to a representative assembly is certainly not central. The *principans* or executive is to be the agent of the representative body, which will provide machinery through which the long tradition against tyranny can be implemented. We have noted that Dante fails to tell us just how the universal ruler can be kept within the bounds of the law to which he must be subordinate. Marsilio fills in this gap and thus lays the foundations for modern doctrines of representation.

But not only does he work out an embryonic theory of representative government, he also deals at some length with the proper jurisdiction of civil or temporal authority. Here there are to be virtually no limits. Anything which affects the community is within the range of its authority, for it is established to ensure the common good. Unlike many early modern doctrines of civil jurisdiction which think of the economy as an autonomous sphere which must be left largely untouched by the polity, Marsilio exempts no aspect of life from control by the political ruler. Legislation may even regulate the number of persons allowed to enter given professions, including the priesthood; for after all, Marsilio reasons, the general objectives of order and peace may be profoundly impaired by failure of the ruler to take positive action in the economic sphere. While the canonists frequently sustain ecclesiastical authority in the realm of prices, interest, and wages (for these matters may directly affect the destiny of the immortal soul), Marsilio strips the Church of all vestiges of jurisdiction in economic affairs.

Although his sketch of secular governance is radical for his times, his attitude to ecclesiastical government is perhaps even more revolutionary. Like every sensitive mind of his day, he is disturbed by the Avignon "captivity" but unlike many he questions the very foundations of those developments which have set up the pope as the direct agent of God.

He first asks himself what is the foundation of Christian Faith. By the time of St. Thomas, of course, the orthodox answer to this question has come to be the Church—and the extreme papalists contend that the pope speaks in the name of the Church. But Marsilio argues that the ultimate foundation is Scripture, which is prior to the Church and therefore of superior authority. When one asks Marsilio who is to interpret Scripture, since Holy Writ is hardly clear at many critical junctures, his answer is equally revolutionary: Its meaning is to be authoritatively given by those who have knowledge and wisdom in these things, the men of intelligence. In this respect, he observes, the University of Paris—his own *alma mater*—may have better insights and scholarship than the Bishop of Rome himself.

Marsilio holds that just as temporal authority is derived from the community and must be held responsible to the representatives of the community, so must papal authority come from the community of the ecclesia and be made accountable to a representative church body. Referring to the old tradition of the ecumenical council, he maintains that it is the Council to which the ecclesiastical community has implicitly committed care of the Faith. It is the General Council, too, to whom the pope must report: He is, in fact, like the prince in the temporal sphere, the agent of the Council and not its master.

As if this doctrine were not extreme enough, Marsilio goes on to assert that the summoning of a General Council should of right belong to the temporal power. He can, of course, cite precedent for secular direction of the Council: One of the most crucial councils in the history of Holy Church, that of Nicea, was presided over by the Emperor Constantine, and that at a time when the emperor was not even a Christian (although Marsilio does not point this out). He apparently gives so vital a role to the secular power partly because he can see no other solution for the problem of Church reform.

If and when the General Council is summoned, he thinks that its general direction should be a prerogative of the emperor. It is apparently the emperor, too, who is to formulate the issues which it must decide and give tone and encouragement to its deliberations.

There is never any doubt in Marsilio about the sweeping powers possessed by temporal authority over the Church as a whole—for its own good, of course. He attacks the doctrine of Boniface VIII that ecclesiastical property is immune from taxation, maintaining, consistently with his general doctrine of the sphere of civil authority, that if the end of the political society is the common good, its ruler must be the judge of whether that good might or might not necessitate imposition of material burdens on the ecclesia. No divided authority about these matters can be tolerated, lest the very order which is sought be impaired.

Perhaps one of the most startling aspects of Marsilio's political-ecclesiastical theory is his elaboration of the way in which the whole body of the Church can and should control the clergy. Any powers the clergy may have, he holds—including their prerogatives over Church courts—are derived from the laity. Just as the pope's universal jurisdiction is one delegated to him by the Church as a whole, so each parish priest may be thought of as simply a delegate of his parishioners. And Marsilio carries out this doctrine literally: The laity in each parish, he maintains, can both appoint and remove the priest.

As a whole, Marsilio's political theory is one of the most radical statements of the entire fourteenth century. It has few if any concessions in it to what might be called the high medieval spirit. Swept away are all barriers of custom, the contractual elements of the feudal system, and the claims of two hundred years of canonical doctrine.

Nor is Marsilio alone in developing views which will later be identified with a radical secularism. His friend, William of Ockham, who is perhaps best known for his part in the great late medieval debate between the nominalists and the realists, is also deeply involved in the political speculations which do so much to undermine the foundations of the papacy.

The Politics of William of Ockham

Earlier we have noted the role of Duns Scotus who, although only a moderate and not a Spiritual Franciscan, had done so much to sustain certain aspects of the Spiritual Franciscan view of property and its relation to the Church.[17] William of Ockham is in somewhat the same tradition, although his tendencies in political thought are more nearly akin to those of Marsilio of Padua than to those of Duns. That Ockham (d. 1347) was looked upon as very dangerous politically is indicated by the fact that he was actually thrown into prison by Pope John XXII and was released only through the efforts of Lewis the Bavarian.

But we cannot understand Ockham as a political thinker unless we first note his place in the history of medieval philosophy. As was suggested earlier, the great problem of the thirteenth century was that of formulating the exact relationship between the domain of philosophy and that of theology, or of reason and faith. Thomas had developed a system which asserted that man could indeed work out demonstrations for the existence of God through reason alone. We can thus *know* that God *is* and revelation simply confirms and supplements our knowledge. Throughout the Thomist scheme, reason and revelation supplement each other, and thus a place exists for both a natural theology and a revealed religion. Thomas was what we usually call a moderate realist with respect to the problem of universals, holding with Aristotle that universals are present in the individual specimens which we observe. Universals, in other words,

17. See p. 259.

are not mere generalizations in which man abstracts common qualities from individuals but are themselves higher-level realities closely related to and shaping the individuals. As a recent writer observed,[18] Thomas presents the view of Aristotle as a mean between two extremes. On one extreme is Democritus, who thinks of knowledge as simply sensation and imagination; while on the other is Plato, who holds that "sensation provides no more than the occasion upon which the understanding climbs to contemplate the spiritual world of forms."

For Thomas, while essences are real, individual existences are real instances of universals. As a recent historian of medieval philosophy has put it, "The order of essence represents in abstraction the ramification and interrelation of universal concepts; the order of existence runs parallel with it and lends to it individuality and reality."[19]

After Thomas, medieval philosophy is characterized by the gradual growth of nominalistic positions which challenge both the extreme realists and those, like St. Thomas, who adopt a moderately realistic position. To some extent, the Dominicans tend to support their greatest philosopher and insist on various versions of realism; while the Franciscans, their rivals, often move in the direction of nominalism.

In general, the transition from a realism characteristic of the High Middle Ages to the nominalism which becomes increasingly important during the declining period, consists in a gradual separation of the world of thought from that of facts; of the inner world of consciousness from the outer universe of sensation. The sphere of Grace, too, instead of being conceived as supplementing the activities of the rational knower, as with Thomas, is now severed from the realm of rationality.

These tendencies become dramatically evident in the philosophy of William of Ockham and in the ethical and political implications of that philosophy. He is perhaps best known for his flat statement that "there is no such thing as a universal, intrinsically present in the things to which it is common."[20] Universals are merely names (hence nominalism, from *nomen,* the Latin for name) and "no universal, except that is such by voluntary agreement, is existent in any way outside of the soul, but everything that can be predicated of many things, is by its nature in the mind either psychologically or logically."[21]

Ockham goes on to apply this nominalistic doctrine to the relation between individual human beings and humanity. If it were true, he contends, that humanity is "different from particular individuals and a part of their essence, one and the same invariable thing would be in many individuals, and so this same numerically one and invariable thing would be at different places, which is false." Thus "that same invariable thing" would "be condemned in Judas and saved in Christ, and hence, there would be something condemned and miserable in Christ, which is absurd." The only true view of the problem of universals is, then, to see individuals alone as real and universals as themselves, "individuals." "Every universal is one singular thing and is universal only by the signification of many things."

While Thomas had held that a "copy" of the external object arises within the soul of him who observes the object, Ockham interprets the ideas which arise in the soul as simply "signs" for the external things. But the signs are of quite a different nature from the outer things and therefore cannot be regarded as copies of the latter.

As things and thought become separated and individuals begin to be conceived as the reality, so, too, does will come to take precedence over intellect in the psychology and ethics of Ockham. In Thomas, as in Aristotle, when man really knows, he wills. True knowledge of the good carries the will with it. Hence the intellect which can grasp the essence of the forms and of final causes is superior in rank to that aspect of the soul which merely executes what the intellect discovers. In the nominalists, however, the relationship between volition and intellect is reversed. The function of the intellect is not to compel the will, as the nominalists charge Thomas with doing, but rather to present to the will the possibilities of choice.

All this can be illustrated further if we turn to the nominalists' conception of will and intellect in God. Thomas holds that God creates only what his intellect tells him is good. This determines the substance of the divine will. In ethical terms and in those of the divine government of the universe, this means that for the realist Thomas, God's commands are subordinate to his perfect comprehension of what is right and that what is right is in turn fixed by the nature of things. Men ought to conform to the will of God for human conduct, not because God commands such action but because what God commands is right and good apart from his command.

As might be expected, Ockham's account of the situation turns Thomas's relationship upside down. Duns Scotus, for example, maintains that that is good which God commands; and Ockham comments that God might through his will have made good something other than what is good now. For Thomas, in other words, God wills the good because it is good apart from his will; for Ockham, the good is commanded by God's will alone and reposes on nothing "in the nature of things."

The implications for ethics and politics of the Ockhamist view of universals and the relationship of intellect to will are momentous indeed and it is not surprising to learn that the great philosopher was excommunicated by Holy Church. If the good cannot be an objective of natural knowledge—that is, of "science" in the Ockhamist sense—there can be no way of rationally establishing norms for human conduct. What God wills as good is good simply because he wills it and our sole source of his will is Revelation or Grace, and not reason.

A recent historian of natural law has put well the implications of nominalism for ethics and law in these words:

> An action is not good because of its suitableness to the essential nature of man—but because God so wills. . . . Law is will, pure will wihout any foundation in reality, without foundation in the essential nature of things.[22]

If universals are unreal, and only individuals can will, and if will takes priority over intellect, then a theory of politics and law cannot consistently be based upon the notion of humanity as a universal operating in and shaping individuals, and law becomes simply the command of an individual (the later "sovereign"). The sharp separation, moreover, between the inner world of consciousness and the outer universe of things leads nominalists like Ockham to confine the realm of the spiritual to the inner life; while the external world is completely released from control by the inner universe. Implicitly, and in part explicitly, Ockham suggests that things of the spirit have nothing to do with the world of sense, which is the external world. Hence the spiritual power—the *ecclesia*—can deal only with man's inner life and can have no power of external compulsion; while the *imperium* or *regnum*, now made master of the entire world of external affairs, can in no sense be subject to binding ecclesiastical pronouncements.

Political authority itself, in this view, arises as the result of a kind of compromise of individual interests, and society is the uneasy product of separate concerns. Ockham's view would deny the organic conception of the political community. Positive law is the result of command, just as is the divine law; and it is the imperative of the lawgiver which defines the good, not the reason-discovered good which prescribes the norms of law.

In Ockham's general position, one sees anticipated a whole series of developments in the history of political thought. He does not spell out in detail the implications of his views nor is he as extreme as his friend Marsilio of Padua. But in the Ockhamite doctrine, and the general philosophy upon which it reposes, one can see a clear foreshadowing of social contract views of the state, the notion of national sovereignty, the separation of Church from state, and the positivist school of law.[23]

Wycliffe and the Politics of Nationalism

One is impressed as one studies the history of ideas by the close relationship between radical conceptions of the Church in the late fourteenth century and the development of the theory of the national state. The latter cannot be understood without the former, so that the historian of political thought is compelled to be also a student of ecclesiastical theory. Moreover, the battle of ideas during the final years of the Avignon papacy cannot be considered apart from the political struggles which center increasingly on ownership of material possessions.

All these observations are particularly illustrated in the politics and political ideas associated with the career of John Wycliffe. A

18. Anne Fremantle, *The Age of Belief*, New York: Mentor Books, 1954, p. 150.
19. D. J. B. Hawkins, *A Sketch of Medieval Philosophy*, New York: Sheed and Ward, 1947, p. 86.
20. William of Ockham, *Commentary on the Sentences of Peter Lombard*.
21. *Ibid.*
22. Heinrich Rommen, *Natural Law*, St. Louis: B. Herder, 1959, p. 59.
23. See A. P. D'Entreves, *Natural Law: An Introduction to Legal Philosophy*, New York: Hutchinson's University Library, 1952, p. 69.

northern Englishman, he was born about 1324 and educated at Oxford. His academic career on the Oxford faculty spanned the period between 1335 and 1374, after which he became increasingly active in practical politics, sustaining the English national cause against the pretensions of the papacy. With the beginning of the Great Schism in 1378, his conception of the Church became even more radical and his denunciations of both popes were filled with vitriolic expressions. By the time of his death in 1384, he had obviously attacked the medieval conception of the Church at so many points that he was in effect both a schismatic and a heretic.

Neither the ecclesiastical nor the political doctrines of Wycliffe can be understood unless we recall some of the major events of English-papal history during the previous century. During the pontificate of Innocent III, it will be remembered, the Pope had been able to force the king to recognize him as feudal suzerain of all England.

It need hardly be said that this subjection of the English monarchy was never a popular one and throughout the thirteenth century many efforts had been made to evade or frustrate papal control. Finally in 1333, payment of all feudal tribute to the pope was suspended—an immensely popular act in an England growing increasingly conscious of its national character. In 1337, the Hundred Years' War with France began and because of the new demands for revenue which ensued, the suspension of payments was even more enthusiastically supported.

In 1351, Parliament enacted the so-called Statute of Provisors, which was designed to limit provisions sent by England to the papacy. In 1353 came the first Statute of Praemunire, which attempted to restrict and define rigidly the jurisdiction of Church courts. By 1365—during the height of Wycliffe's academic career at Oxford—Parliament was adopting a statute which forbade English suits to be carried to the papal courts.

But the political problem was not confined to the questions of resisting papal demands for money and restricting papal jurisdiction. The Black Death of 1349 had profoundly affected the social structure. The number of laborers was drastically reduced and, with the reduction, came a great increase in wages. The "lower orders"—or their members who survived the terrible Plague—now began to acquire a new confidence in themselves and to believe that they might improve both their economic and their social lot. Parliament and the king—who reflected primarily the economic interests of the land-holding classes, the clergy, and the wealthier town-dwellers—attempted in vain, through the Statute of Laborers, to fix maxima for wages.

The general social upheaval began to take a somewhat organized form after the death of King Edward III in 1377. Under the Regency which ruled in the name of the young Richard II, peasant leaders carried on vast demonstrations and asked for an amelioration of the lot of the country dweller. The result was the so-called Peasants' Revolt of 1381 and the widespread repetition of such popular statements of the ideal of social equality as:

When Adam delved and Eve Span,
Who was then the gentleman?

Some of the peasant leaders apparently quoted Wycliffe's doctrines to justify their revolutionary activities, although there is no evidence that Wycliffe himself was associated with the revolt.[24]

Meanwhile, as the stirring antipapal and social politics were developing, Wycliffe was working out the theories which had such an impact not only on the late fourteenth century but also on such fifteenth-century movements as those of the Hussites. Both as an exponent of the idea of the poor Church and as a nationalist, he came more and more to repudiate the foundations of the medieval Church order.

Wycliffe is first of all concerned to argue against the pope's claim to feudal control of England, and his conception of papal-secular relations in the context of English politics has all the flavor of typically medieval argument. He maintains in effect that England could not have become a vassal of the pope because it had been gained by conquest (that of William the Conqueror in 1066) and not by a papal grant. Even if it be assumed, he goes on, that some kind of legitimate feudal relationship existed between pope and king, it has long ago ceased to be. This cessation must have come because the pope violated the basic obligation of a feudal superior to his vassal—that of protection.

It is when we turn to his theory of *dominium* that we encounter the Wycliffe who becomes so explosive a force for his own day as well as for the generation immediately following his death. Like the Spiritual Franciscans, he reverts to the ideal of the "poor church" which allegedly existed—somewhat like the pure nature of the Garden of Eden before the Fall—before the time of Constantine. Churchmen are granted *dominium* in material goods—property rights, in other words—only on condition that they observe the divine law which Wycliffe identifies (unlike Thomas) completely with natural law.

As a vassal of God, the Church must, in return for *dominium*, act with charity, self-control, and love. It cannot devote its goods to aggrandizement or employ its property for purposes of temporal strife. What Wycliffe regards as the feudal principle of mutuality must hold; and he expresses it in a kind of slogan: no *dominium* without *caritas*. In the context of his discussion, this means that if the Church flagrantly misuses its *dominium*—violates, in other words, the principle of charity—it can legitimately be deprived of its temporal goods. And because the temporal ruler intrinsically has the right to control temporal goods in order to carry out his divine temporal functions, it is he who executes the commands of the feudal superior, God, when the Church has violated its feudal obligations.[25]

But his conception of the Church is much broader than the doctrine of ecclesiastical *dominium*, even though the latter may legitimately be called the basis. Theologically, he gives the Augustinian notion of predestination an ethical twist and clearly connects it with the conception of an unorganized church. Men recognize one another's predestined state through the conduct exhibited in practical life and the Church becomes simply the free association of those who extend this mutual recognition.[26] Under such circumstances, most of the sacraments cease to play an important role in Wycliffe's ecclesiastical ideas; and since the sacraments have been inseparably connected with their administration by the Church hierarchy, the Wycliffite will tend—on this ground alone—to think of priests and bishops as not distinguishable in any important respects from the laity.

Why is Wycliffe generally regarded as an important figure in the history of political thought? The answer would seem to be that, although his doctrine as such is not primarily political, one can easily interpret his statements on the Church as having broad social and political implications. And historically they are so regarded, as the history of both Lollardy and the fifteenth-century Hussites shows. His central theory of *dominium*, for example,

is supposed to refer only to the Church. Priests and bishops who utilize their material goods for ends contrary to the purpose for which *dominium* is granted lose their right to the goods. If they become arrogant or act in a manner which the Apostles would never approve, their possessions cease to be theirs. We have here a kind of functional theory of property: Ownership of temporal goods is contingent on their being used only for socially (or divinely) approved functions. And most men in late medieval times can see how this idea corrodes the notion that the Church has and ought to have authority over temporals.

But if the doctrine is applicable to the Church, why is it not also equally valid as against temporal lords? Amidst the complexities of late feudalism and the restlessness of peasants eager to be emancipated from the pressures of their superiors, many men can see no distinction between the theory of *dominium* as applied to the Church and a similar idea when related to temporal lordships. And the individualism stressed in Wycliffe's conception of the Church cannot fail to reinforce this revolutionary tendency.[27]

The Conciliar Movement: Politics and Political Thought

While Wycliffe is struggling to build ideological foundations for national autonomy and incidentally developing bases for social revolution, the inner politics of the Church itself are contributing to its own fundamental transformation. Out of the conflicts of the Avignon period and of the Great Schism which follows, two sharply divergent conceptions of church government struggle for supremacy and in the process profoundly affect men's general po-

24. See particularly George Trevelyan, *England in the Age of Wycliffe, 1368–1520*, New York: Harper & Row, 1963.
25. Note his treatises *De Officio Regis* and *De Civilio Dominio*.
26. Cf. Ernst Troeltsch, *The Social Teaching of the Christian Churches*, vol. 1, p. 360.
27. See Edward Block, *John Wyclif, Radical Dissenter*, San Diego: San Diego State College Press, 1962; Lowrie J. Daly, *Political Theory of John Wyclif*, Chicago: Loyola University Press, 1962; George Trevelyan, *op. cit.*

litical ideas. The first view thinks of the pope as the vital factor in the politics of the Church and gives to the ecclesiastical community only a secondary status. By contrast, the second position, increasingly embraced by those who see no way out of the sad state of the Church except a revolutionary one, exalts the ecclesiastical community and its supposed agent, the General Council.

The pope remained in Avignon from the time of Clement V (1305–1314) to Gregory XI (1370–1378) and during this long period the papacy, partly controlled by the French monarchy,[28] rapidly declined in prestige. Good Christians were scandalized that the Vicar of Christ continued to remain away from the sacred city.

By the middle of the century and from the most diverse sources came pleas that the successors of Peter return to their capital. Scholars in the University of Paris, for example, although they seemed at points to be swayed by national interests, were convinced that only the return of the pope to Rome could make possible the restoration of the Church to a state of health and vigor. And saints like Catherine of Siena directed their eloquence to the same objective.

Much of the agitation, of course, turned not merely on the fact that the papacy was absent from Rome and under the sway of a national monarch but also on the character of the Avignon papacy itself. Although some able and devoted men occupied the chair of Peter from Clement V to Gregory XI, even the best of them seemed unable to control the corruption which became increasingly associated with their Courts; and some of them apparently did not even wish to eliminate it. Somehow, men thought, if the deleterious influences of Avignon could be removed by returning the seat of the pope to Rome, the cancer of ecclesiastical corruption might be eliminated. This may have been a naive view—as subsequent events seemed to show—but that thousands of souls held it there can be no doubt.

The demand for reform of the Church greatly strengthened the claims of temporal authority as a whole. For as men more and more despaired of the Church's self-reformation, they could see no hope except in temporal rulers. The latter, of course, often welcomed the appeal to them, since it gave them opportunities for Church spoliation and domination of which they had hardly ever dreamed before.

When Gregory XI returned to Rome under relatively favorable circumstances (in 1377), most good Christians rejoiced. Now, they thought, the foundations could be laid for a reformed and a revitalized Church under which the ideal of a unified Christendom could be regained. Subversive doctrines like those of Marsilio of Padua and William of Ockham, the hopeful believed, would find few supporters if the Church could be restored to a status like that which it had in the days of Innocent IV. The appeal to a General Council, which had been so widely heard in the early part of the century, would then be stilled.

When the Cardinals met to choose a successor to Gregory XI, there was widespread sentiment among them for a pope who would proceed to the tasks of ecclesiastical reform without undue delay. The new Pope, Urban VI, belonged to the reforming faction of the Church and, while there were disturbances in Rome at the time of his election, most men appeared to believe that he would be accepted and that he would, moreover, succeed in carrying out radical changes. Unfortunately, he was a tactless man and very soon after his election began to quarrel with several cardinals, who resented what they regarded as his dictatorial tactics.

Of course, ecclesiastical and secular politics were almost inextricably combined in the events which followed. The French cardinals (the opponents of Urban) were in some measure influenced by the ambitions of their national monarch, just as several of the cardinals who adhered to the Pope were not immune to Italian jealousy of French prestige. The bluntness and violence of Urban VI, however, continued to promote the rift within the College, until finally the French faction withdrew altogether. Meeting as a separate college, the French Princes of the Church proceeded to denounce the election of Urban VI as illegal (although they had previously clearly recognized its legality) and then to elect a rival Pope, who took the name of Clement VII. Clement established his residence in Avignon, where he was joined by his cardinals.[29]

Thus began the Great Schism which, even more than the Avignon papacy, was to do so much both to weaken the universality of the Church and to pave the way for political theories which would become the keystone of modern life.

With respect to ecclesiastical and political theory, the effects of the Schism were profound indeed. In the first place, it stimulated and encouraged the development of doctrines like those of Wycliffe. But secondly, and of equal importance, it led men within the Church itself to recur to theories similar to the ideas of Marsilio and Ockham.

Wycliffite doctrine, as we have shown, was originally a theory of the nature of the Church and of the relation of the Church to temporal power. But already before the death of Wycliffe, it was becoming merged with vague doctrines of social revolution and, as we have observed, played a part in the Peasants' Revolt of 1381. As the century draws to a close, the "poor preachers" sent out by Wycliffe to attack the property-owning Church become in many instances indistinguishable from what we might regard today as revolutionary agitators.

The revolutionary implications of second-generation Wycliffite teaching are reflected in the Hussites. It is true that not all Hussites push the theory to extremes. The "Calixtines," for example, representing the conservative wing of the movement, are eventually reconciled to the Church when they begin to understand the social and political implications attached to some versions of Hussite theory; and the Moravian Brethren, originally connected with radical Hussitism, later repudiate the appeal to violence which characterizes the extremists. Nevertheless, for a time in the early fifteenth century, it appears likely that the radical wing of the movement—the Taborites, as they come to be called—is about to become the leading exponent of Hussite theory.

Meanwhile, within the limits of Orthodoxy itself, the whole problem of ecclesiastical government becomes acute. With the Great Schism separating good Christians from one another, the cry for reunification of Holy Church continues to increase. But who, under the circumstances, can bring about this much desired result? It appears that men can have little hope in the two pontiffs themselves. And aspiring national kings so frequently benefit from the division of Christendom that few expect help from them. As to the emperor, his power and prestige have been declining since the thirteenth century. Must Christendom, then, accept the Schism as permanent? If so, what then becomes of the cardinal conception of a Christian Church-state or single society?

As men both in high stations and in low reflect on the scandal of disunity, which is inseparably connected in their minds with the problem of reform, they increasingly see hope only in the possibility of a General or Ecumenical Council of the Church. As we have seen, such a council was proposed early in the fourteenth century by Marsilio of Padua and others. Now, however, the pressure for an assembly of bishops and doctors of the Church becomes well-nigh irresistible. And out of the demand for a council emerges a whole body of conciliar theory.

Before examining the theory itself, let us note briefly the nature of the political struggles which lay the groundwork. It is hoped by many that the rival popes may themselves abdicate, thus permitting a fresh election. But neither the Roman pontiff nor his competitor at Avignon is willing to take this step. Each is involved in strengthening his own position; and each, too, is entangled in the meshes of temporal politics. By 1408, the Italian line of popes is represented by Gregory XII and the French by Benedict XIII. Both pontiffs theoretically favor a healing of the schism but by that date it is clear that neither is really serious in his professions. The result is that cardinals from both obediences become disgusted and, uniting for the first time, summon a council of the Church to meet at Pisa in 1409. The Council of Pisa becomes the first of the great conciliar bodies of the time. Its only result, however, is to produce a third pope, Alexander V, whose successor in the Pisan line is John XXIII.

But neither Alexander nor John is successful in securing the abdications of Gregory XII and Benedict XIII; and it becomes increasingly obvious after 1410 that only the intervention of the temporal power can possibly secure a truly General Council and with it the possi-

28. It is easy to exaggerate the degree to which Clement and his successors were actually manipulated by the French king. There is no doubt that during the "Babylonian captivity of the Church" the pope was not as free as he had been in the High Middle Ages. At the same time, however, as Pastor has pointed out, *op. cit.* we should by no means conclude that men like John XXII were always merely puppets.

29. It seems clear, in the perspective of nearly six centuries, that by any standard for defining law, the election of Urban VI was legal and the choice of Clement VII correspondingly illegal.

bility that the schism might be healed. And it is indeed the Emperor Sigismund who eventually puts sufficient pressure on John to force the latter's sanction for a council to meet at Constance in 1414. Pope John promises to attend this council and, presumably, to abide by its decisions.

But soon after the Council convenes, it becomes evident that John XXIII does not regard the assembly as his master. He flees from Constance and is eventually deposed by the Fathers. Gregory XII, meanwhile, has decided to make the great renunciation: Sending his legate to Constance in order to summon it under his allegedly legitimate auspices, he abdicates the papacy immediately after his representative reads the proclamation to the assembly. Benedict XIII, it is true, still remains adamant. But eventually (in 1417) the Council deposes him, thus clearing the way for the choice of a new pope. The Fathers set up a special electoral body, from which emerges the single Pope, Martin V, for whom Christendom has prayed so long.

But the Council, although presumably healing the schism, does little about reform; and while it does ordain that future councils shall be summoned regularly,[30] it is evident very soon after his election that Martin V will be jealous of his asserted prerogatives and very loath to recognize any paramountcy in the Council. Nevertheless, he does obey the conciliar mandates to the extent of summoning another assembly to meet at Siena in 1423. This Council, however, accomplishes nothing and is quite clearly frowned upon by the pope.

Thereafter, popes continue to struggle against the claims of councils, while the latter rise and fall in prestige and authority. In 1439, a council even deposes the pope, Eugenius IV, on grounds of heresy. And an antipope, Felix V, is chosen. Eventually, however, Felix surrenders his claim when the Council of Basel ends in 1449. While calls for a new reform council continue to be heard after Basel, they fall on deaf ears until a generation after the Reformation earth-shakingly disrupts Christendom.

The politics and political thought of the conciliar movement proper may be said to extend from the election of the antipope Clement VII in 1378 to the end of the Council of Basel in 1449.[31]

The roster of conciliarists includes some of the most brilliant minds of the fifteenth century—men like Jean Gerson, who holds the office of Chancellor of the University of Paris; Pierre Cardinal d'Ailly; Gregory of Heimburg; Cardinal Nicholas of Cusa; and Francesco Cardinal Zabarella.[32] While their thought is by no means uniform,[33] it is possible to indicate the many principles which they tend to share with one another and to contrast the viewpoint of the conciliarists as a whole with that which becomes increasingly characteristic of papal partisans in the fifteenth century.

As Figgis has pointed out, the conciliar movement, occasioned as it is by the problems of the Great Schism, tends "to treat the Church definitely as one of a class, political societies."[34] Somewhere in every political society there must be a final adjudication of whether the governors of that society are in fact attaining the ends for which the society is established. The Church exists for the salvation of souls and if its officers, instead of performing acts which conduce to this end, actually pervert souls instead, there must be a way of correcting them. Outside intervention, many conciliarists argue, should not be necessary to correct and hold accountable the officials of the divinely-established ecclesia.

But wherein, ultimately, does final authority in Holy Church repose? Here men like Zabarella have no doubt: The ultimate arbiter of governance in any political society is the community itself. If the divine end of the Church be to ensure the salvation of souls, then only the whole body of the faithful, considered as an organic society, can be said to possess, under Christ, the *plenitudo potestatis*.[35] Salvation depends on the Church and not on any agent of the Church; and if the Church choose to do, it can even decide to make someone other than the Bishop of Rome its earthly head. As for the Apostolic Church, the conciliarists tend to argue that the whole power of the corporate body must have originally been vested in the community. They even go so far as to assert that Saint Peter, whom they accept as first Bishop of Rome, was given his position by consent of the Apostles; and presumably the Apostles might have withheld that consent had they thought it a wise thing to do. The earthly headship of Holy Church, in sum, is a matter of convention and assent by the whole body of the faithful, in whom all political power must ultimately reside. And Nicholas of Cusa adds that many of the prerogatives of the papacy are obviously based on forgery, of which the Donation of Constantine is an excellent example.[36]

Given this view of the Church as a perfect society, with authority basically residing in the community as a whole, it is not surprising that the conciliarists tend to think of the General Council as above the pope. While the prevalent view in the fourteenth century is that no council can be summoned except through the pope (and even the Council of Constance was ostensibly called by John XXIII, the call later being confirmed by Gregory XII), conciliarists like Heinrich von Langenstein,[37] maintain that papal consent is unnecessary to call a council. If the pope does not act, Zabarella argues, the cardinals may do so.

In the whole discussion of the way in which a council is to be summoned, it will be noted, the conciliarists are moving from the custom and convention of the matter (at least as interpreted during the previous two centuries) to a general theory of the nature of the Church as a political society. This appeal from custom and tradition to basic principles is, indeed, highly characteristic of conciliar thought as a whole. There is a strong utilitarian current running all through it: one which, although striving to observe tradition where possible, nevertheless holds that the good of the community (in the case of the Church, the salvation of souls) is the supreme law. The test of right in each instance is to be whether the practice or official involved is in conflict with achievement of that good.

In examining the nature of the ecclesiastical constitution, conciliar thinkers are fond of adverting to both Aristotle and Moses. As they view it, the Church is a divine institution whose constitution must necessarily have the approval of God. But God would approve only a constitution which meets the tests of political right—the framework that, on the whole, is most likely to effect the nonpolitical end of any given community. Now since both Aristotle and the Mosaic principle exalt the idea of a mixed scheme of government, the organization of the Church must be interpreted along those lines. And, in fact, the conciliarists note, it is relatively easy to give the pope the status of constitutional monarch, to see the cardinals as the embodiment of an

30. In its *Decree Frequens*, 1417, The Council of Constance ordered that another Council be held in five years and thereafter every decade.

31. For a scholarly study of the basis of conciliarism, see Brian Tierney, *Foundations of the Conciliar Theory*, Cambridge: Cambridge University Press, 1955.

32. Gerson preached a sermon, *Adorabunt*, on Jan. 6, 1391, in which he asked the kings of France and England to help heal the schism. Although a thorough conciliarist, he can generally be classified as a conservative by comparison with certain other leaders of the movement. But he was one of the most influential.

To show the learning and experience of many conciliarists, we might comment on Francis Cardinal Zabarella. He was a leading canonical writer and became a counsellor of three popes. He negotiated with the Emperor Sigismund on behalf of Pope John XXIII. His *De Schismate*, published in 1403, works out a scheme for ending the "pestiferous schism."

We should not assume that the conciliarists reached their conclusions easily. Gerson, in fact, is rather critical of the proposals for a Council as late as 1396, when he issues his tract *De Schismate vel de Papatu Contendentibus*. See, for example, John B. Morall, *Gerson and the Great Western Schism*, Manchester: Manchester University Press, 1960, p. 42.

On the other hand, a notable conciliarist like Nicholas of Cusa can actually desert the conciliar party. After developing a theory of great force and influence, he defects in 1436, and becomes a papal diplomat. Some suggest that he began to despair of success and felt he might do more for the church by joining triumphant papalism and working for reform from within its councils.

33. A point very rightly emphasized by Tierney's detailed examination. Not all the conciliarists, for example, would define the position of the pope in the same way, some of them granting far greater authority to the papal office than others.

34. Figgis, *op. cit.*, p. 42.

35. Zabarella sharply distinguished between the pope and the whole Church, in that while the former can err, the latter cannot. If the pope and the College of Cardinals should disagree, then the only remedy is to summon a General Council which should consist of the whole congregation of the faithful—the principal heads and prelates, "qui totam congregationem representant." See Walter Ullmann, *The Origins of the Great Western Schism*, London: Burns, Oaks, and Washbourne, 1948, p. 210. In general, Ullmann's work will be found most useful.

36. Nicholas of Cusa's major political work is *De Concordantia Catholica*. In addition to being one of the leading political theorists of the declining Middle Ages, he was also an outstanding philosopher.

37. In *Consilium pacis de unione ac reformatione Ecclesiae in Concilio generali guaerenda*.

aristocratic principle, and to envision the Representative Council as standing for the whole body of the Church.

If these principles are accepted, then the pope cannot on his own authority make law. One aspect of the medieval legal tradition is, of course, the Roman civilian idea that *Quod principi placuit legis habet vigorem* (That which the prince wills has the force of law). Obviously, the conciliarists are in revolt against any such notion and refuse to see the pope as the aphorism's "prince." At the same time, it should also be remembered that the Middle Ages, particularly in the writings of certain canonists, has developed another principle, *Quod omnes tangit ab omnibus approbetur* (That which touches all must be approved by all). The Fourth Lateran Council (1215) had approved this latter rule.[38] The conciliarists now embrace it eagerly and develop the principle that the law of the Church cannot be (as papal apologists are increasingly claiming) simply the dictate of the pontiff. Either the cardinals or the council or both must assent before law can go into effect.

In accordance with the same spirit, many if not most of the conciliarists hold that the council can depose a pope who defies its decrees—a right which the Council of Basel, of course, exercises against Eugenius IV; that similarly a council may declare a pope heretical; that the pope is the mere executive officer of the council (Zabarella); and that the cardinals may establish capitulations (or rules of governance) which will be binding on a yet-to-be elected pontiff. The conciliarists do not, indeed, originate the idea of the capitulation; for such a document was drawn up by the cardinals before the election of Innocent VI in 1352. But there can be little doubt that the principle whereby the pope can be bound to observe preelection rules formulated by the College of Cardinals is entirely within the spirit of conciliar theory as a whole. Indeed, acting partly under the influence of conciliar notions, the College draws up capitulations before the election of Eugenius IV in 1431.[39]

While there is no uniformity among the conciliarists as to the nature of representation in the General Council, there is a strong tendency to assert that laymen as well as clerics have the right to be heard as well as to vote. Several conciliarists maintain that kings, princes, and their ambassadors ought to be seated. Running through the discussion is, of course, the qualitative as well as the quantitative notion of representation—the conception that some segments of the community should count for more than others.[40]

There is also an assertion that the lower clergy should participate in the deliberative process. Traditionally, councils were composed of the higher clergy only—bishops, abbots, and cardinals. Now, however, the Church, for purposes of Council representation, is held to include even ordinary priests. During the Council of Basel, one of the complaints of the pro-papal faction is that inferior clergy are admitted to its sessions, thus adding disproportionately to the weight of opinion against papal claims.

The exaltation of council against pope and the advocacy of representative government in the Church, while foreign to major views of the ecclesia during the High Middle Ages, are not sharply different from conceptions of temporal political organization which are actually embodied in the practices of twelfth and thirteenth centuries. In Leon and Castile, for example, the Cortes has before 1300 become a vital factor in the politics of that country; and during the fourteenth century both the conception and practice of Spanish constitutional government are further developed. The Cortes is more than a supplier of money for royal wars: it governs during the minority of a king; consents to laws made by the monarch; and deals with abuses in administration. And while the English Parliament and French Estates (summoned, it will be remembered, for the first time in 1302 during the controversy between King Philip and Boniface VIII) are in the fourteenth century somewhat behind the Cortes in prerogatives, they are developing additional functions with relative rapidity.

The interconnections between doctrines and practices of ecclesiastical and temporal representation are complex. Most of the conciliarists are not unfamiliar with Spanish, English, and French developments and possibly have them in mind as they work out their conciliar conceptions. Although conciliar views, to be sure, do not envision Councils established on the basis of medieval estates, the differences acknowledged between higher clergy and lower clergy and between clergy and laymen indicate that conciliar thinkers have no intention of homogenizing, as it were, the basis of representation.

It is equally important to suggest the influence of canonical dicta and the example of such orders as the Dominicans on the development of late medieval ideas of both secular representation and ecclesiastical government. The Dominican order, dating back to the thirteenth century, had worked out schemes whereby the various branches of the Order shared in the choice of the Master. According to the constitution:

> The procedure in electing shall be as follows: After the electors have been put in session, the election shall proceed by declaration or secret ballot. But if all of the brethren should settle unanimously on one person, he shall be accepted as Master of the Order. If there is no such acclamation, then one upon whom the majority shall settle in virtue of the election and this constitution shall be considered the Master.[41]

The Dominican constitution also provides for removal of the Master by all members of the order.[42]

Ernest Barker maintains, too, that most of the religious orders of the thirteenth century followed very closely the Dominican legislation.[43]

But while the interaction of earlier ecclesiastical and secular notions of representation, election, and removal must be fully recognized, we should also remind ourselves that in their more extreme proposals, the conciliarists envision the council as playing a much larger role in the governance of the Church than do late medieval parliaments in secular affairs or the governing bodies of the orders with respect to general policy.

Most of the conciliarists deal primarily with the problem of Church governance and only incidentally with conceptions of the temporal order. Nicholas of Cusa, however, seeks to examine both spiritual and temporal authorities on the assumption that they continue to be—as in high medieval doctrine—simply different expressions of a single Christian society. In his *De Concordantia Catholica* he sees the political problem of his day, whether on its temporal or its spiritual side, as one of combining adequate universal leadership with specific methods for gaining the consent of the community. Both temporal and spiritual aspects of society are federal in the sense that neither can dispense with the acquiescence of corporate parts as well as of wholes. The Church is made up of national units, for example, and in secular society municipal and other corporate groups must be taken into account in the gathering of consent.[44]

Just as the principle of consent is to apply to papal activities, so does it become explicitly relevant for the Empire. The emperor is to be subject to similar limitations. Nicholas envisions a revived Empire, with a head bound to consult a standing council.

But schemes like those of Nicholas, however much men might be attracted by their appeal for unity and their ideal of government through positive consent, can make little headway against the hard realities of fifteenth century political conflict. Christendom is dissolv-

38. Innocent III, in summoning the Fourth Lateran Council, had asked the bishops to request other churches besides the cathedral church to send "suitable men on their behalf."
39. When Innocent VI, after his election in 1362, refused to honor the capitulation which he had signed as a cardinal prior to his choice as pope, he alleged that such documents were uncanonical. The cardinals had gone beyond their authority in drafting it, he said, and it purported to limit by human law the power which God had given to the See of Peter. The pope's power was unconditioned by necessity for consent. See Pastor, *op. cit.*, pp. 282–283. It is obvious that such notions as those of Innocent VI were utterly contrary to the letter and spirit of conciliar doctrine.
40. The early Middle Ages, of course, widened the gulf between layman and cleric. Insofar as conciliar theory tends to value the position of the layman, it is questioning the sharp dichotomization of earlier years. With the triumph of the anticonciliar party, the role of the layman becomes correspondingly smaller, until in the twentieth century the Vatican II Ecumenical Council (1962–65) once more stresses that the layman, too, is a vital part of the Church.
41. Francis C. Lehner, ed., *Saint Dominic: Biographical Documents*, Washington, D.C.: Thomist Press, 1964, p. 231.
42. *Ibid.*, p. 236.
43. Ernest Barker, *The Dominican Order and Convocation*, Oxford: Clarendon Press, 1913, p. 30.
44. In Book II, ch. 13, of *De Concordantia Catholica*, Nicholas reiterates that man is spirit, soul, and body. In the church, the corresponding entities are the sacraments, clergy, and faithful, with the latter represented through a General Council. "The force of the law," Nicholas says, "consists in the submission to it by those bound by it." In Bk. II, ch. 14, he remarks: "For if men are by nature powerful and equally free, a valid and ordained authority of any one person, whose power is by nature like that of the rest, cannot be created save by election and consent of the others, just as law is established by consent." Each part of the society, moreover, must be activated by the spirit of consent.

ing, even as an idea (and it has always been rather tenuous as a reality). The emperor has no particular desire to be limited by a permanent council, even though it seems evident that his actual control of affairs will in any event continue to decline. Dynamic political factors, moreover, like the Hussite movement, challenge the very notion of a universal society. Finally, the pope, as we have suggested, is able to take advantage of shifting political circumstance to evade the spirit of the Council of Constance's decrees and to resist the sweeping claims of the Council of Basel.

The result of clever papal diplomacy, operating within a confused political context, is that by the time the Council of Basel adjourns in 1449, the papalist (or curialist) theory of the Church emerges triumphant and the direct influence of conciliarist ideas steadily declines. Pope Eugenius and his successors remove all doubt that the pope is to be regarded as the direct representative of God and that the consent of the community is not essential to legitimate his rule.

What is the significance of the conciliar movement for the history of political thought? In view of the fact that its doctrines are rejected by the post-1449 Church, this may seem to be a somewhat fatuous question.

Yet in a negative sense, the very fact that the conceptions of the conciliarists are disowned by the Church is of great significance for the subsequent development of thought. The triumph of papalism in ecclesiastical government means that pure monarchy is now accepted by the Church as its political basis and that the conciliarist conception of mixed government is cast aside. This fact alone sets an enormously important precedent in an age in which Church government is still looked to as a standard for "temporal" affairs. After 1449, one can no longer cite the divinely established Church as an illustration of God's (and Aristotle's) preference for an ordering of affairs which combines monarchy with aristocracy and democracy. As a matter of fact, when Savonarola, the great Florentine reformer, comes to discuss politics toward the end of the century, he frankly avows that the example of the Church proves pure monarchy to be the best; and he defends the idea of a Florentine Republic only on the ground that circumstances alter cases.[45] With the triumph of anticonciliarist conceptions in the Church, the foundations are laid for the development of the theory of the divine right of kings; for if the pope is indeed the direct agent of God, rather than an official of the community, why does not the same principle hold in secular affairs?

The conciliarists try desperately to avert such an outcome and had they been able to defeat curialist notions within the Church, the subsequent history of both thought and institutions might have been quite different. In an age when it is obvious that characteristically medieval institutions cannot continue, men like Nicholas of Cusa seek to establish new foundations for a universal society by giving due weight to the emerging claims of nationalism while at the same time preserving the medieval ideal of universality. They recognize the new age but hope to maintain the basic values of the old as well.

But while the triumph of curialist ideas of ecclesiastical government helps provide precedents for the doctrine of Divine Right and the refusal to accept Nicholas' views makes easier the divorce of ethics from politics and of national from universal objectives, conciliarist conceptions themselves remain as an important heritage for later generations. Defeated in their own day, they will emerge once more during the Protestant Reformation and will even suggest to some political thinkers of the Counter-Reformation bases for the right of the community to resist tyranny. And the conceptions of representative government found in conciliar theory, however embryonic and poorly developed they may be in some respects, will furnish foundations upon which political philosophers can build two centuries later.[46]

Toward Modern Political Thought

When one reflects on the major streams of thought between 1296 and 1449—on Boniface, Dante, Marsilio, Ockham, Wycliffe, and the conceptions advanced by the conciliar movement—certain major conclusions stand out.

First of all, the speculations of Boniface and Dante were efforts to state the extreme versions of papalist and imperialist thought. At the very time when characteristically medieval institutions and ideas were beginning to be subject to severe attack, two eminent minds, speaking from radically different perspectives, sought to defend them. Both accepted the premise of Christian unity and both continued to see Christendom administered through two separate sets of officials. But whereas Boniface made the pope the arbiter of jurisdictional limits, Dante conferred this prerogative on the emperor.

Secondly, secularist conceptions of the ordering of life were immensely strengthened by men like Marsilio, Ockham, and Wycliffe. Beginning as theorists of ecclesiastical reform, they tended to exalt an autonomous nonecclesiastical power as the means whereby the Church could be reformed. In so doing, they helped provide an ideology for all those tendencies in late medieval life which were moving away from the medieval synthesis. Thus when Ockham stressed the reality of the individual and the nominal quality of the universal, he both expressed and encouraged all those who were increasingly centering their attention on material and temporal concerns to the exclusion of the presumably higher spirituals so exalted by the High Middle Ages; and this very emphasis on the material and temporal paved the way for a decline in ecclesiastical authority.

Thirdly, the doctrines of Marsilio, Wycliffe, Huss, Ockham, and some of the conciliarists could easily be interpreted to sustain the many claims for social revolution which increasingly characterized the fourteenth and fifteenth centuries. Even when their ideas were not intended to provide a defense of revolution, the context in which they were developed and the fact that they did attack ecclesiastical prerogatives facilitated their utilization for broader purposes.

Finally, the controversies and doctrines of the period laid the groundwork for the politics of the Renaissance and Reformation. In part, fourteenth- and fifteenth-century theories represented a partial return to Augustine, with his stress on the individual and his emphasis on the spiritual Church. While none of the thinkers from Boniface to Nicholas of Cusa dared to push the religious realm into an isolated compartment of life, many of them, in their conception of the poor Church, seemed to come close to the idea. If religion is purely a matter of the inner life, as Ockham, Wycliffe, and Marsilio, in their several ways, seemed to teach, then the outer realm is left to its own devices. Material matters, power distribution, and the arrangements of temporal affairs theoretically could be emancipated not only from the institutional Church but also from religiously inspired moral considerations.

As notions like this began to be more widely accepted, the foundations for Renaissance social life and political thought were established. From Marsilio to Machiavelli was not a large jump; and what some have called the pagan idea of the state was reborn long before the author of the *Prince* began to pen his famous lines.

45. See Figgis, *The Divine Right of Kings*, Cambridge: Cambridge University Press, 1914, Appendix.

46. One might well point out, too, that the gist of much conciliarism has been revived in our day by the movement associated with the Second Vatican Council (1962–1965). Vatican II's conception of ecclesiastical politics and government—and the debates associated with their formulation—remind one strongly of the earlier conciliar period. See, in general, Vatican II's *Constitutio Dogmatica De Ecclesia*, Vatican City: 1964; H. Jedin, *Ecumenical Councils of the Church*, New York: Herder and Herder, 1960; and Hans Kung, *Structures of the Church*, Salvator Attanasio, trans., New York: T. Nelson, 1964.

Part II Selected References

(in addition to those mentioned in footnotes)

9. *Christian Attitudes and Politics: Tertullian to Augustine*

ARTZ, FREDERICK B. *The Mind of the Middle Ages, A.D. 200–1500.* New York: Knopf, 1953.

BARTLET, J. V. and A. J. CARLYLE. *Christianity in History.* London: Macmillan, 1917.

BURCKHARDT, JACOB. *The Age of Constantine the Great,* Moses Hadas, trans. Garden City: Anchor Books, 1956.

CANFIELD, LEON HARDY. *The Early Persecutions of the Christians.* New York: Columbia University Press, 1931.

CARLYLE, A. J. AND R. W. CARLYLE. *A History of Medieval Political Theory in the West.* 6 vols. Edinburgh and London: William Blackwood and Sons, 1903–1936. Vol. 1.

CASE, SHIRLEY JACKSON. *The Social Origins of Christianity.* Chicago: University of Chicago Press, 1923.

COCHRANE, CHARLES N. *Christianity and Classical Culture: A Study of Thought and Action from Augustus to Augustine.* Oxford: Clarendon, 1940.

HARDY, E. G. *Christianity and the Roman Government.* London: Allen & Unwin, 1925.

HEERING, G. J. *The Fall of Christianity: A Study of Christianity, the State and War.* J. W. Thompson, trans. New York: Fellowship Publications, 1943.

LECKY, W. E. H. *History of European Morals from Augustus to Charlemagne.* London: Watts, 1911.

MCILWAIN, C. H. *Growth of Political Thought.* New York: Macmillan, 1932.

MILMAN, H. H. *History of Latin Christianity.* 9 vols., 4th ed. London: John Murray, 1883. Vol. 1.

PETRY, RAY C. *Christian Eschatology and Social Thought: A Historical Essay on the Social Implications of Some Selected Aspects in Christian Eschatology to 1500.* Nashville: Abingdon, 1956.

TROELTSCH, ERNST. *The Social Teaching of the Christian Churches.* 2 vols. New York: Macmillan, 1931. Vol. 1.

VOEGELIN, ERIC. "Political Theory and the Course of General History." *American Political Science Review,* August 1944.

WORKMAN, HERBERT H. *Persecution in the Early Church.* 4th ed. London: Epworth Press, 1923.

10. *St. Augustine and the Politics of the Two Cities*

AUGUSTINE. *Basic Writings.* Introduction by Whitney J. Oates. New York: Random House, 1948.

AUGUSTINE. *Confessions.* New York: Boni Liveright, 1927.

AUGUSTINE. *De Doctrina Christiana,* D. W. Robertson, trans. New York: Bobbs-Merrill, 1958.

AUGUSTINE. *De Libero Arbitrio Voluntatis; St. Augustine on Free Will.* Carroll M. Sparrow, trans. Charlottesville: University of Virginia, 1947.

AUGUSTINE. *Divine Providence and the Problem of Evil, a Translation of St. Augustine's De Ordine,* by Robert P. Russell. New York: Cosmopolitan Science & Art Service Co., 1942.

AUGUSTINE. *Anti-Pelagian Writings.* Grand Rapids, Mich.: W. B. Eerdmans, 1956.

AUGUSTINE. *Selected Letters.* James H. Baxter, trans. New York: Harvard University Press, 1953.

CARLYLE, A. J. AND R. W. CARLYLE. *A History of Medieval Political Theory in the West.* 6 vols. Edinburgh: Blackwood, 1936. Vols. 1 and 2.

CHEVALIER, IRENEE. *S. Augustin et la pensee grecque.* Fribourg: Librairie de l'Université, 1940.

CLARK, MARY T. *Augustine, Philosopher of Freedom.* New York: Desceel Co., 1958.

COCHRANE, CHARLES N. *Christianity and Classical Culture: A Study of Thought and Action from Augustus to Augustine.* Oxford: Clarendon, 1940.

CRANZ, EDWARD. "St. Augustine and Nicholas of Cusa in the Tradition of Western Christian Thought." *Speculum* 28 (1953), 297–316.

HARNACK, ADOLF. *Monasticism; Its Ideals and History, and The Confessions of St. Augustine* (two lectures). London: Williams & Norgate, 1901.

HEARNSHAW, F. J. C. *The Social and Political Ideas of Some Great Medieval Thinkers.* New York: Barnes & Noble, 1928.

LEWIS, EWART, ED. *Medieval Political Ideas.* 2 vols. New York: Knopf, 1954.

PAOLUCCI, HENRY, ED. *The Political Writings of St. Augustine.* Chicago: Gateway, 1962.

RICKABY, JOSEPH J. *St. Augustine's City of God; a View of the Contents.* London: Burns, Oates, & Washbourne, 1925.

TROELTSCH, ERNST. *The Social Teaching of the Christian Churches.* 2 vols. New York: Macmillan, 1931. Vol. 1.

11. *Main Currents from Augustine to the High Middle Ages*

ARQUILLIERE, H. *Saint Gregoire VII; Essai sur sa Conception du Pouvoir Pontifical.* Paris: J. Vrin, 1934.

ARTZ, FREDERICK B. *The Mind of the Middle Ages, A.D. 200–1500.* New York: Knopf, 1953.

BARRACLOUGH, GEOFFREY, TRANS. *Medieval Germany, 911–1250. Essays by German historians.* Oxford: Basil Blackwell, 1938.

BECKER, ALFONS. *Studien zum Investiturproblem in Frankreich.* Saarbrücken: West-Ost Verlag, 1955.

CANTOR, NORMAN F. *Church, Kingship, and Lay Investiture in England, 1089–1135.* Princeton: Princeton University Press, 1958.

CARLYLE, R. W. AND A. J. CARLYLE. *A History of Medieval Political Theory in the West.* 6 vols. Edinburgh: Blackwood, 1928–1936.

CARLYLE, A. J. "The Development of the Theory of Authority of the Spiritual Power Over the Temporal Power from Gregory VII to Innocent III." *Revue d'histoire du droit* 5, no. 5 (1923), 33–44.

Correspondence of Pope Gregory VII. Edited by Ephraim Emerton. New York: Columbia University Press, 1932.
CRONNE, H. A., "The Origins of Feudalism." *History*, December 1939, 251–259.
FISHER, H. A. L. *The Medieval Empire*. 2 vols. London: Macmillan, 1898. Ch. 10.
FLICHE, AUGUSTIN. *La Reforme Gregorienne*. 3 vols. Paris: E. Champion, 1924–1937.
GANSHOF, F. L. *Feudalism*. 2nd English ed., Philip Grierson, trans. New York: Harper Torchbooks, 1961.
GIERKE, OTTO. *Political Theories of the Middle Ages*. Frederic Maitland, trans. Boston: Beacon Press, 1958.
HARNACK, ADOLF. *History of Dogma*. 7 vols. Trans. from the 3rd German edition by Neil Buchanan. New York: Russell and Russell, 1958. Vols. 2, 3, and 4.
HEARNSHAW, F. J. C. *The Social and Political Ideas of Some Great Medieval Thinkers*. New York: Barnes & Noble, 1928.
HULL, R. *Medieval Theories of the Papacy*. London: Burns, Oates & Washbourne, 1934.
KERN, F. *Kingship and Law in the Middle Ages*. Oxford: Clarendon, 1948.
LEWIS, EWART. *Medieval Political Ideas*. 2 vols. New York: Knopf, 1954.
MCILWAIN, C. H. *Growth of Political Thought*. New York: Macmillan, 1932.
MILMAN, H. N. *History of Latin Christianity*. 4th ed., 9 vols. London: John Murray, 1883. Vol. 1, Bk. 3, ch. 1 (Gelasius and the Gelasian Doctrine). Vol. 4, Bk. 7, ch. 1, 2, and 3; Bk 7, ch. 1, 2, and 3 (Gregory VII, Henry IV, and Investitures).
ODEGAARD, C. E. "Carolingian Oaths of Fidelity." *Speculum*, July 1941, 284–296.
MACDONALD, ALLAN J. *Hildebrand; a Life of Gregory VII*. London: Methuen, 1932.
MATHEW, ARNOLD H. *The Life and Times of Hildebrand, Pope Gregory VII*. London: F. Griffiths, 1910.
READE, W. H. V. "Political Thought to c. 1300." *Cambridge Medieval History*, vol. 6, ch. 18.
ROUX, A. *Le Pape Saint Gelase Ier; Etude sur sa Vie et ses Ecrits*. Paris: E. Thorin, 1889.
STEPHENSON, C. *Medieval Feudalism*. Ithaca: Cornell University Press, 1942.
TAYLOR, H. O. *The Medieval Mind*. 2 vols., 4th ed. London: Macmillan, 1938. Vol. 1.
TELLENBACH, GERD. *Church, State and Christian Society*. R. F. Bennett, trans. Oxford: Clarendon, 1948.
VILLEMAIN, A. F. *Life of Gregory the Seventh*. London: R. Bentley & Sons, 1874.
VINCENT, MARVIN R. *The Age of Hildebrand*. New York: Christian Literature Co., 1896.
VOOSEN, ÉLIE. Papauté et pouvoir civil à l'époque de Grégoire VII. Gembloux: J. Duculot, 1927.
WHITNEY, JAMES P. "Gregory VII." *English Historical Review* 34 (1919), 129.
WHITNEY, JAMES P. *Hildebrandine Essays*. Cambridge: Cambridge University Press, 1932.
WHITNEY, JAMES P. "Pope Gregory VII and the Hildebrandine Ideal." *Church Quarterly Review* 20 (1910), 414.

12. *Medieval Law and the Political Theory of the Lawyers*

BUCKLAND, W. W. *A Textbook of Roman Law from Augustus to Justinian*. London: Cambridge University Press, 1932.
DE WULF, MAURICE. *Philosophy and Civilization in the Middle Ages*. New York: Dover, 1953.
GÜTERBACK, K. E. *Bracton and His Relation to the Roman Law*. Philadelphia: J. B. Lippincott, 1866.
IMMINK, P. W. A. AND H. J. SCHMELTEMA. *At the Roots of Medieval Society*. 2 vols. Cambridge, Mass.: Harvard University Press, 1958.
JOLOWICZ, H. F. *Historical Introduction to the Study of Roman Law*. Cambridge: Cambridge University Press, 1932.
KAGAN, K. "Bartolus." *Tulane Law Review* 21 (1946), 192.
KANTOROWICZ, HERMANN. *Studies in the Glossators of the Roman Law*. Cambridge: Cambridge University Press, 1938.
KERN, F. *Kingship and Law in the Middle Ages*. Oxford: Clarendon, 1948.
LEE, G. C. *Historical Jurisprudence*. New York: Macmillan, 1900.
LIEBESCHITZ, HANS. *Medieval Humanism in the Life and Writings of John of Salisbury*. London: Warburg Institute, 1950.
MCILWAIN, CHARLES H. *The Growth of Political Thought in the West to the End of the Middle Ages*. New ed. New York: Macmillan, 1953.
MAITLAND, F. W., ED. *Selected Passages from the Work of Bracton and Azo*. London: B. Quaritch, 1895.
MUIRHEAD, J. S. *Roman Law*. London: William Hodge, 1947.
RASHDALL, HASTINGS. *The Universities of Europe in the Middle Ages*. New ed., 3 vols., edited by F. M. Powicke and A. B. Emden. Oxford: Clarendon, 1936.
ROMMEN, HEINRICH. *The Natural Law*. St. Louis: B. Herder, 1947.
SALISBURY, JOHN OF. *Memoirs of the Papal Court*. Introduction by Marjorie Chibnall, trans. London: Thomas Nelson, 1956.
SALISBURY, JOHN OF. *The Metalogicon*. Introduction by David McGarry, trans. Berkeley: University of California Press, 1955.
SCRUTTON, T. E. *The Influence of Roman Law on the Law of England*. Cambridge: Cambridge University Press, 1885.
SMITH, MUNROE. *The Development of European Law*. New York: Columbia University Press, 1928.
TAYLOR, HENRY O. *The Medieval Mind*. 2 vols. Cambridge: Harvard Universtiy Press, 1929. Especially vol. 2, ch. 34, p. 260.

13. *Scholasticism and the Political Mind of St. Thomas Aquinas*

BRENNAN, R. E. *Thomistic Psychology*. New York: Macmillan, 1941.

CANNON, W. R. "Law in Thomas Aquinas." *Religion in Life* 31 (1962), 219–227.

CHESTERTON, G. K. *St. Thomas Aquinas*. London: Hodder & Stoughton, 1933.

CLARKE, W. N. "Platonic Heritage of Thomism," *Review of Metaphysics* 8 (1954), 105–124.

COPLESTON, F. C. *Aquinas*. London: Penguin, 1955.

CRANSTON, MAURICE. "St. Thomas Aquinas as a Political Philosopher." *History Today* 14 (1964), 313–317.

D'ENTREVES, A. P. *The Medieval Contribution to Political Thought*. London: Oxford, 1939.

GILBY, THOMAS. *St. Thomas Aquinas: Theological Texts*. London: Oxford, 1955.

GILBY, THOMAS, ED. AND TRANS. *St. Thomas Aquinas: Philosophical Texts*. London: Oxford, 1952.

GILSON, ETIENNE. *The Philosophy of St. Thomas Aquinas*. Cambridge: W. Heffer & Sons, 1929.

HUTCHINS, R. M. *St. Thomas and the World State*. Milwaukee: Marquette University Press, 1949.

JARRETT, BEDE. *Social Theories of the Middle Ages*. London: E. Benn, 1926.

KILLEEN, S. M. *The Philosophy of Labor According to Thomas Aquinas*. Washington, D.C.: Catholic University of America Press, 1939.

MURPHY, E. F. *St. Thomas' Political Doctrine and Democracy*. Washington, D.C.: Catholic University of America Press, 1921.

PEGIS, A. C. *St. Thomas and the Problem of the Soul in the Thirteenth Century*. Toronto: University of Toronto Press, 1934.

PIEPER, JOSEF, ED. *The Human Wisdom of St. Thomas*. New York: Sheed & Ward, 1948.

PIEPER, JOSEF, ED. "On the Christian Idea of Man." *Review of Politics* 11 (1949), 3–16.

RAND, E. K. *Cicero in the Courtroom of St. Thomas Aquinas*. Milwaukee: Marquette University Press, 1945.

ROLAND-GOSSELIN, B. *La Doctrin Politique de Saint Thomas d'Aquin*. Paris: M. Rivière, 1928.

ROSENTHAL, E. I. J. *Political Thought in Medieval Islam*. Cambridge: Cambridge University Press, 1958.

RUBY, J. E. "Ambivalence of St. Thomas Aquinas' View of the Relationship of Divine Law to Human Law," *Harvard Theological Review* 48 (1955), 101–128.

SIMON, YVES. *Nature and Functions of Authority*. Milwaukee: Marquette University Press, 1940.

WOLFE, MARY JOAN OF ARC. *The Problem of Solidarism in St. Thomas*. Washington: Catholic University Press, 1938.

ZEILLER, J. *L'Idee de l'etat dans Saint Thomas D'Aquin*. Paris: Alcan, 1910.

14. *The Ideologies of the Medieval Sects and the Papal Inquisition*

ANITCHKOF, EUGENE. *Joachim de Flore et les Milieux Courtois*. Rome: Collezione Meridionale Editrice, 1931.

BELPERRON, PIERRE. *La Croisade conte les Albigeois et l'Union de Languedoc a la France*. Paris: Plon, 1945.

BENZ, ERNST. *Creator Spiritus: die Geistlehre des Joachim von Fiore*. Zuerich: Rhein-Verlag, 1957.

BETT, HENRY. *Joachim of Flora*. London: Methuen, 1931.

BOAS, GEORGE. *Essays on Primitivism and Related Ideas in the Middle Ages*. Baltimore: Johns Hopkins University Press, 1948.

BUSSELL, F. W. *Religious Thought and Heresy in the Middle Ages*. London: Robert Scott, 1918.

BUONAIUTI, ERNESTO. *Gioacchino da Fiore: I Tempi, La Vita, Il Messaggio*. Roma: Collezione Mericionale Editrice, 1931.

BUONAIUTI, ERNESTO. *Tractatus super quatuor Evangelia di Gioacchino da Fiore*. Roma: Istituto Storico Italiano, 1930.

COHN, NORMAN. *The Pursuit of the Millennium: Revolutionary Messianism in Medieval and Reformation Europe and Its Bearing on Modern Totalitarian Movements*. Rev. ed. London: Secker and Warburg, 1957; New York: Harper, 1961.

COWLEY, PATRICK. *Franciscan Rise and Fall*. London: J. M. Dent, 1933.

DOUIE, DECIMA L. *The Nature and Effect of the Heresy of the Fraticelli*. Manchester: Manchester University Press, 1932.

EMERY, RICHARD W. *Heresy and Inquisition in Narbonne*. New York: Columbia University Press, 1941.

ENGLEBERT, A. OMER. *St. Francis of Assisi*. Edward Hutton, trans. New York: Longmans, Green, 1950.

GEBHART, EMILE. *Mystics and Heretics in Italy: A History of the Religious Revival in the Middle Ages*, Edward M. Hulme, trans. New York: Knopf, 1923.

HOLMES, E. G. A. *The Holy Heretics: The Story of the Albigensian Crusade*. London: Watts, 1948.

HOLMES, E. G. A. *The Albigensian or Catharist Heresy*. London: Williams & Norgate, 1925.

MAITLAND, S. R. *Facts and Documents Illustrative of the History, Doctrines, and Rites of the Ancient Albigenses and Waldenses*. London: C. J. G. & F. Riyington, 1832.

PETRY, RAY C. *Christian Eschatology and Social Thought: A Historical Essay on the Social Implications of Some Selected Aspects in Christian Eschatology to A.D. 1500*. Nashville: Abingdon, 1956.

SABATIER, PAUL. *Life of St. Francis of Assisi*. Trans. from the 1894 French edition by Louise S. Houghton. New York: Scribners, 1917.

SILBER, ABBA HILLEL. *A History of Messianic Speculation in Israel from the First Through the Seventeenth Centuries*. Boston: Beacon, 1959.

WARNER, HENRY J. *The Albigensian Heresy*. New York: Macmillan, 1922.

15. *The Decline of Medieval Thought and Attitudes*

BETT, HENRY. *Nicholas of Cusa*. London: Methuen, 1932.

BIEL, GABRIEL. *Defensorium Obedientiae Apostolicae et Alia Documenta*. Heiko A. Oberman, Daniel E. Zerfoss, and William J. Courtenay, eds. and trans. Cambridge, Mass.: Harvard University Press, Belknap Press, 1968.

BINNS, L. ELLIOTT. *The History of the Decline and Fall of the Medieval Papacy*. London: Methuen, 1934.

DANIEL-ROPS, HENRI. *The Protestant Reformation*. Vol. 1. Garden City, L.I.: Anchor, 1963.

FLICK, ALEXANDER. *The Decline of the Medieval Church.* New York: Knopf, 1930.

GILL, JOSEPH. *Eugene IV.* Westminster, Md.: Newman Book Shop, 1964.

HOFMANN, GEORG. *Papato, Conciliarismo, Patriarcato (1438–1439) Teologi e Deliberazioni del Concilio di Firenze.* Rome: Case Editrice S.A.L.E.R., 1940.

HUGHES, PHILIP. *A History of the Church.* Vol. 3. New York: Sheed and Ward, 1947.

HUIZINGA, J. *The Waning of the Middle Ages.* London: Edward Arnold, 1924.

JARRETT, BEDE. *Social Theories of the Middle Ages.* Westminster, Md.: Newman Book Shop, 1942.

LAGARDE, GEORGES DE. *La Naissance de l'Esprit, Laique au Declin du Moyen Age.* Vienna: Editions Beatrice, 1934.

LECLER, JOSEPH. *The Two Sovereignties.* New York: Philosophical Library, 1952.

LECLERCQ, J. *Jean de Paris et l'Ecclesiologie du XIIIe Siecle.* Paris: J. Vrin, 1942.

LEWIS, EWART. *Medieval Political Ideas.* 2 vols. New York: Knopf, 1954. Vol. 2.

MILMAN, H. N. *History of Latin Christianity.* 9 vols. London: J. Murray, 1882. Vol. 8, Bk. 13 (End of the Schism and the Councils; leaders of political movements).

NELSON, BENJAMIN N. *The Idea of Usury: From Tribal Brotherhood to Universal Otherhood.* Princeton: Princeton University Press, 1949.

RIVIERE, J. *Le Probleme de l'Eglise et de l'Etat au Temps de Phillippe le Bel.* Paris: E. Champion, 1926.

SALEMBIER, L. *The Great Schism of the West.* London: Kegan Paul, 1907.

SIGMUND, PAUL E. *Nicholas of Cusa and Medieval Political Thought.* Cambridge: Harvard University Press, 1963.

VANSTEENBERGHE, EDMOND. *Le Cardinal Nicolas de Cues.* Paris: H. Champion, 1920.

Dante

CHURCH, R. W. *Dante: An Essay.* London: Macmillan, 1878.

CIOFFARI, VINCENZO. *The Conception of Fortune and Fate in the Works of Dante.* Cambridge: Harvard University Press, 1940.

DINSMORE, CHARLES A. *Life of Dante Alighieri.* Boston and New York: Houghton Mifflin, 1919.

GILBERT, ALAN H. *Dante's Conception of Justice.* Durham: Duke University Press, 1925.

GILSON, ETIENNE H. *Dante the Philosopher.* London: Sheed & Ward, 1948.

KELSEN, HANS. *Die Staatslehre des Dante Alighieri.* Vienna: F. Deuticke, 1905.

READE, W. H. V. *The Moral System of Dante's Inferno.* Oxford: Clarendon, 1909.

ROLBIECKI, JOHN J. *The Political Philosophy of Dante Alighieri.* Washington: Catholic University Press, 1921.

WICKSTEED, P. H. *Dante and Aquinas.* London: J. M. Dent, 1913.

William of Ockham and Marsilio of Padua

BRAMPTON, C. KENNETH. "Marsiglio of Padua. Part I: Life." *English Historical Review* 37 (1922), 501.

CARRE, M. H. *Realists and Nominalists.* London: Oxford, 1946.

D'ENTREVES, A. P. *The Medieval Contribution to Political Thought: Thomas Aquinas,* Marsilius of Padua, Richard Hooker. London: Oxford University Press, 1939.

EMERTON, EPHRAIM. *The Defensor Pacis of Marsiglio of Padua.* Cambridge, Mass.: Harvard University Press, 1920.

GEWIRTH, ALAN. *Marsilius of Padua.* 2 vols. New York: Columbia University Press, 1951.

GUELLUY, ROBERT. *Philosophie et Theologie chez Guillaume d'Ockham.* Louvain: E. Nauwelaerts, 1947.

HAMMAN, G. A. *La Doctrime de l'Eglise et de l'Etat chez Occam.* Paris: Aux Editions franciscaines, 1942.

MARSILIO. *The Defensor Pacis of Marsilius of Padua.* Cambridge: University Press, 1928.

MCKEON, RICHARD, ed. and trans. *Selections from Medieval Philosophers.* Vol. 2: *Roger Bacon to William of Ockham.* New York: Scribner's, 1929–1930.

MOODY, ERNEST A. *The Logic of William of Occam.* New York: Sheed & Ward, 1935.

PREVITE-ORTON, C. W. "Marsiglio of Padua. Part II: Doctrine." *English Historical Review* 38 (1923), 1.

SHEPARD, MAX A. "William of Occam and the Higher Law." *American Political Science Review* 26 (1932), 1005; 27 (1933), 24.

Wycliffe and Huss

BETTS, R. R. "Some Political Ideas of the Early Czech Reformers." *Slavic and East European Review* 31 (1952), 20–36.

CARRICK, JOHN C. *Wycliffe and the Lollards.* Edinburgh: T. & T. Clark, 1908.

GILLETT, E. H. *The Life and Times of John Huss.* Boston: Gould & Lincoln, 1863.

KAMINSKY, HOWARD. "Chiliasm and the Hussite Revolution." *Church History* 26 (1957), 43–70.

KAMINSKY, HOWARD. "Hussite Radicalism and the Origins of Tabor." *Medevalia et Humanistica* 10 (1956), 102–130.

KITTS, EUSTACE J. *Pope John XXIII and Master John Hus of Bohemia.* London: Constable, 1910.

KROFTA, KAMIL. "John Hus." *Cambridge Medieval History,* vol. 8, ch. 2, 1939.

POOLE, REGINALD L. *Wycliffe and Movements for Reform.* London: Longmans, Green, 1896.

RASHDALL, HASTINGS. *John Huss.* Oxford: Clarendon, 1879.

SPINKA, MATTHEW. *John Hus and the Czech Reform.* Chicago: University of Chicago Press, 1941.

TREVELYAN, G. M. *England in the Age of Wycliffe.* London: Longmans, Green, 1904.

WILKINS, HENRY J. *Was John Wycliffe a Negligent Pluralist?* London: Longmans, Green, 1915.

WYCLIFFE, J. *Selected English Writings.* London: Oxford University Press, 1929.

WYLIE, J. H. *The Council of Constance to the Death of John Huss.* London: Longmans, Green, 1900.

part III

THE PROBLEM OF THE INDIVIDUAL FROM THE RENAISSANCE TO THE FRENCH REVOLUTION

With the decline and fall of medieval institutions and thought, Western culture witnessed the release of the individual from status relations. The serf, over the course of centuries, broke his feudal ties. The merchant, very early, conceived himself as separated from the law of the fief. The potential adventurer felt that there were fewer inhibitions on his conduct: in some sense, as a matter of fact, he was free of community ties.

Given an individual increasingly viewing himself as discrete, his relations with other men came gradually to be based on agreement or contract rather than inherited status. His sense of freedom, moreover, led him to revolt against organized religion and its institutions; for while dissent had indeed been present throughout the Middle Ages, it was now much more widespread. Gradually, too, as religious commitments were redefined, faith in science became a real competitor for the allegiance of men.

With the dissolution of many traditional social bonds, the role of the king's estate, relatively weak in the Middle Ages, was magnified greatly. Thus the state—or the estate of the king—more and more became the center of man's collective existence, claiming many of the prerogatives associated with the ancient Roman Empire. It asserted sovereignty and increasingly maintained that other associations existed only on its sufferance. Although the process was a very gradual one, the impact of these developments in general terms was to set the discrete individual over against the state.

The national state came increasingly to sum up the political life of man. The Holy Roman Empire, often shadowy even under the universalist consciousness of the Middle Ages, tended to disappear from man's political awareness. To be sure, it continued to exist in form down to the early part of the nineteenth century, but ever more it became, in the words of the eighteenth-century wit Voltaire, "neither Holy, nor Roman, nor an Empire."

In the nearly four hundred years from the Renaissance to the French Revolution, many medieval institutions—the guild, the empire, feudalism—continued their decline. In their place such characteristic early modern features of life developed as the national state, large-scale commercialism (and, toward the end, the beginnings of industrialism), and the phenomenon of the allegedly discrete individual facing or confronting the nation-state. The French Revolution accented many of these tendencies and accelerated them where they had only partially developed.

All these phenomena were slow in evolving but almost from the beginning their implications were reflected in the history of thought. Thus the Renaissance exemplified in its whole culture the consciousness of individuality. In political theory, this was above all clear in the outlook of Machiavelli, who illustrated a general tendency to separate the spheres of life from one another: hence individual morality, seen by the ancients and even by medieval man as intimately tied to social morality, came often to be studied separately. Each segment of existence had its own principles which were not to be judged by any over-all system such as theology.

In the particularly religious reflection of these tendencies—the Reformation—we have a nice example of how awareness of individuality developed and contributed eventually to radical theories of resistance to the state and equally radical conceptions of democracy. Although Lutheranism was rather conservative socially and politically, its conception of the two realms—the Kingdom of Grace and the Sphere of Power—in some respects resembled Machiavelli's tendency to separate politics from ethics and religion. Calvinism, with its strong consciousness that election was individual, had within it the ingredients for potential personal political activism. Heterodox tendencies in the Protestant Reformation often accented mystical versions of religion which were closely associated with political creeds whose effect was to undermine the status quo.

It is against this background and as a continuation of it that one must view the emergence of social contract theories of the state and society. Although Socrates had suggested an embryonic contract theory of political obligation and Glaucon had seemingly argued for one version of it, ancient political thought, for the most part, rejected full-blown contractualism. In the Middle Ages, of course, there was an implicit contract theory in feudalism; but it so quickly became subordinated to status and inheritance principles that it remained a minor chord. With the growth of early modern philosophical nominalism, the evolution of Reformation theology, and, above all, the development of commerce, the state itself came to be explained and justified in terms of contract. Men saw that commercial relations depended on contract and, since in general they increasingly thought of individuals as discrete, it was but a slight leap to the notion that social bonds and the state were based on agreement among individuals.

Versions of the contract varied, to be sure, but they all took their ostensible point of departure from the belief that only the individual was metaphysically real. Social structures, by contrast, were artificial and were to some extent a product of the combined force of individuals. Man's nature was not social but, in varying degrees, antisocial. While men might agree to establish states and social structures through contract, force was essential to make sure that egoistic men obeyed it. The most extreme version of this view was that of Thomas Hobbes, with what one scholar has called his "possessive individualism." John Locke in many respects provided an outlook similar to that of Hobbes, but sought, not without difficulty, to soften its harsher contours with a vestigial medievalism. Contract theories were often associated with the development of early modern democratic ideas, although we should always remember that contract doctrine does not necessarily entail democracy any more than democratic thought requires contract theory as a foundation.

Meanwhile, the history of general science was reinforcing these tendencies. Beginning with the nominalist and materialist views of the late Middle Ages, many exponents of science came gradually to conceive the universe as a gigantic machine. Political thinkers, using the analogy, tended to think of the state as mechanistic as well as contractual—a view to some extent exemplified in the Constitution of the United States.

Closely associated with these developments was the doctrine of natural rights, which thought of separate individuals as having claims *against* society and the state. It was the individual who was born with rights which in some sense antedated social and political bonds; and the task of the state was to preserve these rights. Whereas medieval natural law doctrines had stressed man's *duties* (to God, to other men, and to groups), the thrust of natural rights conceptions was to minimize obligations.

But just as the classical theological-political theory of the Middle Ages produced its critics in the heretics, schismatics, and nominalists, so evolving individualist and contract theories stimulated rather contrary views. Thus sixteenth and seventeenth century utopists endeavored to recall the notion of the organic community. Those who sought to revive Platonism as an outlook looked with despair on the tendency to exalt social atomism and to think of commercial trading corporations as models for the state. But the attack on contract and individualism did not really come to the forefront until after the middle of the eighteenth century.

Contract theory had a large deductive element in it and was associated historically in some measure with the rationalism of the Cartesians. The critics of individualist and contractualist views were often empiricists, like Montesquieu and Hume. Jean Jacques Rousseau himself, who on one side of his curious intellectual history was a contractualist, was on the other side an admirer of classical Greek political thought; and in the end Rousseau was important in the history of political ideas, not because of his rather tenuous contractualism but rather because he helped revive a version of classical organicism upon which Hegel would build in the nineteenth century.

Meanwhile, the French Revolution broke out and in its contesting ideologies epitomized the growing conflict between natural rights and contract doctrines, on the one hand, and a nascent organicism, on the other. In this, it seemed to reflect the two sides of Rousseau: the individualist, which became a keynote in the outlook of the still-expanding middle classes, and the Plato-like, which animated the slogan of fraternity and provided a basis for the German idealist perspective that owed so much to revolutionary inspiration.

chapter 16

Morality and Politics: Machiavelli and the Renaissance

By the middle of the fifteenth century the danger of schism, whether major or minor, had passed, but the Church still remained basically unreformed. It is true that the popes from Martin V onward attempted minor changes which might be approved by those zealous for reform; and the Councils of Constance and Basel talked much of a fundamental housecleaning, the latter Council appointing a Commission which deliberated for six years. Despite these efforts, however, corruption and most of the conditions which the Spiritual Franciscans had attacked a century before remained highly characteristic of ecclesiastical life.

During the time of Eugenius IV, a well-known Dominican advocate of reform, John Nider, thought that a general ecclesiastical cleansing was unlikely for a long time; "for," said he in his *Formicarius,* "goodwill is wanting among the subjects, the evil disposition of the prelates constitutes an obstacle, and, finally, it is profitable to God's elect to be tried by persecution from the wicked."

Meanwhile, in every area of life—in art, religion, morality, trade, and politics—a new spirit was abroad, particularly in the southern parts of Christendom. The roots of the Renaissance were, of course, to be found in the High Middle Ages themselves, for the recovery of Aristotle and the impact of Arabic learning set in motion forces which were simply accentuated in the fourteenth and fifteenth centuries. Philosophically, a semi-skeptical nominalism began to eat away at the realistic views of an earlier day; and this spirit, which we have seen exemplified in William of Ockham, reinforced other tendencies which in the social realm were removing legal and customary restraints. The weakening of feudal ties helped enlarge the populations of cities and thus encouraged the growth of attitudes characteristic of urban areas in every generation—views hostile to mere tradition and often eager to embrace novelties of all kinds.

It was into this environment that Niccolo Machiavelli was born. The unreformed Church presided over his birth and it remained at his death. He came into the world of the Italian Renaissance and it was upon the basis of his experiences in that world that he worked out his theory of man and of politics; and that theory is with considerable justification said to mark the beginning of modern political thought.

But before we examine Machiavelli's doctrines themselves, let us glance at the fifteenth and early sixteenth century political situation which furnished him so many of the raw materials for his analysis and philosophy.

Politics in the Time of Machiavelli

The political situation in Machiavelli's Italy was in some respects unique. Unlike England and France, Italy was not politically united. While urban viewpoints were becoming more and more significant in both England and France, they developed in the context of increasingly centralized national politics. In Italy, by contrast, not only did culture and ideologies come to be shaped by the cities, but many municipalities were also independent politically. In some measure, it may be said that the Italy of Machiavelli's time revived the spirit of the Greek polis and that the politics which he observed were more like those of ancient Athens, Sparta, and Corinth than they were like the political conditions of England and France.

Yet one must be cautious in making generalizations of this kind, for the actual divisions of Italy were not entirely along city lines and the whole situation was made even more complex because of the Church's peculiar role. There were five major political entities in the Italy of Machiavelli. The Duchy of Milan occupied much of the northern part and, somewhat like an ancient city-state, consisted of the city of Milan and its political allies and tributaries. In the northeast was the ancient Republic of Venice, whose history went back to A.D. 421 and whose constitutional development exhibits one of the most fascinating chapters in the history of politics.[1]

The city of Florence was yet another factor in fifteenth and sixteenth century politics. Like Milan and Venice, it, too, was the central factor in a wider political complex. In greater or lesser degree, depending upon circumstances, Florence dominated Tuscany, even though its authority was often rather tenuous. The political development of Florence, like that of Venice, is instructive of the ways in which Italian city politics resembled, as well as the respects in which they were unlike those of the ancient polis; and Machiavelli himself, in his *History of Florence*, was quite aware of the value of Florentine history for the study of comparative politics.

In the south of Italy, of course, was the Kingdom of Naples. During the time of Machiavelli, it was the object of conflict between France and Spain, a branch of whose royal house claimed the throne of Naples.

But perhaps the most complex role in the politics of Machiavelli's time was played by the states of the Church—the territory in central Italy possessed by the Church and controlled by it either directly or through various forms of feudal tenure. The pope's dual status as spiritual head of the Church universal and at the same time temporal ruler of the states of the Church placed him in an awkward position.

These, then, were the major political divisions. What were the questions about which political struggle revolved?

In the city-states, many of the same controversies with which we are familiar in Greek political history occupied the center of the stage. What was to be the exact influence of the people in the governance of the city and what the prerogatives of the few? In Florence, for example, the Medici family represented the interests of the aristocracy and the Soderini those of the people. Often domestic factions would be supported by outside aid and thus political conflicts turning on the nature of the Florentine constitution would have wide ramifications for Italy or even Christendom as a whole.

Italian cities and states were constantly subject to non-Italian intervention of various kinds. In the first place, the emperor, while a German, continued to maintain a kind of shadowy claim to govern Italy by virtue of the fact that he was theoretically a Roman ruler. And his pretensions, together with rival claims of the pope, had for many years divided Italians into the factions of the Ghibbelines—partisans of the emperor—and the Guelfs—adherents of the pope.

But emperor and pope were not the only contestants, for the kings of France and Spain also played influential roles in Italian life.

The character of the papacy and its occupants also affected politics. Most of these rulers of the Church led lives but little restrained by moral scruples. All had bastard children, Alexander VI openly avowing his. All, in varying degrees, sought to advance their families as rapidly as possible, whether in terms of money or of political power. Thus Alexander VI appointed his son Caesare Borgia Captain-General of Holy Church and instructed him to rid the states of the Church of fief-holders whose positions had been established by previous pontiffs; and Caesare was enriched rapidly both through the direct power of the pope and by means of agreements made with the King of France.

The means used by both ecclesiastical and nonecclesiastical politicians during the period were for the most part not selected because of their conformity to standards of abstract morality but rather because they promised to bring immediate results which were deemed desirable. Thus Pope Sixtus IV assisted in the Pazzi conspiracy which resulted in the cold-blooded murder of several Florentine leaders. And the Republic of Venice had an official poisoner.

The contrast between the religious professions and the conduct of Renaissance rulers was, of course, startling; and it was a subject of constant discussion in both low and high places. Men laughed, for instance, when they heard that Pope Alexander VI gave particular veneration to the Virgin Mary as Mother of Chastity; for not only had the pontiff sired many children prior to his election, but he was alleged as pope to have encouraged the procurement of prostitutes for cardinals and himself. And despite the outcries against simony in ecclesiastical circles, Popes Alexander VI and Julius II virtually bought their way into the papacy, either through money payments or by the offer of political power. While the contrast between religious and moral profession

1. For the evolution of Venice, see W. Carew Hazlitt, *The Venetian Republic: Its Rise, Its Growth, and Its Fall*, 2 vols., London: Adam and Charles Black, 1915. The politics of Venice during the time of Machiavelli are treated in vol. 2, ch. 32–34.

and actual practice is glaring in any age—and is particularly apparent within ruling classes—at no time in human history has it been greater than during the Italian Renaissance.

Machiavelli's Political Biography

Niccolo Machiavelli was born in 1469. Like Dante, he came from a Guelf family background. Aside, however, from the fact that he learned Latin and a little Greek, we know very little about his early life and education. During his twenties he watched the rise to power of Fra Girolamo Savonarola, who sought to inaugurate the reign of Jesus Christ in a city that had been dominated by the Medici; and at the age of twenty-five he saw Charles VIII of France enter the city, encouraged, curiously enough, by the ascetic Friar. Already Machiavelli must have wondered at the strange allies produced by politics—the ambitious Charles VIII holding hands, as it were, with a man who denounced worldly pomp and power and who had a vision much like that of the Spiritual Franciscans. Even more impressive to the young Machiavelli must have been the burning at the stake of Savonarola in 1498, when the papacy and his political enemies united to do away with one who had challenged their right to rule. Was it not his own political ineptitude, Machiavelli wondered, which brought the friar's downfall?

Only a very short time after the execution, Machiavelli was appointed to his first public position—that of Secretary to the City Council. Later he became Secretary to the Council of Ten in charge of military affairs. He was a friend of the Soderini family, which now sought to reestablish popular rule after what it regarded as the undesirably aristocratic government of the Medici and the equally unacceptable administration of the extremist Savonarola. Machiavelli's close relationships with the leading family of the regime led to his appointment as envoy for Florence in a number of external negotiations.

Meanwhile, the Medici had been conspiring to return to power. They finally succeeded in 1512, when the Soderini were overthrown and the aristocracy restored. At first, apparently, Machiavelli believed that he might retain his official position, since he thought of himself as a permanent civil servant. But the Medici were aware of his close relations with the Soderini and undoubtedly thought of him as a partisan official. Hence he was dismissed a short time after the Medici had resumed their direction of affairs. In 1513, the Medici's power in Florence was reinforced when a Medici Pope—Leo X—succeeded the della Rovere Julius II.

From 1513 to 1526, Machiavelli had no connection with the Florentine government. Bitter about his situation, he felt that he had much to contribute and that his friendship with the Soderini ought not to be held against him. So deeply did he resent his political exile, in fact, that he now began an untiring campaign to regain official status. In modern parlance, he sought to "butter up" the Medici, so that they would see him as a valuable servant.

He combined this campaign with literary efforts. During his office-holding period he had long contemplated a literary work which would deal with the principles whereby political power can be gained and maintained. His residence at the court of Caesare Borgia, although very brief, had made him an admirer of the young Borgia's talent for gaining his objectives with maximum efficiency; for unlike many other rulers, Caesare, in Machiavelli's view, knew just when to use force and when to seek the consent of the population. As the fruit of these reflections, *The Prince* and the *Discourses on the First Ten Books of Titus Livius* attempted to show how, under radically differing social and moral conditions, governments ought to conduct themselves. At the same time, Machiavelli's efforts to conciliate the Medici having met with some success, he was given a commission by that family to write the *History of Florence*. In this work, he had an opportunity to apply his framework of analysis to the politics of his own city.

Besides these efforts, he dealt with the whole problem of warfare in *The Art of War* and turned his mind to comic poetry in *Mandragola.*

In many respects, however, his heart was never in his literary work, which he looked upon primarily as a relief from the idleness of political exile. When it became evident, about 1521, that the Medici were becoming more favorable to his pleas for activity, he eagerly embraced the opportunity. Cardinal Giulio dei Medici (the future Clement VII) urged the Council of Eight of Pratica to send him as an envoy to the General Chapter of the Franciscans. As a critic of all friars, Machiavelli jested about this mission but nevertheless performed it in the hope, evidently, that it might lead to reinstatement in political office. The Wool Guild, a little later, charged him with the task of finding it a chaplain and this, too, must have seemed ironical to the author of the *Prince*.

In the spring of 1526, the Medici were so satisfied with his efforts that they finally gave him the office of Secretary to the Superintendents of the Walls. In this capacity he was sent to represent the city before the lieutenant of the pope in the army that had been raised to oppose the Emperor Charles V. That ruler was now menacing Italy with a huge army and Florence, together with other cities, was joining with the pope to resist him. By the spring of 1527, the army of the antiimperial league was still relatively inactive and this in face of the fact that the emperor's troops were now appearing in northern Italy. Again Machiavelli was witnessing what he regarded as incompetency and again he knew that Italy would suffer because of the stupidity of its rulers.

The army of the emperor moved so rapidly and with so little opposition that by May 6 it had entered Rome; and the papal city was given over to systematic looting by Charles' Catholic and Lutheran troops alike. The sack of Rome had immediate repercussions on the politics of Florence. The Pope (Clement VII) was, of course, a Medici; and when news arrived in Florence that his city had been taken, the popular faction felt emboldened enough to attack their own Mediciean rulers. The latter were, therefore, expelled and the democratic party once more took control of affairs.

At this point Machiavelli witnessed the final political irony: he was dismissed from his post as Secretary to the Superintendents on the ground that he had been too pro-Medici! One can well imagine Machiavelli's reaction. But he did not live to write it in a new exile, for he died on June 22.

No one during his lifetime could have predicted that his political reflections would achieve the fame—or perhaps some would say notoriety—they began to have a generation after his death. He was relatively unknown as a thinker while alive, the *Prince* itself not being published until five years after his death. Even within ecclesiastical circles, the impact of his doctrine seems not to have been felt immediately, for not until 1557 did the Pope (Paul IV) place the *Prince* on the Index Expurgatorious. By the end of the sixteenth century, however, he had begun to be widely known in intellectual circles; and in the revolt against all things medieval which characterized both sixteenth and seventeenth centuries, Machiavelli played an important role.

Machiavelli's General Outlook and Method

In some respects, it is difficult to understand why Machiavelli has come to occupy his relatively high place in the history of political ideas. Much of what he says about ideal government, for example, simply carries on the medieval tradition. And his strong emphasis on law is not to be sharply differentiated from that of St. Thomas and the Roman civilian tradition; for while it is true that he appears to discard the natural law outlook, it is also indubitably correct to interpret him as asserting that the ruler should be subject to the positive law.[2] His preference for mixed government, moreover, follows medieval precedents.

Nor are his contributions to method in the study of politics as great as some critics seem to assert. It is not infrequently maintained, for instance, that he attempts to portray political man as he really is, rather than as he ought to be; and that in this respect he differs sharply from such late medieval thinkers as Dante.[3] Yet it is not at all clear that men like St. Thomas and Dante did not think of themselves as also endeavoring to describe man as he really is, whether "existentially" or in potentiality.

Perhaps the most frequent assertion about his place in the history of ideas is that which would make him the first political scientist or at least the first modern political scientist. This contention maintains that before Machiavelli, the study of politics was not empirically oriented: its professors, instead of troubling to observe with care the actual conduct of men and affairs, spent their time building systems of political thought upon premises about human conduct which were never tested in terms of actual behavior. Hence their conclusions were of doubtful validity since their starting points were uncriticized statements of

2. Cf. A. J. Carlyle and R. W. Carlyle, *A History of Medieval Political Theory in the West*, 6 vols., Edinburgh: Blackwood, 1936, vol. 6.
3. This seems to be the position of James Burnham in *The Machiavellians: Defenders of Freedom*, New York: John Day, 1943, ch. 1.

Aristotle, untested assertions of the scriptures, or undemonstrated propositions about human conduct. Machiavelli, by contrast, it is maintained, endeavors to be scientific and to build his system only upon criticized and tested observations of men as they actually behave.

In evaluating these contentions, much depends, of course, on how we define the word scientific. Certainly his method does not embrace the carefully refined techniques used by modern behavioral social scientists. He develops no laboratory schemes, formulates no questionnaires, and systematically interviews no politicians. His knowledge of human beings is derived from his study of history—and particularly his examination of the ancient Roman historian Titus Livius—and from his direct but unsystematized observations of Italian Renaissance politicians. While such sources may be relevant, it is noteworthy that Machiavelli is not very critical in the uses to which he puts Titus Livius nor does he question the correctness of the ancient historian's version of Roman historical development.

His attitude to the ancients is, indeed, one of veneration and in this he is a child of the early Renaissance. Just as artists seek their standards among the ancient Greeks and many philosophers come to venerate Plato, so does Machiavelli think of the political experience of the ancients interpreted through an ancient historian as an almost infallible basis for political generalization. He certainly reflects very little on scientific method and can hardly be called a philosopher of science.

Yet however much we may seek to reject exaggerated claims for Machiavelli, there is certainly some basis for the place he has come to occupy in the history of thought. What is that basis? In large part, we might suggest that it turns on his effort to divorce politics from religion. As the Renaissance develops, there is a tendency in all areas of life to think of each art or science as autonomous. In part the effect of nominalistic philosophy and in some measure the result of the decline of organic conceptions of society, this tendency is everywhere observable. As inner and outer worlds come increasingly to be separated, religion, for example, is identified more and more with the former and less with the universe of economic and political life. As faith in the coordinating role of religion disintegrates, men begin to think of society as a conflict of interests which cannot be appreciably abated.

One of the effects of this splitting up of life is, of course, to free the individual sciences from any central control by theology—to make it possible, in other words, for embryonic studies like Physics and Chemistry to examine physical and chemical phenomena unhindered by Revelation, Aristotle, or St. Thomas. The nominalistic tendency to stress particulars is impatient with dogmatic assertions about wholes; and when the Church presumes to tell Renaissance investigators that what they find is against revelation or nature, they rebel. And the same attitude would be assumed by the artist whose portrayal of nudity might antagonize the moralist.

Machiavelli, then, proceeds to look at politics as if it could be divorced sharply from other human concerns and seeks to discover the inner rules which presumably differentiate it from art, religion, morality, and economic enterprise. This does not mean that he believes there is or ought to be no morality in politics but rather that he assumes politics to have a morality peculiar to itself.

He sees something which we might today call pure politics and seeks to draw out its principles as fully as possible. If this is what is meant by a scientific approach, then Machiavelli is indeed to be regarded as one of the great exemplars of scientific method. But we should carefully differentiate this usage from those which refer to particular techniques for making the study of politics a pure science.

Questions involving method and general outlook can perhaps be more adequately answered only by an examination of his political theory itself.[4]

Political Society: Origins, Nature, and Ends

At the very outset, one should bear in mind that there are not two Machiavellis, as some commentators would have us believe—a Machiavelli of the *Prince* and one of the *Discourses* and the *History of Florence*. Basically, Machiavelli's political thought is a unity built around a political-ethical assumption which he never questions—that any means which will assure the preservation of a state are legitimate. The problem is to discover the means which do in fact preserve it—this is the task which Machiavelli sets before himself in all his political writings.

But granted this integrating factor in Machiavelli's whole system, we should not read him as placing all forms of political society on the same level. The form will tend, he thinks, to follow the general fortune of society; and that fortune is, in turn, shaped by the many interactions of men in responding to ever-present change in human affairs. There are an ebb and flow in political history and limits on the degree to which man is likely to control his destiny. When mankind as a whole have lost *virtu*—that is, their abounding energies and the will to use them—tyranny and the role of princes are the inevitable results; and the very existence of tyrannies in any given historical epoch is an indication that virtu is at a low ebb. On the other hand, when the bulk of mankind have arisen from this depth—as inevitably they do, according to Machiavelli—republics on the Roman model can flourish, bearing within them, of course, the seeds of their own degeneracy. There are rules for government (assuming the supreme end of state preservation) appropriate under a tyranny or principality and other principles appropriate for republics. In his own day, Machiavelli believes, most men have so completely lost virtu, that the tyrannical rule of princes is inevitable and if political objectives are to be accomplished one must think primarily of giving advice to the prince. On the other hand, it is his judgment that republics have greater potentialities for preserving themselves over a longer period of time, even though they, too, are inevitably transmuted into despotisms.

The foundations for this general view will be found in a letter which he writes to Pier Soderini:

> Because the times and human affairs are constantly changing, whereas men do not alter their ideas and their way of life, it comes about that a man will have good fortune at one time, and at another bad. And, in truth, he that should be so wise as to understand the times and the order of things, accommodating himself to them, would always have good fortune, or at least he would preserve himself from bad, and it would come to be true that the wise man should command the stars and the Fates. But since there are no such wise men to be found, man having, in the first place, shortness of sight, and secondly, being unable to rule his nature, it follows that Fortune changes, and thus governs men and subjects them to her yoke.[5]

Order follows disorder, according to a fortune which men can resist but which they cannot ever completely overcome. Political order and liberty having been achieved (and Machiavelli tends to think of liberty as associated with the rule of law), inability to adapt to changing times and the limits of man's nature cause the political society to descend. On the other hand, having reached the depths (identified with the decline of rule under law and the absence of virtu in the mass), reascent is equally inevitable.

Both implicitly and explicitly, he thinks of man as a being, who, while he gives the appearance of goodness (identified by Machiavelli with altruism or concern for beings outside his own ego) is in reality dominated either by desire for self-aggrandizement or by a cowardly love of sloth and a retreat from responsibility. These characteristics embrace what traditional religion has called wickedness. In periods of widespread virtu—that is, epochs in which large numbers of mankind are about equally energetic and able to translate their ambitions into action—a kind of balance of power exists and democratic republics are possible, most men having the will to protect the state which they see as their own protector. On the other hand, when corruption sets in, the other side of human wickedness is revealed—men become cowardly, subservient to superstitions, and lacking in the will to act. In such periods, the few who are energetic and therefore possessed of virtu rule despotically; and the preservation of the state

4. The modern interest in Machiavelli is sufficiently illustrated if we refer to only a few of the titles which have appeared during the past generation. Examples are Federico Bruno, *Romanita e Modernita del Pensiero di Machiavelli*, Milan: Fratelli Bocca, 1951; Carmelo Caristia, *Il Pensiero Politico di Niccolo Machiavelli*, 2nd ed., Naples: E. Jovene, 1951; Herbert Butterfield, *The Statecraft of Machiavelli*, New York: Macmillan 1956; Marcel Brion, *Machiavel*, Paris: A. Michel, 1948; De Lamar Jensen, ed., *Machiavelli: Cynic, Patriot,* or *Political Scientist?*, Boston: Heath, 1960; Leo Strauss, *Thoughts on Machiavelli*, Glencoe: Free Press, 1959; Leonardo Olschki, *Machiavelli the Scientist*, Berkeley, Calif.: Gillick Press; and John H. Whitfield, *Machiavelli*, Oxford: Blackwell, 1947. See also Garrett Mattingly, who interprets Machiavelli as a satirist, "Reappraisals: Machiavelli's 'Prince,' Political Science or Political Satire," *American Scholar*, Autumn, 1958, pp. 1482–1491.
5. Machiavelli, *Draft of a Letter to Pier Soderini*, quoted in Ettore Janni, *Machiavelli*, Marion Enthoven, trans., London: George Harrap, 1930, p. 212.

is dependent on their perspicacity and ability to manipulate the mass.

Machiavelli's account of the origin of the state attributes the first governments, characteristically enough, to chance. Mankind were at first scattered, he suggests, but as they became more numerous (and their increase in numbers was not a planned one), they began, rather unconsciously, to submit themselves to the stronger for self-protection. Government thus had its origin in physical force and the forceful reaction to physical force. It was only after obedience to the stronger became habitual that such distinctions as those between honesty and dishonesty began to arise. Moreover, the rise of so-called justice and the criminal law is merely a by-product of the subordination of most men to the stronger. The state, in other words, was not established to strengthen an objectively existing morality or to implement natural law. Instead, morality and natural law were conceptions which developed only after men began to respond collectively by force to the force which threatened to annihilate them.[6]

It is clear, then, that Machiavelli does not think of political society as natural in the classical Greek sense of that term and that he is equally far from St. Thomas's conception. In the beginning, presumably, the ruler "selected" himself through his sheer ability to dominate. Later, as men became more aware of the reason for rulership, they began to elect their sovereigns; to choose them for their wisdom and justice. Wisdom and justice, of course, Machiavelli always identifies with those maxims and actions that experience has proven conduce to the physical preservation of a given group of individuals or of their ruler. Nonelective sovereignty—inheritance of office by the children of those who have proven wise and just—follows on elective rulership, since presumably men conclude that the children of a wise ruler must inherit their father's virtu.

When this proves not to be the case—when, in other words, sloth and indifference become characteristics of the hereditary ruling class—the now-degenerate governors find themselves objects of jealousy and hatred by their subjects. The prince reacts to this hatred by himself becoming fearful and the princely fear leads him to develop tyrannical habits. He establishes elaborate precautions against possible conspiracy and his rule is founded more and more on naked force—that is, he no longer conceals his violence through religious maxims and pious platitudes. Meanwhile, those who possess virtu lead many a plot against the ruler. Eventually, they are successful and for a time the controls of law are restored in a system which is essentially an aristocracy. In the long run, however, this too, becomes lawless and is transmuted into an oligarchy. The oligarchy provokes rebellion and on this occasion masses of energetic men push forward to control affairs, with popular government under law as the result.

Machiavelli observes that all forms of government are defective—the good ones because they usually flourish for relatively short periods of time and the bad because by their very nature they subvert the preservation of the state. Like Aristotle, he comes to the conclusion that mixed government provides the relatively best scheme; for while it is less good than pure monarchy, aristocracy, or popular government, it also has a tendency to persist longer. It has neither the inherent viciousness of the bad forms nor the brief life of the good ones.

Like the ancient Polybius,[7] he sees in the history of Rome a documentation of the superiority of mixed government. The Roman Republic persisted so long because its founders and rulers were aware that "all men are bad and ever ready to display their vicious nature."[8] The Republic rightly, therefore, made provision for a monarchical principle (consuls), aristocratic (Senate), and popular (comitia and tribunes), knowing that in the competition between and among these institutions both the liberty of the man of virtu and the continuation of the state would be maximized. Machiavelli throughout seems to see liberty in a twofold light: It provides scope for men to exercise their virtu and it provides the most solid foundation for the preservation of the state.

He asks himself to whom the guardianship of liberty can more safely be confided, the aristocracy or the people, and unhesitatingly supports the claim of the people. To sustain this conclusion, he points out that those who wish to preserve their power are more likely to excite passions and disturbances than those who hope to acquire it. If the nobility are the only governors, the very fact that they are a minority leads them to be suspicious of the people; and in the name of greater security they will utilize every means not only to preserve their status but also to extend it. This in turn will provoke the jealousy and resentment of the people all the more.

If the people are not corrupt, their collective judgment is to be preferred to that of the prince. Here Machiavelli differs sharply from Livy, who had argued that nothing was more uncertain than the multitude and that princes were more stable than the mass. On the contrary, the Florentine maintains, "individual men, and especially princes, may be charged with the same defects of which writers accuse the people; for whoever is not controlled by law will commit the same errors as an unbridled multitude."[9]

But his predilection for the people should not lead us to conclude that he has unqualified confidence in them, any more than he reposes unlimited trust in the nobility or the prince. He is above all a relativist; that is, if he had to choose between the people and the prince he would always select the former; and the same would be true if his alternatives were people and nobility. Given his general view of man, however, the one, the few, and the many are all suspect; all of them are but a little way from corruption. While mixed government under a system of positive law may, by granting all three elements a measure of authority, set up maximum safeguards against the corruption of any of them, it can only delay the inevitable degeneracy.

We should guard ourselves against a fatally easy temptation to interpret Machiavelli as holding that the prince, when the people become corrupt, can dispense with their consent. He never asserts this. As a matter of fact, he is forever telling us that the bulk of the people must at least passively acquiesce if the prince is to maintain his status and the state is to remain secure. The consent of the people is qualitatively different in a principality, however, from what it would be under a mixed or popular regime: in the former it is a passive acceptance partly arising out of the general corruption and partly out of deliberate manipulations by the prince; in the latter, it is a more active and virile approbation, which does not, indeed, exclude princely propaganda but which certainly requires a different posture on the part of the ruler.

But how are the tasks of governance to be accomplished? How ought a prince to act in a situation where the mass lack virtu and how ought the consul (or other person responsible for active administration) to conduct himself in a society where a relatively popular government is possible? Machiavelli's answers to these questions have become celebrated and, indeed, they constitute what is most distinctive about his political teaching.

The Strategy and Tactics of Governance

As we have noted, Machiavelli sees political history as an ebb and flow from despotical to popular or semi-popular and mixed regimes. Although he has indicated why he believes that mixed government is preferable to other schemes, he sees all forms as eventually decaying. His task, as an expert in the art of governance, is to make the best of the always poor materials—of moody princes, of an avaricious nobility, and of a people who, while prudent and stable at their best, are always tending to sloth and indifference.

To grapple adequately with these common problems a conception of strategy and tactics is necessary. Machiavelli has only contempt for those who, essaying the task of leadership (whether in a principality or a mixed system), go about it unintelligently. And intelligence in this context is not concerned with the ascertainment of ends (which are fixed) but rather with the manipulation of materials (population, resources, religion, tradition) as means. What, then, are the maxims of political morality which his own experience, his analysis of historical development, and his study of the art of war have taught him?

Public and Private Morality. While he fully recognizes that there are certain maxims of morality which men believe ought to be observed (although he is not interested in giving an account of them, as would a moral philosopher), he holds that whatever may be true of those in private life, it is disastrous if a ruler observes them with any rigidity. While much will depend, of course, on circumstances, in general the ruler should be prepared to disregard all standards which do not conduce to the

6. *Discourses*, Bk. I, ch. 1–12.
7. See Chapter 7, pp. 122–125.
8. *Discourses*, I, 3, 1.
9. *Ibid.*, 1, 58, 3.

maintenance of his own power and to that of the state; and he should never assume that conventionally stated moral standards can always be reconciled with the attainment of public (or political) objectives.[10] The implication is that men even in their private capacities may be forced to disregard the Ten Commandments if they would preserve their lives: and what applies to the individual in his personal relations is even more applicable to the ruler of the state; for if he acts according to "politically" undetermined moral rules in face of external enemies who do not and of subjects who probably will not so act, he may bring about the loss of his own status and the destruction of the state itself.

Yet again we must utter a word of caution about our interpretation at this point. Machiavelli never says that the ruler *must* always ignore customarily accepted moral standards; he emphasizes only that the governor must be *ready* to do so. Wherever possible, the leader will, of course, observe the conventional standards, for this will strengthen his popular support, whether in a tyranny, a popular government, or a mixed regime. Even where he feels compelled to violate conventional beliefs, he will always strive to give the appearance of not doing so; "for the great majority of mankind," he maintains "are satisfied with appearances, as though they were realities, and are often even more influenced by the things that seem than by those that are."[11] One of the reasons he admires the republican Romans so much is that they understood—or at least Machiavelli thinks they understood—this fact.

Let us now note how he applies this general admonition to specific problems of belief and conduct.

Religion. He develops his attitude to religion, of course, at a time when the Church, as we have seen, has become almost the laughing-stock of most men. At the same time, the virtual agnosticism which springs from a system of thought like that of William of Ockham has now penetrated intellectual circles. The existence of God cannot be *known* or proven, Ockham had taught, so that belief in his being is a matter of mere faith. Now Machiavelli undoubtedly shares typical Renaissance attitudes to the Church and is attached to the nominalistic views of the Ockhamites. But he has little, if any, of the faith so essential as a substitute for alleged proofs of the divine existence.

His attitude to the Church and to priests is shown in a letter which he writes to Francesco Guicciardini at the time Machiavelli is on his mission to secure a chaplain for the Florentine Guild of Wool Merchants. In his own letter to which Machiavelli's was a reply, Guicciardini had advised his friend to make haste, lest Machiavelli himself be corrupted by the Friars: "I advise you to expedite this mission with all celerity, for, if you stay in the convent . . . the saintly friars will pass the contagion of their hypocrisy on to you. . . ."[12] In his reply, Machiavelli states that he would like to import a friar who would exemplify all the wickedness of friars in general, for then, perhaps, men would see what hell is really like and set their feet on the road to heaven.

He goes on in the letter to contrast the friars as they are with what they would be if they were genuine followers of St. Francis. "When we realize how much respect and following a bad man attains by hiding his actions under the cloak of religion," he observes, "we can easily conjecture the respect that would accrue to a good man if he sincerely, and not by simulation, followed the muddy path of St. Francis."

Machiavelli is interested not at all in religion as an inner experience, however, and he has but little concern with theology. His is not the kind of mind which would probe the varieties of religious life. His sole involvement is to inquire how religion may be used by the political leader for his own ends; for he sees religious beliefs as perhaps the crucial factor in governance.

He finds the utilization of religion for civic purposes one of the areas in which the Roman Kingdom and Republic succeeded most spectacularly. Thus he observes that Numa Pompilius, the successor to Romulus himself, "finding a very savage people, and wishing to reduce them to civil obedience by the arts of peace, had recourse to religion. . . . "[13] Rome was, indeed, more indebted to Numa, traditional founder of its religion, than to Romulus, who allegedly established the city, "for where religion exists it is easy to introduce armies and discipline, but where there are armies and no religion it is difficult to introduce the latter."[14] Without religion, the discipline so essential for military life would be impossible and of course Machiavelli cannot conceive a political society without an army.

But he is careful to explain that the ruler himself ought to feel free to disregard the dictates of religion, provided he gives the appearance of observing them. There are occasions, in other words, where he can gain the necessary consent and preserve the state only by putting on an elaborate show of religious observance while disregarding it in fact: whether he like it or not, the ruler to retain his position must see religious ceremonies as forms to be manipulated for public or political ends. Thus while Papirius was always careful to take the auspices before battling the Samnites, his public report of them was shaped only by his own judgments as a general: If he thought prospects were good, he always reported the auspices as favorable, whether they were or not. Thus he used superstition to build military morale.

At no point in his whole political analysis is Machiavelli more typically pagan than in his treatment of religion. In effect, he bypasses the Christian centuries completely, and minimizes any independent status for religious belief—it is simply another weapon, like poison, which rulers must cleverly utilize. Rightly employed, it tames men and makes them fit subjects. Distorted, it divides peoples (like those of Italy) who ought to be united.

The Introduction of Reforms. As pointed out earlier, Machiavelli lays great stress on the necessity for periodic changes in laws in order to take account of dynamic factors in social development. He seems to anticipate the cultural lag doctrine of the relationship between material and nonmaterial culture. But Roman experience strongly suggests, he maintains, that those who desire to reform an existing government in a free state—presumably a popular government or mixed form of some kind—should not move hastily. The Romans understood that the new wine must in some measure be poured into old bottles. The forms of the old must be preserved, even though the substance is altered. If both form and substance are changed suddenly, he thinks that civic disruption is likely and with it the possibility that the state itself might fall. In some measure this actually happened in ancient Rome when the radical agrarian legislation of the Gracchi was introduced.[15]

Force and Fraud. One of the most celebrated aspects of his attitude to rulership and politics generally is his inquiry into force and fraud as means for securing reputation and maintaining control of affairs. He is sometimes pictured as one who would give every political leader a vial of poison and then call upon him to use it with great frequency.

Actually, he puts physical force in a relatively secondary position. While he asserts flatly "I believe it to be most true that it seldom happens that men rise from low condition to high rank without employing either force or fraud, unless that rank should be attained either by gift or inheritance,"[16] he also avers that in attaining great fortune (either in material goods or power), cunning and deceit are better than force. Not that the latter is excluded—indeed, failure to use it at crucial junctures may be disastrous—but that often its utilization hinders the attainment of the objective. The life of Cyrus, as revealed by Xenophon, shows clearly that that great monarch could never have attained his high estate without many deceits and frauds. On the other hand, Machiavelli doubts that "there was ever a man who from obscure condition arrived at great power by merely employing open force."[17]

The impression left by Machiavelli's discussion is that while fraud and deceit may be looked upon as ordinary methods of governance and maintenance of power, force is to be regarded as extraordinary. Force, in other words, is to be reserved for circumstances when fraud seems inappropriate and the utilization of force clearly efficacious. On such occasions, however, there are to be no scruples of a religious or moral nature. In his own day, Machiavelli censures Gian Paolo Baglioni, ruler of Perugia, for failing to use force against Pope Julius II and his cardinals, the political enemies of Perugia. The Pope and his College foolishly visited Perugia, and Baglioni had ample opportunity to murder them, but for some reason failed to do so. Yet he clearly ought to have wiped them out.

A judicious measure of fraud and force is particularly necessary, he thinks, when a new prince like Caesare Borgia is endeavoring to establish himself. He has not yet had time to

10. *Prince*, ch. 15.
11. *Discourses*, I, 25, 1–2.
12. F. Guicciardini to N. Machiavelli, May 17, 1521.
13. *Discourses*, I, 11, 1.
14. *Ibid.*
15. See Chapter 7, pp. 120–121.
16. *Discourses*, II, 13.
17. *Ibid.*, III.

develop patterns of habitual obedience nor has he had the opportunity to manipulate ideology for his own ends. Borgia, moreover, was concerned with extremely corrupt populations—those which had become accustomed to disorder and rapine. In order to deal with situations of this kind effectively, he appointed as his governor Messer Ramiro d'Orco, whom Machiavelli characterizes as "a swift and cruel man."[18] Within a relatively short time Don Ramiro had succeeded through his swiftness and cruelty in reducing "the country to peace and unity, thus acquiring the greatest reputation." At the same time, however, Ramiro created many enemies through his necessary use of open force. The result was that good-will—so essential for the prince—began to be lost by Caesare Borgia. What, then, did Caesare do? He wished it to be believed that it was not he, Caesare Borgia, who had instituted the excesses but rather his governor. Therefore, he ordered the murder of Ramiro in order to pacify the people.

Thus Caesare had accomplished two objectives: He had utilized an agent to wipe out by sheer physical force all the enemies of the prince and all the disorderly elements within the cities involved; and order having been attained by these necessary methods, the prince then proceeded to destroy his minister who in process of restoring order had antagonized other elements in the population. The prince himself had the best of everything, as it were: He wiped out his enemies through Ramiro and then gained prestige by murdering his own agent.

Humanity and Benevolence. But while fraud—and, in extraordinary circumstances, assassination and murder—may have to be employed, generosity and acts of kindness will always appeal to the human imagination and hence provide a more substantial base for the governor's power. Violence and ferocity are limited in what they can produce, however much they may be deemed essential in certain circumstances. Human beings are so constituted that, while wickedness is ever lurking beneath the surface, there is normally greater drawing power in what are generally thought of as good acts. At times, Machiavelli waxes eloquent on this theme:

> Provinces and cities which no armies and no engines of war, nor any other efforts of human power, could conquer, have yielded to an act of humanity, benevolence, chastity, or generosity.[19]

Machiavelli makes it clear, however, that in his view both love and fear may be used to move men. Hannibal's career is an example of the utilization of fear just as Scipio's reflects the employment of love. The key to whether either will be successful is, of course, whether the general or politician involved has developed a great reputation. Again and again Machiavelli stresses that in a person of prestige (however that status may have been acquired), much that might otherwise be disastrous may be excused. Thus, as in the careers of both Hannibal and Scipio, reputation "cancels all the errors which a general may commit, either by an excess of gentleness or by too great severity."[20]

In view of the distinction which some political writers appear to make between influence and power, it is instructive to note that Machiavelli apparently thinks of them as practically identical. He virtually uses the terms interchangeably. He is quite certain that in the subtle play of will on will, which he sees as central to politics, the key problem for the ruler is always one of appealing to the emotions, intelligence, and will of the ruled, so that the latter will be ready to do the things which are essential for the preservation of the state and its governor.

The Army and Political Objectives. In carrying out political objectives, a well-disciplined military force is essential and its careful employment by the politician is one of the marks of good Machiavellian statesmanship. The Florentine devotes much of his life to studying the army problem and reaches the conclusion that on the whole a popular militia, recruited from within the state, is the only force which can be trusted. He is bitter about the *condottiere* system of his day, whereby rulers rely mainly on hireling soldiers, whatever their origins. Hired forces offer only a tenuous basis for stable political power, as do foreign auxiliaries.[21] Just as the prince is stronger if he has a substantial foundation in popular consent, so is his necessary utilization of force likely to be the more effective if the militia is composed of natives. Machiavelli is almost passionate in his statement of the notion of a people's militia, seeing in ancient republican Rome the great example of the interrelationship between a people's force and the maintenance and expansion of the state. He thus anticipates much later development in military practice and foreshadows in his thought the development of modern military conscription.

The Impact of Machiavelli

The impact of Machiavelli on political practice and doctrine was significant in the sixteenth and seventeenth centuries and in our own day there has been an important revival of interest in the Florentine. During the sixteenth century, it is obvious that Italian rulers followed his advice in many particulars, either as a result of a study of his works or perhaps as a consequence of circumstances similar to those which had affected Machiavelli himself. And in France, sovereigns like Catherine de Medici were apt devotees of their countryman. The Massacre of St. Bartholomew's eve in 1572 is often cited as an excellent example of Machiavellianism in practice.

Several groups of writers, moreover, were influenced by Machiavelli and may be said to exemplify his spirit. Among them was his friend Francesco Guicciardini, who offered extensive commentaries on the meaning of his friend's work[22] and in his own treatment of politics[23] sought to draw out the implications of Machiavelli's theory.

Another sixteenth-century thinker in the Machiavellian mode was Paolo or Paul Paruta, whose *Perfection of Political Life* and *Political Discourses* deal respectively with philosophical and practical approaches to the study of politics. Paruta was a citizen of Venice and has been described by Janet[24] as the "master of Venetian politics." Like Machiavelli, he was in sharp revolt against many propositions of traditional Western political philosophy. At no point is this more evident than in his repudiation of the Thomist (and Aristotelian) notion that the contemplative is superior to the political life. He suggests, in opposition to the Thomist scheme of values, that the contemplator or philosopher is concerned only with the soul, whereas the active citizen or politicist is interested in the perfection of all man's faculties.[25]

We may cite yet another reflection of the Machiavellian spirit in the thought of Justus Lipsius, whose *Politics* was first published in 1590. Lipsius adopts a traditional attitude to the prince, prescribing for him a rigorous moral regimen and advising him to conduct himself in accordance with all the Christian virtues. Nothing could seem further from Machiavelli. But after he has gone to such great lengths in establishing a moral basis for rulership, he begins to ask himself questions as to whether the ruler can, in fact, measure up to those standards. After all, he remarks, we do not live in the *Republic* of Plato, but rather in a world where men are sometimes evil and designing. Under such circumstances, we must inquire whether the prince cannot, in some measure at least, use ruses and fraud in gaining his objectives. Lipsius then proceeds to analyze three degrees of fraud. In the first, or minimal, the essential note is dissimulation—the ruler does not murder, for example, or engage in other acts of violence. The middle range, by contrast, already smacks of vice—here corruption of various kinds is accepted as a means. In the most extreme kind of fraud, bad faith and positive injustice are countenanced. What will be the attitude of the political moralist to the three species? Lipsius' answer is that he advises the first, under certain circumstances; endures the second; but condemns the third. Venial sins, apparently, are to be permitted in politics, as a concession to human weakness and to public utility. But mortal sins can never be countenanced.[26]

18. *Prince*, ch. 7.
19. *Discourses*, III, 20, 472.
20. *Ibid.*, III, 21, 474.
21. *Prince*, ch. 12–14.
22. *Considerations relatives aux discours de Machiavel sur Tite-Live*, French ed., Paris: Saint Nicolas, 1869.
23. For example, *Del Reggimento di Frenze*, modern ed., Bari: G. Laterza & Figli, 1932. For a modern view of Guicciardini, see Vincent Luciani, *Francesco Guicciardini and His European Reputation*, New York: K. Otto, 1936.
24. Paul Janet, *Histoire de la Science Politique Ses Rapports avec la Morale*, vol. 1, p. 547. Paruta's works include *Discorsi politici*, modern ed., Bologna: N. Zanichelli, 1943, and *History of Venice and the Wars of Cyprus*, Henry, Earl of Monmouth, trans., London: A. Roper and H. Herringman, 1658. For his collected political works see *Opere Politiche di Paola Paruta*, Florence: F. Le Monnier, 1852.
25. One can, of course, question Paruta's interpretation of the classical tradition. Is there not an important distinction, for example, between Aristotle, who sees political activity as a prelude to the life of contemplation, and medieval Christianity, which moves in the direction of separation? And post-Machiavellian thought will attempt a complete separation.
26. Janet, *op. cit.*, p. 564. For a recent interpretation, see Jason L. Saunders, *Justus Lipsius: The Philosophy of Renaissance Stoicism*, New York: Liberal Arts Press, 1955. An early translation of Lipsius is that by W. Jones, *Sixe*

Guiccardini, Paruta, and Lipsius are, then, examples of sixteenth-century thinkers who in some measure and in varying degrees find themselves in agreement with Machiavelli, either in terms of the method which they use in studying politics or in the substance of their teaching.

In a measure, of course, men like Paruta and Lipsius might be counted as severe critics of Machiavelli, insofar as they appear to draw rigid lines with respect to the utilization of certain techniques and strategies in politics. But they could hardly be called anti-Machiavellian thinkers. The latter actually began to appear during the second half of the sixteenth century and almost every generation from then on to the end of the eighteenth century produced several pamphleteers who might best be described as anti-Machiavellian in tendency. As a matter of fact, anti-Machiavels became as much an integral part of political as lyric poetry did of general literature.

Here it will be possible to cite only a few instances of the vast outcry against the Florentine. One of the earliest tracts came from the pen of a Protestant, Innocent Gentillet, who about 1576 excoriated the St. Bartholomew's Massacre which had taken place four years before. He saw in the Massacre an exemplification of Machiavellian morals and politics and proceeded to denounce what he regarded as the theory of the *Prince*.[27]

In addition to Protestant attacks like that of Gentillet, the Jesuits were active in opposing Machiavellian doctrine. In the great movement of the Counter-Reformation, Catholic thinkers sometimes—and with considerable justification—linked certain political tendencies in Machiavelli with Luther's morals and politics. When they directed their shafts against the Florentine, therefore, they were not only criticizing the great antagonist of medievalism in morals and politics but were also undermining, in their view, the political position of the Lutherans. Antonio Possevino (1533–1611) in his attack on the *Prince*[28] is a good instance of that kind of Jesuitical writing which is rather poorly informed on Machiavelli's thought in general, the result being that the alleged refutation is greatly weakened.

In fact, one is impressed in general by the superficial level of much anti-Machiavellian thought. An example is the criticism of Antonio Bosio, who speaks for the papal court. In his two anti-Machiavels,[29] he attempts to show, for instance, that kings who adopt Machiavellian tactics are usually killed by their enemies and suffer from torments of soul.

Throughout the seventeenth and eighteenth centuries, bishops and temporal rulers vied with one another in repudiating the Florentine. Professing horror at his morals, most of them sought to show that Machiavelli was little better than a devil in human form. In fact, the term "old Nick" when used to refer to Satan is probably derived from Machiavelli's first name. In the eighteenth century, two hundred years of anti-Machiavellian treatises were climaxed when King Frederick the Great of Prussia wrote an anti-Machiavel which was noteworthy chiefly because its author was so adept a disciple of the Florentine.

The vehemence with which rulers, either formally or informally, criticized what was thought to be Machiavellian teaching is perhaps an indication of the degree to which the author of the *Prince* had succeeded in exposing the actual methods of ruling classes. In his descriptions of sixteenth-century techniques, as we have seen, he was supremely accurate in sketching the devices of men like Alexander VI, Caesare Borgia, Julius II, and the Medici themselves; and implicitly he was describing as well the ruling class of Venice, French rulers like Cardinal Richelieu and Louis XIV, and British kings like James I. No more than ruling classes of the nineteenth century did princes of the sixteenth and seventeenth appreciate exposure of their methods; and just as Marx stripped off the masks of the Victorian age so did Machiavelli expose the hypocrisy of an earlier epoch.

The Significance and Criticism of Machiavelli

Historically, the significance of Machiavelli is twofold. In the first place, by emphasizing the legitimacy of political study, as such, he helped lay the groundwork for such seventeenth-century inquiries as those of Hobbes, which were to be much more profound psychologically and philosophically than those of Machiavelli. Because he insisted that politics, like art, is an area which, in some measure at least, has its own regularities and patterns, he contributed mightily to that emancipation of science from ecclesiastical control which was to become so characteristic of the early modern age—and of the epoch which followed.

Secondly, however, he must be appreciated historically because he furnishes us with one of the best accounts of the nature of politics in an age when convention and law broke down and the individual was emancipated from many hitherto accepted restraints. Whether or not we adopt his moral and political generalizations as a whole, we can hardly deny that his insight into the politics of his time was remarkable. The man of the sixteenth century, says Machiavelli, had ceased to have roots; and because of this lack of anchorage, he found himself more able both to create and to destroy. His creativity sprang from the exhilaration he felt when he no longer deemed himself bound to the precedents of the immediate past; but his destructive capacity, too, arose from the same source. In both art and politics, the model was a man who ran roughshod over previous restraints in the quest for self-expression; and if in the process he ignored other values, public opinion—and even those whom he wiped out—would understand him. Just as Marx was later one to give us an admirable description of workers alienated from society at the outset of the era of industrialism, so does Machiavelli portray for us a political man who is much more than an abstraction—whose lineaments, in fact, are to be found in actual personages of sixteenth and seventeenth centuries.

But when we have acknowledged our historical debt to Machiavelli on these two scores, there still remains the most perplexing task of all—that of assessing the merits of his moral and political doctrine. And it is particularly with his moral and political theory as it pertains to the alleged exemption of the politician from ordinary standards that we must concern ourselves. While Machiavelli the methodologist can be criticized on many scores by the modern student of scientific procedures, it is far less certain that Machiavelli the political moralist can be legitimately subject to attack.

It is well to observe at the outset that, in greater or lesser degree, political leaders in every age have in fact followed Machiavelli's advice at many points and that, if criticized for doing so, they have resorted to Machiavelli's defense—namely, that the breach of morality was justified by the public interest. As a matter of historical fact, in other words, both ecclesiastical and nonecclesiastical governors have acted as if they believed that the "end justifies the means," assuming the end to be an often poorly defined "general welfare."

While this statement can be most dramatically and sharply illustrated in the realm of international relations, documentation can also be found in domestic politics. In the latter area, it is true, conventional and legal restraints often limit and soften the use of Machiavellian tactics; but the strategies and tactics still remain, nevertheless. As a matter of fact, the common use of military metaphors in the analysis of political life would seem to suggest a widespread belief that not only (in the words of Clausewitz) is warfare an extension of policy or politics but also that politics may be thought of as a kind of war; and just as wholesale deception and some deliberate destruction of life are accepted as legitimate in war (all is fair in love and war) so is there the belief, inarticulate though it may often be, that somehow one is justified in relaxing private morals in the life which resembles warfare.

Examples both of the practice of Machiavellianism and of its implicit or explicit intellectual defense are legion. Thus in the sixteenth century the King of Spain is known to have made several attempts on the life of Queen Elizabeth, despite the fact that he was a pious Catholic and presumably an ardent opponent of Machiavelli. During the reign of James I, an ambassador of that monarch, with only a touch of cynicism, defined a diplomat as one

---

Books of Politickes or Civil Doctrine . . . Which Do Especially Concerene Principalitie, London, 1594.

27. Note an early English version of Gentillet's treatise against Machiavelli, *A Discourse Upon the Means of Wel Governing and Maintaining in Good Peace a Kingdome, or Other Principalitie. Divided into Three Parts, Namely the Counsel, the Religion, and the Policie, which a Prince ought to Hold and Follow. Against Nicholas Machiavell, the Florentine*, Simon Patericke, trans., London: A. Islip, 1602. About the same time, of course, Shakespeare is referring to Machiavelli in *The Merry Wives of Windsor:* "Am I politic? Am I Subtle? Am I a Machiavel?" (Act III, Scene 1); in Henry VI, Pt. 1: "Alencon! That Notorious Machiavel!" (Act V, Scene 4); and in Henry VI, Pt. 3: "I can add colors to the chameleon, change shapes with Proteus for advantages, and set the murderous Machiavel to school." (Act III, Scene 2).

28. *Cautio de iis guae scripsit tum Machiavellus, tum is qui adversus eum scripsit Anti-Machiavellus* (1592).

29. *De robore bellico* (1594) and *De imperio virtutis* (1594).

who was sent abroad "to lie for his country." Double-talk is notoriously characteristic of many politicians, even in so-called democratic nations, where it is often defended on the ground that only by its use can the leader gain political power and hence do good for the community. A well-known American historian has maintained that during the year preceding the United States's entry into World War II, President Franklin D. Roosevelt "repeatedly deceived the American people"; but the historian goes on to defend these deceptions, on the ground that without them the nation might have been seriously injured or even destroyed.[30] Practically every American party convention, moreover, exhibits the viability of Machiavellian arts, even in a society which ostensibly repudiates them.

Why, we may well ask, do men appear to act so often as Machiavelli says they act? And is Machiavelli right in asserting that the ruler ought to conduct himself in accordance with Machiavellian maxims? If we assume that Machiavelli succeeded in describing men as they often do act politically but at the same time eschew Machiavellian maxims for politics, what alternative do we propose? In sum, how should we treat the relationship between morals and politics?

A key issue in discovering an answer to questions of this kind turns on what moral theologians in the Middle Ages called conscience and casuistry. Any general principle of conduct must be applied to specific instances and what the principle implies for a particular case will involve a weighing of many considerations (casuistry). There are many principles of conduct and sometimes it would appear that the observance of one necessitates the violation of another. In such an instance, one must be prepared to decide which moral principle takes precedence—which value has priority.

During World War II, for example, a Protestant pastor living in France rescued many Jews from the Nazis, secluding them in his attic. To prevent the police from being too curious, he drilled his children in deliberate lying: In response to questions from the police, they were to say that their father had no visitors. Their innocence, plus their ability to lie effectively in response to their father's training, possibly saved many a Jewish life. In one sense, the father, who preached the virtue of truth-telling in his sermons, was being Machiavellian. But he justified his actions on the ground that so far as he could see there was a conflict between the command to tell the truth and the command not to kill: had his children told the truth, they might have been guilty of cooperating in the execution of Jews. This illustrates vividly the difficulty of applying two or more general principles to particular cases.

Another problem should be noted in connection with the application of general principles. Inevitably, one must not only consider actions in themselves but must also weigh the probable consequences of given acts; and the prediction of consequences is notoriously difficult. In the case of the Protestant pastor, for example, his decision to lie depended partly on his conclusion that if he were to reveal the hiding place of the Jews they would probably be killed. But they might not have been killed. His violation of the commandment to tell the truth was grounded partly on his prediction (which might be mistaken) that if the Jews were discovered they would be killed. An act, in other words, must be considered not merely in itself and as related to a single moral principle; it must also be weighed in terms of its probable consequences and in relation to other principles which may be involved.

Now in part Machiavelli's alleged immorality can be accounted for in terms of his awareness of the conscience-casuistry problem. He saw with extraordinary vividness that while men might possess very high-sounding principles, the acid test would always come in the application of those principles to particular cases. The politician above all must be acutely aware of the difficulties involved, for upon his decisions depends the welfare of thousands. Although all men are confronted by the problems of casuistry and may by their decisions shape the fate of scores, political leaders are forced to consider the same issues and to make decisions which may affect the happiness of thousands or millions. Thus far, it would seem, we can agree with Machiavelli, and even applaud him.

When, however, he tells us that in his casuistry the politician must place the power of the state and his own power at the summit of his value hierarchy, we may well question exactly what Machiavelli means to imply. In the first place, he is not clear as to which should give way in the event of a conflict. Suppose that the power of the State requires that the ruling class or the prince surrender their power. In such an event, should the ruler give up his position in order to enhance that of the state or should he at all costs endeavor to maintain his own status even though he knows it may weaken that of the state?

If we assume for the moment that he implies state aggrandizement through a princely tyrant, then we might well and legitimately ask whether his prototype of the successful prince, Caesare Borgia, was really successful. Much depends, of course, on the exact connotations of success. If we recur for the moment, however, to the notion that political success means perpetuity in high status over a considerable period of time, then Caesare Borgia was hardly successful. He began the conquest of the Romagna, under a bull of Alexander VI, in 1499, completed it in 1501, and was expelled in 1504. Thus he enjoyed exactly three years of power.[31] After his overthrow, which was accomplished by means of methods which can only be termed Machiavellian (in the opprobrious sense of that term), he fled to Spain. There he took up service under the king of Navarre. He was killed by enemy action in 1507 only six years after his triumph in the Romagna.

It may be said, however, that while Caesare was unsuccessful in maintaining his power and life except for a fleeting moment, he at least established a state which had long endurance. But even this did not take place. His overthrow was accomplished by an alliance between Julius II and the petty tyrants whom Caesare had expelled. With the exile of the Borgias, the tyrants were restored and the consolidated state, which was to have been Caesare's pride, fell into ruins.

As a matter of fact, the career of Caesare Borgia, far from exemplifying either personal or political success—if by those terms we mean a long and full life and the enjoyment of political power in a relatively stable state—can best be used to illustrate the New Testament maxim, "They that take the sword shall perish by the sword."[32]

It is true, of course, that the case for Machiavellian political morality and tactics is not disproved because the methods failed so conspicuously in one instance. But since Machiavelli is so explicit in identifying Caesare Borgia as the model for his prince (while rather lamely explaining his downfall as the result of capricious fortune), it is surely legitimate to ask him whether he will be consistent and hold up the measure of Caesare's success as the standard for all political achievement.

The fact would seem to be that Machiavelli is

himself uncertain about the tactics for which he is so famous. He is torn between his belief that ultimately all stable poiltical authority must root in free consent and, on the other hand, his contention that one must be prepared to utilize tactics which imply deception, fraud, and violence. Basically, he appears to think he is saying that the latter—and particularly violence—are extraordinary remedies and that the former (consent) provides the foundations. But so impressed is he by the apparent need for making exceptions to ordinary rules that he often tends to make fraud and violence the central support for his tactics. Although Figgis is probably exaggerating in attributing to Machiavelli the tendency to make extraordinary remedies into ordinary rules, there is a measure of truth in his statement that "It is not the removal of restraints under extraordinary emergencies that is the fallacy of Machiavelli, it is the erection of his removal into an ordinary and every-day rule of action."[33] Perhaps it was precisely because Caesare Borgia did make ordinary rules of extraordinary remedies that he was so unsuccessful; for if authority is basically a matter of consent, as Machiavelli himself asserts, then any persistent utilization of fraud and violence—such as Machiavelli admired in Caesare Borgia—must weaken the foundations of authority.

But even if we grant, in our casuistry of political morality, that the maintenance of the state—whether in republican Rome, Renaissance Florence, or modern America—requires judicious mixtures of deliberate deception and violence (and, as we have seen, most rulers do, in fact, act as if this were true), we can criticize Machiavelli at a yet more fundamental level. He assumes throughout that the maintenance of the state is an end in itself (at least when he does not seem to be arguing that a

30. Thomas A. Bailey, *The Man in the Street*, New York: Macmillan, 1948, p. 11.
31. For a lively—and pro-Borgia—biography of Caesare Borgia, see Rafael Sabatini, *The Life of Caesare Borgia*, London: Stanley Paul, 1928. Frederic Rolfe's work, *The Borgias*—likewise a defense of the family—should also be consulted.
32. Matthew 26:52.
33. J. N. Figgis, *From Gerson to Grotius*, Cambridge: Cambridge University Press, 1956, pp. 76–77.

given ruler's power is the end). Whether he actually believes this or is simply treating it as an *as if* proposition is uncertain. Throughout, as we have seen, he takes pride in attempting to isolate politics from nonpolitical ends; and it may be that he is asserting that as a *politician* (rather than as a human being) one must consider maintenance of the state as the end. If this is his meaning, one can hold that he recognizes nonpolitical values but does not choose to relate them to what he identifies as political ends. On the other hand, he seems at times to maintain that man is *simply* political and that the profession of nonpolitical ends and values is itself a gigantic deception. If this is his position, then the proposition that the state is an end in itself becomes simply a statement of the only possible real end. At no point is Machiavelli more unsatisfactory than in his ambiguities with respect to this whole issue. And the question is clouded even more because we are never certain as to whether he is asserting that the state is in fact the end or whether it ought to be the end. Do men actually act as if it is the goal or *ought* they to make it the supreme goal?

We might summarize by suggesting that the net impression which Machiavelli leaves is one of a man who succeeded in describing rather vividly the actual political tendencies and methods of his own day and, in considerable degree, of politics in all ages. He saw that most men tend to become lost in the organization; that they often elevate what they proclaim to be means into their ends; that ruling classes do in fact mix deception, fraud, and violence with appeals for consent, claiming that only by so doing can they preserve either themselves or the organization; and that most men, particularly when in positions of status or power, make professions about their conduct which they tend to disregard in practice. Insofar as he purports to be describing politics as they are practiced, Machiavelli is extraordinarily acute and his observations seem to be supported by much historical experience and by direct observation of the contemporary world.

On the other hand, one is frequently uncertain as to whether he is describing the *ought* or the *is*. He is unclear with respect to the objective of his ruler: should the politician seek primarily to enhance and preserve his own power or is his primary objective the maintenance of the state? While Machiavelli clearly thinks that ruling classes must be prepared to combine fraud and violence with appeals for consent, his employment of Caesare Borgia as a model for princes is an unfortunate one; for even if we accept the notion that political power and preservation of the state are ends in themselves, Borgia's use of Machiavellian methods gave him personally only three years of power and ensured the existence of his state for a similarly brief period.

In the end, Machiavelli is seen to be not a profound political thinker but rather a fairly perspicacious journalistic observer of practical politics. His ambiguities and lack of interest in epistemological and moral questions keep him from great profundity of thought; while his capacity and concern for close examination of day to day events makes him somewhat like an early modern newspaperman. Immediate success seems to dazzle him, whether in the killing of Remus by Romulus or the clever assassination of his enemies by Caesare Borgia. But he does not ask himself whether the assassination of Remus was really necessary and what role it and later similar events might have played in the ultimate moral and political deterioration of the Roman people. Nor does he seriously consider the notion that some acts—that of the deliberate killing of a human being, for example—may be morally wrong in themselves.

One reason for his making politics so much a matter of force, violence, and deceit is that he sees the individual of his own day as emancipated from organic relations with his fellows with the result that some men think of themselves as free from all restraints in the pursuit of power while others—the overwhelming majority—tend to be apathetic, alienated, and without civic spirit. One of Machiavelli's political ideals is the unification of Italy, which he despairs of bringing about with the kinds of men he believes are predominant. But we might interpret him as thinking that, given the corrupt nature of most human beings as he observes them, there may be some possibility of unifying Italy if only one can employ the violence and deceit particularly appropriate for a state of degeneration. After all, he sees rulers all about him acting in this way; we may imagine him asking why, if they can utilize methods of this kind for their ends, Italian patriots might not do the same for quite different purposes. To be sure, this interpretation is not without its difficulties. But it is at least worth considering.

Meanwhile, as Machiavelli contemplates the

decline of the medieval community, the rise of the self-centered individual, and what he regards as the low state of man, the Reformation is being born in the North. Many of the Reformers will reach conclusions about human beings and politics not dissimilar to those of Machiavelli. But they will frame their judgments in religious terms and their accent on the individual will be Augustinian in flavor. It may seem startling to bracket Machiavelli with Luther. Yet such an association, if not pushed too far, can be supported in certain respects. As the next chapter will suggest, political ideas of the Renaissance, insofar as they are reflected in Machiavelli, have an affinity with many of those characteristic of the Reformation.

chapter 17

Politics and Morals in the Early Sixteenth Century Reformation

While Machiavelli was seeking to emancipate the study of politics from morals and theology, the fires of the Protestant Reformation were beginning to burn in Germany. A little later they were to be seen in France and Switzerland and eventually the whole of Christendom was to be set aflame.

For the most part, though with some exceptions, problems of politics were matters of secondary consideration in the minds of the reformers. Eventually, however, they were forced to come to grips with them if only because the development of the Reformation itself seemed to be so dependent on the favor of secular princes. Throughout the sixteenth century, religious considerations continued to retain their central place in political discussion, despite Machiavelli's endeavor to shunt them aside.

But it would be a serious mistake to think of the sixteenth-century Reformation as having a uniform political doctrine and ideology. Indeed, the longer one studies it, the more dubious do sweeping generalizations about it appear to be. There were many currents and counter-currents of social and political thought within its ample stream. Here we shall be concerned with Lutheranism, Calvinism, and what might be called the Heterodox Protestantism of the Anabaptists. These tendencies, in turn, must be seen against the background of the Catholic Counter-Reformation, developed to counteract the great revolt and reflected in such movements as the Society of Jesus (Jesuits, 1534) and the great Council of Trent (1545–1563).

Lutheranism: The Two Kingdoms

The life of Luther itself epitomized the late medieval struggles taking place in both ecclesiastical and civil society. Born in 1483 in

Saxony, his father was a worker in the copper mines of that region. He attended the University at Erfurt, studied the Latin classics, and in 1502 was awarded his A.B. degree. By 1505 he had earned his Master's degree.

As in the case of St. Thomas Aquinas, his parents hoped that he would study law, for with the rapid development of commerce and the growth of town life, the legal profession was becoming more and more lucrative. Luther, however, was apparently never strongly attracted by the law. When on a journey by foot, he was struck to the ground, seemingly by a bolt of lightning, he resolved that if God should spare him he would enter a monastery. This he did in 1505. He became an Augustinian and in 1507 was ordained to the priesthood.

He rose rapidly in the Augustinian Order, apparently possessing administrative talents of considerable proportions. After having become a teacher of philosophy at the University of Wittenberg in 1508, he was sent to Rome in 1511 on business for the Augustinians. It was the Rome of Julius II, and Lutheran tradition has handed down many anecdotes turning on Luther's disgust at what he saw during his sojourn there. Julius himself was, of course, a notoriously worldly man, being more fond of the sword than of the Scriptures; and the Rome of his day was hardly noted either for purity of morals or for incorruptibility in politics. All this Luther soon comprehended.

After completing his business, he returned to Wittenberg and in 1512 was made a Doctor of Theology. Meanwhile, he had begun to lecture on the Scriptures. He relied heavily at first on late medieval nominalist views but from those eventually turned to Augustine and then—as was perhaps inevitable in anyone studying Augustine closely—to Paul. It was no doubt this reexamination of St. Paul which initiated the train of thought that was eventually to result in Luther's great stress on faith rather than works.

It was the appearance of Tetzel, a Dominican monk, in Germany which launched Luther on his career of reform. Tetzel, it will be remembered, sold indulgences in order to raise funds for Pope Leo X, who was hard pressed to find enough money for the construction of St. Peter's Basilica. Luther was not alone in regarding the doctrine of indulgences, as popularly understood and as accepted by the popes for their purposes, as antagonistic to the faith. But he was unique in that he dared to attack publicly the popular and papal interpretation. At first, indeed, he sought to protest through regular ecclesiastical channels. When this failed, however, he published the Ninety-five Theses, which may be said to have launched the Reformation.

Luther's public career now began, and with it his involvement in early sixteenth-century politics. After the Ninety-five Theses were published, John Eck sought to answer them. Luther thereupon engaged in a series of debates with Eck and the more he sought to defend his original position, the more radical he became.

In 1520, he published three treatises which laid much of the groundwork for early Reformation thought—the *Appeal to the Christian Nobility; The Babylonian Captivity;* and *The Liberty of the Christian Man.* In the same year he was excommunicated. When the bull of excommunication arrived in Wittenberg, he burned it publicly before a group of students, thus indicating that he was not afraid to cut off his ties with the ancient household of the faith.

Luther's attack on the papacy and on the sacramental system was a heart-thrust at the whole medieval system of religious and political organization. If the Universal Church were no longer needed for administration of the sacraments, as Luther implied, the pope would cease to have that power over princes which was so crucial for the political position of the Church.

The interrelationship between Luther's religious views and the politics of the Empire is shown by the fact that he was summoned to appear, not before the pope, but rather before the Imperial Diet which met at Worms in 1521. There he was subjected to sharp questioning by the ecclesiastical and civil rulers and it was there that he refused to recant.[1]

For the last twenty-five years of his life, Luther was unable to avoid political entanglements of various kinds. The result was that he was impelled to make political pronouncements more frequently than he might have liked, particularly at the time of the Peasants' Revolt in 1525. By the time of his death in 1546, his ties to the world of power relations had become complex indeed.[2]

Luther's Religious Position in General. Since Luther's political and social outlook is so firmly anchored in his religious views, some recapitulation of those ideas would seem to be essential. It may be suggested that they involve the finality of the Bible as an authority in religious matters; the doctrine of justification by faith alone; and the uselessness of external force as a method of keeping men true to the Faith.

1. The Finality of the Bible. Luther thinks of his revolt against Rome as a restoration of true Christianity. The Faith, he believes, has been perverted and corrupted by medieval developments, so that it is not he who is departing from the fold of Christ, but rather the medieval Church.

The central error of Catholicism in departing from Christianity, he believes, has been that of substituting the authority of men—popes, councils, and the Church—for the final authority of the Word of God. It is in Scripture alone that one will find salvation and not in ecclesiastical tradition, canon law, or the decrees of popes. Luther's call is one which bids men to restore Scripture as the standard of religious belief and practice.[3]

In taking this position he repudiates not only the Catholic view that the Church is the primary vehicle for revelation but also any attitude which would establish human reason as the final authority. He sees the old Church as teaching that Scripture is the product of the Church, rather than the direct and presumably self-evident revelation of God.

But it is equally important to remember that Luther, in exalting Scripture, is also repudiating any high place for human reason. One of his objections to scholasticism is that it has a too great confidence in man's capacity through reason to attain religious truth. It seeks to substitute the human mind for God's infallible revelation as stated in Scripture. Thus shortly before his death we find him writing: "Human reason disgraces and insults God. . . . Therefore reason is, in kind and in nature, a ruinous prostitute. . . . See to it, then, that you bridle reason and do not follow her pretty notions. . . ."[4]

To be sure, we should be wary of always taking Luther at face value, particularly when he attacks reason in such terms as "You cursed harlot."[5] At times, he is undoubtedly using hyperbole. Moreover, it may be argued that while he attacks reason in the realm of religion, he supports it in some degree in the social and political realm.

His repudiation of the Church would seem, on the surface, to lead to the finality of individual, as against collective or corporate authority. But his equally emphatic denigration of reason bars this at-first-sight plausible interpretation. In the main, then, Luther appears to think that the Scriptures as the Word of God are self-interpreting—they require neither the experts of the Church nor the corrupt logic and critical capacity of private laymen to explicate their meaning.

Yet curiously enough he is vehement against those who adopt a literalistic interpretation of the Bible, appearing to think that their alleged errors are obvious. Thus some of the Anabaptists of his day interpret the New Testament admonition to "become as little children,"[6] as requiring them to shout for joy and dance in the streets as urchins might do. But Luther treats such acts with scorn. Other literalists maintain that the passage which tells men to "preach . . . upon the housetops"[7] requires exactly that. Again, Luther believes that such views are absurd.

Absurd or not, however, the critic might well point out that in viewing them in this light, Luther is himself using some canon of human reason, which he at other points purports to criticize. How, without employing reason, do we know that the literalistic interpretation is wrong?

This apparent inconsistency in his religious views will, of course, find a parallel in his political outlook and, indeed, it is his later doubt

1. His words before the Diet, "Here I stand," are taken over by Roland Bainton as the title for one of the best-known modern treatments of Luther, *Here I Stand: A Life of Martin Luther*, New York: New American Library, 1962.
2. Although never a systematic political thinker, he had much to say about government in general, for references to this subject alone take up six large columns in the index volume attached to the St. Louis–Walch edition of his works. *Dr. Martin Luther's Saemmtliche Schriften*, 25 vols., Herausgegeben von Dr. Joh. Georg Walch, Neue revidierte Stereotypausgabe, St. Louis: Concordia Publishing House, 1881–1910.
3. Preserved Smith and Charles M. Jacobs, *Luther's Correspondence and Other Contemporary Letters*, 2 vols., Philadelphia: Lutheran Publication Society, 1913–1918, vol. 1, p. 158.
4. *Dr. Martin Luther's Saemmtliche Werke*, 67 vols., Nach den ealtesten Ausgaben kritisch und historisch bearbeitet von Dr. Johann Konrad Irmischer, Erlangen: Heyder, 1826–1854, Vol. 16, pp. 143–145, includes the full quotation.
5. Ewald M. Plass, *This is Luther*, St. Louis: Concordia Publishing House, 1948, p. 42, n. 5.
6. Matthew 18:3.
7. Matthew 10:27.

that the "Word" is in fact self-evident, which will be partly responsible for his exaltation of the state.

2. Justification by Faith. Because the revival of Aristotle had once more given men faith in human rationality (a confidence which had been greatly shaken by Fathers like St. Augustine), scholastic interpretations had tended to stress what man could do through his characteristically human attribute—reason. Late medieval Catholic and Thomas-like doctrine, therefore, was informed by an outlook which stressed the potentialities of men for good works, both in the personal and in the political realm. Grace would complete the work which reason began and the ethic to be discovered by reason in natural law would be rounded out and supplemented by God's superrational and supernatural revelation.

To Luther, however, impressed as he is by the Pauline Epistles as well as by the teachings of St. Augustine, the whole spirit of scholasticism does violence to the view of that final authority—Holy Writ. There man is seen to be, he says, a miserable sinner whose reason has been corrupted by the Fall and the deliverances of whose conscience in ethical matters are equally tainted. If salvation for this creature is at all a possibility—and Scripture clearly teaches us that it is indeed available—then it is to be attained solely through the grace of God given freely to men of faith. If a man is saved it is completely the action of the Holy Spirit which applies the redeeming power of Christ; if, on the contrary, a man is lost, this is to be attributed to his own recalcitrance in resisting the offer of grace.

There is, of course, much more to the doctrine of justification by faith than this statement might suggest, but it is sufficient to indicate the radical difference in outlook between Luther, and, for example, a thinker like St. Thomas. Luther's sharp separation between the inner and the outer life of man is one of the many manifestations of early modern individualism, the stress here being on the subjective holiness associated with inner faith rather than with the outer alleged holiness of works.[8]

3. Christian Faith and the Use of Physical Force. His religious individualism as well as the doctrine of justification by faith make him antagonistic to the employment of physical force. It is impossible, he argues, to change the inward attitude through the use of outward force. The burning of heretics, as heretics, he holds to be utterly contradictory to the Christian Faith. "I condemn masses held as sacrifices and good works," he states at one point, "but I would not lay hands on those who are unwilling to give them up or on those who are doubtful about them, nor would I prevent them by force. I condemn by word only. . . ."[9]

But it should also be noted that there are ambiguities in Luther's attitude. Suppose that unorthodox belief should affect the civil peace, for instance. Or imagine a situation in which resistance to the civil power is taught in the name of religion. What will be his attitude then?

Politics and the Two Realms.[10] Luther's reading of Scripture and particularly the doctrine of justification by faith lead him to conclude that the realm of grace is a fellowship of pure love, untrammeled by external law and, of course, immune from the use of physical force. Among those who are saved and justified by faith and through grace, in other words, the social bond is purely spiritual.

But not all men are justified—and, indeed, as Luther looks out upon the world, he sees little probability that they will ever be. Because of the blighting effects of sin, Scripture tells us, most men need to be governed by external threats and directed by the prince to some kind of earthly felicity. The state is an institution made necessary by sin and at the same time it attempts coercively to combat the effects of sin. Unjustified men are thus governed by the external state for their own temporal good, while the governance of those who are justified and sanctified has become purely a matter of inward control acting under an unlimited love.

Thus Luther launches his celebrated theory of the two realms—the one of grace and the other of power; the one associated with the fellowship of believers, the other established to correct and chastise unbelievers; the one having no punishments, the other permitting even the most cruel scourgings; the one observing the Sermon on the Mount, the other subjected to the harsh laws of Moses; the one a restoration of the innocence characteristic of Eden, the other an exemplification of the awful consequences of the Fall. We see in Luther's general doctrine an obvious return to certain Augustinian views of politics; Thomist-Aristotelian conceptions which would see the state as natural are now superseded by a position which views it once more as the fruit of sin and thus to be sustained only in relation to this fact.

Luther on the State. Because of Luther's deep conviction that the state is to be regarded—in the light of Scripture—as primarily an agency of chastisement and the administration of physical force, it is not surprising to find him describing political life as that which in essence is symbolized by the hangman. Nor are we astonished to learn that he thinks of God as ordaining political institutions: They are as much an expression of divinity as the kingdom of grace and the fellowship of love. Government, he avers, is to be subject to few scruples for it is dealing with sinful men who are essentially rebels against God.

He contrasts his view with that which he attributes to medieval rulers, whom he sees as under the influence of pernicious doctrines which have too much confidence in human reason and natural law. Those rulers, however, confused public with private morality and thought that the prince must be subject to the same self-restraint which governed Christians in their interpersonal relations:

> Of old, under the Papacy, princes and lords, and all judges, were very timid in shedding blood. . . . The executioner had always to do penance, and to apologize beforehand to the convicted criminal for what he was going to do to him, just as if it was sinful and wrong. . . . Thus they were persuaded by monks to be gracious, indulgent, and peaceable. But authorities, princes and lords ought not to be merciful.[11]

The Christian and the State. One of the problems posed by Luther's seemingly sharp dichotomy between the kingdom of grace and the realm of power is, of course, whether the justified and sanctified Christian can legitimately serve the prince who utilizes hanging, drawing and quartering, and many other methods—including, presumably, deceit and fraud—which would appear to be clearly incompatible with those exalted by the Sermon on the Mount. Luther's answer is, on the whole, clear; although, as we shall see, his attitude to the problem of obedience changes somewhat during the latter part of his life. In general, however, he rejects the idea that the Christian can or should withdraw from the state because of its methods. If God has established the state for the chastisement of sinners, then it is the obligation of Christians to assist the ruler in this task.

Luther would thus seem to require of the Christian one standard of morality in private relations and another in public or official roles. A prince, for example, who claims to be sanctified and justified would act vis-à-vis his family, friends, and neighbors in a forgiving way which would be uncalculating and spontaneous. He would not seek to aggrandize himself nor would he be constantly insisting on his rights as against his neighbors. In his role as prince, however, he could, if necessary, completely discard these principles of the Sermon on the Mount and would be governed by few scruples other than those which serve the interests of his divinely established power over his subjects.

Similarly, the Christian subject must have few if any scruples about obeying commands of the prince. Again, in his purely private relations with other Christians he presumably will be governed by the Sermon on the Mount. In his attitude to law and rulership, however, he must be controlled by the necessities of a world in which most men are not justified and sanctified and therefore must be kept in order by the sword. Hence if the ruler commands him to execute a criminal, he will not see in it any violation of the New Testament admonition to forgive one's enemies. If he is required to break a criminal on the wheel and witness his death agonies, he must not complain that the act is un-Christian provided that the ruler has clearly ordered him to preside at the execution.[12]

As Reinhold Niebuhr has put Luther's posi-

8. Note Smith and Jacobs, *op. cit.*, vol. 1, p. 43.
9. *Ibid.*, vol. 2, p. 110.
10. For a more extensive analysis of Luther's political theory, see Luther H. Waring, *The Political Theories of Martin Luther*, New York and London: Putnam, 1910. This work, of course, was written before the recent wave of critical Luther scholarship. For a more recent treatment, see George Wolfgang Farrell, *Faith Active in Love: An Investigation of the Principles Underlying Luther's Social Ethics*, New York: American Press, 1954.
11. *Table-Talk*, edited with an introduction by Thomas S. Kepler, New York: World Publishing, 1952.
12. See *Commentary on St. Paul's Epistle to the Galatians*, Erasmus Middleton, trans., London: B. Blake, 1832.

tion: "He places a perfectionist private ethic in juxtaposition to a realistic, not to say cynical, official ethic."[13] In so doing, we might add, he appears to be developing a teaching—within a radically different context, of course—not unlike that which Machiavelli seems to offer in the *Prince*. But whereas Machiavelli carefully excludes the blessing of God from his public ethic, Luther obviously associates the deity with the sanctification of his own political morality.

The Problem of Obedience. In a sense, we have already suggested Luther's view of obedience and political obligation. Given his analysis of the two realms and of the Christian's relation to them, it would seem that he can offer no possibility for any kind of active resistance.

In 1523, Luther expresses his general position in a treatise called *Secular Authority, to What Extent It Should be Obeyed*. Here he reiterates his view of the sacred character of all temporal rule and vindicates the view that the prince's authority should be free from any ecclesiastical control. Men are to obey the prince because, as Paul had said, the ruler has been appointed by God to correct the wicked and to encourage goodness.

Yet we should beware of making Luther an advocate of passive obedience. He still gives credence to the medieval view that all man-made law binds the individual only to the degree that it is not in violation of God's will as reflected in Scripture or contradictory to the divine insight (Luther even uses the medieval term *Naturlich Recht*) embodied in man's conscience. At this point, evidently, the reason which he so often excoriates in dealing with religious subjects can be a guide. If there is indeed a conflict between God's will and imperial or customary law, the subject is justified in refusing obedience to the latter, even though, as a leading student of Luther's thought puts it, "active resistance is forbidden in all cases."[14] Luther does not suggest the possibility of organized passive resistance.

Two years after the publication of his *Secular Authority*, his general attitude to the state and the social order is put to the test in the great Peasants' Revolt. Restlessness among serfs, as we have seen, was endemic throughout the latter part of the Middle Ages, so that the efforts of German peasants to better their lot in 1525 were by no means unique. The unusual factor in 1525 is that Luther's words in the *Liberty of the Christian Man* and elsewhere could be and are interpreted by many as implying not only emancipation in a religious sense but also freedom from traditional social and political restrictions. Like the quasi-anarchists in the early Church,[15] who thought St. Paul's theory of spiritual freedom in Christ implied that all moral and legal restrictions were abolished, some peasant leaders in Luther's day hold that the Reformer's emphasis on inner freedom means enlarged social liberty as well. This viewpoint is certainly characteristic, as we shall see, of several Anabaptists, and it is implied in the words of a peasant leader to Luther after the Revolt has begun:

> You called all the bishops who would not follow your teaching, idolatrous priests, and ministers of the devil. . . . You called those, "dear children of God and true Christians," who make every effort for the destruction of the bishoprics and the extermination of episcopal rule. You said also that whoever obeyed the bishops was the devil's own servant.[16]

But this is far from Luther's interpretation and during the Peasants' Revolt he reveals not only his insistence on virtually unconditional obedience to the powers that be but also his feeling (for it seems to have represented a real upsurge of emotion) that the ruling princes should be ruthless in the methods they use to secure obedience. In the very year of the war he writes to his friend Nikolaus Amsdorf: "My opinion is that it is better all the peasants be killed than that the magistrates and princes perish, because the peasants took the sword without divine authority. . . . Even if the princes of the world go too far, nevertheless they bear the sword by God's authority. . . . Therefore no pity, no patience, is due the peasants. . . ."[17]

Besides indicating his view that neither active resistance nor revolt are ever justified and that princes must use the sword almost without limit, his attitude to the peasant uprising is an excellent illustration of the two realms theory. At no point during the entire rebellion do we find Luther appealing to the ruling classes in the name of Christian charity or love.

But there is another side to Luther which cannot be ignored and its very existence indicates the complexity of his attitude to politics. While he advocates ruthlessness during the Revolt itself, he is not unaware that government cannot attain any great stability if it relies primarily on threat of physical force. Once the rebellion is crushed and its leaders have been horribly done to death, he appears to take the position that the ruling classes should make some concessions for the sake of harmony and their own continued existence. Here he seems to approach Machiavelli's keen awareness of the need for at least some degree of consent, although, unlike the Florentine, he does not elaborate the method whereby that consent is to be obtained.

Despite this apparent concession to the view that government is based on a kind of consent (whether inner or manipulated from the outside), Luther does not propose concessions before the rebellion is crushed, but only afterwards. Moreover, he appears to advocate reasonableness not primarily because he believes there is some justice in the demands of the peasant leaders but rather because he thinks that the perpetuity of the governing class requires some concessions.[18]

But scholars are by no means agreed about the place they assign to Luther with respect to the Revolt. Some, like McGiffert, hold that he played hardly any role politically and that he is to be exculpated from any share in the brutality of the ruling classes.[19] Others—Grisar, for example[20]—take a kind of middle position, emphasizing his confusions and complexities but by no means excusing him. Still others, notably MacKinnon, cite the words of Luther himself, long after the Revolt: "It was I, Martin Luther, who slew all the peasants during the rising, for I commanded them to be slaughtered."[21]

At a minimum, we might perhaps conclude, Luther is far more disturbed by the active and violent resistance of citizens seeking justice than he is by the equally active and violent repression of rulers endeavoring to preserve their privileges and the status quo.

Although Luther's over-all and basic position with respect to the problem of obedience does not change, it appears that after 1530 he does begin to make some concessions to the view that organized and passive resistance by the princes of the Empire may be permissible. Before 1530, he apparently holds that even if the emperor has taken a coronation oath to observe certain laws which he later violates, the subordinate princes (not to speak of ordinary subjects) have no recourse but to pray to God. The Supreme Authority—the *Obrigkeit*, in Luther's terms—must be obeyed even when it is clearly violating the law of the Empire.

After 1530, however, his conception of the duty to obey is modified in that he begins to

maintain that if there is an imperial law which permits princes and cities to resist or disobey the emperor, they may legitimately do so. But he tends even then to shift the responsibility for giving such advice to the jurists, who presumably know whether there is a law of this kind. Apparently, too, he thinks of the legal right to disobey as attaching only to corporate bodies of various kinds—free cities, for example, princes of the empire, or the electors who under law (if the jurists are right) may even depose the emperor.[22]

When one confronts the task of summarizing Luther's views on political obligation, obedience, and resistance, his own uncertainties and ambiguities must play a large role in the analysis. Although he apparently retains a few medieval notions of natural law and certainly maintains that in a clear conflict between

13. *The Nature and Destiny of Man*, vol. 2, New York: Scribner's, 1943, p. 194.
14. J. W. Allen, *A History of Political Thought in the Sixteenth Century*, 2nd ed., London: Methuen, 1941, p. 27.
15. See p. 154.
16. Quoted by Hartmann Griesar, S.J., *Martin Luther, His Life and Works*, Westminster, Md.: Newman Press, 1960, p. 190.
17. Smith and Jacobs, *op. cit.*, vol. 2, p. 320.
18. For a modern Marxist interpretation of the Peasants' Revolt, see Frederick Engels, *The Peasant War in Germany*, with introduction and appendix by the Institute of Marxism-Leninism, Moscow: Foreign Languages Publishing House, 1956. In general, the Marxist view sees the revolt as of great significance for the class interpretation of history.
19. Arthur C. McGiffert, *Martin Luther: The Man and His Work*, New York: Century, 1912, p. 294.
20. Hartmann Grisar, *op. cit.*
21. Quoted by James MacKinnon, *Luther and the Reformation*, vol. 3, London: Longmans, Green, 1929, p. 209.
22. J. W. Allen thus characterizes Luther's attitude in the letter: "Passive resistance, if resorted to by any large proportion of subjects, would leave any government powerless." *Op. cit.*, p. 27. Apparently Luther is suggesting that without the assistance of the princes, the emperor cannot possibly stand up against thousands of subjects who are thus encouraged by the recalcitrance of their immediate rulers. We must remember, of course, that the emperor must for all practical purposes rely on the cooperation of the princes for any effective action.

Scripture and human law, the subject must obey the former, he is at the same time very loath to challenge any established temporal authority. By and large, he does not ask to see the credentials of a temporal ruler, but seems to assume that the mere fact of widespread acquiescence or successful imposition of rule will confer moral legitimacy.[23] Nor does his post-1530 attitude alter this evaluation substantially.

Thus while the predominant German Lutheran tradition down to recent times may be at fault when it fails to note Luther's hostages to medieval views, it is surely not far wrong when it attributes to Luther a strong tendency to emphasize passive obedience as well as a significant stress on preserving the state-protected economic status quo.

Church and State. Just as Luther's treatment of political obligation tends to leave us rather puzzled in many respects, so does his examination of the relationship between Church and state.

Much of his difficulty in this respect stems from his theory of the Church itself. If one takes his writings at the beginning of the great revolt as the basis for an interpretation, one must reach the conclusion that the objective or empirical Church has lost its significance for Luther. The Word of God as revealed in Scripture will liberate men from the necessity of any coercive ecclesiastical structure like that of the Middle Ages. This seems to be what Luther is saying at the outset of his career. And some of his statements imply that any ecclesiastical organization whatsoever may be unnecessary and perhaps even unscriptural.

From the beginning, of course, he is confronted by those who seek to carry out his doctrine of inner freedom to what they regard as its logical conclusion in the emancipation of the individual not merely from traditional political restrictions but also from authoritative church control. Some of these enthusiasts, as Luther calls them, are essentially mystical and think that when the Reformer speaks of the Word he means what Quakers are later to call the inner light. Interpreted in this way, the Word becomes something which each individual man can gain through his own religious experience, not only in the absence of the Church but also without Scripture (at least Scripture viewed as the final authority). To Luther, however, such views disregard what he conceives to be the truth: Namely, that the Word is reflected in the Scripture.

As the enthusiasts—who include both Anabaptists and others—grow in strength, fortifying themselves with what they regard as good Lutheran doctrine, Luther becomes alarmed. He apparently hopes in the beginning that the mere preaching of the Word as revealed in Scripture will restore the purity of original Christianity while yet not leading to warring sectarian groups. If the Word is one, he believes, it will make itself manifest in a generally perfect agreement among Christians.

But as he witnesses the disturbances connected with Anabaptism and the enthusiasts' interpretation of Scripture, his uncertainty increases as to whether the Church can dispense with some kind of external ordering. At one point he exclaims: "Out of the Gospel and divine truth come devilish lies . . . from the blood in our body comes corruption; out of Luther come Müntzer, and rebels, Anabaptists, Sacramentarians, and false brethren."[24]

Although he might conceivably have become a sectarian, given some of his early language, this would have violated his conviction that the Word is one and would, moreover, have sanctioned all kinds of civil disturbances in the name of an unscriptural religion. At the same time, he cannot bring himself to reinvest the Church itself with the kind of coercive power against which he protested when he revolted against Rome. Where, then, will he find the legitimate coercion which can prevent distortions of the Word and preserve society from the disorder that Luther thinks is engendered when diverse interpretations of the Scripture are publicized? The answer, he thinks, is to be found in the use of the state to promote the faith—or at least in the utilization of its machinery to prevent order-disturbing promulgations of false (that is, unscriptural) faiths.

This would seem to lead, of course, back to the medieval notion that contumacious heretics ought to be killed for their own good as well as the good of society. Yet we have already quoted Luther as repudiating the idea of temporal punishment for unorthodox religious ideas. Now, in giving the state authority to promote the faith through coercion, he would appear to be running counter to his statement that it is impossible to convert to the Word through external force. Does this mean that Luther is to be charged with a glaring inconsistency or at least an ambiguity?

The answer to this question may be found in part if we refer to specific functions which he assigns to the state. He holds, for example, that the public espousal of any religious principles which question the legitimacy of rulership or of traditional social obligations can be suppressed by the state on the ground that such attitudes subvert the civil order itself.[25]

This viewpoint is perhaps understandable, particularly when we remember that Luther is writing in the early part of the sixteenth century; for after all most men of that time still believe that there is a direct connection between what a man says he believes and how he is likely to act. He is simply saying, then, that government should suppress rebellion and disorder by prosecuting the promulgation of doctrines which he thinks are likely to lead to civil strife.

But he then proceeds to go much further than this and argues that it is also the duty of the prince to prosecute those who deny the major propositions of the creed. Here he clearly exemplifies his contention that some religious doctrines are so obviously true (scriptural) that for the prince to allow a public attack on them would mean that the ruler himself is defying the God from whom he obtains his authority.

In views of this kind, Luther appears to be going far beyond the needs of civil order, even if we assume that the utterance of certain kinds of doctrines might indeed lead directly to disorder. It is difficult to see how a denial that Christ died for our sins (a proposition of the creed) could impair public order, for example; nor can modern minds quite see that those who question whether the dead survive are incipient rebels against the prince. Indeed, Luther himself appears to admit that in instances of this kind the government prosecutes not to preserve order but rather to establish that minimum of outward religious conformity which apparently the preaching of the Word is unable to effect but which is nevertheless required by Scripture.

Luther knows that many will assert a conflict between his proclamation that none shall be forced to believe and his constant refrain that the state should punish blasphemy. He asserts however, that there is no such conflict: "By this procedure no one is compelled to believe, for he can still believe what he will; but he is forbidden to teach and blaspheme."[26] At no point in his whole doctrine is his sharp dichotomy between the inner and the outer more manifest; and it is difficult to see how, given this distinction, the government would find any limits whatsoever placed on its authority to suppress expression of allegedly false religious doctrine.[27]

Gradually, then, as Luther comes to think of the state as guardian of the Faith—at least in its public manifestations—he tends to associate faith with his particular version of it.

The result of this concern that the state foster the Faith is that Luther tends to deny civil rights to those who do not hold what he thinks are the true beliefs. At the same time, an unorthodox ruler would presumably have little authority over his orthodox subjects. On the other hand, it is difficult to see what limits Luther could or would put on the authority of an orthodox prince ruling over orthodox subjects—he would be virtually a despot. Whether Luther intended this result or not, it is certainly a plausible outcome of his teaching.

The Impact and Significance of Luther's Political Thought. As might be expected, the general impact of Luther's political ideas on

23. Although it has no direct bearing on the validity of Luther's moral and political position, it is of some interest to note that certain modern scholars trace his extreme fearfulness and social conservatism to traumatic events in his early life. See, for example, Erik H. Erikson, *Young Man Luther*, New York: W. W. Norton, 1958. Erikson suggests that Luther's particular relations with his mother and father played an important role in his subsequent intellectual development.
24. Ernst Troeltsch, *The Social Teaching of the Christian Churches*, vol. 2, p. 492. The "Twelve Articles of the Peasants of Swabia," in which the peasants demanded the liberty to preach the Gospel and the right of congregations to choose their own pastors, constitute a cloak of religion, according to Luther, for what are really revolutionary activities. See MacKinnon, *op. cit.*, vol. 3, pp. 191–192.
25. *Works of Martin Luther with Introduction and Notes*, 6 vols., Philadelphia: Holman, 1915–1932, vol. 4, p. 309.
26. *Commentary on Psalm 82, op. cit.*, pp. 309 ff.
27. When men deny publicly any of the perfectly well-known sections of the Creed, according to one outburst of Luther, their trial is to be summary, for there is no purpose served in arguing with them: "In this case there ought not to be much disputing, but such open blasphemers should be condemned without a hearing and without defense . . . for these common articles of the whole Church have had hearings enough." *Dr. Martin Luther's Werke, Kritische Gesamtausgabe*, vol. 31, Weimar: Boehlhaus Nachfolger, 1883–1939, Pt. I, pp. 209 ff.

the sixteenth century was to discourage those movements of liberation which were so characteristic of the later Middle Ages and early modern times. While initially the implications of his revolt seemed to be favorable to an enlargement of social and political freedom as well as a recognition of inward religious liberty, it soon became apparent that the Reformer was basically conservative in his social outlook. Paradoxically, despite the great changes which his religious teaching and activity wrought, he dreaded change and tended to think that one of the functions of the state was to inhibit it.

He rejected the coercive Church only to exalt the coercion of the state and to give a kind of religious blessing to doctrines which were later to be known as the Divine Right of Kings. His sharp separation between the kingdom of grace and the realm of power provided the basis for that fission between private and public morality which was to characterize so much Lutheran doctrine in the centuries that followed. There was little in Luther's theories which might give his followers hope that the world of politics could be redeemed for positive purposes; for he always tended to think of law and government as primarily negative: they existed to suppress the wicked, punish blasphemers, and guard the Faith against its enemies. He appeared to doubt that the kingdoms of this world could ever be transformed into the Kingdom of Christ by human effort; for his sense of the corruption of human reason was so strong that he at least appeared to see all efforts to eliminate the violence of human affairs as fruitless.

Given the political outlook of Luther himself, it is not surprising that those who took his name should go even further in the direction of political passivity; for followers often tend to exaggerate preponderant tendencies of their prophets. Thus Troeltsch remarks:

> From the political and social point of view, the significance of Lutheranism for the modern history of civilization lies in its connection with reactionary parties; from the religious and scientific standpoint its significance lies in the development of a philosophical theology, which is blended with a religious mysticism and "inward" spirituality, but which, from the ethical point of view, is quite remote from the problems of modern political and social life.[28]

Although Troeltsch is noted as a hostile critic, it is difficult not to agree with at least a qualified version of what he says.

But we should be wary of exaggerating the effect of Luther's teaching, one way or the other, on the development of political practice. Although it is true, for example, that the Lutheran principle of passive obedience became a vital part of German culture, its effect on the positive shaping of such modern movements as twentieth-century National Socialism can easily be overdrawn.[29] Twentieth-century Lutheranism was by no means of one accord in its attitude to the state, for four centuries of development lay between it and Luther's political speculations.

Calvin and the Early Calvinist Outlook

Whereas there were strong mystical tendencies in Luther and a corresponding emphasis on love as against law, Calvin's social and political thought reflects his training in law and the humanities. And while Luther's teaching, in the main, stresses obedience, Calvin's, although beginning with stern injunctions demanding submission to political authority, has within it seeds of revolution and resistance.

Calvin was born in Picardy, France, in 1509 and died in Geneva in 1564. During the first phase of his life, 1509 to 1536, he was subjected to all those influences which built the foundations for his later career as a reformer and social speculator. Luther was molded in considerable measure by monkish learning. Calvin was a student at the University of Paris and later studied law at Orleans. In 1529 came his so-called conversion and by 1531 he was back in Paris as a religious and political polemicist. At the astonishingly early age of 27 (in 1536), he published his most famous work, the *Institutes of the Christian Religion.* This made him a well-known figure but also subjected him to severe criticism from the orthodox. Already in 1535 he was advising King Francis I to do away with Catholicism throughout France.

On his way to Basel, in Switzerland, Calvin met a preacher by the name of William Farel, who urged him to remain in Switzerland and become a teacher of theology. Calvin agreed to do so, after some urging, remarking later that he had been "terrified" by Farel—perhaps the only time in his life that he was frightened by any man.

The two men took up their residence in Geneva, which was a city now sharply divided between Catholic and Protestant political parties. Very early, apparently, Calvin became an important political leader, for in 1537 we read that he was influential in securing the adoption of legislation which required the taking of communion four times a year and which established a system of espionage to ferret out eccesiastical delinquents. Excommunication was used with little restraint, the result being that both Calvin and Farel aroused vitriolic opposition to their leadership. In 1538 the opposition had become so serious that the City Council issued a decree of exile against both men.

Thus began the third major epoch of his life. He took up his residence in Strasbourg, converted an Anabaptist, and, when the Anabaptist died, married his widow. His abilities as a debater were much sought after during the period of exile and in some respects this was one of the most fruitful phases of his career; for he reexamined his whole position on ecclesiastical and political questions and, in effect, prepared himself for the time when he should be able to return to Geneva.

The opportunity came in 1541 and between that date and 1552 his religious and political influence grew steadily. He rebuilt the reputation which had been shattered in 1538 and emerged as the virtual dictator of Genevan affairs. By 1552 his influence was so dominating that the Council of Geneva proclaimed his *Institutes* to be "holy doctrine which no man might speak against."

Both civil and religious authorities did his bidding with little or no protest. St. Thomas's admonition against embodying in the positive law all the dictates of natural and divine law was largely disregarded; and, as James Anthony Froude, the historian, puts it: "At Geneva . . . moral sins were to be treated as crimes to be punished by the magistrate." Within a period of five years after the decree of 1552, under the influence or direction of Calvin, at least fifty-eight sentences of death were meted out against eminent men and sixty-five men were exiled. In 1553, Servetus, who had entered Geneva to discuss theological questions with Calvin and who had been condemned by the Catholic Church, was executed in order to keep the doctrine of Geneva pure.

Geneva was, in effect, a closely-knit Church state, in which the line of division between ecclesiastical and secular authority was almost nonexistent and where the distinction between private and public affairs was virtually wiped out. It was an experiment in the application of those canons of moral and political conduct which we have come to think of as typically

Calvinist; and by the time of his death in 1564 Calvin had provided the text, both in theory and in practice, for that vast religious and sociopolitical movement which bears his name.

Calvin's Legalism. The roots of Calvin's outlook were, like those of Luther, in St. Augustine. Like the German reformer, Calvin revolts against late medieval interpretations of theology and ethics and advocates, as it were, a "back to the Fathers" movement. The stress on man's original sin is even more pronounced, if that is possible, than it is in Luther; so that by himself man can never perform acts which are not corruptions of the original nature with which he had been endowed by God.[30]

But it should be noted that Calvin, in rejecting what he takes to be the Catholic theory of justification by works, states that he means by his repudiation "not that no good works can be done or that those which are performed may be denied to be good but that we may neither confide in them nor ascribe our salvation to them."[31]

Whereas Luther thinks of sin as bodily desire, Calvin sees it as love of self. Luther in effect says that in order to overcome carnal desires one must be given the grace to rise above law and the differentiations worked out in human morality, for these distinctions only remind one the more of the never-ending desires which keep him from God.

Calvin, on the contrary, sees love of self as the sin and discipline as the "way out." The holy life is one which submits itself to rules and regulations and thus overcomes individual tendencies to self-exaltation. Sanctification, which for Luther consists in transcendence of law, for Calvin means obedience to law. Luther's stress on love leads him to identify with the New Testament as the text, so to speak, for the kingdom of grace; while the kingdom of power is animated by the strict legalism of the laws of Moses. Calvin's emphasis on law

28. Troeltsch, *The Social Teaching of the Christian Churches*, vol. 2, p. 577.
29. Cf. William McGovern, *From Luther to Hitler*, Boston: Houghton Mifflin, 1941, one of those who probably overdraw the thesis that Luther and Lutheranism were important factors in the rise of National Socialism.
30. *Institutes of the Christian Religion*, III, 14, 11.
31. *Ibid.*, III, 17, 1.

and submission to it compels him to read the New Testament in the light of the Old Testament's legal requirements. The Elect, for Calvin, are not to operate within the dualistic framework of Luther but rather to bind themselves to conquer the world of egotism and to subordinate all selves—including their own—to the strict code of law enjoined by God. The Elect, as a matter of fact, have as their supreme mission the subjection of sinful societies to the norms which Grace has taught them.

The State and Law. Those norms, as we have seen, are to be found largely in the Old Testament, and the ruler, acting under the aegis of the Elect, is to implement them through the positive law of the state. Calvin, like Luther, seems to interpret the natural law discoverable by reason in terms of divine law revealed in Scripture. The state, then, in this view, is the agency through which the earthly ruler puts into effect the divine code; and because most men are damned and lacking in grace, the ruler must enforce a rigid obedience to the code. So far as one can see, there is no fellowship of love set over against the state in Calvin's thought—there is only discipline under law, with the Elect as the interpreters of the law.

It is not surprising, then, that the general tendency of Calvin's thought is to stress the divine character of the state. This is certainly true at the beginning of his career, when he admonishes those who are disturbed by alleged tyranny to keep in mind that the measures to which they feel opposed are probably enforced as a punishment for their sins. "Wherefore if we are cruelly vexed by an inhuman prince or robbed and plundered by one avaricious," he says, ". . . let us remember our offenses against God which are doubtless chastised by these plagues."[32]

But to a greater degree than Luther, Calvin opens the door for later exceptions to his apparent absolutism. In the first place, his great stress on individual consciousness of election and individual awareness of salvation lead him to emphasize an individualistic interpretation of concsience. If, then, the demands of conscience come into conflict with the commands of political authority, Calvin suggests, with an emphasis more prominent than in Luther, that the individual under those circumstances may disobey, although not resist, the powers that be.

He also opens the way for subsequent doctrines of *corporate* official resistance, as contrasted with disobedience. He suggests, for example, that the lesser magistrates in some situations may be justified in resisting kings who have become tyrannical and by resistance he clearly means something more than a negative refusal to obey the ruler's ordinance.[33] But he does not develop his theory of resistance and it is not until his views are transplanted to another environment and his followers confronted by extraordinarily adverse circumstances that a full-blown Calvinist theory of resistance is worked out.[34]

The Scope and Nature of State and Church Authority. To Calvin, the Church is the Holy Community of the Elect bound together by conviction or certitude of salvation. It is both inward or spiritual and outward or organizational. And while the general theory is that all the Elect share in the government of the Church, the pattern at Geneva is that ministers make the decisions with the usually passive acquiescence of the main body of believers.

There is a strong assertion of the independence of the Church. It is, as the Holy Community, thought to have a life of its own and is in no sense a creature of the state. No more than Luther does Calvin think of himself as establishing a sect: The Church is, on the contrary, to be the integrating factor in society and from it will proceed the admonitions and scriptural interpretations which will govern both individual and corporate life.

Unlike Luther, however, Calvin is not disturbed by the notion of a coercive Church: one, that is, which will excommunicate its members knowing that in so doing they will incur not only religious but also civil penalties. Nor will the excommunicated have an alternative church to which they can turn, for nothing is further from Calvin's idea than that the society should be pluralistic in terms of ecclesiastical organizations. The excommunicated member must suffer for his recalcitrance and cannot be comforted by another religious group.

Within the Church itself, the member's life is subject to minute regulation. The legalistic outlook of Calvin allows the ecclesiastical body to establish standards for his sex life; supervise his amusements; develop rules for the government of his family; and fix criteria for his own periodic and rigorous self-examination. As among the ancient Hebrews, from whom Calvin draws so much of his inspiration, every department of life is theoretically subject to Church regulation; and the upright member of the Genevan church prides himself on the alleged fact that God accompanies him wherever he goes.

It is only by some reference to the theory and practice of the church in Geneva that we can understand the implications of early Calvinist attitudes to the state. It is clear that he does not wish to confuse ecclesiastical with civil authority. It is equally certain, however, that he expects the civil magistrates to follow the advice of the ecclesiastical ministers. In Geneva, it is assumed that civil rulers are of the Elect and that, as such, they follow Church discipline. They are admonished through the ubiquitous sermon as to their duty; and, indeed, the sermon is in Geneva what the papal bull was in medieval terms—the vehicle through which the minister shapes the thought and action of both ruler and subject. In practice, Calvin makes the state subordinate to the Church. By contrast, as we have suggested, Luther tends to subject the Church to the state. In a sense, then, Luther becomes one of the fathers of those tendencies which are later to be called Erastian; while Calvin is the progenitor of early modern theocracies.[35]

We have already noted that Calvin is no advocate of what later comes to be called religious toleration. Here let us simply emphasize that he fully defends the right and duty of the state to prosecute those who challenge the theocracy. His insistence that Servetus be executed is a sufficient indication that he regards not merely overt action but all public expression of allegedly subversive thought as subject to state suppression.

Early Calvinism and the Economic Order. Lutheranism, through its insistence on the "priesthood of all believers" and its attack on the traditional priesthood, had adopted the position that all callings are sacred. The distinction between the sacred and the secular, therefore, which had permeated the ethic of the Middle Ages, was broken down and the good Lutheran could regard a competent butcher in the same light as he might look upon a minister of the Gospel. And we have already noted the vigor with which Luther attacked the apologetic attitude of the Middle Ages to the executioner.

In Calvin we have the same tendency to idealize all useful occupations and to be suspicious of views which would put monk and priest on pedestals. It is true that the Calvinist minister is an enormously powerful figure, as we have seen. But his ecclesiastical and political power does not, in the Calvinist view, give him a peculiarly sacred character.

However, the contexts within which Luther and Calvin develop this view of the calling and the implications which they draw from it differ rather sharply from each other. Luther is thinking within a largely agricultural environment and in terms of a more or less fixed status. When, therefore, he states that every vocation is sacred, he is referring primarily to those occupations associated with rural and small village life: trades and professions which often pass down from father to son and in a social milieu where change is limited if not discouraged. Luther's generally pessimistic attitude to the external world, moreover, leads him to doubt the value of change.

Calvin, however, develops his doctrine of the calling in the context of a rapidly changing life in Geneva. His generally activist attitude to the social order, moreover, tends to make him receptive to social change. The Elect are to demonstrate consciousness of their preferred place in the scheme of things by activity, which will include innovations of various kinds. If the world is to be subjected to the saints, the latter must reveal their kinship to God through exhibition of God-like qualities —imagination, invention, adaptation, and ingenuity of all kinds.

From the very beginning, then, the Calvinist attitude to the social and economic order proceeds along lines that depart from the Lutheran position. The Holy Community must be receptive to change and, through its ministers, will counsel the civil authority to provide expanding opportunities for the saints' vocational energies. Thus Calvin advises the Genevan state to subsidize the cloth and velvet industry and later on his successors do the same with the manufacture of watches.

32. *Ibid.*, IV, 20.
33. The reference occurs in the final (1559) edition of the *Institutes,* IV, 20, 31. Calvin sees the ancient Spartan ephorate as a model, thus obviously thinking of the device as an integral part of the "constitution."
34. See Chapter 18, pp. 333–337.
35. For a more elaborate examination of the problem of church and state in Calvin as compared with Luther, see William A. Mueller, *Church and State in Luther and Calvin: A Comparative Study,* Nashville: Broadman Press, 1954.

But Calvin's receptiveness to economic and social innovations should not be interpreted in any sense as a belief that economic life should be emancipated from moral and legal controls. Like Luther, he preaches against the dangers of Mammon worship; and while he differs from Luther in his acceptance of a money economy, he is as fully aware of the temptations of wealth. The Calvinist saint demonstrates his election by means of his industry but at the same time shows, through his limitations on personal consumption, that he realizes the incompatibility of personal display with election. Hence the tendency of the Calvinist ethic is to encourage production but at the same time to limit personal consumption drastically. The state assists these efforts through development of new industry and, simultaneously, by measures designed to discourage consumption. During the Middle Ages, with their relatively simple economy, the public rules governing economic activity were successful in attaining their objective if they ensured that most men had a bare sustenance. In Calvin's Geneva, the positive law has reached its goal if it encourages the saints to greater activity while at the same time rigorously restricting their consumption. In the latter situation, of course, capital is bound to grow; and with its accumulation, the general conditions essential for a capitalist economy are established.

At the same time, we should remember that Calvinism at Geneva is careful to limit the uses to which capital can be put and the interest rates that may be demanded. Although we see in the theory and practice of early Calvinism a stimulus given by religion to the spirit of capitalism,[36] Calvin and his collaborators are never advocates of utterly unbridled economic enterprise. While the individualism at the heart of their doctrine makes for a spirit of enterprise,[37] they still remain anchored in a medieval tradition which regards the economic sphere as a subordinate aspect of the community. Thus even Geneva forbids the taking of interest from the poor.

In the mixed character of early Calvinism's economic views we seem to see a parallel to its caution on the right of resistance. In both areas its tendency to stress the independence and self-sufficiency of the discrete individual is at war with its inherited organicism. The former, in the doctrine of individual election, thrusts it forward toward theories of resistance and of economic autonomy and competition. The latter, however, so restricts resistance as to make it virtually meaningless; and, in the economic sphere, continues to insist—in principle at least—on the overarching claims of community. The story of late sixteenth-century Calvinism and of its many developments in the seventeenth century is, of course, one of gradually removing this uncertainty and of pushing forward the discrete individual.

The Ubiquity of Calvinism in Politics. During the last decade of Calvin's life, disciples flock to Geneva that they might gain inspiration from the spiritual and temporal master of the city. As they view the Geneva experiment and talk with Calvin, they gain insights into the politics of the Reformation which they might not otherwise have had and which will prove useful in their own nations. Like Rome in the Middle Ages and Moscow in the twentieth century, Geneva becomes the center of an international religio-political movement which will be of enormous importance in subsequent times. Unlike Lutheranism, which remains largely indifferent to the political sphere, Calvinism seems to thrive on political controversy and is never loath to develop its political attitudes beyond those stated by Calvin.

John Knox, for example, who builds largely upon Calvin's political theory, will be of great importance in the working out of the theory of resistance and in the establishment of Calvinist attitudes to politics in Scotland; and through Knox, other British disciples, and the great Puritan movement, the spirit of Calvin will permeate not merely the British Isles but also English colonies in the New World. Men like John Winthrop,[38] although certainly not mere carbon copies of the Genevan reformer, will in considerable measure embody his spirit.

Meanwhile, of course, in the late sixteenth century, international Calvinism increasingly challenges both the religious and the political position of Roman Catholicism and witnesses a remarkable evolution in its own conceptions.

But before we can trace out the ramifications of these doctrines of second-generation Calvinism and of Counter-Reformation Catholicism we must turn to the politics and socio-political theory of what we have termed heterodox Protestantism in the early sixteenth century. These are largely reflected in Anabaptism, which directs its challenges not merely to the ancient Church but also, and with equal vigor, to the mainstream of the Reformation as exhibited in Lutheranism and Calvinism.

The Politics and Social Theory of Anabaptism

To the major reformers and, indeed, to all respectable right-thinking men of the early sixteenth century, the mere utterance of the word Anabaptism usually brought shivers of horror. It was Anabaptist teaching which was in part the occasion for Luther's reaction against the apparent implications of his early Reformation doctrines. To Reformers and Catholics alike, Anabaptism seemed the nadir of depravity and its social and political doctrine utterly subversive of all order and Christian teaching. In many respects—and certainly in the eyes of their opponents—the Anabaptists were sixteenth-century Bolsheviks.[39]

And, indeed, their appeal, like that of modern communism, was in large degree to the lower strata of society. Artisans, peasants, and lower-income groups generally were attracted by their ideology. Taking root in three major geographical areas, their doctrines spread rapidly and were soon alarming the essentially conservative Lutherans, who wondered whether they had given birth to so pestiferous a lot. Indeed, we may see in the opposition of the Anabaptists to the orthodox Reformation the reflection of a class struggle in which relatively well-off intellectuals, feudal lords, and bourgeoisie are met by manual workers, restive serfs, and dissatisfied ministers.

In the German segment of Anabaptism, which centered in such towns as Wittenberg and Zwicken, the ideology was strongly affected by a Christian chiliastic emphasis. It was a friend of Luther, Thomas Münzer—a minister—who is usually looked upon as a co-founder of the movement.[40] He was assisted by a weaver by the name of Nicholas Storch, who added a lower class zest to its early development. The propagandistic aggressiveness of the movement is suggested when we recall that Storch actually appeared on the campus of Luther's own university, Wittenberg, and tried to win over its students; and apparently he had some success in this endeavor, at least down almost to the Peasants' Revolt of 1525. Meanwhile, Münzer had been carrying the message into Bohemia, where he found considerable response in a country which, after all, had given birth to the Hussite movement a century before. Although the causes of the Peasant War of 1525 were many-faceted, it seems certain that some of the peasant leaders had been inspired by Anabaptist ideology. We do know that Münzer, unlike Luther, supported the uprising and that after it was drowned in blood he was executed.

Meanwhile, in Zurich another version of Anabaptism was taking root. Originally its leaders were associated with the Swiss reformer Ulrich Zwingli (1484–1531). But they became dissatisfied with the generally conservative tendencies which he exhibited and in the middle twenties broke away from his leadership. Once they had severed their ties, they became the objects of severe persecution: their leaders were beheaded or drowned and their

36. Cf. R. H. Tawney, *Religion and the Rise of Capitalism*, New York: Harcourt, Brace, 1926, New American Library, 1963; and Max Weber, *The Protestant Ethic and the Spirit of Capitalism*, Talcott Parsons, trans., New York: Scribner's, 1948, 1958.
37. The origins of economic individualism have been treated critically in, for example, H. M. Robertson, *Aspects of the Rise of Economic Individualism*, New York: Kelley & Milman, 1959.
38. The impetus for John Winthrop's emigration to the New World came from one of the early capitalist economic depressions. He was a struggling lawyer, and, like many others, saw greater opportunities in America. In his famous Lay Sermon on board ship, he embodies much of the spirit of Calvin two generations after the latter's death.
39. Modern Marxists like Karl Kautsky have been very much interested in communist ideologies and practices of the Reformation period. See, for example, Kautsky's *Communism in Central Europe in the Time of the Reformation*, J. L. and E. G. Mulliken, trans. London: T. Fisher Unwin, 1897.
40. On Münzer in general, see Otto Brandt, *Thomas Muntzer: Sein Leben und seine Schriften*, Jena: Eugen Diederichs, 1933. For commentaries on his political works, see Carl Hinrichs, *Thomas Muntzer: Politische Schriften mit Kommentar*, Hallische Monographien Nr. 17, herausgegeben von Otto Eissfeldt, Hall: Max Niemeyer, 1950. Münzer's relation to the peasant revolts is treated by M. M. Smirin in *Die Volksreformation des Thomas Münzer und der Grosse Bauernkrieg*, Hans Nichtweiss, German trans., Berlin: Dietz, 1956.

followers subjected to civil restrictions of all kinds.

In the neighborhood of Strasbourg and Münster, yet another Anabaptist circle arose and became perhaps the best-known of all the radical Reformaton groups. Here again, its leaders came largely from the so-called lower orders and included such men as the furrier Melchior Hoffmann and the largely self-educated Bernard Rothmann. Hoffmann had preached Lutheranism in northern Germany and it was not until 1529 that he arrived in Strasbourg, where his religious and political doctrines became more and more extreme. As might have been expected, he eventually died in prison. In the meantime, however, Rothmann had begun to spread a chiliastic Anabaptist theory in Westphalia, where he attacked the corruption of the Catholic hierarchy and argued that the Prince-Bishop of Münster should be overthrown. Attracting many followers, he was able to expel the Bishop in 1532 (about the time the coup de grace was being given to the Zurich Anabaptists) and to take control of the city.

For the next three years, Münster became the Anabaptist haven. From all parts of Christendom, the brethren flocked into the city, many of them apparently believing that the overthrow of Catholic rule betokened that end of political history which their leader Rothmann foretold. But a combination of Catholic and non-Catholic forces was in the meantime being organized to recapture the city for the cause of Orthodoxy. The city was eventually besieged by the army of its bishop and was reduced to rather desperate straits. Its end came in 1535: The city was taken and thousands were tortured and slain.

Despite the physical suppression of the Anabaptists, however, their ideas were not to die. Indeed, the movement as a whole represented something so vital in the tradition of Christendom that even the orthodox were forced to take account of its theories and to answer its propositions.[41]

The Anabaptist Religious Outlook.[42] While there were variations in detail, the religious position of the Anabaptists was essentially one which stressed the independence of the individual even more than did Luther and Calvin.

In fact, this is probably the only characteristic which, in terms of dogma, they have in common with one another. All of them hold that baptism should be reserved for adults who have some awareness of what joining the Christian fellowship might mean. Rejecting infant baptism as a ritual which is meaningless from the viewpoint of individual choice and commitment, they insist that no Christian can countenance it. Harnack calls their revolt against infant baptism "a protest of the independent individual believer against the magic of redemption and the sacramental character."[43]

The religious society, in other words, is to be even more of a holy community than in the thought of Calvin; for the latter, after all, still clings to the idea that the Church is universal, that one can, in other words, be born into it. Anabaptists, by contrast, interpret the priesthood of all believers to signify the abolition of all official churches and the elimination of state sanctions for the purpose of sustaining religious unity.

Besides the doctrine of rebaptism, the Anabaptists also support the notion that religious communions are composed of the laity alone. There are no religious professionals, in the sense of men presumably having a peculiar relation to God by virtue of their office. Here again, they think of themselves as simply carrying out consistently what they take to be Luther's original ideas.

The mystical element in Anabaptist religion is also very strong, although it varies, of course, as between and among the several groups. As in other religious societies with mystical tendencies, this leads Anabaptists to be strongly suspicious of all external authority, whether religious or not.

Within the Anabaptists there are also strong chiliastic currents, which are probably heightened by almost continuous persecution and by a general interpretation of the world as corrupt. These tendencies are very prominent at about the time of the Peasant War[44] and after about 1529 become central among the Anabaptists living in Westphalia. When Münster begins to be subjected to military pressures, it is not difficult for Anabaptists to think of themselves as heralds of a new age and of the struggle with orthodox Catholics and Protestants as the final conflict before God will intervene in human history.

Politics and Morality in Anabaptist Thought.[45] In general, Anabaptists tend to accept the Lutheran dichotomy between the kingdom of grace and the realm of power, but they eschew the interpretation which would require the Christian to participate actively in what is regarded as characteristically political work.

Like the Lutheran, the Anabaptist does, it is true, advocate passive obedience: The Christian must pay his taxes, for example, as a contribution to the maintenance of an order which, after all, is divinely ordained. But because he is a Christian he cannot participate personally in the administration of tasks which are specifically forbidden by Scripture.

Thus there is a strong tendency among most Anabaptists to refuse military service, for has not Holy Writ forbidden the killing of other men? Here the Anabaptist position seems to be similar to that of many of the ancient Church Fathers,[46] who admitted the relative value of the Roman Empire but contended, nevertheless, that they could not countenance the war which seemed to be essential for the protection of the imperial structure. It is an attitude, also, which is not too unlike that taken by the Albigensians during the Middle Ages.

Similarly, no Anabaptist can become a magistrate, take an oath, or participate in the administration of capital punishment. All judging is forbidden by the New Testament, it is argued, and this would bar any Christian from participating in the administration of justice. Oaths, too, are clearly prohibited.

Most Anabaptists support the principle of private property, at the same time emphasizing strongly the moral obligation of mutual aid. It is important to stress this, since their enemies so often claimed that the overwhelming majority wished to uproot property institutions root and branch.[47]

This having been said, however, it must also be pointed out that a considerable minority moved in the direction of a complete communism for themselves, partly on the basis of the precedent established by the early church at Jerusalem. Thus the Hutterites—an offshoot of Anabaptism—hold that the Holy Community can be achieved only by eliminating private property.

It is not difficult to understand why the utopian ideology of the Anabaptists is received by ruling classes and by most Reformers and Catholics with something approaching bitter hatred. For a thousand years, scholars and leaders of the Western world had been constructing an ideology defending class differentiation, feudalism, sharp distinctions between laity and clergy, and private property, despite a doctrine of natural law which, at least until Aquinas, had held that pure nature would exclude class gradations, serfdom, ecclesiastical hierarchies, and private ownership of material goods. Now many Anabaptists appear with an outlook which, in the language of the modern scholar Mannheim,[48] impliedly shatters the old order and the ideology which helps sustain it. In considerable measure, and largely to the degree that they accept a chiliastic position, they think of the dichotomy between grace and power as a relatively temporary one. It will soon be dissolved by divine intervention and the historic political ordering of affairs will give way to a restoration of pure natural law throughout all society. Anabaptist observance of the canons of that law is simply a harbinger of the end; and many Anabaptists see divine intervention taking the form of angelic assistance to the Anabaptist remnant

41. On Anabaptism in general see Richard Heath, *Anabaptism from Its Rise at Zwickau to Its Fall at Münster*, Baptist Manuals, Historical and Biographical, No. 1, edited by George P. Gould, London: Alexander and Shepheard, 1895; and George H. Williams and Angel M. Mergal, *Spiritual and Anabaptist Writers: Documents Illustrative of the Radical Reformation*, vol. 25 of The Library of Christian Classics, London: S.C.M. Press, 1957. On Anabaptism and the economic problem, see Peter James Klassen, *The Economics of Anabaptism, 1525–1560*, The Hague: Mouton, 1964.
42. Franklin Littell examines Anabaptist ecclesiastical conceptions in *The Anabaptist View of the Church*, 2nd ed., Boston: Starr King Press, 1958. General religious ideas are discussed in Adolf Harnack, *History of Dogma*, vol. 7, ch. 3 and 4.
43. Harnack, *op. cit.*, vol. 7, p. 125.
44. The chiliasm of Thomas Münzer and the Peasant Revolt is well-known. See Ernst Bloch, *Thomas Münzer als Theologe der Revolution*, Berlin: Aufbau-Verlag, 1960. Karl Mannheim also devotes not a little attention to Münzer's chiliasm in *Ideology and Utopia*, New York: Harcourt Brace, 1959.
45. E. Belfort Bax, *Rise and Fall of the Anabaptists*, London: S. Sonnenschein, 1903; New York: Macmillan, 1903, remains the best treatment in English of Anabaptist political thought. As a twentieth-century Fabian socialist, Bax is unusually understanding. But his emphasis tends to center on the Munsterites, who hardly represent the majority. One should read him in connection with books like that of Klassen, *op. cit.*, n. 54.
46. See Chapter 9.
47. Klassen, *op. cit.*, stresses that, in fact, most Anabaptists did not attack private property.
48. Karl Mannheim, *op. cit.*

which is standing firm against the temptations of power.

Certainly this viewpoint is accentuated during the last day of Münster, when men who usually repudiate the sword feel that they are justified in taking it up in the final struggle. The tangled and complicated threads of the political history associated with the kingdom of power are to be cut by the small band with assistance from Almighty God; and the utilization of methods characteristic of the realm of power is to be justified on the ground that, after all, the end of history is near and God can suspend his own command against taking the sword. Some such thoughts appear to have run through the minds of men like John of Leyden and Jan Matthys as they fought desperately against the armies of the Catholic bishop.

But this view in turn depends upon a conception of political history held widely by Anabaptist chiliasts—an outlook which connects them with both medieval and ancient apocalyptists. Not very many of the Anabaptists, it is true, have the opportunity, talent, or skill to express themselves fully on the question. But during the last days of Münster the remarkable Bernard Rothmann finds time to state what must have been a widespread Anabaptist attitude to political history and at least a part of his treatise on the general theme has survived.

Rothmann on Earthly and Temporal Power: An Anabaptist Conception of History. As was pointed out earlier, Rothmann appeared near Münster about 1529 and was a leader in the expulsion of the Catholic Bishop in 1532. The Anabaptists were, of course, being constantly criticized by the orthodox, including rulers like Philip of Hesse. To answer such criticisms, Rothmann sketched out *Van Erdesscher Unnde Tytliker Gewalt: Bericht uith Gotlyker Schryfft* (*About Earthly and Temporal Power: Advice From Divine Writ*)[49] in six days, dedicating the finished product to Philip himself but also inditing it to all earthly rulers.

Rothmann believes that the end of political history is near and that the advent of a completely new scheme of things is at hand. Much of his argument, if we discount the traditional religious language, has overtones that remind one of Karl Marx. He is convinced that the subordination of most men to the few powerful has run its course and that the kingdoms of this world are about to end. He probably writes his treatise primarily to preserve his own integrity, rather than because of any belief that ruling classes will see their inevitable doom; for, like his contemporary Thomas More, he has little basic confidence in those who hold power. "Experience has taught me," he caustically remarks, ". . . that it is lost labor to advise the powerful otherwise than in the manner of the court, that is, with grandiloquent, artificial titles and catchwords, lofty and pleasing speech."[50]

Rothmann makes much of the fact that the German word for king (*koenig*) is allegedly derived from "koene," which means haughty. This shows, he thinks, that the German nation has had an excellent insight into the basic nature of political power and this insight confirms and strengthens one's conviction as derived from Scripture. For throughout the history of the world, and however much God's grace might put limitations on the haughtiness of kings, those who rule men have usually tended to rebel against God's restraints. Truly sincere kings he calls "rare game" indeed. Thus the history of political power has consisted in a kind of tension between the purposes of God and the ambitions of the powerful.

When the time has arrived for the end of political history, Rothmann teaches, with many Stoics, that the world is to "perish by fire, that all its impurities are to be purged out and melted by the fire, and will come to naught; thus shall also all earthly power and temporal governments cease and come to naught."[51] The new realm, too, will be an earthly one: A completely new social order is to be established, one which has been foreshadowed, of course, in those groups of Christians who have followed Anabaptist teaching.

Here Rothmann becomes wrathful at all views which interpret the new kingdom only spiritually—an obvious thrust at Lutheran teaching. The new rule is not merely spiritual but is, instead, a concrete system of external relations which will eliminate the old power structure. At this point, it is true, "the learned shocking people snort and threaten." However, "though they snort and murder as they will, nevertheless they shall yet not in the long run be able to stop the truth and to retard God's Word and will."

From an over-all point of view, several things are striking about the thesis which Rothmann develops. In the first place, there is throughout his work an appeal from what we might call Neoplatonic and spiritual interpretations of Christianity to Hebraic emphases which stress the transformation of earthly sociopolitical relations. The Lutheran interpretation of grace and power is given a radically different twist.

Another striking characteristic of Rothmann's doctrine is the appeal to class consciousness. While this is often merely implicit, it sometimes takes overt form. Thus he sees himself as an unlearned man, largely self-taught, who feels obliged to point out the truth to the learned. Throughout his treatment, one gathers the impression that while his opponents are wise in a formal sense, their wisdom is not profound.

In the third place, there is little of that pacifism which for the most part has characterized Anabaptist theory. While the social and political ends of the Anabaptists are certainly revolutionary in a very profound sense, their means, at least as they are revealed in the methods of Münster, are the traditional ones of military violence and retaliation. Rothmann does not tell us in his work how he would reconcile those means with the standards set up by the Sermon on the Mount. Perhaps the only explanation would be that, since he regards the end of history as imminent, the final conflict of the saints is an exception to the general rule of nonviolence and refusal to utilize the physical sword.

The Dissolution and Political Significance of Anabaptism. The Anabaptist utilization of violence at Münster was, of course, not typical of the movement as a whole; although the chiliastic note struck by Rothmann was, as we have seen, a not uncommon feature. After the fall of Münster, the aberrant violence was seen by the remaining Anabaptists in other parts of Christendom as contrary to the mainstream of heterodox Reformation teaching; and when one segment of the movement was reorganized by Menno Simons in 1536, there was a thorough repudiation of military force.

The significance of both Anabaptists and Mennonites (followers of Menno Simons) was that they give a radically different answer to one of the central issues of Renaissance and early Reformation political thought: the question of public versus private morality. Both Machiavelli and Luther had appeared to assert that there was an inevitable and sharp gulf between the two realms; and that the standards which one might establish in the area of personal conduct were not necessarily applicable in that of political relations.

As for Calvin, because he saw salvation as discipline under law rather than, as with Luther, transcendence of law, he conceived of the saints or the elect as dominating the political sphere and eventually subduing it. They were predestined to transform earthly governments through positive action; and while Calvin himself developed no doctrine of the right of resistance (aside from his acceptance of constitutionally ordained collective opposition to the ruler), he did lay the groundwork upon which men like Knox and Beza were to build.

It was the role of the Anabaptists, however, to attack both the Lutheran and the Calvinist position. With Luther, they tended to think of the political or public sphere as irremediably lost; but unlike Luther, they thought it was no responsibility of the saved to help administer an essentially damned society. The Anabaptists could obviously not accept Calvin's view that the saints would and could subdue the kingdoms of this world: their social ethic was one not designed for embodiment in general legislation.

If one looks upon Anabaptism as a utopian ideology, it stands sharply opposed both to the Lutheran encouragement of conformity and to Calvin's conception of transformation. While it appreciates Luther's insistance that the political order cannot be reconciled with the demands of the Sermon on the Mount, it rejects his assertion that Christians must nevertheless assist in its administration. Although it values Calvin's contention that religious faith must reflect itself in the social order as well as in private relations, it rejects his notion that the general social order is subject to basic change; for, it maintains, so soon as one begins to adopt the methods of politics, the ultimate ends for which one is striving begin to be corrupted by the means which one must utilize—those of deceit, coercion, and violence.

The history of Reformation sects after the fall of Münster was profoundly, if indirectly, influenced by these Anabaptist attitudes. While the Mennonites themselves remained relatively few in numbers, their adherents in Holland were often in a position to help in-

49. Translation by Dr. George A. Moore, Chevy Chase, Md.: Country Dollar Press, n.d.
50. Rothmann, *op. cit.*, p. 7.
51. *Ibid.*, p. 25.

fluence the social attitudes of religious and political refugees living in the Netherlands. The later rise of Baptist congregations in Britain, moreover, represented some of the same religious and political views as those which had been reflected among the Anabaptists. By the seventeenth century, it is true, the radical Anabaptism of the sixteenth no longer existed; but the Anabaptist emphases on individual conviction in religion, on the elimination of a professional religious class, and on the value of dissent, were to play vital roles in the rise of seventeenth-century democratic thought.

The Early Reformation and Political Thought

It is not easy to summarize the general impact of the early Reformation on the history of political thought and politics. Frequently we tend to confuse the conceptions of the early Reformers (those before about 1555) with those which emerged later in the sixteenth century. We often forget, moreover, that both Luther and Calvin were still very much under the influence of later medieval thought, particularly with respect to economic questions and to those involving religious toleration.

Actually it would seem clear that, from the political point of view, there were certain respects in which Reformation teaching was ambiguous and contradictory, to say the least. Non-Catholic apologists in modern times, for example, still occasionally talk as if the Reformers were groping for principles of religious toleration. But this is, by and large, to misread them. Neither Luther nor Calvin can legitimately be held up as advocates of toleration.

So, too, on such issues as the prerogatives of the ruler and the problem of resistance, the teaching of the early Reformation does not emerge as a clear and unambiguous one. Luther, as we have pointed out, tends on the whole to give a religious sanction to absolutism and to exalt the secular ruler in a way that had been largely unknown since the days of Pope Gregory I. In Calvin's theory, too, we look in vain for a clear-cut doctrine: Its net effect, despite the theory of resistance by inferior magistrates, is to sustain the prerogatives of absolute ruler. The Anabaptists, with their ethic of a withdrawn perfectionism, operate in a frame of reference which hardly requires them to deal with the problem.

It is only when we consider the early Reformation as a movement which gave great impetus to a kind of generalized individualism that we are on solid ground. In other respects, it is difficult if not impossible to say that there is an early Reformation political doctrine as such. But all the Reformers stressed the primacy of the individual and tended to break with medieval organicist notions. While this emphasis on the individual had diverse implications for Luther, Calvin, and the Anabaptists, it was everywhere of great latent significance. Together with the individualist emphasis present in the Renaissance, it helped establish the foundations for that early modern framework of thought which would increasingly think of political problems in terms of the discrete human being. After the sixteenth century, there was a gradually expanding tendency—reflected particularly in Britain and France but also present in some measure elsewhere—to conceive the individual, not the group or corporation, as the only natural unit of society and government.

chapter 18

The Secular State, Sovereignty, and the Right of Resistance

After the initial phases of the Reformation, which we treated in the previous chapter, it gradually became apparent—although only after much travail—that Catholics could not restore the old order any more than Protestants could wipe out Catholics.

Under these circumstances, political theory began increasingly to turn to such questions as the possibility of a society without religious uniformity; the duty of obedience or resistance to princes not of one's own religious faith; the problem of order in a multifaith society; and the prerogatives of the pope in a society where medieval premises were no longer accepted. Answers to questions of this kind cut across all confessional lines, so that on some issues given Catholics and Protestants would find themselves cooperating against alliances of yet other Catholics and Protestants.

Politics and Social Change in the Sixteenth Century

In many respects, the Protestant Reformation was welcomed by sixteenth-century rulers. In the Germanies, they often made it the occasion for cutting off financial payments which had traditionally been made to Rome but which were very unpopular with both ruling classes and subjects. And we should always remember that hostility to the temporal claims of the papacy had existed in Germany throughout the late Middle Ages.

The progress of the Reformation in England illustrates how complex were the motives which led rulers and people to attack the ancient Church. In England, as is well known, the monarch used the severance from Rome as an excuse for confiscation of Church lands and the seizure of valuable material possessions. Long before, Wycliffe had advocated just such action in the name of ecclesiastical poverty: Now it had become a reality. At the same time, it would be a mistake to think that greed for material goods was the only basis for Henry VIII's action; he was also speaking in the name of a national sentiment which resented foreign control and which had for centuries looked with suspicion on the political claims of the canon lawyers.

This national sentiment, of course, was not unanimous by any means; and the politics of the remainder of the sixteenth century were in considerable degree an exemplification of this fact. During the minority of Edward VI, the guardians of the king had considerable difficulty in enforcing a Protestant uniformity and when Queen Mary ascended the throne in 1553 she was welcomed by a sizable proportion of the population as one who would enforce a Catholic conformity. Her difficulties in reestablishing the old Church on its former footing are well-known and would seem to indicate that English attitudes were as sharply divided as in the days of her brother. Even under Elizabeth, there were significant divisions.

In Scotland, the politics of the Reformation were guided from Geneva itself. John Knox had conferred with Calvin in that city and both inside and outside Scotland he was profoundly influenced by the views of the great Reformer. Knox's objective was to overcome the Catholic rulers of his country, not in order to secure mere toleration for the Presbyterian faith but rather that he might impose Presbyterianism instead. His goal was perfectly clear to his great antagonist, Mary Queen of Scots, who for her part hoped that the followers of Knox could be liquidated in the name of the "true Faith."

In both England and Scotland, then, we find illustrated dramatically what was typical of Reformation politics everywhere: that the Reformers hoped to obliterate Catholics in the name of Reformist uniformity, just as the Catholics thought that they might suppress Protestant dissent in order to restore the medieval order.

After the suppression of the Anabaptists in Münster, Lutherans and Catholics gradually came to the conclusion that, temporarily at least, they should give practical recognition to the political strength of each other. The result was the Peace of Augsburg in 1555, under which the principle of *cuius regio, eius religio* was first given public recognition. This represented the notion that each prince within the Holy Roman Empire could determine whether Lutheranism or Catholicism would be established within his domains. Anabaptism was, of course not mentioned in the Peace, nor was Calvinism: It was assumed that the ruler had only two alternatives.

While Catholics and Lutherans were settling their differences at Augsburg—however temporarily—the series of conflicts between Catholics and Calvinists had begun in earnest. In 1546, Cardinal David Beaton was assassinated by a Scottish Calvinist who announced before he drew his sword that he was killing the Cardinal "because thou hast been, and remain an obstinate enemy against Christ Jesus and his holy Evangel." The whole Calvinist party tended to rejoice at this act, even John Knox being scarcely able to restrain his joy as he described the gory details of the Cardinal's last minutes and the way in which his body was pickled in salt and then buried temporarily in a dunghill.[1] Catholics, of course, were properly horror-stricken and invoked principles of good order and government against their Calvinist opponents.

In France, however, the whole complicated story of Calvinist-Catholic relations showed how Roman Catholics, too, were able to make use of war and assassination for ostensibly religious ends. From 1562 to 1598 there raged, with some interruptions, the so-called Wars of Religion, out of which eventually emerged three major factions.[2] The Huguenots, or French Calvinists, constituted one party and were supported by many of the nobility. The Holy League represented the extreme Catholic position and sought the extermination of the Calvinists as enemies of the monarchy and of the True Religion. Finally, a moderate Catholic alignment, known as the *politiques*, sought to reconcile Calvinists and Catholics in the interests of France's unity and international power.

Here we are not interested in the details of the wars of religion but rather in the methods used and approved by the extreme factions which spoke in the name of religion. The event which most shocked the Calvinists and caused corresponding rejoicing among Catholics was the St. Bartholomew's Day Massacre of Protestants in 1572. The pope celebrated a *Te Deum* in honor of the Massacre and in addition struck a coin to commemorate it.

However, St. Bartholomew's simply strengthened the Calvinist will to resist, perturbed moderate Catholics, and alarmed all those who were seeking some *modus vivendi* in the religious struggle. Far from securing the triumph of Catholicism, the Massacre only exacerbated the violence of the religious conflict. Calvinism at one point actually seemed to grow stronger. Thus in 1576, the King, Henry III, felt compelled to make concessions to the Huguenots. This act, however, led to the foundation of the Catholic Holy League under the leadership of the Duc de Guise. Later Henry proclaimed himself head of the League, although behind the scenes he sought to play off the League against the Huguenots and vice versa, hoping that the dynasty would be strengthened against the menace of the House of Guise.

In 1584, however, the King's brother died, thus removing the last possibility that the throne would be inherited by his immediate family. He thereupon recognized Henry of Navarre as the heir apparent, hence lending the sanction of his prestige to succession of an avowed Protestant to the throne. The response of the Guise family was immediate: It put pressure on the King to attack Henry of Navarre in order to compel the latter to embrace Catholicism. In the ensuing war, while the King and the Duc de Guise were nominal allies, it was evident that the monarch did not feel at ease. In 1587, his forces were defeated by those of Henry of Navarre and the Duc de Guise seized this opportunity to revolt against his reluctant ally. The forces of the Duc de Guise took control of Paris, which precipitated an alliance between Henry of Navarre and the King. The latter was now determined to rid himself of the Guises and, thorough Machiavellian that he was, hired assassins who swiftly eliminated both the Duc de Guise and his brother.

However, Henry III was perhaps not adept enough in the use of means approved by the Florentine. At least he was unable to prevent plots against himself by partisans of the League, for in 1589 he fell victim to an attack by a Dominican monk.

Henry IV thus came to the throne under a cloud and with religious bitterness still intense. Both Huguenots and Catholics seemed to rejoice at the assassination of Henry III, for neither side rejected in principle the means of political murder. Eventually Henry IV changed his faith in order to gain control of Paris and to establish himself firmly on the throne; and in 1598, his Edict of Nantes laid the foundations for a truce between Calvinists and Catholics, with the former being given control of some 200 cities and the boon of toleration. But the end of overt war did not mean that Henry was exempt from assassins' threats, for neither Calvinists nor Catholics were fully satisfied. On nineteen separate occasions, unsuccessful attempts were made on Henry's life by would-be assassins. The twentieth attempt succeeded in 1610.

Meanwhile, the religiopolitical struggle was leading to both successful and unsuccessful attacks on other monarchs. Thus Mary Queen of Scots was executed by Queen Elizabeth; and Elizabeth herself was the object of many conspiracies: She captured some 15 emissaries of Philip II of Spain who confessed that they had been hired by that monarch to murder her. In 1584 William the Silent was assassinated by an extreme Roman Catholic and there were doubtless thousands of Catholics who rejoiced in his act.

The whole conflict between Calvinists and Catholics was in part made bitter because, by contrast with the early Reformation when Luther had to deal only with a corrupt and internally divided Church, the later Protestants had to grapple with a revived Catholicism which had in part purged itself of its late medieval weaknesses and now stood ready to engage in a counter-attack. In 1534, for example, the Society of Jesus (Jesuits) had been founded and it rapidly became a militant and well-disciplined organization in defense of the ancient Faith. Then, too, the Council of Trent (1545–1563), while poorly attended, sought to reexamine Catholic doctrine and to strengthen the Church through a general reform which had been called for since the days of the Avignon papacy.

The generally unsettled political conditions of the century, the appeal to violence by both Calvinists and Catholics, the insistence by most religionists that their particular faith must become the official religion of the state, the tensions developed between rulers of one faith and subjects of another, the new militancy of Catholicism—all these factors taken together furnished the occasion for the central political debate of the late sixteenth century. The issues revolved around whether, under what circumstances, and by what methods resistance to a ruler might be justified.

There are several ways in which one might legitimately classify the political theories of the time. In terms, however, of the problem of resistance as an integrating theme, we might examine, first, the Calvinist formulation of the right of resistance as exemplified by such men as Knox, Duplessis-Mornay, and Buchanan. Then we turn to the Jesuit doctrines of Mariana and Bellarmine. After that, we examine the doctrine of nonviolent resistance of de La Boétie. Finally, we note the arguments against the right of resistance as formulated by thinkers like Bodin, Barclay, and James I.

Calvinism and the Right of Resistance

The assassin of Cardinal Beaton had avowedly killed the ecclesiastic because the latter had allegedly perverted the Gospels as interpreted by the Calvinist faction. But as yet there was no doctrine which justified such actions and, indeed, as we have pointed out, Calvin himself was loath to defend any right of resistance.

In the years between 1546 and 1557, however, the Reformation in Scotland developed to such a point that Scottish Calvinist apologists had to formulate their position under the ever present challenges of monarchs who continued to be Catholic. Moreover, Mary, the queen of England from 1553 to 1558, was a devout Catholic who endeavored to undo all the work of Henry VIII and her brother Edward VI. Scottish reformers viewed the politics of England with interest and alarm, for upon the outcome of the struggle there they thought that Scottish affairs might depend.

In 1557, John Knox, then living on the Continent, began his attack on the rule of Mary of

1. *History of the Reformation in Scotland*, in *The Works of John Knox*, 6 vols., David Laing, collector and ed., Edinburgh: Woodrow Society, 1846, Bk. I, pp. 175–179.
2. See E. Armstrong, *The French Wars of Religion: Their Political Aspects*, 2nd ed., London: Simpkin, Marshall & Co., 1904; and Robert Kingdon, *Geneva and the Coming of the Wars of Religion in France, 1555–1563*, Geneva: E. Droz, 1956.

England in his essay called *The First Blast of the Trumpet Against the Monstrous Regiment of Women.* While this treatise did not purport to be a general argument in favor of the right of resistance, the implications of such a right were certainly there. In general, Knox is concerned with the problem of whether women ought to be rulers. He proposes three "blasts" against their right to govern but never completes the latter two of the attacks. In the first blast, he contends that women are doubly subordinated to men by Scripture. They were, in the first place, clearly subjected to men by nature, since woman was made from man and not man from woman. But in addition, they were responsible for the Fall and hence put under a double subjection; for their subordination to man after Eve ate the furit was a punishment for Eve's temptation of Adam. And Knox also cites Fathers of the Church to support his view.

In addition to Scripture and the Fathers, Knox refers to the pattern of subhuman nature as support for his contentions. As in so many political writers, he seems to think that what allegedly takes place among the beasts constitutes a model for men in their governance of society. "For nature hath in all beastes printed a certeine marke of dominion in the male," he contends, "and a certeine subjection in the female whiche they kepe inviolate."[3]

At no point in the *Regiment of Women,* it is true, does Knox suggest that God-fearing males should resist female rule. But while explicit advocacy of resistance is absent, the principle would seem to be implicit. At one point,[4] for example, he maintains that not even immemorial custom and consent can legitimate the rule of women, in view of the fact that Scripture clearly pronounces against it.

Not until some seven years after the *Regiment* do we find Knox developing a full-fledged theory of resistance. By this time Mary Queen of Scots was on the throne and the Presbyterians of Scotland were restive because of her Catholic sympathies. Knox, indeed, was praying for her, but in a most peculiar way: instead of the usual prayer for prosperity, peace, and long life, he was petitioning God to help the queen overcome her "idolatry." In 1564, the Assembly of the Scottish church met and debated the whole question of resistance to royal authority; for by now it was clear that the battle was joined between Mary and her Catholic nobility, on the one hand, and Knox and his Presbyterian divines, on the other.

The debate took the form of a colloquy between William Maitland, Secretary to Queen Mary, and John Knox. The latter had been charged with insincerity in his prayers for the queen and had openly avowed that her celebration of the Mass was a form of idolatry. During the course of the long discussion between Maitland and Knox, the latter's attitude to resistance was thoroughly explored.[5] It is quite evident that by this time he had advanced beyond the position of the *Regiment of Women.* There he was only implicit in his assertion of the right to resist; here he becomes very explicit.

Knox avers that the thirteenth chapter of Romans, while it demands obedience to the powers that be, makes a distinction between political authority as such and, in the quaint words of Maitland, "the persounis that wer placeit in authoritie."[6] Knox's own statement puts the matter forcefully:

> Godis ordinance is the conservation of mankynd, the punishment of vyce, the mentenyng of vertew, quhilk is in it self holie, just, constant, stable, and perpetuall. But men clad with the authoritie, ar commounlie prophane and unjust; yea, thai ar mutabill and transitorie, and subject to corruption. . . .[7]

He places heavy reliance on the Old Testament to support his theory that, while it is never legitimate to resist genuine political authority as such, it may be a duty as well as a right to oppose a person who claims authority but who in reality does not possess it. Thus he points out that even after Saul had been anointed as king this did not prevent the people from resisting him when he had begun to act in an unking-like way. If a person should take from the law officers a man who had been legitimately convicted of murder, the act would be one of illegitimate resistance—a violation of God's ordinance. If the man is innocent, then the person who takes him away from the law officers is not violating God's commands but rather those of the Devil.

The discussion eventually turns to the exciting question of idolatry, with which offense Knox has accused the queen. Maitland raises two issues: Should the reformers try to suppress the Queen's Mass and can the reformers, by permitting idolatry, be said to be committing it? Knox answers both questions in the affirmative. Both men agree that the idolator must die, but Maitland asks, Who shall do the killing? To this question Knox gives a very specific reply: the "people of God" shall carry out the sentence of death against an idolatrous monarch.

At this point Knox makes a very important statement. When he speaks of resistance and the positive abolition of idolatry, he means, he points out, the act "Of the peopill assembled togidder in one bodie of ane Commonwealth, unto whome God has gevin sufficient force, nocht onlie to resyst, but also to suppress all kynde of opin idolatrie."[8] He seems to suggest that merely individual acts against an idolatrous monarch are inexpedient: a corporate resistance is essential.

Unlike Calvin, however, Knox apparently does not envision this corporate resistance as merely constitutional. While he would undoubtedly argue that traditional "estates of the realm" can legitimately resist an idolatrous monarch in the name of the people, he also envisions the latter acting spontaneously and even in the absence of formal institutions. Thus the whole people conspired against Amasiath, King of Judah, who had become an idolator, and proceeded to establish his son Uzziah on the throne.[9]

Knox's theory of disobedience and resistance is more complex than one might sometimes imagine. We might summarize it by saying that subjects, when they have the power, have a duty to rescue the innocent from the king; that when the king commands a subject to strike an innocent person, the former should refuse to do so; that if a subject executes an innocent person at the command of the king, he is in effect a murderer despite the cloak of alleged royal authority; and that corporate resistance to and deposition of a ruler who violates God's law are fully justified, as is shown by examples from the ancient history of Israel. Implicitly, Knox makes a distinction between acts of individual disobedience—as when a subject rescues an innocent person from the clutches of the king or a Calvinist refuses to obey a law requiring public celebration of the Mass—and those of corporate resistance. The former have in view the keeping of the subject free from direct sin; while the latter is a political act whose objective is the purging of the commonwealth itself.

It is obvious that Knox has gone far beyond Luther and even beyond his great mentor

Calvin. So, too, does George Buchanan, who in 1579 justifies the deposition of Mary Queen of Scots in his celebrated treatise *De Jure Regni apud Scotos*. Like Calvin, Buchanan emphasizes that where constitutional arrangements provide for some form of resistance, there can be no doubt about the right of the people to depose a ruler.

But Buchanan goes beyond constitutional arrangements and tradition in justifying the removal of rulers. He also enunciates a theory of contract. Here he seems to have in mind implicit conceptions of contract in feudalism. Just as the relation between feudal lord and serf is one of reciprocal obligations and rights—protection on the part of the lord and service on that of the serf—so is there an implicit contract between king and people. That there is some such tacit agreement is shown by the coronation oath taken by the king. If, then, the monarch should violate his covenant in any way, the other party to the compact—the people—can depose or even kill him.

Buchanan goes beyond Knox, however—and, indeed, beyond most if not all of the sixteenth-century advocates of resistance—when he justifies individual as well as corporate resistance. While Knox, for example, undoubtedly took great satisfaction in the deaths of men like Cardinal Beaton, the Duc de Guise, and Henry III, he never explicitly suggests an individual right of tyrannicide. But Buchanan would vindicate both individual and corporate resistance to a ruler who has violated divine law.

But it was not only the Scottish Calvinists who were confronted by the problem of resistance. The French Huguenots, too, were perturbed, particularly after the frightful events connected with St. Bartholomew's Eve. In

3. *First Blast of the Trumpet Against the Monstrous Regiment of Women*, in Laing, *op. cit.*, vol. 4, p. 393.
4. *Ibid.*, p. 413.
5. Knox's version of the colloquy is given in his *History of the Reformation in Scotland*, in Laing, *op. cit.*, vol. 2, pp. 427–459.
6. *Ibid.*, p. 435.
7. *Ibid.*, p. 436.
8. *Ibid.*, p. 443.
9. See 2 Chronicles 25:27–28; 26:1–4.

France, a whole political pamphlet literature grew up vindicating the right and duty to resist. In general, this series of tracts, like the great work of Buchanan, grounded its view of royal prerogatives and of the obligations of subjects on both contract and tradition. This is illustrated best of all, perhaps, in Philippe Duplessis-Mornay's *Vindiciae contra Tyrannos*[10] which appeared about the time of Buchanan's treatise. Duplessis-Mornay postulates a dual contract: one between God, on the one hand, and king and people, on the other; while the second contract is between king and people. Under the first contract, king and people promise to observe the true religion and God, for his part, promises them protection so long as they do so. If, however, either the king or the people fail to fulfill their side, God can impose sanctions: He can, for example, stir up the people to revolt against an impious king; or a pious king can be given power by God to chastise an unrighteous people. In the former situation the people are simply appealing from a lower lord, the king, to a higher one, Almighty God. In the second contract, people promise to obey the king so long as the latter acts under the law; while the king, in turn, solemnly recognizes his obligations both to God, as his feudal superior, and to the people, as his inferiors.

Although Duplessis-Mornay thus suggests a very elaborate contract theory—which is obviously based on his understanding of feudal relations—he also looks for evidences of the two contracts in the actual customs and traditions of mankind. He finds that men and rulers have in fact acted as if the contracts were real; that in every kingdom, for example, there is a tradition which asserts that some body or bodies (the estates or the nobility) have the constitutional right to control the king—either by way of assenting to laws or by powers of deposition.

In one sense Duplessis-Mornay is a rather conservative vindicator of resistance, for he makes it clear, as does Knox, that there is no justification for individuals as such resisting the king. Like Calvin, he sees the right as inhering in traditionally established bodies. Theoretically, of course, he might imagine a society in which no such assemblies existed—in which, that is, there would be no organizations to implement the contract on behalf of the people. Actually, however, as we have seen, he suggests that there are such traditional vehicles in every Christian society. At no point, though, does he identify the people with the whole people. Rather does he conceive of them as somehow identical with the estates or even with the nobility or gentlemen.

This aristocratic flavor pervades most of the Huguenot political literature, as a matter of fact, thus perhaps pointing to the fact that men like Duplessis-Mornay are in one sense simply expressing the ideological interests of one segment of the French nobility.

A similar tendency to underline the role of the aristocracy in the theory of resistance is to be noted in Theodore de Beza (1519–1605), French-born successor to Calvin in the leadership of Geneva. In a work first published in 1574,[11] he takes as his point of departure the last edition of Calvin's *Institutes* and certain other of the great reformer's writings.[12] The "lesser magistrates," according to Beza, are intermediate between the sovereign and the people and hold their offices much more from "the Kingdom than from the King."[13] Prominent among the lesser magistrates are the hereditary nobility, elected officials of the towns, and the French estates. Like so many Calvinist theorists of resistance, Beza places great emphasis on covenants and contracts. First, there is the oath taken jointly by the king and people to God, in which they promise to observe all God's laws. And Beza descants on the precedents of the ancient Israelites. A second oath is that between the king and the people, whereby the latter promise to accept the former on condition that he observe certain principles.

If the first oath is broken by the king—if, for example, the sovereign should issue commands against God's will—the people must still uphold their promises to God. They will, if necessary, disregard the king's orders, meanwhile praying to God, who may himself punish the ruler.

If the second contract is broken, the possibility of political resistance, as contrasted with mere disobedience, arises. The lesser magistrates, who are acting as surety for observance of the fundamental laws, can in the last resort carry on armed resistance. If the magistrates fail to act against tyrants, or if they cannot act, Beza opens up the possibility of tyrannicide by the individual. By and large, however, he is suspicious of individual action and stresses throughout resistance by the magistrates who reflect, presumably, a kind of moral consensus on the part of the elite.

Second-stage Calvinism of men like Knox,

Buchanan, Duplessis-Mornay, and Beza tends to say little about what we should today call the common people. Although its pleas for the right of resistance to Catholic rulers and for the positive establishment of Calvinism as the religion of the community will later become a basis for early democracy, this is not true in the sixteenth century. Indeed, and curiously enough to those unfamiliar with the history of political thought, it is to the Jesuits that we must turn for any pleas which could even remotely be called democratic.

Jesuits, the Church, and the Right of Resistance

As suggested earlier, the Society of Jesus became one of the most significant organizations of the sixteenth century. Not only was it a leading arm of the Church in carrying out the objectives of the Counter-Reformation, but several of its prominent members were also responsible for laying the foundations for the predominant modern view of the state.[14] Pressed on the one side by the secularist tendencies of the late sixteenth century and, on the other, by the militancy of Calvinist theologians and political leaders, Jesuit thinkers worked out doctrines which began to conceive state and Church as two separate societies and which appealed from kings and nobles to the mass of commoners. Protestant rulers of the period, such as Queen Elizabeth, feared the Jesuits precisely because their doctrines were so revolutionary in many respects; and in the seventeenth century no charge was more damning to the English dissenting sects than the frequently-heard allegation that they were connected with the Jesuits.

Among all the Jesuit writers of the age, two of the most eminent from the viewpoint of political doctrine were Juan de Mariana and Robert Cardinal Bellarmine.

Mariana's *De Rege et Regis Institutions* (1598) is an excellent expression of the early modern tendency to think in terms of the origins of society rather than in those which would stress its implicit goals. Like the traditional Augustinians, Mariana postulates a state of mankind in which there are no political institutions and in which, presumably, men are utterly free in an individual sense. This situation is brought to an end, however, not because—as in the Augustinian view—vice and crime call forth coercive government but rather by reason of the fact that human beings are menaced by external dangers. They submit themselves to rulers, then, in order to preserve their lives; but in so doing, they give to their governors only that authority essential to effect those purposes which gave rise to the state.

One of the most celebrated chapters in all early modern political literature is that wherein Mariana examines the nature and cure of tyranny. The Greeks had in their popular thought tended to identify the tyrant with the ruler who gained office illegally, although often such a ruler could confer great benefits on the people—as in the case of the Pisistratids. By the time of Mariana the conception of tyranny had become broader: It now included not only those whose titles to rule were defective but also those, whatever their titles, who ruled oppressively. Most political thinkers of the sixteenth century do not hesitate to say that the tyrant in the classical sense might be murdered, although, as we have seen, they are generally distrustful of any claimed right of the individual to resist. At the same time, they are hesitant about justifying tyrannicide in cases involving oppressive rule but not defective titles. It is at this point that Mariana does not hold back. Not only does he argue that such tyrants may be killed—since they have failed to recognize their subjection to law—but he also contends that the mode of killing is largely immaterial. They may be slain, he avers, either openly or by stealth. There is only one line which he draws—and it is a line

10. English translation edited by H. J. Laski as *A Defense of Liberty Against Tyrants*, London: G. Bell, 1924.
11. *Du Droit des Magistrats sur leurs sujets*. Another edition, cited in the text, was published in Lyons, probably in 1579. See also Robert Kingdon, "The First Expression of Theodore de Beza's Political Ideas," *Archiv fur Reformationsgeshichte* 46 (1955), 88–100; and A. Cartier, "Les Idees politiques de Théodore de Bèze d'apres le traité Du Droit des Magistrats sur leurs sujets," *Bulletin de la société d'histoire et d'archeologie* (October 1900), 187–206.
12. Note, for example, Calvin's *Commentary on the Book of the Prophet Daniel,* T. Myers, trans., Edinburgh, 1852.
13. Beza, *Du Droit des Magistrats*, 1579 ed., pp. 31–32.
14. Among them, one might mention Suarez, Molina, Mariana, and Bellarmine.

not unfamiliar to earlier advocates of tyrannicide such as John of Salisbury. Mariana contends that the natural law would forbid any mode of killing which would in effect make the tyrant a suicide. Thus poison administered through food or drink is excluded. At the same time, however—and strangely enough it might seem to the modern mind—Mariana thinks that poison which infects the guilty ruler through clothing does not violate the no-suicide rule; for the condemned does not actually participate in his own death under such circumstances—he only passively accepts a fate which has been prepared for him from the outside.

In Mariana, the whole issue of religious toleration is treated from what we might call a secularist point of view. There is no disposition on his part to require religious uniformity on *religious* grounds; the emphasis is on *political* necessity. No more than one religion should be permitted within a given province, he argues, for to tolerate a competing faith would be to subvert the possibility of civil peace.

The Jesuits help lay the foundations for secular democracy, of course, not merely by providing doctrine which would justify resistance to Calvinist rulers but also by showing the contrast between the exalted position of the pope and the relatively inferior status of the secular ruler. While Jesuit writings are not entirely consistent on the subject, in general they prepare the way for theories which see Church and state as not two distinct functions of a single society but rather as two separate societies.

These tendencies are particularly illustrated in the theories of Robert Cardinal Bellarmine (1542–1621), a Jesuit scholar and churchman whose great mission in life from a political point of view is to defend the power of the pope in temporals. In doing so, of course, he attacks the pretensions of both Catholic and Calvinist rulers, who have begun to think of themselves as immune to outside control.

Bellarmine's great antagonist is William Barclay, who has argued that the pope has no power in temporal affairs. In the process of defending the contrary position, Bellarmine comes to define more exactly the theory of the indirect temporal power of the pope and the circumstances under which subjects may disobey their rulers.[15] Repudiating the view of the extreme canonists which would make the pope the "Lord of the World," Bellarmine identifies his perspective with that of the theologians, who would see papal prerogatives in the temporal sphere as confined to emergencies.[16]

Bellarmine goes on to show that popes have in fact deposed kings and he interprets all such depositions as exercises of the indirect temporal authority. Where they have not utilized the authority, as in the failure of the pope to depose Julian the Apostate, it was not because they did not possess the right to do so but simply because, as he frankly admits, the Church "in its newness not yet did . . . have the strength to check earthly princes."

There is a famous chapter in Bellarmine in which he imagines the people discussing indirect papal temporal authority with the pope.[17] The people are under the impression that they are bound by divine law to obey all temporal rulers and so contend in their arguments with the holder of St. Peter's chair. In one sense, the people seem to espouse Luther's position of passive obedience, while Bellarmine, through the pope, tries to define the conditions under which the people—under guidance of the pope—are bound to disobey their temporal rulers.

It is obvious throughout his argument that Bellarmine assumes the continuance of a single Christendom in which the spiritual and temporal authorities are distinct but united. While both authorities are from God, the pope's prerogatives come from the deity directly, those of the king being derived only by way of the people. And by the people Bellarmine apparently means the whole populus and not merely some minority nobility which stands in the place of the entire community. In this sense, Bellarmine is a much more thoroughgoing democrat—if, indeed, one can use that term in this context—than, for example, Duplessis-Mornay.

It would seem to be clear, then, that Bellarmine is defending a moderate version of the medieval conception of the two-authorities-in-one-society. On this side he is a reactionary in terms of the politics of his day.

Yet the peculiarity of Bellarmine's theories is that, while they obviously exalt medieval conceptions overtly, they also open the door to radically different notions of the relation between temporals and spirituals.

He points out, for example, that before Constantine spiritual and temporal authorities were not only "distinct powers in limits and duties, but also are found to be meanwhile as separate."[18] And he also observes that in his own day "there are many kings and princes outside the church." While he does not spell out the significance of these facts, the implications are relatively clear to those who read the words in the context of his whole system of thought.

By this we mean that whereas he holds up the medieval ideal (as interpreted by him) as the standard, he also acknowledges that the Church must on occasion recognize the objective historical situation for what it is. Thus before Constantine, there could be no harmony within a single society, for the rulers of the Empire were pagans and the Church had no strength to make it otherwise; and even under Julian the Apostate, as we have seen, the failure of the pope to depose Julian is explained in terms of his lack of power to make his authority effective. If ecclesia and regnum were both distinct and separate in the pre-Constantinian period, it is conceivable that they may once more occupy a similar position in the future.

Actually, Bellarmine and other Jesuits are preparing the road for the theory that the state, instead of being a body of lay officials existing side by side with ecclesiastical officials in a single society, is a *societas perfecta;* that is a complete society which exists independently of the existence of the Church. By the same token, the Church, rather than being the ecclesiastical side of a single society, as in the Middle Ages, is increasingly conceived as itself a *societas perfecta.* As these notions develop—and they are only embryonic in Bellarmine—a more nearly modern idea of Church and state is gradually born.[19]

Nonviolent Resistance: Etienne de La Boétie

Men like Mariana and Bellarmine represent what might be termed orthodox Catholic theories of resistance. Only a decade before the French wars of religion began, however, Etienne de La Boétie, alarmed by the religious fissions which have already made their mark and saturated with the writings of the ancients on tyranny, attempts to formulate a theory which will provide a nonviolent way out of the political dilemma.

He was born in 1530, studied law at the University of Toulouse, and eventually was appointed a judge. When in 1562, the Chancellor of France, Michel de L'Hôpital, granted certain liberties to the Protestant minority, the young judge approved—for he was already anticipating rather radical doctrines of religious toleration. His early death in 1563 prevented his witnessing the more horrible results of the wars of religion, even though his imagination and insight had in effect predicted them.

His great essay, *Discours de la servitude volontaire,*[20] written in 1548 when he was only 18, was an attempt to understand the roots of tyranny and to infer from that understanding the best methods of overcoming it. De La Boétie's thesis is that ultimately every structure of tyranny depends primarily on the voluntary submission of hundreds or thousands of men and women. A few men promise to serve the tyrant to realize immediate gain for themselves; and each of these, in turn, has a few hangers-on who likewise expect to profit from their service. The second level of obedience, in turn, is enabled to flourish only because a third, a fourth, a fifth also exist in the hierarchy, until at the bottom a great mass of men are under the illusion that they are being compelled to obey. But basically, it is not the "troops on horseback, it is not the companies afoot, it is not arms that defend the tyrant," Boétie argues; for the force would not be available in the first place unless a great many men obeyed voluntarily to help organize and wield military power.

But if this is true, men need not slaughter their fellows in order to free themselves of tyranny. If the power of the tyrant, in other

15. Major important works of Bellarmine have now been translated into English under the following titles. *Political Excerpts: The Pope* (from the *III General Controversy*), 1575–1585; *Reply to Belloy: Authority of the Pope in Politica,* 1587; and *Power of the Pope in Temporal Affairs,* 1610. All the translations are by George A. Moore and are published by the Country Dollar Press, Chevy Chase, Maryland.
16. *Power of the Pope in Temporal Affairs,* p. 47.
17. *Ibid.,* ch. 31, "Dialogue Between the People Too Much Bound to an Earthly King and the Pope Salubriously Counselling the People."
18. *Reply to Belloy,* "Reply to the Principal Points of the Argument Which Is Falsely Entitled Catholic for the Succession of Henry of Navarre," *op. cit.,* ch. 20, p. 42.
19. Compare J. N. Figgis, *From Gerson to Grotius,* Cambridge: Cambridge University Press, 1956, p. 161.
20. See the English translation by Harry Kurz, published as *Anti-Dictator,* New York: Columbia University Press, 1942.

words, rests ultimately on consent or voluntary servitude, the answer to tyranny and corruption is for those who have given their consent to withdraw it. "Obviously," as de La Boétie puts it, "there is no need of fighting to overcome this single tyrant, for he is automatically defeated if the country refuses consent to its own enslavement: It is not necessary to deprive him of anything, but simply to give him nothing."

This doctrine of voluntary servitude made a deep impression on Michel Montaigne (1533–1592), philosopher and friend of de La Boétie, and he sought to publicize the principle after the death of the latter. During the bitterness of the civil wars, it appeared to be especially relevant, since it combined a theory of resistance with a firm abjuration of violence—something which one will not find in other sixteenth-century theories. But the essay appeared to have little effect in its own day and it was not until the twentieth century that its full significance was realized, in the context of pacifist doctrines like those of Gandhi.

Meanwhile, the groundwork was being laid for the theories of absolutism which rejected all defenses of resistance, whether violent or nonviolent.

The Vindication of Order Against Resistance

While Calvinists like Buchanan and Catholics like Bellarmine were forging theories which undercut the claims of aspiring national monarchs, other thinkers were building doctrines out of which were to emerge such conceptions as the divine right of kings and other principles of early modern absolutism.

But medieval theories of society were not surrendered without vigorous opposition. In Holland, for example, where the Dutch were engaged in a long rebellion against Philip II, several thinkers sought to demonstrate the legitimacy of revolt, basing their contentions on medieval precedents. Thus William the Silent himself in his famous *Apology* calls attention to the fact that the ancestors of Philip attained the throne when in 1369 Pedro the Cruel was deposed; and he asks his readers whether, if the deposition of Pedro was justified, the revolt of the Dutch Republic is not even more legitimate.

About the same time, moreover, Althusius, a naturalized Dutchman, is developing a very elaborate pluralist conception of society, which is more akin to medieval notions than to the emerging sixteenth-century ideas of sovereignty.[21] To Althusius, the significant factor about man is his association-making capacity and tendency. The real unit of society is not the individual, but rather the family group within which the individual is nurtured and without which he would have no being. Along with the family there exist the innumerable associations connected with economic and social life as a whole—guilds, towns, and religious associations which are not called into being by the King but are "natural" to man and have existences apart from that of the state. In an age when the individual is increasingly set up in opposition to the legal notion of a state with sovereignty, Althusius tends to deny the significance of the dichotomy. The claims of nonstate associational life, he insists, are binding on human beings and without a recognition of these claims, the prince can discover no social will to sustain his rule.[22]

But Althusius is in many respects speaking for an age which is passing. Indeed, one of the men whom he criticizes, Jean Bodin, is far more the harbinger of a new age than the Dutch thinker. For Bodin would see both Althusius and William the Silent as exemplars of disorder and would bracket them with such men as Buchanan and Bellarmine. In his *De la Republique* (1576), Bodin is above all concerned to develop the legal conception of sovereignty as a method of buttressing the claims of the French king against both the people and the pope.[23]

He departs radically from all those medieval views which see positive law as anterior to political authority and insists that before we can have a clear statement of the contents of law, we must assume a political authority to define it. This authority can be none other than the king, who is sovereign when he is subject to no higher law-making authority and unbound by any necessity to submit his will to the judgment of Estates or noble orders. Basically, we see in Bodin the development of the doctrine that law is essentially *will* (the will of the monarch) rather than reason; and while he is rather vague about the meaning he ascribes to the term, he thinks of law as the expression of force. The end of political society is order, and order is possible only when authoritative making of rules is confined to one man. Bodin is impatient with all those who would try to discern law in the rules of economic or social groups, except insofar as those rules are made a part of royal decrees.

Yet we should not make the mistake of thinking that Bodin discards all medieval legal categories. His major purpose is to clarify what is implicit in the notion of a positive political order expressing itself in what the medievalists would call human law. Such an order cannot exist, he is maintaining, if the human law is thought of as anterior to the lawmaker. Aside from this, however, Bodin argues that the king continues to remain under divine law, natural law, and *jus gentium*, or the law of nations. But how these laws are to be interpreted is a matter for royal authority and not for the pope or for an emperor. In terms of specifically human law, the monarch ceases to be sovereign when he recognizes a superior law-making or law-interpreting authority.[24]

The desideratum of order is reflected, too, in his attitude to religious toleration. He is, of course, a Catholic and if possible would like to see heresy suppressed. But he is quite aware that Calvinist power is growing and that any attempt to suppress heretics, beyond a certain point, could rend the kingdom. The means of suppression, in other words, could easily destroy the end for which suppression was undertaken—namely, a religious uniformity which might serve as a basis for political harmony. In such a contingency, thinks Bodin, it might be wiser to tolerate the heretics if by so doing the state could be assured some measure of political harmony; it is better to allow a measure of religious dissent than to allow the state to be destroyed completely. Like Mariana, Bodin has in mind, then, the possibility of a secular state, not because it is right to tolerate heretics but because it is expedient.[25]

Bodin's treatment of monarchy and the law is essentially an attempt to develop a "scientific" account of the state and an analytical view of law. While he is, of course, involved in the controversies of the time, his book is less a full polemic than a textbook which he hopes will be the theoretical basis for monarchical power as against the claims of the pope and those who would allege the right of resistance. Much more polemical in the absolutist direction is the treatise of William Barclay—*De regno et Royale Potestate* (*The Kingdom and the Regal Power*)—which was published in 1600, some time after Henry IV had become a Catholic and years after Buchanan and Duplessis-Mornay had developed their theories of disobedience and resistance. A Scotsman, Barclay had long resided in France, where he was a professor of law at a Jesuit institution.

Barclay's arguments for passive obedience and against men like Buchanan, Duplessis-Mornay, and Bellarmine set the stage for much of the seventeenth-century argument turning on the divine right of kings. As a Catholic, Barclay attacks the typical Jesuit argument in favor of papal temporal power and exalts a Gallican (French Nationalist) rather than an ultramontane (exalted papal authority) view of

21. Althusius' major work has been translated into English by Frederick S. Carney as *The Politics of Johannes Althusius*, London: Eyre and Spottiswoode, 1965.
22. Views like those of Althusius are akin to modern pluralist conceptions of H. J. Laski, Leon Duguit, J. N. Figgis, and G. D. H. Cole. See Chapter 28.
23. For interpretations of Bodin see Roger Chauviré, *Jean Bodin, auteur de la "République,"* Paris: E. Champion, 1914; and Beatrice Reynolds, *Proponents of Limited Monarchy in Sixteenth Century France: Francis Hotman and Jean Bodin*, New York: Columbia University Press, 1930.
24. Bodin's *Method for the Easy Comprehension of History* (1566), tends to limit the sovereign more than does his better-known *Six Books of the Republic* (1576). But the general comments in the text reflect the spirit of both volumes. Reynolds, *op. cit.*, has correctly observed that while Bodin in a sense gives absolute authority to the ruler insofar as the latter is placed above all positive law, the King is nevertheless bound by his coronation oath to observe the fundamental laws of the realm, including the Salic law on the succession and the Agrarian law on the inalienability of property. Moreover, "no decision of the king is binding unless it is in keeping with equity and truth" (pp. 117-118). But always, we should remember, these are *moral* commitments of the ruler: the oath apparently does not have the status of law in Bodin's interpretation.
25. In taking this position, Bodin is, of course, simply reflecting the attitude of the French politiques—the faction which, as we have seen, is ardently Catholic but at the same time concerned about the power of the French monarchy and the unity of the state. Among other leading members of the politiques one might mention Michel de l'Hôpital and Pierre Grégoire of Toulouse.

the Church. While his armory of ideological weapons is almost infinite, there is throughout a strong utilitarian strain which contends, against men like Buchanan, that rebellion and resistance always bring in their train more misery than they alleviate. Like Bodin, Barclay is at great pains to show that human law is essentially below the king and not above him.

That which is natural, he contends, can also be shown to be most useful, so that there is basically no conflict between the two, as some might assert.[26] Men are driven by the divine spark within them—nature—to associate themselves with one another and this association is useful to men as individuals. Rulership of some sort arises because the "wild license" of men must be restrained; and it may be established by four methods: imposition by force on the unwilling, election by the community, inheritance, or as a result of the gift of God. The first method results in tyranny, according to Barclay, and is excluded from his conception of kingship altogether. This means that kings, as such, may gain their power only through election, inheritance, or the direct appointment of God.

To support this thesis, he resorts, as do most sixteenth-century polemicists, to Scripture as well as to the secular tradition. Contrary to Buchanan, the ancient Hebrews, when they looked for a ruler, did not seek a tyrant but rather a king. Once they had attained him, Barclay maintains, the Old Testament account clearly shows that the community was required by God to obey him implicitly, even when he was oppressive. For while he was demanded by the community, he was given his authority by God. In a long account, Barclay tries to show that Scriptures never justify rebellion against the king; once his position has been established, his authority is plenary. He is legitimate in the way he obtains power, not in the way he uses it.

Thus the kings of Israel (and presumably all other kings) were, as he puts it, "legitimate, not because they performed their duty honestly and in accordance with the laws, but because they were made by rite and in consequence of the prescription of the laws; in which way an heir is understood to be legitimate."[27] Law is made by kings to control men and is not developed, as Buchanan and others would seem to argue, by men to control kings.

Nor does he confine his vindication of royal prerogatives to any one religious faith. While he attacks Boucher, a Catholic apologist, for defending the assassination of King Henry III, he is equally irritated when the same writer calls Queen Elizabeth "the Anglican harlot." In so doing, Barclay thinks, Boucher has forgotten not only "reverence for princes," which is due even to the "impious," but has also failed to remember "the meaning of the word, public prostitute."[28]

Like Bodin, Barclay thinks he can show that monarchy is the most natural form of government, although he would not, of course, deny that historically there have been other forms. In the first place, he thinks, the necessity for monarchy is proven by the relation of human beings to God. The human spirit is a particle of the divine mind and "so institutes and composes its actions that so far as possible through his terrestrial and muddy medium it may repeatedly echo the very simple nature of its own archetype."[29] The government of the universe is a monarchy and since man has within him the spirit of the universe's monarch, he is forever struggling to set up monarchy in his own society; although he may, of course, often be led astray into mixed forms and into essentially anarchic democracy.

But there is another consideration in favor of monarchical government and that is to be found in the example of the animals themselves. The "cranes follow one in lettered order." Herds of deer always obey a single leader—there is no governing assembly among them; and he recalls a hunt which he attended as a boy in which he was particularly impressed by the fact that "all those stags, in formation on the move, were proceeding" under the guidance of "one leader and ruler going out ahead."[30]

Kingship is intimately related to divinity, he maintains, and therefore the king can in no wise be held responsible and accountable to any but God himself. If he becomes tyrannical, he cannot be resisted by the people but only through an act of God.

But how does God apply sanctions against kings? Barclay wrestles with this question, particularly in light of Scripture. On the one hand, he recognizes that kings have in fact violated their coronation oaths and have acted oppressively, and that in many instances their overthrow by violence can be attributed to God. On the other hand, he stoutly asseverates that those who through their resistance were in effect agents of God cannot be justified. Barclay's formula is that the deity may act in ways which are not permitted to men; but from the perspective of God's law for humanity, those who in the end turn out to be his executioners must themselves be punished by human law.

Barclay's position seems to be that while men can never legitimately take the life of an oppressive ruler, if they nevertheless do so, they may conceivably be acting as officers of God. By contrast, the position of men like Mariana and Buchanan was much simpler and seemingly less filled with paradox: under certain circumstances, they argued, tyrannicide is fully justified and its perpetrator is to be regarded both as an agent of God and as a servant of human well-being. To have taken this uncomplex position, however, Barclay would have had to repudiate the two essential elements of his theory: the notion that the king is completely above the positive law and the idea of passive obedience.

Yet even Barclay is not quite as absolutist as he seems to be. While on the whole there appear to be no holes in his armory of kingly authority, he does apparently admit a few exceptions to the rule of passive obedience. Thus, if the king issues a command contrary to God's moral law, the subject may disobey, provided he be willing to accept the penalty of death: In effect he is not really resisting the king but rather obeying him. Where the king practices a private hatred not only against a few individuals but also acts in such a way as to "tear asunder the body of the Commonwealth, of which he is the head . . . with intolerable savagery," the people can resist. But they must not go "against the king." They can only protect themselves. In resisting mammoth injury to the Commonwealth, Barclay observes, they act in accordance with nature; but if they do violence to the king himself they run counter to nature.

Another exception to the principle of passive obedience is much clearer. When the king commits "that on account of which by his own right he would cease to be king," resistance is in order.[31] But Barclay is careful to point out that this can happen but rarely. As an example, he instances Nero, who, according to Aurelius Victor, decided to destroy both Senate and Roman people and to take up his "seat" elsewhere. In effect, he was deserting the Commonwealth completely.

It is significant that even an absolutist like Barclay can imagine situations in which resistance is legitimated. They appear to show that, absolutist though he is, he yet remains sensitive to some of the arguments of his opponents.

Toward the Seventeenth Century

We might summarize the great controversies involving Calvinist and Catholic polemicists by reminding ourselves, first of all, that the debate about political principles was still largely a reflection of ecclesiastical history. While Machiavelli had sought to separate religion and Church from politics and state and Luther had in part blessed the Machiavellian attempt, ecclesiastical and religious themes could not be eliminated from Calvinist and Jesuit polemics if only because both, on the whole, still thought in terms of the religious rather than the secular state. Although men like Mariana, Bellarmine, and Barclay might vaguely glimpse a political society which would in the name of order admit religious diversity, the principle was by no means fully worked out. On the whole, the end of the sixteenth century witnessed a widespread acceptance of the principle that Christendom would probably never be reunited. At the same time, most thinkers still hoped that the idea of religious uniformity within given parts of the old Christendom could be preserved, if only as a basis for order.

It is in the light of the predominant religious presuppositions that one must view the whole debate about the right of resistance. Initially, neither Calvinists nor Jesuits had any well-rounded theories on the subject, despite the references to lower magistrates in Calvin and the somewhat whiggish doctrines of St. Thomas Aquinas. However, the position of Calvinists under Catholic rulers and of Catholics under Calvinist or other Protestant princes led both sides to speculate more fully on the problem.

But resistance itself was inextricably bound up with the issue of legitimacy. As medieval ties increasingly disintegrated and individuals

26. *The Kingdom and the Regal Power,* George A. Moore, trans., Chevy Chase, Md.: Country Dollar Press, n.d., p. 22.
27. *Ibid.*, p. 77.
28. *Ibid.*, p. 412.
29. *Ibid.*, p. 105.
30. *Ibid.*, p. 107.
31. *Ibid.*, p. 273.

felt themselves even more rootless, the ancient question as to what constitutes legitimacy in a ruler took on new meaning. Closely connected with it was, of course, the problem of political obligation. In both Calvinists and Jesuits there is an acute awareness of the ambiguous character of legitimacy; and while both factions tend still to identify legitimacy in a ruler with his overtly expressed religious faith, there is an equally important tendency to break away from this notion. Barclay, for example, recognizes both Julian the Apostate and Elizabeth as legitimate, even though he abominates their principles; and while Bellarmine argues against the claims of Henry of Navarre on grounds of his heresy, he clearly opens the way for the idea of a legitimacy unconnected with religious faith.

The problem of legitimacy is, of course, closely bound up with other questions as well. It is important to note the large place which contractual ideas play in the sixteenth century discussion. Thus Knox places great stress on covenants and Duplessis-Mornay on the notion of the double contract. Frequently, implicit contractual conceptions are attributed to feudalism, which furnishes analogies both for theorists of resistance like Duplessis-Mornay and for absolutists like Barclay.

Finally, we should note the embryonic presence of democratic conceptions. These can, of course, be easily exaggerated. For the most part, when sixteenth-century thinkers refer to the people, they mean the medieval estates, or even the nobility, as opposed to the king. Yet the very fact that the people are so often appealed to—even by absolutists like Barclay, who admits the elective principle for the original king—is significant, particularly in connection with the right of resistance. The ordinary individual, moreover, begins to take on a new sense of importance when Calvinists like Buchanan and Jesuits like Mariana admit the legitimacy of tyrannicide as well as the right of collective resistance.

In the seventeenth century, while political theory and ideology are still closely connected with ecclesiastical history, the rise of full-blown secularist conceptions of political society makes the connection much more tenuous. And it is in the seventeenth century, too, that we shall find an interaction of natural science with political thought, as well as the development of more solid foundations for democratic theory. We turn to questions of this kind in the chapters which immediately follow.

chapter 19

The New Science and the Contract: Thomas Hobbes

While the debates between those advocating a right of resistance and those insisting on divine right (or some other absolutist doctrine) were maturing, the way was being prepared for one of the most unusual systems of all in the history of political thought. For three centuries Thomas Hobbes has remained a controversial figure throughout the western world. In his own day, he was attacked by almost every faction. In our time, interest in Hobbes has remained lively, with exponents of the "science of politics" seeing in his system a good example of model-making and a contemporary writer even alleging that Hobbes—contrary to most of his interpreters—was something of a traditionalist.[1]

Historically, of course, Hobbes emerged at a time when much political speculation was beginning to be almost completely separated from ecclesiastical history and theological discussions—a process which Machiavelli had initiated and which Hobbes himself was to push to its outer limits. Politics in his hands ostensibly rounded out its autonomy; and contract, which we have already seen as assuming a central place in some of the later Calvinists, became a new basis for absolutism.

Hobbes and the Politics of His Time

Hobbes was born in 1588, at a time when the political uncertainties of the sixteenth century were at their height; and the young Hobbes was no doubt familiar with the attempts made on the lives of Elizabeth, Henry IV, and other rulers. His own insecurities—so central a characteristic of his life—were perhaps deeply affected not only by the events of his time but also by his premature birth and the fact that his father deserted the family at an early age.

After a somewhat bored career at Oxford, he became tutor to William Cavendish in 1608. By this time he was thoroughly conversant with classical Greek learning, which would play a very important, although sometimes a negative role in his later development.[2]

After the death of his first patron, who had become the second Earl of Devonshire, Hobbes continued as tutor to the third Earl, accompanying his pupil on the Grand Tour of the Continent. There he made the acquaintance of Galileo. It was during his travels, too, that he alighted on the 47th proposition of the first book of Euclid,[3] which made so deep an impression on him that he exclaimed, "By God, this is impossible!" He fell in love with geometry thereafter, as did so many others in his day, and this initiated a train of mathematical thought which would deeply affect his political views.

Meanwhile, as Hobbes was being stirred by Euclid and outlying projects for future books, the politics of the world were becoming even more disturbed. The Thirty Years' War, which had broken out in 1608 and was perhaps one of the most senseless wars in history, continued its bloody course until 1648; and as usual in such cases, the original alleged causes of the conflict were by the conclusion of the war largely forgotten. Hobbes was no doubt keenly aware of all this and must have asked himself many times how order, for which he always had such a passionate longing, could be restored.

When the first portents of bloody Civil War between the king and Parliament appeared, Hobbes entered a phase of his life which would extend to the Restoration. He fled back and forth between Britain and the Continent in the effort to preserve his life. Meanwhile, he had published *Elements of Law, Natural and Politique* (1640), in which most of his later doctrines were anticipated. In 1647 appeared *De Cive* and in 1651 the *Leviathan*. Although he sought to present a copy of the latter to the exiled Charles II, the monarch, in indignation, refused to receive him, for Charles was quite aware that Hobbes, while favoring monarchy, grounded his beliefs not on divine right—the current basis for the defense of rule by one and the doctrine so exhalted by the king's grandfather, James I—but rather on the subversive doctrine of contract.[4]

After the Restoration, to be sure, Hobbes gradually accommodated himself to the Stuarts and they to him. However, even his later life, which was, on the whole, not insecure, was occasionally disturbed. After the great fire and plague of 1666, for example, the House of Commons appointed a committee to investigate the causes of the disaster and particularly to inquire into its possible connections with "atheism" and "profanity." The Commons had in mind the works of a former Roman Catholic priest by the name of White, who was allegedly denying the immortality of the soul; but it also thought that "one Thomas Hobbes in *Leviathan*" might through his godlessness have led the deity to visit punishment on London. Fortunately for Hobbes, the affair came to nothing.

By the end of his long life in 1679, he had managed to touch in his writings on the whole range of human knowledge, from physics to politics. And in everything he wrote he was much influenced by the "new science" of his

1. See Howard Warrender, *The Political Philosophy of Hobbes*, London: Oxford University Press, 1957. The import of Warrender's version of Hobbes is certainly to place the seventeenth-century philosopher nearer to St. Thomas Aquinas than the usual interpretation would permit. For a criticism of Warrender's view, see John Plamenatz, "Mr. Warrender's Hobbes," *Political Studies* 5 (1957), 295–308. Warrender replies in *Political Studies* 8 (1960), 48–57.
2. Leo Strauss tends to stress the significance of Hobbes' classical background. See his *The Political Philosophy of Thomas Hobbes*, 2nd ed., Chicago: University of Chicago Press, Phoenix Books, 1963, ch. 3–5.
3. The 47th Proposition of the First Book is "In right-angled triangles, the square on the side subtending the right angle is equal to the squares on the sides containing the right angle."
4. Hobbes' literary works indicate the breadth of his interests. Thus his primarily political works include, in addition to the well-known *Elements of Law, De Cive*, and *Leviathan, Behemoth: History of the Causes of Civil War in England* and *Dialogue Between a Philosopher and a Student of the Common Law of England*. In the latter work he attacks the views of Chief Justice Coke. In *Historia Ecclesiastica*, he criticizes the alleged encroachments of ecclesiastical on civil power. In 1658, he published his treatise on psychology, *De Homine*. In 1674, at the age of 86, he published his *Principles of Geometry*, and at the age of 90 an essay on physics. Meanwhile, he had become embroiled with an Anglican bishop on the problem of freedom of the will.

time, the history of which constitutes an indispensable background for an understanding of his political thought.

The New Science and the Mind of Thomas Hobbes

Although Hobbes lived in an age of violent religious conflict, it was also an epoch in which many of the characteristic attitudes of the ages of faith were being undermined, not merely by the skepticism characterizing most periods of expanding commerce, but also by a new scientific temperament. An intellectual development which had begun in the time of Ockham, or even that of Roger Bacon (in the thirteenth century), and had been accentuated during the Renaissance, was now proceeding at a furious pace. Men struggled toward an altered view of philosophical problems and a radically different perspective on the physical universe.

The growth of science was an expression of the desire to know the natural and to eschew the supernatural, which, in any event, it came to be held, was beyond true knowledge. But how could one study nature? There was great dissatisfaction with the scholasticism of the earlier period on the ground that, while it could prove or refute what was already known and could discuss conceptions of things, it offered no sure way to discover the new or to study "things" in themselves. An older contemporary of Hobbes, Francis Bacon, Viscount Verulam (1561–1626), was particularly antagonistic to what he held were the purely deductive studies of medieval Aristotelianism. Our real understanding of the external world, he maintained, was impeded by four "idols," whose destruction he demanded in the name of true knowledge.[5]

One idol, he contended, was that of the tribe. Men tended to make themselves the measure of the outer world—to read into physical and biological phenomena purely human ends and purposes. Thus Bacon proceeded to attack all teleological ways of looking at nature. A second idol was the cave. All men find, in other words, that their conception of the external world is distorted by the bias which arises from their particular stations in life, their vocations, or their class statuses. The idols of the market had to do with usages of language. Human beings, Bacon asserted, tend to conventionalize meanings of words and then to accept those meanings uncritically. Finally, the idols of the theatre were those stereotyped conceptions which we receive from the past uncritically—we take them simply on the authority of a prestigious figure.

Bacon thought that scientists had to discover methods of guarding against slavery to the four idols. They had to develop what we should today call an empirical approach to nature—to proceed inductively from the particular or concrete to the general, rather than deductively from the general to the particular. Bacon's scheme of causation naturally discards all final causes and, in fact, concentrates on what Aristotle would have called the efficient, material, and formal causes.

But Bacon was unclear as to how the particulars discovered could be related to one another. The purpose of science to him was practical—it was to be developed in order that man might control the external world, not that he might know it as an end in itself. Because of this practical orientation, Bacon was only slightly interested in the value of mathematics, for example, which provides a basis for the ordering of measurable facts. While, therefore, he is important in the history of thought for his attack on traditional and unexamined stereotypes and for his insistence on direct observation, he had but a limited understanding of problems involved in higher-level theoretical constructs.

It was a contemporary of Bacon—Johannes Kepler (1561–1639)—who was in considerable degree responsible for the early modern wedding of empirical observation to mathematics. An astronomer, Kepler was convinced that behind the diverse phenomena that Bacon insisted on observing was an order which could be expressed in terms of mathematical relations. Diversities could be fitted into *principles* or laws of change.

Meanwhile, Galileo Galilei (1564–1642) was beginning to work out the principles of mechanics and to associate them with motion. Experiment, said Galileo, consists in the isolation of simple phenomena in order to measure them. The task of the scientist, according to this mechanistic view, is to discover the most primitive motions, for the more complex ones could be understood only in terms of the simpler out of which they arose. But always the key is quantification. Although Plato had placed great emphasis on the expression of reality in mathematical terms, in this following the Pythagoreans,[6] his use of mathematics was in connection with the Form or idea that lay beyond the motion and change of the world of sense. Now, however, there was being constructed not a mathematical theory of motionless Form but rather a mathematical theory of motion itself.

Bacon had stressed the importance of empirical investigation, Kepler had sought in the motions of the planetary bodies to discover laws of change, and Galileo had emphasized the application of mathematical principles to the motions studied by Kepler. It was René Descartes (1596–1650) who, seizing on the mathematical side of the Galilean statement, concluded that the only rational science was mathematics. So far did Descartes carry this proposition that he came to distrust sense altogether; thus apparently departing radically from the empiricism which had been the foundation for Bacon's speculations. As a matter of fact, the Baconian attack on scholastic deduction had led to an induction that in turn had been fitted into a mathematical framework from which a new emphasis on deduction emerged.

According to Descartes—and even more to some of his disciples—the method of induction should lead, if fruitful, to a single principle in accordance with which experience might be explained. From this single point of certainty, he held, one could then deduce other statements about the external world. These logical deductions would be congruent with the world as it is. As is well known, Descartes reaches his point of metaphysical certainty by doubting his experiences but then concluding that the very process of doubting and dreaming requires a doubter and dreamer. One can at least be certain, then, of the existence of one's consciousness, he holds. And there are also other ideas which are as clear and distinct as one's consciousness of selfhood: these are the ideas which Descartes called innate and they were the basis of true, as contrasted with merely sense knowledge.

The general tendency of Descartes' thought was toward a kind of abstract rationalism. This was even more true of his disciples, the Cartesians, who pushed the notion to extremes. Whereas Descartes through his "synthetic method" hoped that science would, in the words of a commentator, be a "progress in discovery from one intuitive truth to another," the Cartesians "confounded the creatively free intellectual activity . . . with that rigidly demonstrative system of exposition which they found in Euclid's *Text-book of Geometry*."[7]

This position would become a key to an understanding of much eighteenth-century thought, which stressed the possibilities of an abstract reason from which one could deduce the nature of the world of particulars.

By the time of the Cartesians, the new science which had begun with a revolt against the deductionism of scholasticism had come round full circle to a new form of rationalistic deductionism. Instead of deducing the world from Aristotle, however, it was to be derived from the points of certainty associated with the Cartesian approach.

The general bent of the new science and new philosophy of Hobbes' time was to despiritualize nature, to wipe out the distinction between animate and inanimate, and to create a sharp separation between the inner and outer worlds. Whereas the older view had been to impute purposes to natural phenomena, the new outlook erected a mechanical model: natural phenomena could only be explained by searching out their origins in the presumably simple motions from which all others were derivative. But if all nature—including human nature—could be explained mechanistically, there was no longer any basis for the distinction between bodies called animals and bodies called stones. According to Descartes, animal bodies were simply very complex automatisms which, while they might be far more involved than stones, could be explained in the same way. Finally, the inner world was that of qualitative sense experience, while the outer universe was that of mathematically measurable and therefore real bodies. The inner world was what later came to be called merely subjective; while the outer world was real and objective.

As for the relation of this background to Hobbes himself, we may say that the political disorders of his time and of the previous generation furnished the *occasion* for his political philosophy, while the new science and philosophy suggested to him a *method*. The basic elements of his political thought were worked out between 1637 and 1651, the years

5. *Novum Organon Scientiarum* (1629).
6. See Chapter 3, pp. 48–49.
7. Wilhelm Windelband, *A History of Philosophy*, vol. 2, New York and London: Macmillan, 1893, p. 395.

of greatest chaos in Britain. In using the new science and philosophy as the foundation for his method, Hobbes undoubtedly thought that he had discovered the key for unlocking the door to a true political philosophy which would at the same time furnish an irrefutable foundation for political order.

Knowledge and the General Nature of Hobbes' Political Thought

True to the spirit of the new science and philosophy, Hobbes explicitly takes the science of geometry as his model for political and moral knowledge. "Whatsoever things they are in which this present doth differ from the rude simpleness of antiquity," he observes, "we must acknowledge to be a debt which we owe merely to geometry."[8] The "nature of human actions," he goes on, should be as "distinctly known" as the "nature of quantity in geometrical figures."

He sees knowledge as a whole divided into two broad areas–the register of the knowledge of fact, which would embrace both natural and civil history; and, secondly, science, which includes natural philosophy and political and social philosophy. Knowledge of fact is absolute. Knowledge of science is conditional; that is, the scientist is interested in discovering under what conditions certain consequences or motions are likely to occur.

Throughout his analysis of the problem of knowledge, Hobbes makes it clear that he views both the natural and the political worlds as essentially machines. As we shall see, he ridicules all views which would discern nonmechanistic features in either area. He specifically analogizes the understanding of civil government to the comprehension of watches. We know the political world, he avers, by seeking out its roots in the primitive; by looking at the parts which added together constitute the whole.[9]

This mechanistic conception implies, of course, that wholes are not more than the sum totals of their parts. Thus states are aggregates of individuals and persons mere mixtures–and not compounds–of all their physiological and psychological elements, or, in Hobbes' terms, their motions. There is a tendency throughout to a kind of reductionism which would see political events as simply psychological, psychological phenomena as only physiological, and the physiological as physicochemical.

Egoistic Psychology: The Nature of Man

Applying this general view, Hobbes conceives of the human individual in a state of nature as an aggregation of desires or appetites. Contrary to Aristotle and the whole later medieval tradition, this being never seeks society as an end but always only as a means. Men, then, are not political and social animals, as St. Thomas had averred, but rather solitary beasts.

These isolated beings are egoistic: Everything they do has reference to the effect of the proposed action on themselves. They cannot help themselves in this respect for each of them is imprisoned within his own inner consciousness. There each is at first secure, for by nature no one of us can really know anything except one's own inner state of consciousness. This solipsistic tendency in Hobbes' conception reinforces, of course, the psychological theory of men as egoists; for if I can know only my own inner states, then nothing else can really and truly be of concern to me. Every individual is subject to the motions of his mind, which in turn are reflections of the motions or appetites of his body.

Now each of these solitary beings has within him a chief motion or appetite, which is the driving force that leads him to seek power for himself: his self-concern blinds him to the signs which come to him from the external world, so that in pure nature he imagines all things which these signs represent as subordinate to his sway. He is like a king who believes that all creation was meant to do his bidding; and his acts reflect this belief. Thus he is imperious and proud; and all objects which seem to get in the way of his appetite for power are ruthlessly crushed.[10]

But a difficulty arises when men in a state of nature are shocked–and it is a traumatic experience of enormous proportions–into realizing that there are other men who are approximately equal to themselves. They begin to see this when they clash with others in the struggle for power. Originally under the illusion not only that they are the kings of the universe but also that they are immortal, it is the friction between bodies, each of them dominated by lust for dominion, which leads them to realize that there are other powers to be reckoned with.

When men are forced into awareness of the menace of others, they come to fear death at the hands of others. The very rough equality which exists in a state of nature is the basis for insecurity; for while men are not literally equal to one another in all respects, on balance their differences cancel each other out and lead a natural man to conclude that if he can kill another one day a different individual may kill him the following.[11] While each by nature wishes to kill or enslave others, each comes to understand the terrifying fact that he may be subject to a similar terror.

It is the mutual fear which "consists partly in the natural equality of men, partly in their mutual will of hurting"[12] that creates a general atmosphere of anxiety. Neither potential enemy quite knows what the other will do. As the two stand poised, the tension mounts. Torn between the desire to overcome the antagonist and the fear of being killed by him, each man eventually breaks the tension by falling upon the other. "Warre" is the result.[13] And the state of nature is thus characterized by constant and uninterrupted warfare. Man's life is, in Hobbes' words, "nasty, brutish, and short."

Throughout his account of human psychology in nature, it will be noted that Hobbes always assumes discrete individuals as the basis of the power struggle. It is never groups of individuals who are involved. This individualism is, of course, one of the most highly characteristic features not merely of Hobbes but also of most early modern thinkers; and we have seen it growing from the time of the late Middle Ages, sometimes in religious language but increasingly in nonreligious terminology.

Good and Evil, Pleasure and Pain

In a strict sense, of course, there are no morals in a state of nature; for if one views morality as involving some choice, Hobbes' account would permit man no alternatives. Driven by the "restlesse desire of Power after power, that ceaseth onely in Death," the individual cannot help himself—any more than, later on, Marx's capitalist can avoid seeking profits. The good, then, is simply a name which we give to those drives which push us to seek pleasure and to avoid all acts which would frustrate our pleasure. Whatever helps to strengthen the advantages of an individual, in other words, may be called good. Hobbes clearly repudiates the notion that there is a supreme good, or *summum bonum*, despite the venerable history associated with that idea. If the restlessness with which we seek pleasure (power) halts only in death, it is not difficult to see that there is no haven within which we can find peace. Both Plato, who sees the supreme good as contemplation of the Forms, and Augustine, who suggests it is found in seeing God, are wrong.

It is a peculiar feature of Hobbes' thought, however, that while there is no supreme good, there is a supreme evil, or *summum malum*.[14] This Hobbes identifies with the violent death which a man fears he will suffer at the hands of his opponent. Death completely frustrates the restless quest for power and is thus the supreme negation.

Hobbes makes it clear, too, that men merely *appear* to enjoy society as an end in itself. Because of their egoistic constitutions, the good of human social ties is always relative to its ability to enhance the power (and therefore the "good") of the individual. "We do not . . . by nature," Hobbes bluntly asserts, "seek society for its own sake, but that we may receive some honour or profit from it; these we desire primarily, that secondarily."[15]

Altruism is thus in the end the individual's effort to enhance his egoistic pleasure. Pity is really an expression of concern for ourselves and not for others: We imagine ourselves in their places and thus become fearful of disaster befalling ourselves. As a matter of fact, all the alleged social virtues are for Hobbes simply fear for ourselves.

Of what, then, does right consist in the state of nature? Since there is no objective good common to all, it must necessarily be a purely individual attribute. Each man has a right to all that which his power can gain, provided, however, that the pursuit of gain does not lead to his death, which would of course, negate his own striving. Thus each in a state of nature, and subject to the great limiting condition, has a right to seize all the land, to wipe out his opponents, and to take the best women for himself. Each acts, therefore, so that he can

8. *De Cive*, "Epistle Dedicatory."
9. *Ibid.*
10. *Leviathan*, Pt. I, ch. 11.
11. *De Cive*, Pt. I, ch. 1, 3.
12. *Ibid.*
13. *Leviathan*, I, 13.
14. *Ibid.*
15. *De Cive*, I, 1, 2.

gain all the good possible at the expense of his neighbor, while at the same time so conducting himself that he does not destroy the very possibility of that good.

Another great seventeenth-century thinker, Benedict Spinoza (1632–1677), whose position at this and certain other points resembles that of Hobbes, puts the matter in this way: "The natural right of the individual man is thus determined, not by sound reason, but by desire and power."[16] And a little later, he rather strikingly remarks that the "right and ordinance of nature . . . only prohibits such things as no one desires, and no one can attain: it does not forbid strife, nor hatred, nor anger, nor deceit, nor, indeed, any of the means suggested by desire."[17] According to Spinoza, "natural rights of the individual . . . are co-extensive with his desires and power."[18] Hobbes would agree. A man in nature uses others for his own ends, weighing out just enough altruism to make them pliant instruments for his own power.

But the means which may be used for the attainment of his ends are many and various. The question arises, therefore, as to who shall be the judge of the degree to which the proposed means actually conduce to the attainment of the goal. Here the answer of Hobbes is always the same: In the state of nature, each individual must be the final authority as to the utility of methods; for each is equal to everyone else in power.[19]

The Laws of Nature and the Contract

Confronted by the *summum malum* and recognizing as good only the endless and individual pursuit of pleasure and power, natural man searches for principles under which he is least likely to be killed and most likely to be allowed to express his quest for glory. Had it not been for the fear of death, society presumably would never have been established. It is fear, then, which is the creator of all social intercourse whatsoever.

Aware of this, natural man deduces certain laws of nature which will guide him in minimizing possibility of annihilation and maximizing individual honor and power. Here, it should be observed, Hobbes, while using the ancient expression laws of nature, is basing them upon premises radically different from those of the classical position, which had begun with the proposition that human beings were social and political by nature. Hobbes, by contrast, is meaningless unless we see him as assuming exactly the contrary: That men are purely egoistic by nature.

The laws of nature for Hobbes, then, are principles which an egoistic man discerns by a process like that which a mathematician uses in deducing statements from a few basic axioms. There is but a single dictate of reason which somehow natural man discovers: The dictate which advises "us to look to the preservation and safeguard of ourselves." All other laws of nature, according to Hobbes, can be deduced from this principle by as rigorous a process as that which the geometrician employs.[20]

What are the laws deduced? The fundamental one is "that every man ought to endeavour Peace, as far as he has hope of obtaining it; and when he cannot obtain it, that he may seek, and use, all helps, and advantages of Warre."[21] Peace is to be preferred to war, in other words, because war is likely to destroy my own ego, given the fact that other wills are under circumstances of war seeking to kill me physically. A second law of nature is that a man be willing, if others agree, to surrender his right to all things and "be contented with so much liberty against other men, as he would allow other men against himself."[22]

Once men understand that they can preserve themselves only by seeking a society which is unnatural, they covenant among themselves to surrender the natural right to all things and also the right as individuals to judge the best means of extending their egos. Their wills are submitted "to the will of one man, or one council"[23] and they contract with one another "not to resist the will of that one man, or council."[24] But the contract also includes a clause which preserves the right of each man to defend himself if the ruler tries to kill him.[25]

Accompanying the fundamental and second law of nature are certain other laws supposedly deduced from the basic rule. They include such principles as respect for the keeping of covenants; the pardon of offences to those who repent; refusal to hate one another; avoidance of pride; and doing to others what we wish them to do to us. Deduced as they are from our individual egoistic urge to power and physical survival, these laws are not really propositions of morality but rather maxims of prudence.

When men contract with one another to leave the state of nature, they then enter civil society where the equality of nature gives way to subordination to the ruler. But no covenant is made with the ruler himself: He accepts his power from the contractors but makes absolutely no promises to them in doing so. Thus he is free to act in any way he sees fit, subject only to the primary law of nature that he preserve himself. The security of the civil state rests in considerable measure on what Hobbes calls terror; that is, the ruler pools the powers of individuals and is able through this combination to intimidate those who would break the newly developed harmony.[26]

The ruler becomes the sole interpreter of the laws of nature and defines their terms as he sees fit. As a matter of fact, they are not true laws until the ruler translates them into positive rules; for a principle unsanctioned by the sword is not law. Like Bodin, Hobbes is seeking a neat, logically organized social order, with no ragged edges and no doubt as to where authority is lodged. In his search for security, he is rejecting all medieval-like conceptions which would separate spirituals from temporals and see both law and authority as somewhat pluralistic.

His view is made even more starkly clear if we contrast it with a position like that of Sir Edward Coke, a traditionalist who defended the common law against both Parliament and the king. The king, insisted Coke, was under both statutory and common law, even though he was called sovereign. Parliament itself was not to be thought of as sovereign in Hobbes' sense, for in a famous case Coke (in 1610) had said:

> In many cases, the common law will controul acts of Parliament, and sometimes adjudge them to be utterly void: for when an act of Parliament is against common right and reason, or repugnant, or impossible to be performed, the common law will controul it, and adjudge such acts to be void.[27]

Common right, common law, and reason, as used in Coke, would be to Hobbes obfuscations or possibly, as in the *Leviathan,* simply ghosts. Law is will, not reason, and must proceed from and be interpreted by an identifiable and clearly defined sovereign limited only by his own—or, in the case of a Parliament, by its own—version of the so-called laws of nature and prudential considerations. In taking a position radically different from that of medievalists like Coke, Hobbes indicates his sharp break with the past and pushes forward to the modern positivist view of law.

Implications of the Contract: Rebellion and Political Obligation

In the great artificial monster leviathan which Hobbes identifies with the state, it would seem that there can be no justification for revolt or disobedience. Indeed, Hobbes' political treatises can be looked upon from one point of view as a running attack on all those sixteenth-

16. *Tractatus Theologico-Politicus,* R. H. M. Elwes, trans., *Bohn's Philosophical Library, Chief Works of Benedict de Spinoza,* London, 1883; reprinted in *Writings on Political Philosophy* by Benedict de Spinoza, A. G. A. Balz, ed., New York: D. Appleton-Century, 1937, ch. 16, p. 28.
17. *Ibid.*, p. 29.
18. *Ibid.*, preface, p. 11.
19. *De Cive*, I, 1, 8.
20. Warrender, *op. cit.*, distinguishes Hobbes' theory of motivation from his theory of obligation. Motivation, according to this interpretation, has self-preservation as its main aim. But while self-preservation is a "validating condition," it is not a basis of obligation. The validating condition must be satisfied if a ground of obligation is to be operative. Warrender contends that in Hobbes there is a right of self-preservation but that this does not mean a duty to preserve oneself. The "laws of nature" are not maxims for individual self-preservation but rather basic principles for preservation of men in general based on concern for the conservation of society or of men in general. A debate has raged as to whether Hobbes can have a genuine theory of moral and political obligation. Obviously, Warrender thinks that he does have one. For a contrary view, see Thomas Nagel, "Hobbes's Concept of Obligation," *Philosophical Review* (January 1959), 68–83. According to Nagel—and the argument in the present text is similar—Hobbes' so-called theory of obligation is based exclusively on considerations of rational self-interest.
21. *Leviathan*, I, 14.
22. *Ibid.*
23. *De Cive*, II, 5, Art. 7.
24. *Ibid.*
25. *Leviathan*, I, 14.
26. *De Cive*, II, 5, 8.
27. Bonham's case, Coke's Reports, Pt. VIII, 118a. See also Catherin Drinker Bowen, *The Lion and the Throne*, Boston: Little, Brown, 1956, p. 315. On Coke in general, see Herman Block and Hastings Lyon, *Edward Coke, Oracle of the Law*, Boston: Houghton Mifflin, 1929. Hobbes' *Dialogue Between a Philosopher and a Student of the Common Law of England* is, of course, a sharp polemic against Cokian attitudes.

century thinkers—Buchanan, Bellarmine, and Mariana, for example—who in any way seek to justify rebellion or tyrannicide. Psychologically, Hobbes seems to be saying, the individual *cannot* revolt; for have not the "mental bodies in motion" pushed him into approving the contract and, with it, all the resulting consequences of absolutism?

If one presses Hobbes on the constitutional crises of his day and asks whether a sovereign's disregard for historically embedded rights is not a cause for rebellion, his answer would be no. History itself, he would argue, is still a matter of interpretation and once man has covenanted a civil society, the sole interpretative prerogative has been surrendered to the sovereign: History and alleged traditional rights (such as those embodied in Magna Carta) are what the sovereign chooses to make them.

Yet despite the apparent clarity and consistency with which Hobbes rejects any justification for disobedience, one must always point out a fundamental ambiguity about his thought at this point. We have already noted that in the making of the contract he assumes one reservation by those who assent to it, namely, "A Covenant not to defend myself from force, by force, is always voyd."[28] And he goes on to explain this: "Though a man may Covenant thus, *Unlesse I do so, or so, kill me;* he Cannot Coveneant thus, *Unlesse I do so, or so, I will not resist you, when you come to kill me.* For man by nature chooseth the lesser evil, which is the danger of death in resisting."[29]

It requires but little imagination to envision a situation in which there is widespread resistance to executioners sent out by what Mariana might call a tyrannical sovereign. The resisters are successful in killing or disabling all the agents of the sovereign and, in order to make certain that they are not again assaulted, they proceed to attack the sovereign (whether individual or council) himself. They do kill the sovereign, whose police and soldiers immediately begin to obey the successful resisters. In a situation of this kind, Hobbes would have to say that the resisters have become the new sovereign, despite the fact that they had covenanted to obey the former one. The fact that their revolt was successful apparently legitimated the resistance retroactively. This does not mean, of course, that Hobbes vindicates any theoretical right of resistance. Indeed, had the resisters been unsuccessful, the right would have been with the original sovereign as he successfully executed them. What does seem to emerge, however, is Hobbes' clear identification of right with the control of might.

In view of these aspects of Hobbes' theory, it is not surprising that in his own day there were few who were enthusiastic about it. Its ultimate identification of authority with power, of right with might—whether the might of physical force or of public opinion—would not endear him to the monarchists, despite his overwhelming preference for monarchy as a form of government.[30] Most monarchists espoused the divine right of kings precisely because they were searching for a principle which would transcend the shifting sands of power alignments and plebeian opinion. Hobbes failed them because his support of monarchy is in the last analysis solely dependent on the ability of the monarch to prevent successful rebellion. When Cromwell triumphed, Hobbes had no compunctions about taking the oath of allegiance to the Lord Protector, for his success in the use of force had legitimated him.

On the other hand, the Cromwellians and other members of the parliamentary faction could not wax enthusiastic about Hobbes in view of his preference for monarchy, the obviously meterialistic basis for his system, and the strange way (to religious men) in which he manipulated Scripture to suit his purposes.

Implications of the Contract: Religion and Conscience

The full implications of Hobbes' conceptions can perhaps best be understood by turning to his discussion of religion. While he cannot avoid the use of traditional religious terms in most of his political speculations, it is in Parts III and IV of the *Leviathan,* where he treats of the "ecclesiastical commonwealth" and the "kingdom of darkness," that we find the most elaborate examination.

He is, of course, in full revolt against the remnants of medieval scholasticism. But he is also out of sympathy with all views, whether Catholic or Protestant, Platonic or Augustinian, which would ground religious and moral experience on anything objective. All this is obviously consistent with his tendency to accept a solipsistic view of knowledge, his psychological egoism, and his ethical hedonism.

The "kingdom of darkness" is for him that combination of scriptural and philosophical misinterpretations which he associates with scholasticism and with all those views that would see religion as having, in its external observances, an existence independent from that of the civil ruler. He is particularly bitter, as we might expect, in his attack on realistic epistemology. Class names are "ghosts"; "essences" are mere figments of the imagination.[31]

It is clear that Hobbes' attempted refutation of realistic positions has a strictly practical aim: that of eliminating what he regards as the false ideas which prevent men from having a true view of sovereignty and of the basis for civil society. Once the intellectual cobwebs are swept away, he says in effect, men will see clearly that my model of civil society, including the contract, is the only correct one. And when they do envision politics as I see it, they will understand their obligations to the sovereign. From this will flow complete obedience, true order, and the elimination of such discontents as civil wars and factionalism.

With this in mind, he launches into an exposition of his nominalistic view of religion. The whole burden of the argument is to show that, whatever one might think inwardly about the symbols, traditions, and beliefs of religion, any actions or beliefs which are externally expressed are legitimately subject to the sovereign. Like Luther, except with much greater consistency, he thinks of the sphere of religion as an inner one; for in the private consciousness of solipsistic man all kinds of wild imaginings are permissible and no one can say whether they are pious or impious, true or false. As in so many other areas of theological and political speculation, Spinoza expresses Hobbes' thought when he maintains that those who hold sovereign power have rights over everything, whether civil or spiritual.[32] The implication of this view is that when the individual expresses himself publicly or acts publicly in the name of religion, his words and his actions are completely under the authority of the prince. And Hobbes endeavors to prove all this in Biblical terms by one of the most astounding manipulations of scriptural texts of the seventeenth century, or, indeed, of all time.

In his examination of the meaning of church, he has much to say about the etymology of the term ecclesia. He points out its origin in Greek culture as an assembly called by the magistrate. He then goes on to examine its several meanings in the New Testament—as a house, for example, and as the whole "multitude of Christian men, how far soever they be dispersed." But there is only one sense, he argues, in which ecclesia in Scripture can be "taken for one Person; that is to say, that it can be said to have power to will, to pronounce, to command. . . ." We should probably say the objective church, or, with Augustine, the visible church.

It is this latter meaning of the term which interests Hobbes, for he is intent on discovering who summons the church or assembly in this sense. His answer, and the reasons for it,

28. *Leviathan*, I, 14.
29. *Leviathan*, I, 14.
30. In Behemoth, for example, which treats of the cause of the Civil War in Britain, a central theme is the necessity for obedience to the sovereign. But throughout, while Hobbes uses the language of "right," he seems to imply more nearly what we should call prudential reasons. The king has a "right" to obedience of subjects, no matter what he may command, but he should look to the wisdom of his actions lest he encourage an already exacerbated factionalism (William Molesworth, *The English Works of Thomas Hobbes*, 11 vols., London, 1839, vol. 6, pp. 198, 236). What appears to anger Hobbes is that while institutions like the universities teach seditious doctrines which undermine the sovereign's power (*Ibid.*, pp. 212–213), the king himself does not appear to know how to grasp and hold on to the power upon which "right" depends. The failure of the king and the disruptions caused by religious and other factionalism help restore the mutual fear which existed in the state of nature. See F. C. Hood, *The Divine Politics of Thomas Hobbes: An Interpretation of Leviathan*, London: Oxford, 1964, p. 23. See also Strauss, *op. cit.*, pp. 97, 105–106.
31. *Leviathan*, IV, 46.
32. Spinoza develops his argument in the *Tractatus Theologico-Politicus*, ch. 19. Civil rights are designated *jus civile;* spiritual rights *jus sacrum.* In chapter 14, Spinoza contends that fulfillment of God's law requires acts of justice and charity; in chapter 19 he endeavors to show that the meaning of justice and charity can be defined only through the instrumentality of "earthly potentates." Like Hobbes, he ridicules legal and political pluralism. In the *Historia Ecclesiastica*, of course, Hobbes spells out his indictment of the ways in which the ecclesiastical leaders have, in his judgment, encroached on the sovereignty which by right belongs to civil authority.

can be expected: "I define a Church to be, A company of men professing Christian Religion, united in the person of one Sovereign; at whose command they ought to assemble, and without whose authority they ought not to assemble."[33] The legislating, concrete church, then, is itself the creature of the civil sovereign. Indeed, those who distinguish between temporal and spiritual governance are following illusory notions.[34]

This essential union of temporal and spiritual governance, so bluntly espoused in all of Hobbes' political writings, raises, of course, many questions involving traditional religious and political doctrines. It particularly poses issues which concern the meaning and implications of conscience. To the medieval mind conscience was sacred; and while it might be difficult to work out its exact contents—hence the development of casuistry to guide one in applying moral principles to concrete situations—it was the general belief that one committed a sin if one violated the deliverances of the conscience.

Hobbes attacks this doctrine with great vigor. It is, he thinks, a theory "repugnant to Civill Society," for "it dependeth on the presumption" of making the individual himself "judge of Good and Evill."[35] A man's conscience and his "judgment," he argues, are the same thing. And in civil society, no judgments which are made public can be immune to direction of the sovereign.

The full implications of his denial of the principle that "whatsoever a man does against his Conscience, is Sinne" are developed when he discusses the question of what a Christian should do if the prince commands him not to believe in Christ. Hobbes answers that no sovereign can actually do this "because Beleef, and Unbeleef never follow mens Commands. Faith is a gift of God, which man can neither give, nor take away by promise of rewards, or menaces of torture."[36] Here he is clearly reverting to his often-repeated statement that what goes on merely within the consciousness and has no external reflection can literally be of no concern to the sovereign. Suppose, however, that the sovereign commands us to state publicly that we do not believe in Christ. Here the inner belief is denied externally. Surely in this instance we need not obey the command of the prince or senate! And, indeed, there is no doubt that Luther, political absolutist as he tended to be, would have stated that disobedience is justified at this point.

But Hobbes thinks otherwise and argues, on the basis of Scripture, that it is perfectly legitimate to deny Christ on command of the sovereign; for it is the sovereign, not the person who obeys him, who is responsible. The individual is guiltless and, indeed, in his own heart still believes.[37]

It goes almost without saying that, given his general theory, Hobbes would deny that papal excommunications can have any external or civil effect; that Catholics could have any public conscience about obeying the pope rather than the king; and that any church, Protestant or Catholic, could legitimately enforce commands contrary to those of the civil sovereign. Nor is the obligation of absolute obedience confined to the sphere of what used to be called Christendom. Hobbes makes it clear that a Christian living in an infidel land must obey all commands of the infidel prince. Should resistance be offered, the Christian "sinneth against the Laws of God."[38]

Hobbes Viewed Critically

Historically, the criticism of Hobbes began long before his death and continued throughout the subsequent generation.[39] In his own day he was attacked because his doctrine could not without difficulties be used to support the partisan claims of either royalists or parliamentarians; and Catholic partisans found his whole outlook completely anathema. During the second quarter of the eighteenth century men like Bishop Joseph Butler (1692–1752) would direct their onslaughts against Hobbes' logic, psychology, and moral theory.[40] In the late eighteenth and the early nineteenth centuries all those who shared in the revival of organic conceptions[41] would either implicitly or explicitly seek to undermine Hobbes' individualism.

Along what lines can Hobbes' system be criticized? At the outset, we might observe that, unlike Machiavelli, with whom he is often compared, Hobbes seeks to be a systematic thinker. He is keenly aware of semantical, epistemological, and other philosophical problems, even though we may think him inadequate in his treatment of them. Then, too, he is much more conscious of questions involving scientific method than the Florentine.

Hobbes' Attitude to the "Empirical." So anxious is Hobbes to develop a mathematically exact theory of politics that he tends to ignore the differences between a science of abstractions, like that of mathematics, and a study like politics which, wherever it may end, must at least begin with observations of historical phenomena. Yet many of the propositions from which Hobbes begins his process of deduction are neither supported by reference to historical experience nor asserted as self-evident according to the experience of mankind. And Hobbes apparently thinks that his psychological statements are so obvious that he need not bother to support them.

Hobbes is so impressed by Euclidean geometry that despite his posthumously published historical work *Behemoth: The History of the Causes of the Civil Wars of England,* his political discussion tends to be ahistorical. In this, of course, he helps establish a precedent for political ideas down to the latter part of the eighteenth century, when men like Edmund Burke will conduct slashing attacks on merely "abstract reason" in politics. In every age, it would seem, it is difficult to keep in balance "rational" and "empirical" elements.

Egoism and Hedonism. What evidence does Hobbes offer for the alleged fact that all men are basically egoists and only egoists? The answer is none. He simply assumes it as axiomatic—in face of the common belief that such men as Socrates and Christ, for example, when they acted in an apparently altruistic way, were not simply using others for their own ends of power. Hobbes does not even discuss the matter.

When he argues that good is merely a name given to what we desire and that evil is a name which we attach to the pains that we suffer, he would appear to be controverting the common experience of men in using the language. If, following Hobbes, we should say that good is simply pleasure, then it should be possible to substitute the word good for pleasure. But if we do so, we are simply saying pleasure is pleasure, which is obviously tautological. Our language at least seems to suggest that this "reduction" is not what most men mean by good, which is usually regarded as a quality that cannot be equated with anything else. Again, Hobbes makes no effort to refute the commonly held view but simply describes (without citing supporting evidence) his own as the basis for his system.

Throughout his ethical discussion (or what purports to be ethical, since it is difficult to see how an apparent determinist like Hobbes can have a doctrine of ethics), he is, of course, almost obsessed by the idea that one can understand a thing best by taking it apart and reducing it to its simple elements. This is what he purports to do when he says that the so-called altrustic, or other-regarding attitudes, are simply complex disguises for self-interest. The implication is that those things which we normally call goods in themselves—that each person ought to be an end, for example, or that we should do to others what we would like them to do to us—are simply maxims whereby each can most efficaciously attain his own individual pleasure or advantage.

Now this way of thinking is a very old one, of course. It is essentially that used by Thrasymachus and Glaucon in the *Republic.* In modern times, the same way of approaching things is illustrated by those who see religion as originating in fear of the unknown. Similarly, some argue that political institutions originated in primitive intimidation of some men by others; therefore, all political institutions—whatever the rationalizations and complexities—are bottomed on intimidation.

The refutations which Socrates directed against Thrasymachus and Glaucon might also be applied to Hobbes' theory.[42] For like the doctrines of those ancient companions of Socrates, Hobbes' doctrines tend to see in our

33. *Leviathan,* III, 39.
34. *Ibid.*
35. *Ibid.,* II, 29.
36. *Ibid.,* III, 42.
37. *Ibid.*
38. *Ibid.,* III, 43.
39. John Bowle, *Hobbes and His Critics,* New York: Oxford University Press, 1952, studies the philosopher in the context of his own time and discusses the reception of Hobbes' philosophy. See also Sterling Lamprecht, "Hobbes and Hobbism," *American Political Science Review* 34 (1940), 31–53. In addition to noting the way in which Hobbes' doctrine was received, Lamprecht emphasizes the fact that men have read the philosopher with a diversity of questions in mind.
40. Butler criticizes Hobbes' ethical views in his *Sermons on Human Nature* (1726). Against Hobbes, he contends that there are two tendencies operating in man—love of self and benevolence to others. The latter is just as basic as the former. Benevolence, contrary to Hobbes, cannot be reduced to self-love.
41. See Chapter 24, for example.
42. See Chapter 4.

psychological, ethical, and political experience merely primitive "motions" and desire for individual power and advantage. But the phenomena connected with growth cannot be adequately accounted for in this way: mature adults are not simply embryos writ large; the religious faith of a St. Francis cannot be explained by thinking of it as a complex of primitive fears; and the many historical examples of individual sacrifices for the group can with difficulty—if at all—be accounted for wholly in terms of primitive urges or a desire to exalt the ego.

Insofar as Hobbes seems to be inferring the nonexistence of a supreme good because men have differed so widely in their conceptions of the good, he would appear to be making an unwarranted leap. Even assuming the widest variation in individual interpretations of the good, it does not follow that there is no objective order of value. The fact that men have differed widely in their analyses of the physical universe does not mean that there is no physical universe which exists apart from men's subjective consciousness of it. There is a difference between what men think of as good and what *is* good, just as there is a distinction between what men believe to be the nature of the physical universe and what *is* the physical universe. The fact that there may be wide variations in the estimates which men offer as to the weight of a stone does not imply that its weight is simply a name given to our own subjective images.

Even if we assume (which we have not) that widespread agreement on the contents of the good life is an indication of an objectively real moral order, there is more evidence for such an order than Hobbes will admit. Modern anthropology, for example, has come increasingly to stress the values which a wide variety of cultures appear to have in common.[43] All cultures, for instance, tend to value loyalty to the group or groups of which one is a part; the sex act; the public commemoration of marriages, deaths, and individual or group achievements; and the effort to explain natural phenomena, in both magical and scientific terms. While such agreements as to what is good are matched by equally wide cultural variations and individual eccentricities, the extent of agreement is far wider than some of the earlier cultural relativists believed.

"Advantage" and the Contract. It is not easy to see how purely egoistic, constantly warring, advantage-seeking animals can be assumed to have made a contract in the first place. Without interpreting the contract as an historical event but taking it as a necessary presupposition to account for society given Hobbes' conception of self-interest, how could egoistic men have confidence enough in one another to make a contract? Contracts presuppose a minimum degree of trust, as Hobbes ought to have known in view of experience with contracts in the burgeoning commercial society of his day. Yet Hobbes' men at best have only the trust supposedly engendered by fear of violent death. But to say that trust in others arises because we fear them is, as Bishop Butler argued long ago, a clear contradiction, at least as language is ordinarily used: Trust and fear are usually thought of as opposed—if I trust a man, my central attitude to him is not one of fear, despite what Hobbes says. In fact, if one takes Hobbes literally, all culture, civilization, and political order are in the end grounded on men's fears of one another—surely one of the most astounding and implausible propositions in all the history of political thought.

Nature Not Really Abandoned. Despite the sharp gulf he creates between natural and civil society, it turns out that Hobbes does not abandon natural society after all.

This comes about because, again refusing to abandon his egoistic premises, he at one and the same time asserts and denies an obligation to obey the ruler. On the one hand, as we have seen, he claims that by the contract men have surrendered all right of individual judgment and have agreed to obey the sovereign without qualification. The sovereign in civil society is theoretically absolute: He controls all public manifestations of religion, creates or destroys corporations, defines truth, has complete direction of material goods, and exercises authority of life and death over every hitherto independent individual. In all this, the state of nature appears to be utterly abandoned. But this is appearance only, for, on the other hand, Hobbes maintains that men can never covenant not to resist the sovereign when he threatens their lives. If this proposition means what it seems to signify, every man reserves the right, when he enters civil society, to resist all injuries which might lead to his death; and he alone is to interpret when he is in danger of death. This certainly opens the way for that rebellion which Hobbes throughout his long life seemed to be rejecting.

Hobbes is thus really attacking himself. He no sooner gets his egoistic man into civil society (although it is difficult to see how he can do so with consistency, as we have seen) than he takes away both the absolutism and the obligation to obey. In the end, civil society becomes for Hobbes a kind of perpetual contest between, on the one hand, the forces of the egoistic sovereign seeking to retain and expand his power, and, on the other, the potentially large physical and psychological forces of rebellious subjects. Hobbes' so-called principles of obligation turn out to be nonexistent.[44]

The Is and the Ought. Throughout his system, too, there is always a serious doubt whether he is speaking about how men in fact act or how they ought to act or both. His mechanistic framework—which will tend to dominate thought far into the eighteenth century—would seem to be the foundation for these ambiguities and contradictions. On the one hand, he appears to be saying that men are forced by their psychology—primitive movements within them—to make the contract and that once in civil society they *cannot* rebel against the sovereign. On the other hand, he is constantly warning men that they *ought* to obey, which would seem to imply that they might not do so. On the one hand, he maintains that security is the great motivation which pushes men from the state of nature into civil society. On the other hand, he appears to be worried lest men have other values than security. From one point of view, he is undoubtedly attempting to devise a theory of moral and political obligation; yet his mechanistic-determinist-reductionist framework does not permit this, since it would seem to exclude the freedom without which oughts become meaningless.

Domination and Subordination. Hobbes' men are dominion-seeking creatures and there runs through his whole system the notion that the central dynamic of all human beings is the quest for power over others. But this would seem to be a very one-sided assessment that is due, perhaps, to the indelible impression which the rebellion and war of his own day made on Hobbes. Actually, there is as much evidence that men in the mass endeavor to subordinate themselves to others as there is that they seek to dominate. Whatever the explanation for this—and it has constituted an important theme in modern social-psychological literature[45]—it is a question which Hobbes largely ignores. A treatment of it would have drastically changed Hobbes' model.

Sovereignty, Monopoly of Force, and Security. Hobbes is often looked upon, quite correctly, as the philosopher *par excellence* of the modern national state and of the doctrine so often associated with it, that security is attained when a monopoly of force is assigned to the national sovereign. But has national sovereignty, in this sense, actually enhanced security?

The answer is by no means as clear as Hobbes and the Hobbists would like us to believe. A good argument can be made for the proposition that the sovereign national state contributes as much to disorder and insecurity as it does to alleged order and security. Not only do powerful national states provoke wars but they have been less than conspicuously successful even in terms of domestic order; and where they have had a measure of success—as, possibly, in such societies as those of New Zealand and Australia—the relatively great physical security has almost certainly been due to factors, such as a highly developed sense of community, having nothing to do with possession of a legal monopoly of force.

The whole mythology of national sovereignty, which owes so much to Hobbes, ought to be seriously questioned. It should be pointed out, for example, that there is probably less danger of war—and therefore of personal physical insecurity—between Canada and the United States or between Belgium and Holland, which have no common sovereigns in Hobbes' sense, than there is between and among sections of the United States which is ostensibly bound together by sovereignty.

Nor would a common world sovereign, with monopoly of physical force, be likely to fare

43. See, for example, the works of the late Bronislaw Malinowski, who emphasizes, for instance, the universality of science, magic, and religion in *Magic, Science and Religion*, Boston: Beacon Press, 1948.

44. To be sure, it is the burden of modern writers like Warrender, *op. cit.*, to attempt to show the contrary. Much depends on how one defines "theory of obligation." But as ordinarily understood, it seems to me that Hobbes does not and cannot have one. See E. E. Carritt, *Morals and Politics*, London: Oxford University Press, 1935, ch. 3; and Thomas Nagel, *op. cit.*

45. See, for example, Erich Fromm, *Escape from Freedom*, New York: Farrar & Rinehart, 1941.

better. Threat of physical force may, indeed, establish a specious kind of order, as Hobbes saw, but only at the expense of stimulating probable resentment and hence possibly still greater insecurity, which Hobbes did not see.

The Historical Impact of Hobbes

Despite the weaknesses of his system, it is difficult to exaggerate the historical significance of Hobbes' moral and political theory. That significance is twofold: In the first place, he gave philosophical expression to the actual major political and intellectual tendencies of his time and, secondly, the positions which he espoused foreshadowed highly characteristic later attitudes to and theories of morals, law, and politics.

Expression of Seventeenth-Century Tendencies. Whether he was fully aware of it or not, Hobbes was essentially the spokesman for those social and political forces in the seventeenth century which were actually destroying the medieval order and which at the same time were dissatisfied with the achievements of the early Renaissance. These forces included the bourgeois business mentality and all those tendencies which were impatient with traditional interpretations of political phenomena.

Throughout the sixteenth century, businessmen were, of course, becoming increasingly important throughout Western Christendom. They were engaging in that long struggle with agricultural interests which was to culminate in their triumph during the late eighteenth and early nineteenth centuries. *Entrepreneurs* were not bound by the ancient way of doing things and their strong economic motivations, stimulated by past conquests in trade and commerce, led them to seek the individual's emancipation from the last vestiges of medieval restrictions on economic life. They could carry out their enterprises only if they were free to make agreements unhindered by law or tradition. This meant that for them the free contract was seen as the only way in which they could pursue profit with any flexibility. At the same time, they were impatient with the religious wars of the time: Let us get on with the task of profit-making they seemed to say, and suppress these irrelevant conflicts which interfere with commerce.

Now it was but a short step from thinking of all commercial transactions in terms of contract to the thought that all social and political relations were contractual. The image of society held by the sixteenth and seventeenth century businessman became more and more that of an almost infinite complex of contracts voluntarily entered into for the benefit of individual interests. At the same time, he began to think of rulership as primarily designed to secure these interests. One modern writer has characterized this ideology as that of "possessive individualism."[46]

Possessive individualism was sharply contrasted with the traditionalist outlook associated with the landed aristocracy, which, as in ancient Greece, thought of trade and commerce as inferior vocations and of land ownership as a prerequisite for political order. Aristocrats and landowners defended the old; possessive individualists those arrangements of society which were at war with the old. Traditionalists sought an answer to the problem of disorder either in the divine right of kings (itself a revolutionary doctrine in terms of medieval theory) or in a complete return to medieval principles. The ideology of possessive individualism, by contrast, was a wave of the future which rejected both divine right and everything smacking of medievalism.

It was Hobbes, of course, who most fully gave systematic expression to the ideology of possessive individualism (although Locke would later be identified with very similar purposes). His extremism was a recognition both of the fact that the old basis for order was dead and of the necessity for a radical reconstruction. To temporize with natural law (in its classical sense) and tradition was dangerous: The former was too vague and the latter too unsubstantial in a day of revolution.

Hobbes' very atheism and materialism were but frank expressions of often unavowed tendencies within the business community itself. As trade and commerce exercised greater and greater fascination on men, conflicts about religion appeared more and more unreal. The only things real were figures, account books, profit and loss statements, and the multitude of particular transactions always involved in a trading community. While most businessmen remained outwardly pious, it is not at all fantastic to suggest that subconsciously they were already beginning to push the God of tradition aside and to create their own gods in the image of the business contract. Hobbes both expressed their attitude and stimulated its further development.

His whole perspective was calculated to strengthen the image of society and state as essentially business enterprises for the promotion of business interests. To be sure, those in the seventeenth century who welcomed Hobbes' contractual views and his individualist premises must in many instances have wondered what the assertion of state sovereignty would mean in the long run for freedom of contract in the economic arena; for there could be no doubt that all economic associations whatsoever, under Hobbes' doctrine, existed only on sufferance of his sovereign. But this was a matter for the future. Meanwhile, seventeenth-century possessive individualism welcomed Hobbes' vision of the world, since it promised for their profit-seeking enterprises a background of order favorable to their interests.

Impact on Later Generations. But if Hobbes gave theoretical expression to many contemporary tendencies associated with the dissolution of traditional bonds, his system was perhaps even more significant when viewed in relation to later developments, both institutionally and in the realm of theory.

Individual and Hedonism. Hobbes, of course, adumbrated fully the social nominalism which sees in the pleasure-seeking discrete individual human being the only natural human reality. While later seventeenth- and eighteenth-century thinkers were not necessarily as extreme in their expression of this view, Hobbes, in general, set the pattern which would be followed, with some exceptions, until the time of Rousseau, Burke, and Hume. And—far beyond that period—his type of hedonism, dissociated from the contract, would become an ingredient for early nineteenth century utilitarianism which played so vital a role in the development of modern liberalism.[47]

Hobbes and the Sovereign State Concept. The history of the idea of the sovereign national state, whose ruler possesses a monopoly of force, as the textbooks put it, owes much to Hobbes. The central position occupied by physical force in this theory can be explained by virtue of the fact that individuals are held to be basically antisocial and must therefore be intimidated (against their supposed immediate interests) into some kind of order through threat of annihilation. This model of the state still profoundly affects notions of international organization in the twentieth century, as when advocates of a strong United Nations associate strength with possession of an international army which would literally destroy those who might rebel.

Hobbes and Modern Views of Law. Earlier we have pointed out that while there were medieval thinkers who looked upon law as the command of the sovereign—particularly those who shared the Roman legal tradition—most medieval theories of law conceived it to be a discovery rather than something which was made. One looked for the law in reason, or tradition, or the custom of the people. Even the king was for the most part thought of as a kind of detective who found law rather than as a commander who decreed it.

Now Hobbes built upon a radically different tradition—that which ran through some of the Roman jurisconsults and which was present as a minor chord during the Middle Ages. This view, that law is a matter of will rather than reason, came to the forefront again in the fourteenth century and was present, as we have seen, in such nominalists as William of Occam. Hobbes worked out its implications. Later on, and building upon him in the nineteenth century, John Austin will formulate the positivist position which will see law as the dictate of a determinate superior, not, as in St. Thomas, an ordinance of reason. In the twentieth century, men like Hans Kelsen will build upon similar foundations and will thus owe much to Hobbes.

Hobbes and the Extension of State Functions. While Hobbes did not endeavor to lay down a doctrine which would distinguish between the area reserved for public activity as against that which would remain private, he did suggest two notions which played an important role in later politics and thought. By helping establish the foundations of what came to be called the monistic theory of sovereignty and of law as the command of the sovereign, he implied that government need be bound by no tradition-based rights of groups. In the second place, the strong individualist and hedonist emphasis in Hobbes pointed to the idea that, while he himself preferred a monarchical sovereign, there was no bar whatso-

46. C. B. Macpherson, *The Political Theory of Possessive Individualism: Hobbes to Locke,* London: Oxford, 1962, emphasizes Hobbes as an important precursor of Bentham.

47. See particularly Chapter 26.

ever to sovereignty reposing in the majority of individual human beings. Sovereignty could be democratic, in other words; and a democratic sovereign could presumably act in any way it might see fit.

Taken together, these two conceptions were to play important roles in the history of political theory after his death. Individualism and hedonism would be central to eighteenth and nineteenth century utilitarianism; while the notion that the state can be barred by no claimed historic rights or traditions of particular groups would come to be reflected in the French Revolution, early democratic theory, and some versions of socialism. Hobbes' leviathan, from this point of view, became a gigantic beast intent on devouring all lesser social structures in the name of that artificial ordering of human affairs which is so characteristic of the seventeenth-century thinker.

Hobbes and Class Warfare Theories. Because even in civil society, there remains a tension between the ruler and his subjects which is never resolvable except by resort to sheer force, Hobbes may be looked upon as an early modern exemplar of what came later to be called class warfare theories. Indeed, Karl Marx is reported to have muttered, "Hobbes is the father of us all."

It is true, of course, that Hobbes thought he had ended the state of nature. But as we have seen, he really carried it over into the civil state. The ruler (or ruling classes in later doctrines like those of Marx) can act only in accord with his egoistic nature (his own interests), thus seeking to maximize his quest for power while attempting to avoid death at the hands of his subjects; while the subjects, although they have promised to obey the ruler, reserve the natural right to kill his agents if the latter should give evidence of desiring to destroy the subjects' egos. Under such circumstances, of course, the civil order really disguises what later will be called conflict.

Thus while Hobbes by no means developed a class-warfare theory, he did anticipate certain of its main ingredients.

The Seventeenth Century and the Democratic Thrust

At about the time that Hobbes was first formulating his radical possessive individualism, certain of the groups associated with the parliamentary side in the English civil wars were calling upon the spirit of the age for utopian reconstruction and far-reaching democratic revolution. Cromwell himself was not immune to these tendencies and, indeed, his Protectorate and Commonwealth were in some measure influenced by them. But the impetus to utopianism was an old one and the democratic ideas of the seventeenth century reflected both a traditional religious concern and, in considerable degree, the ideologies of groups who felt excluded from the mainstream of seventeenth-century politics. Hobbes' doctrines resembled those of the utopians and democrats insofar as they proposed to provide the basis for an order which would supplant the disorder of the time; but they differed from seventeenth-century democratic notions —despite a frequent common individualism— in many other respects, as we shall see in the next chapter.

chapter 20

The Quest for a Commonweal: Utopianism, Radical Democracy, and Eschatology

While Hobbes was seeking "order" amidst the chaos of his day, other thinkers were searching for a utopian and sometimes a democratic reordering. Hobbes thought he could find an answer in the models provided by the new science. Utopian and democratic thinkers during the period of the British civil wars and the Commonwealth hoped somehow to recapture the ideal of a commonweal despite the central emphasis on individualism so characteristic of thought in the sixteenth and seventeenth centuries.

Oliver Cromwell himself was among those interested in the problem, for as a moderate representative of the parliamentary faction, he had to consider the demands both of the left wing and of the right. The debates as to the nature of the commonwealth reflected both Puritanism (a very ambiguous term at best)—as an expression of seventeenth-century Calvinism—and criticisms of the Puritans. One witnesses also a curious combination of religious sectarianism with appeals to so-called secular considerations.

The Background

After the Wars of the Roses of the fifteenth century, the house of Tudor was eventually triumphant and furnished a line of sovereigns to Britain from 1485 to 1603. Social, economic, and political developments during this long period established the conditions which provoked the establishment of Cromwell's commonwealth and at the same time offered a stimulus for political thought.

Socially and economically, it was an age of revolution in many areas. The enclosure movement, which began in the latter part of the Middle Ages, helped transform the life of Britain. With a steady rise in the price of wool stimulated by demand from the Continent, larger and larger amounts of land were removed from the traditional village common lands and turned into sheep-grazing pasture. Who carried out the enclosures? Largely those who already possessed wealth and who used their power over the crown and Parliament to gain still more in the form of land hitherto regarded as common property: in sum, much of the land was stolen. This meant that thousands of those who formerly lived in the villages had to move to burgeoning cities, there to fend for themselves. The process had already gone far by the time of Henry VIII and was in part the occasion for St. Thomas More writing his great *Utopia* (1516), in which he advocated a kind of patriarchal, nondemocratic communism to reintegrate the isolated individual into an ideal community. More's conception reflected a nostalgia for the Middle Ages and at the same time anticipated many of the problems which were to characterize modern commercialism and industrialism. But More's advice went unheeded and the enclosure movement continued.[1]

Not all those who were forced into the cities could obtain employment, of course. Some joined (or were forced into) the army; but on their return they were confronted with the same issues, since they could no longer live in the village commune. Unemployed men led to increased crime, more brutal punishments, and still greater crime. The old forms of social integration, in other words, were dissolving; but adequate new ones were not created to take their place. Instead, mere repression seemed often to be the answer.

Meanwhile, the development of commerce accentuated the separation of individuals from one another. The spirit of the Renaissance, which released men to create art, also freed them to make money. The new commercial classes found themselves opposed to the ancient feudal landowning classes, on the one

1. More's exact place in the history of thought has been much disputed. For a modern socialist's interpretation see Karl Kautsky's *Thomas More and His Utopia,* new ed., New York: Russsell and Russell, 1959. See also J. H. Henter, *More's Utopia: The Biography of an Idea,* Princeton: Princeton University Press, 1952; and Thomas Stapleton, *Life of Saint Thomas More,* New York: Fordham University Press, 1965.

hand, and to the increasing numbers of the urban poor, on the other. The spirit of later Calvinism furnished a kind of ethic for the commercial capitalists, both economically and politically. Economically, they discovered a religious sanction for their accumulations, while politically they used the individualism implicit in Calvinist religion to attack those who defended the very powerful semifeudal elements.

On the Continent, too, the gradually disintegrating old order created similar problems. The voyages of discovery throughout the sixteenth century had introduced vast quantities of gold into the economy and this, with enormously expanding commerce, made for inflation and for general change and disruption. The apparent certainties of the Middle Ages were no longer present. How could community be revived? How could the individual once more discover a sense of meaning and security?

Questions of this kind puzzled Continental thinkers, particularly since, from the end of the fifteenth century onward, they had been inspired by the reception of Plato's *Republic* in its full text. Plato had led More to have his vision of Utopus establishing a communist society. Now, in the seventeenth century, Plato was in part the stimulus for utopian works like Johann Andreae's *Christianopolis* (1619)[2] and Tommaso Campanella's *City of the Sun* (1623).[3] The first presented a Protestant, somewhat puritanical version of an ideal society. The second, written by an eccentric Catholic monk who had suffered at the hands of the pope's secret police, proposed not merely communism of goods but also planned human reproduction and considerable sexual freedom.

In Britain, Francis Bacon, who did so much, as we have seen,[4] to initiate the new science, followed the Continental thinkers and wrote his *New Atlantis* (1627). Characteristically enough, he found the answer to the malaise of the times in the construction of a community governed by natural scientists—a foreshadowing, perhaps, of the scientism of the twentieth century. Science and technology would somehow redeem mankind.

Meanwhile, the constitutional and political crisis of Britain was becoming more acute. From the accession of James I (1603) to the execution of Charles I (1649), the accelerating struggle between Parliament and the king reflected in part a conflict between the commercial classes, on the one hand, and the aristocratic and landed groups, on the other. The royal party tended to accept the divine right of kings conception as formulated by James I and such theorists as William Barclay.[5] The Parliamentary party was by no means united, religious sectarianism being reflected to some extent in the political divisions. During the period of the Commonwealth itself (1649–1660), Cromwell and his son often found themselves uncertain as to what political position to espouse.

Politics were, of course, enormously influenced by the conceptions of later Calvinism, which we have examined elsewhere.[6] The right of resistance, the notion of the godly community advised by God's ministers, rule by the saints, and a high degree of individualism—all these notions played their role in the years between the beginning of the Civil War (1642) and the Restoration of Charles II (1660). How could the chaos of the times be accounted for? How, in light of early modern utopian and democratic traditions, should life be reordered? Was it possible to reconcile urban and commercial life with true community? Questions of this kind, so reminiscent of the types of issues which confronted classical Greek thinkers, were increasingly asked during the period of the civil wars, the Commonwealth, and the Restoration.

Harrington: Utopia, Land Distribution, and Stability

One of the most influential of the utopian pamphlets with the Civil War as a background was that of James Harrington. Although Harrington would be the first to admit that a multitude of factors were involved in the bloody conflicts that characterized the last years of Charles I's reign, he came to hold that the central one turned on the way land had come to be distributed. And out of this conviction emerged his utopian work *Oceana*.

Born in 1611, Harrington was educated at Oxford and during his early travels on the Continent became interested in the political institutions of many countries, including particularly the city-state of Venice. Steeped as he was in classical history and in the works of Plato and Aristotle, the issue of political stability became an uppermost one in his mind. When he returned from his Continental travels, he took up residence at the court of Charles I, with whom he became well-acquainted. In 1646, when Charles was captured by the parliamentary forces, Harrington was appointed one of his attendants on the journey back to London and captivity. Although the king by now was familiar with Harrington's republican sympathies, their personal relations remained warm; and Harrington attempted to save the monarch from execution, undoubtedly repudiating what Charles A. Beard once called the "devil theory of history."

After the king's execution, Harrington decided to analyze the social and economic factors which in his judgment were largely responsible for the political tumults of the period. But just before the *Oceana* was completed, the manuscript was seized, apparently in the belief that it was a seditious utterance. Through Cromwell's personal intervention, however, it was restored to its author and was published in 1656.

With the coming of the Restoration, Harrington again found himself at odds with the authorities. In 1661, he was arrested and carried to the Tower as a traitor. Never granted a trial nor even given an informal statement of charges against him, he was imprisoned for years, suffered from scurvy, and eventually became mentally ill. Although finally released, he never fully recovered and died in 1677.

Throughout his life, Harrington was puzzled about the relationship between economic and political power, particularly as it shaped the events which appeared to produce the social chaos of his day. He remained unsatisfied with conventional explanations of the Civil War—those, for example, which said that the conflict was due to the wicked factionalism of the times or to rejection of divine right. In his account of political society, he maintains that "dominion is property, real or personal."[7] And he breaks property down into land, money, or goods, the first of which is the more basic and enduring. But if this be true then the way in which land is distributed will, broadly speaking, shape the manner in which political power is organized. Thus if one man owns most of the land, absolute monarchy of some kind is inevitable; if a few, such as the nobility or clergy, possess the bulk of it, mixed monarchy is the result; while if the whole people so divide it that "no one man, or number of men, within the compass of the few or aristocracy" overbalance the great bulk, the dominion will be a "commonwealth."[8]

To Hobbes' classical observation that covenants are worthless without the sword, Harrington replies that the hand which holds the

sword is the militia; that the militia is a beast with a "great belly" which must be constantly fed; and that it cannot be fed without "pastures" which ultimately involve distribution of land. Without the wherewithal for pasture, then, the "public sword" is but "a name or mere spitfrog."[9]

If, then, land is the basic form of property and all dominion rests on property, any interest in political stability will force us to ask what distribution of land and therefore of dominion will most promote our objective. After a rather careful inquiry into historical experience, Harrington concludes that a popular government resting on widespread distribution of land is by far most conducive to political stability. He argues that no commonwealth has ever been conquered by any monarch; for while the Macedonian kings triumphed over the Greek polis, it was only after the latter had ceased to be a commonwealth. Popular governments are less subject to sedition, as is evidenced by Venice and other examples.

In a true commonwealth of this nature, an Agrarian law will make certain that land is widely distributed—this is the foundation, as Harrington calls it. The "superstructure"—and the student of modern political thought will be reminded of Marx at this point—will consist of a law establishing "rotation."

In *Oceana*, the Agrarian law limits land

2. Johann Valentin Andrea, *Republicae Christianopolitanae Descriptio*, 1619. First English translation by Felix Emil Held, *Christianopolis, An Ideal State of the Seventeenth Century*, New York: Oxford University Press, 1916.
3. Tommaso Campanella, *Civitas Solis Poetica: Idea Republicae Philosophiae*, Frankfort, 1623. First English translation by Thomas W. Halliday, in Henry Morely, ed., *Ideal Commonwealths*, London, 1885. On Campanella, see, for example, Edmund G. Gardner, *Tommaso Campanella and his Party*, Oxford: Clarendon, 1923.
4. See p. 346.
5. See pp. 341–343.
6. By the seventeenth century, of course, Calvinism was divided into several schools of thought. Its individualistic tendencies were always a breeding-ground of sectarianism, whether in Europe or in New England.
7. *The Commonwealth of Oceana*, London: George Routledge and Sons, 1887, p. 18.
8. *Ibid.*, p. 19.
9. *Ibid.*, p. 20.

ownership for any family to that which produces a revenue of not more than £2,000 a year. Provision is made, moreover, for dividing the land among several children, rather than passing it on to the eldest son as was true in Britain. The central factor producing the Civil War has been the tendency to concentrate land ownership through the law of primogeniture, with the consequent result that the citizenry as a whole have tended not to have an economic base from which to resist any tendencies to tyranny.

As for the superstructure in *Oceana*, Harrington provides for an elaborate scheme of elections, consultations, and councils. Offices are held for very short terms and even ambassadors are rotated. The objective of all this is to prevent the development of a vested interest in any given office. Through a sharing of offices, it would seem, the stability resulting from a sharing of land is accentuated.

In his own day, the scheme outlined by Harrington in *Oceana* is radical indeed. It anticipates many of the propositions which will be embraced by Jefferson at the conclusion of the eighteenth century. However, we should not forget that not all those dwelling in Oceana are citizens—that is, landholders. Many are simply servants who own no land and who therefore do not share directly in the polity. Although they may acquire land, Harrington apparently does not envision a day when everyone will do so. Thus large masses of the Oceanans are implitly second-class human beings, even though not slaves.

Some have suggested that Harrington's utopia represents the reaction of the seventeenth-century middle classes to aristocratic controls. In a sense, this is true. He is not concerned primarily about the plight of urban artisans or of those who are deprived of employment by the wave of business depressions under early modern capitalism. At the same time, however, we should remember that he is still living in a preponderantly agricultural age, long before the Industrial Revolution. Relative to its times, the utopia represents a rather daring vision which will inspire revolutionists of the future.

Factions in the Civil War and the Commonwealth

While Harrington was writing, the major factional lines in the struggle between king and Parliament are developing. Supporters of the king, of course, while found at all levels of society, are on the whole led by the landed aristocracy and by those who uphold the Church of England. Ranks of the Parliamentary party soon come to be dominated by the Presbyterians, who bring with them all their enthusiasm for Calvinist doctrine in theology and Genevan conceptions of social order. The Presbyterians argue that the Church of England should become Presbyterian while yet retaining its privileged political position. They also contend that sovereignty in the state should be vested in the House of Commons rather than in the King-in-Parliament, as is the traditional view. While revolutionaries in the Knoxian sense, their central idea is that the Revolution is to be a limited one: The existing order should be attacked only insofar as that is necessary to establish the rule of the Presbyterian-Puritan elite; and that elite is composed of fairly well-established lawyers, merchants, and in general, what we should today call members of the middle classes.

In the middle of the Revolution, the most powerful dissenting group is the so-called Independents, consisting of men like Cromwell himself and John Milton. The Independents speak with a strong voice not because they have the largest popular support—indeed, they appear to have been but a relatively minor segment of the prople—but rather because they furnish so many of the leaders of the Revolution. In terms of twentieth-century political terminology, they are generally to the left of the great mass of Presbyterian parliamentarians: Thus they are, on the whole, much more favorable to religious toleration (except for Catholics, of course) and more receptive to some of the political appeals of radical sectarians.

It is from the Baptist congregations that much of the impetus to radical democracy comes.[10] Having some affinities with the great Anabaptist movement of the preceding century, the Baptists believe strongly in the independence of each local congregation, lay the groundwork for radical theories of religious toleration, and tend to sympathize with the social criticisms of the lower middle and lower classes.

From the actual outbreak of war in 1642 to the execution of Charles I in 1649, the general political tendency in parliamentary politics is to become radical. The more conservative parliamentarians, in the beginning, appeal to alleged traditional constitutional rights as the basis for their attack on royal prerogatives, common lawyers insisting that the procedural guarantees worked out by the courts cannot be abrogated by the king and opponents of royal assertions in the realm of finance claiming that parliamentary consent is necessary for the imposition of excises and other taxes.[11] In general, the conservatives base their arguments on such constitutional documents as the Magna Carta and the Petition of Right (1629).

However, Independents like Cromwell go far beyond the initial arguments of the conservatives. As we have seen, he becomes the spokesman for a religious toleration which embraces all except the Catholics and at times is moved by even more radical views within his army. Whereas the conservatives, after their initial successes in the war, seem at times to wish to come to terms with the king and the royal party, Cromwell finds himself torn between the still strong popular monarchist sentiment and the radical republicanism reflected in such groups as the Levellers. Eventually, of course the republicans win the day, the king is executed, and the kingless and lordless Commonwealth is established.

In the latter phases of the War, particularly after 1646, Leveller agitation for more extreme constitutional and political notions increases in intensity. The peculiar fact about it is that it is carried on in the army: Military men are, in effect, urging Parliament to desert its conservative notions and to accept constitutional ideas repugnant to the traditions of the land. Whereas the conservatives are content to ground their claims on an often vague historical tradition that might be appealed to also by the royalists, the Levellers increasingly come to believe that only a specific written constitution can prevent future tyranny.

Just as the Levellers press more conservative Puritans, Presbyterians, and Independents to move in a radical direction, so the Diggers push the Levellers. And on the extreme edges of sectarianism are the Fifth Monarchy men, who reject both Levellers and Diggers as too tame. While in the end, Levellers, Diggers, and Fifth Monarchy men alike will largely fail, theirs is a heritage which will be taken up again in the eighteenth and nineteenth centuries.

Leveller Political Ideology

We may think of the height of Leveller agitation as extending from 1646 to 1649. By the latter year, they had attained some of their objectives but in the end were to find that most of their fundamental propositions had been rejected. The revolution which had begun on a conservative note reached its height with a radical flair and then declined into a more conservative attitude.

The Leveller Richard Overton was the author of the 1646 *Remonstrance of Many Thousand Citizens, and other Free-borne People of England, to their owne House of Commons,* which did much to make sharp and clearcut the issues between the conservatives and the radicals. The pamphlet protests that Parliament has temporized too much: it has claimed to be protecting the liberties of Englishmen but at the same time has not dared to attack the person of the king himself. Parliamentarians tend to blame the king's acts on "evill counsellors," Overton argues, and it is now time that they place the responsibility for "bloody Warre" on Charles.

The *Remonstrance* sets in motion an increasingly detailed series of pamphlets, in which the proposals of the Levellers are spelled out so that none could mistake them. Among these documents, we might mention the *Petition* of March, 1647: *An Appeale from the Degenerate Representative Body of the Commons of England . . .* which was written by Richard Overton in 1647; *An Agreement of the People for A firme and present Peace, upon grounds of common-right and freedome* (1647); and *The Mournfull Cryes of many thousand poor Tradesmen, who are ready to famish through decay of trade* (1648). Although the emphases of these and several other documents differ widely and while in some details there may be inconsistencies, the general import of Leveller proposals is evident: They ask for a reapportioned Parliament to be elected for a very short period, specific limitations on Parliament to be established by a superior law or con-

10. On seventeenth-century democratic political thought in general, see G. P. Gooch, *English Democratic Ideas in the Seventeenth Century,* New York: Harper, 1959. On the influence of the Baptists in particular, see Louise F. Brown, *The Political Activities of the Baptists and Fifth Monarchy Men in England During the Interregnum,* Washington: American Historical Association, 1912.
11. See, for example, Stanley B. Chrimes, *English Constitutional History,* New York: Oxford University Press, 1963.

stitution, religious toleration and a radical alteration in the whole religious situation, the prohibition of military conscription, certain economic changes, and miscellaneous legal and judicial schemes.

Leveller theory is clear that Parliament must be chosen in accordance with actual population distribution by what is the equivalent of a household suffrage. Already many areas which had been populous during the Middle Ages were virtually denuded of their inhabitants; yet they continued to return members to the House of Commons. In the second *Agreement*, the Levellers propose that all this be changed and they prescribe in detail the manner in which membership is to be reapportioned. Impressed, too, by the way in which Parliaments tend to sit for long periods of time, thus losing touch with the community, John Lilburne and his associates increasingly demand short terms, suggesting only one year.

As significant as short terms is the demand that Parliament not be legally sovereign. Unlike many of those struggling against royal prerogative claims, they argue that Parliament, while no doubt a better repository of legislative authority than the crown, ought to be limited by a national agreement defining its powers.[12]

Special mention should be made of the Leveller emphasis on religious toleration, whose status, as we have seen, was very limited indeed at the end of the sixteenth century. Influenced, no doubt, by Baptist notions and in revolt against Presbyterian as well as Anglican intolerance, there is a consistency in their demand which is quite impressive. Thus in the early *Remonstrance*, they maintain that the "Establishment of Religion" is one of the indications that England still remains "under the Norman yoke of an unlawfull Power, from which wee ought to free our selves. . . ." In the third *Agreement*, which on the whole is the most developed Leveller statement, a rigid limitation on Parliament is that the representative body must not have the power "to make any Lawes, Oaths, or Covenants, whereby to compell by penalties or otherwise any person to any thing in or about matters of faith, Religion or Gods worship. . . ."[13] One of the remarkable aspects of the Leveller theory of toleration is that it embraces even the hated Papists—a proposal which very few seventeenth-century Englishmen, including even Cromwell, Milton, and Locke, are ready to espouse. The Levellers even demand that the sequestered lands and goods of Catholics who cannot be shown to have waged war against the commonwealth be immediately returned.[14] The argument of the Levellers against religious persecution is twofold: it is forbidden by the Word of God and it doesn't "work."[15]

Another common theme is the protest against military conscription. It is, they aver, "against our freedome."[16] If a man is to risk his life in war, he himself should decide the "justnesse" of the "cause."[17] Even the army officers protest against conscription for "Forraigne Warre either by Sea or Land."[18] In the third great *Agreement*, it is proposed that Parliament be explicitly forbidden to enact conscription, since it is essential that "every mans Conscience" should be "satisfied in the justness of that cause wherein he hazards his own life, or may destroy an others."[19] In general, the proposition seems to suggest that if a war is just, it will receive adequate support without conscription; and while no Leveller statement explicitly argues the point, it seems to be implied that if conscription is used there must be something unjust about the conflict.

The extreme nature of their criticisms naturally subjects the Levellers to the charge that they desire to make "all things" common—in other words, that they are communists. Coming for the most part from the lower middle classes, however, they protest that they are neither for the communism advocated by economic radicals nor for the preservation of an economic status quo in large part supported by royalists and the respectable upper-middle-class Presbyterians.

Communism, they aver, is not Christian when it is compulsory. It is true that the early church at Jerusalem was communist, but it was a purely voluntary sharing of goods and not one compelled by the public power. Leveller doctrine had always upheld the right of private property: "We profess therefore that we never had it in our thoughts to Level mens estates, it being the utmost of our aime that the Common-wealth be reduced to such a passe that every man may with as much security as may be enjoy his propriety."[20] And in the famous third *Agreement*, they propose that Parliament be forbidden "to render up, or give, or take away any part of this Agreement, nor level mens Estates, destroy Propriety, or make all things Common. . . ."[21]

But the fact that they explicitly reject common ownership and thus turn away from utopias like those of More does not mean that they are satisfied with a commonwealth ruled by wealthy landlords and merchants. They seek economic emancipation for themselves and others largely through the device of removing what they regard as illegitimate restrictions on trade and economic activity. They also propose certain social measures short of communism which they believe will alleviate the economic hardships under which they struggle.

There can be no doubt about their dissatisfaction or, indeed, their class consciousness. This is best brought out in their own words:

> Oh that the cravings of our Stomacks could be heard by the Parliament and City! Oh that the Tears of our poor famishing Babes were botled! Oh that their tender Mothers Cryes for bread to feed them were ingraven in Brasse! Oh that our pined Carkasses were open to every pitifull Eye! Oh that it were known that we sell our Beds and Cloaths for Bread![22]

Despite their disavowals of communism, some Levellers at least propose actions hardly compatible with their general tendency to economic individualism. Thus Richard Overton suggests free schools and public support of hospitals; and, what is of enormous significance, "that all grounds which anciently lay in Common for the poore, and are now impropriate, inclosed, and fenced in, may forthwith (in whose hands soever they are) be cast out, and laid open againe to the free and common use and benefit of the poore."[23]

Leveller proposals are characterized not only by political levelling but also by efforts to provide more specific legal and judicial safeguards for private rights. They write into their proposed agreement provisions which have the sanction of tradition behind them as well as suggestions for novel legal guarantees. Thus they ask that no person be compelled to answer questions which might incriminate him; that punishments be "equall to offences"; that capital punishment be confined to "merther, or other the like hainous offences destructive to humane Society"; and that persons not be penalized for refusing to support financially ministers not of their own faith.[24]

In them, too, we notice an antagonism to the legal profession which is not untypical of utopian thought as a whole. In almost every great literary utopia there is no place for lawyers, who are usually seen as perverting justice and feathering their own nests. Among the Levellers, there is a demand that legal and judicial fees be limited in order that justice might be available to poor as well as rich. They also ask for a rule which would forbid members of Parliament to engage in the private practice of law in order that they "may wholly attend the peoples service therein."[25] In the second *Agreement*, the petitioners go so far as to ask Parliament to rid "this kingdom of those vermine and caterpillars, the Lawyers, the chief bane of this poor Nation."

The bulk of the Leveller demands, however, were not realized during the period of the Protectorate. Confronted as he was by Levellers, Diggers, and Fifth Monarchy men on the left and by the huge conservative Presbyterian center, Cromwell on the whole tended to side with the latter. He was not, it is true, unsympathetic to many Leveller proposals—their pleas for toleration, for example—but in face of the political situation as it actually existed he did not see how he could embrace all of them. The antimonarchical sentiments of the Levellers, to be sure, were realized in the rather nominal republicanism of the Protectorate; and their conception of a written

12. *An Agreement of the Free People of England* (1649), Articles 10–30.
13. *Ibid.*, Article 10.
14. *No Papist War Nor Presbyterian* (1649).
15. *Ibid.*
16. *An Agreement of the People* (1647).
17. *Foundations of Freedom* (1648).
18. *A Petition from His Excellency Thomas Lord Fairfax and the General Councel of Officers of the Army . . . Concerning the Draught of an Agreement of the People* (1649).
19. *An Agreement of the Free People of England*, Article 11.
20. *A Manifestation from Lieutenant Col. John Lilburn, Mr. William Walwyn, Mr. Thomas Prince and Mr. Richard Overton . . .* (1649).
21. *An Agreement of the Free People of England*, Article 30.
22. *The Mournfull Cryes of Many Thousand Poor Tradesmen, who are ready to famish through decay of Trade* (1648).
23. *An Appeale from the Degenerate Representative Body of the Commons of England . . . to the Body Represented, the free people in Generall . . .* (1647).
24. *An Agreement of the Free People of England*, Articles 16, 19, and 23.
25. *To the Supreme Authority of England, The Commons Assembled in Parliament, The earnest Petition of many Free-born People of this Nation* (1648), no. 6.

higher law which would stand above ordinary statutes was given some expression in the Instrument of Government or fundamental law of the Protectorate. On the whole, however, the Levellers were not too happy with the Protectorate and, with their fellow-radicals, the Diggers and Fifth Monarchy men, were constantly pressing the government for bolder action.

The Diggers: True Levellers and Communists

A few months after the execution of King Charles about twenty-five men appeared with spades on St. George's Hill in Surrey. The land there was uncultivated and the men proceeded to dig it up and to plant it with "parsnips, carrots, and beans." The leader of the little band was a man by the name of Everard, a veteran of Cromwell's army but now unemployed; and the men who followed him almost immediately began to be called "Diggers."

They had shown up at St. George's Hill because they had no regular incomes and since the ground was unused they felt they had a right to utilize it. Some of the men had been Levellers but about 1648 had begun to be dissatisfied with Leveller proposals which were believed not to go far enough. The dissidents called themselves "true Levellers," signifying by that term that they proposed to extend egalitarian doctrines to the economic as well as other segments of life.

The goings-on at St. George's Hill were immediately reported to the commander of the army who sent a detachment of troops to break up the little band. The Diggers hoped—as do sectarians in every age—that the masses would rally to their support and that there would be a Digger revolution. But for the most part the masses were quiescent and so the Diggers within a relatively brief time had to give up their efforts to carry out their doctrines in the world of the mid-seventeenth century.

This did not mean, however, that they surrendered the doctrines themselves. Indeed, in January, 1649, Gerrard Winstanley, who was to be the leading theoretician of the Diggers, had published *The New Law of Righteousness* which laid the foundations of official Digger doctrine. And in 1652, he issued his famous *Law of Freedom*,[26] which may be thought of as the Digger utopia. While, therefore, the Digger view of the social order came to naught in practice, its very defeat seemed to stimulate the construction of its well-rounded social ideal.

Digger theory represents in large degree the ideology of landless workers who have no great economic and social status and who burn with a feeling of injustice. They see about them the enclosed lands and they discover that much of the countryside which has been preempted by landowners is kept idle. Reared on the Christian view that the earth belongs to God who gives it to all mankind, the Diggers think it perfectly natural for unused lands to be occupied by those needing them: Positive legal ownership must give way, in their view, to the natural right of men to have access to the basic means of production.

Winstanley's task is to elaborate this position and to show its relation to the social and political developments of the seventeenth century. While by 1649, he is no longer an orthodox Christian, he still accepts much of the medieval social ideology. But he is to be identified not with the Augustinian "relative natural law" but rather with the heterodox medievalist's insistence on observance of the absolute natural law. Thus the very distinction between mine and thine in terms of the basic instruments of production must be discarded. In *The New Law of Righteousness*, he lays down the proposition that until all land is commonly owned and administered, freedom for the ordinary man will remain impossible.

In the same work, he maintains that it should be a rule in political as well as natural society that

> No man shall have any more land than he can labor himself, or have others to labor with him in love, working together, and eating bread together, as one of the tribes or families of Israel, neither giving nor taking hire.[27]

The beginning of the new commonwealth would include the seizure of waste lands by the poor and their cultivation in common. The commonwealth's institutions would be established not by violence but by an appeal to every man's sense of justice and equity. When Diggers do resist the existing authorities in the name of natural authority, they must do so nonviolently in the expectation that even landlords will come to see the moral foundations of their position.

The society which Winstanley sketches out in *The Law of Freedom* reminds one in many respects of More's Utopia. Its bases are the patriarchal family, the common ownership of land, the elimination of trade and a money economy, and a socioeconomic organization built upon the principle that everyone should contribute in accordance with ability and receive in proportion to need. Unlike More, however, Winstanley insists that a commonwealth of this kind cannot be initiated by any Greek-type legislator or Utopus but must rather be built up from below. Even the authority of the father, he contends, is based upon a kind of implicit consent of his children—strange as this may seem.

There is a high degree of decentralization, since Winstanley, like most seventeenth-century democrats, distrusts large-scale organization of any kind. The basis for government will be the parish or town; and each unit will have several officers: peacemakers, overseers, soldiers, taskmasters, and the executioner. The essential tasks of a peacemaker are those of reconciling differences and maintaining the general order. If possible, Winstanley suggests, conflicts between and among individuals should be resolved outside court and the peacemakers will play a large role in this arbitral function. Overseers are economic officers who settle disputes about consumers' goods; supervise the apprenticeship system; direct the organization of the common storehouses; and make sure that all persons contribute something to the common weal.

The soldier is a police officer who may be called upon in time of war to organize the military forces. Most of his work is civil in nature, however, for Winstanley envisions relatively little war-making by his commonwealth. The whole seventeenth-century radical protest against standing armies is reflected in Winstanley's utopia; for he bars all military bureaucracies from his simplified society.

The taskmaster is a kind of prison supervisor, except that Winstanley does not necessarily think that all punishment should be within a prison: It may, on the contrary, consist of compulsory work in any occupation. But only those who have been sentenced for infractions of the law come under the jurisdiction of the taskmaster.

Curiously enough, Winstanley seems to be extraordinarily harsh in his criminal law proposals. While the Levellers appear to look forward to the elimination of the death penalty, he makes death the puunishment for a number of offences. Perhaps his harsh discipline is in part a reaction to what Winstanley regards as the centuries of exploitation to which the people of England have been subjected: he expects the exploiters to resist.

Winstanley, unlike the conservatives, places great emphasis on the positive legislative functions of Parliament: It is not there merely to preserve tradition; indeed, it is to attack all those traditions contrary to reason and equity. But when it repeals old laws or proposes new legislation, it must declare its intentions to the people of the land. If they do not object within one month, it is free to make the final enactment. This necessity for popular consent (and Winstanley is vague as to exactly how it is to be ascertained) he eloquently defends by contrasting it with the parliamentary practices of his own day.

Like certain of the Levellers, he stresses education. The schooling and disciplining of children is to be not merely a family responsibility but also a function of the commonwealth. Every child must be educated in the liberal arts and must also be taught a trade. Thus there will be an educated citizenry and a population able and willing to earn a livelihood.

A well-known passage in the *Law of Freedom* nicely summarizes the essence of Winstanley's moneyless communism:

> The earth is to be planted and the fruits reaped and carried into barns and storehouses by the assistance of every family. And if any man or family want corn or other provision, they may go to the storehouses and fetch without money. If they want a horse to ride, go into the fields in summer, or to the common stables in winter, and receive one from the keepers, and when your journey is performed, bring him where you had him, without money.[28]

26. See George H. Sabine, ed., *The Works of Gerrard Winstanley*, New York: Russell and Russell, 1965.
27. *The New Law of Righteousness: Budding forth to restore the whole Creation from the Bondage of the Curse. Or a glympse of the Earth, wherein dwells Righteousness. Giving an Alarm to silence all that preach or speak from hearsay or imagination*, in Lewis H. Berens, *The Digger Movement in the Days of the Commonwealth as Revealed in the Writings of Gerrard Winstanley*, London: Simpkin, Marshall, Hamilton, Kent & Co., 1906, p. 74.
28. *The Law of Freedom in a Platform: Or, True Magistracy Restored*, in Berens, *op. cit.*, p. 217.

Statements of this kind remind one forcibly of the essentially agrarian outlook of the Diggers. Unhappy with the commercialism of their time, they hoped to reverse those processes which for at least a century and a half had been transforming the life of large parts of western Christendom. But more than that, they expected to restore a hypothetical primitive communism which has ever beckoned those distraught by the complexities of advanced civilization.

Eschatology and Politics: Fifth Monarchy

Every age of acute crisis, as we have frequently noted, gives rise to groups who see politics in the light of an expected end of history itself.

During the Protectorate and Commonwealth, it was the so-called Fifth Monarchy men who discerned in the civil and foreign struggles of the time a sign that Christ's Kingdom was about to arise. Fifth Monarchy ideas during the Cromwellian period, like Leveller conceptions, were closely associated with the development of Baptist congregations.[29] Both the General Baptists, who were non-Calvinist in theology, and the Particular Baptists, who had a Calvinist outlook, tended to emphasize lay activity and democracy and to encourage widespread religious and political speculation. Thoroughly familiar with the Scriptures, some Baptists were markedly impressed by such books as Daniel and Revelation which, with their visions of beasts and bloody conflict, seemed particularly appropriate for the disordered seventeenth century.

There were many public expressions of views which were later to be called by the name Fifth Monarchy. The term itself is related to the Book of Daniel. There the prophet sees four beasts appear, which are taken to symbolize the Assyrian-Babylonian, Persian, Macedonian, and Roman empires.[30] The first three, seventeenth-century eschatologists see, have already disappeared. But the fourth still exists in the form of the Roman Empire and, of course, the Roman Catholic Church. However, there are signs that it, too, is scheduled for death. The long and bloody Thirty Years' War; the civil conflict within England itself; the suffering of the saints under Roman Catholic persecution—all these and many other events are regarded as indications that the fourth beast is approaching destruction. With his passing will come the Fifth Monarchy, which many eschatologists identify with the direct rule of Christ.

Among other items of Fifth Monarchy ideology is the identification of the "little horn" of Daniel[31] with the papacy, which, of course, wars on the saints. While this is perhaps the predominant interpretation of that mysterious passage, it should be emphasized that even here Fifth Monarchists are not unanimous. Some, for example, see the little horn as standing for the rule of the Normans, while others think it means the tyrant Charles I.

As the eschatologic ideology grows during the early years of the Protectorate, the first sign of a division appears as to what it implies for the action of the saints. Perhaps most Fifth Monarchists at first believe that they should merely petition the government of the Protectorate to approximate the rule of the coming Christ: Only the godly should rule, for example, and all church titles should be abolished. This would please the divine king when at last he appears.

But from the beginning there are Fifth Monarchy men who are suspicious of such mild preparations. They doubt that the government will accede to their wishes. By the fifties, some of them have come to believe that they must take a more active role; and the more ardent talk of violent revolution. They cannot abide the temporizing of the Cromwellian administration, which hesitates, in face of a mammoth Presbyterian center, to take measures which would satisfy either Levellers, Diggers, or Fifth Monarchy apologists.

About the same time, too, the Fifth Monarchists begin to lose members, particularly to the Society of Friends (Quakers). While most Friends do not espouse an emphasis on eschatology, it is easy to see why, with their radical egalitarianism and their criticism of hierarchical society, they should attract many Fifth Monarchists. By 1646, in fact, it is clear to some of the latter that they have passed the height of their influence.

This awareness of imminent decline is probably an important factor in leading the extremists to seek a military solution. Convinced as they are that they must establish some approximation of Christ's kingdom if they are to be recognized by Christ on his return, they begin to lose patience. Many of their members, moreover, are in prison and it is feared that others will soon join them if drastic action is not taken. While most Fifth Monarchists apparently continue to believe that Cromwell's government should still be either approached through petitions or overthrown only by prayers to God, the cutting edge of the movement is now increasingly associated with those who contemplate violence. Many plan an uprising, modelling their military strategy on Old Testament precedents.

Before the revolt can take place, however, Cromwell is informed and nips it in the bud (April, 1657).

Thus the perennial attempt to establish the kingdom of God on earth by violence—or at least to prepare the way for it—fails once more. The mass of men, utterly repelled by past violence and plots, accept the Restoration, with all its worldly tawdriness and compromises, as the lesser evil. The ideology of the Fifth Monarchy men largely vanishes, not so much in a blaze of glory as in a feeble heat which is rapidly cooled by the damp cloth of indifference.

Politics and Nonviolence: The Quakers

Just after Charles II returns, there is a rumor that the Fifth Monarchists have revived and that they are threatening to overthrow the government. Some accuse the Society of Friends of having taken over the ideas of Fifth Monarchy men—a not implausible view, since, as we have seen, many eschatologists have been flocking to the Society. But the Friends, of course, utterly reject war and all outward fighting and to distinguish their views from those of the Fifth Monarchy issue their well-know Declaration of 1660. The Declaration is, however, simply one expression of a much broader body of ideas.

Established by George Fox during the Cromwellian period, the Society of Friends embodies certain of the conceptions of the Anabaptists and also has within it a puritanical streak. Its members tend to be mystics and, as such, to question most ecclesiastical and temporal authority. Its principle of nonviolence is grounded on conceptions which it associates—justifiably, as we have seen—with the New Testament and the early days of Christianity.[32] Quakers refuse to join the army or carry swords and do not hesitate to speak to rulers directly (Cromwell, Charles II, James II) about what they regard as social injustice, the infamy of oaths, and the violence of governments.

Although many of them in the beginning appear to be unconcerned about positive conceptions of ordering society (for like most seventeenth-century sects they are highly individualistic), in the second generation they tend increasingly to believe that their pacifistic and, for their day, extremely democratic principles can actually be applied to the social order. Under William Penn, who receives a grant of land in what becomes Pennsylvania, they have an opportunity to put their religious and political faith into practice. The experiment begins in 1682 and, until 1755, Quakers remain in control of the colonial legislature.

Besides exemplifying the radical sectarian democracy so alive in their day, the Pennsylvania Quakers conduct one of the very few experiments in nonviolent government ever recorded. Penn argues that the ethical conceptions of the New Testament can quite literally be implanted in political institutions, despite the tradition since Constantine contrary to

29. See Louise F. Brown, *op. cit.*
30. The first beast is a lion, the second a bear, the third a leopard, and the fourth is described as "dreadful and terrible, and strong exceedingly; and it had great iron teeth: it devoured and brake in pieces, and stamped the residue with the feet of it." (Daniel 7:7.) After the fourth beast appears one "like the Son of Man" who is given "an everlasting dominion, which shall not pass away." (Daniel 7:13, 14.) At the time of the Fifth Monarchy movement—and, indeed, until relatively recently—it was held by both Protestants and Catholics that the lion symbolized the Babylonian Empire, the bear the Medo-Persian, the leopard the Alexandrian or Grecian, and the fourth beast the Roman. The "son of man" image supposedly symbolized the coming of Christ's kingdom on earth. Modern Biblical criticism tends to doubt this interpretation. It places the authorship of Daniel sometime during the Maccabean period and sees the four beasts as symbolizing the Babylonian, Median, Persian, and Alexandrian empires respectively. The "son of man" possibly represents the belief that the kingdom of Israel will ultimately triumph.
31. See Daniel 7:8. The fourth beast in Daniel has ten horns but there arises among them a "little horn" which destroys three of the ten. The little horn has eyes like those of a man and a mouth which speaks "great things." The interpretation of the "little horn" as the pope is not uncommon among seventeenth-century Protestants and, indeed, is not unknown in the twentieth century.
32. See Chapters 8 and 9.

that view. In Pennsylvania there is no army and Penn insists on meticulously fair arrangements with the Indians, even to the extent of paying for land two or three times over if there is the slightest doubt as to its original Indian owner.

The doctrine of nonviolence in Pennsylvania does not necessarily repudiate the use of physical force in all contexts but does insist that if a relatively high level of social justice obtains and instruments of violence are not maintained, group and international violence will not erupt. Implicitly, Quaker doctrine appears to hold, there is an important distinction between the use of mild force in police work—which avoids any intention to kill and is discriminate—and the violence utilized in war and group struggle. The latter is more than restraint, tends to be utterly indiscriminate, and has as its inevitable end-result the killing of human beings.

Whatever the merit of these doctrines, it appears that they worked for a period of two generations, or until the Quakers, inundated by non-Quaker settlers, felt that they had to retire from the legislature. While other colonies were afflicted with Indian wars and massacres, there were no Indian wars in Pennsylvania during the long period between the foundation of the colony and the middle of the eighteenth century; and there is considerable merit in the argument that had the Quakers not become a minority of the population, this experiment in the politics of nonviolence might have been even longer lived.[33]

Even so, it stands as a monument to the radical religious and democratic sectarianism of the times and, with all its shortcomings,[34] as an inerasable challenge to *realpolitik* doctrines of every age. It cannot be denied that the Quaker experimentalists were far more successful, in the usual sense of that term, than the Fifth Monarchy men, with all their appeals to violence.

The Historical Significance of the Utopians and Radical Democrats

The seventeenth century was extraordinarily rich in doctrines which sought, against the background of a developing commercial capitalism and the progressive disintegration of the landed regime, to reexamine the fundamentals of social reordering. Divine right thinkers thought that if only hereditary monarchy could be regarded as absolute and sacred, things would fall in place. Hobbes, on the contrary, saw the answer not in divine right but in a radical individualistic contract doctrine which would discard tradition and rely on self-interest—on possessive individualism. The Parliamentary factions during the Civil War developed several versions of late Calvinist republicanism, seeking to combine them with more conservative doctrines of the rights of Englishmen.

From the viewpoint of the radical utopians and democrats, all these answers were found wanting. Many turned to economic explanations to account for the troubles of the times and to suggest remedies. Some stressed the need for drastic land reform, before political ordering could become stable. Yet others argued for drastic changes in the representative institutions inherited from the Middle Ages. The appeal to violence came to be heard, only to be answered by a radical egalitarian nonviolence.

In their great debate the utopians and radical democrats laid the foundations for the modern dialectic about freedom, equality, democracy, and social change. While later democrats would be selective in building on the foundations of the seventeenth century, the sectarian debate became one of the most vital ingredients in the subsequent history of democratic thought, extending even to our day.

But the sectarians were not, for the most part, academic philosophers: by and large they represented ordinary lower-middle-class or middle-middle-class men. They stood for some of the more extreme egalitarian doctrines of the seventeenth century. Occasioned in considerable degree by a bitter Civil War and standing for rebellion against class stratification, their ideas did not become in their own day or in the subsequent century the beliefs of most men. Indeed, much of their spirit has not yet been accepted in our twentieth-century age.

In the late seventeenth century and through most of the eighteenth century, the general outlook would be keyed to a greater moderation than that reflected in the ideas of men like Winstanley and Penn. Most men were searching for beliefs which would eschew the extremes of divine right or Hobbes-like views, on the one hand, or of radical egalitarianism, democracy, or utopianism, on the other. The period from 1660 onward for about a century would be centrally concerned to establish doctrines of the middle which would be compatible with the continuing development of science and a still-expanding commercialism and at the same time be suspicious of the emotion so often associated with enthusiasts and radical social reformers.

Views of this kind came to be almost inseparably connected with (although not necessarily derived from) the outlook of John Locke. Spurning all fanaticism, seeing religion as reasonable, and endeavoring to offer a less harsh version of social contract thinking than that of Hobbes, Locke continues the tradition of individualism so characteristic of thought since Machiavelli and intellectually becomes a symbol of the eighteenth-century Enlightenment. To his important formulation we turn in the next chapter.

chapter 21

Toward the Eighteenth Century: Locke, the Contract, and Natural Rights

With the death of the Fifth Monarchy movement, the decline in Puritan intensity of conviction, weariness with more than a generation of acute controversy and Civil War, and the Restoration came a search for philosophies of moderation. Divine right theory and Hobbes, in quite different ways, had made order the lodestar of political speculation. The radical democrats and many of the sectarians tended to concentrate on liberty. From 1660 until far into the eighteenth century, men desperately sought for conceptions which, while continuing to preserve individualist premises and the right of resistance, would at the same time give promise of a stability based on something other than sheer force.

The political philosophy of John Locke seemed to respond to this quest. Retaining individualism and contract, it attempted to modify the harshness of Hobbes' egoism and to grant in a limited way some of the claims of groups like the Levellers. Rejecting Hobbes' atheism, it professed to root Christianity in reason. Repudiating in a limited way many

Chapter 20

33. See Isaac Sharpless, *A Quaker Experiment in Civil Government*, Philadelphia: A. J. Ferris, 1898. See also Frederick B. Tolles, *Quakerism and Politics*, Greensboro, N.C.: Guilford College, 1956, for a general discussion of the relation of Friends to the sphere of politics.
34. Critics, of course, have pointed out that the Legislature of Pennsylvania under Quaker control often equivocated and made compromises when faced with demands by the governor for arms. While the legislature never appropriated money for armies as such, it sometimes granted undesignated lump sums to the sovereign and presumably knew that part of the money might be used for military purposes. See Sharpless, *op. cit.*, for a frank treatment of the problems faced by Quaker idealists when confronted with the ambiguities of practical politics.

doctrines of religious intolerance, it stopped far short, nevertheless, of full tolerance.

Locke's doctrine would become an important philosophy for understanding the political mind down to at least 1776, if not in terms of its direct influence then as a significant representative view.

Locke and the Politics of the Seventeenth Century

Locke's career may rather naturally be divided into four periods.[1] During the first, from his birth in 1632 to the age of twenty, when he went up to Oxford to study, many of his basic political attitudes must have been developed. His father was a strong parliamentarian whose philosophy of child discipline reflected a combination of permissiveness and authority which would be echoed in Locke's own political doctrine.

The second phase of his life began in 1652 and ended in 1667. We might term it the period of fundamental higher education, which included the awarding of his M.A. degree, a brief tour of duty as a minor diplomat, study of the ubiquitous Descartes, inquiry into the researches of Sir Robert Boyle (of "Boyle's Law" fame), a sympathetic reading (unlike Hobbes) of the medieval scholastics, training to be a physician, and a fellowship (or studentship) at Oxford.

From 1667 to 1686 he was a tutor and physician to Lord Ashley (later the Earl of Shaftesbury), Secretary to the Council of Trade and Plantations for a brief time, a traveller on the Continent, and a dabbler in the politics of the royal succession. In the latter capacity, he followed the Earl of Shaftesbury in seeking to deprive the Catholic Duke of York (the future James II) of his rights to the throne. Shaftesbury died in 1683, after failing to exclude the duke. When in 1685, James II ascended the throne, Locke became alarmed since he was associated, through the Shaftesburys, with the claims to the throne of the Duke of Monmouth, illegitimate son of Charles II. No Socrates, he fled to Holland under an assumed name, returning later after the suppression of the Monmouth rebellion.

The fourth and last phase of his career began in 1686 and was dominated by writing and publication. For years, he had kept a detailed journal of all his observations known as the "commonplace books." From these jottings he drew to write his influential works, such as the *First Letter Concerning Toleration* (1689) and, in 1690, both the *Two Treatises on Civil Government*[2] and the philosophical *Essay Concerning Human Understanding*. In 1693 came *Some Thoughts Concerning Education* and in 1695 *The Reasonableness of Christianity*. There followed another brief period of public service as executive of the newly established Board of Trade and Plantations (1696).

Locke supported the so-called Glorious Revolution of 1689, of course, and in doing so provided a kind of text for what we might call the whiggish mentality of the first half of the eighteenth century. By the time of his death, in 1704, ideas similar to those he had espoused appeared to have become central to many social thinkers. Even when men did not borrow directly from him, they absorbed many Locke-like views from the climate of opinion that became ubiquitous in the years from 1700 to 1776.

Locke on the Nature of Human Understanding

By the time Locke had begun to mature his reflections on man and nature, the great scientific and philosophical revolution to which we referred in a previous chapter,[3] while proceeding from victory to victory, was also beginning to be questioned. A rather diverse group of thinkers drew out its implications for every area of life. Cartesianism, by distorting certain aspects of Descartes' thought, had produced severe critics like Pierre Gassendi (1592–1655) who levelled his attacks against such propositions as the Cartesian conception of innate ideas and the notion that animals are mere mechanisms. Many were particularly critical of the Cartesian tendency to desert direct observation and to take refuge in *a priori* and deductive thinking.

At the same time, the materialism of thinkers like Hobbes came in for increasing scrutiny. Men like the "Cambridge Platonists" began once more to restress human responsibility and the view that man is more than simply a mechanism.[4]

In religious affairs, the early seventeenth-century tendency for Calvinist approaches to triumph was partly reversed after 1660 when "Latitudinarian" and Arminian[5] views came to the fore. Puritanism, to be sure, still remained an important current in popular life, but it had lost its militancy and had entered a stage of relative quiescence.

These are some of the factors which we must keep in mind if we would understand Locke's general outlook. More critical than Hobbes of some interpretations of the new science, he yet shared Hobbes' concern for the construction of both a theoretical and a practical science and philosophy which would take into account the contributions of thinkers from Bacon to Descartes. Upholding Hobbes' view that there is a gulf between nature and man, he could not, however, accept the former's notion of the enormous breadth of that gulf. In the realm of religious affairs, Locke regarded himeslf as a Christian; but the basis for his Christianity was radically different from that of most of those who used the term.

The keynote of Locke's thought, in short, is its moderation; its effort is to discover valid elements in almost every point of view and to weave these elements into what is not so much a system as it is a tentative suggestion for a system. A twentieth-century commentator on Locke has well said that his writings have "that balanced and tolerant attitude to life which characterized late seventeenth-century England at its best. The prevailing love of cool, disciplined reflection and careful avoidance of excess are mirrored with fidelity on every page."[6]

While we are primarily concerned, of course, with the way in which this moderation and balance are reflected in Locke's political theory, we cannot avoid some inquiry into the metaphysical and epistemological framework of his thought.

To Locke, "The understanding is not much unlike a closet wholly shut from light, with only some little opening left, to let in external visible resemblances, or ideas of things without."[7] "External and internal sensation," he holds, "are the windows by which light is let into this dark room."[8] Carrying on the analogy, he suggests, "Would the pictures coming into such a dark room but stay there, and lie so orderly as to be found upon occasion, it would very much resemble the understanding of a man, in reference to all objects of sight, and the ideas of them."

Thus the senses let in "particular ideas" which lie around the closet ready for action on them by the mind. Gradually the mind becomes familiar with some of these ideas, lodges them in the memory, and gives names to them. The mind then abstracts them, "and by degrees learns the use of general names."[9] From this point on, of course, the human being having been provided his basic stock of ideas through sensation from nature, in turn begins to shape nature by action based on abstractions from the simple ideas originally furnished by nature.

Man's mind is, therefore, passive and there are not, contrary to the Cartesians, any innate ideas. Instead of innate notions, Locke stresses the genuineness of the ideas furnished by the sensations of nature. What we gain from the external world is not an illusion.

But how account for moral experience? It is possible, thinks Locke, to use certain general sensations implanted by nature to construct a body of moral knowledge. All men experience pleasure and pain; and it is these simple experiences which lie at the basis of all genuine moral notions.[10] The sensations of pleasure and pain are, of course, not knowledge but the means furnished by nature for attaining a stock of knowledge about good. Locke, then, like Hobbes, tends to identify the good with that which gives us pleasure and the evil with those things which pain us. Happiness, good, and pleasure are interchangeable terms.

He is quite aware, of course, that we do not

1. Consult, for example, Richard I. Aaron, *John Locke*, Oxford: Clarendon, 1955.
2. The most recent edition of the *Second Treatise* is that by Peter Laslett, Cambridge: Cambridge University Press, 1960, who also contributes an excellent introduction which questions certain hitherto prevalent interpretations. Laslett stresses that the *Second Treatise* was not simply a pamphlet written to "justify" the Glorious Revolution but that it had in fact been written years before.
3. See Chapter 19, pp. 346–348.
4. The Cambridge Platonists are discussed succinctly in Basil Willey, *The Seventeenth Century Background*, New York: Doubleday, Anchor Books, 1953, pp. 139–171. Their relation to Locke is treated at pp. 277–278.
5. "Arminianism" as a general designation of notions which stress "freedom" as against Calvinist "determinism" takes its name from Jacobus Arminius, a Dutch thinker who lived from 1560 to 1609.
6. Aaron, *op. cit.*, p. 1.
7. *Essay Concerning Human Understanding*, Bk. II, ch. 11, no. 17.
8. *Ibid.*
9. *Ibid.*, II, 2, 15.
10. *Ibid.*, I, 3, 3.

always desire the greatest good, for all "present pain, whatever it be, makes a part of our present misery; but all absent good does not at any time make a necessary part of our present happiness, nor the absence of it make a part of our misery."[11] Nevertheless, "a constant Determination to a Pursuit of Happiness" may be thought of as the essential moral nature of man.

Indeed, Locke identifies the pursuit of happiness as the "foundation of liberty," in the sense that insofar as we have "moved" in our wills to search for the highest happiness, our immediate desires no longer determine our wills. We "suspend" those particular desires and thus become more free to pursue "true happiness."[12]

Liberty itself, for Locke, is a "faculty" or "power" to "act or not to act." One is free when one has the power to do what one wills, and willing is "nothing but a power or ability to prefer or choose."[13] When one wills to act in a certain way one uses one's power to choose; and once one has chosen—willed—one is determined by one's will. But it may still be that one does not have the power to do what one wills, in which case one is not free. Thus Locke would say that one can will to walk down town and in so doing one is exercising a "power"; but if one is paralyzed, one has no power to walk, one's power to will cannot be implemented by the power to walk, and hence one is not free. In the social and political realm, this identification of freedom with power can have revolutionary implications: Thus Communists deny that American workers are really free, since they supposedly do not possess, for example, power over the mass media or the economy.

Locke's account of human beings is, like that of Hobbes, basically egoistic, in the sense that all ideas come from personal experience and that all actions must necessarily follow personal experience. At the same time, however, the sensations from the outer world of nature do flow into us without any great trauma or shock, in sharp contrast to Hobbes. This will affect Locke's account of the state of nature and therefore his judgment of political society.

Locke's State of Nature

In Locke's state of nature, each person—as with Hobbes—is the judge of his own actions, since there is no common authority to act in this capacity; and Locke points out that in this sense many men still actually live in the state of nature—people on the frontier, for example, where, whatever the theory, political authority is not really present.

The greatest point of divergence between Hobbes and Locke is that, while both begin with discrete men in the state of nature, Locke's men are never so completely bound up within themselves that they are unaware of the external "reality principle." Hobbes' man, to use Locke's image, must have his closet door battered down by the threat of violent death. Locke's human being, by contrast, is in some measure an intellectually curious and semisocial being *ab initio*.

Because Locke's man is assumed to be rational long prior to the contract, he is able, by and large, to grasp the law of nature. Thus he sees that his liberty is not, in the words of Locke, "license." While each individual has an "uncontrollable" liberty to "dispose of his person or possessions," he has no liberty to "destroy himself, or so much as any creature in his possession, but where some nobler use than its bare preservation calls for it."[14] Here the key words are "some nobler use than its bare preservation." Unlike Hobbes, Locke sees the preservation of human life as a principle primitively inculcated by that reason which is identical with natural law; and men see that the principle means not only one's own individual life but also the lives of others. Contrary to Hobbes, who deduces his so-called laws of nature from our fear for our own lives, Locke sees the respect both for ourselves and for others as deriving directly from a law not deduced from fear of death. At the same time, however, the very fact that Locke speaks of a "nobler use" than "bare preservation" indicates that he thinks the same law of nature may under certain circumstances and in conformity with a higher value dictate that each of us undergo risk of death: This is something which Hobbes will never assert, either in the state of nature or in the civil society.

Locke's espousal of the view that there is a natural religion assists him to reach this conclusion, for he suggests that men can read in the law of nature the fact that they are all the "workmanship of one omnipotent, and infinitely wise maker; all the servants of one sovereign master, sent into the world by his order, and about his business."[15] Men are the property of this omnipotent being. It is in fact because they recognize themselves as creatures of nature's God that they realize it is not within their rights to kill one another.

To be sure, each individual, because there is no common judge, is executive for the application of the law of nature and is given a kind of authority over all others who may be violating the law. But the authority is never arbitrary: The executive has only that measure of control necessary to restrain the violator and to deter others from committing a like offense. He cannot act according to his "passionate heats"; and his retribution is limited to that which "calm reason and conscience dictates." Should the executive act otherwise, he himself would be attacking the law of nature.

The central Lockean conception of man in a state of nature is, of course, that of property. It is the key to his view of law, of politics, of education, and of human personality generally. Generally speaking, property means for him "life, liberty, and estate." It is one's natural right to existence, to move about within the limits of the laws of nature, and to mix labor with natural resources to support oneself.

Natural reason, he maintains, tells us that God has given the earth to mankind in common; for it would be unreasonable to assume that God, having created man, would not have provided for his wherewithal. Revelation confirms what natural reason tells us, as David shows in the Psalms.[16] But while the earth belongs to the human race, it is also true that nature's God cannot be assumed to have given it to men without provision for them to make the best possible use of it. Thus although the fruits and beasts which the earth produces spontaneously must be held to belong to mankind as a whole, the specific ways in which man can make use of these bounties have also to be deduced from the common law of nature. Now it is obvious, according to Locke, that the only way in which mankind can really make use of their common possession is through the application of labor.

But labor, reason tells us, is simply an extension of the individual's body and mind, which reason affirms belong to him alone. Every discrete individual has a property in all his own characteristics: his eyes, his skin coloring, his mental characteristics, his muscular power.[17]

If, however, every human being has a property in his own person, it must also be true that he develops a property in all that with which he mixes his labor. In nature, man is not satisfied unless he exerts himself and he is forever attempting to transform raw nature. As he does so, he extends his personality by changing the products of the earth into things as much his as the color of his eyes.

But Locke also argues that there are two qualifications to this labor theory of property. Material things become an individual's through labor "at least where there is enough, and as good left in common for others"[18]; and insofar as "any one can make use of to any advantage of life before it spoils."[19] Under such circumstances, Locke thinks, natural right and convenience would be virtually identical: Hence most natural men would observe the law of nature, since they could not sell the surplus and all others would continue to share the right to mix their own labor with abundant resources.

All this was changed, however, when men in the state of nature began to value things "both lasting and scarce" which could be hoarded up. Thus gems and metals of various kinds would be acquired in exchange for surplusses which otherwise could not legitimately belong to individuals. Such objects began to have value largely through the "consent of men," since compared with "food, raiment, and carriage," they were relatively useless in a direct sense. As men began to store up precious metals, some naturally acquiring more than others, there was a kind of tacit acquiescence in "a disproportionate and unequal possession of the earth."[20] Locke makes it clear that this grossly unequal distribution of valuable things occurred *before* the contract establishing political society.

Thus unequal distribution is not the creature of civil law but rather of the consent of men in a later development of the state of nature. The no spoilage principle is presumably satisfied through acquisition of precious metals. It

11. *Ibid.*, II, 21, 44.
12. *Ibid.*, II, 21, 52.
13. *Ibid.*, II, 21, 17.
14. Locke, *Second Treatise on Civil Government*, Bk. II, ch. 6.
15. *Ibid.*
16. Locke cites Psalm 115.
17. *Second Treatise*, V, 27.
18. *Ibid.*
19. *Ibid.*, V, 50.
20. *Ibid.*, V, 20.

is interesting to note, however, that his first limitation on private property—that "there is enough, and as good left in common for others"—seems to disappear from view. Theoretically, it would now seem possible for a few men to gain control of the land which in the first stage of nature was possessed by all mankind. At least Locke is not clear as to what happens to the first principle. We may, however, interpret him as saying that when men consented to money they also assented to the consequences which flow from the use of money, including the possibility that through the market and exchange mechanisms some of them may be deprived of adequate property in material goods.

Besides the great emphasis which he gives to property in the state of nature—a subject particularly vital in an age of commercial capitalism—Locke is also concerned to analyze and develop the theory of family right and paternal power. The historical significance of his discussion is that it constitutes his answer to Sir Robert Filmer, who, in his *Patriarchia*, had seemed to identify the power of the father with that of the civil ruler and to make the family—rather than the individual—the basic unit of society.[21] Like Aristotle, Locke takes great pains to show that identification of the father with civil ruler is a false analogy.[22]

Locke's state of nature seems so reasonable and calm that one wonders just why men ever consented to leave it. His answer, in general, is that while men are bound together by a common natural reason, they are at the same time strongly egoistic and always in danger of breaching the peace. While on the whole and on most occasions they respect one another's natural rights and recognize their mutual obligations, their periodic breaches of the peace eventually lead them to contract for entry into the state. The enjoyment of the freedom and security of the state of nature is "very uncertain and constantly exposed to the invasion of others."[23] Breaches of the law of nature are sufficiently frequent to be annoying; and the very fears bred by uncertainty themselves help produce still greater insecurities.[24]

Thus Locke's state of nature is a curious mixture. On the one hand, his natural men generally respect one another, reason telling each that he should not deprive others of life, liberty, and estate. Nor is this respect based simply on calculation of self-interest, as it is in Hobbes: men value one another as ends in themselves. Yet in another sense and to some degree modern critics like Cox[25] are right when they point to a kinship between Hobbes and Locke; for Locke's men breach the peace with sufficient frequency to make the contract extremely desirable.

Political Society: Its General Nature

In making their contract to enter political society, Locke's natural men have an inestimable advantage over those of Hobbes, for since they are already rational in nature and, in a measure, are social as well, it is not difficult to account for their ability to make a contract in the first place; whereas for Hobbes' men, it is hardly believable that beings who are constantly at war with and fear one another could suddenly develop the mutual confidence without which contracts cannot be made. Since Locke's natural men basically trust one another, it is quite understandable how they could psychologically enter into the agreement creating a civil polity. Indeed, as Locke has remarked, they have already been connected with one another through a vast array of non-political contracts. When, therefore, they join together in civil society to protect their property more adequately—life, liberty, and (unequal) estates—the change in certain respects is not a shock.

What natural man surrenders when he enters political society is essentially the right to be his own executive and judge. The legislative of a civil society is the judge established by the contract and the magistrates are essentially the delegates of the legislative. It is the legislative and delegated magistrates who henceforth settle controversies and "redress the injuries that may happen to any member of the commonwealth."[26] The contract authorizes the legislative to make laws for the contracting individuals "as the public good of the society shall require."

Locke argues that we cannot assume the contractors to have created an absolute monarchy. This is so because by definition such a government imposes no restraints on the judgments of the ruler: He still remains in a state of nature, as it were.

But if the contract cannot be held to establish an absolute monarchy, by what, then, are men to be bound when they exchange nature for politic society? The answer is that they agree to be concluded by the majority of all men.

The original contract is a matter of unanimous agreement; but a central aspect of that agreement is that each will accept the decision of the majority as if it were the act of the whole community.[27] Locke's assertion that it is the majority which must conclude seems to be supported by a very curious argument. He contends that every community must move in one direction, or cease to be a community. But in what direction shall it move? It is "necessary," replies Locke that "the body would move that way whither the greater force carries it, which is the consent of the majority."[28] It is not entirely clear what Locke means by greater force, but he seems to have in mind potential physical force, at least in part. Since his natural men are substantially equal, like those of Hobbes, it must be assumed that, on the whole, fifty percent plus one will have greater force (perhaps both physical and psychological) than any minority. While it is conceivable, of course, that a rule of unanimity might be set up, Locke rejects this as in effect restoring the state of nature from whose inconveniences men have sought to escape.

Fragile as its foundations may seem, Locke's basic theory of majority rule is one of the central elements in his conception of political society—and, indeed, a cornerstone of those democratic doctrines which will later owe so much to Locke. The historian of political thought will, of course, note that, unlike Marsilio of Padua, who attempted to combine *qualitative* with *quantitative* weight in his theory of decision-making,[29] Locke at no point deserts purely quantitative criteria—a mark of the development between Marsilio and Locke of the notion of equality. But it should be remembered that Locke's natural men are not equal *economically* when they sign the contract.

Locke is, of course, quite aware of many of the major criticisms which might be directed against his contractualism. To the charge that there is no historical example of a contract, he replies (unlike Hobbes) that there have indeed been men actually living in a state of nature and without politics—and he cites Josephus Acosta's report of the state of nature in the wilds of Brazil.[30] A second objection to the idea of a voluntary contract, which doubts that men ever have any real choice, he answers with his celebrated theory of tacit consent or agreement. While a father's agreement to subordinate himself cannot indeed bind his children, children at the age of discretion can decide to leave a particular commonwealth for another: if they remain in the commonwealth of their birth they have, in effect, consented to the contract.[31]

Political Society: Its Objectives and Powers

By unanimous consent, then, the contract is made and through it power is granted to the majority to conclude all men. So soon as the figurative ink on the contract is dry, the majority must act to establish a legislative power. If it retains the legislative authority itself, the polity is a democracy; if it confers the power on a few and on their heirs, it is an oligarchy; and if on a single person it is a monarchy. Locke himself seems to opt for what some have called a "representative democracy," in which the majority decide to delegate their legislative power to an elected assembly.

The executive is the second power. Unlike many of those who later on will derive much of their inspiration from Locke's political teaching, he himself does not distinguish between the executive and a judiciary. Presumably the latter is regarded simply as a branch of the executive, since it, too, deals with implementation of the laws.

Locke does suggest, however, that there is a third power in the commonwealth which he

21. Locke's point-by-point reply to Filmer will, of course, be found in his *First Treatise on Civil Government*. But the stimulus of Filmer will be noted throughout the *Second Treatise* as well.
22. *Second Treatise,* VI.
23. *Ibid.*, IX, 123.
24. Sir Frederick Pollock refers to Locke's State of Nature as one of "precarious peace."
25. See Richard Cox, *Locke on War and Peace*, Oxford: Clarendon, 1960.
26. *Second Treatise,* VII, 89.
27. Cf. Willmoore Kendall, *John Locke and the Theory of Majority Rule*, Urbana: University of Illinois Press, 1959. There has, of course, been considerable controversy as to exactly what limitations, if any, Locke imposes on his majority.
28. *Second Treatise,* VIII, 96.
29. See Chapter 15, p. 272.
30. Josephus Acosta (1539–1600) was a Jesuit Missionary whose best-known work was perhaps *The Natural and Moral History of the Indies* (1959).
31. *Second Treatise,* VIII, 119.

terms the federative. This may be looked upon as that aspect of public power which has charge of international relations. While it may be administered by the same persons who have charge of the executive power, it can be legitimately differentiated from the latter.

All the powers are, of course, subject to the law of nature, for the more secure implementation of which the contract was made in the first place. Thus the legislative ought not to be arbitrary, for it cannot legitimately go beyond the authority which each person had over himself and others in the state of nature. And in that state, it will be remembered, no man had the right to take his own life or to seize the property—the life, liberty, and estate—of others. In the civil state, it follows, the property of no person can be taken without his own consent, which, in the civil society (by virtue of the contract) means the consent of the majority acting to preserve more fully the general natural right to property.

Locke examines the relation of executive to legislative power-holders at some length. On the whole, he thinks, it is better that the two powers not be vested in the same hands, and this for two reasons: First, the making of laws, as contrasted with their execution, requires only a limited amount of time and, secondly, because union of the two powers may be too large a temptation. By and large, then, the legislative should assemble only for fixed periods and then adjourn to be itself subject to the laws; while the executive should be a permanent on-going authority.

In some respects, indeed, Locke appears to violate this principle, particularly when he comes to discuss the problem of reapportionment. He is scandalized, as were the Levellers, by the lack of proportion between population and representation in the seventeenth century; and he thinks that if the legislative authority does not correct it, the executive can—under the principle *salus populi suprema lex*—redistribute seats. Curiously enough, he justifies such an act by an appeal to rather undefined executive prerogative, which is hard to reconcile with his over-all theory.[32]

If the legislative power should so exceed its natural law rights as to prevent the majority from recalling its acts in an orderly manner, it is obvious that the legal means of redress would have been destroyed: Hence, under these circumstances, there could be no positive "judge on earth." Suppose, however, that the contract has made provision for independent courts which could pass on legislative and executive acts. In such an event, the courts could pronounce laws or decrees *ultra vires;* but the courts, without cooperation of the executive, could not enforce their decrees. If either the legislative or the executive, therefore, failed to respect the judicial orders, the people would again be without a judge on earth.

One can imagine yet another condition: The courts sustain acts of the legislative and executive which violate the contract. Here again, the people would seem to be without positive legal recourse.

Finally, it is possible to conceive of yet another situation in which the majority itself grants arbitrary powers to the legislative. According to Locke, of course, no majority can be imputed to have done so under the laws of nature. But suppose the majority did in fact act in this way. It would seem that again a situation would have been created in which no positive legal recourse would be available: Whatever might be done would have to be revolutionary in nature.

If this interpretation of Locke on executive and legislative powers in relation to political society is correct; if, indeed, there is no foolproof technique whereby either executives or legislators can be held to their commitment to observe the laws of nature, Locke must either counsel passive obedience to illegitimate authority, as did Barclay and, on the whole, Luther, or develop a theory which would justify revolt against the government. As is well-known, he does the latter, which makes him the outstanding philosopher of revolution in early modern times.

Revolution: Its Nature and Justification

The key to his theory of revolution is his likening of usurpation to conquest. Conquest, he maintains, is simply "foreign usurpation," and "usurpation" is "domestic conquest."[33] There is, indeed, one difference, in that conquest may have a limited right on its side (in a just war), while usurpation is never supported by right. The usurper has obtained possession of that to which another, by the Contract, has a right. So soon as the usurpation is determined to be such, it is clear, thinks Locke, that the alleged ruler has no right to be obeyed.

When a ruler gains authority rightfully but at some point exercises power beyond right he becomes a tyrant. Locke thus employs two different terms for the tyranny which many political writers use to designate both illegitimate acquisition of political power and its exercise beyond authorization of law.[34] But whether the individual or council be a usurper or a tyrant, in Locke's terms, the principles which govern the community's relation to them are essentially the same. But does this mean that usurpers and tyrants may not only be disobeyed but also be resisted by force? Earlier[35] we saw the rather involved and often ambiguous answers given to similar questions by St. Thomas, Calvin, Luther, and others.

But Locke's answer seems to be unambiguous. If all branches of the government support the usurpation or tyranny, then the government is really no government and the political community is free to proceed against it. But Locke takes great pains to emphasize that while the government is no more, the political community continues; for the latter is almost never wiped out except in case of foreign invasion. The community thus remains to constitute a new government, through the voice of the majority, whenever the old shall be removed either peacefully or by the exercise of force.

To the objection that this doctrine would make government subject to a fickle opinion and to the "uncertain humour of the people,"[36] Locke replies that most human beings are essentially conservative and that it requires a really fundamental violation of rights to induce them to utilize their natural right to change the government. Revolutions rarely happen "upon every little mismanagement of public affairs": It requires a "long train of abuses, prevarications, and artifices, all tending the same way"[37] even to make men aware that they have a usurping or tyrannical government. Locke thus anticipates the nineteenth century J. S. Mill in arguing that the real danger, if historical experience be the guide, is not that men will utilize their right of revolution irresponsibly but rather that only the most flagrant violations can get them to act at all.

In short, rulers, whether executive or legislative, are regarded by Locke as having powers analogous to those possessed by the "trustee" in private affairs.[38] Trusteeship was, of course, as familiar a concept in private law as contract: in both instances, Locke is transferring private law notions to the realm of the public, thus dramatizing the tendency of all contract thinkers to see society as an aggregation of discrete individuals bound together in public by notions carried over from their individual relations. The state, in one sense, becomes like a gigantic trading corporation whose officers are obviously but the servants of its owners.

At this point, it is well to call our attention once more to the whole implication of the view: Political society, Locke is saying again, is more like a machine with balances and gears than like a biological organism in which the parts have to be accounted for. For Locke, as for Hobbes—and, indeed, for most seventeenth-century thinkers, whether explicitly or by implication—it is the whole and not the parts which must be explained.

The Limitations of Religious Tolerance

Hobbes, as we have seen, was drawn by his own logic into an extreme Erastian position with respect to religion and the church. Such groups as the Levellers, by contrast, were advocates of extreme religious toleration on grounds of both principle and expediency. Locke, as one might expect, attempts to steer a middle ground, not too successfully but, nevertheless, influentially.

To be sure, he is at one with his century in offering only limited toleration, at best. The Peace of Westphalia in 1648 had decided that the prince should choose the religion of his state. The early New England colonies of Plymouth and Massachusetts Bay provided only a very qualified toleration; and while Roger Williams expanded that measure of tolerance in Rhode Island, even he imposed significant limits.[39] Of all those who attempted to apply

32. *Ibid.*, XIV, 160.
33. *Ibid.*, XVII, 197.
34. On the several connotations of the term "tyrant," see Oscar Jaszi and John Lewis, *Against the Tyrant*, Glencoe, Ill.: Free Press, 1957.
35. See Chapters 13 and 17.
36. *Second Treatise*, XIX, 223.
37. *Ibid.*, XIX, 225.
38. *Ibid.*, XIX, 240.
39. See Williams' *The Bloudy Tenent of Persecution* (printed in 1644) and *The Bloudy Tenent of Persecution Yet More Bloudy* (1652). In his famous "ship letter," Williams defended suppression of religious opinions which might hold that Christ's law forbade civil government.

notions of toleration in a principled way, the Quakers in Pennsylvania offer perhaps the outstanding example.[40] Predominantly, toleration tended to be a matter of expediency, as we suggested in an earlier chapter,[41] and even then was usually rather severely restricted.

The intellectual climate within which Locke wrote was such that conceptions of religious toleration were now more widely accepted. This was so in part because passionate devotion to the traditional cults was declining and an air of indifferentism—to be characteristic of most of the eighteenth century—was setting in. Under these circumstances men accepted a certain degree of tolerance because they no longer thought that religious issues were matters of vital importance.

Because Locke's general political theory was informed by individualism and emphasis on the property of the person in liberty, it is not surprising that he should have dealt with the problem at considerable length. Unlike Hobbes, of course, he is no materialist, despite his stress on the origin of all knowledge in sense; nor is he an atheist. His general religious orientation is that of one who believes in the "reasonableness of Christianity,"[42] but who at the same time admits the possibility of revelation—which is, of course, always to be understood in the light of reason.

His first concern, as one might expect, is to ask whether the contract can be held to have committed the "care of souls" to the civil ruler. His answer is in the negative. There has been no such delegation of authority to the magistrate, he argues, because "no man can, if he would, conform his faith to the dictates of another."[43] Faith is a matter of inner belief and it is a sheer impossibility for any other person, ruler or not, to tell me what I do actually believe in face of the fact that I may not really do so.

Thus far, Locke stands on the same ground as Hobbes: Belief not expressed publicly cannot be controlled by the magistrate simply because he cannot get within me to exercise the control. The civil ruler by the contract is confined to outer, civil interests, which Locke identifies with "life, liberty, health, and idolency of body," together with possession of such things as "money, lands, houses, furniture, and the like."

The civil magistrate has control of outward sanctions, of course, and it is legitimate to inquire whether the imposition of penalties on expression of inner beliefs can change the beliefs themselves. In other words, we may grant that the contract could not transfer control of inner beliefs to the ruler; but did it not conceivably delegate control over outward expression of those beliefs? Hobbes, of course, thought it did; Locke, by and large, holds it did not. His reasoning is that the penalties of the civil ruler, while they may historically have been applied against the heterodox, cannot in fact change the inner beliefs of those whose outward expressions have been prohibited. While the magistrate may secure outer conformity, then, he should be under no illusion that he is changing inner belief, which to Locke, contains "all the life and power of true religion."

Locke goes on to make a sharp differentiation between church and civil society. The former, he argues, is simply a voluntary association, the governors of which may indeed have the power to expel its members for failure to observe its rules; at the same time, however, they can have no other coercive powers. The contract establishing the state, by contrast, while entered into voluntarily (and we have noted some of the problems raised by this issue), confers authority on the majority to conclude all members of the society. Once the contract has been entered into, the political community becomes coercive in the sense that its members may be punished for violation of its laws. Locke is a bit vague, however, as to how the punishments of voluntary church and coercive political community actually differ from one another in principle: May not expulsion from my beloved religious community, for example, be to me as coercive and distasteful as a jail sentence imposed by the magistrate?

The fact that there are two governors—Church and state—in matters of conduct may, to be sure, lead to a clash of standards. The magistrate may enjoin something that "appears unlawful to the conscience of a private person." Locke thinks that such situations will be relatively rare, however, if the civil ruler directs all his acts to the public good. When a conflict does arise, the "private person," he contends, must "abstain from the action that he judges unlawful" and accept the punishment which the magistrate inflicts. In such a contingency the individual will have satisfied his conscience but at the same time will be recognizing his obligations under the contract. If the magistrate commands action which is beyond his authority, however, as when he orders men to attend a church not of their own choosing, the individual may apparently (for Locke is not very precise) do all he can to circumvent the law; one infers that he may not only refuse to obey it but may also try to escape its penalties.

Locke's limits on toleration are as important as his grounds for limited tolerance. It is surprising to find that his limitations apply not only to conduct or to actions but also to the mere expression of opinions. "No opinions contrary to human society, or to those moral rules which are necessary to the preservation of civil society," he maintains, "are to be tolerated by the magistrate." His second restriction is against any religious group that arrogates to itself "some peculiar prerogative covered over with a specious show of deceitful words, but in effect opposite to the civil right of the community"—any group, for example, that teaches "that faith is not to be kept with heretics . . . [that] dominion is founded in grace." Thirdly, he would exclude any church "which is constituted upon such a bottom that all those who enter into it do thereby *ipso facto* deliver themselves up to the protection and service of another prince." Fourthly, any who "deny the being of a God" cannot be tolerated because "promises, covenants, and oaths, which are the bonds of human society, can have no hold upon an atheist. The taking away of God, though but even in thought, dissolves all."

These four limitations, taken together, obviously exclude Roman Catholics and atheists; and the first restriction would seem to carry us far beyond even this substantial qualification. Thus while Locke develops one of the most complete theories of religious toleration known to his day, the limitations he imposes are as significant as his defense of the idea itself.

The Strengths and Limitations of Locke

Locke, like Hobbes, both reflected and shaped certain basic tendencies in the thought life of his day, and, indeed, far into the eighteenth century and beyond. But the system itself possesses both strengths and weaknesses.

Empiricism and Rationalism. Many have suggested that there is a basic conflict between Locke the empiricist and repudiator of innate ideas, as presumably reflected in the *Essay Concerning Human Understanding*, and Locke the rationalist, who seems to be more nearly mirrored in the political treatises.

The critic might ask, for example, how natural rights could be derived empirically, even indirectly. Are they not ultimately bottomed on something suspiciously like the innate ideas rejected in the *Essay?* How can they be deduced, even in an ultimate sense, from sensations? Why *should* promises be kept? How, turning to another area, can religious experience be accounted for in sensationalist terms?

Whatever may be the answer to these and similar questions, it is clear that in his politics Locke moves strongly in the direction of what will in the eighteenth century be called rationalism. That is to say, having supposedly established a few basic propositions, he tends to deduce from them other statements about the social and political world without checking specifically against the so-called facts. Or he builds a system of political obligation on a purely hypothetical contract and a rather dubious discrete individual.

This tendency to ignore the empirical in specifics, once he has formulated abstractions from which he makes his deductions, is illustrated very well in his theory of religious toleration. When he excludes Catholics from the state's toleration because of their beliefs, he does not seem to ask whether all men professing that belief—even supposing it to be deleterious to civil society—will actually act on it. Like those who dismissed American "Communist" teachers in the twentieth century because their professed beliefs must "necessarily" lead them to be unobjective in their

40. Thus even Roman Catholics were welcomed in Pennsylvania at a time when they suffered countless civil and educational disabilities in Britain. Only "Christians" could hold office in Pennsylvania, however; this provision, so contrary to the spirit of Quakerism, was possibly written into the Instrument of Government as one of several concessions to Court and public opinion.
41. See Chapters 18 and 20.
42. See his treatise *The Reasonableness of Christianity* (1695).
43. *A Letter Concerning Toleration*, in *Treatise on Civil Government and A Letter concerning Toleration*, edited by Charles L. Sherman, New York: Appleton-Century-Crofts, 1965, p. 173.

teaching, he failed to subject each individual case to the acid empirical test, thus severely restricting his empiricism. In the instance of American "Communists," almost none were visited in their classrooms to see whether their teaching *was* unobjective. Similarly, Locke would condemn a whole class of individuals—Roman Catholics—to intolerance, without inquiring whether or not any given Catholic was disloyal. And he adopts the same attitude with respect to atheists. The reasoning runs somewhat like this: Civil society is a good and cannot exist without promises; those who don't believe in God will not keep their promises; atheists do not believe in God and therefore will not keep promises; atheists are thus a menace in themselves, apart from their overt and concrete acts, and therefore ought not to be tolerated.

Insofar as Locke *is* empirical, of course, he is obviously on sounder ground than Hobbes, who was so impressed by mathematical and deductive models that he seemed to leave the existential world entirely.

Lockean Contract. Locke's theory of the Contract—assuming for the moment that contractual thinking has any validity at all—is much more credible than that of Hobbes. It is more believable, in other words, that men in the state of nature who have some rationality and original awareness of others should enter into a compact than that beings completely bound up within themselves and fearful of all others should do so.

Despite the psychological and logical advantages of Locke over Hobbes, however, the weakness in any contractual theory remains. In what sense, in other words, can one plausibly and usefully suggest that men were or are ever discrete individuals?

There is the problem, too, of the tacit consent theory. If a young man at 21 opts to remain in the society where he has grown up rather than to emigrate, is he acting as a discrete or unprejudiced individual? Surely not—the scales are heavily weighted against his deciding to reject his own society, for he knows its language, has become an integral part of its culture, is adjusted to its customs and laws, and normally might find other ways of life strange and forbidding. To say that he is like the men who, prior to politic society, made the contract, and is therefore consenting freely, is difficult to believe.

Locke is not clear, moreover, as to whether an individual tacitly consenting to the contract has or has not made an irrevocable commitment. Can he decide at any time after attaining his majority whether he wishes to continue his relationship? It is inconceivable, in light of Locke's generally individualistic attitude, that he would argue for a theory of irrevocable commitment. But if this is so, the differences between a voluntary association like the church and the political society based on contract—a distinction which Locke emphasizes—are not as great as he seems to maintain.

To be sure, the notion of contract, if not taken too literally, may sharply symbolize the idea that all governments must observe certain limits if they are to possess the quality of legitimacy. It may also reflect and dramatize the plausible proposition that there are limits to a citizen's political obligations. But the critic might well ask whether these conceptions could not be formulated more directly—by means of traditional natural-law theories, for example.

Nevertheless, if contract is to be used at all, Locke's version, with all its faults, is probably as good as any and better than most.

The Problem of Majority Rule. The doctrine of majority rule, which has become a kind of dogma in modern democratic theory since Locke, has its own difficulties. Its defense is always a bit vague and Locke's vindication is no exception to the rule.

When he says that the majority, after the contract, concludes the society because it represents the greatest force, it is not entirely clear what he means. Physical force? Psychological force? Intellectual force? If he is making a statement of alleged fact and suggesting that in reality fifty percent plus one will, in the long run, determine the general shape of things, we can well ask him how he would prove it. Observations and studies from ancient times to the present seem to have shown that innovations are almost always the work of minorities; that governing classes—whatever the *form* of government—are tiny fractions of the whole; and that the vast mass of mankind are, save perhaps in acute crises, indifferent to public affairs, for the most part acquiescing in what ruling groups determine.[44]

Locke tells us, to be sure, that if we postulate unanimity, we have simply returned to the state of nature. Assuming this to be true, however, it is still possible to imagine men who make the Contract devolving the task of framing the institutions of politic society on a specific minority or on a majority, which, as in

Marsilio, is both qualitative and quantitative. Locke, to be sure, will at this point probably call attention to his principle of equality and argue that majority rule is entailed by it. But why? That all should be consulted in the framing of specific institutions and policies may follow from the notion of equality. But why should the idea that the minority must submit to the majority be an implication? Moreover, even if majority rule can somehow be related to the principle of equality, Locke has argued that, in the state of nature itself, gross economic inequality has already come about. Insofar as the doctrine of majority rule suggests that the greatest force is represented by the majority, it would seem to rest on shaky grounds in view of the obvious fact that in most societies preponderant economic power is at the beck and call of a relatively few persons.

Insofar as majority rule, in Locke's ultimate sense, represents recognition of need for at least the passive acquiescence of the bulk of men if political society is to be stable and law to be implemented, it represents an important insight. But it is unfortunate that Locke—and most of his successors—did not examine the question more closely.

Property. Like majority rule, Locke's conception of property leaves much to be desired. He begins, it will be remembered, by asserting a labor theory subject to the two qualifications of no spoilage and availability of enough for others. Then he accounts for and defends the introduction of money, which enables men to store up values without spoilage. But he is vague as to his second limitation: How will a complex society, given money, continue to assure all men their natural rights to mix their labor with nature? As a matter of fact the implication is that in the second stage of the state of nature, the access of many to natural resources is wiped out through the alleged assent of men to a money economy. When the state of nature is left behind, it is the first stage only, in an economic sense, which is forgotten. Locke's natural right to life, liberty, and estate no longer includes any presumed first-stage right to claim enough natural resources on which one can expend one's labor. Locke does not tell us, moreover, how or when men consented to the money economy before the contract. It seems implausible that they would have consented to abolition of access.

While he begins by defining property very broadly as life, liberty, and estate, in other passages he appears to narrow it and to confine it to a natural or civil right to material possessions. This ambiguity, together with his obvious acceptance of the economic inequalities arising in the second stage of the state of nature, will afford eighteenth and nineteenth century students considerable latitude for interpretation. Predominantly, of course, Locke will be used in such a way as to support the burgeoning institutions of modern capitalism. He also opens the way for the dichotomy between human rights and property rights so characteristic of much later thought.

Locke and the Eighteenth Century

But whatever the critics may have said in his own day and in later generations, Locke both influenced and represented a temper of political thought and opinion which was to become highly important in the eighteenth century. Although some modern scholars, to be sure, have tended to discount his direct influence, indirectly it seemed to permeate much thought. Even when neither direct nor indirect influence can be traced, we may think of Locke as a kind of representative figure for tendencies in eighteenth-century thought. A seventeenth-century figure himself, he appeared to anticipate and epitomize certain major currents of the century of George Washington, Thomas Jefferson, and Voltaire.

Here let us suggest merely a few of the major lines of speculation which Locke either directly or indirectly influenced or which reflected attitudes not dissimilar to his.

In General. Locke's emphasis on cool, calm rationality both influenced and symbolized what we have come to call the Enlightenment, a word which we usually employ to describe both the general and the political thought of the Western world from 1700 to about the French Revolution. To be sure, Locke's teaching was only one element in the development of Enlightenment attitudes. Perhaps it would be more accurate to say that a confluence of factors produced the "Enlightenment" and

44. In modern times, the roles of elites have been considered by such thinkers as Marx, Auguste Comte, Gaetano Mosca, and Vilfredo Pareto.

that Locke's thought more or less accurately reflected that climate of opinion.[45]

We may epitomize this climate by saying that it had confidence in the emancipating power of reason; tended to reject the past, and particularly the Middle Ages; thought of religion in deistic terms—Locke's God of nature; conceived the universe largely as a mechanism, after the model of Sir Isaac Newton, of Hobbes, and of Locke; and thought of intellect as somehow separated from the emotions. These characteristics were true of literature as well as political thought.

It was not until the last three decades of the century that this preponderant climate of opinion began to change, with Rousseau, Burke and Hume.

Contract and Balance. Locke's doctrine and those similar to it, whether or not influenced by Locke, appeared to hold that one could, by observing nature in its primitive or pre-political sense, get clues as to the forms which political society should take. While nature was not based on contract, those who formulated the contract looked to it (and to nature's God) for guidance. The contract sought to make stable in human society that balance and order which one found throughout nature; for Nature was not "red in tooth and claw," as in nineteenth-century evolutionary views, but rather moved toward harmony.

Some have suggested, and with justification, that Alexander Pope's *Essay on Man,* in its social and political aspects, is essentially a poetical version of Locke. It seems plausible to say that Locke, or at least a Lockean climate of opinion, affected the mind of Pope, when he said:

> Thus then to Man the voice of Nature spake—
> "Go, from the Creatures thy instructions take:
>
> . . . .
>
> "Thy arts of building from the bee receive;
> "Learn of the mole to plough, the worm to weave;
>
> . . . .
>
> "Mark what unvary'd laws preserve each state,
> "Laws wise as Nature, and as fix'd as Fate."[46]

When Pope tells us that nature furnished the model for man's political artifact, he speaks forcefully with the voice of Locke.

Among the greatest practical political expressions of Locke's views were the Declaration of Independence, the Constitution of the United States, and the general notions associated with many of the American Founding Fathers. In the Declaration, vindication is sought by an appeal to nature and to nature's God; and the "pursuit of happiness" is lifted directly from Locke. The leading members of the American Constitutional Convention were, of course, thoroughly familiar not only with the political but also with the philosophical Locke.[47] The very notion of a written constitution entered into voluntarily by the sovereign states resembles Locke on the original contract, as does the division of powers within the federal system. While the separation of powers and checks and balances theories owe something, no doubt, to Montesquieu (1689–1755)[48] and, indeed, to a very old tradition in political thought running back at least to Polybius, Locke's inspiration seems to have been the most important source. And the idea that men make political compacts to protect their property runs through the works of the Founding Fathers and the *Federalist Papers,* although property is often interpreted only as estate rather than, in Locke's predominant version, "life, liberty, and estate."

The conception of representative government generally owed not a little to Locke. No advocate of direct "democracy," he saw the representative body as essentially deliberative; and deliberation could be performed with greater effectiveness in a relatively small group than in the citizen body as a whole. Certainly the spirit of Locke—if not always the letter—was an important factor in the growth of late eighteenth-century views of representative government. Those views, of course, were frequently associated with the idea of a restricted franchise based on property qualifications (on the plea that one should have an economic "stake in society" before being admitted to voting rights) but they laid the groundwork for the nineteenth-century "liberal" and "radical" conceptions which included a vastly expanded suffrage.

The notion that the balance of nature could be emulated in political society runs through the writings of Thomas Jefferson. The whole conception of natural rights *against* society is an expression of contractualism, usually in the Lockean sense, and duties *to* society fade in relative importance.

Locke's conception of revolution, so intimately associated with both his view of nature and his idea of contract, was also profoundly influential. As it had been used by some to vindicate the Revolution of 1689 in Britain (although Locke had, of course, written the *Second Treatise* before the deposition of James

II), so was it employed for a similar purpose in the United States nearly a century afterwards; and while not a few assert that Rousseau is more important for understanding the intellectual foundations of the French Revolution than any other thinker, we know that some key figures in that upheaval had read Locke and that others were familiar with his spirit through such men as Voltaire.

Environment and the Shaping of Society. Locke's assertion that the human mind is a *tabula rasa* at birth and that social and political environment shapes the life of man played an enormously important role in the political and educational thought of the eighteenth century. We cannot, of course, attribute the notion solely to Locke, but his was one of the most important formulations. Even when men did not read his *Human Understanding* (and many intellectuals themselves probably did not), its spirit was in the air.

In general, the idea of the *tabula rasa* was important for the notion of progress, which began to occupy a particularly important place toward the end of the seventeenth century and which would be especially significant in the history of modern liberalism, Marxism, and other currents of thought since the French Revolution. Associated with the conception of progress was the widespread belief in the "perfectibility of man," which meant at a minimum that men could, by manipulating the environment, advance increasingly toward moral and political understanding and wisdom and a more nearly ideal practice.

This complex of notions was illustrated during the eighteenth century in the ideas of Richard Price (1723–1791), a radical democrat; Marie Jean, Marquis de Condorcet (1743–1794), who during the French Revolution wrote *Esquisse d'un tableau historique des progres de l'esprit humain,* which predicts in glowing terms the future of mankind; and William Godwin (1756–1836), who in defending the French Revolution (1793) explicitly built his system on Locke's "sensationalism."[49] While Godwin rejected contractualism, he accepted Locke's individualism, pressing the latter in an anarchist direction: Thus he envisioned the possibility—indeed, the inevitability—of a world in which education and enlightened political ideas would produce a society without kings, parliaments, wars, or even death.

Individuality and Harmony. In Locke, too, one finds reflected that search for a new teleology which was so characteristic of speculators after the Restoration. The natural science viewpoint reflected dramatically in Hobbes, as we have seen,[50] cast ridicule on classical Aristotelian and Platonic teleology and sought explanations for things not in their imputed purposes but rather in their origins. Scientific analysis broke things down and purported to explain wholes simply in terms of their parts. Metaphysically, it was the minute particles or corpuscles into which all wholes could be divided which were the units in terms of which thinkers sought to account for larger organizations.

But if this were true, what was the relation of these individuals to one another? Were they completely separable? And if so, were they constantly clashing against one another or were they held together somehow by factors which earlier conceptions of nature could not explain? Was their relation to one another a dynamic or a static one?

It was to questions of this kind that a younger contemporary of Locke, Gottfried Wilhelm Leibniz (1646–1716) sought to respond; and his answers are suggestive for an understanding of Locke and of eighteenth-cen-

45. The many strands of the Enlightenment are treated in such works as Carl Becker, *The Heavenly City of the Eighteenth Century Philosophers,* New Haven: Yale University Press, 1932.
46. *Essay on Man,* Epistle III.
47. See Stanley Elkins and Eric McKitrick, *The Founding Fathers: Young Men of the Revolution,* Washington: Service Center for Teachers of History, 1962; Alfred Hinsey and Winfred A. Harbisan, *The American Constitution: Its Origins and Development,* New York: W. W. Norton and Co., 1963; and Peter Odegard *et al., American Government: Theory, Politics, and Constitutional Foundation,* New York: Holt, Rinehart and Winston, 1961.
48. Baron de Montesquieu would in the eighteenth-century *L'Esprit des Lois* (published in English as *The Spirit of the Laws,* New York: Hafner, 1949) give expression to the old view that separation of powers could guard against tyranny. Locke suggests the same principle. But the task of measuring "influences" on the founders of the American federation would appear to be an almost impossible one.
49. The first portions of Godwin's great work on *Political Justice* are simply a restatement of Locke on *Human Understanding.*
50. See Chapter 19, particularly pp. 346–348.

tury notions which owe much to or at least resemble both Leibniz and Locke.

Essentially, Leibniz tries to restore teleology but in the context of a characteristically individualist framework. His individual units he calls "monads."[51] Each monad is an immaterial force but is at the same time independent of all other monads. Within each the whole universe is mirrored. Thus the differences between one monad and another are not in terms of content but rather in those of the clearness with which the universe is mirrored. Highly active ones represent the whole more distinctly than do relatively passive ones. The force or appetite of each is pushing it from less to more clear reflections of the universe. Thus the primitive forces of each are advancing it in the direction of a goal or purpose.

The ethical implications of Leibniz's metaphysics, which were not fully drawn out by him but which seem to be implicit in his system as well as Locke's, are that every human individual, in studying nature, can perfect himself and in so doing will be reflecting the harmony of the whole. In an ultimate sense, the immaterial forces involved in each ethical monad—each discrete human being, in social terms—cannot, if rightly understood, come into conflict with the forces of other monads. While each human being is self-interested, the very search for true self-interest—the pursuit of happiness, as Locke would say—can only contribute to the harmony or good of the whole, which in this instance is society.

Although Locke is by no means entirely clear in developing themes of this kind, his whole outlook, emphasizing as it does the quest for happiness or pleasure and the compatibility of individual pursuit of happiness with social harmony, lends itself to the automatic harmony conception.[52]

Again, Alexander Pope expresses it in well-known lines:

Nor think, in Nature's state they blindly trod:
The state of Nature was the reign of God. . . .
On their own Axis as the planets run,
Yet make at once their circle round the sun;
So two consistent motions act the Soul;
And one regards Itself, and one the Whole.
Thus God and Nature link'd the gen'ral frame,
And bade Self-love and Social be the same.[53]

Early in the eighteenth century, it came to be held by some that, rightly understood, each individual, in pursuing his own self-interest was actually serving the public good. Thus Bernard Mandeville (1670–1733), in his enormously popular *Fable of the Bees*,[54] could argue that even the human vices of lust and acquisitiveness were almost magically transformed into social welfare: prostitutes seeking their own gain protected the virtue of the wife; and greedy men grasping yet more wealth for themselves added to the gross national product. In general, individual good, individually pursued, even if it seemed cruel to others in the short run, in the long run became socially beneficial. The universe was so constructed that private vices and the self-seeking acts of political leaders became public benefits, without the inconvenience of deliberate social planning. While views of this kind are ridiculed in Voltaire's *Candide*, they become part of the basis for laissez-faire economic views, particularly following the publication of Adam Smith's *Wealth of Nations* (1776). And after that, they will have a long history in early modern liberalism.[55]

Laissez-faire economic views were, of course, very much in the intellectual atmosphere during the last third of the eighteenth century. Thus the French economist François Quesnay (1694–1774) had published in 1758 his *Tableau Économique*, in which he asserted that there is a natural order of things with which the state should interfere as little as possible. All wealth, moreover, is derived from the soil. If the state keeps in mind these principles, it will rule physiocratically (that is, according to nature) and refrain from regulating the economy. The true harmony of nature will then be reflected in the lives of men; and the individual pursuit of wealth will harmonize with the social well-being. The Physiocrats, as they were called, obviously clashed sharply with the "mercantilist" school of thought, which advocated state regulation of the economy in the name of the supposed national interest.[56]

In many respects, Thomas Jefferson can be identified with the Physiocratic approach and its conception that "natural" rather than politically contrived harmony best contributes both to the social and to the individual good. The proposition implies that while the state is necessary for "civilization," it should be guided basically by the fundamental arrangement of things which one will discover in the natural order. "That government is best which governs least" reflects a characteristically individualist sentiment. It should govern least because if it extends its functions it will disturb the natural harmony of the individual and the whole.

Locke's Labor Theory, Economics, and Later Thought. Locke's notion that a mixing of one's labor with nature creates a property in the result was taken up in a sense by late eighteenth and early nineteenth century economists. From them, Marx developed his "labor theory of value," which would become a basis for his radical critique of capitalist society.[57]

Meanwhile, of course, many of Locke's propositions about property, particularly those in which he appears to defend gross inequality of distribution during the second-stage development of the state of nature, would be employed by the ideologists of the capitalist system itself. Middle class and upper class apologists during the early period of industrialism would use a theory of property worked out in an agrarian-commercial civilization to defend their "natural rights" to own factories and industrial tools of production in general. They would think of their claims to property in industrial tools as blessed by nature and by nature's God. They would see what C. B. MacPherson calls "possessive individualism" as vindicated by a Locke-like theory of natural rights.

But the eighteenth century was varied in its political perspectives. It was not only "rationalist" but, especially during the last third of the century, increasingly "empirical," romantic, history-anchored, and enamored of Greek and Roman models. There was a development from what Edmund Burke was to call "abstract rationalism" to an accelerating emphasis on emotion. The growth of empirical viewpoints had been foreshadowed by the thought of Baron de Montesquieu's *L'Esprit des Lois* (1748), in which that remarkable thinker sought to show the influence of culture, climate, and history on the political institutions of a society. Much later, Rousseau would constitute a link between "rationalist" and contract thinking, on the one hand, and romantic and Greek-Roman models, on the other. At about the same time, David Hume would seek to refute all contract thinking, to lay the groundwork for late eighteenth century utilitarianism, and to appeal to "experience" for an explanation of human political behavior. To epitomize tendencies like these in the latter part of the eighteenth century, let us therefore turn next to Jean Jacques Rousseau and then to David Hume.

chapter 22

The Revival of Feeling: Rousseau, Nature, and the Civil State

Rousseau is one of the most complex thinkers in the entire history of political theory and at the same time has been one of the most influential. He seemed to absorb a wide diversity of intellectual tendencies but his ability to digest and integrate them was strictly limited. He

Chapter 21

51. G. W. Leibniz, *The Monadology*, in *The Rationalists: Descartes, Spinoza, Leibniz*, New York: Doubleday, 1962. On the relation of Locke, Leibniz, and others to the theory of automatic harmony, see W. Stark, *The Ideal Foundations of Economic Thought*, New York: Oxford University Press, 1944, pp. 1–50.
52. Basil Willey has thus finely characterized Locke's relation to the theory of individuality and harmony: "The 'State of Nature,' in Locke, is so far from resembling the 'ill condition' described by Hobbes, that it approximates rather to the Eden of the religious tradition, or the golden age of the poets. After Locke, this conception becomes an expression of the current faith that, on the whole, *things if left to themselves* are more likely to work together for good than if interfered with by meddling man." *The Seventeenth Century Background*, London: Chatto & Windus, 1934, p. 265.
53. *Essay on Man*, Epistle III.
54. *The Fable of the Bees* first appeared in 1714. A new edition was issued in 1723. Although obviously social satire, its humor pointed up the widespread and developing view that social harmony and prosperity would be most likely to emerge if men took as their model a presumably unplanned nature.
55. See Chapter 26.
56. On mercantilism, the Physiocratic school, and the early history of modern economic thought, see Eduard Heimann, *History of Economic Doctrines*, London: Oxford University Press, 1945, pp. 22–80.
57. The labor theory of property can, of course, be interpreted either as an *explanation* of economic value or as a normative theory of what the worker *should* receive. Unfortunately, the two meanings have sometimes been confused.

was directly influenced by Locke's viewpoint, yet his writing reflects assumptions and attitudes which Locke would assuredly have repudiated. Like the great majority of eighteenth-century political thinkers down to the time of Edmund Burke (1729–1797), he sought to apply arithmetical and geometrical models to politics; yet at the same time he became one of the founders of the so-called romantic school in literature and politics. Historically, he was looked upon by many French revolutionary leaders and their spiritual descendants as the intellectual defender of the "liberty, equality, and fraternity" which became the slogan of those who overthrew the ancient monarchy and the slogan, too, of one important current of modern democracy; yet he has been termed by certain modern historians of thought the intellectual forbear of twentieth-century totalitarianism.[1] No philosopher of the eighteenth century was more rhapsodical than Rousseau in exalting the virtues of living according to nature, yet his design for civil society, which he opposes to nature, is a complex structure in which natural spontaneity seems to be destroyed.

It is perhaps more true of Rousseau than of most thinkers that we cannot appreciate the full meaning of his words without seeing them in the context of his life experiences. His own emotional turmoil directly conditioned his attitude to nature, for example; and his view of nature, in turn, affected the way in which he saw the civil and political society. Psychologically, his frustrations, engendered partly by the social and political conditions under which he lived, provoked in him those characteristic reactions which we see reflected in his writings.

Rousseau in Eighteenth-Century Society

In an earlier chapter,[2] we pointed out that John Calvin was not only a precocious theologian but also a consummate politician who dominated the city-state of Geneva for many years. When Rousseau was born in Geneva in 1712, much of the legislation fathered by Calvin was still on the statute books and the spirit of the city owed not a little to his inspiration. There can be no doubt, either, that the political Rousseau derived a great deal from the model furnished by the Geneva of his boyhood, despite the fact that his native city was to condemn him severely. Calvin, Geneva, and Rousseau constitute a kind of Trinity in political theory which it would be well to keep in mind as we examine the eighteenth-century Genevan's politics.

Rousseau's mother died in childbirth and his father, in bringing up the boy, followed neither the discipline of conventional education nor that which Jean Jacques was later to advocate in *Emile.* The elder Rousseau, whether from inertia or principle, apparently believed in an utterly unplanned education. Rousseau's father was obviously a man of violent temper: He was sent to prison for an altercation, later fleeing to Lyons. Thereafter, the young Rousseau never saw him again.

The ten-year-old boy was now supervised by his mother's relatives, who provided as tutor for him a Calvinist pastor. In 1724, he was taken into the house of an uncle and a little later was apprenticed to a notary. The notary, however, was apparently not impressed by the future philosopher, for he sent him back to his relatives. A subsequent apprenticeship to an engineer was no more successful. Finally, the boy, who had now reached sixteen, fled from Geneva in 1728. Thereafter he was to wander from place to place and to experience the extremes of the world's rebuffs as well as of its adulations.

His first wanderings were through Italy, where several zealous Roman Catholics sent him to a certain Madame de Warens, a recent convert to the Catholic faith. The impressionable boy was smitten by the attractive woman and it was not long before he followed her example by joining the ancient Church. It is doubtful, however, whether Rousseau was a very good Catholic, although he did attend mass and appear to become very pious. After a brief period as a Count's servant, still further wanderings, and wrought-up emotions, he became Madame de Warens' lover. His mistress was, of course, older than he; and in his *Confessions,* he goes into some detail in describing what must have been a very curious alliance. Later his perennial wanderlust affected him again and in 1740 he journeyed to Lyons, where he became a tutor.

Meanwhile, he had been seeking to develop a new system of musical notations, hoping that he could win not only fortune but fame through it.

For a short period (1743–1744) he was secretary to the French Ambassador to Venice, an occupation which he had obtained through the influence of one of his many women friends. This position, however, was only a brief interlude. In 1712 he had gone to Paris, where he had taken a new mistress (Therese le Vasseur) who would remain with him for a long time and become—according to the *Confessions*—the mother of his five children. The children themselves, he alleges, were all deposited in a foundling hospital.

The middle forties witnessed the beginning of his literary career, when he contributed an article on music to the great *Encyclopaedia*. But his real initiation came in 1749, when, in response to an essay contest of the Academy of Dijon on the subject "Has the progress of sciences and arts contributed to corrupt or purify morals?" he submitted a paper which won the prize. He argued that civilization, contrary to exponents of the "idea of progress," represented a degeneration in morality. The life of nature, in all of its alleged simplicity, was the ideal from which mankind had somehow fallen.[3]

After the Dijon essay, Rousseau continued to speculate on the effects which laws, civilized customs, and political institutions had had on the manners and morals of mankind. He became interested in the information which eighteenth-century amateur anthropologists were gathering about primitive societies and he thought he saw confirmation for his thesis in their researches.

From 1744 to 1756, Rousseau was continuously a resident of Paris and it was during this period that his interest in political questions expanded. His intimate association with the nobility in the capital led him to be impressed by the artificiality of Court life; and he had ample opportunity to make first-hand observations on the monarchical institutions presided over by Louis XV. He thought he saw beneath the glitter of upper-class existence very fragile foundations. This conviction was strengthened when in 1754 he returned to Geneva for a visit: whether correctly or not, he glimpsed in his birthplace a glaring contrast to the life of Paris. He discerned (or professed to discern) simplicity against complexity; reverence and faith opposed to the materialism of Baron D'Holbach,[4] then so popular in Paris; and small-scale virtuous republicanism sharply contrasted with large-scale monarchical bureaucracy. He resolved to leave Paris and return to his native city, whose political climate more nearly fitted his mood.

But this was not to be. In 1756, one of his patronesses, Madame d'Epinay, constructed a rustic lodge for him in a wooded area not far from Paris. Thither he repaired in the early part of 1756 and found the Hermitage (as the house was called) exactly suited to his needs. Communing with nature, he lived very simply and developed still further that sentimental aspect of his character which was to be so well reflected in his educational, religious, and political writings.

Meanwhile, he had become involved in another love affair and had quarreled with his patroness. In December, 1757, therefore, he left the Hermitage and took up his residence in a small cottage in Montmorency. There he continued to live until 1762.

But Rousseau seemed to thrive on emotional turmoil. In fact, his political and educational views were now beginning to reach maturity and the next three years witnessed the completion of his *New Heloise*, the *Social Contract*, and *Emile*. While only the second is political in the strict sense of that term, all three have political overtones.

The publication of the *Social Contract* and *Emile* immediately created difficulties with the authorities, who saw in them subversive tracts which might undermine all contemporary institutions. Thus *Emile* was published in May, 1762, and by June was ordered burned by the Parlement of Paris. The Parlement also decreed the arrest of Rousseau, who was charged with attacks on Christianity.

1. See, for example, Jacob Leib Talmon, *The Origins of Totalitarian Democracy*, New York: Praeger, 1960.
2. See Chapter 17, pp. 320–325.
3 *Discours sur les sciences et les arts.*
4. Baron Paul Henri Dietrich d'Holbach was born in 1723 and died in 1789. One of the leading figures of the Encyclopedists, he had come into prominence at midcentury. D'Holbach's pronounced "materialist" views were common gossip among the salons of Paris and were to be influential in one stream of French revolutionary thought. D'Holbach's most extensive work would be his *Systeme de la nature* (1770). For students of political thought, his *Systeme social* (1773) stands out. The kind of "materialism" espoused by d'Holbach should be carefully distinguished from what Marx and Engels would later call "dialectical materialism." Often d'Holbach's materialism is said to mean that a kind of blind "necessity" rules the world.

After a brief period of exile in Neuchatel, he sought refuge on a little island in the lake of Bienne, which was under the control of the canton of Berne. For a time he appeared to be safe here, not being aware (or forgetting) that the canton had forbidden him access to its territory. When the government of Berne ordered him out of its domains, he made one of the most extraordinary requests in human history: He asked the government to imprison him for life, with right of access to a few books and the privilege of occasional exercise in a garden! After the rejection of this amazing proposal, he eventually found his way to Britain.

His experiences in England were not entirely happy. While he engaged in some study of British institutions, met the king, and had conversations with many eminent people, he soon quarreled with one of his patrons, the Scottish philosopher David Hume.

Meanwhile, his political interests had not lagged. In 1755, the Corsican leader Paoli had defeated the forces of the government of Genoa, which administered the island; and after this it seemed that Corsica was to be independent permanently. The struggles of the Corsicans had impressed Rousseau and he had praised them in the *Social Contract,* remarking that Corsica was the only country where "legislation" (by which he meant the deliberate establishment of new institutions) was still possible. Some at least of the Corsican leaders were impressed and one of them, in 1764, asked Rousseau to produce a scheme of institutions for the new Republic. At one time, apparently, Rousseau hoped to take up his residence in the island in order to become acquainted at first hand with the customs of the people for whom he was to become the legislator. This project fell through. However, he did prevail upon James Boswell, the biographer of the great Dr. Samuel Johnson, to visit the island; and the reflections of Boswell were eventually produced in his *Account of Corsica* (1768). Rousseau himself took seriously his task as a legislator, the result being his *Constitution of Corsica.*[5] Later on, he was to propose institutions for a revived Poland in his *Considerations on the Government of Poland* (1772).[6]

His unhappy experiences in England came to an end in 1767, when he returned to the Continent and spent three years in further wanderings. From 1768 to 1769 he lived in Bourgoin and from 1769 to 1770 in Monquin. At one point he contemplated emigrating to America, where he felt certain that he could really experience the simple life. Eventually, however, he found his way to Paris, where he remained until in 1778 he took up his residence in Ermenoville, which is about twenty miles from the French capital. There he died in the same year.

The life of Rousseau epitomizes some of the most important tensions which are reflected in his thought. For the student of political theory, the most important of these conflicts are those between intellect and feeling; civilization and nature; and the individual and the group. Throughout both his life and his speculations, he seeks to resolve these assumed oppositions but never quite succeeds.

The tension between the life of the mind and that of the passions has been noted at many points. Born into an age of supreme confidence in the human intellect, the circumstances of his life and his own complex personality led him to revolt against views which seemed to ignore or to minimize human emotions. The whole history of his erotic life, for example, mirrors his ultimate belief that what men feel may give them as true an insight into reality as what they speculate about.

As for the tension between civilization and nature, it, too, is obviously reflected in Rousseau's biography. Despite his ostensible repudiation of urban life—which historically has epitomized civilization—he spent a large part of his adult career living in Paris. He thrived in some measure on the adulation of the sophisticated, even while he was endeavoring to make them more "natural." And in his political thought, as we shall see, there is always an unresolved conflict between natural spontaneity and unnatural discipline. In his educational theory, the natural upbringing of Emile is a highly contrived scheme developed by one who is obviously the product of civilization.

We might comment in similar fashion on the tension between individual and group. No social and political thinker can avoid this central problem, of course, but in Rousseau it becomes particularly acute. And again, his life nicely illustrates tendencies in his writings, just as the latter undoubtedly reveal the turmoil of his experiences. His biography shows him as a man forever seeking to make himself independent of others while yet in the end becoming more dependent than ever. On many an occasion he rejected valuable gifts for fear that their acceptance might impair the true freedom which he sought; and he was extremely sensitive to all acts of others which might be deemed condescending. The livelihood he earned by copying music was at best a meager one; but he always preferred it to any possible occupation which might involve him in financial complexities and a close interdependence. Similarly, his nature mysticism can in one sense be looked upon as an effort to substitute emotional dependence on the natural world for what he feared would be a slavish dependence on the group. Yet it is obvious that, more than many men, he was beholden to others both economically and emotionally. All these tensions of his disturbed life are mirrored in his political speculations.

Rousseau's Vision of the Primitive

Given these three major conflicts in his life and thought, the student of Rousseau's political theory is always hard pressed to discover any system in him at all. While it is true that most schemes of thought reveal ragged edges, Rousseau's is particularly subject to this criticism. Nevertheless, as several commentators have pointed out, there would seem to be an over-all pattern, however inconsistently it might be developed. The pattern suggests that mankind first lived in an idyllic state, then became corrupted (just how this was accomplished is a problem for Rousseau), and finally can discover a state of affairs in which their corruption is overcome. F. J. C. Hearnshaw refers to this patterning of Rousseau's thought as a secular version of the Christian doctrine of paradise lost and paradise regained.[7]

The factors leading Rousseau to think of human experience in this way were several. In the first place, he grew up in an environment where he must have become familiar at an early age with the view so powerfully reflected in English literature in the works of Milton; Calvinist Geneva was, indeed, the great center for the doctrine which emphasized the fallen nature of man. At the same time, however, Rousseau was led by the spirit of the Enlightenment to reject the terminology of orthodox religion, both Protestant and Catholic: He could not simply restate the religious view in its own language, even though his patterning is similar. Finally, the prevalent discussion of states of nature—a dialogue by this time more than a hundred years old—provided a framework which enabled him to replace the ancient religious doctrine with a content and language more acceptable to his generation as well as to himself.

Rousseau paints the state of nature as a stage in which inequality is controlled. By this he means that the inequalities associated with differences of physical strength, aptitude, and character are a product of nature and at the same time regulated in a pure state of nature; where political institutions do not interfere, that is to say, only those fit to deal with the rigors of natural living survive at all. Rousseau says, as a matter of fact, that nature handled her children very much as Sparta trained her citizens: If they could not cope with external conditions they were either killed in infancy or died later on.

But besides the natural inequalities which tend to be controlled by nature, there is a second kind of inequality—the moral and political. This is an inequality produced by man revolting against the state of nature and it obviously does not exist in that state. Hence, Rousseau concludes, the primitive state is one in which neither kind of inequality is established.

But if all men are thus equal, what is the positive corollary? It means that they are all equally alert, for one thing. Confronted by the wild beasts and other natural enemies, they keep their wits about them at all times and

5. Although Rousseau began drawing up his *Projet de constitution pour la Corse* in 1765, the work was never completed.
6. The *Considerations sur le guvernement de Pologne* was written just before the first partition of Poland. An envoy of the Polish Assembly, on behalf of that body, had invited Rousseau to make suggestions for encouragement of the Polish spirit and promotion of political stability.
7. F. J. C. Hearnshaw, *The Social and Political Ideas of Some Great French Thinkers of the Age of Reason,* New York: Barnes & Noble, 1950, pp. 186–187. Morley has essentially the same interpretation. Thus in criticizing Rousseau, he even uses the language of Christian doctrine. Rousseau's theory, he avers, has for the base of its argument the "entirely unsupported assumption of there having once been in the early history of each society a stage of mild, credulous, and innocent virtue, from which appetite for the fruit of the forbidden tree caused an inevitable degeneration." John Morley, *Rousseau,* 2 vols., London: Macmillan, 1888, vol. 1, p. 148.

need no leaders to guide them; for it is obvious what they have to do at every state of life. The very fact that they have survived means that they have good health, both physical and mental. They roam the forests—and the earth is literally covered with forests—as comrades, with few if any artifacts and only the kind of knowledge needed for them to survive.

Rousseau thinks that primitive man's major natural virtue is that of pity. From it spring all those qualities which make him understand directly the sufferings of others. Even Mandeville, cynical as he was, had to admit the emotion of pity; and Rousseau waxes eloquent in describing how his savages respond spontaneously to the hardships of others. Reflection is the product of civilization and, because it is associated with and the product of pride, it tends to divide men from one another. Pity, on the contrary, unites them in a vast community of suffering, shared experience, and companionship.

Closely associated with pity is love. Before the complexities of civilization intervened, men and women loved one another without thought for the consequences. Whereas in a civilized state love produces jealousy and often leads to divisions and conflict, the state of nature exhibits it as wholly constructive and irenic. When a man feels the need for a particular woman, he copulates with her under the open sky, without all the restrictions of law and also without the feelings of guilt which arise when the law is violated.

In sum, then, the second *Discourse* maintains,

> Let us conclude . . . that men in a state of nature, wandering up and down the forests, without industry, without speech, and without home, an equal stranger to war and to all ties, neither standing in need of his fellow-creatures nor having any desire to hurt them, and perhaps even not distinguishing them one from another; let us conclude that, being self-sufficient and subject to so few passions, he could have no feelings or knowledge but such as benefitted his situation. . . . If by accident he made any discovery, he was the less able to communicate it to others, as he did not know even his own children.[8]

It will be noted that in this view, the state of nature was an age in which, while progress, in the eighteenth-century sense of the term, was inhibited, so also was vice. Man fulfilled only his real, that is, his immediate wants, and in so doing saved himself the misery which accompanies the quest for knowledge that goes beyond basic concerns.

At this point, however, the student of Rousseau will normally ask why man ever left the state of nature. If he was able to cope with his environment so completely and lived, moreover, in perfect harmony with his fellows how can we account for the development of that civilization which contradicts so many tendencies of nature? Surely there were implicit tendencies within man which, when confronted by the right external circumstances, must have led him to depart from a situation of "free" love, spontaneous action, simplicity, and utter harmony. If there were such tendencies and external circumstances, where were they? In searching for his answer to this question one will find Rousseau's account of the origins of civilization and of its characteristic product, the state.

The Rise of Civilization and the State

His explanation of how men fell from nature is hardly a clear or satisfactory one. In fact, he may be said to have given us three accounts.

In the first, embodied in the first *Discourse*, the inequality is established because men discovered in themselves a diversity of abilities. Why this inequality should become manifest, however, in a natural state where men were largely isolated—except for temporary spontaneous sexual unions—Rousseau does not tell us. Once it was evident, however, that some were strong and some weak, the basis of inequality was established—and with it the possibility of both exploitation and knowledge. Man became "civilized." Science and art enhanced the power of those who already had control by enabling them to extend their manipulations of other human beings; and such inventions as printing, while they did enable us to propagate useful information and sound moral maxims, at the same time perpetuated forever such gross errors as those embodied in the writings of Hobbes and Spinoza.[9] Ideologies exalting power arose; and the struggles of men to exceed one another in prestige, wealth, and authority filled the world with constant war and tumult.

In the second *Discourse* he speculates about the rise of civilization in a somewhat different way; but many of his ambiguities remain. According to this account, geography and accident were the roots of the fall from nature. Some men began to live along the sides of rivers and turned to fishing for a livelihood; others continued to roam through the forests retaining the more primitive and innocent mode of life. Natural catastrophes like earthquakes would disrupt habitual ways of living; and the experience of lightning over the course of centuries would eventually lead man to discover ways of making fire.

Meanwhile, accident and geographical differentiation probably forced men to call on the help of others in certain contingencies and this very primitive interdependence gave birth to crude notions of obligation. Each discovered that others resembled himself and each sought to protect himself against possible disaster by temporary social unions of various kinds. These unions were based upon a kind of primitive enlightened self-interest, each seeing that if his own ego was to be preserved he must be willing to contribute some assistance to the protection of others. Apparently, then, Rousseau sees obligation as rooted in egoism, very much as Hobbes does; and he takes this position despite his formal protestations against the doctrine of Hobbes.

During the period in which accident and geography combined to push men together and to force temporary unions, pity and love underwent modifications. The very factors which led men into a kind of primitive cooperation served to help push such sentiments as spontaneous pity and love into the background; for deliberative and reflective faculties were now developing. Spontaneity was still present, it is true, to a high degree—for the cooperation was still small scale and impermanent—but the shadow of a future state was already apparent.

The great change came, Rousseau thinks, when men discovered metals and began to cultivate the fields. He does not tell us exactly how iron and other metals came to be used, although he suggests that observation of volcanoes might have given clever men the idea of smelting. But whatever the origins of human utilization of metals, it is obvious that specialization of labor entered with it.

With agriculture, Rousseau has less trouble than with metals. Men observed the processes of growth and decay in "raw" nature and, once the reflective epoch had begun, desired to imitate and control the natural processes. Just as spontaneous love and pity receded somewhat in the preceding period, so now, apparently, spontaneous living off the fruits of nature gave way to deliberately cultivated plants. But this in turn led to the idea that he who cultivated the soil—or managed to get others to cultivate it for him—owned it; and thus the conception of private property slowly entered into human consciousness. Rousseau thinks that this was the real beginning of civil society and therefore of civilization:

> The first man who, having enclosed a piece of ground, bethought himself of saying *This is mine*, and found people simple enough to believe him, was the real founder of civil society.[10]

Rousseau's account of the development of civil society from this point on does not differ too radically from that famous passage of Plato's *Republic* in which the philosopher traces out the effects of the division of labor on human society.[11] There is little doubt that Rousseau was very much affected by Plato's conception, even though the eighteenth-century speculator is apparently thinking in historical terms whereas the ancient political theorist was providing a psychological account.

Basically we might say that Rousseau thinks of the whole structure of civil society as "jerry-built." It grew up through a combination of accident and contrivance. It was inevitable once division of labor and private property had arisen; but precisely because it developed bit by bit, rather than as the result of an overall general plan, its rulers were able to hide their manipulations of most men behind a screen which seemed to establish protection and equity for all. Meanwhile, the actual inequalities became more glaring and the slavery of most men to civilization more ubiquitous.

Rousseau himself was perhaps dissatisfied with his own explanations, for at the very outset of the *Social Contract* he professes himself ignorant as to how men had become enslaved. This "no explanation" is in fact his third answer to the problem of how and why men left the state of nature to make a civilization which destroyed their primitive freedom. "Man is born free," Rousseau's well-known

8. Part I of the *Discourse*, in *The Social Contract and Discourses*, G. D. H. Cole, trans., New York: E. P. Dutton, 1927, p. 203.
9. Rousseau apparently refers to such propositions as "might makes right," which he associates with the teachings of Hobbes and Spinoza.
10. Part II of the *Discourse*, Cole translation, *op. cit.*, p. 207.
11. See Chapter 4.

words assert, "and everywhere he is in chains. Many a one believes himself the master of others, and yet he is a greater slave than they." He then asks, "How had this change come about?" The reader is presumably eager to have an explanation as elaborate as that of the second *Discourse*, but Rousseau's answer is an anticlimax: "I do not know." This lame response seems to indicate an enormous dissatisfaction with his former explanations; for had he continued to believe in some definite hypothesis, he would surely have indicated it in at least a brief form.

The Civil State and the Problem of Legitimacy

Although Rousseau in his later political thought does not claim to know exactly how the state of Nature gave way to that of political subjection, he does profess to tell us what can legitimate it. In fact, this is the central question to which he addresses himself; all other issues are strictly subordinate. As we examine his answer, we shall be prepared to find inconsistencies and rather glaring ambiguities, of course, just as we did in treating of his analysis of nature.

He tells us that the first of all societies and the only natural one is the family and that it becomes the model for later political society. Like Locke, he ridicules all those views which would establish legitimacy by grounding it on hereditary right of some kind. He is equally sarcastic about might as the basis of right, rather clearly directing his shafts against Hobbes (although, as we shall see later, there are many points of resemblance between Rousseau's scheme and that of Hobbes). Of course, he remarks, we may have to yield to force; but this is an act of prudence and surely not a maxim of morality. And to those who point out that all power comes from God, he replies: "every disease comes from him too; does it follow that we are prohibited from calling in a physician?"[12] Rousseau thinks of himself as that physician.

If, therefore, no man has authority over others by nature (what Rousseau does with the family, which is admittedly natural, is not clear) and if force can confer no right, what, then, constitutes the basis for legitimate civil subjection?

As he sees it, the problem of legitimacy is "To find a form of association which may defend and protect with the whole force of the community the person and property of every associate, and by means of which, coalescing with all, [he] may nevertheless obey only himself, and remain as free as before."[13] Only such an association, we may interpret Rousseau as saying, will reconcile the pole of solidarity with that of liberty; the tendency of men to belong with their equally important quest for achievement of a uniqueness or eccentricity.

At this point, it is important to note that he does not propose to reverse the process—whatever it may have been—whereby civilization and the state have arisen. The romantic speculator of the *Discourses* and, to some extent of *Emile*, has become the defender of civil society against those who would destroy it.

A legitimate civil state, he argues, implies that men have given up their natural freedom and have exchanged for it a civilized freedom broader and more certain than that which they previously enjoyed. How can this come about?

His answer is that men in the state of nature alienate to the whole community, rather than to a man or an assembly, their natural rights. But in giving up to the community what he had in nature, each associate in effect "gives himself to nobody." Each partner, in other words, acquires rights over all other associates just as they gain rights over him; and since the associates are equal, no one loses by the transaction. As a matter of fact, all gain "more power to preserve what we have."[14] Thus there is a curious transformation which comes about in the civil state based upon right principles: Each man is actually freer and more powerful than he was in the state of nature.

In joining together in the civil state, men implicitly involve themselves in a dual role: Each is a member of the sovereign in relation to other individuals but at the same time is a subject vis-à-vis the sovereign. This implies for Rousseau that the sovereign is unbound by the contract since the reverse would entail the binding of the sovereign by itself. The sovereign itself creates law, that is to say, but cannot be bound by the law it creates. This does not, according to Rousseau, imply that the Community as sovereign will run roughshod over the rights of individuals; for if the whole body of the people possesses sovereignty, it cannot conceivably attack itself.

These statements can be understood better if

we note more exactly what the individual promises to obey when he enters civil society. He alienates his natural liberty, it is true, and thus at first would seem to be enslaving himself without limit. However, the nature of the legitimate community is such that he agrees to conform only to that which is characteristic of the community formed by the contract. This is the general will which emerges with the creation of the "public person," that is, the community. And the general will is that which is common to all members of the community: the will, as it were, which makes the community what it is, as contrasted with the wills of individuals or of other associations.

It is only the command of the general will, therefore, which binds the individual because he has agreed to be bound by it. However, he himself shares in the discovery of the general will through the making of policy; and is thus, as part of the sovereign, a participant in that sovereignty which commands him. This combination of contract and participation thus leads to a situation in which the individual is simply conforming to that which he himself has helped discover. Once the general will is found, therefore, the individual in following it is simply obeying himself. He is as free as he was in a state of nature and has added to the advantages of that state all the products of an ordered civilization—learning, culture, the rule of law, and, what is to Rousseau most important of all, the moral personality that only social and political experience can produce. Only moral freedom, as he puts it, "renders man truly master of himself; for the impulse of mere appetite is slavery, while obedience to a self-prescribed law is liberty."[15]

Despite the fact that Rousseau is constantly referring to the contractual basis of civil society, it would seem obvious that the contract is for him a rather formal device only. He could have stated his doctrine without using the contract by simply contrasting a hypothetical nonsocial man with an equally hypothetical completely socialized man. In doing so, he could have accomplished the same objectives he seeks to attain through the contract device—namely, that man becomes morally responsible only in the group; that the group is more than an arithmetical addition of discrete individuals: it develops a public person, as he puts it; and that freedom in society is inseparably connected with responsibility.

The Nature of the General Will

The social bond, according to Rousseau, is "that which is common" to the diverse interests that arise when man proceeds to leave nature and to develop civilization.[16] No civil society at all could exist without this common interest and sentiment. It is upon this foundation, in fact, that sovereignty rests.

One of the most famous propositions which Rousseau now asserts is that sovereignty is inalienable. That is to say, if the will of the community which expresses sovereignty is to remain general, it must be formulated by the community as a whole and cannot be delegated. Although power can be delegated, will can never be. Elsewhere he illustrates what he means by these two terms in differentiating the decision of a man to walk from the physical strength which enables him to carry out his decision. The first is an act of will, the second an act of power. Presumably no man can devolve the function of policy and decision making on the feet or hands, but, Rousseau seems to be saying, he can, for example, choose various forms of power—that of his own locomotion, for example, or animal strength, or mechanical contrivances. In political terms, will is embodied in legislation; power, by contrast, is government.

The second famous proposition about sovereignty is that it is indivisible. That is to say, all aspects of community action are subordinate to the general will and not independent of it. Sovereignty cannot be split apart: it is either a whole or it is nothing, and the indivisibility of sovereignty is related to its inalienability.

For Rousseau, the general will is the foundation of all public right. But he is careful to point out that this is true only when and if it is truly general. By general he seems to mean that which emerges when informed citizens discuss a policy in public and without any previous agreements as to how they are going to vote.[17] The first condition for the emer-

12. *Social Contract,* Bk I, ch. 3.
13. *Ibid.,* I, 6.
14. *Ibid.*
15. *Ibid.,* I, 8.
16. *Ibid.,* II, 1.
17. *Ibid.,* I, 3.

gence of the general will is that citizens be informed of the issues involved. What this means in exact terms Rousseau does not tell us but presumably he implies that those who are to legislate for the community must have all the relevant facts. Because they cannot alienate their sovereignty, they must, of course, exercise the legislative authority directly. To attempt to confer policy making functions on a representative body, that is, would be to destroy the freedom which he says is not only preserved but enlarged in a legitimate civil society.

Citizens, then, come into the general assembly of citizens fully informed on the questions which they propose to discuss. But before they make their appearance, they will have made no agreements with others as to how they shall cast their ballots. This is an extremely important condition and will have momentous consequences historically. The reason Rousseau bars previous agreements—such as those, for example, which characterize disciplined political parties and pressure groups of various kinds—is that they militate against the generality of the will which might emerge. They do this because generality depends on a large number of plusses and minuses in particular wills cancelling one another out. If the assembly is composed of citizens who have made previous agreements as to how they are going to vote, the number of particular wills is drastically reduced and the danger of particularity dominating the decision is enhanced.

Another and perhaps clearer way of putting Rousseau's thought might be to suggest that the community will be more likely to discover the general will if informed citizens come to the meeting committed only to the proposition that through discussion they will discover common ground. Each appears in the assembly determined to reach a conclusion both better and more general than any he might have tentatively reached outside the meeting. The general will, then, emerges when open-minded but informed citizens meet fact to face seeking answers to common community problems and hoping to reach consensus rather than mere compromise.

Viewed in this way, Rousseau's conception of the general will has much in common with Aristotle's famous vindication of the judgment of assemblies of informed laymen in matters involving policy and aesthetics.[18] Like Aristotle, Rousseau is asserting that something more arises in process of discussion than a combination of individual distorted judgments: The distortions cancel each other out and a new collective judgment arises based on all these judgments and yet transcending them.

If something like this is what Rousseau means by the general will, then there is indeed no conflict between freedom and authority or, as he puts it, "so long as the subjects submit only" to the general will as the expression of "sovereignty," "they obey no one, but simply their own will."[19] But this interpretation of the general will doctrine, it should be observed, does not require a contract: A more viable basis for it is, in fact, the notion that men are by nature social and that they naturally have it within their potentialities to reconcile freedom with "belongingness" and to resolve all conflicts—and without resorting to the subterfuges, fictions, and justification of coercion which, as we shall see, Rousseau employs.

In developing the theory of the general will, Rousseau seems to be constantly torn between seeing it as the expression of a complete consensus, in which case, of course, resort to coercion would seem to be largely unnecessary; and, on the other hand, thinking of it as a majority-interpreted general will which might, of course, require the support of severe coercion. In considerable degree, he seems to be searching for the former formulation. He never attains and supports it with any consistency, however, and, as we shall note, is constantly justifying coercion through devices which can only be called sophistical. This is only one example of the confusions which run through Rousseau, of course, and which lend support to that explication which would see him as a man dominated by his feelings rather than his intellect.

This observation is particularly applicable to his statement that the general will cannot err. This could mean at least two radically diverse things. It could, in the first place, imply that there is an objective order of value and that the general will can never run counter to that order. In effect, this might suggest that the general will—whatever it is—is always the voice of God. On the other hand, Rousseau might conceivably be saying that, while there may or may not be an objective moral order, the only concrete basis for law and morality is the state or the group; and that since the state defines right and wrong it in itself cannot be held to be doing anything but the right: at least, there is no other method of getting at the right except through the general will of the collective sovereign. Rousseau is not at all clear as to which view he holds: We know, of course, that he repudiated the atheism of men like D'Holbach and others but at the same time he has a tendency to think of morality as an eruption of feeling. On the whole, despite his ostensible repudiation of Hobbes, he would seem to be saying that his sovereign cannot err in the same sense that Hobbes' could not commit a wrong: Both the collective sovereign of Rousseau and the monarch or assembly of Hobbes appear to be right in the sense that there is no other discoverable standard of right.

External Prerequisites for Legitimate Civil Societies

Although Rousseau, like most social contract theorists, has often been criticized for his a priori deductive thinking in politics, it is not true that he completely ignores the limitations of men as he actually finds them. At times, indeed, he talks as if a political community expressing its sovereignty through the general will can be constructed under almost any circumstances: The form, as it were, can be imposed on men as they are. One gets the impression in certain passages that it is all a matter of rather arbitrary decision.

Yet there is another strain which seems to indicate that he thinks of the achievement of legitimacy as a nearly impossible task; for he requires so many predisposing personal, geographical, demographic, and economic factors that one can hardly imagine his believing in the probability of their occurrence. In this sense, he is a utopian, as that term is sometimes used. Thus he demands that there be a legislator of god-like proportions; a territory which shall be limited in area but virtually self-sufficient; a very small but well-informed population; and a social economy which will provide no luxuries and produce neither wealthy nor poverty stricken classes.

Rousseau was much impressed by the political speculations and activities of the ancients and this is reflected in the emphasis he places on the legislator. Apparently he is to be modeled on those half-mythical, half-historical figures to whom the ancient Greeks looked for the initiation of their city-states. Thus Rousseau is constantly referring to Lycurgus in a knowing way. But when he comes to draw up

the specifications for the lawgiver who is to set in motion his own ideal institutions, he establishes standards which, as he admits, could be met only by demigods. The legislator must be a man of superior intelligence who would

> see all the passions of men without experiencing any of them; who would have no affinity with our nature and yet know it thoroughly; whose happiness would not depend on us, and who would nevertheless be quite willing to interest himself in ours; and, lastly, one who, storing up for himself with the progress of time a far-off glory in the future, could labor in one age and enjoy in another.[20]

Assuming such a man could be found, his role would be, through force of personality, intelligence, and character, to formulate the ideas upon which basic institutions of the legitimate state would be built and to get those ideas accepted by the community. For while Rousseau apparently thinks of this figure as indispensable for launching the licit civil society, he also believes that the people should have full authority to reject his notions. He is to be a kind of catalytic agent who will lead the people to desire what they should desire. In studying Rousseau's conception of the legislator, it is not without relevance to remind ourselves that he regarded himself as qualified to act as legislator for Corsica and Poland and that he seems never to have doubted his own capacities for this task.

But the legislator would be aware that the territory of the state could not be extensive if legitimacy is to be established. If very large, the sheer task of governing would be too great; if unusually small, it would lack the resources to be relatively self-sufficient.

Just as the territory must be small, so must its population be very limited in numbers. The ratio between population and food supplies must, of course, be taken into consideration, but by and large the population should not exceed a size which would enable every citizen to know all other citizens. Rousseau clearly has in mind a community not much larger than a

18. See Chapter 5, pp. 99–100. Aristotle's discussion is, of course, in *Politics*, Bk. III, Ch. 11.
19. *Social Contract*, II, 4.
20. *Ibid.*, II, 7.

small town; and he thinks that if there is any doubt as to whether the population and territory are too small or too large, the decision ought to favor contraction rather than expansion. He is keenly aware, of course, that the general will, as defined in the previous section, cannot arise in a population large in numbers and complex in structure; and since his main quest is for legitimacy, he must necessarily make all other values subordinate to that of providing the right conditions for its establishment.

He is particularly insistent that his legitimate community dispense with luxuries and that economic gaps between citizens be relatively small. Like both Plato and Aristotle, he argues that moral character and political perspicacity flourish best in societies which do not have to care for an abundance of material goods and in which class and political distinctions based on differences in income are absent.

Throughout his analysis of the conditions essential for the development of the state, one is never quite clear as to whether Rousseau actually believes that the seemingly impossible concatenation of circumstances will arise. When one combines his hallmarks of the legislator with the many other requirements, it is difficult to take him seriously; and, as we have seen, even he admits that his legislative catalyst must be virtually a demigod. Yet the very fact that he rejects democratic government—by which he means the sharing of both administrative and legislative tasks by the whole population—on the ground that it is impracticable[21] indicates that he must at times have had definite conceptions as to what might and might not be possible.

It must be admitted, of course, that, if the general will be defined as complete consensus arrived at after full discussion by an informed people, his conditions—with the possible exception of the semidivine legislator—do seem to be indispensable. The history of modern politics certainly affords little comfort to those who argue that it may be possible to combine an achievement of the general will with large and diverse populations and complex economic systems. Like Thomas Jefferson, Rousseau apparently thinks that man must make a clearcut choice: He must choose between riches, class divisions, complexity, and political illegitimacy, on the one hand, and limited economic goods, homogeneity, simplicity, and political legitimacy, on the other.

Coercion, Government, and the General Will

There is, however, an apparent glaring contradiction in Rousseau's political doctrine. He appears to be searching, as we have seen, for a form of association in which man's freedom will be preserved while at the same time he performs all legitimate social and legal obligations. The interpretation of the general will suggested in the two previous sections implies that a genuine consensus can be reached and that in the implementation of this consensus the problem of severe coercion of the individual would not arise. It would not arise because presumably the individual shared directly in the making of the decision and discussed the issues so thoroughly with his neighbors that a common mind emerged which united men in complete harmony for social purposes, while allowing them to express their unique attributes individually.

Credence is lent to such an interpretation, as we have seen, by Rousseau's admission that "what generalizes the will is not so much the number of voices as the common interest which unites them." This would seem to mean that discussion takes place in the assembly until everyone is satisfied that the common interest which unites them has indeed been found.

Despite the weight of this interpretation, however, Rousseau's political writings are filled with suggestions that men must be coerced and even killed. And, as we shall see, he even provides for the erection of a civil religion which will be sustained in part through the sanction of death. In his treatises on the constitution of Corsica and the government of Poland this emphasis on the alleged necessity of coercion becomes particularly noteworthy, although it is present in his other political writings as well. The man who promises to preserve the presumably absolute freedom of nature despite the existence of civil society turns out in the end to be an advocate of religious persecution. How, we might well ask, does this come about?

The explanation would seem to turn in large part on his conception of the relation between social contract and general will and on a serious ambiguity as to how the general will is to be discovered. He states, it will be remembered, that every person leaving nature for civil society gives an unconditional promise to obey the general will but only the general will. Particular wills seeking to claim obedience have no legitimacy. But how is the individual to distinguish between a decision made by the general will and one dictated by a particular will? How, in modern parlance, is one to differentiate between a law which is alleged to be an expression of the interests of the United States and one which reflects the particular interests of General Motors? Rousseau does not answer questions of this kind with any certainty or clarity.

On the one hand, he seems to require complete consensus before the sovereign can act. Thus "the sovereign, being formed only of the individuals that compose it, neither has nor can have any interest contrary to theirs."[22] It can "injure no one as an individual," presumably because individuals have actually arrived at common goals and policies from which there is no dissent. The liberty which he gains in the civil state is that of "obedience to a self-prescribed law"[23]—which would appear to imply that he has actually assented to the measure which regulates his conduct.

On the other hand are those propositions which appear to identify the general will with the decision of a majority arrived at after discussion in assembly. At no point does Rousseau develop a full-fledged doctrine of majority rule but there are hints that, at least in some of his moods, he advocated one. Hence, in discussing the contractual basis of society, he asks: "If there were no anterior convention, where, unless the election were unanimous, would be the obligation upon the minority to submit to the decision of the majority?"[24] Or again, he maintains, without specifically endorsing majority rule, that "the law of the plurality of votes is itself established by convention, and presupposes unanimity once at least."[25] This would seem to be a kind of indirect, oblique endorsement of majority rule, but it is certainly no specific and unambiguous one.

In his well-known freedom through coercion doctrine, he seems to move in the same direction. In order, he argues, "that the social pact may not be a vain formulary, it tacitly includes this engagement, which can alone give force to the others, that whoever refuses to obey the general will shall be constrained to do so by the whole body."[26] Elsewhere he suggests that when the citizen casts his vote, he is not giving his views as to what public policy ought to be but is rather expressing his own opinion as to what the general will might be. If proven wrong in his judgment of the general will (and how he is proven wrong Rousseau does not clearly indicate), his opinion is shown to have been his own particular will. Or again, since he has promised in the social contract to obey the general will, the society, if it must coerce him to obey its laws, is simply helping him carry out his own rational intent as against his own obdurate action when he violated the law. As one of Rousseau's disciples interprets him,[27] the state is not coercing his real will (that whereby he promised to obey the general will) but is only subduing his false will which is impeding the operation of his rational intent. Thus if the state, through the government, orders a man to be hanged for the violation of its laws, this is no infringement of his freedom; indeed, he is never so free as when he mounts the gallows. "It is in order not to be the victim of an assassin," Rousseau avers, "that a man consents to die if he becomes one."[28] In effect, the killer's true will is enthusiastically cooperative as the hangman adjusts the noose: It is only his apparent will that seems to be less than happy.

This curious doctrine of freedom through coercion is one way by which Rousseau allegedly fulfills his promise to reconcile freedom with the demands of group life. Of course, it is only a government reposing on the general will which can fulfill a man through killing him. But since Rousseau is so vague at many points as to the manner of ascertaining the general will, one can never be quite sure whether the action of the government is carrying out the true will of the victim or engaging in a tyrannical act. In the absence of clear specifications, it would seem that the general will might be discovered by either a majority

21. *Ibid.*, III, 4.
22. *Ibid.*, I, 7.
23. *Ibid.*, I, 8.
24. *Ibid.*, I, 5.
25. *Ibid.*
26. *Ibid.*, I, 7.
27. Bernard Bosanquet, *The Philosophical Theory of the State*, New York: St. Martin's Press, 1899.
28. *Social Contract*, I, 5.

or a minority. Indeed, there is nothing in Rousseau's positive doctrine which would prevent his arguing that under certain circumstances that will might not be better understood by a single individual than by the majority; for even though he does, in another facet of his thinking, argue that generality is more likely to be attained after debate by a large number of individuals, he does not absolutely rule out a minority discerning the common interest through its mystic insight.

It may, of course, be argued that Rousseau justifies the use of force solely to curb momentary passions; that even adopting the interpretation of the general will as complete consensus, we might imagine situations in which the emotions of the moment would lead men to violate the law, in which case coercion would be a kind of educating device only. But this interpretation would seem to be invalid. At no point does he confine the coercive power to acts of passion or momentary lapses. He is never explicitly apologetic about its use; and at some points he seems to relish the thought of coercive power. There is no evidence, for example, that he would be less harsh in his treatment of a conscientious objector to a given law than he would be to one acting solely on the basis of momentary passion.

It is not, of course, the sovereign—that is, the whole body of citizens assembled—which administers coercion. Rousseau does discuss the possibility of conferring executive as well as legislative powers on the sovereign people; but he rejects what he calls the democratic solution as necessitating too small a population to be practicable on other grounds. Hence the general will has a kind of buffer between itself and the particular wills of men likely to rebel against it. This buffer is the government or executive branch. To it the sovereign people delegates power but not will. The power presumably is the agent for effecting the general will. But about the constitutent elements of power Rousseau is again conveniently vague. He seems to identify it at times with physical force, although if we adopt the consensual theory of the general will it would seem most consistent to think of it as an almost automatic emanation of that will: Power then would be the spiritual force so clearly embodied in the contents of the general will that individuals would conform to that will without any of the usual intimidations. If we should accept this consensual theory of power, the main tasks of government in Rousseau's scheme would not be to coerce men but rather, as Communists will later contend, to administer things. Government would then be a device to call men's attention to the general will, which they would spontaneously observe, and to manage collective property in material things.

In his analysis of government, he follows the ancient models and seems to conclude that a mixed form is best. His general test, however, of what is best is a very curious one indeed. "All other things being equal," he asserts, "the government under which, without external aids, without naturalizations, and without colonies, the citizens increase and multiply most, is infallibly the best."[29] This is a strange formulation in view of Rousseau's insistence that the state must be strictly limited in terms of population lest the general will not be discovered.

He goes on to suggest that the general will is the heart of the state and that its government is the brain. Of the two, the brain is the less important, for while the individual may continue to live with little or no brain, the heart is absolutely vital. If the general will can no longer be found, the state itself, as contrasted with its mere government, is dead.

Nevertheless, the disease of the state, Rousseau thinks, usually begins with the government, which has a tendency to usurp the legislative prerogatives of the general will, thus substituting its own particular will or wills for that of the state. Government, he thinks, can "degenerate" in two ways: when it contracts and when the state is dissolved. In the former instance, the contraction is from democracy to aristocracy to royalty. Why this contraction should constitute degeneration we are not told, for in any event the actual government is always a minority; and besides, Rousseau has told us that a democracy is virtually impossible. We seem to have here again one of his common ambiguities. Apparently he means, though, that as the number of governors declines, the danger of particular wills usurping the prerogatives of the general will tends to increase.

When the government does in fact begin to usurp sovereignty, the social compact is broken. In this event, any moral obligation of citizens to obey is wiped out and they follow the behests of the tyrant, if at all, only as a matter of prudence. Presumably a potentially revolutionary situation is created in this event and pure force and expediency take the place of obligation.

According to his own standards for the general will, apparently, all existing governments are illegitimate. The France of Louis XV, the Prussia of Frederick the Great, and even the Britain of George III were all living under tyrants. In none of those nations was there a general will in Rousseau's sense of the term—whether interpreted as consensus or as majority rule after discussion. It is small wonder that the rulers of his day labeled Rousseau a disturber of law and order; nor is it surprising that many leaders of the great French Revolution would later look upon him as their teacher.

Religion and the General Will

As suggested earlier, Rousseau breaks sharply from the deistic tradition of the eighteenth century. Whereas Voltaire (1694–1778) is the intellectual critic of all historic religion and the exponent of an intellectualistic natural religion, Rousseau might be termed a deist of feeling. Like Voltaire and many other eighteenth-century *philosophes*, he cannot accept any of the traditional faiths. But as his picture of the Savoyard Vicar indicates,[30] his religious experience is connected with the heart rather than the head. One can hardly imagine Diderot or Voltaire writing the following passage, for example:

> In fine, the more earnestly I strive to contemplate his infinite essence, the less do I conceive it. . . . The less I conceive it, the more I adore. . . . The worthiest use of my reason is to make itself as naught before thee.[31]

Statements of this kind lend emphasis to that interpretation of Rousseau which sees him as a man who is constantly stressing something beyond reason—something, indeed, which at points seemingly becomes irrational.

It is with an emotion which can only be called religious that he sometimes speaks of the general will: He stands as much in awe of it as the Savoyard Vicar does of God. It is, in fact, a kind of earthly god which must be constantly propitiated. The citizen will look upon it as the great sustainer of order and peace and the guarantor of freedom.

He discerns three kinds of religion. First is purely that of the man: an inner religion of the heart, with no external forms of worship. It is the religion of the Gospel and what Rousseau calls "the natural divine law." It is the true theism. Secondly, there is the religion which identifies civic with religious duties: the kind characteristic of ancient pagan societies. It identifies all the gods outside its own pantheon as civic deities of other nations and when it is at war with other cities its gods are also engaged in struggle. Finally, there is the kind of religion—illustrated chiefly in Roman Catholicism—which divides man between religious and civic duties: there are two authorities and the citizen is in perpetual doubt as to where his allegiance should be on any particular question.

To Rousseau, the latter type of religion is contemptible and utterly wrong-headed. This is so because it constitutes, in essence, a faction which impairs attainment of the general will and obliterates the indispensable civic unity; and, as he puts it, "whatever destroys social unity is good for nothing; and institutions which put man in contradiction with himself are worthless."[32] The dilemmas raised by a multi-group society, to put Rousseau into modern dress, are too great for most men to bear. The implication is that no such religion should be tolerated by the state.

Pagan-like civic religion, on the other hand, has many virtues. It unites citizens to one another and by identifying religious with civic duties helps sustain the general will. Dying for one's country is equated with martyrdom. But it also encourages superstition and "obscures the true worship of the Deity with vain ceremonial." It may also make the nation intolerant and lead it into almost perpetual war.

As for what Rousseau calls the pure religion of the Gospel, it is a noble expression of inner faith uncorrupted either by the political dualism of Roman Catholicism or by the intolerance of pagan religious conceptions. Unfortunately, however, it is other-worldly and has no relevance for politics. It allows the laws to shift for themselves and does not sustain the general will through religious sanctions. Appealing primarily to the inner life, it seems to imply that outer civic bonds are unimportant.

The problem for Rousseau is how to combine

29. *Ibid.*, III, 9.
30. In *Emile*.
31. *Emile*, IV.
32. *Social Contract*, IV, 8.

toleration for a diversity of creeds with religious or quasi-religious sanctions for the institutions of the state. Toleration is essential because the social pact implicitly gives the sovereign no powers which "pass the limits of public utility"; and it cannot be shown that control of opinions is useful for the community. On the other hand, it is extremely important that men be bound to their civic duties through the emotional ties which only religion can provide.

Rousseau's solution for this problem is to establish what he calls a civil religion with a certain minimum belief system. Every citizen shall be asked to believe in God, immortality, "the happiness of the just," "the punishment of the wicked," and the "sanctity of the social contract and of the laws." He thinks of these beliefs as simple and as requiring no commentaries: he fears, apparently, the building up of an elaborate civil theology which might lead to a kind of state church with all of its alleged evils.

He claims that he is not being intolerant in requiring profession of these essential beliefs, for he suggests that if a citizen cannot conscientiously support them he can leave the state or be banished from it. If, however, a citizen does subscribe to them and then later on "believes like an unbeliever in them," he must be punished with death.

The general principle of toleration for religious creeds, as contrasted with the requirement of belief in the civil religion, is qualified by the rule that only those religions should be tolerated which profess belief in toleration of others. Rousseau becomes specific, when he argues that those who aver "Outside the Church no salvation" must be "driven from the State." This is an obvious attack on Roman Catholicism and possibly also on certain of the Protestant sects.

Like Locke, then, Rousseau would exclude Roman Catholics and atheists from toleration. It seems also that he could not allow philosophical anarchists, who could hardly subscribe to the sacred character of the compact and all laws. It should be noted, too, that the grounds for exclusion are not conduct but belief: Rousseau does not use the empirical test and determine whether Catholics, atheists, and anarchists do in fact generally obey the laws; instead, he argues that beliefs implicitly prevent their respecting the general will and that their actions must be assumed to proceed in accord with their alleged beliefs.

Rousseau shows a keen appreciation of the role of religion in the life of men and is shrewd in his observations on historic Christianity. But when he claims to be rejecting what he calls the pagan attitude, he would appear to be deluded. Actually, his civil religion has all the ingredients of the pagan view; for the beliefs inculcated and the sanctions invoked, however simple they may appear, have all the earmarks of those ancient belief-systems which united civic with religious duties.

The whole problem of religion is for him, of course, simply an aspect of the general question which concerns him throughout his political speculations: How can one be free and at the same time belong to society? In religious terms, this is the issue of whether one can follow one's religious conscience while simultaneously sharing with others a kind of religious feeling for the institutions of the state. It must be confessed that Rousseau is as confusing with respect to the religious facet of the civic problem as he is when he deals with the general question itself. When he says, for example, that no one can be compelled to profess belief in the civil religion and then immediately thereafter asserts that one can be expelled from the state for failing to do so, he is engaging in a sophistry reminiscent of Locke's tacit consent theory. When he provides the death penalty for those who behave like unbelievers, without any statement as to what kind of behavior is contrary to professed belief, he opens the gate to an intolerance which he claims to repudiate.

Rousseau as Practical Legislator

Thus far we have been examining Rousseau's political doctrine in terms primarily of its abstract principles and of their relation to major currents of seventeenth- and eighteenth-century thought. We now turn to his interpretation of these principles in the context of his legislation for Corsica and Poland. In some respects Rousseau as legislator helps us understand his general theory but in other instances he seems to make the theory even more ambiguous.

In general, he sees his task as one of prescribing institutions for political societies which are seeking to preserve their identity and promote stability. To carry out his mission, he insists that all the relevant historical and sociological data be provided him and apparently he endeavors to digest these data thoroughly before embarking on his proposals.[33]

As in his other political writings, man in a state of nature is portrayed, on the whole, as limited in vision and lacking in the collective spirit so essential if civilization and civic order are to arise. The problem, as he conceives it, is how to transform these isolated and naive beings into a community possessing a strong sense of social solidarity and a commitment to love of country. How break into the cycle of nature and attain the discipline of political society? He finds the answer in a legislator who will, so to speak, combine the virtues of a Moses, a Lycurgus, and a Numa. The legislator must work out a whole way of life (what the ancients would call a *politeia*) and cause the people to make that way of life uppermost in their consciousness.[34]

To the student of education, as well as of politics, Rousseau's educational doctrine at this point is extraordinarily important. We can take our choice, he says, between education of the man and education of the citizen. In the former, we try to eliminate prejudice and passion and therefore place little emphasis on the study of history. In the latter, however, history becomes the center of study and we deliberately attempt to build in prejudice by stressing the history of the particular nation of which the citizen is a part. And Rousseau has no doubt that education for citizenship must take precedence over education of the man. As with the Plato of the *Laws*, even the play of children must be supervised: they should play together rather than in a solitary way, so that the social and patriotic possibilities will not be frustrated later on.[35] Obviously, this ideal would seem to contradict his position in *Emile*, where he appears to stress spontaneity in play and study, even though the general framework is laid down by the educator.

Like Aristotle, Rousseau the legislator is dubious about complex commercial or industrial societies and seems to make agriculture the center of his economy. An agrarian society, he thinks, promotes attachment to the soil and hence love of country, whereas commercial and industrial societies encourage rootlessness, dissatisfaction, and reliance on the false values of money.[36]

As a practical legislator, the problem of discovering the general will disturbs him not a little. On the one hand, he is convinced that the imprescriptible law of nature cannot justify restricting legislative authority to any particular group;[37] on the other hand, he does not believe that many groups in Poland are yet ready for political liberty. Hence he tolerates serfdom: It is part of the historical situation and must be taken into account by the legislator, who cannot as a practical matter eliminate it overnight. Thus all peasants are excluded from political activity, which would seem to eliminate most of the Polish population.

Those who can participate in decisions are to meet in very small groups and reach conclusions on public policy. Generally speaking, representative government is repudiated, as in the *Social Contract*. To reconcile discovery of the general will with the apparent necessity of large political societies, he suggests a federative scheme, in which the small constituent entities will make fundamental policies, leaving overall execution of policies, in Poland, to an elective king.

Rousseau's proposals for Poland and Corsica are important in his general political outlook because they give us some understanding of how he interprets his more abstract principles and the degree to which he is willing to compromise with the hard facts of political tradition. They also illustrate the inconsistencies which characterize his views everywhere—providing a king for Poland, for example, while yet insisting on a supposedly direct democracy albeit with most of the people excluded.

The emphasis on an intense patriotism having all the hallmarks of a religion reminds us of the *Social Contract*. There is the same spirit of intolerance and a similar stress on coercion.

The Critics Summarized

A large number of the questions and doubts concerning Rousseau's way of thinking have

33. Note the comments of Frederick Watkins, trans., *Rousseau: The Political Writings*, Camden, N.J.: Thomas Nelson, 1953, xxxvi; and of C. E. Vaughan, *The Political Writings of Jean Jacques Rousseau*, 2 vols., New York: Wiley, 1962, vol. 1, p. 82.
34. *Constitutional Project for Corsica*, in Watkins, *op. cit.*, p. 300. Hereafter referred to as *Constitution of Corsica.*
35. *Government of Poland*, pp. 176, 178.
36. *Constitution of Corsica*, pp. 281–283; 297.
37. *Government of Poland*, p. 186.

been suggested in the preceding sections, for it is difficult to develop an exposition of his outlook without simultaneously pointing out the many ambiguities and apparent contradictions characteristic of his system. Here it may be useful to restate and expand the more important of the criticisms.

Rousseau's Ignorance of History and Lack of Empirical Referents. Although Rousseau has many historical references (particularly in the *Constitution of Corsica* and the *Government of Poland*) and pays much respect at many points to the necessity for studying the actual conditions of a society before legislating for it—tendencies in his thought which can be attributed perhaps to the influence of Montesquieu—it is clear from the context that he knew very little history and that what he did know he tended to romanticize. By and large, the criticism applicable to all social contract philosophers can be directed at Rousseau, despite his many eccentricities: it can be charged that all of them proceed in a largely deductive manner from positions which themselves rest on empirically shaky grounds.

The Superfluity of the Contract. In Rousseau we witness an important transition in the history of the social contract notion itself. While throughout he pays obeisance to the doctrine, he has come to think of it as largely superfluous, even though he may not have been fully conscious of his own attitude. In other words, while he still laboriously proves that society is based on contract, at many points he suggests, often rather confusedly, the Aristotelean view that it is prior to the individual. Thus he contends that "the force acquired by the whole" may be "equal or superior to the sum of the natural forces of all the individuals."[38] Yet he never clearly perceives that in subscribing to the notion that society has a personality of its own which presides over both individuals and institutions, he is in effect casting doubt on the individualist and social contract views which he ostensibly embraces.

The Uncertain Nature of the General Will. As we have seen earlier, Rousseau is astonishingly unclear as to the meaning of the general will and even more uncertain as to how it is to be ascertained. On the one hand, it seems to be a kind of consensus arrived at by thorough discussion and without any references to mechanical weighing of numbers. If one draws out the implications of this view, it would seem that coercion would be necessary only on those rare occasions when men become irrational—when, in other words, they forget the policy to which they themselves actually gave consent.

Although Rousseau gives many hostages to this interpretation of the general will—and, indeed, it seems the most plausible view if he is to reconcile "freedom" with the existence of political society—he does not uphold it with any consistency. Indeed, his emphasis on coercion, his apparent vindication of the power of life and death, and his justification for what is in effect religious persecution would seem to point to a rather different version of the general will and its discovery. Thus his doctrine that we must be "forced to be free," as well as his contention that men do not vote their own views on policy matters but rather their own judgment of what the general will might be, seems to imply the idea that the general will is discovered by majority vote and that the minority is, in a way not specified, somehow proved "wrong" by the weight of the majority. His legislation in the *Constitution of Corsica* tends to support this view. Hence he maintains that the minority's true will, despite appearances to the contrary, is expressed by the majority. All the coercive mechanisms which he establishes thus administer not coercion, but actually freedom. By what to the unbeguiled person would seem to be sheer legerdemain Rousseau thus reconciles freedom with political society.

Strength and Weakness in the Small Community. Rousseau rather consistently upholds the view that the general will can be attained only in a very small political community. Hence the only legitimate rule can be that which arises in a society which is probably no more numerous than that of a town of 20,000 souls. The social bond is attenuated as the community becomes more extensive.

Rousseau is here stressing a point almost wholly lacking in other social contract literature. Neither Hobbes nor Locke dealt with the relation of geographical size and number of people to problems of politics. Perhaps they did not do so precisely because they were more or less consistent individualists who thought in great degree mechanistically about the artifact of political society. In Rousseau, however, as suggested previously, the community—despite his protestations to the contrary—is something more than an artificial combination of previously separated individuals. The spirit of the community becomes vital and that spirit somehow lies beyond and entirely apart from contract. Without a community elan the general will ceases to be general and becomes that of the predominant particular will of the moment. Hence it is vital for Rousseau to have a community whose numbers and diversity of particular interests will not inhibit development of a general will.

The very soundness of his position at this point makes all the more remarkable his stress on coercion. If ever an harmonious and at the same time largely spontaneous society is possible, one might seem to find it in Rousseau's small but enlightened community. Yet he appears always to be uneasy lest the harmony and spontaneity fail him; and he resorts to techniques which, while they might conceivably be appropriate for illegitimate civil societies, hardly seem relevant in the limited community. In a community of presumably sympathetic and loving men and women, the harsh overtones of a religious inquisition seem grossly out of place. Rousseau, however, appears to see no problem.

But despite this inconsistency he at least recognizes the interconnections between face-to-face knowledge of one another, strong social bonds, and the general will. What he seems not to be fully aware of is the problem which the breaking up of mankind into parish-like communities would pose for political relations over a wider sphere. If the general will cannot be attained except in a small state, upon what basis will political authority repose in humanity as a whole? Rousseau is not entirely unaware of this issue, for he promises to treat of how the virtues of the small community can be combined with those of the large;[39] and in his proposals for a Polish constitution, as we have seen, he suggests that the reconciliation can best take place through some form of confederation.

But if confederation is the answer, we might well ask him whether its government, too, can possibly rest on the general will, in view of the fact that he repeatedly asserts the indispensability of the small community. How can the wills of many true states be transformed into a general will for the confederacy?

Rousseau and the Problem of Political Obligation. Some scholars, notably Professor Carritt,[40] have contended that, while Rousseau purports to be rejecting Hobbes, in many respects he really carries on the Hobbes tradition. Thus he tends to be a psychological hedonist, making pleasure the hallmark of self-interest for the individual. Rousseau, Carritt goes on, tends, like Hobbes, to identify obligation with self-interest and thus to undercut any distinctive meaning of obligation. If I am obliged to obey the political authority simply because it is my interest to do so, no true theory of obligation (as that expression is usually employed) can be developed.

In some measure, it would seem, the critics are right. Much turns on what we mean by obligation. A great deal, too, depends on what one means by self. Rousseau can be interpreted as recognizing several levels of selfhood. When the individual obeys the political authority, in other words, he may be regarded as submitting to his highest self—reflected in the general will and his own rational will—and suppressing his lowest, which is the self of immediate as against long-run fulfillment. He is thus recognizing an obligation that imposes on him stern demands, in the sense that he renounces present satisfaction for the overall interest—which he shares with others—of social order. Although this may not describe what some philosophers mean by obligation, it would be the line which the defender of Rousseau (and possibly Rousseau himself) might pursue.

The Value of Rousseau's Speculation. Thus far we have on the whole been highly critical of Rousseau's ambiguities and seeming muddleheadedness. Here let us note some respects in which his formulation contributed to the ongoing dialogue.

In the first place, the general will notion expresses an important observation which any realistic student of government must make: that whatever the form of the political society, some basic consensus as to value priorities is a *sine qua non* of any stable system. There must be a kind of over-arching commitment—emotional, intellectual, spiritual—to a way of life before any scheme can operate effectively.

Secondly, the general will conception implies a positive rather than a negative role for political society and this, particularly in a day when the role of the state was widely regarded as that of a restraining force, would seem to be a significant contribution. In this sense, Rousseau

38. *Social Contract*, II, 7.
39. *Ibid.*, III, 15.
40. E. F. Carritt, *Morals and Politics*, London: Oxford, 1935, Part I, ch. 6.

belongs to a stream of thought which will not reach its full flowering until the latter part of the nineteenth century—after the decline of the negative conception of the state.

Finally, although we have argued that he did not really solve the problem, the very fact that he posed the issue of how to discover a form of society in which belongingness and a sense of individuality are reconciled provided an important text for a discussion which is still alive. We do not have the answer today; but we owe to Rousseau the debt of having put the question in such dramatic form.

Rousseau's Influence in Politics and Political Thought

Despite his many weaknesses from the viewpoint of analytical political theory, there can be no doubt about Rousseau's great impact both on practical politics and on political thought. Few great political thinkers have been, to the same degree, the direct inspirers of political factions and few have furnished such an intellectual and emotional armory for diverse political attitudes.

Rousseau's Immediate Impact. Rousseau's immediate influence on those around him was to stimulate and encourage the cult of nature and to sow seeds of unrest about contemporary political institutions. At the same time, he helped give birth to that romantic strain in thought wihch was to counteract in considerable degree the eighteenth-century devotion to reason.

He did not, indeed, originate the cult of nature, but he gave it quite a new meaning. All important thinkers customarily paid tribute to nature, from Alexander Pope to the leaders of the French Revolution. For men like Pope nature was a kind of formal model or intellectual standard; and nature's God, to which the American Declaration of Independence referred, was, as with Voltaire, a necessary assumption if one was to account for the mechanically operating universe.

Rousseau, by contrast, viewed nature not merely as form and reason but also as feeling; and nature's God became to him a deity perceived through the heart. The doctrine of natural rights was given a motive power: Men could now weep about the liberties which had been lost with the rise of a distorted civilization. Those who followed him during his lifetime did, indeed, wax emotional about the beauties of the state of nature in a way which would have been utterly repugnant to men like Locke.

But when countesses and plebeians alike began to shed tears over the remnants of lost innocence, doubts about the whole structure of civilization were given a moving force which, however subtly, soon affected men's attitude to the governments of the day. Institutions had been ridiculed before, of course: Voltaire, the older contemporary of Rousseau, was a past master at the art of sapping and mining. But Voltaire's criticisms, however witty, did not carry the emotional fervor attaching to Roussseau. Moreover, Voltaire was primarily a negative critic, whereas Rousseau proposed an alternative which would presumably combine the best of nature with all the advantages of civilization.

When the general will was combined with Rousseau's tributes to patriotism, the virtues of loyalty, the benefits conferred on mankind by such semimythical figures as Lycurgus, and the wisdom and nobility of simple people, all the ingredients were present for what might be called a romantic view of politics. Just as nature was increasingly viewed through rose-colored emotional spectacles, so were factors which lay beyond reason given a larger place in men's view of society. This was already beginning to take place in Rousseau's own lifetime and later on, of course, would become even more important.

The emotionally favorable connotations attached to Rousseauistic terminology laid the groundwork for demagoguery of all kinds in practical politics, for orators could sway men by appeals to the sovereignty of the people and other expressions, without necessarily subscribing to the idea as Rousseau understood it. It must be confessed, of course, that Rousseau himself assisted the process by his frequently confused language; for in the absence of precise definitions, it was easy to eke out a conception with substantial gusts of feeling. Thus the groundwork was laid for one aspect of practical politics in the French Revolution.

This does not mean, of course, that the romanticism running through Rousseau's thought was entirely one-sided. If it lent itself to irrationalism, it also provided the context within which the ordinary nonintellectual human being could acquire a new dignity. The plowman, artisan, and domestic worker took on aspects of divinity at the hands of Rousseau: Each was as an immortal soul whose nonintellectual tasks were as sacred in the sight of Rousseau's God as the work of the *philosophes.* After reading Rousseau one could no longer despise the ordinary human being. With his contemporary, the English romantic poet Thomas Gray, Rousseau could think of the common man as a being of almost infinite possibilities whose good and evil potentialities alike had been frustrated by circumstances:

Their lot forbade, nor circumscribed alone
Their growing virtues but their crimes confined—
Forbade to wade through slaughter to a throne
Or shut the gates of mercy on mankind.[41]

And William Wordsworth, another poet in the romantic tradition, gave voice a generation later to a sentiment which would have been thoroughly approved by Rousseau:

To me, the meanest flower that blows can give
Thoughts that do often lie too deep for tears.[42]

Rousseauistic romanticism thus provided the emotional fervor which became increasingly characteristic of democratic thought during the latter quarter of the eighteenth century: a quality almost wholly lacking in the tradition which stemmed from men like Locke.[43]

Rousseau's Impact on the French Revolution. It is a commonplace to assert that Rousseau had a profound impact on French Revolutionary politics and thought. But this observation is often a very general one and more frequently than not lacks specific illustrations.

Actually, there were at least two rather distinct although somewhat overlapping intellectual currents reflected during the great turmoil. The first stemmed from *philosophes* like Voltaire and Diderot and included such revolutionaries as Chaumette[44] and Hebert.[45] This was a rationalistic movement which tended in the direction of agnosticism or even atheism. The second tendency owed its inspiration to Rousseau and, while as critical of the old institutions as the Voltairean school, had its own rather dogmatic view about reconstruction.

During the fall of 1793 and immediately thereafter the divergencies of the two schools were manifested in their attitudes to religion. Almost from the outset, of course, it was evident that the Revolution was antagonistic to the claims of the historic Church; and as the radical tendencies grew, many leaders felt that the traditional religion must be destroyed root and branch. There was a wide divergence, however, as to what should take its place. The rationalistic party insisted that only reason could be a legitimate object of worship and proceeded to carry out its views by instituting ceremonies adoring its divinity in the person of a Parisian actress. The Rousseauistic faction professed indignation at this, particularly because the worship of reason implied denial of Rousseau's dogma of the immortality of the soul. In retaliation, leaders of the Mountain like Robespierre established what they called the Festival of the Supreme Being, whose cult included such dogmas as immortality and the reward of the just in another life.

Nor was this controversy a mere plaything of revolutionary fancy. Men were actually executed for denying the doctrines of Rousseau's civil religion. Already in 1790, the Constituent Assembly had decreed the civil constitution of the clergy, which in effect made the church a department of revolutionary government. After the autumn of 1793, the followers of Rousseau were in control of the government and began to enforce his ideas. Thus it was on charges of atheism and a denial of immortality that leaders of the rationalistic faction like Chaumette and Clootz were sent to the guillotine in the spring of 1794, Saint Just[46] claim-

41. *Elegy in a Country Churchyard.*
42. *Ode on Intimations of Immortality from Recollections of Early Childhood.*
43. For a treatment of Rousseau as a romantic, see Irving Babbitt, *Rousseau and Romanticism,* Boston: Houghton, 1919.
44. Pierre Gaspard Chaumette was born in 1763 and executed in 1794. Beginning his career as a botanist, he joined the insurrectionary commune of Paris in 1792 and became its president. Although he opposed the Girondist faction, he was also critical of Robespierre. Aligning himself with Jacques Rene Hebert, he exalted the semi-religious Cult of Reason. Danton and Robespierre united to bring about his death.
45. Jacques Rene Hebert was born in 1755 and, like Chaumette, was executed in 1794 by the combined factions of Danton and Robespierre. An active journalist, Hebert developed a considerable following among the poverty-stricken people of Paris and at one point advocated a rather radical land redistribution.
46. Louis Antoine Leon de Saint-Just was born in 1767 and, with Robespierre, was guillotined in 1794. Avowedly influenced by the writings of Rousseau, he early attached himself to the republican party which demanded the deposition and later the killing of Louis XVI. With Robes-

ing that they were attempting "to destroy all notion of Divinity and base the government of France on atheism."

The influence of Rousseau was manifested throughout the Revolution in a variety of policy-making areas. Many leaders, for example, looked upon the revolutionary turmoil with its destruction of the old as a marvelous opportunity to reconstruct institutions from the bottom up, after the manner suggested by Rousseau. The philosopher, it will be remembered, had said that there were only a few periods in the history of mankind suitable for revolutionary change: those were the epochs when old traditions were losing their hold and when a slight nudge would enable reformers to get their way. In most ages, however, the possibility of creating legitimate government was strictly limited.

After 1790, those into whose hands the destiny of the Revolution increasingly fell thought that Rousseau's golden moment had arrived. The monarchy had been shown to be weak and the nobility were evidently divided. The hold of tradition on the minds of men was seemingly a thing of the past. Now was the time, men of several factions believed, to institute truly fundamental changes. This sentiment was reflected in a decree of the Committee of Public Safety published long after the revolutionists had begun to act in accordance with its dictates. Using language which reminds one of Rousseau, the decree said in part:

> The transition of an oppressed nation to democracy is like the effort by which nature rose from nothingness to existence. You must entirely refashion a people whom you wish to make free—destroy its prejudices, alter its habits, limit its necessities, root up its vices, purify its desires.[47]

Most of the changes wrought by the Revolution were, however, distortions of Rousseau—even taking into account the fact that he can be and has been interpreted in a variety of ways which are sometimes seemingly contradictory. Basically, these distortions stem from the fact that whereas Rousseau envisioned a very small community, the revolutionists were legislating for a complex and numerous body of citizens.

Consider, for example, the notion of popular sovereignty. Rousseau thought of it as inalienable and indivisible, which implied that it could not be delegated. Yet revolutionary leaders sought to combine popular sovereignty with representative institutions. The effect of this in practice was—as Rousseau would have predicted—that the minority sitting in the national and constituent assemblies and particularly the delegates to the Convention came to think of themselves as the people with all the prerogatives which Rousseau vested in his sovereign assembly. In effect, for example, at the height of the Terror, a minority of a minority—the Jacobins—claimed to be the sovereign people with power of life and death; and Jacobin dogma was treated as if it were the voice of God himself.

Similarly, the idea of the general will as applied in revolutionary practice would not have been recognized by Rousseau. Since it was impossible to assemble millions of Frenchmen at a given spot, the search for the general will created problems not envisioned even by Rousseau's rather confused account. Did it repose in the millions of citizens widely separated from one another and therefore not meeting face to face? Or was it to be found in the constituent assembly or in the Convention? If the latter, was it to be expressed by the majority or by a virtually impossible unanimity? Whatever the answer, it would bear only a faint resemblance to Rousseau's conception. Yet many revolutionary leaders insisted on using general will language, thus appealing to the authority of Rousseau without satisfying his conditions. The result was that many laws which were ostensibly reflections of the common interest could realistically be looked upon only as expressions of a predominant particular interest or a combination of particular interests. Statutes creating special revolutionary tribunals, for example, were almost certainly the dictates of a very small minority; and the same observation could probably be made about legislation establishing the civil constitution of the clergy.[48]

Another of Rousseau's ideas which played a considerable role in the whole history of the Revolution was his condemnation of all closely-knit associations except the state. Again, we should remember that this criticism assumed the existence of the parish-like state. However, and once more quite typically, the leaders of the Revolution sought to apply it in a radically different context. Accepting Rousseau's notion that intermediate associations would inhibit the ascertainment of the general will, they frowned on provincial tradition and organization, businessmen's associations, and societies for the benefit of labor. No particular associational wills could be allowed to stand between the individual and the state. Thus the ancient provinces were abolished as administrative units and the departments which took their place were put under the strict control of the central government. It was not until the eighties of the nineteenth century that labor unions came to be fully legalized. In all this, of course, more than Rousseau's dogmas was involved: in one respect, indeed, the revolution was simply extending the work of the monarchy, which had for several centuries battled against the particularism embodied in feudal institutions, provincial loyalties, and the regional *parlements*.

Finally, let us consider Rousseau's preference for direct civic service. He thought that it was much better for each citizen to contribute his labor in such enterprises as road construction than to pay for the services of others through taxation.[49] This would involve the citizen in community responsibilities and heighten his awareness of social questions. It would keep the work of implementing the general will close to those who formulate it, even though, as we have seen, Rousseau repudiates democracy (where legislative and executive functions are completely commingled). In this preference for direct service, ironically enough, he aligns himself with such hated old regime institutions as the corvee (or forced work on the highways).

Here once more, however, Rousseau was thinking of the small intimate community and not of the large and heavily populated eighteenth-century state. Presumably his citizens would do their civic work almost spontaneously, reinforced by the directly observable example of their neighbors.

When revolutionary leaders came to implement Rousseau's conception of direct service, however, their major application was the introduction of the earliest modern-type military conscription. Confronted with the opposition of a Europe aroused by the revolutionists' own aggressiveness, the notion of the nation in arms struck the formulators of policy as not only a correct interpretation of Rousseau but also as an admirable answer to the immediate practical problem. Conscription of a whole nation, one of the most momentous innovations of modern life,[50] was thus introduced under the aegis of the slogan "liberty, equality, fraternity." The casuists who defended the principle could argue that he was freest who was carrying out the general will and that equality of sacrifice and the social solidarity embodied in fraternity were inseparable from freedom. The man who was compelled to take up arms was really being forced to be free. And so began one of the most ubiquitous forms of modern slavery.

Rousseau and German Idealism. One of the most astonishing aspects of Rousseau's influence is the undoubted impact he had on what came to be called the German idealist school of thought. This surprises one because the idealist philosophers—men like Kant, Hegel, and Fichte—were themselves so much more systematic than Rousseau and it might have been thought that they would pay little attention to the rather confused romantic speculator. Yet of Rousseau Kant once said: "At one time I thought that learning could be the glory of humanity and despised the ignorant vulgar: Rousseau put me right. This dazzling vanity is dissipated. I have learned to honour men."[51]

Kant's statement indicates the first particular with respect to which Rousseau's influence made itself felt. It was his reaction to the abstract rationalism of the eighteenth century (and its implicit elitism) which appeared to strike Kant and his successors with so much effect—perhaps precisely because the whole school of idealism itself stemmed originally from that very rationalism. Kant was thus apparently shocked into a realization that man is more than a speculating and logical being: he is also one of feeling and of passionate attachment to other human beings and groups.

That facet of Rousseau's thought which finds contractual conceptions superfluous—which, in fact, implicitly returns to classical Greek

---

pierre, he is usually thought of as the leader of the Reign of Terror.

47. Decree of April 20, 1794.
48. It is always difficult to say just how much popular support lay behind such statutes. Much depends, of course, on what one means by "popular support." Is it to be interpreted as passive acquiescence or as active approval?
49. *Social Contract*, III, 8 and 15.
50. Historically, of course, compulsory military service had characterized several periods. But the French Revolution established it on a national scale, made it systematic, and created a close-knit machinery for administration and enforcement. See Alfred Vagts, *History of Militarism*, New York: W. W. Norton, 1937.
51. In *Nachlass*.

models—was seized upon by Hegel and developed into what is perhaps the most important modern organic view of society and political institutions. The discrete individual, who since at least the time of Machiavelli had played so central a role in the history of political theory, was pushed into the background, to be replaced by a conception which made the political group primary and the individual a product of group action.

Rousseau and Modern Nationalism. Because of his emphasis on group experience and his view of the general will, Rousseau may be looked upon as one of the intellectual forbears of modern nationalism. To be sure, his parochial state was not a nation as nineteenth-century thinkers understood the term. But it was the sentiment which Rousseau thought might arise spontaneously in the small group that nationalists sought to impart to the much larger nation-state. They hoped to give to it at least some of the qualities which Rousseau thought essential for the development of a general will, even though they could not accept his criteria of size and scale. Thus they stressed uniformity of language as an important basis for social cohesion and they sought consciously to encourage and build up the ties of sentiment which Rousseau thought so important. It is easy to see why many think of him as an intellectual ancestor of integral or extreme nationalism.[52]

Rousseau and Democratic Thought. One of the most frustrating problems confronting the historian of thought is that of assessing the place of Rousseau in modern democratic theory. The difficulty arises in part because democracy itself has meant so many things. Although we can identify it rather vaguely with those doctrines which assert that the people should rule, we find a wide variety of interpretations embodied in the particular doctrines themselves.

Broadly speaking, however, modern democratic theory would appear to divide into two streams: the Anglo-American, within which several varieties flourish and which has its theoretical roots in thinkers like Locke and the Levellers of the seventeenth century, and the Continental European, which, while not unconnected with seventeenth-century British speculation, roots to a great degree in French Revolutionary ideology. While Rousseau affected the first stream (through Jefferson and certain eighteenth century English democrats), his major impact was undoubtedly on the second. The Anglo-American tendency in democratic thought has defended the existence of nonstate associations, embodied within it a kind of attenuated medieval natural law doctrine, and looked with suspicion on all assertions that the "general will" can ever be ascertained with any certainty. Continental democratic thought, by contrast, has been throughout a large part of its history either hostile or indifferent to nonstate associations and has placed great emphasis on discovery of the general will. There has been a greater tendency, too, than in Anglo-American thought, to think of the popular voice as somehow morally right as well as politically final; and the emotional overtones exalting the people are far more pronounced. In all these characteristics we can see the authentic spirit of Rousseau.

In the democratic aspects of Marxism, too, we can perhaps catch traces of Rousseau as he is reflected both through the French Jacobin stream and through that associated with German idealism. The proletariat take on the characteristics of Rousseau's sentimentalized people: They become the bearers of a new and legitimate order of things based on their inflexible general will and purpose.

Rousseau and Hume

In the chapter which follows, we turn to the ways in which David Hume affected political thought, with particular reference to the notions of contract and utility.

In personal terms, as we have remarked, Rousseau and Hume clashed over trivialities, in large part because of the former's sensitivity and egocentricity. Intellectually, too, they were widely apart, the romantic and often antiintellectualist Genevan being met by the sceptical Scotsman. At one point, however, Rousseau and Hume seem to come together, in that the first eventually transcends social contract thinking, at least implicitly, and the second develops specific arguments against it. In other terms, Rousseau is the link between the individualist and contractualist thinking of seventeenth and eighteenth centuries and the noncontractualist organismic viewpoint characteristic of much early nineteenth century thought. Hume, in calling attention to the supposed fallacies of contractualist thought, helps pave the way for the several versions of organicism, and in part for some modern conservatism.

chapter 23

Empiricism and the Onslaught on Social Contract: Hume

While Rousseau was meditating in the woods and helping establish the foundations for romanticism and the revival of Greek-like organic conceptions, his great contemporary, David Hume, was preparing a philosophical revolution and in politics delivering what some thought of as body-blows against social contract. After Hume, living social contract doctrine in Europe began largely to disappear. While its offspring seemed to flourish in America, it ceased to have any vital impact in the lands of its birth.

This is not to say that Hume alone was responsible for the death of the tradition which was so closely associated with Hobbes, Locke, and Rousseau. Cultural and economic factors played important roles in establishing the conditions under which men were less likely than before to espouse contractual thinking. Individualistic approaches by no means died, but the weapons used to defend them changed: Whereas contract ideas had been intimately connected with them before, now the tendency almost everywhere was to dispense with the notion of agreement and to turn directly to utility.

But while many cultural, economic, and ideological factors paved the way for the death of contract in popular and semipopular thinking, there can be no doubt that at the philosophical level the role of David Hume was a crucial one.

The Intellectual and Political Worlds of Hume

Hume's life spanned almost exactly the years covered by the earthly existence of Rousseau. Born in Edinburgh in 1711, he came from a family of landed gentry and originally aspired to the bar. After a period of legal study, however, he reached a very firm conclusion that this life was not for him. He acquired, he tells us, "an insurmountable aversion to everything but the pursuit of philosophy and general learning." He seems nevertheless, not to have been as firmly committed as this statement implies, for he did try the life of merchant for a brief period.

The merchant's career, too, proving unsatisfactory, he vowed to leave all activities except scholarship behind him and journeyed to France for reflection and study. There, in 1737, he published his *Treatise of Human Nature* and, in 1741, his *Essays on Moral and Political Subjects*. He evidently hoped for a professorship at the University of Edinburgh when a vacancy occurred in 1745. However, there had already developed a hostility to him for his "scepticism," even in intellectual circles, and a teaching career was thus closed to him.

He became tutor to the half-mad Marquis of Annandale and, later on, secretary to an army officer. In 1748, the year of Montesquieu's *Spirit of Laws*, he published his *Enquiry Concerning the Human Understanding* and in 1751 followed it with the *Enquiry Concerning the Principles of Morals*. By this time, he had become fairly well known in philosophical circles and the defenders of traditional religious and political viewpoints were beginning those attacks that were to make "Humean" an epithet of opprobrium.

Meanwhile, however, he had become Librarian of the Advocate's Library in Edinburgh and had begun work on his *History of England*. That a philosopher of his stature should turn to history was itself something of a phenomenon. The *History* was not in any sense a philosophical treatment, for Hume seems never to have developed an explicit theory of history. Instead, he dealt with his subject rather conventionally, in terms of the reigns of monarchs, and made little effort to discover underlying patterns. The student of Hume's politics must always regret that he made no endeavor to cast his account in a more general mold and that he seemed to be

Chapter 22

52. See Rudolf Rocker, *Nationalism and Culture*, New York: Covici-Friede, 1937, p. 167. See also Chapter 30, pp. 555–560.

satisfied with explanations which today appear somewhat superficial.

In 1757, he gave up his work at the Advocates' Library and by 1763 prepared himself once more to visit France. His only experience as an official came in 1765, when for a brief period he was a secretary in the British Embassy to France. It was at this time that he was brought into touch with the unhappy Rousseau, with results which we have already touched upon.

In 1769, Hume settled in Edinburgh for the last time and it was there that he died in 1776—the year of the Declaration of Independence, Adam Smith's *Wealth of Nations*, and Jeremy Bentham's *Fragment on Government*.

The streams of thought which conditioned and influenced Hume's moral and political theory were as varied as the intellectual history of the eighteenth century itself. He could not, of course, escape Locke and those who espoused Locke's somewhat unsatisfactory epistemology, psychology, and morals. Indeed, Hume's mission was in a sense to make Locke less confusing by drawing out the implications of his empiricism while rejecting what Hume regarded as his rationalistic errors. In terms of psychological doctrine, the impact of both Hobbes and Locke seems to have been to provoke a strong reaction in Hume against their egoistic theories; so that while critics might link Hume with Hobbes in that both were atheists, they had also to recognize that no eighteenth-century thinker was a more vigorous critic of Hobbes' natural man than Hume. Another important factor in Hume's thinking was the system of his fellow Scotsman Francis Hutcheson (1694–1746), who anticipated Hume's application of empiricism to ethical and political questions. There is evidence, too, that he was familiar with Montesquieu, whose analysis he admired, and that he thought of himself, and rightly, as a prime critic of Ralph Cudworth[1] and the whole school of "Cambridge Platonists," who flourished at the close of the seventeenth century.

Hume on Knowing

We have at several points emphasized that although Locke in the *Human Understanding* ostensibly laid the groundwork for a more sophisticated empiricist view of knowledge than that suggested, for example, by Francis Bacon, he was by no means consistent in applying it. All knowledge, he seemed to say, came from sense impressions. At the same time, however, he talked of the law of nature which prescribed principles of property and of justice—a law, it would seem, which by no means could be derived from sensations, even indirectly. Moreover, when he did deal with sense experience, Locke did not subject to any very close analysis the whole cause-effect relationship which we tend to assume as we observe the world about us. Many of the successors of Locke were equally sketchy and apparently inconsistent in these matters; and eighteenth-century rationalism, particularly in the so-called sciences of men (what today we should call the social sciences), was in considerable measure a development of Locke's tendency to deduce the nature of the moral and political world from certain premises which were themselves not subjected to the test of empirical verification. We have noted this tendency in Rousseau,[2] but it was also apparent in many other thinkers.

It was Hume's mission to draw out the implications of empiricism philosophically and, in the area of the moral and political sciences, to apply them as rigorously and consistently as possible.

In matters of fact, Hume argues, there is no way to prove the cause-effect relationship which we assume in our observations of the world. Or, as Hume himself puts it, "in no single instance the ultimate connection of any objects is discoverable either by our senses or reason, and . . . we can never penetrate so far into the essence and construction of bodies as to perceive the principle on which their mutual influence depends."[3] Hence while there is no necessary connection between matters of fact, we build up the idea of regularities of the way in which facts accompany one another. Only observation, however, will discover these regularities: There are no self-evident axioms, whether we are reasoning in the natural sciences or in the sciences of man.[4]

Necessary relations are confined to the world of ideas—to logic and pure mathematics. It is in this area that there are indeed self-evident propositions; and we build our systems by reasoning from these propositions without any reference to the world of sense. Where Locke and his rationalist successors went wrong, however, was in thinking that because there were self-evident principles and necessary connections in logic and mathematics there must also be such propositions and relations in the world of fact.

Hume's well-known scepticism is not the scepticism of the ancients, which doubted the possibility of any knowledge. Rather is it the assertion that our ability to know the world of phenomena is dependent on the contingencies of observation: This fact will always make our understanding of nature and human behavior less certain and more ragged than our comprehension of propositions in logic and mathematics which have necessary relationships to one another.

It should, of course, be made perfectly clear that Hume does not reject reason in repudiating rationalism. Instead, his theory of knowledge bids us spurn what to him was that exaggeration and misuse of reason which he discerns in the eighteenth-century rationalists. There are some things reason cannot do: It cannot, that is to say, act as a substitute for observation and it cannot infuse into our understanding of nature and society the certainty which one can attain within the domain of closed systems of logic and mathematics.

Hume's Views on the Human Psyche

In his psychological views, Hume is a combination of Hobbes and the Scottish moralist Hutcheson. With the former, he tends to think of the passions and human acts in mechanistic terms; with the latter, he places great emphasis on instincts. He is careful, however, not to reduce all passions of soul and body to one or two basic ones and in this respect differs notably from Hobbes.

The passions are, of course, the springs of action which, as we shall see, shape and mold the human organism. But Hume notes two categories of passions—those direct ones which arise out of immediate pleasure and pain and the indirect which are built, so to speak, on the direct. Among the direct passions, he enumerates "desire, aversion, grief, joy, hope, fear, despair, and security."[5] The indirect include "pride, humility, ambition, vanity, love, hatred, envy, pity, malice, generosity, with their dependents."[6]

Hume is, of course, concerned to explain human conduct in terms of the interaction of these passions on one another and to demonstrate the thesis that social behavior exhibits the same regularities which natural scientists discern in their area of study. A great admirer of Newton, he believes that social scientists can do for moral and social phenomena what the great natural scientist did for physics.

In carrying out this task, Hume seeks to account for human behavior in a way which constitutes a radical departure from the ancient Greek classical tradition. Aristotle, for example, thought of human personality as an organic unfolding of potentialities. Hume, however, true to the more mechanistic framework of his thought, suggests explanations in terms of the interaction of the passions with one another and of the organism with its environment. While he does not, it is true, conceive man to be *only* what he discovers in the basic springs of actions, he does tend to think that the human being can best be understood in terms of his psychological origins. Rejecting what he regards as the overly-simplistic psychology of Hobbes, he nevertheless is much closer to the seventeenth-century philosopher than he is to teleological views of the ancients.

There is, however, a basic difference between the psychology of Hobbes and that of Hume. The latter rejects egoism root and branch. We cannot, he contends, reduce the other-regarding attitudes of human beings to self-regarding ones.[7]

Hume seeks to refute the egoistic proposition by invoking what is essentially the principle of Occam's razor. He observes that the mass of mankind at least believe that there are both altruistic and selfish passions and that the

1. Ralph Cudworth (1617–1688) was the Master of Christ's College, Cambridge, from 1654 until his death. A devotee of the Platonism embodied in the so-called School of Alexandria, he stoutly championed the notion that moral ideas are innate. In fact, he appeared to argue that men could comprehend the objective reality of good and evil as exactly as they (supposedly) understand geometry.
2. Chapter 22, p. 406. It was also present in remarkable degree in the political writings of men like William Godwin.
3. *Treatise on Human Nature,* Bk. II, Part III, Sec. 1.
4. *Ibid.*
5. *Ibid.*, II–I, 1.
6. *Ibid.*
7. *Enquiry Concerning the Principles of Morals,* Appendix II.

former cannot be reduced to the latter. The burden of proof, therefore, is on those who would assert that the existence of altruism is an illusion. Hume thinks that no one, least of all Hobbes, has ever shown beyond grave doubts that selfish feelings are in fact the source of what we call altruism. Until, therefore, someone offers better evidence that the common distinction between self-love and love of others is illusory, we are bound to accept the general view of mankind as having some congruence with reality.[8]

He thinks, too, that observation proves animals to be capable of kindness both to their own kind and to the human race. And he wonders whether Hobbists would seek to account for all "*their* sentiments, too, from refined deductions of self-interest." If the exponents of the reductionist view admit benevolence among the beasts, they are under a great burden to show why they adopt one view with reference to subhuman life and another about human beings.

It is the mutual sharing of other-regarding emotions, in fact, which makes possible, Hume maintains, a common moral life. Without it, the conventions of society would not be durable and it would be difficult to account for the way in which societies tend to hold together. The joys and sorrows of others affect a man because he has by nature a sympathy with his fellow-creatures: Observation suggests this pattern and the common opinion of mankind, on the whole, corroborates what the scientist observes.

One of the most celebrated aspects of Hume's teaching is his statement that "reason is, and ought only to be, the slave of the passions, and can never pretend to any other office than to serve and obey them."[9] In making this assertion he is, of course, rejecting the view (common to Greek and Stoic thinking) that the passions can somehow be made subordinate to reason. "A passion," he maintains, "is an original existence or, if you will, modification of existence, and contains not any representative quality which renders it a copy of any other existence or modification."[10] The passion of anger, for example, cannot be in conflict with reason which has to do with discovery of truth. Only that can be contrary to reason which has reference to it.

Attacking the idea that reason can give us ultimate moral standards, Hume goes on to maintain that "it is not contrary to reason to prefer the destruction of the whole world to the scratching of my finger." Reason has nothing to do with our basic value preferences, for the final selections of our goals is in the province of the passions.

The Nature of Moral Experience

Given his theory of knowledge and his psychological doctrine, it is clear that he cannot accept any ethical system which would claim that there are necessary and universal truths. Nor can he hold that moral truths relate to alleged facts which transcend the ordinary empirical world; and thus such notions as the will of God or a supernatural revelation as a basis for conduct would be ruled out. He is clear, however, that our decisions about conduct are somehow related to those springs of actions which are the passions. But what is their exact interrelationship?

At this point it is easy to misconstrue Hume, for he can be interpreted as asserting that moral judgments are simply expressions of personal approval of an act and that they are, moreover, only reactions of feeling. Hume thus seems to anticipate what in the twentieth century has come to be called the emotive theory of ethical judgments, according to which our statements about alleged right and wrong, good, and bad are only outpourings of our emotions of the moment.

But Hume's account of moral experience is in reality much more complex than what usually passes for the emotive theory would allow. While he roots judgments of vice and virtue in the passions, there are certain universals in human behavior which underlie all personal pronouncements. Thus, as he has pointed out in his examination of psychology, every human being has a certain sympathy for other members of the species and members of the opposite sex tend to be attracted to one another. At the same time, however, the intensity of our sympathies is closely related to the nearness of their object: Thus it is universal that the mother responds more quickly to the passion of hunger in her own child than she will to a like desire in the child of another. But if the latter comes to be in close proximity to her over a period of time, her response will gradually approximate that which she makes to her own child. In general, the smaller and more intimately connected the group, the greater the bond of sympathy, and hence of fellow-feeling, which holds it together. The more remote the connections, the less immediate and intense will be our responses.

In their moral sense theory, Hume's predecessors Lord Shaftesbury (3rd Earl, 1671–1713) and Francis Hutcheson had held, in essence, that men were equipped with a moral sense analogous to such faculties as hearing and seeing and that this sense permitted them to distinguish between right and wrong. But it was a natural sense and not something which came from beyond human nature. Thus Shaftesbury and Hutcheson presumably avoided the notion that ethical judgments were a matter of divine revelation or of will.

Now Hume obviously owes much at least to the terminology of Shaftesbury and Hutcheson, but he carefully spurns any notion that the moral sense is cognitive—that it gives us knowledge. When he employs the term, it is with the object of showing that our feelings enter into our judgments of right and wrong and thus provide us with the goals of conduct. Those acts, on the whole, which promote the greatest pleasure in given circumstances tend to be moral; and those, by contrast, which have the effect of producing a net amount of pain we call immoral. But we must not, according to Hume, equate moral goodness with the greatest pleasure principle; for when we pronounce judgments as to what is right and wrong we look to motivations and not to consequences. The consequences are "signs or indications of certain principles in the mind and temper"[11]—while on the whole they give us a clue as to motivations, it is not necessarily an infallible indication: We use it only because we cannot get at motives directly. It is important, thinks Hume, that we keep this in mind, lest we make too easy an identification of good actions (that is, actions which tend to create happiness or pleasure) with laudable motives.

What interests Hume above all is to account for justice—that is, the performance of acts out of a sense of duty and without regard for the consequences. These have come to be equated in a peculiar sense with justice, for it is by no means certain why they should be performed in terms either of individual happiness (pleasure) or of public felicity. Thus when a man of great merit returns a fortune to a miser or a seditious bigot to whom it belongs, he has presumably acted justly, but it is difficult to see how he has benefited either himself or the public. The fortune would be better administered by himself than by the miser or the bigot, from the viewpoint of public interest.[12] Yet we call his act just. If moral value is somehow related to happiness and happiness to pleasure, how can we account for the fact that we approve his conduct?

As one might expect, Hume gives an empiricist answer to the question. Mankind have discovered through experience, he argues, that on the whole it is better to distribute scarce or economic goods to individuals rather than hold them in common. While men do, as we have seen, have a natural sympathy, it becomes attenuated when applied to those not in very close and intimate relations with us; and we have discovered through the give and take of experience that, on the whole, our disquiet is less when scarce goods are distributed according to some over-all general rule than when they are shared directly.

To return to the meritorious man who restores a fortune to the miser. If the act were an isolated one and unrelated to the whole experience of the human race, it would obviously be better, from the viewpoint of net happiness (pleasure), for the money not to be restored. But when we look at the act in the perspective of the universal primary passions combined with the fact of scarce goods and man's tendency to attenuate his sympathy as its objects become remote, the particular act becomes just. That is to say, while the immediate results of the act may not be useful, the observance of the principles upon which the act is based helps to support the whole body of rules which appear essential for stability and social order. And stability and social order are, given the experience of mankind, essential if either individuals or the group are to gain as much happiness as possible and reduce pains and disquiets to the lowest proportions.

What Hume is essentially seeking to show is that "public utility is the *sole* origin of justice, and that reflections on the beneficial consequences of this virtue are the *sole* foundation

8. *Ibid.*
9. *Treatise on Human Nature*, II–III, 3.
10. *Ibid.*
11. *Ibid.*, III–II, 1.
12. *Ibid.*, III–II, 2.

of its merit."[13] He asks us to imagine a situation in which material goods had ceased to be scarce, while at the same time human beings retained substantially the same nature which he has sketched out. Under these circumstances, men would not have to labor for their livelihoods, for nature would provide all they could desire. Would there be any need to provide any partition of goods? Obviously, thinks Hume, this would be superfluous, for, by the hypothesis, "every one has already more than enough." There would be no need for property when there could not possibly be any injury. But if institutions of property would be superfluous so, too, would justice be useless.

On the other hand, Hume suggests, suppose we imagine a state of affairs where goods continue to be limited but where the "mind is so enlarged, and so replete with friendship and generosity, that every man has the utmost tenderness for every man." The sentiment of sympathy, now strongest for ourselves and for those with whom we are in immediate and intimate relations, would become uniformly strong; the distinction between warm sympathy for those within the small closely bound group and lukewarm sentiments for all those outside that group would be abolished through the rise of uniformly warm sentiments for and responses to human beings everywhere. Under such circumstances, justice would be useless.

Justice is thus instrumental. It is a convention whose purpose is to "procure happiness and security by preserving order in society." It presupposes a human nature not egoistic, as with Hobbes, but one in which there is a contrast between strength of sentiment and benevolence for those in my immediate vicinity as over against those remote from me. It also presupposes human desires for material goods far greater than those which nature and human ingenuity can supply. If either of these factors be absent, justice is without utility.

In sum, experience—no doubt through a long trial and error process—teaches us that our common interests (defined in terms of utility) can best be served by what might be called the institutionalization of that experience in the form of conventions. The utility of these conventions, which originally define what men should do in order to provide scope for their passions while simultaneously avoiding the pains caused by a clash of passions, leads to moral approval of the acts enjoined by them. From this approbation there develops a sense of moral obligation, until eventually we come to believe that we should obey the conventional injunctions for their own sake and entirely apart from the immediate consequences which their observance might entail. Our notion of duty thus becomes divorced from the test of utility until social disorder or divisions within the group lead us to recur once more to the utilitarian bases of the conventions.

Hume's discussion of convention and of the social bond immediately puts us into touch with the political aspects of his philosophy. The rise of conventions through collective experience suggests the empirical basis of his politics proper; and his whole account of a moral obligation divorced from the test of consequences raises the question as to whether he will treat political obligation in a similar manner. Moreover, the absence of any resort to promises as a foundation for obligation hints at the vehemence with which he will repudiate social contract.

The Attack on Divine Right and Contract

Living in a day when the French monarch was regarded as ruling by divine right and the British monarch (to those following Locke) by virtue of a contract, Hume repudiates both divine right and the contract. In his repudiation, however, he grants a certain validity to both positions, though not of the kind espoused by partisans of the alternative viewpoints.

In one sense, he argues, all governments are instituted by God. If we believe, that is to say, in a beneficent, omniscient, and omnipotent deity, then all powers that be must somehow be a part of his divine plan for the world. No prince and no republic can rule but by his permission and no monarch or democracy govern except as an agent of his will.[14] Here, we might observe, Hume is restating a constant refrain of many Hebrew and Christian thinkers.

But when either monarchs or republican governments rule by divine right, in this sense of the term, they do so in the same way that every power or force may be said to exist by his permission. Thus governments are not peculiar in this respect. Indeed, Hume would say that every rebellion is divinely ordained and that every monarch who is overthrown by force must have been deposed through the will of God.

Similarly, he argues, there is a certain sense in which the contractualists have a point. If social contract is meant to imply that the first political institutions must have been based on some kind of consent, this is probably true. If we imagine men living in the woods and deserts, loosely organized into tribes and clans but roughly equal to one another, the only way to account for their original submission to political rule is to imagine a kind of voluntary assent or acquiescence. But such men, as we have seen, already lived in primitive social relations; and when some chief led them in forays on remote aggregations, it must originally have been an ad hoc relation between the temporary ruler and those who followed him. Formal and continuous political relations had not yet come about and after the particular purpose had been achieved, the primitive chief no doubt ceased to occupy a position of superordination. During his short tenure, he was obeyed largely because of a free and spontaneous awareness that it was in the public interest that men follow him.

Meanwhile, however, the interests of the men of limited sympathetic responses had not only led them to begin a distribution of material goods but almost insensibly had driven them into the notion of promises. The observance of promises was originally connected very obviously with apparent social and individual interests to be served. Just as the institution of private property arose because men found it useful, so the obligation of promises was initially indistinguishable from their utility.[15] The same tendency of the human mind which divorced the obligation to respect property right from its original utility gradually, in the course of experience, separated the obligation to keep promises from the usefulness of keeping them. Thus the basis of fidelity—the keeping of promises—is ultimately the same as that of justice—respect for the property of others. The one is not derived from the other but both are examples of those artificial moral duties which we come to accept when we understand their necessity for human society.[16]

Now Hume thinks of the obligation to obey rulers as being on a parity with fidelity and justice. The duty to obey, even if we assume that there was originally a kind of rough consent, arises not from a contract of agreement; instead, both contract and the obligation to obey are bottomed in utility.

As a matter of fact, Hume thinks, political institutions could not have arisen as a result of a contract if only because it requires the services of government to promote an exact observance of contractual obligations. The interests which led men to see that it is desirable to keep promises also induced them to establish political subordination as a method of implementing contracts.

The Origin of Government and the Explanation of Obedience

What, then, in a more positive sense, is the origin of political institutions and the explanation for men's submission to rulers? In general, as we have seen, Hume argues that utility—defined in terms of the pleasure-pain principle—is the answer. But the exact origin and explanation need to be spelled out.

At the outset he asks why, if men perceive the utility of property distribution—justice—and find it so obviously connected with the implementation of their interests, they need civil institutions at all. One would think, he observes, that disorder could not arise if all men were aware of the close connection between their lives and interests, on the one hand, and the observance of justice, on the other. Yet they felt obliged to submit to rulers.

He finds the explanation in a distinction which, it will be remembered, he made in his psychological and moral discussion. He had observed that what is contiguous to us in time and space moves us more powerfully than that which is remote: Our wills and passions are directed more certainly by that which is immediate than by that which "lies in a more distant and obscure light."[17]

It is, then, this conflict between our remote commitment to sustain society through the observance of justice and fidelity and our tendency to succumb to pressures close at hand which leads us to set a few men to act as governors. Yet it is still difficult to see how men could do this, for how can they, if incapable of preferring the remote to the contiguous, "consent to anything which would

13. *Enquiry Concerning the Principles of Morals.* Sec. 3.
14. See *Of the Original Contract.*
15. *Treatise on Human Nature*, III–II, 5.
16. *Of the Original Contract.*
17. *Treatise on Human Nature*, III–II, 7.

oblige them to such a choice and contradict in so sensible a manner their natural principles and propensities"?

Hume's anwer to this question is that the very infirmity in human nature corrects itself. That is to say, while remote duties do not move one as do immediate passions, one can nevertheless be more impartial and clear-sighted about the remote than about the immediate. This is reason, improperly so called. We see that some artifice is necessary to "render the observance of the laws of justice our nearest interest, and their violation our most remote." Hence we set aside magistrates, who, being indifferent to the immediate passions of most men, "have no interest, or but a remote one, in any act of injustice."[18]

But while this may be regarded as the general or remote origin of government—hence a certain validity to the consent theory—once institutions are established, particular rulers may arise through a diversity of methods. On the whole, he thinks, historical experience indicates that almost all governments originate in conquest, rebellion, or violence of some kind. This fact, of course, leads us to ask what is the true distinction between legitimate and illegitimate government, for upon this differentiation depends our view of political obligation in any given instance.

By and large, thinks Hume, all those governments are legitimate which manage to survive over a long period of time. The common opinion of mankind, at least, would suggest this answer and in such matters human consensus is to be preferred to the judgments of erudite philosophers. A dynasty founded on what is clear usurpation will, if it manages to persist, eventually evoke sentiments of loyalty on the part of descendants of those who regarded it as illegitimate. Hume is not clear as to whether the sentiment of loyalty precedes the firm establishment of a government or whether its stability comes prior to the sentiment. Possibly we can interpret him as suggesting an interaction—tendencies to stability evoke sentiments of loyalty just as the latter will promote stability.

It is not at all clear, however, as to what Hume is endeavoring to show. If he means to demonstrate that men in fact tend to accept a government which has been established for a long time and that the custom of obedience gives rise to sentiments of loyalty, he can make a good case for his contention. If, however, he is suggesting that men *ought* to obey an authority simply because it is firmly established, regardless of the character of that government, he is maintaining a more dubious proposition. He has a tendency to be ambiguous and to equate the moral legitimacy of a government with the fact that it has managed to survive. When, for example, he asserts that "Right to authority is nothing but the constant possession of authority, maintained by the laws of society and the interests of mankind,"[19] the critic might legitimately ask whether there is any government in "constant possession of authority" which can ever, according to his view, be contrary to the "laws of society and the interests of mankind."

While long possession is the first and best basis for political right, Hume believes that present possession also provides an excellent claim. He seems to be saying that just as in private relations "possession is nine points of the law," as we usually maintain, so in the ruler-subject situation, a *de facto* power to gain obedience confers a certain kind of right. Those who possess the power, he contends, are to be obeyed, other things being equal. Here again, it would seem, Hume makes hardly any distinction between legitimacy and ability to coerce or manipulate men.

And the same observation can be made when we note that he thinks of conquest as another source of legitimacy. Akin to the doctrine of present possession, the right of conquest yet seems to have a greater sway over men's minds than does the claim of a usurper; for men, Hume thinks, "are more apt to ascribe a right to successful violence betwixt one sovereign and another than to the successful rebellion of a subject against his sovereign."[20]

He appears to be describing titles to authority in descending order. That is, if there is no long possession, then present possession will (or should?) take precedence. If no one is in clear present possession, then a foreign conqueror could make his claim. In the absence of any of these, however, hereditary succession will have great claim and after hereditary succession positive laws will carry weight. Of course, if long possession, present possession, hereditary succession, and positive law unite to support a given ruler, his title is as strong as it could ever be. Often, however, we are forced to make decisions as between rival claims and in any given instance, Hume admits, they will be difficult.

On the whole, however, Hume seems to reaffirm the proposition that effective possession of ability to command confers the right to command. He looks to the actual way in which men have behaved politically and his discussions of long possession, present possession, hereditary succession, and positive law are simply generalizations on human experience. We have noted throughout an ambiguity about whether Hume is saying that men *should* conduct themselves in this way or that, or whether, on the contrary, they *do* in fact view political right in the way he describes.

Hume on Revolution

Writing as he does on the eve of a generation of revolution, it is not surprising that Hume is concerned about the legitimacy of revolt. In his analysis, however, while he begins by asserting the right to revolt under certain circumstances, he concludes that a given revolt is to be justified only if and when it is thoroughly successful. Or rather, following his political morality in general, those revolts which are successful men tend to think of as right and Hume either does not or feels he cannot inquire into these conclusions of the bulk of mankind. He accepts without question the common judgment as the correct one.

He begins by pointing out that the elevation of men to positions of superior power and authority does not make them superior in nature to the remainder of the human race. While they presumably acquire a more immediate interest in the "execution of justice" than those not occupying positions in government, the "irregularity of human nature" makes it probable that their passions may at times lead them into an "excess of cruelty and ambition." When this takes place, he thinks, "our general knowledge of human nature, our observation of the past history of mankind, our experience of present times" will lead us to make exceptions to the rule that those in authority should be obeyed.

Beyond this, however, it is impossible to go in stating principles which might guide us in approving or disapproving a particular revolt: Even philosophy cannot give us particular rules. The people always retain the "right of resistance," Hume contends, but immediately gives as the reason for this assertion, "since it is impossible, even in the most despotic governments, to deprive them of it." This means, apparently, that in despotisms, no less than in other political relations, the right is retained because self-preservation is always an overriding interest and if enough believe that their self-preservation is involved they will probably gain the power to carry out the act of successful revolt. There is no hint in all this, however, that any revolt which is unsuccessful could be vindicated: Hume would probably think of it as *ipso facto* unjustified.

Nor will he accept the notion, made popular in systems like Locke's political philosophy, that it is the entire community in whom the right to revolt is vested. Every legitimate revolution, he thinks, is the work of a minority; and while the people may, indeed, acquiesce in the result, they really have no choice. Thus the much-touted Glorious Revolution was the work of only the majority of the seven hundred in the convention which decided to invite William of Orange. Realistically, once William had been summoned, it became treason to resist him; yet the community had in no wise been consulted about the event. While Hume has, of course, admitted a kind of general consent to political institutions as a whole, any particular change in them—at least historically speaking—must always be thought of as the work of a few. And what has been true as a matter of fact is also right—Hume does not exactly say that the fact makes the right but he does clearly imply a curious coincidence.

Hume's further analysis of the revolution of 1689 strengthens our contention that, while he insists on the right of revolution, the right is almost wholly dependent on the might which lies behind it. Legitimacy, in other words, is conferred retroactively. Nothing could, of course, be further from the view of those who, like Jefferson, rooted the right of revolution on some such natural rights doctrine as Locke's.

Specifically, Hume discusses the question whether the deposition of James II should also have deprived his infant son of the right to the succession. "Reason" tells us that if the father "forfeits" the throne through misdeeds, the son should not share the father's fate—he should, it would seem, "remain in the same situation as if the king were removed by death."[21] But revo-

18. *Ibid.*
19. *Ibid.*, III–II, 10.
20. *Ibid.*
21. *Ibid.*

lutions overthrow allegedly reasonable conclusions; and thus the infant son was swept away along with the father. In the event, the result was apparently legitimated by the fact that William retained the throne and that the line of sovereigns established as a result of the Revolution managed to survive.

At this point Hume injects a highly characteristic note into his political thinking, one which would seem to flow directly from his psychological and moral thought. He suggests that William's very title to the throne was established not primarily by his ancestors but rather by his successors. Although his *right* to the throne was challenged in his own lifetime, the Revolution which led to his claim was vindicated by the fact that his successors in the line established by the Revolution continued to rule without serious challenge. Thus the principle of long possession retroactively established William's right to the throne many years after he himself was dead.

In his whole analysis of retroactive legitimacy, it will be noted, Hume once more exhibits his tendency to accept the judgment of history (interpreted largely in terms of the predominant social forces) as final. What men have in fact pronounced to be legitimate is legitimate; and the political philosopher is not so much concerned to work out his own standards of legitimacy as to discover that which men, through their actions, have regarded as right.

Hume's Conservative Political Temper

We can say of Hume that, while he is a revolutionary in the history of philosophy, he is essentially what later came to be called a conservative in his political outlook. And this conservatism, in some measure at least, flows in part from his epistemology and his moral theory.

Essentially, Hume is contending that all we can really *know* about the right or the good is what most men have held to be right or good—that is, the actions deemed by the bulk of mankind to give pleasure, or, more indirectly, to promote society which in turn makes possible the extension of pleasure and the avoidance of pain. Throughout our discussion of his morality and politics we have noted his equation of what men hold to be good with the good itself; and it has been equally apparent that he does not venture to state what he himself thinks of as the norm, apart from the opinion of mankind.

Given these foundations, it is not surprising to find him always pleading against novelty and appealing for moderation. He distrusts, moreover, the idea of great leaders changing patterns of the past, holding that the sphere within which individuals can effectively act is always highly restricted by the traditions of the community: In fact, he contends, the form of political society is the vital factor, despite Pope's famous lines, "For forms of government let fools contest, Whate'er is best administered is best."[22] As a good empiricist, Hume naturally contends that we can discern certain regularities in human political conduct no less than in the behavior of the natural world;[23] but unlike many modern empiricists, he does not see the knowledge thus gained as the basis upon which radical reform measures can be built. Instead, he appears to reach the conclusion that one must always move slowly, lest we disturb disadvantageously such equilibria as have been achieved. The firm opinions of most men as to what is politically right constitute the severe limits within which we must carry out such measures as might be approved by the reformer; and those opinions themselves are usually changed with difficulty.

As an illustration of his attitude, we may take Hume's discussion of the problem of popular government and of its possible applicability to eighteenth-century Britain. He thinks that the experience of republican Rome clearly demonstrates that "democracy without a representative" leads to disorder, anarchy, and unhappiness. At the same time, however, he argues that when the people are "dispersed in small bodies" they may act reasonably and for the "public interest." There is no doubt that he would see a representative democracy as a possibility. But to those who would attempt to move in this direction under the circumstances of his time, he utters a restraining word:

> It is needless to reason any farther concerning a form of government which is never likely to have place in Great Britain, and which seems not to be the aim of any party amongst us. Let us cherish and improve our ancient government as much as possible, without encouraging a passion for such dangerous novelties.[24]

While he does not tell us what his attitude would be should a party amongst us begin to advocate a thorough-going democracy, his general position in morals and politics would lead one to conclude that if such a group did arise and were successful over a period of time, he would deem it to be both morally and politically right: Its success would vindicate its position.

This is not to say that Hume completely repudiates all speculative projects for reform. Indeed, he himself sketches out certain proposals for an ideal commonwealth,[25] among them being decentralized government, an administrative Senate of one hundred members, and county assemblies in which the final legislative power will reside; and it is interesting that he makes no provision for a monarchy.

Despite this concession to utopian speculation, however, the general thrust of Hume's political theory is to concentrate on explanations of the springs of the passions, of commonly held moral ideas, and of political institutions as they are. He is always more interested in accounting for what men are than in projecting what they should or even can be; and throughout his social and political outlook runs an emphasis on the dangers of innovation to social order. He is constantly appealing to experience as against the a priori reasonings and speculations of the philosophers.

Hume's Theory in Perspective

In his moral theory, as we have seen, Hume is a utilitarian and a hedonist. Ultimately, in other words, that course of conduct is right which leads to pleasurable consequences. But Hume's view is more complicated than that of some eighteenth-century utilitarians and hedonists in that he admits both egoistic and altruistic motives, attempts to account for our moral approval of acts which obviously do not give us pleasure, and suggests that that is right which the mass of men, rather than a given individual, hold to be right.

Given his psychological and moral notions, it is thus much easier for Hume to account for political society than it is for Hobbes or even Locke and Rousseau. It is less difficult because he rejects an egoistic psychology and does not try to reduce altruistic emotions to those of egoism. When he defends the irreducibility of benevolence to mere selfishness by pointing out that all of us feel emotions of approval for actions in literature which cannot possibly affect our egos, he undercuts much of the historically fashionable argument of Hobbes'

followers. He admits, of course, that our so-called unselfishness may be a species of self-deception, but immediately asks himself "how does this affect the argument?" If, in other words, we are deluding ourselves about our benevolence, we must then ask ourselves why men believe it necessary to pretend that they are benevolent.

Now Hume was not the first modern speculator to reason thus about egoistic psychology but he was certainly one of the most significant of the major thinkers. After him, it became more and more difficult—despite the persistence of egoism in many circles—to conceive the human being as dominated wholly by selfishness. And Hume's refutation of Hobbes no doubt played its role in preparing the way for the group theories of human personality and of politics which were to make their appearance with Hegel a generation after the Scottish philosopher's death.

Hume's equation of the right with what the bulk of mankind think to be right, while consistent with his general outlook, really evades the question of whether what the mass think to be right and good is in fact so. It is difficult, of course, to see how Hume could have reached any other conclusion, given his denial that the good can be known. In effect, he is saying, we must take the word of the majority which is ultimately shaped in its attitude by its passions. The results for Hume's politics are clear: the firmly established way is "best" because it is established; we adopt revolutionary attitudes at our peril; and we can often never know whether a given government is legitimate until the following generation (through the test of long possession).

Historically, it was perhaps Hume's refutation of social contract which became most significant. Here again, while others had moved in the same direction, his general philosophical eminence and the succinctness with which he phrased the refutation carried great

22. *Essay on Man*, Bk. III.
23. See his essay *That Politics May be Reduced to a Science*.
24. *Of the First Principles of Government*.
25. In his essay the *Idea of a Perfect Commonwealth*.

weight with subsequent generations. After him, the theory was gradually undermined.

In place of the social contract, Hume's account of political society erected hedonistic utility and habit. The former provided the ultimate basis for the establishment of political relations and obligation, while the latter explained in an immediate sense men's tendencies to obey. Here again, however, as in his general moral theory, Hume appears to think that because he has given a genetic account of political obligation—because, in other words, he has provided us a kind of natural history of the subject—he has also told us why we *should* obey. By equating obligation with interest or utility, he has raised—but not answered—the question as to why he uses the term moral at all. Even if he has explained how we have come to value what he calls justice as an end in itself (despite its often painful immediate results), he has failed to tell us what political righteousness is. In effect, although by a somewhat different route, he has adopted a Glauconian position and has told us that the quest for political justice—in any sense other than that of the norms established by tradition, convention, or mass sentiment—is a fruitless one.

But whatever the weakness of Hume's account of political obligation and society, his latent conservative attitude is present throughout. True, he never developed it at great length. He did, however, provide a framework for it: he doubted that we could "know" right and wrong apart from how men defined them.

The impact of Hume on later generations was at least threefold. In the first place, he laid the foundations for the characteristically modern view that, while there are necessary relations between logical and mathematical ideas, there are no necessary cause-and-effect relations between and among facts. Secondly, in his principle of utility, he both reflected and helped shape the foundations of much modern moral and political thought, particularly in early liberalism. Finally, with Rousseau and Edmund Burke, he helped lay the groundwork for views which, in Hegel, would help revive interest in history and the notion of the organic community.

The first view led to a great stress on discovery of correlations by actual examination of the patterning of facts. And out of this emerged in the social sciences the very strong emphasis on empiricism which has particularly characterized the American scene. At times, this perspective tended to forget that the concepts with which we view the facts cannot themselves be derived from the facts—and a kind of raw empiricism was the result. But at any rate, the rationalistic deductionism of the Cartesians was repudiated.

In his moral and political views, the emphasis on utility in accounting for men's actual conduct and in providing standards for it was, of course, not new. But Hume provided for it a context of signal importance when he sought to combine hedonism and utility with a nonegoistic conception of man. Not all later utilitarians, to be sure, would adopt this peculiar combination, many reverting to a Hobbes-like egoism. But British utilitarianism did accept for example, Jeremy Bentham (1748–1832)—Hume's rejection of contract and his hedonism; and some utilitarians at least appeared, with Hume, to cast doubt on any easy reduction of altruistic to purely egoistic passions.

Finally, with Rousseau and, later, with Burke, Hume helped lay the foundations for views which, in men like Hegel, would constitute an important turning point in the history of political thought. Rousseau's stress on emotion and sentiment as bases of community had undercut the abstract rationalism of the contractualism to which he had ostensibly appealed. Hume, by emphasizing habit as the explanation of men's near-universal actual tendency to obey established powers, also sapped and mined rationalistic views. As for Edmund Burke, to whose views we shall refer in greater detail in Chapter 27, his teaching after the French Revolution had the effect of reviving interest in history as the source of both the sentiment and the habit which came increasingly to be regarded as the basis of a nation's constitution. In varying ways, all three thinkers (Hume, with his rejection of egoism) reflected a growing tendency to question the individualist orientation which had been so central during the previous three hundred years.

All three, too, were groping for a theory which would adequately reconcile the claims of individuality and freedom with the demands of social life. All wrote on the eve or at the beginning of the great Industrial Revolution which, by magnifying economic interdependence and the role of technology, would suggest a political doctrine more organic in character.

It was G. W. F. Hegel who systematically sought to develop an organismic conception of this kind. As we shall see in the next chapter, his idealist doctrine will build on classical Greek thought, on Hume's repudiation of contract theories, on the historicism of men like Burke, and on many facets of Rousseau. After Hegel's death, his theory will become the text or point of departure for some of the most significant currents in the political thought of modern times.

Part III Selected References

(in addition to those mentioned in footnotes)

16. *Morality and Politics: Machiavelli and the Renaissance*

BLEZNICK, D. W. "Spanish Reaction to Machiavelli in the Sixteenth and Seventeenth Centuries." *Journal of the History of Ideas,* 19 (October, 1958), 542–550.

BURCKHARDT, JACOB. *The Civilization of the Renaissance in Italy.* S. G. C. Middlemore, trans. New York: Phaidon Publishers, 1950.

DYER, LOUIS. *Machiavelli and the Modern State.* Boston: Ginn and Co., 1904.

FERRARA, ORESTES. *The Private Correspondence of Niccolo Machiavelli.* Baltimore. Johns Hopkins University Press, 1929.

FREDERICK THE GREAT. *Anti-Machiavel.* London: T. Woodward, 1741.

JENSEN, DE LAMAR. "Machiavelli: Cynic, Patriot, or Political Scientist?" In R. W. Greenlaw and D. E. Lee, *Problems in European Civilization.* Boston: D. C. Heath and Co., 1960.

KOZHUKHAROV, KONSTANTIN D. "Niccolo Machiavelli." Reprinted from *National University Law Review* 10, no. 2 (1930).

LAISTNER, M. L. W. *The Greater Roman Historians.* Berkeley: University of California Press, 1963.

MARCU, VALERIU. *Accent on Power: The Life and Times of Machiavelli.* New York: Farrar & Rinehart, 1939.

MAZZEO, J. A. "Cromwell as Machiavellian Prince in Marvell's 'An Horatian Ode.'" *Journal of the History of Ideas,* 21 (January–March, 1960), 1–17.

MEINECKE, FRIEDRICH. *Machiavellism.* New York: F. A. Praeger, 1957.

MORLEY, JOHN. *Machiavelli.* London: Macmillan, 1897.

MUIR, DOROTHY E. *Machiavelli and His Times.* London: William Heinemann, 1936.

PASTOR, LUDWIG. *The History of the Popes from the Close of the Middle Ages.* Trans. from the German. Edited by Frederick I. Antrobius. London: Kegan Paul, 1891.

PULVER, JEFFREY. *Machiavelli.* London: Herbert Joseph, 1937.

RITTER, GERHARD. *The Corrupting Influence of Power.* F. W. Pick, trans. London: 1952.

ROEDER, RALPH. *The Men of the Renaissance.* New York: Viking Press, 1933.

SCHEVILL, FERDINAND. *Medieval and Renaissance Florence.* Vol. 2. New York: Harper, Harper Torchbooks, 1960.

VILLARI, PASQUALE. *The Life and Times of Niccolo Machiavelli.* London: Unwin, 1898.

WALSH, P. G. *Livy, His Historical Aims and Methods.* Cambridge: Cambridge University Press, 1961.

17. *Politics and Morals in the Early Sixteenth-Century Reformation*

AGATE, LEONARD D. *Luther and the Reformation.* New York: Dodge Publishing Co., 1914.

BOEHMER, HEINRICH. *Luther and the Reformation in the Light of Modern Research.* New York: G. Bell & Sons, 1930.

CARLSON, EDGAR M. *The Reinterpretation of Luther.* Philadelphia: Westminster Press, 1948.

COHN, NORMAN. *The Pursuit of the Millennium: Revolutionary Messianism in Medieval and Reformation Europe and Its Bearing on Modern Totalitarian Movements.* Rev. ed., London: Secker and Warburg, 1957; New York: Harper, 1961.

DAVIS, RUPERT E. *The Problem of Authority in the Continental Reformers.* London: Epworth Press, 1946.

HARKNESS, GEORGIA E. *John Calvin: The Man and His Ethics.* New York: Holt, 1931.

HEARNSHAW, F. J. C. *The Social and Political Ideas of Some Great Thinkers of the Renaissance and the Reformation.* London: G. G. Harrap, 1925.

KRAMM, HANS. *The Theology of Martin Luther.* London: J. Clark, 1947.

LECLER, JOSEPH. *Toleration and the Reformation.* 2 vols. T. L. Westow, trans. New York: Association Press, 1960.

LUTHER, MARTIN. *Whether Soldiers, Too, Can Be Saved.* A. J. Holman and Charles M. Jacobs, trans. In *Works of Martin Luther,* edited by Henry E. Jacobs, vol. 5. Philadelphia: A. J. Holman and Castle Press, 1931.

Luther's Works. 51 vols. Edited by Jaroslav Pelikan and Helmut T. Lehmann. Philadelphia: Muhlenberg Press; St. Louis: Concordia Publishing House, 1955.

MACKINNON, JAMES. *Calvin and the Reformation.* London: Longmans, Green, 1936.

Mennonite Encyclopaedia: A Comprehensive Reference Work on the Anabaptist-Mennonite Movement. 4 vols. Edited by Harold S. Bender *et al.,* Scottdale, Pa.: Mennonite Publishing House, 1955–1959.

MURRAY, ROBERT H. *Erasmus and Luther: Their Attitude to Toleration.* London: Society for Promoting Christian Knowledge, 1920.

MURRAY, ROBERT H. *The Political Consequences of the Reformation: Studies in Sixteenth Century Political Thought.* London: E. Benn, 1926.

PREUS, HERMAN A. *The Communion of Saints: A Study of the Origin and Development of Luther's Doctrine of the Church.* Minneapolis: Augsburg Publishing House, 1948.

SCHAPIRO, JACOB SALWYN. *Social Reform and the Reformation.* New York: Columbia University Press, 1909.

SMITH, PRESERVED. *The Age of the Reformation.* New York: Holt, 1920.

STEPHENSON, GEORGE M. *The Conservative Character of Martin Luther.* Philadelphia: United Lutheran Publishing House, 1921.

VOLLMER, PHILIP. *John Calvin: Theologian, Preacher, Educator, Statesman.* Philadelphia: Heidelberg Press, 1909.

WALKER, WILLISTON. *John Calvin.* New York: Putnam, 1906.

WARING, LUTHER HESS. *The Political Theories of Martin Luther.* New York: Putnam, 1910.

WILLIAMS, GEORGE H. AND ANGEL M. MERGAL. *Spiritual and Anabaptist Writers: Documents Illustrative of the Radical Reformation.* London: S. C. M. Press, 1957.

WOLLIN, SHELDON S. "Politics and Religion: Luther's Simplistic Imperative," *American Political Science Review* 50 (1956), 24–42.

ZWEIG, STEFAN. *The Right to Heresy: Sastellio Against Calvin.* New York: Viking Press, 1936.

18. *The Secular State, Sovereignty, and the Right of Resistance*

ALLEN, J. W. *A History of Political Thought in the Sixteenth Century.* 2nd ed. London: Methuen, 1941.

ARMSTRONG, E. "The Political Theory of the Huguenots." *English Historical Review* 4 (1889), 13–40.

BAIRD, H. M. *History of the Rise of the Huguenots in France.* Vols. 1 and 2. New York: Scribner's, 1879.

CHURCH, W. F. *Constitutional Thought in Sixteenth Century France.* Cambridge, Mass.: Harvard University Press, 1941.

FIGGIS, J. N. *The Theory of the Divine Right of Kings.* Cambridge: Cambridge University Press, 1896.

GIERKE, OTTO. *Natural Law and the Theory of Society, 1500–1800.* Ernest Barker, trans. Boston: Beacon Press, 1958.

HEARNSHAW, F. J. C. *The Social and Political Ideas of Some Great Thinkers of the Renaissance and the Reformation.* London: Harrap, 1925.

HUDSON, W. "Democratic Freedom and Religious Faith in the Reformed Tradition." *Church History,* September 1949, 177–194.

MERCIER, C. "*Les théories politiques des Calvinistes en France au cours des guerres de religion.*" *Bulletin de la société de l'histoire du protestantisme français* 83 (1934), 225–260; 381–415.

MESNARD, P. *L'essor de la philosophie politique en France au seizième siècle.* Paris: Boivin, 1936.

NEALE, J. E. *The Age of Catherine de Medici.* New York: J. Cape, 1943.

Political Works of James I. Edited by C. H. McIlwain. Cambridge: Harvard University Press, 1918.

Politics of Johannes Althusius. Frederick S. Carney, trans. London: Eyre and Spottiswoode, 1965.

SALUTATI, C. *De Tyranno.* Ephraim Emerton, trans. In *Humanism and Tyranny: Studies in the Italian Trecento.* Cambridge, Mass.: Harvard University Press, 1925.

STEEHOLM, CLARA AND HARDY STEEHOLM. *James I of England.* New York: Covici-Friede, 1938.

TILLEY, A. A. *The French Wars of Religion.* London: Society for Promoting Christian Knowledge, 1919.

TROELTSCH, ERNST. *The Social Teachings of the Christian Churches.* New York: Macmillan, 1931.

WILLON, DAVID H. *King James VI and I.* London: Jonathan Cape, 1963.

19. *The New Science and the Contract: Thomas Hobbes*

BALZ, ALBERT G. *Idea and Essence in the Philosophies of Hobbes and Spinoza.* New York: Columbia University Press, 1918.

BIDNEY, DAVID. *The Psychology and Ethics of Spinoza.* New Haven: Yale University Press, 1940.

BROWN, J. M. "A Note on Professor Oakeshott's Introduction to the Leviathan." *Political Studies* 1 (1953), 53–64.

BROWN, STUART M. "Hobbes: The Taylor Thesis." *Philosophical Review* 68 (1959), 303–323.

CATLIN, G. E. G. *Thomas Hobbes as Philosopher, Publicist, and Man of Letters.* Oxford: Clarendon, 1922.

DUFF, ROBERT. *Spinoza's Political and Ethical Philosophy.* Glasgow: J. Maclehose & Sons, 1903.

GOOCH, G. P. *Hobbes.* Proceedings of the British Academy, vol. 15. London: British Academy, 1939.

GOUGH, J. W. *The Social Contract.* London: Oxford University Press, 1957.

GRAHAM, WILLIAM. *English Political Philosophy from Hobbes to Maine.* London: E. Arnold, 1899.

JAMES, CHARLES W. *Chief Justice Coke.* New York: Scribner's, 1929.

KROOK, DOROTHEA. "Mr. Brown's Note Annotated." *Political Studies* 1 (1953), 216–227.

LAIRD, JOHN. *Hobbes.* London: E. Bern, 1934.

MCKEON, RICHARD P. *The Philosophy of Spinoza: The Unity of his Thought.* New York: Longmans, Green, 1928.

MINTZ, S. I. *The Hunting of Leviathan.* Cambridge: Cambridge University Press, 1960.

OLIVER, PETER. *Saints of Chaos.* New York: W. F. Payson, 1934.

PENNOCK, J. ROLAND. "Hobbes's Confusing Clarity: The Case of Liberty." *American Political Science Review* 54 (1960), 428–436.

PETERS, RICHARD. *Hobbes.* London: Penquin, 1956.

STEPHEN, LESLIE. *Hobbes.* New York Macmillan, 1904.

TAYLOR, A. E. "The Ethical Doctrine of Hobbes." *Philosophy* 13 (1938), 406–424.

WOODBRIDGE, F. J. E. *The Philosophy of Hobbes.* Minneapolis: H. W. Wilson, 1903.

20. *The Quest for a Commonweal: Utopianism, Radical Democracy, and Eschatology*

AMES, RUSSELL. *Citizen Thomas More and His Utopia.* Princeton: Princeton University Press, 1949.

BACON, FRANCIS. *New Atlantis.* Oxford: Clarendon Press, 1915.

BERNERI, MARIE LOUISE. *Journey Through Utopia.* London: Routledge & Paul, 1950.

BERNSTEIN, EDWARD. *Cromwell and Communism.* London: Allen & Unwin, 1930.

CHAMBERS, RAYMOND W. *Thomas More.* London: J. Cape, 1935.

FOX, GEORGE. *Journal.* 2 vols. London: Friends Bookshop, 1902.

GOOCH, G. P. *English Democratic Ideas in the Seventeenth Century.* Cambridge: Cambridge University Press, 1927.

HARRINGTON, JAMES. *The Commonwealth of Oceana.* London: G. Routledge & Sons, 1887.

HARRINGTON, JAMES. *The Art of Law-giving.* London: H. Fletcher, 1659.

HERTZLER, J. O. *The History of Utopian Thought.* New York: Macmillan, 1926.

HOLORENSHAW, HENRY. *The Levellers and the English Revolution.* London: Gollancz, 1939.

HOOKER, RICHARD. *The Laws of Ecclesiastical Polity.* London: J. M. Dent, 1925.

The Leveller Tracts (1647–1653). Edited by William Haller and Godfrey Davies. New York: Columbia University Press, 1944.

MILTON, JOHN. *Areopagitica.* New York: Macmillan, 1927.

MORGAN, ARTHUR E. *Nowhere Was Somewhere: How History Makes Utopias and How Utopias Make History.* Chapel Hill: University of North Carolina Press, 1946.

PEASE, THEODORE C. *The Leveller Movement.* Washington: American Historical Association, 1916.

PETEGORSKY, DAVID. *Left-Wing Democracy in the English Civil War.* London: V. Gollancz, 1940.

ROSS WILLIAMSON, HUGH. *John Hampden: A Life.* London: Hodder & Stoughton, 1933.

SAURAT, DENIS. *Milton: Man and Thinker.* New York: Dial Press, 1925.

21. *Toward the Eighteenth Century: Locke, the Contract, and Natural Rights*

BECKER, CARL L. *The Heavenly City of the Eighteenth-Century Philosophers.* New Haven: Yale University Press, 1932.

BERLIN, ISAIAH. "Hobbes, Locke and Professor Macpherson." *Political Quarterly* 35 (1964), 444–468.

BROGAN, A. P. "John Locke and Utilitarianism." *Ethics* 69 (1959), 79–93.

BUCHDAHL, GERD. *The Image of Newton and Locke in the Age of Reason.* London and New York: Sheed and Ward, 1961.

BURY, J. B. *The Idea of Progress: An Inquiry Into Its Origin and Growth.* New York: Dover Publications, 1955.

CASSIRER, ERNST. *The Philosophy of the Enlightenment.* Princeton: Princeton University Press, 1951.

CRANSTON, MAURICE. *John Locke.* London: Verry, 1957.

GODWIN, WILLIAM. *Political Justice.* London: G. G. J. and J. Robinson, 1793.
GOUGH, JOHN W. *John Locke's Political Philosophy.* Oxford: Clarendon, 1950.
HAZARD, PAUL. *European Thought in the Eighteenth Century.* J. Lewis May, trans. New Haven: Yale University Press, 1954.
HEFELBOWER, SAMUEL G. *The Relation of John Locke to English Deism.* Chicago: University of Chicago Press, 1918.
JAMES, DAVID G. *Life of Reason: Hobbes, Locke, Bolingbroke.* New York: Longmans, Green, 1949.
LAMPRECHT, STERLING P. *The Moral and Political Philosophy of John Locke.* New York: Russell and Russell, 1962.
LARKIN, PASCHAL. *Property in the Eighteenth Century with Special Reference to England and Locke.* London: Longmans, Green, 1930.
MCLACHLAN, HERBERT. *The Religious Opinions of Milton, Locke, and Newton.* Manchester: Manchester University Press, 1941.
MACLEAN, KENNETH. *John Locke and English Literature of the Eighteenth Century.* New York: Russell and Russell, 1962.
MOULDS, H. H. "John Locke and Rugged Individualism." *American Journal of Economics* 24 (1965), 97–109.
POLLOCK, SIR FREDERICK. *Locke's Theory of the State.* London, 1904.
RITCHIE, DAVID G. *Natural Rights.* London: Swan Sonnenschein, 1903.
SALVADORI, M., ED. Locke and Liberty. London: Pall Mall Press, 1960.
SELIGER, M. "Locke's Theory of Revolutionary Action." *Western Political Quarterly* 16 (1963), 548–568.
STRAUSS, LEO. "Locke's Doctrine of Natural Law." *American Political Science Review* 52 (1958), 490–501.
THOMPSON, C. "John Locke and New England Transcendentalism." *New England Quarterly* 35 (1962), 435–457.
YOLTON, J. W. "Locke and the Seventeenth-Century Logic of Ideas." *Journal of the History of Ideas* 16 (1955), 431–452.
WISHY, B. "John Locke and the Spirit of '76." *Political Science Quarterly* 73 (1958), 414–425.
WOODCOCK, GEORGE. *William Godwin: A Biographical Study.* London: Porcupine Press, 1946.

22. *The Revival of Feeling: Rousseau, Nature, and the Civil State*

BECKER, CARL. *The Heavenly City of the Eighteenth Century Philosophers.* New Haven: Yale University Press, 1936.
BOYD, WILLIAM. *The Educational Theory of Jean-Jacques Rousseau.* London: Longmans, Green, 1911.
CASSIRER, ERNST. *The Philosophy of the Enlightenment.* Princeton: Princeton University Press, 1951.
CASSIRER, ERNST. *Rousseau, Kant, Goethe.* Princeton: Princeton University Press, 1945.
CHARPENTIER, JOHN. *Rousseau, the Child of Nature.* New York: Dial Press, 1931.
COBBAN, ALFRED. *Rousseau and the Modern State.* London: Allen & Unwin, 1934.
CUENDET, W. *La Philosophie Religieuse de Rousseau.* Geneva: A. Jullien, 1913.
DAVIDSON, THOMAS. *Rousseau and Education According to Nature.* New York: Scribner's, 1902.
FAGUET, E. *La Politique Comparée de Montesquieu, Rousseau, et Voltaire.* Paris: Societe Francaise d'Imprimerie et de Librairie, 1902.
FAGUET, E. *Rousseau Penseur.* Paris: Societe Francaise d'Imprimerie et de Librairie, 1912.
FAGUET, E. *Vie de Rousseau.* Paris: Societe Francaise d'Imprimerie et de Librairie, 1911.
HAZARD, PAUL. *European Thought in the Eighteenth Century.* J. Lewis May, trans. New Haven: Yale University Press, 1954.
HENDEL, CHARLES W. *Jean-Jacques Rousseau, Moralist.* London and New York: Oxford University Press, 1934.
HÖFFDING, HAROLD. *Jean-Jacques Rousseau and His Philosophy.* London: Oxford University Press, 1930.
HUDSON, W. H. *Rousseau and Naturalism in Life and Thought.* New York: Scribner's, 1903.
JOSEPHSON, MATTHEW. *Jean-Jacques Rousseau.* New York: Harcourt, Brace, 1932.
LINCOLN, CHARLES H. "Rousseau and the French Revolution." *Annals of the American Academy of Political and Social Science* 10 (1897), 54–72.
MAYO, HENRY B. *An Introduction to Democratic Theory.* New York: Oxford University Press, 1960.
MOWAT, ROBERT B. *Jean-Jacques Rousseau.* Bristol: Arrowsmith, 1938.
OSBORN, ANNIE MARION. *Rousseau and Burke: A Study of the Idea of Liberty in Eighteenth Century Political Thought.* New York: Oxford University Press, 1940.
PEYRE, HENRI MAURICE. "The Influence of Eighteenth Century Ideas on the French Revolution." *Journal of the History of Ideas* 10 (1949), pp. 63–87.
ROLLAND, ROMAIN, ANDRÉ MAUROIS, AND EDOUARD HERRIOT. *French Thought in the Eighteenth Century.* London: Cassell, 1953.
STEPHEN, LESLIE. *English Thought in the Eighteenth Century.* 2 vols. New York: Putnam, 1876.
TUVESON, ERNEST LEE. *Millennium and Utopia: A Study of the Background of the Idea of Progess.* Berkeley: University of California Press, 1949.
VAUGHAN, C. E. *Studies in the History of Political Philosophy Before and After Rousseau.* Edited by A. G. Little. London: Longmans, Green, 1925.
WILLIAMS, ALFRED. *The Concept of Equality in the Writings of Rousseau, Bentham, and Kant.* New York: Columbia University Press, 1907.
WRIGHT, ERNEST H. *The Meaning of Rousseau.* London: Oxford University Press, 1929.

23. *Empiricism and the Onslaught on Social Contract: Hume*

CORSI, MARIO. *Natura e società in David Hume.* Florence: La Nuova Italia, 1953.
DELEUZE, GILLES. *Empirisme et subjectivité; essai-*

sur la nature humaine selon Hume. Paris: Presses universitaires de France, 1953.
HEDENIUS, INGEMAR. *Studies in Hume's Ethics*. Uppsala and Stockholm: Almqvist and Wiksells Boktryckeri, 1937.
HUTCHESON, FRANCIS. *A Short Introduction to Moral Philosophy*. Glasgow: R. Foulis, 1747.
KYDD, RACHEL M. *Reason and Conduct in Hume's Treatise*. London: Oxford University Press, 1946.
LASKI, HAROLD J. *Political Thought in England*. London: Oxford University Press, 1920.
MASSNER, ERNEST C. *The Forgotten Hume*. New York: Columbia University Press, 1943.
PRICE, HENRY H. *Hume's Theory of the External World*. Oxford: Clarendon, 1940.
RITCHIE, DAVID G. *Natural Rights*. London: Swan Sonnenschein, 1903.
STEPHEN, LESLIE. *English Thought in the Eighteenth Century*. 2 vols. New York: Putnam, 1876.
VAUGHAN, C. E. *Studies in the History of Political Philosophy Before and After Rousseau*. Edited by *A. G. Little*. London: Longmans, Green, 1925.
VLACHOS, GEORGES. *Essai sur la politique de Hume*. Athènes: Institut Francais, 1955.

part IV

MAJOR CURRENTS SINCE 1789: REVOLUTION, THE NATION-STATE, AND INDUSTRIALISM

We may think of political thought since Hume as responding essentially to three major issues: the ideology of the French Revolution; the problem of the nation-state, particularly as its citizenship and participation bases are broadened with the development of democratic thought in its several versions; and the question of industrialism. Every major current of modern political thought makes some effort to grapple with these interrelated challenges and in the process finds itself debating, criticizing, or applauding the other currents. From this point of view, the period since the French Revolution can be regarded as a single unit in which discussion, while inevitably related to the dialectic of previous centuries, is nevertheless peculiarly concerned about the three characteristically modern phenomena.

It has often been said that one cannot remain neutral about the French Revolution, and the history of thought since 1789 seems to support this thesis. The ideology of the Revolution symbolized for many a new era in the history of mankind. For others, however, it represented an undermining of all the principles upon which any order must be built. The great trinity of liberty, equality, and fraternity was not, of course, self-interpreting, and much of modern thought has been devoted to drawing out its implications and suggesting limitations and qualifications. The Revolution, moreover, became the great inspiration for other modern attempts to change social structures fundamentally, as with the western European upheaval of 1848, the Russian social earthquakes of 1905 and 1917, and the Spanish affair of the 1930s. For some, the Revolution was aborted and merely middle class and needed to be completed by other violent acts in the name of those outside the middle classes; for others, the violence of the Revolution betrayed it and raised the question whether violence could ever be a vehicle for fundamental change.

The national state, which emerged as the basic unit of political life with the decline of medieval institutions, became, to an even greater degree than in the previous period, the center of men's loyalties after the French Revolution. With the extension of the franchise in the nineteenth and twentieth centuries, larger and larger numbers of men and women began to identify with the national state and its mythology. For many, nationalism became a kind of religion, somewhat like the civic cult suggested by Rousseau; and it was in the name of democratic nationalism that countless civil and foreign wars were fought in the nineteenth and twentieth centuries. The attack on the nation-state, too, became significant with the development of ideas which saw the class as more basic than the state or which argued for some kind of a world synthesis. Industrialism, with its vast international ties, posed the question whether the national state could possibly be reconciled with the world economic interdependence so intimately associated with rapid technological change.

Finally, the many phenomena connected with imperatives of industrialism—particularly in its capitalist guise—dramatically portrayed issues as old as political thought itself. The ancient world, as we have pointed out, was acutely aware of what happened when man moved from pastoral and agrarian forms of economic life to the more complex interdependence of commercial and urbanized societies; in Book II of the *Republic*, it will be remembered, Plato had graphically posed the problem that economic development at fever heat created for any society which sought to keep purely economic values subordinate to social and spiritual goals. In general, ancient and medieval thinkers sought to limit economic development, lest its imperatives completely engulf and dominate men, destroying the possibility of human community in the process.

What was a nightmare for the ancients became for modern man an existential reality: with the development of complex technology, ties to traditional communities were disrupted, alienation of men from one another and from their creations developed, and a widespread belief grew up that technological change was in itself a good. Technological and industrial growth, to be sure, vastly increased the material goods of life; but it also challenged man's capacity to subordinate material to nonmaterial values. Throughout the nineteenth and twentieth centuries, change in itself often came to be regarded as desirable; process and flux were central to many systems of thought; and traditional positions which sought to gain a measure of certainty in social life were often viewed with suspicion. The acceptance of industrialism involved a vastly more complex division of labor and a correspondingly great development of bureaucracy to perform the tasks of coordination. Ironically enough, while men paid increasing lip-service to democracy, their very acceptance of industrialism and the centrality of technology seemed to make its achievement much less likely.

How did modern political thinkers respond to the central questions posed by the French Revolution, the problem of the national state, and the ubiquity of industrialism with its imperatives?

One of the earliest responses took the form of a reexamination of the individualist premises so central from Machiavelli to the latter quarter of the eighteenth century. G. W. F. Hegel, whose views were profoundly affected by the Revolution, by Rousseau, by Kantian philosophy, and by classical Greek ideas, sought in his organicist political theory to come to grips with the spirit of the Revolution, the problems of social change and interdependence, and the question of the national state. Hegel initiated intellectually that central tendency of nineteenth-century thought which saw collective life as forever in flux and human history as progressively enlarging liberty. Later nineteenth-century theories of biological evolution would fall into a similar pattern insofar as they were to be applied to social and political life. Both Hegelianism and evolutionary doctrine tended to find their models in organic analogies rather than in the mechanical similitudes so characteristic of the seventeenth and eighteenth centuries.

It was out of Hegelianism that Marxism emerged. But just as Hegel's philosophy was in part a response to and in part a critique of Lockean or Locke-like individualism, so was Marxism rooted not merely in the Kantian-Hegelian stream of thought but also in the history of British economic theory. Like nineteenth-century liberalism, Marxism sought to examine the French Revolution critically and, even more, to suggest the impact which industrial capitalism would have on man's effort consciously to control his collective affairs. In a sense, like Rousseauistic thought, Marxism tried to answer the question of how one could remain free and still belong to others. It also carried on the long tradition of viewing experience as a triadic pattern—from prehistory, to history, to a posthistorical epoch. In developing a class interpretation of politics, Marxism tended to negate the nation-state orientation of Hegelianism.

Meanwhile, the discussion of modern culture carried on by the Hegelian-Marxist thrust had been challenged. Liberalism, seeking to build on the originally individualist Utilitarianism of the early nineteenth century and, in part, on persisting contract ideas in the United States, endeavored to preserve individual liberty as the central value. In considerable measure, by contrast with Hegelian thought, its early models stayed mechanistic (although there was also a "liberal" interpretation of Hegel). At first not particularly democratic, by the middle of the nineteenth century it was increasingly annexing democratic to liberal ideas. In the beginning, the liberal tradition sought to preserve for economic life a large measure of autonomy; later, however, the new liberalism which emerged triumphant after the eighties viewed much state regulation as an enlargement of liberty. Like Hegelian and Marxist thought, both the old and the new liberalism tended to think of technology and industrialism as basically progressive in nature—contributing, that is, to the enlargement of freedom. The historian of thought must be impressed by the ways in which Hegelian organicism helped shape the new liberalism—an excellent example of the never-ending dialogue going on between and among the currents of modern political thought.

While modern political thought has basically tended to think of all change as "progressive" and therefore desirable, there has been an important stream questioning this proposition. The history of modern conservatism, beginning with Edmund Burke in the late eighteenth century, has to some extent exemplified this dubiety about progress. Questioning a widespread belief that man can rationally control his collective affairs beyond rather narrow limits, a central thrust of conservatism has been to rely upon tradition, not reason and speculation, as the guide to political action and development. Conservative thought has been critical of the notion that politics is the key to human life; instead, it stresses permanent emotional bonds—hence it has been hostile to Utilitarian liberalism—and the solidarity supposedly developed in small groups. Like liberalism, however, conservative thought has itself undergone a change in emphasis: while in the beginning it sought to retain agrarian-type restrictions on economic life, its later stress was to limit state control of the economy.

Industrialization appeared to many thinkers to pose the question not of economic individualism versus collectivism but rather the issue of one form of collectivism versus another. The imperatives of interdependence and technology were such, it was maintained, that collective ownership and administration of material goods were inevitable. But what form should they take and for what ends should they be developed? Questions of this kind were often put by non-Marxist socialist thought. Marxism has been vague about the precise nature of a socialist and communist society, preferring to concentrate on process and political analysis. Non-Marxist socialism, from its beginnings in nineteenth-century utopian movements, has emphasized not merely explanation but also concrete goals. Like most modern thought, it was in part inspired by certain tendencies in the French Revolution but also had roots in the British and American empirical tradition and in religious perspectives. Akin to liberal thought in its stress on personal liberty, some versions of it moved in the direction of anarchism and antistatist thought. Like Marxism, it was internationalist and cosmopolitan in principle, but when its exponents actually gained political power, it tended to take on a nationalist coloration.

The very imperatives which industrialism and the national state apparently set up—such as domination by technology, expansion of national state activity, bureaucracy, and the persistence of international violence—emphasized the difficult question of whether political authority could be justified at all. Unlike other streams of modern political thought, anarchism answered in the negative; and antistatism tended to move in the same direction, although with greater hesitancy and ambiguity. In both anarchism and antistatism, too, there has been a very strong strain of pacifism and a tendency to identify violence with centralized state institutions. But both anarchism and antistatism are loosely defined terms and can be understood only in the context of specific currents of thought. Thus, one tendency seeks to reconcile complex industrial society with anarchist and antistatist principles; while another denies emphatically that this is possible.

But the very complexities which have puzzled all modern political thinkers have led some to despair. How, they asked, can man cut through the labyrinthian paths of industrialism? How can one really espouse an ideology of equality when inequality appears to be dictated by social necessity? How, indeed, can one hope to discover answers by sheer intellect? In view, too, of twentieth-century insights into human personality, such as the Freudian, is it not evident that politics itself—in the sense of an attempt rationally and consciously to control collective affairs—is an impossibility? Questions of this kind have been asked by many schools of thought; but Fascism and National Socialism probably epitomized best all answers which either negate reason or hold it in low esteem. In the twentieth century doctrines of blood and soil, of the omnicompetent tribal-type society, and of racism, reason itself was repudiated and a kind of ethical nihilism exalted. The mainstream of Western political thought was denied and Plato's rational soul, which had played such an important role throughout history, was trampled into the dust. But students of modern political thought should always remember that National Socialism and Fascism were simply extreme epitomizations of many ubiquitous currents in all modern politics—racism, for example, the naive belief in violence as an instrument for social change, and the ubiquitous idolization of the nation-state.

chapter 24

Hegel, Organicism, and Modern Political Thought

In earlier chapters we have seen how Hume developed a thorough-going critique of contract doctrines[1] and have also suggested that even in Rousseau, who ostensibly bases his political philosophy on contract, the necessity for it is dubious.[2] Later, when we touch on Edmund Burke, we shall point out that while a certain amount of lipservice is paid to the ubiquitous contractualism, history and tradition loom so large that contract is virtually wiped out.[3] And we shall see that the whole philosophy of Utilitarianism had as one of its incidental foundations a denial of anything smacking of contractualism.[4]

Meanwhile, however, the history of German political speculation was to introduce a fresh factor into the stream of Western thought. It shared the critical attitude to contract of men like Hume while at the same time building on certain elements of Rousseau. But perhaps its central mission was to develop a revived respect for community as something more than an artifact: Here, obviously, it again had affinities with Rousseau. Basically, however, German idealism represented, at its apex, an endeavor to turn back the stream of individualism which had persisted, in varying forms, since the declining period of the Middle Ages. Whereas the seventeenth century, reflecting the progress of this individualism, had asked how one could account for the community, German idealism will in effect turn the question around and ask itself how one can explain the experience of individuality. In putting this query, it will try to give new meaning to the vexing word freedom and will provide yet another answer to the problem which puzzled

1. Chapter 23.
2. Chapter 22.
3. Chapter 27.
4. See Chapter 26.

Rousseau: How the individual could at one and the same time be free and yet belong. Questions like this are among the central issues which concerned Hegel, to whom this chapter is devoted.

The Development of Hegel's Outlook

Hegel's life may be divided into four phases.[5] The first extends from his birth in 1770 to the end of his young manhood in 1800. The second continues until 1806, when his career is interrupted by the Napoleonic wars. In the third, which ends in 1818, we can think of him as developing those modes of thought which later generations are to term typically Hegelian. Finally, from 1818 to his death in 1831 is the period within which he builds up his enormous influence at the University of Berlin.

There was nothing particularly remarkable about Hegel's young manhood. Born into the middle-class home of a Swabian government official, he must have been subjected to the typical influences of the time. Germany, of course, was still divided into many political entities and the spirit of modern German nationalism had not yet been born. German thought during this epoch—and, indeed, down to the period of the Napoleonic wars—was still characterized by a rather cosmopolitan spirit and was yet to be influenced by the romanticism which we associate with it in the second decade of the nineteenth century. However, we should never forget that in his late teens, Hegel read about the great events in France and there is evidence that these were not without influence on his subsequent development.

From 1788 to 1793, Hegel studied at the theological seminary of the University of Tübingen and here for the first time he seems to have been caught up in the budding Romantic movement. F. W. J. Schelling,[6] another very influential German thinker in the early nineteenth century, was also a student at Tübingen, where he apparently began that intellectual pilgrimage which was to lead to his transcendentalist philosophy.

Overlapping his study at Tübingen, Hegel was a tutor in Berne, Switzerland from 1791 to 1796 and in the latter year became a teacher at Frankfort, where he remained until 1800. In this period, apparently, a reaction set in against his theological training—not a surprising development in view of Hegel's rapidly developing critical intelligence. In philosophy, of course, the overshadowing influence in the Germany of the time was the thought of Immanual Kant and Hegel participated for a time in the idolization accorded Kant by most young German intellectuals. Certainly no name in Western philosophy stood higher than that of Kant and for Hegel not to have been shaped by his mighty system would have been astounding.

In 1801, the second phase of his life began, when he accepted a professorship at the University of Jena. Now, seemingly for the first time, he entered into a thorough study of political questions. Hitherto, he had been concerned with general philosophy and with religion. During the Jena epoch, however, he was increasingly fascinated by the study of constitutional law and gave close attention to German legal institutions. At the same time, a key word of his political philosophy—consciousness (*bewusstsein*)—came more and more to occupy a central place in his thinking. In reacting to the eighteenth-century empiricism of men like Hume and against the sensationalism so central in the orientation of many thinkers after Locke, he began to attach increasing significance to spirit (*geist*) and the ways in which spirit becomes conscious of itself. Just before the end of this second period of his life, he finished writing one of his greatest works, *The Phenomenology of the Spirit*, in which he developed the consciousness theme in all of its ramifications.

The invasion of Napoleon in 1806 brought an end to Hegel's labors at the University of Jena. Escaping to Bavaria, he edited a newspaper for about two years before becoming Rector of the Latin School (high school) at Nürnberg in 1808. Now began his reflections on what was to become his celebrated *Logic*, which constitutes so central a part of his whole attitude to law and politics.

Meanwhile, the spirit of early nineteenth-century German nationalism had been developing, largely under the influence of the Napoleonic invasions. But nationalism as we know it in the modern world was born only after great travail. Even when it was learned that Napoleon was appearing with his armies, for example, Goethe's response was to ask how he could find the French ruler: Napoleon was so remarkable a man, the poet said, that he had always desired to meet him. This kind of attitude was hardly compatible with a nationalistic outlook. But when J. G. Fichte gave his

Addresses to the German Nation and the University of Berlin was founded (1810), we may say that the old cosmopolitanism was dying.[7] The intellectual, military, and political factors which were to lead to German unification and particularism were now present.

Earlier, as we have seen, Hegel had come under the influence of the late eighteenth-century Romantic movement and his reading of Rousseau had done nothing to discourage him. This earlier romanticism was now combined, in his mind, with a growing consciousness of German nationality which he could hardly help but share with men of his generation. Everywhere a renewed interest in German history, literature, law, and political institutions was arising; and scholars were asking themselves whether there were not characteristically German ways of looking at social and political institutions.[8]

It is not surprising that in this atmosphere he should have worked out political views which tended to make their center the development of consciousness through the national state. As his philosophy of history took shape, he thought that he could discern in human affairs a pattern which made freedom the central theme of man's spirit. In the years from 1805 onward, in fact, he was seeking a synthesis which would fit a quest for the "rights of man and the citizen" so emphasized by the French Revolution into his growing awareness of historical and cultural factors as vital in human experience.

Meanwhile, Hegel had been awarded a professorship at the University of Heidelberg. This was in 1816. In 1818, he was called to the newly founded but already influential University of Berlin. At Berlin, during the last phase of his life, he became one of the most prominent voices in the shaping of the new Germany. Long before his death in 1831, students were already beginning to quarrel about what he really meant; and only a few years after his death, the young Marx was to come under the spell of his teaching.

We can perhaps best understand his place in the history of political thought if we look first at the basis of his politics in the phenomenology of spirit and the logic, then turn to his theories of right and the state, and after that endeavor to understand his philosophy of history. We conclude by suggesting his very great impact on nineteenth and twentieth-century thought and evaluating certain major criticisms of his system.[9]

Phenomenology and Logic

The key to Hegel's philosophy of man and politics lies in his so-called "logic" and his "phenomenology of spirit." The former, as it has been observed, is really a "logic of ontology" (or being) and the latter an attempt to

5. For the biography of Hegel consult André Cresson, *Hegel, sa vie, son oeuvre, avec un exposé de sa philosophie,* Paris: Presses universitaires de France, 1949.
6. Schelling (1775–1854) came to be known as a synthesizer of such apparently diverse systems as those of Kant, Spinoza, Leibniz, Fichte, Bruno, and Plotinus. Like many nineteenth-century thinkers, including Hegel, he developed a doctrine of evolution. There was, he thought, a continuous process of evolution in both inorganic and organic worlds. He had a profound influence on Goethe and many other early-nineteenth-century thinkers.
7. Johann Gottlieb Fichte (1762–1814), like Hegel, was immensely influenced by the Kantian system; but unlike Kant, he became an ardent German nationalist. In some respects, his *Closed Commercial State* is an anticipation of later utopian socialist thought, but within the context of a nationalist framework.
8. Thus Friedrich Karl von Savigny (1779–1861), who became professor of jurisprudence at the University of Marburg in 1803 and professor of jurisprudence at the University of Berlin in 1810, was very influential in developing the historical approach to jurisprudence. Associated with the romantic school of thought, Savigny helped shape the mind of Jacob Grimm (1785–1863) who, with his brother Wilhelm Carl (1786–1859), did so much for the science of philology, the study of mythology, and the revival of interest in German history. The brothers Grimm also published *Kinder- und Hausmärchen*—usually known in English as *Grimm's Fairy Tales*—which, by making available traditional folk and fairy tales, did much to stimulate investigation of the "folk mind." It is not without significance that many of the fairy tales are in effect political parables.
9. The literature on Hegel and Hegelianism is enormous. Here we might mention as particularly relevant Jakob Hommes, *Krise der Freiheit: Hegel, Marx, Heidegger,* Regensburg: F. Pustet, 1958; Sidney Hook, *From Hegel to Marx,* London: Victor Gollancz, 1936; Robert Mackintosh, *Hegel and Hegelianism,* New York: Scribner's, 1903; Herbert Marcuse, *Reason and Revolution: Hegel and the Rise of Social Theory,* 2nd ed., New York: Humanities Press, 1954; Franz Rosenzweig, *Hegel and der Staat,* Munich and Berlin: R. Oldenbourg, 1920; and Eric Weil, *Hegel et l'etat,* Paris: J. Vrin, 1950.

describe the development of man's consciousness (*bewusstsein*) of nature and himself. The logic purports to tell us how we think in general, while the phenomenology is the "science of the experience of consciousness." In the former, we get the pattern of thought about existence, in the latter an analysis of man's experience of the natural world about him and of his relationship to himself and to his fellows. Throughout, it will be noted that Hegel, as idealist, thinks of the central factor in the shaping of man's individual and collective life as the development of reason.[10]

In the logic, Hegel appears to maintain a proposition which violates previous conceptions of the word, in that he suggests that any given truth also contains its negation or opposite. Within the dialectic of thought—and "dialectic," of course, reminds us of Plato—there is a self-movement of the notion, in which every incomplete idea gets lost in a more complete one. Every assertion about the world has within it an implicit attack on the assertion; and what is implicit becomes explicit. The mind in its infantile stage begins by conceiving pure "being" (*sein*), a kind of empty absolute which is undifferentiated. It is the abstract category of immediateness, in which relationships and relativity are not yet present. At this level, the mind holds that every thing is an independent factor or substance.

But the very notion of being implies nonbeing, from which emerges the apprehension that in reality all is neither being nor nonbeing but rather a kind of union of the two, or "becoming." What appeared to be absolute turns out in the end to be simply a process of attaining more comprehensive levels of understanding.

Thus we see that the objective world—whose relation to the merely inner life had so disturbed the seventeenth and eighteenth centuries—is really also subjective: In the very process of vanishing, the initial assertion of objectivity is purified by our inner subjectivity which was latent in the original assertion. Our awareness of being is corrected by latent "not-beingness" so that the "idea" is truly "becomingness." Becoming thus is the more comprehensive idea in which both being and not-being are lost. It is this idea of becoming, then, which represents a kind of chemical compound of supposedly objective life with mere intellect and will. So soon as the mind thinks it has achieved a final understanding of the world, however, and thus actually attained being once more, the process is renewed and the new level of comprehension is seen to be merely an initiating factor leading to its negation, to what some students of Hegel have called a new synthesis, and thus to a repetition of the process.

The actual reality, therefore, according to Hegel, is neither being nor its opposite but rather the process of becoming and disappearing. The only absolute, we may interpret Hegel as saying, is the reality of no absolute—and here the reader will note more than an echo of the ancient Heraclitus. The recognition of this process by the mind constitutes its gradual consciousness not only of the external universe but also of its own internal world. It is this union of the external or objective with the internal or subjective in "becoming" or "process" which may be said to be the pattern that sums up human consciousness in all of its ramifications.

But the problem of tracing out this consciousness is a complicated one. In general, as thought moves through partial antinomies and contradictions, its awareness is enlarged. The awareness reflects movements both from the bottom upward and from the top downward. That is to say, the individual or subjective consciousness is expanded as it comprehends the lack of finality in its individuality; and the universal which is reflected in the so-called individual is itself developing along with the individual. In other terms, as the individual thinks dialectically he is reflecting the process going on in the universal spirit (*geist*) which transcends mere individuality.

The process is thus one whereby man becomes aware that the sharp gulf which, since the early modern period, thinkers had erected between the outer and inner worlds, is in reality nonexistent. The phenomenology of spirit treats of the process whereby the real unity of outer and inner develops. It shows, in other words, how the whole complex of institutions which constitutes the life of man permeates his alleged inner character and how, at higher and higher levels of awareness, he becomes conscious of the process itself. The history of man, of course, and the life of the state are integral parts of this process and, indeed, play central roles in the analysis of consciousness as a whole.

In general, the movement of spirit in the world begins with man's consciousness of things. Before, that is to say, he is aware of himself, the world appears to him simply one. It is undifferentiated. Presumably, this is the lowest level of consciousness—that which lacks the purification which will set in with its negation. Here modern psychologists would seem to agree with Hegel (if, indeed, the suggestion did not come from him originally) when they observe that the child is at first unaware of his own separateness from others. This is what we mean by absence of differentiation. But it is not only in children that this takes place: any new phenomenon tends to appear to all of us primarily as object until we later become aware of the so-called subjective or conceptual elements entering into our judgments of it. Our sense experiences seem to us certain. Thus Hegel does not deny that knowledge begins with experience even though he does reject the notion that all knowledge can be comprehended within sense experience. Sense experience, so to speak, constitutes, as with Plato, the occasion and the initiating factor in knowledge but it does not furnish all the ingredients.

As one might anticipate, the consciousness of things is followed by the differentiation of self from things. The very awareness of things with which we begin, in other words, has within it the germ of self-consciousness. Hence, at a primitive level (and thus Hegel is implicitly directing his attacks at much of the philosophy of the seventeenth and eighteenth centuries), we do in fact go through the phase of separating self from things. But consciousness does not, rightly analyzed, stop at this point.

For no sooner is consciousness of things opposed to consciousness of self than we begin to comprehend, however vaguely, the way in which the two are held together. This higher level of consciousness is reason. Through it, consciousness of things and consciousness of self are brought together.[11]

But reason is no sooner aware of itself than it sees that in it the whole life of the spirit is reflected. "When reason 'observes,' this pure unity of ego and existence, the unity of subjectivity and objectivity, of for-itself-ness and in-itself-ness—this unity is immanent, has the character of implicitness or of being; and consciousness of reason *finds itself*."[12]

It is at the level of spirit, of course, that we have reflected the institutions and attitudes of the moral and political orders. Consciousness here, as a matter of fact, is awareness of what Hegel calls concrete ethical actuality or *wirklichkeit*. The whole complex of the ethical world or of social righteousness (*sittlichkeit*) is the body of established institutions, mores, and folkways into which the individual is born and through which the universal spirit impresses itself on the individual consciousness. But here objective universality meets its contradiction in the interests which groups and individuals also pursue and which conflict with that aspect of the process that is seeking general stability. Another way of putting it, in general, is to say that the ethical world is reflected both in the customs and conventions which bind men together in community and in the individuality which as one moment of ethical consciousness pursues what it takes to be its own ends. As consciousness develops, however, we are increasingly aware that the universal and the individual are really one.

It is at this level of *sittlichkeit* that Hegel's detailed analysis of institutions occurs and to it we shall return in the next section. Suffice it to note here that the antinomies and contradictions which he discerns in his *logic* are repeated as he seeks to show the unity of objective and subjective in the world of human conduct. The dialectic which is integral to thought is literally reflected in behavior, which is the mirror of thought.

It is the state, of course, which Hegel thinks of as the highest embodiment in the concrete of the union of universal and individual in the ethical world. For the state pushes man's consciousness up yet another notch in the sense that it is the most complex level of collective self-consciousness. Just what this implies in greater detail we shall again note in the section which follows.

10. Hegel is not, of course, the only early-nineteenth-century philosopher to make consciousness and its development the center of his thought. J. G. Fichte, for example, thinks of evil essentially as sloth, lack of awareness, refusal to reflect, and failure to act in accordance with ideals. Idealism as a philosophy—whether in Hegel or in Fichte and others—concentrates its attention on the development of awareness, which is regarded as the basic factor in human history.
11. *Phenomenology of the Spirit*, 2 vols., J. B. Baillie, trans., New York: Macmillan, 1910, p. 277.
12. *Ibid.*, p. 457.

Meanwhile, we should observe that beyond the level of spirit, as Hegel analyzes the phenomenology of the spirit, stands religion in its various guises. He develops a threefold classification: natural religion, religion as art, and revealed religion. It is not our main objective to work out all the implications of this categorization except again to emphasize that the dialectic pattern is at work here as well, partial insights evoking yet other partial perspectives which in turn give rise to more comprehensive understanding.

Finally, the realm of religion itself but mirrors absolute knowledge. At this very highest of the levels of consciousness, the self is aware that it is all existence. Philosophical knowledge, moreover, enables the self to understand the realm of the spirit. And spirit understood at this level returns to the beginning point of consciousness—sense experience. It has, in other words, as one might interpret Hegel, become so "knowledgeable" that it sees the initial sharp dichotomy between "sense" and "self" or objective and subjective as illusory.[13]

Having examined briefly the pattern ("logic of ontology") and the general account of consciousness which constitute the framework and context of Hegel's political theory, let us now turn to a closer examination of the theory itself.

Sittlichkeit: Consciousness and Context

The key to the theory, as we have suggested earlier, is the notion of *sittlichkeit,* or social righteousness. But before this level of consciousness is reached, Hegel suggests that there is an awareness of abstract right, which is negated by subjective morality. Let us note how they stand opposed to each other and yet reflect in their very opposition the search for a universal which will transcend both of them. In so doing, we should always remember that Hegel is attempting to analyze moral and political experience logically and not, at this point, to look at it in terms of historical development. We should remind ourselves again that the problem before him is the apparent conflict between man as belonging and man as an individual and between man in his relation to the world outside himself and man as subjectively conscious. The problem is similar to that which Rousseau set for himself but Hegel's account is a much subtler, more detailed, and (for all his difficulties with language) a clearer analysis than that which the French thinker offered.[14]

It will be remembered that in his outline of phenomenology, Hegel suggested that we first experience things and then become aware of ourselves as subjective beings. Following out this pattern, we first experience right as abstract and only then do we become aware of the sphere of morality, in which right is viewed from the viewpoint of subjective duty and conscience. In both moments, of course we are only dimly aware that the experiences through which we are moving reflect a yet higher level, which will be that of the ethical world or social righteousness.

In treating of abstract right, Hegel observes that at this level, the individual is pitted against the external world. He exerts his power to acquire material goods which will support him and that which he gains by his power is his. At this primitive point, in other words, there is something like Locke's mixing of labor with natural resources and the right attached to it.

But the right to material goods is purely the result of accident and depends on arbitrary wishes, fortuitous circumstances, and the particular talents of the individual involved. Here possession is arbitrary will. But the conception of "mine" arises only after we have relinquished the material goods acquired arbitrarily and regained them through agreement of others: thus the idea of contract is born. Hegel remarks that if the human race consisted of only one person, the very idea of property could not arise; from the beginning, therefore, property depends on contract and contract on property, and both depend on the mutual recognition by human beings of one another. It is out of the interaction of possession and contract that the consciousness of injustice and crime emerges.

However, Hegel emphasizes, the common will which arises from contract and mutual recognition of one another is still at a very primitive level. Common will should not be confused with universal will which springs from the nature of man as a rational being. In the universal will, nothing is arbitrary; whereas at the level of common will and contract, there is a type of agreement (based, perhaps, on a kind of balance of power) to respect the arbitrary or fortuitous gains of each.

But the fact that the common will foreshadows, and indeed partly expresses, the universal will, does not mean that it cannot be objectively wrong. Indeed, the very fact that the idea of the particular will based on accident and caprice can exist means not only that it can reflect right (in a universal sense) but that it can be distorted into wrong. At this level, indeed, right and wrong are both accidental.

Punishment on this plane can hardly be anything but vengeance or unreflecting retaliation. And unreflecting retaliation, Hegel goes on, will be met by counter vengeance: There is thus set up a cycle of violence and counter violence which seems to be endless. But the very idea that the cycle appears to continue forever leads to the thought of the opposite: namely, the possibility that punishment may be other than vengeful and that some kind of norm can be established which will be passionless. The thought which can imagine an alternative to vengeance takes us into the realm of morality, which, as we have seen, Hegel identifies with the subjective or inner experience of right.

Let us attempt to see more explicitly what he really means by morality. He suggests, first of all, that whereas abstract objective right arose as a result of caprice, morality implies a reflective subjective will which can itself change the external world. Hence arises the notion of purpose. But secondly, the very idea of purpose implies the conception of individual responsibility. So soon, however, as the will holds itself responsible, it is drawn into great difficulties, for the external world, which it hopes to change, is a complicated set of relationships which the will tries to affect. But changing these relationships at any point produces both calculable and incalculable consequences: The former, presumably, are intended by the will; the latter are not. When the subjective will sees this, the conception of responsibility limited by knowledge arises. Hence the theory of responsibility comes to hold that I am responsible only for those consequences which might reasonably have been anticipated as a result of my knowledge.

At this pole of experience, then, the element of intention, inseparably connected with knowledge, plays a large role. We become aware of the universal character of an act and of its relation to the welfare or happiness of him who performs the act. Hegel thinks that this recognition of the subjective element of right is closely connected with the rise of Christianity and that it is also reflected in the idea of individual conscience and in such modern movements as those associated with Romanticism.

But no sooner does the notion of universality suggest itself to the conscience than a problem arises. At the pole of morality, we now have a glimpse of the universal or essential will of humanity and of the goal of uniting it with the particular will of the individual man. We see that the end is a harmony between the individual will and the universal will. But the good at this level is a kind of vague ideal of duty. We are commanded to seek the good as a universal and the individual becomes conscious of this imperative. The imperative is, in fact, categorical.

It is at this point that a reference to Immanuel Kant is inevitable, for we have noted that in his intellectual development Hegel became dissatisfied with the great idealist's moral theory. Kant had held that the universe is divided into two parts: The world of things as they are in themselves and, by contrast, the universe as it appears to be.[15] The latter aspect of the universe, he taught, is always colored by our own subjectivity. When we seek to learn about the physical world, for example, we must use frameworks which reflect our own measuring rods, so to speak. Thus we use such rods as quality and quantity and we develop such conceptions as cause and effect. We utilize the conceptions of space and time and in the process inevitably erect barriers in our own minds to an understanding of the world of phenomena. The very notions which seem to be indispensable for an understanding, in other words, impose on the external world characteristics developed not by that external world but rather generated by the mind of man. We

13. *Ibid.*, p. 806.
14. In general, consult Hegel's *Philosophy of Right*, London: George Bell, 1896. For a systematic exposition of Hegel's scheme, see Hugh A. Reyburn, *The Ethical Theory of Hegel: A Study of the Philosophy of Right*, Oxford: Oxford University Press, 1968.
15. Immanuel Kant, *Critique of Pure Reason* and *Critique of Practical Reason*, 2nd ed., Max Müller, trans., New York: Macmillan, 1927; 6th ed., T. K. Abbott, trans., New York: Longmans, Green, 1909.

study the world of society and nature with our own constructs, in other words. We can even look at man in this way: He, too, is simply a phenomenon.

Now, Kant goes on, we know this world of phenomena through reason and sense experience and the kind of knowledge we obtain is always hypothetical. Thus science is a series of propositions such as "if *xyz* under circumstances *bbc*, then *aqy*." At this level of knowledge, too, the "oughts" which we can discern always take the form of hypothetical imperatives. Thus we say that if our ends are such and such, then our knowledge of phenomena is such that we must do so and so if we are to attain those ends. Here cause and effect are crucial, as they are in the whole realm of phenomena.

But Kant also held that there is another world reflected above all in man's moral experience. This is the world of things as they are, and "knowledge" of it (different certainly from the "cognition" of the phenomenal world) is gained through intuition. The utilization of will is a free act, by contrast with the acts characteristic of the phenomenal world. And it is in connection with acts of will that the notion of duty arises. When we use the term "ought" in this sense, we are asserting that our duty has a quality about it which has nothing to do with the universe of appearance. As a moral entity, the human being participates in the world of "things as they are" and is thus emancipated–in this respect–from that of "things as they appear." As Kant himself puts it: "Obligation expresses a sort of necessity . . . which occurs nowhere else in nature. It is impossible that anything in nature *ought to be* other than in fact it is."[16]

The moral will is, therefore, real, Kant holds, and we are obliged to obey it. In fact, he goes on, "There is nothing in the world–nay, even beyond the world, nothing conceivable–which can be regarded as good without qualification, saving alone a good will."[17] We must obey it categorically: It escapes the cycle of the hypothetical. We cannot understand its contents by reference to the phenomenal world but only by reference to itself. It is unconditioned by circumstances and contingencies. Thus we all recognize certain imperatives intuitively: That we should not lie, for example. Here honesty is to be followed, not because it brings results that we approve but rather because it is right in itself and we perceive that it is right through our faculty of moral intuition.

From the general notion that men do participate in the realm of "things as they are" Kant deduces that men should never be treated merely as means. To do so would be to deny that the only end valuable in itself is a good will. When a man is treated only as a means to power or glory or the satisfaction of other men, his essential worth as a participant in the free world of things as they are is denied.

Now it is Kant's notion of the categorical imperative as thus briefly outlined which Hegel finds defective. He obviously shares much of Kant's view in the sense that he regards the binding character of the "ought" as a direct or intuitive perception; and we have already seen that at the level of morality, he conceives man's experience to be one of comprehending the universal command to develop the welfare of every individual. Where he finds Kant defective, however, is in the earlier philosopher's alleged failure to tell us how we can discover the concrete details or the substance of our binding duty. A modern thinker has expressed a similar dissatisfaction with Kant:

> Granted that I know my duty, Kant tells me why I ought to do it. He reveals, in fact, the source and authority of moral obligation, but he does not tell me how I am to know it.[18]

The abstract ideal of Duty, in other words, however well accounted for (and Hegel does not seem to question Kant's account in its basic essentials), is formal only. It will not tell an inquirer what his duty is. It is purely subjective and tells us only that we should do right and seek the happiness of all men as individuals. The specific contents of duty, Hegel complains, are really, so to speak, left up in the air. Kant gives us an account of subjective conscience which may be admirable and he tells us that we should follow its guidance. But he fails to fill the house of conscience, as it were, with the furniture of details. It is at this point that Hegel calls upon the conception and reality of social righteousness to supply the deficiency.

Sittlichkeit is reflected in the whole body of complex relations revealed in such institutions as the family and the educational system. The "ethical world," Hegel goes on, is a "living good" which has been willed by the increasingly self-conscious work of men acting in actual historical circumstances. As the individual transcends the mere morality, which, as we have seen, Hegel identifies with subjectivity, he is guided to his true selfhood and comes to a genuine knowledge of himself through the operations of historic institutions. As a member of the family, for example, content is given to morality: He now knows not only that he should perform his duty but begins to have some idea of the contents of that duty. He is no longer up in the air, as it were, but has his feet on the ground.

But it should not be assumed that the social righteousness inherent in historical and cultural institutions destroys individuality. On the contrary, Hegel develops the theme that the individuality we experience at the pole of mere morality is a false or at least an incomplete one: Implicitly it is seeking completion or fulfillment. It is lost in its own subjectivity and is the prey of illusions. Only when it becomes aware of its relations to the ethical world and sees that the principles of social righteousness must become a part of itself does it fulfill itself.

But how does this come about? True to his general proposition that all is becoming and never being, Hegel tells us that we should think of the acquiring of true selfhood as a continuous process. The subjective quest for contents in duty is met by the deposits of the whole ethical world, which proceed to fill up the vessel of subjectivity. Meanwhile, however, social righteousness itself has been evolving; and the subjectively real, having been enlightened by social righteousness as it was, is now anxious to embrace the somewhat new commands of the ever-moving ethical world. The growth of the self, in other words, is a never-ending one, in which both the dictates of an ever-changing social righteousness and the yearning for contents to fill up mere morality play their respective roles.

In the ethical world itself, conflict occupies an important function in shaping both the contents of social righteousness and, thereby, the selfhood of the individual. The two basic poles of this conflict are the family, which stands for natural society in Hegel's scheme, and the civil society, which includes social and economic institutions viewed primarily from the viewpoint of subjectivity. Let us note a little more fully how the dialectic process works out both in the family and in civil society.

The Family and Consciousness of Selfhood. For Hegel the family is essentially the outpost of the ethical spirit in its natural form. That is to say, the family is biologically natural, due to the helplessness of children and their need for care. But, as one might expect, it is also the nurturing ground for those tendencies which will enable man to escape the biologically natural.

This escape potentiality is present in all three aspects of the family process—in marriage, in family fortune, and in education. Marriage, the physical union of male and female, is biological but it is also spiritual. The passions become subordinated to the imperatives of a common life—the ethical spirit shaping even the passions to its own ends. As this transformation is wrought, the selfhood of both husband and wife advances from its earlier status and begins to comprehend the true selfhood which is always in process of becoming.

It is assisted in this by the common property of the family, which, because it is common and is intimately connected with the spirit of love that develops, gives a material base to advancing consciousness of self.

The third aspect of family—education—has to do with the children who embody in visible form, as it were, the "invisible" love which is the basis of marriage. But within the educational function itself are the germs of the family's dissolution. That education is most successful which develops in the offspring the yearning for independence, which encourages the pole of subjectivity. The organic unity of the family, in other words, through its very activity, provokes its opposite—consciousness of subjective individuality. Here Hegel seems to be suggesting a paradox: that that family is most successful which leads to its timely dissolution; for when the children, now presumably acquiring subjective consciousness, depart from the home, they enter a civil society in which the world is now viewed as one of conflict between the pole of indi-

16. *Critique of Practical Reason*, trans. and with an introduction by Lewis White Beck, Indianapolis: Bobbs-Merrill, 1956.
17. *Ibid.*
18. C. E. M. Joad, *Guide to the Philosophy of Morals and Politics*, New York: Random House, 1937, p. 214.

vidual self-interest and that of social order. At this level of consciousness, which leaves behind the natural family, the tension between subjectivity and objectivity is as yet unresolved.

The Civil Society and Consciousness of Selfhood. Let us note a little more fully just what Hegel implies by this tension.

In the family, he is saying, the sense of separateness from the pole of order grows slowly. We become aware of ourselves as apart from other members of the family but by and large, until adolescence, we are tied to it by economic, ethical, and social cords which seem utterly natural. But then comes the revolt for which the family has presumably prepared us. This is the period at which we tend to become aware of the religious problem, for example; and the subjective idea of duty takes hold on us. The order of the family no longer seems natural and we become restless to be out in the world. We strain at the leash, we attack our parents, we become impatient to make our own livelihoods.

Thus the civil society is born, and it stands in many ways over and against the family. From the perspective of the individual in civil society, all law, for example, appears to be an external imposition on our (subjectively conceived) individuality. Our own interests, we think, are opposed to those of the whole. Indeed, the whole is thought of as simply a minister for our own wants and needs. The state appears to be an artifact. Insofar as the good of society is thought of at all, it is conceived to be the sum total of individual goods or interests individually pursued.

We will note in this description many of the propositions with which we have become familiar in seventeenth- and eighteenth-century thought. The interpretations which many placed on Locke, for example, might well be those of Hegel's civil society. And Mandeville's *Fable of the Bees*, Hegel would undoubtedly say, reflects very well the stage of consciousness reached by those who cannot yet see beyond the level of civil society. In other words, Hegel is not denying a certain validity to the statements of men like Adam Smith: Sociopolitical society, seen from one perspective, does indeed appear to be one of tension between order and authority, on the one hand, and individuality, on the other. It is, in fact, inevitable that our consciousness must be aware of the apparent tension before it can grasp the fact that beyond the tension lies a higher or more complete reality to which the tension is in fact subordinated.

Nevertheless, there is no question about the conflict between the natural family order and the civil society. The former stresses harmony and sharing; the latter, antagonism. Hegel discerns three "moments" of civil society which help to shape the emancipated individual and at the same time foreshadow the higher level of consciousness which unites subjective with objective poles. These "moments" have to do with man's wants, the administration of justice, and the corporations.

Hegel thinks that man's movement toward universality is shown by the very multiplication of wants so characteristic of him. With specialization of labor, wants are refined and extended and spiritual wants, often pushed aside when pressure for a mere material livelihood is great, come into play. The multiplication of wants thus leads to man's emancipation, in the sense that freedom is a spiritual factor and involves full consciousness of the world as it is. This consciousness cannot be developed without the material base implied in multiplication of material wants. Freedom and spirit are therefore foreshadowed in the apparently crass desires exhibited by men.

This judgment that multiplication of wants represents progress at every level is confirmed when we note Hegel's categories of workers. He discerns three basic divisions. Tillers of the soil are bound to nature and have very little place for reflection and enhanced consciousness. Hence, a purely agricultural society will exhibit a relatively low level of awareness and therefore of freedom. The industrial class, however, is less dependent on nature in a direct sense and can develop reflective potentialities. Finally, there is a class which is assigned to care for the general interests of all civil society. Members of this class are relieved of the necessity for productive labor in the immediate sense; and, relying either on family fortune or on state salaries, seek to discover a general interest amidst the clashes which inevitably occur between agricultural and industrial interests.

But the very conflict of interests always present gives rise to the consciousness of a possible general interest under which administration of justice can be subsumed. At the level of civil society, crime comes to be conceived as a public offense, whereas it has hitherto been thought of as purely private. Law arises to objectify right; and the court of justice presumably reflects a reason unaffected by particularized interests. Yet the special interests will still conceive themselves as at war with the incipient idea of the general interest.

This conflict is emphasized in the third "moment" of civil society, that of corporations and corresponding police power. In general, we may identify the corporation (in Hegel's sense) with special interest groups based largely on economic considerations. The police are called into being as agents of the purely mechanical order of civil society. The assumption throughout is of a society in which private individuals and corporations are pursuing their own interests in their own way. But even here the dialectic is at work. While each interest group seeks its own ends in its own way, some of those ends are remote and others are immediate. The latter, of course, can be seen from the perspective of the particular interest involved. The former, however, become involved in conditions and contingencies which no one group can control. Thus, interpreting Hegel, we may say that an industrial corporation can plan the use of its materials and labor-power for the market it anticipates. But its material goods are themselves the fruit of remote conditions—wars or absence of wars in foreign lands; the degree of order existing or likely to exist; the conditions of foreign trade, and so on. Now the very self-interest of the private individual or corporation, therefore, necessitates some nonprivate regulation of these remote conditions. Thus from apparent selfishness arises a body of law which goes beyond the selfish and foreshadows the higher union in which tension between private and public will be seen in a larger context.

Throughout this discussion, in other words, Hegel is suggesting that the very notion of private enterprise entails that of some public regulation if only because the ideas with which private enterprisers deal—property, contract, and so on—require authoritative definition. The conception of a particular interest, to use another expression, immediately evokes its opposite—that of a universal interest.

In his treatment of industrial development—a phase of civil society—Hegel is keenly aware of the contradictions involved. Thus, as wealth accumulates, the tendency is for the few wealthy to be separated more sharply than before from the many who, relatively speaking, are poor. And while the poor may be better off in a material sense as a result of the industrialization process, their perspectives tend to become narrower as specialization increases. They are dependent on the few who possess the wealth. While greater abundance would seem to create possibilities for the enlargement of liberty, the narrowing of perspectives characteristic of industrialism tends to decrease man's ability to appreciate it. The dependence of the many and their feeling of separation or alienation from the community—accompaniments, Hegel contends, of industrialism—create a proletarian mentality (Hegel uses the term *Pöbel*) that, in its very consciousness of helplessness, accentuates the process of economic concentration.

Hegel clearly foreshadows the Marxian view that at one stage the development of industry tends not only to proletarianize the mentality of most men but also to deprive them of steady work. Concentration of economic power and the pursuit of immediate self-interest on the part of those who control the wealth creates a contradiction in that the stability of purchasing power of the many is undermined. Unemployment of men is matched by unemployment of resources. It is in situations of this kind that trade and commerce with distant lands develop to dispose of material surpluses and at the same time reemploy men. And trade, while initially undertaken to advance particular interests, becomes the vehicle through which civilization is advanced. Intellectual horizons are broadened and with their enlargement can come a greater awareness of the unity of subjective and objective worlds.

More specifically, this means that, in terms of human consciousness, the notion of man as governed by external factors—forces beyond his control, law as external, the police as coercive, and so on—which is characteristic of civil society, gives way to the consciousness that he is, or may be, self-governing. In the idea of self-government, that is to say, the union of morality and social righteousness attains its highest level.

Another way of putting this is to suggest that both the family and civil society have ends which are limited. To fulfill themselves they need the authority of the universal state, in which the human consciousness becomes aware of itself both as a director of nature and as a free spirit. It is at the level of the state that the imposed and external government of the civil society and the primarily natural government of the family are seen to be expressions of the higher self-government implicit in the state.

The Nature of the State

Much has been written about Hegel on the state that is misinformed. In the twentieth century particularly, certain writers seem to wish to pin on the nineteenth-century thinker responsibility for both world wars and for the insane nationalism of our times.[19] There have even been those who would associate the name of Hegel with the philosophy of National Socialism.[20]

Some of the confusion about Hegel's doctrine is due to a misunderstanding of his teaching. When he speaks of the state as an idea, he means that which any given so-called state of history—the "existential" state—is presumably striving to achieve. Historic states make no sense, he is saying, or have no meaning, unless we interpret them as striving, however awkwardly and corruptly, to attain the goal of a consciously and rationally controlled collective life. The implicit *telos* of the existential state (and again we must remind ourselves of Hegel's enormous debt to ancient Greek conceptions) is the life of reason applied to the common life of man. Hence the state is indeed the "march of God" (Hegel's expression), if God be looked upon as evolving reason.

Hegel does seem to suggest at times, to be sure, that the idea of the state has come to its final resting-place in a particular state—the Prussia of his day, for example. To the extent that he is guilty of this, he is, of course, contradicting his own basic argument.

By and large, however, the role of historical states in his system of thought is that of *suggesting* the pure idea of the state. To use Plato's image, existing so-called states are the shadows which point to a reality beyond them. The idea of the state is the ethical spirit conceived as the deliberately developed, self-conscious will of collective man. Among its characteristics are self-knowledge and the direction of action in accordance with that knowledge. In the idea of the state, merely erratic passions are purged and the whole life of man is organized to fulfill its true or rational ends. As the idea develops, moreover, genuine personal liberty is enlarged.

Now Hegel thinks that this ethical spirit flourishes in two ways. Unreflectingly, it permeates what we should today call the folkways and mores of every given people. At this level, we may say, the individual does that which is right because he has not even discovered an apparent conflict between his own individuality and what the right commands. The question has not been raised for him.

But obviously the full import of the ethical spirit cannot be understood until we reach the reflective level. Here the individual subjectivity has become aware of an apparent conflict between its own morality and subjection to civil society, on the one hand, and the ethical spirit on the other. This very awareness of conflict calls into being the state, in which man seeks to express his aspirations for rationality. He sees that he himself cannot develop his own true self without the support and guidance of the ethical spirit. But because he has become reflective and can never again become unreflective, he sees also that this ethical spirit must be embodied in concrete organized form.

As the idea of self-conscious, deliberate rational action develops, the notion of the state grows with it. The quest for universality and rationality in the selfhood of the person exhibits the effort of organized society to develop universality and rationality in the state. This process is reflected downward through civil society and the family and through morality and abstract right. Thus, as the person is shaped through the moments of abstract right in tension with morality and of family in conflict with civil society, his true selfhood comes more into view and with it his awareness of the state as the crucial factor in that selfhood. As he becomes increasingly aware of the contents of duty through the activity of the state, he becomes free in the sense that he now knows that upon which the development of his selfhood is dependent. Or, as Hegel puts it at one point, "Freedom is Necessity transfigured."

Statements of this kind have been the basis for much jest at Hegel's expense, and with some justification, as we shall see. But here it is our task to understand rather than to criticize. When Hegel says that freedom is necessity transfigured, he is essentially challenging that view of human personality which sees the individual only in his "moment" of subjectivity, which thinks of him as a discrete entity for whom the life of the organized community is a kind of excrescence or artifact. Here above all we see revealed his utter revolt against the complex of traditions stemming from Hobbes and Locke and his repudiation of such political theories as those embodied in early Benthamite Utilitarianism.

The view which conceived the individual to be discrete thought of freedom in negative terms: It was essentially freedom from restrictions of state and society, which tended to be regarded as extraneous factors in the life of man. For Hegel, however, freedom is increasing awareness of the one-sided illusion of discreteness and a growing consciousness that the true self which one is seeking is inseparably connected with the idea of the state as the struggling embodiment of collective rationality. The idea of true selfhood is inseparably intertwined with that of statehood.

From this perspective, it is not surprising to find Hegel denying that the state is primarily instrumental: This is another of the illusions of those who look at politics only from the viewpoint of morality and civil society. Instead, the state is the end of man.

Here again, we should be clear about Hegel's meaning. When he uses "state" in this context, he implies the idea of the state: the idea, that is to say, of the rationally organized community in which the unreflective ethical spirit has given way to the reflective and man has ceased to be the plaything of nature and instead has realized the life of the spirit. Individuality, or personality, has become fully itself only in the state as thus conceived.

But while Hegel distinguishes between the idea of the state and actual so-called states, he does not ignore the latter. In some sense, they reflect the idea of the state just as actual families are shadows of the idea of the family. We see in each actual state, in other words, a hint as to what it is endeavoring to become, just as we note in each individual, however much he may be under the illusion of discreteness, some notion as to that for which he is implicitly striving.

In his view of actual states, Hegel, of course, finds the dialectic at work, as one might expect. Thus the idea of the state is reflected in some measure in every particular state. But it is also revealed in the relationships of states to one another. Finally, it shows itself in the world spirit of humanity as a whole. In the latter respect, it is revealed in the struggles of human history, and we shall treat Hegel's theory of the state in history in the next section.

In every particular state, there are three phases of activity which reflect its "becomingness." In the legislative power, each phase possesses the capacity to define the universal in law. Here, presumably, the unreflective spirit gives way to increasing self-consciousness about universals. In defining the universal as law, of course, the legislative power will inevitably be guided by the sense of right developed by the nation over the course of history. Hegel's legislator, in other words, does not *will* law in any arbitrary sense: He is always bound, and must necessarily be bound, by the ethical genius of the people for whom he is legislating. The legislator, as it were, becomes self-conscious about those customs and patterns of conduct in a given nation which should be given the status of law, with all of its sanctions. He recognizes those aspects of the *volksgeist* (spirit of a people) which are striving to become law; and he defines them as clearly as possible. Here Hegel is giving expression to the ancient German view of law as history or as custom, as against that aspect of the Roman tradition which conceived of law as the will of the imperator. Law as the dictate of the ruler will, of course, be emphasized by analytical jurists such as John Austin (1790–1859), and the historical conception associated with Hegel and jurists like Friedrich Karl Savigny (1779–1861) will stand opposed to all those schools which stem from positions like Austin's.

Because certain later interpreters of Hegel give the impression that he was an absolutist, it is important to note at this point his attitude to the problem of constitutional government. He is an admirer of the British constitution,[21] and observes—this, of course, is in strict conformity with his general theory of law—that con-

19. Thus John Dewey's *German Philosophy and Politics*, New York: Holt, 1915, was used by many during World War I to help document the notion that the basic idea-structure of imperial Germany—the structure allegedly so responsible for German precipitation of the war—was Hegelian.
20. During World War II, William McGovern's *From Luther to Hitler*, New York: Houghton Mifflin, 1941, was designed to trace far back into the German past the roots of National Socialism.
21. See, for example, his essay *The Philosophy of Right*, London: George Bell, 1896.

stitutions must be conceived to be growths rather than artificial structures. They are true expressions of the *sittlichkeit* embodied in the *volksgeist* of every nation.

The second aspect of every particular state is executive power. Hegel attaches very great importance to it as the agency which applies universals to individual cases. It includes both the judicial and the civil service organization of a given state. Because the idea of the state presumably implies the union of objective with subjective, the executive embodies this function in a very significant way.

Finally, there is the power of ultimate decision, which Hegel identifies with that of the prince or sovereign. It is the sovereign who unites the various powers of the state. Apparently he means that neither legislative nor executive power can be thought of as having ultimate authority: They are simply means for carrying out the sovereignty of the state as a whole.

Hegel thinks of the state as possessing personality. As a thing of the spirit, this must necessarily be so. It is the highest embodiment of that which is most distinctive of man and will, therefore, itself be a person with a selfhood and distinct characteristics. It has, as it were, a life of its own and is in no sense the result of any merely mechanical addition of its parts. Its personality extends beyond the life of any given generation and is rooted in all the struggles of the past.

Just as Hegel is a constitutionalist, so is he an advocate of the separation of church and state, the former being wholly a reflection of subjective consciousness,[22] whereas the latter, as we have seen, is the union of the objective and the subjective.

Yet here again we should be cautious in our interpretation. When he comes to an analysis of actual states with one another—*Das äussere Staatsrecht*—he lays it down that no one state can be a complete political entity unless it is recognized by other states. The personality of the state and its moral character, in other words, require for their full development the presence of other states; just as the growth of individual personality, as we have seen, cannot be separated from the presence and mutual relations of the whole complex of individuals. Thus while an actual state is a growing personality, it can never be independent in the sense of isolation; and, indeed, its very personality is a contingent thing, insofar as it is dependent on acknowledgement of other actual states.

Because of this contingency, the national spirit of any particular state is necessarily restricted. While for any given people it is the concrete embodiment of *sittlichkeit*, it is itself subordinate to the evolution of the universal or world spirit, which is reflected in universal history.

As we have suggested earlier, the return to the significance of history for political thought came to be increasingly emphasized toward the end of the eighteenth century after a long period in which history was deemed to be of relatively little importance for those whose thinking was primarily *a priori* and deductive. When, therefore, Hegel works out his theory of universal history, he allies himself in some measure with this revised early modern historicism and, in a more remote sense, with what might be called the Hebraic stream of Western political thought.

Universal History: Its Nature and Significance

In treating his theory of history,[23] we should remember that he is interested essentially in the chief hallmarks of each culture or nation and not in the accidents or details. The latter are important only to illustrate what, to the eye of the philosopher, seems to be the major theme of human history.[24] That theme is the development of the idea of freedom in all of its implications. Since prehistory is by definition the epoch in which human reflection was minimal, there being no formal recorded account of human affairs, Hegel is interested primarily in historical mankind—that is, the human race since written records in some form have been kept. But history in this sense is primarily confined, he thinks, to two continents, Asia and Europe, with the ancient Egyptian culture added. Thus most of Africa and all of the Americas are excluded.

Hegel maintains, too, that history, as he understands it, is the story primarily of men organized in some form of state-life. Thus only where there is a hierarchically arranged system of governance and a scheme of superordination and subordination will history exist. Mere tribalism, unless incipient state-elements are also present in considerable degree, is of no interest to the philosopher of history as such. Here it should be clearly remembered that Hegel is talking of *particular* historical states in which the *idea* of the state may be present in embryo but where it is, of course, not developed.[25]

There is another ideological observation by Hegel that we should keep in mind. Matter to him signifies the reverse of spirit. In the former, consciousness is nonexistent and to the degree that man remains enchained to it, he is not free. On the other hand, spirit can be present in varying degrees in the life of man. It exists, as we have seen, in its objective form—where consciousness is of the external world—and in its subjective guise, in which we are self-conscious. Now just as consciousness of the external is logically prior to our subjective consciousness, so is it prior chronologically. In history, therefore, we see, according to Hegel, the growth of subjective freedom as perhaps the central theme. The civilizations in which man is conceived to be subordinate to the external world, whether of nature or of social organization, precede those in which the human being becomes aware of subjective individuality and its concomitant morality. Yet without the latter, freedom cannot be born.

Hegel therefore tries to show, in his survey of Asian and European civilization, how consciousness of subjective freedom developed over the course of centuries and millennia. He does this by means of an analysis of five state-cultures which to him have constituted the central vehicles through which the idea of freedom has passed—the Chinese, the Indian, the Persian, the Greek, and the German.

He discerns the essence of Chinese history (and we should always remember that he is writing before 1831) to be rigidity and great stress on externalities. The emphasis is on observance of externally imposed rules and on obedience to tradition and carefully defined etiquette. The duty of child to parent and the importance of outward manners are matched by an elaborate bureaucratic system in the empire. Hegel devotes great attention to the traditional Chinese civil-service system, emphasizing that anyone, whatever his status at birth, can rise through competence to the highest ranks in the civil service. But while anyone can rise, only the ruler, or emperor, is possessed of any idea of subjective freedom.[26]

In India, the same general pattern is to be observed, despite the many points at which superficial differences between it and China may be discerned. Hegel gives considerable attention, for example, to the caste system, for which there is no exact analogue in Chinese history. Men become differentiated, as he puts it, in Indian history, by contrast with Chinese history, but any awareness of themselves as subjective beings, any notion of individuality, is at best embryonic. Subjective freedom, we may interpret Hegel as suggesting, although it may make a kind of dim appearance in Indian culture, does not become a central theme.

The same is true of Persia, except that here the germ of subjective freedom is somewhat larger. (By "Persia" he means the whole of the ancient Middle or Near East, including Syria, Babylonia, Assyria, Israel, and Egypt.) In general, he sees Persia as a kind of middle ground between China and India, on the one hand, and Greece and Germany on the other. In it are born the religions of Zoroaster and of Jehovah, the former with its emphasis on the struggle between Light and Darkness and the latter with important germs of the idea of subjective freedom.

By "Greece" Hegel really signifies the whole Greco-Roman civilization, since he seems to imply that culturally Rome tends to be an offshoot of Greece. Here he seeks to show that in the purely Greek aspect of Greece, the general notion of democracy is born and with it the conception of citizenship. Men are no longer merely subjects, in other words, as in the Orient, but actually are conceived to have a kind of subjective free-

22. For a study of the early development of Hegel's religious ideas, see Paul Asveld, *La penseé religieuse du jeune Hegel: Liberté et alienation*, Louvain: Publications Universitaires de Louvain, 1953.
23. In general, consult Hegel's *Philosophy of History*, J. Sibree, trans., New York: Colonial Press, 1899. The Introduction provides the general framework and the remainder of the study seeks to illustrate his major propositions by reference to the concrete events of human experience.
24. For a recent study of the problem of meaning in history, including the Hegelian interpretation, see Karl Löwith, *Meaning in History*, Chicago: University of Chicago Press, 1949.
25. *Philosophy of History*, *op. cit.*, pp. 55–79.
26. *Ibid.* Because all are subordinate to the emperor and are not conceived to have autonomy, subjective consciousness, except for the ruler, is out of the question (pp. 116–138).

dom which is to be connected and in tension with the external politics of the polis. But not all are free, even in Greece; for there are the vast masses of slaves who were still not regarded as possessed of subjective freedom. In the imperial regimes which succeed ancient Greek classical civilization, of course, the possibility of an intimate civic life is destroyed. Under the domination of Rome, the consciousness of subjective freedom born in Greece retreats more and more within itself. An inner world is conceived to exist in sharp opposition to the outer world controlled by Roman despotism. And in this inner world, some begin to suggest, all are free. This is characteristic of the Stoic view, of course, but is to become particularly true of the Christian position.[27]

In fact, it is in the spiritual climate of the despotic Roman Empire that Christianity finds a fertile soil. Severed from their relatively brief period of citizenship in the Greek world, men find themselves once more subjected to dominations and powers and yearning for the assurance of a subjectivity which will emancipate them. This Christianity provides.

Hegel then proceeds to show how the development of Christianity in the German world which succeeds the Roman may be considered as a further growth of the idea of subjective freedom. He traces this out through the early period of German history, after its contact with the Romans, and into the Middle Ages. The development reaches a kind of culminating point, he thinks, in the Protestant Reformation. The loose alliances among the Germans, he argues, were particularly conducive to the notion of freedom. "The German confederations have their being not in a relation to a mere external aim or cause, but in a relation to the spiritual self—the subjective inmost personality."[28]

Because of this, German history becomes predestined, as it were, to carry on the notion of subjective freedom first revealed in its potentialities by the Christian religion in the late Roman Empire. But the process is a long and indirect road, for in a sense the barbarian spirit is obviously also antithetic to Christianity. Barbarian passions are confronted by a religion which demands the cessation of violence; and at first the religion seems only to exacerbate the very untamed emotions it is supposed to control. But Hegel seems to imply that in the very conflict between religion and passion, there is forged a greater and greater awareness of subjective freedom, which is the prelude to the union of subjective and objective that is the idea of the state.

Throughout his analysis of history, he stresses the notion of development: things are shaped into different forms, which in turn are always changing. Development, in Hegel's words, "involves . . . the existence of a latent germ of being—a capacity or potentiality striving to realize itself."[29] This is revealed par excellence in the realm of the spirit, whose theatre is human history. But it is also a characteristic of organized natural objects. Thus even nonhistorical phenomena are not wholly dependent on outside forces but also have within them the potentiality for inner growth toward that which they ought to become. But there is an important distinction between merely natural events and those which are historical. The former are revealed, as Hegel puts it, in "a direct, unopposed, unhindered manner." The latter, by contrast, are "mediated by consciousness and will." Since human beings are both *natural* and *historical*, the potentialities which we call human are first developed in the unhindered natural way; but as spirit grows within man, he finds himself split, as it were, between the "free-flowing" natural aspect and the "consciousness and will" characteristic of history. It is in the realm of spirit that man discovers the only freedom he can ever know; in the process, he transcends merely natural and externally imposed development.

When one realizes fully that he is not merely an individual but that he is literally an outpost of all the historical forces which have developed in human experience, the tendency, present in individualists like Kant, to see the individual as coerced by history, will disappear. The newly discovered consciousness will teach each person the reality of the world historical spirit within him; and in the end, laws, institutions, and even the machinery of direct coercion will be seen to be not devices to enslave man but rather as the effort of collective humanity to emancipate itself.

Because Hegel's philosophy of history will be the point of departure for much that is in Karl Marx, it should be emphasized that the earlier thinker does not purport to see the patterns of the future. He is no fortune teller, in other words, but confines himself to an analysis of the patterns he discerns in the past and to their import for the idea of freedom, which, as we have seen, he takes to be the central theme of the whole historical process.

Another caution is essential. Not only does Hegel not venture to predict the details of the future, he does not even maintain that human history has been a process which moves toward freedom without interruption. While, in general, he thinks that he sees a general tendency for the idea of freedom to expand, this development is not without its tribulations and setbacks. The process would seem to be a kind of spiral in which the development of human consciousness overcomes the shackles of the past, to some degree, only to find that it must be checked before it resumes its progress. As one who opposes a priori approaches to politics, Hegel stresses the extraordinary difficulty of discovering the social devices which will ensure progress in Freedom:

> There must be institutions adapted, political machinery invented, accompanied by appropriate political arrangements—necessitating long struggles of the understanding before what is really appropriate can be discovered—involving, moreover, contentions with private interests and passions, and a tedious discipline of these latter, in order to bring about the desired harmony.[30]

But if right and duty are in substance to be found in *sittlichkeit*, how can change take place? If everyone subjectively wills the conceptions of duty embodied in positive custom and law, how account for what Hegel calls world historical figures who help remold the objective basis for law? What is the role of leadership when Freedom is defined as necessity transfigured? Hegel's answer to questions of this kind is to remind us of the "becomingness" of *sittlichkeit* and to see leaders as those who can comprehend whither the world historical spirit is moving at any particular time. While most men achieve freedom by conformity to the apparently stable social righteousness, there are always some who see how its patternings are potentially changing into something other than they seem to be at present. These leaders, often when pursuing their own private interests, in effect become agents of the world historical spirit which is working for change. But the mark of true leadership is that it understands both the potentialities for and the historic or cultural limits on possible change. Caesar was such a figure, as was Napoleon: Each may have been moved initially by supposedly subjective passions but each comprehended also the possibilities as well as the limits of change, thus uniting the subjective with the objective and promoting the enlargement of freedom.

The general picture which emerges in any assessment of this view of political history is that of a humanity having a collective becoming which is best reflected in the expression "progress toward but also frustration of freedom." This progress consists of an increasing awareness that true freedom demands the subordination of aberrant subjective wills (whether of followers or leaders) to the objectively rational embodied in the historical scheme and specifically contained in the evolving idea of the state. As men submit to this objective reason, which is objective freedom (the principles underlying the necessary development of things), they attain genuine subjective freedom.

In the view of a recent philosopher of freedom,[31] Hegel's notion of liberty may be called "compulsory rational freedom," in the sense that freedom is identified with the discipline of the passions by the understanding. This conception is to be sharply contrasted with definitions of freedom which think of it as the removal of constraints of various types. In effect, Hegel is saying that each person as he develops in the historical process becomes free to the extent that he understands the process and submits to it; and even world historical figures must do this, although the role assigned them by the universal spirit is somewhat different from that of nonleaders. Since the state is regarded as the highest relative embodiment of Rationality, this subordination is basically to the institutions reflecting the idea of the state. Here we see reflected once more a Rousseau-like view that there is or can be a harmonization of individuality and collectivity in the discovery of a general will. For Rousseau's general will, we can substitute Hegel's

27. *Ibid.*, pp. 317–318.
28. *Ibid.*, p. 353.
29. *Ibid.*, p. 55.
30. *Ibid.*, p. 24.
31. See Maurice Cranston, *Freedom: A New Analysis*, London: Longmans, Green, 1953. See also Mortimer Adler, *The Idea of Freedom*, New York: Doubleday, 1958.

idea of an understanding of the historical process.

From yet another perspective, Hegel is providing us with a theodicy or a justification of the ways of God to man in human history. The apparently irrational aspects of the historical process—and every age provides its own apt illustrations—are, when seen in the light of the development of spirit, either accidental irrelevancies or actual moments in the dialectical development of human thought and action.

Hegel's theodicy, of course, has much in common with the ancient Hebrew prophetic view and is an excellent example of the persistence of certain themes in the history of political thought for thousands of years. In both the Hebrew and the Hegelian view, history assumes a central place (by contrast with the classical Greek conception which tends to discern no particular progress in the imposition of what Plato called the Forms) and in both it is held that history, somehow, must make sense. But an important distinction between the Hegelian position and that of the ancient prophetic conception would seem to be that while, for the Hebrews, Yahweh acts through history although he himself is perfection, Hegel's God would appear to be identified with the *geist* of the process itself.

This Hegelian theodicy, then, is hardly the classical Christian one. All important Christian thinkers, it is true, had been puzzled by similar problems: They, too, tried to explain man's frequent alienation from the process as well as from God. But in solving the problem, they always assumed that, while God's work was visible in the process, He also was not to be thought of as contained wholly within it. Hegel's notion seems to make of God a kind of relative divinity and not the Absolute of traditional Jewish-Christian theology.[32]

The Historical Impact of Hegel

While the whole Hegelian theory of politics is subject to severe criticism—and has accordingly been analyzed and attacked many times since Hegel's death—it is difficult to exaggerate its enormous historical significance for modern political philosophy and, indeed, for the growth of the social sciences in general. In this section, we indicate the general lines of Hegel's influence on subsequent generations, reserving for the section which follows a criticism of his system.

In the History of German Political Thought. When Hegel appeared on the scene of German speculation, the predominant attitude to politics was still that of the Enlightenment associated with men like Kant and with the cosmopolitanism of the eighteenth century. The national state meant little if anything to the cosmopolitans, including the great Goethe. There were yet to be born that sentiment of nationalism and that drive toward national unity which were to characterize so much of German politics during the nineteenth century.

But with Hegel all this began to change. This is not to say that Hegel initiated the radical departure from the eighteenth century but rather that he gave expression to it in his political philosophy and that the philosophy itself helped to consolidate the marked shift in attitude. While we often date the intellectual birth of modern German nationalism from Johann G. Fichte's *Reden an Die Deutsche Nation,* lectures delivered during 1807–1808, Fichte's efforts were at a somewhat different level from those of Hegel. Fichte's call was for a national rejuvenation and for unity. It had many topical references. Hegel, by contrast, wrote for the long run and endeavored to state the significance of nation-statehood in universal terms.

In the process of doing so, to be sure, he verged at times on appearing to rationalize and even to divinize all the acts of the Prussian monarchy. And modern critics like Karl Popper make much of statements from Hegel which seem to make Prussia the highest development of the world spirit. There can be no doubt that Hegel at points can be quoted to this effect, which probably pleased the Prussian king. Yet the main thrust of his argument for nineteenth-century German thought was to see the struggle for existential statehood as a phase or reflection of his philosophy of history in general—which surely cannot be reduced merely to special pleading.

The German disciples of Hegel soon began to quarrel among themselves, dividing into conservative Hegelians and liberals, each group having its own subdivisions. Conservatives stressed those aspects of the Hegelian system which identified duty with conformity to *sittlichkeit* as it was; while liberals, of course, emphasized the "becomingness" of social righteousness and its potentialities for change and even revolution.

Whether they called themselves liberal or

conservative, German thinkers, students, and prominent politicians popularized certain Hegelian terms, which then affected thought in general. Thus *bewusstsein,* or consciousness, became almost a household word among intellectuals after the Napoleonic wars and from then on down to our own day. While liberal thought in Britain, France, and the United States had its roots in Locke, Jefferson, Bentham, Mill, and Rousseau, Hegel became one of the great watchwords for German liberalism. While American and British thought tended to take the discrete individual as their point of departure, Germany, under the influence of men like Hegel and Fichte, was stressing organismic views. Nor was this merely a matter of nineteenth-century thought—it penetrated deep into the twentieth century, shaping German ideas in many areas of life.

Some Ramifications of the Idea. But while Hegelian approaches to politics were characteristically German in many respects, they were by no means confined to Germany.

There can be little doubt, for example, that the Hegelian emphasis on the centrality of history as the record of the human spirit with which one must come to grips profoundly altered the attitude of many to the past. Of course, there was fertile soil prepared by circumstance as well as by such thinkers as Edmund Burke, and it is difficult to assess the degree to which Hegel directly affected ideas and the degree to which he simply gave expression to conceptions which were in the air both in Germany and elsewhere. The very notion of evolution or development owed much, however, to the Hegelian spirit; and the relativism of the idea of becoming was attractive to large numbers of thinkers who were so impressed by the constancy of social change, particularly as industrialism spread its tentacles throughout the Western world. Later on in the nineteenth century, of course, this evolutionary view of things—which often purported to discover obligatory norms for human behavior in the way that man had developed during the past—was to be reinforced from the perspective of Darwinian biological theory, which seemed to confirm, deepen, and strengthen many aspects of Hegel's system.

So, too, in the realm of legal thought did Hegel's scheme both reinforce and help shape important intellectual currents. At several points, we have stressed the medieval German view of law, which saw legal norms as essentially the deposit of the way of life of a people rather than merely the dictate of the legislator or ruler.[33] After the reception of the Roman law into German courts this view became modified and with the Enlightenment tended to recede. But with the post-Napoleonic period and the enormous influence of Hegel's political philosophy, the ancient emphasis on law as the expression of a people's general spirit received a new impetus. In Germany itself, there was a revolt against Roman law notions and an endeavor to revive tribal legal conceptions. This movement—often associated with jurists like Friedrich von Savigny (1779–1861)—naturally derived much inspiration from Hegel who, with the iteration of the view that law is the expression of a kind of group mind, tended to oppose those definitions (like that of John Austin) which thought of it as the deliberate will of a ruler or which (like those of the natural-law thinkers) saw it as the expression of a rather abstract reason. In areas other than Germany, the historical view of law gained for itself great respect, men like Sir Henry Sumner Maine (1822–1888) giving it a form which was to be profoundly influential in both nineteenth and twentieth centuries.

In general, the role of Hegel's thought during the last three-quarters of the nineteenth century was to provide a philosophical basis for those views which underlined the indispensability of community for the experience of individuality and which thought of the latter as, in some sense, derived from the former. In this respect as well as others Hegel influenced such diverse thinkers as the anarchist P. J. Proudhon (1809–1865) and the founder of the rising science of sociology, Auguste Comte (1798–1857). Comte's conception of progress in history—from the theological phase, to the metaphysical, to the positive—reminds one of

32. If this is indeed a correct interpretation of Hegel's supposed divinity his view would seem to have much in common with that of the late H. G. Wells who, in *God the Invisible King,* London: Macmillan, 1917, adumbrates a kind of God who evolves with human experience. Wells may have been influenced, of course, by Hegel, directly or indirectly, since he stands squarely in that stream of thought which was so profoundly affected by the nineteenth century's "process" conceptions—whether Hegelian, Darwinian, or Spencerian.

33. See Chapters 11 and 12.

Hegel, although quite divergent from it in many respects. All those currents of thought which developed notions of a group mind or which spoke in terms of national characters owe not a little to Hegel. And wherever the culture concept makes an explicit appearance, Hegel is not far away.

Hegel and Marx. More specifically, it is obvious that Marx and the Marxians, while owing much to other streams of thought as well, build explicitly on Hegelian concepts. Although Marxian political thought is treated elsewhere,[34] it is appropriate at this point to stress the general indebtedness of Marx and Engels to Hegel. Whether in the conception of the historical dialectic, the significance of history, the relativity of the right and the good, or the notion of the group or class mind, the Hegelian foundations for Marxist thought are ubiquitous.

Hegel and Non-Marxian Thought. In the realm of political speculation, we may immediately recognize the Hegel-Marx connection but fail at the same time to note the impact of Hegel on important non-Marxian streams.

Let us take, for example, the political doctrine of John Dewey. Dewey was, during his early teaching career, very much affected by Hegel; and his later thought obviously contains many Hegelian overtones. If we regard Dewey as a "process" philosopher, for instance, or if we look at him as one who stresses the nonabsolute character of moral values, we obtain some notion of the degree to which he is reflecting Hegel. Like Hegel, too, he stresses the way in which the culture shapes the individual; and he calls attention to the constantly shifting scene within the context of which each person must make his decisions.

Dewey became the inspiration for a whole group of thinkers who tended to think of the group as the basic factor in politics. Thus A. F. Bentley, in the early part of the twentieth century, wrote a book[35] which became virtually a text for those who, later in the century, developed what was to be called the "group theory" of politics. The Hegel-Dewey-Bentley relationship is perfectly evident to anyone who studies the basis of the group theory.

So, too, in the realm of social psychology, George Herbert Mead—perhaps one of the most influential university thinkers of twentieth-century America—obviously owes much to Hegel.[36] To the degree that Mead sees mind as a deposit of group experience and in the measure that he develops a mirror theory of personality—so that one's own view of oneself is dependent on how others view one—he is using Hegel as a foundation.

To trace out the influence of Hegel on other political thinkers would itself constitute a major task. One might mention, for example, Benedetto Croce and the theory of liberal Hegelianism; or, in a sharply different direction, the self-avowed Hegelian Giovanni Gentile, who became associated with Mussolini's Fascism.

The Problem of Hegel and National Socialism. One of the vexing issues of twentieth-century historical interpretation has been the degree to which we may attribute the foundations of National Socialism and Fascism to Hegel. During World War I, there was a whole school of propagandists which sought to pin the blame for Germany's alleged aggression on certain tendencies in German thought which the propagandists associated particularly with Hegel.[37] And in World War II likewise, there were those who believed that an Hegelian cast of mind was behind much of the thought known as National Socialism. Specifically, interpreters of this school tended to argue that an alleged Hegelian emphasis on authority had become a part of the warp and woof of German politics and political thought and thus made it easier for an authoritarian regime to evoke a favorable response. Some sought also to associate the National Socialist glorification of war with the name of Hegel; and others called attention to the undoubted fact that certain well-known Fascists were avowed Hegelians.

Now these charges are very difficult to evaluate. In their simple and naive form, which they sometimes took at the level of propaganda, they must be rejected; for the one-to-one causal relationship usually implied is far too simple to be reconciled with the undoubted complexities of thought in its relationship to politics. Moreover, the Hegelian way of looking at political phenomena is so foreign to typical British and American modes of thought that it is often difficult to translate Hegel's idiom into language which British and Americans can understand.

But if we minimize these factors for the moment and seek to interpret Hegel's influence in all of its complexity and without prejudice, the picture becomes very cloudy indeed. If the critics imply that Hegel was in any sense a racist, the reply must be that nothing could be more foreign to his thought.

While he may be legitimately charged at times with making generalizations on the basis of too little evidence, none of those generalizations point to anything resembling what later was to be called racism.

As for the connection between Hegel and nationalist ideology, there can be no doubt, as we have seen, that it was a rather direct one. Whether he would have approved of the extreme nationalism which was sometimes defended in his name is, however, extremely doubtful; for we must remember that he always held that every nation had its own peculiar contribution to make to the development of "spirit"—a position hardly compatible with those versions of nationalism which would exalt the concentration of all the virtues in a given nation.

But with respect to war, it cannot be denied that Hegel does provide a basis for those views (including National Socialism and Fascism) which think of it as inevitable and even desirable. The very fact that he saw the nation-state as the basic unit of world history meant that in their struggles the several national states might come to physical blows. Hegel thought of this as part of the dialectical process which would apparently continue indefinitely. Why he could not envision a situation in which the very dialectic partly embodied in war could lead to the ultimate establishment of a world state, with the dialectical struggle transferred to a nonphysical level, is something of a mystery.

However, it was only by distorting the full Hegel that either National Socialism or Fascism could legitimately make him appear to support their ideologies as a whole. While Hegel on war did appear in a limited way to sustain them, Hegel on authority could hardly do so. Hegel was a constitutionalist, as we have seen, and it is very difficult to fit him into any scheme which exalts the arbitrary and which, moreover, talks of "blood and soil" as the basis of life. To be sure, there is that within him, as we have seen, which distrusts abstract reason; but this distrust is always because abstract reason is incomplete and not because it is not an essential part of consciousness.

Hegel and the Development of Democratic Thought. Hegel was no democrat (although a constitutionalist and an admirer of the British constitutional system), but his whole mode of thought would have a not inconsiderable influence on the development of democratic thought during the nineteenth century. In earlier chapters, we have noted the beginnings of modern democratic theory and have seen how, in the seventeenth century, it was closely connected with individualist outlooks such as those of Locke and the radical sectarian democrats. In the eighteenth century, of course, a new element entered the picture with Rousseau. Meanwhile, nineteenth-century democratic thought was to be intimately associated with the rise of Utilitarianism in Britain[38] as well as with the continuation of Lockean approaches in the United States. How does Hegel fit into this complex pattern?

In the middle of the nineteenth century, British democratic thinkers like John Stuart Mill are to become increasingly dissatisfied with the rather primitive Utilitarianism which constituted their heritage. They will search for correctives and in doing so will turn to German thought, with its large Hegelian element; and while Mill himself can hardly be said to embody much of what we should call Hegelianism, later English contemporaries do exactly that. For example, one of those dissatisfied with the Lockean-utilitarian heritage will be Thomas Hill Green. Green will seize upon German speculation, and particularly the system of Hegel, seeking to build part of it into a scheme of liberal democratic thought which he will deem to have more solid foundations than the older systems. Green was very explicitly influenced not only by Hegel but also by Rousseau, and it is through him that what we might call the revised version of democratic thought will be established.[39]

34. See Chapter 25.
35. *The Process of Government* (1908), recent ed., Evanston, Ill.: Principia Press, 1949.
36. See his *Mind, Self and Society from the Standpoint of a Social Behaviorist*, Chicago: University of Chicago Press, 1934; *Movements of Thought in the Nineteenth Century*, Chicago: University of Chicago Press, 1936; and *The Philosophy of the Present*, Chicago: Open Court, 1932.
37. See John Dewey, *German Philosophy and Politics*, *op. cit.*, and L. T. Hobhouse, *The Metaphysical Theory of the State*, New York: Barnes and Noble, 1960.
38. See Chapter 26.
39. See Green's *Lectures on the Principles of Political Obligation*, Ann Arbor: University of

A Critique of Hegel's Political Thought

Here let us deal first with the permanent values of Hegel's system and then turn to the serious questions which can be put to him as a political thinker.

What Is Living in Hegel's Political Theory? In the previous section we have suggested some of the many ways in which Hegel influenced later generations of political thinkers. At this point, it would seem useful to sum up those aspects of his system which possess greatest merit and which possibly have kept Hegel alive as a thinker. We may identify those elements as (1) the plausibility of his conception of human personality; (2) the utility of the notion of "social righteousness"; (3) the relevance of the "dialectical" conception; (4) the importance of understanding social reality.

(1) Few thinkers in modern times have been as concerned as Hegel with the problem of understanding human personality in community.

Hegel is rebelling essentially against the model—so frequent in the seventeenth and eighteenth centuries—which pictures society and state as gigantic machines and the individual, correspondingly, as also mechanistic. And while there are fallacies in his own position, he would seem to be essentially right in suggesting that, if we must have models at all, the community is more like a biological organism than it is like a machine. The state, that is to say, is the kind of whole which is more than the sum total of all its parts; and personalities growing in the state are shaped by this whole to such a degree that in some sense and to a certain extent it is the whole which makes them.

Now without going to the lengths to which Hegel would carry us in this conception, it must be admitted that there is much to be said for it. As over against all contractual views, that is, Hegel is saying that the individual has no choice: He is born into a community with established ways of doing things and, indeed, at birth the "he" is simply an organized physical entity whose spiritual potentialities are drawn out and developed by the whole complex of institutions, practices, laws, and traditions which constitute the whole of the community.

But we can go further. No modern thinker has been more aware than Hegel that personality is not only a deposit of community but also that consciousness of one's relation to the world exists at varying levels and that it depends also, at least partly, on the way in which others view one.

While we shall argue that Hegel presses organic analogies too far in his account of the state, there is, nevertheless, something to be said for his view that even individual thought is in some sense a reflection of a more universal thought. Although there is a measure of validity in Bertrand Russell's parody of Hegel—when one goes around Cape Horn and thinks, "there is Cape Horn," it is really not oneself who is thinking but a universal thinking "Cape Horny" thoughts[40]—yet it is certainly true that one's own speculations are an inseparable part of all those which have gone before and will follow. In some sense, one is not alone, in other words, but is a moment in a kind of "dialectic" which has continued from the beginning of human history.

(2) As for the conception of *sittlichkeit*, Hegel conceived of it as an answer to what he regarded as the extreme subjectivism of Kant who, according to Hegel, had told us why we should do our duty but was extremely vague as to how our duty could be discovered.

Out of this notion emerged the idea of "my station and its duties," a phrase developed by F. H. Bradley, one of Hegel's leading British disciples.[41] I can discover what is right, in other words, by finding out the particular role established for me by the whole complex of social righteousness. And I am free when, having discovered this role, I perform it in a conscientious and thorough manner. I shall, of course, be required to fill many roles, but they are all subsumed in the end under the state, which as we have seen, is the rational organizing principle seeking to be embodied in the over-all organization of society.

In the next sub-section we shall be critical of this notion of social righteousness. Here, however, let us note its merits. In one sense, it is simply a development of Aristotle and as such has the merits of the Aristotelian position. For most men and women, at least, to be moral or righteous implies a cheerful adoption of the roles assigned to them by society in their several directions. If we attempt to spurn these roles, we shall become alienated and less than men. Our very "holiness" (wholeness) as human beings, in other words, depends upon our fitting into the roles which social righteousness has assigned us.

If it be objected that the roles assigned to us

by social righteousness are not morally right, Hegel would reply that at any given moment, the morally right must be identified with social righteousness; for if the whole process embodies rationality and yet is incomplete, that is relatively right which is contained in *sittlichkeit*. To think otherwise, is to follow the will-o'-the-wisp of a false subjectivity.

We should remember, of course, that *sittlichkeit* is not *being* but always *becoming*. Hence our duties to the state will always be shifting somewhat and never frozen. New experiences redefine the "right" in given instances. And leaders, as we have seen, may find in *sittlichkeit* radical possibilities for change. It would be a grave mistake, therefore, to think of Hegel as establishing a static situation in which change has been exorcised. Quite the reverse: he would be critical of all those views —and among them he would probably include the Platonic and Aristotelian—which seem to look forward to a kind of still-life picture of things.

(3) Although only the dedicated Hegelian would accept all of Hegel's dialectical position—whether at the level of logic or of history—with proper qualifications, if one does not push it too far, the notion of a dialectic process in politics and society can constitute a useful framework within which to think. Certainly at the level of thought, and specifically of political thought, the confrontation of opposites or the posing of conflicting interpretations is the very essence of speculation.

The clashing of institutions and organizations in the political process and in history can also be usefully subsumed under some such scheme as Hegel proposes, provided, again, that we do not use it mechanically. While there is always an ambiguity about the use of the word "opposite," the conflicts between family and economy, subjective and objective, law as external and law as internal, external versus internal polity, judiciary versus executive would seem to be perennial in our political experience; and Hegel's suggestion that these conflicts shape both our ideas and actions and at the same time constitute the means of social change is a viable hypothesis.

(4) As for the importance of understanding social reality, Hegel, with the Marxists, shows a justifiable impatience with those students of politics and political reformers who think that society can be transformed largely by the imposition of abstract blueprints. The whole Hegelian discussion of consciousness, in fact, is pointed in the direction of comprehending the complex relations which arise in political society.

But while an understanding of the process imposes severe limits on what we can do (and some critics of Hegel would allege that he in effect asserts that we can do nothing because of these limits), it also affords us the only possibility for knowing *how* we can affect the process. The very limits constitute the basis for opportunities, as it were. By and large, in other words, Hegel may be interpreted as not being against social reform (although there is undoubtedly a very conservative side to him) but rather as insisting that it proceed intelligently—with a full awareness of the complexities imposed by the *sittlichkeit* and *volksgeist* (spirit of a given people).

What Is Dubious About Hegel's Doctrine? Earlier we suggested that while Hegel has had an enormous impact on the modern world historically, his system, analytically speaking, is subject to serious attack. Here let us note a few of the points at which that attack would seem most valid. They may be summarized as (1) the limits of the organic analogy; (2) the dubiety about the notion that the state has a real personality; (3) the tendency—at times—to absorb society into state; (4) the apparent conflict between the view of history as process and change and Hegel's seeming identification of the nation-state as the final form of human organization; (5) the ambiguities and apparent contradictions in his conception of the philosophy of history.

(1) As we have noted, one of the most

Michigan, 1967, where the connection with Hegel is made very explicit indeed. See also Chapter 26.

40. See Bertrand Russell's essay, *Philosophy and Politics*, Cambridge: Cambridge University Press, 1947. See also Russell's *History of Western Philosophy*, New York: Simon and Schuster, 1945, pp. 730–746, where Russell gives an unsympathetic and, at many points, an unfair account of Hegel's thought. Russell is an excellent example of the British and American writers who seem to put forth only a minimum effort to understand a man whose approach is so foreign to their own.

41. F. H. Bradley, *My Station and Its Duties*, recent ed., New York: Liberal Arts Press, 1951.

important contributions of Hegel historically lay in his revival of a version of the organic view of society and state. They are, he reiterates, more like biological organisms than machines. But in developing this analogy, Hegel would appear to push it much too far, particularly insofar as he seems to imply that the individual is *merely* an outpost, as it were, of the state.

Throughout this history, we have observed the perennial revival of organic theories in various forms but Hegel's is perhaps the most thorough-going of all. It is probably true, of course, that if we have to use analogies in thinking about society, the biological organism is more useful than the machine. The biological similitude recognizes that individuals are not discrete and that personality is to a great degree social. The individual is born into a social whole or wholes which impress their marks on him: they are a necessary condition for his becoming a human being. Like the cells of a human body, individuals do subserve ends much broader than their own; and all their actions are conditioned by the roles assigned to them by society and state, somewhat as the organs of the human body fulfill roles or offices given them by the organism as a whole. Society and state continue beyond the lifetimes of given individuals and impose their stamps on generations yet unborn: thus the conceptions and practices of the ancient Roman jurists affected what men would become in Hegel's own day. In the United States, the office of President shapes its holder; yet that office is the product of no one generation. In many respects, societies are more than the sum totals of their parts and the individual is from one point of view a "deposit" of the whole complex of historical factors into which he is born. Certainly the idea that we contract as disparate individuals for the organization of a society is, at a minimum, a gross oversimplification.

But when this has been admitted, we ought also to point out the severe limitations to which the organic view, in its Hegelian form, must be subjected. Organs of the human body have no ends of their own; human beings in society and state do have such ends—ends, moreover, which cannot legitimately be regarded simply as incomplete or partial versions of state or social ends. While one cannot become a person except in a human group, this does not mean that personality is not more than a social deposit. Although society and state are not contractual in a literal sense, the existence of individual members is logically prior to the existence of society; but it is not true that the organs of the body are logically prior to the biological entity—instead, body and organ seem logically to entail each other somewhat as a triangle and its angles are related. The significance and importance of the individual aspect of human personality in its relation to society and state are infinitely greater than any imagined individuality of an organ or cell in relation to the body.

(2) Subject to similar criticism is the tendency for Hegel to attribute personality to the state. So impressed is he by the organic view that he endows the state with attributes which we usually impute only to individual human beings. Indeed, he thinks of it as the "march of God," and God as a kind of thinking, experiencing, debating person in whom all other persons live and move and have their being through the historical process.

But if we cast doubt on any extreme use of the organic analogy, we must likewise question seriously any attribution of personality to the state. When we attempt to identify what we mean by personality, we usually think of will, reason, and purpose. Now to what degree can we really say that the state possesses will, reason, and purpose? There is, no doubt, a certain autonomy in social and political processes which is beyond the capacity of any given generation to alter in a radical sense: Hence, from one point of view, all of us are subjected to a complex of institutions and customs which do have a "life of their own," as we say. We cannot simply contract them away, in other words, but we ourselves are, in fact, to some degree, their products. Perhaps we can say that there are will-like elements in the social and political patterns to which we are subjected. But to endow these with what we usually call personality is again to take literally what can be only a limited though useful analogy.

To think of the state in Hegel's extreme way tends to make individual personalities largely illusory. Since all real thought and will are to be found in the political process or state, which is conceived to be the guardian of *sittlichkeit*, Hegel cannot really develop a theory of moral and political obligation. As Carritt points out, if the source and desideratum of all morality is the state, there is no standard by which the individual can measure acts of specific governments or rulers; for the tendency of the Hegelian is to say that whatever is rational or moral is real (that is, is embodied in the complex of *sittlichkeit* and its protector the state).[42]

But, we may ask, if the state is endowed with personality—and, indeed, is the only true personality—why do not all groups have the same attribute? Hegel says that in association a will emerges which is the will of the association and not merely a kind of mixture of the wills of individuals. But if this be admitted, why is the state peculiar in this respect? After all, churches, schools, trade unions, chambers of commerce, and a wide variety of other organizational forms flourish, a fact which is readily admitted by Hegel, as we have seen. But how does it happen that they, too, do not have personalities and wills? Hegel is silent at this point. As a matter of fact, there have been significant political theorists—modern pluralists like J. N. Figgis and Harold Laski, for example—who have asserted just this: that so-called nonstate associations owe their existence to the independent associative tendency in man and that they develop group quasi-personalities much like the so-called personality which Hegel attributed to the state.[43]

(3) This leads us to observe that Hegel and many of the modern idealists who follow him tend to identify the state with society in a rather confusing way. He seems to imply that all the rich variety of associative life can be subsumed under the rubric of the state, that the social roots of personality are to be made equivalent to state roots.

It is true, of course, that he discusses, rather elaborately—as we have seen—the role of familial and economic organization in the shaping of human personality and in the development of *bewusstsein*. But always he seems to be saying that these are, somehow, lower orders of reality than the state and are, indeed, creatures of it. The state shapes them to its ends; and any ends they may profess to have of their own, if rightly understood, are simply ingredients of state ends. Certainly this has been the tendency of many who profess to speak in his name, if not of Hegel himself.[44]

The error in Hegel's thinking would seem to be that, while he rightly stresses the enormous importance of the idea of the state as the principle of emerging or would-be rationality and a decisive factor in shaping personality, he thinks he must also assert that all other associations and all persons are completely absorbed in the purposes of the state and that their supposedly independent purposes and ends are illusory. There is no direct way of refuting an Hegelian when he makes assertions of this kind; but we can reply that in our judgment our trade unions and our persons have ends apart from state ends and that these ends, too, are significant in themselves.

(4) As we have seen, Hegel thinks of all history as process in which nothing "is" but is only becoming. Political forms change. Within any given form exists a kind of contradiction so that one might expect that which apparently exists today to become transformed tomorrow.

In view of this stress on process and change, it is indeed astonishing to find Hegel often apparently thinking of the nation-state as the final and highest form of political organization. In effect, he would seem to be asserting, there are two exceptions to the rule that all is becoming and not being. The first is that the nation-state form persists, despite the decline of given nation-states, and the second is that war as an institution continues.

This position is all the more astonishing when we remember that Hegel is very careful to trace out changes in political forms of the past. He is acutely aware, for example, of the distinction between the empire form and the city-state form of the ancient past. How he then came to accept, as he apparently did, the nation-state as the highest political expression of the world spirit is one of the mysteries of the Hegelian position.

In viewing the nation-state as sovereign, moreover, he appears to imply a way of life, a culture, and a decision-making process which are separate and distinct in each nation-state from other nation-states. But this is, in fact, never true. There are relations between and among individuals which cut across nation-state lines and associations which are genuinely international in nature. Each nation-state in its policies is, moreover, profoundly conditioned

42. See Edward Carritt, *Morals and Politics*, Oxford: Clarendon, 1935, and *Ethical and Political Theory*, Oxford: Clarendon, 1947.
43. See, for example, J. N. Figgis, *Churches in the Modern State*, London: Longmans, Green, 1913.
44. See, for example, Bernard Bosanquet, *The Philosophical Theory of the State*, New York: St. Martin's, 1923.

by what other nation-states do. Thus in the twentieth century it has sometimes been observed that the foreign policy of the United States is as much made by the Soviet Union as by the United States. It is true that Hegel does, in some measure, seem to recognize all this when he points out that a nation-state requires recognition by others before it can possess statehood, just as individual recognition by other men is required for personality to exist. But he seems to forget all this in much of his discussion and to stress all too frequently the alleged separateness and conflict of nation-states.

(5) Finally, Hegel has been charged by Benedetto Croce,[45] who in many respects finds the Hegelian system a suggestive one, with philosophical errors in his very conception of the philosophy of history. In considerable degree, it would seem, Croce's criticism is justifiable.

Croce's questions about Hegel can best be put in his own words. After pointing out that every historical judgment must consist of both intuitive and logical elements, Croce goes on to say:

> From this historical gnoseology, it follows that every progress of philosophical thought is translated into a progress of historical knowledge, since we understand far more adequately what were truly the historical facts of Dante's composition of his poem, when we know better what poetry and artistic creation are. But we also gather that the attempt would be vain to resolve those historical affirmations into abstract philosophic affirmations. That would be to absorb the whole and complete fact in what is merely the condition of the fact. History can give rise to a conceptual science of an empirical character, as when we pass from it to a sociology that proceeds by types and classes; but for that very reason, it is not absorbed by that conceptual science, of which it remains the presupposition or the basis. Conversely, history can give rise to philosophy, when we pass from the historical consideration of the particular to the theoretical elements, which are at the bottom of that consideration; but, for that very reason, it cannot be said to be absorbed in that philosophy, which is its presupposition and its basis. A philosophy of *history*, understood not as the elaboration of this abstract philosophy, but as *history of a second degree*, a history obtained by means of that abstract philosophy, is a contradiction in terms.[46]

Yet, Croce argues, this is exactly what Hegel attempts to do. He posited the idea of a philosophy of history and in so doing he had to negate the history treated by historians—a requirement of his logical presupposition. Croce charges Hegel with claiming to know what the facts must be even before he seeks historical data. The latter, then, simply fill in specific dates and names of persons. While he does profess quite often a respect for fact, this stands in conflict with his apparent assertion that history can be understood *before* the data are gathered, simply through the logic. "If a philosophy of history be created," Croce goes on, "then this accidental and individual, and the historical and empirical method, are not recognized and are refuted."[47]

Croce is also very critical of Hegel's tendency to think that only those facts are valuable which represent the history of the state. All other facts are accidental or nonessential and have nothing to do with history as Hegel defines it. Truth is that of the spirit and external existence is of no concern to the historian. But this, Croce observes, really sets up the notion of two kinds of facts—historical facts on the one hand and unessential facts on the other. This is a pernicious distinction, argues the Italian philosopher, and yet has been maintained by most Hegelians.[48]

Hegel and His Opponents

The criticisms of Hegel in the nineteenth century took several forms, both explicit and implicit. Among the former, the most important were often those which were themselves profoundly influenced by Hegelian teaching. As for the implicit criticisms, we may include many of those views which continued to be dubious about positions reposing on organismic conceptions of society and which often took their point of departure, in one form or another, from the thought of individualists like Hobbes and Locke.

Some of the most vociferous explicit critics of Hegel who were at the same time deeply enamored of his thought were Karl Marx, Friedrich Engels, and their intellectual and spiritual descendants. Building on a reinterpretation of Hegel which was a product of their criticism, they were to become among the most influential political thinkers of the nineteenth and twentieth centuries. Men had to come to grips with their arguments and to react either positively or negatively. To them we turn in the chapter which immediately follows.

As for the implicit critics, perhaps the most important were the early modern Utilitarians. Rooted in the individualist-hedonist tradition, their outlook constituted an important factor in the shaping of primitive liberal thought. Later liberal ideas, however, would be influenced by both Hegelian and Marxist streams, thus illustrating once more the never-ending dialectic so characteristic of the history of political ideas in general. Following our examination of Marxism, it would seem particularly appropriate to show how this significant development in liberal thought took place.

chapter 25

Marx, the Marxists, and Modern Politics

The name Karl Marx has been one of enormous importance for more than a hundred years and promises to be invoked for yet another century. Since 1848, outlooks on the political world calling themselves Marxist have shaped the thought patterns of millions; and even those who have been violently opposed to the Marxist way of looking at politics and history have been forced to grapple with the questions raised by Marx, Engels, and their successors. The sheer bulk of the critical literature in many languages has reached astounding proportions.

The Genesis of the System

When Marx was born in 1818 at Treves, in southwestern Germany near the border of Luxembourg,[1] Hegel was just beginning the final phase of his career as a professor in the University of Berlin. The intellectual basis for German nationalism was being established and the post-Napoleonic world was searching for a political stability that seemed always to escape it. In Britain, industrialism was far advanced and the condition of the working class which Marx was later to describe so graphically was

Chapter 24

45. In *What Is Living and What Is Dead in the Philosophy of Hegel?*, Douglas Ainslie, trans., London: Macmillan, 1915.
46. *Ibid.*, pp. 136–137.
47. *Ibid.*, p. 142.
48. *Ibid.*, pp. 146–147.

Chapter 25

1. On the life of Marx, see, for example, Franz Mehring, *Karl Marx: The Story of His Life*, Ann Arbor: University of Michigan Press, 1962; and Isaiah Berlin, *Karl Marx: His Life and Environment*, New York: Oxford University Press, 1963.

becoming one of increasing dependence on the owners of capital.

Marx was born into a middle-class family on both sides of which could be found rabbis. In the Germany of the time, however, converts to Christianity had had considerable social and professional advantages and when Karl was six his father and mother followed a widespread practice among Jews of the time by becoming Protestants.

Marx's father was a lawyer and hoped that his son would follow him in his profession. When he entered the University of Bonn, in 1835, it was presumably with the legal calling in mind. However, at Bonn he was subjected to other intellectual influences and was already beginning to be torn away from his father's objectives. In addition, he fell in love (incidentally, with a member of the upper bourgeoisie), which distressed his family and distracted him from his studies.

When Marx transferred to the University of Berlin in 1836, Hegel had been dead for only five years and his influence was still overwhelming. Marx studied jurisprudence and steeped himself in the philosophy of Hegel. He became involved in the debates of the young Hegelians at the University and already the first stirrings of his later revolt against the domination of Hegel were revealed. However, he found it difficult to concentrate on formal academic study: The world of external struggle already began to press in upon him; he was determined to marry, and the necessity of earning a living became more and more imperative. The criticisms by Ludwig Feuerbach of Hegelian philosophy were reinforcing his tendencies to revolt. In 1841, however, he was awarded the Ph.D. by the University of Jena for a thesis *On the Difference Between the Democritean and the Epicurean Natural Philosophy*.

In the same year, he issued an attack on the Prussian state censorship, in this joining many young Germans of the time who looked forward to a liberal, free, and united nation. Taking up the career of journalism, he continued to contribute to the *Rheinische Zeitung* until that journal was suppressed because of its opposition to the status quo. Throughout this period, it should be emphasized, Marx read widely. Contrary to some hostile interpretations of him, he was thoroughly familiar with the great humanist tradition in Western culture and became interested for a time even in theological questions.[2]

Undoubtedly this strong humanist concern was a leading factor in his so-called revolt against religion, about which later critics were to wax so eloquent. In 1843, in his *Introduction to a Critique of the Hegelian Philosophy of Right*, we find him beginning that process of reversing Hegel in which he was to take so much pride. "Man," he averred, "makes religion; religion does not make man." Religion had come to be the way in which oppressed people expressed themselves when they were hopeless about improving their conditions in life; and it was used by their oppressors to lull them into acquiescence in and acceptance of the status quo—"It is the opium of the people."

Marx's increasingly bitter attacks on conditions in Germany made him no longer welcome there and in 1844 he began the exile from his native land which was to persist throughout the remaining part of his life. In that year he met Friedrich Engels in Paris and their lifelong friendship and collaboration began. Engels' father was a wealthy manufacturer with interests in both Germany and Manchester; and Engels himself combined broad intellectual interests with considerable business and administrative acumen. In France, the two new friends published *The Holy Family*, which was in part an attack on the utopian mentality. But their political agitation made them unwelcome in France and they now took up residence in Brussels. There *The German Ideology* was published in 1846.

Meanwhile, the post-Vienna world was beginning to break up. Already in 1830, a series of revolutions had changed the dynasty in France and had had repercussions on many other states. Rulers everywhere were feeling insecure as the middle classes and even some workingmen gained a new self-confidence. Although many thought that the spirit of the French Revolution had been killed in the post-1815 reaction to it, events now appeared to demonstrate that it was very much alive. Thus when the revolutions of 1848 swept the Western world they represented the fruits of the previous half generation of development. In France, the junior Bourbon dynasty was toppled without seeming difficulty and the revolutionary spirit made itself felt in Germany, Austria, Italy, and even the papal States. In Brussels, Marx watched all these events with the greatest interest because they seemed to him to foreshadow even greater disturbances. When asked by the Communist League to draft a declaration of principles for that socialist organization, Marx and Engels produced the *Communist Manifesto*, in which the disturbances of the time were fitted into a broadly conceived philosophy of history that used a framework not unlike the one developed by Hegel. The *Manifesto* was the fruit of the general revolutionary spirit; but it was also influential in stimulating and encouraging that spirit.

Again, however, Marx found himself clashing with the exponents of the existing order and moved to England as a place of exile. There he remained until his death; and it was there that his great investigation of capitalist industrial society was carried on.

Particularly after 1865, Marx's home in London became a center for discussion of politics. Exiles from all over Europe visited him and he became increasingly interested in the practical politics of revolution. In 1864, he had been one of the guiding spirits in the foundation of the International Workingmen's Association, which federated proletarian parties and movements from a number of nations. Originally very broadly based, it included anarchists, socialists, and others who could not be legitimately classified under either label. Within the Association, these diversities in political views caused enormous fissions, particularly between the anarchists, led by Mikail Bakunin, and the Socialists, led by Marx. Eventually the struggle between Marx and Bakunin became so bitter that the Association was allowed to die but not before the anarchists had been expelled.

In his adventures into the realm of practical politics, Marx exhibited certain personal characteristics that were to impose their stamp for many years upon the movements which bore his name. There remains to be written a full-fledged psychological study of him as man and thinker. In the conflict with Bakunin, he seemed to be utterly violent and ruthless: Unless he could control affairs on his own terms, he would not cooperate with others. He insisted on centralized control of all the groups which called themselves Marxist, thus establishing a precedent for twentieth-century movements which invoked his name. There was a strong tendency to intolerance running through his character. Compromise he appeared to spurn as a weakness. Yet curiously enough he was the epitome of gentleness and kindness in his relations with children and in his family life.

In the latter part of his life, Marx seemed always to be hoping that the events of the time foreshadowed the coming "final revolution." Thus he saw the revolt of the Communards in France at the conclusion of the Franco-Prussian War as setting the pattern for imminent overturn of all existing systems of rule.[3] So convinced was he that capitalism was doomed that he appeared to look for its death momentarily.

After his death in 1883, Engels carried on his work, publishing the second and third volumes of *Das Kapital* and such significant Marxist treatises as *Socialism: Utopian and Scientific* (1877). While at some points Engels appears to depart from Marx's view, the differences between the two men are no more significant than the apparent contradictions and ambiguities occurring in the writings of Marx himself.

There are various ways in which one might approach the Marx-Engels analysis. Here, however, it would seem most fruitful to ask ourselves, first, what the political goals of Marx and Engels appeared to be; second, to inquire into the philosophical and scientific basis of the original Marxian system; and, third, to note the means for the conquest of power which Marx thought were indicated by the philosophical and scientific analysis. Of these elements, the second is by far the more significant in the eyes of Marx himself and will therefore occupy a correspondingly large place in our treatment.

The Political Goals of Marx and Engels

Marx and Engels—and most Marxists since—were very suspicious about any exact formulation of political ideals.

We might ask in the beginning why nineteenth-century Marxist thought and, for the most part, its twentieth-century descendants, have spurned what they call "utopianization." The answer would seem to lie basically in the historical circumstances and ideological context out of which the system arose. Marx began his inquiries at a time when utopian socialism was establishing its foundations in the Western world. Robert Owen had worked

2. See Erich Fromm, *Marx's Concept of Man*, New York: F. Ungar, 1961.
3. See his essay "The Civil War in France," to be found in Karl Marx, *The Paris Commune*, New York: New York Labor News Co., 1945.

out a scheme which, generally speaking, provided for a kind of planned community; and Owen had actually attempted to put it into practice on a limited basis. Proudhon, although usually classified as an anarchist, envisioned a system of society which in many respects can be thought of as a kind of decentralized socialism. During the Revolution of 1848, there were many proposals for collective ownership of property and great attention was given to the elaboration of details.[4] And the schemes of Fourier and Cabet are excellent examples of the utopian socialist mentality around the middle of the century.[5]

A frequent characteristic of utopian proposals was their emphasis on small experimental colonies which would test the ideals in microcosm in the hope that the schemes would later be adopted on a large scale. Thus there were many Fourierist and Cabetist communities in the United States, and in New Harmony, Indiana, Robert Owen's son endeavored to implement Owenite socialism.

Very early in the evolution of their thought, Marx and Engels took issue with the utopians. In an early treatise, Marx vigorously attacked the schemes of Proudhon,[6] and Engels later tried to elaborate the distinction between utopian and scientific thought.[7] In their polemics against the utopians, Marx and Engels often became quite bitter.

Yet an over-all picture of the Marx-Engels position must initially recognize their great indebtedness to the utopians. It was the utopian socialist stream of thought which helped to arouse their interest in the reordering of industrial society.

Perhaps it was precisely because they were so sympathetic with the moral principles of the utopians that Marx and Engels criticized them so vigorously. For utopian socialism, they argued, while right in its moral indignation, never went much beyond the stage of preaching. It was almost entirely lacking in an understanding of the dynamics of history and sought to impose a pattern without comprehending the relativities of a given social and political situation. Moreover, insofar as it stressed experimental colonies, it did not recognize that radically different economic and social systems could not long flourish in the midst of a culture organized along diametrically opposed lines: A private-property capitalist culture would soon engulf the feeble efforts of the utopians.

The problem, as Marx and Engels saw it, was not that of working out detailed schemes for the ideal society but rather of understanding the political and historical process and the limits which that process imposed on the revolutionary and reformer. What was needed was a scientific study of society, in other words, similar to the scientific approaches which Darwin was developing in biological study.[8]

So great was the stress of Marx and Engels on science, in fact, that they ostensibly repudiated altogether any pretense to be moralists. Although they could not carry out this self-assigned role consistently and their conception of science was a curious one (as we shall see), they at least held it up as an ideal.

For them to have worked out a full-fledged picture of the ideal society would, then, have appeared a contradiction of their main objective. By and large, they contended, history would itself shape the nature of the new society: the important problem was to comprehend where history was taking the world and how one could accentuate the process. To artificially impose a pattern on the process was unscientific.

In general, the Marx-Engels view of history is colored and conditioned by the threefold patterning which we have seen running through all Western political thought, whether in a religious or a secular guise. Broadly speaking, in other words, Marx and Engels accept the notion—which we discovered in such diverse writers as St. Augustine and Rousseau[9]—that human experience is triadic. There is an uncorrupt phase before power and property relations arise; an historical epoch, which includes the rise of the state and of property; and a posthistorical era, in which paradise is somehow regained and the tension between freedom and authority, so characteristic of history, is eliminated. The third phase is the ideal, whether in heaven or on earth, to which human experience apparently points.

It is to be an era foreshadowed by the last phases of history. In the preliminary stage, each will receive from the common store in accordance with "deed" (that is, contribution to society), rather than under the hit-or-miss system of fate and fortune which is the hallmark of historical relations. The right of inheritance will presumably be wiped out in this stage and increasingly an accelerated proportion of all production will be reserved for social purposes: replacement of capital, expansion of capital equipment, social insurance of all kinds, and general administration. The number of free services—parks, playgrounds, education, health, and so on—will expand. The element of coercion, so characteristic of history, will decline as collective services increase, presumably because man's material needs are now much better satisfied and the tensions out of which coercion arises have drastically declined. As coercion virtually disappears the way is prepared for the final stage, which will, so to speak, cap the climax.

In this final or truly communist state of society, contribution will be in accordance with ability and distribution will be in proportion to need. Thus deed is changed to need; and while Marx, Engels, and, after them, Lenin are very vague as to who judges need, the implication is that each individual appraises his own need. He has been disciplined in the preliminary stage to be self-restrained and to be concerned for the common weal, so that no external check on his own judgment is required.

Because of this discipline, in fact, all external forms of coercion now disappear. The hierarchical civil service, which Marx and Engels think of as an important weapon of coercion, disappears, as do the army, navy, and police. In their place, spontaneous co-operation cares for public need and for such slight restraints as are required in a communist society. Somehow, too, all the advantages of specialization of labor (high production, for example) are present without such disadvantages as alienation of man from man and of man from the product of his work.

It is difficult to discover whether Marx and Engels envisioned this state of affairs coming about in the relatively near future or whether they thought that it was to be the result of centuries of evolution. At times the first conclusion seems plausible, while at other points the second appears more legitimate. And professed Marxists in the twentieth century are no less uncertain. Thus at various times in the history of Soviet Marxist thought, both versions have been held.

What is clear, however, is that Marxism thinks of the final stage as being a temporal epoch. It is not, that is to say, a paradise to be attained beyond time, as with much medieval thought, nor is it to be regarded as a mere utopian standard by which to judge contemporary society—as some interpretations of Rousseau might hold. Thus it shares the characteristics of what Professor Voegelin calls the Gnostic mentality of modern times—belief in inevitable progress and attachment to the notion that the dilemmas of power and coercive relations can be transcended in the here and now.[10]

The Marxist View of Human History

Putting the ideal aside, Marx and Engels concentrate most of their effort on an analysis of the historical process and an effort to formulate in theoretical terms the nature and logic of capitalist economics. Taken together, these two elements constitute the foundation for their predictions of the future course of the world. In this section we center our attention on their analysis of the historical process, reserving the next for a discussion of their economic ideas.

The historical conceptions are inseparably connected with Hegelianism. As we noted in the preceding chapter, Hegel thinks of history as a patterned phenomenon in which aware-

4. An older work is still valuable in connection with the "utopian" socialists. See Richard Ely, *French and German Socialism in the Nineteenth Century*, New York: Harper, 1883.
5. For a recent critical appraisal of some of these schemes, see Marie Louise Berneri, *Journey Through Utopia*, London: Routledge and Paul, 1950.
6. See *The Poverty of Philosophy*, Moscow: Foreign Languages Publishing House, 1956.
7. See *Socialism: Utopian and Scientific*, Chicago: C. H. Kerr, 1903. Note the following from Engels: "To speculate on how a future society might organize the distribution of food and dwellings leads directly to utopia. The utmost we can do is to state from our understanding of the basic modes of production up to now that with the downfall of the capitalist mode of production certain forms of appropriation which existed in society hitherto will become impossible." Friedrich Engels, *Selected Works*, vol. 5, Moscow: Foreign Languages Publishing House, 1961, pp. 632–633.
8. Both Darwinism and Marxism, of course, placed a great emphasis on the flux of things. In terms of the ancient Greek debate on the permanent versus the changing, they took their stand with Heraclitus as against Parmenides.
9. See Chapters 10 and 22. Other thinkers could also be cited.
10. See Eric Voegelin, *The New Science of Politics*, Chicago: University of Chicago Press, 1952. Note also Voegelin's series *Order and History*, Baton Rouge, La.: Louisiana State University Press, 1956.

ness of the union of objective and subjective progressively develops. In this manner, freedom, in its only meaningful sense, is enlarged. Ideas, rather than things, are the ultimate substance from which things emanate.

A central proposition of the Hegelian thesis is, as we have suggested, that the individual is not ultimately real, for individuality can be explained only in terms of the universal operating in the group and particularly in the state. Individuality as usually understood (by classical social contract thinkers, for example) has merely a low-level reality status. Only the state, as idea, the universal, and the rational, may be thought of as actually possessing first-order status.

Now Marx, as we have seen, early became attracted by the Hegelian viewpoint. It had affinities (as well as important differences) with the Hebrew prophetic conception of human development and it ostensibly provided ethical and political guidance (by contrast with Kant's "subjectivism"). It recognized, Marx thought, the subsidiary nature of human individuality in history and it provided the basis for a theory of conflict.

But just as Hegel was dissatisfied with Kant's subjectivism, so was Marx uneasy about Hegel's idealism. Whereas Hegel tended to say that things or matter are mere emanations of minds, Marx maintained that mind itself is a kind of reflection of things—that is, of the external world of production and distribution of material goods. Our thought patterns, in other words, are shaped by the necessity of getting a living and the institutions which have grown up around getting and spending. The primary fact is that man must live before he can think and this remains the dynamic principle in human experience: With changes in methods of gaining a livelihood, man's whole intellectual and spiritual expression is altered. Ultimately, religion, politics, art, and other reflections of the intellectual and aesthetic life are molded in their contours by the ways in which the mode of producing material goods shifts.[11]

Marx himself has said that he placed Hegel on his feet, meaning that whereas the earlier thinker made *mind* the dynamic factor, the Marxist sees in the changing organization of *things* the basic stuff out of which history is made.

Individual and Class. But while Marx apparently reverses the relations of the Hegelian system, he clearly retains Hegel's conception of the individual's subordinate role. The shift from Hegel to Marx in this respect is simply that for Marx the individual is imprisoned in the class mind whereas for Hegel he was an emanation of the state mind. For Marx and Engels (and their Marxist successors), the class takes the place of the state.

But what is a class? Marx apparently means that social and intellectual differentiations arise which owe their existence to the fact that men find themselves in varying relations to the mode of production at a given period of history and tend to act in accordance with the interests thus established. Owners of capital equipment, in other words, will tend to think differently from those who merely contribute labor. Possessors of land in a feudal epoch will, by and large, have a world outlook sharply differentiating them from serfs.

Although classes differentiate themselves in relation to the mode of production, we should not assume that Marx means by mode of production something wholly tangible or literally material. The productive methods of a given age are composed of natural forces—material goods available, geographical position, and so on—and the human mind—state of technology, human organization, and similar ingredients. When the Marxist speaks of mode of production, then, he is referring to a kind of interpenetration of matter and mind, with the brute necessities of material existence forcing the mind to develop technological and organizational devices.[12]

Dialectical Materialism, Class, and Human History. The Marx-Engels view can be better understood if we picture it as operating dynamically in the concrete events of history.

But in this connection we should remember that it is a conception of history and not of prehistory. As we indicated earlier, the Marxist outlook adopts the familiar triadic picture of a state before history, history itself, and posthistory, the achievement of communism. Classes, presumably, developed only in history, being absent (or largely so) in prehistory and in its communist consummation. Marx and Engels are strongly influenced in their version of prehistory by the writings of the American anthropologist Lewis Henry Morgan (1818–1881),[13] who alleged that primitive cultures exhibit a state of communism and classlessness.

All this changes, however, when the primitive division of labor (between man and woman) gives way to more complex relations. Simple and spontaneous relations between human beings and to the work that sustains them are no longer possible. The immediate interests of now-separated men no longer coincide with the general interest of all in a livelihood and in maintenance of life. The clever and powerful come to control access to means of production and reduce others to a subordinate status. Systems of coordination arise to hold together in a tenuous fashion a humanity whose class interests are now alienating them from one another. And with systems of coordination, the phenomenon of the state arises.

Marx and Engels see the state as the device whereby the predominant class in any historical epoch seeks to provide an order which will enhance its own interests. In other terms, those who control the means of production (landowners, merchant capitalists, industrial capitalists, and so on) will tend to mold the political institutions and the predominant mythology (belief system) of the age. The ruling class will develop an ideology making appeals to the public interest in order to delude both itself and the subordinate classes into believing that its control is for the best interests of all.

The whole spiritual life of men will, in fact, be colored by the class-ridden culture. In the Middle Ages, for example, God becomes a kind of feudal lord who sustains the set of relations established by the predominant land-controlling classes. Under industrial capitalism, religion is called into the service of the owners of machines who now constitute the predominant class and who use religion as a cloak to sustain their rule. Educational systems, too, become primarily agents of propaganda for the successful economic class. Knowledge itself is relative to the class interests of those who control the mode of production.

But no ruling class historically, Marx and Engels teach, has been immune to decay from within and to attack from without. In fact, human history is essentially the story of how class succeeds class in positions of power, prestige, and spiritual control. Just as Hegel thinks of the history of the idea as reflected in the struggles of national cultures, so Marx and Engels see material culture changing and propelling the rise of new classes to power. In fact, the very efforts of a given class to maintain itself prepare the way for its downfall: The thesis, borrowing from some interpretations of Hegel, provokes its opposite, from which emerges a synthesis and a new thesis.

Marxist thought purports to be able to analyze any epoch in history according to this scheme. Thus ancient Greek history after about the eighth century B.C. can be fruitfully subjected to a class and dialectical materialist analysis. So, too, can medieval history.

But while the historical analysis can be applied to any aspect of man's experience, Marx and Engels are naturally most concerned to use it for comprehending what is going on under conditions of industrial capitalism. Modern capitalism arises, they think, as the feudal way of life breaks down. In its first phase, the predominant class is composed of merchants who buy their way into positions of power when the feudal system is no longer able to function. In its second aspect, it is the owners of the complex machines developed by the industrial process who occupy the crucial role. Through their possession of machines, which have become essential for the productive process, they can initially dictate conditions of labor and can manipulate legal and political institutions in such a way as to benefit themselves as a class. Yet in the long run, the very activities whereby they endeavor to consolidate their power and status provoke a rising class antithesis destined to overthrow them.

11. These notions are developed in several important Marxist treatises. See particularly *The German Ideology*. In the preface to the second edition of *Capital* (1873), Marx asserts: "My own dialectical method is not only fundamentally different from the Hegelian dialectical method, but is the direct opposite. For Hegel, the thought process (which he actually transforms into an independent subject, giving to it the name of 'idea') is the demiurge (creator) of the real; and for him the real is only the outward manifestation of the idea. In my view, on the other hand, the idea is nothing other than the material when it has been transposed and translated inside the human head."
12. For an excellent analysis of these issues, see G. D. H. Cole, *The Meaning of Marxism*, London: V. Gollancz, 1950.
13. Morgan was a lawyer who studied intensively the customs and traditions of American Indians. In 1851, he published his first work, *The League of the Iroquois*, Rochester: Sage & Bros. In 1870 came his *Systems of Consanguinity and Affinity of the Human Family*, Washington, D.C.: Smithsonian Institution. His most philosophical treatise was *Ancient Society*, New York: Holt, 1877.

Let us note a little more specifically how this takes place.

The great characteristic of industrialism in its earlier phases is the uprooting of men from the soil and their attachment to the machine. They move from the traditional village community, with its agricultural economy, to the town, there to become the hired employees of the capitalist who owns the machines. But in severing their connections with the village community they also cut their ties with nature; it thus becomes impossible for them to rely for a livelihood directly upon the soil. If they are discharged by their employer in the city, they can hardly take up residence in the country again. Thus they are forced to work on the capitalist's own terms or face the threat of starvation. This is particularly true because initially they are unorganized, isolated, and unconscious of their place in the industrial process as a whole.

However, the very process which enables the employer to dictate the terms under which they shall labor for him also, however imperceptibly at first, begins to change the status of both employee and employer. Originally isolated when they start operating the machine, the "proletariat" (an old Latin term signifying those who are good for nothing except to reproduce themselves) find themselves working side by side and subject to "socialization": They exchange experiences, rely upon one another for assistance, and gradually come to see that their interests as workers set them apart from the employer's interests. In sum, the industrial capitalist scheme itself helps promote the solidarity of the working class and this solidarity becomes the foundation for an eventual overthrow of the scheme.

Meanwhile, however, growing awareness of common interests leads to organization and organization to an intensified class struggle. Workers in unions and, where possible, political parties, may be expected to exert pressures both in the industrial and in the political realm.

But while this development of class consciousness by the workers has been taking place, the dialectic has also been at work among owners of capital. The very pressures of competition among themselves (and early industrialism is characterized by the ideology and practice of entrepreneurial competition), as well as the increasing power of self-conscious labor, have begun to transform the nature of capitalism. Each employer seeks to minimize costs and to maximize gain (Marx and Engels assume that profit is the end-all of the owners of capital under industrialism); to do so, each attempts to introduce more efficient methods of production, which implies that machinery will increasingly do the work that men have done in the past. But if one employer discovers a way to cut costs through introduction of more machinery, others will have to follow suit or find their profits approaching zero. There is thus set up a scramble to increase relative proportions of what Marx calls constant capital (largely machinery) and to reduce those of variable capital (labor power). In the struggle, the weaker competitors go under and the stronger increase their relative strength. Capitalism, which in the beginning was competitive, now tends in the direction of a stifling of competition, where this permits an enhancement of constant capital.

The process on the capitalist side is accentuated through pressures exerted by organized labor as well as by more demanding legal standards. Both tend to put a premium on lowered costs of production and greater use of constant rather than variable capital. Meanwhile, as small entrepreneurs are squeezed out, the size of the proletariat grows and the number of capitalists declines. Marx and Engels envision a kind of split in the middle classes, with the large bourgeoisie increasing their relative wealth and power and the petty bourgeoisie losing their stake in ownership and becoming mere hired employees.

The economic theory through which Marx attempts to account for this process in specific terms we shall turn to in the next section. Here, however, let us note the Marxist prognosis. As the polarization of the class structure proceeds and the misery of the proletariat is accentuated (whether in absolute or relative terms is unclear and is still a subject of dispute among students of Marx), severe crises become characteristic of capitalist culture. Unused machinery and unused labor power will characterize these crises, as well as a growing rigidity in prices which will make it more difficult for capitalists to adjust to changing demand and supply. In an effort to overcome the crises, a temporary way out will be found in export of consumers' and later of capital goods which cannot be consumed in the crisis-ridden domestic market. This, however, can provide only a temporary remedy at best and can be accomplished only at the expense of accentuating political crises. Thus Lenin makes competition of capitalist nations for raw materials and markets a major if not the main cause of modern imperialism and war.[14]

Although the final crisis of the capitalist world can be postponed, the inevitable working out of the dialectical process, Marxist doctrine holds, dooms it to destruction. This is not basically because some external force will crush capitalist economies and politics but rather because owners of capital in a quasi-monopolistic situation and confronted by increasingly self-conscious organized workers will find their markets shrinking and their machines idle. Capitalism, which Marx and Engels praise so highly as initially a great creator of material abundance,[15] will in its declining stages not know what to do with the very abundance which it has created. In their ceaseless search for profit, the controllers of capitalist culture will fail to see that the very quest is undermining the ability of the system to use the goods it has created.

In the declining epoch of capitalism, the Marxist analysis goes on, ruling classes will tend to become desperate. While they have never been loathe to use physical force to sustain their order—thus following all ruling classes in history—at the height of capitalist control such force was usually minimal or covert. Now, however, in the declining phase, one might expect use of overt force to come to the fore as rulers, desperate by reason of their inability to maintain profit and the assumptions of the system, turn to fruitless repression. The use of force will not avail them because by now the bankruptcy of the system will have become so obvious and the self-consciousness of the proletariat—and their organization as well—so clear that the socialist phase of industrial evolution will ensue. This is the period in which state power will be seized by the fully aware proletariat, the engines of justice will be turned against the remaining functions of the capitalists, and the last vestiges of capitalism will be wiped out. In the thought of Marx and Engels, this socialist episode is apparently to be rather brief in time, for the way will have been prepared for it through the virtual collapse of the old order. In Lenin, notably, there seems to be the suggestion that the socialist period may be rather extended. But, long or short, it will be followed by the communist society to which reference has been made in the preceding section.

In terms of the dialectic analysis, communism is, as it were, the final synthesis. This is to say, the synthesis will not constitute a new thesis to be followed by another class antithesis. This is so because all class lines have now been destroyed through socialist production and the triumph of the proletariat, whose interest is identical with the interest of all mankind. At the level of propaganda, this thought is expressed in the well-known lines of the great Marxist hymn *The International:*

'Tis the final conflict, let each stand in his place,
The International Party will be the human race.

At this point, then, as was suggested earlier, history—defined in the Marxist sense as class conflict—comes to an end. Conflict, no doubt, will continue to exist, but it will not be class conflict and hence will no longer be historical.

Marxist versus Hegelian Dialectic. Throughout the Marxist analysis, both striking similarities to and equally important differences from the Hegelian view are notable. The similarities include the idea of dialectic both as logic and in history; the assumption of human perfectibility in history; the belief that generalizations about historical tendencies somehow enlighten one as to one's duties and obligations; the great stress on evolving consciousness as a key to understanding; and the idea that the individual mind is essentially simply an outpost of a group or social mind. But differences are equally significant: Marxism sees the dynamic factor in the movement of "things," or the mode of production, Hegelianism sees it in the motions of "spirit"; Marxism identifies the group mind with the class rather than the nation-state; and finally, Marxism, unlike Hegelianism, purports to be able to predict the future in considerable detail.

Marxism and Religion. The Hegelian system,

14. See V. I. Lenin, *Imperialism*, New York: International Publishers, 1939. In his analysis, Lenin was anticipated by the British Liberal economist John Atkinson Hobson, who discussed imperialism in economic terms. See his *Imperialism*, Ann Arbor: University of Michigan Press, 1965. (Originally published 1902.)
15. See *The Communist Manifesto*, New York: New York Labor News Co., 1959.

as we have suggested, is heretical from the viewpoint of the major religious tradition in Western culture in that it thinks of God and man as evolving together in terms of growing self-consciousness. Divinity, or spirit, is, as it were, a part of the process and is reduced from the status of *being* to that of *becoming*. With this view as a background, it is not surprising that Marx and Engels should become hostile to religion in its orthodox sense. In the very act, too, of "setting Hegel on his feet" and making the dialectic materialist, one might expect them to reject the primary of the spiritual, whether in Hegel's or in the orthodox sense.

This attitude is revealed in an early letter which Marx writes to Hermann Wagener, assistant judge in the Prussian ecclesiastical courts. Writing in 1847, Marx remarks that

> the social principles of Christianity have now had eighteen hundred years for their development, and do not need any further development at the hands of Prussian consistorial councillors. The social principles of Christianity find justifications for the slavery of classical days, extol medieval serfdom, and are ready in case of need to defend the oppression of the proletariat.[16]

Religion, Marx and Engels consistently teach, tends to become merely political—to be used as an instrument by which a given ruling class helps sustain itself in power. Historically, Marxists attempt to show, religious convictions are employed to sustain the morality of the age and morality is always class morality and not human morality: Whatever the formulations of the moralist and however universal they may appear, in practice they become slogans of class rule; or the gulf between moral-religious principles and actual practice is rationalized by various devices including the postulation of original sin.

Another way of putting the Marxist position is to say that class struggles inevitably make political weapons of religion and morality. Try as they may to avoid it, men find themselves reducing such notions as God, truth, right, and love to class divinities, class truths, class right, and class love. It has often been observed in the twentieth century that "God" in a world of nation-states tends to be restricted by the nationalist shibboleths of each state involved.[17] While men talk of a universal God or good, in effect they identify God with the power interests of Germany, or Britain, or the United States. With his class interpretation, Marx is making the same observation about the effect of class antagonisms on religious and moral beliefs.[18]

The whole Marxist attitude to religion and morality is in effect a harsh description of the fact that men talk loudly about the brotherhood of man and the fatherhood of God but live in societies where these notions cannot be implemented because of the distortions wrought by class divisions. Given this analysis, Marx is saying that a religion which is imprisoned by class bias cannot make universalist moral teaching relevant in the world of the actual. It therefore takes refuge in the world of spirit and comforts its devotees by assuring them that all will be different in the afterlife.[19]

Yet the very vehemence of the Marxist rejection—so unscientific in its tone—perhaps reflects a profound commitment to many of the professed moral beliefs associated with traditional religion. In certain respects the Marxist attitude resembles that of the ancient Hebrew prophets who, in endeavoring to restore faith in a universal divine being, often seemed to reject all religion as conventionally practiced. This is not the only parallelism between Marx and men like Jeremiah and the second Isaiah but it is certainly one of the most striking.[20]

Marx and the Idea of Community. In his analysis of industrialist capitalism, one of the central observations of Marx concerns the psychological loss of community on the part of those who have been reduced to the status of mere "hands" by the industrial process. The impersonalism of the industrial life—the worker is now a kind of cog in a complex process which he does not understand—is an important ingredient in this loss of community.

As the working class gradually develops a consciousness of increasing solidarity and of its common interests, a kind of half-community is developed. But it is still only a partial and distorted version, for being built on the antagonism of class struggle, it is not "human." To be sure, this has been true of all historical situations; but it seems to be accentuated in an industrial capitalist environment. And even in the twilight sort of community engendered by increasing awareness of the class struggle, the worker remains alienated from the tools of his labor and from the product of his work.[21]

Just as men have lost religion and human morality in a history dominated by class stratification, so, too, have they lost community. Only the consummation of the historical process in the final synthesis will make possible full human morality and complete human community.

The Economic Analysis of Capitalist Society

Earlier it was said that Marx's analysis of past and present consists of two parts: his view of history which reposes on a modified Hegelianism, and his account, in economic terms, of the way in which industrial capitalism will destroy itself. We now turn to the second aspect of this analysis.

The economics of capitalism, of course, are closely related to Marx's view of the historical process as it applies to the evolution of capitalism. The theory of history suggests the general patterning and the economic theory purports to explain how in specific terms the capitalist system moves toward its own fatal destiny. One can accept the former without necessarily agreeing with the latter.

He builds his scheme on foundations laid down by British economists like Adam Smith and David Ricardo. The history of British economic thought had been one which, in writings like those of Thomas Malthus, had stressed the pressure of population on resources and had argued that wages in a free economy would always tend to approximate a subsistence level. With every advance in production would come a disproportionate increase in population that would more than counterbalance the additional resources and income. British economics had, moreover, come to develop a labor theory of value, which maintained in essence that the value of a commodity was due to the quantity of labor employed in its production.[22]

Marx fits a version of the subsistence theory of wages and the labor theory of value into his own general economic theory. Wages he roughly identifies with variable capital, in the sense that they constitute the basis for value. Buildings and machinery are constant capital and, given the labor theory of value, are simply "stored up" or "frozen" or "congealed" labor. In general, the history of capitalism is one in which the capitalist owners increase proportions of constant capital (primarily machinery) in relation to variable capital in order to prevent the rate of profit from falling to zero, as, according to Marx and Engels, it tends to do in the process of capitalist maturation.

Let us see more explicitly how this takes place and what may be expected to be its results. Initially, of course, the capitalist has an enormous advantage over the worker in the sense that he owns the tools which are indispensable if the worker's labor is to be used in an industrial society. The workers are unorganized and their bargaining power vis-à-vis the capitalist is not great. They must work virtually on the capitalist's own terms. Their own labor is a commodity and the capitalist owner buys it for the wages essential barely to

16. Quoted in Otto Rühle, *Karl Marx: His Life and Work*, Eden Paul and Cedar Paul, trans., New York: Viking Press, 1929, pp. 121–122.
17. See Carlton J. H. Hayes, *Essays on Nationalism*, New York: Macmillan, 1926.
18. See *Anti-Duhring*, New York: International Publishers, 1935, p. 105.
19. A position similar to that of the late Archbishop William Temple, *Nature, Man, and God*, New York: Macmillan, 1934. Actually, Temple maintains, the true nature of Christianity is to be "the most materialistic religion in the world" in the sense that it emphasizes the created world and the close relation between body and spirit (p. 478). See also Alexander Miller, *The Christian Significance of Karl Marx*, New York: Macmillan, 1947.
20. Atheism in general is often, if not usually, a vigorous protest against the tendency of professed religionists to defy and thus make sacred their own concepts and ideas. Notions regarded as sacred are beyond criticism. The so-called atheist is thus protesting against what is essentially a form of idolatry.
21. "In what does this alienation of labour consist? First, that the work is *external* to the worker, that it is not a part of his nature, that consequently he does not fulfill himself in his work but denies himself, has a feeling of misery, not of well-being, does not develop freely a physical and mental energy, but is physically exhausted and mentally debased. The worker therefore feels himself at home only during his leisure, whereas at work he feels homeless. His work is not voluntary, but imposed, *forced labor*. . . . Finally, the alienated character of work for the worker appears in the fact that it is not his work but work for someone else, that in work he does not belong to himself but to another person." *Economic and Philosophical Manuscripts* (1844), *Marx-Engels Gesamtausgabe*, I, 3, 85.
22. See Thomas Malthus, *Essay on the Principles of Population* (London, 1798); David Ricardo, *The Works of David Ricardo*, London: Cambridge University Press, 1951; and Adam Smith, *The Wealth of Nations*, New York: Modern Library, 1937.

hold body and soul together. But the commodities which the variable capital of labor is able to produce, in conjunction with the constant capital of the capitalist, are far greater in value than the commodities which the capitalist must provide to sustain the physical life of labor. The worker, in other words, produces his "keep" in far fewer hours of labor than the capitalist can require him to work. The hours necessary to provide the commodities essential for his support Marx calls "necessary labor time." The difference between the hours which he must contribute to the capitalist and the necessary labor time which provides his own support is known as surplus labor time, and the value created by this time is called surplus value.

Thus if the wage contract calls for 16 hours of labor and the amount of work necessary to provide the worker's support is only nine hours, seven hours constitutes surplus labor time or surplus value. This is taken by the capitalist and out of it comes his profit.

Now in the preceding section we have seen that the capitalist is subject to two kinds of pressures: those of his competitor and those of the workers who through organization and legislative activity press upon the resources of the capitalist. Both types of pressure tend to force the capitalist to reduce his costs in order to prevent his own liquidation as a capitalist. One of the major ways in which he responds to this pressure is to increase the ratio of constant (machines) to variable (labor) capital. Through this method he hopes to meet the competition of other capitalists and also to counteract the beginning of organized workers' power.

Perhaps an illustration will show what Marx means. Let us assume that the constant capital of an enterprise is valued at $10 million and the variable capital at $15 million. If we assume a total surplus value of $2 million, the rate of profit is 8 percent ($2 million divided by the investment of $25 million). The rate of surplus value, which is related to the variable capital only, is about 13.3 percent ($2 million divided by $15 million).

In the effort to increase his total profits (the pursuit of which, let us remember, constitutes the moving force of capitalism), the capitalist decides next year to increase his constant capital to $15 million, which he thinks will enable him to reduce variable capital to $10 million. His total surplus value, let us assume, remains at $2 million. It would have fallen had he not taken the precaution of increasing the relative amount of constant capital and decreasing that of variable capital. Profit rate remains eight percent. But with the same profit and profit rate, the rate of surplus value (which is the rate, it will be remembered, of exploitation) has gone up—from 13.3 percent to 20 percent.

Although the capitalist's profit rate remained constant in the second illustration, he is alarmed because it did not increase. The following year he increases his constant capital to $20 million, which enables him to decrease his variable capital to $7.5 million. Surplus value increases to $2.1 million. Profit rate falls to a little more than 7.6 percent. But rate of surplus value (exploitation) mounts to 28 percent.

The gist of the statement is that as the capitalist increases the ratio of constant to variable capital in the effort to maximize profits, he exploits labor more intensively but finds that his profits do not increase. Instead, over the long run, they will decline. Thus the capitalist must exploit with increasing intensity if he is to prevent the rate of profit from declining still more drastically. Fearful that the profit rate might sink to zero, he frantically promotes efficiency and introduces more machinery only to find that his mounting ratio of exploitation brings declining gains in terms of percentages of profit.

Thus the very process of substituting constant capital for variable capital appears to undermine the basis of the capitalist system. Yet the capitalist is helpless: He must act in this way or else find himself out of business very soon. His actions help postpone the day of general collapse but they cannot avert it forever.

Meanwhile, of course, machines themselves are becoming more complex and therefore expensive. Single capitalists, by contrast with the early days of industrialism (when men like Robert Owen accumulated their own capital and became rich almost overnight[23]) can no longer accumulate enough resources from their own savings to buy the machines. Moreover, the stronger capitalists are beginning to buy out the weaker ones and to enlarge units of production. Resources for purchase of constant capital must be gathered from many sources through such devices as the joint stock limited liability company. As units of industry become larger through stronger units absorbing the weaker and the imperatives of complex machinery putting their pressures on all capitalists, early competitive capitalism gives way to semimonopolistic capitalism.

At the same time, as the rate of exploitation increases, capitalism begins to undergo a series of crises. These are produced because the sheer quantity of goods produced by the accelerating ratio of constant capital cannot find a market. True, subsistence wages for the worker now means something quite different than in primitive capitalism, for the cultural standard of subsistence has advanced. But the potentialities for production are always several steps ahead of possibilities for consumption, given the framework of the capitalist system, the imperatives of profit seeking, and the increasing rate of exploitation. Unused capital equipment is matched by vast unemployment and a tendency for purchasing power to shrink.

But while consumers in highly developed capitalist nations find it increasingly difficult to buy the goods they produce, vast undeveloped areas remain for capitalist exploitation in other parts of the world. The owners of machines, now banded together in semimonopolies, seek markets for their products abroad and to some degree this postpones the day of collapse. Manufactured products are exchanged for cheap raw materials and the terms of trade always favor the highly developed industrial capitalist nations. Later on, capital goods themselves are exported to build up the industrial capitalist potentialities of those areas not yet subject to the factory system. But the export of capital goods, too, only postpones the day of collapse, since eventually the machines exported will be producing goods that will compete with those of the highly developed and older industrial countries.

As small capitalists and shopkeepers are squeezed out, they sink into the proletariat, that is, become wage workers, and there they tend to take on the characteristic world outlook of proletarians. Thus the proletarian class is vastly enlarged in numbers and the real owners and controllers of the machines become fewer. With every move of the former to increase the intensity of exploitation, the danger grows of crises arising from unemployment and unused resources. The proletariat becomes more miserable either absolutely or relatively (Marxist teaching on this point is by no means clear).[24] Sharpened in their class consciousness and increasing in political power through sheer weight of numbers, they see that the capitalist system which in the beginning performed wonders far beyond those carried out by the builders of the pyramids[25] can no longer function: With its periodic crises, its vast unused resources, and its incapacity to distribute the goods to those who need them, its day of collapse is imminent and it must give way to the socialism which precedes the final stage of communism.

As we noted in the preceding section, it is at this stage of the evolution of capitalism that Marxists—and particularly men like Lenin—suggest that imperialism and war result, as capitalist-controlled states compete with one another to avert the collapse. Basically, it is the accelerated pace of exploitation initiated in order to sustain the profit rate which is thus at the root of international violence, just as it constitutes the foundation of domestic violence. Some twentieth-century Marxists have associated this mature capitalism with the rise of Fascist and National Socialist movements of various kinds.[26]

The Strategy of Marxist Politics

If history is destined to produce first a socialist and then a communist economy and polity, it has often been asked, then why need the Marxist concern himself with strategy and tactics? If the capitalist, so to speak, in the

23. For the life of Robert Owen, consult his autiobiography, *The Life of Robert Owen,* New York: Knopf, 1920, and G. D. H. Cole, *Robert Owen,* London: E. Benn, 1925.
24. There has been a considerable debate among students of Marx as to whether the "immiseration" of the proletariat implies a poorer economic position in absolute terms or only in relation to what the ruling classes are taking from the gross national product. Since the history of capitalist economic societies has witnessed a steady over-all increase of the working class's real income, the tendency to interpret Marx in relativistic sense is understandable.
25. See *The Communist Manifesto, op. cit.*
26. During the twenties and thirties of the twentieth century, for example, Italian Fascism was explained by Marxist analysts as a kind of last-ditch stand by the capitalist owners of industry.

very process of sustaining his status, is undermining the basis of capitalist order, what possible role can a Marxist political movement have?

The answers to questions of this kind are not entirely clear. On the one hand, Marx argues that men "make their own history"; on the other hand, much of the analysis would seem to indicate that human beings have their history made for them by factors which are largely beyond their control. A similar problem arises, of course, in connection with the politics of Hegelianism; but at least Hegel does not purport to foretell the future in detail.

Perhaps the best solution for the problem is to follow those students of Marx who have suggested that, while the general pattern is laid down and can be known—both in the past and for the future—human beings can, through their understanding, help to speed it up. Although communism is inevitable, in other words, careful analysis of the historical process will tell us how, under given contingencies, we can hasten its development.

Certainly Marx, Engels, and their successors have acted as if certain political strategies were to be preferred to others and they have seemed to suggest that there are contingencies in political history when men might either hasten or retard development. The foundation of the First International itself may be looked upon as an exemplification of these beliefs, as may the many parties which have professed adherence to the Marxist outlook. Men, the doctrine appears to argue, have the capacity either to cooperate with the process or, through ignorance and mistaken belief, to slow down the rapidity of its motions.

This granted, the specific and over-riding issue in Marxist political thought has been whether the process can best be assisted by operating within traditional political systems or rather by acting outside them. Generally speaking, the former position might be described as evolutionary and the latter as revolutionary. But in any given interpretation, the two positions may conceivably be combined.

Marx himself is hardly consistent and certainly he is not without serious ambiguities. In the *Communist Manifesto*, much of the tone is revolutionary in nature: capitalist rulers are to "tremble" at their imminent fate.[27] And in his comments on the civil war in France[28] there is likewise an accent on drastic and relatively sudden change. On the other hand, Marx also stresses the contention that socialism will not be established until, in the full maturity of its development, industrial capitalism has been weakened by the internal crises to which we have referred. It is foolish to expect socialized means of production until capitalism has passed from the competitive era to the semi-monopolistic epoch of debility. In elaboration of this view, Marx and Engels generally expect socialism to be first established in a highly industrial country and not in one which is still largely agricultural in nature. And in his classical conflict with Bakunin in the First International, Marx in 1868 takes the position that his followers should seek to use whatever political machinery is available to them in their respective countries.[29]

On the whole, while the language of Marx and Engels is often violent and bitter, their main tendency is to press for parliamentary politics wherever the possibility for it exists. Socialists are to support extended suffrage, utilization of the initiative and referendum, and working-class solidarity in winning of elections. This does not mean, of course, that they will participate in nonsocialist governments; but it does imply that they will take their seats as elected members of Parliaments, using the legislative assemblies as forums for advocacy of their views. Parliamentary politics, Marx and Engels hold, can greatly assist in building proletarian consciousness of its mission and in so doing serve to advance the cause of socialism.

Associated with this view is the idea that industrial society in its capitalist phase will always give rise to parliamentary institutions, political party systems, and the struggle for political power by means of elections. Like nineteenth-century liberalism, the Marx-Engels doctrine sees the wave of the future in the establishment of liberal political systems.

This tendency to link parliamentary institutions with the rise of industrial capitalism and to suggest that working class parties should act for a time within the assumptions of parliamentarianism should not be interpreted to mean that Marx and Engels repudiate all illegal methods. Tactics must be fitted to the contingencies. A careful study of the dialectical process will help indicate the means which are likely to be most successful. And certainly proletarian parties, once they gain power, may have to use force to suppress the vestiges of capitalism which refuse to submit to the new order. Meanwhile, nevertheless, all isolated tactics of violence are to be spurned, as are most collective acts which employ violence.

With respect to the details of how parliamentary life can and should be used to advance the cause of socialism, Marx and Engels offer little guidance, and what there is seems to be subject to a variety of interpretations. If one studies the history of the Social Democratic movements in Germany and France—both of them avowedly Marxist until the period after World War II—one finds considerable differences of opinion about specific strategies. Down to World War I there does seem to be agreement on the proposition that no Socialist should enter a nonsocialist cabinet lest he surrender his socialist principles in the compromises of politics. But between this extreme and no participation in the parliamentary process there can be many positions of an intermediate nature.[30]

Despite the room for maneuver which Marxist theory seemingly allows, one is still impressed in the end by the fact that a kind of mechanical determinism underlies much of the thought stemming from Marx and Engels. The workers will be forced to adopt revolutionary positions by external circumstances. Whether through parliamentary tactics or violent direct action, they will inevitably come to an awareness of the gulf which lies between them and capitalist owners and will be impelled to appropriate action.

Schools of Marxist Thought

Thus far in our analysis we have been concerned primarily with a reconstruction of what Marx and Engels themselves taught. In general, we have referred to other Marxist thinkers only when they appeared with some measure of certainty to have expressed the thought of the original formulators. Now, however, we must devote some attention to the several schools of Marxist interpretation and to their ramifications in practical politics.

We are from the outset confronted with the fact that the system of Marx and Engels has been used for a diversity of purposes and that its ramifications differ in accordance with the purposes for which it is employed. Some thinkers will seize on certain aspects of the system and ignore others, thus modifying the context within which one can speak of Marxism. Others turn Marx's thought into a series of slogans for ends of political power: hence there is a kind of vulgar Marxism that becomes a political weapon rather than a system

of thought. Some accept what they take to be Marx's system uncritically; others are critical.

Over and above any classification of Marxist schools, we should also note the impact of Marx's thought on social science in general. Like Hegelianism, Marxism has profoundly affected the way in which social scientists analyze political and social problems.

Keeping these considerations in mind, let us

27. Thus the *Manifesto* says: "A spectre is haunting Europe—the spectre of Communism. All the Powers of old Europe have entered into a holy alliance to exorcise this spectre; Pope and Czar, Metternich and Guizot, French radicals and German police-spies. . . . Where is the party in opposition that has not been decried as communistic by its opponents in power? Where the Opposition that has not hurled back the branding reproach of Communism, against the more advanced opposition parties, as well as against its reactionary adversaries? . . . Communism is already acknowledged by all European Powers to be itself a Power" [p. 11]. . . . "Let the ruling classes tremble at a Communist revolution. The proletarians have nothing to lose but their chains. They have a world to win. Working men of all countries unite!" [p. 66]. Karl Marx and Friederich Engels, *The Communist Manifesto, op. cit.*
28. *The Civil War in France* (1848). Much earlier, after the fall of Vienna in 1848, he had commented: "The fruitless butcheries which have occurred since those June and October days will convince the peoples that there is only one means of shortening, simplifying, and concentrating the torturing death agonies of society—only one means—revolutionary terrorism." *Neue Rheinisch Zeitung,* November 6, 1848, quoted in Max Beer, *Life and Teaching of Karl Marx,* London: L. Parsons, 1921, p. 50.
29. Compare with other words of Marx: "Even where there is no prospect whatsoever of their being elected, the workers must put up their own candidates in order to preserve their own independence, to count their forces, and to bring before the public their revolutionary attitude and standpoint." *Selected Works,* vol. 1, Moscow: Foreign Languages Publishing House, 1961, p. 114.
30. On Marxian Socialist politics in Germany and France, see, for example, Samuel Bernstein, *The Beginnings of Marxian Socialism in France,* New York: Russell, 1965; G. D. H. Cole, *A History of Socialist Thought,* London: Macmillan, 1953; David Caute, *Communism and the French Intellectuals, 1914–1960,* New York: Macmillan, 1964; and John Plamenatz, *German Marxism and Russian Communism,* New York: Harper and Row, 1965.

divide our analysis into two broad sections. In the first, we note briefly some of the tendencies in what we call critical and scholarly Marxism—that which is not directly connected with struggles in the political realm (although obviously any critical use of Marx will indirectly affect politics). The second division will identify schools of Marxist thought more or less directly related to the struggle for power in the realm of practical politics. The two divisions are not mutually exclusive, it should be emphasized, for some names could legitimately appear in both.

Critical and Scholarly Marxism. "Marxism of the chair," as it might be called, tends to see Marx and Engels as part of the whole tradition of Western social and political thought and to use them as points of departure for understanding both historical and modern society. It may reject considerable segments of the teaching, as it understands it, and yet hold that Marx's system is almost indispensable for a full comprehension of the social and political world.

In the realm of economic theory, to use only one example, the writings of Joan Robinson are an instance of critical and scholarly Marxism.[31] Similarly, in the analysis of the economist H. D. Dickinson we find a like indebtedness to the framework of Marx and Engels.[32] And in the multifarious works of the British socialist G. D. H. Cole,[33] one has a particularly good example of how many of the essentials of Marx's conceptions of history, politics, and economic life affect and shape an important socialist thinker. Cole rejects significant segments of Marx's economic theory—for example, the doctrine of surplus value—while yet building on his moral and social teaching. And in the Untied States, economists like Paul Sweezy are critical Marxists in their economics and politics.[34]

Biographers like Isaac Deutscher work within the framework of Marx's theory, while not feeling obliged to follow him—or his proclaimed disciples—in all respects.[35] And psychiatrists like Erich Fromm, in developing the humanist implications of Marx, follow the nineteenth-century thinker in considerable degree on such themes as alienation. Marx, as Fromm portrays him, was essentially a humanist in revolt against the dehumanizing processes of modern capitalist industrialism and was seeking to restore to man his dignity as a whole human being.[36]

The spirit of critical and scholarly Marxists is well reflected in words of the late C. Wright Mills. They work, he says,

> . . . in Marx's own tradition. They understand Marx, and many later Marxists as well, to be firmly a part of the classic tradition of sociological thinking. They treat Marx like any great nineteenth century figure, in a scholarly way; they treat each later phase of Marxism as historically specific. They are generally agreed that Marx's work bears the trademarks of the nineteenth century society, but that this general model and his ways of thinking are central to their own intellectual history and remain relevant to their attempts to grasp present-day social worlds.[37]

Marxism and the Struggle for Power. Broadly speaking, we may discern two distinct tendencies in the politicians' Marxism since Marx. One we might term scoial democracy and the other Bolshevism.

1. Social Democracy. Social democracy arose in the latter part of the nineteenth century and its theoretical center lay largely in Germany and Austria. Even before the death of Marx, the Social Democratic Party of Germany had been born and after his death, particularly after the repeal of the repressive Bismarckian laws, it grew rapidly. Between 1899 and 1914, mass socialist movements were confederated on an international basis in what was called the Second International, which in a series of conferences sought to stimulate common action and thinking on political questions.

The great theoretical conflict within the ranks of social democracy before 1914 centered on the degree to which Marxian socialists could cooperate with the nonsocialist state and particularly with the German state. There was a fission between the so-called Orthodox Marxists, whose theoretical leader was Karl Kautsky, and the Revisionists, led by Eduard Bernstein. Kautsky argued that cooperation with and actions within the nonsocialist state should be minimal, lest the revolutionary objectives of the movement be forgotten.[38] The revolution can best be advanced, Kautsky maintained, by accenting the gulf between the socialist state and the communist post-historical period, on the one hand, and the existing order, on the other. This does not suggest that Marxists cannot organize political parties and engage in political propaganda within the framework of the bourgeois state; nor does it mean that they should not accept seats in parliament. It does, however, imply wariness about any active cooperation with nonsocialist groups.

Revisionism, by contrast, suggested that the primary task of the Marxist political movement was to build workers' organizations with a view to concrete immediate gains. While revolutionary objectives, to be sure, are implicit in Marxism, its practical politics must be accommodated to the exigencies of the political context within which it is developing. Socialist parties, cooperating with unions and the cooperative movement, will accent the immediate improvement of working conditions, on the assumption that as the material circumstances of workers improve, so, too, will their political power.[39]

If it is possible to summarize briefly the distinction between Kautsky's and Bernstein's world view, we might say that the former stresses the eschatological element in Marxism and the latter the gradualist tendency. As we have seen, both emphases are present in Marx and Engels, without their becoming very clear as to what they imply in terms of tactics.

In the years immediately before World War I, international socialism seriously debated its attitude to war, for many foresaw that given the arms competition between Britain and Germany, a world war was very likely.[40] Views differed quite widely, all the way from positions like those of Keir Hardie, the great Scottish parliamentary leader, who advocated the general strike, to outlooks which, while not condoning war, would leave each national movement free to determine its own position in the event of crisis. The result was a compromise, which appeared to suggest that in general socialist movements should use whatever methods seemed most appropriate—not excluding the general strike—to prevent war, while at the same time encouraging the maximum of international conciliation.

In the event, as is well known, very few socialists, whether Marxists or non-Marxists, stood out against the war. French socialist leaders like Jean Jaurés and radical Marxists like the Germans Rosa Luxembourg and Karl Liebknecht did, indeed, refuse to acquiesce; and the Italian and American socialist movements as a whole joined them. But the broad picture was one of socialist acceptance.

The whole discussion of Marxism and war illustrates the fact that the theory of Marx and Engels is, to say the least, ambiguous on the issue. If the workers have no country, as the *Communist Manifesto* proclaims, then it would seem that highly developed Marxist movements—as the French, German, and Austrian were in 1914—could have nothing in them of bourgeois patriotism and chauvinism. Lacking patriotism and claiming international working-class solidarity to be far more significant than any national cause, they would presumably ignore calls to the national colors for the purpose of killing one another. World War I could have been prevented if highly developed Marxist movements had acted as Marx impliedly said they would act: there would have been few soldiers to join the armies of the major powers. Yet the fact remains that ties of nationalism were much stronger than those of class solidarity. This would seem to cast serious doubt on any theory of historical development which makes economic determinism the key to an explanation of human conduct. Although economic considerations undoubtedly play an enormous role, it may well be questioned whether men

31. See her *Essay on Economics and Marxism*, New York: St. Martin's, 1967, and *On Re-Reading Marx*, Cambridge: Students Bookshop, 1953.
32. See his the *Economics of Socialism*, London: Oxford University Press, 1939.
33. See particularly his the *Meaning of Marxism*, London: Victor Gollancz, 1948.
34. Paul M. Sweezy, *The Theory of Capitalist Development: Principles of Marxian Political Economy*, New York: Oxford University Press, 1942.
35. See Deutscher's *Stalin*, London: Oxford University Press, 1949. See also his *Trotsky*, vol. 1, *The Prophet Armed: Trotsky 1879–1921;* vol. 2, *The Prophet Unarmed: Trotsky 1921–1929;* vol. 3, *The Prophet Outcast: 1929–1940*. New York: Oxford University Press, 1954, 1959, 1963.
36. See Erich Fromm, *Marx's Concept of Man*, New York: F. Ungar, 1961.
37. *The Marxists*, New York: Dell, 1962, p. 98.
38. For Kautsky's views, see *The Class Struggle*, Chicago: C. H. Kerr, 1910; *The Dictatorship of the Proletariat*, Ann Arbor: University of Michigan, 1964; *The Road to Power*, Chicago: S. A. Bloch, 1909; *The Social Revolution*, Chicago: C. H. Kerr, 1903.
39. For an elaboration of Bernsteinism, see Eduard Bernstein, *Evolutionary Socialism: A Criticism and Affirmation*, London: Independent Labour Party, 1907; and Peter Gay, *The Dilemma of Democratic Society: Eduard Bernstein's Challenge to Marx*, New York: Collier Books, 1962.
40. The conferences were at Stuttgart in 1907, Copenhagen in 1910, Bale in 1912, and Brussels in 1914.

always act out of motives of economic interest or whether, even if they do, they always recognize the direction in which their economic interests lie.

2. Bolshevist Marxism. Bolshevist Marxism arose early in the twentieth century when, in a conference of the Russian Social Democratic Party (1904), the majority (*bolshevik*) faction of the moment shaped the program. The minority (*menshevik*) was defeated. The ideological struggle between the two factions had been incipient for some time and the doctrine and practice of both would be elaborated still further in the years before the Russian Revolution of 1917.

In general, the Menshevik outlook tended to be aligned with that of Western social democracy, possibly in its Kautskyan version. Accent was on evolution of bourgeois industrialism, and its corresponding parliamentarianism, before a revolutionary situation could develop. To the Menshevik mind, Russia in 1905, with the first or preliminary revolution, and in 1917, with the second, was ready for an overturn of tsarist institutions and the inauguration of bourgeois liberalism but was unprepared historically to move directly into a socialist phase as the gateway to communism. The task of Marxism was to encourage the elimination of the semi-feudalism so characteristic of Russia and the establishment of liberal institutions.

The greatest theorist of the Bolsheviks, Vladimir Lenin (1870–1924), thought otherwise, at least after World War I had led to an undermining of the Russian bureaucracy. True, Marx and Engels could be quoted at length to support the thesis that socialism would be established first in a highly industrialized society. But Lenin stressed that, given unprecedented historical circumstances, the theory of Marxism could sustain the proposition that with proper guidance drastic change might come in an economically backward nation like Russia. In fact, by 1917, Lenin was arguing that the intermediate state of bourgeois liberal parliamentarianism could be bypassed.[41]

Lenin's theory was in part developed as a result of his practical experience with the revolutionary forces which came more and more to the fore after 1916. To be sure, his writings had for some time stressed the possibility of sharp and drastic social and political change. But it was only after 1916 that the full implications of the doctrine were worked out. Between that date and his death in 1924, Lenin formulated the mature theory of Bolshevism which then became, at least ostensibly, the official creed of the Soviet Union.

Four basic principles of the theory seem to stand out:

(1) While Lenin does not deny that a mature capitalism—one which has passed through the stage of bourgeois industrial liberalism and has become semimonopolistic—can give birth to socialism, he also maintains that with an appropriate objective situation and a party organization constructed along Bolshevist lines, socialism can also be imposed on a feudal structure. The appropriate objective situation must involve a severe crisis in the existing political ordering—a crisis possibly produced by war and including among its ingredients a state of desperation among the peasantry.

(2) The Marxist party must be a tightly organized, centralized structure operated by men devoting virtually their whole lives to the task. Revolution is as demanding as any profession, Lenin is saying.

Lenin works out a theory of guidance and of representation in some respects astonishingly like that of elitists in any generation. The proletariat virtually reflect the interests of the peasants because in the long run most peasants will be forced by the dialectic into the proletariat; and even if they are not, the proletariat through their more highly developed consciousness understand the movements of history much better than the peasants can be expected to do. As for the party, it basically represents the proletariat, since its consciousness of the historical situation is much broader and more intense than that of workers as a whole. Thus a very small minority is ultimately responsible for taking advantage of the objective situation. It speaks, however, in the name of the true interests of the great majority.

But the party to act effectively must be closely knit and this involves, according to Lenin, the principle of "democratic centralism." By this he means that while proposed policies are discussed thoroughly within party ranks before decisions are made, once the policy has been adumbrated, it must be applied uniformly by a central administrative machinery.

(3) Lenin's doctrine is very clear in its defense of violence as a political weapon. Since all morality prior to communism is class morality and the proletariat, even in a backward country, are the bearers of the idea of a classless society, any means are justified which

appear to conduce to the end of socialism and then of communism. Thus guided by the party and its leaders, it is legitimate for the proletariat to dissolve a freely elected Constituent Assembly chosen by the Russian people in 1917; for the assembly is dominated by opponents of Bolshevism and hence is against the best interests of both workers and peasants. So, too, violence may be justified against agencies of capitalist states and against all opponents of a Bolshevist-controlled political society.

(4) Finally, Lenin's analysis of imperialism and war becomes an integral part of Bolshevik doctrine. We have already suggested that Lenin builds his theory of imperialism on the foundations of Marx's theory of mature capitalism. He holds that major capitalist powers tend to divide the underdeveloped world among themselves in the frantic effort to secure markets for consumers and then for capital goods. This means that backward areas cannot expect to develop economically along the lines characteristic of older capitalist nations: Instead they must, like the small proletarian class in Russia, initiate revolutionary activity despite the absence of highly developed capitalism. Fortunately, from the viewpoint of Marxian socialism, the very factors which lead to capitalist imperialism also engender the crises out of which Bolshevik revolution can emerge. Imperialism inevitably makes for war among the capitalist powers themselves and war both weakens capitalist structures and creates opportunities—because of ensuing disorder and undermining of imperialist controls—for the tightly disciplined Bolshevik cadres.[42]

The apparent success of Lenin's doctrine, pragmatically speaking, made it to a degree unsurpassed by any other political outlook the official creed of many governments. Although liberalism and utilitarianism are often said to be the guidelines of Western governments during the last century, they are in many respects much vaguer than the ideas which Lenin set forth and they have not, moreover, been embodied in authoritarian political parties. Leninism, in form at least, becomes a kind of religious creed for those multitudes of human beings who live under regimes professing it.

But a political doctrine which also becomes a religious creed is always subject to the emendations of time and circumstance. Just as the religion of the New Testament came to be encrusted with vast accretions of cultural and ideological barnacles not originally attached to it, so has Leninism been modified by circumstance, expediency, and the exigencies of rapidly changing conditions. As the original theory of Marx became the text for a diversity of interpretations, so did the Leninist gospel come to have somewhat different meanings for Lenin's successors.

(a) Leninism-Stalinism may be said to be the tendency in Soviet ideology which prevailed in the period between 1927 and the death of Joseph Stalin in 1953. The years between Lenin's death in 1924 and 1927 were marked by a severe struggle for power between Leon Trotsky, Lenin's great associate during the Revolution, and Josef Stalin, who had become General Secretary of the Soviet Communist party before the death of Lenin. By 1927, it was clear that Stalin had won and by 1932 he had consolidated his position in the Soviet Union to such a degree that overt opposition had been stilled. In the process, "Trotskyism" became distinguished from "Stalinism."

Stalinism is not a political theory so much as it is a series of propositions which appeared to govern the actions of the Soviet government from the thirties to Stalin's death and which permeated many interpretations of Leninism long after his passing. Stalinism suggests that it is possible to build socialism in one country (the Soviet Union) and that, indeed, this is essential if the ultimate international objectives of Marxism-Leninism are to be accomplished. The revolution must be consolidated in the

41. That this position was contrary to Lenin's prewar attitude is pointed out by Bertram Wolfe. At the time of the 1904–1905 revolutionary disturbances, Lenin said: "The present degree of economic development in Russia . . . make the immediate, complete emancipation of the working class impossible. Only the most ignorant people can ignore the bourgeois character of the present democratic revolution. . . . Whoever wants to approach socialism by any other path than that of political democracy will inevitably reach the most absurd and reactionary conclusions." Quoted in Bertram D. Wolfe, *Three Who Made a Revolution*, Boston: Beacon Press, 1948, pp. 292–293.

42. For an elaboration of Leninist theory, see V. I. Lenin, *Imperialism: The Highest Stage of Capitalism*, New York: International Publishers, 1937, *State and Revolution*, New York: International Publishers, 1943, and *What Is To Be Done?*, New York: International Publishers, 1939.

Soviet Union; immediate interests of men must succumb to their long run interests as interpreted by Stalinist Bolshevik leaders; and the Soviet state must be strengthened militarily to battle external enemies who would frustrate the gains of the revolution. All this implies economically a rapid development of industrialization; very harsh treatment of the peasantry, who are to be either uprooted rapidly and sent into the city or forced to join agricultural collectives; justification of terror as a political weapon; and the elimination of internal party democracy.

Perhaps the greatest distinction between Leninism and Leninism-Stalinism is that the latter is much more rigid and dogmatic than the former. There is a flexibility about Leninism, an openness, which is absent in the spirit of Leninism-Stalinism. To be sure, this openness is purely relative, for all Bolshevism is implicitly dogmatic and authoritarian. Nevertheless, Stalinism pushes such qualities to their extremes.[43]

(b) Leninism-Trotskyism is Leninism dethroned and critical of the political ideology which retains political power. Basic foundations of both Trotskyism and Stalinism remain alike in that both repose on Bolshevik principles. But Trotskyism, no longer enchurched in the Soviet Union, tends to stress the necessity for an international and permanent revolution. It becomes an ideology which, while highly critical of bureaucratic tendencies in the Soviet Union (which it believes distort socialist achievements), still believes that the Revolution in 1917 accomplished fundamental changes in the social order. The Soviet Union becomes for Trotskyism a perverted workers' state.[44]

(c) Leninism-Khrushchevism may be said to have been the official ideology of the Soviet Union from 1955 to 1964. The years immediately following Stalin's death in 1953, like those after Lenin's demise, were devoted to a reshuffling of power relations within the Soviet State. The triumphant ideology was that associated with the name of Nikita Khrushchev. Rebelling against what it thought of as the "errors" of Stalin,[45] it claims to restore Leninism in its unperverted form. It particularly denounces the "cult of personality" which is associated with Stalinism.

Thus it accents greater freedom of discussion within the party and casts doubt on the extreme centralization of economic planning which had become such a hallmark of Stalin's rule. Stalinism, it argues, while preserving something of Lenin's original doctrine, departs from it in a number of ways, notably in the way it justifies departure from the rule of law.

Broadly speaking, Khrushchev's interpretation of Leninism may be said to constitute an ideology for a Soviet Union primarily concerned to maintain a long period of peace in order to carry out its economic plans. It is, in other terms, the ideology for a stabilized "workers' state."

In its essentials, the ideology remained predominant even after the deposition of Nikita Khrushchev in the fall of 1964.

(d) Leninism-Maoism designates the Chinese cultural version of Leninism which assumed control of China under the name of the Chinese People's Republic in 1949. Led by Mao Tse-tung, the Chinese Communist movement had struggled for years, first within the Chinese nationalist forces, then against them, and always against foreign control. Born in 1893, Mao had grown up in a peasant household, became a teacher, and flirted briefly with anarchism. Bitter against foreign exploitation of China as were so many young Chinese, he was one of the founders of the Chinese Communist movement after World War I. The movement was never thoroughly supported by the Soviet Union, perhaps because it felt a challenge to its own leadership. Even during the 1930s, when all Chinese factions were preoccupied with the Japanese occupation, Chinese Communist agitators found only a qualified sustenance in Russia. Only after 1950, as a matter of fact, did official Soviet leadership under Stalin actually accord a tentative blessing to the Chinese movement as authentic Communism.

Mao's theory of revolution is dominated by his Chinese nationalism. In a sense, he adopts Leninism because he sees in it the only way to organize an effective force which will unify China and eliminate foreign control: His doctrines in the end spring from this source and Leninism becomes a convenient ideological weapon for the achievement of his goal. On numerous occasions he has frankly recognized the peculiar nature of Chinese Communism.

Because the revolution is national, its base must repose on that class which constitutes the overwhelming mass of the people—the peasantry. Hence throughout his theoretical career, Mao stresses stimulation of the peasantry to spontaneous action against foreign oppressors and rich landlords; and when finally the revolution is successful in 1949, he systematically encourages revenge against rich landlords. To be sure, the Russian Revolution makes its appeal to peasants as well as industrial workers, but pure Leninist theory always thinks of the proletariat as the vanguard. Maoist-Leninism, by contrast, stresses, first, spontaneous action by the peasantry; then, power having been won, guidance by the authoritarian party. In certain respects, Maoism is a kind of peasant-Leninist ideology.

This is not to say that, established in power, Maoist theoreticians do not look beyond the peasantry, but rather that active support by the peasants constitutes the starting point. Once political power is gained, land is distributed to the poor and middle peasants and is taken away from rich landlords, who are liquidated either functionally or physically. In some respects, Mao carries the strategy of terror, implicit in original Leninism, still further. Thus he writes:

> Every Communist must grasp the truth: "Political power grows out of the barrel of a gun." . . . Experience in the class-struggle of the era of imperialism teaches us that the working class and the toiling masses cannot defeat the armed bourgeois and landlords except by the power of the gun; in this sense we can even say that the whole world can be remoulded only with the gun.[46]

Through terror, stiff-necked resistance to necessary reordering of China can be overcome and the people molded into a single unit fit to develop the nation economically, to destroy the power of the landlord class, and to expel the last foreigner.

The Appeals of Marxism. The ubiquity of the Marxist impact on the world has been due both to the grand sweep of the system itself and to the fact that it has filled a vacuum in thought. The system dealt with some of the most important questions confronting mankind at a time when men were searching for a new basis of community in light of the disintegration of old community forms. Men were uprooted from the soil, where they had lived in traditional village communities for many centuries, and suddenly forced into an urban life which was something of an artifact. Their traditional moorings were gone and they were searching for new schemes of integration.

Into the breach stepped Marxism. As social science it dealt, as C. Wright Mills has observed, with many of the broad, macrocosmic issues, whereas much other nineteenth and twentieth century social and political inquiry

confined itself to what many regarded as trivial, fragmented questions.[47] While it may have obtained this large view at the expense of what some called strict science, it boldly set forth to explore areas which were largely untouched by others.

In emphasizing man's alienation under industrialism, Marxism touched a phenomenon directly experienced by many. The political philosophy of individualism appeared to think that discrete, isolated men were natural. Marxism denied this and with its foundations in the Hegelian philosophy of community sought to show that isolation and alienation could not be regarded as ends of the human quest, however much they might be regarded as inevitable in a given phase of existence. This emphasis in Marxism on the restoration of community and meaning was to be found not only in its vision of the goal of history but also in its conception of the means for organizing the proletariat. Working-class movements and political parties —not excluding bolshevik Marxist parties— provided their members with a sense of solidarity among themselves and of oneness against the outside world. Psychologically,

43. For discussions of Stalinism, see Isaac Deutscher, *Stalin, op. cit.*, John E. Turner, "The Problem of Political Succession," in James B. Christoph, *Cases in Comparative Politics*, Boston: Little, Brown, 1965; and Merle Fainsod, *How Russia is Ruled*, Cambridge, Mass.: Harvard University Press, 1964.
44. The doctrines of Trotskyism are created in Leon Trotsky, *Dictatorship vs. Democracy (Terrorism and Communism)*, *A Reply to Karl Kautsky*, New York: W. P. A., 1922, *In Defense of Marxism*, New York: Pioneer Publishers, 1942, and *The Permanent Revolution* New York: Pioneer Press, 1931.
45. See Khrushchev's address before the Twentieth Congress of the Communist Party of the Soviet Union, 1956. On February 25 Khrushchev said: "Stalin originated the concept 'enemy of the people.' . . . This term made possible the use of the most cruel repression, violating all norms of revolutionary legality, against anyone who in any way disagreed with Stalin, against those who were only suspected of hostile intent. . . . The formula 'enemy of the people' was specifically introduced for the purpose of physically annihilating such individuals."
46. See Mao Tse-tung, *Selected Works*, London: Lawrence and Wishart, 1954, pp. 153–154.
47. C. Wright Mills, *The Marxists*, New York: Dell, 1962.

communism was born for one when one joined the movement: recognized by others as an authentic outpost of future dialectical changes, the member acquired a new status in his own eyes.

All this was preeminently true of the appeal of bolshevik Marxism to the "underdeveloped" areas of Europe, Asia, South America, and Africa. Having never experienced a bourgeois capitalist parliamentary phase of historical development and yet noting what industrial technology could accomplish, men in underdeveloped areas who had been deprived of their ancient community life by the inroads of Western imperialism turned to Leninism as the basis for a new integration. Peasants all over the world began to be conscious of the fact that highly industrialized nations of the West had taken advantage of their economic and social weakness and various versions of Leninism spoke to their condition. By the middle of the twentieth century, the appeal of bolshevik Marxism had by no means subsided.

It was not, then, merely the economic poverty of men which conditioned them for the several forms of Marxism. It was above all the social message which seemed relevant; for Marxism as ideology suggested that their isolation and alienation could be overcome. Ireland, for example, has been desperately poor economically during the twentieth century; but Marxism has made virtually no inroads into either the cities or the countryside. The reason for this is not far to seek: old community forms in Ireland have survived with amazing persistence and modern ways have developed with sufficient slowness to permit new community life to develop. Moreover, the persistence of the traditional religion in more than a formal sense has strengthened the community rootage of the Irish. By contrast, other areas also desperately poor but lacking Ireland's strong community and religious consciousness have been attracted by Marxism.

Religion should be singled out for special consideration in this connection. Where emotional and intellectual adherence to a religious faith is still vital and other elements of community anchorage are also present, it is unlikely that Marxism will have great impact on the politics of a people. Human existence under such circumstances still has meaning. On the other hand, Marxism is usually influential where traditional religious faiths have lost their appeal and social change is so rapid that new community anchorages have no opportunity to develop. For Marxism is not only a science and a philosophy, it also has many of the characteristics of a religion.

Evaluation and Criticism of Marxism

As it has permeated the world of scholarship and politics, Marxism has provoked severe and searching attacks on its theory and ideology. Literature critical of Marxism has by now become so voluminous that here it will be possible to provide only a partial analysis of the main questions which are raised.

Negative Criticisms. The attack began in Marx's own day and has been elaborated in detail against a background of twentieth-century experiences, particularly those growing out of the actions of governments ostensibly governed by Marxist principles.

1. Dialectical Materialism. It has been suggested by the British philosopher C. E. M. Joad that even if it could be shown that dialectical materialism is in some metaphysical sense true—and the demonstration is, of course, virtually impossible—it does not follow automatically that the theory can be applied in a practical way to the processes of history. Yet most Marxists, including Marx and Engels themselves, appear to believe that this can be done.

But if we try to use dialectical conceptions for practical purposes, we immediately discover that there can be no certain result. We are confronted, in the actual interpretation of historical events with a bewildering array of apparent forces—religious, political, economic, personal, biological. While some may, indeed, be more significant than others—thus we might hypothesize that a man's method of earning a livelihood is far more important in shaping his conduct than is the color of his hair—to say that all are determined (and Marx does use the word in certain of his writings) by the mode of production would appear to be a very hazardous undertaking.[48]

It is true, of course, that in his later interpretations, Engels grants a certain autonomy to spiritual factors.[49] That is to say, while it is the method of production which fundamentally determines conflicting ideologies, religions, political institutions, law, and even art, these expressions of human history become somewhat independent of the forces of production and in turn modify the basic economic factors. But to the degree that Engels grants an autonomous role to the realm of spirit, the critic will observe, he is in effect denying a strict economic determinism and hence casting doubt on some of his own early formulations.

2. Marx-Engels' Forecasts. In their forecasts of what would happen in the mature development of capitalism, Marx and Engels can be shown to have been frequently wrong and this observation has been used by critics to cast doubt on their whole theoretical structure. This might not be a significant criticism except for the fact that Marx and Engels, as we have seen, take pride in their ability to forecast the future. Their conception of science, as was observed earlier, embraces the idea that the investigator can validate not only if-then propositions but also can foretell what will happen as capitalism develops. They assert their power to formulate and support both hypothetical statements and macrocosmic forecasts.

Now whatever the basis of these forecasts, several have not been substantiated by the course of history. Here let us note only three.

Marx and Engels maintain that in the course of industrial capitalist development, a polarization of classes will inevitably take place. The middle groups will be wiped out functionally and psychologically, most of them becoming proletarianized and a few others joining the increasingly small numbers of capitalist owners. But this, it can be persuasively argued, has not taken place. As Lewis Corey and other critics have pointed out,[50] the fact seems to have been that while the old middle class (shopkeepers, small businessmen) has indeed tended to disappear, a whole new middle class has entered the historical scene. This new class is composed of the vast numbers of professional or "service" people, most of whom are salaried. Although it is true that this new class does not consist, for the most part, of private self-employed entrepreneurs, it is equally true that it is not an element in the proletariat. Nurses, administrators, accountants, social workers, teachers, medical technologists, and other similar specialists, however one might characterize them positively, most certainly do not share the outlook either of the owning classes or of the proletariat.

Another forecast in which they have apparently been proved wrong by actual developments is their general prediction that the proletariat would become more miserable. True, they are ambiguous as to precisely what they mean by the term. Do they mean economic misery in an absolute sense or only in a relative one? If the former, there is no doubt that they are in error; for the course of capitalist development has resulted in a general advance in the real income of the working classes. This has happened in every country possessing an advanced technology. If they mean relative misery, there is also room for doubt; for while the working classes' relative share of industrial nations' income may not have increased,[51] it has not substantially decreased either. If "miserable" implies a judgment in the realm of psychology or world outlook, there is, of course, room for diversity of interpretation. But whatever Marx and Engels meant by their prediction, they do not appear to have been remarkably perceptive.

Finally, the Marx-Engels forecast of the chronological order in which socialist revolutions will take place would seem to be at worst almost totally mistaken and at best very ambiguous. By and large, as we have seen, they argue that socialism (and then communism) will arise first in the most highly developed industrial capitalist order. While logically this forecast would seem to flow from their general conception of historical development, it simply has not been corroborated by actual events. The Marxist revolution—or at least what professed to be one—first took place in a highly agrarian society and secondly in an even more highly non-industrial culture.

3. Surrender of Power by the Proletariat. Marx and Engels argue, it will be remembered, that once the last vestiges of capitalism have been swept away in the stage of socialism, the rulers of the State at that time will then give

48. See *Guide to the Philosophy of Morals and Politics*, New York: Random House, 1938, p. 715.
49. See particularly *Socialism: Utopian and Scientific*.
50. See Lewis Corey, "The New Middle Classes," *Antioch Review* (Spring, 1945), 68–83.
51. Thus in the United States the lower 50 percent of income earners have received approximately 25 percent of the income since before World War I. The figure has remained remarkably stationary, despite New Deal legislation and other factors which might have been expected to alter distribution in a fundamental way.

up their power and thus inaugurate communism. But it is difficult to see why this would be so. Admittedly, according to the Marx-Engels interpretation, no previous ruling class has acted in this way. The action of the proletarian governors would be *sui generis*. Presumably they would renounce power because classes will have been abolished. But what reason is there to assume that a new class will not begin to arise as the old one fades out? This has happened throughout history. Why, then, will the socialist period be an exception? While there may be no private owners, on what premise can we contend that the coordinators and managers who would presumably still be needed would not start their career as a separate class?

The point can perhaps be made clearer if we examine what has actually taken place in the Soviet Union. Although the Soviet Union is undoubtedly not exactly what Marx and Engels envisioned, nevertheless its rulers for more than fifty years have purported to act in the name of Marx's ideology. They have proclaimed that the Revolution of 1917 inaugurated Lenin's version of the dictatorship of the proletariat. They have also asserted, on numerous occasions, that the purpose of this dictatorship is to liquidate all classes and ultimately the state itself. Under these circumstances, one might expect state bureaucracy to decline, however gradually, since presumably the "class enemy" would become progressively less menacing. But this has certainly not taken place within the Soviet Union. On the contrary, with increasing industrialization have come a more extensive bureaucracy and other phenomena characteristic of the state.

The phenomenon of a continued state apparatus in the Soviet Union, to be sure, can be accounted for in many ways: external pressures, traditions inherited from Czarist days, and the imperatives established by increasingly complex division of labor. But the fact remains that an allegedly socialist revolution, with its dictatorship, has not in more than a generation been able to produce a decline.

4. Ends and Means. Many modern critics have pointed out that Marxist means often appear to set up ends directly contrary to professed objectives.[52] Although Marxist theory about means is at many points ambiguous, as we have seen, it certainly does not exclude violence and, in its bolshevik versions, positively endorses it. Moreover, the notion in Leninism that a very small elite circle knows what is best for both the proletariat and the population as a whole suggests that before the vast masses can enter the promised land they must be forced and cajoled into it by those who understand their true interests.

Now it may be seriously questioned whether the means of action in political affairs can be sharply separated from the ends without distorting the latter or even destroying them. Thus the professed ends of Marxist ideology are a free, spontaneous society without state, bureaucracy, war, police, or systematically organized physical coercion. But the means frequently (although not always) exalted—partially in Marx and Engels but more fully in Lenin—include temporary repression, dictatorship, and overt violence. Is it possible, the critic will ask, that spontaneity can be encouraged by dictatorship and free cooperation by violence of various kinds? Experience seems to show that violence promotes counterviolence; and that unless there is a deliberate effort not to retaliate in kind, the chain of violence and counterviolence is a well-nigh endless one.

In making these observations, however, we should not forget that Marxists are not alone in failing to take seriously the organic relationship between means and ends. The Western democratic tradition, too, has frequently asserted the necessity for violence. Jefferson, for example, at one point argued that periodic violence is essential to preserve liberty;[53] and throughout the nineteenth century violent methods were justified by democrats in attaining national independence. In the twentieth century, very few democratic theorists and ideologists condemned violence against Germany in the two world wars; and in the forties, fifties, and sixties of the century it is probable that most supporters of the Western "free world" would have justified the use of violence in attempts to overthrow Soviet and Chinese governments. Indeed, only those who espouse a pacifist or Gandhian position would argue otherwise.

5. Ambiguities About the End. The critic can easily raise almost unanswerable questions about Marxist conceptions of communism. Once he gets beyond such generalities as "from each according to his ability, to each according to his need," the Marxist is confronted by such problems as the reconciliation of extreme industrialism with the apparent absence of any permanent system of coordination of work; the difficulty of imagining how man can be freed from the trammels of divi-

sion of labor; and the dubious proposition that once material goods are abundant, social conflict will be virtually eliminated. And the Marxist tends to be of little help in clarifying these issues because he refuses to become specific and often takes refuge in the statement that history will reveal the solutions.

The proposition that production of material goods in abundance and their distribution according to need will destroy most serious social conflicts is open to serious question. It rests, of course, on the Marxist belief that power conflicts are all basically economic. But this, as we have seen, is suspect. Men will often struggle for glory even though they know that it will involve great economic loss. Human beings, the critic will urge, are not simply calculating economic animals, as Marx (and many liberals as well) seems to imply. The quest for power, glory, subordination, or security cannot be reduced to economic factors alone but includes complex psychological and sociological dimensions.

The Positive Contributions. During the fifties and sixties, it was customary for many writers living in Western Europe and the United States to blame all the political difficulties of the times on Marx's teaching. In the United States particularly Marxist theory has been distorted in such a way as to obscure its real contributions. Yet the fact remains that when all the negative criticisms have been taken into account, several of its propositions continue to have a large measure of validity.

1. The Centrality of the Economic Factor in Politics. Although we have argued earlier that all the manifold aspects of politics could not be derived simply from one, this is not to say that some are not more important than others. Among these, the economic undoubtedly stands out. It is above all because Marxism emphasizes the significance of the economic factor and attempts to show particularly how it relates to the development of politics under industrialism that it must remain for many years one of the two or three most significant theoretical systems of modern times.

2. Marx as an Economic Historian. However much Marx as an economic theorist may be criticized, as an economic historian of the early stages of industrial capitalism he remains unexcelled. His descriptions of the way in which an early capitalist culture will affect the worker, both economically and psychologically, can be applied not merely to nineteenth-century industrialism but to most primitive

industrial capitalist systems, including those in the twentieth century.

3. The Class-Struggle Thesis. Although Marx and Engels push the class-struggle analysis beyond what most students would accept, it still constitutes a proposition of enormous significance and utility in political study. Classes may not be as homogeneous as extreme Marxists pretend them to be, but at the heart of the argument there is a large element of validity. Lower-income groups do tend, for example, to be aware of interests rather sharply distinguished from those possessing large incomes, as election analyses in the United States and elsewhere will show. Correlations between income level and political preferences are frequently rather close.

We know, too, that the general ways of life of human beings vary in considerable degree with their class status. Thus the sexual mores of the lower classes, most studies tend to show, are quite different in many respects from those of upper-income groups.[54] There is some evidence, moreover, than even the kind of mental illness one is likely to have can be correlated with one's class status.[55] Attitudes to the state, to political power, and to religion, too, are heavily conditioned by class position. Sociology in general and political sociology in par-

52. For a general discussion of ends and means in politics, see Aldous Huxley, *Ends and Means,* New York: Harper, 1937.
53. Note the words of his famous letter to James Madison, 1787: "The late rebellion in Massachusetts has given more alarm than I think it should have done. Calculate that one rebellion in thirteen states in the course of eleven years is but one for each state in a century and a half. . . . *No Country should be so long without one.* Nor will any degree of power in the hands of government prevent insurrections." [Italics added.] *The Works of Thomas Jefferson,* vol. 2, edited by H. H. Washington, New York: T. MacCoun, 1884, pp. 327–333.
54. By and large, lower-income groups will profess less toleration for deviation from orthodox sexual practices than higher-income groups. See Alfred Kinsey, *Sexual Behavior in the Human Male,* Philadelphia: Saunders, 1948, and *Sexual Behavior in the Human Female,* Philadelphia: Saunders, 1953.
55. Note, for example, the evidence in A. B. Hollinshead and F. C. Redlich, *Social Class and Mental Illness.* New York: Wiley, 1958, which was a study of New Haven, Connecticut.

ticular have come to emphasize rather strongly propositions of this kind.

4. The Economic Forecasts of Marx. Although the critics have justifiably called attention to many errors in Marx's economic forecasts, it remains true that his general understanding of the major lines of capitalist development was startling. He foresaw the rise of monopolistic combinations and the large role they would play in more mature capitalism. While certain critics accuse him of rigidity, Marx was far less dogmatic than some of his professed followers have been. Capitalism, he thought, would not always be what it had been in the nineteenth century: The dialectical process would not stop. Fresh appraisals of the economic process would be required and one could not always apply inflexibly the formulas which may have been suitable for the nineteenth century.

For those who would accept too easily the allegedly new capitalism of the mid-twentieth century, Marx would have this to say: Although the form may be new, the underlying tendencies of monopoly capitalism connect it with the capitalism of an earlier era. While the absolute economic standard of living has increased a century after the *Communist Manifesto*, Marx would undoubtedly ask us to look at relative distribution of goods. In the United States, while the middle ranges have been somewhat enlarged, the general picture (even with graduated income taxes) is not remarkably different. We should hasten to add, of course, that in the land which first professed to have applied Marxism, the same observation can be made.

5. Marx the Moral Prophet. Paradoxically, while Marx wished to be remembered primarily as a scientist, it is perhaps as a kind of prophet that he ranks even higher. He could never remain the pure scientist or philosopher, but must explode in indignation against the exploitation of man by man and of helpless creatures by highly organized power manipulators. In so doing, Marx carries on the tradition of ancient Hebrew prophecy as exemplified in such men as Amos, Jeremiah, and the two Isaiahs. He shows that with all its initial merits, industrial capitalism has demanded a fearful price of human beings and that this great wrong must be righted—using as the criterion of right the very tradition of religious ideals which Marx legitimately criticizes men for not observing.

Essentially, as Reinhold Niebuhr has observed, Marxism is a protest against the hypocrisy of all those who occupy seats of power and who tend to mold the major lines of a given culture. Marx's insight into the rationalizations which ruling groups develop to sustain their own power and privileges has never been excelled. Although the whole Western moral and political tradition has frequently emphasized the theme, it remained for Marx and Engels to develop it most fully in the context of the accelerated change so characteristic of the politics of industrialism.

6. Values in the Communist Vision. Although earlier we were critical of the vagueness with which Marxism formulates the ideal of the posthistorical epoch, much in the ideal would appear to stand up under critical scrutiny. There would seem to be a certain self-evident truth in such propositions as that each should contribute in accordance with his ability; that each should receive in accordance with need; that men ought to cooperate freely and spontaneously; and that they should be freed from economic concerns not as an end in itself but rather that they might then pursue the really important questions of human life and destiny. It is difficult to deny the Marxist contention that for most human beings history up to now has consisted in large degree of men's efforts to sustain life at a bare subsistence level; that human struggles, including military conflicts, have been strongly shaped by the economic struggle; and that man was made for better things.

7. Emancipation from Domination of the Material. Critics of Marx—particularly those who term him "godless" and an "enemy of religion"—often condemn him for what they call his materialism. As we have seen, however, this is not materialism in the simple, traditional interpretation but rather dialectical materialism. In this qualified sense, then, Marx suggests that man's history has been bound to the forces of production. And we have earlier suggested the limitations of this kind of explanation.

However, the view of some religious critics that Marx exalts materialism in a normative sense is almost totally wrong. He is passing a judgment on the history which up to now has made man the prey of material forces and suggesting that that same history will emancipate him from their thralldom. Insofar as he exemplifies the role of a moral prophet, he is holding out hope that human experience will cease to be materialist and will instead come to reflect that primary concern about things of mind and spirit which has always been held up as the goal by the major prophets. In this normative sense, Marx is very much a non-materialist: Man may no longer be enslaved by matter but will instead live in the spirit.

8. The Value of Marxist Atheism. In denying God, Marx is essentially protesting against the tendency in human history to create God in the image of a man still so largely subservient to material factors. Each age must produce its atheists in this sense of the term if men are to preserve a sense of tension between what is and what ought to be. Because every epoch, as Marx teaches, is tempted to endow its own class-biased system with divine qualities, the atheist or iconoclast is essential to destroy the false divinity.

Hegel, Marxism, and Liberalism

At the very time the Hegelian and Marxist systems were taking root, an analytic and normative doctrine of politics known as "liberalism," and later as "liberal democracy," was also beginning to shape the outlook of the world. Like the Hegelian and Marxist doctrines, the liberalism of the early nineteenth century underwent considerable changes in formulation and application during the course of about one hundred fifty years. Less pretentious and perhaps more unsystematic than either Hegelianism or Marxism, liberalism in great degree was antagonistic to them; yet ironically enough, its later development was to be significantly influenced by their analyses.

Liberal ideas were highly important in all parts of the world between 1800 and our own day. To their development and theoretical roots we turn in the next chapter.

chapter 26

The Modern Liberal Tradition

While Hegel was formulating the propositions which signified a return in some sense to classical Greek conceptions, the basis for what came to be known as liberalism was being laid in Britain, France, and the United States.

The term itself, like so many in the political lexicon, is not entirely satisfactory. But it has persisted so long and appears to be so ineradicable that any treatment of political theory since 1800 seems obliged to employ it. During the course of more than a century and a half, however, it has undergone a considerable substantive transformation and has not been unaffected by both Hegelian and Marxist streams of thought, as well as by other rivulets which have flowed into its somewhat eclectic ocean.

Evolution

The movement and body of thought to be characterized as liberalism had its roots in a diversity of intellectual and social strands. Here we note some of its antecedents in British, American, and French thought, leaving the analysis to subsequent sections.

The British strain goes back at least to the seventeenth century, with the conceptions of Locke and other social contract thinkers and also with such popular movements as the Levellers.[1]

In the eighteenth century, as we have seen, contract conceptions began to decline in Britain and on the Continent,[2] and those whose point of departure was some kind of individualism had to turn to other frameworks. The major revision came in the doctrines of the Utilitarians who, while repudiating both natural law and social contract, sought to provide a base for legal reform and (later) representa-

1. See Chapter 20.
2. See Chapters 22 and 23.

tive democracy in a moral doctrine which stressed the consequences of acts in terms of a calculus of pains and pleasures.

Meanwhile, in the British American colonies, contract notions persisted and, indeed, seemed to be strengthened in the eighteenth century. The United States was founded in considerable measure on doctrines of social contract, as is evidenced in the words of the Declaration of Independence and in the constitutional and political theory of the Constitution. Along with social contract ideas went deistic religious notions and the conception, associated with men like Jefferson, that an understanding of the "springs" of men's actions would lead to the release of the true human being from the bonds of irrational tradition and prejudice.

In France, currents of thought preceding the French Revolution were highly important in shaping the modern liberal tradition. The atmosphere of rational inquiry, associated with many of the Encyclopaedists and with men like Voltaire, gave birth to political ideas highly critical of the feudal tradition. And in thinkers like Condorcet (1743–1794), who wrote during the Revolution, belief in the possibility of almost infinite human progress received one of its classical expressions. Leaders like Mirabeau represented a moderate liberal viewpoint; and the Girondin faction in revolutionary politics can be thought of as carrying on this tradition.

The liberal tendencies in French Revolutionary thought were, of course, important in the shaping of modern German liberalism. In reaction to Napoleon, statesmen like Baron von Stein, proceeded to attack the bastions of feudalism in order to provide a basis for resistance against the French; and the foundation of the University of Berlin in 1810 was a symbol of the rise of German liberalism as well as of nationalism. Hegel himself, as we have suggested, was profoundly affected by the liberal strain in French Revolutionary thought; and freedom—key word for all liberals—occupied a central place in his whole political philosophy.[3]

Given foundations of this kind, what was the subsequent history of liberal thought in epitome?

In Britain, the moral foundations for the movement were developed on bases established by Jeremy Bentham (1748–1833), changes elaborated by James Mill (1773–1836), and serious modifications worked out by John Stuart Mill (1806–1873). By the time the latter had finished his work, Bentham's propositions had been greatly attenuated, except in form.

The philosophical foundations of British liberalism were also profoundly affected by the impact of Hegelian thought. This was particularly notable in the writings of T. H. Green (1836–1882), who in effect tried to combine elements of the British liberal tradition stemming from Locke and Bentham with the organicism of Hegel and Rousseau. The fusion of mature Millian with Hegelian emphases made the liberalism of the later nineteenth century rather different than that of 1832.

Early liberalism was not necessarily democratic. In the United States, for example, the Founding Fathers tended to be suspicious of unmitigated popular rule and were fearful that Locke's property—defined in its narrow sense—might be endangered by the cupidity of the masses. Early American liberals often defended property qualifications for voting, contending that only those who had an economic "stake in society" could be trusted with political power. Even Jefferson was only a contingent democrat, associating the possibility of democracy with the preservation of a nonurban society. It was not until relatively late in the nineteenth century that the rather vague formulations of Jacksonian democracy gave ideological expression to such contemporary movements as expansion of the suffrage and the growth of confidence in popular rule. Eventually most American leaders—including such diverse personalities as Martin Van Buren and Abraham Lincoln—associated themselves with Jacksonian democracy, thus helping to marry the very powerful early liberal impulse to the sweep of democratic sentiment.[4] Later on, in the Progressive and Populist movements, this marriage became even firmer. With the growth of liberal democracy or democratic liberalism, however, was associated a general defense of the capitalist economic system, although there were, to be sure, quasi-socialist aspects of some Progressivism. The political philosophy of the American New Deal in the thirties of the twentieth century was a peculiar combination of early liberalism, later progressivism, and the attempt to make capitalism compatible with the ideology of Jeffersonianism.

In Britain, early Utilitarianism which constituted much of the basis of liberal thought, was originally not democratic. It sought, to be sure, to liberate from the trammels of the past and to stress human freedom; but it did not advocate popular rule. The shift to democratic liberalism began about 1830, was solidified in the thought of men like John Stuart Mill, and confirmed in such politicians as W. E. Gladstone and, in the twentieth century, David Lloyd George.

In France, too, the development of liberal thought and practice in a democratic direction was relatively slow. Although the slogans of the French Revolution seemed to be both democratic and liberal, the reaction to it after 1815 often accented the liberalism and depreciated the democracy. If the revolutions of 1830 and 1848 be regarded as expressions of the middle-class liberal spirit, their predominant thrusts were hardly democratic. To be sure, they represented demands for a greater sharing of political power and for regimes of constitutionalism. But men like Guizot,[5] who described themselves as liberals, were hardly democrats. As in the United States and Britain, widespread democratic liberalism was a development of the latter part of the century; and in general it was associated with a middle-class economic outlook.

In Germany, as we have suggested, the liberals and conservatives contended with each other about their interpretation of Hegel. In the beginning, the democratic element was a relatively minor chord; and the conditions of German politics down to the Weimar regime tended to make the Marxian socialists (or social democrats) major bearers of the democratic tradition. While early liberalism, to be sure, was modified by democratic elements, the latter were often not central.

By World War I, both European and American liberalism had undergone substantial changes in their attitudes to the state and in the philosophical basis for their outlooks. We may summarize these changes as, in general (and subject to many exceptions), the movement away from highly discrete individualism (in Britain and the United States particularly) to a form of thought affected in some measure by Hegelian organicism; a shift from an often rather rigid hostility to state intervention in economic life to a kind of pragmatic collectivism (as with liberals like David Lloyd George, Woodrow Wilson, and Benedetto Croce); and development from a position having no necessary connection with democracy to one often linking liberalism with democracy, the result being what some have called a theory of liberal democracy. As a general rule, these characteristic changes per-

sisted in the liberalism of the period following World War I.[6]

The Development of Liberal Theory: Search for a Definition

This brief survey of the evolution of modern liberalism suggests the difficulty of defining the term and of discerning common threads running through its propositions.

In the first place, it is not easy to discover any one thinker who may be said to epitomize liberal thought. There is, for example, no liberal theorist quite the equivalent of Marx. Because much liberal thought, particularly in its later phases, is rather vague and eclectic, the varieties of self-proclaimed liberals are numerous. This very eclecticism opens liberalism in the twentieth century to criticisms coming from a diversity of viewpoints. Thus both Marxists and Fascists have attacked what they call liberalism; yet the image of the liberal for the Marxist may be quite different from that for the Fascist. The difficulty is compounded because liberals have usually professed to reject strongly dogmatic statements: they thus open themselves up to polemics from more

3. For the subsequent history of the idea of freedom in Germany, see Leonard Krieger, *The German Idea of Freedom*, Boston: Beacon Press, 1957.
4. On the theory of Jacksonian Democracy, see Lee Benson, *The Concept of Jacksonian Democracy*, New York: Atheneum Press, 1964; Joseph Blau, *Social Theories of Jacksonian Democracy*, New York: Hafner Publishing Co., 1947; and Walter Hugins, *Jacksonian Democracy and the Working Class*, Stanford, Calif.: Stanford University Press, 1960.
5. Francois Pierre Guizot (1787–1874) was an historian who associated himself with the early French liberal movement in the years following 1815. In this period, he held various public offices and lectured at the Sorbonne. After the enthronement of Louis Philippe in 1830, he became a strong supporter of that ruler, holding high office under him for a number of years. He became increasingly conservative and even less than in his earlier days could he be said to have been a democrat.
6. On the rise of liberalism consult such works as Guido De Ruggiero, *History of European Liberalism*, Boston: Beacon Press, 1959 and H. J. Laski, *The Rise of European Liberalism*, New York and London: Allen & Unwin, 1936.

authoritatively stated outlooks. Any discussion of liberal theory must somehow come to grips with these ambiguities, whether of liberalism itself or of its detractors.

The clue to part of the problem of definition may be found in a second consideration which should be central in any study of liberalism—namely, the fact that the word has been used to designate both a spirit and a series of specific propositions about the nature of the state, of morals, and of the limits of state action. As a spirit, it has stressed such commitments as the high-order value of liberty; receptivity to change; openness to experimentation in social and political affairs; distrust of mere tradition as a guide; the possibility of rationality in collective life; and the potentiality for moral and political progress. John Morley, one of the greatest of modern liberals, has perhaps best expressed this spirit:

> Such ideas are these: that the conditions of the social union are not a mystery, only to be touched by miracle, but the results of explicable causes, and susceptible of constant modification; that the thoughts of wise and patriotic men should be perpetually turned towards the improvement of these conditions in every direction; that contented acquiescence in the ordering that has come down to us from the past is selfish and anti-social, because amid the ceaseless change that is inevitable in a growing organism, the institutions of the past demand progressive readaptation; that such improvements are most likely to be secured in greatest abundance by limiting the sphere of authority, extending that of free individuality, and steadily striving after the bestowal so far as the nature of things will ever permit it, of equality of opportunity.[7]

In terms of its specific propositions, liberalism began historically as a revolt against status relationships which it associated with the remnants of feudalism. It called for a society more largely based on free contracts. Philosophically, it tended to spurn the Platonic and Aristotelian traditions and to ground its revolt against the old ways of ordering society on the appeal to utility in Britain and on social contract notions in the United States. Later on, the very principle of utility, which in the beginning seemed to justify its revolt against state and tradition controlled human life, was turned to the support of state intervention. And both social contract and utilitarian principles were undermined by a modified Hegelianism, which in itself served to weaken the early dogmas against public regulation of the economic order. Hence, as we have seen, liberal propositions of the twentieth century often differed quite widely from those of the early nineteenth.

Because recent (or twentieth-century) liberalism appears to differ so widely in the specific applications of its spirit, some liberals deny that there is any connection between the nineteenth-century version and that which goes by the name in our day. Thus Senator Eugene J. McCarthy, an American liberal thinker and practicing politician, affirms this position in a recent work.[8] And on the surface there seems much to be said for it. If both philosophical foundations and specific applications in the realms of law and politics have changed, why, it may be asked, connect the liberalism of 1850 with that of 1970?

The answer would seem to lie in the common spirit which animates both. Tenuous as the connection may be at times, there does seem to be a sense in which the liberalism of Mill's middle phase and that of the post–World War II period can be said to be one. But it is liberalism of the spirit which constitutes the binding tie, and not necessarily (and sometimes not at all) the liberalism of specific propositions, whether of philosophical foundations or of legislation.

In order to understand and illustrate the link as well as the discontinuities between nineteenth- and twentieth-century liberalism, a somewhat more detailed treatment is essential. We begin with the early utilitarian analysis which was primarily British but which was also influential in France and the United States. Then we examine the transformation of the early utilitarian liberal view by John Stuart Mill and Thomas Hill Green. Finally, let us say a word about the relation of liberalism to the idea of progress and to twentieth century politics and political thought.

The Early Utilitarian View

The economic and social context for the rise of early utilitarianism, and hence of the foundations for nineteenth-century liberalism, is the development of commercial and industrial capitalism. Commercial capitalism had brought to the fore an economic class which challenged the traditional domination of the conservative land-owning classes and, in ideological terms, its political philosophy in Britain came to be that associated with social contract conceptions. The free and discrete individual, emancipated from custom and at liberty to pursue his own interest in his own way, became the image which dominated commercial capitalist thought. Medieval restrictions and ecclesiastical regulations had to go.

The great commercial capitalist impetus was still in effect during the very early days of utilitarianism. But already the merchant was beginning to transform himself into an industrialist and by 1800, we may say that industrial capitalism had begun its victorious progress. Meanwhile, political speculation was discarding social contract (with the exception of the United States) and was searching for a new formulation which would avoid the pitfalls of both traditional natural law and early modern contractual notions.

We have already traced out at some length[9] the rise of the conception of the discrete individual in the context of declining medieval institutions and thought. Here we must reiterate the gradualness of that decline. For most men, the image of man in society remained medieval long after the institutions characteristic of medieval life had begun to be undermined. On the other hand, the institutions themselves persisted for many years after their raison d'etre had gone. Even in Britain, the seat of commercial enterprise and the pioneer in industrial capitalism, legal institutions, for example, still reflected modes of thought and action characteristic of an agrarian way of life rather than of commercialism, let alone industrialism.

It was into this situation that Jeremy Bentham (1748–1833) was born. Trained to be a lawyer, he early gave up practice of the law in order to examine the basis of law and pursue the task of legal reform. At first, he believed that a mere appeal to his utilitarian principles would lead the enlightened despots (Joseph II, for example, or Frederick II) of the late eighteenth century and the oligarchical government of Britain to institute what he regarded as indispensable changes in the law. After a generation of arduous effort, however, he concluded that the only way in which genuine legal reform along utilitarian lines would come about would be through a radically transformed political machinery. Hence, in the latter period of his life, Bentham became a champion of parliamentary reform and an extended suffrage, dying just after the enactment of the great Reform Bill of 1832. Many attributed much of the impetus for the Reform Bill to disciples of Bentham who carried out in the domain of politics what Bentham speculated about in the quiet of his rather secluded life.[10]

It is curious that Bentham's great call to legal reform—and his first statement of utilitarian principles—should have occurred in the same year as the American Declaration of Independence and the publication of Adam Smith's *Wealth of Nations*. Thus the *Fragment on Government* became one of the triad of 1776 utterances which constitute the beginnings of modern liberalism. The *Fragment* was the rallying-cry for all those who for many years had criticized law and justice; the *Declaration*, with its commitment to a very un-Benthamite natural rights doctrine, became the great inspiration for early political liberalism; while the *Wealth of Nations* helped to build the foundations of primitive economic liberalism.

For a half century after 1776 Bentham continued to elaborate the theory of utilitarianism, notably in the *Principles of Morals and Legislation* (1789). And Benthamism both influenced and was influenced by similar tendencies in French and Swiss thought. So confident was Bentham in his doctrine that at one point he advertised that he would draw up a new code of laws for any nation on earth: Utilitarianism could be applied, he seemed to suggest, in a diversity of cultures, traditions, and psychological contexts. When eventually his disillusionment with ruling classes of the day impelled him to consider a broadening of the suffrage and a reform of Parliament, he still clung to the basic tenets of his doctrine of morals and legislation.

Bentham's rejection of contract, natural rights, and natural law is not unlike that of Hume. All of them are mere fictions or lies which have no useful purpose but rather serve

7. *On Compromise*, London: Chapman and Hall, 1874, pp. 125–126.
8. See Eugene J. McCarthy, *Frontiers in American Democracy*, New York: Harcourt, 1960.
9. See Chapter 15 particularly.
10. On Bentham and early utilitarianism, see Elie Halévy, *The Growth of Philosophic Radicalism*, Boston: Beacon Press, 1955; and Leslie Stephen, *The English Utilitarians*, vol. 1, *Bentham*, and vol. 2, *James Mill*, London: Duckworth, 1900, and New York: Kelley, 1968.

to becloud the actual issues which confront mankind. So, too, he can see no value in mere tradition or the santification allegedly conferred by time: Thus his attack on the common law and on Blackstone as its great exponent is based in considerable measure on his allegation that the law enshrines principles and practices which have no possible usefulness. Bit by bit the legal and judicial structure has grown without rime or reason, Bentham argues, and what infuriates him is that men like Blackstone should endeavor to applaud this nefarious growth. The delays of the law, the devices used by lawyers to prolong a case for years—and the reader will remember Dickens' graphic picture in *Bleak House*—the unnecessarily obscure language, the ferocious punishments (some two hundred offenses are still punishable by death)—all these characteristics of late eighteenth-century life become the objects of his biting criticism. He is particularly shaken by the use of legal fictions, which, of course, occur in every legal system, whether common law or Roman, but which Bentham thinks of as dishonesties that make the law still more cumbrous and unuseful.[11]

One of his central contentions emphasizes the ambiguities in the existing law, which befuddle the layman and enable the lawyer to accumulate wealth as a result of endless litigation. Bentham sees ambiguities as basically the product of judicially created law.

Instead of judge-made law, Bentham advocates codification, which he believes will simplify legal principles and make them understandable. If the code is drawn up carefully and with due regard to coherence, he suggests, there will be precious little need for judicial elaboration or interpretation. The growth of legal obscurantism can be nipped in the bud, so to speak.

But what principles should govern the development of codes? If there are, contrary to Jefferson, no natural rights, and if classical natural law is itself a kind of superstition, how shall the legislator be guided? Bentham's answer is "by a pleasure-pain" calculus which makes right and wrong turn only on the consequences of given acts.

The identification of pleasure with good and of pain with evil is, of course, an ancient notion. In its early modern form, it was restated by Hobbes[12] and, in fact, is perhaps the major note in moral thought during the seventeenth and eighteenth centuries. The idea that consequences of acts should be decisive in making moral judgments is also old and, in fact, in less extreme forms plays a role in systems reposing fundamentally on natural law bases (the scheme of St. Thomas Aquinas, for example). What Bentham does is to make the pleasure-pain and consequences desiderata the center of his moral and political thought and he obscures the fact that he has resorted to other principles.

In deciding whether or not a proposed act is right, he tells us, we should keep in mind the fact that human springs of action turn on the search for happiness defined as pleasure and the avoidance of unhappiness which is identified with pain. Intelligent action, then, will be based on an informed judgment as to the probable consequences of any decision in terms of pleasure and pain.

When we ask Bentham the meaning of "pleasure" and "pain," he replies that we simply take the word of individual human beings about what is pleasurable and what painful. Moreover, there can be no qualitative distinctions between pleasures and pains; only quantitative desiderata can be considered. Quantitative standards include such factors as intensity, propinquity, and duration. Thus we may interpret Bentham as saying that the pleasure of a striptease performance and of a Beethoven symphony cannot be differentiated in terms of an intrinsic "good" or "better" but only as measured by such factors as the nearness of the pleasure, its intensity, and its time-span.

Moreover, he goes on, pleasures and pains are not to be differentiated in terms of the persons experiencing them. Each person is to count for one and no more than one—the pleasures (or pains) of a duke, other things being equal, are to be rated no more highly than those of a commoner. Here again, we note continuity from Hobbes to Bentham. In this sense, too, Bentham's utilitarianism reposes on radically democratic foundations.

Bentham assumes that he is dealing with discrete individuals, each of whom can discover his own best interests in light of the pleasure-pain-consequences principle. But how are these discrete individuals held together in society? And what is the role of the legislator? It is not easy to see how self-interested, separate individuals can be transmuted into aggregates of men and women setting up as their goal the "greatest happiness of the greatest number." But such is Bentham's assertion. The legislator is to be guided by hedonistic utilitarianism in formulating statutes and, above all, in proposing the repeal of statutes which do not serve that principle.

Ideally, one supposes, Bentham would have his legislator conducting constant and meticulous surveys attempting to discover the exact effect of legislation on the pleasures and pains of individuals. If it can be shown, for example, that the incidence of a given law is to enhance pain, then the law must be repealed, regardless of its antiquity and its alleged conformity with natural law or the national interest.

And as a matter of fact, this is precisely what Benthamite utilitarians attempted to do. They noted, for instance, that over two hundred crimes were punishable by death and decided to examine whether the death penalty actually served to deter crime (as was alleged by those who appealed to antiquity, precedent, natural law, or "common sense"). At public executions for pick-pocketing, the Benthamites discovered an extraordinarily high incidence of pocket-picking, which led them to infer that the public execution had little effect in preventing the crime for which the offender was being killed. But if the death penalty and public executions could not be shown to prevent crime (and the burden of proof must be on those who advocated the death penalty), then it would seem that the mode of punishment must be strongly criticized. As a result, and in considerable degree through direct Benthamite agitation, the number of crimes punishable by death was drastically reduced and public executions were abolished.

This is only one example of the application of Benthamite principles to practical questions of legislation. In general, we may say that early Utilitarianism was an important factor in undermining much traditional legislation and thus in liberating the individual from conditions which presumably impaired the maximization of his pleasure. And liberalism in its early stages is thus a movement and an outlook implying freedom from any restrictions which cannot be justified by the pleasure-pain or "felicific" calculus.

Implicitly, too, although he does not recognize it at first, Bentham is driven increasingly in the direction of political democracy. In the beginning, as we have noted, he appears to think that governments of any kind whatsoever can be persuaded to institute legal reforms according to utilitarian principles. But later he becomes grievously disillusioned and presses for a wider basis of political rule. In a sense, of course, this thrust toward democracy is latent in his whole system of thought, based as it is on such notions as the discrete individual, equality, and the apparent belief that each individual can judge his own best interests.

Yet it is obvious that in trying to establish new directions, Bentham (and the Benthamite liberals) fell into other traps. It has often been pointed out, for example, that while repudiating natural law principles in explicit terms, he reimports something like them implicitly. Thus such notions as "each shall count for one and no more than one" cannot be sustained through utilitarian methods: They are either intuited premises or mere feelings. So, too, the critic will ask why *quantitative* desiderata should be the only ones considered in working with the "felicific" calculus. Does Bentham really believe, the critic may inquire, that there is no *qualitative* difference between the so-called pleasures of sense and what the classical tradition might have termed the life of contemplation; or rather does he spurn qualitative differentials because they are too vague and lacking in objectivity?

Early utilitarianism bristles with questions of this kind. As a body of ideas moving men to eliminate outworn statutes and conventions, it may have been quite effective. But as a moral and political philosophy, it is very sketchy, ambiguous, and generally inadequate.

The Development and Modification of Utilitarian Liberalism

Because of its incompleteness and frequent superficiality, early utilitarianism came under attack from several sources. In part, Hegel's shafts are directed at it. Early nineteenth-century conservatives, too, criticize its lack of any feeling for the historical dimension of morals and politics. But it is within the ranks of utilitarian liberalism itself that we must look for some of the more eloquent statements.

Perhaps the ablest and most thoughtful nineteenth-century utilitarian liberal is John Stuart Mill (1806–1873). Mill was brought up on the

11. On legal fictions as an expression of the theory of fictions in general, see Hans Vaihinger, *The Philosophy of "As If"* new ed., London: Routledge and Kegan Paul, 1952.
12. See Chapter 19.

utilitarian gospel as interpreted by his father James, a disciple of Bentham. But before he died, he so modified and developed it that some critics suggest it virtually disappeared.

In many ways, Mill was an eclectic. Precocious, highly disciplined, and an insatiable delver into a diversity of streams of thought, it is not easy to place him in any neat category of political speculation. As the late Harold Laski once put it,

> No one can appreciate Mill who does not realize how wide are the influences which went into the formation of his thought. Not merely Bentham and James Mill, but Coleridge and Saint-Simon, Comte, and Tocqueville, were streams that emptied themselves into the central ocean.[13]

Although Mill to the end of his life claimed to remain a utilitarian, the meaning of the term at his hands is certainly modified drastically. To be sure, he emerges still making the maximization of pleasure and the minimization of pain the ultimate end; but in the process he discards one Benthamite proposition after another.

In the first place, he stresses factors of cultural relativity. Institutions which might be justified (by utilitarian principles, of course) at one cultural level might have to be rejected at another. One must maintain a sense of perspective with respect to historical factors which shape a culture and limit the degree to which one can apply utilitarian liberal principles. Whereas Bentham appears to think in terms of abstractions, Mill stresses that general principles can often be applied only to a limited degree in face of the often obdurate (and, from Bentham's point of view, silly) resistance of human beings conditioned by history to think in other ways or limited in their possibilities by economic and social factors. Thus, while Mill is a strong advocate of representative government, he also argues that it is perhaps not desirable for all states of society and all cultural levels.

He questions Bentham's assertion, too, that we can and ought to pursue happiness directly. Perhaps in the long run all human effort does indeed aim at happiness (defined as balance of pleasure over pain) but in the short run we must often make choices which may produce the reverse of happiness. "The only chance," he tells us in his *Autobiography*, "is to treat, not happiness, but some end external to it, as the purpose of life."[14]

But insofar as he remains a utilitarian (and one must stress that he himself believed he never departed from Benthamite foundations), it is in quite a different sense from that of Bentham, or even of his father James. He attacks the notion, for example, that all pleasures and pains are qualitatively at the same level. Some, he asserts, are higher in the scale than others. How, then, do we know which are at the top and which below? Mill's reply is that we consult those men who have experienced all levels of pleasure from the sensual to the intellectual and spiritual. We shall find, he believes, a virtual unanimity of judgment that intellectual and spiritual pleasures are intrinsically more to be desired than pleasures of mere sense; and we should thus accept the judgment of those who presumably have tasted all levels. Here Mill is obviously attempting to retain a kind of empiricism in arranging pleasures in an hierarchical scale. Still repudiating natural law, he yet realizes that utilitarianism takes pride in the objectivity of its judgments.

The implications of this qualitative distinction are far-reaching for Mill's moral and political theory. As we shall see, he deduces from this revisionist utilitarianism the proposition that those capable of enjoying the higher pleasures are more valuable than those who presumably do not have this capacity. But he will also argue that political authority should reside in the people as a whole. One of the great problems in his theory of representative government will be the reconciliation of an ethical theory which appears to stress hierarchy with a political commitment that, on the surface at least, seems to emphasize equality.

His vital contribution to the debate about freedom consists in his assertion that the rise of democracy can be a deadly thrust at freedom itself. This is true because the tendency is to think that if the people are their own rulers they will not be likely to curb their own liberties. Not so, argues Mill. When men believe they no longer have a highly differentiated ruling class to attack, they tend to accept restrictions on liberty more readily; for they can rationalize the limitations on the ground that they are self-imposed. Moreover, even if the restrictions are not formally established by statute, they tend increasingly to be set up by public opinion.

At no point in his whole system of thought does Mill reason so acutely and with so much prophetic insight into the nature of modern industrial democratic society. One might almost think that he is writing in the twentieth century, with its mass engulfment of individual eccentricity, its McCarthyism, and its "people's democracies." Mill, more than any other nineteenth-century thinker—liberal or nonliberal—is sharply aware of these potentialities. His is a voice crying out against those versions of democracy—some of them Rousseauistic in inspiration—which would tend to equate it with suppression of diversity of opinion.

But more than this, Mill believes it essential to argue the case for freedom in a positive sense. In this respect, he repeats certain individualist propositions while at the same time going beyond them. Freedom is a good (presumably to be justified on utilitarian grounds) in terms of both action and expression (or opinion):

> The sole end for which mankind are warranted, individually or collectively, in interfering with the liberty of action of any of their number, is self-protection. The only purpose for which power can be rightfully exercised over any member of a civilized community, against his will, is to prevent harm to others. His own good, either physical or moral, is not a sufficient warrant.[15]

The only exceptions to this rule, Mill believes, are those which involve children (who have not attained the maturity of their faculties) and "backward" states of society in which the race may be thought of as in its "nonage."

The modern critic will, of course, question Mill's sharp distinction between actions which affect only oneself and those which may do harm to others. What, it might be asked, does *not* affect others in a complicated and highly organized society? And can any individual action affect merely the actor?

However, it is with respect to opinion and free expression that Mill will continue to stand for a long time as the epitome of the liberal spirit. Later liberalism will, following Mill himself, seriously modify what seem to be the implications of his doctrine of freedom of action. But although his theory of freedom of expression has been severely criticized also,[16] particularly by those concerned with the rise of totalitarianism in the twentieth century, it still stands out as one of the ablest and most viable expressions of all liberal thought.

It is illegitimate for either government or mass pressure to interfere with the free expression of unorthodox viewpoints, he contends, for three basic reasons.

The first is that the unorthodox opinion may be true while the accepted view may be invalid. Of all utilitarian liberals, Mill's is perhaps the best example of a mind which doubts the possibility of any one view being true. But in the event that one version is the complete truth, he is asking us why we assume the orthodox expression to possess that quality. Does the support of numbers guarantee the truth or validity of an opinion?

But secondly, he maintains, even if we assume that the accepted opinion is true, we still ought not to suppress the contrary expression; for the full meaning of the orthodox words and beliefs (which are "true" by the hypothesis) cannot be understood, either intellectually or emotionally, unless they are confronted with their opposite. A religious faith unchallenged becomes dead, even if we assume that its propositions are entirely true and that the opposing dogma is entirely false. Western democratic beliefs, Mill would say today, need to be challenged openly by Communist doctrine, on peril of becoming dessicated. No paraphrase can do justice to Mill's own words:

> He who knows only his own side of the case, knows little of that.
>
> All Christians believe that the blessed are the poor and humble, and those who are ill-used by the world; that it is easier for a camel to pass through the eye of a needle than for a rich man to enter the kingdom of heaven; that they should judge not, lest they be judged; that they believe these things. They do believe these things. They do believe them, as people believe what they have always heard lauded and never discussed. But in the sense of that living belief which regulates conduct, they believe these doctrines just up to the point to which it is usual to act upon them.[17]

But it is unlikely, according to Mill, that either the unorthodox or the orthodox belief system is entirely true. Thought and expression, he believes, probably never completely grasp the whole. The very fact that a received opinion is questioned probably means that it is

13. In the Introduction to the Oxford edition of Mill's *Autobiography*, Oxford: Oxford University Press, 1924, pp. xiv–xv.
14. *Ibid.*, p. 121.
15. *On Liberty and Representative Government*, R. B. McCollum, ed., Oxford: Basil Blackwell, 1946, pp. 8–9.
16. See, for example, James Feibleman, *Positive Democracy*, Chapel Hill: University of North Carolina Press, 1940.
17. *On Liberty*, *op. cit.*, pp. 32–36.

at least partially untrue. It needs the challenge to help refine away elements of untruth and invalidity.

Mill will hear of few if any exceptions to absolute freedom of expression. Although he does accept the law of slander and libel (which he believes can be defended on utilitarian grounds), it must be very explicitly defined and can apparently deal with only the most explicit acts of defamation or of narrowly factual untruths.

Modern governments have never really accepted Mill's doctrine of expression. So, too, mass opinion for the most part—as Mill clearly foresaw—is frequently hostile to freedom of expression, whether in the West or in the East. Always at some point "dangerous thoughts"—an expression utilized by certain modern authoritarian Japanese governments—must be eliminated from the body politic.[18]

So far does Mill carry out his doctrine of individual liberty that he appears to value eccentricity almost as an end in itself. He waxes eloquent in defense of the unusual and of departures from the common norm. It is not doing him an injustice to say that he would value strange dress, curious personal action, and unusual speech habits if only because he is so distrustful of uniformities in any realm of life.

He is not only eloquent in defense of eccentricity, however. He is indignant, too, that half of mankind—the women—have been so long in subjection to the other half.[19] He asks himself how this subservience, whether of law or custom, can be justified on Millian utilitarian grounds. His reply is an emphatic assertion that it cannot be upheld. While women are differentiated from men biologically and naturally are more closely related to children in their formative beginning years, this cannot possibly justify their exclusion from the suffrage, from the professions, and from all the avenues open to men historically. Mill's defense of equality between the sexes is perhaps the most effective ever penned and it epitomizes utilitarian liberalism at its best.[20]

Both his relativism and his radically modified utilitarianism are admirably illustrated in his theory of representative institutions. The problem of representation is a central one in liberal theory and, indeed—at least in a very broad sense—in all political thought. The conflicts involved in the conciliar movement were, as we have pointed out, in considerable measure those which turned on representation.[21] In the seventeenth century, Locke and the Levellers found it of vital importance.[22]

Mill cannot adopt Rousseauistic notions which would deny the possibility of representing wills. He asks himself where in the last analysis political authority in the community must rest and his answer is in the whole body of adult members. Political decisions affect all (as the canon lawyers would have put it) and this demands that all be consulted. But how will the assent of the community be conveyed?

In answering this question, Mill advocates a system of actual representation that builds on the precedents of British constitutional history. All members of the community—including women—are to have the franchise. But since he has argued in his modified utilitarian principles that some are of greater value to the community than others, he maintains that these more valuable individuals should have extra votes (thus those who hold degrees from universities will carry greater weight than others). Moreover, because he is so impressed by the necessity for a full reflection of minority voices, he strongly advocates the Hare system of proportional representation, which had only recently been suggested by Thomas Hare.

In his upper chamber Mill would include experienced statesmen who would perform the work of revision and criticism.

When he discusses the functions of the representative body, Mill again demonstrates that moderation and eclecticism which run through his political thought generally.[23] On the one hand, he criticizes those who would make the body of representatives the actual government; on the other hand, he is equally critical of those who might wish to reduce Parliament to a kind of advisory status. In his judgment, the central function of the representative body is to control the government, not to govern directly. The government (or Cabinet) will presumably reflect the general political complexion of the lower house; and once it has been chosen, it will be given a relatively free hand, subject, of course, to the dismissal, criticism, and assent powers of Parliament.

But thus far we have been concerned mainly with what might be described as the mechanical aspects of Mill's doctrine of representation. We have not, except incidentally, spoken of the basic or underlying justification for representative nondespotic government in general.

Nor have we explicitly noted the ways in which the diverse aspects of Mill's scheme illustrate his peculiar version of utilitarian liberalism. Here three considerations would seem to be in order: the relation of representative government to stages of cultural development; the general defense of nondespotic, popular government; and the over-all vindication of Mill's own version of representation.

Mill is emphatic in arguing that the ideal of representative government is not necessarily appropriate for all levels of culture. Thus a stone-age way of life is incompatible with it, as are primitive historical stages. Then, too, without a certain minimum of economic resources, it is doubtful whether representative institutions could be maintained. Unlike Bentham, Mill is constantly stressing historical factors as conditioning the probable success or failure of institutions. At the same time, he believes that representative institutions are indispensable in the kinds of national cultures characteristic of Western civilization and assuming the values of his drastically modified utilitarian liberalism.

For where the ideal of individual liberty has come to the fore and where the pursuit of happiness—as with Locke and Jefferson—is made a central value, only representative institutions within the context of nondespotic government can help implement the prime moral considerations. A despotism conceivably could be good, in the sense that it might provide security and material benefits to the population; but it would not thereby be justified. For the primary and acid test of good government, within Mill's framework, is whether it tends to increase the sum of good qualities in the governed. And what is the essence of those good qualities? To Mill they are the characteristics we associate with an active rather than a passive personality type. The passive personality accepts and does not originate; the active, by contrast, raises questions, exhibits imagination, objects, and innovates. If therefore the encouragement of the latter be the desideratum —and Mill has no doubt on this score, given his qualitative utilitarianism—any political system which reposes on despotism, however benevolent, and which does not establish representative institutions, is simply ruled out. This is true because human personality cannot develop (beyond its primitive stages) unless it is called upon to be a participant in community governance. It must exert itself not only in purely individual matters—making a living, personal development, and so on—but also in affairs concerning the community's weal.

But while considerations of this kind may vindicate popular participation and representative institutions in general, what propositions can be put forth for Mill's scheme in particular? There are many systems of representative government. Why is Mill's the best? Keeping in mind the propositions of his moral theory and his vindication of liberty, Mill's answer is that his system constitutes the proper combination for blending popular assent with qualitative differences; majority rule with emphasis on the value of a strong minority voice; and general insight into common affairs with specialized expertise.

Can Mill be termed a democrat? The answer depends on how one defines the term. If it means one who argues that the community has the moral right, through majority rule, to make any political decision it desires, the answer must be in the negative; for Mill certainly implies that in acting, the community must respect such values as a nearly absolute freedom of expression, representation for minorities, and the qualitative superiority of some pleasures to others. If, on the other hand, democracy means that the community's governors are in principle dismissable by it (through an ostensibly representative body),

18. The ridiculous lengths to which violations of Mill's principles may lead were expressed facetiously in the British tabloid *The Word* (c. 1948 or 1949):
    Your Honor, this book is a bucket of swill,
    It portrays a young couple alone on a hill.
    And a woman who lived in a shoe as a house
    With her brood, but not once does it mention her spouse.
    I submit that this book is obscene, vile and loose,
    I demand its suppression. Its name? Mother Goose.
19. Cf. *The Subjection of Women*, New York: Appleton, 1869.
20. Thus in the United States, despite great strides in the direction of equality, there still remains extensive discrimination against women in many of the professions.
21. See Chapter 15.
22. See Chapters 20 and 21.
23. See, in general, *Representative Government*, Ch. 5.

then Mill would qualify as a democrat. In principle, however, Mill's scheme is much closer to what Aristotle would call a polity than it is to any Rousseauistic version of democracy.

Unlike Rousseau, Mill does not purport to be able to reconcile our freedom with our sense of belonging. He sees the struggle between claimed political authority and freedom as a perpetual one and has no formula for eliminating the conflict. At best, he proposes a system in which dissenters can express themselves without hindrance in the hope, but no certainty, that their voices will somehow help in arriving at a decision which is more widely acceptable. Despite his consciousness of Hegelian and other organicist streams of thought, Mill remains essentially an individualist emphasizing the tension between ostensible authority and personal liberty.

So pronounced is Mill's stress on intellectual and political dissent, that critics in his day (and ours) sometimes charged that the full adoption of his principles could only encourage social disorder and even civil war. But Mill rejects all such criticisms. The real problem, he is constantly arguing, is not to keep men from revolting and dissenting. Rather is it to stimulate them to question the existing order of things. By and large, he contends, the history of mankind is one of a kind of herd morality in which incipient individualism is discouraged and all are expected to conform. But mankind ought not to be a herd. Those, therefore, who call into question existing customs and laws and who live as intellectual and spiritual rebels constitute the lever whereby others can be elevated to greater heights of development.

But at no point, perhaps, are the tensions within Mill's thought more apparent than in the economic realm. He begins more or less as an advocate of laissez faire, sharing in general the belief of early utilitarian liberals that abstention by the state from control of the economic order (except for a few general regulations) will on the whole best conduce to the greatest happiness of the greatest number. But there is nothing in utilitarian liberalism which necessarily implies an inflexible attitude to economic issues. And if it can be clearly shown that regulation, or even state ownership of productive mechanisms, will enlarge liberty and promote a greater balance of pleasure, utilitarian liberalism can in principle reverse its early position.

This is in substance the evolution which takes place in Mill. From being a utilitarian exponent of laissez faire, he comes in the end to espouse a position very close to that of an undogmatic socialism. He sees clearly that the tendency of mid-nineteenth-century industrial capitalism is to enhance the wealth and power of the few and increase the gulf between the proletarian and the owner of capital. And he is quite aware of the "land question," which becomes the center of Henry George's attack on unearned increment.[24] By the time he prepares the third edition of his *Political Economy*,[25] he is favoring public ownership of land and is raising the question of the desirability of social ownership of basic means of production. For gross economic and social inequality is to him intolerable.[26]

In many respects, it is these views of Mill on the economic issue which become the foundation for the tendency of later liberalism to be receptive to state intervention. This does not mean that Mill is perfectly consistent or sure of himself in the statement of his final principles. But there can be no doubt that, in this respect at least, he is moving rapidly in the direction of what we might call an inchoate kind of Fabian socialism.[27] In doing so, he anticipates a new generation of thinkers, who, while retaining much of what we have termed "liberalism of the spirit," begin to reject the laissez-faire views of their spiritual ancestors.

Old Versus New Liberalism: Spencer and Green

The contrast between old as against new versions of liberalism, substantively speaking, can perhaps best be summarized by referring to the systems of Herbert Spencer (1820–1903) and Thomas Hill Green (1836–1882).

Spencer's sociology is a peculiar and rather uncertain compound of explanatory and normative analysis. He sees Western society since the Middle Ages as having evolved from a system of status to that of contract. Although the process is not yet complete in his own day, he thinks that it is moving rapidly to consummation.[28] In a system of status, such as that of the Middle Ages, men are born and remain in fixed positions; the element of social dynamics, as Spencer terms it, is minimal; individual freedom of movement and experiment is almost nonexistent; law tends to take the form of custom; autocracy is the rule in politics; and warfare appears to be endemic. With the gradual rise of industrialism, however, this pattern changes: Contract takes the place of status as the central regulating factor; old systems of class are broken up; rapid change in social relations now comes to the fore; the individual is freed to pursue his own ends in his own way; law tends to become simply multifarious free agreements among individuals; the state gradually disappears; and warfare is increasingly eliminated.

The peculiar feature about Spencer's analysis (and it is to be followed by a host of evolutionary sociologists and ethicists) is that it proceeds from description and explanation to the establishment of norms: because the movement of history is in the direction of contract and the disappearance of the state, Spencer maintains, it is right that human affairs be regulated solely by contract and that the state vanish.

It is not surprising, therefore, that Spencer should view the tendencies of the new liberalism, as reflected in the later Mill, with great alarm. It is, he thinks, attempting to reverse the natural development of things and to restore the world to some kind of a status system. The natural evolution of industrialism, he believes, is in the direction of weeding out the unfit (those incapable of surviving through their own efforts) and eventually producing a race of supermen. But with the new liberalism advocating factory legislation, public health measures, and public education, the very foundations of liberalism—as Spencer interprets them—are undermined.

State intervention, by and large, will simply afford greater scope than in private organizations for "the love of power, the selfishness, the injustice, the untruthfulness" which bring those organizations "to disaster." Once one initiates the habit of state interference, moreover, there is a tendency to rely more and more on it, until the individual freedom presumably exalted by liberalism eventually disappears. While state intervention may seem to be justified by its "proximate" or immediate effects, if we consider it in its long-run implications, it constitutes a proposal "to improve life by breaking through the fundamental conditions to life."[29]

However one evaluates Spencer's position as a whole, it is obvious that he takes very seriously the proposition that there is an "individual" who is discrete and who can somehow be "self-made." Spencer's individual, in other words, is not a convenient abstraction used by social scientists for analytical purposes and then corrected for nonindividual characteristics but an actual entity who in Spencer's judgment can and ought to arise. Hence his bitterness against the new liberals of all varieties and his appeal from the new to the old. To him, the Spencerian version of liberalism is the only correct one: All others are spurious and have surrendered to state slavery.

The new liberalism, however, cannot be dismissed so easily. Several years before Spencer penned his diatribe against the liberal "interventionists" (his great outburst against the new liberals was first published in 1884), the Oxford philosopher Thomas Hill Green was working on the problem of a political philosophy which would somehow take account of the great stream of Hegelian criticism while yet not abandoning the spirit of the liberal position. The result was a moral and political theory reposing on a modified version of Rousseauistic-Hegelian organicism.[30] Maintaining, with the British tradition of individualism, the primacy of the individual, Green yet argues that the very characteristics of individuality depend for their background and sustenance on organic relations with the group. Rousseau was right when he stressed the element of will as the basis of social

24. *Progress and Poverty*, 4th ed., New York: H. George & Co., 1887; Modern Library edition, 1938. *Progress and Poverty* first appeared in 1879. It is interesting to note the many references which George makes to the economics of John Stuart Mill. He points out that Mill approves the principle that the community, and not private individuals, should reap the economic rent of land. But he chides Mill for being unwilling to carry out the principle consistently.
25. *Principles of Political Economy*, 3rd ed., 2 vols., London: 1852.
26. See his *Autobiography*, preface by Harold Laski, London: Oxford University Press, 1935, p. 196.
27. See Chapter 28.
28. See Spencer's *Principles of Sociology*, New York: Appleton, 1896 and *The Data of Ethics*, New York: Appleton, 1892.
29. See Herbert Spencer, *Man versus the State*, London: Williams & Norgate, 1910, 105.
30. See Green's *Prolegomena to Ethics*, 5th ed., Oxford: Clarendon, 1906 and his *Lectures on the Principles of Political Obligation*, London: Longmans Green, 1895.

cohesion; and will, not force, becomes for Green the foundation of the state. Although the state cannot make men good directly, since good actions must be voluntary, it very emphatically can do so indirectly by removing the external impediments to free choice and hence to good decisions.

Freedom to him is "a positive power or capacity of doing or enjoying something worth doing or enjoying, and that, too, something that we do or enjoy in common with others." Freedom in this sense is the fruit of civilization and not the result of savagery or the natural state; and if we inquire into the matter we shall see that the real capacities of the "savage" "do not admit of comparison with those of the humblest citizen of a law-abiding state." The uncivilized human being, to be sure, is not the slave of man—and here Herbert Spencer is right—but he just as emphatically is the slave of nature and finds his powers (and hence, to Green, his freedom) circumscribed by the hazards and arbitrary attributes of nature.

In light of these considerations, Green thinks of freedom of contract—which Spencer makes the center of his analysis—as a good, to be sure, but only an instrumental or subsidiary good. If "freedom in the positive sense" is "liberation of the powers of all men equally for contributions to a common good," then no one has a right to do anything (even with his "own") which contravenes this end. As a matter of fact, one's very property rights are products of the state and of the group: They do not exist in a savage state and are created in the civilized state as instruments for enlarging man's powers; they are not, however, ends in themselves and are always subject to rational regulation for the increase of freedom.

It is in these terms that Green justifies a considerable degree of state intervention and regulation. Legislation dealing with labor, education, and health will always involve some restriction of freedom of contract and yet may in the end vastly increase the ability of most men to achieve their true selves (the reader will note here the Hegelian overtones). And Green even argues that state prohibition of the liquor traffic may conceivably be justified if it removes temptation from the worker as he walks home with his paycheck from his factory: If he is not tempted to drink by the presence of a dram-shop, his higher powers will remain intact and hence his capacity for acting "freely" (that is, rationally).[31]

Within the liberal tradition, Spencer's old liberalism and Green's new liberalism become the basis for two diverse currents of thought on the economic order down to our own day. On the whole, for example, the writings of Herbert Hoover indicate a modified survival of Spencerian attitudes.[32] So, too, do those, like Friedrich von Hayek, the Austrian economist, who appeal for at least a partial restoration of the market economy.[33] The liberal, according to Hayek, is concerned about the direction of movement; and because he is interested in the possibilities of spontaneous change, is more attracted by the ideal of market controls than either the conservative or the collectivist liberal.

On the other hand, Green and the later Mill are reflected in what is perhaps the predominant school of liberal thought in the twentieth century. The Liberal party of Great Britain, for example, has long ago given up any dogmatic rejection of all collectivism, although it is certainly not socialist. This is true, too, of most liberal movements on the continent of Europe. In the United States, liberal politicians like Eugene McCarthy and Chester Bowles have written treatises which suggest that state controls of the economy, as well as state ownership under certain circumstances, may be required by liberal beliefs.[34]

At this point, too, it is appropriate to note the influence of Keynesian economics on modern liberal attitudes to public policy. Shortly after World War I, the British economist John Maynard Keynes, in a very influential but highly technical treatise,[35] dealt in a rather original way with business cycle phenomena. Overly simplified, his thesis holds that a major factor in causing economic depressions is the problem of hoarding or saving. By this he means that if all money received as wages, salaries, interest, rent, and profits were immediately spent either for consumers' goods or for investment, there would be no tendency for economic depressions to occur; for what is received as income would quickly absorb the goods produced, thus allowing no opportunity for the creation of unemployed men and resources. But this does not happen under all circumstances. Savings and investment, for example, may and often are carried out by different groups: the former are not immediately turned into the latter. This means that the value of the goods produced will exceed the value of money available to purchase them. If this gap persists, unemployment is the result and the spiral downward, once begun, is difficult to stop.

The public-policy implications of this proposition are fairly obvious. If when private hoarding increases substantially, the government should deliberately unbalance its budget, it would, other things being equal, counteract the drying up of private investment and purchasing power. Economic declines could thus be averted. What is more, this could presumably take place primarily through a manipulation of fiscal policy rather than through direct government control or collectivism. The government, when depression threatened, would compensate through public spending for the decline in private expenditures. Once the system began to function again, the public budget could again be balanced.

Public policy based upon these ostensibly Keynesian principles appeals to many modern liberals because it seems to make the role of government an indirect one and thus presumably limits the degree of collectivism. If government expenditures in traditionally public areas—like education, highways, and public works—can be increased when the private sector of the economy threatens to collapse and reduced when hoarding has begun to decline, socialism can be avoided; while at the same time one of the industrial capitalist defects most criticized by socialists can be corrected. In the United States and Great Britain, political liberals of the Mill-Green tradition have built upon propositions of this kind, which they tend to think of as a kind of *via media* between socialism, on the one hand, and the laissez-faire position of early liberalism, on the other.[36]

Liberalism and the Idea of Progress

We have argued that there is a liberalism of the spirit and also a liberalism which may be defined in substantive terms. In spirit, it has been suggested, liberal political thought is open to experimentation and innovation, is not enamored of tradition, and has tended to have great confidence in the human capacity for reason. Out of this spirit emerges its general attitude to the problem of human progress.

During the nineteenth century, liberal thinkers, by and large, either espouse some version of the inevitability of progress or at least argue strenuously for the possibility of progress. And by progress, they generally mean a gradual enlargement of man's rational control of

his collective destiny, endless technological development, an increase of individual freedom, the liberation of nationalities, and the eventual elimination of war. In an age when evolutionary doctrines, whether Hegelian, Marxian, Darwinian, or Spencerian, were ubiquitous, it would have been surprising if liberalism had taken any other position.

Quite often nineteenth-century versions of liberal progress see the very spread of industrialism itself as the vital factor. With industrialism come increases in wealth, the growth of commerce, closer ties among nations, moral advancement, the development of representative institutions, the multiplication of national states, international federation, and the abolition of war. Many a nineteenth-century liberal's faith is represented in these lines from Tennyson's *Locksley Hall:*

And I dipt into the future, far as human eye could see,
Saw a vision of the world and all the wonders that would be,
Saw the heavens fill with commerce, argosies of magic sails,
Pilots of the purple twilight, dropping down with costly bales.
Heard the heavens fill with shouting, and there rained a ghastly dew
From the Nations' aerial navies, grappling in the central blue.

. . . .

31. Note especially Green's lecture "Liberal Legislation or Freedom of Contract" in R. L. Nettleship, ed., *Works of T. H. Green,* London: Longmans Green, 1888, particularly pp. 370–376.
32. See, for example, Herbert Hoover's *American Individualism* and *The Challenge to Liberty,* New York: Scribner's, 1934.
33. See Friedrich von Hayek, *The Road to Serfdom,* Chicago: University of Chicago Press, 1944 and *The Constitution of Liberty,* Chicago: University of Chicago Press, 1960.
34. Eugene J. McCarthy, *op. cit.;* and Chester Bowles, *The Coming Political Breakthrough,* New York: Harper, 1959.
35. See John M. Keynes, *General Theory of Employment, Interest and Money,* New York: Harcourt Brace, 1936.
36. See, for example, J. K. Galbraith, *The Affluent Society,* Boston: Houghton, 1958. In this volume, which was very influential in the America of the late fifties, particularly among liberals, Galbraith argues the necessity for an expansion of the public sector while maintaining a balance between public and private expenditures.

Till the war-drums throbbed no longer, and the battle flags were furled
In the Parliament of Man, the Federation of the World.

To be sure, thinkers like Jefferson and John Stuart Mill heavily qualify their faith (Jefferson through his agrarianism and Mill in his profound awareness of the limitations of popular government)—a fact which is often forgotten. Despite these qualifications, however, the general principle remains that early and middle liberalism are almost inseparably bound up with rather optimistic views about the future. This is reflected, for example, in the thought of a man like L. T. Hobhouse, who is a very sophisticated liberal indeed.[37] Most liberals before World War I envision the gradual spread of parliamentary institutions and the decline of autocratic government everywhere. For them, with some exceptions, it is almost unthinkable that there should be retrogression.

With the aftermath of World War I, however, the accent on progress is abated somewhat and in the post World War II epoch it becomes still more muted. The complication of factors leading to the rise of Fascism, the seeming irrationalism of a large part of mankind (illustrated in twentieth-century events and analyzed in such streams of thought as Freudianism), and the apparent inability or unwillingness of mankind to bring the technological process under rational control—all this serves to circumscribe the optimism so characteristic of the nineteenth century. What remains by the middle of the twentieth century is a kind of limited optimism, no longer stressing inevitability but rather reasserting possibilities. The militancy of the nineteenth century is gone.

These observations apply, although perhaps with somewhat less force, even to the United States. Born in the eighteenth century and affected profoundly by both Lockean optimism and the eighteenth-century Enlightenment, the nation for many years was dominated by the liberal accent on progress—despite strong dissent by men like John C. Calhoun and many in the Adams family. The United States was to be a departure from the enslavement of past history: It would avoid bureaucracy, war, the corruption of cities, and the degradation of man supposedly characteristic of the European experience. Economic and other difficulties would be overcome and every advance in technology meant, almost automatically, moral and political progress. Beliefs of this kind characterized the predominant liberalism of American thought, even in the face of such phenomena as the Civil War, World War I, and the great economic depression of the thirties.

By the thirties of the twentieth century, however, many of these beliefs began to be seriously questioned, although not rejected entirely. Men like Reinhold Niebuhr popularized a gloomier view of man, stressing the relevance of the myth of original sin and pointing out the enormous cruelties and irrationalities of political history.[38] The liberal, he and others argued, saw man superficially; and liberalism, whether rooted in the eighteenth-century tradition of men like Locke or in nineteenth-century utilitarianism, failed to grasp the paradoxes of human history. Men were passionate and capricious; and great knowledge could and would be utilized as easily for destruction as for amelioration and improvement. Every step in progress entailed the possibility of an even greater fall.

Criticisms of this kind bore a strong family resemblance to many of the traditional viewpoints characteristic of modern conservative thought. The dialogue between liberal and conservative perspectives has been virtually a continuous one for nearly two hundred years. And without an appreciation of the conservative outlook, to which we turn in the next chapter, our understanding of liberalism itself tends to be limited.

chapter 27

The Modern Conservative Tradition

Like liberalism, modern conservatism is not easy to define in a few words. As is true of liberalism, it has included both a spirit and a series of substantive propositions or attitudes to public policy.

Its spirit—which connects the conservatism of the late eighteenth century with that of our own day—can be epitomized in the words of John Morley:

> Such ideas are these—that the social union is the express creation and ordering of the Deity; that its movements follow his mysterious and fixed dispensations; that the church and the state are convertible terms; . . . that conscience, if perversely and misguidedly self-asserting, has no rights against the decrees of the conscience of the nation; that it is the most detestable of crimes to perturb the pacific order of society either by active agitation or speculative restlessness; that descent from a long line of ancestors in great station adds an element of dignity to life, and imposes many high obligations.[1]

But while the spirit of conservatism may have remained essentially the same throughout the past two centuries, its attitudes to public and particularly to economic policy have changed several times. Like the substantive conflict between the old and the new liberal, typical conservative perspectives on specific questions of legislation have gone through a slow evolution. This makes an historical approach to modern conservatism of special importance; for only through a somewhat careful account of the circumstances in which it developed and the factors which affected its changes in emphasis can one fully understand it.

Evolution

We may think of its development in terms first of its eighteenth-century origins and, secondly, of its nineteenth and twentieth century evolution. In the process, we shall note, as in the case of liberalism, how it interacted with other currents of modern political thought.

Origins. Although several thinkers in the ancient and medieval worlds can be termed conservative in the generic meaning of the term—and thus both Aristotle and St. Thomas Aquinas have often been so described[2]—the beginning of modern conservatism was inseparably associated with attitudes to life characteristic of the semifeudal land-owning classes as they confronted the initial phases of the Industrial Revolution and the world-shaking events of the great Revolution in France. Then, too, the origins of modern conservatism must be connected very intimately with a rejection of that individualism which, as we have seen, was the hallmark of the history of political thought from Machiavelli to Rousseau. Hume helped lay the groundwork for much modern conservative thought.

But perhaps the greatest figure in its beginning was Edmund Burke (1729–1797).[3] Born in Ireland, he was for many years a member of the House of Commons, sitting for a "pocket" borough during the early part of his career.

Chapter 26

37. See L. T. Hobhouse, *Social Evolution and Theory*, New York: Columbia, 1911; *Liberalism*, London: Williams and Norgate, 1911; and *Elements of Social Justice*, London: Allen & Unwin, 1922.
38. One of Niebuhr's most impressive criticisms of many liberal beliefs was his *Moral Man and Immoral Society*, New York: Scribner, 1932. See also his *The Nature and Destiny of Man*, 2 vols., New York: Scribner, 1941–1943.

Chapter 27

1. *On Compromise*, *op. cit.*, pp. 123–124.
2. See Chapters 5 and 13.
3. Problems arising from Burke's political philosophy have been explored in many works. Among older treatments, one might mention William Hazlitt, *Political Essays*, London: W. Hone, 1819; Leslie Stephen, *History of English Thought in the Eighteenth Century*, 2 vols., New York: Putnam, 1876; and J. MacCunn, *The Political Philosophy of Edmund Burke*, London: E. Arnold, 1913. More recent general works include those by Charles Parkin, *The Moral Basis of Burke's Political Thought*, Cambridge University Press, 1956 and Francis P. Canavan, *The Political Reason of Edmund Burke*, Durham: Duke University Press, 1960.

Later he was a member for Bristol but his independent attitude to his constituents, which was the occasion for stating one aspect of his doctrine of representation, led him to lose his seat. He attacked the attitude of the British government to the revolting American colonies, on the ground that while a legal right to coerce the Americans may have existed, ties of sentiment and historic connections, together with sheer expediency, should have kept the government from using that right. Burke opposed any alteration in the system of representation for Parliament (unlike Locke, it will be remembered), on the ground that the scheme was the product of centuries of evolution and virtually represented the community because of deep-rootedness in the culture.

When the French Revolution broke out in 1789, Burke soon became hostile, for he saw in it a violent break with the historical continuity of the French nation and therefore likely to produce disastrous results. To him, the Revolution was the product of the erroneous deductive reasoning so characteristic of eighteenth-century thought.

It was in 1794 that the Old Whigs—to whom Burke adhered—aligned themselves with the followers of the younger William Pitt, thus separating themselves from the so-called New Whigs who were led by men like Charles James Fox. The New Whigs tended to take a favorable attitude to the Revolution, while the Old Whigs—who constituted the beginning of the British Conservative party—based their outlook on Burke's criticisms of the Revolution. By the time of his death, Burke had become the symbol of everything against which the Revolution supposedly stood. In addition, his writings laid out a series of propositions which have usually been characterized as a platform for modern conservative thought.

Burke's thought represented a violent reaction to what he called abstract reason and metaphysics in politics. All political propositions must, he maintained, be seen in the light of concrete experience and not be accepted merely because they are logical deductions from acceptable statements. Thus while Parliament had the abstract right to tax the American colonies, men should ask whether the exercise of that right would not destroy many precious associations built up during the course of centuries. Parliament could in the abstract pass any legislation it desired; but to exercise that right under all circumstances might be utterly foolish. So, too, those who advocated reform of Parliament had to ask themselves whether their proposals, while logically they may have been excellent, suited the experience of the British people. All theories in morals and politics, in other words, had to be subjected to two questions: Do they suit man's nature in general, and do they suit his nature as modified by habits?

Naturally, Burke became a leading opponent of all contract theories, or rather, like Rousseau, he so redefined contract that it bore little resemblance to its historic signification. For Burke the contract was between the dead, the living, and generations yet unborn. Men were born into society and could not be conceived as discrete individuals. Like Hume, Burke was constantly appealing to history and experience in his reasoning. Along with Hegel, he did as much as any early modern figure to revive history as a basis for political judgments, after the centuries in which it had been virtually ignored by contract and other individualist thinkers.

Because he repudiated metaphysical thinking, then, Burke turned to prejudice and tradition as guides. However absurd the custom, he seemed to say, if it suited the spirit of the nation, it must be retained.[4] Political society is held together by habit patterns, prejudices, and traditions which transcend deliberative acts of any given group of persons.

Religion was for Burke the best example of a prejudice essential to any civil society; and the questioning of traditional religion was the supreme instance of that unlimited discussion against which he set his will. The British constitution, he argued, was intimately bound up with the established religion; and it was one of his bitterest complaints against the rationalist philosophers of France—men like Voltaire and Rousseau, who in Burke's mind sowed the seeds of Revolution—that they pursued "the utter extirpation of religion" with a "fanatical fury."[5]

In the end, Burke's attachment to prejudice both as an explanation for civil society and as a guide to policy rests upon the possible conflict which he discerned between peace and truth. He placed so high a value on the former—and by the term he apparently meant the absence not only of physical conflict but also even of serious verbal clashes—that he made the primary test of whether truth should be spread abroad the likelihood or unlikelihood that it might ruffle the peace. Truth was uncertain at best, whereas the existence of a stable peace was a fact that could not be doubted.[6]

To be sure, Burke was not opposed to all reform. Thus he advocated Catholic emancipation and proposed successfully the elimination of many sinecure positions at the royal court. But reform, in his judgment, had to move slowly, should not rend the fabric of the nation, and should not run counter to the most basic prejudices. One of the problems Burke never did resolve, of course, was how to distinguish between legitimate reform proposals and those which might be regarded as illegitimate. Thus restrictions on Catholics were very old, as were the patterns of a "rotten" and "pocket" borough-dominated Parliament. Yet Burke proposed eliminating the former and opposed reforming the latter. But then, with his distrust of abstract reasoning it probably was difficult for him to establish criteria.

In his attitude to the theory of representation, one finds a sharp contrast to the evolution of liberal attitudes. The latter, as we have seen,[7] tended from the time of Locke to the twentieth century, to stress actual representation in accordance with population and sometimes even proportional representation. Burke, by contrast, argued that a community need not be represented through delegates of its own choosing but that its true will might be better reflected by a long-standing aristocracy or small group having roots in the national mind and understanding the communal spirit. This view has come to be called the theory of "virtual" representation and it has an astonishing resemblance to Lenin's doctrine that a small disciplined Communist minority is, under certain historical circumstances, the best interpreter of the true will of a nation.

There was also a strong emphasis in Burke on property and its defense. Property ought somehow to be given great weight in the counsels of the nation, even more than ability; for, by contrast with ability, "property is sluggish, inert, and timid" and must be guarded against the clever men who are always ready to seize it. In his stress on property, Burke reminds one of another great eighteenth-century conservative, John Adams; and like most defenders of long-standing property relations, he does not inquire into the conditions under which material goods were originally acquired —even robbery appears to be vindicated if its fruits are sanctified by long-standing tradition and custom.

It is obvious that Burke was no democrat, even in a qualified sense of the term. Men's duties, to him, are more important than their rights; and their duties are defined not merely by legislation but, more importantly, by the spirit of every particular nation. The representative, even if chosen by the community through an electoral process, must never think of himself as a mere delegate, voting in accordance with every whim of his constituents; rather he must cast his ballot in accordance with his best insight and with his own particular evaluation of experience.[8]

Historically, Burke contributed not a little to eighteenth-century political discussion by emphasizing the serious limitations of contract theories, even though it is doubtful whether his own rather romantic "organic" doctrine is more nearly adequate. His impact on nineteenth and twentieth century conservative thought was, of course, considerable. In effect, he helped found the Conservative party of Britain and, directly or indirectly, assisted in shaping nineteenth-century romantic conservatism. By denouncing abstract reason (in contrast to reason working closely with an historical tradition and limited by it), he helped inspire all those political movements from his day to ours which distrust change and lack confidence in man's speculative capacity.

Nineteenth and Twentieth Century Currents. After Burke, the revolt against the French Revolution produced several important

4. Thus running through Burke's *Reflections on the Revolution in France* (1790) is the idea that while many of the practices against which the revolutionists complained might, indeed, have violated canons of logic or "abstract reason," they were nevertheless, to be defended simply because they were old and well-established.
5. *Letters on a Regicide Peace* (1796).
6. *Speech on the Relief of Protestant Dissenters* (1773).
7. See Chapters 21 and 26.
8. Thus while the incipient radical democracy of the time was beginning to contend that the representative is a kind of delegate who must reflect the views of his constituents, Burke stood adamant for the view that he ought not to sacrifice "his unbiased opinion, his mature judgment, his enlightened conscience . . . to you, to any man, or to any set of men living." *Address to the Electors of Bristol* (Nov. 3, 1774).

movements of thought having affinities with his outlook. Thus there was the so-called Catholic Reaction, reflected intellectually in the writings of such men as Joseph Marie de Maistre[9] and the Viscount de Bonald. De Maistre stands out as one of the greatest critics of the French Revolution, as an important defender of the Middle Ages against their eighteenth-century detractors, and, above all, as an advocate of a revived papacy. To him, the only hope for world order and stability lay in an expansion of papal prerogatives which could check the forces of liberal nationalism released by the Revolution. De Bonald became an ardent defender of the principle of monarchy against those in the revolutionary tradition who wished it utterly abolished. The Catholic Reaction was also embodied in the teachings of Pope Pius IX (1846–1878), who, although he had begun his pontificate as a liberal, quickly turned to a conservative outlook when he became alarmed by the Revolution of 1848. In his encyclical *Quanta Cura* and in the *Syllabus of Errors,* both issued in 1864, Pius denounced such liberal "errors" as the notions that the church should be separated from the state, that the state should not prefer one religion over another, that there ought to be liberty of speech and the press, and that the pope should be reconciled to modern progress and civilization. The latter reference was undoubtedly to the writings of such liberal Catholics as Hughes Felicite Robert de Lamennais,[10] who advocated some kind of accommodation to the principles of the French Revolution.

Associated with much of the conservatism of the first half of the nineteenth century was a revived interest in the Middle Ages. The eighteenth century had tended to look down on the Middle Ages as an epoch of unmitigated superstition. Conservatives in the nineteenth century, in their revolt against everything they connected with eighteenth-century thought, felt obliged to rescue the medieval period from the disgrace to which it had been consigned by many of the *philosophes.* From the viewpoint of conservatism, the Enlightenment was not enlightened.[11]

The exaltation of the Middle Ages was often accompanied by a rejection of industrialism and praise of an agrarian way of life. As the Industrial Revolution corroded the economic and political power base of land-owning aristocrats, conservatives tended to align themselves with the old order, while liberalism, as we have seen, was almost inseparably linked with the new.

Indeed, the association of conservatism with an agrarian society and of liberalism with industrialism had a certain logic both in the nineteenth century and in later generations. After all, if suspicion of change is the hallmark of conservatism, the most congenial atmosphere would seem to be a way of life—the agrarian—in which the imperatives for change are not great. Under industrialism, by contrast, change—whether as a result of technological dynamics, of allegedly automatic forces, or of deliberate planning—tends to be endemic. From this point of view, the development of industrialism made conservatism as a political philosophy, at least to the liberals, increasingly archaic.

The clash between nineteenth-century liberalism and conservatism can be illustrated in a number of ways. In the first place, the conservative temper was violently opposed to utilitarian morals and politics, which it regarded as an over-simplification both of human nature and of the dilemmas of choice which confront man. Moreover, utilitarianism tended to reduce man to a mere economic creature. Secondly, conservatism stressed the family as against the individual. Thirdly, it became a kind of apologist for the imperial tradition, in contradistinction to much liberalism that tended to look forward to the day when empire would be no more. Fourthly, while liberalism was often espoused by men who were either agnostics or who thought that the church should not be formally connected with the state, conservatism tended to sustain religion as an important ingredient in state life.

The working out of attitudes of this kind may be illustrated in the history of nineteenth-century conservatism by noting that much of the impetus for factory legislation came from conservatives and not liberals. Men like the seventh Earl of Shaftesbury (1801–1885), inheriting a high Tory view of the state, thought that it was the obligation of the law to establish standards for economic life, at the very time that utilitarian liberals were pleading the cause of free enterprise. To be sure, not all conservatives shared Shaftesbury's views—some were laissez-faire exponents themselves—but a sufficiently large number did support them to make Herbert Spencer's statement that Toryism is akin to Socialism have a measure of truth.[12]

Grounds for the conservative support of economic legislation were rooted in the medieval tradition that the lord looks after "his own"—the conception of noblesse oblige was thus applied to relations between the state and the proletarian victim of the industrial process. The proletarian was helpless and only the assistance of public authority could preserve him and his family. Here the conservative emphasis on authority and hierarchy is particularly illustrated; and it is to be sharply contrasted with the utilitarian basis upon which later liberal ideas of state intervention are often to repose.

Although the repeal of the Corn Laws was moved by Sir Robert Peel, a conservative, much of the mid-century conservative temper was utterly antagonistic to the idea of free trade—and, indeed, has continued to be opposed to it. The opponents of repeal argued that agriculture was a mainstay of the organic nation and that free trade would destroy it in the interests of industrialism. Notoriously, the conservative outlook and the agricultural way of life have been associated historically and this occasion was no exception. With the repeal of the Corn Laws, industrialism did indeed receive a great stimulus and liberalism marched along with it.

Later British conservatives like Benjamin Disraeli tended to support strongly the claims of empire and to think of it in terms of a mission of the colonizing power to those in need of development. End-of-the-century imperialism is illustrated in the poetry of Kipling, the plea for a British Empire protected by imperial preference tariffs, and, in the United States, by the conservative claim that America's mission is that of civilizing and educating those peoples whom the fortunes of war brought within its control.

Meanwhile, as liberals more and more take on the mantle of state interventionism in economic affairs—the theoretical basis for which we have noted before—and socialism enters increasingly into the realm of practical politics, much conservatism appears to argue that intervention has gone far enough. Thus in British politics, professed conservatives before World War I oppose the liberal taxation measures of Lloyd George and much of the increasing pressure for an expansion of social services. Perhaps we can say that the spirit of conservatism, which is one of caution and suspicion of innovation, in some respects puts a damper on another of its historical elements—that of noblesse oblige and the claims of high authority. At any rate whereas men like Shaftesbury were arguing for state intervention, against the liberals, in the first half of the nineteenth century, by the second decade of the twentieth, conservative leaders look with suspicion on further state activity in the economic order.

Yet never do they discard the early nineteenth-century view completely. In practical politics, indeed—at least in Britain—they often vie with the socialists after World War I in proposals for increasing state ownership and intervention. Thus the great Central Electricity Board for the wholesale distribution of electric power is the product of a Conservative government in 1926. And after World War II, the Conservative governments which succeeded the Labour regime of 1945–1951 repealed almost none of the socialist measures of their predecessors.

Although it is sometimes said that conservatism has historically been hostile to the claims of democracy—the writings of the late nineteenth and early twentieth century conservative W. H. Mallock seemed to illustrate this—even this statement cannot be made without serious qualifications. True, Burke opposed the democracy of the French Revolution and the conservative generally rejected the arguments of those who advocated parliamentary reform, at least down to 1832. On the other hand, that

9. De Maistre's great classic is *Du Pape*, vol. 3 of *Oeuvres Completes*, Lyon: Libraire Generale Catholique et Classique, 1891, in which he suggests that only the restoration of medieval papal authority can eliminate revolution and stabilize the world.
10. See his *Paroles d'un Croyant, Oeuvres Posthumes*, Paris: 1856, for a classical statement of "liberal" Catholicism in which Lamennais attempts to reconcile the spirit of the French Revolution with Catholicism.
11. Among the leaders of the Romantic movement associated with early nineteenth-century conservatism, one might mention Sir Walter Scott and Francois Rene de Chateaubriand.
12. Shaftesbury was a member of the House of Commons during most of the period between 1826 and 1851. He was active in seeking to improve the lot of the mentally ill and in 1833 first proposed to limit the working day for factory laborers to ten hours. After a long struggle—during which many of his opponents were liberals—he had the satisfaction of seeing the ten hour day become law in 1847.

strain in conservative political philosophy which emphasizes the organic character of the national community and the importance of a community of interest between government and governed provides the ground for Benjamin Disraeli's conception of Tory democracy in the sixties and seventies; and a Conservative British government is responsible for a substantial enlargement of the electorate in 1867.

In the United States, it has been argued by some, there has never really been a conservative tradition as that term is used in Europe and particularly in Britain.[13] Virtually all Americans, this view maintains, have been liberals. This statement is based at least partially on the proposition that European conservatism historically has been associated with defense of the land-owning semifeudal way of life. Since the United States never knew feudal structures in any major degree—including the close interweaving of church and state—conservatism has been absent by definition.

But if we think of conservatism as that political temper which looks with some suspicion on human nature and which fears innovation, there has certainly been an important conservative strain. In many respects, the political outlook of men like John C. Calhoun was conservative in this sense. A defender of the Aristotelian notion of natural slavery and of the idea of a kind of preordained social subordination, he reminds one in certain respects of Burke. His strong distrust of simple majority rule and his espousal of concurrent majority rule pitted him against the rising tide of liberal democracy. It is also highly instructive to note that once the Constitution of the United States had been adopted, it came after about a generation to be widely venerated and only rarely changed. The awe with which most Americans today regard the Constitution makes it a sacred document, which surely reflects a kind of practical Burkeanism in the American people.

After World War II, the United States exhibited the phenomenon of the new conservatism which may be described as a movement that sought to adapt many of the categories of Burke's thought to the analysis of modern and particularly of American conditions. While the new conservatism—as reflected in writers like Russell Kirk—often seemed to be rather vague and contradictory, there appear to have been certain common themes. One was the great value assigned, as with Burke, to tradition.[14] "We must think," Russell Kirk once asserted orally in the presence of this writer, "through the graveyard." Then, too, a whole school of American historiography highly critical of the economic and conflict theories associated with Charles Beard, sought to restore more organic and patriotic interpretations of the American experience.[15] Much of this view embodied values which historically have been thought of as conservative: It was suspicious of debunking, for example, and stressed the organic continuity of American history; and it alleged that serious conflicts had rarely, if at all, disturbed this continuity. Then, too, the post–World War II writings of men like Walter Lippmann, which underlined the supposed importance of traditional restraints on mass action and seemed to stress a kind of elitist hierarchical principle, can be fitted into the conservative tradition.[16]

In the ideological battle with Soviet Communism, many throughout the Western world sought refuge in what they thought were the traditional values of Western culture. Upon these values, and upon these alone, they appeared to think, could be built an ideology militant enough to combat what the conservatives thought of as the abstract rationalism, the antireligious proclivities, and the materialism of Marxism.

But much self-proclaimed conservatism of the post–World War II vintage was not at all clear as to the ultimate basis for its outlook. In the American versions, for example, there has frequently been no distinction drawn between the spirit of conservatism and the specific public policy proposals espoused by conservatives. There has been a lack of awareness on the part of many that conservatives have during the course of history advanced contradictory policy proposals. Thus much alleged American conservatism—that of Barry Goldwater, for example—seemed to be simply a series of attacks on New Deal legislation and a diatribe against all nonmarket economies, and this in face of the fact that not a little historical conservatism has been highly suspicious of the free market.[17]

Human Nature and the Role of Politics

It is, in fact, singularly difficult to offer any systematic exposition of modern conservatism without recognizing many exceptions. Beyond such sweeping statements as that quoted from Lord Morley, any organization of its principles must be highly tentative. Perhaps the best way to understand its general drift is to use the British conservative tradition as the basis, on the very good ground that in that tradition one will find the principles most fully articulated. Let us note, then, the conservative's attitude to human nature and the role of politics; the defense of property; attitudes to functions of the state; and the problem of patriotism and the international order.

The modern conservative mind, in taking its point of departure from Burke, distrusts all simple views of human nature. And it is particularly dubious about the foundations of utilitarian liberalism. Unlike the latter, it insists that the individual exists in the context of a whole network of group relations and cannot be abtsracted from them. Moreover, the hedonistic utilitarian standard for legislation, even as revised by J. S. Mill, is to it too mechanical: No simple formula is possible and the only guide can be a kind of intuitive interpretation of the national tradition. Skeptical as he is of abstract rationality, the conservative maintains that reason is to be trusted only when guided by the values provided in the corporate heritage, which itself cannot be questioned without grave danger.

Early in his career, the great British statesman Benjamin Disraeli took up this theme and sought to vindicate the Burkean view against the onslaughts of the Benthamites. Castigating the new school of utilitarian statesmen, he argues that its propositions spring from the "fallacy" of thinking "that theories produce circumstances, whereas the very converse of this proposition is correct and circumstances indeed produce theories."[18] Reforms, he goes on, if needed, must be limited and guided by the essential "principles of ancestral conduct." Theories of legislation, such as Bentham has offered, are utterly pernicious; for they spurn these guides and reject the experience which is revealed in the actual and empirically discoverable practices of a people. Utilitarians, he maintains, have "superficial minds" in that they show no respect for "precedent," do not cling "to prescription," and fail to revere "antiquity."

Implicit in positions such as those of Disraeli is the belief that political history must be seen in the perspective of broader and more fundamental human concerns. Liberals and radicals put too great a trust in the state and are forever seeking to make over human nature. Human nature is primarily reflected in nonpolitical concerns such as the family, play, and small group activities. There are severe limits to what may be expected of political action and it is in recognition of this fact that conservatism supposedly differs from both the liberal and the socialist traditions.

Thus in a well-known twentieth-century exposition of conservatism, the author, a prominent politician, maintains that "Conservatives do not believe that political struggle is the most important thing in life. In this they differ from Communists, Socialists, Nazis, Fascists, Social Creditors, and most members of the British Labour Party."[19] The limitations of politics, he goes on, are partly inherent in the method (difficulties of large-scale organization and similar problems) but also arise "because man is an imperfect creature with a streak of evil as well as good in his inmost nature." Any attempt to implement utopia by political methods can only result in human beings being degraded by ambitious governments which forget their own alleged raison d'être.

And another modern conservative suggests the same notion when he criticizes the progressives who, he argues, think that if only they can control the state, the world can be remolded to their hearts' desires. They assume that the state will then "act directly on the spiritual and moral plane." But politics can never take the place of personal development, the establishment of right family ties, and the

13. See Louis Hartz, *The Liberal Tradition in America*, New York: Harcourt, 1955.
14. Note the works of Russell Kirk, particularly *The Conservative Mind*, Chicago: Regnery, 1953; *Program for Conservatives*, Chicago: Regnery, 1954; *Intelligent Woman's Guide to Conservatism*, New York: Devin-Adair, 1957.
15. See, for example, Eric F. Goldman *et al.*, *Charles A. Beard: An Appraisal*, Lexington: University of Kentucky Press, 1954.
16. See Lippmann's *Essays in the Public Philosophy*, New York: New American Library, 1956.
17. See particularly Barry Goldwater, *The Conscience of a Conservative*, Shepardsville, Ky.: Victor Pub. Co., 1960; the American journal *National Review;* and, for the history of conservatism, Peter Viereck, *Conservatism: From John Adams to Churchill*, Princeton, N.J.: Van Nostrand, 1956.
18. Benjamin Disraeli, *Vindication of the English Constitution*, London: Saunders & Otley, 1835.
19. Quintin Hogg, *The Case for Conservatism*, London: Penguin Books, 1947, p. 10.

nonpolitical effort to fulfill duty. Political methods such as those usually espoused by nonconservatives, and especially Marxists, involve an always self-defeating effort to "set up the Kingdom of God by force."[20]

In short, the conservative seems to be saying that there is a flow of life forever beyond the possibility of political manipulation and particularly of control based upon abstract reason or hedonistic utilitarianism. Society is a natural organism of which politics (thought of as deliberate efforts at social control) can constitute only an infinitesimal part.

In this sense, most modern conservatives suggest that they have a religious view of history and of social cohesion. That is to say, they believe that our ability to comprehend more than a small segment of the whys and wherefores of human social action is strictly limited: most historical experience, then, cannot be fully accounted for but must be viewed with a kind of religious awe.

Conservatism and Property

Modern conservatism has usually been associated, and quite rightly, with the defense of private property. This defense reposes on various grounds but certainly one of the most basic is that the gaining and possessing of material goods, like family and the concrete relations of person to person, are an expression of man's basic nature. To be sure, the state can regulate; but it is unjust for it to take material goods from one person in order to directly benefit another.

To do so, many conservatives argue, deprives the person of his ability to stand up against political power. In a sense, it is to rob the individual of a kind of dress without which he would stand naked against that impersonal entity known as the state. Thus in the nineteenth century, Samuel Taylor Coleridge, the great conservative essayist and poet, wrote to one of his friends:

> The pretence of considering persons not states, happiness not property, always has ended, and always will end, in making a new State or corporation, infinitely more oppressive than the former; and in which the real freedom of persons is as much less, as the things interfered with are more numerous and more minute.[21]

Quintin Hogg, one of the most articulate of twentieth-century conservatives, has perhaps spoken for the majority of conservatives when he bottoms the defense of private property on four grounds. First, property is, he maintains, essential for the development of personality. Second, it helps safeguard the family, which is the natural unit of society. Thirdly, it helps the community in that it provides an incentive for labor of those who might not respond to nonmaterial incentives. Finally, it provides a guarantee that economic power will be somewhat dispersed and will thus ensure that all power will not devolve on the state.[22]

We cannot, the conservative seems to be saying, discuss liberty in the abstract. Rather must we clothe it with the material power which is implied in the institutions of private property. Eliminate these institutions and, whatever the abstract doctrine may be, liberty as against the state will become precarious.

There would seem at this point, however, to be a considerable ambiguity in conservative conceptions. Is the property of everyone in material goods to be defended, regardless of how it was acquired? What legitimizes property? Simply possession? Or positive law? Do material goods acquired by robbery become legitimized if the robber can hold on to them long enough to acquire them by what conservatives call (and defend) as prescription? The conservative answer to questions of this kind is unclear. So, too, is it less than satisfactory—as many socialists have pointed out—on the problem of what to do if and when (as is true of most modern societies) most men have few if any property rights in material goods. If property is so valuable, is it not our obligation to make it universal? Yet how can this be done unless we are willing to limit the property of some in order to provide access to material goods for those who are deprived—a principle which many conservatives seem to reject?

Conservatism and the Functions of the State

Because the conservative stresses such basic social units as the family and expresses the conviction that politics ought to be a relatively small segment of human life, it would be surprising if he should view with favor any large accretion of functions in the state. On the whole, he emphasizes the principle that where cooperative action can effectively take place in voluntary associations or in local governments, the national state government should not assume such prerogatives in these fields.

In the nineteenth century, Coleridge exemplifies the problem in his discussion of the proportion of "free and permeative" life to "organized powers."[23] By the former, he means the scope allowed to persons, to voluntary social groups, and to localities. By the latter, he appears to suggest highly rigid and fixed schemes such as those characteristic of central political institutions. He argues that the ancient Greek democracies suffered from an excess of the former emphasis, while the Venetian Republic fell victim to the latter. And men like Coleridge obviously have in mind the example of revolutionary France as an instance similar to that of Venice.

In the twentieth century, Hogg carries on the discussion initiated by Burke and Coleridge.[24] Maintaining that political liberty is "nothing else but the diffusion of power," he argues that while conservatism supports the principle of central authority when the state appears to be in danger of disintegration, the modern problem is essentially that of too much centralization. Socialism reposes, he declares, on the principle of "concentration of power"; conservatism, as applied to conditions of the twentieth century, on that of "diffusion of power."

Working out the implications of these principles, most conservatives would place great stress on the rule of law and the limitations of national tradition as frameworks within which such functions as are permissible can be exercised. When the state does act, it must do so according to time sanctioned means and not by novel methods: Shortcuts which seek to bypass channels of nonarbitrary action are always to be deplored. Thus those in the major tradition of conservatism would undoubtedly reject techniques used by the late Senator Joseph McCarthy in the United States[25] even though they would apparently share his repudiation of communist ideology. Liberty, as the conservative might put it in other terms, is best assured by strict adherence to procedural due process and obeisance to traditional ways of doing things.[26]

Beyond this caution and its general insistence on the limited place of politics in human life, conservative political doctrine is not too clear. One of the best twentieth-century formulations is perhaps that of Lord Hugh Cecil.[27] He stresses the spiritual sphere of human nature which lies beyond the prerogatives of the state; he contends that while every individual is in a sense the product of the state (as Hegelians will argue), yet in his spiritual dimensions, the individual has potentialities for "independence of all surrounding conditions." Religiously speaking, the power of grace exists only within the individual human soul and not in any corporate body. The state must conform to the moral standards set up by this personal spiritual consciousness.

Given these general propositions, Cecil goes on, it can be laid down that the state ought never to commit an injustice, even for the good of the community. This means that it cannot punish the innocent, for example, whatever the alleged justification. It cannot, as a result, "intervene directly to regulate the amount of wealth which an individual may be permitted to acquire." Although it may regulate trade and industry for the common benefit, it ought not to do so unless it can be shown that voluntary effort has been exhausted; for in the end it is better even for the state if men can accomplish their legitimate objectives without its help: voluntary action builds the strength of individuals, whereas state action may have a tendency to sap it. And Cecil asks whether the workman would really have benefitted had the state in the nineteenth century intervened directly rather than (as it did) simply allowing factory workers to make their striking material gains through the voluntary efforts of trade unions. This does not mean, however, that state regu-

20. See Kenneth Pickthorn, *Principles and Prejudices*, London: Signpost Books, 1943.
21. Letter to Daniel Stuart, October 30, 1814, in E. H. Coleridge, ed., *The Letters of S. T. Coleridge*, Boston: Houghton, Mifflin, 1895, pp. 634–639.
22. Hogg, *op. cit.*
23. See Samuel Taylor Coleridge, *On the Constitution of the Church and State According to the Idea of Each*, Henry Nelson Coleridge, ed., London: W. Pickering, 1839, ch. 10 and 11.
24. Hogg, *op. cit.*, ch. 10.
25. On McCarthy's methods, see, for example, Jack Anderson and Ronald W. May, *McCarthy: The Man, The Senator, The "Ism,"* Boston: Beacon Press, 1952; William F. Buckley, *McCarthy and His Enemies: The Record and Its Meaning*, new ed., Chicago: H. Regnery, 1961; James Rorty and Moshe Doctor, *McCarthy and the Communists*, Boston: Beacon Press, 1954; and Richard H. Rovere, *Senator Joe McCarthy*, New York: Harcourt, Brace, 1959.
26. See Hogg, *op. cit.*, ch. 13.
27. See his *Conservatism*, London: T. Butterworth, 1912, ch. 6.

lation is not to be embraced on many occasions; for Cecil is as opposed to the laissez-faire principles of early modern liberalism as he is to what he regards as the dogmatically interventionist ideas of socialism. No general conservative formula can be developed, however, aside from the one which asserts that no individual must be treated unjustly or in an oppressive way. "Subject to the counsels of prudence," he adds, "and a preference for what exists and has been tried over the unknown, Conservatives have no difficulty in welcoming the social activity of the State."

That Cecil's interpretation of conservatism as it affects social legislation is at odds with certain other views which also claim support of the conservative tradition goes almost without saying (in the United States, for example, conservatism is often associated with an almost dogmatic opposition to extended social legislation). But that it fairly reflects the general view of such organizations as the British Conservative party in the twentieth century would also appear to be true.

In certain respects, the conclusions reached by Cecil are not too far removed from those of Thomas Hill Green,[28] although their premises may at points be radically different. Both, for example, conceive of the role of the state as that of a "remover of hindrances." Even in terms of their basic frameworks of thought, they seem to have much in common, in that both repudiate the discrete and abstract individualism associated with early utilitarianism.

Conservative Loyalties and Patriotism

Burke in the eighteenth century had spoken of the "little platoon" as the basis of all wider allegiances. We must first learn to love the family in depth, that is to say, or the county, before a sentiment of loyalty to the nation can develop; and without the sentiment of national patriotism, conservatives since Burke have generally held, it is far-fetched to believe that there can be any higher allegiances. Whereas the thrust of early utilitarianism—and hence of much liberalism—is toward an abstract individualism, on the one hand, and an equally abstract humanity on the other, conservatism in its emphasis on tradition and the social character of individuality has distrusted both abstractions.

During the nineteenth century, as we have noted, this attitude is closely connected with the Romantic movement, which revives interest in the Middle Ages, stresses emotion rather than reason, and argues that human beings sacrifice for things beyond themselves only when they have very concrete and comprehensible groups into which their loyalties can be caught up. One cannot, the conservative says, die for an abstraction, nor can one live for it. Human life is much more than reason and a political philosophy which does not take this into account will be grossly inadequate.

"The patriot," says Samuel Taylor Coleridge, "knows that patriotism itself is a necessary link in the golden chain of our affections and virtues, and turns away with indignant scorn from the false philosophy or mistaken religion which would persuade him that cosmopolitanism is nobler than nationality, and the human race a sublimer object to love than a people."[29] And in the twentieth century, Lord Balfour echoes the same sentiment: "Loyalties to a country, a party . . . a tribal chief, . . . may be ill-directed: they often are. Nevertheless, it is such loyalties that make human society possible; they do more, they make it noble."[30]

Although most conservatives would deny that tribal and national loyalties exclude allegiance to ideals beyond the provincial, the general drift of the argument would seem to be a strong conservative bias for any given set of national loyalties whenever these come into conflict with newer and untried ideals (for example, a preference for the British Empire as over against the League of Nations or the United Nations; and for national tradition as contrasted with European or Western civilization). In times of war, we might note, conservative conscientious objectors are rare. Indeed, a leading twentieth-century expositor of conservatism maintains that this must necessarily be so. The conservative, he reasons, will accord very high rank to the traditional society which is the national state. He will give every benefit of the doubt to his national government when it is at war and will generally believe that it is likely to be more nearly right than the enemy government. He will value its collective wisdom far above his own individual tendency to doubt the righteousness of the cause. If because of his religion, he finds he cannot give full cooperation in a war, he will accept the consequences and not try to evade them; for he cannot object to material suffering if, as he alleges, he is taking his stand out of nonmaterial motives.[31]

The conservative seems to be saying that

while the citizen is morally obliged at all times to do the right, the right is far more likely to lie in the decisions of his own national state than it is in those of the opposing state or of neither. Why this should be true is unclear, but it is presumably because the "collective wisdom" of national tradition enshrines a more comprehensive understanding than that of a mere individual. But then, the critic might ask, how would a conservative act in the opposing nation? Can each nation be more right than its opponent? To this we are vouchsafed no certain answer.

What does emerge is a reiteration of the general conservative theme that the conventional act is to be preferred to the untried or unconventional one.

But when one inquires why this should be true, one reaches the conclusion that conservatism is basically skeptical about the possibility of a moral and political knowledge or reason which could be used as a platform from which to attack the conventional. Conservatism distrusts man's claims to be able to transcend the conventional wisdom of any given society. At this point, certainly, it is at war both with liberal philosophy and with socialism.

Conservatism and Liberalism in Perspective

As political outlooks, modern liberalism and conservatism may be said to exhibit certain common traits. Here let us conclude by identifying three.

In the first place, neither is what might be called a tight political doctrine. By this we mean that each is more or less a tendency rather than a series of closely knit propositions which, taken together, exclude others. Thus while conservatism in its spirit is suspicious of abstract reason, it does not exclude reason altogether; and although liberalism places the accent on individual freedom and stresses the possibility of innovation, it does not reject entirely (at least in its later developments) the dependence of individuality on the group and the value of experience. So, too, in their substantive policy statements, both liberalism and conservatism support given measures and attitudes more or less or in general, leaving much to contingency and to evaluation of circumstances. Within each stream, moreover, there have been rather wide variations in application. Although individual liberals and conservatives might prove exceptions to these observations, the general propositions hold.

Because liberalism and conservatism are more nearly tendencies in thought rather than tightly knit systems, our second observation should not be surprising: The spirits of both will be reflected, in some measure, in political movements and systems of thought which, as such, are neither conservative nor liberal. Thus some Hegelians have been conservative and others liberal; and even in socialist movements, there is a sense in which conservatism and liberalism contest the field. While both have constituted specific political philosophies, in other words, it is equally true to say that their general outlooks transcend the explicitly labelled philosophies or the political parties involved.

Finally, it should be emphasized that as more or less articulate political philosophies (however loosely constructed) and specific movements, liberalism and conservatism have been united in accepting the basic elements of the property system characteristic of modern Western societies. To be sure, both have been willing at times to modify that system in particular circumstances; but neither has challenged it root and branch. Indeed, there is some validity to the often-repeated assertion that, during the nineteenth century at least, liberalism was essentially an ideology of the middle classes; and conservatism came more and more to take on like overtones as its original defense of feudal-like institutions began to be overcome. True, in thinkers like Mill, a fundamental critique of property institutions is begun. But this occurs late in his career and may be regarded as an exception to the general rule. For the most part, a certain system of property—what might be called private capitalism—is assumed without serious challenge; and both conservatives and liberals then proceed from this point to examine their systems of politics.

To get beyond this assumption one must turn, as in a previous chapter, to the Marxian system. Or one can examine the various ver-

28. See pp. 499–500.
29. *The Friend*, Section I, Essay 13.
30. See "Nationality and Home Rule," in Balfour's *Opinions and Arguments*, London: Hodder and Stoughton, 1927.
31. For the full argument, see Pickthorn, *op. cit.*

sions of non-Marxian socialism and anarchism —as we propose to do in the two chapters which follow. Non-Marxian socialism both borrows from and is highly critical of liberalism; while anarchism and antistatism constitute a fundamental critique of political authority, whether espoused by liberal, conservative, or socialist.

chapter 28

Non-Marxian Socialism

What is meant in the modern world by a socialist outlook on politics? In certain respects this is as difficult to answer as similar questions inquiring about liberalism and conservatism. For Marxism, as we have seen, socialism is generally held to be that stage of sociopolitical evolution which immediately precedes the rise of communism. But not all socialists are Marxists. And those who are not are themselves divided in many different ways.

In this chapter, we sketch out the development of non-Marxian socialist ideas and movements in modern politics and then attempt to analyze certain major propositions which they appear to share.

The Development of Socialist Thought and Ideology

Socialists themselves, when they seek to trace the antecedents for modern systems which go by that name, often point out that something in the nature of the socialist outlook is very old.[1] Thus Max Beer, himself a Marxist, thinks of Plato as in some sense anticipating many of the arguments of nineteenth and twentieth century socialism.[2] And Karl Kautsky sees a kind of non-Marxian socialism in St. Thomas More.[3] Others have identified socialist tendencies among the early Christians, within certain groups in the Middle Ages, and in such ancient empires as that of the Incas in Peru.[4]

The more immediate foundations of modern socialist political thought, however, may be discovered in seventeenth-century British thought, in the evangelical movements of the eighteenth century, and in certain French revolutionary and postrevolutionary currents.

Seventeenth-century British philosophy and political thought included several elements which would assist later socialism in constructing its analysis. Its hedonism, to be woven into the utilitarianism of the nineteenth century, tended to stress human satisfactions as the criterion for politics. Hobbes in his construction of the Leviathan, suggested that his great artificial beast could remold the whole social universe and tame natural man. Locke in his labor theory of property could be employed by later socialists to point out how far modern society had strayed from the time when all had access to the land and to natural resources; and Locke, moreover, in his justification of revolution, built up a doctrine which could be of great service to socialists as well as liberals. Finally, the various egalitarian currents of the seventeenth century—the Diggers, for instance, and radical religionists like many of the Quakers and Baptists—although often sidetracked in subsequent years, undoubtedly remained the basis of an important tradition upon which the socialist doctrines of industrial Britain could build.[5]

Rousseau himself, while living before the industrial age, may be said to have played some role in helping to shape Western culture's receptivity to socialist principles. Contradictory as he was, he helped to revive the idea of the organic community and in his suggestion that public and private interests could be reconciled, he anticipates many later socialist arguments. Although the Rousseau-influenced French Revolution itself was primarily bourgeois in nature, there were radical currents that remained utterly dissatisfied with its limits.[6]

It may seem strange to include the evangelical movement of the eighteenth century as part of the background for modern socialism but the inclusion is not without merit. Although men like John Wesley were high Tories, the movement they founded awakened many to a greater degree of social and political consciousness and the tradition thus set in motion was important as an inspiring factor in the lives of nineteenth and twentieth century British socialists. Building upon the evangelical concern for human souls, it was but a short step for twentieth-century men like Arthur Henderson and J. Ramsay MacDonald to embrace socialism as a means to provide the decent life which industrial capitalism was denying the rank and file. Evangelicalism, moreover, helped provide an emotional depth so essential if socialism in the practical political arena was to break through the assumptions of traditional politics. W. E. H. Lecky, the nineteenth-century British historian, has remarked

that John Wesley "saved" Great Britain from a French Revolution;[7] but he might also have added that Britain was saved from a French Revolution only that it might embrace a kind of evolutionary socialist doctrine which became so characteristic of it between 1890 and the post–World War II years.

We usually say that modern socialist thought begins in the period just before and immediately after the Napoleonic wars, when, with the continued spread of industrialism and at the same time the dislocations wrought by war, many became concerned about what they thought were the injustices being inflicted on the working classes. Others, envisioning a widespread discontent erupting into violence, were exercised by the fear that a revolution might bring disaster to Britain.

In the context of the times, there was good ground for many of these fears. Unemployment was mounting, an unreformed Parliament appeared to be utterly indifferent, and peaceful unemployed demonstrators, as at Peterloo in 1819, were attacked by government troops. All the respectable political discussions of the eighteenth century appeared irrelevant to conditions of these times.

Poets in many instances grasped the situation better than politicians. Thus the great mystic

1. Thus Alexander Gray in *The Socialist Tradition*, New York: Harper Torchbook, 1968, goes back to the time of Moses in his treatment of socialist antecedents.
2. In *Social Struggles in Antiquity*, London: L. Parsons, 1922.
3. Russell Ames, *Citizen Thomas More and His Utopia*, Princeton, N.J.: Princeton University Press, 1949; *Ibid.*, *Karl Kautsky*, New York: Russell & Russell, 1959; and Jack Heter, *More's Utopia: Biography of an Idea*, Princeton, N.J.: Princeton University Press, 1952.
4. On "practical" models for many socialist utopias, see Arthur E. Morgan, *Nowhere Was Somewhere*, Chapel Hill: University of North Carolina Press, 1946.
5. On the philosophical foundations of British socialism, see Adam Ulam, *The Philosophical Foundations of English Socialism*, Cambridge, Mass.: Harvard University Press, 1951.
6. Among the radicals was Francois Noel Baboeuf. See David Thomson, *The Baboeuf Plot*, London: K. Paul, Trench, Trubner, 1947.
7. W. E. H. Lecky, *History of England in the Eighteenth Century*, London: Longmans, Green, 1918–1925.

poet William Blake had long called for a radical reorientation to social and religious issues and in scathing terms had questioned the existing social order. He had proclaimed:

I shall not cease from mental fight,
Nor shall my sword rest in my hand,
Till I have built Jerusalem
In England's green and pleasant land.[8]

And Percy Bysshe Shelley, burning with indignation after the massacre at Peterloo, had called for a fundamental egalitarianism and nonviolent resistance to what he regarded as the inequities of the times:

Stand ye calm and resolute,
Like a forest close and mute,
With folded arms and looks which are
Weapons of unvanquisht war.
And if then the tyrants dare
. . . .
Let them ride among you there,
Slash, and stab, and maim, and hew,—
What they like, that let them do.
With folded arms and steady eyes,
And little fear, and less surprise
Look upon them as they slay
Till their rage has died away.[9]

But poetic expressions like those of Blake and Shelley did not and could not formulate any detailed analysis of the conditions responsible for the plight of the unemployed and of the industrial workers generally. The earliest socialist discussion of questions of this kind came from Robert Owen, a wealthy manufacturer, who was acquainted at first hand with the business cycles of industrialism and also with the difficulties faced by those thousands who worked the machines and who had severed their connections with the soil. In his *New View of Society*, Owen had in 1813 attempted a diagnosis and proposed a remedy; and in the subsequent year he had continued the theme in his *Lectures on the Rational System of Society*. Thereafter, he was to be known as a socialist social reformer.

Meanwhile, in France, various schemes for utopian socialist experimentation were being launched. Francois Marie Fourier (1772–1837), the son of a linen draper who had lost his fortune under the Revolutionary Convention of 1793 and had then worked as a clerk and at various odd jobs, was beginning a remarkable series of speculations on the nature of the social world. Interwoven with elaborate cosmological views involving cycles and vibrations, Fourier's social and political analysis included much shrewd observation of human nature.[10] Existing civilization and society, he argued, are characterized by the mutual enmity of men against one another and the problem for the social reformer is how to eliminate this Hobbesian situation. Etienne Cabet offered similar criticisms.

Both Cabet and Fourier inspired numerous followers to set up experimental colonies in which the proposals of the masters would be given a trial. In the United States, for example, Fourierist and Cabetist efforts were serious and persistent and extended over a period of several decades. Although Cabet had hoped to achieve political office in France, and with it the possibility of remolding French economic life in a socialist direction, he never succeeded politically. Efforts to establish Cabetist colonies were, therefore, in a certain sense, a second-best alternative. Eventually most of the Fourierist as well as the Cabetist colonies collapsed, sometimes through inadequate practical knowledge and at other points because of personal jealousies of various kinds.[11]

The thrust of Saint-Simonism, a sociopolitical outlook shaped by the works of Saint-Simon[12] was also in a socialist direction. Stressing the fact of human solidarity, it sought to reorder the community so that the tendency to human cooperation could find full vent. In the writings of Pierre-Joseph Proudhon, too, one will find semi-socialist ideas, although Proudhon is usually described as an anarchist.[13]

While utopian conceptions were flourishing, other expressions of socialist thought also made their appearance. Christian Socialism, for instance, developed out of the religious concerns of Charles Kingsley[14] and of Frederick D. Maurice. As its designation implies, it based its doctrines on what it took to be the spirit of the New Testament. In the United States, John Humphrey Noyes, revolting against a rather narrow Calvinist environment, developed "perfectionist" socialism and for a generation (at Oneida, New York) was the leading spirit in a communal experiment that successfully combined common ownership of material goods with a complex or common marriage system.[15] Noyes argued vehemently that what he called "Bible Communism" was clearly indicated by the gospels and that private property institutions and monogamic marriage, being closely interrelated, must both be abolished.

All streams of socialist thought, in some measure, supported one another during the middle years of the nineteenth century. Thus, while Marxism criticized utopian socialism with great vigor, it also owed not a little to it. And the challenge of Marxism to other varieties of socialist thought was often equally evident.

It should be pointed out, too, that most nineteenth century socialism was developed within a context of evolutionary doctrines. Marxism itself, as we have noted, saw in the very tendencies of history themselves an inevitable achievement of socialism and then communism. And many other socialists, like the liberals, could not resist adapting social interpretations of Darwinism to the ends of socialist ideology; just as Spencer saw "contract" emerging as the universal way of conducting human affairs, so they foresaw the day when contract would be superseded through the more or less irresistible laws of social evolution. The fangs of the state would be pulled, so to speak, and it would become only an agency for cooperation, with its coercive aspects fading into the background.

An excellent illustration of socialist eclecticism is to be found in the writings of the American novelist and publicist Edward Bellamy (1850–1898). He was very much influenced by the context of Darwinian evolutionary and Marxist doctrines. Yet he built his propositions in the climate of American culture and in part took his point of departure from conditions peculiar to the United States. Bellamy was very much disturbed by the long period of economic depression in American life which persisted, with but few interruptions, throughout the seventies and eighties.

It was with this background that he penned his two socialist classics, *Looking Backward* (1888) and *Equality* (1897). Although hardly a Marxist, he drew on his knowledge of Marx in his analysis of the tendencies of capitalism. Like Marx, too, he tended to think of socialism as the product of the evolution of the highly centralized state. Bellamy's socialist society is one of the most centrally controlled ever projected. While Marx envisioned "from each according to his ability to each according to his deed" as the principle which would govern under socialism, Bellamy provided a system of equal incomes. Throughout his writings ran a strong current of moral indignation at the increasingly great disparities between the possessing and the working classes.

His writings were enormously popular until World War I. Toward the end of the nineteenth century, his proposals became the basis for political action in the so-called nationalist movement of the United States. And his doctrine of how socialism would evolve under American conditions was not uninfluential in the outlook of the American Socialist party, which was founded at the turn of the century.

Meanwhile, the foundations of the most powerful non-Marxian socialist movement of modern times—that of Great Britain—were being established. Intellectually, it owed not a little to seventeenth-century thought and to the modified utilitarianism of John Stuart Mill. Since Mill approached the socialist position toward the end of his life, we can think of at

8. In the preface to *Milton*, 1804 (published in 1808).
9. *The Mask of Anarchy*, Stanzas 79, 84, and 85.
10. See particularly F. M. C. Fourier, *Selections from the Works of Fourier*, Julia Franklin, trans., London: S. Sonnenschein, 1901; and F. M. C. Fourier, *Fourier, 1772–1837*, Intro. et choix par Jacques Debû-Bridel, Geneva: Traits, 1947.
11. On nineteenth-century socialist colonies, particularly those set up by Fourier and Cabet, see G. D. H. Cole, *op. cit.*, vol. 1; Frank Manuel and Fritzie Manuel, eds., *French Utopias: An Anthology of Ideal Societies*, New York: Free Press, 1966; Max Beer, *The General History of Socialism and Social Struggles*, vol. 1, New York: Russell & Russell, 1957; and Harry Laidler, *Social-Economic Movements*, New York: Thomas Y. Crowell, 1947.
12. Claude Henri, Comte de Saint-Simon (1760–1825), was allegedly descended from Charlemagne. He fought in the American Revolution, was sympathetic with the objectives of the French Revolution (although for the most part politically inactive), and after many travels worked out a system of thought which attempted to apply Christianity to the organization of society. His best known and most influential work, *Le nouveau christianisme*, was written in 1825. The Saint-Simonians became an important religio-political sect.
13. See Chapter 29.
14. See Stanley E. Baldwin, *Charles Kingsley*, Ithaca, N.Y.: Cornell University Press, 1934; H. Laidler, *op. cit.*; and Robert B. Martin, *The Dust of Combat: A Life of Charles Kingsley*, New York: W. W. Norton, 1960.
15. See Charles Nordhoff, *The Communistic Societies of the United States* (1875), New York: Schocken Brooks, 1966; Robert A. Parker, *A Yankee Saint: John Humphrey Noyes and the Oneida Community*, New York: Putnam's, 1935; and S. Person and D. D. Egbert, eds., *Socialism and American Life*, vol. 1, Princeton, N.J.: Princeton University Press, 1952.

least one aspect of British socialism as springing almost directly from him. At the same time, the cultural environment out of which it grew had been profoundly shaped by the Non-Conformist and particularly the evangelical religious tradition. Although Marx himself had lived and worked in Britain for many years, his influence on the mainstream of British socialism was to be very slight indeed.

The beginnings of the British movement may be traced to the development of trade unionism, the rise of the Fabian Society, and the gradual disillusionment with the Liberal party as a vehicle for political action.

For many years, trade unionism had been subject to a multitude of legal restrictions, so that it was not really until after the middle of the nineteenth century that industrial workers began to organize more or less freely. Originally, many were attached politically to the Liberal party, which was responsible for the Reform Act of 1884 that extended the suffrage virtually to a manhood basis.

While the trade union foundations were being laid, there was an important minority among British intellectuals who were becoming utterly dissatisfied with both Liberal and Conservative politics. At the same time, they were dubious about Marxism. British Marxism itself established in 1884 a political arm in the Social Democratic Federation which was under the leadership of H. M. Hyndman. In the same year, the non-Marxian socialists organized the Fabian Society, whose purpose it was to discuss socialist ideas and particularly to seek applications of those ideas to the concrete realities of British society.[16]

One of the greatest of British socialist thinkers, Sidney Webb, joined the Fabian Society a year after its founding and his early career illustrates a not untypical background. Born in 1859, Webb had worked in a broker's office, had then joined the Civil Service, and later on had passed the bar examinations. Meanwhile, he had carried on intensive study in the British Museum Reading Room and at Birkbeck College, London University. After joining the Fabian Society, he was quickly made a member of its executive committee. In 1892, he was elected a member of the London County Council, having now resigned from the Civil Service. Thereafter, his career until his death in 1947 was a mixture of public service (including two terms as a Cabinet Minister) and prolific writing.

Other intellectuals prominent in the early history of the Fabian Society were Annie Besant, H. G. Wells, and George Bernard Shaw. The Society was noted for the pamphlets which it published on a wide variety of topics having to do with socialist theory and practice. And throughout the history of the British socialist movement, the Society has acted more or less as its "brain trust."

British socialists became increasingly disillusioned with the Liberal party as a vehicle for political action. They saw that the party was still essentially the mouthpiece of middle-class views and that it continued to defend private capitalism. Reflecting this growing dissatisfaction was the foundation, under Keir Hardie's leadership, of the Scottish Labour party in 1888 and its successor, the Independent Labour party, in 1893. Finally, in 1900 a Labour Representation Committee, broadly reflecting all the labor criticism of Liberal politics, was set up. Out of it emerged the British Labour party which eventually came to be regarded as the leading socialist political action group and which, even before World War I, was beginning to elect members of Parliament.

The socialism of the Labour party was very catholic in nature. It ranged all the way from a minor Marxist strain to a trade unionism of the "pork chop" variety.[17] It included both those who advocated a highly centralized version of the socialist society and those, immediately after World War I, who proposed drastic decentralization and even the abolition of the state. The latter called themselves "guild socialists."

During World War I, several leaders of the movement opposed the war but in so doing probably contributed to the party's popularity during the years of postwar disillusionment with the conflict. After the peace treaty, socialist sentiment increased and with it the strength of socialist organization; and in 1924, the party, with the support of the Liberals, formed its first government. After five years of intervening Tory rule, it established its second Administration in 1929, only to find itself split in 1931 over issues arising out of the economic depression. A coalition government succeeded the Labour regime and it was not until 1945, in the aftermath of World War II, that the party was again able to constitute a Cabinet, this time with an absolute majority in the House of Commons. Then followed the enactment of many measures partially establishing a socialist framework for British life. When finally the Conservatives succeeded Labour in 1951, a substantial segment of British industrial and commercial life had been nationalized and free services of a socialist character (the National Health Service, for example) had been extended.

Following defeat of the Labour party in 1951 there set in a period of self-criticism and reevaluation. A group of Fabians, for example, produced the *New Fabian Essays*,[18] which attempted to take stock of current socialist theory, particularly in light of Labour's administrative experience. Many were disillusioned with the results of nationalization and increasingly asked whether nationalization could be equated with socialization. This introspective mood characterized British socialists down to the sixties of the twentieth century, and even after a new Labour government had been installed.

In the meantime, non-Marxian approaches to socialism were developing in other parts of the world. In Norway, for example, the Labor party had originally been largely Marxist in orientation. But by the forties, many of the Marxist tendencies had receded into the background. Although movements elsewhere on the Continent were still Marxist—except for West Germany, where the Social Democrats officially rejected their historic Marxist commitment—the reformist Marxist approach which by the thirties was becoming more and more central was frequently indistinguishable from the gradualist socialism of Britain. In the United States, there were strong Marxist elements in the American Socialist party down until the twenties; but on the whole after World War I, non-Marxian currents waxed and Marxist tendencies waned.

An important factor affecting the character of socialism in many parts of the world was the fission caused by the formation of the Third International in 1919. This world association of Marxist parties was avowedly Leninist in orientation and its establishment engendered great bitterness in the socialist movement as a whole. Many of the most ardent Marxian socialists joined the communist movement and hence the Third International. There were left in the old socialist parties, then, many of the least dogmatic Marxists as well as a higher percentage of non-Marxian socialists. In France, the majority of socialists, together with the party newspaper, were acquired by the Communists. In the United States, the American Socialist party, which had steadily grown until World War I, found itself greatly reduced in numbers and particularly in Marxist membership.

Outside the Leninist and later the Trotskyist dominated parties, then, the tendency was for the lines between Marxian and non-Marxian socialism to be blurred, at least in considerable degree. Although many Continental parties in the twenties, thirties, and forties repeated Marxist slogans and professed adherence to Marx-Engels theory, their actions in the realm of practical politics were usually not sharply differentiated from those of the British Labour party.

After World War II, the growing rigidity of the split between the Eastern Communist world and the Western nation-states tended to accentuate the gulf between Leninist-Stalinist Communists and Western-type socialists (whether Marxian or non-Marxian). And as the ideological battle became more vitriolic the tendency to reconciliation between Western Marxists and non-Marxists was strengthened. Non-Marxian socialist ideas helped shape non-Leninist Marxist notions and in some measure Marxist conceptions had their impact on non-Marxist socialism. The Christian socialism of the Continent and Marxian socialism seemed to be far less separated than in the days before World War I or even during the period between the two world wars.

The ideological struggle not only brought Marxists and non-Marxists closer together in the West, it also appeared to make the gulf between socialism and a generally non-socialist culture less great, at least in practice. In France, for example, many socialists supported French colonialism in Africa, despite traditional socialist attacks on imperialism. In Britain, the programmatic positions of the Conservative and Labour parties sometimes became almost indistinguishable after the mid-fifties, much to the consternation of the socialist left wing.

16. On the early development of the Fabian Society, see Edward R. Pease, *The History of the Fabian Society*, London: Burns & MacEachern, 1963.
17. "Pork Chop" trade unionism concentrates on immediate economic gains and tends to have little concern for over-all political objectives.
18. R. H. S. Crossman ed., *New Fabian Essays*, London: Turnstile Press, 1952.

Where socialists were successful in their political campaigns and called upon to form governments—as in Britain—they frequently found that traditional socialist principles were very sharply at odds with the supposed short-run interests of the national state which they felt called upon to defend in their new political role. As more and more compromises appeared to be forced upon them by situations existing in the world after 1945, revolutionary changes receded into the background.

Writing a few years before his death, the long-time British theoretician G. D. H. Cole commented on what he regarded as the sad state to which much democratic socialism had been reduced as a result of its compromises and what it thought of as the imperatives of office. He pointed out that the international spirit of early socialism had been lost and that socialism was becoming nationalist in its outlook. In its struggle with communism, moreover, it often glossed over the elements of validity in the communist argument. While Cole detested the "suppression of all free thinking which Communists not only regard as needful but seem positively to admire," he also rejected the designation "democratic socialist" if this meant

> renouncing the Socialist Revolution and reducing socialism to a set of independent national electoral movements designed to gain parliamentary majorities with support of non-socialist voters. I do not deny the need for parliamentary action but I do deny that socialism means no more than a number of national endeavors to advance gradually and constitutionally toward the welfare state.[19]

Cole's statement probably represented fairly well the views of those socialist critics who by the mid-fifties and the early sixties of the century were unhappy not necessarily with basic socialist theory but rather with the compromises which socialist parties had made in their quest for political power.

The Criticism of Modern Capitalism

Although the analysis of non-Marxian socialists is by no means uniform, there is a sufficiently large body of propositions held in common to provide us with a picture that is on the whole true to the several outlooks represented.

We begin by noting the socialist critique of modern capitalism.

Sidney and Beatrice Webb, among the greatest of non-Marxist socialist thinkers, suggest four basic points in the indictment of capitalist civilization: The divorce of most men from ownership of the instruments of production leads to the great mass living in penury; the contrast between the penury of the many and the luxury of the few is made glaring; personal freedom of the propertyless is greatly restricted by virtue of their position in the socioeconomic order; and, finally, the capitalist mode of organizing production and distribution of commodities is scientifically unsound.

By "capitalist civilization," the Webbs mean that "particular stage in the development of industry and legal institutions" in which most laborers are divorced from ownership of tools, "in such a way as to pass into the position of wage-earners, whose subsistence, security and personal freedom seem dependent on the will of a relatively small proportion of the nation." The minority is composed of those who legally own and control the land and machinery and, through them, control the labor-force of the community, their objective being individual and private gain.

Developing the argument, the Webbs contend that in primitive societies poverty is due to the scarcity of natural resources. In a capitalist civilization, however, it is primarily produced by the fact that those who own the tools can dictate, within broad limits, to those who have only their labor to contribute. Profit-seeking becomes the dynamic force of the society; and private ownership of the means of production by those intent on profit leads to great disparity in income, inefficient consumption of wealth (through war, fashion, and sheer waste), and a shrinking of effective demand (since income distribution is greatly skewed, the workers cannot buy back the goods they produce). Moreover, the whole system of social status is affected: men and women who are made wealthy through the laws or inheritance or through capitalist ownership tend to be given social deference simply by reason of their wealth and not because of any intrinsic merit. Money-getting becomes the central value of the society and children grow up in an atmosphere of servility to those who have been fortunate enough to gain and hold money.[20]

In the kind of culture described by the Webbs along these lines, there develops what Tawney calls the "acquisitive society."[21]

Acquisition of material goods becomes an end in itself, rather than a means. We forget the purpose of accumulation, which is presumably to sustain life. The man who has inherited or gained through ownership or manipulation several hundred thousand dollars does not stop at this point but rather seeks a million. Property, in the pregnant words of Tawney, becomes functionless. That is, whereas in earlier ages, one needed a certain amount of property in material goods to perform one's function in life—the carpenter needed tools, for example, in addition to enough consumer goods to support himself—property under capitalism is no longer subordinate to a professional or vocational end but is regarded as itself the goal.

The owning classes, of course, by virtue of their control of vast properties, tend to dominate politics. They alone have the money so essential in modern political campaigns. They shape art through their patronage. They establish the standards which even the nonowning classes adopt; hence one of the chief objectives of the workers is to become like the owner.[22]

Socialism at this point is highly critical of modern liberalism, in that the latter still appears to work basically within the premises of a capitalist culture. Most liberals, that is to say, do not propose any fundamental changes in property relationships, however much they may have abandoned their early nineteenth century devotion to laissez-faire principles. They still seem to think that such liberal values as personal freedom and the individual quest for happiness (in J. S. Mill's qualitative pleasure sense) can be implemented within a property-order whose overwhelming tendency is to discourage them. How, for example, can a businessman imprisoned in a scheme which imposes the imperatives of profit and yet more profit pursue the qualitatively superior goals so emphasized by Mill?

Despite all liberal reform measures, moreover, basic distribution of income still remains highly skewed in favor of the upper ten percent. Thus in the United States, post–World War II socialists have pointed out,[23] the upper tenth of income recipients obtain approximately 28 percent of the income, after taxes; and this figure is not markedly different from the 30 to 31 percent they obtained in 1910. The lower tenth, as a matter of fact, actually received less than in 1910—about one percent in 1955, as against 2 percent in 1910. While the middle tenths increased their shares slightly, the distorted distribution of income emphasized by the Webbs remains fundamentally the same.

The third point in the indictment by the Webbs is that a capitalist culture inevitably leads to gross inequality in personal freedom; and with this statement most other socialist theoreticians would undoubtedly agree. Because men live under conditions where property in material goods tends to measure worth, ownership by a small minority and skewed income distribution have the effect of restricting the liberty of most men, despite an ideology of equality. Thus most capitalist societies claim that men are equal under law; but this is a purely formal equality: the poor man is not the equal of the rich, for example, in payment of bail, access to the ablest lawyers, satisfaction of fines, and impact of fees. The rich are overwhelmingly more likely to be acquitted of criminal charges than the poor and have enormous advantages in civil litigation as well.

In a capitalist culture such as that of the United States, moreover, it is obvious that medical services are in large degree dependent on the status of one's income; and even where free medical services are available, one has to swear to one's pauperdom in order to obtain them. The very wealthy and the very poor conceivably have no problem; but the middle groups, having neither the money of the wealthy nor the extreme poverty of the pauper, have the threat of penury hanging over them in the form of astronomical medical bills.

19. G. D. H. Cole, "A New Socialist Program—Why the Old Has Failed," *Nation*, April 23, 1955, p. 345.
20. For the development of this argument in full, see Sidney and Beatrice Webb, *Decay of Capitalist Civilization*, New York: Harcourt, Brace, 1923.
21. See R. H. Tawney, *The Acquisitive Society*, London: Allen & Unwin, 1920, and *Equality*, London: Allen & Unwin, 1952.
22. With much justification, Socialists often point to attitudes common among American workers who tend to insist that their union leaders' salaries equal those of corporation executives and whose values do not appear to differ greatly from those of the middle class.
23. See, for example, Gabriel Kolko, *Wealth and Power in America*, New York: Praeger, 1962.

Nor is this all. Most men find themselves placed in the position of being used as instruments for another's end. The profit-making employer shapes not only the economic environment but also claims the right to mold the worker's social and cultural life as well. In the United States, it is increasingly the custom for corporations to attempt to regulate (informally, of course) what the worker (or even the executive) shall wear, how he shall think, and even what kind of family life he shall lead. In a modern capitalist environment, too, with the expense of equipment constantly mounting, the number of newspapers declines drastically, thus leaving the shaping of the public mind to the relatively few men who control and dominate the publishing business.[24] The power of big advertisers in the communications industry is a typical example of irresponsible control of the social and mental environment. Actually, most have been deluded into believing that they possess freedom, when in reality they have only its hollow shell.

The Webbs call attention to one of the classical post–World War I apologists for capitalism in support of their (and the socialists') thesis. In 1920, J. M. Keynes, a political liberal, wrote:

> The immense accumulations of fixed capital which, to the benefit of mankind, were built up during the half-century before the war, could never have come about in a society where wealth was divided equitably.
>
> Thus this remarkable system depended for its growth on a double bluff or deception. On the one hand the labouring classes accepted from ignorance or powerlessness, or were compelled, persuaded, or cajoled by custom, convention, authority, and the well-established order of society into accepting, a situation in which they could call their own very little of the cake, that they and nature and the capitalists were co-operating to produce. And on the other hand the capitalist classes were allowed to call the best part of the cake theirs and were theoretically free to consume it, on the tacit underlying condition that they consumed very little of it in practice. The duty of "saving" became nine-tenths of virtue and the growth of the cake the object of true religion.[25]

The system that was thus built up by "cajolery" depends for its continuation on the preservation of the myth that most men can be free under a scheme of things in which they do not control the tools of production or receive an equitable share in consumers' goods. Once this myth is broken, the absence of freedom under capitalism will be clearly seen.

Non-Marxian socialism at this point is, of course, not wholly different in its observations from Marxism. For both, such "formal" freedoms as due process, freedom of expression, and freedom to choose one's own occupation are in large degree counteracted by the economic imperatives established in a capitalist culture. To make freedom more than formal requires a fundamental shift in property relations. Marxism, to be sure, pushes economic determinism further than non-Marxian socialism: in fact, the latter can hardly be called determinist in the usual sense of the term. Insofar as this is true, then, the non-Marxian will never argue that political freedoms are ever wholly nominal, even under capitalism; and he will certainly not contend that we are justified in suspending legal and political liberty for the end of economic transformation. But even when this is fully recognized, the parallelism between Marxist and non-Marxian positions is striking.

Finally, the very basis of capitalist civilization is said to be scientifically unsound as a basis for organizing production and distribution of commodities. By this socialists mean that besides its tendency to destroy freedom, to separate men economically and socially, and to reduce human personality to a thing, capitalism shows itself more and more incapable even of economizing: As it develops, waste is encouraged, for example, and its periodic economic slumps and peaks become more severe. Let us see more explicitly what this implies.

Because of the distorted income distribution, the tendency to produce outruns ability to consume for economic purposes. A great premium, therefore, is placed on selling and the cost of distributing goods rises far beyond what it ought to be. In the effort to cut costs of production and maximize gain, as well as to purchase complex machinery, consolidation is encouraged and hence a quasi-monopoly capitalism. Under these circumstances, the competitive regulation of prices is greatly limited and monopolistic price fixing encouraged: Administered prices of oligopolies are substituted for strict market prices. But when this takes place, it is often to the immediate advantage of the oligopoly to keep prices up when business falls off rather than reduce prices and have a larger sales volume. Actions of this kind, naturally, lead to unemployment of both men and resources.

To illustrate criticisms of this kind, socialists

often point to the United States after World War II. On a number of occasions there were economic recessions in which, while unemployment mounted, prices remained the same or even increased. Thus in the depression of 1957 to 1958, the price level was practically stationary in the face of stagnation. Classical theory had held that with mounting unemployment, competitors would be compelled to reduce prices in order to get rid of goods; and this in turn would provoke full employment once more when the old goods had been sold. But in 1957 to 1958 and on other occasions, semi-monopoly control of prices enabled corporations in many instances to make higher profits by keeping up prices on a reduced volume of goods.

Thus capitalism eventually finds itself in a position that tends to defeat the ostensible purposes of an economy. The very quest for profits leads to the wastes of an elaborate system of middlemen; periodic and severe depressions; and the conspicuous consumption of luxury items by those in the upper income groups, the lower income groups in the meantime being deprived. War itself is another method of absorbing the goods which capitalism produces but does not know how to consume economically.

Again we may use the United States as an example of what socialists argue about war. It is pointed out that the only times when this country has had reasonably full employment since 1929 have been epochs of war or of widespread preparation for war. After the stock-market crash of 1929, the United States experienced a depression which lasted almost exactly ten years. As late as December, 1939, there were still 9,000,000 unemployed. Then began the war orders of Europe and within a few months, the number of unemployed was greatly reduced. When the United States itself entered the war, unemployment was virtually wiped out, reaching a low point of fewer than half a million. After the war, immediate economic catastrophe was averted because purchasing power stored up during the war could be released for consumers' goods which could under postwar circumstances be produced. But after this gave out, the unemployed again began to mount and only the Korean War, according to some analyses, helped save the situation. After the Korean War there were several periods of less than full employment (even by the generous standards under which normal employment is defined). The Vietnamese War was again a period of full employment.

It is important to stress that socialists are not maintaining that this problem of the economy's dependence on war cannot be solved. What they are contending is that it cannot be solved within the assumptions accepted by a capitalist economy and civilization. There is nothing inherent in the structure of a complex economy as such which requires gigantic waste and periodic breakdowns. It is the capitalist nature of the economy which sets up these imperatives.

Again, the socialist emphasizes that liberal solutions—those, that is to say, within the limits of assumptions such as those which governed Franklin D. Roosevelt or David Lloyd George or John Kennedy—cannot help in any basic way. This is so because the liberal, as socialist critics interpret him, accepts the institutions and practices out of which crises in the capitalist order grow: private ownership of land, for example, and the premises and expressions of semimonopolistic private economic institutions. Although liberalism, to be sure, is no longer a free market ideology and will sanction a certain measure of public collectivism, the fundamentals it leaves unaltered. Socialist critics of the American New Deal, for example,[26] argue that it was basically designed to strengthen the structure of American capitalism by making the economic system

24. On the problem of consolidation in the publishing business, see R. M. Hutchins, ed., *A Free and Responsible Press*, Chicago: University of Chicago Press, 1947. See also the *Report of the Royal Commission in Great Britain*, London: H.M. Stationery Office, 1949; J. Edward Gerald, *The British Press Under Government Economic Controls*, Minneapolis: University of Minnesota Press, 1956; and Frank Hughes, *Prejudice and the Press*, New York: Devin-Adair, 1950.
25. *The Economic Consequences of the Peace*, London: Macmillan, 1920, pp. 16–17.
26. American socialist criticisms of the New Deal will be found in Norman Thomas' books *America's Way Out*, New York: Macmillan, 1931; *As I See It*, New York: Macmillan, 1932; *The Choice Before Us*, New York: Macmillan, 1934; *After the New Deal, What?* New York: Macmillan, 1936; *Democracy's Dictatorship*, New York: Macmillan, 1937; and *Democratic Socialism*, New York: League for Industrial Democracy, 1953.

more acceptable to those who had begun to have doubts during the period of the great economic depression. Keynesian economic policies, moreover, upon which so many liberals rely, while they may serve to restrict the depths to which economic depression may go, do virtually nothing about distorted income distribution, land speculation, and the system of values exalted by an industrial capitalist society.

On ethical, social, political, and economic grounds, then, capitalist civilization is found wanting. It promotes an inequality incompatible with socialist democratic goals; it leads to enormous waste, particularly in its more mature stages; it encourages resort to war, even if it does not cause it; it tends to destroy personal freedom for the great majority; it exalts money-getting as a goal and a status symbol; and, in the end, it does not know how to use constructively the vast quantities of material goods which its machines can produce.

Evolution and Socialism

One of the important features which distinguishes non-Marxian from Marxian approaches is the more or less consistent belief of the former that socialist institutions can develop in a peaceful and orderly way. With liberalism, socialism tends to share the view that parliamentary institutions can become effective instruments for the remolding of society. True, they are in considerable measure dominated by capitalist owning and administrative classes; but with the growth of political awareness on the part of the masses and the increasingly obvious inability of capitalist institutions to function for the ends which any economic system must carry out, Parliaments and Congresses which developed so largely in the historical context of modern capitalism can be transformed into socialist instrumentalities. And some socialists have even argued that this development is inevitable.

Socialists differ, however, on the precise way in which this evolution can or will take place. In general, nineteenth-century thinkers, as one might expect, seem to think of it as inevitable. Since World War I, however, exponents of socialism have increasingly questioned this and have instead suggested that, while the evolution is possible, it is certainly not inevitable.

Let us note briefly the development of these positions.

Many of the utopian socialists of the nineteenth century appeared to reason that small-scale experiments of a socialist or communist character would be so successful that they would become models for rapidly evolving socialist institutions everywhere. When the American J. H. Noyes, for example, first set up the Oneida experiment, he definitely believed it would attract so much interest that others would emulate it, so that within a relatively brief period of time America would be dotted with socialist colonies. With these as a base, then, socialists could shape the larger politics of the nation. Fourier and Cabet, too, shared similar conceptions.

Although the great wave of socialist colonization was disillusioning in terms of its effect on political society, socialist thinkers did not surrender the idea of inevitability, which seemed to be woven into the very basis of most nineteenth-century British and American thought. When Edward Bellamy came to formulate his notions of socialist evolution in 1887, for example, he conceived the process to be one in which giant industrial corporations would become even larger. With their growth, popular consciousness of the problem of making them accountable would also expand. At the same time, the reduction of the number of industrial units would pave the way for the single socialist corporation which, in Bellamy's conception, would arise with hardly any injurious shock. Here the transformation of state and society is seen to be the result of developments made inevitable by the nature of capitalism itself; and when Congress eventually recognizes the accomplished fact, it is a purely formal act.[27]

In British socialist theory, the notion of inevitability emerges at many points in the writings of H. G. Wells, although sometimes the evolution is associated with considerable violence before the essential reasonableness of socialism emerges triumphant. In his pre-World War I socialist utopia,[28] for example, the double (or duplicate) of the earth is the scene of the rise of planned socialist institutions. By and large they develop when mankind decided that they have had enough of the muddle of private property institutions and the national state. The institutions of the world utopia somehow emerge out of the ruins to which the old way of life has reduced itself.

But perhaps the notion of inevitability is best illustrated in the writings of Sidney and Beatrice Webb. Although in the latter part of their lives the note was somewhat muted, in their prime, they appeared not to doubt the development of socialism through slow evolution and gradual transformation of older institutions. It is to them that we owe the expression "the inevitability of gradualness." Much of their life was devoted to the study of local institutions,[29] the history of the cooperative movement,[30] and the general examination of social organization, particularly in Great Britain. From this detailed analysis, they develop the thesis that institutions change, slowly, to be sure, but nevertheless inevitably. Political and social institutions adapt themselves to the evolving imperatives of human need. As private collectivism, in the form of the corporation, supplants free competitive individual enterprise, governmental institutions must and do broaden their functions to embrace the new situation.

Following this line, the development of socialism is not the end-product of dramatic storming of barricades or even of spectacular legislating but rather of slow inch-by-inch movements of institutions. Men can, to be sure, guide these movements to some extent but, at least in the British context, the Webbs appear to think that they are already tending in a socialist direction.

There is thus a strong current in non-Marxian thought which matches the Marxist belief that "history is on our side." It is never, perhaps, as pronounced among non-Marxians as Marxists but it is sufficiently prominent to deserve emphasis. At the level of practical politics, it is frequently a more or less implicitly held belief: Thus when Eugene V. Debs was running for President of the United States, he was often met by questions which began "When socialism comes . . . ," the initial word being *when* rather than *if*.

Although this stress by no means dies out after 1919, we can perhaps identify the beginning of its decline with the end of World War I. By the thirties and forties, socialists are not so sure that out of capitalist institutions will emerge a socialist society. The experience of Fascist and National Socialist regimes during the twenties and thirties leads many to wonder whether the old notion of evolution as a straight line from individual enterprise to semi-monopoly to socialism is not grossly over-simplified. In the forties, for example, these doubts are symbolized by James Burnham, who asks whether bureaucratic non-socialist collectivism may not be the "wave of the future."[31] Although Burnham comes from the Trotskyite tradition, non-Marxians often ask similar questions.

Public and Social Ownership and Administration

But what would be the nature of the socialist transformation?

As its general criticism of capitalist civilization implies, it seeks a reversal of all those tendencies which it condemns in capitalist culture. Specifically, it hopes to establish institutions that will release modern man from such phenomena as the quest for money as an end, the insecurities associated with the business cycle, economic and social inequality, capitalist restrictions on freedom, and the waste so intimately associated with capitalism. Because it is not an outlook based on economic determinism, it does not hold that radical transformation of the economy will automatically eliminate the social and political evils of capitalism; but it does maintain that basic economic changes can do much to achieve this goal.

27. It was difficult for men like Bellamy, as it was difficult for other late nineteenth-century thinkers, to believe that the course of social evolution could possibly be in directions which they thought to be undesirable. During the same epoch, philosophers like John Fiske (in books such as *Through Nature to God*) and men of the cloth like Henry Drummond (in *The Accent of Man*) were also reading their own norms into the very nature of the historical process.
28. See *A Modern Utopia*, New York: Scribner, 1905.
29. See Sidney Webb, *The History of Local Government*, London: Longmans, Green, 1906.
30. See Sidney Webb, *The Constitutional Problems of a Co-operative Society*, London: The Fabian Society, 1923; Beatrice (Potter) Webb, *The Co-operative Movement in Great Britain*, London: Allen & Unwin, 1930; Sidney and Beatrice Webb, *The Consumer's Co-operative Movement*, London: Longmans, Green, 1921, and *A Constitution for the Socialist Commonwealth of Great Britain*, London: Longmans, Green, 1920.
31. James Burnham, *The Managerial Revolution*, New York: John Day, 1941.

We may discern three interrelated elements in non-Marxian socialist objectives: The proposal for public and social ownership, democratic controls and democratic objectives, and internationalism. In this section, let us turn to the first.

Basically, socialists argue, once a culture has opted for any large measure of industrialism, it has also implicitly chosen some form of collective ownership and administration of the tools of production. Thus within the relatively brief time span of modern industrial capitalism, private individual ownership of tools—characteristic of the early period—has given way to private corporate ownership and administration. Individual ownership of capital equipment becomes increasingly impossible with development of complex machinery, the purchase of which makes imperative the pooling of individual resources. But the collectivist corporation is still private in the sense that it is not regarded, under capitalism, as an entity accountable to the community as a whole. While its activities obviously affect millions of persons, it is largely treated, in law and theory, as if it were simply a private person with private objectives. Thus it can own and manipulate land, fix prices (in effect), and coerce individuals through its control of resources. Capitalist apologetics insist that it is in a different category from such great traditional public institutions as the post office or public parks. Yet it becomes more and more an instrument of a private government that shapes human destiny as much as many institutions formally recognized as public.

The basis for public and social ownership is, then, the fact that gigantic industrial and commercial entities are already performing functions which affect millions of persons; and socialists argue that this should be formally recognized by assimilating the corporation to the status of a fully public institution. It would then be accountable to the democratic assembly (however organized) and would exist not to make private profit but to render service to the community.

Full public character would, moreover, facilitate the planning so essential if the complexly divided labors of industrialism are to be coordinated for the social good. Conflicts between private and public interests would be minimized in a system where private profit has been abolished.

Along with public and social ownership of the productive and distributive instruments of an industrial community would go a similar form of ownership and control of land and natural resources. Here the socialist argument is that since land is very limited in extent, it should never be the object of speculation and private trading as it is to so large an extent in a capitalist civilization. Basic title would be vested in the community which might, of course, lease out the land for periods of time on conditions to be laid down by public law.

But while all socialists are agreed on the general principles of public and social ownership, they differ considerably about the exact form it should take. In its early development, "public" for the socialist often means state or government. About the time of World War I, however, a version known as guild socialism seriously attacked this emphasis on the state and proposed producers' guilds as alternative instruments. The guilds would be held together very loosely by a coordinating committee; but the state as such would supposedly be abolished. Guild socialism obviously had much in common with certain versions of anarchism and antistatism, which will be treated in the next chapter. During the thirties and forties of the twentieth century both American and British socialist theory increasingly used the term social to indicate the variety of forms which socialist ownership and control might assume. Thus many suggested a combination of producers' association, consumers' cooperative, local government, and central government administration.[32]

Increasing distrust of purely government ownership and administration after 1920 was engendered by a number of factors. One was the general movement known as pluralism which affected the history of political thought between 1917 and 1933: It attacked monistic notions of sovereignty, argued that associations do not derive their life from the state, and, in general maintained that human personality is likely to develop most freely in a society where voluntary associations are encouraged and direct state administration is peripheral.[33] Another factor was undoubtedly a growing fear that reliance on the state might lead to forms of national socialism taking on certain characteristics of fascist states. Finally, scholarly studies in bureaucracy and oligarchy—such as those of Roberto Michels and Gaetano Mosca[34]—suggested that if socialism were to be democratic, it must devolve as much authority as possible on nonstate or local government groups: This would, it was believed, limit the tendency for centralized state bureaucracy to dominate and control industry for its own ends and would also curtail the rigidity of thinking and action which the studies associated with elaborate and centralized administrative machines. At any rate, it is important to note that socialists themselves anticipated many of the nonsocialist criticisms which were to be leveled at socialist theory after 1941.

In Sidney and Beatrice Webb's *Constitution for the Socialist Commonwealth of Great Britain,* for example, which appeared just after World War I,[35] many of the questions raised by pluralists and guild socialists are well recognized. Thus there is a strong accent on local administration, emphasis on use of the already strong consumers' cooperatives in retail distribution, and recognition of regional administration. Bellamy a generation earlier had proposed gigantic national corporations and a highly integrated framework of administration. But the Webbs spurn such a scheme of organization. True, some services are to be administered nationally through tripartite boards in which workers, administrators, and government will have a voice; but the burden of proof, so to speak, is to be put on those who would establish nationally managed industries and distributive systems. Only where local or cooperative operation is unfeasible or out of place (because of the wide ramifications of the service, for example) will the national board system be operative.

When the Labour Government of 1945 came to plan its program, its emphasis at first seemed often to be on centralization. But experience—with nationalized coal, for example—gradually led it to provide considerable administrative decentralization in many areas.

Non-Marxian socialists usually give great attention to the problem of controlling industries and services which have become public or social and this has been particularly true since governments dominated by socialist ideology attained office. Actual experience with administration has often dramatized the tendency of bureaucracy to set up ends of its own, forgetting the purposes for which it has been established.

Overwhelmingly, non-Marxian socialists plead for democratic controls but the precise meaning attached to the expression varies. In Bellamy's scheme, only those who have retired (at the age of 45) have the suffrage and vote for the national Congress, which acts as the controlling body. Before retirement age men are merely economic rather than political. The assumption is that so long as they are active in the "industrial army"—the highly coordinated and planned productive machine—they should not be put in the position of trying to regulate affairs in which they presumably have special interests. Once retired, they can be impartial and just. It should be noted, too, that democracy for Bellamy operates primarily at the national level: A kind of democratic centralism is established and the problem which exercises later socialists—that of devolution and flexibility—hardly crosses Bellamy's consciousness.

By the time of the Webbs, democratic controls imply a whole complex of machinery designed to reconcile freedom with planning, central direction with local autonomy, and representation of special interests with reflection of the general interest. The Webbs propose that the national legislative body be split into two—a social parliament and a political parliament. The latter would be responsible for foreign affairs, defense, and justice; the former for finance and the vast proliferation of new social services and publicly owned industries. In the political parliament, Cabinet government would remain unimpaired, but the social parliament would administer its concerns through committees, after the manner of British local government bodies.[36] Detailed

32. On guild socialism see G. D. H. Cole, *Guild Socialism,* London: L. Parsons, 1920, and *Guild Socialism Restated,* New York: Frederick A. Stokes, 1921.
33. On pluralism see J. H. Figgis, *Churches in the Modern State,* London: Longmans, Green, 1914; and Harold Laski, *Studies in the Problem of Sovereignty,* New York: Fertig, 1968.
34. For example, Roberto Michels' *Political Parties,* New York: Hearst's International Library, 1915, which tended to show that even where, as in the Social Democratic party of Germany, the formal commitment was to democracy, the imperatives of complex organization and "efficiency" established rule by a very small elite.
35. Sidney and Beatrice Webb, *A Constitution for the Socialist Commonwealth of Great Britain,* London: Longmans, Green, 1920.
36. In Great Britain, municipal councils carry on their administration by means of committees chosen from among members of the councils. Each committee will have general oversight of

management of each national service would be delegated by the proper committee to a National Board on which important special interests (those of the workers, for example) would be represented.

In the Webbs' proposals as well as in those of others, one of the most important questions concerns the effort to combine responsibility to the community with business efficiency. Nationalized and socialized services must be accountable to the community, since this objective has loomed large in the major arguments for public or social ownership. On the other hand, if the resources of the community are not to be wasted and creative effort is to be encouraged, day to day operations should, it is argued, be free of detailed political inspection. The formula devised in the several British nationalized industries is that while the Cabinet minister responsible can be questioned in the House of Commons about general policy questions, business operations must be under the control of the National Board involved. Moreover, while the minister can give general directions to the National Board, he is supposed to leave the Board free to conduct day to day activities and to organize the whole industry within very broad guidelines.[37]

In the United States, recent non-Marxian socialists have usually suggested that publicly owned industries might well be controlled by Boards representing workers within the industry, consumers of the product of the industry, and the government as the trustee of the public interest. Thus some socialists have criticized the method whereby the governing board of the TVA is selected. Instead of all its members being appointed by the President of the United States, as at present, only a third should be designated by him, the remainder to be representative of workers and consumers.[38]

Throughout all the discussion of control, there has been an increasing emphasis on the notion that public and private interests will never be completely reconciled, even in a socialist society. Public or social ownership and control does not mean that differences between producers' and consumers' perspectives will not continue, for example; nor does it imply that there may not be a serious tension between the ideal of public accountability and business and professional autonomy. The problem, many would argue, is to ensure that the major interests be reflected openly and that there be adequate machinery for peaceful resolution of conflict.

It is at this point, perhaps, that non-Marxian socialism will differ most profoundly from the picture of communism as painted by Marxists. In the latter, differences between particular and general interests are apparently virtually wiped out; or, at a minimum (and as we have seen, the vision is often rather blurred), they are reduced so much that any given individual will not wish to act in ways contrary to a hypothetical general interest. Most currents of non-Marxian socialism, however, do not envision the attainment of any such society. Tensions between the particular and the general appear to be regarded as inseparable from human affairs; and if we are democrats, non-Marxists seem to be saying, the human being regarded as an end in himself must be as highly respected as the human being seen as a kind of cell in the social organism. One ought never to reduce the one to the other.

Ends and Values

But public and social ownership and administration are usually not regarded by non-Marxian socialism as ends in themselves. They are advocated because it is believed that the ends of socialists can best be implemented under these circumstances. One of those ends is, of course, the extension of democratic controls into all areas of collective life and in the preceding section we have noted a few of the ways in which democratic control might be assured.

What are some of the other ends which non-Marxians seem to share? And how would they be attained under conditions of public or social ownership with machinery for democratic control and consultation?

The ends can be derived by implication from socialist critiques of capitalist civilization. A socialist society would presumably remedy the deficiencies of capitalism as seen by the socialist critic.

Aside, then, from the end of democratic controls, other socialist values which could be implemented might be listed as a measure of economic stability; a combination of consumers' freedom with socialist planning; a more equitable distribution of income; a vast extension of free services; and a transformation of values.

A Measure of Economic Stability. As noted earlier, a major socialist criticism of capitalist culture has been that it has not been able to avoid the distorted and false prosperity of "boom" periods and the waste of human and natural resources characteristic of "bust" years. Technically equipped to produce an abundance of goods, capitalism periodically fails to do so and even when it does produce them cannot, within its assumptions, distribute them. Socialists argue that such a system is both economically unsound and ethically outrageous.

In a socialist society, the argument continues, stability would be produced by a number of devices. In the first place, since land and natural resources would be owned by the community, the speculation so often associated with them under capitalism would be abolished and with it those features of instability which are encouraged by speculation of various kinds. Secondly, the principle of social ownership and production for use rather than profit would ensure that a very large proportion of everything produced could be immediately consumed, thus avoiding the piling up of surpluses and their depressing effect on the economy. Thirdly, a measure of central planning of production and distribution would make possible rapid adjustments of prices and production to demand as well as ensure, over-all, a measure of coordination between supply and demand. Fourthly, because repair and expansion of capital equipment, retirement incomes, medical care, and other services would be planned for beforehand and would be a first charge on the social budget, consumers could spend virtually all they earned on purchase of all the goods produced during a given year, thus obviating the need for much private saving and with it the possibility that some of it might be hoarded. Finally, a more equitable distribution of income would contribute to the end by reducing any possibility that a few would save without the savings being immediately transformed into investments. Although the major purpose of income redistribution is social and ethical, it would thus incidentally contribute to stability.

A Combination of Consumers' Freedom with Socialist Planning. In the history of socialist thought there has been much discussion about the role which a price system might or might not play in a socialist society. Some socialists—notably many of the utopians—have argued for the abolition of the price system altogether and for distribution of income in kind. But most modern socialists would attempt to combine nonmarket with market controls in the economy. Over-all, they argue, there should be a system of public planning within which would be made such basic decisions as to how much shall be produced, how resources shall be allocated, and how rapidly capital equipment shall be expanded. Within these limits, a price system would continue to operate to reflect current demands.

If, during a given planning period, a commodity does not sell at a given price as rapidly as predicted, the planning authority could lower the price and thus encourage its sales. If, on the other hand, the commodity sells faster than anticipated, the Planning Board would presumably raise the price. Prices, in other words, within the limits of the planning scheme and the system of social ownership, would serve to indicate producer and consumer preferences. But the adjustment of prices would be a public function carried out in accordance with publicly stated principles: "sticky" prices, so characteristic of semimonopolistic capitalism, would be ruled out since the machinery for adjustment would operate within the glare of publicity and with private-profit-making corporations abolished.[39]

A More Equitable Distribution of Income. Socialists criticize capitalist distribution of income on a number of grounds: It separates men from one another by providing an eco-

---

a given department, whose permanent professional head will be selected from the municipal civil service. A given committee will also recommend legislation to the full council. According to this system, then, executive and legislative prerogatives are merged.

37. On the problem of combining community responsibility and accountability with business autonomy, see V. V. Ramanadhan, *Problems of Public Enterprise*, Chicago: Quadrangle Books, 1959; Michael Shanks, ed., *The Lessons of Public Enterprise*, London: Jonathan Cape, 1963; A. H. Hanson, ed., *Nationalization*, London: Allen & Unwin, and William Robson, ed., *Problems of Nationalized Industry*, London: Allen & Unwin, 1952.
38. See the works of Norman Thomas and, for example, the Socialist party platforms of 1960 and 1964.
39. In the thirties of the twentieth century, there was widespread discussion of this problem. See, for example, the essays by Benjamin Lippincott, Fred Taylor, and Oscar Lange, printed in Benjamin Lippincott, ed., *On the Economic Theory of Socialism*, Minneapolis: University of Minnesota Press, 1938.

nomic base for class differentiations; it distorts consumer demand in favor of the luxury items which can be insisted upon by the rich; it is in considerable degree built upon factors which have nothing to do with contributions of those involved and certainly not with their need; and it enables the few to influence unduly the politics of the community.

For all these reasons, socialists have suggested radically different principles of income distribution. Sometimes they have argued for literal equality, as with Bellamy and, in the twentieth century, with George Bernard Shaw.[40] It is impossible, so part of this argument would hold, to determine with any accuracy the contributions of individuals, particularly in a complex technological society where individual contributions play smaller relative roles and the fact of cooperative organization (beyond differentiated individual capacities) becomes central in the productive process. Since this is true, the best rule would seem to be equality.

But most twentieth-century socialism is not egalitarian in this sense. By and large, it argues simply for principles and practices of distribution which will reduce drastically the gap obtaining in capitalist societies between lowest and highest incomes. This reduction will be facilitated by a socialist system of production, the argument goes on, for the assembly to which planners would be accountable could suggest maxima and minima within which particular enterprises would work. Since speculation in land and natural resources will have been abolished, the preservation of a socialist scheme of distribution will be facilitated.

Most socialist thinkers would accept, within these limits, the possibility of incentive salaries or wages. At the same time, it is usually argued, major incentives in a socialist society will not be economic but rather social and spiritual: social, in that one's desire to do good work will be reinforced by the standards of the group to which one belongs; spiritual, in the degree that a fully socialized educational system, by helping individuals discover their true vocations, will tend to eliminate the phenomenon of "square pegs in round holes"—men will work because they enjoy their occupation and not by reason of external incentives.[41]

The Extension of Free Services. Although most modern socialist theory envisions a considerable sector remaining within the price system, it also argues for a vast extension of free services and goods. These would be services and goods which are so indispensable to a reasonable standard of life for all that it would be most convenient and economical to distribute them without the intermediation of prices or fees. They would be a first-order charge on the social budget and would be provided for before any monetary income would be distributed. Examples are greatly extended educational systems, medical services, legal services, recreation, burial schemes, and possibly even free bread. These would be in addition to such free services as are usually provided even under capitalist cultures—police and fire protection, for example, highways, parks, and many others.

Some socialists see an extension of free services as providing a kind of basic minimum standard of life for creative persons who prefer to live on a budget barely sufficient for a livelihood rather than work at regular income-producing work. Thus the artist or poet might elect to exist on the common minimum in order to provide the leisure necessary for creativity.[42]

A Transformation of Values. Socialists contend that the theory of a socialist society involves much more than changes in organization and in the mechanics of collective life. A central point in their critique of capitalist culture is that the moral and religious professions which that culture makes are impossible to fulfill within the imperatives established by the profit system and its context. Brotherhood becomes a mockery when, as is often true, the choice seems to be between economic death and acts which violate respect for the person but which appear to be essential for business survival. Love for neighbor is meaningless in a context where money values become central.

Socialist doctrine maintains that the very establishment of socialist institutions would help release men from the stranglehold of the existing system, so that they would be confronted with alternatives compatible with both survival and morality. In the realm of law and legal protection, a socialized profession would provide services in accordance with need rather than in relation to income, thus establishing an economic foundation for justice which is lacking today. Justice would no longer depend on size of income but upon the merits of the case.

New institutions would, then, in themselves encourage greater observance of the moral ideals which most men in Western culture have held up but which capitalist institutions belie. At the same time, the socialist argument continues, machinery of government and economy is not enough. Thus there may be adequate channels whereby resources can be publicly allocated and administered; but the values which guide the public assembly may give cheap entertainment a priority over education and immediate sense pleasure may take precedence over child welfare, to the consternation of most socialists. More than social, economic, and political reorganization is required if the goals of socialism are to be implemented: a transformed sense of values must also actually govern conduct. And to achieve this requires education and widespread discussion; a different spirit as well as radically altered institutions.

The International Problem and Socialist Thought

Modern socialism developed within the context of the nation-state and among its most acute problems, both in theory and in practice, has been the determination of its attitude to the national state. In the abstract, both Marxists and non-Marxians have been internationalists or even, as with H. G. Wells, advocates of cosmopolitanism—which implies a discarding of the nation-state altogether.[43] But within the limits of this common distrust of the nation-state there have been wide variations.

Socialist criticism of the nation-state has centered on its role in the making of modern war and its inadequacy as a political unit within an industrial culture. Men like Keir Hardie, before World War I, have particularly stressed the former; and at one point Hardie advocated a general strike against any state making war. There was, in fact, widespread socialist sentiment for such action before 1914. In the United States, the Socialist party under the leadership of Eugene V. Debs opposed American entrance into the war and officially continued its opposition (despite many resignations) after the United States had become a combatant. Debs served a term in prison for his outspoken statements and many other American socialists were also prosecuted.[44]

Like Marxian socialism, non-Marxian views see modern war as intimately bound up with industrial capitalism; and while non-Marxian theory, by and large, would reject extreme economic determinist interpretations, it would tend to suggest that the modern state is frequently dominated in its war-making by the capitalist classes which have most to gain. Although the undermining of capitalism, most modern socialists argue, would not automatically eliminate war, so long as the nation-state continues to be the major form of political organization, it would remove one of the major factors in the encouragement of military conflict.

The nation-state, too, is a grossly inadequate form for administration of industrial culture, particularly under socialist conditions. Hence non-Marxian socialism emphasizes that in a socialist society, the nation-state ought to be transcended. Economic planning must be international. Running through most of the utopian projections of H. G. Wells, for example, is this theme.

Thus socialist theory is not enamored of the idea of national sovereignty. By and large, the national state is seen to be a political form which in the long run should disappear as the supreme object of human political allegiance.

When confronted by the exigencies of practical politics, however, political parties dominated by socialist views have often hesitated. In the interest of immediate political gain, they have frequently compromised seriously with their internationalist professions; and once in office, they have not seldom become simply trustees for a "national interest" that has been shaped by non-socialist policies. The history of

40. For Bellamy's arguments, see *Looking Backward*, Boston: Houghton Mifflin Co., 1931, ch. 9, and *Equality*, New York: D. Appleton, 1897, ch. 13. For Shaw's views, see *An Intelligent Woman's Guide to Capitalism and Socialism*, London: E. Benn, 1929.
41. For discussions of incentives within a socialist system, see Bellamy, *op. cit.;* Sidney and Beatrice Webb, *A Constitution for the Socialist Commonwealth of Great Britain, op. cit.;* and R. H. Tawney, *Equality, op. cit.*
42. A theme, for example, in H. G. Wells, *A Modern Utopia.*
43. The great utopias of Wells such as *A Modern Utopia*, *Men Like Gods*, and *A Dream* are all world societies; and throughout his political works there is great impatience with what he is constantly calling the militant national state.
44. For Debs' biography, see, for example, Ray Ginger, *The Bending Cross*, New Brunswick, N.J.: Rutgers University Press, 1949.

the British Labour party will nicely illustrate this problem. Aside from the fact that it officially supported both world wars, it has often found itself in seeming opposition to its own professed economic internationalism. In office, for example, it has been torn between the immediate needs of stable national economic planning, on the one hand, and an internationalism which would involve cooperation with nations not having socialist objectives. To pursue the latter course, many socialists maintain, would endanger the objectives of the former. Thus the exigencies of the quest for political power and conflicts between immediate and long run goals have served to weaken much socialist internationalism. Just as a French socialism ostensibly Marxist in character has often supported French imperialism, so have non-Marxian socialists appeared to abandon much of their internationalism and cosmopolitanism when confronted by the imperatives of gaining office or defending the immediate interests of their nation-states.

While this must be admitted, it should also be pointed out that much of the impetus in the struggle against imperialism has come from non-Marxian socialists. To be sure, many Fabians supported the Boer War, or at least did not oppose it (unlike the Liberal leadership). But by and large modern socialists have undergirded Asian and African anticolonialism; and socialist ideals have been an important ingredient in the gradual disintegration of the British Empire and its transformation into a Commonwealth of Nations.

Currents of Criticism

Non-Marxian socialism, like Marxism, has been subjected to a variety of criticisms during the past generation. Although some of the criticisms apply to Marxism as well as non-Marxian socialism, they will be treated here primarily in the context of the latter.

We may classify the criticisms as those which stem from a Marxist perspective; those which argue the incompatibility of socialism with freedom; the tendencies which see socialism as out of date; and socialist self-criticisms, particularly those which arise out of experience with office in Great Britain.

Marxist Attacks. The Marxist critique, built as it is on a more rigid doctrinal scheme, attacks non-Marxian socialism on the ground that its social and political analysis is inadequate. In fact, non-Marxists are not really socialists.

In the United States, for example, the theories stemming from the Socialist Labor party, a professedly Marxist group,[45] suggest that accounts of human society which do not build on Marx's propositions cannot explain typical twentieth-century phenomena. Imperialism, for example, which to the non-Marxist arises out of a whole complex of factors—including capitalist exploitation, a kind of will to power on the part of the large national state, and possibly even rival personal ambitions—is to the Marxist simply the "last stage of capitalism" and is reducible to economic explanations.

In the Leninist tradition, too, non-Marxist views are suspect. They are simply another expression of capitalism; for non-Marxists, stressing evolution rather than revolution, inevitably surrender the essentials of socialism in their slavish observance of parliamentary forms. Leninism is hostile to the stress placed by most non-Marxian socialists on civil liberties and procedural due process; for it argues that these should be used simply as instruments in the struggle for power and should be discarded when revolutionary parties believe it in their interest to do so. By and large, the Leninist perspective on the British Labour party would be that the latter is not socialist at all but rather reformist within a framework accepting capitalist institutions.

The basic conflict between Marxist-Leninists and non-Marxian socialists roots, perhaps, in the tendency of the former to stress unicausal explanations of history, while the latter emphasize multicausal accounts. Because Leninism professes to see politics, religion, and culture, as shaped ultimately by economic factors, it gives very little credence to the non-Marxist view that noneconomic elements may in some sense be autonomous. If one sees politics and law, for example, as having a measure of independence—however much they may be heavily conditioned by economic factors—one will be suspicious of all notions of freedom which see it arising only out of economic relations; one will instead think of liberty as a product of many ingredients which mutually support one another but which cannot be reduced to any single factor.

Planning and Freedom. Since socialism, whatever its particular expression, always involves a great measure of public planning, it becomes the target of all those attacks which claim an incompatibility between planning and individual freedom.

Criticisms on this score are relatively old but acquired a new importance in the forties and fifties of the twentieth century. In 1942, Friedrich von Hayek, the well-known Austrian economist, summarized the gist of the contentions in semipopular form.[46] Von Hayek's basic argument centered on the allegation that planning, once initiated, tends to invade every aspect of life. We cannot, that is to say, seek to plan one segment of human existence, without finding that in order to sustain our partial planning we must move into other realms as well. Eventually, then, initiatives from individuals—which repose on the existence of a realm immune from social planning—dry up. Individuals find themselves imprisoned in a network of rules and regulations made by the planners, so that freedom in any meaningful sense disappears. A similar thesis has been suggested by another well-known Austrian economist, Ludwig von Mises.[47]

Closely connected with arguments like that of von Hayek is the criticism which would associate socialism with an expanding bureaucracy and in turn with the wiping out of individuality. Planning per se reduces human beings to mere instruments and elaborately graded civil services are the means for accomplishing this objective. Moreover, all wholesale social engineering such as that involved in radical planning inevitably tends to create what Karl Popper calls a "closed society."[48] That is to say, not only are restrictions placed on human action in the interests of the over-all scheme but thought and spiritual expression are affected as well. Large-scale planning, the critic seems to be asserting, sets up imperatives of its own which have not been intended by the planners but which are, nevertheless, inherent in the central idea.

Running through all the criticism is the fear expressed by men like von Hayek, von Mises, and Popper that a socialist society would combine political with economic power. That is, nonsocialist societies generally make a careful distinction between the government and private industry; in law and custom, the sphere of the former is severely demarcated and its direct control of the latter strictly limited. In a socialist society, by contrast, the same groups which administer the political area of life will also direct the economic. In a nonsocialist society, the private economic segment constitutes a kind of countervailing power to the public political sector and individual freedom is supposedly protected through their conflicts.

The reply to criticisms of this kind challenges the critics' definition of freedom, argues that the extension of freedom requires planning, and denies that because a certain aspect of community life is planned political direction of all aspects is inevitable.[49]

Freedom is not separable from community organization, the reply maintains. When the critics set freedom over against organization, as they seem to do, they are beclouding the fact that liberty of movement and of initiative cannot be abstracted from the way in which social and political relations are ordered.

In fact, an industrial society requires considerably more planning if freedom is to have any reality for vast masses of human beings. The great bulk of mankind, it is contended, are hungry and if they are to be fed, organization and planning are indispensable. Hungry men, moreover, cannot be free. Life organized wholly in accordance with the market calculus soon finds the regulation of competition giving way to the rule of the most powerful private entrepreneurs who are not responsible to the general community. Public planning is an effort of the community to reverse the disasters to freedom brought about by irresponsible private planning (preemption of land by the few, for example), "sticky" prices which

45. On the Socialist Labor party, see Morris Hillquit, *History of Socialism in the United States*, New York: Funk & Wagnalls, 1910; and Henry Kuhn and O. M. Johnson, *The Socialist Labor Party During Four Decades: 1890–1930*, New York: New York Labor News Co., 1931.

46. See Friedrich von Hayek, *The Road to Serfdom*, Chicago: University of Chicago Press, 1944.

47. See Ludwig von Mises, *Omnipotent Government*, London: G. Routledge & Sons, 1945.

48. Karl Popper, *The Open Society and Its Enemies*, 2 vols., Princeton, N.J.: Princeton University Press, 1963.

49. Among the most important treatises critical of the critics freedom-planning arguments are Barbara Wootton, *Freedom Under Planning*, Chapel Hill: University of North Carolina Press, 1945; and Herman Finer, *The Road to Reaction*, Chicago: Quadrangle Books, 1963.

prevent the rapid adjustments that classical economic theory postulates, waste of human and natural resources, and an income distribution setting up barriers between human beings. True, it might in the abstract be possible to deindustrialize and thus restore a somewhat more flexible and unbureaucratic market economy; but this would itself involve deliberate planning and would, moreover, necessitate a vast reduction in the standard of living and probably of the population.

Finally, the reply concludes, there is nothing in either the psychological nature of things or the social and political structure which necessarily entails planning in all areas of life simply because it has begun in some. As a matter of fact, traditional states have always planned some things—the police, military defense—but this did not mean that, for example, family life would also be planned. Law, custom, and a sense of the fitness of things can interpose barriers to the extension of planning. Most modern socialists, moreover, suggest that market controls—through the limited operation of a price system—will be combined with nonmarket planning: the two ways of governing economic life will support and at the same time check each other. Planning will make for a more rapid adjustment of prices to demand and the partial use of a price system will interpose a barrier to any planning that might take on arbitrary tones.

The very accountability and responsibility associated with public planning, moreover, would create an atmosphere different from that characteristic of the private and largely irresponsible oligopolistic capitalist planning: the latter, as a matter of fact, is far more likely to stifle freedom, initiative, and spontaneity—by reason of its very immunity from public control—than is a public system subject to all the legitimized scrutiny of the community.

Bureaucracy, to be sure, constitutes a problem of serious proportions in any complex economy. But this is true whether the economy be socialist or oligopolistic capitalist; and the former is much more likely to be able to cope with it—because of the element of public accountability and responsibility—than the latter. Decentralization within the limits of an over-all planning system, the development of adequate legislative organs at both central and local levels, and a certain measure of competition between socialized institutions are some of the devices which socialists envision to keep bureaucratically administered agencies from forgetting their raison d'être.

Modern Liberalism and Socialism. As we have seen, modern liberalism is much more receptive to collectivist views than was its ancestor of a hundred years ago. Nevertheless, it sharply differentiates itself from socialism.

It is not easy to identify its specific criticisms of socialism, however, if only because there is nothing approaching an authoritative statement dealing with the liberal position. In general, however, if we take the attitude of the Liberal party in Britain and the theory associated with the New Deal (and its successors) in the United States as the basis, liberalism would seem to doubt the necessity for the radical transformation called for by socialism. Sympathizing with many socialist criticisms of capitalism, it would argue, nevertheless, that they can be met with less hazard to liberal values by means that are not characteristically socialist.

Thus the liberal suggests that public and social ownership is unnecessary to gain the objective of economic stability. An application of Keynesian public policy measures can accomplish the objective. Indirect controls, he maintains, are better than direct ones; for they allow much more room for private initiative and responsibility, values which liberalism makes central.

Or again, extension of democratic controls can best be accomplished not by the radical overhaul proposed by the socialist but rather by a kind of pragmatic working out of extensions through trade union bargaining, regulatory statutes, and a realization by industrial managers that consultations with their workers are advantageous economically.

To socialist criticisms of power distribution, liberals tend to reply that use of graduated income taxes can correct the more egregious disparities in income distribution. Once more, the liberal argues for indirect controls.

By and large, we may summarize, liberalism is much less definite than socialism in its criticisms and proposals for capitalist society and for the state associated with it. But inheriting as it does a tradition against state authority, it tends to be doubtful about any radical extension of public functions, and its major criticisms of socialism are often animated by this distrust.

Socialist Self-Criticisms. Previously it was pointed out that socialism at the beginning of the twentieth century tended to be more complacent about its outlook than it did in the forties and fifties. In the meantime, nonsocialist collectivist systems—notably in Germany and Italy—had dramatized the fact that public control and administration could be used for ends grossly contrary to those of traditional socialism; and the experiences of the Labour Government in Great Britain (1945–1951) had raised serious questions involving earlier ideological positions and ways of administering a socialist society.

Experience with Fascism led socialists after the thirties to stress increasingly that collective public ownership did not necessarily mean *state* ownership. But of still greater importance, socialist theory after 1940 places an even greater emphasis than before on the ends for which social ownership shall be used: the goals must be democratic and egalitarian to be socialist.

The tenure of the Labour Cabinet produced critical reactions on the part of some socialist thinkers.[50] Among them we may note a questioning of the dogma of nationalization, discussion of the best mode for organizing collectively owned enterprises, and an inquiry into the problem of reconciling public accountability with the presumed value of business autonomy and efficiency.

Increasingly, socialist thinkers have emphasized that mere nationalization of an industry does not mean that it is socialized; and they have also suggested that older interpretations mistakenly thought of nationalization as a kind of cure-all. Nationalization is not the equivalent of socialization because the latter involves ends for which nationalized industries may or may not be used and modes of organization which may or may not be employed. Nationalization, for example, can be used to buttress a state primarily devoted to war; but this would hardly be socialization. A nationalized scheme, moreover, in which workers in the industry were not consulted could hardly be thought of as being socialized. Of even greater importance is the fact that some British socialists (their critics call them right-wingers) have increasingly asked whether all important modes of production and distribution *ought* to be publicly owned; perhaps, the argument goes, socialist ends could be better achieved without formal ownership.

As for organization of collectively owned enterprises, socialist criticisms have centered on absence of effective workers' control and advice and the allegation of too much centralization. Left-wing critics particularly are often disillusioned on the first score, claiming that nationalization as actually practiced seems often to differ only slightly, if at all, from private capitalist organization. As one coalminer is said to have put it, "There's still the bloody boss." The machinery for workers' consultation, the critic argues, is often purely nominal; and ordinary laborers by and large have hardly any voice in selection of managers.

Finally, there has been vigorous debate about what should be the ideal relation between a public business enterprise and the democratic principle of public accountability and responsibility. As we have seen, the theory of nationalized industries under the Labour Government was that each enterprise must be given a considerable latitude for business experimentation without interference from the elected House of Commons or the Cabinet responsible to it. At the same time, the industry must be responsible in an overall sense to the political organs of the community. Criticism has centered on the precise definition of these spheres, many of the critics alleging that the responsibility and accountability side is minimized: Here again, seemingly, the actual administration of nationalization tends to be assimilated to the capitalist notion of business autonomy. British socialists have by no means resolved the question of how public accountability and democratic responsibility can be reconciled with business freedom, assuming the latter to be desirable.

It should not be assumed, however, that self-criticisms of this kind mean that those who offer them have ceased to be socialists. The critics still accept the basic socialist analysis of capitalism, for example, and continue to support the ends of socialism, together with its traditional major means.

Throughout their careers, however, modern Marxism and non-Marxian socialism, together with conservative and liberal outlooks, have been subject to basic attacks by the several schools of anarchist thought. Although the

50. See R. H. S. Crossman, ed., *New Fabian Essays, op. cit.*

affinities between socialism and anarchism are often striking, their differences are also highly important. While anarchism, with some exceptions, has never been popular as a political outlook, its propositions are so fundamental to any understanding of modern thought that we turn next to it and to its affiliate, antistatism.

chapter 29

Anarchism and Antistatism: Evolution and Doctrines

Although the term "anarchism" is of modern coinage, the central anarchist attitude has been upheld at many points in the history of political thought. Thus Lao-tze (sixth century B.C.), if not an anarchist, was very close to being one.[1] Some of the early Cynics approximated the position. And during the Middle Ages, the more revolutionary interpretations of such movements as the Joachimites and the Spiritual Franciscans had close affinities. In an earlier chapter,[2] we have pointed out that the primitive Anabaptists, although difficult to interpret from the viewpoint of social doctrine, sometimes expressed positions antagonistic to political authority.

But the history of modern anarchist theory and politics is in a sense a rather distinctive chapter. It is only since the eighteenth century that anarchism and antistatism (which we might identify with a kind of near-anarchism) have become self-conscious, developed more or less unique schools of thought, and became relatively important factors in some segments of practical politics. Perhaps this has been in part a reaction to the ubiquity of the national state as a factor in all aspects of life, to the imperatives of industrialism which seem to press for more and more coordination and hence political authority, to the impersonalism so characteristic of industrial culture, and to a mass violence which in the modern age has often become endemic.

In general, anarchism (*an:* without, *archy:* authority) rejects authority and particularly political authority; antistatism, while it may be less clear in its position than anarchism proper, moves in the same general direction.

1. On Lao-tze's political conceptions, see William Pott, *Chinese Political Philosophy*, New York: Knopf, 1925.
2. See Chapter 17.

Modern anarchism originated in the same social and intellectual climate that gave birth to early liberalism. The philosophy of Locke, at least in some of its aspects, was an important ingredient, as was the Enlightenment attitude of the eighteenth century. Locke's theory contributed the argument that man is shaped by the environment; and the Enlightenment, building partly on Locke, furnished the general spirit of optimism about human nature that is an essential ingredient of much anarchism. There was, of course, an anarchist strain in some of the French revolutionary thinkers, although it did not become central.

It was the nineteenth century, however, which constituted the real seedbed for anarchist thought and politics. The Romantic movement in literature was sometimes fertile ground, as with Percy Bysshe Shelley.[3] In the United States, the romantic current present in some versions of Transcendentalism was on occasion associated with a near-anarchist position, as with Emerson and to a still greater degree with Thoreau.

The reaction to the centralism and militarism of the French Revolution laid the groundwork for an important segment of nineteenth-century antistatist thought, for from one point of view men had clamored for "liberty, equality, and fraternity," only to find themselves enchained far more than under the old regime to a highly centralized state.

Meanwhile, a fundamental division within anarchists themselves began to be dramatized. This rift developed because one school of thought moved in the direction of an absolute individualism, akin in some respects to primitive utilitarian liberalism, whereas the other centered more on the possibilities of communal cooperation. Opposing the individualists in the nineteenth century were the communist anarchists. In many respects close to the Marxists, they nevertheless differed sharply with the latter about the role of the state in social evolution.

During the years between 1880 and 1914, the very term anarchism came to be associated in many minds over a large part of the world with crimes of violence. The Haymarket riots of 1886 in the United States led to the conviction and killing by the state of several anarchists. The language of Johann Most, a German revolutionist who had taken up residence in the United States, seemed to corroborate the connection of the outlook with violence—despite the fact that Most had never committed an act of violence himself. So widespread did the identification with violence become that many cursory observers of politics came to suspect anarchists whenever political violence broke out. The statutes of the United States began to reflect this opinion, American immigration and naturalization laws, for example, more or less assuming that all anarchists must be violent conspirators.

In many instances, however, professed anarchists knew very little about the political crimes committed, which were sometimes the work of mentally unbalanced persons only vaguely familiar with the political philosophy of anarchism. Most anarchists, as a matter of fact, did not espouse violence as an ordinary political technique.

The heyday of modern anarchism was the generation immediately before World War I. It was in this epoch that its major lines of argument were developed and that social and political conditions were most favorable for its growth. It was in this period, too, that quasi-anarchist or antistatist views, such as those reflected in anarchosyndicalism and in the political outlook of Tolstoy, were established.

World War I and its immediate aftermath witnessed a decline in both anarchism and anarchosyndicalism, although the politics of pacifist antistatism developed more fully. We can perhaps explain the general decline of anarchism and anarchosyndicalism in terms of the greater drawing power of a better organized socialism and of the hope that the Bolshevik Revolution of 1917 might achieve anarchist goals—a hope which was, of course, to be quickly shattered.[4] Pacifist antistatism, as with Gandhi's conceptions in India, represented a

3. While Shelley was no systematic political thinker, the anarchist implications of his poetry are obvious, whether in *Queen Mab* or in *The Mask of Anarchy*.
4. The American anarchist Emma Goldman was one of the first to be completely disillusioned by Leninist communism—long before most Western liberals became critical. See her *My Disillusionment in Russia*, New York: Doubleday, Page, 1923 and *My Further Disillusionment in Russia*, Garden City: Doubleday, 1924.

note of antiindustrialism as well as antiimperialism in a so-called underdeveloped region of the world.

In the politics of Spain, anarchism continued to play a large role through the period of the great civil war (1936–1938) but after the triumph of Franco, although it was still relatively strong, it had to go underground.

After World War II, there appeared to be some recrudescence of anarchist thought. Disillusionment with the state and the war was undoubtedly a factor, as was suspicion of old socialist and liberal panaceas. Even in the United States, such notable journals as *Politics* espoused an anarchist point of view. And the pacifist antistatism of Gandhi, at least in some of its facets, aroused a new interest. Antistatism in general represented a fundamental revulsion against totalitarian tendencies of twentieth-century politics and thought.

One problem of anarchist and antistatist thought from the very beginning has been that there is such a variety of interpretations. To spell out these divergencies fully entails a breakdown into the several schools of thought which have evolved during the nineteenth and twentieth centuries.

For convenience, we may divide our treatment into classical anarchism, antistatism, and recent currents in anarchism and antistatism. Chronologically, classical anarchism evolves between the end of the eighteenth century and World War I; antistatism is typically an expression of the twentieth century; and by recent currents we suggest illustrations of anarchist and antistatist thought in the period since World War II. The three divisions, of course, overlap and are closely interrelated both to one another and to other major streams of political thought since the French Revolution.

Classical Anarchism

The major currents of classical anarchist thought are the individualist, the mutualist-federalist, and the communist. In their development through the nineteenth century, the foundations are laid for typical classical anarchist positions since World War I.

Individualist Anarchism. Locke's philosophy, as we have seen, exerted a profound influence on many currents of thought throughout the eighteenth century. It is to his inspiration that we owe the foundations of individualist anarchism; for William Godwin (1756–1836) argued in his great treatise *Political Justice* (1793) that if, as Locke said, men are blank slates at birth, then enlightenment and a radical alteration of political institutions might literally reshape the whole nature of man.[5]

Writing in reply to Burke's *Reflections on the Revolution in France*, Godwin defended the revolutionary impulse but made the basis of his political view utilitarianism rather than natural rights or the social contract. Men can become so enlightened that they can learn what their obligations are at any given moment in time: They will be guided only by their understanding of what they owe to men and will prefer the virtuous to the unvirtuous. They must repudiate all promises, for to contract to perform an act in the future limits my ability to act at the time in the interests of utility and my own view of duty. To promise to obey even the baton of an orchestra conductor is to Godwin a species of wickedness.

When men fully understand that they are potentially free and enlightened, each will pursue the right as he sees it and the separate quests for righteousness will not lead to conflict—for there is a universal norm which each can discover for himself. Once this norm is understood, political rule will decline and disappear, its final stages taking the form of highly decentralized assemblies and juries. War will vanish as men learn to be frank and open in their dealings with one another. Each will see that he is entitled only to the goods of the earth absolutely necessary for his own support; and if perchance he comes into possession of more than this, he will give it away. There will thus not be a communism of material goods but rather a highly developed personal Calvinist-like trusteeship acting in accordance with the universal standard of righteousness which each can discover.

Godwin envisions the state collapsing, then, as men become enlightened. And there is almost a limitless progress in store. With the arbitrary restraints of law and political institutions removed (without violence), man's imaginative capacities will have full reign and he can eventually become literally immortal. Tyrants can no longer tyrannize, since the obedience of their potential subjects will have been withdrawn. In the end, opinion, not force, will be seen to be the most powerful factor in political affairs.

Godwin, of course, had an immense influence on his son-in-law Percy Shelley, much of whose poetry reflects individualist anarchist views. The individual rises above the trammels of political subjection and comes into his own. And in the *Masque of Anarchy*, written after the Peterloo massacre of 1819, Shelley envisions a situation where, through nonviolent noncooperation, unarmed masses undercut the authority of government and bring about revolution.

After Shelley, individualist anarchism is sometimes severed from Godwin's norm of general happiness. The individual still pursues emancipation from the state and all institutions but seems no longer to seek for a universal standard, which itself is regarded as slavery. This view is perhaps best illustrated in Max Stirner (1806–1856). Born Johann Caspar Schmidt, he was a meek and mild mannered teacher in a Berlin academy for young women and his only significant work, *The Ego and His Own,* published in 1843, achieved little notoriety during the author's lifetime.[6] It was only later in the century, when anarchism became associated with violent deeds, that the book was resurrected as a kind of textbook for one kind of anarchist doctrine.

In a sense, Stirner carries nineteenth-century individualist views to their logical end—to goals which even the most radical liberals would have repudiated. The egoist, in his view, is the man who has been released from a sense of obligation to any social entities, and, above all, the state. All association is suspect, as with Godwin, for whether it takes the compulsory form of the state or the voluntary expression so exalted by some anarchists, it inhibits free expression of the "I." Stirner even commiserates with ruling classes: They are bound by their obligations to the state and their freedom is in many respects even more restricted than that of their subjects. The only union which Stirner's doctrine will admit is that in which the force of each ego utilizes other egos for its own ends without sacrificing any sense of its own "I-ness." All society is purely slavery, if one takes Stirner literally. Individual "power" confers egoistic "right," as the term is defined by the German thinker.[7]

Stirner conceives the basic problem to be one of the ego imposing its own slavery by accepting thought systems as well as schemes of law and order which trammel it. I am, so to speak, forced by myself to bow the knee when I imprison myself in orderings of logic and commitments to ideals no less than when I swear allegiance to a prince.

In the United States, perhaps the ablest exponent of individualist anarchism was Benjamin R. Tucker (1854–1939).[8] Like Stirner, although with far less violent overtones, Tucker holds individual pleasure, egoistically conceived, to be the supreme desideratum. But unlike Stirner, he thinks of contractual devices in a very loose sense as providing a substitute for political institutions. Presumably the building of the contractual society is accomplished by men concerned for their own egos, of course, and apparently the only sanction is to be a consciousness that if the contract is not met, the ego will suffer. Nevertheless, it will be noted that Tucker does not follow Godwin in repudiation of promises.

Tucker's teaching on property institutions is that the individual pleasure can be expressed in terms of possessions. There is no limitation on them other than the restrictions imposed by the individual's own power and his concern for his ego. Apparently, too, Tucker would affirm the prerogative of group ownership, but only within the limitations of his egoism and strict contractualist views. There is something very much akin to Herbert Spencer's conceptions in Tucker, although without the latter's elaborate sociology and philosophy of history.

The difficulty of classifying anarchist thought is illustrated emphatically when we turn to Tucker's conception of the means of social change. Like Stirner, he is dubious about revolutionary methods in the orthodox sense; for they imply subordination of the individual and an implicit if not explicit endorsement of the state. Nor can he embrace the optimistic creed of thinkers like Godwin, who appear to assume a gradual transformation of institutions in the anarchist direction. And he obviously

5. On Godwin's life and political theories, see Ford K. Brown, *Life of William Godwin,* New York: E. P. Dutton, 1926 and George Woodcock, *William Godwin,* London: Porcupine Press, 1946.
6. For an English translation, see *The Ego and His Own,* B. R. Tucker, trans., New York: Boni and Liveright, 1907.
7. *Ibid.,* 247.
8. Much of Tucker's thought is reflected in *Individual Liberty,* New York: Vanguard, 1926, a collection of the essays which had appeared under his name over a long period of time. See also his *Instead of a Book,* New York: B. R. Tucker, 1893.

rejects orthodox legislative methods. In certain respects, and rather surprisingly considering his premises, he appears to argue that the best hope lies in revolutionary breaches of the law carried on without violence. Thus he praises the Russian Revolution of 1905, which he considers as having taken place largely without violence and in a spirit calculated to break the fetters of political institutions permanently.[9]

There is in the general position of individualist anarchism one of the most radical of all critiques of modern politics. Unlike early nineteenth-century liberals, whom they apparently resemble so much, individualist anarchists can hardly be said to be rationalizing bourgeois property institutions. In the last analysis, too, liberals had an enormous confidence in the state insofar as they relied on it to enforce the contracts which in their model would constitute the binding ties of the developing industrial society. But individualist anarchists either repudiate contracts altogether, as with Godwin and Stirner, or, with Tucker, refuse to confide in any state for their implementation. And by contrast with most mutualist and communist anarchists, the individualists appear to recognize what Nicholas Berdyaev calls the slavery of any society, whether of the state or of allegedly "voluntary association."[10]

Mutualist or Federalist Anarchism. The history of mutual or federalist anarchism is largely the story of Pierre Joseph Proudhon and his enormous influence, both positive and negative, on the nineteenth century.

The career of Proudhon illustrates many of the curious contradictions characteristic of the doctrine which he taught. Born in 1809, in Besancon, eastern France, his life spans the period between the onset of reaction to the Great Revolution and the beginning of the decline of Napoleon III. In his mature years, he was involved in the Revoluion of 1848 and even sat in parliament, contrary to his principles.

He came to his anarchist views after he learned that his brother had been killed while in military training. This made a profound impression on him: The state, he thought, had taken advantage of his brother's poverty and had in effect slain him. He thus became disillusioned with the centralized state structure—which was so much a product of the French Revolution itself.

During the course of his residence in Paris in the forties, Proudhon became acquainted with the young Karl Marx and with another of the great nineteenth-century anarchists, Mikhail Bakunin. Proudhon carried on long discussions with both men and it was perhaps these personal interchanges which left such a deep impression on Marx; for while Proudhon and Marx were to become political enemies, there is no doubt about the French writer's influence on the great nineteenth century communist.

It was in 1846 that Proudhon published his book on poverty.[11] Marx was incensed by the work, partly because he believed that Proudhon had misinterpreted Hegel. His *Poverty of Philosophy* attacked Proudhon in terms which many deemed unfair. Proudhon, in turn, was stung by Marx's vitriol and is said to have called the German "the tapeworm of socialism."

Proudhon's life was characterized by many clashes with the law, as in 1858, when he was sentenced to three years in prison for publishing his critical study on the church.[12] Earlier, he had attacked Louis Napoleon and fled to Belgium to escape prosecution.

In 1863, he published one of his most significant political theory volumes, in which he outlined his federalist principles.[13] And by the time of his death in 1865 he had managed to complete another important treatise, on the political consciousness of the laboring classes.[14]

Although in many respects he is the heir of eighteenth-century optimism and believes in the perfectibility of man, Proudhon emphasizes that perfectibility does not mean that mankind will ever be perfect. Human beings are capable of impartial concern for justice, but also have enormous potentialities for injustice. The conflict between the thrust to injustice and possibilities for justice simply mirrors a general universe in which gigantic cosmic forces are forever contending with one another. Like the ancient Heraclitus, Proudhon sees no One behind the Many. Instead, struggle and change appear to underlie both cosmic and sociopolitical life.

Justice, he holds, is "respect, spontaneously felt and mutually guaranteed, for human dignity, in whatever person and under whatever circumstances we find it compromised, and to whatever risk its defense may expose us." Because he rejects justice as transcendent just as he repudiates the notion of a God, he comes to conceive of just principles as arising out of the mutual conflict between alternative notions of justice. The interaction of human wills and conceptions, Hegel-like, eliminates the false principles and discovers the true foundations. Justice tends to be identified with equality.

Like Marx, he stresses the importance of eliminating economic barriers which stand in the way of justice as equality. The great bar to justice is property, which destroys spontaneity and is, in Proudhon's startling expression, robbery.

But when he associates property with theft, he does not mean, as some of his more superficial critics imagine, that all private ownership of material goods is to be eliminated. On the contrary, his constant appeal is from property, as he defines it, to "possession." Property is connected with seizure of surplus value by the owning class, which is supported by the state. As he looks about him in the France of the July Monarchy and of the second Empire, Proudhon sees the whole structure of law and bureaucracy sustaining property, in this sense, by sheer force.

The task of the revolutionist, he thinks, is to restore possession while eliminating property. He appears to have a kind of unmodified Lockean conception of things when he argues that for dignity of personality, every man must be able to control his own dwelling and the land and tools he needs for his work. He can then maintain his family in what Proudhon calls poverty—that is, in fundamental necessities of life with a few modest luxuries.

The goal which Proudhon generally espouses is a society of many independent producers, each in possession of his own tools of work and beholden neither to landlords—who would be nonexistent—nor to industrial entrepreneurs.

But he is not unaware of the rise of industry. His experience in the relatively advanced industrial city of Lyons forced him to take account of it, even had he been unconscious of it before. In the end, then, he does allow for limited industry. Because individual ownership of tools would be impossible, as machines become more complex, some kind of collective possession would seem to be essential. Hence Proudhon modifies his general pattern sufficiently to allow for common ownership of tools by all those who work within a particular industry.

Given his society of small producers' units (whether individual or collective), how would relations between them be regulated? Proudhon's answer is "by contract." Each unit will provide what it can best produce and exchanges of products will be arranged by mutually satisfactory agreements. In fact, the only general norm allowable is that "contracts must be lived up to." Here we note in Proudhon a very warm tribute to the allegedly bourgeois respect for contracts. If we ask him what is to prevent some units from taking advantage of their superior strength to contract with weaker ones for the latter's absorption, his answer is that a kind of balance of power between and among units will prevent such an eventuality.

Obviously, in a scheme of this kind, which pushes contractualism to the nth degree—and hence, from this point of view is to be sharply distinguished from the anarchism of Godwin and Stirner—there can be little if any room for the state. "Government of man by man is slavery," as Proudhon puts it.[15] Authority would seem to be in inverse ratio to the level of intellectual development which a society has attained. The existence of the state implies vertical regulation of various kinds, rather than the horizontal contractualism suggested by Proudhon's mutualism. The state is the great defender of property and the destroyer of possession.

Nor is Proudhon much impressed by the distinction traditionally made between forms of government. In his day, of course, the devotees of progress look to democracy as the scheme which will carry out Rousseau's dream of a reconciliation between freedom and belonging. Not so, argues Proudhon. Democracy

9. *Individual Liberty*, 78–79.
10. See Nicholas Berdyaev, *Slavery and Freedom*, London: G. Bles, The Centenary Press, 1943. See also his *The Realm of Spirit and the Realm of Caesar*, Donald A. Lowrie, trans., London: Gollancz, 1952.
11. *La Philosophie de la Pauvreté*, in *Oeuvres Complètes*, C. Bouglé and H. Moysset, eds., Paris: M. Rivierre, 1923–52.
12. *De la Justice dans la Revolution et dans l'Eglise*, Paris: Garnier freres, 1858.
13. *Du Principe Federatif et de la Necessite de Reconstituer le Parti de la Revolution*, Paris: E. Dentu, 1863.
14. *De la Capacite Politique des Classes Ouvrieres*, 2nd ed., Paris: 1865.
15. Quoted by Paul Eltzbacher, *Anarchism*, New York: B. R. Tucker, 1908, p. 47.

can only lead to exaltation of the state and to the destruction of all those tendencies to mutualism which he desires to implement. The state, whether democratic or not, is always subjugating the individual and thus compounds the evil wrought by property. By voting, the individual effectively surrenders his sovereignty. By abstaining, he retains it. And Proudhon implies that the road to anarchism is to be paved in part through the development of mass conscientious abstention from the political act of casting a ballot.

For the state, Proudhon would substitute federalism, which seems to imply mutualism extended into the realm of over-all regulation. Instead of being managed bureaucratically or vertically, general (what are now called political) concerns would come under the contractual principle.

His differences from many other anarchists center on his great respect for contract and his stress on family life. Anarchists stemming from the Godwinian tradition would indubitably repudiate the former, arguing that it substitutes for the vertical controls of the state the equally onerous, if self-imposed, promises of a different character. I ought not to be bound, the Godwinian would maintain, by my previous promises but only by what is right according to my best insights of the moment. But Proudhon's scheme makes contract central. As for the family, it is the nurturing ground for personal autonomy—or self-government—wtihout which an anarchist society is impossible.

But he shares with other anarchists a vigorous disapproval of one of the central characteristics of nineteenth-century politics—nationalism. Seeing in "authoritarian nationalism" a denial of all the values of "justice," he views the nation-state of the previous four hundred years as one of the central factors inhibiting the growth of the spontaneous life.

Achievement of the anarchist society is to Proudhon the task of revolution. But he is wary of following the Jacobins in their interpretation of its meaning: They went wrong, he believes, in attempting to utilize political methods such as universal suffrage. The radical transformation of society cannot be wrought by means which are essentially tied to the present order of things.

Nor can basic change be achieved by war or institutionalized violence of any kind.[16] He thinks that a major task of nineteenth-century revolution is the elimination of militarism, which is so closely associated with the nation-state. War fastens the chains of the nation-state even more firmly and prevents the emancipation of man. To be sure, Proudhon does sanction spontaneous violence, both to dramatize the cause of anarchism before the revolution and to redress imbalances of power after it. But he would make a sharp distinction between the highly organized mechanical violence of the state and the violent demonstrations which might help promote working-class solidarity and thus prepare the way for the anarchist revolution. Then, too, although he believes that the general balance of power would on the whole continue to be maintained under federalism and mutualism, it might still be necessary occasionally to resort to violent demonstrations lest any one constituent unit become too powerful.

Proudhon is important in the history of anarchist thought because of his enormous influence not only on anarchists of all schools but also on the intellectual life of even his opponents. Thus the communist anarchists drew inspiration from his writings, as did the Marxists. Even where other anarchists departed from his analysis, they acknowledged their debt to him.

Communist Anarchism. Mutualist-federalist anarchism was in many respects the philosophy of those who were dubious about industrialism, recognizing that if one accepted it wholeheartedly one was driven in the direction of state centralization. Communist anarchism, by contrast, purported to be able to reconcile industrialism with anarchism. Federalist anarchism, in its dubiety about complex division of labor, may be said to be primitivist in nature; communist anarchism, by contrast, is progressive, in the sense that it shares much of the assurance of nineteenth-century liberalism and Marxism about the supposedly beneficent effects of industrial progress.

Two thinkers stand out as formulators of communist anarchist doctrine—Mikhail Bakunin (1814–1876), characterized by G. D. H. Cole as "if not the founder of modern anarchism at least its outstanding leader when it was first shaping itself into . . . [a] movement,"[17] and Peter Kropotkin (1842–1921). Taken together, their lives span more than a century and exemplify the development of communist anarchism from a period of relatively close, though tense, association with Marxism, to a sharp break with the followers of Marx.

Bakunin came from a family of Russian

landed proprietors and very early was influenced by Hegel, Ludwig Feuerbach, Wilhelm Weitling, and, of course, Proudhon. The revolutionary events of 1848 moved Bakunin as they did so many other radicals, yet at this time he was something of a pan-Slavist, thinking that the Slavic races were destined to lead a movement toward universal human emancipation. For some twelve years—1849 to 1861—Bakunin spent his life in prisons and Siberia. Once released, he became the center of conspiratorial activities in many parts of the world. For a time, he seemed to come under the spell of the Russian nihilist movement, and particularly of Sergei Nechayev (1847–1882), whose *Principles of Revolution* appeared to advocate violence and terror as ends in themselves.[18] Although scholars are still debating Bakunin's precise relation to Nechayev, there can be no doubt that Bakunin during his middle years was the inspiration for many riots having ostensibly political ends.

The best-known episode in Bakunin's political development is, perhaps, his great struggle with Marx over control of the International Workingmen's Association. Eventually, as we have suggested earlier, Marx's followers managed to move the Association headquarters to Philadelphia and thus effectively kill it; for they feared that if it remained in Europe, Bakuninists would obtain permanent control. The center of the Bakuninist-Marxist debate was the great anarchist's insistence on decentralist principles against the centralizing tendencies of the Marxists.

Any attempt to summarize Bakunin's political ideas is subject to the danger that they may be overly simplified and made to look more consistent than they actually are. Thus modern Bakuninists like Maximoff[19] seem to edit Bakunin in such a way as to remove the paradoxes and contradictions which undoubtedly exist in his thought. Bakunin is not so much a systematic thinker as he is a propounder of scattered notions which have been profoundly influential.

As, in many respects, a child of the eighteenth century, Bakunin admires the primitivist phases of Rousseau even while repudiating his statist aspects. He builds, too, on what he conceives to be Darwinian propositions. Man is an animal who throughout most of his history has submitted to such institutions as the state and such authorities as God primarily because of fear. Knowledge, however, and particularly the understanding of evolution—which Bakunin interprets as a combination of Hegelian and Darwinian struggle—can, and, indeed, will emancipate man.

The state has been inevitable, for it is the reflection of all man's fears. Each man guards his own existence and the strongest impose the state in order to dominate others and thus presumably to provide for their own security. Whatever its particular form, then, the state partly represents the quest for domination, which is itself the product of anxiety. The so-called wickedness of man, which conservatives and liberals claim justifies the state, is itself largely the product of illusions which have been fostered by class-dominated cultures. Anarchism, by calling upon men to rebel against all authority, seeks to free them from these illusions and to call forth their potential ability to cooperate spontaneously.

In his more positive proposals, Bakunin links together atheism and anarchism. Idolization of the state is considered an expression of belief in the authority of God, which is the reflection of ignorance as well as fear. God, in some sense, is a projection of the authority of the state. Thus if a truly anarchist world is to come into being, religious practices and political institutions must be bracketed together as objects of repudiation.

Like most communists, Bakunin is loath to spell out the details of a free society; for spontaneity cannot be imprisoned within set forms. He does suggest—and here he follows Proudhon—that the principle will be federative. The basic unit will be the small neighborhood group, which might be either geographical or functional (economic, intellectual, artistic). These small associations would apparently be bound to one another very loosely at the level of national cultural committees and these in turn would cooperate with similar associations throughout the world. The state and law

16. For his attitude to war and military institutions, see his *War and Peace*, New York: Harper & Bros., 1886.
17. G. D. H. Cole, *History of Socialist Thought*, London: Macmillan, 1953–1960, v. 2, p. 213.
18. The early twentieth-century anarchist Paul Elzbacher agrees with this judgment. See his *Anarchism*, ch. 6.
19. See G. P. Maximoff, ed., *The Political Philosophy of Bakunin*, New York: Free Press, 1953.

would give way to norms expressed by a kind of spontaneous general will.

Unlike Proudhon, Bakunin leaves little room for private property: The principal modes of production, land, and the distributive machinery will be collectively owned.

He has an amazing faith that spontaneous activity by workers and peasants can undercut state authority. In this work, violence will necessarily play a part. Students of Bakunin have debated for many years whether he really advocates wholesale extermination such as is reflected in the words of the *Principles of Revolution:* "We recognize no other activity but the work of extermination, but we admit that the forms in which this activity will show itself will be extremely varied—poison, the knife, the rope, etc." On the whole, it would seem, Bakunin himself—as contrasted with Nechayev, the main author of *The Principles*—does not go this far, although some passages in his writings appear to refute this.[20]

He attacks the beliefs of the Marxists that before the state withers away, it must first be conquered and used. For revolutionists to utilize the state, he argues, is to corrupt themselves; since there is no reason to assume that they, any more than others, will surrender state authority voluntarily.[21]

Like Bakunin, Kropotkin sprang from the Russian landed aristocracy. Spending his early life in Siberia, he became a student of biology and was impressed by the role of cooperation in the evolution of life. While many social Darwinists were suggesting that nature is "red in tooth and claw," Kropotkin was arguing that cooperation within species was far more significant than competition.

Very early he began to revolt against authority, perhaps because of his experiences with the military in Siberia. Military authority is almost always the most pernicious form of rule, as many anarchists have discovered. Also playing a vital role in Kropotkin's development were the nihilists, with whom he became acquainted during his residence in St. Petersburg. The term itself had been coined by Ivan Turgenev in his great novel *Fathers and Sons* (1862), where it was stated that "A Nihilist is a man who submits to no authority, who accepts not a single principle on faith merely, however high such a principle stands in the eyes of men." Alexander Herzen, the famous Russian liberal exile, had characterized Nihilism as a doctrine which advocated "the most complete freedom—nihilism is science without dogmas . . . a rejection of metaphysics, a denial of absolute morality, a relativism of principle . . . it is a philosophy of despair, hopelessness and disbelief."[22]

Kropotkin was tempted by a brilliant career in science but chose instead to work for political emancipation, which sometimes involved his own imprisonment and later his exile in England. After the Russian Revolution of 1917, he returned to the Soviet Union but was soon disillusioned by Leninism and died a despairing man.

Kropotkin is undoubtedly the most learned and cultured of all the classical anarchists. He was widely read and drew upon a vast array of thinkers for his views. Like Herbert Spencer and Bakunin, he was profoundly influenced by doctrines of biological evolution. But his was a much more sophisticated version of communist anarchism than that of Bakunin.

The central proposition of Kropotkin's political philosophy is that solidarity and mutual aid have been as important in animal and human evolution as competition—indeed, even more so. Species are preserved and extended not primarily by conflict within themselves but rather by cooperation in the effort to adapt to the demands of nature.[23] Although sub-human creatures cannot be assumed to reason, they know through a native tendency implanted within them that certain kinds of conduct enhance the species' life, while other actions may be expected to inhibit it. Individuality itself is sacrificed to this end. Even in human societies, corrupted as they are by the rise of the state, there are innumerable evidences that thousands of men know mutual aid to be best for this goal.[24] There is a natural feeling of sympathy within the breast of every man for other men and women and this becomes the basis upon which a sound theory of society must be bottomed.

Like so many social Darwinists, he seems to think that norms for ethical and political life can somehow be derived from statements about the way in which biological evolution took place.

He does not, to be sure, confine himself to prehuman evolution. Against Hobbists and competitive Darwinists, he argues that men began their existence in relatively large bands of cooperating beings,[25] and not in isolated families. Communal marriages, for instance, were not uncommon among primitive groups.

Referring to the history of civilization, he instances the medieval city as an example of a way of life based on near-anarchist principles. Before its degeneracy set in, the medieval urban community was a complex of freely cooperating men and women who in their guilds and other corporate groupings had little need for the state or the mechanisms of law. Under such circumstances, men were judged for infractions of common standards by fellow-beings who knew them well rather than by remote and impersonal devices. Thus, Kropotkin implies, something analogous to an enlarged family ethic existed. All this was changed with the beginning of sharp separation socially between well-established families; the development of Roman law, with its rigid and remote impersonalism; the increasing influence of the centralized church; and finally the development of the state, which absorbed spontaneous social life and tended to destroy the well-springs of creativity in the medieval city.[26]

One of the most fascinating aspects of Kropotkin's analysis is his account of the ways in which state life is related to modern individualism and the absence of a sense of social obligation. At first it might seem that the claims of the centralized state would be antagonistic to the individualistic spirit. But Kropotkin makes a sharp distinction between the development of vertical obligations to the state, which are sanctioned by the legal and impersonal mechanisms of bureaucracy, and the feeling of horizontal obligation that existed before the state began its conquest of autonomous civic life. Thus the good citizen in the modern state pays his taxes and feels no sense of responsibility for his fellow human beings; for with his fulfillment of political obligations, he tends to think that all responsibilities have been met.[27] Individualism and state power thus go hand in hand.

Like most anarchists, he hesitates to develop a blueprint for release from what he calls the "triple alliance" of the military chief, the Roman judge, and the priest.[28] But there are certain guidelines which the anarchist can suggest for the revolutionized system of human relations.[29] The means of production, which have been developed during the course of centuries by all humanity, must belong to the human race as a whole. Inequality and private property can have no place in an anarchist society. Administration and control of means of production will be vested in associations or communes of producers.

All goods thus produced would be placed in a common pool, from which men would draw in accordance with need. In suggesting this free distribution of goods and services, Kropotkin is obviously simply extending vastly what already exists: most modern states distribute parks and police and fire services without charge; Kropotkin is saying that bread, housing, and eventually every good and service would be allocated in the same way. Thus slavery to the false values of money would be abolished, as would the whole wages system which is part of it. Kropotkin stresses that in an anarchist society, mental and physical work will and can be combined, so that the tendency in capitalist society for laborers by hand to be separated from workers by brain will be over-

20. For a not unsympathetic treatment of this aspect of Bakunin's belief system, see George Woodcock, *Anarchism*, Cleveland: Meridian Books, 1962, pp. 172–175.
21. For Bakunin's political philosophy in general, see Maximoff, *op. cit.;* E. H. Carr, *Michael Bakunin*, London: Macmillan, 1937; Alexander Herzen, *My Past and Thoughts*, 6 vols., London: Chatto and Windus, 1924–47, vol. 5; Woodcock, *op. cit.;* Elzbacher, *op. cit.;* E. Pyziur, *The Doctrines of Anarchism of M. A. Bakunin*, Milwaukee: Marquette University Press, 1955; Samuel Rezneck, "The Political and Social Theory of M. Bakunin," *American Political Science Review*, May 1927; and Eric Voegelin, "Bakunin's Confessions," *Journal of Politics*, February 1946. Bakunin's own major political work is *God and the State*, New York: Mother Earth, 1916, or volume 1 of *Oeuvres*, Paris: P. V. Stock, 1895–1913.
22. See Vasilii V. Zenkovsky, *History of Russian Philosophy*, 2 vols., George L. Kline, trans., New York: Columbia University Press, 1953, vol. 2, p. 296.
23. See, for example, his *Anarchist Morality*, London: 1890. *Freedom* Pamphlets, No. 6, n.d.
24. Peter Kropotkin, *Mutual Aid: A Factor in Evolution*, London: Heinemann, 1902.
25. *Ibid.*, 79.
26. *Ibid.*, pp. 218 ff. In many respects, Kropotkin's account of the medieval city is corroborated by the well-known Belgian historian Henri Pirenne in his *Medieval Cities*, New York: Doubleday, 1956. See also Kropotkin, *The State: Its Historic Role*, London: 1903, p. 25 (New Printing, London: Freedom Press, 1943).
27. *Mutual Aid*, *op. cit.*, pp. 223 ff.
28. *The State*, *op. cit.*, p. 25.
29. In *The Conquest of Bread*, London: Chapman and Hale, 1906 (also New York: Vanguard, 1926), Kropotkin develops most fully his conception of the anarchist society.

come. For the mental health of any given person, both manual and intellectual labor must be seen as essential.[30]

Like so many anarchists, he embraces a kind of mystique of revolution. On the one hand, change obeys certain laws of social evolution which appear to be beyond individual control. On the other hand, the workers and self-conscious minorities which arouse them can do much to hasten and ensure success. Education is important and, in general, Kropotkin thinks that the revolution will come about nonviolently. Although he once supported a resolution of an anarchist congress that endorsed the necessity of violence, as he grew older he very much doubted that mass violence could be reconciled with the achievement of anarchist goals. Actually, it appears, resort to violence would largely be ruled out if one accepts Kropotkin's premises about the cooperative nature of man. This is particularly true if one adopts the view, apparently characteristic of Kropotkin, that the state is built on violence: Utilization of violence by anarchists, it might be argued, would simply set in motion new state-like tendencies. Kropotkin, however, is not always consistent; and it remained for the antistatist doctrines of Gandhi to work out a more nearly complete theory of nonviolence.

Communist anarchism was the most influential version of anarchist theory. Many of the "propagandists of the deed", who resorted to assassinations at the turn of the century, claimed to be disciples of Bakunin, even though a large proportion had perhaps not even read him.[31] The very powerful anarchist movement of Spain tended to be explicitly Bakuninist and became a large factor in practical politics both before and after the overthrow of Alfonso XIII in 1931.[32] In fact, Bakuninist anarchism and orthodox Marxism emerged as the most influential movements in Spanish politics. Even under Franco, the underground anarchist movement remained significant.

As for anarchism in the United States, while some of it stemmed from native anarchists like Josiah Warren (1798–1874) and Benjamin Tucker, the mainstream has been Bakuninite or Kropotkinite, with the former tending to give way to the latter. Perhaps the two most influential American anarchists in the twentieth century were Emma Goldman (1869–1940)[33] and Alexander Berkman (1870–1936).[34] Both began as disciples of Bakunin but in the latter part of their lives embraced views more nearly resembling those of Kropotkin.

The appeal of communist anarchism lay perhaps in its communist goal combined with its repudiation of the state as means. Marx had seemed to suggest goals similar to those of Kropotkin but, in embracing the state and "political" methods, had led many to believe that his means contradicted his ends. In its rather rigid repudiation of state and political methods, communist anarchism appeared, in some measure, to correct Marx; and during the controversies turning on the meaning of Marxism in mid-twentieth century, many have pointed to Bakunin and Kropotkin as being more nearly correct than Marx. The rise of totalitarianism—whether of the right or the left—has seemed to vindicate a Bakuninite-Kropotkinite position.

Modern Antistatism

In the development of modern political ideas, several schools of thought have been antistatist without necessarily avowing themselves anarchist. There was, of course, an antistatist thread in early modern liberalism, which, as we have seen, seemed to believe that a large segment of life could be ordered through automatic processes and without collective deliberation.

Here we illustrate the form of antistatism closely associated with anarchism in terms of anarchosyndicalism and Gandhian pacifism.

Anarchosyndicalism. Anarchosyndicalism was a movement in political thought and practical politics which reached its heyday in France in the decade just before World War I and in the United States during the period between 1914 and the middle twenties.

If any one figure can be said to be the philosopher of French anarchosyndicalism it is that of Georges Sorel (1847–1922). An engineer, Sorel was long interested in the problems of society and during the latter part of his life was particularly influenced by the philosophy of Henri Bergson (1859–1941). Bergson's theory represented a revolt against evolution interpreted in a mechanistic way and an effort to discover the holistic elements in the evolutionary process. In his formulation, he sees social and political development—and, indeed, all organic growth—as directed by a vital force or *elan vital* which is more than the sum total of all possible physiological, social, and psychological elements that go to make up the organism. It is the kind of whole which shapes the parts—somewhat as in certain aesthetic theories the whole of a painting is said to shape the parts composed of particular lines or combinations of colors.[35] A similar position was worked out later by the South African philosopher Jan Christiaan Smuts (1870–1950).[36]

At the turn of the century, then, Sorel was meditating on conceptions of this kind and the fruits of his reflections were embodied in what became a kind of classic for anarchosyndicalist revolutionaries, *Reflections on Violence* (1906).[37] Throughout the argument, couched often in difficult and obscure language, runs the theme of "will" and "emotion" giving us more profound clues to human character and potentialities than reason. Socially and politically, the implication is that men, and particularly revolutionaries, can be moved to action only by great myths which transcend rational formulation and, like Bergson's *elan vital*, direct the course of change.

In the development of his theme Sorel has much to say of violence. But when he uses the term, it is to be interpreted much differently from our usual language. Violence for him means the struggle of men to overcome the stasis or static condition which tends to capture them in ordinary civilized bourgeois life. Struggle and change are imperatives if the vital force of human evolution is to possess men. But what evokes this violence? Only complete devotion to a myth which lies beyond reason, he thinks. During the early ages of Christianity, this galvanizing force for Christians was the belief in the Second Coming of Christ: This impressed itself upon all their actions and made them heroes and martyrs.

What, then, asks Sorel, is the great myth which can arouse revolutionaries and enable them to burst the bounds of bourgeois culture? It is the myth of the general strike: the organized withdrawal of labor by the vast mass of proletarians. Whether the general strike actually materializes in its full form is immaterial; what is important is that the workers *believe* in its efficacy. There is something in this doctrine which reminds one of William James' essay *The Will to Believe*. Developing his analysis, Sorel argues that "myths are not descriptions of things, but expressions of a determination to act." He identifies a utopia as purely intellectual, whereas a myth is the device essential if men are to achieve the new society embodied in the utopia. In other terms, we may think of Sorel as suggesting that the myth is that which generates the power to implement the authority of the intellectual vision.

Violence bottomed upon commitment to the myth will lead to "moral uplift of both workers and employers," in the words of one student of Sorel.[38] Morality in this sense apparently means the overcoming of the complacency and indifference which tend to set in under any regime—a complacency and peace exalted by conservatives like Burke but which ought to be anathema to the revolutionist.

Like anarchists in general, Sorel stresses the frustrations of legislative efforts in achieving fundamental change. Yet without a powerful myth to sustain those who would transcend bourgeois culture, the inertia of modern industrial society is such that the proletariat easily succumb to the blandishments of parliamentary politicians.

In what we might call the practical politics of

30. See his *Fields, Factories, and Workshops*, London: T. Nelson, 1912.
31. Ernest A. Vizitelly, *The Anarchists*, London: John Lane, 1911 and other writers early in the twentieth century tended to make all "propagandists of the deed" anarchists.
32. For the history of Spanish anarchist thought and practice, see Gerald Brenan, *The Spanish Labyrinth*, New York: Macmillan, 1943, ch. 7 and 8, and Eduardo Comin Colomer, *Historia del Anarquismo Espanol*, 2 vols., Barcelona: Editorial, AHR, 1956.
33. On the evolution of her anarchist views, see Emma Goldman's autobiography *Living My Life*, New York: Knopf, 1931. See also Richard Drinnon, *Rebel in Paradise*, Chicago: University of Chicago Press, 1962.
34. See Alexander Berkman, *What is Communist Anarchism?*, New York: Vanguard, 1929 and *Now and After: The ABC of Communist Anarchism*, New York: Vanguard, 1929.
35. See Bergson's *Creative Evolution*, Arthur Mitchell, trans., New York: Modern Library, 1944.
36. See Jan Christiaan Smuts, *Holism and Evolution*, New York: Viking, 1961.
37. Georges Sorel, *Reflections on Violence*, T. E. Hulme, trans., New York: B. W. Huebsch, 1914; also an ed. trans. by Hulme and J. Roth, Glencoe: Free Press, 1950. See also Irving L. Horowitz, *Radicalism and the Revolt Against Reason: The Social Theories of Georges Sorel*, New York: Humanities, 1961.
38. Max Nomad, *Aspects of Revolt*, New York: Bookman Associates, 1959, p. 66.

French anarchosyndicalism,[39] revolutionary action is thus confined to the direct action efforts of the *syndicats* or trade unions. It is they who accustom workers to the strike technique and they who educate for the coming general strike which overturns bourgeois parliamentary and authoritarian institutions. In the actual practice of French syndicalism, many means are approved, including the factory slow-down, sabotage (in which the functioning of machinery may be impaired by throwing sand into it or using one's *sabots,* or wooden shoes), and the industrial strike. But all are looked upon as subordinate to the coming general strike.

Assuming the anarchosyndicalist outlook to be triumphant, how would the new society be organized? Apparently solely on the basis of producers' *syndicats,* which would have complete charge of production, distribution, and, loosely confederated, of the few tasks of general governance to be performed in such a society. As in the case of guild socialism, whose ideal is so similar, syndicalism holds that the state will wither away.[40]

About the time that anarchosyndicalism came to the forefront in French affairs, an American anarchosyndicalist movement and political philosophy were also taking shape. The Industrial Workers of the World (I.W.W.) was founded in 1908 as an expression of this outlook.[41] In terms of their social background, members of the Industrial Workers often came from the migratory worker classes who had been spurned by the regular trade unions and by American society generally. Although the political ideology of the I.W.W. resembles that of French anarchosyndicalism at many points, there was apparently no direct connection between the two movements.

In the politics of American labor, the I.W.W. was a pioneer in arguing for industrial unionism. At a time, in the early twentieth century, when most American unions were organized along "craft" lines, it contended that the nature of modern industry, with its masses of workers not trained to any particular craft, demanded organization on the basis of whole industries rather than on that of particular skills.

But besides being a pioneer in industrial unionism, the I.W.W. sought to stress the necessity for looking beyond the immediate goals psychology of American labor. For the most part, American unionism has not been political in the sense that it has conceived of unionism as part of a movement which goes beyond "pork-chop" or economic ends. In the philosophy of Samuel Gompers (1850–1924), for example, orthodox unionism seemed to suggest an aloofness from any partisan politics and a concentration on better wages and working conditions, thinking of these ends as somewhat isolated from problems involving the general organization of society.[42]

In terms of its analysis and goals, the I.W.W. is somewhat like French anarchosyndicalism. Industrial society is to be transformed through the use of direct action and particularly by adapting the strike weapon to revolutionary ends. In one of his essays, Jack London, the American novelist, describes how this will come about.[43] After long preparation, industrial unions all over the nation call a general strike. They have accumulated food and made due provision for a long siege. On the day of the strike, plutocrats, owners, and political rulers wake up to find themselves paralyzed. And thus the revolution begins.

Politics, as Industrial Workers ideology understands it, is abolished after the revolution. Such rules as are necessary for the administration of industry are developed by the workers themselves through their unions. And these unions are in turn tied to other unions through very loose federal ties. Finally, there is one big union which presumably acts for the few purposes where general integration is necessary. It is obvious that I.W.W. thought, like French syndicalist theory, regards man as primarily a producer; as such, he manages his work and plans his collective life. That his roles might be multiple (he might, also, for example, be a citizen in the traditional sense, as well as a consumer) never seems to occur to anarchosyndicalist thinkers, so impressed are they by the overwhelmingly central role of production.

Throughout all anarchosyndicalist conceptions runs a very strong egalitarian thread. Thus, officials in the I.W.W. are strictly limited in their terms of office and cannot be paid more than the average worker. Few organizations have ever equalled the I.W.W. in its horror of bureaucracy and its insistence that any bureaucratic tendencies must be nipped in the bud, even at the expense of possible immediate efficiency and gains in membership.

As most unions turned increasingly to bureaucratic techniques for maintenance and extension of membership (in the United States the check-off, union shop, and closed shop are examples, all of which are characteristically rejected by the I.W.W.), anarchosyndicalist unions found they could no longer compete. Culture and social factors also contributed to their decline. In France, the disintegration was assisted by the rise of Communism, which had no hostility to bureaucracy; while in the United States, the sharp drop in immigrant labor and a corresponding development of cultural homogeneity undoubtedly were important.

But while anarchosyndicalism as such found itself losing strength, other political movements began to embody something of its spirit, particularly with respect to its anti-statist outlook.

Gandhian Pacifist Antistatism. Although Gandhian pacifist antistatism, so far as we know, has no direct connections with anarchosyndicalism, many of the historical problems in the light of which it developed its doctrine were similar, as were its analyses. Anarchosyndicalism despaired of using regular political machinery to achieve its aims; Gandhian pacifism, confronted by a firmly entrenched imperialist regime in an underdeveloped nation, had to go outside regular legislative channels. Both anarchism in general and anarchosyndicalism in particular centered much of their discussion on the problem of means in politics; for Gandhi, the question of means became central. Finally, Gandhi, like classical anarchism and anarchosyndicalism, had little confidence in the modern state.[44]

Mohandas K. Gandhi (1869–1948) was born into an Indian middle-caste family and, in Britain, educated for the bar. At first rather conventional in his outlook, he came gradually, in light of his experiences as a lawyer in South Africa and a great diversity of intellectual influences, to work out a theory of nonviolent action, a conception of the economy, and a view of politics which differentiated him from liberals, socialists, Marxists, and conservatives and placed him more nearly in the category of what might be called critical antistatism. During his leadership of the Indian Congress Party in its struggle against British imperialism, his conceptions were further refined. At the time of his death by assassination, his formulations about the political world were still undergoing change, for he seemed to be always open to new experiences and to re-interpretation of old ones.

Among the intellectual influences which shaped Gandhi were the Hindu Scriptures, the New Testament, Henry David Thoreau, John Ruskin, and Leo Tolstoy. The Hindu and Christian Scriptures gave him a profound religious base for his political views, although in some respects he seemed to interpret Hindu Scriptures in rather eccentric ways. Thoreau's essay *On the Duty of Civil Disobedience* posed for him in dramatic terms the problem of political obligation. Ruskin's *Unto This Last*, about which he speaks frequently in his autobiography, helped confirm him in the value of simplicity and the necessity for closeness to nature.

As a young man, Gandhi had exchanged letters with Leo Tolstoy (who died in 1910) and the quasi-anarchist views of the two men were to become strikingly similar. Tolstoy had, of course, undergone an intellectual revo-

39. On the history of French anarchosyndicalism, see Majorie R. Clark, *A History of the French Labor Movement, 1910–1928*, Berkeley, Calif.: University of Californa Press, 1930; and Jean Maitron, *Histoire du mouvement en France (1880–1914)*, Paris: Societe Universitaire d'editions et de librairie, 1951.
40. See G. D. H. Cole, *Guild Socialism*, London: L. Parsons, 1920, and *Guild Socialism Re-Stated*, New York: Frederick A. Stokes, 1921.
41. For the history and ideology of the Industrial Workers of the World, consult Paul Brissenden, *The IWW*, New York: Russell and Russell, 1957; Joyce Kornbluh, *Rebel Voices, an IWW Anthology*, Ann Arbor: University of Michigan Press, 1964; and Fred Thompson, *The IWW, Its First Fifty Years, 1905–1955*, Chicago: IWW, 1956.
42. See Gomper's autobiography, *Seventy Years of Life and Labor*, New York: Dutton, 1925, new ed. 1957.
43. See "The Dream of Debs," in Jack London, *Essays of Revolt*, New York: Vanguard, 1928.
44. On Gandhi's political philosophy in general, see his *An Autobiography: The Story of My Experiments With Truth*, Boston: Beacon Press, 1957; *Speeches and Writings of Mahatma Gandhi*, 4th ed., Madras: G. A. Natesan and Co., n.d.; *Satyagraha in South Africa*, Stanford: Academic Reprints, 1954; *Towards Non-Violent Socialism*, edited by Bharatan Kumarappa, Ahmedabad: Navajivan Publishing House, 1951. See also Biman Bihari Majumdar, ed., *The Gandhian Concept of the State*, Calcutta: M. C. Sarkar and Sons, 1957; Vishwanath Prasad Verma, *The Political Philosophy of Mahatma Gandhi and Saryodaya*, Agra: Lakshmi Nayain Agaywal, 1959; and K. G. Machruwala, *Gandhi and Marx*, Ahmedabad: Navajivan Publishing House, 1951.

lution during the last thirty years of his life, and, while he never called himself an anarchist, he certainly approached the position in practice. Basing his political views on his interpretation of the Sermon on the Mount, he reached the conclusion that if one is commanded to love one's enemies, to turn the other cheek, to go two miles instead of one, and not to judge others, all political society must be repudiated. One must refuse to pay taxes, serve on juries, go to war, and, in general, participate in complex civilization, whose agent is the violent state.[45]

Although Tolstoy's political position was not the determining factor in Gandhi's political philosophy—for Gandhi was far too independent to allow another to shape his own views—it is striking to summarize the ways in which the outlooks of the two men were similar. Both espoused the principle of celibacy; both were vegetarians; both were highly critical of complex technology and civilization; both rejected capitalism and Marxism; both developed doctrines of nonviolence; both were highly critical of the state; and both denied that material had any necessary connection with moral progress. It is perhaps in his development of practical political techniques that Gandhi is to be most sharply distinguished from Tolstoy.

With Indian religionists generally, Gandhi holds that a central imperative of human life is *ahimsa*, or noninjury, nonviolence. While there is always an element of *himsa* in life, men are required to discover those modes of existence and organization which will reduce it to the lowest possible point. This is particularly true in politics, where violence in the past has played so central a role. The transformation we are asked to bring about in the political sphere is a revolution of *means* and not primarily of *ends*. Do not talk to me of ends, Gandhi once said, speak only of means and the ends will care for themselves. While this was undoubtedly a hyperbolical statement, it does point to the central element in his political teaching. Like John Dewey, Gandhi holds that there is an organic interrelationship between means and ends and that the former cannot be sharply separated from the latter.

The central mission of Gandhi was, then, not merely to win independence of India from Britain but to work out political means which would not violate the ends he sought or set up new ends which he would disapprove. Those means he characterizes as *satyagraha*, soul power or truth power. The world is to be transformed fundamentally only through satyagraha within the general notion of *ahimsa.*

Satyagraha is both a principle and a technique. As a principle, it seeks to exalt the highest moral standards in politics—and politics for Gandhi is regarded as simply an expression of one's religion. As a technique, satyagraha entails a series of steps to bring about social change—steps which Gandhi works out with great care and tests in his many political struggles from the beginning of the century to his death.

At the beginning, the satyagraha politician will seek to employ any constitutional methods available—legislation, petition, journalism. Later on, if these methods seem ineffective, he will turn to agitation and organization for more direct action. Still later, he may issue ultimata—specific demands which, if not met, will be followed by nonviolent sanctions. Meanwhile, members of the movement will purify themselves through such means as fasting and meditation—attempt, in other words, to eliminate egoistic motivations. If the demands have not been met by a set time, direct action proper will begin, which may include demonstrations, boycotts, and similar activities. Finally, as a last resort, civil disobedience (either individual on the part of a leader or mass, collective disobedience) may become the ultimate sanction. Throughout all satyagraha activities, Gandhi emphasizes the need for commitment to the ethic of nonviolence.

In analyzing the doctrine, one is impressed by the fact that it includes both a noncoercive and a coercive element. In the first, all the resources of reason and appeals to conscience are utilized. In the second, with the threat of sanctions, one goes beyond reasoning, even at the expense of inconvenience (although not physical injury) to the opponent. Ethically, Gandhi seems to hold, there is an important difference between violent and nonviolent coercion.[46]

It is a doctrine of nonretaliatory conflict which repudiates the killing of human beings under all circumstances. At the same time, it is an effort to work out a theory of nonviolent power in which the stress is on reopening channels of genuine communication so that those in disagreement can once more discuss and deliberate. A careful distinction is made between firm opposition to certain acts of the opponent and hatred of or serious injury to the opponent himself. Gandhi is a vigorous exponent of the principle of discussion and debate for resolution of conflict; but at the same time he does not believe that genuine discussion—such as is postulated by liberal democracy—can take place if the participants are grossly unequal in power. But power can take many forms and, in Gandhi's view, violence is one of the least efficacious of them as well as the least moral: it always leaves scars which impede that unity and agreement without which human community is impossible. Love, Gandhian philosophy argues, is one of the most powerful forces that can be employed, even in politics.

One notes in the development of Gandhi's propositions elements that remind one of the sixteenth-century De la Boetie[47] and also of the anarchist Benjamin Tucker. The difference is that Gandhi has spelled out more explicitly the details of direct action. In common with classical anarchists, however, he always tends to assume a situation in which legislative or orthodox political methods will not be sufficient, so that direct action of some kind must be resorted to. The state itself—even the so-called democratic state of modern times—is always tending to create a rigidity or stasis which only the traumatic experience of direct action can overcome.

Unlike many anarchists, Gandhi does not repudiate organization and even tightly knit organization. All his campaigns are carried on through a proliferation of committees and subcommittees and with much planning. Indeed, Gandhi thinks of the *satyagraha* organization itself as constituting the germs of an alternative government: The *satyagrahis* will obey it increasingly and the regular government will thus dry up for want of functions.

Gandhi differs from progressive anarchists, however, in questioning seriously the value of industrialism. Because the imperatives of complex technology tend to separate man from his work and human beings from primitive nature, something is lost in the process. Too much division of labor promotes irresponsibility and moral inertia, for we can always blame others for the weaknesses of society. Gandhi does not spurn all technology, and he fully understands that an underdeveloped nation must industrialize to some extent. But he would try to confine technology to simple contrivances like the sewing machine, develop economic autonomy in the village, and stress the improvement of rural life. Only a few complex machines would be accepted and these would be owned by the sketchy central organization which Gandhi envisions.[48]

He sees India and other nations as being related to one another primarily through organizations of villages and small towns. With limited technology, large cities are unnecessary and undesirable. The village or town could govern itself on a face-to-face noncoercive basis and each village would send delegates to a loosely structured regional and then a national organization. Internationally, Gandhi implies a very unrigid confederation based on these autonomous vilages and towns. Policing would be local, unarmed, and nonviolent.

One criticism of communist anarchism has always been that it (and Marxism, too) professes to have its cake and eat it too; that is, it seems to accept complex industrialism but rather inadequately tries to show how complexity in technology can be combined with decentralization in politics. Critics have rightly wondered just how this can be done. Gandhi

45. Tolstoy's political position is stated in many of his later works. See particularly *The Kingdom of God Is Within You*, vol. 20, Tolstoy Centenary Edition, London: Oxford, 1935; the novel *Resurrection*, Leo Wiener, trans., rev., ed. by F. D. Reeve, New York: Heritage Press, 1963; *My Religion*, New York: Crowell, 1885; and *The Slavery of Our Times*, New York: Dodd, Mead, 1900. See also Aylmer Maude, *The Life of Tolstoy: Later Years*, London: Archibald Constable, 1910.
46. The concept of nonviolent coercion is analyzed by the American sociologist Clarence Marsh Case in *Non-Violent Coercion*, New York: Appleton-Century, 1923. For a further discussion of nonviolent power, see Richard Gregg, *The Power of Non-Violence*, New York: Schocken, 1966.
47. See Chapter 18, pp. 339–340.
48. Although generally suspicious of complex technology, Gandhi was no dogmatist. "I would make intelligent exceptions," he once said. "Take the case of the Singer's sewing machine. It is one of the few useful things ever invented. . . ." "But," said the questioner, "if you make an exception of the Singer's sewing machine and your spindle, where would these exceptions end?" "Just where they cease to help the individual and encroach upon his individuality. The machine should not be allowed to cripple the limbs of man." From an article by Shri Mahadev Desai in *Harijan*, subsequently reprinted as a preface to the new edition of Gandhi's *Hind Swaraj* in 1938.

does not fall into this trap. He sees clearly that if one is to eliminate centralized political institutions, one must be willing to accept strictly curtailed technology and perhaps a lower standard of living in the economic sense. This he is willing to do, for in terms of his religious and moral values—the emphasis on small community, on personalism, on responsibility, and on nonviolence—he thinks it is a small price to pay.

After his death, the politics of India did not move in his direction and Gandhi's political ideas guided only a small sect in the land of his birth. They have not been without great influence elsewhere, however, as in the theories of Martin Luther King and the civil rights movement in the United States.[49] However, Gandhi's conceptions have usually been adopted selectively; very few have been willing to accept his drastic critique of industrialism, of the national state, and of the violence which he associates with centralized power structures and with industrialism itself.

Yet in the end his may prove to be one of the most prophetic voices in modern political thought.

Recent Currents in Anarchism and Antistatism

Although we have emphasized the general decline of anarchist notions between the two world wars, there have not been wanting indications that since World War II anarchist and antistatist notions have had some recrudescence.

In the United States, anarchist thought after World War II was reflected in journals like *Resistance* and *Why?* and above all in the well-edited *Politics*. In a day when men were beginning to line up either for or against the United States or the Soviet Union in the so-called Cold War, *Politics* attacked both power blocs. It was one of the most vigorously antimilitarist journals ever published. In 1957, the journal *Liberation* was established by a group, led by A. J. Muste, having a generally pacifist and antistatist outlook; it had a not inconsiderable influence on the American "left."

In Britain, the spearhead of the formal anarchist movement was the so-called *Freedom* group—those who continued to edit Kropotkin's old journal. The journal itself was open to a wide variety of anarchistlike views and discussion groups in London pursued classical anarchist themes in the realms of sex, law, colonialism, and disarmament. *Freedom* anarchists were by no means united on all issues, least of all on such questions as the legitimacy of violence. Thus when the editors praised David Pratt for his attempt on the life of the racist Prime Minister Verwoerd of South Africa, not all agreed.[50]

In general, *Freedom*'s commentaries on men and events in the post-World War II world took positions which are not surprising to those familiar with classical anarchism. Thus by and large they were hostile to organized religion as well as to the authority of the state. They reacted unfavorably to identity cards as a violation of individual liberty,[51] pointing out that emergency regulations tend to become permanent in an authoritarian environment. Advocating wide latitudes in sexual matters, they saw all repressive sex legislation as a reflection of an illegitimate State concern with spontaneity in human life. They viewed sympathetically such experiments as the Summerhill school in Britain, where external discipline is completely eliminated and children are not even required to attend classes.[52] They supported "direct action" for peace (boarding nuclear-powered submarines, for example) and mass demonstrations such as the Aldermaston marches; but they argued that such activities did not go far enough. In the spring of 1963, it was a group of anarchists, Spies for Peace, which was responsible for passing out leaflets showing exactly where certain emergency government shelters for wartime were located.

One of the most important theorists of anarchism since World War II was the British art critic Herbert Read. Coining the term the "politics of the unpolitical," he sees Christ as the exemplar par excellence of this position and the Sermon on the Mount as its best expression. In modern times, he maintains, six figures stand out among those continuing the tradition: John Ruskin, Peter Kropotkin, William Morris,[53] Leo Tolstoy, Mohandas Gandhi, and Eric Gill.

Read argues that the "politics of the unpolitical" cannot be associated with the word "democracy" as that term is usually understood in the twentieth century. Even in Rousseau's theory, democracy in its full sense is possible only in a very small community. In modern states, democratic parliamentary politics become essentially the politics of centralization and monopoly, regardless of the party in power. We should turn, he goes on, to natural society for guidance—the family, guilds of workers, and associations of friends. All central authority, including Parliament, must be abolished. Arbitration will settle all disputes among guilds.[54]

On another occasion, he contrasts politics with poetry. The former, particularly in its modern form, tends to be totalitarian, in that it seeks for the hegemony of the reason, to which all that is merely sensuous must be strictly subordinate. Hence, for Hegel, art is always subordinate to the intellect and thus to politics. "The moments of creation," suggests Read, "are still and magical, a trance or reverie in which the artist holds communion with forces which lie below the habitual level of thought and emotion. That is what the man of action, the politician and fanatic, cannot appreciate."[55]

From this point of view, anarchism becomes the most appropriate political outlook for the artist and poet: only anarchism recognizes what Read calls the universalism of truth which is beyond the arbitrary and has nothing to do with the "man-made system of government." Anarchism, in short, "denies the rule of kings and castes, of churches and parliaments."[56]

Not unlike the doctrine of Read is that of Paul Goodman, the anarchist implications of whose writings became increasingly evident in the fifties of the twentieth century. Criticizing the world of centralized culture and politics along the lines of classical anarchism, Goodman has been concerned to reunite man's work with the rest of life; to plan small, decentralized communities in which there will be an integration of manual with intellectual labor and agricultural with industrial; and to establish modes of instruction and learning that will overcome the apathy and destruction of spontaneity which he identifies with modern education.[57]

From the viewpoint of psychoanalytical approaches, the teaching of Wilhelm Reich (1897–1957) has been lauded by many anarchists. Trained as a Freudian, Reich later came to reject some of Freud's propositions, at least as they were developed during the last part of his life. A controversial figure among physicians, Reich's theories led him to clash with the laws of the state, the result being that he died in prison after being convicted of fraudulent use of the mails.[58] His books were ordered burned by an American court.

The key to his position is the relation he discovers between freedom of sexual practice and liberty in the social and political arena. When men and women are unable (either because of their own "character armor" or by reason of external restraints) to give free vent to their sexual energies, the result, socially and politically, is a highly authoritarian culture, which reaches its culmination in Fascist politics. To will freedom in a political sense, without unrestrained expression of libidinal impulses, is an impossibility. Hence the fundamental revolution libertarians call for in human society must begin with an attack on sexual repression.

In the specifically political aspects of his argument, Reich seeks to show that in the most authoritarian of modern systems, those of Fascism and Communism, sexual repressions and restrictions are closely associated with the enhancement of authority. In Germany, for example, National Socialism built upon the heritage of the authoritarian family with very limited opportunity for sexual expression; in Italy, Catholic culture established similar norms, even though they were frequently vio-

49. See Martin Luther King, *Stride Toward Freedom*, New York: Harper, 1958. See also King's semiautobiographical sketch, "Pilgrimage to Nonviolence," *Christian Century*, April 13, 1960, in which he specifically avows the influence of Gandhi on his thinking.
50. See *Freedom*, April 16, 1960.
51. *Ibid.*, July 7, 1951.
52. See A. S. Neill, "Summerhill Education vs. Standard Education," *Anarchy* 11 (January 1962), 29–32.
53. Morris's well-known agrarian anarchist novel was *News from Nowhere*, London: Longmans, Green, 1901.
54. See Herbert Read, *The Politics of the Unpolitical*, London: Routledge, 1946.
55. *Poetry and Anarchism*, London: Freedom Press, 1947, p. 17.
56. *Ibid.*, pp. 60–61.
57. See Paul and Percival Goodman, *Communitas: Means of Livelihood and Ways of Life*, Chicago: University of Chicago Press, 1947. See also Paul Goodman, *Growing Up Absurd: Problems of Youth in the Organized System*, New York: Random House, 1961, and *Utopian Essays and Practical Proposals*, New York: Random House, 1962.
58. Reich died in 1961. For his theories as applied to politics, see *The Mass Psychology of Fascism*, T. P. Wolfe, trans.; New York: Orgone Institute Press, 1946. See also *The Sexual Revolution*, T. P. Wolfe, trans., New York: Orgone Institute Press, 1945.

lated in practice. In the Soviet Union, the revolution initially sought to establish free sexual expression and it was precisely during this period that political authority gave greatest promise of withering away. Later, when the Soviet Union reintroduced difficult divorce and imposed new restrictions on sexual conduct, the authority of the state began once more to be exalted.

In developing this thesis, it is obvious that Reich is sharply differing from the later Freud in his analysis of civilization and politics. Freud argues that libidinal repression, with all its pain and sorrow, is the price we pay, so to speak, for the presumed values of civilization.[59] Reich, in sharp contrast, does not assume a fixed fund of libidinal energy but rather that with direct sex expression the fund can be extended indefinitely. Full achievement of "orgasmic potency" (genital sexuality) means a more abundant life in every way, including an enhancement of creativity and imagination.

Whatever we may think of recent currents of anarchist thought, it is clear that they are directed to problems which, while always present in political life, have been accentuated by the industrialist cultures and political structures increasingly characteristic of both Western and Eastern worlds since World War I. It is against the bureaucratic, repressive, impersonal, and warlike character of those structures that anarchism and antistatism are radical protests. Perhaps never before in history have slogans of freedom and democracy been more widespread. Yet it is precisely in this period that mass annihilation, the herding of millions of men into concentration or refugee camps, the acceptance of an ethic of power as an end, and the worship of the state have been most ubiquitous. This incongruity between slogan and fact provided an admirable point of departure for anarchist thought; and there seemed to be ample grounds indeed for a revival of classical anarchist and antistatist positions.

In 1948, George Orwell gave literary form, in his novel *Nineteen Eighty-Four,* to the kind of politics which anarchists for a hundred years had been criticizing. Orwell's state is one in which the individual has become a zero and even the writing of "history" is under centralized political control. War is endemic and is defended in the name of peace.

But long before Orwell wrote, the politics of Fascism and National Socialism had dramatically portrayed in extreme guise tendencies which were present in almost all nation-states. Hegelianism, Marxism, Liberalism, Conservatism, Non-Marxian Socialism, and Anarchism had been, generally speaking, united by one factor—their emphasis on man's possibilities for reason, even when, as in Conservatism, they distrusted merely "abstract reason." In the political doctrines of Fascism and National Socialism, however, one sees epitomized all those trends in speculation since the French Revolution which had exalted nihilism and utter irrationality and had rejected the guidance even of tradition. In a sense, as we shall see in the next chapter, political man turned upon himself and sought to repudiate the quest for freedom and responsibility.

chapter 30

Fascism and National Socialism: Antecedents and Doctrines

Out of nineteenth-century thought came liberalism, Marxism, and the anarchist philosophies akin in part to both. But the nineteenth century was also the seedbed of political philosophies which were to provide major critiques of Marxism and liberalism alike. Indeed, it was in the very soil from which both sprang that roots of the critical outlooks developed. And among those views none were more fraught with grave consequences for twentieth-century life and politics than Fascism and National Socialism.

In this chapter we first inquire into the antecedents of Fascism and National Socialism in nineteenth- and early-twentieth-century nationalism and related phenomena. We then turn to analyses of Italian Fascism and German National Socialism. Finally, we ask ourselves in what measure Fascism and National Socialism furnished valid criticisms of the political outlooks with which they are most sharply contrasted.

Nationalism: Facets and Related Phenomena

Many scholarly efforts in recent years have been devoted to ferreting out the alleged roots of Fascism and National Socialism in a diversity of thought currents. In this first section of the analysis, however, we are not so much concerned with those currents in the specific contexts of German and Italian politics as we are with the general atmosphere of thought and practice which provided materials for the construction of Fascist philosophies of life. For neither Fascism nor National Socialism can be looked upon as springing solely from Italian and German soil: They were also extreme expressions of certain cultural phenomena which transcended purely national environments.

Of these phenomena, perhaps the most significant was nationalism, both as a complex of popular attitudes and practices and as the basis for more grandiose systems of thought. But in saying this, we should be careful to recognize that nationalism could be and was associated with a wide diversity of political systems and outlooks. It was only when it became connected with certain other relatively independent tendencies in culture and thought that it provided intellectual foundations for the Fascism and National Socialism of recent times. Here let us recall some of the major elements in the evolution of nationalism and then turn to parallel aspects of thought which would become important in forging Fascist and National Socialist systems.

The Evolution of Modern Nationalism. The evolution of modern nationalism in thought and practice has been a slow, tortuous, and complex affair; and any brief summary is likely to do injustice to its many facets.[1] At the outset of early modern political history, as we have observed,[2] the forging of what were later to become nation-states was characterized by the expansion of the estate of the king at the expense of subroyal and feudal estates. In this expansion, the king was often assisted by the self-interested actions of the rising middle classes, eager as they were to eliminate rules which inhibited their economic development and to overcome the inherited power of the landed aristocracy. With the exception of Germany and Italy, the great nation-states of the Western world had been established by the end of the eighteenth century, having overcome the particularism of province, region, and feudal estates. The stage was then set for nineteenth-century evolution of democratic

Chapter 29

59. See his *Civilization and Its Discontents,* Joan Riviere, trans., New York: Doubleday, 1958.

Chapter 30

1. On the evolution of nationalism, see Carlton J. H. Hayes, *The Historical Evolution of Modern Nationalism,* New York: R. R. Smith, 1931; and Hans Kohn, *The Idea of Nationalism,* New York: Macmillan, 1944, and *Nationalism: Its Meaning and History,* Princeton; Van Nostrand, 1955.
2. See Chapter 15.

nationalism, which owed so much to the impetus of the French Revolution.

The first phase of nationalist evolution, then, consists of the complex of developments which established the general notion and fact of the nation-state. This epoch may be said to have extended from about the fourteenth century to the end of the eighteenth. In it, the fissiparous tendencies of feudalism had to be overcome and in political terms this involved a strengthening of the royal power and authority. But the establishment of the nation-state was also a victory over the universalist tendencies of the Middle Ages–those institutions and patterns of thought, enshrined in civil and canon law traditions, which embodied the general heritage of the Roman Empire.

The nation-state thus represented a victory over the feudal tradition, on the one hand, and the universalist thrust in Western culture, on the other. On the side of its political theory, its philosophers developed the idea of sovereignty to express its view of law as the will of the national sovereign.

The model of the nation-state down to the middle of the eighteenth century was one of royal personal sovereignty in the cultural environment of an increasing national consciousness. True, this kingly sovereignty was qualified to some degree in British society and, in other ways, by French and Spanish institutions as well. Nevertheless, the model was not seriously impaired.

The great ideological change in the model—and the one which inaugurated the second phase in the evolution of modern nationalism—came with the writings of men like Rousseau in the eighteenth century. Here sovereignty, which remained national, was to be transferred from the prince of the traditional model to the whole community. True, Rousseau thought of his "people" as inhabiting a very small territory, and as being few in number.[3] But the precedent had been established for shifting sovereignty—or final authority—from the one to the many. And the French revolutionists regarded it as one of their great missions to translate the notion of popular sovereignty from Rousseau's small community to the nation-state.

In making this translation, they were helping to establish the ideological foundations for nineteenth-century militant nationalism. Its extreme form, reflected in some measure in the Revolution itself, disregarded traditional internal social and political divisions, tended to question voluntary associations, attacked ecclesiastical autonomy, and romanticized the collectivity known as the people.

More specifically, the philosophy of nationalism was formulated by men like Hegel,[4] Johann Gottlieb Fichte, and Giuseppe Mazzini. Hegel provided it with a theory of history in which the nation-state was looked upon as the vehicle through which the evolving world spirit manifests itself. Fichte, addressing himself to the problem of German nationhood, elaborated the relationship between philosophical idealism and nationality. Mazzini, as a philosopher of Italian national unity, attempted to formulate a view which saw nationalism as the indispensable prelude to some form of internationalism. Below the level of systematic thought, the nationalist spirit was attached to rather diverse political attitudes: thus there was the conservative nationalism associated with some of the Hegelians and with British leaders like Disraeli; the liberal nationalism characteristic of men like Guizot; the democratic nationalism of Mazzini; and, under the Third French Republic, the effort of royalists to combine nationalist ideology with devotion to traditional monarchical institutions. In the United States, a spirit of nationalism was in part developed to provide an ideological basis for rapid assimilation of culturally diverse immigrants.[5]

Under the banners of the several types of nationalism, new nation-states were either born or reborn (Greece, Ireland, Italy, Rumania, Czechoslovakia, Poland) and languages long since nearly dead (as with Gaelic) were revived to provide a cultural basis for national claims. Many of the wars of the nineteenth and twentieth centuries were waged to liberate nations then under foreign political control, the implication being that every nation should also constitute a state. The process continued far into the twentieth century, as Asian and African nations aspired to statehood after the manner of their European and American predecessors. The multi-nation-state was held to be anathema.

As traditional religions declined, nationalism often took their place, becoming the effective final commitment for millions of human beings. Carlton Hayes rightly points out that a "religion of nationalism" came to characterize almost every modern state.[6] Sometimes aided and abetted by high toned philosophers and in most areas encouraged by journalism, official propaganda, and popular culture, this religion had its own martyrs, priests, rituals, and appeals to the irrational. Its martyrs were those who had died in wars of national liberation, its priests the intellectuals and journalists who developed its mystique. Its rituals consisted of patriotic exercises, rigidly defined ceremonies for paying homage to the flag, gun salutes for presidents and kings, national holy days, religious services at tombs of unknown soldiers, and national creeds repeated by rote.

By the beginning of World War I, indeed, the religion of nationalism had become so ubiquitous that political beliefs and philosophies which challenged it in fundamental terms were swept aside in periods of crisis. Karl Marx, for example, was notoriously pro-German at the time of the Franco-Prussian War, despite the fact that he had asserted in the *Communist Manifesto* that the workers had no country. And even an anarchist cosmopolitan like Kropotkin became a partisan of Russia during World War I. The great Socialist parties, all of whom were pledged to the principle of international class solidarity, collapsed like jerrybuilt shacks before the nationalist hurricanes in 1914.

One cannot study the history of nationalism during the past hundred years without being impressed by the fact that it apparently appealed to something basic in human beings—to nonrational sentiments, even in the face of intellectual professions which often moved in a contrary direction; to emotions so primitive that even carefully trained minds succumbed; to perhaps the search for a way of life which might swallow up and overcome the frustrations of individualism. In its extreme forms, which have been called "integral nationalism," (reflected in the writings of Charles Maurras, for example), it appeared at times to become outrightly irrational and to spurn all efforts to establish any form of internatinal order that might limit the prerogatives of the nation-state.

From one point of view, nationalism can be seen (certainly in its integral forms) as a revolt against that current in the Western intellectual tradition which stresses the possibility of rationality and which searches for norms of conduct such as those embodied in "natural law." In fact, it has been plausibly argued that there has always been a tension between modes of looking at the collective life of mankind as in some sense a unity and, by contrast, approaches which stress its diversities.[7] Nationalism, in this view, would be the modern version of the rebellion against schemes of thought which think of the whole race of men as unified.

But while nationalism has been one of the most significant factors in modern political ideology and the history of institutions, certain other parallel developments must also be understood if we are to comprehend Fascism and National Socialism in their historic context. Among these parallel doctrines and attitudes, racism takes a high rank.

Racist Currents in Modern Thought. One student of racism terms it a "modern superstition."[8] That it is decisively modern can hardly be doubted. Although many previous thinkers had emphasized diversity of culture in their studies of political phenomena—Montesquieu, for example—"race" as the center of attention was largely a nineteenth-century attitude.

Among the first formulators of racist doctrine was Charles de Gobineau (1816–1882), who laid down many of the lines which others were to develop. In general, racists thought that color differentiations among men might be external indications of intellectual and moral distinctions having great significance. Many held that the "white" race was superior to the "yellow" and "black" races; and some sought to distinguish racial types within the white race itself. Studies of language systems in the nineteenth century innocently abetted the development of racism by providing plausible criteria for social differentiation; and physical anthropology contributed to it by suggesting ways in which skulls and physiognomies of alleged races could be distinguished from one another. This is not to say that the majority of language and anthropology stu-

3. See Chapter 22.
4. See Chapter 24.
5. Cf. D. W. Brogan, *The American Character*, New York: Knopf, 1956.
6. *Essays on Nationalism*, New York: Russell and Russell, 1966.
7. See Ernest Barker, Introduction to Otto Gierke, *Natural Law and the Theory of Society*, Ernest Barker, trans., Cambridge: University Press, 1934; Boston: Beacon Press, 1957, paperback.
8. Jacques Barzun, *Race: A Study in Modern Superstition*, New York: Harcourt, Brace, 1937. See also Hannah Arendt, *The Origins of Totalitarianism*, New York: Harcourt, Brace, 1951, Part I.

dents were racists, but rather that their studies furnished materials upon which expositors of racist doctrines were to build.

Contributing to the racist mentality at the popular level was the great movement for emancipation of Jews, which was one of the fruits of liberalism. For centuries, Jewish life had often been confined to ghettoes and Jews had been restricted as to the occupations they could pursue. Often there was legal discrimination of various types. As industrialism and liberalism grew, old patterns of life and thought were shaken up and ancient restrictions on the Jews tended to break down, at least in western and central Europe (and in the United States they never existed, at any rate in rigid form). But emancipation had its own perils: It meant that Jews were now moving in non-Jewish circles, where they could become visible objects for prejudice and jealousy. This was particularly true because many Jews were associated in the public mind with money and banking; and when the non-Jewish middle class tended to be pinched financially, it was easy to associate their plight with an alleged Jewish conspiracy. Because the Jews maintained ties of international solidarity, moreover, it was not difficult for ardent nationalists to claim that they had no primary loyalty to the nation-states of which they were residents.

In many parts of the world, however, hostility directed at Jews had nothing to do with a new consciousness of Jewishness brought about by emancipation movements. In much of Eastern Europe, for example, antisemitism had been built into the fabrics of the largely rural societies: In part, this was a result of Christian prejudices against Jews for religious reasons and in some degree an expression of opposition to eccentricities of any kind. In Russia, governments frequently made use of antisemitic prejudices to promote support for themselves; and the anti-Jewish *pogrom* of a semiofficial character became in effect an institution of respectable standing.

Antisemitism as a reflection of racism assumed many guises. Thus the Protocols of the Elders of Zion, which were ultimately to be shown to be a forgery, supposedly revealed an international plot of Jews to take control of the world.[9] Periodically since the end of the nineteenth century, the Protocols have been revived and have apparently been taken as genuine by millions of human beings. Again, much latent antisemitism was revealed in the whole complicated Dreyfus affair,[10] in which a Jewish officer in the French army was falsely accused of treasonable activities.

Even in the United States, supposedly founded on principles of egalitarianism, antisemitism was at least a covert factor in politics. In the late nineteenth- and early twentieth-century progressive movement, for example, there were antisemitic undertones in the propaganda of some midwestern leaders. Here the antisemitism was associated with the alleged position of Jews in the world of international finance; and the bitterness of Midwesterners against Wall Street control could easily become antisemitic.[11]

Aside from its antisemitic expressions, racism took many other forms. Thus a German writer of British ancestry, Houston Stewart Chamberlain (1855–1927), sought to show the alleged superiority of the Nordic to other races.[12] And it may have been significant that his book was introduced by a British peer, Lord Redesdale. In the United States, eminent scholars like the political scientist John W. Burgess apparently held to a somewhat similar version of Nordic or Anglo-Saxon supremacy.[13] Often Social Darwinism took on overtones of racist doctrines, the significant struggle for survival being conceived in terms of conflicts between white, yellow and black races.[14]

Nor were racist attitudes and thinking confined to works of propaganda and learned treatises. They actually affected legislation. In Australia, for example, colored peoples were excluded altogether from immigration and this policy has persisted, with few if any changes, down to our own day. In the United States, too, racist thinking is evident in statutory provisions: in the Chinese exclusion laws of the nineteenth century, in state statutes restricting the rights of Orientals to own land, in the Act of 1924 which forbade immigration to those ineligible for naturalization (primarily Orientals—a policy which was modified only after World War II), and in the National Origins principle of the basic immigration law.

Feeling and Will in Modern Thought. Both nationalism and racism have been in some measure reflections of an important emphasis on emotion and will in major currents of modern thought. This stress had helped to shape the context not only of racism and nationalism but also of the political doctrines of Fascism and National Socialism. In suggesting this, however, we should make clear that those who have tended to point out the significance of feeling and will have not necessarily—or even, perhaps, usually—been extreme nationalists, racists, or Fascists. In some instances, indeed, there may be a direct relation between them and philosophies of integral nationalism and Fascism; but it is usually very difficult to show this connection. And many thinkers exalting the emotions and will have been hostile to Fascism and National Socialism. The whole problem is referred to here because any understanding of Fascism and National Socialism must take account of the general climate of opinion to which they could appeal; and that climate in the twentieth century was often strongly conditioned by doctrines emphasizing the irrationality of man.

In the nineteenth-century's revolt against the eighteenth-century's abstract rationalism, there were many elements. But undoubtedly one of the most important was the romantic current which in considerable measure roots in Rousseau. As a rebellion against form and order, its expressions were various: in literature, we have the poetry of Wordsworth; in music, the symphonies of Beethoven and Wagner; in religion, the subjectivism of Kierkegaard. In pre-World War I psychological thought, systems like those of Freud tended, in the eyes of many of their interpreters, to make reason merely rationalization and to stress as the vital factor in human life the deep and largely unconscious libidinal impulses. True, expositors of the psychology of the unconscious did not necessarily exalt "thinking" through the libido as the norm —indeed, many thought of the problem as a revolt against domination by the unconscious —but their analyses served to popularize the notion that men do in fact act largely in response to deeply felt desires rather than to standards worked out by reason; many concluded, therefore, that possibilities for rational ordering were severely limited.

The best that we can do, many came to believe, is to impose some kind of a tentative scheme on the aberrant emotions but without any hope that things can be ordered in the classical (Platonic, natural law) sense. Indeed, if one thinks of ethical standards as simply expressions of the emotions, as one school of modern moral thought tends to do,[15] then there are no rational (or universally intuited) forms to impose. One moves from day to day, adjusting things to one another according to hunches or simply by acts of will.

In some measure, the whole approach of pragmatism in philosophy is closely associated with the revolt of emotion and will against reason and form. While there is a diversity of schools within the pragmatic current, all seem to hold that the test of a thing is its practicality measured in terms of goals which arise out of experience or are accepted as the result of an act of will. In the thought of the American pragmatist William James, for example, the "will to believe" in a given set of standards or commitments can, if persisted in, become a "truth" for the individual involved, even though others may not see it as a truth. The emphasis here is obviously on "will" rather than on "reason" or allegedly objective standards.[16] But if will can in some sense become the source of truth, traditional conceptions of universality are obviously discarded and, logi-

9. On the Protocols, see John S. Curtiss, *An Appraisal of the Protocols of Zion,* New York: Columbia University Press, 1942; Sergyei A. Nilus, *World Conquest Through World Government: The Protocols of the Learned Elders of Zion,* Victor E. Marsden, trans., London: Britons, 1963; Benjamin Segel, *The Protocols of the Elders of Zion: The Greatest Lie in History,* New York: Block, 1934; and Hugo Valentin, *Anti-Semitism,* A. G. Chaten, trans., New York: Viking Press, 1936.
10. See Wilhelm Herzog, *From Dreyfus to Petain: The Struggle of a Republic* New York: Creative Age Press, 1947; M. Josephson, *Zola and His Time,* New York: Macauley, 1928; and Pierre Dreyfus, *The Dreyfus Case,* edited by D. C. McKay, New Haven: Yale University Press, 1937.
11. See S. M. Lipset, "The Sources of the Radical Right," in Daniel Bell, ed., *The Radical Right,* New York: Doubleday, 1964, pp. 309–310.
12. See his *Foundations of the Nineteenth Century,* John Lees, trans., London: J. Lane, 1912.
13. See, for example, Louis Snyder, *The Idea of Racism,* New York: Van Nostrand, 1962, pp. 86–87.
14. See, for example, Madison Grant, *The Passing of the Great Race,* New York: Scribner, 1916, new ed. 1918, 1921; and Lathrop Stoddard, *The Rising Tide of Color Against White World Supremacy,* New York: Scribner's, 1920.
15. See, for example, Charles L. Stevenson, *Ethics and Language,* New Haven: Yale University Press, 1944. Stevenson is often looked upon as one of the leading twentieth-century expositors of the notion that ethical views are simply emotive.
16. See William James, *The Will to Believe,* New York: Longmans, Green, 1897.

cally, it would seem, the truth belongs to those having the strongest wills. Elaborate systems of ideals are discarded.[17]

Again, it should be emphasized that there is no one-to-one relationship between currents of thought noted here and the political doctrines of Fascism and National Socialism. But that there are close affinities at certain points we can hardly doubt.[18]

The Cult of Violence. In some measure and at certain points, almost every modern body of political ideas has felt it legitimate to appeal for violence. In the Marxist system, as we have seen, violence may under certain circumstances play a constructive role in ushering in the socialist and then the communist society. This is true above all in the bolshevik version of Marxism; and both Lenin and Trotsky seem to think of violence in a revolutionary situation not merely as inevitable but also as desirable.[19] The ideologies of Stalinism and Maoism are likewise associated with the notion that violence can be a vehicle for bringing about a communist world order.

In anarchism, too, as we have pointed out, there is an important tradition of violence.[20] And while Georges Sorel uses the term in a peculiar way, there can be no doubt that under certain circumstances he approves its utilization in the sense normally understood: Certainly French anarchosyndicalism was not averse to its employment as an industrial-political weapon.

What students often forget, however, is the fact that in the Western democratic tradition itself violence plays a not inconsiderable role, both in theory and in practice. In the thought of Thomas Jefferson, for example, violent rebellion appears to be a kind of tonic: "A little rebellion," Jefferson writes on the occasion of Shay's Rebellion, "now and then, is a good thing, and as necessary in the political world as storms in the physical. . . . It is a medicine necessary for the sound health of government."[21] Or again: "What country can preserve its liberties, if its rulers are not warned from time to time, that this people preserve the spirit of resistance? Let them take arms. . . . The tree of liberty must be refreshed from time to time with the blood of patriots and tyrants."[22]

Although Jefferson's words may be regarded by some as hyperbolical, they are perhaps less so when read in the light of the actual relationship of violence to struggles having as their avowed objective the achievement of democracy. Thus the use of violence was exalted by many of the most pronounced advocates of liberty, equality, and fraternity during the French Revolution. The whole conscious use of terror as a weapon in politics begins its modern career with the triumph of the Mountain and of Robespierre.

During the nineteenth century, those who led wars for national liberation, which were usually associated with democracy, had few scruples about using violence. To be sure, they attacked their opponents for resort to violence; but they appeared to think that its employment was quite justified when the ends were national independence and democracy.

Curiously enough, the very employment of violence for national liberation and democracy was paralleled not infrequently by professed democrats' using it to destroy the independence of Asians and Africans. Thus France, the avowed champion of liberty, equality, and fraternity, conquered Indo-China only a few years after its republicans had overthrown the yoke of the third Napoleon. Imperialism, while by no means an exclusively democratic phenomenon, was often condoned by professed democrats.

But the cult of violence has transcended particular political ideologies, whether Marxist, anarchist, or democratic. In some measure, it has been built into the very mystique of the modern state. Thus since the French Revolution, the state has tended more and more to adopt military conscription as a fundamental institution. Its leaders have not hesitated to pledge the lives of whole populations for the most nebulous goals. Its test for patriotism, more frequently than not, has been the degree to which individuals are willing to pledge themselves to programs of mass killing.[23]

These, then, have been important elements in the soil out of which the philosophies and practices of Fascism and National Socialism grew. Integral nationalism, racism, the revolt against reason and exaltation of feeling and will, and the cult of violence were ubiquitous factors in modern culture and thought. They cut across divisions of political thought and were embedded in institutions and practices both east and west.

Italian Fascism: Evolution, Main Currents, and Analysis

As one of the latest modern nations to achieve statehood, as a power which was frustrated in its World War I goals, as a relatively poor area economically, and as a country of strong localism and particularism, Italy provided many of the ingredients which, when combined with certain of the general factors noted previously, made the rise of Fascism possible.

Although Italy emerged from World War I on the victorious side, it had been frustrated in its ambitions. Its military forces had hardly shown themselves the equals of the British and French; and while the nation had gained territorially as a result of the war, the accretions were not nearly as great as many had desired (Fiume, for example, was to be a free city, rather than to be annexed to Italy). Frustrations of this kind, in the context of modern nationalist thought, could easily provide the basis for an authoritarian policy.

Then, too, a country basically poor in natural resources and worn out by war found after the end of the conflict that the newly organized Communist movement was growing in its northern industrial areas. Poverty had been sufficiently overcome through industrialization to enable men to see that still more could be done; and Communist political organization proved to be an attractive vehicle for this outlook. This, of course, alarmed the middle classes and helped contribute to an atmosphere of fear upon which Fascism would build.

Finally, the fissiparous nature of Italian life and politics was an easy target for ardent nationalists, many of whom thought that there must be a short cut which would truly unify the nation. It has often been said that the modern Italian is highly individualist in his proclivities and tends to be apolitical.[24] This is particularly true of the peasant, deprived as he is of most of the amenities and resentful of landlords and of politicians from Rome. Regional loyalties, too, remain strong; for until very recently Italy was split up into many segments, with the Venetian and the Tuscan, for example, being widely separated both geographically and culturally from the Neapolitan.

It was in this context of national frustration, psychological inferiority feelings, economic dislocation, and political fissiparousness that Fascism arose. Its leading politician and theoretician was Benito Mussolini (1883–1945). Mussolini had been born into a family originally having anarchist sympathies but he grew up as a socialist. Entering journalism, he eventually—after a period of residence in Switzerland where he sometimes attended the lectures of Vilfredo Pareto, the theorist of elitist rule[25] —became editor of the Italian Socialist journal *Avanti*. Mussolini was always something of an enigma, however, even to his friends. He was mercurial and unpredictable.[26] After the Socialist party decided to oppose entry of Italy into World War I, thus becoming one of the few Socialist parties to maintain prewar convictions, Mussolini became alienated from the party. He took up the cause of Italian entry and when Italy finally joined the allies he saw

17. But see John Dewey, *Outline of a Critical Theory of Ethics*, New York: Hillary House, 1957, and, with James H. Tufts, *Ethics*, rev. ed., New York: Holt, 1932. Consult also Dewey's *Human Nature and Conduct*, New York: Holt, 1922, and *Liberalism and Social Action*, New York: Putnam, 1935. For a criticism of antiformalists and pragmatists, see Morton White, *Social Thought in America: The Revolt Against Formalism*, New York: Viking Press, 1949.
18. Thus W. Y. Elliott suggests that there is a close relation between pragmatism, on the one hand, and Fascism, on the other. See *The Pragmatic Revolt in Politics*, New York: Macmillan, 1928.
19. See V. I. Lenin, *The State and Revolution*, London: Allen & Unwin, 1919; and Leon Trotsky, *History of the Russian Revolution*, London: Allen & Unwin, 1919, and *My Life*, New York: Scribner, 1930; see also, V. I. Lenin, *What Is to Be Done? Burning Question of Our Movement*, New York: International Publishers, 1939; and L. Trotsky, *Dictatorship vs. Democracy (Terrorism and Communism): A Reply to Karl Kautsky* (New York: Worker's Party of America, 1922).
20. See Chapter 29.
21. Letter to James Madison, January 30, 1787.
22. Letter to Col. Smith, November 13, 1787.
23. Cf. Alfred Vagts, *A History of Militarism: Civilian and Military*, New York: Meridian Books, 1959.
24. In part, this is the theme of Carlo Levi's novel *Christ Stopped at Eboli*, Frances Frenaye, trans., New York: Farrar, Strauss, 1947, in which the villager is portrayed as a kind of quasi-anarchist.
25. See Vilfredo Pareto, *Mind and Society*, 4 vols., Arthur Livingston, ed., Andrew Borgiarro, trans., New York: Harcourt, Brace, 1935.
26. For Mussolini's biography, see Margherita Sarfatti *The Life of Benito Mussolini*, Frederic Shyto, trans., New York: Stokes, 1925; and Benito Mussolini, *My Autobiography*, New York: Scribner's, 1928. See also *The Fall of Mussolini: His Own Story*, Frances Frenaye, trans., New York: Farrar, Strauss, 1948.

service at the front. He returned from the war with the conviction that something new in Italian life was needed and out of this conviction were born the organizations originally called the *Fasci di Combattimento*.

The years 1920 to 1922 were characterized by the rapid rise and fall of Italian cabinets. The fissiparous tendencies of Italian politics in general were particularly marked during these years of national inferiority feelings and uncertainty. Only the Communists appeared to know where they were going, the Socialists having lost prestige and power not only because of the Communist secession but also because opinion, due to their war attitudes, classified them as unpatriotic. It was a time when the industrial owning classes sought for firm political solutions in a context of Communist seizure of factories, unstable governments, and widespread absence of consensus.

Increasingly, the Fascist groups following Mussolini seemed to offer an answer: Not that they supported anything in particular but that they were against the phenomena so distasteful to the propertied classes.

This is not to say, however, that the Fascist movement did not meet obstacles. In the first place, the middle classes and certainly the nobility were by no means united: There was something disreputable about the "black shirts," as Mussolini's followers came to be known, if only because their methods were unorthodox. But secondly, serious efforts were undertaken to build up a political grouping which would transcend the divisions of the older parties and offer some hope for a new alignment, while at the same time not using violent means. This resulted in the establishment of the Popular party (Popolari), founded by the highly educated priest Dom Luigi Sturzo and which appealed particularly to the overwhelmingly preponderant Roman Catholic religious beliefs of Italians. Offering a program of moderate social reform and building upon the social encyclicals of Leo XIII, the Populists for a time seemed to be growing rapidly.[27]

In the end, however, the efforts of the Populists and their allies were insufficient to stem the tide of Fascism. Confronted by his apparent inability to form long-lasting cabinets, on the one hand, and by the threatening marches and demonstrations of the Fascists, on the other, King Vittorio Emmanuel III in 1922 finally asked Mussolini to become Prime Minister at the head of a coalition government.

Once established as leader of the government, Mussolini proceeded to take advantage of his status by gradually making the position of his coalition partners untenable. Initially, Parliament continued to be elected under the old constitution and the Mussolini cabinet was subject to the usual interpollations and criticisms in the Chamber and Senate. But outside the parliamentary chambers, Fascist bands made old forms of political life increasingly impossible. Political opponents were physically mistreated and men like the Socialist deputy Matteoti were murdered.

The result was that by 1924, the Fascists dominated the government and were able to reform the electoral system in such a way as to assure their control of the Chamber of Deputies without the support of other parties. Eventually an elaborate scheme was worked out whereby the party receiving the largest number of votes obtained two-thirds of all the seats in the Chamber of Deputies.

Still later in the development of the regime, Mussolini's firm control of Parliament enabled him to propose and get adopted a scheme which abolished the Chamber of Deputies altogether and substituted for it a Chamber of Fasces and Corporations. This body was chosen by the Fascist party and by the corporations which had been set up to control and coordinate economic life and which were ostensibly representative of both workers and employers. Thus a species of functional (or economic) representation was—at least in form—substituted for the old system of geographical representation.[28]

But long before this, the regime had taken other measures to establish itself firmly. Thus it developed a system of secret police, reformed municipal government to put it more directly under the control of the central government, expanded the army and navy, and initiated a scheme of public works to provide employment for the workless.

Since one of the leading opposition political parties under the pre-Fascist administration had been the Catholic-inspired Popolari, the Fascist regime from 1924 onwards began to seek some kind of accommodation with the Church. Ever since seizure of the states of the Church by the Italian government, which culminated in the capture of Rome in 1870, the popes had refused to be reconciled to their position as subjects of the Italian state. The Bishops of Rome had proclaimed themselves prisoners of the Vatican and had announced that they would not leave until a measure of their temporal sovereignty was restored. The Fascist regime felt that if it could settle the question of Italian State–Catholic Church relations, it would eliminate part of the hostility of Catholics to its activities.

For its part, the Church had no objection to the establishment of closer relations with the state, provided that the issue of temporal sovereignty could be satisfactorily resolved. In Catholic theory, the form of government is a matter of indifference, provided the rights of the Church are respected and the natural law not openly violated. With both state and Church thus favorable to a settlement, negotiations were brought to a successful conclusion in 1929, when the Vatican Accords were signed by Mussolini and Pope Pius XI.[29] These recognized temporal sovereignty of the popes over a miniscule bit of soil in Rome (including St. Peter's and the Vatican, together with certain other papal residences) and provided for cooperation between Church and state in education. While the Accords did not in the end eliminate all Church-state tension—for controversies about education and the Catholic lay movement known as Catholic Action erupted in the thirties—the reestablishment of temporal sovereignty did serve for a time to alleviate certain major problems.

In the realm of foreign relations, the history of the Fascist regime was one of an endeavor to revive Italian prestige and to promote military power. An ideology of Italian imperialism, Fascism insisted on firmer control of such colonies as Tripoli (conquered before World War I) and agitated to expand Italian sovereignty in all areas where Italian was spoken. And in 1935 the Italians began the conquest of Ethiopia, where Italian arms in an earlier period (during the nineties) had been unsuccessful. The King of Italy was proclaimed Emperor of Ethopia. When Italy entered World War II in 1940, its troops invaded Albania and deposed its king; and the Italian king now had the title King of Albania added to his honors.

Meanwhile, Fascist philosophers and politicians, among whom Mussolini stood out, had developed a theory of politics and society within which the events of political history from 1924 to 1940 must be seen. And since the theory was to find emulators in other parts of the globe, its significance became universal, not only in the years before World War II but also in those following that conflict.[30]

Origins. The theory combined virtually all the general elements noted earlier, with the exception of racism. It never became racist, although slight gestures in that direction were made during World War II, on the insistence, in all probability, of Adolf Hitler. Some Fascist thinkers were undoubtedly familiar with the general theory of pragmatism and it is said that Mussolini was an admirer of Georges Sorel with his emphasis on the role of mythology.

In terms of peculiarly Italian origins, the influence of Machiavelli on Mussolini was apparently considerable.[31] The modern Italian saw in the conditions of twentieth-century politics parallels to those of the Renaissance affairs with which Machiavelli was concerned; and the emphasis of Machiavelli on the necessity for decisive action and the exertion of will was also appealing.

Mussolini's brief contact with Pareto, too, was of some importance. As an elitist theorist who emphasized the significance of self-con-

27. See Margo Hentze, *Pre-Fascist Italy: The Rise and Fall of the Parliamentary Regime*, London: Allen & Unwin, 1939; Denis Smith, *Italy: A Modern History*, Ann Arbor: University of Michigan Press, 1959; and Cecil Sprigge, *The Development of Modern Italy*, New Haven: Yale University Press, 1944.
28. Federico, *A History of Italian Fascism*, Muriel Grindred, trans., London: Weidenfeld & Nicholson, 1963; James Meehan, *The Italian Corporative System*, Cork, Ireland: Cork University Press, 1944; and William Welk, *Fascist Economic Policy*, Cambridge, Mass.: Harvard University Press, 1938.
29. On the politics and theory of church-state relations in Italy, see D. A. Binchy, *Church and State in Fascist Italy*, London: Oxford University Press, 1941.
30. For elaborations of Italian Fascist theory, see Benito Mussolini, *The Political and Social Doctrine of Fascism*, New York: Carnegie Endowment for International Peace, 1955; Giovanni Gentile, *The Genesis and Structure of Society*, H. S. Harris, trans., Urbana: University of Illinois Press, 1960. See also Henry S. Harris, *The Social Philosophy of Giovanni Gentile*, Urbana: University of Illinois Press, 1960; and Alfredo Rocco, *The Political Doctrine of Fascism*, New York: Carnegie Endowment for International Peace, 1926. Consult also Herman Finer, *Mussolini's Italy*, New York: Holt, 1935.
31. Mussolini's doctoral thesis dealt with Machiavelli.

fidence in politics, he had a definite impact on the young Italian politician.

Not without intellectual influence also was one version of Italian Hegelianism. In saying this, however, we should be careful not to connect all schools of the Hegelian outlook with Fascist theory. Benedetto Croce, for example, who remained a stout opponent of Fascism, was a leader of one wing of the Italian Hegelian movement. Eventually, however, Croce parted company with another important Hegelian, Giovanni Gentile,[32] who became Mussolini's Minister of Education and an important formulator of Fascist ideas.

General Outlook. The general outlook of Fascism, rooted as it was in a pragmatic temper and in a fundamental suspicion of intellect, distrusted any action which followed merely abstract theory. Instead, Mussolini argues, those having a consciousness of mission and the will to act on it should first seize political power and then, in the context of actual experience, formulate their doctrine. The will must precede speculation and cannot be rigidly bound by it.

Unlike Leninist Communism, with which it is sometimes compared, Italian Fascist theory is much more the product of successful political action than a conscious guide to that action. To be sure, this distinction between Fascism and bolshevism can be exaggerated, in view of the fact that Lenin has often been legitimately charged with improvising "theory" to fit the exigencies of the quest for power; but even when this has been admitted, Fascist doctrine remains much more of a rationalization for *faits accomplis* than does bolshevism.

Fascist Criticisms of Non-Fascist Theories and Practice. In his negative comments on what he deems to be modern liberalism and liberal democracy, Mussolini stresses its social atomism, its doctrine of liberty, and its practical results in governments which cannot act and which, in fact, become paralyzed.

The social atomism of liberalism consists in its false belief that human beings are isolates which somehow have a life of their own that can exist apart from the state. This is the assumption of J. S. Mill, according to Mussolini, and also of later liberal thinkers, including the Italians. But it is utterly without foundation. The individual is essentially bound up in his life with the state, whose ends are prior to and whose existence is the condition for individual existence.

It is not surprising, then, that in their theory of human liberty, liberalism and liberal democracy should proceed to construct doctrines equally false. Because they begin with individual isolates, they think that somehow the freedom of all these isolates from controls is the primary value. In economic policy, the liberals have a misplaced faith in the notion that individual pursuits of gain will somehow add up to the social good. And an equally unfounded statement is the assertion that freedom of expression (speech, press) is necessarily compatible with the highest ends of man.

Finally, the fruits of liberalism are best revealed in the inability of political systems founded on its principles to carry on the tasks of governance. Social atomism and the liberal doctrine of freedom have led governments to abdicate, according to Mussolini, and parliaments to become mere talking-shops. Wherever one turns, there is a paralysis of the political will or the will to power and it could not be otherwise, given the premises upon which liberals build. For they think that by talk and appeal to intellect they can govern, in face of the obvious fact that true government results only when men of will break through the never-ending talk and impose the order for which men hunger.

Similarly, Fascist theory is highly critical of all schools of Marxism, seeing in it to some degree yet another version of liberalism. Marxism, by appealing to men's particular interests and denying the existence of a general or public interest, breeds all the conditions out of which political chaos arises. It aids and abets class struggle and class consciousness, whereas the task of the man of will is to evoke by his intuitive understanding and action a popular response to his call for class collaboration.

The Fascist View of Man. Fundamentally, according to Fascism, man is essentially an emotional creature who attains his true nature only when the few men of will organize his life in the state. He is not, in other words, the rationally calculating being postulated by the classical economists and the liberals. In the absence of a leadership conscious of its own call to rule, he is something like a lost sheep without a shepherd. With that leadership, however, he is ennobled and fulfilled.

There is in Mussolini's view something very much like the position attributed to Friedrich Nietzsche who, according to Windelband, in exalting the "will for power," suggests that that is a "will for mastery, and the most important mastery is that of man over man. . . . All the brutality of trampling down those who may be in the way, all the unfettering of the primitive beast in human nature, appear here as the right and duty of the strong."[33]

This is a position which, of course, has little in common with the psychology and ethics associated with most traditional Christianity and we have already seen how it conflicts with both liberalism and Marxism. Any religion which stresses abnegation of the will to power or which exalts the ideology of perpetual peace is anathema to the founders of Italian Fascism.

The Role of the State. Leaders of will, the doctrine continues, by that fact become the bearers of the soul or spirit of the state, without which, as we have seen, the individual is lost. While liberalism would seek for a life of men outside the state, Fascism insists that the entire energy of men must be absorbed within the state.

Fascism is not primarily concerned with law and the state, for the state is not essentially a legal entity. Instead, it is spiritual and is, indeed, invested with personality. It is the nation realizing its oneness; for without the state, a nationality cannot be one. Or, as Giovanni Gentile put it, several years before he became a leading official in Mussolini's cabinet, the nation

> must . . . act in such a manner as to realise its own personality in the form of the State beyond which there is no collective will, no common personality of the people. And it must act seriously, sacrificing the individual to the collective whole, and welcoming martyrdom, which in every case is but the sacrifice of the individual to the universal, the lavishing of our own self to the ideal for which we toil.[34]

The implications of views like this are several. In the first place, all nonstate associations owe not only their legal recognition to the state but also their very being, social and spiritual. Because the state is ultimately their creator, it can also destroy them at will. They are completely at its mercy. Doctrinally speaking, this is why, despite the Vatican Accords of 1929, state and church so frequently clashed.

The Fascist doctrine implies, in the second place, that the family, considered as a peculiar form of association with both biological and social implications, has no independent right to exist. It is assimilated to the idea of the association in general and therefore is at the mercy of the state. In Fascist theory, one of its most important functions is to furnish soldiers for the state.

A third implication is the tendency to adopt a literal version of the notion that the individual is simply a cell in the higher personality of the state. The biological analogy is, as we have seen, a very old one. But only in Fascist theory does it seem to become, not merely a simile, but also an ostensibly direct description.

Attitude to Economic Life. Since the state is central in Fascist theory, one might expect the liberal thesis of the autonomy of economic life to be questioned. And such, indeed, is the case. In theory, while economic interest groups are to reflect their wills in a kind of tentative way, the final word must be with the state and its leader, who ostensibly embodies the best in all interest groups and has the capacity to discern the public interest.

One might expect that this view would tend to deprecate schemes of representation that think of man primarily as a producer rather than as a citizen. But the fact remains that as Mussolini's Fascist thought developed, it came more and more to insist on a system of economic representation and to argue against the old scheme of political representation. Eventually, as we have seen, federations and confederations of employers and employees constituted a large part of the base for the Chamber of Fasces and Corporations, which took the place of the old conventionally organized Chamber of Deputies.

This inconsistency never entirely disappears. In theory, the scheme of economic representation has much in common with anarchosyndicalism, at least up to a point; and Mussolini was, as we have seen, an admirer of Sorel. In practice, of course, the system of corporations

32. On Gentile, see Giovanni Gentile, *op. cit.*, Henry Harris, *The Social Philosophy of Giovanni Gentile*, Urbana: University of Illinois Press, 1960; Roger Holmes, *The Idealism of Giovanni Gentile*, New York: Macmillan, 1937; and Patrick Romanell, *Croce vs. Gentile; a Dialogue on Contemporary Italian Philosophy*, New York: S. F. Vanni, 1947.
33. Wilhelm Windelband, *A History of Philosophy*, vol. 2, New York: Harper Torchbooks, 1958, p. 679.
34. Giovanni Gentile, *The Reform of Education*, Dino Bigongiari, trans., New York: Harcourt, Brace, 1922, p. 13.

was largely directed and coordinated by the Fascist Grand Council, composed of men of will selected finally by Mussolini.[35] As nearly as one can determine, the theory maintains that political man entered the picture only after the apparently irreconcilable economic differences have been expressed through syndicates, confederations, and corporations. The economic debate, it may be suggested—although this is not said in so many words in Fascist literature—is somewhat analogous to the briefs of opposing lawyers before a judge. The conflicts formalized through the corporate machinery are resolved, after a hearing, by the leader or his deputies, who may be assumed to rise above the conflict as such and yet to take into consideration opposing positions before making a ruling. The decision of the Fascist leader is never a compromise, however, but always an insight into the true public interest.

Actual experience with the corporate state appears to show that this "above the battle" status of the leader was far from being a fact. By and large, the government of Italy under the Fascist regime seemed to favor employer interests, even while it was proclaiming its conflict-transcending position. While both strikes and lockouts were prohibited by law, there can be little doubt that under the circumstances, the claims of labor suffered most.

The Place of War in Fascist Ideology. One of the most characteristic features of Italian Fascism was its exaltation of war. One might, indeed, expect this if one take seriously certain anarchist views which hold that "war is the health of the state":[36] the state, this position argues, depends for its existence and status on the continuation of war. Since Fascism is obviously an ideology proclaiming the centrality of the state, it would, quite consistently, insist on an ideology of war.

In this, of course, Fascism is not unique. During the generation previous to Mussolini, as well as in his own day, ideologists of diverse political views, operating within the context of the "cult of violence" previously noted, had argued in varying ways for the inevitability and desirability of war. Thus many Social Darwinists had taken up the theme. About the time of Mussolini's march on Rome, the eminent American biologist Raymond Pearl was contending that the biological nature of man made war inescapable;[37] and at the height of Italian Fascism's prestige, the noted British anthropologist Sir Arthur Keith was writing: "Nature keeps her human orchard healthy by pruning; war is her pruning hook."[38] And one could go on.[39]

No modern political creed has, however, emphasized the alleged glory and desirability of war more than Fascism. According to it, man achieves his highest reaches of personality only through war. War weeds out the frail of heart and is used by men of will to establish themselves. It solidifies the state and calls forth most dramatically the sacrifices whereby the individual is subordinated to the universal. Its spirit combats the materialism and pursuit of gain which have been too largely the hallmarks of modern life. Through war the national state tests its mettle and its larger destiny is achieved.

In its whole ideology of war, Fascism nicely exhibits that revolt against reason of which its outlook as a whole is so emphatic an exemplification. While war and preparation for war have constituted very substantial elements in the political writings of many of the most eminent Western thinkers—notably in those of Plato, for example—usually this has occurred in a context which thinks of war as subordinate to reason and as a means to peace. In Fascist thought, however, war appears to be almost an end itself, along with the state. For Fascism, theoretical "natural" limits on human action, so stressed in classical political thought, are seemingly obliterated.

National Socialism: Development and Main Currents

Like Fascism, National Socialism was partly the outgrowth of the general factors noted in Section 1 and in some measure an expression of conditions peculiarly associated with German culture and development.

The latter may be summarized as the Lutheran political tradition; certain characteristic features of German thought as it developed in the nineteenth century; and the particular economic and political context of German thought and practice after World War I.

How much weight to give to the Lutheran political tradition is still being debated. Some would stress it,[40] while others would doubt whether it can be regarded as an important element. All things considered, it would seem that we must grant a measure of significance to the fact that a very high percentage of the German people were reared in the Lutheran outlook and that that tradition did emphasize, in Luther's theory of the two realms,[41] a doctrine of virtual passive obedience.

When the age of nationalism dawned in Germany during the Napoleonic wars, the national idea assumed many forms. Much of it was rooted in the ideology of the French Revolution. On the other hand, there came to be, particularly after the time of Bismarck, an important current attached to monarchical notions. The final unification of Germany, many held, was essentially a matter of "blood and iron" and was accomplished under the aegis of the monarchy. Thus much German nationalism under the Empire and after its overthrow in 1918 came to be an exemplification in a peculiar sense of the idea of authority reposing on strict obedience, with the army exalted as its instrument. And in the minds of some Hegelians—although by no means all—this theme was connected with the state theory of Hegel.

Perhaps because force appeared to play a central role in the rather late unification of Germany, the function of military violence was more closely studied—and approved—than in other national contexts. The nineteenth-century views of Clausewitz, which looked upon war as simply the continuation of politics, and the militarist strain in men like von Treitschke[42] had been duly noted by some scholars at the time of World War I.

The strain of romanticism in the modern German tradition must also be reckoned with. Essentially a protest against positivism in science, it was often closely connected with nationalism. In the operas of Wagner, it took the form of developing ancient German religious myths; and in such diverse fields as art, law, and the fairy tale, it often sought to exalt the peculiar virtues of German folk culture as over against the universals in Western culture. This was the outlook, in varying degrees and with different emphases, of men like Paul de Lagarde, Guido von List, Alfred Schiller, and Julius Langbohn, among others. In some thinkers, the Jews were thought of as enemies —symbols of the city life and materialism that were opposed to the life force of nature. And there was a tendency to glorify the life of action rather than that of thought. Although a recent writer may be exaggerating, he is partly right in suggesting that

> In Germany, the recovery of the unconscious in reaction against the dominant positivist ideology formed the groundwork for the German form of 20th century totalitarianism. The reaction combined the deep stream of German romanticism with the mysteries of the occult as well as with the ideals of deed. . . .[43]

In this context, elaborate racist doctrines might be expected. Houston Stewart Chamberlain was read by many National Socialist pamphleteers and, indeed, one of them gave his antisemitic tract a Chamberlain-like title.[44]

But most attitudes characteristic of National Socialism would have had far less acceptance had it not been for the particular complex of economic and political events that characterized post World War I German life. The elements of National Socialist ideology, that is to say, were latent in modern German culture, some of them, indeed, extending back through the centuries. But they would not have become

35. For details of the Italian corporate scheme, see Paul Einzig, *The Economic Foundations of Fascism*, London: Macmillan, 1934; and George L. Field, *The Syndical and Corporative Institutions of Italian Fascism*, New York: Columbia Press, 1938. See also Carmen Haider, *Capital and Labor Under Fascism*, New York: Columbia University Press, 1930. Max Ascoli, *Fascism For Whom?*, M. A. and Arthur Feiler, trans., New York: W. W. Norton, 1938, and William G. Welk, *Fascist Economic Policy*, Cambridge: Harvard University Press, 1938.
36. Cf. *War and the Intellectuals: Essays by R. S. Bourne 1915–1919*, Carl Resek, ed., New York: Harper & Row, 1964.
37. See Raymond Pearl, *Studies in Human Biology*, Baltimore: Williams & Wilkins, 1924.
38. Arthur Keith, *The Place of Prejudice in Modern Civilization*, New York: John Day, 1931.
39. Many of the views are summarized in Pitirim Sorokin, *Contemporary Sociological Theories*, New York: Harper, 1928, ch. 6.
40. See William McGovern, *From Luther to Hitler*, Boston: Houghton, Mifflin, 1941.
41. See Chapter 17.
42. See Heinrich von Treitschke, *History of Germany in the Nineteenth Century*, by Eden and Cedar Paul, trans., London: Jarrold, 1915–1919; and *Selections from Treitschke's Lectures on Politics*, Adam L. Gowans, trans., New York: Frederick A. Stokes, 1914. See also Ernest Barker, *Nietzsche and Treitschke: The Worship of Power in Modern Germany*, London: Oxford University Press, 1914.
43. G. L. Mosse, "The Mystical Origins of National Socialism," *Journal of the History of Ideas* (1961), 22: 81–96.
44. See Alfred Rosenberg, *The Myth of the Twentieth Century*, Munich: Hoheneichen, 1935; and Albert Chandler, *Rosenberg's Nazi Myth*, Ithaca: Cornell University Press, 1945.

the basis for a powerful movement had it not been for the peculiar conditions of the years 1918 to 1933.

Following military defeat, German leadership had to deal with the great inflation of the early twenties, which destroyed the savings and self-confidence of a considerable section of the middle class. After 1924, however, economic conditions became relatively stable—despite rather high unemployment—and it appeared that Germany had overcome some of its more serious economic difficulties. True, its economy was still basically capitalist and thus potentially subject to all the fluctuations characteristic of modern capitalism. But there is little reason to suppose that the outlook of National Socialism would have become popular had it not been for the second great wave of economic depression which set in after the American stock market crash of 1929. This wiped out much of what had been gained during the previous six years, multiplied the unemployed, and reduced a substantial proportion of the German people to a state of both economic and psychological insecurity. It was in this environment of the early thirties that National Socialism began to make its political gains.

The politics of the years 1918 to 1933 are closely related to economic factors. The political doctrine of the Weimar Constitution, established on the ruins of the old monarchy, was that of a moderate constitutional state with some provision for development of a socialist sector. For a time, the Social Democratic party was prominent in the affairs of the Republic, providing its first President, Friedrich Ebert. It was the Social Democrats, together with strong trade union activity, which frustrated the serious attempt of Wolfgang Kapp and his military followers to seize control of the government in 1920: through a general strike and with careful discipline, the trade unionists simply refused to cooperate, thus reducing the Kappists to impotence.

Politics after 1920 were characterized by a multiparty system and by coalition governments led often by members of one of the middle-of-the-road groups, usually the Center (or Roman Catholic) party. On the right were the Nationalists, who advocated restoration of the monarchy. On the left, the Communists adopted a Leninist approach. Even during the period of the early twenties, when inflation was rife, the moderates retained control, sustained by the power of the trade unions and by a general aversion to disorder. Thus Adolf Hitler's attempt to gain power in 1923 through a *putsch* had almost no support; and throughout the remaining part of the twenties, in fact—indeed, down to 1932—National Socialism remained a relatively minor current politically.[45] To be sure, governments after 1930 frequently resorted to legislation by decree, under Article 48 of the Constitution, as parties found it increasingly impossible to develop a measure of consensus in the Reichstag. But even the use of decree powers might have been relatively temporary had it not been for the worsening economic situation.

Economically, Germany was subjected to all the pressures engendered by the crash of 1929. As unemployment mounted, with politicians of the center appearing to be able to do little if anything about it, political repercussions began to be felt after 1930: Communism seemed to grow, the Nationalist and National Socialist movements took on new confidence, and breaches of the law became more frequent, especially after 1931. But down to the end of 1931, the national Parliament was overwhelmingly opposed both to the Nationalist and to the National Socialist movements. In 1932, however, the economic situation steadily worsened, street clashes between National Socialists and Communists became more frequent, and, what was even more indicative of a trend, Social Democrats began to desert to the National Socialists, on the one hand, and Communists on the other. Much of the appeal of National Socialism was to the younger generation, confronted as it was with prospects of unemployment and lack of opportunity for exercise of its talents. The older generation of Social Democrats in large degree remained attached to the revisionist Marxism of the twenties. Meanwhile, trade union organization and Social Democratic party alike had tended to lose flexibility and capacity to adapt to changing situations, and the bureaucratic spirit in the party which the political scientist Michels had discerned early in the twentieth century[46] became even more characteristic. By contrast, National Socialism seemed to many to be imaginative, flexible, and clear-headed, combining the socialism so popular for the previous generation and a half with a nationalist outlook that seemingly took account of existing political reality.

Despite a rapid increase in National Socialist strength after 1931, however, the party never received a majority at an unmanipulated election. Only after Hitler had been appointed

Chancellor (early in 1933), at the head of a coalition of National Socialists and Nationalists, and had been in power for some months, did National Socialism come to be accepted at elections. But by that time, electoral contests were no longer free. The National Socialist government survived until the military defeat of Germany in 1945.

Meanwhile, the ideology of National Socialism had been formulated by its leader, Adolf Hitler, aided and abetted by men like the racist Alfred Rosenberg and the master of propaganda, J. P. Goebbels. Within the party itself, there were originally several conflicting currents; and it was only after the great purge of 1934 (in which many prominent leaders of the party lost their lives) that a more or less uniform outlook developed. Even then, however, there were stresses and strains in the inner circle and the movement was held together not so much by commitment to an ideology as by the charismatic personality of Hitler himself, combined with the hope for status and power on the part of many members.

In fact, one of the first questions that any student of National Socialist ideology must ask himself is whether there was any such thing. The case for the contrary is a powerful one and was stated during the thirties by a former member of the party, Herman Rauschning. National Socialism, according to Rauschning, represented essentially the spirit of nihilism.[47] By this he means that its ideology was almost wholly an invention to gain power and was not taken seriously by its leaders. The basic impulse in the movement was to attain a "complete liberation from the past, on which to build a totalitarian despotism."[48]

There is a large measure of validity in Rauschning's argument. More perhaps even than Italian Fascism, we may think of National Socialism as rooted in sheer feeling and as shaping its overt doctrine in accordance with the exigencies of the quest for power. Thus in considerable degree it may be considered nihilistic.

But we should beware of pushing this interpretation too far. Every movement (even the most principled) in the realm of practical politics is pushed by its quest for power in the direction of nihilism; in the process of organization, its principles are to some extent forgotten.[49] No doubt National Socialism exemplified this tendency in an extreme form. Alleged doctrines tend to become mere rationalizations, to be discarded when no longer useful. At the same time, however, every movement is also captured by the notions it professes and finds it difficult to discard them even in the face of practical exigencies.

Keeping in mind these considerations, we may think of the National Socialist outlook as consisting of five strands: the doctrines of "blood and soil," Aryan supremacy and anti-semitism, *Gleichschaltung*, economy, and international order.

Blut und Boden. There can be little doubt that *blut und boden*—blood and soil—constitutes the basic strand. The term means many things but all of them add up to a rejection of reason and form and an exaltation of feeling.

First of all, German life has been distorted, according to Hitler and his theorists, by modern emphases on liberalism, universalism, and Marxism. All of these outlooks have rejected the only firm foundation for the life of a people—consciousness of kinship by blood and closeness to the soil of the Fatherland. Like Mussolini, Hitler criticizes liberalism for stripping man of his status as a product of the group. Universalism and Marxism would dilute the intensity of group feelings, as would, according to some National Socialist pamphleteers, traditional Christianity.

The doctrine of blood and soil implies that beneath the upper layers of life in society—such artifacts as universal legal norms, absence of race consciousness, divisions along class lines—there lies a primitive and tribal sense of oneness which it is the task of National Socialism to resurrect. The literature of National Socialism is filled with appeals to folkish foundations for collective life: Thus it proclaims law to be the dictate of the folk rather than of

45. Thus down to 1931, it was able to muster only about a dozen votes in the Reichstag. See William Shirer, *The Rise and Fall of the Third Reich*, New York: Simon & Schuster, 1960.
46. Roberto Michels, *Political Parties*, Eden Paul and Cedar Paul, trans., New York: Hearst's International Library, 1915.
47. Herman Rauschning, *The Revolution of Nihilism*, E. W. Dickes, trans., New York: Alliance, 1939.
48. *Ibid.*, p. 12.
49. Cf. Eric Hoffer, *The True Believer*, New York: Harper, 1951.

reason; racial ties of blood to be superior to economic self-interest; and solidarity with one's folk to be the true social cohesion as over against a class solidarity exalted by Marxists but produced by an effete, industrialized civilization. To think with one's blood becomes the hallmark of National Socialist doctrine.

Folkish doctrine includes a strong emphasis on the family and on the alleged virtues of rural existence. As a protest against urban life, the natural ties of the rural countryside are often appealed to.

Aryan Supremacy and Antisemitism. The antecedents for National Socialist race doctrine have already been noted. It is perhaps the most distinctive element in the ideology; for, as we have seen, racism is absent in Italian Fascism.

In *Mein Kampf*, Adolf Hitler dwells at length on the notion of Aryan supremacy and on his repudiation of Jewishness. He describes how when he was living in Vienna he first became aware of the East European Jews, with their beards and strange dress. He brooded on this almost endlessly and later his expert on "racial science," Rosenberg, worked out at great length the implications of antisemitic ideology.

Aryan supremacy is apparently grounded on a mixture of biological and cultural factors which make the Aryan—reflected in truest form by the Nordic races like Germans and Scandinavians—the epitome of imagination, intelligence, and capacity for morality. This is demonstrated historically in cultural achievements and in military prowess. But Aryan hegemony is threatened in the modern world by the yellow races and by such impure breeds as the Slavs. Therefore, it behooves all Nordic Aryans to develop a spirit of solidarity if they are to preserve the inestimable advantages of their superiority for the world.

National Socialist racist doctrine is expressed through legislation prohibiting marriage between Jews and Aryans; reducing and then excluding Jews in the learned professions; forcing them to wear distinctive badges; confiscation of property for minor offenses; and eventually—in World War II—physical annihilation. Legislation and administration are such, moreover, that mob action against Jews is encouraged; and judges, instructed to think racially, must adjudicate accordingly.

Gleichschaltung. National Socialism shares with Italian Fascism a repugnance for ragged edges in the organization of collective life. Because it repudiates the notion that individuals can or ought to have ends apart from those of the folk, it looks with suspicion on all organizations and institutions that are not strictly subordinate to the folkish state.

It is at this point that the doctrine of *gleichschaltung* enters the picture. All life is to be coordinated by the state, which is the representative of the folk. This means that associations and groups of every kind and purpose must be directly related to state ends and permeated by the folk spirit. No segment of human existence must be allowed to escape.

The thrust of National Socialist doctrine is thus to eliminate all distinctions between public and private realms and all tensions between state and nonstate associations. The latter become, in fact, simply instrumentalities of the state. The most intimate details of what has hitherto been regarded as private life are theoretically subject to the scrutiny of the folk.

All this is illustrated nicely in the theory and practice of the Third Reich itself. The state is subject to the leadership principle (*Der Fuehrer Prinzip*) in very much the same way noted in Italian Fascism; direction and authority proceed from the top downward, the assumption being that the leader at every level is the best interpreter of the folkish spirit. The leadership notion is encouraged and reinforced by the central position given to the National Socialist party (N.S.D.A.P.), which is the sole political party allowed and which is not so much a party in the traditional Western sense of the term as an elite that provides the intensive direction of the state. Within the party itself, of course, the leadership principle is also central.

From folkish state and party radiate out the several kinds of organizations and associations subject to their guidance. Labor unions, for example, become agencies of the state for enforcing ideology and norms among working people. The several economic estates coordinate production and distribution and youth organizations are likewise subjected to central control. Music and art, too, are organized under the supervision of the Reich's cultural agencies.[50]

The Economy. On its road to political power, the socialism side of National Socialism constituted one of its greatest appeals, particularly after the onset of the great depression. Its doctrine was calculated to establish economic and social security for the millions who had been deprived of it, first by the great inflation following World War I and then by the post-1929 collapse.

And National Socialism is indeed highly critical of the capitalist structure which it associates with liberalism. In its party platforms, it promises to better the lot of the worker and the small business by breaking cartels and developing public responsibility of economic enterprise. It is critical of the ideology of laissez faire and insists on a positive economic policy guided by the state. In some of its statements, as a matter of fact, it reminds one very strongly of German social democracy.[51]

Certainly the thrust of its doctrine is toward a planned economy and one in which both natural and human resources will be fully utilized. Like Italian Fascism, it is impatient with the policy of drift which it associates with liberal parliamentary democracy.

But in at least two respects, its economic ideology is far removed from that of social democracy. In the first place, its leadership principle is extended to the economy in quite thorough fashion and this means, in practice, that in considerable measure the large industrialists who controlled business life under the Weimar Republic continue to do so (in their capacity as economic *fuehrers* of the "new order") under National Socialism. True, they are subject to the exacting and often arbitrary demands of state and party and their freedom of action in relation to the economy as a whole is greatly circumscribed. Nevertheless, vis-à-vis the ordinary worker, they continue in their accustomed role and if anything are even more powerful than before; for they now have the full sanction of public authority behind their position. Everything in the ideology of National Socialism is against the conception of workers' control in industry as it is against the notion of parliamentary control generally. Basic decisions of both policy and administration are to be made at the summit and the workers are to obey.

A second important respect in which National Socialist economic doctrine differs from social democracy lies in the end for which the economy supposedly exists. Generally speaking, the purpose of National Socialist autarchy or self-sufficiency in the economy is to facilitate military strength. Autarchy implies that so far as possible the state will depend only on the resources of its own economy; and if it must have economic relations with other states, the commercial intercourse will be carried on by the state itself rather than by independent entrepreneurs. Too great dependence on others will frustrate the military ends of the state by subjecting it to the uncertainties of foreign supplies and markets.

In practice, the autarchic planning principles espoused by National Socialism provided an admirable basis for wiping out unemployment. Vast highway, public works, and military programs were set in motion and soon idle men and idle resources were no more.

The International Order. Like Fascism, National Socialist thought exalts the heroic qualities of the military and thinks of the life of the camp as one to which all should aspire. Connecting its international with its *blut und boden* position, it sees the autarchic, strongly military national state as the fruit of the deepest emotional yearnings of the folk soul. In the life of the self-sufficient armed state, the collective psyche fulfills its mission; and in struggling against inferior races and peoples it attains its primary goal.

Given this outlook, it is not surprising to find National Socialism fundamentally hostile to international organization. It rises to power as a protest against what it believes to be the unjust dictate of the Treaty of Versailles, which it thinks of as having kept Germany in thrall during the years before it gains control of the state. Its goals cannot be reconciled with the ideals of the League of Nations and its disarmament efforts.

Beyond this, the ideology of National Socialism becomes rather vague and resorts to what Sorel would no doubt think of as political mythology. It sees its Third Reich as the successor to the Second Reich established by Bismarck as well as to the First Reich which it identifies with the Holy Roman Empire of the German people. Interestingly enough, millennarian imagery enters at this point: The Third Reich, once established, will continue a thousand years and will stand as the symbol of

50. For a description of the coordination, see William Ebenstein, *The Nazi State*, New York: Farrar & Rinehart, 1943.

51. See Fritz Ermarth, *The New Germany: National Socialist Government in Theory and Practice*, Washington, D.C.: Digest Press, 1936; and, J. E. Nordskog, "Is Nazism Socialism?" in *Sociology and Social Research* 23 (1939) 455-465.

resistance to inferior races and as the exemplar of Nordic virtues. It will repudiate the vague and sentimental internationalism of Christianity, liberalism, and democracy, and breed a race of virtuous soldiers who will carry on the tradition of the ancient Germans.

To some extent, there is an affinity between National Socialism and the world historical views of Oswald Spengler, whose writings were so popular during the twenties and early thirties. Spengler sees in the modern world a decline of the West with the rise of rootlessness and a tendency to cosmopolitanism—world outlooks which deprecate attachments to particular groups and which exalt a kind of undifferentiated universalism.[52]

Although Spengler's outlook and that of National Socialism cannot be equated, it would seem that both reflect in some degree a strong reaction to internationalism and to what both discern as a tendency to level cultures and nations. Just as both would submerge the individual in the national soul, so each would appear to repudiate the quest for a world spirit to which all national souls could be held in bondage.

Evaluation of Fascism and National Socialism

Neither Fascism nor National Socialism can be thought of as political philosophies, in the traditional sense. Both, in greater or lesser degrees, repudiate reason and both are suspicious of systematic thought and the categories of logic.

But both are certainly ideologies, which because they have been widely accepted, either passively or actively, must be assumed to express something concerning man and his aspirations that has remained unsatisfied in other political outlooks. What is it, then, about Fascism and National Socialism which has both repelled and attracted twentieth-century man?

The repulsion can be accounted for by reason of the fact that Fascism and National Socialism do, as Rausching emphasizes, go so far in the direction of utter nihilism. There is something about the human spirit which calls for principles and which rejects outlooks that seem to place scant value upon them. This is partly what is meant when the classical tradition tells us that man is a rational animal: Historically, at least, he has tended to be uneasy about action which could not at least claim some principle as its cause. But Fascism and National Socialism, in appealing primarily to emotion—even though we have contended that they were not utterly without principle—have tended to deny this aspiration. In disparaging the ideal of rationality, they have attempted to discredit a major current in the whole cultural tradition.

At the same time, Fascism and National Socialism—or variants of them—are not dead; nor can they be defeated by war. For in their emotional expression, they reflect a basic and to some degree a valid criticism of and an understandable dissatisfaction with modern versions of the rational tradition. Distorted as this criticism may seem to be, it is worth emphasizing.

First of all, their stress on emotion represents to many a valid protest against views of life and politics which would completely destroy the feeling and intuitive man. About some versions of liberalism and Marxism, for example, there has been a flavor of the mechanistic—a tendency to reduce the human being to a piece of machinery manageable by scientists who understand psychology and sociology. Against this tendency, Fascism and National Socialism have raised their banners of objection and have found a ready response.

Secondly, they have constituted violent expressions of man's frustrations in his quest for community. The alienation of human beings from a sense of community has been a commonplace theme in modern thought. Yet all solutions to the problem seem to leave a sense of dissatisfaction. Fascism and National Socialism, in seeking a kind of resurrection of the tribal, may not have provided an answer either; but certainly this factor must be considered in weighing their appeal and in evaluating them as ideologies.

Finally, both Fascism and National Socialism, having gained support under conditions of economic disorder, legitimately criticized a world in which men had but barely glimpsed the possibilities of planning for abundance. Fascist planning, to be sure, subordinated economic planning to what could only be called demonic ends; but in the very dramatization of these ends, it raised the question as to why the resources of the earth could not be employed for nondemonic purposes. The ideology of Fascism represented simply an extreme form of planning for destruction—an end which is exalted by most of the so-called Great Powers in our own day, with their swollen military budgets, their disregard for human life, and their euphemistic language in which peace is achieved by war and military conscription is a species of freedom. But then contemporary Great Powers—which may be defined as nation-states having great killing capacity—in effect re-pose the question made dramatic by Fascist ideology: Why do men submit to planning for destruction instead of joining together to demand planning for abundance?

This question, in turn, may be related to a still broader one: Is there a kind of collective subconscious desire for both slavery and death? Perhaps in grappling with this query, we may discover clues to some of the puzzles and paradoxes of the human condition.

Part IV Selected References

(in addition to those mentioned in footnotes)

24. *Hegel, Organicism, and Modern Political Thought*

AVINERI, S. "Problem of War in Hegel's Thought." *Journal of the History of Ideas* 22 (1961), 463–474.

AVINERI, S. "Hegel and Nationalism." *Review of Politics* 24 (1962), 461–484.

BOSANQUET, BERNARD. *The Philosophical Theory of the State.* 3rd ed. London: Macmillan, 1920.

CARRITT, E. F. *Morals and Politics.* Oxford: Clarendon, 1935. Ch. 9.

FINDLAY, JOHN N. *Hegel: A Re-Examination.* New York: Collier Books, 1962.

FOSTER, MICHAEL B. *The Political Philosophies of Plato and Hegel.* Reprint. New York: Russell and Russell, 1965.

FRIEDRICH, CARL J. ED. *The Philosophy of Hegel.* New York: Modern Library, 1965.

GOLDSTEIN, L. J. "The Meaning of State in Hegel's Philosophy of History." *Philosophical Quarterly* 12 (1962), 60–72.

HECKSCHER, G. "Calhoun's Idea of Concurrent Majority and the Constitutional Theory of Hegel." *American Political Science Review,* August 1939. (Vol. 33, pp. 585–590.)

HEGEL, GEORG W. F. *Political Writings.* T. M. Knox, trans., introductory essay by Z. A. Pelczynski. Oxford: Clarendon, 1964.

HEGEL, GEORG W. F. *Reason in History: A General Introduction to the Philosophy of History.* New York: Liberal Arts Press, 1953.

HEGEL, GEORG W. F. *Philosophy of Right.* Trans. and notes by T. M. Knox. Oxford: Clarendon, 1958.

HEGEL, GEORG W. F. *The Philosophy of History.* With prefaces by Charles Hegel and by J. Sibree, trans., and a new introduction by C. J. Friedrich. New York: Dover, 1956.

HOBHOUSE, L. T. *The Metaphysical Theory of the State.* Reprint. New York: Barnes & Noble, 1960.

HOOK, SIDNEY. *From Hegel to Marx.* Reprint. Ann Arbor: University of Michigan Press, 1962.

KANT, IMMANUEL. *The Critique of Practical Reason.* Chicago: University of Chicago Press, 1949.

KANT, IMMANUEL. *The Idea of a Universal History on a Cosmopolitical Level.* Hanover: Dartmouth College Press, 1927.

KAUFMANN, WALTER A. *Hegel: Reinterpretation, Texts and Commentary.* Garden City: Doubleday, 1965.

Chapter 30

52. Oswald Spengler, *The Decline of the West,* New York: Knopf, 1939, and *The Hour of Decision,* Charles Atkinson, trans., New York: Knopf, 1934.

KAUFMANN, WALTER A. "Hegel's Early Anti-theological phase." *Philosophical Review* 63 (1954), 3–18.

LEE, O. "Method and System in Hegel." *Philosophical Review* 48 (1939), 3–18.

LINDSAY, A. D. *Kant*. London: E. Benn, 1934.

LOWITH, KARL. *From Hegel to Nietzsche*. New York: Holt, 1964.

MCTAGGART, J. M. E. *Studies in the Hegelian Dialectic*. 2nd ed. New York: Russell and Russell, 1964.

MARCUSE, HERBERT. *Reason and Revolution: Hegel and the Rise of Social Theory*. London: Oxford, 1941; Boston: Beacon, 1968.

MERZ, J. T. *History of European Thought in the Nineteenth Century*. Vols. 3 and 4. London: W. Blackwood & Sons, 1903–1914.

MORRIS, G. S. *Hegel's Philosophy of the State and of History*. Chicago: Griggs, 1887.

MUELLER, G. E. "Hegel Legend of Thesis-Antithesis-Synthesis." *Journal of the History of Ideas* 19 (1958), 411–414.

MURE, G. R. G. *The Philosophy of Hegel*. New York: Oxford, 1965.

PLAMENATZ, JOHN. *Man and Society*, 2 vols. New York: McGraw-Hill, 1963.

POPPER, KARL. *The Open Society and Its Enemies*. Vol. 2. London: G. Routledge & Sons, 1945.

REISS, H. S., ED. *The Political Thought of the German Romantics, 1793–1813*. London: Blackwell, 1955.

RUSSELL, BERTRAND. *Philosophy and Politics*. Cambridge: Cambridge University Press, 1947.

SANDERS, W. J. "Logical Unity of John Dewey's Educational Philosophy Compared with the Dialectic of G. W. F. Hegel." *Ethics* 50 (1940), 424–40.

SMITH, C. I. "Hegel on War." *Journal of the History of Ideas* 26 (1965), 282–285.

STACE, W. T. *The Philosophy of Hegel*. New York: Dover, 1955.

STERN, FRITZ R. *Politics of Cultural Despair: A Study in the Rise of the Germanic Ideology*. Berkeley: University of California Press, 1961.

TUCKER, R. C. "Cunning of Reason in Hegel and Marx." *Review of Politics* 18 (1956), 269–295.

VAUGHAN, CHARLES E. *Studies in the History of Political Philosophy Before and After Rousseau*. Manchester: University of Manchester Press, 1925; New York: Russell, 1960.

WILKINS, B. T. "James, Dewey, and Hegelian Idealism." *Journal of the History of Ideas* 17 (1956), 332–346.

25. *Marx, the Marxists, and Modern Politics*

Biography, Development, and General

BARON, S. H. *Plekhanov, the Father of Russian Marxism*. Stanford: Stanford University Press, 1963.

BEER, MAX. *The Life and Teachings of Karl Marx*. Boston: Small, Maynard, 1924.

BERDIAEV, N. A. *The Origins of Russian Communism*. Ann Arbor: University of Michigan Press, 1955.

BERLIN, ISAIAH. *Karl Marx: His Life and Environment*. New York: Oxford University Press, 1963.

BYCHOWSKI, G. *Dictators and Disciples from Caesar to Stalin*. New York: International Universities Press, 1948.

CANNON, JAMES P. *The History of American Trotskyism*. New York: Pioneer, 1944.

COLE, G. D. H. *A History of Socialist Thought*. 7 vols. London: Macmillan, 1953.

CORNU, A. *Origins of Marxist Thought*. Springfield, Ill.: Charles C Thomas, 1957.

DEUTSCHER, ISAAC. *The Prophet Armed*. [Trotsky.] New York: Oxford University Press, 1954.

DEUTSCHER, ISAAC. *The Prophet Unarmed: Trotsky, 1921–1929*. New York: Oxford University Press, 1959.

DEUTSCHER, ISAAC. *The Prophet Outcast: Trotsky 1929–1940*. New York: Oxford University Press, 1963.

FOX, RALPH. *Lenin: A Biography*. London: Victor Gollancz, 1933.

GRAY, ALEXANDER. *The Socialist Tradition: Moses to Lenin*. London: Longmans, Green, 1946.

HOWE, IRVING. *The American Communist Party: A Critical History*. New York: Praeger, 1962.

KAUTSKY, KARL. *Frederick Engels: His Life, His Work and His Writings*. Chicago: C. H. Kerr, 1899.

LAFARGUE, PAUL. *Karl Marx: His Life and Work*. New York: International Publishers, 1943.

MAYER, GUSTAV. *Friedrich Engels: A Biography*. New York: Knopf, 1936.

MEHRING, FRANC. *Karl Marx: The Story of His Life*. London: Allen & Unwin, 1955.

NOMAD, MAX. *Political Heretics, from Plato to Mao-tse-Tung*. Ann Arbor: University of Michigan Press, 1963.

NOMAD, MAX. *Apostles of Revolution*. Boston: Little Brown, 1939; New York: Collier, 1961.

PAYNE, P. *Mao Tse Tung*. New York: Secker and Warburg, 1950.

ROSENBERG, ARTHUR. *A History of Bolshevism from Marx to the First Five Year Plan*. London: Oxford University Press, 1934.

ROSENBERG, ARTHUR. *Democracy and Socialism: A Contribution to the Political History of the Past 150 Years*. New York: Knopf, 1939.

RÜHLE, OTTO. *Karl Marx, His Life and Work*. New York: Viking Press, 1929.

SALVADORI, M. *A Brief History of the Communist Movement in the Twentieth Century*. New York: Holt, 1952.

SCHLESINGER, RUDOLF. *Marx: His Time and Ours*. London: Routledge & Paul, 1950.

SCHWARTZ, B. *Chinese Communism and the Rise of Mao*. Cambridge, Mass.: Harvard University Press, 1951; New York: Harper Torchbooks, 1967.

SERGE, VICTOR. *Memoirs of a Revolutionary (1901–1941)*. Peter Sedgwick, trans. New York: Oxford University Press, 1963.

SOUVARINE, BORIS. *Stalin: A Critical Survey of Bolshevism*. New York: Alliance, 1939.

TRAGER, F. N., ED. *Marxism in Southeast Asia*. Stanford: Stanford University Press, 1960.

ULAM, ADAM B. *The Unfinished Revolution: An Essay on the Sources of Influence of Marxism and Communism*. New York: Random House, 1960.

WILSON, EDMUND. *To the Finland Station*. New York: Harcourt, Brace, 1940; Doubleday, Anchor, 1953.

WOLFE, BERTRAM D. *Marx and America.* New York: John Day, 1934.

Exposition and Doctrine: Marx and Engels

ENGELS, FRIEDRICH. *The Condition of the Working Class in England.* New York: Macmillan, 1958.
ENGELS, FRIEDRICH. *Herr Eugen Dühring's Revolution in Science.* New York: International Publishers, 1935.
ENGELS, FRIEDRICH. *The Peasant War in Germany.* New York: International Publishers, 1926.
ENGELS, FRIEDRICH. *Socialism, Utopian and Scientific.* E. Averling, trans. New York: International Publishers, 1945.
MARX, KARL. *The Civil War In France.* Moscow: Foreign Languages Publishing House, 1948.
MARX, KARL. *Capital.* 4th ed. Eden and Cedar Paul, trans. New York: Dutton, 1930.
MARX, KARL. *The Civil War in the United States.* New York: International Publishers, 1937.
MARX, KARL. *Critique of the Gotha Programme.* New York: International Publishers, 1938.
MARX, KARL. *Economic and Philosophic Manuscripts of 1844.* Martin Milligan, trans. Moscow: Foreign Language Publishing House, 1959.
MARX, KARL. *The Eighteenth Brumaire of Louis Bonaparte.* New York: International Publishers, 1963.
MARX, KARL. *A History of Economic Theories.* Edited by Karl Kautsky, Terence McCarthy, trans. New York: Langland, 1952.
MARX, KARL. *The Poverty of Philosophy.* Moscow: Foreign Language Publishing House, 1956.
MARX, KARL. *A World Without Jews,* Introduction by D. D. Runes. New York: Philosophical Library, 1959.
MARX, KARL, AND FRIEDRICH ENGELS. *Basic Writings on Politics and Philosophy.* Edited by Lewis Feuer. Garden City: Doubleday, 1959.
MARX, KARI, AND FRIEDRICH ENGELS. *Capital, the Communist Manifesto and Other Writings.* New York: Modern Library, 1952.
MARX, KARL, AND FRIEDRICH ENGELS. *The Essential Left: Four Classic Texts on the Principles of Socialism.* London: Allen & Unwin, 1961.
MARX, KARL, AND FRIEDRICH ENGELS. *The German Ideology.* Parts I and II. Edited by R. Pascal. New York: International Publishers, 1947.
MARX, KARL, AND FRIEDRICH ENGELS. *Letters to Americans, 1848–1895.* Leonard Mins, trans. New York: International Publishers, 1953.
MARX, KARL, AND FRIEDRICH ENGELS. *Marx and Engels on Malthus: Selections from the Writings of Marx and Engels Dealing with the Theories of Thomas Malthus.* Edited by Robert Meek. New York: International Publishers, 1954.
MARX, KARL, AND FRIEDRICH ENGELS. *On Religion.* Introduction by Reinhold Niebuhr. New York: Schocken Books, 1964.
MARX, KARL, AND FRIEDRICH ENGELS. *On the Theory of Marxism.* Selections from Marx, Engels, Lenin, and Stalin. New York: International Publishers, 1948.

Exposition, Doctrine, and Criticism: Since Engels

BELL, D. "The Rediscovery of Alienation, Some Notes Along the Quest of the Historical Marx." *Journal of Philosophy* 56 (1959), 933–952.
BENNETT, J. C. *Christianity and Communism Today.* New York: Association Press, 1950.
BERNSTEIN, EDUARD. *Evolutionary Socialism: A Criticism and Affirmation.* London: Independent Labour Party, 1907; New York: Schocken, 1961.
BOBER, M. *Karl Marx's Interpretation of History.* Cambridge: Harvard University Press, 1948.
BUBER, MARTIN. *Paths in Utopia.* New York: Macmillan, 1950; Boston: Beacon, 1958.
CHEN, JEROME. *Mao and the Chinese Revolution.* London: Oxford University Press, 1965.
CORNFORTH, M. *Materialism and Dialectical Method.* Cambridge: Harvard University Press, 1948.
DE LEON, DANIEL. *Socialist Landmarks; Four Addresses.* New York: New York Labor News Co., 1952.
DE MAN, HENRI. *The Psychology of Socialism.* London: Allen & Unwin, 1928.
DOBB, MAURICE H. *On Marxism Today.* London: Hogarth Press, 1932.
FISCHER, GEORGE. *Science and Politics: The New Sociology in the Soviet Union.* Ithaca: Cornell University Press, 1964.
FISCHER, LOUIS. *The Life and Death of Stalin.* New York: Harper, 1952.
FROMM, ERICH. *Marx's Concept of Man.* New York: Ungar, 1961.
FROMM, ERICH. *Beyond the Chains of Illusion: My Encounter with Marx and Freud.* New York: Simon and Schuster, 1962.
HEIMANN, EDUARD. *Reason and Faith in Modern Society: Liberalism, Marxism, and Democracy.* Middleton, Conn.: Wesleyan University Press, 1961.
HOOK, SIDNEY. *From Hegel to Marx: Studies in the Intellectual Development of Karl Marx.* New York: Reynal and Hitchcock, 1936.
HOOK, SIDNEY. *Towards the Understanding of Karl Marx; A Revolutionary Interpretation.* New York: John Day, 1933.
HUNT, R. N. C. *The Theory and Practice of Communism.* New York: Macmillan, 1950.
KAUTSKY, KARL. *Terrorism and Communism; A Contribution to the Natural History of Revolution.* London: Allen & Unwin, 1920.
KELSEN, HANS. *The Political Theory of Bolshevism.* Berkeley: University of California Press, 1948.
KHRUSHCHEV, NIKITA. *The Anatomy of Terror: Khrushchev's Revelations About Stalin's Regime.* Washington: Public Affairs Press, 1956.
LENIN, VLADIMIR I. *Collected Works of V. I. Lenin.* Only authorized edition by Lenin Institute, Moscow. New York: International Publishers, 1927.
LENIN, VLADIMIR I. *Imperialism, the State and Revolution.* New York: Vanguard, 1927.
LENIN, VLADIMIR I. *Lenin on War and Peace.* Peking: Foreign Languages Press, 1960.
LENIN, VLADIMIR I. *The Letters of Lenin.* Edited and translated by Elizabeth Hill and Doris Modie. London: Chapman and Hall, 1937.
LEWIS, JOHN. *Marxism and the Open Mind.* London: Routledge and Paul, 1957.
LONDON, JACK. *The War of the Classes.* New York: Grosset and Dunlap, 1912.

MAO TSE-TUNG. *On the Correct Handling of Contradictions Among the People.* New York: New Century Publishers, 1957.
MAO TSE-TUNG. *On Peoples Democratic Rule.* New York: New Century Publishers, 1950.
MAO TSE-TUNG. *The Political Thought of Mao Tse-Tung: Anthology.* New York: Praeger, 1963.
MALLOCK, W. H. *A Critical Examination of Socialism.* London: J. Murray, 1908.
MARCUSE, HERBERT. *Soviet Marxism, A Critical Analysis.* New York: Columbia University Press, 1958.
MASHRUWALA, K. *Gandhi and Marx.* Ahmedabad: Marajiran Publishing House, 1951.
MAYO, H. B. *Democracy and Marxism.* New York: Oxford University Press, 1955.
MEYER, A. G. *Leninism.* Cambridge, Mass: *Harvard* University Press, 1957.
MITRANY, DAVID. *Marx Against the Peasant: A Study in Social Dogmatism.* Chapel Hill: University of North Carolina Press, 1951.
PAPPENHEIM, F. *The Alienation of Modern Man: An Interpretation Based on Marx and Tonnies.* New York: Monthly Review Press, 1959.
PETERSON, ARNOLD. *Bourgeois Socialism, Its Rise and Collapse in America.* New York: New York Labor News Co., 1951.
PLAMENATZ, JOHN. *Man and Society.* 2 vols. New York: McGraw-Hill, 1963.
PLEKHANOV, G. V. *Anarchism and Socialism.* Chicago: C. H. Kerr, 1912.
ROBINSON, JOAN. *An Essay on Marxian Economics.* New York: St. Martin, 1967.
SEE, HENRI E. *The Economic Interpretation of History.* New York: Adelphi, 1929; Franklin, 1966.
SWEEZY, PAUL M. *The Theory of Capitalist Development: Principles of Marxian Political Economy.* New York: Oxford University Press, 1942.
TROTSKY, LEON. *In Defense of Marxism.* New York: Pioneer Publishers, 1942.
TROTSKY, LEON. *Lenin.* New York: Minton, Balch, 1925.
TROTSKY, LEON. *Lessons of October.* New York: Pioneer Publishers, 1937.
TROTSKY, LEON. *The History of the Russian Revolution.* Max Eastman, trans. New York: Simon and Schuster, 1932.
TUCKER, ROBERT C. *Philosophy and Myth in Karl Marx.* Cambridge: Cambridge University Press, 1961.
WETTER, G. A. *Dialectical Materialism: A Historical and Systematic Survey of Philosophy in the Soviet Union.* New York: Praeger, 1958.
WILLIAM, MAURICE. *The Social Interpretation of History: A Refutation of the Marxian Economic Interpretation of History.* Long Island City: Sotery Publishing Co., 1921.

26. *The Modern Liberal Tradition*

BAUMGARDT, D. *Bentham and the Ethics of Today.* Princeton: Princeton University Press, 1952.
BENTHAM, JEREMY. *A Fragment on Government* and *An Introduction to the Principles of Morals and Legislation.* Oxford: Clarendon, 1948.
BERTHOLD, S. M. *Thomas Paine, America's First Liberal.* Boston: Meador Publishing Co., 1938.
BRINTON, CRANE. *The Shaping of Modern Thought.* Englewood Cliffs: Prentice-Hall, 1963.
BULLOCK, ALAN, AND MAURICE SHOCK, EDS. *The Liberal Tradition from Fox to Keynes.* London: Adam and Charles Black, 1956.
BURY, J. B. *The Idea of Progress.* London: Macmillan, 1920; New York: Dover, 1955.
CROCE, BENEDETTO. *History as the Story of Liberty.* New York: W. W. Norton, 1941.
DAVIDSON, WILLIAM L. *Political Thought in England: The Utilitarians from Bentham to J. S. Mill.* New York: Holt, 1916.
DEWEY, JOHN. *The Public and Its Problems.* New York: Holt, 1927.
HALLOWELL, JOHN. *The Decline of Liberalism as an Ideology.* Berkeley and Los Angeles: University of California Press, 1943.
HARTZ, LOUIS. *The Liberal Tradition in America.* New York: Harcourt, Brace, 1955.
HOBHOUSE, L. T. *The Metaphysical Theory of the State.* New York: Barnes & Noble, 1960.
HUGHES, H. STUART. *Consciousness and Society: The Re-orientation of European Social Thought, 1890–1930.* New York: Knopf, 1961.
JEFFERSON, THOMAS. *Writings of Thomas Jefferson.* New York: G. P. Putman, 1904–1905.
KAYSER, ELMER L. *The Grand Social Enterprise: A Study of Jeremy Bentham in His Relation to Liberal Nationalism.* New York: Columbia University Press, 1932.
KEETON, GEORGE W., AND GEORGE SCHWARZENBERGER, EDS., *Jeremy Bentham and the Law.* London: Stevens, 1948.
KEYNES, JOHN MAYNARD. *The End of Laissez-Faire.* London: L. and V. Woolf, 1926.
KEYNES, JOHN MAYNARD. *Essays in Persuasion.* New York: Harcourt, Brace, 1932.
LAFONTAINERIE, FRANCOIS DE, ED. AND TRANS. *French Liberalism and Education in the Eighteenth Century.* New York: McGraw-Hill, 1932.
LINDSAY, A. D. *The Modern Democratic State.* New York: Oxford University Press, 1962.
LIPPMANN, WALTER. *Public Opinion.* New York: Harcourt, Brace, 1922.
LUNDIN, HILDA G. *The Influence of Jeremy Bentham on English Democratic Development.* Iowa City: State University of Iowa Press, 1920.
MABBOTT, J. D. *The State and the Citizen.* London: Hutchinson, 1948.
MACCUNN, JOHN. *Six Radical Thinkers.* London: E. Arnold, 1907.
MACIVER, R. M. *The Web of Government.* New York: Macmillan, 1947.
MACK, M. *Jeremy Bentham: An Odyssey of Ideas.* New York: Columbia University Press, 1963.
MALONE, DUMAS. *Jefferson and His Time.* Boston: Little, Brown, 1948.
MARTIN, KINGSLEY. *French Liberal Thought in the Eighteenth Century.* London: Turnstile Press, 1954.
MAYO, HENRY B. *An Introduction to Democratic Theory.* Chicago: University of Chicago Press, 1956; New York: Oxford University Press, 1960.
MORGAN, CHARLES. *The Liberty of Thought and the Separation of Powers.* Oxford: Clarendon, 1948.
OSTROGORSKI, M. *Democracy and the Organization of Political Parties.* New York: Macmillan, 1902.
PENNOCK, J. ROLAND. *Liberal Democracy: Its Merits and Prospects.* New York: Rinehart, 1950.
RITCHIE, DAVID G. *Natural Rights.* New York: Humanities, 1952.

SCHAPIRO, J. SALWYN. *Liberalism and the Challenge of Fascism: Social Forces in England and France (1815–1870)*. New York: McGraw Hill, 1949.

SCHILPP, PAUL A., ED. *The Philosophy of John Dewey*. New York: Tudor, 1951.

SELDEN, A., ED. *Agenda for a Free Society: Essays on Hayek's Constitution of Liberty*. London: Hutchinson, 1961.

SMITH, ADAM. *The Wealth of Nations*. New York: Modern Library, 1937.

SOLTAU, ROGER. *French Political Thought in the Nineteenth Century*. London: E. Benn, 1931.

TUVESON, ERNEST L. *Millennium and Utopia: A Study of the Background of the Idea of Utopia*. Berkeley: University of California Press, 1949.

VAUGHAN, C. E. *Studies in the History of Political Philosophy Before and After Rousseau*. London: Longmans, Green, 1925. N.Y.: Russell, 1960.

WILLIAMS, ALFRED T. *The Concept of Equality in the Writings of Rousseau, Bentham, and Kant*. New York: Columbia University Press, 1907.

WOLLHEIM, R. "Democracy." *Journal of the History of Ideas* 19 (1958), 225 ff.

27. *The Modern Conservative Tradition*

BAUMANN, AUTHUR A. *Burke: The Founder of Conservatism*. London: Eyre and Spottiswoode, 1929.

BAYLE, FRANCIS. *Les Idees Politiques de Joseph de Maistre*. Paris: Editions Domat Montchrestien, 1945.

BURKE, EDMUND. *Burke's Politics*. Edited by R. J. S. Hoffman and Paul Levack. New York: Knopf, 1949.

BURKE, EDMUND. *Letters*. Edited by Harold Laski. London: Oxford University Press, 1922.

COBBAN, ALFRED. *Edmund Burke and the Revolt Aganist the Eighteenth Century*. London: Allen & Unwin, 1929.

CALHOUN, JOHN C. *A Disquisition on Government* and *A Discourse on the Constitution and Government of the United States*. Edited by Richard K. Cralle, New York: D. Appleton, 1854.

DEBONALD, VISCOMTE. *Considerations sur la Revolution Francaise*. Paris: 1907.

DOWER, ROBERT S. "Thomas Carlyle." In F. J. C. Hearnshaw, ed., *The Social and Political Ideas of Some Representative Thinkers of the Victorian Age*. New York: Barnes and Noble, 1933, pp. 31–52.

FEILING, KEITH. "Coleridge and the English Conservatives." In F. J. C. Hearnshaw, ed., *The Social and Political Ideas of Some Representative Thinkers of the Age of Reaction and Reconstruction, 1815–1865*. New York: Barnes and Noble, 1949, pp. 68–81.

FLINT, ROBERT. *History of the Philosophy of History*. London: W. Blackwood, 1893.

FRISH, M. J. "Burke and the New Conservatives." *New Republic*, April 23, 1956.

GRAHAM, WILLIAM. *English Political Philosophy from Hobbes to Maine*. London: E. Arnold, 1899.

LONGEE, R. W. *Paul de Lagarde: A Study of Radical Conservatism in Germany*. Cambridge, Mass.: Harvard University Press, 1961.

MACCUNN, JOHN. *The Political Philosophy of Burke*. New York: E. Arnold, 1913.

MALLOCK, W. H. *The Limits of Pure Democracy*. London: Chapman and Hall, 1918.

MAXWELL, CONSTANTIA. "Chateaubriand and the French Romantics." In F. J. C. Hearnshaw, ed., *The Social and Political Ideas of Some Representative Thinkers of the Age of Reaction and Reconstruction, 1815–1865*. New York: Barnes & Noble, 1949, pp. 29–51.

MONTMORENCY, J. E. G. DE. "Sir Henry Maine and the Historical Jurists." In F. J. C. Hearnshaw, ed., *The Social and Political Ideas of Some Representative Thinkers of the Victorian Age*. New York: Barnes & Noble, 1933, pp. 31–52.

MORLEY, JOHN. *Biographical Studies*. London: Macmillan, 1923.

MORLEY, JOHN. *Burke*. London: Macmillan, 1904.

MORLEY, JOHN. *Critical Miscellanies*. 4 vols. London: Macmillan, 1886–1908.

NEWMAN, BERTRAM. *Edmund Burke*. New York: Knopf, 1924.

ORTEGA Y GASSET, JOSÉ. *The Revolt of the Masses*. New York: Norton, 1932 (also Norton paperback).

REYNOLDS, ERNEST F. *Edmund Burke: A Christian Statesman*. London: S.C.M. Press, 1948.

SIBLEY, M. Q. "Burke and the New Ancestor Worship." *New Republic*, April 23, 1956.

SOLTAU, ROGER. *French Political Thought in the Nineteenth Century*. London: E. Benn, 1931.

VAUGHAN, C. E. *Studies in the History of Political Philosophy Before and After Rousseau*. London: Longmans, Green, 1925; N.Y.: Russell, 1960.

WHITE, R. J., ED. *The Conservative Tradition*. New York: New York University Press, 1957.

WILSON, FRANCIS GRAHAM. *The Case for Conservatism*. Seattle: University of Washington Press, 1951.

28. *Non-Marxian Socialism*

General Development and Biography

ANGRAND, PIERRE. *Etienne Cabet et la Republique de 1848*. Paris: Presses Universitaires de France, 1948.

ARMAND, F. *Fourier*. Paris: Editions Sociales Internationales, 1937.

BEER, MAX. *A History of British Socialism*. London: National Labour Press, G. Bell and Sons, 1921.

BOOTH, ARTHUR J. *Saint-Simon and Saint-Simonism*. London: Longmans, Green, 1871.

BOUGLE, C. ET ELIE HALEVY, EDS. *Doctrine de Saint-Simon*. Paris: Riviere, 1924.

CALVERTON, V. F. *Where Angels Dared to Tread*. Indianapolis: Bobbs-Merrill, 1941.

CARRE, PAUL. *Cabet: de la Democratie au Communisme*. Lille: Imprimerie Le Bigot Freres, 1903.

COLE, G. D. H. *The Life of Robert Owen*. London: Macmillan, 1930.

COLE, G. D. H. *Communism and Social Democracy, 1914–1931*. London: St. Martin's Press, 1958.

COLE, G. D. H. *A History of Socialist Thought*. 7 vols. London: Macmillan, 1959. Particularly vols. 1, 2, and 5.

COLE, G. D. H. *A Short History of the British Working Class Movement, 1789–1937*. New York: Humanities, 1960.
COLE, MARGARET. *Beatrice Webb*. New York: Harcourt, Brace, 1946.
DEANE, H. A. *The Political Ideas of Harold J. Laski*. New York: Columbia University Press, 1955.
DURKHEIM, EMILE. *Socialism and Saint Simon*. Yellow Springs, Ohio: Antioch Press, 1958.
ELY, RICHARD. *French and German Socialism in the Nineteenth Century*. New York: Harper, 1883.
FOURIER, CHARLES. *Oeuvres Complètes*. Paris: Librairie Sociétaire, 1841–1848.
GIDE, CHARLES AND CHARLES RIST. *History of Economic Doctrines from the Time of the Physiocrats to the Present Day*. Boston: D. C. Heath, 1915.
GRAY, ALEXANDER. *The Socialist Tradition from Moses to Lenin*. London: Longmans, Green, 1947.
GUTHRIE, WILLIAM B. *Socialism Before the French Revolution*. London: Macmillan, 1907.
HARRINGTON, MICHAEL. *The Accidental Century*. New York: Macmillan, 1965.
HINDS, W. A. *American Communities*. 3rd ed. Chicago: C. H. Kerr, 1908.
KIRKUP, THOMAS. *A History of Socialism*. 3rd ed. London: Black, 1906.
LENS, SIDNEY. *Radicalism in America*. Philadelphia: Crowell, 1966.
MACHENZIE, N. J. *Socialism: A Short History*. London: Longmans, Green, 1950.
MADISON, CHARLES. *Critics and Crusaders: A Century of American Protest*. New York: Holt, 1947.
MARTIN, KINGSLEY. *Harold Laski*. London: Victor Gollancz, 1957.
MOULIN, L. *Socialism in the West*. London: Victor Gollancz, 1948.
NOYES, JOHN HUMPHREY. *History of American Socialisms*. New York: Hilary House, 1961.
SHAW, ALBERT. *Icaria: A Chapter in the History of Communism*. London: G. P. Putnam, 1884.
SHINE, HILL. *Carlyle and the Saint-Simonians*. Baltimore: Johns Hopkins University Press, 1941.
TRACEY, HERBERT, ed. *The British Labour Party*. 3 vols. London: Caxton, 1949.
TYLER, ALICE F. *Freedom's Ferment*. Minneapolis: University of Minnesota Press, 1944.
WELLS, H. G. "My Socialism." *Contemporary Review* 94 (1908), 161–181.

Theory, Ideology, and Criticism

AHMAD, L. A., ED. *Philosophy of Socialism*. Allahabad, India: Kitab Mahal, 1947.
ALLEN, DEVERE. "Socialism: Gateway to Democracy." *Annals of the American Academy of Political and Social Science* 53 (1935), 74–82.
ATKINSON, F. J. "Saving and Investment in a Socialist State." *Review of Economic Studies* 15, no. 2 (1947–1948), 78–83.
BECKWITH, B. P. *The Economic Theory of a Socialist Economy*. Palo Alto: Stanford University Press, 1949.
BECKWITH, B. P. *The Modern Case for Socialism*. New York: Meador, 1946.
BLANSHARD, PAUL. "Socialist and Capitalist Planning." *Annals of the American Academy of Political and Social Science* 162 (1932), 6–11.
CARPENTER, EDWARD. *Towards Democracy*. New York: M. Kennerley, 1912.
COLE, G. D. H. *Studies in Class Structure*. London: Routledge & Paul, 1955.
DICKINSON, H. D. "The Economic Basis of Socialism." *Political Quarterly* 1 (1930), 561–572.
DURKHEIM, EMILE. *Le Socialisme: Sa Definition, Ses Debuts, La Doctrine Simonienne*. Paris: F. Alcan, 1928.
ELLIS, HAVELOCK. "Individualism and Socialism." *Contemporary Review* 101 (1912), 519–528.
FELLNER, ERNST. "The Psychology of Socialism." *Hibbert Journal* 46 (1948), 138–145.
GAY, PETER. *The Dilemma of Democratic Socialism*. New York: Columbia University Press, 1953.
GEORGE, HENRY. *Progress and Poverty*. New York: Doubleday, 1925.
HARDIE, J. KEIR. *From Serfdom to Socialism*. London: G. Allen, 1907.
HAYEK, FRIEDRICH A. "Socialist Calculation: The Competitive Solution." *Economica* New Series 7 (1940), 125–149.
HERBERG, WILL. "Collectivism: Totalitarian or Democratic?" *The Commonweal*, February 22, 1946.
HILLQUIT, MORRIS. *Socialism in Theory and Practice*. New York: Rand School, 1946.
HOFF, T. J. B. *Economic Calculation in Socialist Society*. London: Hodges, 1949.
KNIGHT, FRANK H. "Socialism: The Nature of the Problem." *Ethics* 50 (1940), 253–289.
LASKI, HAROLD. *Socialism and Internationalism*. London: Fabian Society, 1947.
LOUCHEN, W. AND J. HOOT. *Comparative Economic Systems*. New York: Harper, 1948.
MALLOCK, W. H. *A Critical Examination of Socialism*. London: Murray, 1908.
MILLS, C. WRIGHT. *Power, Politics, and People*. Edited by Irving L. Horowitz. New York: Oxford, 1963.
SHAW, GEORGE BERNARD. *An Intelligent Woman's Guide to Socialism and Capitalism*. London: Constable, 1928.
SHAW, GEORGE BERNARD, ED. *Fabian Essays in Socialism*. Boston: Ball Publications, 1908.
SCHUMPETER, J. A. *Capitalism, Socialism and Democracy*. New York: Harper, 1947.
SINCLAIR, W. A. *Socialism and the Individual*. New York: Oxford University Press, 1955.
STRACHEY, JOHN. *Contemporary Capitalism*. London: Gollancz, 1956.
THOMAS, IVOR. *The Socialist Tragedy*. London: Latimer House, 1949.
THOMAS, NORMAN. *A Socialist's Faith*. New York: Norton, 1951.
ULAM, ADAM B. *Philosophical Foundations of British Socialism*. Cambridge, Mass.: Harvard University Press, 1951.
VON MISES, LUDWIG. *Socialism*. New Haven: Yale University Press, 1951.

29. *Anarchism and Antistatism: Evolution and Doctrines*

General Development and Biography

BOWLE, JOHN. *Politics and Opinion In the Nineteenth Century*. London: J. Cape, 1954. Ch. 6.
BRAILSFORD, H. N. *Shelley, Godwin, and Their Circle*. New York: Holt, 1913.

COLE, G. D. H. *A History of Socialist Thought.* 7 vols. London: Macmillan, 1959. Particularly vol. 2, ch. 12.

GRYLLS, ROSALIE G. *William Godwin and His World.* London: Odhams, 1953.

HOBSBAWM, ERIC J. *Primitive Rebels: Studies in Archaic Forms of Social Movement in the Nineteenth and Twentieth Centuries.* Manchester: Manchester University Press, 1959.

HUMPHREY, RICHARD. *Georges Sorel, Prophet Without Honor.* Cambridge: Harvard University Press, 1951.

LEON, DERRICK. *Tolstoy: His Life and Work.* London: Routledge, 1944.

MARTIN, JAMES J. *Men Against the State.* De Kalb, Ill.: Adrian Allen Associates, 1953.

NANDA, B. R. *Mahatma Gandhi.* Boston: Beacon Press, 1959.

PEERS, E. ALLISON. "Bakunin and Spanish Anarchism." *Studies* 27 (1938), 136–141.

PREU, J. "Swift's Influence on Godwin's Doctrine of Anarchism." *Journal of the History of Ideas* 15 (1954), 371–383.

REDPATH, THEODORE. *Tolstoy.* London: Bowes and Bowes, 1960.

THOMAS, HUGH. *The Spanish Civil War.* New York: Harper, 1961.

TOLSTOY, ALEXANDRA. *Tolstoy: A Life of My Father.* New York: Harper, 1958.

WOODCOCK, GEORGE AND IVAN AVAKUMOVIC. *The Anarchist Prince: A Biographical Study of Peter Kropotkin.* London: Boardman, 1950.

ZENKER, E. V. *Anarchism: A Criticism and History of Anarchist Theory.* New York: G. P. Putnam, 1897.

Theory and Criticism

ABRAHAM, J. H. "Religious Ideas and Social Philosophy of Tolstoy." *International Journal of Ethics* 40, (1929), 105–120.

BASCH, VICTOR. *L'Individualisme Anarchiste,* Max Stirner. Paris: F. Alcan, 1904.

BONDURANT, JOAN. *Conquest of Violence.* Princeton: Princeton University Press, 1958.

CHAMBERLAIN, JOHN. "Blueprints for a New Society: Dream of Anarchism." *New Republic,* September 13, 1939.

COMFORT, ALEX. *Authority and Delinquency in the Modern State.* London: Routledge & Paul, 1950.

FLEISHER, DAVID. *William Godwin: A Study in Liberalism.* London: Allen & Unwin, 1951.

GODWIN, WILLIAM. *Enquiry Concerning Political Justice and Its Influence on Morals and Happiness.* 3 vols., 1793 ed. Edited by F. E. L. Priestly. Toronto: University of Toronto Press, 1946.

GODWIN, WILLIAM. *Caleb Williams.* New York: Holt, Rinehart & Winston, 1960.

GOLDMAN, EMMA. *Anarchism and Other Essays.* New York: Mother Earth Publishing Association, 1911.

KROPOTKIN, PETER. *Mutual Aid: A Factor in Evolution.* London: W. Heinemann, 1904.

KROPOTKIN, PETER. *Kropotkin's Revolutionary Pamphlets.* Edited by Roger Baldwin. New York: Vanguard, 1927.

KROPOTKIN, PETER. *Fields, Factories, and Workshops.* London: Hutchinson, 1898.

KROPOTKIN, PETER. *The Great French Revolution, 1789–1793.* 2 vols., N. F. Dryhurst, trans. New York: Vanguard, 1927.

KVITKO, DAVID. *A Philosophic Study of Tolstoy.* New York: Columbia University Press, 1927.

LU, SHI YUNG. *The Political Theories of P. J. Proudhon.* New York: M. R. Gray, 1922.

MACKAY, JOHN H. *The Anarchists.* George Schumm, trans. Boston: B. R. Tucker, 1891. A novel.

MAJIADAR, B. B., ED. *The Gandhian Concept of the State.* Calcutta: Sarakar and Cons, 1957.

MALATESTA, ERRICO. *Scritti.* 3 vols. Geneva: 1934–1936.

MONRO, DAVID H. *Godwin's Moral Philosophy: An Interpretation.* London: Oxford University Press, 1953.

MORRIS-JONES, W. H. "Mahatma Gandhi–Political Philosopher?" *Political Studies* 8 (1960), 16–36.

NAG, KALIDAS. *Tolstoy and Gandhi.* Putna: Pustak Bhandar, 1950.

ORWELL, GEORGE. *Homage to Catalonia.* Boston: Beacon, 1952.

PLEKHANOV, GEORGE. *Anarchism and Socialism.* Eleanor Aveling, trans. London: Twentieth Century Press, 1895.

PLOWMAN, MAX. *Bridge Into the Future.* London: A. Dakers, 1944. Letters.

PROUDHON, P. J. *The General Idea of Revolution in the Nineteenth Century.* J. B. Robinson, trans. London: Freedom Press, 1923.

RECLUS, ÉLISÉE. *L'Évolution, La Révolution et L'Idéal Anarchique.* 4th ed. Paris: P. V. Stock, 1898.

REICHERT, WILLIAM O. "Toward a New Understanding of Anarchism." *Western Political Quarterly* 20 (1967), 856–865.

RITTER, ALAN. *The Political Thought of Pierre-Joseph Proudhon.* Princeton: Princeton University Press, 1969.

ROCKER, RUDOLF. *Anarcho-Syndicalism.* London: Secker & Warburg, 1938.

RUSSELL, BERTRAND. *Proposed Roads to Freedom.* New York: Holt, 1919.

SHAW, GEORGE B. *The Impossibilities of Anarchism.* London: Fabian Society, 1903.

SIBLEY, MULFORD Q. "Gandhi, the Technological Problem, and the Economic Order." Khadi Gramodyog 15 (1969), 631–642..

TOLSTOY, LEO. *The Law of Love and the Law of Violence.* New York: R. Field, 1948.

TOLSTOY, LEO. *The Kingdom of God and Peace Essays.* London: Oxford, 1936.

TOLSTOY, LEO. *Resurrection.* New York: Dodd, Mead, 1900; Penguin Books, 1966.

VARNA, V. P. *The Political Philosophy of Mahatma Gandhi and Sawadaya.* Agra: Lakshin, 1959.

YARROWS, V. S. "Philosophical Anarchism: Its Rise, Decline, and Eclipse." *American Journal of Sociology* 41 (1936), 470–483.

30. *Fascism and National Socialism: Antecedents and Doctrines*

Development and Biography

BUTLER, ROHAN D. *The Roots of National Socialism, 1783–1933.* London: Faber and Faber, 1941.

CARSTEN, FRANCIS L. *The Rise of Fascism.* Berkeley: University of California Press, 1967.

CHABORD, FREDERICO. *A History of Italian Fascism.* Muriel Grindrod, trans. London: Weidenfeld and Nicolson, 1963.

CROSS, COLIN. *The Fascists in Britain.* London: Barrie and Rockliff, 1961.

EISENBERG, DENNIS. *The Re-Emergence of Fascism.* London: MacGibbon and Kee, 1967.

GOEBBELS, P. J. *The Goebbels Diaries, 1942–43.* Edited by Louis Lochner. New York: Doubleday, 1948.

GUÉRIN, DANIEL. *Fascism and Big Business.* Frances and Mason Merrill, trans. New York: Pioneer Press, 1939.

HALPERIN, SAMUEL W. *Mussolini and Italian Fascism.* Princeton: Van Nostrand, 1964.

HEIDEN, KONRAD. *Hitler: A Biography.* New York: Knopf, 1936.

HEIDEN, KONRAD. *Der Führer: Hitler's Rise to Power.* Boston: Houghton Mifflin, 1944.

HEIDEN, KONRAD. *A History of National Socialism.* New York: Knopf, 1935; Fertig, 1968.

KOHN, HANS. *The Mind of Germany: The Education of a Nation.* New York: Scribner's, 1960.

LONG, WELLINGTON. *The New Nazis of Germany.* Philadelphia: Chilton, 1968.

PLUMYÈNE, JEAN AND R. LASIERRA. *Les Fascismes Français, 1923–1963.* Paris: Editions du Seuil, 1963.

RIDLEY, FRANCIS A. *The Papacy and Fascism.* London: M. Secker, Warburg, 1937.

ROSENBERG, ALFRED. *Memoirs.* Eric Posselt, trans. Chicago: Ziff-Davis, 1949.

SCHAPIRO, J. SALWYN. *Liberalism and the Challenge of Fascism: Social Forces in England and France, 1815–1870.* New York: McGraw-Hill, 1949.

TALMON, J. L. *Political Messianism.* New York: Praeger, 1960.

TAUBER, KURT P. *Beyond Eagle and Swastika: German Nationalism Since 1945.* Middletown, Conn.: Wesleyan University Press, 1967.

VERMEIL, E. *The German Scene (Social, Political, Cultural): 1890 to the Present.* London: George C. Harrop, 1956.

WEBSTER, RICHARD A. *Christian Democracy in Italy, 1860–1960.* London: Hollis and Carter, 1961.

Theory, Ideology, and Criticism

ARENDT, HANNAH. *On Revolution.* New York: Viking Press, 1963.

BRZEZINSKI, Z. "Totalitarianism and Rationality." *American Political Science Review* 50 (1956), 751–763.

BRINTON, CRANE. "The National Socialist Use of Nietzsche." *Journal of the History of Ideas* 1 (1940), 131–150.

CASSINELLI, C. W. "Total Ideology and Propaganda." *Journal of Politics* 22 (1960), 68–95.

COBBAN, ALFRED. *Dictatorship: Its History and Theory.* New York: Scribner's, 1939.

COHEN, CARL. *Communism, Fascism and Democracy, The Theoretical Foundations.* New York: Random House, 1962.

FLORINSKY, M. T. *Fascism and National Socialism: A Study of the Economic and Social Politics of the Totalitarian State.* New York: Macmillan, 1936.

FRAENKEL, ERNEST. *The Dual State: A Contribution to the Theory of Dictatorship.* Translated by E. A. Shils with the collaboration of Edith Lowenstein and Klaus Knorr. New York: Oxford University Press, 1941. Octogon, 1968.

FRIEDRICH, C. J., ED. *Totalitarianism.* Cambridge, Mass.: Harvard University Press, 1959.

GERMINO, D. L. *The Italian Fascist Party in Power.* Minneapolis: University of Minnesota Press, 1959.

GILBERT, G. M. *The Psychology of Dictatorship: Based on an Examination of the Leaders of Nazi Germany.* New York: Ronald, 1950.

GREGOR, A. JAMES. *The Ideology of Fascism.* New York: Free Press, 1969.

HEIDEGGER, MARTIN. *German Existentialism,* Dagobert Runes, trans. New York: Wisdom Library, 1965.

HEIMANN, EDUARD. *Communism, Fascism or Democracy?* New York: W. W. Norton, 1938.

HITLER, ADOLF. *My New Order.* Edited and with a commentary by Raoul de Roussy de Sales. New York: Reynal and Hitchcock, 1941. Speeches.

HITLER, ADOLF. *Mein Kampf.* Unabridged. New York: Stackpole, 1939.

HITLER, ADOLF. *The Speeches of Adolf Hitler: April 1922 to August, 1939.* Norman H. Baynes, trans. London: Oxford, 1942.

HUDAL, ALOIS. *Die Grundlagen des Nationalsozialismus.* Leipzig: J. Gunther, 1937.

International Council for Philosophical and Humanistic Studies. *The Third Reich.* Published with the assistance of UNESCO. New York: Praeger, 1955.

KNELLER, GEORGE F. *The Educational Philosophy of National Socialism.* New Haven: Yale University Press, 1941.

KOLLENREUTER, O. *Volk und Staat in der Weltanshauung des Nationalsozialismus.* Berlin: Pan-Verlagsgesellschaft, 1935.

LLOYD, ROGER B. *Revolutionary Religion: Christianity, Fascism, and Communism.* New York: Harper, 1938.

MUNBY, D. L. *The Idea of a Secular Society and Its Significance for Christians.* London: Oxford University Press, 1963.

NEUMANN, FRANZ. *Behemoth: The Structure and Practice of National Socialism.* New York: Oxford University Press, 1944; Harper Torchbooks, 1966.

NOLTE, ERNEST. *Theorien über Faschismus.* Köln, Berlin: Kiepenheuer u. Witsch, 1967.

PINSON, K. S., ED. *Essays on Anti-Semitism.* New York: Conference on Jewish Relations, 1946.

REICH, WILHELM. *The Mass Psychology of Fascism.* New York: Orgone Institute Press, 1946.

ROSENBERG, ALFRED. *Der Mythus des 20. Jahrhunderts.* München: Hoheneichen, 1935.

TILLICH, PAUL. *Christianity and the Encounter of the World Religions.* New York: Columbia University Press, 1963.

TIMASHEFF, N. S. *Three Worlds: Liberal, Communist, and Fascist Society.* Milwaukee: Bruce, 1946.

UNGARI, PAOLO. *Alfredo Rocco e L'ideologia Giuridica del Fascismo.* Brescia: Morcelliana, 1963.

VON MISES, LUDWIG. *Omnipotent Goverment: The Rise of the Total State and Total War.* New Haven: Yale University Press, 1944.

part V

IN PERSPECTIVE: SOME PERENNIAL ISSUES OF POLITICAL THOUGHT

chapter 31

No attempt to summarize major currents in the history of political ideas can possibly do justice to their ramifications and their relations with one another. Here, however, we may, by way of a brief recapitulation, call attention to a few central issues which have persisted from the dawn of political thought until the present day—issues, moreover, which are likely to continue for generations to come.

Approaches to Politics

One cannot see, feel, smell, or touch politics. Sense experience, apparently, will tell us only indirectly about it. How, then, can we understand and explain its movements and set up goals or ends? Questions of this kind have puzzled political thinkers from the very outset of speculation.

In the beginning, efforts to understand were largely mythological and unsystematic, as with the Egyptians and the Hebrews. They were also closely connected with religious consciousness; and the social order was seen as an extension of the cosmic. The Hebrews saw cosmic significance in the concrete experiences of history and sought their standards and goals in interpretations of a presumed Covenant with Yahweh. With the Greeks, systematic and rational approaches came to the fore and flowered in the classical period. With Plato, the forms were metaphysical realities, ethical norms, and analytical constructs; and while Aristotle tended to stress existential experience or empirical observation more than Plato, in the end his basic premises were very similar to those of the earlier thinker. Aristotle emphasized that a thing could be understood in two senses: by breaking it down into its parts, as in what we today would call science; and in terms of its implicit end (*telos*) which could be comprehended by a combination of empirical observation and reason.

During the Christian centuries, much thinking was a series of deductions from presumably authoritative documents—the Bible, the Code, canon law, and, later on, Aristotle. With conceptions of natural law went the notion that standards of right and wrong were indeed objective rather than purely subjective or merely emotional. Presuppositions tended to be those of philosophical realism, as with St. Thomas Aquinas.

With the decline of the Middle Ages and the rise of nominalism, sense observation and empirical analysis once more came to the fore and mere deductions from the authority of Aristotle were ostensibly rejected by men like Machiavelli, Hobbes, and Locke. Although no one argued that sense experience could tell one about politics directly, it was contended that one could at least infer things about the political world from one's sense experience and that, under the guidance of pleasure and pain, sense could help provide standards for morality. Seventeenth-century science, presumably based on induction rather than deduction, established models for many. Yet what began as an emphasis on the empirical with men such as Bacon ended, with the development of mathematical approaches, in the so-called rationalistic tendencies of the Cartesians who were emulated by thinkers like Hobbes. Except for a few (Montesquieu, for example) who stressed the empirical study of comparative politics and cultures, deduction from certain supposed truths or self-evident propositions characterized eighteenth-century thought down to the last quarter of the century. Politics tended to be divorced from the study of history. With Hume, Rousseau, Burke, and others, however, a new groping for empirical foundations began.

In the nineteenth century, the pleasure-pain calculus and the test of consequences were exalted by Utilitarians, who rejected natural law, natural rights, and social contract notions. About the same time, however, a radically different view arose with Hegelianism, which emphasized historical approaches combined with modified classical organic models. In the biological evolutionary theories of the nineteenth century, many thought they saw fruitful models not only for the explanation of political phenomena but also for the discovery of norms: The process of evolution, as with Spencer, supposedly provided guidance for what men ought to do and be. The rise of the science of sociology encouraged many twentieth-century analysts of politics to study in more exact terms such phenomena as the "iron law of oligarchy," the tendency to bureaucracy, and the historical and sociological roots of law. For many, the formulation of goals for politics became relatively unimportant since, it was argued, the really controversial issues turned on questions of means. Emotivist theories of ethics had their impact, as men rejected natural law and tended to question whether reason could provide norms. For many, physics and psychology became models of what a science of politics should be.

Always, as in the past, rationalistic and deductive approaches have been in tension with empirical and inductive attempts to understand, although each might be said to rest on a faith beyond demonstration; and while it has been widely recognized that any study must involve both, enthusiasts for the one or the other have often forgotten this. Although the basic thrust of twentieth century political study has tended to an examination of what ostensibly *is* rather than of what *ought to be,* we can perhaps say that the most comprehensive vision recognizes that the two are most fruitfully pursued together: value judgments must inevitably affect what we study in the sense that what we deem important or significant will be shaped by them; and if, as Aristotle argued, politics is a practical science, we seek not merely to *know* but also to *do* or *act* for explicitly defined purposes which must somehow be defended or vindicated.

The Problem of Liberty

Mortimer Adler has identified at least three senses in which the word "freedom" has been used during the history of thought.[1] It is connected with the notion of indeterminacy of will, with the conception that individuals ought to be allowed to do what they desire, and with the idea that we have liberty only when we do what we ought to do. The first notion can be called freedom of the will; the second, freedom as self-realization; the third, freedom as self-perfection.

All three positions can be illustrated in the history of thought related to politics. The assumption of freedom of the will has seemed necessary if we are to speak of what men ought to do and thus to establish a morality; for if men's wills are completely bound, to suggest what they ought to do would appear to be meaningless. Among the ancient Hebrews, the prophetic theory of history could preserve both the omnipotence and the goodness of Yahweh only by asserting man's freedom either to observe or to rebel against the will of God for history. Political history became the story of man's frequently mistaken choices or his deliberate defiance of God. St. Augustine was puzzled by the same issue; and we have seen how he resolved it along similar lines: God's omniscience does not mean that he dictates man's choices. In general, orthodox thought followed this line. But in thinkers like Hobbes, it would appear, freedom of the will is doubtful; for if we interpret him (and many of those whom he influenced) as a reductionist, then man's alleged acts of free choice, when rightly understood, are simply resultants of matter in motion. And much modern so-called scientific thought has tended to take this position, although the notion that there is indeterminacy in the movements of molecules has for some seriously undermined the idea that either matter or mind is strictly determined.

Freedom as self-realization identifies the idea with the removal of external obstacles to the individual's doing what he desires to do. Laws, customs, and physical restraints which keep one from acting as one wishes are seen, by and large, as antagonistic to freedom. On the whole, this definition has been associated with individualist perspectives on politics. Some groups among the early Christians appeared to stress it; and it was against them that Paul uttered his warnings in the thirteenth chapter of Romans. During the Middle Ages, some of the sectarians held to this notion and by the end of that epoch, commitment to philosophical nominalism led certain thinkers to conceive of freedom in this light. The Renaissance, too, moved in a similar direction. In modern times, certain currents of liberalism, insofar as they denied the possibility of discovering objective norms for human action, appeared to subscribe to it. Legislation was seen as a device to ensure that every individual had an opportunity to do what he desired, so long as he did not directly

1. Mortimer J. Adler, *The Idea of Freedom,* 2 vols., New York: Doubleday, 1958.

interfere with others. Views which stressed rights rather than duties tended to define freedom as self-realization rather than self-perfection.

Finally, freedom has been thought of as the state in which alleged lower elements in human personality are subordinated to its higher or rational levels. One has no claim to do what one desires—since desire might take the form of aberrant passions which enslave—but only what one ought to do. If the lower elements of the self are in control, the person would not in fact be free, since he would be subject to the servitude of blind emotion, arbitrariness, and personality disintegration. Law and social constraints could thus help the individual suppress his lower elements and release his higher self; they could, in fact, enlarge freedom. Obviously, the idea of liberty as self-perfection has had a long history. It was the core of Platonic-Aristotelian views and remained central in most natural law theory during the Middle Ages. In more modern times, it was restated in an influential way by Hegelian thought and helped shape the new liberalism as formulated by thinkers like Thomas Hill Green. In general, where organic views of political society have been emphasized, freedom has been seen as self-perfection: hence Rousseau's notion of "forcing" men to be "free" is not untypical of this position.

In varying ways, then, the development of political thought has attempted to wrestle with these three conceptions of freedom or combinations of them. Each has been relevant for views of human personality, which in turn have affected conceptions of what is or ought to be going on in politics. Marx illustrated nicely the intersection of the three conceptions of fredom. Most men, he seemed to say, have historically not been free; but when the historical process is complete, they will have liberty in all three senses: They will be able to make significant choices and what they choose will be both what they desire to choose and what they ought to choose.

An issue which in modern times often came to the forefront was that of the relationship between equality and freedom. Some conservatives alleged that there was a fundamental conflict between the two, since liberty would eventually lead to an exhibition of the inequalities between and among men. A coerced equality, whether of status or economic distribution, would, on the other hand, undermine liberty. Here again, of course, much depended on how the two terms were defined. Socialists did not deny that in a certain sense, particularly in the economic realm, freedom as self-realization would have to be curtailed in favor of a kind of equality; but they argued also that under socialist conditions men would be freed to pursue the central values of the humanist tradition. Curtailment of economic liberty was a small price to pay for this boon.

The history of the idea of freedom has been accompanied by many brutal wars and revolutions supposedly waged in its name. Yet most of those who fought these wars and revolutions have had only the vaguest notions of what the term might mean—certainly an example of the melancholy blindness so characteristic of human history.

Political Obligation

The problem of one's obligation to the community is an aspect of the general question of obligation; and it presupposes freedom, in some or all senes of that term. One may have obligations to oneself, to others, and to the community or communities. Political obligation may be thought of as peculiarly related to the latter; but since issues of obligation are always interrelated, it cannot be divorced sharply from the former two senses. It has always been closely connected, too, with problems of defining justice or righteousness; consent; relations between person and group; legitimacy and authority; and justifications for civil disobedience, resistance, and revolution.

In prepolitical societies, presumably, questions of obligation did not arise, for it was assumed that one obeyed the age-long patterns of the fathers. Among some of the ancients, once politics arose, one had to obey the ruler because his authority was simply an extension of that of the gods. The notion of the Covenant and the idea of the righteous king were intimately bound up with the principles of obligation among the ancient Hebrews; and Yahweh supposedly released men on occasion from obligations, as in the case of Jeroboam's secession. For Socrates, merely living in a community over a long period created a presumption that one should respect its demands and not evade its penalties for wrong-doing. In Plato, rule according to the Form of Justice—which entailed both happiness and holiness—created the greatest degree of obligation on the part of the individual: In the highest sense, one was obliged to obey because one was persuaded of the rationality of the appeal; and even in the law-commonwealth, rules obliged because of this. In the New Testament, Paul suggested an obligation to obey to the extent that the ruler sought to ensue the good and for the sake of the community with which every individual was inseparably connected. Possession of sheer force, of course, could never create obligation, whether for Plato or for Paul.

St. Augustine sought to identify legitimate rule with justice but appeared to conclude that under most earthly regimes one had to settle for something far less: so long as the ruler preserved a modicum of order—for a wide variety of ends—he had a certain claim on obedience, given the fact of original sin. During much of the Middle Ages, obligation was associated with the claims of custom, which was often held to embody a kind of rough justice. While temporal rule arose out of sin, it was by God's Providence also a corrective for sin. For many, papal authority was designed to oversee the fulfillment of obligations and could on occasion release men from duties which would otherwise be regarded as binding. With St. Thomas, human laws which were unjust by the standards of natural law did not bind in conscience: they were, in fact, not laws.

With the rise of contractual conceptions, alleged consent through contract—under the assumption that promises were always binding (which, of course, might well be questioned by the critic)—became an ostensible foundation for obligation, although this was qualified in various ways. For Hobbes, one was not obliged to obey if the ruler sought to take one's life; for Locke, obligation ceased when he invaded the individual's natural right to property (life, liberty, and estate). Locke's view was profoundly influential in modern conceptions justifying revolution and, in conjunction with Rousseau's ideas, may be said to underly the defense of revolution from 1789 to the present day. In early Utilitarianism, obligation turned on whether the ruler promoted a balance of pleasure over pain; but some have held that the primitive Utilitarians did not or could not have a true conception of obligation.

The rise of modern organic conceptions in Rousseauistic, Hegelian, and other streams of thought placed great emphasis on the debt which every individual owed to the community for his very life and personality: Contract theories, with their discrete individualism, had failed to recognize this debt; and organic notions therefore rejected grounding of obligation in any views resembling contractualism. Since personality was social, the person could not be his true self without a conformity to the norms developed by the group: rightly understood, there was no conflict between liberty and the claims of community.

But the history of thought has always been puzzled by the issue of conflict of loyalties. If the claims of one group conflict with those of others or of individual ends, which should take precedence and according to what principles? The ancient tragedians saw this as an almost insoluble question. For Stoics, a universal commonwealth of reason was postulated as a norm by the standards of which conflicting temporal loyalties could be measured; and Christianity in some measure carried on this tradition. Some modern views made the norms enunciated by the national state definitive, with the claims of other associations being assigned a secondary role: The state always represented the social good and other associations only particular goods. But pluralism—whose history goes back at least to the Middle Ages—argued that the state as such could have no greater legitimate claims on the individual than the other associations of which he was a member.

Throughout much of the history of obligation, the notion of conscience was debated, with some—particularly in the organic tradition—seeing it primarily as a kind of social deposit of communal norms and others arguing its individualistic nature. Yet others saw in conscience both a social phenomenon and at the same time a guide which transcended the groups which were so important in its development. Some saw conscience as reason, while others conceived it, in part at least, as transrational.

The Problem of Law

We have emphasized at many points certain controversies about law. Here we select three by way of recapitulation: the definition and sources of law; its significance; and its potentialities.

The history of political thought witnessed

many efforts to define law and to identify its sources. Classically, its norms were derived from reason and from nature as teleologically conceived. This was true in Plato and Aristotle and in the medieval tradition of natural law. Principles of law could be deduced from the *telos,* or purpose of collective humanity, from insightful legislators, from Holy Writ, or even from a kind of collective reason embodied in custom. In modern times, however, there was a greater tendency to associate the term with will—that was law which was the express will of the ruler, said a tradition sharply illustrated in Hobbes and John Austin; the law was binding, in other words, not because it conformed to norms of reason or nature but because it was willed by an individual or body widely accepted as a political superior. In part, the modern tendency—which had antecedents in the theory of Roman law—was an attempt analytically to separate morality from law in the interests of clarity. For many natural-law thinkers, positive alleged laws which violated natural law were not law; for modern analytical views, such statements would still be law but unjust law.

As for the significance of law, in the classical tradition there was an acute awareness of the limitations of law; for by its very nature, Plato held, it had to categorize men who were individually unique and thus "tyrannize" over them. On the other hand, it was widely recognized that if pure wisdom was unlikely to be found in rulers—who historically have usually had conflicting private interests and have been far from infallible—the law was a kind of second-best device. Where respected, it at least checked potential tendencies to tyranny in men. This ambivalence about law has characterized the history of political thought down to our day, with many utopian political treatises seeking to banish law and lawyers altogether and anarchists placing law and political authority in the same category.

Political thinkers have varied considerably from one another in their views as to the potentialities for law. Some, like St. Augustine, conceived it to be a clumsy but necessary restraining factor in controlling evil men: its positive uses were few, if any. Men like Locke, Jefferson, and others hoped to limit its scope rather drastically, in the belief that the basic harmony among men could best be promoted with minimal legal restraints. On the other hand, there has been an equally long tradition in the history of thought which would see law as an instrument for regulating a wide variety of human acts in the name of both social harmony and individual freedom (usually freedom as "self-perfection"). Plato's *Laws* illustrated this attitude as did many conceptions of the Puritans who, by contrast with St. Thomas Aquinas, tended to think that everything which was morally wrong should be legally prohibited.

In modern times, of course, all these controversies continue against a background in which larger and larger proportions of positive law tend to become public—with growing interdependence and complexity—and the role of private law, relatively speaking, tends to be less important.

Who Governs and Who Should Govern?

Since the dawn of political consciousness, men have sought to identify those who in fact govern the community. They have also endeavored to state who should govern.

With respect to the first question, analysis in ancient times was quite aware that in considerable degree Fate, Fortune, or other forces beyond human control were the actual governors. The ancient Hebrews saw history as a combination of uncoordinated human choices with factors which escaped direction by the human mind. Plato spoke of "accident" legislating. Machiavelli sought to relate the actions of his prince to the overwhelming role which fortune played. And recognition of this fact has been present in early modern and modern political thought. While men may aspire to control their collective destiny, they have thus far not succeeded. At the same time, they have sought to do so from the very beginning and one of the problems of political thought has been to identify the human governors who actually operate within the limits of fortune. Both Plato and Aristotle were quite aware that those who nominally governed were often controlled by others outside the visible governing process: Thus an ostensibly democratic assembly might be dominated by the military or by the wealthy; or formal rule by an aristocracy might be belied by the over-reaching influence of the mob. Where sharp distinctions of wealth existed, the city might in fact be two cities—one of the rich and another of the poor: the sense of community required for political governance would be absent. Roman thinkers, too, were quite conscious that the nominal lines of authority in the late Republic and during the Empire were often not reflective of actual power relations. In seventeenth century thinkers, there was often a keen awareness that while the king might ostensibly rule, he was often the prisoner of those who controlled the land. In modern times, of course, men like Marx and some of the anarchists sought to interpret rulership in class terms and to suggest that the predominant class at any period of history manipulated the symbols and instruments of law and justice in order to ensure the economic or psychological interests of the governing class. Throughout the history of political thought, major thinkers have been conscious that an evanescent public interest or social good was often in bitter conflict with the particular interests of those who governed.

As for the problem of who *should* govern, the classical tradition answered the *aristoi* or the best—if they could be found; and the best were identified with those presumably fitted by native capacity and education for the tasks of discovering the norms of righteousness and implementing them. A few could possess what Aristotle called "intellectual virtue": most men were capable, perhaps, only of the lesser moral virtue. In general, this has been a persistent position in the history of political ideas. In modern times, for example, it has been identified with certain versions of conservatism, with one stream of Hegelian thought, and with Leninist versions of Marxism. In some varieties of the Rousseauistic tradition, it is a specially equipped individual who can best interpret the general will.

On the other hand, an equally important tradition in political thought has doubted the possibility of finding an identifiable group best qualified to govern or suggested that, even if it could be discovered, the many should be associated with it in some way. Some have suggested that governance is not really a matter for special expertise but is rather a question of over-all insight. Even if the governors supposedly have a certain expertness, those who control them ought to be the general community. Aristotle argued that the many laymen might make better political and aesthetic judgments than the supposedly expert few, for their varied insights built upon diverse experiences would, when pooled, in an assembly discussion, provide a kind of wisdom not available to the few. This so-called democratic tradition took various forms and has been reflected in many thinkers whose particular expressions might differ widely from one another; thus it was stated in several canonical thinkers of the Middle Ages, in many of the conciliarists, in a large number of the sectarians from the fourteenth through the seventeenth centuries, and in such modern writers as John Stuart Mill.

But the difficulties of implementing a fully democratic order, together with the claimed undesirability of doing so, have led some to argue for mixed schemes of various types. Essentially, it has been maintained, some men will in the nature of things always gain disproportionate wealth or demonstrate greater ability. Positions of status, moreover, tend to be inherited in one way or another. It would seem desirable, in the interests of accountability, realism, and a greater modicum of political stability, to ensure that such groups, even though minorities, should be represented in the governing councils, along with the many. A blending of wealth, status, and ability with mere numbers appeared to be the desideratum, given the goals of relative stability and responsibility. This tendency was reflected in Plato's scheme of the *Laws;* in Aristotle's polity; in the reflections of Polybius on Roman affairs; in some of the theorists of Church government during the Middle Ages; in Montesquieu, John Adams, and the American Constitution during the eighteenth century; and in John Stuart Mill during the nineteenth.

But whether the form of rule be by the best, the wealthy, those of inherited social status, or by the many, there has always arisen the question of precisely how rulers should be related to the community as a whole. Obviously, if the community could actually and literally govern itself in all senses, the issue would not arise, since governors and governed would always be identical. But in the absence of such a state, various theories of representation and choice have been offered and debated. Should rulers be elected, chosen by lot, or somehow designated by God to stand in the place of the community? Both election and lot were defended by Plato and Aristotle, in varying proportions. In the theory of the Roman law, the Imperator was the representative person who reflected the populus that had delegated its plenary authority to him. The medieval theory of estates assumed functionally differentiated bodies—nobility, clergy, burgesses. To Hobbes, the monarch or parliamentary body gained authority through a contract that bound contracting individuals but not the representative person or assembly. Some doctrines enunciated a theory of virtual representation: thus Rousseau argued that under certain circumstances an individual might best reflect the public weal; and Burke contended that a traditionally established elite might, even though not elected according to any rational scheme, reflect the true spirit of the community. In the nineteenth and twentieth centuries, non-Marxian socialists have argued the virtues of geographical versus functional (economic group) representation. Certain types of guild socialists have stoutly maintained the superiority of the latter, given the large role which economic interests play in modern industrialized societies. Then there have been thinkers who have sought to combine geographical with functional types.

In the modern discussion of rulership, one of the most astonishing and widely accepted propositions was the notion that the majority should rule. Why this should be was rarely explored except in such vague and unsatisfactory formulations as that of Locke. Majority rule, generally speaking, was simply taken for granted and took on many of the characteristics of a sacred doctrine.

Accountability and Responsibility

Akin to the questions of who does rule and who should rule has been the issue of how rulers can be controlled and held accountable. In ancient Egyptian thought, the Pharaoh was accountable and responsible only to God. Among the ancient Hebrews, the notion grew up that the king must have the assent, under the Covenant, of both Yahweh and the people: If either were to be withdrawn, his authority would be suspect. And Yahweh's ordinances for history established the way in which, through historical forces only indirectly related to the issue, the ruler would be deposed if he violated the Covenant. In classical Greek thought, tyrannicide was sanctioned and it was asserted that if, in fact, rulers exceeded their proper moral limits, their days were numbered: Nemesis would follow *hubris*. In Greek democratic thought, of course, all free citizens sat in the Assembly and in principle had to validate all proposals of public policy and hear reports of officials. In Roman theory, consuls were to be controlled through short terms; and the balances and built-in frictions of the constitution would serve to preserve both liberty and accountability. In imperial Roman theory, the imperator's *auctoritas* was derived from the *populus*, but the doctrine was ambiguous as to how the populus could hold the imperator accountable, this becoming an important theme in the medieval context. Medieval thinkers did, on occasion, justify tyrannicide, although only within carefully prescribed limits supposedly derived from natural law. Conciliar and canon law thinkers sought to develop a concept of accountability to representative Church councils.

The early modern period was characterized by development of doctrines of divine right, on the one hand, and of resistance to illegitimate authority, on the other. In the first, the king was accountable only to God and in the event of tyranny the main recourse of the community was to pray to God for deliverance. Doctrines of resistance, whether by Jesuits or Protestants, at first seemed to justify resistance only by select groups, such as the lesser magistrates. Later, with the growth of democratic thought, the scope of legitimate resistance and the numbers of those who could participate were enlarged.

In the various modern theories connected with liberal democracy, non-Marxian socialism, and other currents, an effort was made to spell out specific methods for keeping rulers and administrators within the law, removing them, criticizing their actions, and holding them accountable. At the same time, it became widely recognized in the twentieth century that the tendency to bureaucracy and oligarchy was so overwhelming that all merely mechanical and formal efforts to control and direct the governing process—whether in so-called private corporations or in public bodies—were inadequate. In the absence of a firm and persisting public spirit taking a constant interest in collective affairs, the likelihood was that control of affairs—insofar as it was possible at all—would tend in fact to be devolved on a relatively few men: this certainly was the implication of elitist analyses such as those of Michels, Mosca, Pareto, and others. Various anarchist and antistatist tendencies in thought sought yet more radical answers to accountability and responsibility by arguing for a high degree of functional or geographical decentralization; and some anarchists—rather dubiously, according to their critics—thought that this decentralism could be reconciled with a high degree of industrialism. As for Fascism and National Socialism, they could plausibly be interpreted as nihilistic, antirational viewpoints which dismissed accountability and responsibility and sought refuge in vague formulae appealing to mass emotion—they symbolized a wide spectrum of modern attitudes which sought, in the words of Fromm, "escape from freedom."

By the middle of the twentieth century, it was evident to large numbers of competent observers that the problems of control and responsibility were still enormous. Whether one lived in a nominally democratic or a nondemocratic society, always rulers tended to be sharply separated from ruled; fortune and the imperatives of technology appeared to overwhelm efforts to control affairs as a whole; and the vast mass of the community seemed not to have acquired that strong sense of civic responsibility which nineteenth-century theorists of progress—whether liberal, socialist, or Marxist—assumed they would develop under the stimulus of increased leisure and wide accessibility of public education.

Division of Labor, Technology, and Control of Change

From the days of the ancient Hebrews, who were concerned about man's tendency to idolize his creations and thus to enslave himself, political thinkers have seen extreme division of labor and human technique as often creating obstacles to the good life. Beyond a moderate division of labor and limited technology, Plato and Aristotle argued, it is impossible to subordinate man's inventions to the true goals of human existence: economic and technological forces tend to become blind and to escape over-all or political control; men become the victims of that which they have created. Being subjected to legislation by accident and fortune, men find the political quest frustrated. The answer of the classical thinkers was to attempt to limit commerce and urbanization in the interests of emphasizing characteristically human (in the teleological sense) objectives—aesthetic and intellectual contemplation. Men could, to be sure, be human only with a measure of division of labor and a certain development of the tool-making art; but beyond this point they would tend to become teleologically inhuman. The task of the political thinker was to discover this optimum point at which genuinely human beings could live in communities which made the good life central.

In late classical civilization, of course, large cities and extensive commerce seemed to illustrate the dangers against which the classical thinkers had warned. Philosophies of alienation like Cynicism and, to some degree, early Christianity, were reactions. In the Christian centuries, with their reversion to more primitive forms of collective life, thinkers like St. Augustine, through the elaboration of myths such as the Fall of Man, still warned against man's tendency to subordinate himself to his own creations, thus subverting his soul. Pride in achievement became the source of all the deadly sins. A too rapid social change and a too complex division of labor tempted men to believe that they could escape the judgment of God for placing material values at the center of existence. In the High Middle Ages, warnings of this kind were epitomized in the philosophy of strict regulation of economic life.

It was only with early modern development, however, that the ancient and medieval attitudes began to be undermined radically. With the rise of confidence in science came a greater faith in the possibilities of expanding technique; and social change was now regarded increasingly not with dread but rather with hope. Many came to believe that technological development and commercial expansion could be achieved without undermining such values as community, brotherhood, and humility. In the eighteenth and nineteenth centuries, it was held by exponents of the idea of progress, Marxists, and most liberals that, while technology might have posed a danger in the past, its very perfection in modern times would not only make for material abundance but would also destroy alienation, class discrimination, and exploitation. Social change, so suspect in the eyes of the ancients, would almost inevitably produce the framework within which technique would remain a slave of man and not become his master. Some speculators who developed the doctrine of cultural lag came to believe that, while in the past non-material culture (control, politics, coordination) had always lagged behind material developments, in the future the nonmaterial would catch up.

For the most part, statements of this kind, variously expressed, became premises of modern political thought. Only a few dissented—some of the primitivist anarchists, for instance, and thinkers like Tolstoy and Gandhi. Yet modern economic-political life has so far not demonstrated man's capacity to avoid the alienation process which philosophers of progress like Marx had described in historical terms. Everywhere—in developed and underdeveloped nations alike—the speed of technological change seemed to paralyze men for its control: They became the prey of those very forces against which the classical political philosophers had warned them. Would this fever heat development of division of labor, technology, economy, and society—a pace never before known in the history of mankind—confirm the judgments of the ancients or confound them? By the middle of the twentieth century, the answer was by no means certain: There was little evidence that the views of Plato and Aristotle had been effectively refuted in terms of modern experience. While many modern critics of Plato charged that he had hoped virtually to halt the flux of things in the name of a static good life, the modern Platonist might with considerable justification assert that twentieth-century idolization of flux and change was completely destroying the possibilities of community, equity, mental health, and justice. The pace was so furious, it might plausibly be contended, that despite the vast proliferation of legislation modern men were more under the control of mere "accident" than the ancients.

Property in Material Goods

The history of political thought has evidenced a kind of ambivalence about the principle of private property in material goods. On the one hand, community of material goods has been exalted as an expression of community in general; and private property has been defended with extreme reluctance or not at all. Thus among the ancient Hebrews, the prophets living in an age of commercialism looked back longingly to an earlier epoch when there was supposedly a greater sharing of material goods. In Greece, too, the belief persisted that in generations long past, the divisiveness associated with private property during the classical age had not existed. There was a keen awareness of the conflict between private economic interest and the public good, as is reflected in the dialogues of Plato. Most of the early Church Fathers were quite hostile to private property. In the first portion of the Middle Ages, communism was supposed to have been characteristic of Eden, private property being regarded as the product of sin even though it was also its correction. To Rousseau and Marx, of course, the rise of private property represented the beginning of class divisions and alienation; and true community could develop only when men either were not sharply separated by maldistribution of goods or lived under conditions where private property was abolished altogether. And certain of the anarchist schools shared a similar position.

On the other hand, private property has been defended as an extension of personality, as essential if men were to develop a sense of responsibility, and as needed to enable them to exercise the virtue of charity. In Aristotle, of course, private possession was natural although its use should be common. With the revival of classical learning in the thirteenth century, St. Thomas came to argue that property was added to Nature by man's reason, although its use, as with Aristotle, should be common. Locke, of course, symbolized the developing middle classes' sense of property rights: in the broad sense, indeed, property meant life, liberty, and estate. In the narrow meaning of property in material goods, those raw materials were one's own with which one mixed one's labor, subject to there being enough left for others and to assurance that none would be spoiled. But the invention of money supposedly qualified the limitations of the latter notion and, as actually interpreted through much of the history of subsequent thought, Locke's principle came to mean that a kind of sacred character was given to property. In the eighteenth century and through much of the nineteenth, certain schools of thought elevated the struggle for private possession of material goods into a principle of social and moral progress which none might question. But Marx, later liberalism, non-Marxian socialism, and most anarchism carried on a counterattack which had considerable success.

Ancient classical thought held that distribution of material goods depended on the nature of the constitution: Thus democracy tended to the principle of equality. In his discussion of distributive justice, Aristotle examined the nature of principles governing allocation of resources under alternative schemes. Throughout his analysis, he always assumed that property in material things would and should be distributed according to certain ethical-political standards and that it should not be a matter of mere happenstance. In general, medieval thought continued the same tradition. In modern times, however, the notion arose—as part of individualist approaches to politics—that distribution could best be left to the play of market forces: A rough kind of justice, it appeared to be argued, would result. But gradually this market conception began to be undermined, under increasingly complex industrialism, by characteristically modern notions of planning: socialist, liberal, and some conservative theories tended to abandon sole reliance on the market.

Many thinkers made a distinction between property in producers' or capital goods and that in consumers' goods. Often the former was to be publicly or socially owned and administered, while the latter would still be privately possessed. Much socialist thought took this position, arguing that it was property which conferred power to control others that ought to be public and subordinate to the community.

The problem of justice in distribution has puzzled thinkers from the very outset of thought. In the communist tradition, of course, the notion of distribution according to need has been central—as with the early church at Jerusalem, the ancient Essenes, certain medieval sects, ultimate Marxist goals, and many others. Equality became cardinal for some, as in certain groups during the French Revolution and modern thinkers like Edward Bellamy and George Bernard Shaw. Yet others argued for a functional theory in which each would have only those goods necessary to enable him to carry out his basic role in society: much medieval thought turned on this view and such modern thinkers as R. H. Tawney have restated it.

Spirituals and Temporals

In ancient organic notions of society, a central problem of politics turned on the question of whether it was possible to order collective affairs so that spiritual ends—learning, for example, aesthetic appreciation, and the ideal of right living—would remain central. It was assumed in ancient Israel and in the Greek city-state that the purpose of politics was not merely to preserve life but to ensure a good life. The legislator hoped to develop an environment in which men could act morally and where—at least in Athens—man's most characteristic attributes, the spiritual and intellectual, would be ends and not merely means. Ethics was one side of the coin and politics the other; and man's eternal destiny was closely linked with the political.

With the Babylonian captivity of the Jews, however, the notion that one could, in some measure, separate spiritual from merely temporal goals began to arise. The nub of the church idea was suggested; for the Jews, now lacking political independence, turned inward and thought of themselves as in a measure separated from secular society. With the growth of Cynicism and similar systems, this feeling of separation on the part of many was enhanced. In Christianity, the infant Church was seen as a group of pilgrims only partially tied to the concerns of the general society. Man's individual eternal salvation, many seemed to say, could be separated from his social and political welfare here below: His legal servitude need not mean that he was not spiritually free and his state of economic poverty did not imply that he might not be rich in treasures of heaven. As conceptions of this kind developed, society came to be thought of as divided between two authorities, one of which presided over the state of the soul while the other was concerned with the body. Although it was recognized, to be sure, that soul and body constituted an interrelated complex, still it was argued that two kinds of governance were appropriate. While in the earlier days of Christianity, the good Christian was not supposed to participate actively in war, the magistracy, and coercion, he might now do so with the sanction of both spiritual and temporal authority. Those who sought perfection, of course—particularly the monks—could renounce concupiscence of the eyes, of the flesh, and of status and power; but the bulk of mankind, given the fact of sin, had to be satisfied with more limited moral objectives. Later in the Middle Ages, those who controlled the central spiritual authority often came to say that temporal rule must be completely subordinate to the pope, thus in effect undermining the two-authority idea.

With early modern thought, there was a tendency to pursue the study of ethics separately from that of politics and also the beginning of a decline in religious perspectives.

As science developed, orthodox religious commitments waned. When no religious group could gain predominance, the idea of toleration arose. Religious indifferentism was also partly responsible for the growth of doctrines of religious toleration: What one professed about spirituals, men seemed to say, had no bearing on social welfare or political controversy. Or, as the slogan became, "religion is a purely private matter."

By the eighteenth and nineteenth centuries and far into the twentieth, views of this kind had become central, even among most members of religiously orthodox groups. But in the meantime, the private pursuit of traditional religions was paralleled by the quasi-religious and often intolerant demands of the national state. While professing to be only temporal, it tended, particularly after the nineteenth century, to make the same kinds of claims on its subjects that the Medieval Church had made. Allegiance to it was to be primary. Philosophies centering on nationalism increasingly made the state an object of devotion beyond all rational inquiry—a process which culminated in the totalitarian views of twentieth century National Socialism and Fascism.

Although in so-called democratic theory, there was an area of human conduct which the state could not invade—oral and written expression, for example, and religious worship and exercises—the state arrogated to itself, as did the Medieval Church at its height, the prerogative of determining where the line was to be drawn. Thus a constitution might guarantee religious freedom, but a group could not practice polygamy even though it regarded plural marriages as a divine command. And nowhere was the claim to exemption from military service regarded as an indisputable right of the individual: it was always a privilege extended by the state for its own ends.

Education

Education is an excellent example of an issue which has been political from the beginning and which poses dramatically the problem of where spirituals and temporals intersect. Classical Greek speculation, of course, was keenly aware of the centrality of education for any study of politics: It became, in fact, overriding in the political treatises of Plato. Vital in the socialization process, education in turn affects such questions as cohesiveness, sense of community, possibilities of active civic participation, and many others. In the history of utopian thought, as with Thomas More, Campanella, H. G. Wells, and others, the Platonic emphasis on education has usually been followed; and in modern theories of liberalism, Marxism, and non-Marxian socialism it is equally important.

Although education is thus important for civic purposes, it should never be forgotten that it may also serve to liberate the individual from prejudice and to encourage independence of thought. In some measure, its civic function—to pass on and preserve a tradition and a social belief system—is at war with its liberating role, which is one of questioning tradition, of unsettling beliefs, and, potentially, of encouraging revolution. The greatest political thinkers—from ancient to modern times—have recognized this conflict between the roles of education; but it can hardly be said that they have successfully suggested a framework for peaceful co-existence. The tension would seem to be a perennial one. Teaching in a political community is forever attempting, on the one hand, to cultivate civic myths—such as nationalism, the superiority of the proletariat, or the virtues of capitalism—and, on the other, to break away from those myths.

The Problem of Violence

For some four thousand years, thinkers have been perturbed and fascinated by violence. It has played a central part in political speculation of all types. The ancient prophets were puzzled as to why Yahweh permitted it and particularly why he allowed the Hebrews to be destroyed by out-groups like the Assyrians and Babylonians. Many concluded that while violence was not allowed to men, Yahweh could use it for his own ultimate purposes. In ancient Greece, the tragedians saw collective man as caught up in the network of violence and counterviolence and yet somehow defying it. Although Socrates enunciated the principle that it was not legitimate for any man to injure another, whether friend or enemy, classical Greek thinkers were never able to get beyond the idea that the city must be seen as beleagured by other cities and that violence was an inevitable concomitant of inter-city life—hence the large role which the military played in both Plato and Aristotle. With the rise of Christianity, the tension between the violence of general society and the demands of the

Gospel was acute. For a century and a half, at least, Christians said no to the demands of organized violence; and in works like Origen's *Contra Celsum* their position was spelled out in detail.

With the compromises of subsequent centuries, the dualistic ethic established two standards—one for clerics, who were to refrain from bloodshed, and another for laymen, who might be called upon to kill, even in the name of the Faith. Collective violence and war were seen as the fruit of original sin; and while they might be checked by such devices as the Truce of God, it would be blasphemy to believe that they could be wiped out. Later on, philosophical elaborations of the distinction between just and unjust wars endeavored to provide standards.

With the rise of the modern state, the doctrine arose that the state had—or should have—a monopoly of legitimate violence, legitimacy to be determined by the state itself. In early modern doctrines of resistance, of course, theories like those of De La Boetie maintained that the most effective opposition to tyranny was nonviolent noncooperation which preserved morality and at the same time grappled with political reality. In certain of the early modern sects, like the Quakers, nonviolence was elevated to a principle; and Quakers actually founded a rather successful commonwealth which for two generations at least partially demonstrated the possibilities of a wholesale commitment to nonviolence.

The extensive modern wars of eighteenth, nineteenth, and twentieth centuries, together with the spread of tyranny and the development of revolutionary ideologies, have reposed the issues of violence and nonviolence. An important stream of anarchist thought was in effect committed to nonviolence; and in the thought of Gandhi, nonviolent resistance to tyranny and invasion, together with decentralization, became central. Meanwhile, various cults of violence were associated with the development of modern political thought: that of Bakunin in the nineteenth century, for example, and those of Lenin and Mao Tse-tung in the twentieth. It is one of the most vital political and ethical issues of our day.

It would seem that critics of the nation-state raise an important question when they ask whether its structure—despite the hopes of Hobbes and its other idolizers—really provides great assurance against internal violence: thus some of the bloodiest wars of the nineteenth and twentieth centuries have been civil conflicts. On the other hand, some of the most peaceful relations have developed between and among men living under diverse sovereignties and having no common state structure—Canadians and Americans, for example, or Danes and Swedes. In modern thought about world order—whether liberal, Marxist, conservative, or non-Marxian socialist—observations of this kind should have great relevance, particularly for those who see a World State as in itself a possible answer to violence. Meanwhile, it is a serious question whether the modern state has not, on the whole—at least in its Great Power form—been as responsible for the deaths of human beings, particularly in war, as it has been for their protection. This is, at least, a debatable issue, as many anarchists, antistatists, and pacifists have suggested.

Concluding Reflections

We have seen political speculation moving from a context of tribe and intimate community to one of universal empire; from a period in which it was assumed that religion and politics were interwoven to a period in which society was conceived to be a single entity divided between two distinct but cooperating authorities; from a body of thought which, in general, was dominated by varying organic models to outlooks which were often characterized by discrete individualism conditioned by "force" and contract theories of sovereignty; and from an epoch when belief in mutual automatic adjustment of individual desires and social goals was widespread to an age (since the Great Revolution) when men, while still clinging to automatic adjustment concepts, were at the same time seeking to discover a new basis for organic community which would overcome individual alienation.

The student of human affairs can develop many observations from this long story. Here we note only three in conclusion:

First, no given image of the political world, whether in normative or in analytical and empirical terms, seems to get at the whole truth. The dialectic so characteristic of the history of political ideas would seem to be essential if we are to catch even a vague glimpse of an elusive reality. *Both* Hobbes and Burke are essential. Past and "present" merge as we see the story from this perspective: thus classical political theory, treated in the context of peculiar social and political conditions, is highly relevant for us in the twentieth century—for example, in illustrating the theory and practice of small community, in raising the problem of relating frenetic and unlimited economic development to the purposes of human beings as more than economic animals, and in exhibiting the major tendencies of historical politics when freed from the governance of principle. Or again, we no sooner think we have an answer to the vexing issue of political obligation than we begin to doubt it and find in the ebb and flow of theories of obligation a kind of macrocosm of what is going on in our minds. With Augustine, we can see merit in the notion that existential states are little more than piratical bands (particularly when we see them in the context of concrete historical events); but with Hegel, we can perhaps also see them as implicitly striving to transcend their piratical character.

Secondly, the history of political ideas gives us perspective on such questions as the interrelations of rational, empirical, and normative approaches. It suggests that they ought to be pursued together if we are interested in *political* or practical philosophy and not merely in what Aristotle called theoretical science. In ages accenting "abstract reason" we have seen how "empiricist" critics begin to attack what they think of as an overemphasis on merely *a priori* and deductive methods. On the other hand, in periods of raw empiricism, the "rationalists" have attempted to correct the balance by their stress on the necessity for concepts of some kind before we even begin to examine the empirical domain. Indeed, the problem of definition is so basic that it would seem to be prior to any assessment of so-called facts. As for normative considerations, we have observed them permeating a wide diversity of systems in a variety of historical contexts: in the teleological conceptions of the classical Greeks, which tend to merge the "is" and the "ought" in an ultimate reality quite different from ordinary sense experience; in the valuations of what is important to consider and emphasize in a political theory—thus in ages of disorder like the sixteenth century and possibly our own time, one finds the historical context affecting valuations, in the sense that men address themselves centrally to questions like authority, resistance, passive obedience, and civil disobedience; and in the search for new teleologies which seems to follow emphases—like Hobbes' view—that appear to discount purpose and the possible existence of an objective moral order.

Finally, one cannot help but be impressed by the limitations of political thinking in any age. The difficulties of language, for example, immediately set up bars to expression of thought. Diverse conceptions of "reality" from the very outset may separate thinkers. In their ultimate contours, all schemes of political thought—as, indeed, all frameworks of thought in general—depend upon diverse faiths beyond reason. Often, in their final reaches, as Reinhold Niebuhr has suggested, every system of thought that endeavors to take account of all factors and avoid the sin of oversimplification appears to end in a series of paradoxes. Elijah Jordan has suggested, undoubtedly with hyperbolical intent, "Man must do his own political thinking, yet cannot; such is the surd of politics."[2]

Despite observations of this kind, we should remember that thought is man's only salvation in the political realm: the gods will not provide answers for the riddle of consciously and deliberately controlling human collective destiny, and man has long ago passed the point where he can rely on instinct or rigid tradition. In his very attempt to think politically lies his fulfillment.

2. Elijah Jordan, *Theory of Legislation,* Indianapolis Progress Publishing Co., 1930, p. 25.

INDEX

70 71 72 73 7 6 5 4 3 2 1